D1572992

Florida Edition

GLENCOE LITERATURE

The Reader's Choice

Florida Edition

GLENCOE LITERATURE

The Reader's Choice

Program Consultants

Beverly Ann Chin

Denny Wolfe

Jeffrey Copeland

Mary Ann Dudzinski

William Ray

Jacqueline Jones Royster

Jeffrey Wilhelm

Course 4

Glencoe McGraw-Hill

New York, New York   Columbus, Ohio   Chicago, Illinois   Peoria, Illinois   Woodland Hills, California

Acknowledgments

Grateful acknowledgment is given authors, publishers, photographers, museums, and agents for permission to reprint the following copyrighted material. Every effort has been made to determine copyright owners. In case of any omissions, the Publisher will be pleased to make suitable acknowledgments in future editions.

Acknowledgments continued on page R154.

The Standardized Test Practice and FCAT Test-Taking Strategies pages in this book were written by The Princeton Review. Through its association with McGraw-Hill, The Princeton Review offers the best way to help students excel on standardized assessments.

The Princeton Review is not affiliated with Princeton University or Educational Testing Service.

Glencoe/McGraw-Hill

A Division of The ***McGraw·Hill*** *Companies*

Copyright © 2003 by The McGraw-Hill Companies, Inc. All rights reserved. Except as permitted under the United States Copyright Act of 1976, no part of this publication may be reproduced or distributed in any form or means, or stored in a database or retrieval system, without the prior written permission of the publisher.

Printed in the United States of America

Send all inquiries to:
Glencoe/McGraw-Hill
8787 Orion Place
Columbus, OH 43240

ISBN 0-07-828593-3
(Student Edition)

ISBN 0-07-828601-8
(Teacher Wraparound Edition)

3 4 5 6 7 8 9 10 027/055 06 05 04 03

Florida Edition
Book Overview

Florida Advisory Board

Bonnie Valdes, M.S. (Reading Education), is one of twelve Master Trainers for Project CRISS (Creating Independence through Student-owned Strategies), training thousands of educators across the United States. A senior advisor for *Glencoe Literature: The Reader's Choice,* and a Reading teacher for more than thirty years, Bonnie Valdes is currently an independent educational consultant. From 1989 to 2002, she was Secondary Reading Resource Teacher/Project CRISS Coordinator for the Pinellas County Schools District Office in Largo, Florida. She has also developed FCAT preparation training materials for middle and high school educators.

Linda Damsky, M.A. (TESL/Bilingual Education), has been an educator since 1977. She is presently ESOL Testing Coordinator, Pinellas County Schools. She is also a national CRISS trainer, a National Board Certified Teacher in English as a New Language, and a well-known presenter at TESOL conferences.

Roxana Hurtado is Area Coordinator for FLaRE (Florida Literacy and Reading Excellence) in Dade and Monroe Counties. She is a Language Arts teacher at W. R. Thomas Middle School, where she has served as Language Arts Department Chairperson. A former President of the Dade County Council of Teachers of English, she was also a member of Florida's Instructional Materials Committee for Language Arts and Composition, K–8 (2000–2001).

ReLeah Cossett Lent, M.S., an educator in Florida since 1978, is the Area I Coordinator for FLaRE (Florida Literacy and Reading Excellence) at the University of Central Florida. She is a nationally recognized educator and the coauthor of *At the Schoolhouse Gate: Lessons in Intellectual Freedom.*

Ruth E. Rigby, M.Ed., is a longtime English Language Arts and Reading educator, currently serving as President of the Florida Council of Language Arts Supervisors, Commissioner of the Reading Commission of the National Council of Teachers of English, and member of the FLaRE (Florida Literacy and Reading Excellence) advisory board. She is past president of the Florida Council of Teachers of English.

Linda Thompson, M.Ed., was Secondary Language Arts, Speech, Journalism, and Foreign Language Specialist for Florida's Escambia County School District for thirteen years. Before that, she was an English teacher for more than twenty years. She is a CRISS trainer and a 6+1 Traits™ of Writing trainer. Her professional activities include membership on the Florida Curriculum Frameworks Writing Team, the FCAT Writing Committee, and the FCAT Prompt Writing and Review Committee. She has won numerous awards, including three Teacher of the Year awards.

Florida Instructional Mentor Team

Diane Bondurant
Executive Secretary of FCTE
Language Arts Chairperson
Lake Region High School
Eagle Lake, Florida

Lynn Brennan
Former Supervisor of Middle School Education
Hillsborough County Public Schools
Tampa, Florida

Frank De Varona
Visiting Associate Professor
Department of Curriculum and Instruction
Florida International University
Former Assistant Superintendent
Miami-Dade County Public Schools

Nadia Findlater
Language Arts/Reading Department Chairperson
Kissimmee Middle School
Kissimmee, Florida

Mercedes Naranjo
Language Arts Chairperson
Doral Middle School
Miami, Florida

Terry H. Savell
English Teacher
Head of Reading Team
Bay High School
Panama City, Florida

Ann Still-Chapman
Supervisor of Secondary Language Arts
Pasco County Schools
Land O' Lakes, Florida

Luisa Suarez
Language Arts/ESOL Teacher
ESOL Department Chairperson
Howard A. Doolin Middle School
Miami, Florida

Denise Kit Weir
Assistant Principal
Murray Middle School
Stuart, Florida

Letter to Students

Dear Student,

Welcome to ***Glencoe Literature: The Reader's Choice.*** In this lively collection of classic and contemporary literature, you will find much to amuse, surprise, delight, engage, and inform you. A wide variety of selections—including poems, plays, short stories, essays, autobiographies, and news articles on a broad range of themes—offers you the chance to hear talented authors in all their diversity, as well as to experience and learn about the people, places, and ideas that moved them.

The literature selections in your book are grouped into six units, each focusing on a particular genre of writing. The selections include questions and activities that will stretch your ability to read and think. Through your answers and work, you will gain an understanding of the selections as well as learn to analyze and appreciate each genre. You will also have a chance to respond to selections in a personal journal—to connect them to your experiences and raise questions of your own.

In addition, each unit is subdivided by theme. With every theme, you will complete an extended project and longer writing assignment along with many other individual, partner, and group activities. Keep your graded, completed assignments in a portfolio or as your teacher directs. Share your progress with your parents or guardians and also talk with them about the literature you are reading. Discuss your thoughts about the characters, themes, and other aspects of your reading. Complete the **Survey of Reading Habits** on page FL16 to gain a better understanding of your own reading habits, processes, and attitudes.

To guide you in your classwork and to prepare you for the real world, the Florida Department of Education has created content and performance standards for you—the **Sunshine State Standards** and the **Florida School Improvement Goal 3 Standards.** We have included them on pages FL9–FL14 and page FL15. Take time to read over the standards with your teacher and family. Then outline steps that you can take to help you achieve the standards both in and outside the classroom.

Later in the year, you will be taking the **Florida Comprehensive Assessment Test (FCAT)** to measure your achievement. On pages FCAT1–FCAT16 at the back of this book, you will find strategies for taking the FCAT to help you get the best results.

We hope that you enjoy ***Glencoe Literature: The Reader's Choice*** and that the lessons help you not only to master standards but to learn more about yourself and the world you live in.

Sincerely,

The Editors

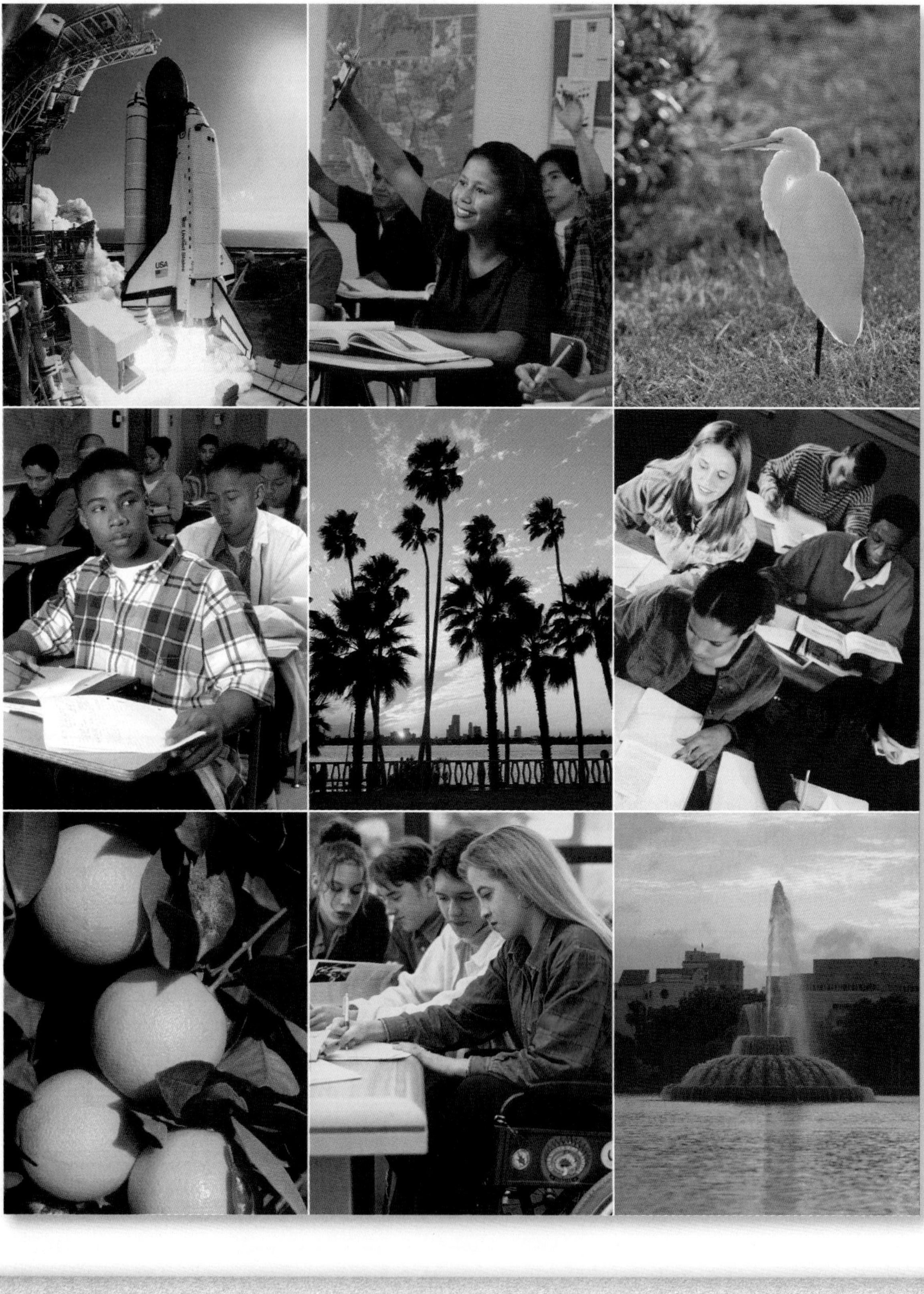

Left to right: (*t*) Corbis; Jose L. Pelaez/Corbis Stock Market; PhotoDisc; (*c*) Michael Newman/PhotoEdit; Creatas; Jamie Marcial/SuperStock; (*b*) EyeWire; Ian Shaw/Stone; Corbis.

FLORIDA
Sunshine State Standards
Literature

Strand A: Reading

Standard 1: Use the reading process effectively.

Reaching the following benchmarks will help you achieve this standard.

Benchmark LA.A.1.4.1:

Select and use prereading strategies that are appropriate to the text, such as discussion, making predictions, brainstorming, generating questions, and previewing to anticipate content, purpose, and organization of a reading selection.

Benchmark LA.A.1.4.2:

Select and use strategies to understand words and text and to make and confirm inferences from what is read, including interpreting diagrams, graphs, and statistical illustrations.

Benchmark LA.A.1.4.3:

Refine vocabulary for interpersonal, academic, and workplace situations, including figurative, idiomatic, and technical meanings.

Benchmark LA.A.1.4.4:

Apply a variety of response strategies, including rereading, note taking, summarizing, outlining, writing a formal report, and relating what you read to your own experiences and feelings.

Standard 2: Construct meaning from a wide range of texts.

Reaching the following benchmarks will help you achieve this standard.

Benchmark LA.A.2.4.1:

Determine the main idea and identify relevant details, methods of development, and their effectiveness in a variety of types of written material.

Benchmark LA.A.2.4.2:

Determine the author's purpose and point of view and their effects on the text.

Benchmark LA.A.2.4.3:

Describe and evaluate personal preferences regarding fiction and nonfiction.

Benchmark LA.A.2.4.4:

Locate, gather, analyze, and evaluate written information for a variety of purposes, including research projects, real-world tasks, and self-improvement.

Benchmark LA.A.2.4.5:

Identify devices of persuasion and methods of appeal and their effectiveness.

Benchmark LA.A.2.4.6:

Select and use appropriate study and research skills and tools according to the type of information being gathered or organized, including almanacs, government publications, microfiche, news sources, and information services.

Benchmark LA.A.2.4.7:

Analyze the validity and reliability of primary source information and use the information appropriately.

Benchmark LA.A.2.4.8:

Synthesize information from multiple sources to draw conclusions.

Strand B: Writing

Standard 1: Use writing processes effectively.

Reaching the following benchmarks will help you achieve this standard.

Benchmark LA.B.1.4.1:

Select and use appropriate prewriting strategies, such as brainstorming, graphic organizers, and outlines.

Benchmark LA.B.1.4.2:

Draft and revise writing that

a) is focused, purposeful, and reflects insight into the writing situation

b) has an organizational pattern that provides for a logical progression of ideas

c) has effective use of transitional devices that contribute to a sense of completeness

d) has support that is substantial, specific, relevant, and concrete

e) demonstrates a commitment to and involvement with the subject

f) uses creative writing strategies as appropriate to the purposes of the paper

g) demonstrates a mature command of language with freshness of expression

h) has varied sentence structure

i) has few, if any, convention errors in mechanics, usage, punctuation, and spelling.

Benchmark LA.B.1.4.3:

Produce final documents that have been edited for

a) correct spelling

b) correct punctuation, including commas, colons, and common use of semicolons

c) correct capitalization

d) correct sentence formation

e) correct instances of possessives, subject/verb agreement, instances of noun/pronoun agreement

f) intentional use of fragments for effect

g) correct formatting that appeals to readers, including appropriate use of a variety of graphics, tables, and charts

h) illustrations in both standard and innovative forms.

Standard 2: Communicate ideas and information effectively.

Reaching the following benchmarks will help you achieve this standard.

Benchmark LA.B.2.4.1:

Write text, notes, outlines, comments, and observations that demonstrate comprehension and synthesis of content, processes, and experiences from a variety of media.

Benchmark LA.B.2.4.2:

Organize information using appropriate systems.

Benchmark LA.B.2.4.3:

Write fluently for a variety of occasions, audiences, and purposes, making appropriate choices regarding style, tone, level of detail, and organization.

Benchmark LA.B.2.4.4:

Select and use a variety of electronic media, such as the Internet, information services, and desktop publishing software programs, to create, revise, retrieve, and verify information.

Strand C: Listening, Viewing, and Speaking

Standard 1: Use listening strategies effectively.

Reaching the following benchmarks will help you achieve this standard.

Benchmark LA.C.1.4.1:

Select and use appropriate listening strategies according to the intended purpose, such as solving problems, interpreting and evaluating the techniques and intent of a presentation, and taking action in career-related situations.

Benchmark LA.C.1.4.2:

Describe, evaluate, and expand personal preferences in listening to fiction, drama, literary nonfiction, and informational presentations.

Benchmark LA.C.1.4.3:

Use effective strategies for informal and formal discussions, including listening actively and reflectively, connecting to and building on the ideas of a previous speaker, and respecting the viewpoints of others.

Benchmark LA.C.1.4.4:

Identify bias, prejudice, or propaganda in oral messages.

Standard 2: Use viewing strategies effectively.

Reaching the following benchmarks will help you achieve this standard.

Benchmark LA.C.2.4.1:

Determine main concept and supporting details in order to analyze and evaluate nonprint media messages.

Benchmark LA.C.2.4.2:

Understand factors that influence the effectiveness of nonverbal cues used in nonprint media, such as the viewer's past experiences and preferences, and the context in which the cues are presented.

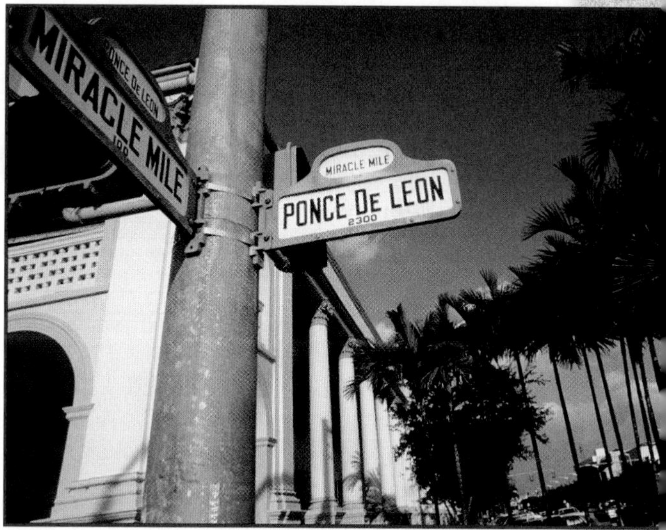

Standard 3: Use speaking strategies effectively.

Reaching the following benchmarks will help you achieve this standard.

Benchmark LA.C.3.4.1:

Use volume, stress, pacing, enunciation, eye contact, and gestures that meet the needs of the audience and topic.

Benchmark LA.C.3.4.2:

Select and use a variety of speaking strategies to clarify meaning and to reflect understanding, interpretation, application, and evaluation of content, processes, or experiences, including asking relevant questions when necessary, making appropriate and meaningful comments, and making insightful observations.

Benchmark LA.C.3.4.3:

Use details, illustrations, analogies, and visual aids to make oral presentations that inform, persuade, or entertain.

Benchmark LA.C.3.4.4:

Apply oral communication skills to interviews, group presentations, formal presentations, and impromptu situations.

Benchmark LA.C.3.4.5:

Develop and sustain a line of argument and provide appropriate support.

Strand D: Language

Standard 1: Understand the nature of language.

Reaching the following benchmarks will help you achieve this standard.

Benchmark LA.D.1.4.1:

Apply an understanding that language and literature are primary means by which culture is transmitted.

Benchmark LA.D.1.4.2:

Make appropriate adjustments in language use for social, academic, and life situations, demonstrating sensitivity to gender and cultural bias.

Benchmark LA.D.1.4.3:

Understand that there are differences among various dialects of English.

Standard 2: Understand the power of language.

Reaching the following benchmarks will help you achieve this standard.

Benchmark LA.D.2.4.1:

Understand specific ways in which language has shaped the reactions, perceptions, and beliefs of the local, national, and global communities.

Benchmark LA.D.2.4.2:

Understand the subtleties of literary devices and techniques in the comprehension and creation of communication.

Benchmark LA.D.2.4.3:

Recognize production elements that contribute to the effectiveness of a specific medium.

Benchmark LA.D.2.4.4:

Effectively integrate multimedia and technology into presentations.

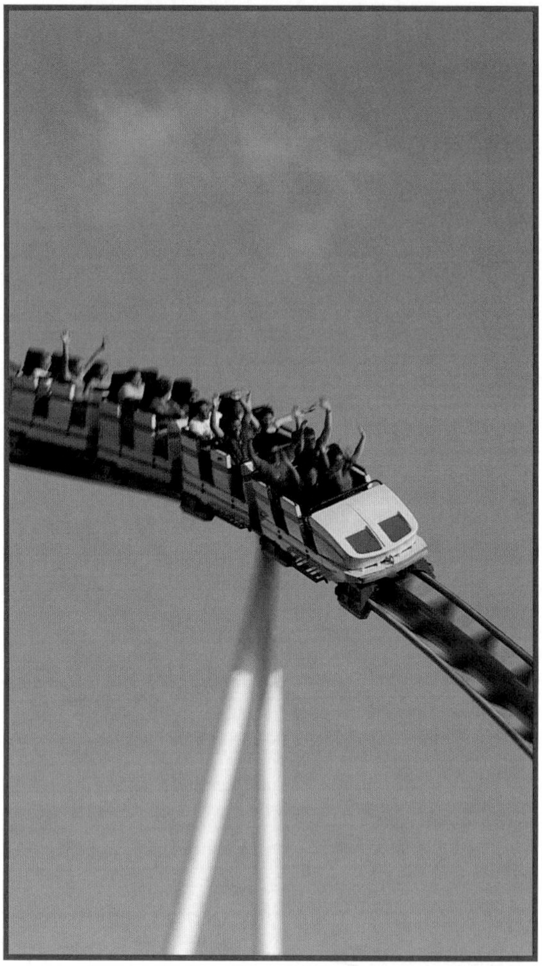

Benchmark LA.D.2.4.5:

Critically analyze specific elements of mass media with regard to the extent to which they enhance or manipulate information.

Benchmark LA.D.2.4.6:

Understand that laws control the delivery and use of media to protect the rights of authors and the rights of media owners.

Strand E: Literature

Standard 1: Understand the common features of a variety of literary forms.

Reaching the following benchmarks will help you achieve this standard.

Benchmark LA.E.1.4.1:

Identify the characteristics that distinguish literary forms.

Benchmark LA.E.1.4.2:

Understand why certain literary works are considered classics.

Benchmark LA.E.1.4.3:

Identify universal themes prevalent in the literature of all cultures.

Benchmark LA.E.1.4.4:

Understand the characteristics of major types of drama.

Benchmark LA.E.1.4.5:

Understand the different stylistic, thematic, and technical qualities present in the literature of different cultures and historical periods.

Standard 2: Respond critically to fiction, nonfiction, poetry, and drama.

Reaching the following benchmarks will help you achieve this standard.

Benchmark LA.E.2.4.1:

Analyze the effectiveness of complex elements of plot, such as setting, major events, problems, conflicts, and resolutions.

Benchmark LA.E.2.4.2:

Understand the relationships between and among elements of literature, including characters, plot, setting, tone, point of view, and theme.

Benchmark LA.E.2.4.3:

Analyze poetry for the ways in which poets inspire the reader to share emotions, such as the use of imagery, personification, and figures of speech, including simile and metaphor; and the use of sound, such as rhyme, rhythm, repetition, and alliteration.

Benchmark LA.E.2.4.4:

Understand the use of images and sounds to elicit the reader's emotions in both fiction and nonfiction.

Benchmark LA.E.2.4.5:

Analyze the relationships among author's style, literary form, and intended impact on the reader.

Benchmark LA.E.2.4.6:

Recognize and explain those elements in texts that prompt a personal response, such as connections between one's own life and the characters, events, motives, and causes of conflict in texts.

Benchmark LA.E.2.4.7:

Examine a literary selection from several critical perspectives.

Benchmark LA.E.2.4.8:

Know that people respond differently to texts based on their background knowledge, purpose, and point of view.

FLORIDA SCHOOL IMPROVEMENT

Goal 3 Standards

In Language Arts, you use and develop a variety of important skills. Many of these skills, however, are useful even beyond your Language Arts class. Skills such as finding and organizing information, for example, can help you in other classes, in life at home, in your community, and in a career.

Florida's Goal 3 standards, listed below, highlight a number of such skills that are useful in all subject areas and in your life beyond school.

STANDARD 1 ❧ *Information Managers*

You will be able to locate, comprehend, interpret, evaluate, maintain, and apply information, concepts, and ideas found in literature, the arts, symbols, recordings, video and other graphic displays, and computer files in order to perform tasks and/or for enjoyment.

STANDARD 2 ❧ *Effective Communicators*

You will be able to communicate in English and other languages using information, concepts, prose, symbols, reports, audio and video recordings, speeches, graphic displays, and computer-based programs.

STANDARD 3 ❧ *Numeric Problem Solvers*

You will be able to use numeric operations and concepts to describe, analyze, disaggregate, communicate, and synthesize numeric data, and to identify and solve problems.

STANDARD 4 ❧ *Creative and Critical Thinkers*

You will be able to use creative thinking skills to generate new ideas, make the best decision, recognize and solve problems through reasoning, interpret symbolic data, and develop efficient techniques for lifelong learning.

STANDARD 5 ❧ *Responsible Workers*

You will be able to display responsibility, self-esteem, sociability, self-management, integrity, and honesty.

STANDARD 6 ❧ *Resource Managers*

You will be able to appropriately allocate time, money, materials, and other resources.

STANDARD 7 ❧ *Systems Managers*

You will be able to integrate your knowledge and understanding of how social, organizational, informational, and technological systems work with your abilities to analyze trends, design and improve systems, and use and maintain appropriate technology.

STANDARD 8 ❧ *Cooperative Workers*

You will be able to work cooperatively to successfully complete a project or activity.

STANDARD 9 ❧ *Effective Leaders*

You will be able to establish credibility with your colleagues through competence and integrity and help your peers achieve their goals by communicating your feelings and ideas to justify or successfully negotiate a position that advances goal attainment.

STANDARD 10 ❧ *Multiculturally Sensitive Citizens*

You will be able to appreciate your own culture and the culture of others, understand the concerns and perspectives of members of other ethnic and gender groups, reject the stereotyping of yourself and others, and seek out and utilize the views of persons from diverse ethnic, social, and educational backgrounds while completing individual and group projects.

STANDARD 11 ❧ *Involvement of Families*

Families will share the responsibility of accomplishing the standards set in Goal 3 throughout your education from preschool through 12th grade.

FLORIDA

Survey of Reading Habits

How does reading figure into your life? By honestly considering what you think and how you feel about the process of reading, you can make some important discoveries about yourself.

On a separate sheet of paper, answer the following questions about your reading habits, processes, and attitudes.

1. What makes someone a good reader? Are you a good reader? Explain.

2. Do you do most of your reading in school or out of school?

3. What was the last book you read for pleasure? Did you enjoy it? Why?

4. What are some of the best books you have ever read? What magazines and newspapers do you enjoy reading?

5. What advantage do good readers have in school? In a career? In daily life?

6. What do you do when you read a sentence or passage you don't understand? What are some other reading strategies you use when you read?

7. What do you think of people who read a lot?

8. Would you like to improve your reading skills? Would you like to spend more time reading? Explain.

9. How is the way you read a textbook different from the way you read a story or novel?

10. How do you feel about the reading you do for school? What would make your reading at school more enjoyable?

GLENCOE LITERATURE

The Reader's Choice

Program Consultants

Beverly Ann Chin
Denny Wolfe
Jeffrey Copeland
Mary Ann Dudzinski
William Ray
Jacqueline Jones Royster
Jeffrey Wilhelm

Course 4

Glencoe McGraw-Hill

New York, New York   Columbus, Ohio   Woodland Hills, California   Peoria, Illinois

Acknowledgments

Grateful acknowledgment is given authors, publishers, photographers, museums, and agents for permission to reprint the following copyrighted material. Every effort has been made to determine copyright owners. In case of any omissions, the Publisher will be pleased to make suitable acknowledgments in future editions.

Acknowledgments continued on page R154.

The Standardized Test Practice pages in this book were written by The Princeton Review, the nation's leader in test preparation. Through its association with McGraw-Hill, The Princeton Review offers the best way to help students excel on standardized assessments.

The Princeton Review is not affiliated with Princeton University or Educational Testing Service.

Senior Program Consultants

Beverly Ann Chin is Professor of English, Director of the English Teaching Program, Director of the Montana Writing Project, and former Director of Composition at the University of Montana in Missoula. In 1995–1996, Dr. Chin served as President of the National Council of Teachers of English. She currently serves as a Member of the Board of Directors of the National Board for Professional Teaching Standards. Dr. Chin is a nationally recognized leader in English language arts standards, curriculum, and assessment. Formerly a high school English teacher and adult education reading teacher, Dr. Chin has taught in English language arts education at several universities and has received awards for her teaching and service.

Denny Wolfe, a former high school English teacher and department chair, is Professor of English Education, Director of the Tidewater Virginia Writing Project, and Director of the Center for Urban Education at Old Dominion University in Norfolk, Virginia. For the National Council of Teachers of English, he has served as Chairperson of the Standing Committee on Teacher Preparation, President of the International Assembly, member of the Executive Committee of the Council on English Education, and editor of the SLATE Newsletter. Author of more than seventy-five articles and books on teaching English, Dr. Wolfe is a frequent consultant to schools and colleges on the teaching of English language arts.

Program Consultants

Jeffrey S. Copeland is Professor and Head of the Department of English Language and Literature at the University of Northern Iowa, where he teaches children's and young adult literature courses and a variety of courses in English education. A former public school teacher, he has published many articles in the professional journals in the language arts. The twelve books he has written or edited include *Speaking of Poets: Interviews with Poets Who Write for Children and Young Adults* and *Young Adult Literature: A Contemporary Reader.*

Mary Ann Dudzinski is a former high school English teacher and recipient of the Ross Perot Award for Teaching Excellence. She also has served as a member of the core faculty for the National Endowment for the Humanities Summer Institute for Teachers of Secondary School English and History at the University of North Texas. After fifteen years of classroom experience in grades 9–12, she currently is a language arts consultant.

William Ray has taught English in the Boston Public Schools; at Lowell University; University of Wroclaw, Poland; and, for the last fourteen years, at Lincoln-Sudbury Regional High School in Sudbury, Massachusetts. He specializes in world literature. He has worked on a variety of educational texts, as editor, consultant, and contributing writer.

Jacqueline Jones Royster is Professor of English and Associate Dean of the College of Humanities at The Ohio State University. She is also on the faculty of the Bread Loaf School of English at Middlebury College in Middlebury, Vermont. In addition to the teaching of writing, Dr. Royster's professional interests include the rhetorical history of African American women and the social and cultural implications of literate practices.

Jeffrey Wilhelm, a former English and reading teacher, is currently an assistant professor at the University of Maine where he teaches courses in middle and secondary level literacy. He is the author or co-author of several books on the teaching of reading and literacy, including *You Gotta BE the Book* and *Boys and Books*. He also works with local schools as part of the fledgling Adolescent Literacy Project and is the director of two annual summer institutes: the Maine Writing Project and Technology as a Learning Tool.

Teacher Reviewers

Rahn Anderson
Arapahoe High School
Littleton Public Schools
Littleton, Colorado

Linda Antonowich
West Chester Area School District
West Chester, Pennsylvania

Mike Bancroft
Rock Bridge High School
Columbia, Missouri

Luella Barber
Hays High School
Hays, Kansas

Lori Beard
Cypress Creek High School
Houston, Texas

Hugh Beattie
Bergenfield Public School District
Bergenfield, New Jersey

Patricia Blatt
Centerville High School
Centerville, Ohio

Edward Blotzer III
Wilkinsburg High School
Pittsburgh, Pennsylvania

Ruby Bowker
Mt. View High School
Mt. View, Wyoming

Darolyn Brown
Osborn High School
Detroit, Michigan

Rob Bruno
Atholton High School
Columbia, Maryland

Mary Beth Crotty
Bridgetown Junior High
Cincinnati, Ohio

Susan Dawson
Sam Barlow High School
Portland, Oregon

Thomas A. Della Salla
Schenectady City School District
Schenectady, New York

Sandra Denton
East High School
Columbus, Ohio

Charles Eisele
St. John Vianney High School
St. Louis, Missouri

Mel Farberman
Benjamin Cardozo High School
Bayside, New York

Caroline Ferdinandsen
San Joaquin Memorial High School
Fresno, California

Tye Ferdinandsen
San Joaquin Memorial High School
Fresno, California

Randle Frink
East Rowan High School
Salisbury, North Carolina

Pamela Fuller
Capital High School
Charleston, West Virginia

Tara Gallagher
River Hill High School
Columbia, Maryland

June Gatewood
Rio Americano
Sacramento, California

Ellen Geisler
Mentor High School
Mentor, Ohio

Leslie Gershon
Annapolis Senior High
Mitchellville, Maryland

Kim Hartman
Franklin Heights High School
Columbus, Ohio

Charlotte Heidel
Gaylord High School
Gaylord, Michigan

Keith Henricksen
Sutton Public Schools
Sutton, Nebraska

Patricia Herigan
Central Dauphin High School
Harrisburg, Pennsylvania

Azalie Hightower
Paul Junior High School
Washington, D.C.

Bobbi Ciriza Houtchens
San Bernardino High School
San Bernardino, California

Cheri Jefferson
Atholton High School
Columbia, Maryland

Marsha Jones
Seymour High School
Seymour, Indiana

Cheryl Keast
Glendale High School
Glendale, California

Glenda Kissell
Littleton High School
Littleton, Colorado

Jan Klein
Cypress Lake High School
Fort Myers, Florida

Beth Koehler
Nathan Hale High School
West Allis, Wisconsin

Sister Mary Kay Lampert
Central Catholic High School
Portland, Oregon

Elaine Loughlin
Palo Duro High
Amarillo, Texas

Tom Mann
Franklin Heights High School
Columbus, Ohio

Carolyn Sue Mash
Westerville North High School
Westerville, Ohio

Eileen Mattingly
McDonough High School
Pomfret, Maryland

Wanda McConnell
Statesville High School
Statesville, North Carolina

Victoria McCormick
John Jay High School
San Antonio, Texas

Sandra Sue McPherson
McKeesport Area High School
McKeesport, Pennsylvania

Jill Miller
Odessa High School
Odessa, Texas

Karmen Miller
Cypress Falls High School
Houston, Texas

Catherine Morse
Shelby High School
Shelby, Ohio

Tom Omli
Rogers High School
Puyallup, Washington

John O'Toole
Solon High School
Solon, Ohio

Helen Pappas
Bridgewater-Raritan High School
Bridgewater, New Jersey

Jill Railsback
Seymour High School
Seymour, Indiana

Doug Reed
Franklin Heights High School
Columbus, Ohio

Mary Jane Reed
Solon High School
Solon, Ohio

Dorlea Rikard
Bradshaw High School
Florence, Alabama

Diane Ritzdorf
Arapahoe High School
Littleton, Colorado

Leonor Rodriguez
Breckenridge High School
San Antonio, Texas

Susanne Rubenstein
Wachusett Regional High School
Holden, Massachusetts

Steve Slagle
San Gabriel High School
San Gabriel, California

Tammy Smiley
Littleton High School
Littleton, Colorado

Carol Smith
Moses Lake School District
Moses Lake, Washington

Helen Spaith
Franklin Heights High School
Columbus, Ohio

Marsha Spampinato
High School of Enterprise,
Business, and Technology
Smithtown, New York

Nora Stephens
Huntsville High School
Huntsville, Alabama

David Stocking
Wachusett Regional High School
Holden, Massachusetts

Mark Tavernier
Norfolk Public Schools
Norfolk, Virginia

Martin Tierney
Bishop Dwenger High School
Fort Wayne, Indiana

Elysa Toler-Robinson
Detroit Public Schools
Detroit, Michigan

Megan Trow
Sprague High School
Salem, Oregon

Joseph Velten Jr.
Archbishop Wood High School
Warminster, Pennsylvania

Margaret Wildermann
McDonough High School
Pomfret, Maryland

Kathy Young
Walnut Ridge High School
Columbus, Ohio

Mary Young
Greenville High School
Greenville, Illinois

Book Overview

Reference Section

Contents

UNIT ❧ ONE

The Short Story

indicates world literature

CONTENTS

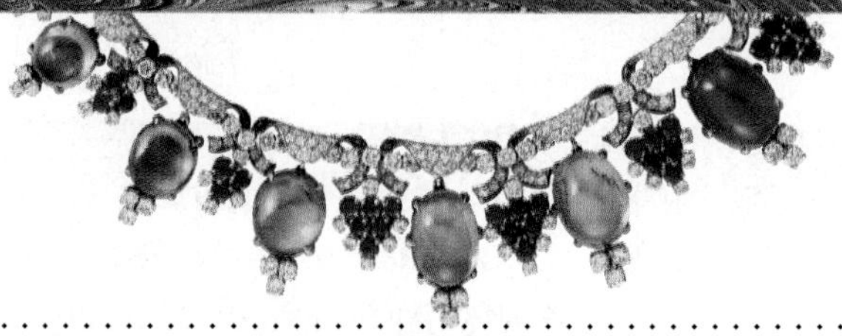

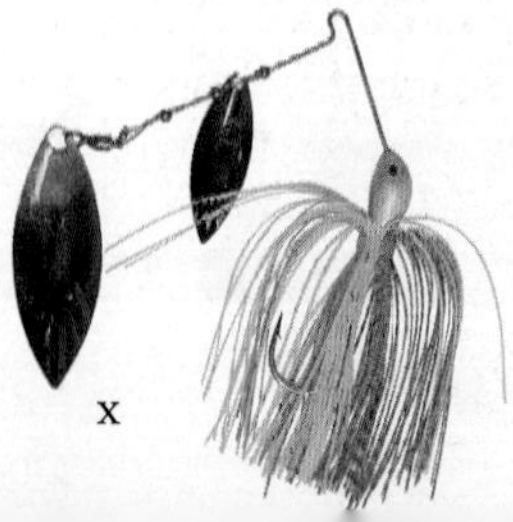

UNIT TWO

Nonfiction

UNIT THREE

Poetry

Theme 8 Inspirations

UNIT FOUR

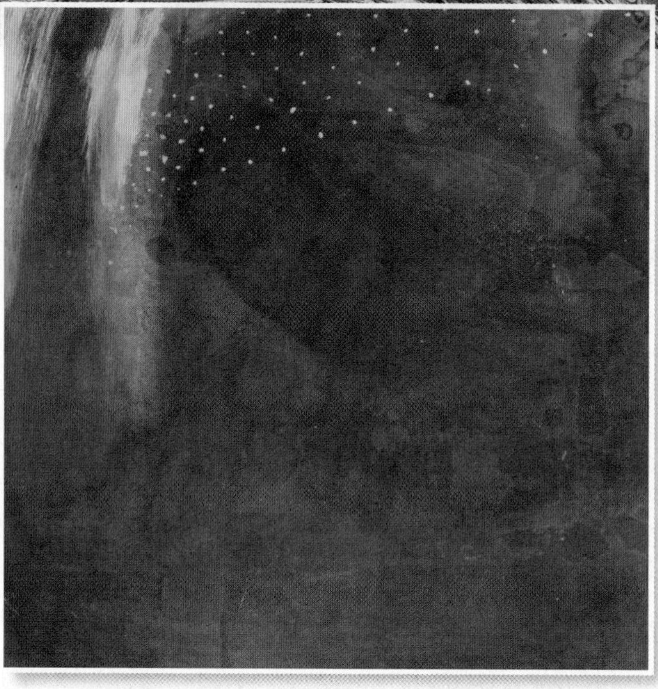

UNIT SIX

Science Fiction and Fantasy

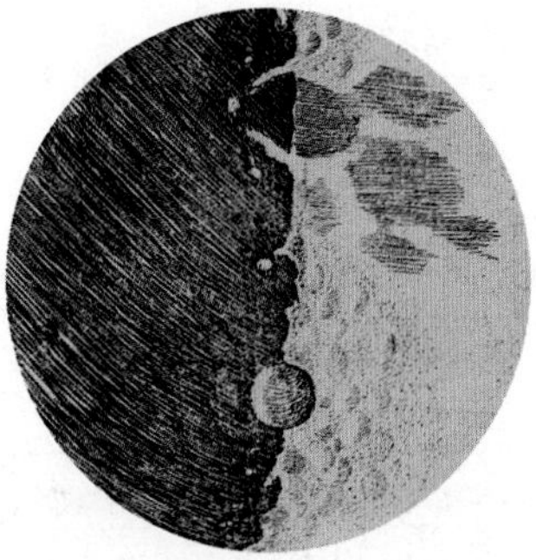

Reference Section

Features

MEDIA connection

COMPARING *selections*

Interdisciplinary Connection

Genre Focus

Active Reading Strategies

Literature FOCUS

Writing Workshop

Skills

Grammar Link

Listening, Speaking, and Viewing

Reading & Thinking Skills

Technology Skills

Vocabulary Skills

Writing Skills

Skill Minilessons

GRAMMAR AND LANGUAGE

READING AND THINKING

VOCABULARY

Enter: The Muse, 1994. Debby West. Acrylic on canvas, 30 x 24 in. Gallery Contemporanea, Jacksonville, FL.

UNIT ONE

The Short Story

"In the country of the story the writer is king."

—Shirley Jackson

Genre Focus

The Short Story

When you talk about sports, you use sporting language. You discuss penalty shots, goaltending, touchbacks, power serves, and use other terms that relate to sports. Literature analysis has its own language, too, and learning to use it will help you see how short stories are put together and what makes them work.

A short story is a short piece of fiction containing elements described in the chart on these pages. Look at how a story you probably already know, the children's tale "Little Red Riding Hood," can be analyzed in terms of these elements.

● For more on elements of short stories, see **Literary Terms Handbook,** pp. R1–R13.

SHORT STORY ELEMENTS	MODEL: "Little Red Riding Hood"
Setting Setting is the time and place of the story's action. Setting includes ideas, customs, values, and beliefs.	The story takes place in the woods a long time ago.
Characters Characters are the actors in a story's plot. They can be people, animals, or whatever the writer chooses. ● The **protagonist** is the main character. ● The **antagonist** is in conflict with the main character. Not all stories have antagonists.	The characters are Little Red Riding Hood, the big bad wolf, the grandmother, and the woodsman. **protagonist:** Little Red Riding Hood **antagonist:** the big bad wolf
Point of View Point of view refers to the relationship of the **narrator,** or storyteller, to the story. ● In **first-person point of view,** the narrator is a character in the story, referred to as "I." ● In **third-person limited point of view,** the narrator reveals the thoughts of only one character, referring to that character as "he" or "she." ● In **third-person omniscient point of view,** the narrator knows everything about the story's events and reveals the thoughts of all the characters.	"Little Red Riding Hood" is traditionally told from the **third-person omniscient point of view:** the narrator explains what Little Red Riding Hood is doing as well as what is happening to her and to her grandmother.

Theme

Theme is the central idea or message of a story, often a perception about life or human nature.

- **Stated themes** are directly presented in a story.
- **Implied themes** must be inferred by considering all the elements of a story and asking what message about life is conveyed.

The theme of "Little Red Riding Hood" is **implied.** While the narrator does not directly state a message, the reader can infer it: be suspicious of things (and people) that do not appear the way they should.

Plot

Plot is the sequence of events in a story. Each event causes or leads to the next. Plot is often created through **conflict,** a struggle between opposing forces.

- An **external conflict** is one between a character and an outside force, such as another character, nature, society, or fate.
- An **internal conflict** takes place within the mind of a character who is torn between opposing feelings or between different courses of action.

In "Little Red Riding Hood," the conflict is **external**—Little Red Riding Hood versus the big bad wolf. The events that make up the plot of "Little Red Riding Hood" are shown in the diagram below.

Most plots develop in five stages.

- **Exposition** introduces the story's characters, setting, and conflict.
- **Rising action** occurs as complications, twists, or intensifications of the conflict occur.
- **Climax** is the emotional high point of the story.
- **Falling action** is the logical result of the climax.
- **Resolution** presents the final outcome of the story.

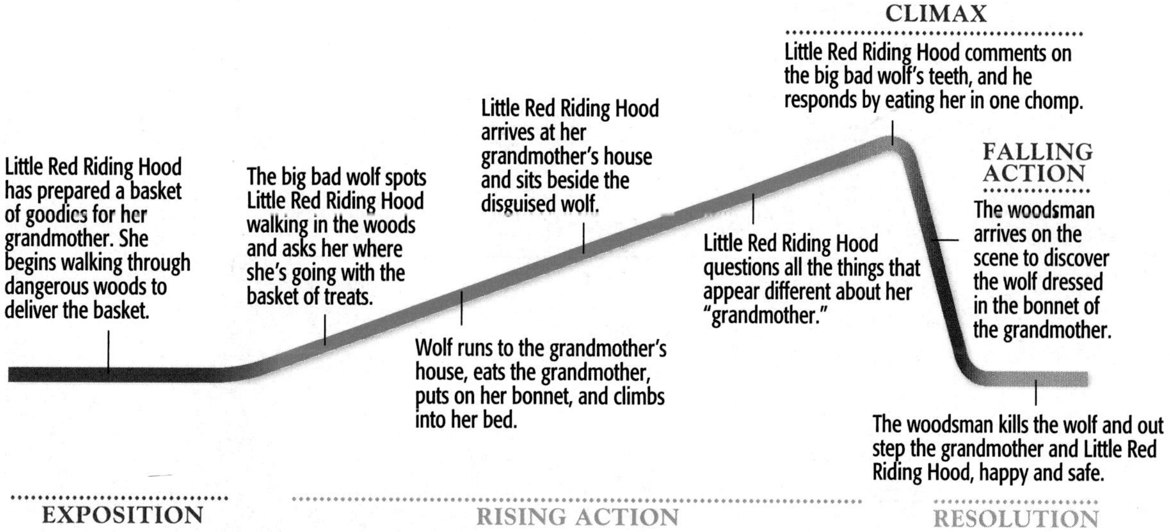

CLIMAX
Little Red Riding Hood comments on the big bad wolf's teeth, and he responds by eating her in one chomp.
Little Red Riding Hood has prepared a basket of goodies for her grandmother. She begins walking through dangerous woods to deliver the basket.
The big bad wolf spots Little Red Riding Hood walking in the woods and asks her where she's going with the basket of treats.
Little Red Riding Hood arrives at her grandmother's house and sits beside the disguised wolf.
Wolf runs to the grandmother's house, eats the grandmother, puts on her bonnet, and climbs into her bed.
Little Red Riding Hood questions all the things that appear different about her "grandmother."
FALLING ACTION
The woodsman arrives on the scene to discover the wolf dressed in the bonnet of the grandmother.
The woodsman kills the wolf and out step the grandmother and Little Red Riding Hood, happy and safe.
EXPOSITION
RISING ACTION
RESOLUTION

Active Reading Model

Active Reading Strategies

The Short Story

How can you get the most from your reading? Effective readers are active readers. As they read, they have conversations with themselves about the text; they get involved. Don't be a passive reader! Use the strategies below to help you read short stories actively and effectively.

● For more about related reading strategies, see **Reading Handbook,** pp. R78–R107.

PREDICT

Make educated guesses about what will happen next by combining clues in the story with what you already know. Predicting helps you anticipate events and stay alert to the less obvious parts of a story.

Say to yourself . . .

- I think the title might mean . . .
- I think this character is going to . . .
- *Now* I think he or she will . . .
- My first prediction doesn't match what I read. Now I think . . .

CONNECT

Draw parallels between the people, places, and events in the story and the people, events, and places in your own life.

Ask yourself . . .

- How would the main character act in my situation?
- How would I act in the main character's situation?
- When have I felt the same way as this character?
- What parts of my life does this remind me of?
- What other stories does this remind me of?

QUESTION

Ask yourself questions to help you clarify the story as you go along.

Ask yourself . . .

- Do I understand what I've read so far?
- Why did he or she say that?
- What's going on here?
- What does this mean?

VISUALIZE In your mind, form pictures of what is happening in the story. Pay attention to the details the writer gives you, and make them a part of your reading experience.

Ask yourself . . .
- How does this scene, character, or object look?
- Who is in this scene?
- Where are the characters in relation to one another and to their surroundings?

EVALUATE Form opinions and make judgments about the story while you are reading–not just after you've finished.

Ask yourself . . .
- Does this turn of events make sense?
- Is this character believable?
- What is particularly effective about this writer's style?
- Do I agree with this idea?

REVIEW Pause every page or two to think about your reading. Summarize events in a story or rephrase difficult language to help you understand and remember what you've read.

Say to yourself . . .
- So far, . . .
- In other words, . . .

RESPOND Respond *while* you are reading. React to different parts of the story.

Say to yourself . . .
- I like this character because . . .
- I'd like to ask the writer why . . .
- I wish I could see this place because . . .

Applying the Strategies

1. Read the next story, "The Gift of the Magi," using the Active Reading Model in the margins.
2. Choose a story you have not read and practice using all of these strategies. Write comments on stick-on notes and put them in the margins of the story as you read or take notes on a separate piece of paper.

Before You Read

The Gift of the Magi

Reading Focus

The nineteenth-century novelist George Eliot once wrote, "One must be poor to know the luxury of giving." What do you think she meant? Do you agree with her?

Discuss In a small group, discuss the quotation. You might begin by restating the quotation in your own words. Then share ideas about whether or not you agree with its message.

Setting a Purpose Read to learn how a young married couple discovers the true meaning of gift-giving.

Building Background

The Time and Place

This story takes place in New York City around 1900. Most of the action occurs in the main characters' dingy, inexpensive flat, or apartment. The story begins on the afternoon of Christmas Eve and ends shortly after 7:00 P.M. on the same day.

Did You Know?

According to the gospel of Matthew in the New Testament of the Bible, the Magi were the three wise men who came from the East to visit the newborn baby Jesus. The Magi brought precious gifts of gold, frankincense, and myrrh for the child. Over time, the Magi have come to be associated with the practice of giving gifts.

Vocabulary Preview

imputation (im′ pyə tā′ shən) *n.* an accusation; p. 7
parsimony (pär′ sə mō′ nē) *n.* stinginess; p. 7
instigate (in′ stə gāt′) *v.* to stir up or cause to happen; p. 7
depreciate (di prē′ shē āt′) *v.* to lessen the price or value of; p. 9
prudence (pro͞od′ əns) *n.* cautious, good judgment; p. 10
ravage (rav′ ij) *n.* a destructive action or its results; p. 10
coveted (kuv′ i təd) *adj.* desired strongly; wished for longingly; p. 13

Meet O. Henry

William Sydney Porter, who used the pen name O. Henry, published his first story while he was in jail. He had been convicted of embezzling money from the bank where he worked, some say in order to pay his dying wife's medical bills. O. Henry became a popular writer of short stories known for their plot twists and surprise endings. O. Henry's own life ended with a "twist"—his funeral was somehow scheduled in the same church at the same time as someone else's wedding! The O. Henry Award honors the authors of the best stories printed each year in American magazines.

O. Henry was born in 1862 and died in 1910. This story was published in the New York Sunday World *in 1905.*

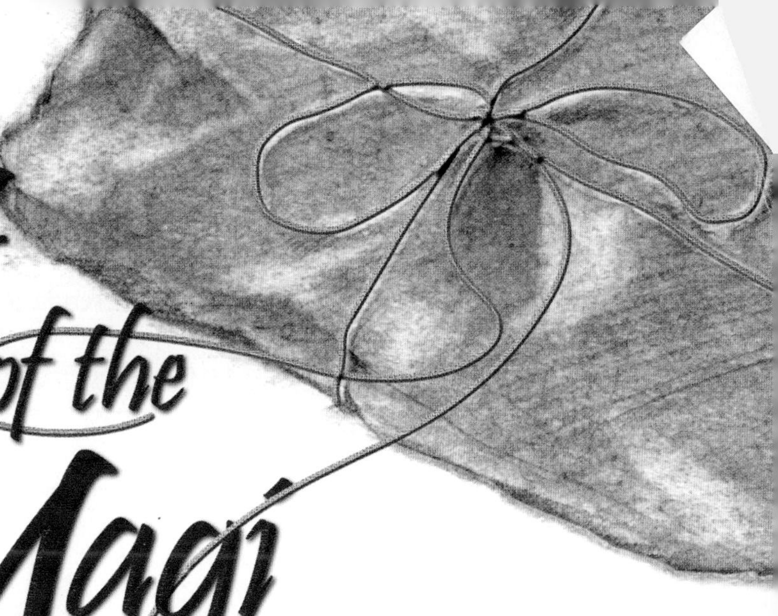

The Gift of the Magi

O. Henry

ONE DOLLAR AND EIGHTY-SEVEN CENTS. That was all. And sixty cents of it was in pennies. Pennies saved one and two at a time by bulldozing the grocer and the vegetable man and the butcher until one's cheeks burned with the silent imputation of parsimony that such close dealing implied. Three times Della counted it. One dollar and eighty-seven cents. And the next day would be Christmas.

There was clearly nothing to do but flop down on the shabby little couch and howl. So Della did it. Which instigates the moral reflection that life is made up of sobs, sniffles, and smiles, with sniffles predominating.

Active Reading Model

While the mistress of the home is gradually subsiding from the first stage to the second, take a look at the home. A furnished flat at $8 per week. It did not exactly beggar description, but it certainly had that word on the lookout for the mendicancy squad.[1]

In the vestibule below was a letter-box into which no letter would go, and an electric button from which no mortal finger could coax a ring. Also appertaining[2] thereunto was a card bearing the name "Mr. James Dillingham Young."

QUESTION

Why might the narrator be describing the vestibule?

1. O. Henry is making a play on words here. To *beggar* is to defy or go past the limits of something. A *mendicancy squad* consists of the authorities who deal with mendicants, or beggars.
2. Here, *appertaining* means "belonging or relating."

Vocabulary

imputation (im′ pyə tā′ shən) *n.* an accusation
parsimony (pär′ sə mō′ nē) *n.* stinginess
instigate (in′ stə gāt′) *v.* to stir up or cause to happen

Active Reading Model

REVIEW

What do you know about Jim and Della so far?

The "Dillingham" had been flung to the breeze during a former period of prosperity when its possessor was being paid $30 per week. Now, when the income was shrunk to $20, the letters of "Dillingham" looked blurred, as though they were thinking seriously of contracting to a modest and unassuming[3] D. But whenever Mr. James Dillingham Young came home and reached his flat above he was called "Jim" and greatly hugged by Mrs. James Dillingham Young, already introduced to you as Della. Which is all very good.

3. *Unassuming* means "not bold or boastful."

Woman at Her Toilet. Edgar Degas (1834–1917). Oil pastel on paper. The Hermitage, St. Petersburg, Russia.
Viewing the art: What do you think Della and this woman each think about having long hair?

Della finished her cry and attended to her cheeks with the powder rag. She stood by the window and looked out dully at a gray cat walking a gray fence in a gray backyard. Tomorrow would be Christmas Day, and she had only $1.87 with which to buy Jim a present. She had been saving every penny she could for months, with this result. Twenty dollars a week doesn't go far. Expenses had been greater than she had calculated. They always are. Only $1.87 to buy a present for Jim. Her Jim. Many a happy hour she had spent planning for something nice for him. Something fine and rare and sterling—something just a little bit near to being worthy of the honor of being owned by Jim.

There was a pier-glass[4] between the windows of the room. Perhaps you have seen a pier-glass in an $8 flat. A very thin and very agile person may, by observing his reflection in a rapid sequence of longitudinal strips, obtain a fairly accurate conception of his looks. Della, being slender, had mastered the art.

Suddenly she whirled from the window and stood before the glass. Her eyes were shining brilliantly, but her face had lost its color within twenty seconds. Rapidly she pulled down her hair and let it fall to its full length.

Now, there were two possessions of the James Dillingham Youngs in which they both took a mighty pride. One was Jim's gold watch that had been his father's and his grandfather's. The other was Della's hair. Had the Queen of Sheba lived in the flat across the airshaft, Della would have let her hair hang out the window some day to dry just to depreciate Her Majesty's jewels and gifts. Had King Solomon[5] been the janitor, with all his treasures piled up in the basement, Jim would have pulled out his watch every time he passed, just to see him pluck at his beard from envy.

So now Della's beautiful hair fell about her, rippling and shining like a cascade of brown waters. It reached below her knee and made itself almost a garment for her. And then she did it up again nervously and quickly. Once she faltered for a minute and stood still while a tear or two splashed on the worn red carpet.

On went her old brown jacket; on went her old brown hat. With a whirl of skirts and with the brilliant sparkle still in her eyes, she fluttered out the door and down the stairs to the street.

Where she stopped the sign read: "Mme. Sofronie.[6] Hair Goods of All Kinds." One flight up Della ran, and collected herself, panting. Madame, large, too white, chilly, hardly looked the "Sofronie."

Active Reading Model

VISUALIZE
What does the view from the window look like?

CONNECT
Of what things are you or your family most proud?

VISUALIZE
Stop and form a detailed mental image of Della and her beautiful, long hair.

PREDICT
What do you think Della is going to do?

4. A *pier-glass* (pēr′ glas) is a tall, narrow mirror designed to be hung between two windows.
5. The Bible says that the *Queen of Sheba* visited *King Solomon,* bearing gifts that included great quantities of gold, spices, and jewels. Solomon is famous as the wisest and wealthiest man of his time.
6. *Mme. Sofronie* (mə dam′ sō frō′ nē)

Vocabulary
depreciate (di prē′ shē āt′) *v.* to lessen the price or value of

Active Reading Model

RESPOND

How do you feel about Della and what she did for Jim?

"Will you buy my hair?" asked Della.

"I buy hair," said Madame. "Take yer hat off and let's have a sight at the looks of it."

Down rippled the brown cascade.

"Twenty dollars," said Madame, lifting the mass with a practiced hand.

"Give it to me quick," said Della.

Oh, and the next two hours tripped by on rosy wings. Forget the hashed[7] metaphor. She was ransacking the stores for Jim's present.

She found it at last. It surely had been made for Jim and no one else. There was no other like it in any of the stores, and she had turned all of them inside out. It was a platinum fob chain simple and chaste[8] in design, properly proclaiming its value by substance alone and not by meretricious[9] ornamentation—as all good things should do. It was even worthy of The Watch. As soon as she saw it she knew that it must be Jim's. It was like him. Quietness and value—the description applied to both. Twenty-one dollars they took from her for it, and she hurried home with the 87 cents. With that chain on his watch Jim might be properly anxious about the time in any company. Grand as the watch was, he sometimes looked at it on the sly on account of the old leather strap that he used in place of a chain.

Did You Know?
A *fob chain* is attached to a pocket watch and worn hanging from a pocket.

When Della reached home her intoxication gave way a little to prudence and reason. She got out her curling irons and lighted the gas and went to work repairing the ravages made by generosity added to love. Which is always a tremendous task, dear friends—a mammoth task.

Within forty minutes her head was covered with tiny, close-lying curls that made her look wonderfully like a truant schoolboy. She looked at her reflection in the mirror long, carefully, and critically.

"If Jim doesn't kill me," she said to herself, "before he takes a second look at me, he'll say I look like a Coney Island[10] chorus girl. But what could I do—oh! what could I do with a dollar and eighty-seven cents?"

7. O. Henry pokes fun at himself here. His metaphor is *hashed,* or mixed, because it combines parts of the familiar phrases "rose-colored glasses" and "on gossamer wings."
8. Here, *chaste* means modest.
9. *Meretricious* means cheap, showy.
10. *Coney Island* is a famous beach and amusement park in Brooklyn, New York.

Vocabulary
prudence (pro͞od′ əns) *n.* cautious, good judgment
ravage (rav′ ij) *n.* a destructive action or its results

Active Reading Model

At 7 o'clock the coffee was made and the frying pan was on the back of the stove hot and ready to cook the chops.

Jim was never late. Della doubled the fob chain in her hand and sat on the corner of the table near the door that he always entered. Then she heard his step on the stair away down on the first flight, and she turned white for just a moment. She had a habit of saying little silent prayers about the simplest everyday things, and now she whispered: "Please God, make him think I am still pretty."

The door opened and Jim stepped in and closed it. He looked thin and very serious. Poor fellow, he was only twenty-two—and to be burdened with a family! He needed a new overcoat and he was without gloves.

Jim stopped inside the door, as immovable as a setter at the scent of quail. His eyes were fixed upon Della, and there was an expression in them that she could not read, and it terrified her. It was not anger, nor surprise, nor disapproval, nor horror, nor any of the sentiments that she had been prepared for. He simply stared at her fixedly with that peculiar expression on his face.

QUESTION
What do you think Jim might be thinking?

Della wriggled off the table and went for him.

"Jim, darling," she cried, "don't look at me that way. I had my hair cut off and sold it because I couldn't have lived through Christmas without giving you a present. It'll grow out again—you won't mind, will you? I just had to do it. My hair grows awfully fast. Say 'Merry Christmas!' Jim, and let's be happy. You don't know what a nice—what a beautiful, nice gift I've got for you."

"You've cut off your hair?" asked Jim, laboriously, as if he had not arrived at that patent[11] fact yet even after the hardest mental labor.

CONNECT
Think about a time when you were nervous about the way you looked. What happened?

"Cut it off and sold it," said Della. "Don't you like me just as well, anyhow? I'm me without my hair, ain't I?"

Jim looked about the room curiously.

"You say your hair is gone?" he said, with an air almost of idiocy.

"You needn't look for it," said Della. "It's sold, I tell you—sold and gone, too. It's Christmas Eve, boy. Be good to me, for it went for you. Maybe the hairs of my head were numbered," she went on with a sudden serious sweetness, "but nobody could ever count my love for you. Shall I put the chops on, Jim?"

Out of his trance Jim seemed quickly to wake. He enfolded his Della. For ten seconds let us regard with discreet scrutiny some inconsequential object in the other direction.[12] Eight dollars a week or a million a

11. Here, Jim tries to grasp the obvious *(patent)* fact that Della has cut her hair.
12. *[For ten seconds . . . other direction.]* O. Henry suggests that we give the couple privacy by examining some object on the other side of the room, as if we were physically in the couple's home.

Active Reading Model

PREDICT

What do you think will be in the package?

year—what is the difference? A mathematician or a wit would give you the wrong answer. The Magi brought valuable gifts, but that was not among them. This dark assertion will be illuminated later on.[13]

Jim drew a package from his overcoat pocket and threw it upon the table.

"Don't make any mistake, Dell," he said, "about me. I don't think there's anything in the way of a haircut or a shave or a shampoo that could make me like my girl any less. But if you'll unwrap that package you may see why you had me going a while at first."

White fingers and nimble tore at the string and paper. And then an ecstatic scream of joy; and then, alas! a quick feminine change to hysterical tears and wails, necessitating the immediate employment of all the comforting powers of the lord of the flat.

13. *[This dark assertion . . . later on.]* O. Henry promises to explain, later, his statement in the preceding sentence.

Cross Streets of New York, 1899. Everett Shinn. Charcoal, watercolor, pastel, white chalk, and Chinese white on paper, 21½ x 29¼ in. Corcoran Gallery of Art, Washington, DC.

Viewing the art: Look closely at this piece of art. How does the mood of this painting compare with the mood of "The Gift of the Magi"?

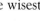

Did You Know?
This *comb* is designed both to fasten and adorn a woman's hair. Ordinary combs are used only to smooth and arrange it.

Active Reading Model

For there lay The Combs—the set of combs, side and back, that Della had worshipped for long in a Broadway window. Beautiful combs, pure tortoise shell, with jewelled rims—just the shade to wear in the beautiful vanished hair. They were expensive combs, she knew, and her heart had simply craved and yearned over them without the least hope of possession. And now, they were hers, but the tresses that should have adorned the coveted adornments were gone.

But she hugged them to her bosom, and at length she was able to look up with dim eyes and a smile and say: "My hair grows so fast, Jim!"

QUESTION
Why does Della say this?

And then Della leaped up like a little singed cat and cried, "Oh, oh!"

Jim had not yet seen his beautiful present. She held it out to him eagerly upon her open palm. The dull precious metal seemed to flash with a reflection of her bright and ardent spirit.

"Isn't it a dandy, Jim? I hunted all over town to find it. You'll have to look at the time a hundred times a day now. Give me your watch. I want to see how it looks on it."

Instead of obeying, Jim tumbled down on the couch and put his hands under the back of his head and smiled.

"Dell," said he, "let's put our Christmas presents away and keep 'em a while. They're too nice to use just at present. I sold the watch to get the money to buy your combs. And now suppose you put the chops on."

REVIEW
Take a moment to summarize what has happened in the story.

The Magi, as you know, were wise men—wonderfully wise men—who brought gifts to the Babe in the manger. They invented the art of giving Christmas presents. Being wise, their gifts were no doubt wise ones, possibly bearing the privilege of exchange in case of duplication. And here I have lamely related to you the uneventful chronicle of two foolish children in a flat who most unwisely sacrificed for each other the greatest treasures of their house. But in a last word to the wise of these days let it be said that of all who give gifts these two were the wisest. Of all who give and receive gifts, such as they are wisest. Everywhere they are wisest. They are the Magi.

EVALUATE
The narrator says that people like Jim and Della are the wisest of gift-givers. Do you agree or disagree? Why?

Vocabulary
coveted (kuv′ i təd) *adj.* desired strongly; wished for longingly

Responding to Literature

Personal Response

Were you surprised by the outcome of the story? Explain why or why not.

Active Reading Response

Look back at the kinds of strategies described in the Active Reading Model notes on pages 4 and 5. Which strategy do you use most often? Find three places in the story where you could apply it.

Analyzing Literature

Recall

1. What is Della doing at the beginning of the story and why?
2. Which possessions do Della and Jim value most?
3. What is Jim's initial reaction to Della when he arrives home?
4. What gifts do the couple give each other?
5. According to the narrator, who were the Magi?

Interpret

6. This story begins on Christmas Eve. Why is this aspect of **setting** so important to the story? (See Literary Terms Handbook, page R11.)
7. What do Della's and Jim's sacrifices tell you about their relationship?
8. Della compares the watch chain to Jim: "Quietness and value–the description applied to both." Does this description apply to Jim when he enters the flat? Why?
9. What is both wonderful and terrible about each gift? Use details from the story to explain the **irony** of the situation. (See Literary Terms Handbook, page R7.)
10. Why might the narrator refer to Della and Jim as the Magi?

Evaluate and Connect

11. What does this story say to you about giving gifts?
12. During O. Henry's time, his stories were praised for their surprise endings and plot twists, but later generations of readers criticized them. What is your opinion of the surprise ending in this story? Explain your answer.
13. If you could give Della and Jim some advice, what might you tell them?
14. Do you think the story's message is valuable to today's readers? Why or why not?
15. This is a story that many people remember for a long time after they read it. In your opinion, what makes it so memorable?

Literary **ELEMENTS**

Point of View

Point of view refers to the relationship of the narrator to the story. This story uses the **third-person omniscient point of view,** which means that the narrator is not a character in the story, but someone who stands outside the story and comments on the action. A third-person omniscient narrator knows everything about the characters and the events and may reveal details that the characters themselves could not reveal.

1. What does the narrator know that the characters don't know? Cite specific lines from the story as evidence.
2. The narrator comments on the characters and events in this story. How would the story change if the narrator were not to comment?
3. What is the narrator's opinion of the characters and their actions? Use details from the story to support your answer.

- See **Literary Terms Handbook,** p. R10.

Literature and Writing

Writing About Literature

Exploring the Theme Theme is the main idea of a work of literature, often a perception about life or human nature. With a partner, discuss the theme of "The Gift of the Magi." Write the theme in your own words across the top of a sheet of notebook paper. Then work together to write an explanation of how this theme is made clear through the words and actions of the main characters.

Personal Writing

Changing Your Mind? Think about your response to the Reading Focus on page 6. Now that you have read this story, have you changed your mind about what the quotation by George Eliot might mean? Has the story helped you better understand the quotation? Explain your answer in your journal.

Extending Your Response

Literature Groups

Do You Agree? The narrator contradicts himself at the end of the story, saying first, "And here I have lamely related to you the uneventful chronicle of two foolish children in a flat who most unwisely sacrificed for each other the greatest treasures of their house." Then he says, "Let it be said that of all who give gifts these two were the wisest. Of all who give and receive gifts, such as they are wisest." With your group, discuss which of these statements is closer to your views about Della and Jim. Do you think there might be truth in both statements? Share your opinions with the rest of your classmates.

Listening and Speaking

What They Did for Love With a partner, interview several adults to find out about the greatest sacrifices they ever made for love. Ask for their permission to tape the stories. Then select your favorite and play it for other pairs.

Interdisciplinary Activity

Mathematics: Adding It Up O. Henry wrote: "One dollar and eighty-seven cents. . . . And 60 cents of it was in pennies." Is this mathematically possible? When O. Henry wrote this story in 1905, two- and three-cent coins were still in use. Can you think of three different variations of old-fashioned coins and bills that would add up to O. Henry's total?

Reading Further

If you'd like to read more by O. Henry, you might enjoy these works:

Short Stories: "A Retrieved Reformation," which can be found in the collection *41 Stories,* shows how love can reform a criminal.

"The Cop and the Anthem" and "The Last Leaf," from the collection *The Best Short Stories of O. Henry,* both feature beloved, simple characters and twisting plots.

Viewing: *The Gift of Love* is a film adaptation of "The Gift of the Magi."

Save your work for your portfolio.

Skill Minilessons

GRAMMAR AND LANGUAGE • Varying Sentence Structure

One way that O. Henry creates interest is by varying his sentences. He uses long and short sentences; complex, simple, and compound sentences; sentences with unexpected word order; and even sentence fragments. Note how varied the sentences are in this passage: "As soon as she saw it she knew that it must be Jim's. It was like him. Quietness and value–the description applied to both. Twenty-one dollars they took from her for it, and she hurried home with the 87 cents."

PRACTICE Rewrite the following passage. Vary the sentences.

> You can give extra-special gifts. Extra-special gifts don't have to cost a lot of money. These gifts come from the heart. They do have a cost. They may require sacrifice. They show your love.

APPLY Review a piece of your writing. Do any sections seem dull or flat? Try rewriting them using varied sentence structure.

● For more about sentences, see **Language Handbook,** p. R42.

READING AND THINKING • Asking Questions

"The Gift of the Magi" includes some unusual vocabulary and complex sentence structures that can make the story difficult to understand. Asking yourself questions as you read, however, can help you clarify the story's meaning. Stop and ask questions such as: "What is happening now?" and "What does this mean?" When you're not sure of the answers, you can use any or all of the following strategies: you can look up unfamiliar words in a dictionary, restate a sentence in your own words, or reread difficult passages.

PRACTICE Write questions you might ask yourself–and strategies for answering them–to check your understanding of this sentence from the story: "It was a platinum fob chain simple and chaste in design, properly proclaiming its value by substance alone and not by meretricious ornamentation–as all good things should do."

APPLY Reread the story, applying the questioning strategy as you go. Jot down a list of your questions.

● For more about related reading strategies, see **Reading Handbook,** pp. R78–R107.

VOCABULARY • Unlocking Meaning

Coming across a new word can be like dealing with algebra, crossword puzzles, and life. You use what you know to figure out what you don't know. For example, since you know that *ravage* can be a noun that means "a destructive action or its results," you can conclude that as a verb it means "to destroy violently." Also, the noun *ravager* means "violent destroyer."

An unfamiliar word may have no resemblance to a word you already know. To determine its meaning, you can rely on context clues, look up the word in a dictionary, or ask someone for help. Sometimes, however, a new word is just another form of a familiar one or one that shares a root with a word you know. In these situations, it is helpful to use the knowledge you already have.

PRACTICE Use what you know about the vocabulary words in "The Gift of the Magi" to figure out what each word in the left column means. Match each to its meaning.

1. covetous	a. sensible and careful
2. depreciation	b. one who urges or causes an action
3. instigator	c. a decrease in the value of something
4. impute	d. strongly desiring what belongs to another
5. prudent	e. to consider to be guilty of; blame

Theme 1 Matters of Life and Death

Danger wears numerous faces and threatens us in many ways—our pride, our happiness, our safety, even our lives can be at stake. The selections in this theme examine some of the ways people face their fears about life and death, both real and imagined. Have you ever encountered death? If so, how did the experience change the way you look at life? How did it change your hopes and fears?

THEME PROJECTS

Listening and Speaking

Pitch a Movie Films often deal with life or death incidents. If you made a movie, what kind of drama would you want to depict?

1. Create an idea for a movie about a life or death situation, using the characters, plot, or setting from at least two stories in this theme for inspiration.
2. Prepare to convince others that your idea is a good one by outlining the plot of the movie, describing where and how it will be filmed, and compiling a cast of characters.
3. Present your ideas to the class as you might present them to a film-studio president.

Interdisciplinary Project

Art Sometimes, worlds of meaning can be expressed in a single moment.

1. Consider the moment in each story that best conveys an attitude about life or death.
2. Choose the moment that seems most meaningful to you. Reread the story in which it occurs, visualizing the action and physical details.
3. Make a three-dimensional model of that moment, representing as accurately as possible the setting of the story, the appearance of the characters, and the mood of the scene.

Not Drowned, 1984. Maria Chevska. Oil on canvas, 91.5 x 76 cm. Collection of the artist.

Before You Read

The Open Window

Reading Focus

People often make assumptions about others on the basis of their first impressions. Has your first impression of someone ever turned out to be wrong?

Quickwrite Write about a time when you were mistaken about a first impression. Describe the assumptions you made the first time you met someone, and tell what you learned about him or her later on.

Setting a Purpose Read to find out what happens when two characters act on their first impressions of each other.

Building Background

The Time and Place
This story takes place in the early 1900s, at an English country house set on an estate with hunting grounds. It begins on a late October afternoon and ends at twilight the same day.

Did You Know?
At the time of this story, hunting was a popular amusement among the upper classes. In "The Open Window," the men are hunting snipe, which are wetland game birds. Bird dogs, such as spaniels, were brought along on a hunt to flush out birds resting in the brush and then to retrieve the felled birds.

Vocabulary Preview

self-possessed (self′ pə zest′) *adj.* in control of oneself; composed; p. 19
duly (do͞o′ lē) *adv.* rightfully; suitably; p. 19
moor (moor) *n.* a tract of open, rolling, wild land, often having marshes; p. 20
infirmity (in fur′ mə tē) *n.* a weakness or ailment; p. 20
imminent (im′ ə nənt) *adj.* likely to happen soon; p. 21

Meet Saki

A master of surprise, H. H. Munro even took a rather surprising pen name when he chose the single name *Saki* (sä′ kē). Full of cleverness and wit, his stories make readers both laugh and cringe as they read about the deceptions and cruelties that supposedly civilized people inflict on one another. In 1914 Saki joined the army to fight in World War I. He said that he was glad to be in the trenches, so far from "all the thousand and one horrors of civilization." Saki's stories and three novels have been published in the volume *The Complete Works of Saki*.

H. H. Munro was born in 1870 in Burma, lived in England, and was killed in France in 1916 while fighting in World War I. This story was first published in Beasts and Super-Beasts *in 1914.*

THE OPEN WINDOW

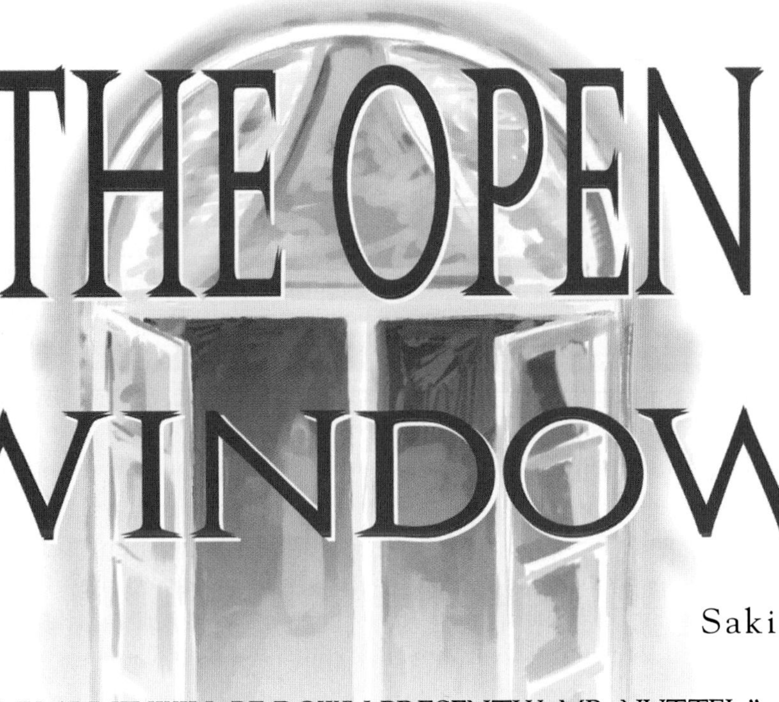

Saki

"MY AUNT WILL BE DOWN PRESENTLY, MR. NUTTEL," said a very self-possessed young lady of fifteen; "in the meantime you must try and put up with me."

Framton Nuttel endeavored to say the correct something which should duly flatter the niece of the moment without unduly discounting the aunt that was to come. Privately he doubted more than ever whether these formal visits on a succession of total strangers would do much towards helping the nerve cure which he was supposed to be undergoing.

"I know how it will be," his sister had said when he was preparing to migrate to this rural retreat; "you will bury yourself down there and not speak to a living soul, and your nerves will be worse than ever from moping. I shall just give you letters of introduction to all the people I know there. Some of them, as far as I can remember, were quite nice."

Framton wondered whether Mrs. Sappleton, the lady to whom he was presenting one of the letters of introduction, came into the nice division.

"Do you know many of the people round here?" asked the niece, when she judged that they had had sufficient silent communion.

"Hardly a soul," said Framton. "My sister was staying here, at the rectory,[1] you know, some four years ago, and she gave me letters of introduction to some of the people here."

He made the last statement in a tone of distinct regret.

"Then you know practically nothing about my aunt?" pursued the self-possessed young lady.

"Only her name and address," admitted the caller. He was wondering whether Mrs. Sappleton was in the married or widowed state. An undefinable something about the room seemed to suggest masculine habitation.

"Her great tragedy happened just three years ago," said the child; "that would be since your sister's time."

1. A *rectory* is the house in which a priest or minister lives.

Vocabulary

self-possessed (self′ pə zest′) *adj.* in control of oneself; composed

duly (do͞o′ lē) *adv.* rightfully; suitably

"Her tragedy?" asked Framton; somehow in this restful country spot tragedies seemed out of place.

"You may wonder why we keep that window wide open on an October afternoon," said the niece, indicating a large French window[2] that opened on to a lawn.

"It is quite warm for the time of the year," said Framton; "but has that window got anything to do with the tragedy?"

"Out through that window, three years ago to a day, her husband and her two young brothers went off for their day's shooting. They never came back. In crossing the moor to their favorite snipe-shooting ground they were all three engulfed in a treacherous piece of bog. It had been that dreadful wet summer, you know, and places that were safe in other years gave way suddenly without warning. Their bodies were never recovered. That was the dreadful part of it." Here the child's voice lost its self-possessed note and became falteringly human. "Poor aunt always thinks that they will come back some day, they and the little brown spaniel that was lost with them, and walk in at that window just as they used to do. That is why the window is kept open every evening till it is quite dusk. Poor dear aunt, she has often told me how they went out, her husband with his white waterproof coat over his arm, and Ronnie, her youngest brother, singing, 'Bertie, why do you bound?' as he always did to tease her, because she said it got on her nerves. Do you know, sometimes on still, quiet evenings like this, I almost get a creepy feeling that they will all walk in through that window—"

She broke off with a little shudder. It was a relief to Framton when the aunt bustled into the room with a whirl of apologies for being late in making her appearance.

"I hope Vera has been amusing you?" she said.

"She has been very interesting," said Framton.

"I hope you don't mind the open window," said Mrs. Sappleton briskly; "my husband and brothers will be home directly from shooting, and they always come in this way. They've been out for snipe in the marshes today, so they'll make a fine mess over my poor carpets. So like you men-folk, isn't it?"

She rattled on cheerfully about the shooting and the scarcity of birds, and the prospects for duck in the winter. To Framton it was all purely horrible. He made a desperate but only partially successful effort to turn the talk on to a less ghastly topic; he was conscious that his hostess was giving him only a fragment of her attention, and her eyes were constantly straying past him to the open window and the lawn beyond. It was certainly an unfortunate coincidence that he should have paid his visit on this tragic anniversary.

"The doctors agree in ordering me complete rest, an absence of mental excitement, and avoidance of anything in the nature of violent physical exercise," announced Framton, who labored under the tolerably wide-spread delusion that total strangers and chance acquaintances are hungry for the least detail of one's ailments and infirmities, their cause and cure. "On the matter of diet they are not so much in agreement," he continued.

"No?" said Mrs. Sappleton, in a voice which only replaced a yawn at the last moment. Then she suddenly brightened into

2. A *French window* is a pair of door-like windows hinged at opposite sides and opening in the middle.

Vocabulary

moor (moor) *n.* a tract of open, rolling, wild land, often having marshes

infirmity (in fur′ mə tē) *n.* a weakness or ailment

alert attention—but not to what Framton was saying.

"Here they are at last!" she cried. "Just in time for tea, and don't they look as if they were muddy up to the eyes!"

Framton shivered slightly and turned towards the niece with a look intended to convey sympathetic comprehension. The child was staring out through the open window with dazed horror in her eyes. In a chill shock of nameless fear Framton swung round in his seat and looked in the same direction.

In the deepening twilight three figures were walking across the lawn towards the window; they all carried guns under their arms, and one of them was additionally burdened with a white coat hung over his shoulders. A tired brown spaniel kept close at their heels. Noiselessly they neared the house, and then a hoarse young voice chanted out of the dusk: "I said, Bertie, why do you bound?"

Framton grabbed wildly at his stick and hat; the hall door, the gravel drive, and the front gate were dimly noted stages in his headlong retreat. A cyclist coming along the road had to run into the hedge to avoid imminent collision.

"Here we are, my dear," said the bearer of the white mackintosh,[3] coming in through the window; "fairly muddy, but most of it's dry. Who was that who bolted out as we came up?"

"A most extraordinary man, a Mr. Nuttel," said Mrs. Sappleton; "could only talk about his illnesses, and dashed off without a word of good-bye or apology when you arrived. One would think he had seen a ghost."

"I expect it was the spaniel," said the niece calmly; "he told me he had a horror of dogs. He was once hunted into a cemetery somewhere on the banks of the Ganges by a pack of pariah[4] dogs, and had to spend the night in a newly dug grave with the creatures snarling and grinning and foaming just above him. Enough to make any one lose their nerve."

Romance[5] at short notice was her specialty.

Gabrielle Vien as a Young Girl, 1893. Armand Seguin. Oil on canvas, 88 x 115 cm. Musée d'Orsay, Paris.

Viewing the painting: What does this girl's facial expression convey? What qualities might the girl in this painting share with the niece in the story?

3. A *mackintosh* is a heavy-duty raincoat.

4. The *Ganges* is a river in northern India. A *pariah* is one who is shunned or despised by others. In India, where dogs are not highly regarded, packs of wild dogs are considered pariahs.

5. Here, *romance* means "tales of extraordinary or mysterious events."

Vocabulary

imminent (im′ ə nənt) *adj.* likely to happen soon

Responding to Literature

Personal Response

How did you respond to the main characters in the story? Describe your reactions in your journal.

Analyzing Literature

Recall

1. Why does Framton Nuttel visit Mrs. Sappleton?
2. What does Vera learn about Mr. Nuttel before she begins her story?
3. What "tragedy" does Vera describe?
4. What causes Mr. Nuttel to run from Mrs. Sappleton's house?
5. What do you find out about Vera at the end of the story?

Interpret

6. What makes Mr. Nuttel a rather unusual visitor? Use details from the story to describe him.
7. How does Vera use the information she learns about Mr. Nuttel to her advantage?
8. What makes Mr. Nuttel especially susceptible to Vera's story?
9. Describe the author's **tone** in the scene of Mr. Nuttel's "headlong retreat." What words or events help create the tone? (See Literary Terms Handbook, page R13.)
10. What three words do you think best describe Vera? Give reasons for your answer.

Evaluate and Connect

11. What was your first impression of Vera? Did it change? Compare your experience of learning about Vera with the experience you described in the Reading Focus on page 18.
12. Would you describe this story as humorous? Why or why not? Use details or events from the story to support your opinion.
13. The author subtly plays with the theme of hunting in this story. How is Vera like a hunter and Mr. Nuttel like her prey?
14. Would you like to be friends with Vera? Why or why not?
15. **Theme Connections** How does this story connect to the theme of this section–"Matters of Life and Death"?

Literary ELEMENTS

Plot

The sequence of events in a story is called its **plot.** The plot begins with the **exposition,** or the introduction of the characters, the setting, and the conflict. **Rising action** occurs as complications, twists, or intensifications of the conflict occur. This action leads up to the **climax,** or emotional high point of the story. The climax gives way rapidly to its logical result in the **falling action,** and finally to the **resolution,** in which the final outcome is revealed.

1. Summarize the exposition and rising action of "The Open Window."
2. What is the climax of the story? How do you know?
3. Explain how the author intended to surprise his readers in the story's resolution. Was the ending effective? Why or why not?

- See **Literary Terms Handbook,** p. R9.

Literary Criticism

"The cruelty is certainly there," writes critic Elizabeth Drew about Saki's stories, "but it has nothing perverted or pathological about it. . . . It is the genial heartlessness of the normal child, whose fantasies take no account of adult standards of human behavior." In a small group, discuss whether this quotation applies to "The Open Window" and to Vera.

Literature and Writing

Writing About Literature

Examining Irony Situational irony exists when the outcome of a situation is the opposite of someone's expectations. Review the conversation Vera has with Mr. Nuttel before Mrs. Sappleton enters the room. Then write a paragraph explaining what is particularly ironic about that scene.

Creative Writing

Once Upon a Time . . . Take ten minutes or so to write a story about the next person who might walk through the door of your classroom. Explain who will walk in; then explore what will happen next and describe the effect the person will have on the class. Check that your story is believable by sharing it with a partner.

Extending Your Response

Literature Groups

Discussing Theme Who or what is this story really about? Is it about Framton Nuttel? Vera? the open window? Or is it about something else altogether? Discuss your ideas about the story's theme with your group. Together, search for details in the story that help you decide on the theme. Then compare your ideas with those of other groups.

Internet Connection

Hunting Down Facts Hunting remains a popular pastime in today's society. What laws govern hunting in your state? When is the hunting season? Which animals can be hunted and which are protected? Use a search engine to find Web sites and other on-line documents devoted to some of these aspects of hunting.

Performing

Gossip! With a partner, role-play a scene between Vera and one of her close friends. Vera should tell her friend about how she amused herself at Framton Nuttel's expense. Be sure to explore both Vera's feelings about the situation and her friend's reaction to the news. Alternatively, you might role-play a conversation between Framton Nuttel and his sister after the events of the story. What will he tell her? How will she react?

Save your work for your portfolio.

Skill Minilesson

VOCABULARY • Compound Words

The word *chalkboard* is a compound word, a word made up of two other words with separate and distinct meanings. You probably know what the compound means because you know the meaning of its parts. You can determine the meaning of many, not all, compound words by thinking about the meaning of their parts. For example, if you are self-possessed, you possess (and, therefore, control) yourself. Self-discipline is discipline applied to oneself.

• For more about compound words, see **Language Handbook,** Spelling, p. R56.

PRACTICE Use your knowledge of the words that form the compounds in the left column to match each with its definition.

1. breakneck
2. self-made
3. lackluster
4. slide fastener
5. rubberneck

a. dull
b. a device like a zipper
c. extremely dangerous
d. to look all around
e. successful through one's own efforts

Before You Read

Before the End of Summer

Reading Focus

Was there something you were afraid of when you were younger that no longer frightens you? Or perhaps there was an event you dreaded, such as giving a speech or going to a funeral, that turned out to be not as bad as you had thought it would be.

Sharing Experiences With a partner, discuss your childhood fear and what helped you overcome it. If you are discussing a particular event, explore why the event turned out to be better than you had anticipated.

Setting a Purpose Read to discover how a boy learns to cope with serious fears.

Meet Grant Moss Jr.

Like the main character in his story, Grant Moss Jr. was a quiet boy who grew up in the small southern town of Winchester, Tennessee. His aunt Luella, a dedicated teacher, influenced him greatly. Despite the fact that he published numerous stories, Moss later described himself primarily as a teacher, not a writer. He taught college English for twenty-two years. Afterwards, he retired to his hometown, where he lived into his eighties.

Grant Moss Jr. was born in 1910. This story, his first, was originally published in the New Yorker *magazine in 1960.*

Building Background

The Time and Place

"Before the End of Summer" takes place in the early 1900s in a rural farming community.

Did You Know?

- At the time of the story, many homes had no electricity or running water. Telephones and cars were not common, and television did not yet exist. Houses were far apart, and neighbors depended on one another for help, information, and company. Children in these areas had not only a great amount of personal freedom but also much responsibility. Children often had to care for younger brothers and sisters, tend the livestock, and do other household chores.
- In the early 1900s, African Americans had limited employment opportunities. As a result, many worked in the homes or on the land of wealthier white families. Friends or relatives cared for their children, since daycare did not exist. Parents who were day workers returned to their children each night, but parents who worked as live-in help saw their children only on their days off.

Vocabulary Preview

rawboned (rô′ bōnd′) *adj.* thin or very lean; p. 29
plait (plāt) *n.* a braid, as of hair; p. 31
sultrier (sul′ trē ər) *adj.* more hot and humid; p. 33

Before the End of Summer

Grant Moss Jr.

When Dr. Frazier came, Bennie's grandmother told him to run down to the spring and wade in the stream that flowed from it across the pasture field to Mr. Charley Miller's pond, or play under the big oak tree that stood between her field and Mr. Charley Miller's. He started along the path, but when he was about midway to the spring he stopped. He had waded in the stream and caught minnows all that morning. He had played under the oak tree all yesterday afternoon. He had asked his grandmother to let him walk the mile and a half down the road to James and Robert Lee Stewart's to play, but she had not let him go. There was nothing he wanted to do alone. He wanted someone to play with. He turned and went back and crept under the window of his grandmother's room. Their voices floated low and quiet out into the cool shade that lay over the house.

"How long will it be?" he heard his grandmother say.

"Before the end of summer."

"Are you sure?"

"Yes. You should have sent for me long ago."

"I've passed my threescore and ten years. I'm eighty-four."

What did they mean? Perhaps he ought not to be listening.

"How will it come? Tell me, Doctor, I can stand it."

"There will be sharp, quick pains like the ones you've been having. Your heart cannot stand many more attacks. It grows weaker with each one, even though you're able to go about your work as you did before the attack came. I'm going to leave you a prescription for some pills that will kill the pain almost instantly. But that's about all they will do. When an attack comes, take two with a glass of water. They'll make you drop off to sleep. One time you won't wake up."

Now Bennie understood. But he could not turn and run away.

There was a brief silence. Then his grandmother said, "Don't tell Birdie nor anybody else."

"But you can't stay here alone with the child all day long. Why, he's only ten years old."

"I know. . . . Doctor, there ain't anyone to come stay with me. Birdie must go to the Fieldses' to work. You know it's just Birdie, the boy, and me. I got no close kin. My husband, my three sons, and my other daughter's been dead for years now. You see, I know death, Doctor. I know it well. I'm just not use to it."

"No one is," Dr. Frazier said.

"Here's what I want to do. I'll go on just like before. There ain't nothin' else for me to do. When an attack comes, I'll take the two pills and I'll send Bennie runnin' down the road for May Mathis. She'll come. May will come. I know nobody I'd rather have set beside me than May. I knowed her all my life. Me and her done talked about this thing many times. It's July now. July the seventh. Then August—then September. But here I go runnin' on and on. Let me get your money. You've got to be paid. You've got to live."

"Please," Dr. Frazier said.

"No harm meant."

Anne Washington Derry, 1927. Laura Wheeler Waring. Oil on canvas, 20 x 16 in. Gift of the Harmon Foundation, National Museum of American Art, Washington, DC.

Viewing the painting: What qualities might this woman have in common with Bennie's grandmother?

In a moment, Bennie heard them walking out onto the porch through the door of her room. Then he could see them as they crossed the yard to the gate, where Dr. Frazier's horse and buggy stood. He was a little man, with a skin that was almost black. He climbed into his buggy and started up the road toward the town, which was three miles away, and she stood and looked after him. Her back was to the house. People said that

Bennie's grandmother had Indian blood in her veins, for she had high cheekbones and her nose was long and straight, but her mouth was big. Her eyes seemed as though they were buried way back in her head, in a mass of wrinkles. They danced and twinkled whenever they looked at him. She was a big woman, and she wore long full skirts that came all the way to the ground.

She closed the gate and started back to the house, and it came to Bennie that he was alone with her, and that she was going to die soon. He turned and ran noiselessly across the back yard, through the back gate, and down the path to the spring.

When he reached the spring, he kept running. He ran across the pasture field and up the hill to the barbed-wire fence that divided his grandmother's land from Mr. Charley Miller's. He threw himself to the ground and rolled under the fence, picked himself up on the other side, and ran through Mr. Charley Miller's field of alfalfa and into the woods, until at last he fell exhausted in the cool damp grass of a shaded clearing.

His grandmother was going to die. She might even be dead now. She was going to lie cold and still, in a long black casket that would be put into a hearse that would take her to church in town. The Reverend Isaiah Jones would preach her funeral. People would cry, because people liked his grandmother. His mother would cry. He would cry. And now he was crying, and he could not stop crying.

But at last he did, and he sat up and took from his pocket the clean white rag that his grandmother had given him to use as a handkerchief and dried his eyes. He must get up and go back to the house. He would have to be alone with his grandmother until his mother came home from the Fieldses' after she had cooked their supper. And he must tell no one what he had heard Dr. Frazier say to his grandmother.

He found her sitting in her big rocking chair, her hands clasped in her lap. "You been gone a long time," she said. "The water bucket's empty. Take it and go fill it at the spring. Time for me to be gettin' up from here and cookin' supper."

When he got back from the spring, he found her laying a fire in the kitchen stove.

It was nearly dark when he saw his mother coming, and he ran to meet her. She looked at him closely and said, "Bennie, why on earth did you run so fast?"

He could only say breathlessly, "I don't know." He added quickly, "What did you bring me?" Sometimes she brought him a piece of cake or pie, or the leg of a chicken from the Fieldses'. Today she did not have anything.

It was a long time before he went to sleep that night.

The next day, he stayed outdoors and only went into the house when his grandmother called him to do something for her. She did not notice.

On Sunday, his mother did not go to the Fieldses'. In the morning, they went to church. That afternoon, Mr. Joe Bailey drove up to the house in his horse and buggy to take Bennie's mother for a buggy ride. She had put on her pretty blue-flowered dress and her big wide-brimmed black straw hat with the red roses around its crown and the black ribbon that fell over the brim and down her back. She looked very pretty and as pleased as she could be. Bennie wanted to go riding with them. Once, he had asked Mr. Joe if he could go along, and Mr. Joe had grinned and said yes, but Bennie's mother had not been pleased at all, for some reason. This Sunday, after they had gone, his grandmother let him walk the mile and a half down the road to play with James and Robert Lee Stewart.

He knew that his grandmother was preparing to die. He came upon her kneeling in prayer beside her bed with its high headboard that almost touched the ceiling. As she sat in her rocking chair, she said the Twenty-third Psalm. He knew only the first verse: "The Lord is my shepherd; I shall not want."

Now he felt toward his grandmother the way he felt toward certain people, only more so. There was a feeling that made people seem strange—a feeling that came from them to you—that made you stand away from them. There was Miss Sally Cannon, his teacher. You did not go close to Miss Sally. She made you sit still and always keep your reader or your spelling book open on your desk, or do your arithmetic problems. If she caught you whispering or talking, she called you up to the front of the room and gave you several stinging lashes on your legs or across your back with one of the long switches that always lay across her desk. You did not go close to Miss Sally unless you had to. You did not go close to Dr. Frazier or the Reverend Isaiah Jones. Teachers, doctors, and preachers were special people.

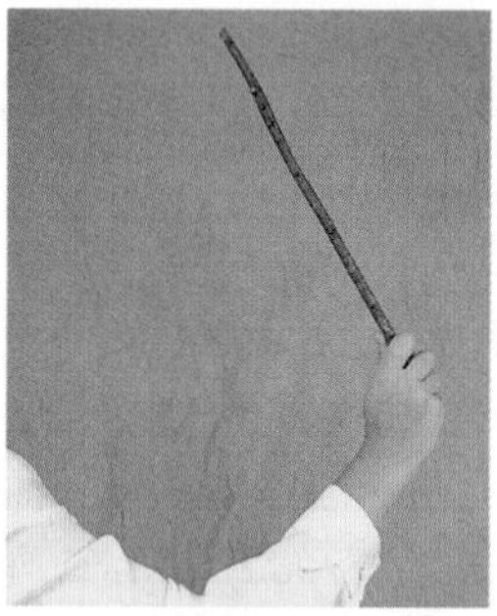

Did You Know?
A *switch* is a slender, flexible rod or stick used for whipping.

You did not go close to white people, either. Sometimes when he and his grandmother went to town, they would stop at the Fieldses'. They would walk up the long green yard and go around the big red brick house, with its tall white columns, to the kitchen, where his mother was; it always seemed a nice place to be, even on a hot summer day. His mother and his grandmother would chuckle over something that Miss Marion Fields or Mr. Ridley Fields had done. They would stop smiling the minute Miss Marion came into the room, and they would become like people waiting in the vestibule of a church for the prayer to be finished so they could go in. He knew that he acted the same way.

Miss Marion had light-brown hair and light-brown eyes. His grandmother said that she was like a sparrow, for she was a tiny woman. She always wore a dress that was pretty enough to wear to church. The last time he was at the Fieldses', Miss Marion came into the kitchen. After she had spoken to his grandmother, she turned to him. He was sitting in a chair near the window, and he felt himself stiffen both inside and outside. She said, "I declare, Birdie, Bennie's the prettiest colored child I ever did see. Lashes long as a girl's. Is he a good boy, Hannah?"

"He's a quiet child," his grandmother said. "Sometimes I think he's too quiet, but he's a good child—at least when I got my eyes on him." They all laughed.

"I'm sure Bennie's good," Miss Marion said. "Be a good boy, Bennie. Eat plenty and grow strong, and when you're big enough to work, Mr. Ridley will be glad to give you work here on his place. We're so glad to have your mother here with us. Now, be good, won't you?"

"Yes, Ma'am," he answered.

"Birdie, give him a piece of that lemon pie you baked for supper. Well, Hannah, it's been nice talking with you again. Always stop on your way to town."

Two weeks to the day after Dr. Frazier's visit, Miss May Mathis came to see his grandmother. She was much shorter than his grandmother—a plump woman, who always wore long black-and-white checked gingham dresses that fell straight down from her high full breasts to her knees and then flared outward. Her chin was sharp, with folds of flesh around it. Her nose was wide and flat. She had small, snapping black eyes. Her skin was like cream that had been kept too long and into which hundreds of tiny black specks had fallen.

As she came into the yard, she asked Bennie if his grandmother was at home. She said she would sit on the porch, where it was cool. He ran into the house to tell his grandmother that she was there.

His grandmother put away her sewing and went out on the porch. "May, I'm glad you come. I've been lookin' for you," she said.

"I'd been here sooner, but my stomach's been givin' me trouble lately. Sometimes I think my time ain't long."

"Hush—hush! You'll live to see me put under the ground."

"Well, the day before yesterday I spent half the day in bed. I thought I'd have to send John for you," Miss May answered, and she went into a long account of the illness that troubled her.

Bennie got up from the edge of the porch and ran around the house. The two old women paid no attention to his going. He knew what his grandmother would say to Miss May. She would tell Miss May how she wanted to be dressed for burial. She would name the song she wanted to be sung over her. He had heard the same conversation many times. Now it was different. What they were talking about would soon "come to pass," as his grandmother would say. Miss May did not know, but he knew.

He went out of the back gate and down the path to the spring. He waded in the stream awhile, catching minnows in his hands and then letting them go. He went across the pasture field. He broke off a persimmon bush to use as a switch, and he chased his grandmother's cow about the pasture a bit. But the cow was old and soon grew tired of moving when he hit her with the switch. Then he went to the big oak tree that stood between the fields and sat down. He stayed there until he saw Miss May Mathis going out of the front gate.

The July days went slowly by, one much like another. It grew hotter and hotter.

One day when he walked into the house after playing a long time in the stream and the pasture field, he found his grandmother quietly sleeping in her big rocking chair. He saw a bottle full of big white pills on the dresser. It had not been there when he left the house. An empty glass stood beside the pills. He felt too frightened to move. Her breast was rising and falling evenly. She stirred and then opened her eyes.

She seemed dazed and not to see him for a moment. Then her lips curved into a queer smile, and a twinkle came into her eyes. "Must have dropped off to sleep like a baby," she said. "Run outdoors and play. I'll set here awhile and then I'll get up and start supper."

Later on, she called him and asked if he could make out with milk and cold food from dinner. She left the milking for his mother to do when she came home from the Fieldses'. But the next morning his grandmother was all right, and he thought that she was not going to die that summer, after all.

One morning, a little after his mother had gone to the Fieldses', Mr. John Mathis drove up. He turned his horse and buggy around to face the way he had come. Then he walked up the path to the house. He was a tall, rawboned man with a bullet-shaped head, and he looked exactly like what he was—a deacon[1] in a church.

1. In some Christian churches, a *deacon* is a congregation member who helps the priest or minister in either worship services or the church's business affairs.

Vocabulary
rawboned (rô′ bōnd) *adj.* thin or very lean

© Estate of Grant Wood/Licensed by VAGA, New York, NY.

Study for American Gothic. Grant Wood (1892–1942). Watercolor. Private collection.

Viewing the painting: How does the house in this painting compare with the one described in the story?

"What is it, John?" Bennie's grandmother asked.

"It's May. She was sick all day yesterday. Last night I had to get the doctor for her. Jennie Stewart's there now."

"I'll be ready to go in a minute," his grandmother said.

On the way to the Mathises', Bennie sat on the back of the buggy. His grandmother and Mr. John said only a few words. When they reached the house, his grandmother told him to keep very quiet and to be good, and she went inside at once. There were people on the porch, and people continued to come and go. It was midafternoon, and still his grandmother had not come from within the house. A Ford car drove up to the gate. In it were Philomena Jones and her mother. Philomena was a year younger than Bennie. She had a sharp little yellow face, big black eyes that went everywhere, and she wore her hair in two long plaits. "Come on," she said, "and let's play something." When they were out of hearing of the grown-up people, she said, "Miss May going to die."

"How do you know?"

"I heard my mama say she was. She's old. When you're old you have to die."

Next, Philomena said, "Your mama's tryin' to catch Mr. Joe Bailey for a husband. Mama said it's time she's getting another husband if she's ever going to get one."

"You stop talkin'!" Bennie told her.

"She said your pa's been dead nine years now and if your mama don't hurry and take Mr. Joe Bailey—that is, if she can get him—she may never get a chance to marry again."

"If you don't stop talkin', I'll hit you!"

"No, you won't. I'm not scared of you, even if you are a boy, and I'll say what I want to. Mama said, 'Birdie Wilson's in her forties, if she a day, and if a woman lets herself get into her forties without marryin', her chance are mighty slim after that.' I'm goin' to marry when I'm twenty."

"Nobody'd want you. You talk too much."

"I don't, neither."

"I won't play with you. I'm goin' back to the porch," he said.

Philomena stayed in the yard a little longer. She carried on an imaginary conversation with a person who seemed as eager to talk as she. After a while, she ran back to the porch and sat down and gave her attention to what the grown-up people were saying, now and then putting in a word herself.

Then his grandmother came out from the house. People stopped talking at the sight of her face. "May's gone," she said.

The people on the porch bowed their heads, and their faces became as though they were already at Miss May Mathis's funeral.

His grandmother looked very tired. After a moment, she said, "The Lord giveth and the Lord taketh. Blessed be the name of the Lord." There was a silence. Then she spoke again. "I thought May would do for me what I have to do for her now." She turned and went back into the house. Some of the women rose and followed her.

The people who remained on the porch spoke in low voices. Someone wondered when the funeral would be. Someone wondered if Miss May's sister Ethel, who lived in St. Louis, would come. Someone hoped that it would not rain the day of the funeral.

Then Mr. John Mathis and Bennie's grandmother came out on the porch. Mr. John said, "Hannah, you done all you could do. May couldn't have had a better friend. You're tired now. I'll send you home."

At home, his grandmother seemed not to notice him. Her eyes seemed to be taking a great sad rest. She sent him to the spring to get water to cook supper.

As he walked down the path, he thought about his grandmother. He felt more sorry for her than he felt fear of her. Miss May Mathis was dead; he could not run and get her now.

On Sunday afternoon at two o'clock at the Baptist Church, Miss May Mathis's funeral service was held. There was a procession of buggies, surreys, and even a few automobiles from the house to the church. Mr. Joe Bailey came and took Bennie's mother, his grandmother, and him to church. The funeral was a long one. He sat beside his

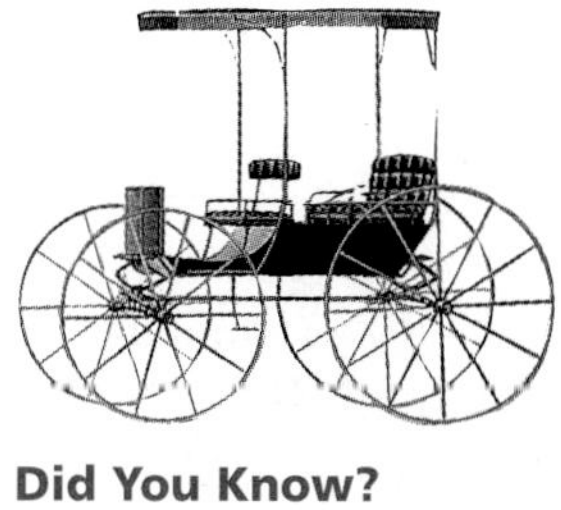

Did You Know?
A *surrey* is a light, four-wheeled carriage that seats two passengers and usually has a top.

Vocabulary
plait (plāt) *n.* a braid, as of hair

grandmother and listened to the prayers, the songs, and the sermon, all the time dreading the moment when the flowers would be taken from the gray casket, the casket would be opened, and the people would file by to see the body for the last time.

The Reverend Isaiah Jones described Heaven as a land flowing with milk and honey, a place where people ate fruit from the tree of life, wore golden slippers, long white robes, and starry crowns, and rested forever. The Reverend Isaiah Jones was certain that Miss May Mathis was there, resting in the arms of Jesus, done with the sins and sorrows of this world. Bennie wondered why Mr. John covered his face with his hands, and why Miss May's sister Ethel, who had come all the way from St. Louis, cried out, and why people cried, if Miss May was so happy in this land. It seemed that they should be glad for her, so glad they would not cry. Or did they cry because they were glad? He could not understand. The Reverend Jones said that they would see Miss May on the Resurrection morning.[2] Bennie could not understand this, either.

At last the gray casket was opened, and people began to file by it. And at last he was close. His mother went by, and then Mr. Joe. Now his grandmother. The line of people stopped, waiting expectantly. His grandmother stood and looked down on Miss May for a long time. She did not cry out. She simply stood there and looked down, and finally she moved on. Now he was next. Miss May Mathis looked as though she had simply combed her hair and piled it on top of her head, put on her best black silk dress, pinned her big old pearl brooch to its lace collar, picked up a white handkerchief with one hand, and then decided that instead of going to church she would sleep a little while. As he looked down on her, he was not as afraid as he'd thought he would be.

Outside the church, as the procession was forming to go to the graveyard, Dr. Frazier came up to his grandmother and asked how she was.

"As well as could be expected, Doctor," his grandmother said. And then, in a low voice, "I've had only one."

"You got through it all right."

"Yes."

"And this?"

"I've managed to get through it."

"You will be careful."

"Yes."

"Now?"

"He'll have to go to the Stewarts'."

They did not know that he understood what they were talking about, even if none of the other people around them did. He heard two women whispering. One said to the other, "It's wonderful the way Aunt Hannah took it." He felt very proud of his grandmother.

Now his grandmother's footsteps were slower as she moved about the house and yard. He kept the garden and the flower beds along the yard fences weeded, the stove box full of wood, the water bucket full all the time, without her having to ask him to do these things for her. He overheard her say to his mother, "Child does everything without being told. It ain't natural."

"Reckon he's not well?" his mother asked anxiously.

"Don't think so. He eats well. Maybe the trouble is the child don't have nobody to play with every day. He'll be all right when fall comes and school starts."

2. *Resurrection morning* refers to the time when, according to some Christian religions, all human dead will rise again to life before the last judgment.

August came, and it grew hotter. The sun climbed up the sky in the morning and down the sky in the evening like a tired old man with a great load on his back going up and down a hill. Then one hot mid-August day dawned far hotter and sultrier than the one just past. It grew still hotter during the early part of the morning, but by midday there was a change, for there was a breeze, and in the west a few dark clouds gathered in the sky. His grandmother said, "I believe the rain will come at last."

About three o'clock, the wind rose suddenly. It bent the top of the big oak tree that stood in the yard. There were low rumbles of thunder.

"Bennie, Bennie, come! Let's get the chickens up!" his grandmother called to him.

By the time all the chickens were safe in the henhouse and chicken coops, it was time to go into the house and put the windows down. The wind lifted the curtains almost to the ceiling. They got the windows down. His grandmother went into the kitchen. He went out on the porch. He wanted to watch the clouds, for he had never seen any bigger or blacker or quite so low to the earth—he was sure they must be touching the ground somewhere. He wanted to see what the wind did to the trees, the corn, and the grass.

At last the rain fell, first in great drops that were blown onto the edge of the porch by the wind and felt cool and good as they touched his face. They made him want to run out into the yard. Then the rain came so quickly and so heavily, and with it so much wind, that it came up on the porch and almost pushed him back into the house. The thunder roared and there were flashes of lightning.

"Bennie, Bennie, where are you?" his grandmother called, and when he went inside she said, "Set down—set down in the big chair there or come into my room if you want to. I'm goin' to just set in my rocker."

"I'll stay here," he said, and he went to the big chair near the fireplace and sat down.

"There—there—just set there. I'll leave the door open."

He tried to keep from thinking what might happen if his grandmother had one of her spells, but he could not. He went to the fireplace. The back of the fireplace was wet; water stood on it in drops that looked like tears on a face. He stood and looked at it awhile, then he sat down in the big chair. There was nothing else to do but to sit there.

He heard her cry out. The cry was sharp and quick. Then it was cut off.

She called him. "Bennie! Bennie!" Her voice was thick.

He could not move.

"Bennie!"

He went into the room where she was.

She sat on the side of her bed. She was breathing hard, and in one hand she had the bottle of white pills. "Get me a glass of water. One of my spells done come over me."

He went into the kitchen and got a glass from the kitchen safe and filled it with water from the bucket that sat on the side table. Then he went back to her and gave her the water.

She took it and put two pills in her mouth and gulped them down with the water. She was breathing hard. "Pull off my shoes," she said.

As he was unlacing the high-top shoes she always wore, she gave a little cry. He felt her body tremble. "Just a bit of pain. Don't worry. I'm all right," she said. "It's gone," she added a moment later.

When he got her shoes off, he lifted her legs onto the bed, and she lay back and closed her eyes. "Go into the front room," she said, "and close the door behind you and

Vocabulary

sultrier (sul′ trē ər) *adj.* more hot and humid

stay there until the storm is past. I'm goin' to drop off to sleep—and if I'm still asleep when the storm is over, just let me sleep until your mama comes. Don't come in here. Don't try to wake me. 'Twon't do me no harm to take me a long good sleep."

He could not move. He could only stand there and stare at her.

"Hear me? Go on, I tell you. Go on—don't, I'll get up from here and skin you alive."

He crept from the room, closing the door after him.

He went to the big chair and sat down. He must not cry. Crying could not help him. There was nothing to do but to sit there until the storm was past.

The rain and the wind came steadily now. He sat back in the big chair. He wondered about his mother. Was she safe at the Fieldses'? He wondered if the water had flowed into the henhouse and under the chicken coops, where the little chickens were. If it had, some of the little chickens might get drowned. The storm lasted so long that it began to seem to him that it had always been there.

At last he became aware that the room was growing lighter and the rain was not so hard. The thunder and lightning were gone. Then, almost as suddenly as it had begun, the storm was over.

He got up and went out on the porch. Everything was clean. Everything looked new. There were little pools of water everywhere, and it was cool. There were a few clouds in the sky, but they were white and light gray. He looked across the field toward Mr. Charley Miller's, and he opened his eyes wide when he saw that the storm had blown down the big oak tree. He started to run back into the house to tell his grandmother that the storm had blown the tree down, and then he stopped. After a minute, he stepped down from the porch. The wet grass felt good on his bare feet.

He felt his grandmother in the doorway even before he heard her call. He turned and looked at her. She had put on her shoes and the long apron she always wore. She came out on the porch, and he decided that she looked as though her sleep had done her good.

He remembered the tree, and he cried, "Look—look, Grannie! The storm blowed down the tree between your field and Mr. Charley Miller's."

"That tree was there when me and your grandpa came here years and years ago," she said. "The Lord saw fit to let it be blowed down in this storm. I— I—" She broke off and went back into the house.

He ran into the house and said to her, "I'm goin' down to the spring. I bet the stream's deep as a creek."

"Don't you get drowned like old Pharaoh's army,"[3] she said.

The storm drove away the heat, for the days were now filled with cool winds that came and rattled the cornstalks and the leaves on the oak tree in the yard. There were showers. The nights were long and cool; the wind came into the rooms, gently pushing aside the neat white curtains to do so.

One morning when he went into the kitchen to get hot water and soap to take to the back porch to wash his face and hands, he found his mother and grandmother busy talking. They stopped the moment they saw him. His mother's face seemed flushed and uncomfortable, but her eyes were very bright.

"Done forgot how to say good mornin' to a body?" his grandmother said.

3. In the Bible, Israelites leaving Egypt are pursued by *Pharaoh's army* to the edge of the Red Sea. There, God (through Moses) divides the water to allow the Israelites to cross on dry land and then closes it, drowning Pharaoh's men.

Portrait of Willie Gee, 1904. Robert Henri, Oil on canvas, 311/4 x 261/4 in, Newark Museum, NJ. Viewing the painting: How would you describe the expression on the face of this child? Finish reading the story and then think about when Bennie might have had a similar expression.

"Good mornin', Grannie. Good mornin', Mama."

"That's more like it."

"Good mornin', Bennie," his mother said. She looked at him, and he had a feeling that she was going to come to him and take him in her arms the way she used to do when he was a little boy. But she did not.

His grandmother laughed. "Well, son, Mr. Joe Bailey went and popped the question to your mama last night."

His mother blushed. He did not know what to say to either of them. He just stood and looked at them.

"What you goin' to say to that?" his mother said.

All he could think to say was "It's all right."

His grandmother laughed again, and his mother smiled at him the way she did when he ran down the road to meet her and asked her to let him carry the packages that she had.

"When will they be married?" he asked.

"Soon," his mother said. "Where will they livehere?"

"That ain't been settled vet," his grandmother said. "Nothin' been settled. They just got engaged last night while they were settin' in the front room and you was sleepin' in your bed. Things can be settled later." She gave a sigh that his mother did not hear. But he heard it.

He poured water from the teakettle into the wash pan

and took the pan out on the back porch and washed and dried his hands. He looked across the fields and hills. The sun had not come up yet, but the morning lay clear and soft and quiet as far as his eyes could see.

His mother was going to marry Mr. Joe Bailey. He did mind a little. He knew that was what she wanted. He liked Mr. Joe. When Mr. Joe smiled at him, he always had to smile back at him; something seemed to make him do so.

After his mother had gone to the Fieldses', he and his grandmother sat down to breakfast at the table in the kitchen. His grandmother never ate a meal without saying grace. Usually she gave thanks just for the food that they were about to eat. This morning she asked the Lord to bless his mama, Mr. Joe, and him, and she thanked the Lord for answering all her prayers.

As they ate, she talked to him. She spoke as though she were talking to herself, expecting no answer from him, but he knew that she meant for him to listen to her words, and he knew why she was talking to him. "Joe Bailey will make your mama a good husband and you a good father to take the place of your father who you never knew. The Lord took your father when your father was still young, but that was the Lord's will. Joe Bailey will be good to you, for he is a good man. Mind him. Don't make trouble between him and your mama. Hear me?"

"Yes, Ma'am."

"Don't you worry about where you'll stay. You'll be with your mama. Hear me?"

"Yes'm."

She sat silent for a moment, and then she added, "Well, no matter if your mama is going to marry Mr. Joe Bailey. We got to work today just like we always has. No matter what comes, we have to do the little things that our hands find to do. Soon as you finish eatin', go to the spring and get water and fill the pot and the tubs."

August drew toward its close, but the soft cool days stayed on, and they were calm and peaceful. His grandmother cooked the meals, and washed and ironed their own clothes and those that his mother brought home from the Fieldses' and Mr. Charley Miller's. Sometimes Bennie wondered if she had put from her mind the things that Dr. Frazier had said to her that day he listened under the window. Sometimes it seemed to him that he had never crept close to the window and listened to her and Dr. Frazier. The summer seemed just like last summer and the summer before that.

One day near the end of the month, Mr. John Mathis stopped by the house on his way to town. He was on horseback, riding a big black horse whose sides glistened. He hailed Bennie's grandmother, and she came out on the porch to pass the time of day with him.

"Ever see such a fine summer day, John?" she said.

"It's not a summer day, Hannah. It's a fall day. It's going to be an early fall this year."

"Think so?" his grandmother asked. Her face changed, but Mr. John did not notice.

"I can feel it. I can feel it in the air. The smell of fall is here already." Then they fell to talking about the church and people they knew.

She stood on the porch and watched Mr. John ride up the road on his big black horse. Often that day, she came out on the porch and stood and looked across the fields and hills.

When Bennie went outside for the first time the next morning and looked around him, he did not see a single cloud in the sky. The quiet that lay about him felt like a nice clean sheet you pull over your head before you go to sleep at night that shuts out everything to make a space both warm and cool just for you. The day grew warm. A little after midday, clouds began to float across the sky, but for the most part it remained clear and very blue. He played in the yard under the oak tree, and then he went down to the spring and played. In the afternoon, he rolled his hoop up and down the road in front of the house. He grew tired of this and went and sat under the tree.

He was still sitting under the tree when his grandmother cried out. She gave a sharp sudden cry, like the cry people make when they've been stung by a bee or a wasp. He got to his feet. Then he heard her call. "Bennie! Bennie!"

He ran into the house and into her room.

She sat in her big rocking chair, leaning forward a little, her hands clutching the arms of the chair. She was breathing hard. He had never seen her eyes as they were now. "Water—the pills—in the dresser."

He ran into the kitchen and got a glass of water and ran back to the room and gave it to her and then went to the dresser and got the bottle of pills. He unscrewed the top and took out two of them and gave them to her.

She put the pills in her mouth and gulped them down with water. Then she leaned back and closed her eyes. At last she breathed easier, and in a few moments she opened her eyes. "Run and get—get Miss— No, go get your mama. Hurry! Your grandmother is very sick."

It was a long way to the Fieldses'—even longer than to the Stewarts'! He stood still and looked at her. She was a big woman, and the chair was a big chair. Now she seemed smaller—lost in the chair.

"Hurry—hurry, child."

"Grannie, I'll stay with you until you go to sleep, if you want me to," he heard himself say.

"No! No! Hurry!"

"I heard you and Dr. Frazier talking that day."

"Child! Child! You knew all the time?"

"Yes, Grannie."

"When I drop off to sleep, I won't wake up. Your grandmother won't wake up here."

"I know."

"You're not afraid?"

He shook his head.

She seemed to be thinking hard, and at last she said, "Set down, child. Set down beside me."

He pulled up the straight chair and sat down facing her.

"Seems like I don't know what to say to you, Bennie. Be a good boy. Seems like I can't think any more. Everything leavin' me—leavin' me."

"I'll set here until you go to sleep, and then I'll go and get mama."

"That's a good boy," she said, and she closed her eyes.

He sat still and quiet until her breath came softly and he knew that she was asleep. It was not long. Then he got up and walked from the room and out of the house.

He did not look back, and he did not run until he was a good way down the road. Then suddenly he began to run, and he ran as fast as he could.

Responding to Literature

Personal Response

Were you surprised by what happened at the end of the story? Why or why not?

Analyzing Literature

Recall

1. Which character first said "before the end of summer"? What was the person referring to?
2. How did Bennie first react to Dr. Frazier's conversation with Grannie?
3. What did Grannie do when her friend May died?
4. Describe Bennie and Grannie's life as "August drew toward its close"?
5. At the end of the story, what did Bennie say when Grannie told him to get his mother?

Interpret

6. What might "the end of summer" **symbolize,** or represent? Explain your answer. (See Literary Terms Handbook, page R12.)
7. What do Bennie's actions after overhearing the doctor's conversation with Grannie tell you about how he was feeling at the time?
8. How did May's death affect Bennie's feelings about Grannie?
9. After Grannie hears that it is going to be an early fall, the narrator says, "Often that day, she came out on the porch and stood and looked across the fields and hills." Why do you suppose she does this?
10. In the last scene, what do we learn about Bennie and Grannie and their relationship through their **dialogue,** or conversation?

Evaluate and Connect

11. Bennie changes and grows during this story. How does the author show him changing? Use specific details from the story to explain your answer.
12. Think about your response to the Reading Focus on page 26. Was your way of overcoming fear different from Bennie's? How?
13. What can you infer about the relationship between Joe Bailey and Bennie's mother? What clues in the story help you to learn about them?
14. Stories often contain **foreshadowing**–clues that hint at events that will happen later. How does what happens during the storm foreshadow later events? What other instances of foreshadowing can you find?
15. What lesson about life or human nature does the author communicate through this story? Do you agree with this message? Why or why not?

Literary ELEMENTS

Characterization

Characterization is the method a writer uses to reveal a character's personality. A writer can describe someone's personality, or show it through the character's words, thoughts, or actions. The writer can also reveal a character's personality through the words, thoughts, or actions of other characters.

1. How would you describe Grannie? What words and actions best illustrate Grannie's character?
2. Do you learn about Grannie through her own words, thoughts, and actions; through those of another character; or through both? Explain your answer.
3. What methods of characterization does the author use to show how Bennie changes from the beginning to the end of the story? Use evidence from the story to support your answer.

- See **Literary Terms Handbook,** p. R2.

"Access to the basic tools of the information age is no longer a luxury for our children. It is a necessity."
—Al Gore

"The push to net-connect every school is an educational disaster in the making."
—David Gelernter

No—Learn First, Surf Later

by David Gelernter, *Time*, May 25, 1998

Quack medicine comes in two varieties: "irrelevant but harmless" and "toxic." The Administration's plan to wire American classrooms for Internet service is toxic quackery.

The push to net-connect every school is an educational disaster in the making. Our schools are in crisis. Statistics prove what I see every day as a parent and a college educator. My wife and I have a constant struggle to get our young boys to master the basic skills they need.

The Internet, said President Clinton in February, "could make it possible for every child with access to a computer to stretch a hand across a keyboard to reach every book ever written, every painting ever painted, every symphony ever composed." Pardon me, Mr. President, but this is demented. Most American children don't know what a symphony *is*. If we suddenly figured out how to teach each child *one* movement of *one* symphony, that would be a miracle.

And our children are overwhelmed by information even *without* the Internet. The glossy magazines and hundred-odd cable channels, the videotapes and computer CDs in most libraries and many homes—they need *more* information? It's as if the Administration were announcing that every child must have the fanciest scuba gear on the market—but these kids don't know how to swim, and fitting them out with scuba gear isn't just useless, it's irresponsible; they'll drown.

And it gets worse. Our children's attention spans are too short already, but the Web is a propaganda machine for short attention spans. The instant you get bored, click the mouse, and you're someplace else. And while the Web is full of first-rate information, it's also full of lies and garbage.

Still, imagine a well-run, serious school with an Internet hookup in the library for occasional use by students under supervision who are working on research projects; would that be so bad? No. Though it ranks around 944th on my list of important school improvements, it's not bad. But if children are turned loose to surf, then Internet in the schools won't be a minor educational improvement, it will be a major disaster.

Analyzing Media

1. What is each writer's motivation for writing? How does each writer try to convince readers to share his point of view?
2. Which writer's argument is more convincing to you? Explain why.

Before You Read

The Lady, or the Tiger?

Reading Focus

Have you ever felt as if you were "caught between a rock and a hard place"—where you needed to make a choice between two courses of action and neither option seemed quite right?

Journal In your journal, write about this difficult situation. What were the advantages and disadvantages of each course of action? How do you know you made the right choice in the end?

Setting a Purpose Read to learn about a difficult choice that's a matter of life and death.

Building Background

The Time and Place

Like a fairy tale that takes place "once upon a time," this story has a purposely vague setting.

Did You Know?

During the Middle Ages in England, guilt or innocence was decided through a practice known as an ordeal. An accused person was physically tested, and the outcome determined guilt or innocence. The accusers believed that supernatural forces controlled what happened. For instance, in the ordeal by water, the accused person was tied up and thrown into deep water. A person who floated was thought to be guilty; a person who sank was considered innocent. Unfortunately, those who sank often drowned before they could be hauled back up.

Vocabulary Preview

impartial (im pär′ shəl) *adj.* not favoring one side more than another; fair; p. 46

emanate (em′ ə nāt′) *v.* to come forth; p. 46

dire (dīr) *adj.* dreadful; terrible; p. 46

fervent (fur′ vənt) *adj.* having or showing great intensity of feeling; passionate; p. 47

imperious (im pēr′ ē əs) *adj.* extremely proud and controlling; p. 47

novel (nov′ əl) *adj.* new and unusual; p. 47

presume (pri zo͞om′) *v.* to take upon oneself without permission or authority; dare; p. 50

Meet Frank R. Stockton

Frank Stockton's father wanted his son to be a doctor, but the boy became a wood-engraver, an inventor, and a writer instead. Most of Stockton's early work was written for children, but he later turned his attention to short stories and novels for adults. His collected works fill twenty-three volumes, but he is remembered mainly for the short story "The Lady, or the Tiger?" This story was extremely popular; it was even made into an operetta! The story's unusual ending created a flurry of letters to the author that continued throughout his life.

Frank R. Stockton was born in 1834 and died in 1902. This story was first published in Century *magazine in 1882 and collected in* The Lady, or the Tiger? *in 1884.*

The Lady, or the Tiger?

Frank R. Stockton

IN THE VERY OLDEN TIME, there lived a semibarbaric king, whose ideas, though somewhat polished and sharpened by the progressiveness of distant Latin neighbors, were still large, florid, and untrammeled,[1] as became the half of him which was barbaric. He was a man of exuberant fancy, and, withal, of an authority so irresistible that, at his will, he turned his varied fancies into facts. He was greatly given to self-communing; and, when he and himself agreed upon any thing, the thing was done. When every member of his domestic and political systems moved smoothly in its appointed course, his nature was bland and genial;[2] but whenever there was a little hitch, and some of his orbs got out of their orbits, he was blander and more genial still, for nothing pleased him so much as to make the crooked straight, and crush down uneven places.

Among the borrowed notions by which his barbarism had become semified[3] was that of the public arena, in which, by exhibitions of manly and beastly valor, the minds of his subjects were refined and cultured.

But even here the exuberant and barbaric fancy asserted itself.[4] The arena of the king was built, not to give the people an opportunity of hearing the rhapsodies[5] of dying gladiators, nor to enable them to view the inevitable conclusion of a conflict between religious opinions and hungry jaws, but for purposes far better adapted to widen and develop the mental energies of the people. This vast amphitheater, with its encircling galleries, its mysterious vaults, and its unseen passages, was an agent of poetic justice, in which crime

1. The king's ideas are somewhat uncivilized *(semibarbaric)*; they are very showy *(florid)* and unrestrained *(untrammeled)*.
2. The king himself is generally agreeable and mild *(bland)* and pleasantly cheerful *(genial)*.
3. *Semified* is a made-up word meaning "reduced in half or made partial."
4. Here, *asserted itself* means "exercised its influence; insisted on being recognized."
5. *Rhapsodies* are enthusiastic expressions of emotion.

was punished, or virtue rewarded, by the decrees of an impartial and incorruptible chance.

When a subject was accused of a crime of sufficient importance to interest the king, public notice was given that on an appointed day the fate of the accused person would be decided in the king's arena,—a structure which well deserved its name; for, although its form and plan were borrowed from afar, its purpose emanated solely from the brain of this man, who, every barleycorn[6] a king, knew no tradition to which he owed more allegiance than pleased his fancy, and who ingrafted on every adopted form of human thought and action the rich growth of his barbaric idealism.

When all the people had assembled in the galleries, and the king, surrounded by his court, sat high up on his throne of royal state on one side of the arena, he gave a signal, a door beneath him opened, and the accused subject stepped out into the amphitheater. Directly opposite him, on the other side of the enclosed space, were two doors, exactly alike and side by side. It was the duty and the privilege of the person on trial, to walk directly to these doors and open one of them. He could open either door he pleased: he was subject to no guidance or influence but that of the aforementioned impartial and incorruptible chance. If he opened the one, there came out of it a hungry tiger, the fiercest and most cruel that could be procured, which immediately sprang upon him, and tore him to pieces, as a punishment for his guilt. The moment that the case of the criminal was thus decided, doleful iron bells were clanged, great wails went up from the hired mourners posted on the outer rim of the arena, and the vast audience, with bowed heads and downcast hearts, wended slowly their homeward way, mourning greatly that one so young and fair, or so old and respected, should have merited so dire a fate.

Did You Know?
An *amphitheater* is a circular structure with rising tiers of seats around a central open space.

But, if the accused person opened the other door, there came forth from it a lady, the most suitable to his years and station that his majesty could select among his fair subjects; and to this lady he was immediately married, as a reward of his innocence. It mattered not that he might already possess a wife and family, or that his affections might be engaged upon an object of his own selection: the king allowed no such subordinate arrangements to interfere with his great scheme of retribution and reward.[7] The exercises, as in the other instance, took place immediately, and in the arena. Another door opened beneath the king, and a priest, followed by a band of choristers, and dancing maidens blowing joyous airs on golden horns and treading an epithalamic measure, advanced to where the pair stood, side by side; and the wedding was promptly and cheerily solemnized.[8] Then the gay brass

6. The *barleycorn* is an old unit of measure equal to the width of one grain of barley—about a third of an inch. This phrase is similar to "every inch a king" and means that he was kingly in every way and in every part, top to bottom.

7. The king's plan for giving out punishment *(retribution)* and *reward* was of primary importance, and everything else was less important *(subordinate)*, including family values.

8. *Epithalamic* (ep′ ə thə lā′ mik) refers to a song in honor of a bride and groom. When a wedding is *solemnized,* it is celebrated with a formal ceremony.

Vocabulary

impartial (im pär′ shəl) *adj.* not favoring one side more than another; fair
emanate (em′ ə nāt′) *v.* to come forth
dire (dīr) *adj.* dreadful; terrible

bells rang forth their merry peals, the people shouted glad hurrahs, and the innocent man, preceded by children strewing flowers on his path, led his bride to his home.

This was the king's semibarbaric method of administering justice. Its perfect fairness is obvious. The criminal could not know out of which door would come the lady: he opened either he pleased, without having the slightest idea whether, in the next instant, he was to be devoured or married. On some occasions the tiger came out of one door, and on some out of the other. The decisions of this tribunal were not only fair, they were positively determinate:[9] the accused person was instantly punished if he found himself guilty; and, if innocent, he was rewarded on the spot, whether he liked it or not. There was no escape from the judgments of the king's arena.

The institution was a very popular one. When the people gathered together on one of the great trial days, they never knew whether they were to witness a bloody slaughter or a hilarious wedding. This element of uncertainty lent an interest to the occasion which it could not otherwise have attained. Thus, the masses were entertained and pleased, and the thinking part of the community could bring no charge of unfairness against this plan; for did not the accused person have the whole matter in his own hands?

This semibarbaric king had a daughter as blooming as his most florid fancies, and with a soul as fervent and imperious as his own. As is usual in such cases, she was the apple of his eye, and was loved by him above all humanity. Among his courtiers was a young man of that fineness of blood and lowness of station common to the conventional heroes of romance who love royal maidens. This royal maiden was well satisfied with her lover, for he was handsome and brave to a degree unsurpassed in all this kingdom; and she loved him with an ardor[10] that had enough of barbarism in it to make it exceedingly warm and strong. This love affair moved on happily for many months, until one day the king happened to discover its existence. He did not hesitate nor waver in regard to his duty in the premises. The youth was immediately cast into prison, and a day was appointed for his trial in the king's arena. This, of course, was an especially important occasion; and his majesty, as well as all the people, was greatly interested in the workings and development of this trial. Never before had such a case occurred; never before had a subject dared to love the daughter of a king. In after-years such things became commonplace enough; but then they were, in no slight degree, novel and startling.

The tiger-cages of the kingdom were searched for the most savage and relentless beasts, from which the fiercest monster might be selected for the arena; and the ranks of maiden youth and beauty throughout the land were carefully surveyed by competent judges, in order that the young man might have a fitting bride in case fate did not determine for him a different destiny. Of course, everybody knew that the deed with which the accused was charged had been done. He had loved the princess, and neither he, she, nor any one else

9. Usually, *tribunal* refers to a group of judges or a place of judgment. Here, it is "the king's semibarbaric method of administering justice," and its outcome is absolutely final *(determinate)*.

10. *Ardor* means intense passion.

Vocabulary

fervent (fur′ vənt) *adj.* having or showing great intensity of feeling; passionate
imperious (im pēr′ ē əs) *adj.* extremely proud and controlling
novel (nov′ əl) *adj.* new and unusual

thought of denying the fact; but the king would not think of allowing any fact of this kind to interfere with the workings of the tribunal, in which he took such great delight and satisfaction. No matter how the affair turned out, the youth would be disposed of; and the king would take an aesthetic pleasure in watching the course of events, which would determine whether or not the young man had done wrong in allowing himself to love the princess.

The appointed day arrived. From far and near the people gathered, and thronged the great galleries of the arena; and crowds, unable to gain admittance, massed themselves against its outside walls. The king and his court were in their places, opposite the twin doors,—those fateful portals, so terrible in their similarity.

Mona Vanna, 1866. Dante Gabriel Rossetti. Oil on canvas, 88.9 x 86.4 cm. Tate Gallery, London.

Viewing the painting: How would you describe this woman's personality?

All was ready. The signal was given. A door beneath the royal party opened, and the lover of the princess walked into the arena. Tall, beautiful, fair, his appearance was greeted with a low hum of admiration and anxiety. Half the audience had not known so grand a youth had lived among them. No wonder the princess loved him! What a terrible thing for him to be there!

As the youth advanced into the arena, he turned, as the custom was, to bow to the king: but he did not think at all of that royal personage; his eyes were fixed upon the princess, who sat to the right of her father. Had it not been for the moiety[11] of barbarism in her nature, it is probable that lady would not have been there; but her intense and fervid soul would not allow her to be absent on an occasion in which she was so terribly interested. From the moment that the decree had gone forth, that her lover should decide his fate in the king's arena, she had thought of nothing, night or day, but this great event and the various subjects connected with it. Possessed of more power, influence, and force of character than any one who had ever before been interested in such a case, she had done what no other person had done,—she had possessed herself of the secret of the doors. She knew in which of the two rooms, that lay behind those doors, stood the cage of the tiger, with its open front, and in which waited the lady. Through these thick doors, heavily curtained with skins on the inside, it was impossible that any noise or suggestion should come from within to the person who should approach to raise the latch of one of them; but gold, and the power of a woman's will, had brought the secret to the princess.

11. A *moiety* (moi′ ə tē) means "a half."

And not only did she know in which room stood the lady ready to emerge, all blushing and radiant, should her door be opened, but she knew who the lady was. It was one of the fairest and loveliest of the damsels of the court who had been selected as the reward of the accused youth, should he be proved innocent of the crime of aspiring to one so far above him; and the princess hated her. Often had she seen, or imagined that she had seen, this fair creature throwing glances of admiration upon the person of her lover, and sometimes she thought these glances were perceived and even returned. Now and then she had seen them talking together; it was but for a moment or two, but much can be said in a brief space; it may have been on most unimportant topics, but how could she know that? The girl was lovely, but she had dared to raise her eyes to the loved one of the princess; and, with all the intensity of the savage blood transmitted to her through long lines of wholly barbaric ancestors, she hated the woman who blushed and trembled behind that silent door.

When her lover turned and looked at her, and his eye met hers as she sat there paler and whiter than any one in the vast ocean of anxious faces about her, he saw, by that power of quick perception which is given to those whose souls are one, that she knew behind which door crouched the tiger, and behind which stood the lady. He had expected her to know it. He understood her nature, and his soul was assured that she would never rest until she had made plain to herself this thing, hidden to all other lookers-on, even to the king. The only hope for the youth in which there was any element of certainty was based upon the success of the princess in discovering this mystery; and the moment he looked upon her, he saw she had succeeded, as in his soul he knew she would succeed.

April Love, 1855. Arthur Hughes. Oil on canvas, 88.9 x 49.5 cm. Tate Gallery, London.

Viewing the painting: Compare and contrast this painting with the one on page 48. Which woman seems more like the princess, and which seems more like the lady behind the door?

Then it was that his quick and anxious glance asked the question: "Which?" It was as plain to her as if he shouted it from where he stood. There was not an instant to be lost. The question was asked in a flash; it must be answered in another.

Her right arm lay on the cushioned parapet[12] before her. She raised her hand, and made a slight, quick movement toward the

12. Here, the *parapet* is a low wall or railing around the royal "box seats."

right. No one but her lover saw her. Every eye but his was fixed on the man in the arena.

He turned, and with a firm and rapid step he walked across the empty space. Every heart stopped beating, every breath was held, every eye was fixed immovably upon that man. Without the slightest hesitation, he went to the door on the right, and opened it.

Now, the point of the story is this: Did the tiger come out of that door, or did the lady?

The more we reflect upon this question, the harder it is to answer. It involves a study of the human heart which leads us through devious mazes of passion, out of which it is difficult to find our way. Think of it, fair reader, not as if the decision of the question depended upon yourself, but upon that hot-blooded, semibarbaric princess, her soul at a white heat beneath the combined fires of despair and jealousy. She had lost him, but who should have him?

How often, in her waking hours and in her dreams, had she started in wild horror, and covered her face with her hands as she thought of her lover opening the door on the other side of which waited the cruel fangs of the tiger!

But how much oftener had she seen him at the other door! How in her grievous reveries[13] had she gnashed her teeth, and torn her hair, when she saw his start of rapturous delight as he opened the door of the lady! How her soul had burned in agony when she had seen him rush to meet that woman, with her flushing cheek and sparkling eye of triumph; when she had seen him lead her forth, his whole frame kindled with the joy of recovered life; when she had heard the glad shouts from the multitude, and the wild ringing of the happy bells; when she had seen the priest, with his joyous followers, advance to the couple, and make them man and wife before her very eyes; and when she had seen them walk away together upon their path of flowers, followed by the tremendous shouts of the hilarious multitude, in which her one despairing shriek was lost and drowned!

Would it not be better for him to die at once, and go to wait for her in the blessed regions of semibarbaric futurity?

And yet, that awful tiger, those shrieks, that blood.

Her decision had been indicated in an instant, but it had been made after days and nights of anguished deliberation. She had known she would be asked, she had decided what she would answer, and, without the slightest hesitation, she had moved her hand to the right.

The question of her decision is one not to be lightly considered, and it is not for me to presume to set myself up as the one person able to answer it. And so I leave it with all of you: Which came out of the opened door,—the lady, or the tiger?

13. Something that is *grievous* causes great grief or worry; *reveries* are daydreams.

Vocabulary

presume (pri zo͞om′) *v.* to take upon oneself without permission or authority; dare

Responding to Literature

Personal Response

What was your first reaction to the end of the story?

Analyzing Literature

Recall

1. In the kingdom described in the story, what happens after a person is accused of a crime?
2. For what crime was the young man thrown into prison?
3. When the young man was in the arena, what did the princess do, and what did he do?
4. What did the princess know about the lady behind one of the doors?
5. What question does the narrator ask at the end of the story?

Interpret

6. Why did the people in the community support the king's method of administering justice? Do you agree that the method is fair? Explain.
7. Why were the young man's actions considered a crime?
8. What do the young man's actions in the arena tell you about his relationship with the princess?
9. What would motivate the princess to send the young man to his death? What would motivate her to save his life?
10. In your opinion, why does the story end without an answer to the question?

Evaluate and Connect

11. The **narrator,** the person telling the story, directly addresses readers at the end. What is the effect of this technique? Explain.
12. Think about your response to the Reading Focus on page 44. How would you compare your situation with that of the princess or with that of the young man? Explain how your situation was similar and how it was different.
13. In what ways is the king's justice like flipping a coin to decide an important question?
14. Why is the princess described as "semibarbaric" rather than barbaric or civilized? In what ways does her *semi*barbaric nature make her decision more difficult?
15. Most stories end by telling you what happens to the main characters. This story leaves it open for the reader to decide. What is your opinion of this type of ending?

Literary ELEMENTS

Conflict

Every story revolves around a **conflict,** or struggle, between two opposing forces. An **external conflict** is one between a character and an outside force, such as another character, nature, society, or fate. An **internal conflict** takes place within the mind of a character who is torn between different courses of action.

1. What conflicts does the young man have? Are his conflicts external or internal? Support your answers with details from the story.
2. What internal conflict does the princess have? Include specific lines from the text in your explanation.
3. Why is the princess's internal conflict so important to the story?

- See **Literary Terms Handbook,** p. R3.

Literature and Writing

Writing About Literature

Review Imagine that you are a literary critic, and write a review of this story, analyzing its strengths and weaknesses. Which parts of the story are the most effective? Which scenes are the most vivid? Which parts do you think are the least effective? Be sure to provide a plot summary and details about specific lines or scenes from the story.

Creative Writing

And the Decision Is . . . Write a new ending for the story in which you reveal the princess's decision and show the effects of her decision on all the characters. What happens to the young man? How does she feel about it? What does the king do next? Be sure to use descriptive details, and try to match the style of the rest of the story.

Extending Your Response

Literature Groups

Merely a Trick? Some people might dismiss "The Lady, or the Tiger?" as a trick on the reader because of its ending. Writer M. Griffin disagrees. Griffin insists that the epilogue "raises the story above the level of a 'trick'" and gives the story dignity by examining both human strength and human weakness. With your group, discuss and debate Griffin's opinion. Draw conclusions about whether Griffin was right or wrong and share them with the rest of the class.

Learning for Life

Convince Me! Imagine how the young man felt as he awaited his "trial" in the king's arena. As the young man, write a persuasive memo to either the king or the princess. The purpose of the memo is to persuade the receiver to spare your life.

Interdisciplinary Activity

Civics: On Trial In a small group, review what the narrator of "The Lady, or the Tiger?" says about how the people in the kingdom behave on trial days. Discuss what is similar and what is different about how people today react to trials covered in the media. Share your conclusions with the class.

Reading Further

If you'd like to read more by Frank R. Stockton, you might enjoy these works:

Short Story Collection: *The Best Short Stories of Frank R. Stockton* is a volume of timeless stories that show what happens when witty inventiveness is applied to absurd situations.

Novel: *The Casting Away of Mrs. Lecks and Mrs. Aleshine* is an adventure about two widows who set out on a relaxing retirement cruise to Japan only to become shipwrecked on a deserted island.

Save your work for your portfolio.

Skill Minilessons

GRAMMAR AND LANGUAGE • Using Adjectives

Frank R. Stockton uses descriptive adjectives in "The Lady, or the Tiger?" to make his meaning more precise. Contrast the sentence below with the quotation from the story that follows:

- This amphitheater, with its galleries, its vaults, and its passages, was an agent of justice, in which crime was punished, or virtue rewarded, by the decrees of chance.
- "This vast amphitheater, with its encircling galleries, its mysterious vaults, and its unseen passages, was an agent of poetic justice, in which crime was punished, or virtue rewarded, by the decrees of an impartial and incorruptible chance."

Note how much more you know about the scene and situation in the second sentence because of the adjectives Stockton used.

PRACTICE Rewrite the following sentence, adding adjectives to make the nouns more precise.

The king entered the arena, sat down in his chair, and waited for the man to choose one of the doors.

APPLY Review a piece of your writing. Revise it by adding descriptive adjectives where they are needed to make your meaning more precise.

● For more about adjectives, see **Language Handbook,** p. R37.

READING AND THINKING • Visualizing

Sometimes a writer uses vivid words and phrases to create scenes that you can visualize, or picture in your mind. Such scenes often contain specific sensory details. Visualizing can add to your reading pleasure and to your overall understanding of a literary work. By visualizing, you can experience a scene as if you were there watching it happen. For example, picture this scene from "The Lady, or the Tiger?" as if you were seeing it in a movie: "Then the gay brass bells rang forth their merry peals, the people shouted glad hurrahs, and the innocent man, preceded by children strewing flowers in his path, led his bride to his home." Can you see and hear the scene?

PRACTICE Review "The Lady, or the Tiger?" and look for a scene that is easy to visualize. On your paper, identify it and describe the details that you picture in your mind.

APPLY Review a piece of your own writing that contains a description of a person or place. Rewrite that section, adding vivid details to help readers visualize it.

● For more about related reading strategies, see **Reading Handbook,** pp. R78–R107.

VOCABULARY • Multiple-Meaning Words

Some words have more than one meaning. For example, in "The Lady, or the Tiger?" the word *presume* means "to take upon oneself without permission or authority." However, *presume* can also mean "to accept as true until proven otherwise." Another word that has multiple meanings is *partial.* Sometimes, *partial* means "not whole." Other times, it means "favoring one side more than another." Which meaning of *partial* do you think the word *impartial* is related to?

You may be able to tell that a familiar word has multiple meanings when it's used as a different part of speech than you're accustomed to. For example, in the sentence "What a novel approach," the word *novel* is used as an adjective, not as a noun. Although a dictionary provides all of a word's meanings, you'll have to use the context–the sentence or paragraph that the word appears in–to figure out which meaning applies to the word you're reading.

PRACTICE Write two sentences for each word below. Use a different meaning for the word in each of the two sentences.

1. partial
2. presume
3. novel

INTERDISCIPLINARY CONNECTION

MATHEMATICS

Is It Probable, or Is It Only Possible?

The young man in "The Lady, or the Tiger?" had a difficult decision to make. Behind one door stood a vicious tiger, ready to attack. Behind the other stood a beautiful woman, ready to marry. Since there were only two doors to choose from, there were only two possible outcomes. The probability that he would pick the woman was 1 out of 2.

What Are the Odds?

Event	Odds Against
Going into overtime in an NBA game	23 to 1
The kickoff being returned for a touchdown in football	45 to 1
Being born on Friday the 13th	213 to 1
Being an identical twin	273 to 1
Getting a hole in one in golf	3,708 to 1

Understanding Probability

To figure probability, you divide the number of desired outcomes by the number of possible outcomes. The mathematical equation looks like this:

$$\frac{\text{number of desired outcomes}}{\text{number of possible outcomes}} = \text{probability}$$

Imagine that on a multiple-choice test question, you have no idea which of four possible answers is correct. The probability that you will guess correctly is

$$\frac{1 \text{ (desired outcome)}}{4 \text{ (possible outcomes)}}$$

Since $1 \div 4 = .25$, you have a 25% chance of choosing correctly. The probability of your choosing the wrong answer is 3 out of 4, or 75%! If you can rule out one of the four options, the probability of your selecting the correct response increases from 25% to 1 in 3, or 33%.

What Are the Odds?

Odds are probabilities that are expressed in the form of a ratio: the probability of the event occurring to the probability of it not occurring. If you were guessing among those four multiple-choice answers, the odds *in favor of* guessing right are 1 to 3—one chance that you will answer correctly to three chances that you will not. The odds *against* answering right are 3 to 1.

A clear understanding of odds might discourage many people from playing their states' lottery games. For example, a game in which you pick 6 out of 44 numbers correctly would have odds of 7,059,051 to 1. So, while it is *possible* to win these games of chance, it is certainly not very *probable*.

Activity

Imagine that you are playing a board game with your friends and the best roll of the die is a 6—you get to move ahead 6 spaces! What is the probability that you will roll a 6 in your first turn? (Express your answer in a percentage.) What are the odds against rolling a 6? (Express your answer as a ratio.)

Reading & Thinking Skills

Making Inferences

Imagine that a new student has joined your class, and you notice a St. Louis Cardinals sticker on her folder. You conclude that she likes baseball, and you bring up the topic during your first conversation. You have made an **inference,** a conclusion based on what you know.

As a reader, you must also make inferences. You must look for clues in description and dialogue that can help you understand ideas that the author is implying, but not directly stating. Often you will also use information from your own experiences to help you make inferences and draw conclusions. For example, the narrator in "The Lady, or the Tiger?" says that the king "was a man of exuberant fancy, and, withal, of an authority so irresistible that, at his will, he turned his varied fancies into facts. He was greatly given to self-communing; and, when he and himself agreed upon any thing, the thing was done." From these statements, you can infer that the king has absolute power and control over his empire.

Sometimes the information you use to make inferences will be incomplete, or will conflict with other information. Be sure to base any inferences you make on clues from the text along with what you already know. You will probably find, after finishing a story, that some of your inferences are off target, but many are right on!

- For more about inference, see **Reading Handbook,** pp. R78–R107.

EXERCISE

Read the following paragraph from "The Secret Life of Walter Mitty" by James Thurber, a story that appears later in the book. Then answer the questions that follow.

> **Walter Mitty stopped the car in front of the building where his wife went to have her hair done. "Remember to get those overshoes while I'm having my hair done," she said. "I don't need overshoes," said Mitty. She put her mirror back into her bag. "We've been through all that," she said, getting out of the car. "You're not a young man any longer." He raced the engine a little. "Why don't you wear your gloves? Have you lost your gloves?" Walter Mitty reached in a pocket and brought out the gloves. He put them on, but after she had turned and gone into the building and he had driven on to a red light, he took them off again. "Pick it up, brother!" snapped a cop as the light changed, and Mitty hastily pulled on his gloves and lurched ahead.**

1. What can you infer about Walter Mitty's personality? What clues tell you this?
2. What can you infer about Mitty's relationship with his wife? What did you use to make this inference?

Before You Read

The Leap

Reading Focus

Think of a story from history, literature, or your own life in which someone "rose to the occasion" and acted with great strength or courage.

Draw It! Create a cartoon strip or other illustration of the act. You may wish to include a caption to help others understand what happened and who was involved.

Setting a Purpose Read to find out how a woman's acts of strength and courage affect the course of her daughter's life.

Building Background

The Time and Place

This story is set in a small New Hampshire town just after World War II (in the late 1940s).

Did You Know?

Until the 1950s, most circus troupes performed in huge canvas tents that they carried with them as they traveled from town to town. The main circus tent, or "big top," was large enough to hold one or more performance rings as well as grandstands for hundreds of spectators. It was supported by wooden poles that were held in place by thick wires staked into the ground. Portable tents enabled circus troupes to perform in even the smallest towns. However, the tents proved to be dangerous. With walls of flammable canvas and dirt floors covered with sawdust, circus tents sometimes became the scenes of terrible fires.

Vocabulary Preview

commemorate (kə mem′ ə rāt′) *v.* to preserve the memory of; p. 58
hover (huv′ ər) *v.* to remain suspended in the air in one place; p. 59
extricate (eks′ trə kāt′) *v.* to release from entanglement or difficulty; set free; p. 60
constricting (kən strikt′ ing) *adj.* restricting; limiting; p. 61
perpetually (pər pech′ o͞o əl ē) *adv.* constantly; unceasingly; p. 61
comply (kəm plī′) *v.* to act in accordance with another's request; p. 63
tentative (ten′ tə tiv) *adj.* hesitant; uncertain; p. 63

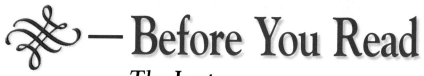

Meet Louise Erdrich

Along the way to becoming an award-winning author, Louise Erdrich remembers taking "some really crazy jobs." She weeded beet fields, taught poetry at prisons, served as a lifeguard, and waved the signal flag at road construction sites. A Chippewa Indian, Erdrich feels that she owes her interest in writing to her Native American roots. "People in [Native American] families make everything into a story," she says. "People just sit and the stories start coming, one after another. I suppose that when you grow up constantly hearing the stories rise, break, and fall, it gets into you somehow."

Louise Erdrich was born in 1954. This story was first published in 1990.

THE LEAP

Louise Erdrich

Au Cirque, 1976. Marc Chagall. Oil on canvas, 48 x 43¼ in. Private collection.

MY MOTHER is the surviving half of a blindfold trapeze act, not a fact I think about much even now that she is sightless, the result of encroaching and stubborn cataracts. She walks slowly through her house here in New Hampshire, lightly touching her way along walls and running her hands over knickknacks, books, the drift of a grown child's belongings and castoffs.

She has never upset an object or as much as brushed a magazine onto the floor. She has never lost her balance or bumped into a closet door left carelessly open.

It has occurred to me that the catlike precision of her movements in old age might be the result of her early training, but she shows so little of the drama or flair one might expect from a performer that I tend to forget the Flying Avalons. She has kept no sequined costume, no photographs, no fliers or posters from that part of her youth. I would, in fact, tend to think that all memory of double somersaults and heart-stopping catches had left her arms and legs were it not for the fact that sometimes, as I sit sewing in the room of the rebuilt house in which I slept as a child, I hear the crackle, catch a whiff of smoke from the stove downstairs, and suddenly the room goes dark, the stitches burn beneath my fingers, and I am sewing with a needle of hot silver, a thread of fire.

I owe her my existence three times.

I owe her my existence three times. The first was when she saved herself. In the town square a replica tent pole, cracked and splintered, now stands cast in concrete. It commemorates the disaster that put our town smack on the front page of the Boston and New York tabloids.[1] It is from those old newspapers, now historical records, that I get my information. Not from my mother, Anna of the Flying Avalons, nor from any of her in-laws, nor certainly from the other half of her particular act, Harold Avalon, her first husband. In one news account it says, "The day was mildly overcast, but nothing in the air or temperature gave any hint of the sudden force with which the deadly gale would strike."

I have lived in the West, where you can see the weather coming for miles, and it is true that out here we are at something of a disadvantage. When extremes of temperature collide, a hot and cold front, winds generate instantaneously behind a hill and crash upon you without warning. That, I think, was the likely situation on that day in June. People probably commented on the pleasant air, grateful that no hot sun beat upon the striped tent that stretched over the entire center green. They bought their tickets and surrendered them in anticipation. They sat. They ate caramelized popcorn and roasted peanuts. There was time, before the storm, for three acts. The White Arabians of Ali-Khazar rose on their hind legs and waltzed. The Mysterious Bernie folded himself into a painted cracker tin, and the Lady of the Mists made herself appear and disappear in surprising places. As the clouds gathered outside, unnoticed, the ringmaster cracked his whip, shouted his introduction, and pointed to the ceiling of the tent, where the Flying Avalons were perched.

They loved to drop gracefully from nowhere, like two sparkling birds, and blow kisses as they threw off their plumed helmets and high-collared capes. They laughed and flirted openly as they beat their way up again on the trapeze bars. In the final vignette[2] of

1. Here, *tabloids* are newspapers with pages half the size of an ordinary newspaper page. They contain brief news articles and many pictures.

2. A *vignette* (vin yet′) is a short scene, sketch, or incident.

Vocabulary

commemorate (kə mem′ ə rāt′) *v.* to preserve the memory of their act, they actually would kiss in midair, pausing, almost hovering as they swooped past one another. On the ground, between bows, Harry Avalon would skip quickly to the front rows and point out the smear of my mother's lipstick, just off the edge of his mouth. They made a romantic pair all right, especially in the blindfold sequence.

That afternoon, as the anticipation increased, as Mr. and Mrs. Avalon tied sparkling strips of cloth onto each other's face and as they puckered their lips in mock kisses, lips destined "never again to meet," as one long breathless article put it, the wind rose, miles off, wrapped itself into a cone, and howled. There came a rumble of electrical energy, drowned out by the sudden roll of drums. One detail not mentioned by the press, perhaps unknown—Anna was pregnant at the time, seven months and hardly showing, her stomach muscles were that strong. It seems incredible that she would work high above the ground when any fall could be so dangerous, but the explanation—I know from watching her go blind—is that my mother lives comfortably in extreme elements. She is one with the constant dark now, just as the air was her home, familiar to her, safe, before the storm that afternoon.

From opposite ends of the tent they waved, blind and smiling, to the crowd below. The ringmaster removed his hat and called for silence, so that the two above could concentrate. They rubbed their hands in chalky powder, then Harry launched himself and swung, once, twice, in huge calibrated[3] beats across space. He hung from his knees and on the third swing stretched wide his arms, held his hands out to receive his pregnant wife as she dove from her shining bar.

It was while the two were in midair, their hands about to meet, that lightning struck the main pole and sizzled down the guy wires, filling the air with a blue radiance that Harry Avalon must certainly have seen through the cloth of his blindfold as the tent buckled and the edifice[4] toppled him forward, the swing continuing and not returning in its sweep, and Harry going down, down into the crowd with his last thought, perhaps, just a prickle of surprise at his empty hands.

Did You Know?
A *guy* is a rope, cord, or cable used for steadying, guiding, or holding something. In this case, *guy wires* hold the main pole of the tent steady.

My mother once said that I'd be amazed at how many things a person can do within the act of falling. Perhaps, at the time, she was teaching me to dive off a board at the town pool, for I associate the idea with midair somersaults. But I also think she meant that even in that awful doomed second one could think, for she certainly did. When her hands did not meet her husband's, my mother tore her blindfold away. As he swept past her on the wrong side, she could have grasped his ankle, the toe-end of his tights, and gone down clutching him. Instead, she changed direction. Her body twisted toward a heavy wire and she managed to hang on to the braided metal, still hot from the lightning strike. Her palms were burned so terribly that once healed they bore no lines, only the blank scar tissue of a quieter future. She was lowered, gently, to the sawdust ring just underneath the dome of the canvas roof,

3. Here, *calibrated* means "precisely timed and measured."

4. An *edifice* is a building or other structure (here, the tent), especially a large, impressive one.

Vocabulary
hover (huv′ ər) *v.* to remain suspended in the air in one place

which did not entirely settle but was held up on one end and jabbed through, torn, and still on fire in places from the giant spark, though rain and men's jackets soon put that out.

Three people died, but except for her hands my mother was not seriously harmed until . . .

Three people died, but except for her hands my mother was not seriously harmed until an overeager rescuer broke her arm in extricating her and also, in the process, collapsed a portion of the tent bearing a huge buckle that knocked her unconscious. She was taken to the town hospital, and there she must have hemorrhaged,[5] for they kept her, confined to her bed, a month and a half before her baby was born without life.

Harry Avalon had wanted to be buried in the circus cemetery next to the original Avalon, his uncle, so she sent him back with his brothers. The child, however, is buried around the corner, beyond this house and just down the highway. Sometimes I used to walk there just to sit. She was a girl, but I rarely thought of her as a sister or even as a separate person really. I suppose you could call it the egocentrism[6] of a child, of all young children, but I considered her a less finished version of myself.

When the snow falls, throwing shadows among the stones, I can easily pick hers out from the road, for it is bigger than the others and in the shape of a lamb at rest, its legs curled beneath. The carved lamb looms larger as the years pass, though it is probably only my eyes, the vision shifting, as what is close to me blurs and distances sharpen. In odd moments, I think it is the edge drawing near, the edge of everything, the unseen horizon we do not really speak of in the eastern woods. And it also seems to me, although this is probably an idle fantasy, that the statue is growing more sharply etched, as if, instead of weathering itself into a porous mass, it is hardening on the hillside with each snowfall, perfecting itself.

It was during her confinement in the hospital that my mother met my father. He was called in to look at the set of her arm, which was complicated. He stayed, sitting at her bedside, for he was something of an armchair traveler and had spent his war quietly, at an air force training grounds, where he became a specialist in arms and legs broken during parachute training exercises. Anna Avalon had been to many of the places he longed to visit—Venice, Rome, Mexico, all through France and Spain. She had no family of her own and was taken in by the Avalons, trained to perform from a very young age. They toured Europe before the war, then based themselves in New York. She was illiterate.

It was in the hospital that she finally learned to read and write, as a way of overcoming the boredom and depression of those weeks, and it was my father who insisted on teaching her. In return for stories of her adventures, he graded her first exercises. He bought her her first book, and over her bold letters, which the pale guides of the penmanship pads could not contain, they fell in love.

5. To *hemorrhage* (hem′ ər ij) is to bleed heavily or excessively—in this case, probably because of internal injuries.

6. *Egocentrism* means "viewing everything in relation to oneself; self-centeredness."

Vocabulary

extricate (eks′ trə kāt′) *v.* to release from entanglement or difficulty; set free

I wonder if my father calculated the exchange he offered: one form of flight for another. For after that, and for as long as I can remember, my mother has never been without a book. Until now, that is, and it remains the greatest difficulty of her blindness. Since my father's recent death, there is no one to read to her, which is why I returned, in fact, from my failed life where the land is flat. I came home to read to my mother, to read out loud, to read long into the dark if I must, to read all night.

Once my father and mother married, they moved onto the old farm he had inherited but didn't care much for. Though he'd been thinking of moving to a larger city, he settled down and broadened his practice in this valley. It still seems odd to me, when they could have gone anywhere else, that they chose to stay in the town where the disaster had occurred, and which my father in the first place had found so constricting. It was my mother who insisted upon it, after her child did not survive. And then, too, she loved the sagging farmhouse with its scrap of what was left of a vast acreage of woods and hidden hay fields that stretched to the game park.

I owe my existence, the second time then, to the two of them and the hospital that brought them together. That is the debt we take for granted since none of us asks for life. It is only once we have it that we hang on so dearly.

I was seven the year the house caught fire, probably from standing ash. It can rekindle, and my father, forgetful around the house and perpetually exhausted from night hours on call, often emptied what he thought were ashes from cold stoves into wooden or cardboard containers. The fire could have started from a flaming box, or perhaps a buildup of creosote inside the chimney was the culprit.[7] It started right around the stove, and the heart of the house was gutted. The babysitter, fallen asleep in my father's den on the first floor, woke to find the stairway to my upstairs room cut off by flames. She used the phone, then ran outside to stand beneath my window.

When my parents arrived, the town volunteers had drawn water from the fire pond and were spraying the outside of the house, preparing to go inside after me, not knowing at the time that there was only one staircase and that it was lost. On the other side of the house, the superannuated[8] extension ladder broke in half. Perhaps the clatter of it falling against the walls woke me, for I'd been asleep up to that point.

As soon as I awakened, in the small room that I now use for sewing, I smelled the smoke. I followed things by the letter then, was good at memorizing instructions, and so I did exactly what was taught in the second-grade home fire drill. I got up, I touched the back of my door before opening it. Finding it hot, I left it closed and stuffed my rolled-up rug beneath the crack. I did not hide under my bed or crawl into my closet. I put on my flannel robe, and then I sat down to wait.

Outside, my mother stood below my dark window and saw clearly that there was no

Did You Know?
An *extension ladder* has two or more sections joined together by a sliding mechanism that allows the ladder to be extended to its total length.

7. *Creosote* (krē′ ə sōt′), an oily liquid that comes from the tar in wood and coal, would be a natural suspect as the *culprit,* or guilty party, in a chimney fire.
8. Something that is *superannuated* has been set aside as too old and out-of-date to use.

Vocabulary
constricting (kən strikt′ ing) *adj.* restricting; limiting
perpetually (pər pech′ o͞o əl ē) *adv.* constantly; unceasingly

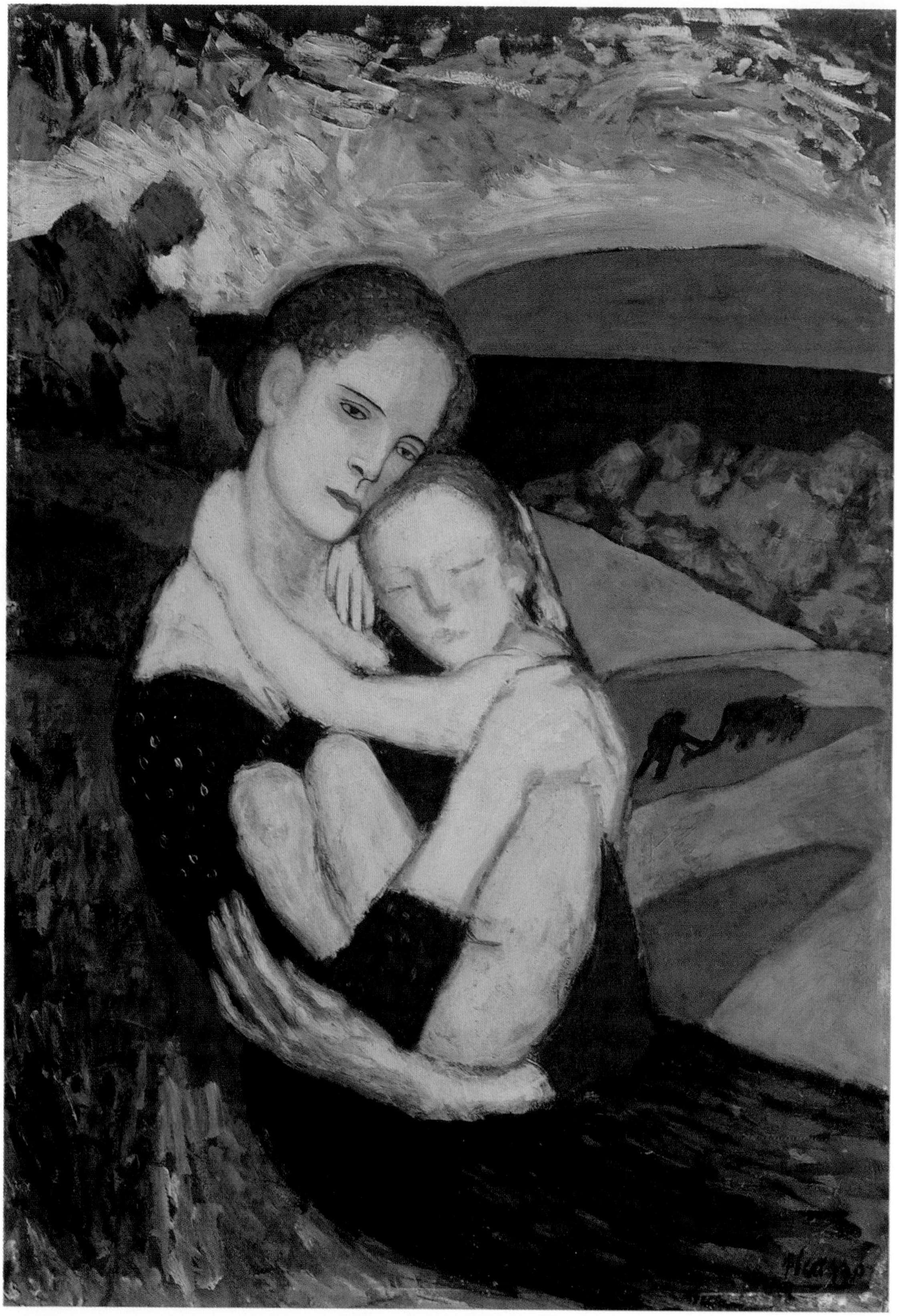

La Maternité, 1901. Pablo Picasso. Oil on burlap. Private collection.

Viewing the painting: How does this painting reflect the relationship of the mother and the daughter in the story?

rescue. Flames had pierced one side wall, and the glare of the fire lighted the massive limbs and trunk of the vigorous old elm that had probably been planted the year the house was built, a hundred years ago at least. No leaf touched the wall, and just one thin branch scraped the roof. From below, it looked as though even a squirrel would have had trouble jumping from the tree onto the house, for the breadth of that small branch was no bigger than my mother's wrist.

Standing there, beside Father, who was preparing to rush back around to the front of the house, my mother asked him to unzip her dress. When he wouldn't be bothered, she made him understand. He couldn't make his hands work, so she finally tore it off and stood there in her pearls and stockings. She directed one of the men to lean the broken half of the extension ladder up against the trunk of the tree. In surprise, he complied. She ascended. She vanished. Then she could be seen among the leafless branches of late November as she made her way up and, along her stomach, inched the length of a bough that curved above the branch that brushed the roof.

Once there, swaying, she stood and balanced. There were plenty of people in the crowd and many who still remember, or think they do, my mother's leap through the ice-dark air toward that thinnest extension, and how she broke the branch falling so that it cracked in her hands, cracked louder than the flames as she vaulted with it toward the edge of the roof, and how it hurtled down end over end without her, and their eyes went up, again, to see where she had flown.

I didn't see her leap through air, only heard the sudden thump and looked out my window. She was hanging by the backs of her heels from the new gutter we had put in that year, and she was smiling. I was not surprised to see her, she was so matter-of-fact. She tapped on the window. I remember how she did it, too. It was the friendliest tap, a bit tentative, as if she was afraid she had arrived too early at a friend's house. Then she gestured at the latch, and when I opened the window she told me to raise it wider and prop it up with the stick so it wouldn't crush her fingers. She swung down, caught the ledge, and crawled through the opening. Once she was in my room, I realized she had on only underclothing, a bra of the heavy stitched cotton women used to wear and step-in, lace-trimmed drawers. I remember feeling light-headed, of course, terribly relieved, and then embarrassed for her to be seen by the crowd undressed.

I was still embarrassed as we flew out the window, toward earth, me in her lap, her toes pointed as we skimmed toward the painted target of the fire fighter's net.

I know that she's right. I knew it even then. As you fall there is time to think. Curled as I was, against her stomach, I was not startled by the cries of the crowd or the looming faces. The wind roared and beat its hot breath at our back, the flames whistled. I slowly wondered what would happen if we missed the circle or bounced out of it. Then I wrapped my hands around my mother's hands. I felt the brush of her lips and heard the beat of her heart in my ears, loud as thunder, long as the roll of drums.

Vocabulary

comply (kəm plī′) *v.* to act in accordance with another's request
tentative (ten′ tə tiv) *adj.* hesitant; uncertain

Responding to Literature

Personal Response
In your opinion, what is the most dramatic event in this story? Why? Share your thoughts with a classmate.

Analyzing Literature

Recall

1. What caused the disaster at the circus, and what happened to the Flying Avalons?
2. How did the narrator's parents meet, and what trade did they offer to each other?
3. Why has the narrator moved back in with her mother?
4. Why was the narrator unable to escape the burning house?
5. To what does the **title** of the story refer? Keep in mind that a leap can be literal, as in a big jump, or it can be figurative, as in a leap of faith.

Interpret

6. In your opinion, why didn't the mother save her circus costume or other souvenirs from her days as a trapeze artist?
7. Why might the mother have wanted to stay in the town where the disaster happened and to live in her husband's old family home?
8. What comparisons do you think the narrator would make between her life and her mother's? Find evidence in the story to support your ideas.
9. Why might it have seemed natural to the mother to tear off her outer garments before the rescue?
10. **Theme Connections** How do each of the "leaps" in this story fit into the theme "Matters of Life and Death"?

Evaluate and Connect

11. Evaluate the author's use of **foreshadowing**–clues about upcoming events–to build suspense.
12. The narrator refers to reading as a "form of flight." Do you agree? Give reasons for your answer.
13. Do you think the mother's rescue of her daughter was realistic? Why or why not?
14. The narrator says that she felt relief and embarrassment when she saw her mother climb through the window. Explain whether these emotions are typical of a seven-year-old child in this situation.
15. Reread the story's final paragraph. What do you suppose was the author's purpose in ending her story this way?

Literary ELEMENTS

Flashback
A **flashback** is a literary device in which an earlier episode, conversation, or event is inserted into the chronological sequence of a narrative. Information revealed in a flashback helps readers understand a character's situation. Often presented as a memory of the narrator or of another character, a flashback may be sparked by one or more cues, such as a sound or odor associated with a prior experience or a visit to a related setting.

1. How do a sound, an odor, and a certain setting work together to spark the narrator's memory at the beginning of "The Leap"?
2. Identify the main flashbacks in the story, and tell how they are related to one another. Where in the story does the narrator return to the present?
3. Do you think "The Leap" would have been more or less dramatic if the author had used strict chronological order instead of flashback to tell her story? Give reasons for your opinion.

- See **Literary Terms Handbook,** p. R5.

Literature and Writing

Writing About Literature

Comparing Events This story revolves around two dramatic events. What similarities can you find between the two events? Why might the author have created these similarities? Write a paragraph or two describing the parallels between the two events and analyzing the effectiveness of the author's technique.

Personal Writing

That's Incredible! Think about the artwork you created in the Reading Focus on page 56. What motivated the person you depicted to act the way he or she did? In your journal, compare that person's motivation to do something extraordinary or unexpected with the mother's motivation in "The Leap." What connections can you make?

Extending Your Response

Literature Groups

Thoughts While Falling The narrator discovers that her mother is right: "As you fall there is time to think." We learn what the narrator is thinking as she and her mother fall to the firemen's net below, but we never hear the mother's thoughts. Discuss and debate what thoughts might have run through the mother's mind as she and her daughter leaped from the burning house to safety. Work together to write the mother's inner monologue. Be sure to consider her knowledge, experience, and point of view as you write her thoughts. Share your monologue with other groups.

Learning for Life

On-the-Spot Reporting The narrator quotes from a newspaper account of the circus fire. Imagine that you are a radio news reporter on the scene of the burning house. Create a news report to present the facts to your class. Make the report authentic, factual, and dramatic.

Interdisciplinary Activity

Sports: The Flying Trapeze Conduct research on the flying trapeze act, using library resources, CD-ROMs, and the Internet. What kind of training do the performers receive? What physical and mental skills or attributes are required? Give an oral report.

Save your work for your portfolio.

Skill Minilesson

VOCABULARY • Analogies

An analogy is a type of comparison that is based on the relationships between things or ideas. Some analogies are based on synonyms.

lucky : fortunate :: lovely : attractive

Lucky is a synonym for *fortunate; lovely* is a synonym for *attractive.*

To finish an analogy, decide what relationship exists between the first two things or ideas. Then apply that relationship to another pair of words.

● For more about analogies, see **Communications Skills Handbook,** p. R77.

PRACTICE Complete the analogies below.

1. command : order :: comply :
   a. obey b. agree c. defy
2. steady : regular :: constricting :
   a. building b. binding c. painful
3. marvel : wonder :: extricate :
   a. punish b. liberate c. soothe
4. careful : cautious :: tentative :
   a. obedient b. bold c. doubtful

Before You Read

The Most Dangerous Game

Reading Focus

According to Rainsford, a character in "The Most Dangerous Game," "The world is made up of two classes–the hunters and the huntees."

Quickwrite Might the world also be divided into adults and children? winners and losers? rich and poor? Write about what would happen if any two of these groups were to switch places.

Setting a Purpose Read to learn how it might feel to change places with the "other class."

Building Background

The Time and Place

This story is set in the early 1920s on a small lush island in the Caribbean Sea.

Did You Know?

Long before the world became aware that many species of wild animals were seriously endangered, big-game hunting was considered a great sport for "gentlemen and kings." Hunters would hire guides to take them deep into jungles to stalk, trap, and shoot big game. These adventurers were primarily interested in the "trophy aspect" of hunting; they usually kept only the animals' heads, which they hung on the walls of their homes and hunting lodges.

Vocabulary Preview

tangible (tan′ jə bəl) *adj.* capable of being touched or felt; p. 68

quarry (kwôr′ ē) *n.* anything that is hunted or pursued, especially an animal; p. 70

discern (di surn′) *v.* to detect or recognize; make out; p. 71

condone (kən dōn′) *v.* to excuse or overlook an offense, usually a serious one, without criticism; p. 75

scruple (skrōō′ pəl) *n.* an uneasy feeling or hesitancy to act that arises from moral or ethical considerations; p. 75

diverting (di vur′ ting) *adj.* amusing; entertaining; p. 78

deplorable (di plôr′ ə bəl) *adj.* very bad; regrettable; p. 78

imperative (im per′ ə tiv) *adj.* absolutely necessary; p. 79

zealous (zel′ əs) *adj.* very eager; enthusiastic; p. 79

Meet Richard Connell

When asked when he first began writing, Richard Connell couldn't remember a time in his life when he didn't write. The son of a newspaper owner, Connell was paid to cover sporting events for the paper when he was only ten years old. At sixteen, he had become the paper's city editor. As an adult, Connell wrote novels, short stories, and movie screenplays. Critics consider "The Most Dangerous Game" his masterpiece.

Richard Connell was born in 1893 and died in 1949. This story, first published in 1925, was made into a movie in 1932.

The Most Dangerous Game

Richard Connell

"OFF THERE TO THE RIGHT—somewhere—is a large island," said Whitney. "It's rather a mystery—"

"What island is it?" Rainsford asked.

"The old charts call it 'Ship-Trap Island'," Whitney replied. "A suggestive name, isn't it? Sailors have a curious dread of the place. I don't know why. Some superstition—"

"Can't see it," remarked Rainsford, trying to peer through the dank tropical night that was palpable as it pressed its thick warm blackness in upon the yacht.

Sea Piece by Moonlight. Caspar David Friedrich (1774–1840). Oil on canvas, 25 x 33 cm. Museum der bildenden Künste, Leipzig, Germany.

"You've good eyes," said Whitney, with a laugh, "and I've seen you pick off a moose moving in the brown fall bush at four hundred yards, but even you can't see four miles or so through a moonless Caribbean night."

"Nor four yards," admitted Rainsford. "Ugh! It's like moist black velvet."

"It will be light enough in Rio," promised Whitney. "We should make it in a few days. I hope the jaguar guns have come from Purdey's. We should have some good hunting up the Amazon. Great sport, hunting."

"The best sport in the world," agreed Rainsford.

"For the hunter," amended Whitney. "Not for the jaguar."

"Don't talk rot, Whitney," said Rainsford. "You're a big-game hunter, not a philosopher. Who cares how a jaguar feels?"

"Perhaps the jaguar does," observed Whitney.

"Bah! They've no understanding."

"Even so, I rather think they understand one thing—fear. The fear of pain and the fear of death."

"Nonsense," laughed Rainsford. "This hot weather is making you soft, Whitney. Be a realist. The world is made up of two classes—the hunters and the huntees. Luckily, you and I are hunters. Do you think we've passed that island yet?"

"I can't tell in the dark. I hope so."

"Why?" asked Rainsford.

"The place has a reputation—a bad one."

"Cannibals?" suggested Rainsford.

"Hardly. Even cannibals wouldn't live in such a God-forsaken place. But it's gotten into sailor lore,[1] somehow. Didn't you notice that the crew's nerves seemed a bit jumpy today?"

Sometimes I think evil is a tangible thing . . .

"They were a bit strange, now you mention it. Even Captain Nielsen—"

"Yes, even that tough-minded old Swede, who'd go up to the devil himself and ask him for a light. Those fishy blue eyes held a look I never saw there before. All I could get out of him was: 'This place has an evil name among seafaring men, sir.' Then he said to me, very gravely: 'Don't you feel anything?'—as if the air about us was actually poisonous. Now, you mustn't laugh when I tell you this—I did feel something like a sudden chill.

"There was no breeze. The sea was as flat as a plate-glass window. We were drawing near the island then. What I felt was a—a mental chill; a sort of sudden dread."

"Pure imagination," said Rainsford. "One superstitious sailor can taint the whole ship's company with his fear."

"Maybe. But sometimes I think sailors have an extra sense that tells them when they are in danger. Sometimes I think evil is a tangible thing—with wave lengths, just as sound and light have. An evil place can, so to speak, broadcast vibrations of evil. Anyhow, I'm glad we're getting out of this zone. Well, I think I'll turn in now, Rainsford."

"I'm not sleepy," said Rainsford. "I'm going to smoke another pipe up on the afterdeck."

"Good night, then, Rainsford. See you at breakfast."

1. Accumulated traditions and beliefs about a particular subject are called *lore.*

Vocabulary

tangible (tan′ jə bəl) *adj.* capable of being touched or felt

"Right. Good night, Whitney."

There was no sound in the night as Rainsford sat there but the muffled throb of the engine that drove the yacht swiftly through the darkness, and the swish and ripple of the wash of the propeller.

Rainsford, reclining in a steamer chair, indolently puffed on his favorite briar.[2] The sensuous drowsiness of the night was upon him. "It's so dark," he thought, "that I could sleep without closing my eyes; the night would be my eyelids—"

An abrupt sound startled him. Off to the right he heard it, and his ears, expert in such matters, could not be mistaken. Again he heard the sound, and again. Somewhere, off in the blackness, someone had fired a gun three times.

Rainsford sprang up and moved quickly to the rail, mystified. He strained his eyes in the direction from which the reports had come, but it was like trying to see through a blanket. He leaped upon the rail and balanced himself there, to get greater elevation; his pipe, striking a rope, was knocked from his mouth. He lunged for it; a short, hoarse cry came from his lips as he realized he had reached too far and had lost his balance. The cry was pinched off short as the blood-warm waters of the Caribbean Sea closed over his head.

He struggled up to the surface and tried to cry out, but the wash from the speeding yacht slapped him in the face and the salt water in his open mouth made him gag and strangle. Desperately he struck out with strong strokes after the receding lights of the yacht, but he stopped before he had swum fifty feet. A certain cool-headedness had come to him; it was not the first time he had been in a tight place. There was a chance that his cries could be heard by someone aboard the yacht, but that chance was slender, and grew more slender as the yacht raced on. He wrestled himself out of his clothes, and shouted with all his power. The lights of the yacht became faint and ever-vanishing fireflies; then they were blotted out entirely by the night.

Rainsford remembered the shots. They had come from the right, and doggedly he swam in that direction, swimming with slow, deliberate strokes, conserving his strength. For a seemingly endless time he fought the sea. He began to count his strokes; he could do possibly a hundred more and then—

Rainsford heard a sound. It came out of the darkness, a high screaming sound, the sound of an animal in an extremity of anguish and terror.

He did not recognize the animal that made the sound; he did not try to; with fresh vitality he swam toward the sound. He heard it again; then it was cut short by another noise, crisp, staccato.

"Pistol shot," muttered Rainsford, swimming on.

Ten minutes of determined effort brought another sound to his ears—the most welcome he had ever heard—the muttering and growling of the sea breaking on a rocky shore. He was almost on the rocks before he saw them; on a night less calm he would have been shattered against them. With his remaining strength he dragged himself from the swirling waters. Jagged crags appeared to jut up into the opaqueness; he forced himself upward, hand over hand. Gasping, his hands

Did You Know?
Crags are steep, rugged, protruding rocks or cliffs. Here, the crags jut up into the darkness *(opaqueness)* of the night.

2. *Indolently* means "lazily"; a *briar* is a tobacco pipe made from the fine-grained wood of the root of a Mediterranean shrub.

raw, he reached a flat place at the top. Dense jungle came down to the very edge of the cliffs. What perils that tangle of trees and underbrush might hold for him did not concern Rainsford just then. All he knew was that he was safe from his enemy, the sea, and that utter weariness was upon him. He flung himself down at the jungle edge and tumbled headlong into the deepest sleep of his life.

When he opened his eyes he knew from the position of the sun that it was late in the afternoon. Sleep had given him new vigor; a sharp hunger was picking at him. He looked about him, almost cheerfully.

"Where there are pistol shots, there are men. Where there are men, there is food," he thought. But what kind of men, he wondered, in so forbidding a place? An unbroken front of snarled and ragged jungle fringed the shore.

He saw no sign of a trail through the closely knit web of weeds and trees; it was easier to go along the shore, and Rainsford floundered along by the water. Not far from where he had landed, he stopped.

Some wounded thing, by the evidence, a large animal, had thrashed about in the underbrush; the jungle weeds were crushed down and the moss was lacerated; one patch of weeds was stained crimson. A small, glittering object not far away caught Rainsford's eye and he picked it up. It was an empty cartridge.

"A twenty-two," he remarked. "That's odd. It must have been a fairly large animal, too. The hunter had his nerve with him to tackle it with a light gun. It's clear that the brute put up a fight. I suppose the first three shots I heard was when the hunter flushed his quarry and wounded it. The last shot was when he trailed it here and finished it."

He examined the ground closely and found what he had hoped to find—the print of hunting boots. They pointed along the cliff in the direction he had been going. Eagerly he hurried along, now slipping on a rotten log or a loose stone, but making headway; night was beginning to settle down on the island.

Bleak darkness was blacking out the sea and jungle when Rainsford sighted the lights. He came upon them as he turned a crook in the coast line, and his first thought was that he had come upon a village, for there were many lights. But as he forged along he saw to his great astonishment that all the lights were in one enormous building—a lofty structure with pointed towers plunging upward into the gloom. His eyes made out the shadowy outlines of a palatial chateau;[3] it was set on a high bluff, and on three sides of it cliffs dived down to where the sea licked greedy lips in the shadows.

"Mirage," thought Rainsford. But it was no mirage, he found, when he opened the tall spiked iron gate. The stone steps were real enough; the massive door with a leering gargoyle for a knocker was real enough; yet above it all hung an air of unreality.

Did You Know?
A *gargoyle* is an outlandish or grotesquely carved figure.

He lifted the knocker, and it creaked up stiffly, as if it had never before been used. He let it fall, and it startled him with its booming loudness. He thought he heard steps within; the door remained closed. Again

3. A *palatial chateau* (sha tō′) is a magnificent, palace-like mansion.

Vocabulary
quarry (kwôr′ ē) *n.* anything that is hunted or pursued, especially an animal

Rainsford lifted the heavy knocker, and let it fall. The door opened then, opened as suddenly as if it were on a spring, and Rainsford stood blinking in the river of glaring gold light that poured out. The first thing Rainsford's eyes discerned was the largest man Rainsford had ever seen—a gigantic creature, solidly made and black-bearded to the waist. In his hand the man held a long-barreled revolver, and he was pointing it straight at Rainsford's heart.

Out of the snarl of beard two small eyes regarded Rainsford.

"Don't be alarmed," said Rainsford, with a smile which he hoped was disarming.[4] "I'm no robber. I fell off a yacht. My name is Sanger Rainsford of New York City."

The menacing look in the eyes did not change. The revolver pointed as rigidly as if the giant were a statue. He gave no sign that he understood Rainsford's words, or that he had even heard them. He was dressed in uniform, a black uniform trimmed with gray astrakhan.[5]

"I'm Sanger Rainsford of New York," Rainsford began again. "I fell off a yacht. I am hungry."

The man's only answer was to raise with his thumb the hammer of his revolver. Then Rainsford saw the man's free hand go to his forehead in a military salute, and he saw him click his heels together and stand at attention. Another man was coming down the broad marble steps, an erect, slender man in evening clothes. He advanced to Rainsford and held out his hand.

In a cultivated voice marked by a slight accent that gave it added precision and deliberateness, he said: "It is a very great pleasure and honor to welcome Mr. Sanger Rainsford, the celebrated hunter, to my home."

Clay, 1986. Thomas Kennedy. Pastel on sand paper, 24 x 20 in. Private collection.

Viewing the art: In what way might this man remind you of General Zaroff? Explain.

Automatically Rainsford shook the man's hand.

"I've read your book about hunting snow leopards in Tibet, you see," explained the man. "I am General Zaroff."

Rainsford's first impression was that the man was singularly handsome; his second was that there was an original, almost bizarre quality about the general's face. He was a tall man past middle age, for his hair was a vivid white; but his thick eyebrows and pointed military mustache were as black as the night from which Rainsford had come.

4. *Disarming* means "tending to remove fear or suspicion; charming."

5. *Astrakhan* is the woolly skin of young lambs and is named after a region in Russia.

Vocabulary

discern (di surn′) *v.* to detect or recognize; make out

His eyes, too, were black and very bright. He had high cheek bones, a sharp-cut nose, a spare, dark face, the face of a man used to giving orders, the face of an aristocrat. Turning to the giant in uniform, the general made a sign. The giant put away his pistol, saluted, withdrew.

"Ivan is an incredibly strong fellow," remarked the general, "but he has the misfortune to be deaf and dumb. A simple fellow, but, I'm afraid, like all his race, a bit of a savage."

"Is he Russian?"

"He is a Cossack,"[6] said the general, and his smile showed red lips and pointed teeth. "So am I."

"Come," he said, "we shouldn't be chatting here. We can talk later. Now you want clothes, food, rest. You shall have them. This is a most restful spot."

Ivan had reappeared, and the general spoke to him with lips that moved but gave forth no sound.

"Follow Ivan, if you please, Mr. Rainsford," said the general. "I was about to have my dinner when you came. I'll wait for you. You'll find that my clothes will fit you, I think."

It was to a huge, beam-ceilinged bedroom with a canopied bed big enough for six men that Rainsford followed the silent giant. Ivan laid out an evening suit, and Rainsford, as he put it on, noticed that it came from a London tailor who ordinarily cut and sewed for none below the rank of duke.

The dining room to which Ivan conducted them was in many ways remarkable. There was a medieval magnificence about it; it suggested a baronial hall of feudal times with its oaken panels, its high ceiling, its vast refectory tables where twoscore men could sit down to eat.[7] About the hall were the mounted heads of many animals—lions, tigers, elephants, moose, bears; larger or more perfect specimens Rainsford had never seen. At the great table the general was sitting, alone.

"You'll have a cocktail, Mr. Rainsford," he suggested. The cocktail was surpassingly good; and, Rainsford noticed, the table appointments were of the finest—the linen, the crystal, the silver, the china.

They were eating *borscht*, the rich, red soup with whipped cream so dear to Russian palates. Half apologetically General Zaroff said: "We do our best to preserve the amenities of civilization here.[8] Please forgive any lapses. We are well off the beaten track, you know. Do you think the champagne has suffered from its long ocean trip?"

"Not in the least," declared Rainsford. He was finding the general a most thoughtful and affable host, a true cosmopolite.[9] But there was one small trait of the general's that made Rainsford uncomfortable. Whenever he looked up from his plate he found the general studying him, appraising him narrowly.

"Perhaps," said General Zaroff, "you were surprised that I recognized your name. You see, I read all books on hunting published in English, French, and Russian. I have but one passion in my life, Mr. Rainsford, and it is the hunt."

"You have some wonderful heads here," said Rainsford as he ate a particularly well cooked *filet mignon*. "That Cape buffalo[10] is the largest I ever saw."

---

6. The *Cossacks* are a people of southern Russia (and, now, Kazakhstan). During czarist times, Cossack men were famous as horsemen in the Russian cavalry.

7. The words *medieval, baronial,* and *feudal* all relate to the Middle Ages. A *refectory table* might be found in a baron's castle; it is a long, wooden table with straight, heavy legs.

8. *Borscht* (bôrsht) is a soup made from beets. Here, *palates* means "tastes or likings," and *amenities* means "agreeable features, or niceties."

9. *Affable* means "friendly and gracious." A *cosmopolite* (koz mop′ ə līt′) is a gracious and sophisticated person.

10. The African *Cape buffalo* is a large, often fierce buffalo with heavy, downward-curving horns.

"Oh, that fellow. Yes, he was a monster."

"Did he charge you?"

"Hurled me against a tree," said the general. "Fractured my skull. But I got the brute."

"I've always thought," said Rainsford, "that the Cape buffalo is the most dangerous of all big game."

For a moment the general did not reply; he was smiling his curious red-lipped smile. Then he said slowly: "No. You are wrong, sir. The Cape buffalo is not the most dangerous big game." He sipped his wine. "Here in my preserve on this island," he said in the same slow tone, "I hunt more dangerous game."

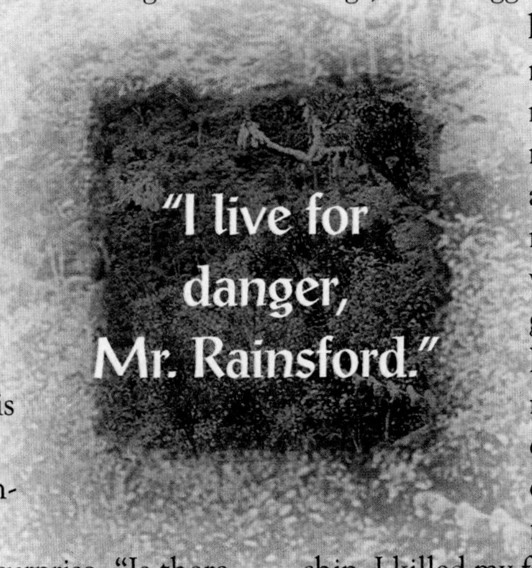
"I live for danger, Mr. Rainsford."

Rainsford expressed his surprise. "Is there big game on this island?"

The general nodded. "The biggest."

"Really?"

"Oh, it isn't here naturally, of course. I have to stock the island."

"What have you imported, general?" Rainsford asked. "Tigers?"

The general smiled. "No," he said. "Hunting tigers ceased to interest me some years ago. I exhausted their possibilities, you see. No thrill left in tigers, no real danger. I live for danger, Mr. Rainsford."

The general took from his pocket a gold cigarette case and offered his guest a long black cigarette with a silver tip; it was perfumed and gave off a smell like incense.

"We will have some capital hunting, you and I," said the general. "I shall be most glad to have your society."

"But what game—" began Rainsford.

"I'll tell you," said the general. "You will be amused, I know. I think I may say, in all modesty, that I have done a rare thing. I have invented a new sensation. May I pour you another glass of port?"

"Thank you, general."

The general filled both glasses, and said: "God makes some men poets. Some He makes kings, some beggars. Me He made a hunter. My hand was made for the trigger, my father said. He was a very rich man with a quarter of a million acres in the Crimea, and he was an ardent sportsman. When I was only five years old he gave me a little gun, specially made in Moscow for me, to shoot sparrows with. When I shot some of his prize turkeys with it, he did not punish me; he complimented me on my marksmanship. I killed my first bear in the Caucasus[11] when I was ten. My whole life has been one prolonged hunt. I went into the army—it was expected of noblemen's sons—and for a time commanded a division of Cossack cavalry, but my real interest was always the hunt. I have hunted every kind of game in every land. It would be impossible for me to tell you how many animals I have killed."

The general puffed at his cigarette.

"After the debacle in Russia I left the country, for it was imprudent for an officer of the Czar to stay there.[12] Many noble Russians lost everything. I, luckily, had invested heavily in American securities, so I shall never have to open a tearoom in Monte Carlo or drive a taxi in Paris. Naturally, I continued

---

11. *Crimea* (krī mē′ ə) is a region in the southern part of the former Russian empire near the Black Sea. *Caucasus* (kô′ kə səs) refers to both a region and a mountain range between the Black and Caspian seas.
12. A *debacle* (di bä′ kəl) is a disastrous defeat. Zaroff refers to the 1917 revolution that overthrew the Czar, an event that made it unwise *(imprudent)* for him to stay in Russia.

to hunt—grizzlies in your Rockies, crocodile in the Ganges, rhinoceroses in East Africa. It was in Africa that the Cape buffalo hit me and laid me up for six months. As soon as I recovered I started for the Amazon to hunt jaguars, for I had heard they were unusually cunning. They weren't." The Cossack sighed. "They were no match at all for a hunter with his wits about him, and a high-powered rifle. I was bitterly disappointed. I was lying in my tent with a splitting headache one night when a terrible thought pushed its way into my mind. Hunting was beginning to bore me! And hunting, remember, had been my life. I have heard that in America business men often go to pieces when they give up the business that has been their life."

"Yes, that's so," said Rainsford.

The general smiled. "I had no wish to go to pieces," he said. "I must do something. Now, mine is an analytical mind, Mr. Rainsford. Doubtless that is why I enjoy the problems of the chase."

"No doubt, General Zaroff."

"So," continued the general, "I asked myself why the hunt no longer fascinated me. You are much younger than I am, Mr. Rainsford, and have not hunted as much, but you perhaps can guess the answer."

"What was it?"

"Simply this: hunting had ceased to be what you call 'a sporting proposition.' It had become too easy. I always got my quarry. Always. There is no greater bore than perfection."

The general lit a fresh cigarette.

"No animal had a chance with me any more. That is no boast; it is a mathematical certainty. The animal had nothing but his legs and his instinct. Instinct is no match for reason. When I thought of this it was a tragic moment for me, I can tell you."

"Instinct is no match for reason."

Rainsford leaned across the table, absorbed in what his host was saying.

"It came to me as an inspiration what I must do," the general went on.

"And that was?"

The general smiled the quiet smile of one who has faced an obstacle and surmounted it with success. "I had to invent a new animal to hunt," he said.

"A new animal? You're joking."

"Not at all," said the general. "I never joke about hunting. I needed a new animal. I found one. So I bought this island, built this house, and here I do my hunting. The island is perfect for my purposes—there are jungles with a maze of trails in them, hills, swamps—"

"But the animal, General Zaroff?"

"Oh," said the general, "it supplies me with the most exciting hunting in the world. No other hunting compares with it for an instant. Every day I hunt, and I never grow bored now, for I have a quarry with which I can match my wits."

Rainsford's bewilderment showed in his face.

"I wanted the ideal animal to hunt," explained the general. "So I said: 'What are the attributes of an ideal quarry?' And the answer was, of course: 'It must have courage, cunning, and, above all, it must be able to reason.'"

"But no animal can reason," objected Rainsford.

"My dear fellow," said the general, "there is one that can."

"But you can't mean—" gasped Rainsford.

"And why not?"

"I can't believe you are serious, General Zaroff. This is a grisly joke."

"Why should I not be serious? I am speaking of hunting."

"Hunting? Good God, General Zaroff, what you speak of is murder."

The general laughed with entire good nature. He regarded Rainsford quizzically. "I refuse to believe that so modern and civilized a young man as you seem to be harbors romantic ideas about the value of human life. Surely your experiences in the war—"

"Did not make me condone cold-blooded murder," finished Rainsford stiffly.

Laughter shook the general. "How extraordinarily droll you are!" he said. "One does not expect nowadays to find a young man of the educated class, even in America, with such a naive, and, if I may say so, mid-Victorian[13] point of view. It's like finding a snuff-box in a limousine. Ah, well, doubtless you had Puritan ancestors. So many Americans appear to have had. I'll wager you'll forget your notions when you go hunting with me. You've a genuine new thrill in store for you, Mr. Rainsford."

"Thank you, I'm a hunter, not a murderer."

"Dear me," said the general, quite unruffled, "again that unpleasant word. But I think I can show you that your scruples are quite ill founded."

"Yes?"

"Life is for the strong, to be lived by the strong, and, if needs be, taken by the strong. The weak of the world were put here to give the strong pleasure. I am strong. Why should I not use my fist? If I wish to hunt, why should I not? I hunt the scum of the earth—sailors from tramp ships—lascars,[14] blacks, Chinese, whites, mongrels—a thoroughbred horse or hound is worth more than a score of them."

"But they are men," said Rainsford hotly.

"Precisely," said the general. "That is why I use them. It gives me pleasure. They can reason, after a fashion. So they are dangerous."

"But where do you get them?"

The general's left eyelid fluttered down in a wink. "This island is called Ship-Trap," he answered. "Sometimes an angry god of the high seas sends them to me. Sometimes, when Providence is not so kind, I help Providence a bit. Come to the window with me."

Rainsford went to the window and looked out toward the sea.

"Watch! Out there!" exclaimed the general, pointing into the night. Rainsford's eyes saw only blackness, and then, as the general pressed a button, far out to sea Rainsford saw the flash of lights.

The general chuckled. "They indicate a channel," he said, "where there's none; giant rocks with razor edges crouch like a sea monster with wide-open jaws. They can crush a ship as easily as I crush this nut." He dropped a walnut on the hardwood floor and brought his heel grinding down on it. "Oh, yes," he said, casually, as if in answer to a question, "I have electricity. We try to be civilized here."

"Civilized? And you shoot down men?"

A trace of anger was in the general's black eyes, but it was there for but a second, and he said, in his most pleasant manner: "Dear me, what a righteous young man you

13. Zaroff feels that Rainsford is quaint *(droll)*, innocent and unsophisticated *(naive)*, and old-fashioned *(mid-Victorian)*.

14. *Lascars* are sailors from India.

Vocabulary

condone (kən dōn′) *v.* to excuse or overlook an offense, usually a serious one, without criticism

scruple (skrōō′ pəl) *n.* an uneasy feeling or hesitancy to act that arises from moral or ethical considerations are! I assure you I do not do the thing you suggest. That would be barbarous. I treat these visitors with every consideration. They get plenty of good food and exercise. They get into splendid physical condition. You shall see for yourself tomorrow."

"What do you mean?"

"We'll visit my training school," smiled the general. "It's in the cellar. I have about a dozen pupils down there now. They're from the Spanish bark *San Lucar* that had the bad luck to go on the rocks out there. A very inferior lot, I regret to say. Poor specimens and more accustomed to the deck than to the jungle."

Did You Know?
A *bark* has from three to five masts, all but one of which are rigged with four-sided sails. The last mast has both three- and four-sided sails.

He raised his hand, and Ivan, who served as waiter, brought thick Turkish coffee. Rainsford, with an effort, held his tongue in check.

"It's a game, you see," pursued the general blandly. "I suggest to one of them that we go hunting. I give him a supply of food and an excellent hunting knife. I give him three hours' start. I am to follow, armed only with a pistol of the smallest caliber and range. If my quarry eludes me for three whole days, he wins the game. If I find him"—the general smiled—"he loses."

"Suppose he refuses to be hunted?"

"Oh," said the general, "I give him his option, of course. He need not play that game if he doesn't wish to. If he does not wish to hunt, I turn him over to Ivan. Ivan once had the honor of serving as official knouter[15] to the Great White Czar, and he has his own ideas of sport. Invariably, Mr. Rainsford, invariably they choose the hunt."

"And if they win?"

The smile on the general's face widened. "To date I have not lost," he said. Then he added, hastily: "I don't wish you to think me a braggart, Mr. Rainsford. Many of them afford only the most elementary sort of problem. Occasionally I strike a tartar.[16] One almost did win. I eventually had to use the dogs."

"The dogs?"

"This way, please. I'll show you."

The general steered Rainsford to a window. The lights from the windows sent a flickering illumination that made grotesque patterns on the courtyard below, and Rainsford could see moving about there a dozen or so huge black shapes; as they turned toward him, their eyes glittered greenly.

"A rather good lot, I think," observed the general. "They are let out at seven every night. If anyone should try to get into my house—or out of it—something extremely regrettable would occur to him." He hummed a snatch of song from the *Folies Bergère*.[17]

"And now," said the general, "I want to show you my new collection of heads. Will you come with me to the library?"

"I hope," said Rainsford, "that you will excuse me tonight, General Zaroff. I'm really not feeling well."

"Ah, indeed?" the general inquired solicitously.[18] "Well, I suppose that's only natural, after your long swim. You need a good, restful night's sleep. Tomorrow you'll feel like

15. As the Czar's *knouter* (nou′ tər), Ivan was in charge of administering whippings and torture. A knout is a whip made of leather straps braided together with wires.

16. To *strike a tartar* is to take on someone who is stronger or abler.

17. The *Folies Bergère* (fô lē′ ber zher′) is a music hall in Paris, famed for its variety shows.

18. *Solicitously* means "in a caring or concerned manner."

a new man, I'll wager. Then we'll hunt, eh? I've one rather promising prospect—" Rainsford was hurrying from the room.

"Sorry you can't go with me tonight," called the general. "I expect rather fair sport—a big, strong black. He looks resourceful—Well, good night, Mr. Rainsford; I hope you have a good night's rest."

The bed was good, and the pajamas of the softest silk and he was tired in every fiber of his being, but nevertheless Rainsford could not quiet his brain with the opiate of sleep. He lay, eyes wide open. Once he thought he heard stealthy steps in the corridor outside his room. He sought to throw open the door; it would not open. He went to the window and looked out. His room was high up in one of the towers. The lights of the chateau were out now, and it was dark and silent, but there was a fragment of sallow moon, and by its wan light he could see, dimly, the courtyard; there, weaving in and out in the pattern of shadow, were black, noiseless forms; the hounds heard him at the window and looked up, expectantly, with their green eyes. Rainsford went back to the bed and lay down. By many methods he tried to put himself to sleep. He had achieved a doze when, just as morning began to come, he heard, far off in the jungle, the faint report of a pistol.

General Zaroff did not appear until luncheon. He was dressed faultlessly in the tweeds of a country squire. He was solicitous about the state of Rainsford's health.

"As for me," sighed the general, "I do not feel so well. I am worried, Mr. Rainsford. Last night I detected traces of my old complaint."

To Rainsford's questioning glance the general said: "Ennui.[19] Boredom."

Then, taking a second helping of *Crêpes Suzette*, the general explained: "The hunting was not good last night. The fellow lost his head. He made a straight trail that offered no problems at all. That's the trouble with these sailors; they have dull brains to begin with, and they do not know how to get about in the woods. They do excessively stupid and obvious

Did You Know?
Crêpes Suzette (krāps′ so͞o zet′) are thin pancakes rolled and heated in a sweet sauce flavored with orange or lemon juice and brandy.

19. ***Ennui*** (än wē′)

things. It's most annoying. Will you have another glass of *Chablis*,[20] Mr. Rainsford?"

"General," said Rainsford firmly, "I wish to leave this island at once."

The general raised his thickets of eyebrows; he seemed hurt. "But, my dear fellow," the general protested, "you've only just come. You've had no hunting—"

"I wish to go today," said Rainsford. He saw the dead black eyes of the general on him, studying him. General Zaroff's face suddenly brightened.

He filled Rainsford's glass with venerable *Chablis* from a dusty bottle.

"Tonight," said the general, "we will hunt—you and I."

Rainsford shook his head. "No, general," he said, "I will not hunt."

The general shrugged his shoulders and delicately ate a hothouse grape. "As you wish, my friend," he said. "The choice rests entirely with you. But may I not venture to suggest that you will find my idea of sport more diverting than Ivan's?"

He nodded toward the corner to where the giant stood, scowling, his thick arms crossed on his hogshead of a chest.

"You don't mean—" cried Rainsford.

"My dear fellow," said the general, "have I not told you I always mean what I say about hunting? This is really an inspiration. I drink to a foeman worthy of my steel—at last." The general raised his glass, but Rainsford sat staring at him.

"You'll find this game worth playing," the general said enthusiastically. "Your brain against mine. Your woodcraft against mine. Your strength and stamina against mine. Outdoor chess! And the stake is not without value, eh?"

"And if I win—" began Rainsford huskily.

"I'll cheerfully acknowledge myself defeated if I do not find you by midnight of the third day," said General Zaroff. "My sloop will place you on the mainland near a town." The general read what Rainsford was thinking.

"Oh, you can trust me," said the Cossack. "I will give you my word as a gentleman and a sportsman. Of course you, in turn, must agree to say nothing of your visit here."

"I'll agree to nothing of the kind," said Rainsford.

"Oh," said the general, "in that case—But why discuss that now? Three days hence we can discuss it over a bottle of *Veuve Cliquot*,[21] unless—"

The general sipped his wine. Then a businesslike air animated him. "Ivan," he said to Rainsford, "will supply you with hunting clothes, food, a knife. I suggest you wear moccasins; they leave a poorer trail. I suggest, too, that you avoid the big swamp in the southeast corner of the island. We call it Death Swamp. There's quicksand there. One foolish fellow tried it. The deplorable part of it was that Lazarus followed him. You can imagine my feelings, Mr. Rainsford. I loved Lazarus; he was the finest hound in my pack. Well, I must beg you to excuse me now. I always take a siesta after lunch. You'll hardly have time for a nap, I fear. You'll want to start, no doubt. I shall not follow till dusk. Hunting at night is so much more exciting than by day, don't you think? *Au revoir*,[22] Mr. Rainsford, *au revoir*." General Zaroff, with a deep, courtly bow, strolled from the room.

20. *Chablis* (sha blē′) is a white wine.

21. *Veuve Cliquot* (vœv klē kō′) is a French champagne.

22. *Au revoir* (ō rə vwär′) is French for "good-bye," or "until we meet again."

Vocabulary

diverting (di vur′ ting) *adj.* amusing; entertaining

deplorable (di plôr′ ə bəl) *adj.* very bad; regrettable

Rainsford had fought his way through the bush for two hours. "I must keep my nerve. I must keep my nerve," he said through tight teeth.

He had not been entirely clear-headed when the chateau gates snapped shut behind him. His whole idea at first was to put distance between himself and General Zaroff, and, to this end, he had plunged along, spurred on by the sharp rowels of something very like panic. Now he had got a grip on himself, had stopped, and was taking stock of himself and the situation. He saw that straight flight was futile; inevitably it would bring him face to face with the sea. He was in a picture with a frame of water, and his operations, clearly, must take place within that frame.

Did You Know?
A *rowel* is a wheel with sharp radiating points, as on the end of a rider's spur.

"I'll give him a trail to follow," muttered Rainsford, and he struck off from the rude path he had been following into the trackless wilderness. He executed a series of intricate loops; he doubled on his trail again and again, recalling all the lore of the fox hunt, and all the dodges of the fox. Night found him leg-weary, with hands and face lashed by the branches, on a thickly wooded ridge. He knew it would be insane to blunder on through the dark, even if he had the strength. His need for rest was imperative and he thought: "I have played the fox, now I must play the cat of the fable." A big tree with a thick trunk and outspread branches was near by, and, taking care to leave not the slightest mark, he climbed up into the crotch, and stretching out on one of the broad limbs, after a fashion, rested. Rest brought him new confidence and almost a feeling of security. Even so zealous a hunter as General Zaroff could not trace him there, he told himself; only the devil himself could follow that complicated trail through the jungle after dark. But, perhaps the general was a devil—

An apprehensive night crawled slowly by like a wounded snake, and sleep did not visit Rainsford, although the silence of a dead world was on the jungle. Toward morning when a dingy gray was varnishing the sky, the cry of some startled bird focused Rainsford's attention in that direction. Something was coming through the bush, coming slowly, carefully, coming by the same winding way Rainsford had come. He flattened himself down on the limb, and through a screen of leaves almost as thick as tapestry, he watched. . . . That which was approaching was a man.

He was General Zaroff. He made his way along with his eyes fixed in utmost concentration on the ground before him. He paused, almost beneath the tree, dropped to his knees and studied the ground. Rainsford's impulse was to hurl himself down like a panther, but he saw that the general's right hand held something metallic—a small automatic pistol.

The hunter shook his head several times, as if he were puzzled. Then he straightened up and took from his case one of his black cigarettes; its pungent incenselike smoke floated up to Rainsford's nostrils.

Rainsford held his breath. The general's eyes had left the ground and were traveling inch by inch up the tree. Rainsford froze there, every muscle tensed for a spring. But the sharp eyes of the hunter stopped before they reached the limb where Rainsford lay;

Vocabulary
imperative (im per′ ə tiv) *adj.* absolutely necessary
zealous (zel′ əs) *adj.* very eager; enthusiastic

a smile spread over his brown face. Very deliberately he blew a smoke ring into the air; then he turned his back on the tree and walked carelessly away, back along the trail he had come. The swish of the underbrush against his hunting boots grew fainter and fainter.

The pent-up air burst hotly from Rainsford's lungs. His first thought made him feel sick and numb. The general could follow a trail through the woods at night; he could follow an extremely difficult trail; he must have uncanny powers; only by the merest chance had the Cossack failed to see his quarry.

Rainsford's second thought was even more terrible. It sent a shudder of cold horror through his whole being. Why had the general smiled? Why had he turned back?

Rainsford did not want to believe what his reason told him was true, but the truth was as evident as the sun that had by now pushed through the morning mists. The general was playing with him! The general was saving him for another day's sport! The Cossack was the cat; he was the mouse. Then it was that Rainsford knew the full meaning of terror.

"I will not lose my nerve. I will not."

He slid down from the tree, and struck off again into the woods. His face was set and he forced the machinery of his mind to function. Three hundred yards from his hiding place he stopped where a huge dead tree leaned precariously on a smaller, living one. Throwing off his sack of food, Rainsford took his knife from its sheath and began to work with all his energy.

The job was finished at last, and he threw himself down behind a fallen log a hundred feet away. He did not have to wait long. The cat was coming again to play with the mouse.

Following the trail with the sureness of a bloodhound came General Zaroff. Nothing escaped those searching black eyes, no crushed blade of grass, no bent twig, no mark, no matter how faint, in the moss. So intent was the Cossack on his stalking that he was upon the thing Rainsford had made before he saw it. His foot touched it, the general sensed his danger and leaped back with the agility of an ape. But he was not quick enough; the dead tree, delicately adjusted to rest on the cut living one, crashed down and struck the general a glancing blow on the shoulder as it fell; but for his alertness, he must have been smashed beneath it. He staggered, but he did not fall; nor did he drop his revolver. He stood there, rubbing his injured shoulder, and Rainsford, with fear again gripping his heart, heard the general's mocking laugh ring through the jungle.

"Rainsford," called the general, "if you are within sound of my voice, as I suppose you are, let me congratulate you. Not many men know how to make a Malay man-catcher. Luckily, for me, I, too, have hunted in Malacca.[23] You are proving interesting, Mr. Rainsford. I am going now to have my wound dressed; it's only a slight one. But I shall be back."

When the general, nursing his bruised shoulder, had gone, Rainsford took up his flight again. It was flight now, a desperate, hopeless flight, that carried him on for some hours. Dusk came, then darkness, and still he pressed on. The ground grew softer under his moccasins, the vegetation grew ranker, denser; insects bit him savagely. Then, as he stepped forward, his foot sank into the ooze. He tried to wrench it back, but the muck sucked viciously at his foot as if it were a giant leech. With a violent effort, he tore his feet loose. He knew where he was now. Death Swamp and its quicksand.

His hands were tight closed as if his nerve were something tangible that someone in the darkness was trying to tear from his grip. The softness of the earth had given him an idea. He stepped back from the quicksand a dozen feet or so and, like some huge prehistoric beaver, he began to dig.

Rainsford had dug himself in in France when a second's delay meant death. That had been a placid pastime compared to his digging now. The pit grew deeper; when it was above his shoulders, he climbed out and from some hard saplings cut stakes and sharpened them to a fine point. These stakes he planted in the bottom of the pit with the points sticking up. With flying fingers he wove a rough carpet of weeds and branches and with it he covered the mouth of the pit. Then, wet with sweat and aching with tiredness, he crouched behind the stump of a lightning-charred tree.

Did You Know?
A *sapling* is a young tree.

He knew that his pursuer was coming; he heard the padding sound of feet on the soft earth, and the night breeze brought him the perfume of the general's cigarette. It seemed to Rainsford that the general was coming with unusual swiftness; he was not feeling his way along, foot by foot. Rainsford, crouching there, could not see the general, nor could he see the pit. He lived a year in a minute. Then he felt an impulse to cry aloud with joy, for he heard the sharp crackle of the breaking branches as the cover of the pit gave way; he heard the sharp scream of pain as the pointed stakes found their mark. He leaped up from his place of concealment. Then he cowered

23. The *Malay* are a people of southeast Asia, and *Malacca* (mə lak′ ə) is their home region.

back. Three feet from the pit a man was standing, with an electric torch in his hand.

"You've done well, Rainsford," the voice of the general called. "Your Burmese tiger pit has claimed one of my best dogs. Again you score. I think, Mr. Rainsford, I'll see what you can do against my whole pack. I'm going home for a rest now. Thank you for a most amusing evening."

At daybreak Rainsford, lying near the swamp, was awakened by a sound that made him know that he had new things to learn about fear. It was a distant sound, faint and wavering, but he knew it. It was the baying of a pack of hounds.

Rainsford knew he could do one of two things. He could stay where he was and wait. That was suicide. He could flee. That was postponing the inevitable. For a moment he stood there, thinking. An idea that held a wild chance came to him, and, tightening his belt, he headed away from the swamp.

Land's End–Cornwall, 1888. William Trost Richards. Oil on canvas, 62 x 50 in. The Butler Institute of American Art, Youngstown, OH.

Viewing the painting: What might it feel like to stand at the edge of cliffs like these?

The baying of the hounds drew nearer, then still nearer, nearer, ever nearer. On a ridge Rainsford climbed a tree. Down a watercourse, not a quarter of a mile away, he could see the bush moving. Straining his eyes, he saw the lean figure of General Zaroff; just ahead of him Rainsford made out another figure whose wide shoulders surged through the tall jungle weeds; it was the giant Ivan, and he seemed pulled forward by some unseen force; Rainsford knew that Ivan must be holding the pack in leash.

They would be on him any minute now. His mind worked frantically. He thought of a native trick he had learned in Uganda. He slid down the tree. He caught hold of a springy young sapling and to it he fastened his hunting knife, with the blade pointing down the trail; with a bit of wild grapevine he tied back the sapling. Then he ran for his life. The hounds raised their voices as they hit the fresh scent. Rainsford knew now how an animal at bay[24] feels.

He had to stop to get his breath. The baying of the hounds stopped abruptly, and Rainsford's heart stopped, too. They must have reached the knife.

He shinned excitedly up a tree and looked back. His pursuers had stopped. But the hope that was in Rainsford's brain when he climbed died, for he saw in the shallow valley that General Zaroff was still on his feet. But Ivan was not. The knife, driven by the recoil of the springing tree, had not wholly failed.

Rainsford had hardly tumbled to the ground when the pack took up the cry again.

"Nerve, nerve, nerve!" he panted, as he dashed along. A blue gap showed between the trees dead ahead. Ever nearer drew the hounds. Rainsford forced himself on toward that gap. He reached it. It was the shore of the sea. Across a cove he could see the gloomy gray stone of the chateau. Twenty feet below him the sea rumbled and hissed. Rainsford hesitated. He heard the hounds. Then he leaped far out into the sea. . . .

When the general and his pack reached the place by the sea, the Cossack stopped. For some minutes he stood regarding the blue-green expanse of water. He shrugged his shoulders. Then he sat down, took a drink of brandy from a silver flask, lit a cigarette, and hummed a bit from "Madame Butterfly."[25]

24. *At bay* refers to the position of a cornered animal that is forced to turn and confront its pursuers.

25. *Madame Butterfly* is an Italian opera by Giacomo Puccini.

General Zaroff had an exceedingly good dinner in his great paneled dining hall that evening. With it he had a bottle of *Pol Roger* and half a bottle of *Chambertin*. Two slight annoyances kept him from perfect enjoyment. One was the thought that it would be difficult to replace Ivan; the other was that his quarry had escaped him; of course the American hadn't played the game—so thought the general as he tasted his after-dinner liqueur. In his library he read. At ten he went up to his bedroom. He was deliciously tired, he said to himself, as he locked himself in. There was a little moonlight, so, before turning on his light, he went to the window and looked down at the courtyard. He could see the great hounds, and he called: "Better luck another time," to them. Then he switched on the light.

A man, who had been hiding in the curtains of the bed, was standing there.

"Rainsford!" screamed the general. "How in God's name did you get here?"

"Swam," said Rainsford. "I found it quicker than walking through the jungle."

The general sucked in his breath and smiled. "I congratulate you," he said. "You have won the game."

Rainsford did not smile. "I am still a beast at bay," he said in a low, hoarse voice. "Get ready, General Zaroff."

The general made one of his deepest bows. "I see," he said. "Splendid! One of us is to furnish a repast[26] for the hounds. The other will sleep in this very excellent bed. On guard, Rainsford. . . ."

He had never slept in a better bed, Rainsford decided.

26. *Repast* means "meal; feast."

Responding to Literature

Personal Response

What thoughts or feelings did you experience while reading? Share them with a partner.

Analyzing Literature

Recall

1. How did Rainsford end up on Ship-Trap Island? What is the meaning of the island's name?
2. Why had General Zaroff become bored with hunting, and what did he do to solve the problem?
3. Summarize the "rules" of General Zaroff's game.
4. Describe three tricks that Rainsford used while being hunted.
5. How did Rainsford win the game, and what happened to Zaroff at the end of the story?

Interpret

6. Explain the **irony** of Rainsford's thoughts: "All he knew was that he was safe from his enemy, the sea. . . ." (See Literary Terms Handbook, page R7.)
7. Why is Zaroff so excited to have Rainsford play his "game"?
8. *Game* can mean both "contest" and "an animal to be hunted." Use each definition to explain two possible meanings of the **title.**
9. Did Rainsford's knowledge, experience, and training as a hunter help him win the game? Explain your answer.
10. What do you think Zaroff meant when he said to himself at the end of the game, ". . . of course the American hadn't played the game. . . ."

Evaluate and Connect

11. Theme Connections In what ways does the story illustrate the theme "Matters of Life and Death"?
12. Connell uses **hyperbole,** or exaggeration, when he writes about Rainsford: "He lived a year in a minute." How does the exaggeration help describe Rainsford's feelings?
13. Evaluate Rainsford's final act. Do you think he did the right thing? What might you have done in his situation?
14. Review the quotation in the Reading Focus on page 66. Did Rainsford's attitude about hunters and huntees change by the end of the story? Explain.
15. Would you recommend this story to a friend? Explain why or why not.

Literary ELEMENTS

Setting

The **setting** of a story is the time and place in which the events occur. Ideas, customs, values, and beliefs can also be part of a setting.

Often the setting helps create an atmosphere or mood. This story takes place in the 1920s in different parts of Ship-Trap Island, including the dense jungle, Death Swamp, and General Zaroff's lavish home.

1. Why do you think the author chose an island setting for this story?
2. Describe the interior of Zaroff's home. What mood does this setting help create? How does the setting of the house create a different mood from that of the jungle just outside?
3. Describe a scene from the story that you felt was particularly exciting or suspenseful. How did the time of day and the place in which the scene was set add to the suspense and action?

- See **Literary Terms Handbook,** p. R11.

Literature and Writing

Writing About Literature

Comparing Characters In what ways are Rainsford and Zaroff alike and in what ways are they different? Consider such factors as their interests, knowledge, attitudes, and backgrounds. Write at least two paragraphs to compare and contrast them.

Creative Writing

What Happens Next? The story ends abruptly. What do you think might happen next? Does Rainsford stay on the island? If so, what does he plan to do there? Does he leave the island? If so, how? Does he continue to hunt? Write an epilogue to the story; show what becomes of Rainsford.

Extending Your Response

Literature Groups

Casting Call If your group were casting a movie based on "The Most Dangerous Game," which actors would you select to play Zaroff, Rainsford, and Ivan? Carefully consider the personality, physical appearance, speech patterns, and approximate age of each character. Write up a cast list and compare it with those of the other groups.

Performing

You're On! With a partner, select your favorite scene from the story. You might choose the scene that you find most exciting, or a scene that gives insight into the minds of the characters. Rehearse the scene until you feel that you have mastered all of its details. Then perform your scene for your classmates.

Interdisciplinary Activity

Mathematics: Create a Daily Schedule The story clearly indicates the passage of time from the opening scene to the closing scene. Create a daily schedule listing all the events as they occur on each day and night. Use specific times when possible. Use your schedule to estimate how many hours pass from the time Rainsford falls from the ship to the time he confronts Zaroff in his bedroom.

Save your work for your portfolio.

Skill Minilesson

VOCABULARY • Etymology

The etymology of a word is its history—where it came from and what it originally meant. Some words took a direct route from their original languages to English. For example, *zealous* is simply the adjective form of *zeal,* which comes from the Greek word *zēlos,* meaning "zeal." Looking into that word's etymology does not add to your understanding of the word.

Some words have fascinating etymologies that do add to your understanding, however. The word *scruple,* for example, comes from the Latin word *scrupulus,* which means "a small stone." A *scrupulus* was a really tiny stone, only a twenty-fourth of an ounce. Imagine walking around with such a small stone in your shoe. Would it make you uncomfortable? Would it stop you from, say, running? If so, you would be a sensitive person. That's why the "small stone" that creates discomfort about certain behaviors is known as a scruple.

PRACTICE Use a dictionary to look up the etymologies of *quarry, diverting* (from *divert*), and *deplorable* (from *deplore*). A word's etymology is usually given along with its definition. Then, for each word, briefly describe something that the etymology helps you to understand about the word.

Before You Read

The Cask of Amontillado

Reading Focus

Have you ever done something you knew you shouldn't have done, and gotten away with it? Think about how you felt about the experience.

Discuss Which is worse–the guilt you feel when you get away with something or the consequences you face when caught? Share your experiences and opinions with a partner.

Setting a Purpose Read to learn how revenge affects one avenger.

Building Background

The Time and Place

This story is set in the 1800s during Carnival season in an unnamed town in Italy. Much of the story occurs in the Montresor (môn′ tre sôr′) family's wine cellar.

Did You Know?

- Carnival is a celebration involving costume parades, feasting, and festivity that takes place mainly in Roman Catholic regions during the weeks before Lent, usually in January or early February.
- Catacombs are underground cemeteries found throughout the Mediterranean region; most lie just outside Rome, Italy. A series of narrow passageways and steep staircases–sometimes descending as many as four stories below ground–are lined with recesses or niches into which the bodies were laid. The passageways measure only about eight feet high and are less than three feet wide! It is estimated that the catacombs near Rome stretch sixty to ninety miles and that as many as 750,000 people are buried there.

Vocabulary Preview

preclude (pri klo͞od′) *v.* to prevent; make impossible; p. 87
impunity (im pū′ nə tē) *n.* freedom from punishment, harm, or bad consequences; p. 87
accost (ə kôst′) *v.* to approach and speak to, especially in an aggressive manner; p. 88
explicit (eks plis′ it) *adj.* definitely stated; clearly expressed; p. 89
implore (im plôr′) *v.* to ask earnestly; beg; p. 91

Meet Edgar Allan Poe

"From childhood's hour I have not been/As others were—I have not seen/As others saw—"

So wrote Edgar Allan Poe in his poem "Alone." Indeed, Poe had a unique vision of the dark side of life—terror, suspense, mystery, madness, and phantoms were his literary specialties. Poe began writing professionally when he was only eighteen, but his works never gained him the recognition or money he longed for. Only after his death did Poe's fiction, poetry, essays, and reviews gain popularity and critical acclaim.

Edgar Allan Poe was born in 1809 and died in 1849. This story was first published in 1846.

The Cask of Amontillado

Edgar Allan Poe

THE THOUSAND INJURIES of Fortunato[1] I had borne as I best could; but when he ventured upon insult, I vowed revenge. You, who so well know the nature of my soul, will not suppose, however, that I gave utterance to a threat. *At length* I would be avenged; this was a point definitively settled—but the very definitiveness with which it was resolved, precluded the idea of risk. I must not only punish, but punish with impunity. A wrong is unredressed when retribution overtakes its redresser. It is equally unredressed when the avenger fails to make himself felt as such to him who has done the wrong.[2]

It must be understood, that neither by word nor deed had I given Fortunato cause to doubt my good-will. I continued, as was my wont, to smile in his face, and he did not perceive that my smile *now* was at the thought of his immolation.[3]

He had a weak point—this Fortunato—although in other regards he was a man to be respected and even feared. He prided himself on his connoisseurship[4] in wine. Few Italians have the true virtuoso spirit. For the most part their enthusiasm is adopted to suit the time and opportunity—to practice imposture upon the British and Austrian *millionnaires*. In painting and gemmary Fortunato, like his countrymen, was a quack—but in the matter of old wines he was sincere. In this respect I did not differ from him materially: I was skilful in the Italian vintages myself, and bought largely whenever I could.

1. *Fortunato* (fôr′ to͞o nä′ tō)
2. *[A wrong is . . . done the wrong.]* These sentences might be rephrased this way: "A wrong is not avenged if the avenger either is punished for taking revenge or doesn't make the wrongdoer aware that he is taking revenge."
3. Here, *immolation* means "death or destruction."
4. *Connoisseurship* (kon′ə sur′ ship) is expert knowledge that qualifies one to pass judgment in a particular area.

Vocabulary

preclude (pri klo͞od′) *v.* to prevent; make impossible
impunity (im pū′ nə tē) *n.* freedom from punishment, harm, or bad consequences

Crispino and Scapino, 1864. Honoré Daumier. Oil on panel, 60.5 x 82 cm. Louvre Museum, Paris.

Viewing the painting: What secret do these men share? If they were to represent the main characters in this story, who would be Montresor, and who would be Fortunato?

It was about dusk, one evening during the supreme madness of the carnival season, that I encountered my friend. He accosted me with excessive warmth, for he had been drinking much. The man wore motley.[5] He had on a tight-fitting parti-striped dress, and his head was surmounted by the conical cap and bells. I was so pleased to see him, that I thought I should never have done wringing his hand.

I said to him: "My dear Fortunato, you are luckily met. How remarkably well you are looking today! But I have received a pipe of what passes for Amontillado,[6] and I have my doubts."

"How?" said he. "Amontillado? A pipe? Impossible! And in the middle of the carnival!"

"I have my doubts," I replied; "and I was silly enough to pay the full Amontillado price without consulting you in the matter. You were not to be found, and I was fearful of losing a bargain."

"Amontillado!"

"I have my doubts."

"Amontillado!"

"And I must satisfy them."

"Amontillado!"

"As you are engaged, I am on my way to Luchesi.[7] If anyone has a critical turn, it is he. He will tell me——"

"Luchesi cannot tell Amontillado from Sherry."

"And yet some fools will have it that his taste is a match for your own."

"Come, let us go."

"Whither?"

"To your vaults."

"My friend, no; I will not impose upon your good nature. I perceive you have an engagement. Luchesi——"

5. *Motley* is the multicolored costume of a court jester or clown.
6. A *pipe* is a wine barrel that holds 126 gallons. *Amontillado* (ə môn′ tē yä′ dō) is a kind of pale, dry sherry from Spain.

7. *Luchesi* (lo͞o kā′ sē)

Vocabulary

accost (ə kôst′) *v.* to approach and speak to, especially in an aggressive manner

"I have no engagement;—come."

"My friend, no. It is not the engagement, but the severe cold with which I perceive you are afflicted. The vaults are insufferably damp. They are encrusted with niter."[8]

"Let us go, nevertheless. The cold is merely nothing. Amontillado! You have been imposed upon. And as for Luchesi, he cannot distinguish Sherry from Amontillado."

Thus speaking, Fortunato possessed himself of my arm. Putting on a mask of black silk, and drawing a *roquelaure* closely about my person, I suffered him to hurry me to my palazzo.[9]

Did You Know?
A *roquelaure* (rôk ə lor′) is a knee-length cloak popular in the 1700s.

There were no attendants at home; they had absconded to make merry in honor of the time. I had told them that I should not return until the morning, and had given them explicit orders not to stir from the house. These orders were sufficient, I well knew, to insure their immediate disappearance, one and all, as soon as my back was turned.

I took from their sconces two flambeaux,[10] and giving one to Fortunato, bowed him through several suites of rooms to the archway that led into the vaults. I passed down a long and winding staircase, requesting him to be cautious as he followed. We came at length to the foot of the descent, and stood together on the damp ground of the catacombs of the Montresors.

The gait of my friend was unsteady, and the bells upon his cap jingled as he strode.

"The pipe?" said he.

"It is farther on," said I; "but observe the white web-work which gleams from these cavern walls."

He turned toward me, and looked into my eyes with two filmy orbs that distilled the rheum of intoxication.[11]

"Niter?" he asked, at length.

"Niter," I replied. "How long have you had that cough?"

"Ugh! ugh! ugh!—ugh! ugh! ugh!—ugh! ugh! ugh!—ugh! ugh! ugh!—ugh! ugh! ugh!"

My poor friend found it impossible to reply for many minutes.

"It is nothing," he said, at last.

"Come," I said, with decision, "we will go back; your health is precious. You are rich, respected, admired, beloved; you are happy, as once I was. You are a man to be missed. For me it is no matter. We will go back; you will be ill, and I cannot be responsible. Besides, there is Luchesi——"

"Enough," he said; "the cough is a mere nothing; it will not kill me. I shall not die of a cough."

"True—true," I replied; "and, indeed, I had no intention of alarming you unnecessarily; but you should use all proper caution. A draft of this Medoc[12] will defend us from the damps."

Here I knocked off the neck of a bottle which I drew from a long row of its fellows that lay upon the mold.

"Drink," I said, presenting him the wine.

8. *Niter* is a salt-like substance found in cool, damp places.
9. A *palazzo* (pə lät′ sō) is a mansion or palace.
10. *Sconces* are wall brackets that hold candles or torches, and *flambeaux* (flam′ bō′) are lighted torches.
11. *[filmy orbs . . . intoxication]* This phrase describes Fortunato's eyes as clouded and watery from excessive drinking.
12. *Medoc* (mā dôk′) is a French red wine. A *draft* is the amount taken in one swig or swallow.

Vocabulary
explicit (eks plis′ it) *adj.* definitely stated; clearly expressed

He raised it to his lips with a leer. He paused and nodded to me familiarly, while his bells jingled.

"I drink," he said, "to the buried that repose[13] around us."

"And I to your long life."

He again took my arm, and we proceeded.

"These vaults," he said, "are extensive."

"The Montresors," I replied, "were a great and numerous family."

"I forget your arms."

"A huge human foot d'or, in a field azure; the foot crushes a serpent rampant[14] whose fangs are imbedded in the heel."

"And the motto?"

"Nemo me impune lacessit."[15]

"Good!" he said.

The wine sparkled in his eyes and the bells jingled. My own fancy grew warm with the Medoc. We had passed through walls of piled bones, with casks and puncheons[16] intermingling, into the inmost recesses of the catacombs. I paused again, and this time I made bold to seize Fortunato by an arm above the elbow.

Did You Know?
Arms is short for "coat of arms," an arrangement of figures and symbols on or around a shield that, along with a motto, represents one's ancestry.

"The niter!" I said; "see, it increases. It hangs like moss upon the vaults. We are below the river's bed. The drops of moisture trickle among the bones. Come, we will go back ere it is too late. Your cough——"

"It is nothing," he said; "let us go on. But first, another draft of the Medoc."

I broke and reached him a flagon[17] of De Grâve. He emptied it at a breath. His eyes flashed with a fierce light. He laughed and threw the bottle upward with a gesticulation I did not understand.

I looked at him in surprise. He repeated the movement—a grotesque one.

"You do not comprehend?" he said.

"Not I," I replied.

"Then you are not of the brotherhood."

"How?"

"You are not of the masons."[18]

"Yes, yes," I said; "yes, yes."

"You? Impossible! A mason?"

"A mason," I replied.

"A sign," he said.

"It is this," I answered, producing a trowel from beneath the folds of my *roquelaure*.

"You jest," he exclaimed, recoiling a few paces. "But let us proceed to the Amontillado."

"Be it so," I said, replacing the tool beneath the cloak, and again offering him my arm. He leaned upon it heavily. We continued our route in search of the Amontillado. We passed through a range of low arches, descended, passed on, and descending again, arrived at a deep crypt,[19] in which the foulness of the air caused our flambeaux rather to glow than flame.

At the most remote end of the crypt there appeared another less spacious. Its walls had been lined with human remains, piled to the vault overhead, in the fashion of the great catacombs of Paris. Three sides of this interior crypt were still ornamented in this manner. From the fourth the bones had been thrown down, and lay promiscuously upon the earth, forming at one point a mound of some size.

---

13. To *repose* is to lie at rest, either sleeping or in death.
14. The Montresor family's coat of arms includes a golden foot on a sky-blue background and a snake rising up.
15. The *motto* is Latin for "Nobody provokes me with impunity."
16. *Casks* and *puncheons* are large containers for storing liquids.
17. The *flagon* is a narrow-necked bottle with a handle.
18. Here, *masons* is short for "Freemasons," an organization of stonecutters and bricklayers that was formed in the Middle Ages. By the time of this story, the masons had become a social group with secret rituals and signs.
19. A *crypt* is a burial chamber.

Within the wall thus exposed by the displacing of the bones, we perceived a still interior recess, in depth about four feet, in width three, in height six or seven. It seemed to have been constructed for no especial use within itself, but formed merely the interval between two of the colossal supports of the roof of the catacombs, and was backed by one of their circumscribing walls of solid granite.

It was in vain that Fortunato, uplifting his dull torch, endeavored to pry into the depth of the recess. Its termination the feeble light did not enable us to see.

"Proceed," I said; "herein is the Amontillado. As for Luchesi——"

"He is an ignoramus," interrupted my friend, as he stepped unsteadily forward, while I followed immediately at his heels. In an instant he had reached the extremity of the niche,[20] and finding his progress arrested by the rock, stood stupidly bewildered. A moment more and I had fettered[21] him to the granite. In its surface were two iron staples, distant from each other about two feet, horizontally. From one of these depended a short chain, from the other a padlock. Throwing the links about his waist, it was but the work of a few seconds to secure it. He was too much astounded to resist. Withdrawing the key I stepped back from the recess.

"Pass your hand," I said, "over the wall; you cannot help feeling the niter. Indeed it is *very* damp. Once more let me *implore* you to return. No? Then I must positively leave you. But I must first render you all the little attentions in my power."

"The Amontillado!" ejaculated my friend, not yet recovered from his astonishment.

"True," I replied; "the Amontillado."

As I said these words I busied myself among the pile of bones of which I have before spoken. Throwing them aside, I soon uncovered a quantity of building stone and mortar. With these materials and with the aid of my trowel, I began vigorously to wall up the entrance of the niche.

I had scarcely laid the first tier of the masonry when I discovered that the intoxication of Fortunato had in a great measure worn off. The earliest indication I had of this was a low moaning cry from the depth of the recess. It was *not* the cry of a drunken man. There was then a long and obstinate silence. I laid the second tier, and the third, and the fourth;

20. Here, the *extremity of the niche* (nich) is the farthest spot inside the recess.
21. *Fettered* means "bound with chains or shackles; restrained."

Vocabulary
implore (im plôr′) *v.* to ask earnestly; beg

COMPARING *selections*

The Most Dangerous Game and The Cask of Amontillado

COMPARE **CHARACTERS**

Montresor and General Zaroff share certain qualities, yet they are different in many ways.

1. How are their actions, attitudes, and personality traits alike and different? Use a Venn diagram like the one shown to record your group members' ideas as you discuss.

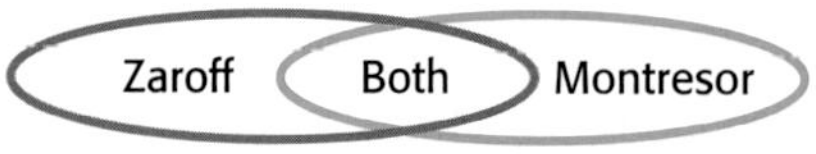

2. Zaroff and Montresor use similar strategies to attract Rainsford and Fortunato. How does each man use a shared interest to lure and trap his "guest"?

COMPARE **SUSPENSE**

To build tension and excitement, writers often give just enough information to make the reader question "What will happen next?" This rising tension is called **suspense.** Write an evaluation of Connell's and Poe's strategies for building suspense. First, compare and contrast how they use setting and plot development. Based on your comparison, tell which author you feel is more effective in building suspense. Support your evaluation with reasons and examples from their stories.

COMPARE **EXPERIENCES**

Imagine that Fortunato and Rainsford could discuss their experiences.

- With a partner, consider the following questions: In what ways are Fortunato and Rainsford similar? What is different about their personalities and actions?
- Consider what the two characters might have to say to one another. Then, write a dialogue between the two characters, exploring the similarities and differences in their experiences.
- Rehearse your conversation and perform it for the class.

Vo•cab•u•lar•y Skills

Using Familiar Words to Understand New Words

If you were asked to give a commentary on the subject of incivility, would you know what to do? (Hint: What do *comment* and *civil* mean?)

By thinking about words you know, you can often figure out the meaning of words you don't know. Apply this strategy to the above sentence. Did the hint help you guess that you were asked to present a series of remarks or observations on the subject of impolite behavior?

Many new words you hear or read will be similar to words you already know. Some new words will simply have a familiar prefix or suffix attached to a familiar base word. Others will remind you of words you already know. Often this similarity is a clue to a word's meaning.

EXERCISE

Use familiar words to figure out the meanings of the underlined words below. On a separate piece of paper, write the letter of the word that completes each unfinished sentence.

1. Zaroff demonstrated an amazing amount of ferocity.

   The meaning of *ferocious* indicates that *ferocity* means

   a. cruelty. b. cleverness. c. stubbornness.

2. Montresor built an impenetrable wall.

   The meaning of *penetrate* indicates that something *impenetrable* cannot be

   a. destroyed. b. noticed. c. passed through.

3. Fortunato's guise at the carnival was that of a court jester.

   The meaning of *disguise* indicates that *guise* means

   a. appearance. b. behavior. c. manner of speaking.

4. Too late, Fortunato ascertained his fate.

   The meaning of *certain* indicates that *ascertained* means

   a. dreaded. b. tried to change. c. knew for sure.

5. Bennie is resolute about not telling his grandmother's secret.

   The meaning of *resolution* indicates that *resolute* means

   a. unhappy. b. determined. c. brave.

6. The king's decision to imprison his daughter's beloved was unalterable.

   The meaning of *alter* indicates that something *unalterable* is

   a. unbelievable. b. unchangeable. c. unreasonable.

MEDIA connection

Magazine Articles

Do you enjoy looking at pictures of famous people—even when it's clear they didn't pose for the photographs? The photographers say they are only doing their jobs, but their subjects often yearn for privacy.

To Protect Their Baby

by Liz Smith—*Good Housekeeping*, May 1996

Now that [Alec Baldwin and Kim Basinger], two high-profile actors, are brand-new parents, their lives seem to be defined by their six-month-old baby girl, Ireland Eliesse Baldwin.

Liz Smith: When the baby was only three days old and you were bringing her home from the hospital, a photographer tried to videotape you outside your house. It turned into an unfortunate confrontation, and the paparazzo claims you hit him. How does having the baby make you feel about privacy now?

Kim Basinger: I've always wanted a lot of land to live on. I'm a country girl, and I've never gotten used to lots of people around me. I love California, but we feel like prey here.

Alec Baldwin: There's a difference between being in legitimate forums where press and photographers are supposed to be, and being stalked. We make ourselves available, and we go to places where we're going to encounter the press. We're as nice as can be and we do what people expect. But with this guy coming after the baby. . . . Just think about it: He was waiting for us in front of our house. He was very odd-looking, and he continued to insist on photographing us, even after I said very nicely, "Don't do it." I went to push the camera out of his hand, and I inadvertently hit him in the face. He says I punched him. Now he's suing me.

Smith: You've said that you would arrange to be photographed with the baby at the right time and place. But you didn't want to do it with somebody who comes up on the street.

Baldwin: We wanted to get used to having the baby first. She was only three days old!

Basinger: We were in New York in front of the hotel one day and someone started snapping pictures. [The baby] is very frightened of flashbulbs, and she's very jumpy. I don't want to put her through that now. Babies' fears when they're small are of falling and of loud noises. So the less ruckus the better for her. I want her to have a really peaceful existence.

Secrets of the Paparazzi

American Photography,
July/August 1992

"The children of celebrities are a gray area for me. Sometimes the stars will complain. They'll say, 'We'll pose for you, but we don't want the kids shown.' The reality is, we wouldn't photograph the kids if the public didn't want to see them."
—*Nick Elgar, New York photographer*

"You should expect battle scars in this business. . . . If you're playing the big boys' game you're sometimes going to get hurt."
—*Dave Hogan, London photographer*

"For stakeouts, I never park in front of people's houses—you should park down the street. You don't want to lose the element of surprise."
—*Russell Turiak, New York photographer*

Analyzing Media

1. Do you think famous people have the same privacy rights as everyone else? Why or why not? What is your reaction to the photographers' comments?
2. How would you feel if a photographer took pictures of you and your family without your prior consent?

Before You Read

Blues Ain't No Mockin Bird

Reading Focus

Have you ever felt as if your privacy had been invaded? Perhaps someone read your diary or came into your room without knocking.

Journal Write about the incident in your journal. How did you feel? What–if anything–did you say to the person who intruded?

Setting a Purpose Read to learn about a dramatic response to an invasion of privacy.

Building Background

The Time and Place

The characters in this story probably live in a poor rural county in the South, during the late 1940s or 1950s. It is winter, near Christmas, but the weather is still mild enough to play outdoors.

Did You Know?

- Blues is an American original–a style of music with its roots in the rural South. The blues were first sung by African Americans as a way to express their troubles. "Singing the blues" means singing with deep feeling, often with sadness, about life's experiences. The blues can express a range of other emotions too, from anger to joy.
- The mockingbird is a songbird that mimics, or imitates, the songs of other birds. While it communicates with other mockingbirds using songs of its own, it mimics other sounds as a survival mechanism. For example, it hides from its predators by mimicking their calls. The mockingbird is also highly territorial, fiercely defending its nest and environment by swooping down on its enemies.

Vocabulary Preview

In some dialects, the "g" sound is not pronounced at the ends of words ending in *-ing.* Here are some examples from the story.

Dialect	Standard English
stompin	stomping
filmin	filming
buzzin	buzzing

Meet Toni Cade Bambara

Toni Cade Bambara says, "My mother never interrupted either my brother or me if we were daydreaming. She recognized that as important work to do." In fact, throughout her childhood, Bambara was encouraged to be creative, and she wrote on any slip of paper she could find. Her mother and other grownups in her life not only encouraged her writing and daydreaming, they also said she had an important role in life. As proof of that special role, Bambara went on to publish short stories, essays, screenplays, and novels that reflect her African American heritage.

Toni Cade Bambara was born in 1939 and died in 1995. This story was first published in 1971.

Blues Ain't No Mockin Bird

Toni Cade Bambara

THE PUDDLE HAD FROZEN OVER, and me and Cathy went stompin in it. The twins from next door, Tyrone and Terry, were swingin so high out of sight we forgot we were waitin our turn on the tire. Cathy jumped up and came down hard on her heels and started tap-dancin. And the frozen patch splinterin every which way underneath kinda spooky.

"Looks like a plastic spider web," she said. "A sort of weird spider, I guess, with many mental problems." But really it looked like the crystal paperweight Granny kept in the parlor. She was on the back porch, Granny was, making the cakes drunk. The old ladle dripping rum into the Christmas tins, like it used to drip maple syrup into the pails when we lived in the Judson's woods, like it poured cider into the vats when we were on the Cooper place, like it used to scoop buttermilk and soft cheese when we lived at the dairy.

"Go tell that man we ain't a bunch of trees."

"Ma'am?"

"I said to tell that man to get away from here with that camera." Me and Cathy look over toward the meadow where the men with the station wagon'd been roamin around all mornin. The tall man with a huge camera lassoed to his shoulder was buzzin our way.

"They're makin movie pictures," yelled Tyrone, stiffenin his legs and twistin so the tire'd come down slow so they could see.

"They're makin movie pictures," sang out Terry.

"That boy don't never have anything original to say," say Cathy grown-up.

By the time the man with the camera had cut across our neighbor's yard, the twins were out of the trees swingin low and Granny was onto the steps, the screen door bammin soft and scratchy against her palms. "We thought we'd get a shot or two of the house and everything and then—"

"Good mornin," Granny cut him off. And smiled that smile.

"Good mornin," he said, head all down the way Bingo does when you yell at him about the bones on the kitchen floor. "Nice place you got here, aunty. We thought we'd take a—"

"Did you?" said Granny with her eyebrows. Cathy pulled up her socks and giggled.

"Nice things here," said the man, buzzin his camera over the yard. The pecan barrels, the sled, me and Cathy, the flowers, the printed stones along the driveway, the trees, the twins, the toolshed.

"I don't know about the thing, the it, and the stuff," said Granny, still talkin with her eyebrows. "Just people here is what I tend to consider."

Camera man stopped buzzin. Cathy giggled into her collar.

"Mornin, ladies," a new man said. He had come up behind us when we weren't lookin. "And gents," discoverin the twins givin him a nasty look. "We're filmin for the county," he said with a smile. "Mind if we shoot a bit around here?"

"I do indeed," said Granny with no smile. Smilin man was smiling up a storm. So was Cathy. But he didn't seem to have another word to say, so he and the camera man backed on out the yard, but you could hear the camera buzzin still. "Suppose you just shut that machine off," said Granny real low through her teeth, and took a step down off the porch and then another.

©Elizabeth Catlett/Licensed by VAGA, New York, NY.

Sharecropper, 1970. Elizabeth Catlett. Linoleum cut, 26 x 22 in. Hampton University Art Museum, Hampton, VA.

Viewing the art: How would you describe the personality of this woman? How might she be similar to or different from Granny?

"Now, aunty," Camera said, pointin the thing straight at her.

"Your mama and I are not related."

Smilin man got his notebook out and a chewed-up pencil. "Listen," he said movin back into our yard, "we'd like to have a statement from you . . . for the film. We're filmin for the county, see. Part of the food stamp campaign. You know about the food stamps?"[1]

1. *Food stamps* are coupons issued by the government to people with low incomes, who use the stamps, as if they were cash, to buy food at stores.

Granny said nuthin.

"Maybe there's somethin you want to say for the film. I see you grow your own vegetables," he smiled real nice. "If more folks did that, see, there'd be no need—"

Granny wasn't sayin nuthin. So they backed on out, buzzin at our clothesline and the twins' bicycles, then back on down to the meadow. The twins were danglin in the tire, lookin at Granny. Me and Cathy were waitin, too, cause Granny always got somethin to say. She teaches steady with no let-up. "I was on this bridge one time," she started off. "Was a crowd cause this man was goin to jump, you understand. And a minister was there and the police and some other folks. His woman was there, too."

"What was they doin?" asked Tyrone.

"Tryin to talk him out of it was what they was doin. The minister talkin about how it was a mortal sin,[2] suicide. His woman takin bites out of her own hand and not even knowin it, so nervous and cryin and talkin fast."

"So what happened?" asked Tyrone.

"So here comes . . . this person . . . with a camera, takin pictures of the man and the minister and the woman. Takin pictures of the man in his misery about to jump, cause life so bad and people been messin with him so bad. This person takin up the whole roll of film practically. But savin a few, of course."

"Of course," said Cathy, hatin the person. Me standin there wonderin how Cathy knew it was "of course" when I didn't and it was *my* grandmother.

After a while Tyrone say, "Did he jump?"

"Yeh, did he jump?" say Terry all eager.

And Granny just stared at the twins till their faces swallow up the eager and they don't even care any more about the man jumpin. Then she goes back onto the porch and lets the screen door go for itself. I'm lookin to Cathy to finish the story cause she knows Granny's whole story before me even. Like she knew how come we move so much and Cathy ain't but a third cousin we picked up on the way last Thanksgivin visitin. But she knew it was on account of people drivin Granny crazy till she'd get up in the night and start packin. Mumblin and packin and wakin everybody up sayin, "Let's get on away from here before I kill me somebody." Like people wouldn't pay her for things like they said they would. Or Mr. Judson bringin us boxes of old clothes and raggedy magazines. Or Mrs. Cooper comin in our kitchen and touchin everything and sayin how clean it all was. Granny goin crazy, and Granddaddy Cain pullin her off the people, sayin, "Now, now, Cora." But next day loadin up the truck, with rocks all in his jaw, madder than Granny in the first place.

"I read a story once," said Cathy soundin like Granny teacher. "About this lady Goldilocks who barged into a house that wasn't even hers. And not invited, you understand. Messed over the people's groceries and broke up the people's furniture. Had the nerve to sleep in the folks' bed."

"Then what happened?" asked Tyrone. "What they do, the folks, when they come in to all this mess?"

"Did they make her pay for it?" asked Terry, makin a fist. "I'd've made her pay me."

I didn't even ask. I could see Cathy actress was very likely to just walk away and leave us in mystery about this story which I heard was about some bears.

"Did they throw her out?" asked Tyrone, like his father sounds when he's bein extra nasty-plus to the washin-machine man.

"Woulda," said Terry. "I woulda gone upside her head with my fist and—"

2. In some Christian teachings, a *mortal sin* is one so terrible that it causes the death of the soul and results in eternal damnation.

"You woulda done whatcha always do—go cry to Mama, you big baby," said Tyrone. So naturally Terry starts hittin on Tyrone, and next thing you know they tumblin out the tire and rollin on the ground. But Granny didn't say a thing or send the twins home or step out on the steps to tell us about how we can't afford to be fightin amongst ourselves. She didn't say nuthin. So I get into the tire to take my turn. And I could see her leanin up against the pantry table, starin at the cakes she was puttin up for the Christmas sale, mumblin real low and grumpy and holdin her forehead like it wanted to fall off and mess up the rum cakes.

Behind me I hear before I can see Granddaddy Cain comin through the woods in his field boots. Then I twist around to see the shiny black oilskin[3] cuttin through what little left there was of yellows, reds, and oranges. His great white head not quite round cause of this bloody thing high on his shoulder, like he was wearin a cap on sideways. He takes the shortcut through the pecan grove, and the sound of twigs snapping overhead and underfoot travels clear and cold all the way up to us. And here comes Smilin and Camera up behind him like they was goin to do somethin. Folks like to go for him sometimes. Cathy say it's because he's so tall and quiet and like a king. And people just can't stand it. But Smilin and Camera don't hit him in the head or nuthin. They just buzz on him as he stalks by with the chicken hawk slung over his shoulder, squawkin, drippin red down the back of the oilskin. He passes the porch and stops a second for Granny to see he's caught the hawk at last, but she's just starin and mumblin, and not at the hawk. So he nails the bird to the toolshed door, the hammerin crackin through the eardrums. And the bird flappin himself to death and droolin down the door to paint the gravel in the driveway red, then brown, then black. And the two men movin up on tiptoe like they was invisible or we were blind, one.

Did You Know?
A *chicken hawk* is any hawk that preys on chickens.

"Get them persons out of my flower bed, Mister Cain," say Granny moanin real low like at a funeral.

"How come your grandmother calls her husband 'Mister Cain' all the time?" Tyrone whispers all loud and noisy and from the city and don't know no better. Like his mama, Miss Myrtle, tell us never mind the formality as if we had no better breeding than to call her Myrtle, plain. And then this awful thing—a giant hawk—come wailin up over the meadow, flyin low and tilted and screamin, zigzaggin through the pecan grove, breakin branches and hollerin, snappin past the clothesline, flyin every which way, flyin into things reckless with crazy.

"He's come to claim his mate," say Cathy fast, and ducks down. We all fall quick and flat into the gravel driveway, stones scrapin my face. I squinch my eyes open again at the hawk on the door, tryin to fly up out of her death like it was just a sack flown into by mistake. Her body holdin her there on that nail, though. The mate beatin the air overhead and clutchin for hair, for heads, for landin space.

The camera man duckin and bendin and runnin and fallin, jigglin the camera and scared. And Smilin jumpin up and down swipin at the huge bird, tryin to bring the hawk down with just his raggedy ole cap.

3. Here, the *oilskin* is a coat made of cloth treated with oil to make it waterproof.

Granddaddy Cain straight up and silent, watchin the circles of the hawk, then aimin the hammer off his wrist. The giant bird fallin, silent and slow. Then here comes Camera and Smilin all big and bad now that the awful screechin thing is on its back and broken, here they come. And Granddaddy Cain looks up at them like it was the first time noticin, but not payin them too much mind cause he's listenin, we all listenin, to that low groanin music comin from the porch. And we figure any minute, somethin in my back tells me any minute now, Granny gonna bust through that screen with somethin in her hand and murder on her mind. So Granddaddy say above the buzzin, but quiet, "Good day, gentlemen." Just like that. Like he'd invited them in to play cards and they'd stayed too long and all the sandwiches were gone and Reverend Webb was droppin by and it was time to go.

They didn't know what to do. But like Cathy say, folks can't stand Granddaddy tall and silent and like a king. They can't neither. The smile the men smilin is pullin the mouth

Our House, 1994. Jessie Coates. Acrylic on Masonite, 3½ x 5 in. Private collection.

Viewing the painting: How does this painting compare with the setting described in the story?

back and showin the teeth. Lookin like the wolf man, both of them. Then Granddaddy holds his hand out—this huge hand I used to sit in when I was a baby and he'd carry me through the house to my mother like I was a gift on a tray. Like he used to on the trains. They called the other men just waiters. But they spoke of Granddaddy separate and said, The Waiter. And said he had engines in his feet and motors in his hands and couldn't no train throw him off and couldn't nobody turn him round. They were big enough for motors, his hands were. He held that one hand out all still and it gettin to be not at all a hand but a person in itself.

"He wants you to hand him the camera," Smilin whispers to Camera, tiltin his head to talk secret like they was in the jungle or somethin and come upon a native that don't speak the language. The men start untyin the straps, and they put the camera into that great hand speckled with the hawk's blood all black and crackly now. And the hand don't even drop with the weight, just the fingers move, curl up around the machine. But Granddaddy lookin straight at the men. They lookin at each other and everywhere but at Granddaddy's face.

"We filmin for the county, see," say Smilin. "We puttin together a movie for the food stamp program . . . filmin all around these parts. Uhh, filmin for the county."

"Can I have my camera back?" say the tall man with no machine on his shoulder, but still keepin it high like the camera was still there or needed to be. "Please, sir."

Then Granddaddy's other hand flies up like a sudden and gentle bird, slaps down fast on top of the camera and lifts off half like it was a calabash cut for sharing.

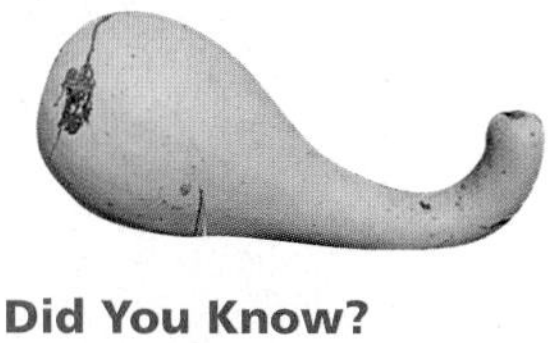

Did You Know?
A *calabash* is a gourdlike fruit of a tropical American tree.

"Hey," Camera jumps forward. He gathers up the parts into his chest and everything unrollin and fallin all over. "Whatcha tryin to do? You'll ruin the film." He looks down into his chest of metal reels and things like he's protectin a kitten from the cold.

"You standin in the misses' flower bed," say Granddaddy. "This is our own place."

The two men look at him, then at each other, then back at the mess in the camera man's chest, and they just back off. One sayin over and over all the way down to the meadow, "Watch it, Bruno. Keep ya fingers off the film." Then Granddaddy picks up the hammer and jams it into the oilskin pocket, scrapes his boots, and goes into the house. And you can hear the squish of his boots headin through the house. And you can see the funny shadow he throws from the parlor window onto the ground by the string-bean patch. The hammer draggin the pocket of the oilskin out so Granddaddy looked even wider. Granny was hummin now—high, not low and grumbly. And she was doin the cakes again, you could smell the molasses from the rum.

"There's this story I'm goin to write one day," say Cathy dreamer. "About the proper use of the hammer."

"Can I be in it?" Tyrone say with his hand up like it was a matter of first come, first served.

"Perhaps," say Cathy, climbin onto the tire to pump us up. "If you there and ready."

Responding to Literature

Personal Response

What images from the story linger in your mind? Share your response with a classmate.

Analyzing Literature

Recall

1. Explain what the two men are doing on the Cain family's property.
2. Until now, where has the Cain family lived? How does their current home differ from the places the family has lived before?
3. Summarize Granny's experience on the bridge.
4. What happens to the two hawks? Explain why.
5. Who is the **narrator,** or person telling the story?

Interpret

6. How would you describe Camera and Smilin's initial attitude toward Granny and the rest of the family?
7. Toward the end of the story, Granddaddy Cain says to the men, "You standin in the misses' flower bed. This is our own place." Explain what this reveals about his character and the family's values.
8. What does Granny's story about the man's suicide attempt reveal about her and her reaction to the men?
9. How are the two hawks like Granny and Granddaddy Cain? How are they like Camera and Smilin? Consider what kind of message the hawks' deaths might have sent to these men.
10. How might the story have been different if it had been told from Camera's **point of view?** (See Literary Terms Handbook, page R10.)

Evaluate and Connect

11. Do you think "Blues Ain't No Mockin Bird" is an appropriate **title** for this story? Why or why not?
12. The narrator says that Granny "always got somethin to say. She teaches steady with no let-up." Does the narrator think she is a good teacher? Do you think so? Support your opinion with evidence from the story.
13. Why do you think Toni Cade Bambara gave Granddaddy only fifteen words to say? Do you feel you got to know this character? Explain.
14. In your opinion, why did the author choose to tell the story from the point of view of a child?
15. Think about your response to the Reading Focus on page 97. Compare your response to the situation with Granny's response to the film crew.

Literary ELEMENTS

Dialect

People who live in a specific region or who belong to a specific group may use **dialect,** a variation of a standard language. Their speech may contain different sounds, words, or sentence structures from the speech used by other groups or in other regions. Consider how the use of dialect in "Blues Ain't No Mockin Bird" helps readers learn about the story's setting and its characters.

1. Rewrite in Standard English each of the following examples of dialect from the story. Think about what is lost when the dialect is removed.
   a. Granny always got somethin to say.
   b. Let's get on away from here before I kill me somebody.
   c. I woulda gone upside her head with my fist.
2. The first words Granny speaks in the story are "Go tell that man we ain't a bunch of trees." What does she mean? Why does she say it this way?
3. How did the dialect affect your reading and understanding of the story? How does dialect make the story's characters and events seem more real?

- See **Literary Terms Handbook,** p. R4.

Literature and Writing

Writing About Literature

Analyzing Minor Characters Granny and Granddaddy Cain are the main characters of "Blues Ain't No Mockin Bird." What are readers told about the story's minor characters, Camera and Smilin? What can you infer about them? How do Camera and Smilin help you learn more about the main characters and their values? Write several paragraphs analyzing the importance of these minor characters to the story.

Creative Writing

Telling a Tale With a partner, discuss how Cathy's retelling of Goldilocks connects to the action of the story. What would she say is the moral of that story? Discuss other fairy tales with which you are familiar and brainstorm about ways those tales teach valuable life lessons. Then write your own story in which you connect a fairy tale to your own life experience.

Extending Your Response

Literature Groups

Defending Your Position Granny and Granddaddy Cain confront Smilin and Camera in different ways. Granny uses words; Granddaddy uses actions. In your opinion, do actions speak louder than words? Debate this question using information from the story to defend your position.

Learning for Life

Memo to the Boss Think about the story from Camera and Smilin's point of view. How did they first perceive the Cain family, and what did they think after they left the family's property, unable to complete the assignment? What will they tell their supervisor when they return to the office with the ruined film? Draft a memo Camera and Smilin might write to their boss explaining what happened and why. Include their recommendations for how the county should proceed with its plan to document the food stamps campaign.

Listening and Speaking

Interview With a tape or video recorder, interview relatives, friends, and teachers. Ask them to relate a story about a time when they have been imposed upon. Ask how they reacted to the situation and how the situation made them feel. Use the interviews to stimulate class discussion about the way people should treat one another.

Reading Further

If you'd like to read more by Toni Cade Bambara, you might enjoy these short stories:

"Raymond's Run" tells about a girl who is a track star and takes care of her brother. "Happy Birthday" shows the loneliness of a girl who celebrates her birthday by herself. Both of these stories can be found in the collection *Gorilla, My Love.*

"The War of the Wall," from the collection *Deep Sightings and Rescue Missions,* shows what happens when a strange artist visits two boys' neighborhood.

Save your work for your portfolio.

Skill Minilessons

GRAMMAR AND LANGUAGE • Using Gerunds

A gerund is a verb form that ends in *-ing* and is used in the same way a noun is used. In the sentence "Tyrone stopped swinging," the word *swinging* is a gerund: an *-ing* form of the verb *swing* that functions as a noun in the sentence. Gerunds can be subjects, direct objects, indirect objects, objects of prepositions, predicate nominatives, and appositives.

Don't confuse gerunds with present participles, which are verb forms that act as adjectives. When you come across a verb form ending in *-ing,* ask yourself what function it is serving in the sentence. For example, in the sentence "Filming rural families was the goal of Camera and Smilin," *filming* is a gerund because it acts as a subject. In the sentence "Filming rural families, Camera and Smilin felt out of place," *filming* is a participle modifying Camera and Smilin.

PRACTICE Find the gerund in each sentence. Then, write a sentence using the same gerund.

1. The men were busy with filming.
2. The twins enjoyed playing on the swing.
3. Speaking up is really no problem for Granny!
4. At the end of the story, Granny shows a sign of happiness–humming as she works.

● For more about gerunds, see **Language Handbook,** p. R39.

READING AND THINKING • Varying Reading Rates

Do you consider yourself a fast reader or a slow one? Perhaps your reading rate varies depending on what you read. For example, you might race through a suspenseful thriller, or you may slowly savor a descriptive poem. Other factors may also affect how quickly you read. You may find that you read the beginning of a story slowly. Once you have the characters and the conflict straight, you may be able to pick up speed. However, difficult vocabulary, unexpected events, and even changes in sentence structure may cause you to slow down again. A writer's use of language may also affect your reading rate.

PRACTICE Monitor your reading rate as you reread the story. When does it speed up or slow down? Give reasons why you vary your rate at particular points.

● For more about related reading strategies, see **Reading Handbook,** pp. R78–R107.

VOCABULARY • Analogies

An analogy is a type of comparison that is based on the relationships between things or ideas. Some analogies are based on a relationship that could be called "worker and tool."

plumber : wrench :: barber : scissors

A *plumber* uses a *wrench*; a *barber* uses *scissors.* The first word in each pair names a worker. The second names a tool used by that worker.

To finish an analogy, decide what relationship exists between the first two things or ideas. Then apply that relationship to another pair of words and see if it is the same.

PRACTICE Complete each analogy.

1. photographer : camera ::
   a. farmer : crop
   b. baker : bread
   c. dressmaker : needle
   d. rancher : steer
   e. journalist : newspaper
2. gardener : shovel ::
   a. lawyer : defendant
   b. singer : opera
   c. teacher : school
   d. actor : play
   e. doctor : stethoscope

● For more about analogies, see **Communications Skills Handbook,** p. R77.

Grammar Link

Avoiding Sentence Fragments

A fragment is a piece of something. If you read two pages of a book, you have read a fragment of it. A **sentence fragment** is a word or group of words that is only part of a sentence.

Problem 1 A fragment that lacks a subject, a verb, or both

Jim had few possessions. *Treasured his old watch.* [lacks a subject]
Christmas was coming. *Jim desperate for a gift for Della.* [lacks a verb]
Her beautiful, long hair. [lacks both]

Solution Add the missing subject and/or verb.

Jim treasured his old watch.
Jim was desperate for a gift for Della.
Della loved her beautiful, long hair.

Problem 2 A fragment that is a subordinate clause

Edgar Allan Poe was a great writer. Whose horror stories won him fame.

Solution A Rewrite the fragment as a complete sentence, eliminating the subordinating conjunction or the relative pronoun and adding words necessary to make a complete thought.

Edgar Allan Poe was a great writer. His horror stories won him fame.

Solution B Combine the fragment with a sentence.

Edgar Allan Poe was a great writer whose horror stories won him fame.

People often speak in sentence fragments: "Right after lunch." "What?" The meaning of a spoken fragment is often clear to your listener in the context of your conversation. Writers, however, must be careful; sentence fragments that leave out information can be confusing!

● For more about sentence fragments, see **Language Handbook,** p. R14.

EXERCISE

Rewrite this paragraph. Use the strategies above to correct the sentence fragments.

Toni Cade Bambara was born in Harlem. New York. Looked up to women in her community. Who traveled and returned home with stories from around the country and the world. As a young girl, she was also inspired by women. Who were active in their churches. And by women who were members of the Ida B. Wells Club. These women were historians and journalists. Courageously spoke out on behalf of all women. Bambara's mother, however, perhaps her greatest inspiration.

Writing Workshop

Personal Writing:
Responding to a Short Story

Reading a short story can transport you to another world, inspiring new thoughts and feelings in the process. It can make you look deeply at your own life, thus creating new awareness of the world around you. Responding to short stories in writing is one way to explore your reactions to them. **Follow the process described on these pages to write your personal response to a story you've read.**

- As you write your personal response, refer to the **Writing Handbook,** pp. R58–R71.

EVALUATION RUBRIC

By the time you complete this Writing Workshop, you will have

- presented your personal responses to a story
- written an introduction that is appropriate for your audience and purpose
- elaborated your response with details and quotations from the story
- concluded with a summary of your responses and their relevance to your audience
- presented a response to a story that is free of errors in grammar, usage and mechanics

The Writing Process

PREWRITING

PREWRITING TIP

Jot down your initial responses in a private journal so that you have a record of your honest feelings.

Explore ideas

Use these questions to help you articulate your reactions to a story in this theme.

- Which of the stories most affected you? Why did it affect you so much?
- Which aspects of the story made the strongest impressions on you?
- Which parts of the story reminded you of your own life experiences?
- What new understanding of life and death did you gain from the story?
- What do you think you will remember about the story a month from now? Why?

Consider your purpose

In addition to exploring your own thoughts and feelings, you might want to respond to a story in order to communicate something to others. For example, you may want your response to convince someone that the story is worth reading, or you may want your response to describe an emotion that is difficult to explain.

Choose an audience

Will you address your response to someone who has already read the work? Will you write for someone who has had an experience similar to the one the author describes? Do you want to address a large group of readers or a particular friend or family member? The content and style of your response will depend on what you decide. For example, you'll have to include a summary of the story for those who aren't familiar with it. If you're writing for family members or close friends, you may want to capture their interest by connecting the story to their life experience.

Make a plan

How will you organize your response into a form that readers can follow and understand? You can't go wrong if you provide the basic essay elements of introduction, body, and conclusion. Ask yourself the following questions to help you frame your response.

		STUDENT MODEL
Introduction	Focus on your reader and the story: What work are you responding to? Who is your audience? Why are you addressing this audience?	I want to share my response to "The Leap" with teenagers like me because we can learn a lot about decision making from the mother in the story.
Body	Focus on your responses: What were your strongest responses? Why did you have these responses? Which passages made you respond as you did?	The story made me realize that even when you are terrified, it is possible to make life and death decisions. (The mother leaping from the tree to the burning house to save her daughter.)
Conclusion	Focus on your reader and your work: Why have you written this response for this particular reader?	My friends and I will probably have times in our lives when we will have to make instant critical decisions. I hope that when we do, we have the strength and courage of the mother in the story.

Complete Student Model on p. R108.

Create a graphic like the one below to help you plan the structure of your response.

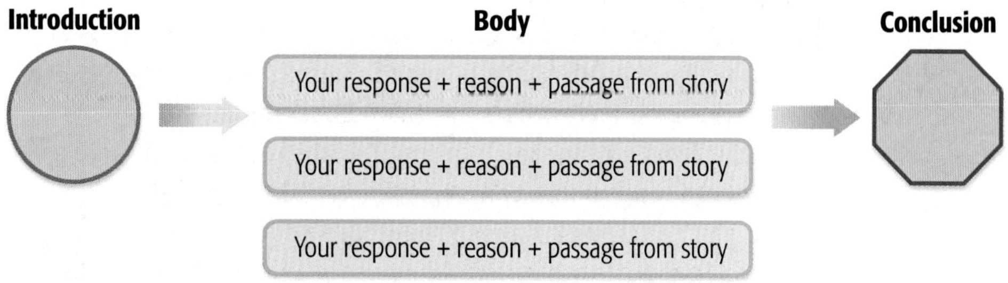

DRAFTING

DRAFTING TIP

Draft the body first, because it's the heart of your response. Use the introduction and conclusion to frame the body.

Expect surprises as you draft

You may find that you don't quite know how to express your feelings when you start drafting. You may even find that you're not completely sure what all your reactions are. That's fine. At this stage in the process, you're still exploring your responses. You're using writing as a way of discovering what you think and feel. You are having an inner discussion with yourself and recording it as you go. Therefore, your ideas may change as you write. Let that work for you. Let your first thoughts lead you to new thoughts.

Write your draft

As you write, refer to your plan to make sure that you develop an introduction, body, and conclusion. Concentrate on getting your responses down, not on phrasing them perfectly. You can always change a draft later. You can also change your original plan any time you discover new ideas.

STUDENT MODEL

I felt an overwhelming sense of awe when I read about how the mother saved her daughter from the fire that was burning their home. It seemed like either mother or daughter or both would surely die. I couldn't believe that anyone could be so brave. I don't know whether I could jump right into a fire like that or whether my friends could make such a brave, quick decision. What made the mother risk her life? I was amazed by how she took control of the situation. There was no time to think, to weigh the risks. Her child was in danger, and she jumped. I could almost hear the branch snap as it broke, "so that it cracked in her hands, cracked louder than the flames as she vaulted with it toward the edge. . . ."

I still need to think about the last sentence of the story: "As you fall there is time to think." How much time can you have when you fall? Does she mean falling from a trapeze or falling in other ways, like how being in trouble can sometimes make you feel like you're falling? I guess there will probably be times in my life when I will have to make such quick critical decisions. I just hope that I have as much strength and courage as this mother did.

Complete Student Model on p. R108.

REVISING

REVISING TIP

Save all versions of your work. As you revise, you may find solutions to new problems in your old work.

Take another look

Put your draft aside for a while after you finish it. Then take a mental leap and imagine that you are your audience. Read your draft as if you were seeing it for the first time. As you read, mark places that need improvement. Then leap back into the role of writer and use the **Rubric for Revising** to guide you as you revise your draft.

STUDENT MODEL

"The Leap" [by Louise Erdrich,] is about a [remarkable] woman who risks her life to save her daughter. The mother ~~is blind~~ [has lost her eyesight as a result of cataracts], but even without sight her life is ~~one~~ [a reflection] of precise vision and courage. The dexterity and skill she developed as a young trapeze artist saved a life ~~more than~~ [not] once[, but twice]. Reading this story left me stunned by her courage and [physical] skill, and it convinced me that even when you are terrified[,] you can [and do] make life-and-death decisions.

Complete Student Model on p. R108.

RUBRIC FOR REVISING

Your revised personal response to a short story should have

- ☑ an introduction that identifies the title and author of the story to which you are responding
- ☑ enough explanation about the story to make your response understandable to your audience
- ☑ reasons and quotations from the story that elaborate the main points of your response
- ☑ vivid words and sentences that communicate clearly
- ☑ a conclusion that emphasizes your main point and your reasons for sharing your response

Your revised personal response to a short story should be free of

- ☑ confusing or contradicting information
- ☑ dull or uninteresting details
- ☑ errors in grammar, usage, and mechanics

Read your response aloud

Read your work aloud to a friend, a family member, or a classmate. (It's best not to give your listener a written copy, since you haven't edited it yet.) As you read, your partner should focus on *what* you've written. You should focus on *how* you've written it. When you're done, ask your partner for an immediate response. Then go through the **Rubric for Revising** together. Make notes right on your draft, and refer to the notes as you revise.

Polish your sentences

The final step in the revision process is to make sure your sentences are working for you and not against you. In other words, your sentences should communicate your ideas clearly and directly. They should not confuse readers or leave them guessing. Take time to reread each sentence carefully and revise those that don't say exactly what you want them to. Sometimes you may need to rewrite a sentence two or three times until it gets your point across in the clearest manner. Your effort will pay off. Any piece of writing is only as good as its individual sentences.

EDITING/PROOFREADING

PROOFREADING TIP

Use the **Proofreading Checklist** on the inside back cover of this book to help you mark errors that you find.

When you are satisfied with the content of your response, edit it for errors in grammar, usage, mechanics, and spelling. The Grammar Link on page 107 has more on sentence fragments.

Grammar Hint

Eliminate fragments. Make sure that every sentence has a subject and a verb.

NO SUBJECT: *Did not survive.*
CORRECT: *The baby did not survive.*
NO VERB: *Books a constant part of her life.*
CORRECT: *Books became a constant part of her life.*

For more about fragments, see **Language Handbook,** p. R14.

Complete Student Model

For a complete version of the model developed in this workshop, refer to Writing Workshop Models, p. R108.

STUDENT MODEL

I was struck, by how she took control of the situation. With no time to think about the consequences, This woman acted because it was necesary to save the life of her child.

Complete Student Model on p. R108.

PUBLISHING/PRESENTING

PRESENTING TIP

Add an illustration that captures the mood of your response.

How you present your response depends, of course, on your audience. For an audience of one close friend, you might include your response in a note or letter. If you are writing for your classmates, you might mount your response on a bulletin board devoted to student work. In any case, check it for mistakes one last time.

Reflecting

When you write a response to a work of literature, you join the "grand conversation" between writers and readers. In your journal, reflect upon what it means to be part of this exchange. Then, consider how you can draw on your strengths the next time you write. What will you do differently?

Save your work for your portfolio.

Theme 2 Filling a Void

When there's a hole in our clothing, we either mend or replace the garment. But what action do we take when we discover a hole in our lives? The selections in this theme show many different ways people try to mend the holes, or fill the voids, in their lives. What is the thing you—or the people you know—yearn for most?

THEME PROJECTS

Performing

Act It Out Have you ever wished you could meet someone you read about or watched on screen? Now you can give your characters the chance to do just that.

1. Make a list of the characters in this theme who are particularly interesting to you. Choose no more than one character from each story.
2. Write a skit in which two of the characters meet each other. You may base your skit on what might happen if one of the characters entered the story of the other, or you may create a totally new scenario.
3. Perform your skit for the class.

Listening and Speaking

Finding Fulfillment There are many different ways to find fulfillment in life.

1. Identify the void that each main character in this theme faces.
2. Interview your friends and family members to find out how they might fill these voids. Be sure to take notes. You may want to use a hand-held tape recorder to collect quotes.
3. Which suggested paths to fulfillment were similar to those actually taken by the characters in the stories? Compare the responses you've gathered with those of your classmates. Which suggestions were recorded most often?

Two Figures (Menhirs), 1964. Dame Barbara Hepworth. Stone sculpture, 756 x 635 x 330 mm. Tate Gallery, London.

MEDIA connection

Comic Strip

Do you play an active role in your daydreams, or do you dream about other people and places? As you can see in the comic below, Calvin is a space explorer in his daydreams.

Calvin and Hobbes

by Bill Watterson

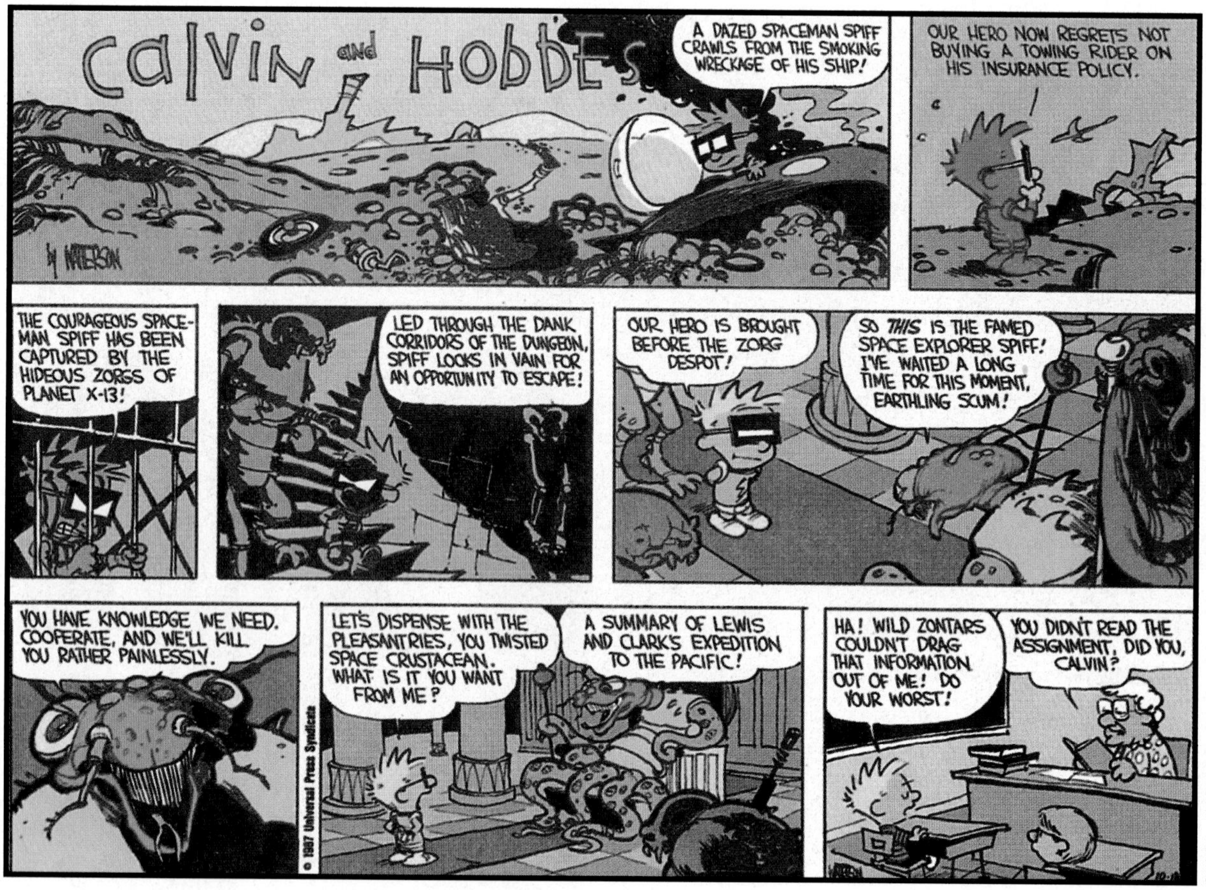

CALVIN & HOBBES ©1987 Watterson. Dist. by UNIVERSAL PRESS SYNDICATE. Reprinted with permission. All rights reserved.

Analyzing Media

1. What are some possible reasons for Calvin's vivid daydream? What might he be trying to avoid? Explain.
2. The teacher's question becomes a part of Calvin's daydream. At the same time, her voice brings him back into reality. How do your surroundings lead you into daydreams? How do they wake you up?

Before You Read

The Secret Life of Walter Mitty

Reading Focus

What are some reasons why you daydream?

Connect It! Think about what you are doing when you daydream. For example, you might daydream while watching a boring movie or while being scolded by an adult. Make a diagram like this one to help you find relationships between *when* you daydream and *why*.

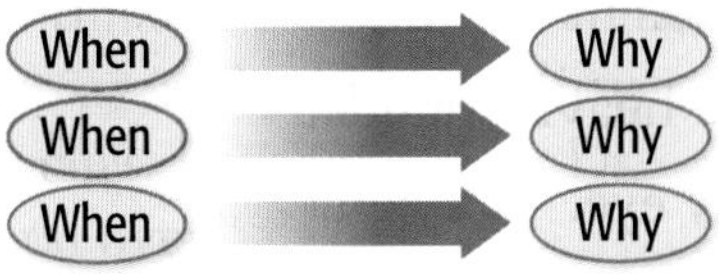

Setting a Purpose Read to learn when and why Walter Mitty daydreams—and what he daydreams about.

Building Background

The Time and Place

This story takes place in Waterbury, Connecticut, a suburb of New York City. It is winter, sometime after World War I.

Did You Know?

This story includes a person's daydreams about heroic real-life situations, but many of the details of these situations are invented. For example, one daydream includes an eight-engine Navy hydroplane, but there is no such thing. Its commander orders full strength from the turrets to get out of a storm, but turrets are structures on which guns rotate; they have nothing to do with engine power. Other fractured facts include a medical diagnosis of obstreosis in the ductal tract—a disease that cannot afflict humans in a part of the body that doesn't even exist—and a reference to a 50.80 caliber pistol, which in reality would be bigger than a cannon!

Vocabulary Preview

distraught (dis trôt′) *adj.* very upset; confused; p. 117
haggard (hag′ ərd) *adj.* having a worn and tired look; p. 117
craven (krā′ vən) *adj.* extremely cowardly; p. 118
insolent (in′ sə lənt) *adj.* so rude or proud as to be offensive; p. 118
insinuatingly (in sin′ ū āt′ ing lē) *adv.* in an indirect way; p. 118
pandemonium (pan′ də mō′ nē əm) *n.* wild uproar; p. 119
disdainful (dis dān′ fəl) *adj.* showing scorn for something or someone regarded as unworthy; p. 120

Meet James Thurber

When he was six years old, James Thurber stood with an apple on his head while his older brother aimed a homemade arrow at the fruit. The arrow pierced Thurber's left eye, blinding him in that eye. As Thurber grew older, the vision in his right eye grew increasingly worse, but this didn't prevent him from living a successful life. In 1927 he began writing for *The New Yorker* magazine, delighting readers with his humorous stories, essays, and cartoons. Although Thurber was completely blind in his later years, he continued his job at *The New Yorker* until the end of his life.

James Thurber was born in 1894 in Columbus, Ohio, and died in New York City in 1961. This story was published in My World—and Welcome to It *in 1942.*

Literature and Writing

Writing About Literature

Character Sketch Brainstorm a list of character traits that Walter Mitty exhibits in this story, using a chart like the one below to help you organize your thoughts. Be sure to include a sentence or an incident from the story that illustrates each character trait. Then write a brief character sketch of Mitty, using the information in your chart. Compare your sketch with those of other students.

	Character traits	Examples
Mitty's public life		
Mitty's private life		

Creative Writing

Mitty Steps Up to Bat Walter Mitty's daydreams are usually triggered by something he sees or by another character's words. Use your imagination to write a daydream that Walter Mitty might have as he passes a baseball diamond or a university or visits any other site of potential drama. As you're writing your passage, try to include some of the elements that link the daydreams with the narration in the story.

Extending Your Response

Literature Groups

Critique the Critic Literary critic Carl M. Linder once remarked that in this story, Thurber touched upon one of the major themes in American literature: the conflict between individual and society. Do you agree that this story is about a conflict between an individual and society? Debate this question within your group and try to reach a consensus. Explain your opinions to the rest of the class, using specific passages or details from the story to support your opinions.

Learning for Life

Your Dream Job Daydream for a few minutes about a job that you might like to have some day. Then write a job description listing the education, experience, and abilities that you believe one must have for your dream job. Also describe the opportunities for advancement this job may offer.

Listening and Speaking

Dramatic Reading With a small group, organize and present a dramatic reading of "The Secret Life of Walter Mitty." Select a director and a person to create sound effects and then assign actors to play the different roles. (In order to perform the daydream sequences, some actors may need to play the parts of two or more characters.) Rehearse the story until you can perform it smoothly and then present it to the class.

Reading Further

You might enjoy these works by James Thurber:

Collections: *The Thurber Carnival* includes some of Thurber's best stories and drawings.

Fables for Our Times puts a humorous twist on classic poems and fables such as "Little Red Riding Hood."

Children's Story: *Many Moons* is the story of a young princess who wanted the moon and her father's efforts to get it for her.

Literary Criticism

"Mitty's fantasies," comments critic Anthony Kaufman, "may reveal a longing for the heroic, but much of the delight of the story comes from our perception of how formulaic, superficial, and false to life they really are." Is this how you perceive Mitty's fantasies? Write a short paragraph in which you explain whether you agree with Kaufman's assessment.

Save your work for your portfolio.

Skill Minilessons

GRAMMAR AND LANGUAGE • Capitalizing Proper Nouns

A proper noun is the name of a particular person, place, thing, or idea. Proper nouns should always be capitalized. Types of proper nouns include names of people and their titles (e.g., Queen Elizabeth); names of ethnic groups, national groups, and languages (e.g., Chinese); historical events (e.g., Vietnam War); and geographical terms (e.g., Midwest). Note the capitalization of names and places in this sentence from "The Secret Life of Walter Mitty":

> ". . . there are two specialists here, Dr. Remington from New York and Mr. Pritchard-Mitford from London."

PRACTICE On your paper, rewrite the following paragraph. Capitalize each proper noun.

> In one daydream, walter mitty becomes captain mitty. The time is world war I, and the place is germany. Mitty imagines he is flying against von richthofen, whom he mistakenly calls von richtman, the famous aviator known as the red baron.

APPLY Review a piece of your writing. List the proper nouns and tell why each should be capitalized.

● For more about capitalization, see **Language Handbook,** p. R45.

READING AND THINKING • Sequence of Events

In stories, events often take place in chronological sequence, or in the order in which they actually occur. Sometimes, though, a writer uses flashbacks or other devices to relate a story's events out of chronological sequence. In "The Secret Life of Walter Mitty," Mitty's daydreams transport him to another place and time. Thurber uses ellipses and obvious clues as to the time and place to signal changes in the sequence of events. Writers also use verb tense and transition words or phrases, such as *before, earlier that morning,* or *once,* to indicate shifts in sequence.

PRACTICE Find a passage in the story where Thurber relates events out of chronological order without using ellipses to signal the change. What words and phrases help readers understand the order of events?

APPLY Review another story and analyze the way the author ordered the events. Is the story told in strict chronological order? Do characters describe events that occurred in the past? Note how the author signals changes in the sequence of events.

● For more about reading strategies, see **Reading Handbook,** pp. R78–R107.

VOCABULARY • Synonyms

Synonyms are words that have the same or nearly the same meaning. The words *cheerful, delighted, glad, pleased, joyous,* and *ecstatic* are all synonyms for the word *happy.* We need different words to describe one emotion because that one emotion has many nuances, or shades of meaning.

Paying attention to the differences that exist between many synonyms will help you communicate more clearly and better understand what you read. For example, *insolent* and *sassy* are synonyms, but they do not mean exactly the same thing. A sassy remark may not be respectful, but it is usually light and cheerful. An insolent remark, on the other hand, is extremely rude and deliberately insulting.

PRACTICE For each word given, choose the synonym that best matches its precise meaning.

1. craven	a. hesitant	b. spineless
2. pandemonium	a. riot	b. disturbance
3. disdainful	a. haughty	b. proud
4. distraught	a. bewildered	b. distracted
5. haggard	a. tired	b. drained

Grammar Link

Avoiding Run-on Sentences

When people "run on" in conversation, they talk too long without pausing or stopping. A **run-on sentence** has the same problem; it "runs on" instead of pausing or stopping where it should. You can spot a run-on sentence by noticing main clauses–groups of words that have both a subject and a verb and can function as sentences.

Main clauses must always be separated from each other with an end mark of punctuation, with a semicolon, or with a comma and a coordinating conjunction.

Problem 1 A comma splice, or two main clauses separated only by a comma
Walter Mitty's daydreams are funny, they are also interesting.

Solution A Replace the comma with an end mark of punctuation, such as a period or a question mark, and begin the new sentence with a capital letter.
Walter Mitty's daydreams are funny. They are also interesting.

Solution B Place a semicolon between the two main clauses.
Walter Mitty's daydreams are funny; they are also interesting.

Solution C Add a coordinating conjunction after the comma.
Walter Mitty's daydreams are funny, but they are also interesting.

Problem 2 Two main clauses with no punctuation between them
Mitty hated his weekly trips into town he always forgot something.

Solution A Separate the main clauses with an end mark of punctuation, such as a period or question mark, and begin the second sentence with a capital letter.
Mitty hated his weekly trips into town. He always forgot something.

Solution B Separate the main clauses with a semicolon.
Mitty hated his weekly trips into town; he always forgot something.

Solution C Add a comma and a coordinating conjunction between the main clauses.
Mitty hated his weekly trips into town, and he always forgot something.

● For more about run-on sentences, see **Language Handbook**, p. R15.

EXERCISE

Correct the run-on sentences below as you rewrite them on your own paper. Apply the strategies shown above.

1. Everyone has daydreams, few of us have daydreams as detailed as Mitty's.
2. Reality is too dull for Mitty he escapes into his imagination.
3. Walter Mitty wakes from his dreams noises from the street rouse him.
4. Walter Mitty imagines himself to be a surgeon, he also dreams he's a pilot.
5. I know how Mitty feels I also daydream when someone is yelling at me.

MEDIA connection

Web Site

Have you ever seen an unfamiliar insect and said, "Eeeeew, what's *that?*" If you're interested in entomology, the study of insects, you'll find lots of information on the World Wide Web.

Mystery Bugs

Address: www.uky.edu

Can you identify the mystery bugs? We now offer two categories of mystery pictures: Novice and Expert. Try your hand at guessing the names of these insects!

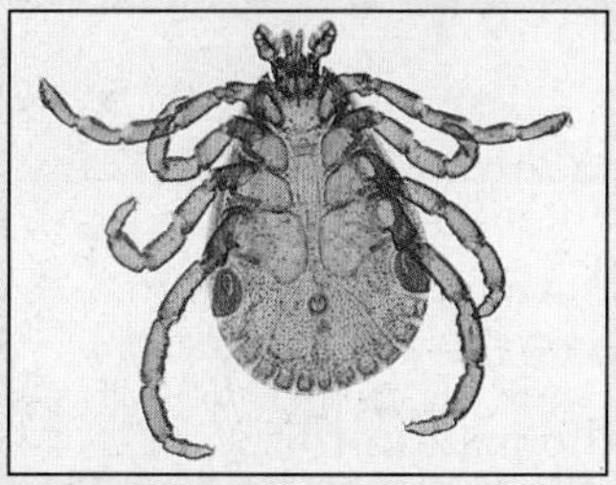

Novice

(Text Hint)

Mystery Picture Hint: Novice

This arthropod is a pest to domestic animals and humans. It is an external parasite that feeds on blood. It has a broadly oval, unsegmented body and eight short legs. After it has fed it can balloon up to twelve times its normal weight. It is the primary vector of Rocky Mountain Spotted Fever.

Expert

(Text Hint)

Mystery Picture Hint: Expert

These tiny wingless insects have distinctive heads and a hump-backed appearance. Their name comes from a forked structure attached to the underside of the abdomen which acts as a spring to flip them into the air. This behavior gives them the appearance of tiny fleas. They live in rich soil or leaf litter, under bark or decaying wood, or associated with fungi. Many are scavengers, feeding on decaying plants, fungi, molds, or algae.

Send a message with your best guess(es) to our mailbox by clicking here.

Past Mysteries

Look here for a list of mystery pictures from the first to the most recent!

University of Kentucky Department of Entomology

Return to *UK Department of Entomology Youthfacts*

Return to *UK Department of Entomology homepage*

Analyzing Media

The photographs of these insects have been enlarged many times. How does seeing them so large–and with so much detail–affect your understanding of them?

Before You Read

Gaston

Reading Focus

How do you feel about insects? Think about cockroaches, ladybugs, mosquitoes, butterflies, and ants. Do you feel the same way about all insects?

Sharing Ideas Consider why you feel the way you do about particular insects and share your reasons with your classmates. Which insects do people have different opinions about? Did your attitude about a particular insect change after hearing other people's opinions?

Setting a Purpose Read to learn about a father's and daughter's reactions to an insect.

Building Background

The Time and Place

The events in "Gaston" take place in Paris, France, one hot afternoon in August, sometime in the 1950s or early 1960s.

Did You Know?

Did you ever see a cat investigating a new room and think that it was curious about its surroundings? Attributing human qualities and characteristics to animals or inanimate objects is called anthropomorphism. People frequently anthropomorphize animals or things so that they can better relate to them. You anthropomorphize a lion if you say that it is brave. You anthropomorphize your computer if you say that it is smart.

Vocabulary Preview

kilo (kē′ lō) *n.* short for *kilogram,* a unit of measure in the metric system equal to 1,000 grams (about 2.2 pounds); p. 127

flawed (flôd) *adj.* faulty; imperfect; blemished; p. 127

precisely (pri sīs′ lē) *adv.* exactly; p. 128

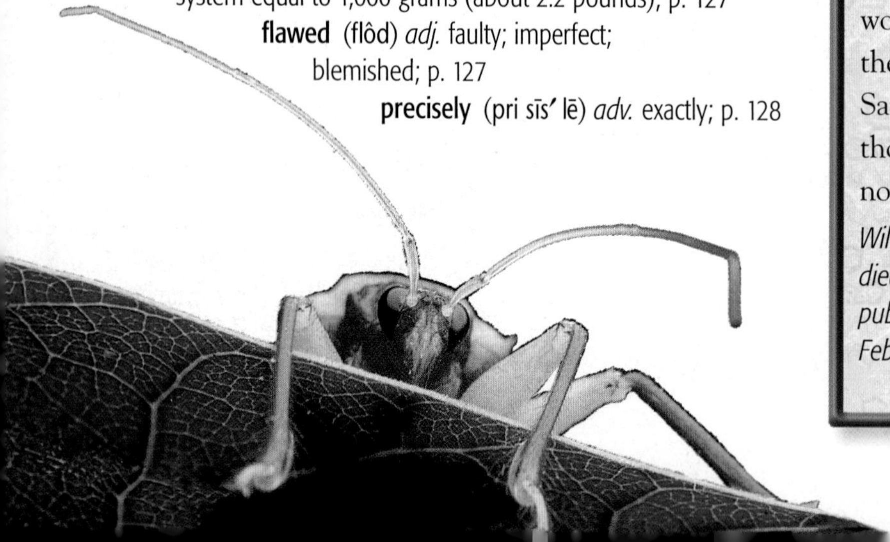

Meet William Saroyan

Like the man in this story, William Saroyan (sə roi′ ən) had a huge mustache and a vivid imagination. After his divorce, he moved to Paris, France, where his children visited him often. Saroyan wrote stories, plays, novels, memoirs, and songs. The dialogue and emotions of his characters are very realistic, perhaps because much of his work is based on his own experiences. His play *The Time of Your Life* won two major awards, including the prestigious Pulitzer Prize. Saroyan turned the prize down, though, believing its donors were not qualified to judge art.

William Saroyan was born in 1908 and died in 1981. "Gaston" was first published in the Atlantic Monthly *in February 1962.*

Gaston

William Saroyan

THEY WERE TO EAT PEACHES, as planned, after her nap, and now she sat across from the man who would have been a total stranger except that he was in fact her father. They had been together again (although she couldn't quite remember when they had been together before) for almost a hundred years now, or was it only since day before yesterday? Anyhow, they were together again, and he was kind of funny. First, he had the biggest mustache she had ever seen on anybody, although to her it was not a mustache at all; it was a lot of red and brown hair under his nose and around the ends of his mouth. Second, he wore a blue-and-white striped jersey[1] instead of a shirt and tie, and no coat. His arms were covered with the same hair, only it was a little lighter and thinner. He wore blue slacks, but no shoes and socks. He was barefoot, and so was she, of course.

He was at home. She was with him in his home in Paris, if you could call it a home. He was very old, especially for a young man—thirty-six, he had told her; and she was six, just up from sleep on a very hot afternoon in August.

That morning, on a little walk in the neighborhood, she had seen peaches in a box outside a small store and she had stopped to look at them, so he had bought a kilo.

Now, the peaches were on a large plate on the card table at which they sat.

There were seven of them, but one of them was flawed. It *looked* as good as the others, almost the size of a tennis ball, nice red fading to light green, but where the stem had been there was now a break that went straight down into the heart of the seed.

He placed the biggest and best-looking peach on the small plate in front of the girl, and then took the flawed peach and began to remove the skin. When he had half the skin off the peach he ate that side, neither of them talking, both of them just being there, and not being excited or anything—no plans, that is.

1. A *jersey* is a sweater or shirt, usually a close-fitting pullover, made of machine-knitted fabric.

Vocabulary

kilo (kē′ lō) *n.* short for *kilogram,* a unit of measure in the metric system equal to 1,000 grams (about 2.2 pounds)

flawed (flôd) *adj.* faulty; imperfect; blemished

The Pink Bow. Alice Beach Winter (1877–1970). Oil on canvas, 24 x 20 in. Private collection.

Viewing the painting: What might this child have in common with the little girl in the story?

The man held the half-eaten peach in his fingers and looked down into the cavity, into the open seed. The girl looked, too.

While they were looking, two feelers poked out from the cavity. They were attached to a kind of brown knob-head, which followed the feelers, and then two large legs took a strong grip on the edge of the cavity and hoisted some of the rest of whatever it was out of the seed, and stopped there a moment, as if to look around.

The man studied the seed dweller, and so, of course, did the girl.

The creature paused only a fraction of a second and then continued to come out of the seed, to walk down the eaten side of the peach to wherever it was going.

The girl had never seen anything like it—a whole big thing made out of brown color, a knob-head, feelers, and a great many legs. It was very active, too. Almost businesslike, you might say. The man placed the peach back on the plate. The creature moved off the peach onto the surface of the white plate. There it came to a thoughtful stop.

"Who is it?" the girl said.

"Gaston."[2]

"Where does he live?"

"Well, he *used* to live in this peach seed, but now that the peach has been harvested and sold, and I have eaten half of it, it looks as if he's out of house and home."

"Aren't you going to squash him?"

"No, of course not, why should I?"

"He's a bug. He's *ugh*."

"Not at all. He's Gaston the grand boulevardier."[3]

"Everybody hollers when a bug comes out of an apple, but you don't holler or *anything*."

"Of course not. How would *we* like it if somebody hollered every time we came out of our house?"

"Why *would* they?"

"Precisely. So why should we holler at Gaston?"

"He's not the same as us."

2. *Gaston* (gas tôn′)
3. Here, *boulevardier* (bo͞ol var dyā′) is a man about town, a worldly person who frequently goes to fancy restaurants and clubs, mainly in an effort to be seen.

Vocabulary
precisely (pri sīs′ lē) *adv.* exactly

"Well, not exactly, but he's the same as a lot of other occupants of peach seeds. Now, the poor fellow hasn't got a home, and there he is with all that pure design and handsome form, and nowhere to go."

"Handsome?"

"Gaston is just about the handsomest of his kind I've ever seen."

"What's he saying?"

"Well, he's a little confused. Now, inside that house of his he had everything in order. Bed here, porch there, and so forth."

"Show me."

The man picked up the peach, leaving Gaston entirely alone on the white plate. He removed the peeling and ate the rest of the peach.

"Nobody else I know would do that," the girl said. "They'd throw it away."

"I can't imagine why. It's a perfectly good peach."

He opened the seed and placed the two sides not far from Gaston. The girl studied the open halves.

"Is *that* where he lives?"

"It's where he used to live. Gaston is out in the world and on his own now. You can see for yourself how comfortable he was in there. He had everything."

"Now what has he got?"

"Not very much, I'm afraid."

"What's he going to do?"

"What are *we* going to do?"

"Well, we're not going to squash him, that's one thing we're *not* going to do," the girl said.

"What *are* we going to do, then?"

"Put him back?"

"Oh, *that* house is finished."

"Well, he can't live in our house, can he?"

"Not happily."

"Can he live in our house *at all?*"

"Well, he could *try,* I suppose. Don't you want to eat a peach?"

"Only if it's a peach with somebody in the seed."

"Well, see if you can find a peach that has an opening at the top, because if you can, that'll be a peach in which you're likeliest to find somebody."

The girl examined each of the peaches on the big plate.

"They're all shut," she said.

"Well, eat one, then."

"No. I want the same kind that you ate, with somebody in the seed."

"Well, to tell you the truth, the peach I ate would be considered a bad peach, so of course stores don't like to sell them. I was sold that one by mistake, most likely. And so now Gaston is without a home, and we've got six perfect peaches to eat."

"I don't want a perfect peach. I want a peach with people."

"Well, I'll go out and see if I can find one."

"Where will I go?"

"You'll go with me, unless you'd rather stay. I'll only be five minutes."

"If the phone rings, what shall I say?"

"I don't think it'll ring, but if it does, say hello and see who it is."

"If it's my mother, what shall I say?"

"Tell her I've gone to get you a bad peach, and anything else you want to tell her."

"If she wants me to go back, what shall I say?"

"Say yes if you want to go back."

"Do you want me to?"

"Of course not, but the important thing is what you want, not what I want."

"Why is *that* the important thing?"

"Because I want you to be where you want to be."

"I want to be here."

"I'll be right back."

He put on socks and shoes, and a jacket, and went out. She watched Gaston trying to find out what to do next. Gaston wandered around the plate, but everything seemed wrong and he didn't know what to do or where to go.

The telephone rang and her mother said she was sending the chauffeur to pick her up because there was a little party for somebody's daughter who was also six, and then tomorrow they would fly back to New York.

"Let me speak to your father," she said.

"He's gone to get a peach."

"*One* peach?"

"One with people."

"You haven't been with your father two days and already you *sound* like him."

"There *are* peaches with people in them. I know. I saw one of them come out."

"A *bug?*"

"Not a bug. Gaston."

"*Who?*"

"Gaston the grand something."

"Somebody else gets a peach with a bug in it, and throws it away, but not him. He makes up a lot of foolishness about it."

"It's not foolishness."

"All right, all right, don't get angry at me about a horrible peach bug of some kind."

"Gaston is right here, just outside his broken house, and I'm not angry at you."

Peaches and Almonds, 1901. Auguste Renoir. Oil on canvas, 31.1 x 41.3 cm. Tate Gallery, London.

Viewing the painting: In your opinion, would these peaches satisfy the little girl in the story? Why or why not?

"You'll have a lot of fun at the party."

"OK."

"We'll have fun flying back to New York, too."

"OK."

"Are you glad you saw your father?"

"Of course I am."

"Is he funny?"

"Yes."

"Is he crazy?"

"Yes. I mean, no. He just doesn't holler when he sees a bug crawling out of a peach seed or anything. He just looks at it carefully. But it *is* just a bug, isn't it, *really?*"

"That's all it is."

"And we'll *have* to squash it?"

"That's right. I can't wait to see you, darling. These two days have been like two years to me. Good-bye."

The girl watched Gaston on the plate, and she actually didn't like him. He was all *ugh,* as he had been in the first place. He didn't have a home anymore and he was wandering around on the white plate and he was silly and wrong and ridiculous and useless and all sorts of other things. She cried a little, but only inside, because long ago she had decided she didn't like crying because if you ever started to cry it seemed as if there was so much to cry about you almost couldn't stop, and she didn't like that at all. The open halves of the peach seed were wrong, too. They were ugly or something. They weren't clean.

The man bought a kilo of peaches but found no flawed peaches among them, so he bought another kilo at another store, and this time his luck was better, and there were *two* that were flawed. He hurried back to his flat and let himself in.

His daughter was in her room, in her best dress.

"My mother phoned," she said, "and she's sending the chauffeur for me because there's another birthday party."

"Another?"

"I mean, there's *always* a lot of them in New York."

"Will the chauffeur bring you back?"

"No. We're flying back to New York tomorrow."

"Oh."

"I liked being in your house."

"I liked having you here."

"Why do you live here?"

"This is my home."

"It's nice, but it's a lot different from our home."

"Yes, I suppose it is."

"It's kind of like Gaston's house."

"Where *is* Gaston?"

"I squashed him."

"Really? Why?"

"Everybody squashes bugs and worms."

"Oh. Well. I found you a peach."

"I don't want a peach anymore."

"OK."

He got her dressed, and he was packing her stuff when the chauffeur arrived. He went down the three flights of stairs with his daughter and the chauffeur, and in the street he was about to hug the girl when he decided he had better not. They shook hands instead, as if they were strangers.

He watched the huge car drive off, and then he went around the corner where he took his coffee every morning, feeling a little, he thought, like Gaston on the white plate.

Responding to Literature

Personal Response

Would you have done what the girl did to Gaston at the end of the story? Explain why or why not.

Analyzing Literature

Recall

1. Describe the **setting** of the story.
2. Who is Gaston? What does he look like?
3. Why wouldn't the girl eat any of the peaches?
4. What did the girl do after she talked to her mother on the phone?
5. How did the girl and her father say good-bye?

Interpret

6. What are some differences you can infer between the girl's usual home and that of her father?
7. In what way was the father's reaction to Gaston unusual? What does this suggest about him?
8. Why does the girl's attitude toward Gaston keep changing?
9. According to the narrator, the little girl no longer cried out loud because she thought that "if you ever started to cry it seemed as if there was so much to cry about you almost couldn't stop." What does this statement imply about the little girl's frame of mind and her feelings about her family life?
10. What do you learn about the father from the way the story ends?

Evaluate and Connect

11. On the phone, the mother tells the girl that her father's story about Gaston is foolishness. Do you agree or disagree with the mother's assessment? Explain.
12. Do you think both parents are good parents? Support your answer with evidence from the story.
13. Think about your response to the Reading Focus on page 126. Has this story's use of anthropomorphism changed your point of view in any way? Explain.
14. Evaluate Saroyan's use of **dialogue,** or conversation between characters, in this story. How does the dialogue help you get to know the characters?
15. **Theme Connections** How would you describe the void that exists in each of the three characters' lives?

Literary ELEMENTS

Exposition

Exposition is the introduction of the characters, the setting, or the situation at the beginning of a story. The details a writer chooses to include in the first few paragraphs are important, because they set the tone for the rest of the work. For example, in the first paragraph Saroyan describes the father as a "man who would have been a total stranger except that he was in fact her father." This statement gives readers an early insight into the relationship between the man and his daughter.

1. What do you learn about the two main characters in the first sentence of the story?
2. What are the first details you know about the father? What can you infer about him from these details?
3. What do you learn about the setting in the second paragraph?

- See **Literary Terms Handbook,** p. R5.

Literary Criticism

According to one critic, "Saroyan's work conveys a powerful sense of not being at home in the world." With a partner, discuss whether you think this sense is conveyed in "Gaston."

Literature and Writing

Writing About Literature

Making Comparisons The story ends with this sentence about the father: "He watched the huge car drive off, and then he went around the corner where he took his coffee every morning, feeling a little, he thought, like Gaston on the white plate." In what ways is the father like Gaston? Write a comparison using details from the story to support your ideas.

Creative Writing

You're Invited Compose a note that the father in this story might write to his daughter, in which he invites her to Paris for another visit. In order to persuade her to make the trip, remind her of how fun the last visit was and how good it felt to get to know her. You may even want to suggest how the next visit might be different. In your writing, try to mimic the way the man speaks in the story.

Extending Your Response

Literature Groups

You Be the Judge Imagine that a judge is determining whether the mother or the father will have full custody of the little girl or whether they will have joint custody. Using details from the story to support your opinion, argue for one of the three options. Try to reach an agreement on where–and with whom–the girl should live.

Interdisciplinary Activity

Biology: Going Buggy Choose an insect to research and prepare a brief report of your findings. In your report, describe your subject, identify its habitat, and discuss its impact on humans. Include a sketch or photo as a visual aid. You may want to begin your research on the Internet, looking for sites about your particular insect.

Internet Connection

The City of Lights Many writers and artists have been attracted to Paris. Search the Internet for information about Paris and its art community. First, look at travel sites for general information. Then, narrow your search to Web pages of Parisian art museums, cultural centers, or theaters. Report your findings to the class.

Reading Further

You might enjoy these works by William Saroyan:

Novel: *The Human Comedy* tells about a young boy determined to become the fastest messenger in the West during World War II.

Story: "Mystic Games," from the book *Madness in the Family,* tells about a boy who outwits his uncle.

Save your work for your portfolio.

Skill Minilesson

VOCABULARY • Clipped Words

Many English words are short forms of longer words; for example, *kilo* is short for either *kilogram* or *kilometer.* (To know which meaning *kilo* has, you need to consider the context.) The long form of some clipped words, such as *bike, gas, exam,* and *lab,* may be just as familiar as the short form. Some long forms are less familiar; *van,* for example, was shortened from *caravan. Pants* comes from the word *pantaloons.*

PRACTICE Match each clipped word in the left column with its original form in the right column.

1. flu	a. curiosity
2. wig	b. gabble
3. curio	c. influenza
4. sport	d. periwig
5. gab	e. disport

Before You Read

And Sarah Laughed

Reading Focus

Which would be more of a challenge, living with someone who was unable to hear or living with someone who was unwilling to listen?

Quickwrite Spend ten minutes writing an answer to the question above.

Setting a Purpose Read to learn about how a person who can hear becomes a person who can listen.

Building Background

The Time and Place

The story is set in a small rural community, possibly in the Midwest, in the early to mid-1900s.

Did You Know?

Today, American Sign Language, or ASL, is the fourth most-used language in the United States. It consists of hand signs representing words or phrases and a manual alphabet used to spell out words or names that have no sign. At the time of this story, few people used sign language. Throughout most of the twentieth century, deaf children were taught to speak and to read lips. It was mistakenly thought that using sign language would set the deaf apart from their peers and alienate children from their hearing parents. As a result, communication between deaf and hearing people was sometimes very difficult. In the 1960s, however, American Sign Language became more accepted, and today it is offered as a course of study in some high schools and colleges. Rather than separating deaf people from hearing people, ASL has improved communication between the two groups.

Vocabulary Preview

reticence (ret′ ə səns) *n.* the tendency to keep one's thoughts and feelings to oneself; p. 136
strident (strīd′ ənt) *adj.* loud, harsh, and shrill; p. 139
inflection (in flek′ shən) *n.* change or variation in the tone or pitch of the voice; p. 140
anguish (ang′ gwish) *n.* extreme mental or emotional suffering; p. 143
vindictive (vin dik′ tiv) *adj.* wanting revenge; p. 144

Meet Joanne Greenberg

"My ambition in life is to keep on writing, getting better all the time, until I hit eighty-five, and then coast."

Joanne Greenberg grew up in Brooklyn, New York, and later moved to Manhattan. In spite of the city's dense population and its cultural diversity, Greenberg felt isolated. The theme of isolation is apparent in much of her work, including the novel *I Never Promised You a Rose Garden*, which she wrote under the pseudonym Hannah Green. Greenberg—a wife, mother, and interpreter for the deaf—is the author of many acclaimed short stories and novels.

Joanne Greenberg was born in 1932. "And Sarah Laughed" was published in Rites of Passage *in 1972.*

And Sarah Laughed

Joanne Greenberg

SHE WENT TO THE WINDOW EVERY FIFTEEN MINUTES to see if they were coming. They would be taking the new highway cutoff; it would bring them past the south side of the farm; past the unused, dilapidated outbuildings instead of the orchards and fields that were now full and green.

It would look like a poor place to the new bride. Her first impression of their farm would be of age and bleached-out, dried-out buildings on which the doors hung open like a row of gaping mouths that said nothing.

All day, Sarah had gone about her work clumsy with eagerness and hesitant with dread, picking up utensils to forget them in holding, finding them two minutes later a surprise in her hand. She had been planning and working ever since Abel wrote to them from Chicago that he was coming home with a wife. Everything should have been clean and orderly. She wanted the bride to know as soon as she walked inside what kind of woman Abel's mother was—to feel, without a word having to be said, the house's dignity, honesty, simplicity, and love. But the spring cleaning had been late, and Alma Yoder had gotten sick—Sarah had had to go over to the Yoders and help out.

Now she looked around and saw that it was no use trying to have everything ready in time. Abel and his bride would be coming any minute. If she didn't want to get caught shedding tears of frustration, she'd better get herself under control. She stepped over the pile of clothes still unsorted for the laundry and went out on the back porch.

The sky was blue and silent, but as she watched, a bird passed over the fields crying. The garden spread out before her, displaying its varying greens. Beyond it, along the creek, there was a row of poplars. It always calmed her to look at them. She looked today. She and Matthew had planted those trees. They stood thirty feet high now, stately as figures in a procession. Once—only once and many years ago—she had tried to describe in words the sounds that the wind made as it combed those trees on its way west. The little boy to whom she had spoken was a grown man now, and he was bringing home a wife. *Married. . . .*

Did You Know?
The *poplar* tree is in the willow family and has pale, ridged bark and broad leaves. Often, rows of tall, dignified *(stately)* poplars are grown as a windbreak.

Ever since he had written to tell them he was coming with his bride, Sarah had been going back in her mind to the days when she and Matthew were bride and groom and then mother and father. Until now, it hadn't seemed so long ago. Her life had flowed on past her, blurring the early days with Matthew when this farm was strange and new to her and when the silence of it was sharp and bitter like pain, not dulled and familiar like an echo of old age.

Matthew hadn't changed much. He was a tall, lean man, but he had had a boy's spareness then. She remembered how his smile came, wavered and went uncertainly, but how his eyes had never left her. He followed everything with his eyes. Matthew had always been a silent man; his face was expressionless and his body stiff with reticence, but his eyes had sought her out eagerly and held her and she had been warm in his look.

Sarah and Matthew had always known each other—their families had been neighbors. Sarah was a plain girl, a serious "decent" girl. Not many of the young men asked her out, and when Matthew did and did again, her parents had been pleased. Her father told her that Matthew was a good man, as steady as any woman could want. He came from honest, hard-working people and he would prosper any farm he had. Her mother spoke shyly of how his eyes woke when Sarah came into the room, and how they followed her. If she married him, her life would be full of the things she knew and loved, an easy, familiar world with her parents' farm not two miles down the road. But no one wanted to mention the one thing that worried Sarah: the fact that Matthew was deaf. It was what stopped her from saying yes right away; she loved him, but she was worried about his deafness. The things she feared about it were the practical things: a fall or a fire when he wouldn't hear her cry for help. Only long after she had put those fears aside and moved the scant two miles into his different world, did she realize that the things she had feared were the wrong things.

Now they had been married for twenty-five years. It was a good marriage—good enough. Matthew was generous, strong, and loving. The farm prospered. His silence made him seem more patient, and because she became more silent also, their neighbors saw in them the dignity and strength of two people who do not rail[1] against misfortune, who

1. *Rail* means "to complain bitterly."

Vocabulary
reticence (ret′ ə səns) *n.* the tendency to keep one's thoughts and feelings to oneself

River Fields, 1983. Walter Hatke. Oil on linen, 23½ x 38¼ in. Collection of The Chase Manhattan Bank, New York.

Viewing the painting: How would you describe the mood of this painting? How well does the painting reflect the mood of the story? Explain.

were beyond trivial talk and gossip; whose lives needed no words. Over the years of help given and meetings attended, people noticed how little they needed to say. Only Sarah's friend Luita knew that in the beginning, when they were first married, they had written yearning notes to each other. But Luita didn't know that the notes also were mute. Sarah had never shown them to anyone, although she kept them all, and sometimes she would go up and get the box out of her closet and read them over. She had saved every scrap, from questions about the eggs to the tattered note he had left beside his plate on their first anniversary. He had written it when she was busy at the stove and then he'd gone out and she hadn't seen it until she cleared the table.

The note said: "I love you derest wife Sarah. I pray you have happy day all day your life."

When she wanted to tell him something, she spoke to him slowly, facing him, and he took the words as they formed on her lips. His speaking voice was thick and hard to understand and he perceived that it was unpleasant. He didn't like to use it. When he had to say something, he used his odd, grunting tone, and she came to understand what he said. If she ever hungered for laughter from him or the little meaningless talk that confirms existence and affection, she told herself angrily that Matthew talked through his work. Words die in the air; they can be turned one way or another, but Matthew's work prayed and laughed for him. He took good care of her and the boys, and they idolized him. Surely that counted more than all the words—words that meant and didn't mean—behind which people could hide.

Over the years she seldom noticed her own increasing silence, and there were times when his tenderness, which was always given without words, seemed to her to make his silence beautiful.

She thought of the morning she had come downstairs feeling heavy and off balance with her first pregnancy—with Abel. She had gone to the kitchen to begin the day, taking the coffeepot down and beginning to fill it when her eye caught something on the kitchen table. For a minute she looked around in confusion. They had already laid away what the baby would need: diapers, little shirts and bedding, all folded away in the drawer upstairs, but here on the table was a bounty of cloth, all planned and scrimped for and bought from careful, careful study of the catalogue—yards of patterned flannel and plissé,[2] coat wool and bright red corduroy. Sixteen yards of yellow ribbon for bindings. Under the coat wool was cloth Matthew had chosen for her; blue with a little gray figure. It was silk, and there was a card on which was rolled precisely enough lace edging for her collar and sleeves. All the long studying and careful planning, all in silence.

She had run upstairs and thanked him and hugged him, but it was no use showing delight with words, making plans, matching cloth and figuring which pieces would be for the jacket and which for sleepers. Most wives used such fussing to tell their husbands how much they thought of their gifts. But Matthew's silence was her silence too.

When he had left to go to the orchard after breakfast that morning, she had gone to their room and stuffed her ears with cotton, trying to understand the world as it must be to him, with no sound. The cotton dulled the outside noises a little, but it only magnified all the noises in her head. Scratching her cheek caused a roar like a downpour of rain; her own voice was like thunder. She knew Matthew could not hear his own voice in his head. She could not be deaf as he was deaf. She could not know such silence ever.

So she found herself talking to the baby inside her, telling it the things she would have told Matthew, the idle daily things: Didn't Margaret Amson look peaked[3] in town? Wasn't it a shame the drugstore had stopped stocking lump alum[4]—her pickles wouldn't be the same.

Abel was a good baby. He had Matthew's great eyes and gentle ways. She chattered to him all day, looking forward to his growing up, when there would be confidences between them. She looked to the time when he would have his own picture of the world, and with that keen hunger and hope she had a kind of late blooming into a beauty that made people in town turn to look at her when she passed in the street holding the baby in the fine clothes she had made for him. She took Abel everywhere, and came to know a pride that was very new to her, a plain girl from a modest family who had married a neighbor boy. When they went to town, they always stopped over to see Matthew's parents and her mother.

Mama had moved to town after Pa died. Of course they had offered to have Mama come and live with them, but Sarah was glad she had gone to a little place in town, living where there were people she knew and things happening right outside her door. Sarah remembered them visiting on a certain spring day, all sitting in Mama's new front room. They sat uncomfortably in the genteel[5] chairs, and Abel crawled around on the floor as the women talked, looking up every now and then for his father's nod of approval. After a while he went to catch the sunlight that was glancing off a

2. *Plissé* (pli sā′) is a cotton fabric with a crinkly finish.

3. Margaret Amson looked pale and sickly *(peaked).*

4. *Alum* (al′ əm) is a chemical compound that is used to purify water and stop bleeding as well as in pickle-making.

5. Here, *genteel* means "elegant; stylish."

crystal nut dish and scattering rainbow bands on the floor. Sarah smiled down at him. She too had a radiance, and, for the first time in her life, she knew it. She was wearing the dress she had made from Matthew's cloth—it became her and she knew that too, so she gave her joy freely as she traded news with Mama.

Suddenly they heard the fire bell ringing up on the hill. She caught Matthew's eye and mouthed, "Fire engines," pointing uphill to the firehouse. He nodded.

In the next minutes there was the strident, off-key blare as every single one of Arcadia's volunteer firemen—his car horn plugged with a matchstick and his duty before him—drove hellbent for the firehouse in an ecstasy of bell and siren. In a minute the ding-ding-ding-ding careened in deafening, happy privilege through every red light in town.

"Big bunch of boys!" Mama laughed. "You can count two Saturdays in good weather when they don't have a fire, and that's during the hunting season!"

They laughed. Then Sarah looked down at Abel, who was still trying to catch the wonderful colors. A madhouse of bells, horns, screaming sirens had gone right past them and he hadn't cried, he hadn't looked, he hadn't turned. Sarah twisted her head sharply away and screamed to the china cats on the whatnot shelf as loud as she could, but Abel's eyes only flickered to the movement and then went back to the sun and its colors.

Did You Know?
A *whatnot shelf* is an open shelf for displaying trinkets and ornaments.

Mama whispered, "Oh, my dear God!"

Sarah began to cry bitterly, uncontrollably, while her husband and son looked on, confused, embarrassed, unknowing.

The silence drew itself over the seasons and the seasons layered into years. Abel was a good boy; Matthew was a good man.

Later, Rutherford, Lindsay, and Franklin Delano came. They too were silent. Hereditary nerve deafness was rare, the doctors all said. The boys might marry and produce deaf children, but it was not likely. When they started to school, the administrators and teachers told her that the boys would be taught specially to read lips and to speak. They would not be "abnormal," she was told. Nothing would show their handicap, and with training no one need know that they were deaf. But the boys seldom used their lifeless voices to call to their friends; they seldom joined games unless they were forced to join. No one but their mother understood their speech. No teacher could stop all the jumping, turning, gum-chewing schoolboys, or remember herself to face front from the blackboard to the sound-closed boys. The lip-reading exercises never seemed to make plain differences—"man," "pan," "began."

But the boys had work and pride in the farm. The seasons varied their silence with colors—crows flocked in the snowy fields in winter, and tones of golden wheat darkened across acres of summer wind. If the boys couldn't hear the bedsheets flapping on the washline, they could see and feel the autumn day. There were chores and holidays and the wheel of birth and planting, hunting, fishing, and harvest. The boys were familiar in town; nobody ever laughed at them, and when

Vocabulary
strident (strīd′ ənt) *adj.* loud, harsh, and shrill

Edith Holman Hunt, 1876. William Holman Hunt. Red and black chalk on paper, 54.3 x 37.4 cm. National Gallery of Canada, Ottawa.

Viewing the art: What personal qualities or characteristics does this woman seem to possess? Which of these qualities might Sarah possess?

Sarah met neighbors at the store, they praised her sons with exaggerated praise, well meant, saying that no one could tell, no one could really tell unless they knew, about the boys not hearing.

Sarah wanted to cry to these kindly women that the simple orders the boys obeyed by reading her lips were not a miracle. If she could ever hear in their long-practiced robot voices a question that had to do with feelings and not facts, and answer it in words that rose beyond the daily, tangible things done or not done, *that* would be a miracle.

Her neighbors didn't know that they themselves confided to one another from a universe of hopes, a world they wanted half lost in the world that was; how often they spoke pitting inflection against meaning to soften it, harden it, make a joke of it, curse by it, bless by it. They didn't realize how they wrapped the bare words of love in gentle humor or wild insults that the loved ones knew were ways of keeping the secret of love between the speaker and the hearer. Mothers lovingly called their children crow-bait, mouse-meat, devils. They predicted dark ends for them, and the children heard the secrets beneath the words, heard them and smiled and knew, and let the love said-unsaid caress their souls. With her own bitter knowledge Sarah could only thank them for well-meaning and return to silence.

Vocabulary

inflection (in flek′ shən) *n.* change or variation in the tone or pitch of the voice

Standing on the back porch now, Sarah heard the wind in the poplars and she sighed. It was getting on to noon. Warm air was beginning to ripple the fields. Matthew would be ready for lunch soon, but she wished she could stand out under the warm sky forever and listen to birds stitching sounds into the endless silence. She found herself thinking about Abel again, and the bride. She wondered what Janice would be like. Abel had gone all the way to Chicago to be trained in drafting.[6] He had met her there, in the school. Sarah was afraid of a girl like that. They had been married quickly, without family or friends or toasts or gifts or questions. It hinted at some kind of secret shame. It frightened her. That kind of girl was independent and she might be scornful of a dowdy mother-in-law. And the house was still a mess.

From down the road, dust was rising. Matthew must have seen it too. He came over the rise and toward the house walking faster than usual. He'd want to slick his hair down and wash up to meet the stranger his son had become. She ran inside and bundled up the unsorted laundry, ran upstairs and pulled a comb through her hair, put on a crooked dab of lipstick, banged her shin, took off her apron and saw a spot on her dress, put the apron on again and shouted a curse to all the disorder she suddenly saw around her.

Now the car was crunching up the thin gravel of the driveway. She heard Matthew downstairs washing up, not realizing that the bride and groom were already at the house. Protect your own, she thought, and ran down to tell him. Together they went to the door and opened it, hoping that at least Abel's familiar face would comfort them.

6. Here, *drafting* involves drawing or designing plans for machinery or buildings.

They didn't recognize him at first, and he didn't see them. He and the tiny bride might have been alone in the world. He was walking around to open the door for her, helping her out, bringing her up the path to the house, and all the time their fingers and hands moved and spun meanings at which they smiled and laughed; they were talking somehow, painting thoughts in the air so fast with their fingers that Sarah couldn't see where one began and the other ended. She stared. The school people had always told her that such finger-talk set the deaf apart. It was abnormal; it made freaks of them. . . . How soon Abel had accepted someone else's strangeness and bad ways. She felt so dizzy she thought she was going to fall, and she was more bitterly jealous than she had ever been before.

The little bride stopped before them appealingly and in her dead, deaf-rote voice,[7] said, "Ah-am pliizd to meet 'ou." Sarah put out her hand dumbly and it was taken and the girl's eyes shone. Matthew smiled, and this time the girl spoke and waved her hands in time to her words, and then gave Matthew her hand. So Abel had told that girl about Matthew's deafness. It had never been a secret, but Sarah felt somehow betrayed.

They had lunch, saw the farm, the other boys came home from their summer school and met Janice. Sarah put out cake and tea and showed Abel and Janice up to the room she had made ready for them, and all the time the two of them went on with their love-talk in their fingers; the jokes and secrets knitted silently between them, fears told and calmed, hopes spoken and echoed in the silence of a kitchen where twenty-five years of silence

7. Janice's *deaf-rote voice* is mechanical-sounding because, without ever having heard speech, she learned to speak by technically memorizing how to produce sounds.

Share Cropper, 1937. Jerry Bywaters. Oil on Masonite, 29¼ x 23½ in. Dallas Museum of Art, TX.

Viewing the painting: What does this farmer's expression suggest about his thoughts? How might his thoughts compare with Matthew's?

had imprisoned her. Always they would stop and pull themselves back to their good manners, speaking or writing polite questions and answers for the family; but in a moment or two, the talk would flag, the urgent hunger would overcome them and they would fight it, resolutely turning their eyes to Sarah's mouth. Then the signs would creep into their fingers, and the joy of talk into their faces, and they would fall before the conquering need of their communion.

Sarah's friend Luita came the next day, in the afternoon. They sat over tea with the kitchen window open for the cool breeze and Sarah was relieved and grateful to hold to a familiar thing now that her life had suddenly become so strange to her. Luita hadn't changed at all, thank God—not the hand that waved her tea cool or the high giggle that broke into generous laughter.

"She's darling!" Luita said after Janice had been introduced, and, thankfully, had left them. Sarah didn't want to talk about her, so she agreed without enthusiasm.

Luita only smiled back. "Sarah, you'll never pass for pleased with a face like that."

"It's just—just her ways," Sarah said. "She never even wrote to us before the wedding, and now she comes in and—and changes everything. I'll be honest, Luita, I didn't want Abel to marry someone who was deaf. What did we train him for, all those special classes? . . . *not* to marry another deaf person. And she hangs on him like a wood tick all day . . . " She didn't mention the signs. She couldn't.

Luita said, "It's just somebody new in the house, that's all. She's important to you, but a stranger. Addie Purkhard felt the same way and you know what a lovely girl Velma turned out to be. It just took time. . . . She's going to have a baby, did she tell you?"

"Baby? Who?" Sarah cried, feeling cold and terrified.

"Why, *Velma.* A baby due about a month after my Dolores'."

It had never occurred to Sarah that Janice and Abel could have a baby. She wanted to stop thinking about it and she looked back at Luita whose eyes were glowing with something joyful that had to be said. Luita hadn't been able to see beyond it to the anguish of her friend.

Luita said, "You know, Sarah, things haven't been so good between Sam and me. . . . " She cleared her throat. "You know how stubborn he is. The last few weeks, it's been like a whole new start for us. I came over to tell you about it because I'm so happy, and I had to share it with you."

She looked away shyly, and Sarah pulled herself together and leaned forward, putting her hand on her friend's arm. "I'm so happy for you. What happened?"

"It started about three weeks ago—a night that neither of us could get to sleep. We hadn't been arguing; there was just that awful coldness, as if we'd both been frozen stiff. One of us started talking—just lying there in the dark. I don't even know who started, but pretty soon we were telling each other the most secret things—things we never could have said in the light. He finally told me that Dolores having a baby makes him feel old and scared. He's afraid of it, Sarah, and I never knew it, and it explains why he hates to go over and see them, and why he argues with Ken all the time. Right there beside me he told me so many things I'd forgotten or misunderstood. In the dark it's like thinking out loud—like being alone and yet together at the same time. I love him so and I came so close to forgetting it. . . . "

Sarah lay in bed and thought about Luita and Sam sharing their secrets in the dark. Maybe even now they were talking in their flower-papered upstairs room, moving against the engulfing seas of silence as if in little boats, finding each other and touching and then looking out in awe at the vastness all around them where they might have rowed alone and mute forever. She wondered if Janice and Abel fingered those signs in the dark on each other's body. She began to cry. There was that freedom, at least; other wives had to strangle their weeping.

When she was cried out, she lay in bed and counted all the good things she had: children, possessions, acres of land, respect of neighbors, the years of certainty and success. Then she conjured[8] the little bride, and

8. Sarah called to mind *(conjured)* an image of Janice.

Vocabulary

anguish (ang′ gwish) *n.* extreme mental or emotional suffering saw her standing in front of Abel's old car as she had at first—with nothing; all her virtues still unproven, all her fears still forming, and her bed in another woman's house. Against the new gold ring on the bride's finger, Sarah threw all the substance of her years to weigh for her. The balance went with the bride. It wasn't fair! The balance went with the bride because she had put that communion in the scales as well, and all the thoughts that must have been given and taken between them. It outweighed Sarah's twenty-five years of muteness; outweighed the house and barn and well-tended land, and the sleeping family keeping their silent thoughts.

The days went by. Sarah tortured herself with elaborate courtesy to Janice and politeness to the accomplice son, but she couldn't guard her own envy from herself and she found fault wherever she looked. Now the silence of her house was throbbing with her anger. Every morning Janice would come and ask to help, but Sarah was too restless to teach her, so Janice would sit for a while waiting and then get up and go outside to look for Abel. Then Sarah would decide to make coleslaw and sit with the chopping bowl in her lap, smashing the chopper against the wood with a vindictive joy that she alone could hear the sounds she was making, that she alone knew how savage they were and how satisfying.

At church she would see the younger boys all clean and handsome, Matthew greeting friends, Janice demure[9] and fragile, and Abel proud and loving, and she would feel a terrible guilt for her unreasonable anger; but back from town afterwards, and after Sunday dinner, she noticed as never before how disheveled[10] the boys looked, how ugly their hollow voices sounded. Had Matthew always been so patient and unruffled? He was like one of his own stock, an animal, a dumb animal.

Janice kept asking to help and Sarah kept saying there wasn't time to teach her. She was amazed when Matthew, who was very fussy about his fruit, suggested to her that Janice might be able to take care of the grapes and, later, work in the orchard.

"I haven't time to teach her!"

"Ah owill teeech Ja-nuss," Abel said, and they left right after dinner in too much of a hurry.

Matthew stopped Sarah when she was clearing the table and asked why she didn't like Janice. Now it was Sarah's turn to be silent, and when Matthew insisted, Sarah finally turned on him. "You don't understand," she shouted. "You don't understand a thing!" And she saw on his face the same look of confusion she had seen that day in Mama's fussy front room when she had suddenly begun to cry and could not stop. She turned away with the plates, but suddenly his hand shot out and he struck them to the floor, and the voice he couldn't hear or control rose to an awful cry, "Ah ahm dehf! Ah ahm dehf!" Then he went out, slamming the door without the satisfaction of its sound.

If a leaf fell or a stalk sprouted in the grape arbor, Janice told it over like a set of prayers. One night at supper, Sarah saw the younger boys framing those dumb-signs of hers, and she took them outside and slapped their

9. Here, *demure* (di myoor′) means "quiet and shy."

10. *Disheveled* (di shev′ əld) means "untidy or rumpled."

Vocabulary
vindictive (vin dik′ tiv) *adj.* wanting revenge

hands. "*We* don't do that!" she shouted at them, and to Janice later she said, "Those . . . signs you make—I know they must have taught you to do that, but out here . . . well, it isn't our way."

Janice looked back at her in a confusion for which there were no words.

It was no use raging at Janice. Before she had come there had never been anything for Sarah to be angry about. . . . What did they all expect of her? Wasn't it enough that she was left out of a world that heard and laughed without being humiliated by the love-madness they made with their hands? It was like watching them undressing.

The wind cannot be caught. Poplars may sift it, a rising bird can breast it, but it will pass by and no one can stop it. She saw the boys coming home at a dead run now, and they couldn't keep their hands from taking letters, words, and pictures from the fingers of the lovers. If they saw an eagle, caught a fish, or got scolded, they ran to their brother or his wife, and Sarah had to stand in the background and demand to be told.

One day Matthew came up to her and smiled and said, "Look." He put out his two index fingers and hooked the right down on the left, then the left down gently on the right. "Fwren," he said, "Ja-nuss say, fwren."

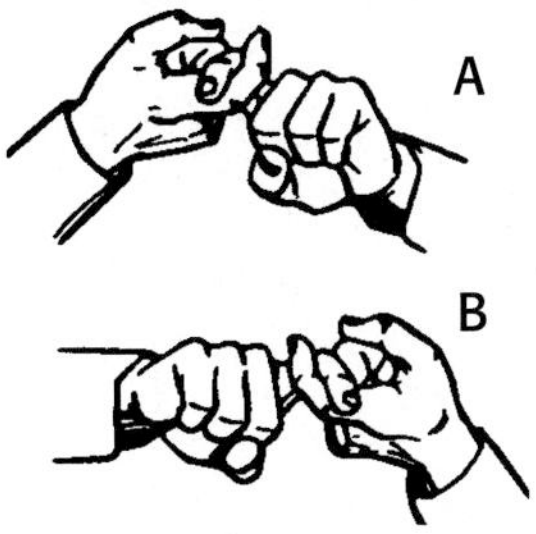

Did You Know?
This is the hand sign for "friend" *(fwren).*

To Sarah there was something obscene about all those gestures, and she said, "I don't like people waving their hands around like monkeys in a zoo!" She said it very clearly so that he couldn't mistake it.

He shook his head violently and gestured as he spoke. "Mouth eat; mouth kiss, mouth tawk! Fin-ger wohk; fin-ger tawk. E-ah" (and he grabbed his ear, violently), "e-ah dehf. *Mihn,*"[11] (and he rapped his head, violently, as if turning a terrible impatience against himself so as to spare her) "*mihn not* dehf!"

Later she went to the barn after something and she ran into Lindsay and Franklin Delano standing guiltily, and when she caught them in her eye as she turned, she saw their hands framing signs. They didn't come into the house until it was nearly dark. Was their hunger for those signs so great that only darkness could bring them home? They weren't bad boys, the kind who would do a thing just because you told them not to. Did their days have a hunger too, or was it only the spell of the lovers, honey-honeying to shut out a world of moving mouths and silence?

At supper she looked around the table and was reassured. It could have been any farm family sitting there, respectable and quiet. A glance from the father was all that was needed to keep order or summon another helping. Their eyes were lowered, their faces composed. The hands were quiet. She smiled and went to the kitchen to fix the shortcake she had made as a surprise.

When she came back, they did not notice her immediately. They were all busy talking. Janice was telling them something and they all had their mouths ridiculously pursed with the word. Janice smiled in assent and each one showed her his sign and she smiled at each one and nodded, and the signers turned to one another in their joy, accepting and begging acceptance. Then they saw Sarah standing there; the hands came down, the faces faded.

She took the dinner plates away and brought in the dessert things, and when she went back to the kitchen for the cake, she

11. Matthew says only his hearing is impaired; his mind *(mihn),* or intellect, is fine.

began to cry. It was beyond envy now; it was too late for measuring or weighing. She had lost. In the country of the blind, Mama used to say, the one-eyed man is king. Having been a citizen of such a country, she knew better. In the country of the deaf, the hearing man is lonely. Into that country a girl had come who, with a wave of her hand, had given the deaf ears for one another, and had made Sarah the deaf one.

Sarah stood, staring at her cake and feeling for that moment the profundity[12] of the silence which she had once tried to match by stuffing cotton in her ears. Everyone she loved was in the other room, talking, sharing, standing before the awful, impersonal heaven and the unhearing earth with pictures of his thoughts, and she was the deaf one now. It wasn't "any farm family," silent in its strength. It was a yearning family, silent in its hunger, and a demure little bride had shown them all how deep the hunger was. She had shown Sarah that her youth had been sold into silence. She was too old to change now.

An anger rose in her as she stared at the cake. Why should they be free to move and gesture and look different while she was kept in bondage to their silence? Then she remembered Matthew's mute notes, his pride in Abel's training, his face when he had cried, "I am deaf!" over and over. She had actually fought that terrible yearning, that hunger they all must have had for their own words. If they could all speak somehow, what would the boys tell her?

She knew what she wanted to tell them. That the wind sounds through the poplar trees, and people have a hard time speaking to one another even if they aren't deaf. Luita and Sam had to have a night to hide their faces while they spoke. It suddenly occurred to her that if Matthew made one of those signs with his hands and she could learn that sign, she could put her hands against his in the darkness, and read the meaning—that if she learned those signs she could hear him. . . .

She dried her eyes hurriedly and took in the cake. They saw her and the hands stopped, drooping lifelessly again; the faces waited mutely. Silence. It was a silence she could no longer bear. She looked from face to face. What was behind those eyes she loved? Didn't everyone's world go deeper than chores and bread and sleep?

"I want to talk to you," she said. "I want to talk, to know what you think." She put her hands out before her, offering them.

Six pairs of eyes watched her.

Janice said, "Mo-ther."

Eyes snapped away to Janice; thumb was under lip: the Sign.

Sarah followed them. "Wife," she said, showing her ring.

"Wife," Janice echoed, thumb under lip to the clasp of hands.

Sarah said, "I love. . . ."

Janice showed her and she followed hesitantly and then turned to Matthew to give and to be received in that sign.

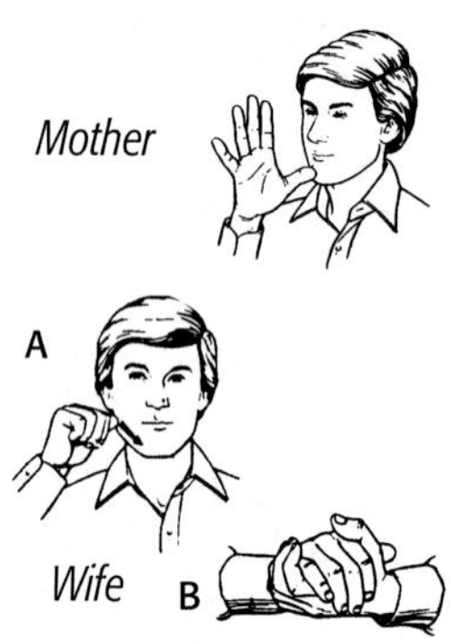

Did You Know?
These are the signs for *mother* and *wife.*

12. Here, *profundity* refers to the intensity of Sarah's feelings.

Responding to Literature

Personal Response

Which scenes from the story linger in your mind? Record your impressions in your journal.

Analyzing Literature

Recall

1. At the beginning of the story, whose arrival is Sarah expecting?
2. Describe Matthew, Sarah's husband.
3. How does Sarah find out that Abel is deaf?
4. What happens between Luita and Sam that changes their lives?
5. What signs does Sarah learn at the end of the story?

Interpret

6. In your opinion, why is Sarah so nervous at the beginning of the story? What does this say about her?
7. Do you think Sarah and Matthew are a good match for each other? Explain why or why not, using details from the story.
8. What are some reasons why Sarah would "cry bitterly, uncontrollably," when she realizes Abel is deaf?
9. How does Luita's news affect Sarah? Why do you think Sarah feels as she does?
10. What do the signs that Sarah first chooses to learn reveal about her character and what is important to her?

Evaluate and Connect

11. **Theme Connections** What has been the void in Sarah's life? Do you think she will be able to fill it? Explain.
12. A story's **title** often gives clues as to what is important. When and where in the story did Sarah laugh, and why is that scene significant?
13. Think about your response to the Reading Focus on page 134. In what ways is Sarah "deaf" to her family and their needs?
14. Did your feelings toward Sarah change from the beginning to the end of the story? At what points did you empathize with Sarah? At what points did you feel critical of her?
15. What can you learn from this story about the importance of being open to change?

Literary ELEMENTS

Irony

Irony is a contrast between reality and appearance. **Situational irony** exists when the actual outcome of a situation is the opposite of the expected outcome. **Dramatic irony** exists when the reader knows something that a character does not know. Explain what is ironic about each of the following quotations from "And Sarah Laughed." Are any of these examples of situational or dramatic irony?

1. She wanted the bride to know as soon as she walked inside what kind of woman Abel's mother was—to feel, without a word having to be said, the house's dignity, honesty, simplicity, and love.
2. Their neighbors saw in them the dignity and strength of two people who do not rail against misfortune, who were beyond trivial talk and gossip; whose lives needed no words.
3. With a wave of her hand, [Janice] had given the deaf ears for one another, and had made Sarah the deaf one.

- See **Literary Terms Handbook,** p. R7.

Literature and Writing

Writing About Literature

Book Jacket Imagine that "And Sarah Laughed" will be reprinted and published as a book. Write the copy, or written manuscript, for the book jacket. For the cover, write two or three sentences to catch a buyer's eye. Then write a summary of the story for the inside flap. Finally, for the back cover, write a brief critical review of the story in which you consider its strengths and weaknesses. Look at a real book jacket for guidance. Consider inventing quotations from critics for the back cover and create an appealing design–with original artwork–for the front. Display your book jackets on a class bulletin board.

Personal Writing

I Don't Understand Have you ever been in a situation where people were speaking a language you did not understand? Do freewriting for five or ten minutes about how you felt–or about how you imagine that you would feel–in such a situation. Then consider how Sarah felt about being unable to understand her family's sign-language conversation. Write a paragraph or two comparing your experience with Sarah's.

Extending Your Response

Literature Groups

Wherein Lies the Conflict? Do you think that the main conflict Sarah faces in this story is internal or external? In other words, does the conflict exist in her mind because she is torn between opposing feelings and goals, or is she struggling against some outside force, such as another person, nature, society, or fate? Debate this question, using evidence from the story to back up your opinions. Try to reach a consensus within your group and then share and discuss your conclusions with other groups.

Internet Connection

Sign-On for Sign Language Use a search engine to find Web sites or home pages about deaf culture and ASL, American Sign Language. Uncover the history of ASL, use the Web to learn how to sign a message to a friend, and discover what other sign languages exist. Share your findings with your classmates.

Performing

Body Language Think of different ways mimes and other actors use their bodies and expressions to communicate. With a partner, think of nonverbal ways that you could communicate to a person that you like him or her. If you prefer, you may think of a different emotion or a phrase to communicate. Practice your "signs" and then present them to the class.

Reading Further

If you liked this story, you might enjoy these other works about people living with deafness:

Novel: *Tell Me How the Wind Sounds,* by Leslie D. Guccione, describes the friendship and romance between a young hearing girl and her deaf friend, Jake.

Nonfiction: *Everyone Here Spoke Sign Language,* by Nora Ellen Groce, is the story of how both deaf and hearing islanders on Martha's Vineyard spoke sign language.

Speak to Me! by Marcia Calhoun Forecki, tells of a single mother's struggle to raise her deaf son.

Literary Criticism

One reviewer observes that in the novel *The Far Side of Victory*, Greenberg writes about "how hard it is to know the people you love–and how that knowledge, once gained, must be tenderly held." Write a letter to the reviewer, explaining how this theme is likewise developed in the story "And Sarah Laughed." Be sure to provide details from the story to support your ideas.

Save your work for your portfolio.

Skill Minilessons

GRAMMAR AND LANGUAGE • Using Semicolons

In writing, a semicolon can be used to join two closely related main clauses that might otherwise stand alone as complete sentences ending with a period. The semicolon helps readers understand that the ideas connect, as do the main clauses in the following sentence from "And Sarah Laughed": "Matthew had always been a silent man; his face was expressionless and his body stiff with reticence, but his eyes had sought her out eagerly and held her and she had been warm in his look." Notice that the second main clause does not begin with a capital letter.

● For more about semicolons, see **Language Handbook,** p. R47.

PRACTICE Combine the following pairs of sentences using a semicolon. Note how the ideas are closely related.

1. Matthew was deaf. He never heard Sarah's voice.
2. Sarah missed her husband. She missed talking to him.
3. Sirens and bells were ringing. The racket was tremendous.
4. Matthew knew sign language. He learned it from Janice.
5. Sarah felt jealous. Everyone could communicate except her.

READING AND THINKING • Problem and Solution

One strategy you can use to help you understand stories is to think about them in terms of problems and solutions. Ask yourself these questions:

- What is the main problem?
- Who has it?
- What solutions are tried?
- What happens as a result?

Often, a story contains more than one problem. For example, one problem in "And Sarah Laughed" is that Sarah misses talking and sharing verbally. She expects that her new baby, Abel, will be the solution to her problem, but her hopes are dashed when she discovers that he too is deaf.

PRACTICE What other problems and solutions can you find in the story "And Sarah Laughed"? Make a list of three or more problems and then try to solve each by answering the four bulleted questions in the left column.

APPLY Reread the last few sentences in "And Sarah Laughed." Describe the problem and the solution that they address.

● For more about reading strategies, see **Reading Handbook,** pp. R78–R107.

VOCABULARY • The Latin Root *flect*

The Latin root *flect* (or *flex*) comes from *flectere,* which means "to turn, bend, or curve." An *inflection,* therefore, is a kind of turn or bend, usually in one's tone of voice. A *reflective* pause indicates that someone is turning a subject over in his or her mind before speaking.

Recognizing this root when you see it in an unfamiliar word can help you get a general sense of the word's meaning. Recognizing it in a familiar word can help you understand the word when it's used in an unfamiliar way.

PRACTICE What, do you suppose, is the meaning of each underlined word below?

1. After I did pull-ups, my arm flexor muscles were sore.
2. We slanted the blinds to deflect the sunlight.
3. A flexuous path went through the woods.
4. Many people genuflect when they approach an altar or greet a monarch.

Before You Read

Elena

Reading Focus

What makes family members feel close to one another? What makes them feel distant from one another?

Chart It! Think about your own experiences or those of your friends as you fill in a chart like the one shown.

Family members feel close when . . .	Family members feel distant when . . .

Setting a Purpose Read to identify with a mother's efforts to communicate with her children and thus feel closer to them.

Building Background

Did You Know?

- People who are "bilingual" can speak a foreign language as fluently as they can speak their "native" or "primary" language. In the United States, most schools provide programs to help English language learners feel more comfortable among an English-speaking population. Both children and adults usually make a lot of mistakes when they begin learning a second language because the new language has different rules for word and sentence structure. Eventually, the speaker makes fewer and fewer mistakes, and the new language feels more natural.
- Most young children can learn a new language quickly and easily, but adults acquire new language skills much more slowly and are often frustrated by the learning process. Researchers believe that young children may process new linguistic information more easily because their brains and cognitive functions are still developing.
- Pat Mora says, "Although I am bilingual, I am English dominant, which means that I feel I can express myself with more confidence in English than in Spanish. I love the Spanish language, but my educational experience has been completely in English. In my last book of poems for adults, *Agua Santa,* I did write a *corrido,* a border ballad, in honor of my father in Spanish."

Meet Pat Mora

"We want those words to fly right off the page into the reader's heart."

For Pat Mora, the most difficult thing about being a writer is "facing the gap between what I hope to write and what I write." She keeps a disciplined schedule, spending as much time as possible at her desk writing. Mora is interested in the ways families preserve their heritage—their language and traditions. She writes often about her own and her family's experiences living near the Mexico–United States border. Mora has written prize-winning books of poetry for adults, a book of essays, a memoir, and many books for children.

Pat Mora was born in 1942 and grew up in El Paso, Texas. This poem was published in her first book, Chants, *in 1985.*

La Cocinera, 1922. Leopoldo Romanach. Oil on canvas, 90.2 x 122 cm. Private collection.

Elena

Pat Mora

My Spanish isn't enough.
I remember how I'd smile
listening to my little ones,
understanding every word they'd say,
their jokes, their songs, their plots.
Vamos a pedirle dulces a mamá. Vamos.°
But that was in Mexico.
Now my children go to American high schools.
They speak English. At night they sit around
the kitchen table, laugh with one another.
I stand by the stove and feel dumb, alone.
I bought a book to learn English.
My husband frowned, drank more beer.
My oldest said, "*Mamá*, he doesn't want you
to be smarter than he is." I'm forty,
embarrassed at mispronouncing words,
embarrassed at the laughter of my children,
the grocer, the mailman. Sometimes I take
my English book and lock myself in the bathroom,
say the thick words softly,
for if I stop trying, I will be deaf
when my children need my help.

6 Let's ask Mama for some candy. Let's go.

Responding to Literature

Personal Response
What feelings or thoughts did you experience while you were reading this poem?

Analyzing Literature

Recall and Interpret

1. Who is the **speaker** in "Elena"? What kinds of memories does the speaker recall? (See Literary Terms Handbook, page R12.)
2. How has the speaker's life changed since she left Mexico? Why, do you think, is she now thinking about the way things used to be?
3. How does each parent react to the changes in the family's life? What do the parents' reactions suggest about each of them and about their relationship with each other?
4. In your opinion, why does the speaker lock herself in the bathroom to learn English?
5. What motivates the speaker? How does she feel about her children?

Evaluate and Connect

6. Why might the poet have included Spanish words in her English-language poem?
7. Will this poem change your attitude toward people struggling to learn a new language? Explain.
8. Why is "Elena" an appropriate **title** for this poem? List two other possible titles.
9. Read over your response to the Reading Focus on page 150. After reading this poem, what else might you add to the chart?
10. **Theme Connections** What is the void in the speaker's life? Do you think she can fill it? Give reasons for your answer.

Literary **ELEMENTS**

Diction
Diction refers to a writer's choice of words and the arrangement of those words in phrases, sentences, or lines of a poem. Poets generally consider their words' meaning and sound as well as the images and associations the words suggest. Poets are also careful in their arrangement of words on a page. Each word in a poem is carefully placed to illuminate mood or meaning.

1. The speaker says that she feels "dumb" and worries that she will be "deaf." Why do you think the poet chose these words?
2. Why might the poet have placed the word "embarrassed" at the beginning of two lines in a row?
3. The speaker describes speaking English as saying "thick words." What does this phrase suggest?

- See **Literary Terms Handbook,** p. R4.

Extending Your Response

Literature Groups
Finding Your Place Have you ever experienced a time when you, like the speaker in the poem, felt dumb and alone because you did not understand something? What kind of situation might make you feel that way? How do your experiences compare with those of the speaker? Discuss these questions with your group. Write a brief summary of a common experience.

Creative Writing
A Different Point of View Think about how the language barrier affects each of the members of Elena's family and how it affects their relationships with one another. Then write a poem from the perspective of Elena's husband or one of her children. Be sure to use diction that would be appropriate for your speaker.

Save your work for your portfolio.

COMPARING *selections*

And Sarah Laughed and *Elena*

COMPARE **CONFLICTS**

Both Sarah and Elena, the speaker of the poem, have problems communicating with their families. They also are troubled by the ways in which their family members communicate with one another.

1. How are their problems alike? How are they different?
2. How are Sarah's and Elena's emotional responses similar and different? How does the personality of each character affect her response?
3. In your opinion, how successful will each woman be at remedying the situation? Explain.

La Cocinera, 1922 (detail).

Edith Holman Hunt, 1876 (detail).

COMPARE **EMOTIONS**

Both Sarah and Elena feel sad and isolated within their own families. Such feelings are often expressed in songs. With a partner or on your own, write the lyrics for a song or rap that expresses how one or more of the characters in these works might feel or how you would feel in a similar situation. Try to include such elements as rhythm, rhyme, repetition, or imagery in your lyrics. If you wish, you may perform your song or rap for the class.

COMPARE **RESPONSES**

Imagine that Sarah and Elena could visit your classroom.

- Working with a partner, choose a role to play, Sarah or Elena. Together, give a presentation to the class about living with and adapting to differences within the family.
- As the characters, describe your situations and how you are handling them.
- End the presentation with a question-and-answer session in which you respond to your classmates' questions. Be sure to respond as the character, not as yourself.

Writing Skills

Using Elaboration

If a friend tells you that he is sad, you may not have a clear understanding of what he's feeling. If that person goes on to explain that his stomach has felt tight ever since his dog died, your understanding of his emotion probably deepens. That's because your friend has used **elaboration**–or concrete details–to support his claim. To see how one writer uses elaboration to support and develop her ideas in writing, read the paragraph below from an essay analyzing the character of Sarah from the story "And Sarah Laughed."

> **Although she loved and respected her husband, Sarah often felt sad and lonely during her first twenty-five years of married life. She had no one with whom she could share her emotions, and that made her feel even more isolated. When she longed for the sounds of laughter and conversation, she "told herself angrily that Matthew talked through his work." And when neighbors told her that her sons hardly seemed deaf, "Sarah wanted to cry to these kindly women." She wanted to tell them about all the communication they take for granted with their own children, and which she missed with her own. Instead, "with her own bitter knowledge Sarah could only thank them for well-meaning and return to silence."**

The main idea in this paragraph is that Sarah felt sad and lonely. *Sad* and *lonely* are abstract words–they refer to things that can't be seen or touched. The writer has developed these ideas with reasons and opinions, specific incidents, and quotations from the story.

The types of details you choose to develop your ideas will often depend on the purpose and form of your writing. The box on this page lists types of elaboration you might use.

Types of Elaboration

- facts and statistics
- sensory details
- incidents
- examples
- reasons and opinions
- quotations

EXERCISES

1. Choose an emotion or abstract idea and describe it in writing. Use at least two different types of elaboration to explore and develop your subject.
2. Write a paragraph in which you describe a family member. Enliven your description by using incidents, quotations, or sensory details as elaboration.

Before You Read

American History

Reading Focus

Have you ever met a person whom you liked right away, but something prevented the friendship from growing?

Sharing Ideas With a partner, discuss your experience and list some reasons why friendships can fail to develop. As a team, present your conclusions to the class.

Setting a Purpose Read to learn about a special friendship—and the forces that prevented it from growing.

Building Background

The Time and Place

"American History" takes place in an urban neighborhood in Paterson, New Jersey, where the Puerto Rican tenement known as El Building is located. It is November 22, 1963, the day that President John F. Kennedy is killed.

Did You Know?

Most Americans who were alive in 1963 can remember exactly what they were doing when they learned that President Kennedy had been killed by an assassin's bullet. Throughout the country, people from all walks of life reacted to the news with disbelief and deep sorrow. Kennedy—the youngest man to be elected President of the United States—was a dynamic, popular leader who energized the American people and instilled in them a sense of hope for the future. During his brief term, Kennedy urged Congress to pass sweeping civil rights legislation, saying, ". . . race has no place in American life or law." His campaign slogan was "A Time for Greatness," and many Americans believed Kennedy fulfilled this promise once he took office.

Vocabulary Preview

profound (prə found′) *adj.* significant; deep; intense; p. 156
discreet (dis krēt′) *adj.* showing good judgment; cautious; p. 158
vigilant (vij′ ə lənt) *adj.* alert and watchful for danger or trouble; p. 159
enthrall (en thrôl′) *v.* to hold spellbound; fascinate; p. 159
elation (i lā′ shən) *n.* a feeling of great joy; ecstasy; p. 161
solace (sol′ is) *n.* relief from sorrow or disappointment; comfort; p. 162

Meet Judith Ortiz Cofer

Judith Ortiz Cofer realized the importance of language early in her life. She spent the first part of her childhood in Puerto Rico, where she spoke Spanish. Then she moved to the United States, where she had problems in school because she could speak little English. However, Ortiz Cofer says, "I quickly built up my arsenal of words by becoming an insatiable reader of books." Today, she is an award-winning author of poems, essays, novels, and short stories.

Judith Ortiz Cofer was born in 1952 in Puerto Rico. She grew up in Paterson, New Jersey, the setting of this story.

American

Judith Ortiz Cofer

I ONCE READ IN A *RIPLEY'S BELIEVE IT OR NOT* column that Paterson, New Jersey, is the place where the Straight and Narrow (streets) intersect. The Puerto Rican tenement known as El Building was one block up from Straight. It was, in fact, the corner of Straight and Market; not "at" the corner, but *the* corner.

At almost any hour of the day, El Building was like a monstrous jukebox, blasting out *salsas*[1] from open windows as the residents, mostly new immigrants just up from the island, tried to drown out whatever they were currently enduring with loud music. But the day President Kennedy was shot, there was a profound silence in El Building; even the abusive tongues of viragoes,[2] the cursing of the unemployed, and the screeching of small children had been somehow muted. President Kennedy was a saint to these people. In fact, soon his photograph would be hung alongside the Sacred Heart and over the spiritist altars that many women kept in their apartments. He would become part of the hierarchy of martyrs[3] they prayed to for favors that only one who had died for a cause would understand.

On the day that President Kennedy was shot, my ninth grade class had been out in the fenced playground of the Public School Number 13. We had been given "free" exercise time and had been ordered by our P.E. teacher, Mr. DePalma, to "keep moving." That meant that the girls should jump rope and the boys toss basketballs through a hoop at the far end of the yard. He in the meantime would "keep an eye" on us from just inside the building.

It was a cold gray day in Paterson. The kind that warns of early snow. I was miserable, since I had forgotten my gloves and my knuckles were turning red and raw from the jump rope. I was also taking a lot of abuse from the black girls for not turning the rope hard and fast enough for them.

"Hey, Skinny Bones, pump it, girl. Ain't you got no energy today?" Gail, the biggest of the black girls who had the other end of the rope yelled, "Didn't you eat your rice and beans and pork chops for breakfast today?"

1. *Salsas* are Latin American dance tunes.
2. *Viragoes* (vi rä′ gōz) are bad-tempered, scolding women who, here, use coarse or insulting *(abusive)* language.
3. The *hierarchy* (hī′ə rär′ kē) *of martyrs* (mär′ tərz) is the ranking of those who have suffered or died for their religion.

Vocabulary

profound (prə found′) *adj.* significant; deep; intense

The other girls picked up the "pork chop" and made it into a refrain: "pork chop, pork chop, did you eat your pork chop?" They entered the double ropes in pairs and exited without tripping or missing a beat. I felt a burning on my cheeks, and then my glasses fogged up so that I could not manage to coordinate the jump rope with Gail. The chill was doing to me what it always did, entering my bones, making me cry, humiliating me. I hated the city, especially in winter. I hated Public School Number 13. I hated my skinny flat-chested body, and I envied the black girls who could jump rope so fast that their legs became a blur. They always seemed to be warm while I froze.

There was only one source of beauty and light for me that school year. The only thing I had anticipated at the start of the semester. That was seeing Eugene. In August, Eugene and his family had moved into the only house on the block that had a yard and trees. I could see his place from my window in El Building. In fact, if I sat on the fire escape I was literally suspended above Eugene's backyard. It was my favorite spot to read my library books in the summer. Until that August the house had been occupied by an old Jewish couple. Over the years I had become part of their family, without their knowing it, of course. I had a view of their kitchen and their backyard, and though I could not hear what they said, I knew when they were arguing, when one of them was sick, and many other things. I knew all this by watching them at mealtimes. I could see their kitchen table, the sink and the stove. During good times, he sat at the table and read his newspapers while she fixed the meals. If they argued, he would leave and the old woman would sit and stare at nothing for a long time. When one of them was sick, the other would come and get things from the kitchen and carry them out on a tray. The old man had died in June. The last week of school I had not seen him at the table at all. Then one day I saw that there was a crowd in the kitchen. The old woman had finally emerged from the house on the arm of a stocky middle-aged woman whom I had seen there a few times before, maybe her daughter. Then a man had carried out suitcases. The house had stood empty for weeks. I had had to resist the temptation to climb down into the yard and water the flowers the old lady had taken such good care of.

Did You Know?
A *fire escape* is a fireproof stairway attached to an outside wall of a building.

Green Roofscape Vessel, 1986. Lidya Buzio. Burnished earthenware, 18 x 12½ in. Collection of Dawn Bennett & Martin J. Davidson.

Viewing the art: How well does this artwork capture the setting of "American History"? Explain.

By the time Eugene's family moved in, the yard was a tangled mass of weeds. The father had spent several days mowing, and when he finished, I didn't see the red, yellow, and purple clusters that meant flowers to me from where I sat. I didn't see this family sit down at the kitchen table together. It was just the mother, a red-headed tall woman who wore a white uniform—a nurse's, I guessed it was; the father was gone before I got up in the morning and was never there at dinner time. I only saw him on weekends when they sometimes sat on lawn chairs under the oak tree, each hidden behind a section of the newspaper; and there was Eugene. He was tall and blond, and he wore glasses. I liked him right away because he sat at the kitchen table and read books for hours. That summer, before we had even spoken one word to each other, I kept him company on my fire escape.

Once school started I looked for him in all my classes, but P.S.[4] 13 was a huge, overpopulated place and it took me days and many discreet questions to discover that Eugene was in honors classes for all his subjects; classes that were not open to me because English was not my first language, though I was a straight A student. After much maneuvering I managed "to run into him" in the hallway where his locker was—on the other side of the building from mine—and in study hall at the library, where he first seemed to notice me but did not speak; and finally, on the way home after school one day when I decided to approach him directly, though my stomach was doing somersaults.

I was ready for rejection, snobbery, the worst. But when I came up to him, practically panting in my nervousness, and blurted out: "You're Eugene. Right?" He smiled, pushed his glasses up on his nose, and nodded. I saw then that he was blushing deeply. Eugene liked me, but he was shy. I did most of the talking that day. He nodded and smiled a lot. In the weeks that followed, we walked home together. He would linger at the corner of El Building for a few minutes then walk down to his two-story house. It was not until Eugene moved into that house that I noticed that El Building blocked most of the sun and that the only spot that got a little sunlight during the day was the tiny square of earth the old woman had planted with flowers.

I did not tell Eugene that I could see inside his kitchen from my bedroom. I felt dishonest, but I liked my secret sharing of his evenings, especially now that I knew what he was reading, since we chose our books together at the school library.

4. Here, *P.S.* stands for *public school.*

Vocabulary

discreet (dis krēt′) *adj.* showing good judgment; cautious

One day my mother came into my room as I was sitting on the windowsill staring out. In her abrupt way she said: "Elena, you are acting 'moony.'" *Enamorada*[5] was what she really said—that is, like a girl stupidly infatuated. Since I had turned fourteen and started menstruating my mother had been more vigilant than ever. She acted as if I was going to go crazy or explode or something if she didn't watch me and nag me all the time about being a señorita[6] now. She kept talking about virtue, morality, and other subjects that did not interest me in the least. My mother was unhappy in Paterson, but my father had a good job at the blue jeans factory in Passaic, and soon, he kept assuring us, we would be moving to our own house there. Every Sunday we drove out to the suburbs of Paterson, Clifton, and Passaic, out to where people mowed grass on Sundays in the summer and where children made snowmen in the winter from pure white snow, not like the gray slush of Paterson, which seemed to fall from the sky in that hue. I had learned to listen to my parents' dreams, which were spoken in Spanish, as fairy tales, like the stories about life in the island paradise of Puerto Rico before I was born. I had been to the Island once as a little girl, to grandmother's funeral, and all I remembered was wailing women in black, my mother becoming hysterical and being given a pill that made her sleep two days, and me feeling lost in a crowd of strangers all claiming to be my aunts, uncles, and cousins. I had actually been glad to return to the city. We had not been back there since then, though my parents talked constantly about buying a house on the beach someday, retiring on the island—that was a common topic among the residents of El Building. As for me, I was going to go to college and become a teacher.

But after meeting Eugene I began to think of the present more than of the future. What I wanted now was to enter that house I had watched for so many years. I wanted to see the other rooms where the old people had lived and where the boy I liked spent his time. Most of all, I wanted to sit at the kitchen table with Eugene like two adults, like the old man and his wife had done, maybe drink some coffee and talk about books. I had started reading *Gone with the Wind*.[7] I was enthralled by it, with the daring and the passion of the beautiful girl living in a mansion, and with her devoted parents and the slaves who did everything for them. I didn't believe such a world had ever really existed, and I wanted to ask Eugene some questions, since he and his parents, he had told me, had come up from Georgia, the same place where the novel was set. His father worked for a company that had transferred him to Paterson. His mother was very unhappy, Eugene said, in his beautiful voice that rose and fell over words in a strange, lilting way. The kids at school called him the Hick and made fun of the way he talked. I knew I was his only friend so far, and I liked that, though I felt sad for him sometimes. Skinny Bones and the Hick, was what they called us at school when we were seen together.

The day Mr. DePalma came out into the cold and asked us to line up in front of him was the day that President Kennedy was shot. Mr. DePalma, a short, muscular man with slicked-down black hair, was the science

5. *Enamorada* (en äm′ ər ä′ dä)

6. *Señorita* (sen′ yə rē′ tə) is Spanish for young lady.

7. *Gone with the Wind* is a romantic novel about the South during and after the Civil War.

Vocabulary

vigilant (vij′ ə lənt) *adj.* alert and watchful for danger or trouble

enthrall (en thrôl′) *v.* to hold spellbound; fascinate

teacher, P.E. coach, and disciplinarian at P.S. 13. He was the teacher to whose homeroom you got assigned if you were a troublemaker, and the man called out to break up playground fights, and to escort violently angry teenagers to the office. And Mr. DePalma was the man who called your parents in for "a conference."

That day, he stood in front of two rows of mostly black and Puerto Rican kids, brittle from their efforts to "keep moving" on a November day that was turning bitter cold. Mr. DePalma, to our complete shock, was crying. Not just silent adult tears, but really sobbing. There were a few titters from the back of the line where I stood, shivering.

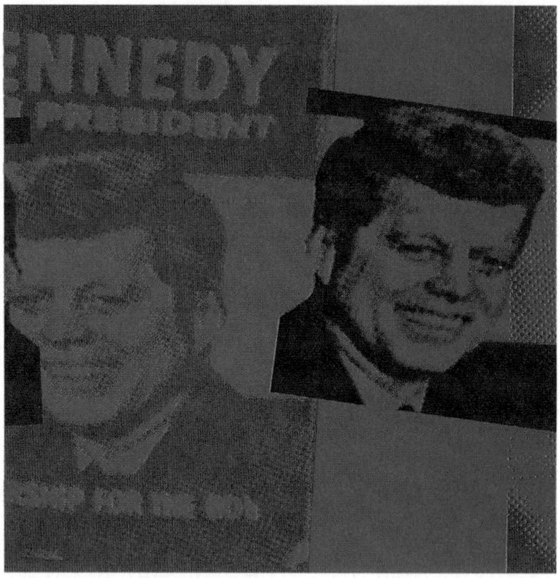

Flash–November 22, 1963, 1968. Andy Warhol. Silkscreen on paper, from a portfolio of 11 screenprints, colophon and text, 21 x 21 in. The Andy Warhol Foundation, Inc.

Viewing the art: **Can you imagine why Elena might think of Kennedy this way–in harsh colors and abstract shapes? Explain.**

"Listen," Mr. DePalma raised his arms over his head as if he were about to conduct an orchestra. His voice broke, and he covered his face with his hands. His barrel chest was heaving. Someone giggled behind me.

"Listen," he repeated, "something awful has happened." A strange gurgling came from his throat, and he turned around and spit on the cement behind him.

"Gross," someone said, and there was a lot of laughter.

"The president is dead, you idiots. I should have known that wouldn't mean anything to a bunch of losers like you kids. Go home." He was shrieking now. No one moved for a minute or two, but then a big girl let out a "yeah!" and ran to get her books piled up with the others against the brick wall of the school building. The others followed in a mad scramble to get to their things before somebody caught on. It was still an hour to the dismissal bell.

A little scared, I headed for El Building. There was an eerie feeling on the streets. I looked into Mario's drugstore, a favorite hangout for the high school crowd, but there were only a couple of old Jewish men at the soda bar, talking with the short order cook in tones that sounded almost angry, but they were keeping their voices low. Even the traffic on one of the busiest intersections in Paterson—Straight Street and Park Avenue— seemed to be moving slower. There were no horns blasting that day. At El Building, the usual little group of unemployed men were not hanging out on the front stoop, making it difficult for women to enter the front door. No music spilled out from open doors in the hallway. When I walked into our apartment, I found my mother sitting in front of the grainy picture of the television set.

She looked up at me with a tear-streaked face and just said: *"Dios mío,"*[8] turning back to the set as if it were pulling at her eyes. I went into my room.

8. ***Dios mío*** (dē′ os mē′ ō) is Spanish for *My God.*

Though I wanted to feel the right thing about President Kennedy's death, I could not fight the feeling of elation that stirred in my chest. Today was the day I was to visit Eugene in his house. He had asked me to come over after school to study for an American history test with him. We had also planned to walk to the public library together. I looked down into his yard. The oak tree was bare of leaves, and the ground looked gray with ice. The light through the large kitchen window of his house told me that El Building blocked the sun to such an extent that they had to turn lights on in the middle of the day. I felt ashamed about it. But the white kitchen table with the lamp hanging just above it looked cozy and inviting. I would soon sit there, across from Eugene, and I would tell him about my perch just above his house. Maybe I would.

In the next thirty minutes I changed clothes, put on a little pink lipstick, and got my books together. Then I went in to tell my mother that I was going to a friend's house to study. I did not expect her reaction.

"You are going out *today*?" The way she said "today" sounded as if a storm warning had been issued. It was said in utter disbelief. Before I could answer, she came toward me and held my elbows as I clutched my books.

"*Hija,*[9] the president has been killed. We must show respect. He was a great man. Come to church with me tonight."

She tried to embrace me, but my books were in the way. My first impulse was to comfort her, she seemed so distraught, but I had to meet Eugene in fifteen minutes.

"I have a test to study for, Mama. I will be home by eight."

"You are forgetting who you are, *Niña.*[10] I have seen you staring down at that boy's house. You are heading for humiliation and pain." My mother said this in Spanish and in a resigned tone that surprised me, as if she had no intention of stopping me from "heading for humiliation and pain." I started for the door. She sat in front of the TV, holding a white handkerchief to her face.

I walked out to the street and around the chain-link fence that separated El Building from Eugene's house. The yard was neatly edged around the little walk that led to the door. It always amazed me how Paterson, the inner core of the city, had no apparent logic to its architecture. Small, neat, single residences like this one could be found right next to huge, dilapidated apartment buildings like El Building. My guess was that the little houses had been there first, then the immigrants had come in droves, and the monstrosities had been raised for them—the Italians, the Irish, the Jews, and now us, the Puerto Ricans, and the blacks. The door was painted a deep green: *verde*, the color of hope. I had heard my mother say it: *Verde-Esperanza.*[11]

I knocked softly. A few suspenseful moments later the door opened just a crack. The red, swollen face of a woman appeared. She had a halo of red hair floating over a delicate ivory face—the face of a doll—with freckles on the nose. Her smudged eye makeup made her look unreal to me, like a mannequin seen through a warped store window.

"What do you want?" Her voice was tiny and sweet-sounding, like a little girl's, but her tone was not friendly.

9. *Hija* (ē′ hä) is Spanish for *daughter.*

10. *Niña* (nēn′ yä) is Spanish for *girl.*

11. Translated directly, *Verde-Esperanza* (vār′ dā es pe rän′ zə) is Green-Hope.

Vocabulary

elation (i lā′ shən) *n.* a feeling of great joy; ecstasy

"I'm Eugene's friend. He asked me over. To study." I thrust out my books, a silly gesture that embarrassed me almost immediately.

"You live there?" She pointed up to El Building, which looked particularly ugly, like a gray prison with its many dirty windows and rusty fire escapes. The woman had stepped halfway out, and I could see that she wore a white nurse's uniform with "St. Joseph's Hospital" on the name tag.

"Yes. I do."

She looked intently at me for a couple of heartbeats, then said as if to herself, "I don't know how you people do it." Then directly to me: "Listen. Honey. Eugene doesn't want to study with you. He is a smart boy. Doesn't need help. You understand me. I am truly sorry if he told you you could come over. He cannot study with you. It's nothing personal. You understand? We won't be in this place much longer, no need for him to get close to people—it'll just make it harder for him later. Run back home now."

I couldn't move. I just stood there in shock at hearing these things said to me in such a honey-drenched voice. I had never heard an accent like hers except for Eugene's softer version. It was as if she were singing me a little song.

"What's wrong? Didn't you hear what I said?" She seemed very angry, and I finally snapped out of my trance. I turned away from the green door and heard her close it gently.

Our apartment was empty when I got home. My mother was in someone else's kitchen, seeking the solace she needed. Father would come in from his late shift at midnight. I would hear them talking softly in the kitchen for hours that night. They would not discuss their dreams for the future, or life in Puerto Rico, as they often did; that night they would talk sadly about the young widow and her two children, as if they were family. For the next few days, we would observe *luto*[12] in our apartment; that is, we would practice restraint and silence—no loud music or laughter. Some of the women of El Building would wear black for weeks.

That night, I lay in my bed, trying to feel the right thing for our dead president. But the tears that came up from a deep source inside me were strictly for me. When my mother came to the door, I pretended to be sleeping. Sometime during the night, I saw from my bed the streetlight come on. It had a pink halo around it. I went to my window and pressed my face to the cool glass. Looking up at the light I could see the white snow falling like a lace veil over its face. I did not look down to see it turning gray as it touched the ground below.

12. *Luto* (lo͞o′ tō) is Spanish for *mourning.*

Vocabulary

solace (sol′ is) *n.* relief from sorrow or disappointment; comfort

Responding to Literature

Personal Response

How do you feel about what happens to Elena at Eugene's house? Write your thoughts in your journal.

Analyzing Literature

Recall

1. Use details from the story to describe Elena's neighborhood.
2. What does Elena enjoy looking at from her window?
3. What common interests and conditions help to develop a friendship between Elena and Eugene?
4. How does each adult character react to the death of President Kennedy? How do Elena and her classmates react?
5. Why does Elena feel particularly happy on the day the story takes place, and particularly sorrowful that night?

Interpret

6. How does Elena feel about her home and about Eugene's home? Do her perceptions of her home change after Eugene's family moves into the house next door? Explain your answers.
7. In your opinion, why is Elena interested in the daily habits of the old Jewish couple, and later of Eugene's family?
8. What roles do diversity, prejudice, and unkindness play in this story?
9. Why might the adult characters respond to Kennedy's death differently than the younger characters?
10. What factors might have led Eugene's mother to react as she did to Elena? Use details from the story to support your opinion.

Evaluate and Connect

11. **Theme Connections** Explain how this story fits the theme, "Filling a Void." Consider what might be missing from each character's life.
12. Do you think that the author expressed the feelings of a ninth-grade girl realistically? Support your response with details from the story as well as from your own experience.
13. In your opinion, why did the author title this story "American History"?
14. A **character trait** is a habit, a physical attribute, or an attitude that helps to define a character. Why might Ortiz Cofer have given Eugene's mother the character trait of a tiny and sweet-sounding voice?
15. Think about your response to the Reading Focus on page 155. Did your experience have anything in common with Elena's? What was different?

Literary ELEMENTS

Main and Minor Characters

The important characters in a piece of fiction are called **main characters;** all others are **minor characters.** The central conflict in a story always involves one or more of the main characters. Minor characters help move the plot along by interacting with the main characters. In this story, Elena is a main character and her mother is a minor character.

1. In your opinion, what makes Elena the main character? Use information from the story to support your answer.
2. What purpose did the author have for creating the minor character Mr. DePalma? In your opinion, does his presence as a character enhance or detract from the story?
3. Who are the other minor characters in this story? Why might they have been included?

- See **Literary Terms Handbook,** p. R2.

Literature and Writing

Writing About Literature

Connecting Fiction to History Why do you suppose Ortiz Cofer chose this date in history as a setting? (You may want to reread the Building Background section on page 155.) Think about what Kennedy's death might have meant to many Americans, especially minorities. Then think about what has also died for Elena. Write a brief analysis, making connections between the story and the historical events it includes. Use details and examples from the story to support your ideas.

Creative Writing

In Another's Shoes Elena learned an extremely painful lesson in this story. Reread the last paragraph. What is Elena feeling? Put yourself in her shoes and write a journal entry about the events of the day and how they affected you.

Extending Your Response

Literature Groups

Shades of Gray A symbol is an object, a person, a place, or an experience that represents something else, especially something abstract. In this story, Judith Ortiz Cofer uses the colors white and gray to symbolize feelings or perceptions that Elena has about her life and surroundings. Work together to list each item in the story that is identified as being either white or gray. Discuss and debate what each color might signify. Also discuss the items in the story that have more vivid colors and decide what those colors might symbolize. Share your ideas with the class.

Interdisciplinary Activity

Social Studies: Being Different In this story, Elena encounters problems because she is Puerto Rican. Identify and research a group of people in history who have endured trials and challenges because of their culture, race, or ethnic heritage. Summarize your findings for your classmates. Can you conclude what might be learned from the experiences of these people?

Learning for Life

Advice and Problem-Solving Elena tells the reader that her friendship with Eugene was the "only . . . source of beauty and light" for her that school year. With a partner, role-play a conversation a friend, teacher, or relative might have with Elena. Discuss Elena's attitude about her physical appearance, her school, her home, and her neighborhood and brainstorm ideas about how she might gain more satisfaction from each.

Reading Further

If you'd like to read more by Judith Ortiz Cofer, you might enjoy these works:

Poem: "Some Spanish Verbs," from *The Latin Deli,* was inspired by the author's childhood experiences in Puerto Rico.

Short Story: "Bad Influence," from *An Island Like You,* tells about a teenaged girl who matures during a summer vacation with her grandparents.

Essay: "The Myth of the Latin Woman: I Just Met a Girl Named Maria," from *The Latin Deli,* examines racial and ethnic stereotypes.

Literary Criticism

Reviewer Nancy Vasilakis writes that the narratives in Ortiz Cofer's *An Island Like You: Stories of the Barrio* "have universal resonance in the vitality, the brashness, the self-centered hopefulness, and the angst expressed by the teens." Working with a partner, make a list of examples of youthful vitality, brashness, self-centered hopefulness, and angst you can find in "American History." Then discuss whether you think that the story has "universal resonance."

Save your work for your portfolio.

Skill Minilessons

GRAMMAR AND LANGUAGE • Combining Sentences

A paragraph that contains many simple sentences often seems choppy and dull. You can make your writing more interesting by using sentences with either compound subjects or compound predicates. Notice how combining the following simple sentences improves their flow.

Choppy: He had few other friends. So did I.

Compound subject: *He* and *I* had few other friends.

Choppy: He sat at the table. He read books.

Compound predicate: He *sat* at the table and *read* books.

● For more about sentences, see **Language Handbook,** pp. R42–R43.

PRACTICE Combine each of the following pairs of sentences by using a compound subject or a compound predicate. You may change verb forms and omit words as necessary.

1. The old man sat in the garden. His wife sat with him.
2. My mother was unhappy in Paterson. His mother was too.
3. I read *Gone With the Wind.* I discussed it with Eugene.
4. Mr. DePalma came outside. He asked us to line up.
5. El Building stood at the corner. It shaded his yard.

READING AND THINKING • Clarifying

Good readers know that their understanding of a story will change as they read. They often ask themselves questions or review earlier events. For example, Elena says that she liked Eugene "right away because he sat at the kitchen table and read books for hours." If you ask yourself *why* this would make her like him, you might say that she, too, must spend time reading and that this shared interest would lead her to feel an immediate connection with him. You have now *clarified* her motive and are ready to continue reading.

● For more about related reading strategies, see **Reading Handbook,** pp. R78–R107.

PRACTICE Answer each clarifying question below.

1. When Elena meets Eugene, she is "ready for rejection, snobbery, the worst." Why? What had happened to her in the past?
2. After she met Eugene, she "began to think of the present more than of the future." Why?
3. Students make fun of the way Eugene talks. Why?
4. Elena is unable to feel "the right thing" about President Kennedy's death. What does this mean?
5. Elena considers telling Eugene about her "perch." Why has she not told him already?

VOCABULARY • Analogies

An analogy is a comparison based on the relationships between things or ideas. Some analogies are based on a relationship that could be called "degree of intensity."

infatuated : fond :: furious : displeased

To be *infatuated* is to be extremely *fond;* to be *furious* is to be extremely *displeased.* The first concept in each pair is more intense than the second.

To complete an analogy, decide what relationship exists between the meanings of the first two words. Then apply that relationship to another pair of words.

PRACTICE Choose the word pair that best completes each analogy.

1. elation : pleasure ::
   a. misery : happiness
   b. terror : fear
   c. jealousy : anger
   d. silliness : stupidity
   e. sorrow : gladness
2. interest : enthrall ::
   a. gladden : sadden
   b. weigh : measure
   c. select : choose
   d. moisten : soak
   e. grab : take

● For more about analogies, see **Communications Skills Handbook,** p. R77.

Technology Skills

Internet: Searching for Information

According to a 1998 estimate, there were 1.76 billion Web pages on the Internet at that time! The number is even larger today. Every hour, new sites and new pages increase the amount of available information. To find your way around a body of knowledge as enormous and fast-growing as the Internet, you need a tool that helps you search.

Subject Guides and Search Engines

Subject guides and search engines are programs that help you find Web documents that relate to the information you need. A **subject guide** (also called a directory) takes you to specific sites by way of subject categories and various levels of subcategories. Through this hierarchy of categories–sometimes called a subject tree–you start with a general subject area and gradually narrow it down to sites for a specific topic. Subject guides are especially useful when you are looking for general information or when you're not sure exactly what information will best meet your needs.

SELECTED SEARCH TOOLS

	Name	Uniform Resource Locators (URLs)
Filtered Search Engines and Subject Guides	Answers.Com	http://www.answers.com
	Homework Central	http://www.homeworkheaven.com
	Infoplease	http://www.infoplease.com
	Kids Search Tools	http://www.rcls.org/ksearch.htm
	StudyWeb	http://www.studyweb.com
	Yahooligans!	http://www.yahooligans.com
Subject Guides and Search Engines	AltaVista	http://www.altavista.com
	Excite	http://www.excite.com
	Infoseek	http://www.infoseek.com
	Lycos	http://www.lycos.com
	Magellan	http://www.mckinley.com
	WebCrawler	http://www.webcrawler.com
	Yahoo!	http://www.yahoo.com

With a **search engine,** you type one or more keywords relating to your topic. The engine then searches for those words in millions of Web pages and gives you a list of sites containing those words. A brief description of each site helps you decide how relevant it is to your needs. Some search engines also rate each site for you. Other search engines concentrate on a single kind of information. For example, Govbot is an engine that searches government databases. Search engines are most useful when you've narrowed down your topic to something specific. If you type in an overly general term (literature, for example), you'll get references to hundreds of thousands of specific sites–far too many to be useful. In reality, the distinction between subject guides and search engines is less important today. Most search engines contain subject categories, and most subject guides have a search engine feature. Whichever search tool you use, many of the hits–references to specific sites–will not be of interest to you. You must still browse through each hit's description to see if it's what you need.

Searching Safely and Efficiently

Some search sites have filters that screen for distracting or unsuitable materials. These tools can often speed up your search. Filtered sites include both search engines and subject guides.

TECHNOLOGY TIP

A Boolean search lets you combine keywords with indicators such as *AND, OR,* and *NOT* to narrow a search. For example, to find sites on Edgar Allan Poe's poetry, you might type: poe AND (poems OR poetry).

ACTIVITIES

1. Explore the search tools listed in the chart.
   - Use your browser to log on to the World Wide Web.
   - Click the "Search" button on your browser. Notice to which search engine it takes you. Click again. Which engine loads now?
   - Connect to at least three different search tools from each of the two groups on the chart. Read through any search tips or FAQS (frequently asked questions) the tool contains. Then try doing a few subject or keyword searches. Note which tools you think will be most useful to you.
   - Compare your results with those of others in your class. Work with a group or as a class to make a chart of pros and cons for the various search tools.
2. Use a search engine to find information about a specific topic.
   - Type the URL of one of the listed search engines into your browser. Then enter these keywords: kennedy + assassination.
   - Spend a few minutes browsing through the descriptions to find sites that might tell you about John F. Kennedy's assassination in Dallas. Ignore sites that focus on such topics as conspiracy theories; stick with the *facts.*
   - Use the search engine and the sites it finds to answer the following questions:
     a. What is the URL for the National Archives and Records Administration's John F. Kennedy Assassination Records Collection?
     b. On what site can you listen to a RealAudio radio broadcast reporting the assassination?
     c. Where can you download an image of the front-page coverage of the assassination from the *Fort Worth Star-Telegram*?
     d. Where can you find a picture of the "magic bullet"?
     e. Who was Abraham Zapruder?

Before You Read

The Necklace

Reading Focus

"Honesty is the best policy" is a common saying. Why do people sometimes ignore this good advice?

Discuss With a partner, brainstorm a variety of circumstances under which people may decide not to tell the truth. What are the likely consequences of each case of dishonesty? Do any of the circumstances justify, or excuse, hiding the truth?

Setting a Purpose Read to discover the long-term effects of a well-meaning deception.

Building Background

The Time and Place

This story is set in Paris, France, in the late 1800s.

Did You Know?

In the nineteenth century, a rigid class structure defined Parisian society. At the top of the social ladder were the aristocrats. They had enormous wealth, large estates, and many servants. Below this small, privileged group was a middle class consisting of merchants, clerks, and others. The middle class generally lived in modest homes or apartments and could afford one or two servants. Although household budgets were often tight, custom forbade middle-class women from working outside the home. Below this class was the huge number of peasants and servants who worked for the rich or farmed the land. While the rich had yearly incomes of hundreds of thousands of francs, during the late 1800s the average worker earned fewer than 900 francs a year.

Vocabulary Preview

incessantly (in ses′ ənt lē) *adv.* endlessly; constantly; p. 169
disconsolate (dis kon′ sə lit) *adj.* so unhappy that nothing can comfort; hopeless and depressed; p. 169
vexation (vek sā′ shən) *n.* anger, annoyance, or distress; p. 170
pauper (pô′ pər) *n.* a very poor person, especially one supported by public charity; p. 171
aghast (ə gast′) *adj.* filled with fear, horror, or amazement; p. 173
gamut (gam′ ət) *n.* the entire range or series of something; p. 174
privation (prī vā′ shən) *n.* the lack of the comforts or basic necessities of life; p. 174

Meet Guy de Maupassant

Writing about life's "inexplicable, illogical, and contradictory catastrophes" made Guy de Maupassant (gē də mō pä sän′) famous as a master of the short story. Some of his best work was drawn from his experiences fighting in the Franco-Prussian War and from the time he spent working as a civil servant. When he achieved fame and fortune as a writer, however, Maupassant put the working world behind him and lived an extravagant life, eventually falling into debt. His six novels and over three hundred short stories paint a picture of French life at the end of the nineteenth century.

Guy de Maupassant was born in 1850 and died in 1893. This story was first published in 1884.

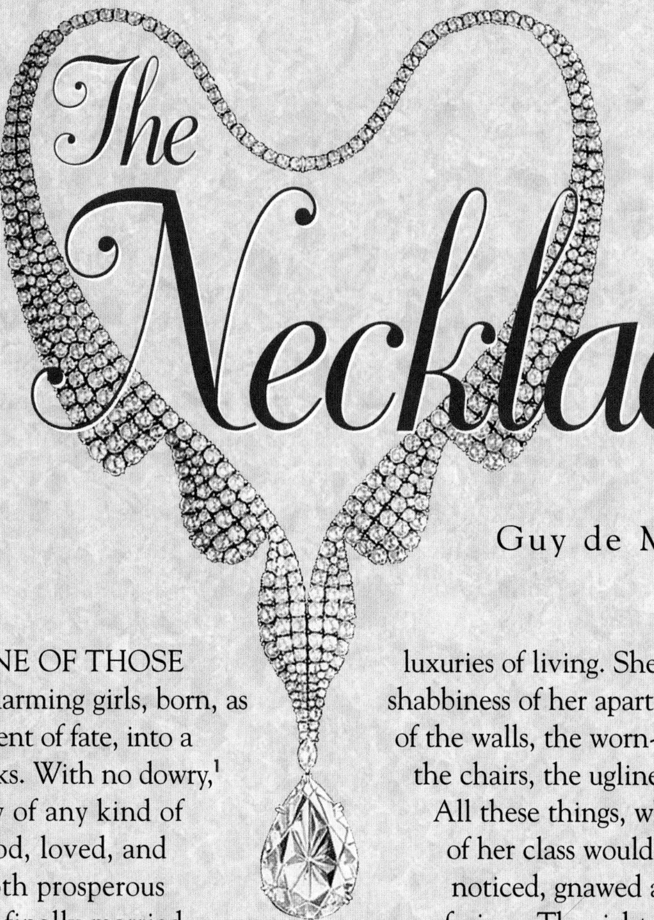

The Necklace

Guy de Maupassant

SHE WAS ONE OF THOSE pretty and charming girls, born, as if by an accident of fate, into a family of clerks. With no dowry,[1] no prospects, no way of any kind of being met, understood, loved, and married by a man both prosperous and famous, she was finally married to a minor clerk in the Ministry of Education.

She dressed plainly because she could not afford fine clothes, but was as unhappy as a woman who has come down in the world; for women have no family rank or social class. With them, beauty, grace, and charm take the place of birth and breeding. Their natural poise, their instinctive good taste, and their mental cleverness are the sole guiding principles which make daughters of the common people the equals of ladies in high society.

She grieved incessantly, feeling that she had been born for all the little niceties and luxuries of living. She grieved over the shabbiness of her apartment, the dinginess of the walls, the worn-out appearance of the chairs, the ugliness of the draperies. All these things, which another woman of her class would not even have noticed, gnawed at her and made her furious. The sight of the little Breton[2] girl who did her humble housework roused in her disconsolate regrets and wild daydreams. She would dream of silent chambers, draped with Oriental tapestries and lighted by tall bronze floor lamps, and of two handsome butlers in knee breeches, who, drowsy from the heavy warmth cast by the central stove, dozed in large overstuffed armchairs.

She would dream of great reception halls hung with old silks, of fine furniture filled with priceless curios,[3] and of small, stylish, scented sitting rooms just right for the four o'clock

1. A *dowry* is money or property that a woman brings to her husband at the start of a marriage.

2. *Breton* (bret′ ən) refers to someone or something from the French province of Brittany.

3. *Priceless curios* are rare or unusual ornamental objects that are very valuable.

Vocabulary

incessantly (in ses′ ənt lē) *adv.* endlessly; constantly

disconsolate (dis kon′ sə lit) *adj.* so unhappy that nothing can comfort; hopeless and depressed chat with intimate friends, with distinguished and sought-after men whose attention every woman envies and longs to attract.

When dining at the round table covered for the third day with the same cloth, opposite her husband, who would raise the cover of the soup tureen, declaring delightedly, "Ah! a good stew! There's nothing I like better . . ." she would dream of fashionable dinner parties, of gleaming silverware, of tapestries making the walls alive with characters out of history and strange birds in a fairyland forest; she would dream of delicious dishes served on wonderful china, of gallant compliments whispered and listened to with a sphinxlike[4] smile as one eats the rosy flesh of a trout or nibbles at the wings of a grouse.

Did You Know?
A *tureen* is a deep dish used for serving soup or other food at the table.

She had no evening clothes, no jewels, nothing. But those were the things she wanted; she felt that was the kind of life for her. She so much longed to please, be envied, be fascinating and sought after.

She had a well-to-do friend, a classmate of convent-school days whom she would no longer go to see, simply because she would feel so distressed on returning home. And she would weep for days on end from vexation, regret, despair, and anguish.

Then one evening, her husband came home proudly holding out a large envelope.

"Look," he said, "I've got something for you."

She excitedly tore open the envelope and pulled out a printed card bearing these words:

"The Minister of Education and Mme. Georges Ramponneau beg M. and Mme. Loisel[5] to do them the honor of attending an evening reception at the Ministerial Mansion on Friday, January 18."

Instead of being delighted, as her husband had hoped, she scornfully tossed the invitation on the table, murmuring, "What good is that to me?"

"But, my dear, I thought you'd be thrilled to death. You never get a chance to go out, and this is a real affair, a wonderful one! I had an awful time getting a card. Everybody wants one: it's much sought after, and not many clerks have a chance at one. You'll see all the most important people there."

She gave him an irritated glance and burst out impatiently, "What do you think I have to go in?"

He hadn't given that a thought. He stammered, "Why, the dress you wear when we go to the theater. That looks quite nice, I think."

He stopped talking, dazed and distracted to see his wife burst out weeping. Two large tears slowly rolled from the corners of her eyes to the corners of her mouth; he gasped, "Why, what's the matter? What's the trouble?"

By sheer will power she overcame her outburst and answered in a calm voice while wiping the tears from her wet cheeks:

"Oh, nothing. Only I don't have an evening dress and therefore I can't go to that affair. Give the card to some friend at the office whose wife can dress better than I can."

4. *Sphinxlike* means "mysterious," referring to a creature in Greek mythology that killed anyone who could not answer its riddle.

5. *Georges Ramponneau* (ram pə nō′); *Loisel* (lwä zel′). The abbreviations *M.* and *Mme.* are the French versions of *Mr.* and *Mrs.* and stand for *Monsieur* (mə syœ′) and *Madame* (mə dam′).

Vocabulary
vexation (vek sā′ shən) *n.* anger, annoyance, or distress

He was stunned. He resumed, "Let's see, Mathilde.[6] How much would a suitable outfit cost—one you could wear for other affairs too—something very simple?"

She thought it over for several seconds, going over her allowance and thinking also of the amount she could ask for without bringing an immediate refusal and an exclamation of dismay from the thrifty clerk.

Finally, she answered hesitatingly, "I'm not sure exactly, but I think with four hundred francs I could manage it."

He turned a bit pale, for he had set aside just that amount to buy a rifle so that, the following summer, he could join some friends who were getting up a group to shoot larks on the plain near Nanterre.

However, he said, "All right. I'll give you four hundred francs. But try to get a nice dress."

As the day of the party approached, Mme. Loisel seemed sad, moody, and ill at ease. Her outfit was ready, however. Her husband said to her one evening, "What's the matter? You've been all out of sorts for three days."

And she answered, "It's embarrassing not to have a jewel or a gem—nothing to wear on my dress. I'll look like a pauper: I'd almost rather not go to that party."

He answered, "Why not wear some flowers? They're very fashionable this season. For ten francs you can get two or three gorgeous roses."

"I'll look like a pauper: I'd almost rather not go to that party."

She wasn't at all convinced. "No . . . There's nothing more humiliating than to look poor among a lot of rich women."

But her husband exclaimed, "My, but you're silly! Go see your friend Mme. Forestier[7] and ask her to lend you some jewelry. You and she know each other well enough for you to do that."

She gave a cry of joy, "Why, that's so! I hadn't thought of it."

The next day she paid her friend a visit and told her of her predicament.

Mme. Forestier went toward a large closet with mirrored doors, took out a large jewel box, brought it over, opened it, and said to Mme. Loisel: "Pick something out, my dear."

At first her eyes noted some bracelets, then a pearl necklace, then a Venetian cross, gold and gems, of marvelous workmanship. She tried on these adornments in front of the mirror, but hesitated, unable to decide which to part with and put back. She kept on asking, "Haven't you something else?"

"Oh, yes, keep on looking. I don't know just what you'd like."

All at once she found, in a black satin box, a superb diamond necklace; and her pulse beat faster with longing. Her hands trembled as she took it up. Clasping it around her throat, outside her high-necked dress, she stood in ecstasy looking at her reflection.

Then she asked, hesitatingly, pleading, "Could I borrow that, just that and nothing else?"

"Why, of course."

6. *Mathilde* (mä tēld′)

7. *Forestier* (fô res tyā′)

Vocabulary

pauper (pô′ pər) *n.* a very poor person, especially one supported by public charity

The Hunt Ball, 1885. Julius L. Stewart. Phototype, colored after a painting. Private collection.

Viewing the art: What might you find particularly exciting about this party if you were Mme. Loisel?

She threw her arms around her friend, kissed her warmly, and fled with her treasure.

The day of the party arrived. Mme. Loisel was a sensation. She was the prettiest one there, fashionable, gracious, smiling, and wild with joy. All the men turned to look at her, asked who she was, begged to be introduced. All the Cabinet officials wanted to waltz with her. The minister took notice of her.

She danced madly, wildly, drunk with pleasure, giving no thought to anything in the triumph of her beauty, the pride of her success, in a kind of happy cloud composed of all the adulation,[8] of all the admiring glances, of all the awakened longings, of a sense of complete victory that is so sweet to a woman's heart.

She left around four o'clock in the morning. Her husband, since midnight, had been dozing in a small empty sitting room with three other gentlemen whose wives were having too good a time.

He threw over her shoulders the wraps he had brought for going home, modest garments of everyday life whose shabbiness clashed with the stylishness of her evening clothes. She felt this and longed to escape, unseen by the other women who were draped in expensive furs.

Loisel held her back.

"Hold on! You'll catch cold outside. I'll call a cab."

But she wouldn't listen to him and went rapidly down the stairs. When they were on the street, they didn't find a carriage; and they set out to hunt for one, hailing drivers whom they saw going by at a distance.

They walked toward the Seine,[9] disconsolate and shivering. Finally on the docks they found

8. Here, *adulation* means "plentiful praise; flattery."

9. The *Seine* (sen) is a river that flows through Paris.

one of those carriages that one sees in Paris only after nightfall, as if they were ashamed to show their drabness during daylight hours.

It dropped them at their door in the Rue des Martyrs,[10] and they climbed wearily up to their apartment. For her, it was all over. For him, there was the thought that he would have to be at the Ministry at ten o'clock.

Before the mirror, she let the wraps fall from her shoulders to see herself once again in all her glory. Suddenly she gave a cry. The necklace was gone.

Her husband, already half undressed, said, "What's the trouble?"

She turned toward him despairingly, "I . . . I . . . I don't have Mme. Forestier's necklace."

"What! You can't mean it! It's impossible!"

They hunted everywhere, through the folds of the dress, through the folds of the coat, in the pockets. They found nothing.

He asked, "Are you sure you had it when leaving the dance?"

"Yes, I felt it when I was in the hall of the Ministry."

"But if you had lost it on the street we'd have heard it drop. It must be in the cab."

"Yes, quite likely. Did you get its number?"

"No. Didn't you notice it either?"

"No."

They looked at each other aghast. Finally Loisel got dressed again.

"I'll retrace our steps on foot," he said, "to see if I can find it."

And he went out. She remained in her evening clothes, without the strength to go to bed, slumped in a chair in the unheated room, her mind a blank.

Her husband came in about seven o'clock. He had had no luck.

He went to the police station, to the newspapers to post a reward, to the cab companies, everywhere the slightest hope drove him.

That evening Loisel returned, pale, his face lined; still he had learned nothing.

"We'll have to write your friend," he said, "to tell her you have broken the catch and are having it repaired. That will give us a little time to turn around."

She wrote to his dictation.

At the end of a week, they had given up all hope.

And Loisel, looking five years older, declared, "We must take steps to replace that piece of jewelry."

By Firelight, 1889 (detail). Frank W. Benson. Oil on linen, 40 x 32½ in. Private collection.

Viewing the painting: How would you describe the mood of this painting? How does it reflect the mood of Mme. Loisel after the ball?

10. A Paris street, *Rue des Martyrs* (ro͞o dā mär tĕr′) translates as "Street of Martyrs." A martyr is a person who suffers greatly or sacrifices all for a belief, principle, or cause.

Vocabulary

aghast (ə gast′) *adj.* filled with fear, horror, or amazement

The next day they took the case to the jeweler whose name they found inside. He consulted his records. "I didn't sell that necklace, madame," he said. "I only supplied the case."

Then they went from one jeweler to another hunting for a similar necklace, going over their recollections, both sick with despair and anxiety.

They found, in a shop in Palais Royal, a string of diamonds which seemed exactly like the one they were seeking. It was priced at forty thousand francs. They could get it for thirty-six.

They asked the jeweler to hold it for them for three days. And they reached an agreement that he would take it back for thirty-four thousand if the lost one was found before the end of February.

Loisel had eighteen thousand francs he had inherited from his father. He would borrow the rest.

He went about raising the money, asking a thousand francs from one, four hundred from another, a hundred here, sixty there. He signed notes, made ruinous deals, did business with loan sharks, ran the whole gamut of moneylenders. He compromised the rest of his life, risked his signature without knowing if he'd be able to honor it, and then, terrified by the outlook for the future, by the blackness of despair about to close around him, by the prospect of all the privations of the body and tortures of the spirit, he went to claim the new necklace with the thirty-six thousand francs which he placed on the counter of the shopkeeper.

When Mme. Loisel took the necklace back, Mme. Forestier said to her frostily, "You should have brought it back sooner; I might have needed it."

She didn't open the case, an action her friend was afraid of. If she had noticed the substitution, what would she have thought? What would she have said? Would she have thought her a thief?

"You should have brought it back sooner; I might have needed it!"

Mme. Loisel experienced the horrible life the needy live. She played her part, however, with sudden heroism. That frightful debt had to be paid. She would pay it. She dismissed her maid; they rented a garret under the eaves.[11]

She learned to do the heavy housework, to perform the hateful duties of cooking. She washed dishes, wearing down her shell-pink nails scouring the grease from pots and pans; she scrubbed dirty linen, shirts, and cleaning rags which she hung on a line to dry; she took the garbage down to the street each morning and brought up water, stopping on each landing to get her breath. And, clad like a peasant woman, basket on arm, guarding sou[12] by sou her scanty allowance, she bargained with the fruit dealers, the grocer, the butcher, and was insulted by them.

11. A *garret under the eaves* would be a small attic apartment.
12. The *sou* (so͞o) is a French coin worth about one-twentieth of a franc.

Vocabulary

gamut (gam′ ət) *n.* the entire range or series of something
privation (prī vā′ shən) *n.* the lack of the comforts or basic necessities of life

Each month notes had to be paid, and others renewed to give more time.

Her husband labored evenings to balance a tradesman's accounts, and at night, often, he copied documents at five sous a page.

And this went on for ten years.

Finally, all was paid back, everything including the exorbitant[13] rates of the loan sharks and accumulated compound interest.

Mme. Loisel appeared an old woman, now. She became heavy, rough, harsh, like one of the poor. Her hair untended, her skirts askew,[14] her hands red, her voice shrill, she even slopped water on her floors and scrubbed them herself. But, sometimes, while her husband was at work, she would sit near the window and think of that long-ago evening when, at the dance, she had been so beautiful and admired.

What would have happened if she had not lost that necklace? Who knows? Who can say? How strange and unpredictable life is! How little there is between happiness and misery!

Then one Sunday when she had gone for a walk on the Champs Élysées to relax a bit from the week's labors, she suddenly noticed a woman strolling with a child. It was Mme. Forestier, still young-looking, still beautiful, still charming.

Did You Know?
The *Champs Élysées* (shäɴ zā lē zā) is a fashionable, tree-lined avenue in Paris.

Mme. Loisel felt a rush of emotion. Should she speak to her? Of course. And now that everything was paid off, she would tell her the whole story. Why not?

She went toward her. "Hello, Jeanne."

The other, not recognizing her, showed astonishment at being spoken to so familiarly by this common person. She stammered, "But . . . madame . . . I don't recognize . . . You must be mistaken."

"No, I'm Mathilde Loisel."

Her friend gave a cry, "Oh, my poor Mathilde, how you've changed!"

"Yes, I've had a hard time since last seeing you. And plenty of misfortunes—and all on account of you!"

"Of me . . . How do you mean?"

"Do you remember that diamond necklace you loaned me to wear to the dance at the Ministry?"

"Yes, but what about it?"

"Well, I lost it."

"You lost it! But you returned it."

"I brought you another just like it. And we've been paying for it for ten years now. You can imagine that wasn't easy for us who had nothing. Well, it's over now, and I am glad of it."

Mme. Forestier stopped short. "You mean to say you bought a diamond necklace to replace mine?"

"Yes. You never noticed, then? They were quite alike."

And she smiled with proud and simple joy.

Mme. Forestier, quite overcome, clasped her by the hands. "Oh, my poor Mathilde. But mine was only paste.[15] Why, at most it was worth only five hundred francs!"

13. *Exorbitant* means "beyond what is reasonable or fair; excessive."
14. *Askew* (ə skyo͞o′) means "crooked; to one side."
15. Here, *paste* is a hard, brilliant glass used to make artificial jewels.

Responding to Literature

Personal Response

What went through your mind at the end of the story? Discuss your thoughts with a classmate.

Analyzing Literature

Recall

1. At the beginning of the story, why is Madame Loisel unhappy with her life?
2. How does Madame Loisel react to the party invitation?
3. In what way does Madame Loisel's big night out prove to be both a triumph and a disaster for her?
4. How do the Loisels pay for the necklace's replacement?
5. What is the last thing you learn about the necklace?

Interpret

6. Compare Madame and Monsieur Loisel's attitudes toward their situation in life. How are they different?
7. Monsieur Loisel sacrifices his savings to buy a new dress for his wife. What does this tell you about his feelings for her?
8. The disaster brings many external changes to the life of Madame Loisel. How do you think it affects her emotionally?
9. In your opinion, why do the Loisels decide not to tell Madame Forestier about the loss? What does this tell you about their **characters?**
10. Describe the **irony** of the Loisels' situation. (See Literary Terms Handbook, page R7.)

Evaluate and Connect

11. Think about your response to the Reading Focus on page 168. Do you think "honesty is the best policy" is the moral of this story? Why or why not?
12. Do you find this story believable? Explain your answer.
13. **Theme Connections** According to the narrator, why does Madame Loisel feel there is a void in her life at the beginning of the story? Do you agree with this explanation?
14. Do you think it was admirable or foolish for the Loisels to try to replace the necklace? Give reasons for your opinion. If you were in their shoes, what would you have done?
15. What questions would you like to ask Maupassant after reading this story?

Literary ELEMENTS

Symbol

A **symbol** is an object, a person, a place, or an experience that represents something else, usually something abstract. In this story, for example, a fancy evening dress is a symbol of class and distinction. A symbol may have more than one meaning, or its meaning may change from the beginning to the end of a literary work. Consider the importance of the diamond necklace as a symbol in this story.

1. What does the necklace represent when Madame Loisel first sees it in its black satin box?
2. What does the necklace symbolize after Madame Loisel discovers that it is lost?
3. How does the meaning of the symbol change when it is revealed that the diamonds in the necklace were fake?

- See **Literary Terms Handbook,** p. R12.

Literary Criticism

According to one reviewer, Maupassant had a "remarkable ability to suggest character with one deft stroke of the pen–a single phrase, a couple of well-chosen verbs." Make a list of the "well-chosen verbs" and phrases that cleverly bring the character of Mme. Loisel to life. Then use your list to write a brief essay discussing what makes Maupassant's diction so effective.

Literature and Writing

Writing About Literature

Analyze a Relationship What kind of marriage do Monsieur and Madame Loisel have? Is theirs a marriage between equals? Does one partner take advantage of or mistreat the other, or do the two make sacrifices for each other, fulfilling their duties as husband and wife? Write a few paragraphs analyzing the couple's relationship. Be sure to support your opinions with details from the story.

Personal Writing

Neither a Borrower nor a Lender Be Write about a time when you or someone you know got into trouble by lending or borrowing something. Describe what happened and explain what you learned from the experience. How was the experience similar to or different from that of Madame Loisel?

Extending Your Response

Literature Groups

Reading Minds What do you suppose the original necklace meant to Madame Forestier? Do you think she knew that Madame Loisel thought that the diamonds were real? What was Madame Forestier's motivation for not disclosing the true value of the necklace at the time Madame Loisel borrowed it? Would Madame Loisel have wanted to wear the necklace if she had known that it was fake? Why or why not? Discuss these questions with your group, and share your conclusions with other groups.

Interdisciplinary Activity

Social Studies: Changing Roles Using this story and the information provided in Before You Read, page 168, as a starting point, research women's roles in late nineteenth-century France. Investigate how class structure affected the way women lived and the things they valued. Then, do research to find out what is similar and different about the way women live today. Using your personal experience in addition to your research findings, organize your ideas in a chart like the one below. If you wish, you may change the categories listed across the top of the chart. Compare your completed chart with those of others.

	Work	Money	Relationships with Men
Nineteenth-century French women			
Women in the United States today			

Performing

Meet Madame Loisel With a partner, discuss how Madame Loisel might carry herself at the beginning of the story. For example, imagine how she might walk, hold her head, or greet strangers. Also consider what her characteristic hand gestures might be. How do you suppose she carried herself on the night of the party? After she arrives home? At the end of the story? Perform your movements for the class. Ask your audience to determine what stage of Madame Loisel's life you are presenting.

Reading Further

If you would like to read more stories by Guy de Maupassant, try these works in *Fifteen by Maupassant*:

"Simon's Papa," about a fatherless boy who invents an imaginary dad.

"On the River" is a tale of psychological terror and suspense.

Save your work for your portfolio.

Skill Minilessons

GRAMMAR AND LANGUAGE • Commas with Items in a Series

A group of three or more related words, phrases, or clauses in a sentence is called a series. Use a comma to separate the elements in a series. Notice how Guy de Maupassant uses commas to punctuate this sentence: "And she would weep for days on end from vexation, regret, despair, and anguish."

PRACTICE On your paper, punctuate the following sentences that include items in a series.

1. She had neither fine clothes jewels nor outer wear.
2. Her house had dingy walls worn chairs and ugly curtains.
3. She went to the fruit dealers to the grocer and to the butcher.
4. She was elegant graceful smiling and wild with joy.
5. They hunted for the necklace through the folds of her dress through the creases of her wraps and in all her pockets.

APPLY Review a piece of your writing. Check for items in a series and revise the punctuation if necessary.

● For more about commas in a series, see **Language Handbook,** p. R27.

READING AND THINKING • Summarizing

By summarizing, or restating the basic meaning of what you read as you go along, you can keep track of characters, events, and other story details. Begin by identifying the key character and the key action or idea in a passage. Then say to yourself, or jot down, the essential meaning of the passage without including its many details. For example, reread the first paragraph of "The Necklace." The key character is a woman; the key idea is that because she was born into the middle class–and therefore unlikely to marry a man of great wealth and fame–she married a clerk.

PRACTICE On your paper, summarize this passage from "The Necklace."

> "Mme. Loisel experienced the horrible life the needy live. She played her part, however, with sudden heroism. That frightful debt had to be paid. She would pay it. She dismissed her maid; they rented a garret under the eaves."

● For more about reading strategies, see **Reading Handbook,** pp. R78–R107.

VOCABULARY • Unlocking Meaning

What if you learned what the word *jewel* means but couldn't use that knowledge to understand the word *jewelry?* Luckily, you don't learn words one at a time. You use what you know about word structure–prefixes, suffixes, and roots–to increase your vocabulary by many words each time you unlock the meaning of a new word. You use this knowledge when you make connections between unfamiliar words and words you already know. For example, in "American History," *solace* means "comfort." If you recognize *solace* in *disconsolate,* you might realize that in "The Necklace," *disconsolate* means something like "unable to be comforted."

PRACTICE Use what you know about vocabulary words in "The Necklace" to figure out what each word in the left column means. Match each word to its meaning.

1. cessation	a. poverty
2. ghastly	b. annoying, troublesome
3. deprive	c. a stopping
4. vexatious	d. to take away or to keep from having
5. pauperdom	e. horrible, frightful

INTERDISCIPLINARY CONNECTION

EARTH SCIENCE

Diamonds Are Forever

Mme. Loisel is not alone in her desire for diamonds. The hardest natural substance in existence, the diamond has been prized throughout history. Diamonds have been collected by kings and queens, flaunted by movie stars, and treasured by romantics as symbols of love and commitment.

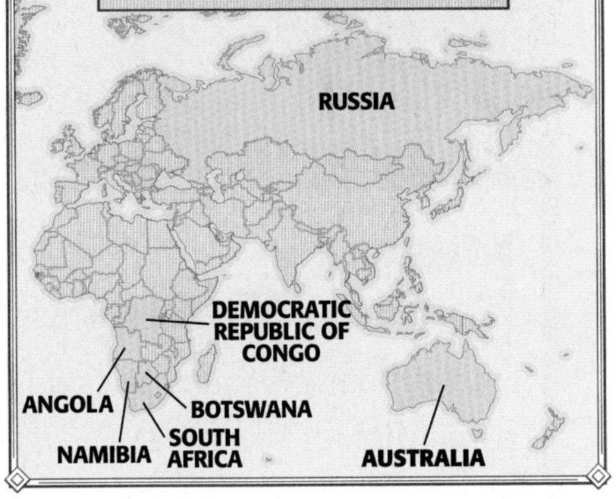

The most highly esteemed gem in the world actually has its origins in a very humble substance. Diamonds are made of carbon, the same element present in soft, black charcoal. Under extremely great pressure and high temperatures, carbon atoms can bind together tightly and evenly to form carbon crystals, or diamonds.

This crystallization occurs far beneath the earth's surface. Some diamonds may have been formed as deep as 125 miles below ground. Volcanic activity eventually forces diamond-carrying rocks to rise. Although some diamonds have been found along the banks of rivers and streams, most diamonds are mined. Tons of rock may be dug out and destroyed to produce one small diamond.

After they are mined, gem-quality diamonds are carefully cut to bring out their brilliance. Diamonds that are too flawed to be used as gems are used in industry, where their hardness is valued. Diamonds are used in many kinds of cutting and drilling tools, and vinyl records are played with diamond needles.

There are so many uses for industrial diamonds that natural supply cannot keep up with demand. Therefore, scientists have studied nature's process and imitated it, heating and compressing carbon until it forms synthetic diamonds. These human-made diamonds are not beautiful enough to be used as gems, however.

Of course, imitation gem-quality diamonds exist. Some are created from less expensive clear gemstones, while others are manufactured from human-made substances such as glass. An imitation diamond, which is softer than a real one, may show scratches and other signs of wear with time. Real diamonds, which may already be millions of years old, will probably remain brilliant for millions more.

Activity

Research a gemstone such as ruby, jade, emerald, or opal. Find out about the structure of its crystals, its hardness, its uses, and the places where it is found. Prepare a brief illustrated report.

Before You Read

The Winner

Reading Focus

Have you ever been told to look at the bright side or to make the best of a situation? Have you ever given someone else this advice? What happened?

Quickwrite Jot down your answers to these questions and tell whether you think "looking on the bright side" is good advice.

Setting a Purpose Read to see how important attitude can be when it comes to winning and losing.

Building Background

The Time and Place

"The Winner" takes place some time before 1967 in Kalasanda, a small eastern African village in the kingdom of Buganda.

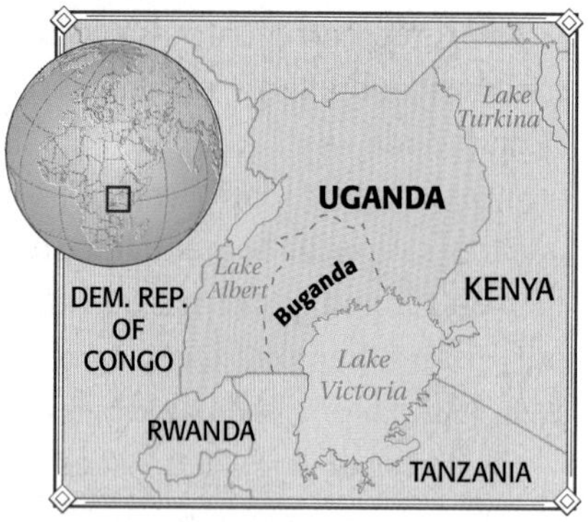

Did You Know?

Once a rich and powerful kingdom, Buganda fell under British rule in 1894 and became part of an independent Uganda in 1967. English is the official language, and Swahili and Luganda are widely spoken. However, no language is understood by everyone; each of the more than forty ethnic groups in Uganda speaks its own language! Most Ugandans are subsistence farmers, growing their own sweet potatoes, corn, millet, and plantains for food. Customs such as the football pool, or betting on soccer, are a holdover from the days of British occupation.

Vocabulary Preview

converge (kən vurj′) *v.* to come together at a place; meet; p. 181

unpretentious (un′ pri ten′ shəs) *adj.* modest; simple; not showy; p. 181

obscurity (əb skyoor′ ə tē) *n.* the state of being undistinguished or not well known; p. 182

obliterated (ə blit′ ə rāt′ əd) *adj.* blotted or rubbed out; p. 183

incredulity (in′ krə dōō′ lə tē) *n.* an unwillingness or inability to believe something; disbelief; p. 184

Meet Barbara Kimenye

Acclaimed as a journalist and columnist for the paper *Uganda Nation*, Barbara Kimenye has also published collections of short stories and numerous books for children. Kimenye was once a private secretary for the kabaka, or king, of Buganda. She spent ten years freelancing in London, England, before returning to Uganda in 1986. Today, Kimenye lives in Nairobi, Kenya. Her recent publications include two novels for African teenagers about the impact of AIDS on victims and their families. She has also written *The Modern African Vegetable Cookbook*.

Barbara Kimenye was born in Uganda in 1929. "The Winner" is from the short story collection Kalasanda, *which was first published in 1965.*

The Winner

Barbara Kimenye

WHEN PIUS NDAWULA[1] WON the football pools,[2] overnight he seemed to become the most popular man in Buganda. Hosts of relatives converged upon him from the four corners of the kingdom: cousins and nephews, nieces and uncles, of whose existence he had never before been aware, turned up in Kalasanda by the busload, together with crowds of individuals who, despite their downtrodden appearance, assured Pius that they and they alone were capable of seeing that his money was properly invested—preferably in their own particular businesses! Also lurking around Pius's unpretentious mud hut were newspaper reporters, slick young men weighed down with cameras and sporting loud checked caps or trilbies[3] set at conspicuously jaunty angles, and serious young men from Radio Uganda who were anxious to record Pius's delight at his astonishing luck for the edification[4] of the Uganda listening public.

The rest of Kalasanda were so taken by surprise that they could only call and briefly congratulate Pius before being elbowed out of the way by his more garrulous[5] relations. All, that is to say, except Pius's greatest friend Salongo,[6] the custodian of the Ssabalangira's[7] tomb. He came and planted himself firmly in the house, and nobody attempted to move him. Almost blind, and very lame, he had tottered out with the aid of a stout stick. Just to see him arrive had caused a minor sensation in the village, for he hadn't left the tomb for years. But recognizing at last a chance to house Ssabalangira's remains in a state befitting his former glory, made the slow, tortuous journey worthwhile to Salongo.

Nantondo hung about long enough to have her picture taken with Pius. Or rather, she

1. *Pius Ndawula* (pī′ əs n′ dä′ wo͞o lä)
2. Outside the United States, soccer is called *football.* A *pool* is a kind of organized betting in which the winner or winners get all of the accumulated bets.
3. A *trilby* is a soft felt hat with a narrow brim and deeply creased crown.
4. *Edification* means "moral enlightenment or instruction."
5. *Garrulous* (gar′ ə ləs) means "tiresomely talkative."
6. *Salongo* (sä lon′ gō)
7. The *Ssabalangira* (s′ sa′ bä′ lan gē′ rə) is the head of the princes in the royal clan of Buganda. He governs the day-to-day affairs of the clan while the kabaka, or king, handles the affairs of state.

Vocabulary

converge (kən vurj′) *v.* to come together at a place; meet
unpretentious (un′ pri ten′ shəs) *adj.* modest; simple; not showy

managed to slip beside him just as the cameras clicked, and so it was that every Uganda newspaper, on the following day, carried a front-page photograph of "Mr. Pius Ndawula and his happy wife," a caption that caused Pius to shake with rage and threaten legal proceedings, but over which Nantondo gloated as she proudly showed it to everybody she visited.

"Tell us, Mr. Ndawula, what do you intend to do with all the money you have won . . . ?"

"Tell us, Mr. Ndawula, how often have you completed pools coupons . . . ?"

"Tell us . . . Tell us . . . Tell us . . ."

Pius's head was reeling under this bombardment of questions, and he was even more confused by Salongo's constant nudging and muttered advice to "Say nothing!" Nor did the relatives make things easier. Their persistent clamoring for his attention, and the way they kept shoving their children under his nose, made it impossible for him to think, let alone talk.

It isn't at all easy, when you have lived for sixty-five years in complete obscurity, to adjust yourself in a matter of hours to the role of a celebrity, and the strain was beginning to tell.

Behind the hut—Pius had no proper kitchen—gallons of tea were being boiled, while several of the female cousins were employed in ruthlessly hacking down the bunches of *matoke* from his meager plantains,[8] to cook food for everybody. One woman—she had introduced herself as Cousin Sarah—discovered Pius's hidden store of banana beer, and dished it out to all and sundry as though it were her own. Pius had become very wary of Cousin Sarah. He didn't like the way in which she kept loudly remarking that he needed a woman about the place, and he was even more seriously alarmed when suddenly Salongo gave him a painful dig in the ribs and muttered, "You'll have to watch that one—she's a sticker!"

Everybody who came wanted to see the telegram that announced Pius's win. When it had arrived at the Ggombolola[9] Headquarters—the postal address of everyone residing within a radius of fifteen miles—Musisi had brought it out personally, delighted to be the bearer of such good tidings. At Pius's request he had gone straight away to tell Salongo, and then back to his office to send an acknowledgment on behalf of Pius to the pools firm, leaving the old man to dream rosy dreams. An extension of his small coffee *shamba*,[10] a new roof on his house—or maybe an entirely new house—concrete blocks this time, with a veranda perhaps. Then there were hens. Salongo and he had always said there was money in hens these days, now that the women ate eggs and chicken; not that either of them agreed with the practice. Say what you liked, women who ate chicken and eggs were fairly asking to be infertile! That woman Welfare Officer who came round snooping occasionally, tried to say it was all nonsense, that chicken meat and eggs made bigger and better babies. Well, they might look

Did You Know?
A *veranda* is a long porch, usually with a roof, that extends along one or more sides of a house.

8. *Matoke* (mə tō′ kə) is a name for the fruit of the *plantain,* a type of banana that is eaten cooked.

9. *Ggombolola* (g′ gom′ bō lō′ lä)

10. The word *shamba* can refer to a garden, farm, or plantation.

Vocabulary
obscurity (əb skyoor′ ə tē) *n.* the state of being undistinguished or not well known

bigger and better, but nobody could deny that they were fewer! Which only goes to show.

But news spreads fast in Africa—perhaps the newspapers have contacts in the pools offices. Anyway, before the telegram had even reached Pius, announcements were appearing in the local newspapers, and Pius was still quietly lost in his private dreams when the first batch of visitors arrived. At first he was at a loss to understand what was happening. People he hadn't seen for years and only recognized with difficulty fell upon him with cries of joy. "Cousin Pius, the family is delighted!" "Cousin Pius, why have you not visited us all this time?"

Pius was pleased to see his nearest and dearest gathered around him. It warmed his old heart once more to find himself in the bosom of his family, and he welcomed them effusively.[11] The second crowd to arrive were no less well received, but there was a marked coolness on the part of their forerunners.

However, as time had gone by and the flood of strange faces had gained momentum,[12] Pius's *shamba* had come to resemble a political meeting. All to be seen from the door of the house was a turbulent sea of white *kanzus* and brilliant *busutis*,[13] and the house itself was full of people and tobacco smoke.

The precious telegram was passed from hand to hand until it was reduced to a limp fragment of paper with the lettering partly obliterated: not that it mattered very much, for only a few members of the company could read English.

"Now, Mr. Ndawula, we are ready to take the recording." The speaker was a slight young man wearing a checked shirt. "I shall ask you a few questions, and you simply answer me in your normal voice." Pius looked at the leather box with its two revolving spools, and licked his lips. "Say nothing!" came a hoarse whisper from Salongo. The young man steadfastly[14] ignored him, and went ahead in his best BBC[15] manner. "Well, Mr. Ndawula, first of all let me congratulate you on your winning the pools. Would you like to tell our listeners what it feels like suddenly to find yourself rich?" There was an uncomfortable pause, during which Pius stared mesmerized[16] at the racing spools, and the young man tried frantically to span the gap by asking, "I mean, have you any plans for the future?" Pius swallowed audibly, and opened his mouth to say something, but shut it again when Salongo growled, "Tell him nothing!"

The young man snapped off the machine, shaking his head in exasperation.[17] "Look here, sir, all I want you to do is to say something—I'm not asking you to make a speech! Now, I'll tell you what. I shall ask you again what it feels like suddenly to come into money, and you say something like, 'It was a wonderful surprise, and naturally I feel very pleased'—and will you ask your friend not to interrupt! Got it? Okay, off we go!"

The machine was again switched on, and the man brightly put his question, "Now, Mr. Ndawula, what does it feel like to win the pools?" Pius swallowed, then quickly chanted in a voice all off key, "It was a wonderful

11. *Effusively* (i fū′ siv lē) means "with excessive emotion, without restraint."
12. Here, *momentum* means "force or speed."
13. *Kanzus* (kän′ zūs) are men's white, ankle-length, long-sleeved garments, and *busutis* (bu sū′ tēs) are women's long, multicolored cotton dresses decorated with needlework.
14. *Steadfastly* means "faithfully; steadily."
15. The *BBC* is the British Broadcasting Corporation.
16. *Mesmerized* means "spellbound" or "hypnotized."
17. *Exasperation* is a state of anger or great irritation.

Vocabulary

obliterated (ə blit′ ə rāt′ əd) *adj.* blotted or rubbed out surprise and naturally I feel very happy and will you ask your friend not to interrupt!" The young man nearly wept. This happened to be his first assignment as a radio interviewer, and it looked like being his last. He switched off the machine and mourned his lusterless future, groaning. At that moment Cousin Sarah caught his eye. "Perhaps I can help you," she said. "I am Mr. Ndawula's cousin." She made this pronouncement in a manner that suggested Pius had no others. The young man brightened considerably. "Well, madam, if you could tell me something about Mr. Ndawula's plans, I would be most grateful." Cousin Sarah folded her arms across her imposing bosom, and when the machine again started up, she was off. Yes, Mr. Ndawula was very happy about the money. No, she didn't think he had any definite plans on how to spend it—with all these people about he didn't have time to think. Yes, Mr. Ndawula lived completely alone, but she was prepared to stay and look after him for as long as he needed her. Here a significant glance passed between the other women in the room, who clicked their teeth and let out long Eeeeeeehs! of incredulity. Yes, she believed she was Mr. Ndawula's nearest living relative by marriage. . . .

Pius listened to her confident aplomb[18] with growing horror, while Salongo frantically nudged him and whispered, "There! What did I tell you! That woman's a sticker!"

Around three in the afternoon, *matoke* and tea were served, the *matoke*, on wide fresh plantain leaves, since Pius owned only three plates, and the tea in anything handy—tin cans, old jars, etc.—because he was short of cups, too. Pius ate very little, but he was glad of the tea. He had shaken hands with so many people that his arm ached, and he was tired of the chatter and the comings and goings in his house of all these strangers. Most of all he was tired of Cousin Sarah, who insisted on treating him like an idiot invalid. She kept everybody else at bay, as far as she possibly could, and when one woman plonked a sticky fat baby on his lap, Cousin Sarah dragged the child away as though it were infectious. Naturally, a few cross words were exchanged between Sarah and the fond mother, but by this time Pius was past caring.

Yosefu Mukasa and Kibuka called in the early evening, when some of the relatives were departing with effusive promises to come again tomorrow. They were both alarmed at the weariness they saw on Pius's face. The old man looked utterly worn out, his skin gray and sickly. Also, they were a bit taken aback by the presence of Cousin Sarah, who pressed them to take tea and behaved in every respect as though she were mistress of the house. "I believe my late husband knew you very well, sir," she told Yosefu. "He used to be a Miruka chief in Buyaga County. His name was Kivumbi." "Ah, yes," Yosefu replied, "I remember Kivumbi very well indeed. We often hunted together. I was sorry to hear of his death. He was a good man." Cousin Sarah shrugged her shoulders. "Yes, he was a good man. But what the Lord giveth, He also taketh away." Thus was the late Kivumbi dismissed from the conversation.

Hearing all this enabled Pius to define the exact relationship between himself and Cousin Sarah, and even by Kiganda standards it was virtually nonexistent, for the late Kivumbi had been the stepson of one of Pius's cousins.

"Your stroke of luck seems to have exhausted you, Pius," Kibuka remarked, when he

18. *Aplomb* (ə plom′) means "self-confidence; assurance; poise."

Vocabulary

incredulity (in′ krə dōō′ lə tē) *n.* an unwillingness or inability to believe something; disbelief

Jeanne, Martiniquaise, 1938. Loïs Mailou Jones. Oil on canvas, 24 x 28½ in. Collection of the artist.

Viewing the painting: How would you describe this woman? With which character in the story might you compare her? Why?

and Yosefu were seated on the rough wooden chairs brought forth by Cousin Sarah.

Salongo glared at the world in general and snarled, "Of course he is exhausted! Who wouldn't be with all these scavengers collected to pick his bones?"[19] Pius hushed him as one would a child. "No, no, Salongo. It is quite natural that my family should gather round me at a time like this. Only I fear I am perhaps a little too old for all this excitement."

Salongo spat expertly through the open doorway, narrowly missing a group of guests who were preparing to bed down, and said, "That woman doesn't think he's too old. She's out to catch him. I've seen her type elsewhere!"

Yosefu's mouth quirked with amusement at the thought that "elsewhere" could only mean the Ssabalangira's tomb, which Salongo had guarded for the better part of his adult life. "Well, she's a fine woman," he remarked. "But see here, Pius," he went on, "don't be offended by my proposal, but wouldn't it be better if you came and stayed with us at Mutunda for tonight? Miriamu would love to have you, and you look as though you need a good night's rest, which you wouldn't get here—those relatives of yours outside are preparing a fire and are ready to dance the night away!"

"I think that's a wonderful idea!" said Cousin Sarah, bouncing in to remove the tea cups. "You go with Mr. Mukasa, Cousin Pius. The change will do you as much good as the rest. And don't worry about your home—I shall stay here and look after things." Pius hesitated. "Well, I think I shall be all right here—I don't like to give Miriamu any extra work. . . ." Salongo muttered, "Go to Yosefu's. You don't want to be left alone in the house with that woman—there's no knowing what she might get up to . . . !"

19. Salongo compares people to *scavengers,* animals such as hyenas and vultures that feed on dead, decaying flesh.

"I'll pack a few things for you, Pius," announced Cousin Sarah and bustled off before anything more could be said, pausing only long enough to give Salongo a look that was meant to wither him on the spot.

So Pius found himself being driven away to Mutunda in Yosefu's car, enjoying the pleasant sensation of not having to bother about a thing. Salongo too had been given a lift to as near the tomb as the car could travel, and his wizened old face was contorted[20] into an irregular smile, for Pius had promised to help him build a new house for the Ssabalangira. For him the day had been well spent, despite Cousin Sarah.

Pius spent an enjoyable evening with the Mukasas. They had a well-cooked supper, followed by a glass of cool beer as they sat back and listened to the local news on the radio. Pius had so far relaxed as to tell the Mukasas modestly that he had been interviewed by Radio Uganda that morning, and when Radio Newsreel was announced they waited breathlessly to hear his voice. But instead of Pius, Cousin Sarah came booming over the air. Until that moment the old man had completely forgotten the incident of the tape recording. In fact, he had almost forgotten Cousin Sarah. Now it all came back to him with a shiver of apprehension. Salongo was right. That woman did mean business! It was a chilling thought. However, it didn't cause him to lose any sleep. He slept like a cherub,[21] as if he hadn't a care in the world.

Because he looked so refreshed in the morning, Miriamu insisted on keeping him at Mutunda for another day. "I know you feel better, but after seeing you yesterday, I think a little holiday with us will do you good. Go home tomorrow, when the excitement has died down a bit," she advised.

20. Salongo's face is shriveled or withered (*wizened*) and twisted (*contorted*) in a smile.
21. In this context, *cherub* means "a sweet, innocent child."

Soon after lunch, as Pius was taking a nap in a chair on the veranda, Musisi drove up in the landrover, with Cousin Sarah by his side. Miriamu came out to greet them, barely disguising her curiosity about the formidable[22] woman about whom she had heard so much. The two women sized each other up and decided to be friends.

Meanwhile, Musisi approached the old man. "Sit down, son," Pius waved him to a chair at his side. "Miriamu feeds me so well it's all I can do to keep awake."

"I am glad you are having a rest, sir." Musisi fumbled in the pocket of his jacket. "There is another telegram for you. Shall I read it?" The old man sat up expectantly and said, "If you'll be so kind."

Musisi first read the telegram in silence, then he looked at Pius and commented, "Well, sir, I'm afraid it isn't good news."

"Not good news? Has somebody died?"

Musisi smiled. "Well, no. It isn't really as bad as that. The thing is, the pools firm say that owing to an unfortunate oversight they omitted to add, in the first telegram, that the prize money is to be shared among three hundred other people.

Pius was stunned. Eventually he murmured, "Tell me, how much does that mean I shall get?"

"Three hundred into seventeen thousand pounds won't give you much over a thousand shillings."[23]

To Musisi's astonishment, Pius sat back and chuckled. "More than a thousand shillings!" he said. "Why, that's a lot of money!"

22. Here, *formidable* (fôr′ mi də bəl) means "impressive by reason of strength or power."
23. Uganda uses the British monetary units of *pounds* and *shillings,* a carryover from its days as part of the British Empire. To get an idea of the difference in Pius's winnings, imagine that the original prize was $17,000. Divided by 300 people, his actual share would be only about $57.

"But it's not, when you expected so much more!"

"I agree. And yet, son, what would I have done with all those thousands of pounds? I am getting past the age when I need a lot."

Miriamu brought a mat onto the veranda and she and Cousin Sarah made themselves comfortable near the men. "What a disappointment!" cried Miriamu, but Cousin Sarah sniffed and said, "I agree with Cousin Pius. He wouldn't know what to do with seventeen thousand pounds, and the family would be hanging round his neck forevermore!"

At mention of Pius's family, Musisi frowned. "I should warn you, sir, those relatives of yours have made a terrific mess of your *shamba*—your plantains have been stripped—and Mrs. Kivumbi here," nodding at Sarah, "was only just in time to prevent them digging up your sweet potatoes!"

"Yes, Cousin Pius," added Sarah. "It will take us some time to put the *shamba* back in order. They've trodden down a whole bed of young beans."

"Oh, dear," said Pius weakly. "This is dreadful news."

"Don't worry. They will soon disappear when I tell them there is no money, and then I shall send for a couple of my grandsons to come and help us do some replanting." Pius could not help but admire the way Sarah took things in her stride.

Musisi rose from his chair. "I'm afraid I can't stay any longer, so I will go now and help Cousin Sarah clear the crowd, and see you tomorrow to take you home." He and Sarah climbed back into the landrover and Sarah waved energetically until the vehicle was out of sight.

"Your cousin is a fine woman," Miriamu told Pius, before going indoors. Pius merely grunted, but for some odd reason he felt the remark to be a compliment to himself.

All was quiet at Pius's home when Musisi brought him home next day. He saw at once that his *shamba* was well-nigh wrecked, but his drooping spirits quickly revived when Sarah placed a mug of steaming tea before him, and sat on a mat at his feet, explaining optimistically how matters could be remedied. Bit by bit he began telling her what he planned to do with the prize money, ending with, "Of course, I shan't be able to do everything now, especially since I promised Salongo something for the tomb."

Sarah poured some more tea and said, "Well, I think the roof should have priority. I noticed last night that there are several leaks. And while we're about it, it would be a good idea to build another room on and a small outside kitchen. Mud and wattle is cheap enough, and then the whole place can be plastered. You can still go ahead and extend your coffee. And as for hens, well, I have six good layers at home, as well as a fine cockerel.[24] I'll bring them over!"

Did You Know?
Wattle is a framework of poles, branches, or twigs, woven together and used in building walls, fences, or roofs.

Pius looked at her in silence for a long time. She is a fine looking woman, he thought, and that blue *busuti* suits her. Nobody would ever take her for a grandmother—but why is she so anxious to throw herself at me?

"You sound as if you are planning to come and live here," he said at last, trying hard to sound casual.

Sarah turned to face him and replied, "Cousin Pius, I shall be very frank with you.

24. A *cockerel* (kok′ ər əl) is a rooster less than a year old.

Six months ago my youngest son got married and brought his wife to live with me. She's a very nice girl, but somehow I can't get used to having another woman in the house. My other son is in Kampala,[25] and although I know I would be welcome there, he too has a wife, and three children, so if I went there I wouldn't be any better off. When I saw that bit about you in the paper, I suddenly remembered—although I don't expect you to—how you were at my wedding and so helpful to everybody. Well, I thought to myself, here is somebody who needs a good housekeeper, who needs somebody to keep the leeches off, now that he has come into money. I came along right away to take a look at you, and I can see I did the right thing. You do need me." She hesitated for a moment, and then said, "Only you might prefer to stay alone . . . I'm so used to having my own way, I never thought about that before."

Pius cleared his throat. "You're a very impetuous[26] woman," was all he could find to say.

A week later, Pius wandered out to the tomb and found Salongo busily polishing the Ssbalangira's weapons. "I thought you were dead," growled the custodian, "it is so long since you came here—but then, this tomb thrives on neglect. Nobody cares that one of Buganda's greatest men lies here."

"I have been rather busy," murmured Pius. "But I didn't forget my promise to you. Here! I've brought you a hundred shillings, and I only wish it could have been more. At least it will buy a few cement blocks."

Salongo took the money and looked at it as if it were crawling with lice. Grudgingly he thanked Pius and then remarked, "Of course, you will find life more expensive now that you are keeping a woman in the house."

"I suppose Nantondo told you," Pius smiled sheepishly.

"Does it matter who told me?" the custodian replied. "Anyway, never say I didn't warn you. Next thing she'll want will be a ring marriage!"

Pius gave an uncertain laugh. "As a matter of fact, one of the reasons I came up here was to invite you to the wedding—it's next month."

Salongo carefully laid down the spear he was rubbing upon a piece of clean barkcloth and stared at his friend as if he had suddenly grown another head. "What a fool you are! And all this stems from your scribbling noughts and crosses[27] on a bit of squared paper! I knew it would bring no good! At your age you ought to have more sense. Well, all I can advise is that you run while you still have the chance!"

For a moment Pius was full of misgivings. Was he, after all, behaving like a fool? Then he thought of Sarah, and the wonders she had worked with his house and his *shamba* in the short time they had been together. He felt reassured. "Well, I'm getting married, and I expect to see you at both the church and the reception, and if you don't appear, I shall want to know the reason why!" He was secretly delighted at the note of authority in his voice, and Salongo's face was the picture of astonishment. "All right," he mumbled, "I shall try and come. Before you go, cut a bunch of bananas to take back to your good lady, and there might be some cabbage ready at the back. I suppose I've got to hand it to her! She's the real winner!"

25. *Kampala,* in southern Uganda, is the nation's capital and largest city.

26. An *impetuous* (im pech′ o͞o əs) person is impulsive, acting suddenly and with little thought.

27. *Noughts* (nôts) and *crosses* refers to *o*'s and *x*'s, the way bets are marked on the football pools' entry form.

Responding to Literature

Personal Response

Were you pleased with the outcome of the story? Explain why or why not.

Analyzing Literature

Recall

1. What do Pius's relatives do when the news spreads that Pius has won the football pools?
2. Who is Cousin Sarah, and why is Pius wary of her at first?
3. Explain what relationship Salongo has to Pius, and why he, too, is interested in Pius's good news.
4. What does Pius say and do when he learns that he won much less money than he expected? What does Sarah say?
5. What happens at the end of the story?

Interpret

6. What human weaknesses does the author make fun of in this story? Explain your answer.
7. Compare and contrast Cousin Sarah with Nantondo or with one of Pius's other visitors or relatives.
8. In your opinion, why is Salongo so suspicious of the media and of Pius's family and Cousin Sarah? What do his suspicions reveal about his character?
9. When and why does Pius's opinion of Sarah begin to change? Did your opinion of her change as well? Explain.
10. What will Sarah and Pius each gain from their partnership?

Evaluate and Connect

11. Kimenye relies heavily on **dialogue** to end the story. How does Pius's final conversation with Salongo help to reveal Pius's character? How has he changed from the beginning of the story?
12. Do you think the portrayal of Pius's family is realistic? Explain.
13. Think about your response to the Reading Focus on page 180. How do Pius and Sarah make the best of their situations?
14. Do you think this story is humorous, serious, or both? Describe your impressions.
15. In what ways is Bugandan society, as portrayed in "The Winner," similar to and different from contemporary American society? Cite details from the story to support your opinion.

Literary ELEMENTS

Flat and Round Characters

Characters who reveal just one personality trait are called **flat characters.** Nantondo, for example, is a flat character–all the reader learns about her is that she pushes her way into the newspaper photograph. Characters who show varied and sometimes contradictory traits are called **round characters.** Salongo is a round character because many of his traits are revealed, including his self-interest, his concern for Pius, and his ability to respond graciously to news he did not wish to hear.

1. Is Cousin Sarah a round or flat character? Give reasons for your answer.
2. Identify two additional flat characters in "The Winner," and explain their role in the story.

- See **Literary Terms Handbook,** p. R2.

Literary Criticism

A critic notes that in Barbara Kimenye's books for children, "her characters [are shown] in a positive light despite their negative environment." Do you think that this is also true of Kimenye's characters in "The Winner"? Jot down your thoughts in your journal and include examples from the story to support your ideas. Then share your notes with a partner.

Literature and Writing

Writing About Literature

Considering Conflict Choose a conflict between two characters that you feel is particularly significant to the story. In one or two paragraphs, explain what the conflict is and how it is resolved. Then tell why the conflict is important to the plot of the story.

Creative Writing

The Winner, Take Two Imagine that you could rewrite "The Winner," taking the story and its characters in a different direction. What changes would you make? Create a new plot outline for the story, beginning with the same exposition: the same characters, setting, and initial event. Then, briefly relate the events that will make up the rising action, the climax, and the resolution.

Extending Your Response

Literature Groups

And the Winner Is . . . Do you agree with Salongo when he says that Cousin Sarah is "the real winner"? Why or why not? In a group, decide how you think the author of this story might define winning and write the definition down on a piece of paper. Then discuss who the winners and losers might be in this story, keeping track of your ideas in a chart like this one. Share your "winning" definition and your conclusions about the characters with another group.

Character's Name	Winner or Loser?	Why?

Interdisciplinary Activity

Art: Create a Cartoon Plan and sketch a single cartoon or a series of frames representing a scene from this story. For example, you might show the relatives eating Pius's food and drinking his stores of banana beer, or you might depict the inner thoughts as well as the words that pass between Salongo and Pius during a conversation. Use speech bubbles to show characters' thoughts and dialogue or write a caption to sum up the scene.

Learning for Life

Persuading Others Some people say that lotteries make poor people poorer. Others say that lotteries open doors for a few lucky winners, while generating funds for important government services. Conduct research into a state lottery system and learn what you can about these two points of view. Were your own beliefs about the lottery swayed one way or the other on the basis of your findings? Give a persuasive talk to your class, explaining why the lottery system should either be continued or terminated.

Reading Further

For more by African authors, try these works:

Short Stories: "The Late Bud," by Ama Ata Aidoo, is about a rebellious young girl living in the Ghanaian countryside; "The Test," by South African writer Njabulo Ndebele, is about a dilemma faced by a group of teenaged boys. Both stories may be found in *Rites of Passage: Stories About Growing Up by Black Writers from Around the World,* edited by Tonya Bolden.

Children's Story: *Moses and the Ghost,* by Barbara Kimenye, is one of a series of adventure tales about a mischievous and energetic boy named Moses.

Save your work for your portfolio.

Skill Minilessons

GRAMMAR AND LANGUAGE • Concrete and Abstract Nouns

A **concrete noun** names an object that occupies space or that can be recognized by any of the senses, such as "car." An **abstract noun** names an idea, a quality, or a characteristic, such as "freedom." The following sentence from "The Winner" contains the abstract noun *afternoon* (something you cannot see, smell, touch, taste, or hear); it also contains many concrete nouns, which are underlined.

> "Around three in the afternoon, *matoke* and tea were served, the *matoke,* on wide fresh plantain leaves, since Pius owned only three plates. . . ."

PRACTICE On your paper, identify the nouns in this passage. Label them *abstract* or *concrete.*

> He saw at once that his *shamba* was well-nigh wrecked, but his drooping spirits quickly revived when Sarah placed a mug of steaming tea before him, and sat on a mat at his feet, explaining optimistically how matters could be remedied.

APPLY In "The Winner," find five more concrete nouns and five more abstract nouns.

- For more about nouns, see **Language Handbook,** p. R40.

READING AND THINKING • Making Inferences

When you make inferences as you read, you draw logical conclusions, combining clues from the text with what you already know from experience or other reading. For example, when the photograph of Pius and Nantondo appears in the newspaper with the caption "Mr. Pius Ndawula and his happy wife," Pius is enraged and threatens to take legal action. From this you may infer that Pius is single—and he likes it that way!

PRACTICE On your paper, make an inference on the basis of each of the following pieces of information about the characters and situations in "The Winner."

1. Pius's many relatives assured him that they knew the proper way for him to invest his winnings.
2. The first visitors to arrive at Pius's hut did not happily greet the arrival of additional visitors.
3. Musisi offers to read the telegram aloud.
4. Pius's visitors wreck his home and eat all his food.
5. At the end of the story, Salongo sends Pius home with bananas and a cabbage for Cousin Sarah.

- For more about reading strategies, see **Reading Handbook,** pp. R78–R107.

VOCABULARY • The Latin Root *cred*

The Latin root *cred* comes from the verb *credere*, which means "to trust or believe." Therefore, when you come across the word *incredulity* (which contains the negating prefix *in-*), you can guess that it has to do with not trusting or believing. Amazing events, extremely good news, and really bad excuses can all cause you to feel *incredulity*—an unwillingness or inability to believe. Similarly, a store owner will give you *credit* if he or she trusts you to pay for your goods later. Recognizing the *cred* root in an unfamiliar word can help you get at least a general sense of the word's meaning.

PRACTICE Briefly state what you'd guess is the meaning of each underlined word.

1. It is easy to trick an innocent and credulous child.
2. I don't give much credence to the stories that appear in *that* tabloid paper!
3. If you place credit in what your doctor says, you are more likely to follow his or her advice.
4. "The Boy Who Cried Wolf" is about a child who loses his credibility by frequently lying.

Writing Workshop

Descriptive Writing: Character Study

In descriptive writing, you use words that appeal to the senses to share your impressions of people, places, and things. You might use descriptive writing in a classified ad to describe a bike that you want to sell, or in a short story to portray a character or setting. **In this workshop, you will write a character study that uses description to bring a person to life on the page.**

- As you write your character study, refer to the **Writing Handbook,** pp. R58–R71.

EVALUATION RUBRIC

By the time you complete this Writing Workshop, you will have
- written an introduction that presents your main impression of a character
- described scenes and incidents that elaborate your main impression
- revealed your character's thoughts, feelings, and physical appearance through anecdote, dialogue, and descriptive detail
- concluded by alluding to your main impression
- presented a character study that is free of errors in grammar, usage, and mechanics

The Writing Process

PREWRITING

PREWRITING TIP

Close your eyes and visualize your character. Then open your eyes and list the adjectives that come to mind.

Explore ideas

Do you want to depict a real person, a character from one of this theme's stories, or a character of your own invention? Use the questions below to begin exploring your subject's personality.

- How can appearance reveal personality? (Consider how the father looks in "Gaston.")
- How can thoughts reveal personality? (Consider Mitty's daydreams in "The Secret Life of Walter Mitty.")
- How can the spoken word reveal personality? (Consider Eugene's mother's speech to the narrator in "American History.")

Choose your audience and decide how to reach it

Will you share your character study with an audience who knows your subject? Or will you intrigue readers by describing someone who is a stranger to them? Consider how you'll present your finished work. The style and form your writing takes will vary according to the method and audience you choose. The Publishing/Presenting section on page 196 gives some options.

Understand your purpose

Your goal in writing a character study is to make your readers feel that they know the subject as well as you do. Depending on your audience, you may have other goals as well; for example, you may wish to inform, entertain, or persuade your readers.

Explore your impressions

Use the early stages of the writing process to explore your impressions of your subject. If you plan to write about a real person, interview or observe him or her. If your character is fictional, imagine yourself talking to or watching him or her.

Make a plan

The best way to organize a character study is in order of impression. Lead off with your main impression of the character. Then describe scenes or incidents–each in a separate paragraph–that best convey that impression. Repeat the process if you'd like to include more than one main impression in your character study.

Use a picture-frame graphic organizer like the one on this page to help you visualize the structure of your character study.

- In the center, jot down your main impression of the character. Focus on what your character is really like.
- In each side of the frame, write notes for scenes or incidents that will convey the main impression. You may want to include
  – descriptions of facial features, expressions, style of dress, speech, and mannerisms
  – descriptions of behavior toward other people
  – thoughts and feelings

STUDENT MODEL

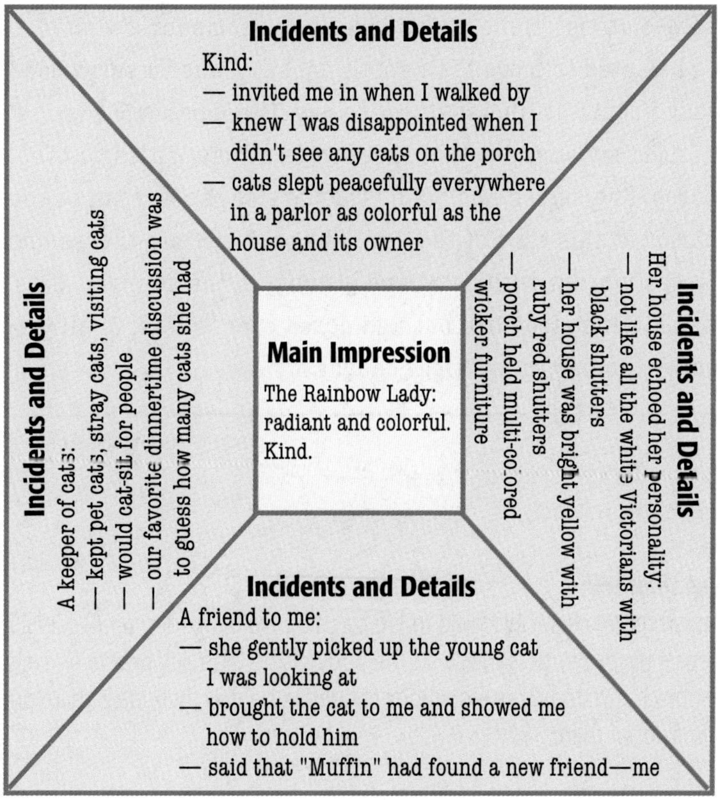

Complete Student Model on p. R109.

DRAFTING

DRAFTING TIPS

If you don't like to face a blank page, dictate the first few words or sentences into a tape recorder. Transcribe them, and you're on your way.

If you completed a frame graphic during Prewriting, use the notes in the center of the organizer for your introduction and conclusion. Use the notes in the side panels in the body paragraphs.

Drafts and rehearsals

A draft is a little like a rehearsal for a play. Actors and directors use rehearsals to experiment, trying out ideas and developing the characters in the play. The director tries to allow as many rehearsals as the actors need to feel confident enough to perform for an audience.

Drafts are your rehearsals. Experiment. Explore the character. Remember that each draft is temporary, written to be replaced by the next one.

Write your draft

As you write, refer to your plan but feel free to change it. Drafting is a time for quickly getting thoughts on paper. Don't try to edit yourself at this point and don't stop to look up words or facts. You'll polish your work later.

STUDENT MODEL

It was a bright and cool October day as I walked by the Rainbow Lady's house. I tried to see if I could catch a glimpse of some of her cats. I was so busy looking for cats that I did not see the Rainbow Lady sitting right there. She stood up, wearing a beautiful cloud of green and blue. She smiled at me. "Hello, would you like to come for a visit?"

I wanted to more than anything, but I was so surprised that I couldn't find anything to say. The Rainbow Lady noticed my surprise that there were no cats sitting on the porch. She smiled and said, "They prefer the warmth of the parlor at this time of the day." She took me into the parlor. It was vibrant with color and glowing in the sunlight. Cats and kittens stretched out and dozed everywhere. Of all the cats, a young orange tiger caught my eye.

Complete Student Model on p. R109.

Show rather than tell

As you write, make the character come to life by using dialogue, descriptive detail, and anecdotes that reveal his or her personality. In the body of the draft, it's best to leave your opinions of the subject unstated. Those opinions should lie behind the details that you show the reader, not in front of them.

REVISING

Take another look

When your draft is finished, set it aside until you can look at it with fresh eyes. When you return to it, read it quickly, put it aside again, and think about the impression the character will make on your audience. Then reread the draft slowly and mark places where you can improve the effect. Use the **Rubric for Revising** to guide you as you revise.

Read your draft aloud

Read the body of your character study aloud to someone. (Keep the written copy to yourself at this stage, since it's still in development.) Ask your listener for his or her main impression of your subject. Then read the introduction and conclusion and compare your impressions with those of your listener. Finally, go through the **Rubric for Revising** together, noting your listener's comments. Refer to those comments when you revise but don't feel that you have to use them all. This is your writing. Shape it as you wish.

REVISING TIP

Tighten the focus. If a detail doesn't support the impression you want to make, delete it or replace it with one that does.

STUDENT MODEL

Before I moved here, I came from a small, ~~boring~~ New England town where ~~everything seemed the same.~~ the days, years, and even most of the people tended to blend together. However, there was one woman in our town who stood out from all the rest, and her name was Vivian Esther. She was tall and her silver gray hair was always neatly braided, often with flowers. A radiant complexion showed only the faintest hint of spider-like wrinkles around her eyes. We kids called her the "Rainbow Lady" because she wore dazzling green and yellow skirts graced with cool pink and warm orange blouses. ~~We have no idea why she wore such odd shoes.~~ She turned out to be as kind as she was colorful.

Complete Student Model on p. R109.

RUBRIC FOR REVISING

Your revised character study should have
- ☑ an introduction that presents your main impression of a character
- ☑ body paragraphs that includes scenes or incidents that support your main impression
- ☑ dialogue, description, and anecdotes that reveal the character's personality and appearance
- ☑ vivid verbs and adjectives that enliven your descriptions
- ☑ a conclusion that complements your introduction

Your revised character study should be free of
- ☑ details that do not support your impression of the character
- ☑ passages that tell your opinion of the character without showing his or her qualities
- ☑ errors in grammar, usage, and mechanics

EDITING/PROOFREADING

TECHNOLOGY TIP
Spell check is helpful, but it can't detect misused homonyms such as *there* and *their.* Check for those types of mistakes yourself.

When your character study presents the character as you want it to, use the **Proofreading Checklist** on the inside back cover of this book to help you mark errors in grammar, usage, mechanics, and spelling.

Grammar Hint

Take special care to make subjects and verbs agree in number when a phrase separates them.

INCORRECT: *The cats in the yard was very pretty.*
CORRECT: *The cats in the yard were very pretty.*

- For more about subject-verb agreement, see **Language Handbook,** p. R16.

Complete Student Model

For a complete version of the student model, see **Writing Workshop Models,** p. R109.

STUDENT MODEL

The crisp, yellow clapboard house with the saging [g] roof tiles ~~were~~ was easily identified.

Complete Student Model on p. R109.

PUBLISHING/PRESENTING

PRESENTING TIP
Illustrate your character study with a portrait of your subject.

Present your character study in a way that suits the audience you want to reach. For the students in your class, you might "introduce" your character as if you were at a dinner where the character will receive an award. Or join together with your classmates to create a magazine of character studies. For an audience of local readers, you might submit your work as a "profile" for the opinion page of the local newspaper.

Reflecting

Consider whether you could use your character sketch as a starting place for a short story. Before you put it away, read it again. If you were to make one more draft, what would you change? Why? Instead of revising the study again, plan to use your answer to improve your next piece of writing.

Save your work for your portfolio.

Theme 3 Looking Back

People don't experience events just once. Instead, they relive them again and again in their memory. When you look back, long-past occurrences can gain importance or shift in meaning. The selections in this theme include characters who remember specific events from their pasts that color their present lives. What do you think is more real, the way an event actually happens or the way you remember it?

THEME PROJECTS

Interdisciplinary Project

History: Communities Past Just as an individual can look back, citizens can reflect on local, national, and global events from the past.

1. Identify where and when three of the stories in this theme take place.
2. Research what affected life in each setting—current events, trends in the arts and media, jobs and technologies.
3. Using both words and images, present your findings. You may want to create a poster or other visual display.

Multimedia Project

Author Presentation Create a multimedia presentation about one author from this theme.

1. Gather information and images about your chosen author.
2. Make a visual such as a time-line to present interesting facts about the author's life.
3. Organize and present your work.

Untitled. Joel Peter Johnson (b. 1962). Oil and acrylic on board.

Before You Read

The Bass, the River, and Sheila Mant

Reading Focus

The Roman general Scipio Africanus wrote, "I am never less at leisure than when at leisure, nor less alone than when I am alone." What do you think he meant?

Discuss With a small group of classmates, discuss the meaning of this quotation and whether it might hold true for some people today.

Setting a Purpose Read to learn how one person feels about his leisure-time activity.

Building Background

The Time and Place

This story is set in the early 1960s on and around the Connecticut River, which runs the border between New Hampshire and Vermont.

Did You Know?

The largemouth black bass of New England likes warm, slow-moving rivers and muddy-bottomed, weedy lakes. During the day, it swims in the deeper, shaded areas of the water, moving into shallower areas at night. The average largemouth bass lives about eight years, measures just over fourteen inches long, and weighs one and a half pounds–but some bass weigh as much as eleven pounds! Most bass fishers are passionate about their sport: the fish are challenging to catch but delicious to eat.

Vocabulary Preview

pensive (pen′ siv) *adj.* thinking deeply, often sadly; p. 200
dubious (do͞o′ bē əs) *adj.* skeptical; feeling doubt; p. 202
filial (fil′ ē əl) *adj.* appropriate to a son or daughter; p. 203
surreptitiously (sur′ əp tish′ əs lē) *adv.* secretly or slyly; p. 203
inhibition (in′ i bish′ ən) *n.* a restraint on one's natural impulses; p. 203
lithe (līth) *adj.* limber; bending easily; p. 205

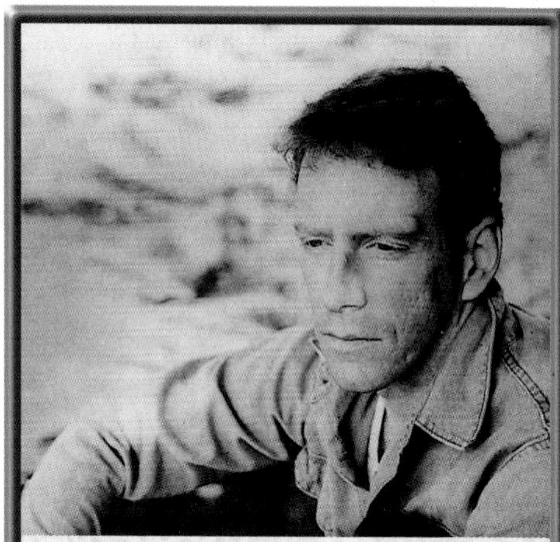

Meet W. D. Wetherell

Fishing enthusiast W. D. Wetherell has been hooking readers since the early 1980s. Having tried every job from movie extra to tour guide, Wetherell eventually found his calling as a full-time writer of short stories, essays, and novels. Wetherell has said that his work is ". . . a testament of faith—in the power of art in general, and in the importance of fiction in particular." His works often focus on the complexity of human dreams and disappointments. His work has earned him many prestigious awards, including the O. Henry Award for fiction.

W. D. Wetherell was born in 1948. This story appears in a prize-winning collection of short stories, The Man Who Loved Levittown.

The Bass, the River, and Sheila Mant

W. D. Wetherell

THERE WAS A SUMMER IN MY LIFE when the only creature that seemed lovelier to me than a largemouth bass was Sheila Mant. I was fourteen. The Mants had rented the cottage next to ours on the river; with their parties, their frantic games of softball, their constant comings and goings, they appeared to me denizens[1] of a brilliant existence.

"Too noisy by half," my mother quickly decided, but I would have given anything to be invited to one of their parties, and when my parents went to bed I would sneak through the woods to their hedge and stare enchanted at the candlelit swirl of white dresses and bright, paisley skirts.

Sheila was the middle daughter—at seventeen, all but out of reach. She would spend her days sunbathing on a float my Uncle Sierbert had moored in their cove, and before July was over I had learned all her moods. If she lay flat on the diving board with her hand trailing idly in the water, she was pensive, not to be disturbed. On her side, her head propped up by her arm, she was observant, considering those around her with a look that seemed queenly and severe. Sitting up, arms tucked around her long, suntanned legs, she was approachable, but barely, and it was only in those glorious moments when she stretched herself prior to entering the water that her various suitors found the courage to come near.

1. A *denizen* (den′ ə zən) is an inhabitant, or occupant.

These were many. The Dartmouth heavyweight crew[2] would scull[3] by her house on their way upriver, and I think all eight of them must have been in love with her at various times during the summer; the coxswain would curse at them through his megaphone, but without effect—there was always a pause in their pace when they passed Sheila's float. I suppose to these jaded twenty-year-olds she seemed the incarnation of innocence and youth,[4] while to me she appeared unutterably suave, the epitome of sophistication.[5] I was on the swim team at school, and to win her attention would do endless laps between my house and the Vermont shore, hoping she would notice the beauty of my flutter kick, the power of my crawl. Finishing, I would boost myself up onto our dock and glance casually over toward her, but she was never watching, and the miraculous day she was, I immediately climbed the diving board and did my best tuck and a half for her, and continued diving until she had left and the sun went down and my longing was like a madness and I couldn't stop.

Did You Know?
The *coxswain* (kok′ sən) steers the boat and directs the timing of the team's oar strokes.

It was late August by the time I got up the nerve to ask her out. The tortured will-I's, won't-I's, the agonized indecision over what to say, the false starts toward her house and embarrassed retreats—the details of these have been seared from my memory, and the only part I remember clearly is emerging from the woods toward dusk while they were playing softball on their lawn, as bashful and frightened as a unicorn.

Sheila was stationed halfway between first and second, well outside the infield. She didn't seem surprised to see me—as a matter of fact, she didn't seem to see me at all.

"If you're playing second base, you should move closer," I said.

She turned—I took the full brunt of her long red hair and well-spaced freckles.

"I'm playing outfield," she said, "I don't like the responsibility of having a base."

"Yeah, I can understand that," I said, though I couldn't. "There's a band in Dixford tomorrow night at nine. Want to go?"

One of her brothers sent the ball sailing over the leftfielder's head; she stood and watched it disappear toward the river.

"You have a car?" she said, without looking up.

I played my master stroke. "We'll go by canoe."

I spent all of the following day polishing it. I turned it upside down on our lawn and rubbed every inch with Brillo, hosing off the dirt, wiping it with chamois until it gleamed as bright as aluminum ever gleamed.[6] About five, I slid it into the water, arranging cushions near the bow so Sheila could lean on them if she was in one of her pensive moods, propping up my father's transistor radio by the middle thwart[7] so we could have music

2. *Dartmouth heavyweight crew* refers to one of the rowing teams from Dartmouth College in Hanover, New Hampshire.
3. Here, *scull* means "propel by rowing."
4. The narrator imagines that the college men, being dulled by long experience *(jaded)* with women, see Sheila as the personification or purest form *(incarnation)* of adolescent innocence.
5. The narrator believes Sheila is polished and gracious (*suave*) beyond words *(unutterably)* and the *epitome* (i pit′ ə mē), or perfect example, of mature, worldly experience.
6. *Brillo* is the brand name of a steel-wool pad used to scrub and clean, and *chamois* (sham′ ē) is a very soft, absorbent leather used to dry and polish.
7. In a canoe, a *thwart* is a brace running from side to side.

Vocabulary
pensive (pen′ siv) *adj.* thinking deeply, often sadly

Country House with Canoe, 1996. Ed Labadie. Watercolor on paper, 17½ x 10½ in. Collection of the artist.

Viewing the painting: How well does the scene in this painting match your image of the story's setting?

Siri, 1970. Andrew Wyeth. Tempera on panel, 30 x 30½ in. Brandywine River Museum, Chadds Ford, PA.

Viewing the painting: How might the girl in the painting be like Sheila Mant? How might she be different from Sheila?

when we came back. Automatically, without thinking about it, I mounted my Mitchell reel on my Pfleuger spinning rod and stuck it in the stern.

I say automatically, because I never went anywhere that summer without a fishing rod. When I wasn't swimming laps to impress Sheila, I was back in our driveway practicing casts, and when I wasn't practicing casts, I was tying the line to Tosca, our springer spaniel, to test the reel's drag, and when I wasn't doing any of those things, I was fishing the river for bass.

Too nervous to sit at home, I got in the canoe early and started paddling in a huge circle that would get me to Sheila's dock around eight. As automatically as I brought along my rod, I tied on a big Rapala plug, let it down into the water, let out some line and immediately forgot all about it.

It was already dark by the time I glided up to the Mants' dock. Even by day the river was quiet, most of the summer people preferring Sunapee or one of the other nearby lakes, and at night it was a solitude difficult to believe, a corridor of hidden life that ran between banks like a tunnel. Even the stars were part of it. They weren't as sharp anywhere else; they seemed to have chosen the river as a guide on their slow wheel toward morning, and in the course of the summer's fishing, I had learned all their names.

I was there ten minutes before Sheila appeared. I heard the slam of their screen door first, then saw her in the spotlight as she came slowly down the path. As beautiful as she was on the float, she was even lovelier now—her white dress went perfectly with her hair, and complimented her figure even more than her swimsuit.

It was her face that bothered me. It had on its delightful fullness a very dubious expression.

"Look," she said. "I can get Dad's car."

"It's faster this way," I lied. "Parking's tense up there. Hey, it's safe. I won't tip it or anything."

She let herself down reluctantly into the bow. I was glad she wasn't facing me. When her eyes were on me, I felt like diving in the river again from agony and joy.

Vocabulary
dubious (do͞o′ bē əs) *adj.* skeptical; feeling doubt

I pried the canoe away from the dock and started paddling upstream. There was an extra paddle in the bow, but Sheila made no move to pick it up. She took her shoes off, and dangled her feet over the side.

Ten minutes went by.

"What kind of band?" she said.

"It's sort of like folk music. You'll like it."

"Eric Caswell's going to be there. He strokes number four."[8]

"No kidding?" I said. I had no idea who she meant.

"What's that sound?" she said, pointing toward shore.

"Bass. That splashing sound?"

"Over there."

"Yeah, bass. They come into the shallows at night to chase frogs and moths and things. Big largemouths. *Micropetrus salmonides*,"[9] I added, showing off.

"I think fishing's dumb," she said, making a face. "I mean, it's boring and all. Definitely dumb."

Now I have spent a great deal of time in the years since wondering why Sheila Mant should come down so hard on fishing. Was her father a fisherman? Her antipathy[10] toward fishing nothing more than normal filial rebellion? Had she tried it once? A messy encounter with worms? It doesn't matter. What does, is that at that fragile moment in time I would have given anything not to appear dumb in Sheila's severe and unforgiving eyes.

She hadn't seen my equipment yet. What I *should* have done, of course, was push the canoe in closer to shore and carefully slide the rod into some branches where I could pick it up again in the morning. Failing that, I could have surreptitiously dumped the whole outfit overboard, written off the forty or so dollars as love's tribute.[11] What I actually *did* do was gently lean forward, and slowly, ever so slowly, push the rod back through my legs toward the stern where it would be less conspicuous.

It must have been just exactly what the bass was waiting for. Fish will trail a lure sometimes, trying to make up their mind whether or not to attack, and the slight pause in the plug's speed caused by my adjustment was tantalizing enough to overcome the bass's inhibitions. My rod, safely out of sight at last, bent double. The line, tightly coiled, peeled off the spool with the shrill, tearing zip of a high-speed drill.

Four things occurred to me at once. One, that it was a bass. Two, that it was a big bass. Three, that it was the biggest bass I had ever hooked. Four, that Sheila Mant must not know.

"What was that?" she said, turning half around.

"Uh, what was what?"

"That buzzing noise."

"Bats."

She shuddered, quickly drew her feet back into the canoe. Every instinct I had told me to pick up the rod and strike back at the bass, but there was no need to—it was already solidly hooked. Downstream, an awesome distance downstream, it jumped clear of the water, landing with a concussion heavy enough to ripple

8. Eric *strokes,* or rows, in the *number four* position in the racing scull.
9. The narrator probably means to say *Micropterus salmoides* (mī crop′ tə rəs sal moi′ dēz), the scientific name for the largemouth bass.
10. *Antipathy* (an tip′ ə thē) means "intense dislike."
11. Here, a *tribute* is a payment showing devotion, respect, or gratitude.

Vocabulary

filial (fil′ ē əl) *adj.* appropriate to a son or daughter
surreptitiously (sur′ əp tish′ əs lē) *adv.* secretly or slyly
inhibition (in′ i bish′ ən) *n.* a restraint on one's natural impulses

the entire river. For a moment, I thought it was gone, but then the rod was bending again, the tip dancing into the water. Slowly, not making any motion that might alert Sheila, I reached down to tighten the drag.

While all this was going on, Sheila had begun talking and it was a few minutes before I was able to catch up with her train of thought.

"I went to a party there. These fraternity men. Katherine says I could get in there if I wanted. I'm thinking more of UVM or Bennington.[12] Somewhere I can ski."

The bass was slanting toward the rocks on the New Hampshire side by the ruins of Donaldson's boathouse. It had to be an old bass—a young one probably wouldn't have known the rocks were there. I brought the canoe back out into the middle of the river, hoping to head it off.

"That's neat," I mumbled. "Skiing. Yeah, I can see that."

"Eric said I have the figure to model, but I thought I should get an education first. I mean, it might be a while before I get started and all. I was thinking of getting my hair styled, more swept back? I mean, Ann-Margret?[13] Like hers, only shorter."

She hesitated. "Are we going backwards?"

We were. I had managed to keep the bass in the middle of the river away from the rocks, but it had plenty of room there, and for the first time a chance to exert its full strength. I quickly computed the weight necessary to draw a fully loaded canoe backwards—the thought of it made me feel faint.

"It's just the current," I said hoarsely. "No sweat or anything."

12. *UVM* refers to the University of Vermont at Burlington; *Bennington* is a small, private college, also in Vermont.

13. *Ann-Margret* is an actress and singer who was a young, glamorous movie star at the time of the story.

I dug in deeper with my paddle. Reassured, Sheila began talking about something else, but all my attention was taken up now with the fish. I could feel its desperation as the water grew shallower. I could sense the extra strain on the line, the frantic way it cut back and forth in the water. I could visualize what it looked like—the gape of its mouth, the flared gills and thick, vertical tail. The bass couldn't have encountered many forces in its long life that it wasn't capable of handling, and the unrelenting tug at its mouth must have been a source of great puzzlement and mounting panic.

Me, I had problems of my own. To get to Dixford, I had to paddle up a sluggish stream that came into the river beneath a covered bridge. There was a shallow sandbar at the mouth of this stream—weeds on one side, rocks on the other. Without doubt, this is where I would lose the fish.

"I have to be careful with my complexion. I tan, but in segments. I can't figure out if it's even worth it. I wouldn't even do it probably. I saw Jackie Kennedy[14] in Boston and she wasn't tan at all."

Taking a deep breath, I paddled as hard as I could for the middle, deepest part of the bar. I could have threaded the eye of a needle with the canoe, but the pull on the stern threw me off and I overcompensated—the canoe veered left and scraped bottom. I pushed the paddle down and shoved. A moment of hesitation . . . a moment more. . . . The canoe shot clear into the deeper water of the stream. I immediately looked down at the rod. It was bent in the same, tight arc—miraculously, the bass was still on.

14. *Jackie Kennedy* (1929–1994), President John F. Kennedy's wife, was admired by many as a role model and style setter.

The moon was out now. It was low and full enough that its beam shone directly on Sheila there ahead of me in the canoe, washing her in a creamy, luminous glow. I could see the lithe, easy shape of her figure. I could see the way her hair curled down off her shoulders, the proud, alert tilt of her head, and all these things were as a tug on my heart. Not just Sheila, but the aura[15] she carried about her of parties and casual touchings and grace. Behind me, I could feel the strain of the bass, steadier now, growing weaker, and this was another tug on my heart, not just the bass but the beat of the river and the slant of the stars and the smell of the night, until finally it seemed I would be torn apart between longings, split in half. Twenty yards ahead of us was the road, and once I pulled the canoe up on shore, the bass would be gone, irretrievably gone. If instead I stood up, grabbed the rod and started pumping, I would have it—as tired as the bass was, there was no chance it could get away. I reached down for the rod, hesitated, looked up to where Sheila was stretching herself lazily toward the sky, her small breasts rising beneath the soft fabric of her dress, and the tug was too much for me, and quicker than it takes to write down, I pulled the penknife from my pocket and cut the line in half.

15. Here, Sheila's *aura* is a sort of atmosphere or quality that the narrator senses around her.

With a sick, nauseous feeling in my stomach, I saw the rod unbend.

"My legs are sore," Sheila whined. "Are we there yet?"

Through a superhuman effort of self-control, I was able to beach the canoe and help Sheila off. The rest of the night is much foggier. We walked to the fair—there was the smell of popcorn, the sound of guitars. I may have danced once or twice with her, but all I really remember is her coming over to me once the music was done to explain that she would be going home in Eric Caswell's Corvette.

"Okay," I mumbled.

For the first time that night she looked at me, really looked at me.

"You're a funny kid, you know that?"

Funny. Different. Dreamy. Odd. How many times was I to hear that in the years to come, all spoken with the same quizzical, half-accusatory tone Sheila used then. Poor Sheila! Before the month was over, the spell she cast over me was gone, but the memory of that lost bass haunted me all summer and haunts me still. There would be other Sheila Mants in my life, other fish, and though I came close once or twice, it was these secret, hidden tuggings in the night that claimed me, and I never made the same mistake again.

Vocabulary

lithe (līth) *adj.* limber; bending easily

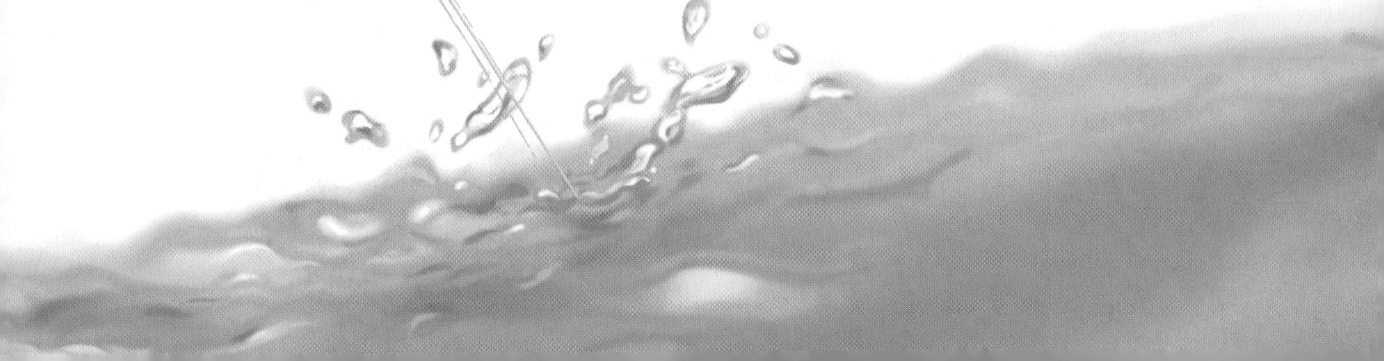

Responding to Literature

Personal Response

Did you find this story to be humorous or serious? Or was it, perhaps, a little of both? Describe your impressions.

Analyzing Literature

Recall

1. How old is the narrator? How old is Sheila Mant?
2. Which of the narrator's special hobbies or skills does he openly reveal to Sheila, and which does he keep secret?
3. What does Sheila talk about on the way to Dixford?
4. Explain why the narrator says, ". . . it seemed I would be torn apart between longings, split in half."
5. How does the narrator's date with Sheila end?

Interpret

6. What makes Sheila Mant so attractive to the narrator, and why is she "all but out of reach"?
7. How would you describe the importance of fishing to the narrator? Use details from the story to support your answer.
8. What does Sheila's **dialogue** reveal about her? (See page R4.)
9. In your opinion, why does the narrator make the choice he does?
10. Explain the meaning of the last line of the story. Be sure to explain what the "hidden tuggings" are and what "mistake" the narrator never made again.

Evaluate and Connect

11. In what ways is the narrator like a bass caught on Sheila Mant's "hook"?
12. How does the author create sympathy for the narrator?
13. In your experience, when do people feel free to be themselves, and when do they try to be someone they're not?
14. Think about your response to the Reading Focus on page 198. Do you think that the narrator would agree with Scipio Africanus? Explain.
15. Do you think that the narrator made the right choice in putting aside his interests for Sheila? When do you think it is appropriate to put aside one's own interests for another, and when might it be wrong to do so?

Literary ELEMENTS

Falling Action and Resolution

In a story's plot, the **falling action** shows what happens to the characters after the climax. In "The Bass, the River, and Sheila Mant," the falling action begins after the narrator chooses between Sheila and the bass. The **resolution** is the part of the plot that concludes the falling action. It suggests or reveals the final outcome of the conflict.

1. What events make up this story's falling action?
2. In your opinion, is Sheila's comment that the narrator is a "funny kid" part of the falling action or part of the resolution? Why?
3. Did you find the resolution surprising, or was it predictable? Explain your answer.

- See **Literary Terms Handbook,** pp. R5 and R10.

Literary Criticism

One critic writes that W. D. Wetherell's "often surprising offerings read like fables." What does "The Bass, the River, and Sheila Mant" have in common with a fable? Why might Wetherell have chosen to write in this style? Write an analysis of the story, using specific examples to support your ideas about its fable-like style.

Literature and Writing

Writing About Literature

Analyzing Author Purpose Why do you think W. D. Wetherell might have wanted to tell this story? Do you think that his goal might have been to reveal how painful adolescent crushes can be–and how fleeting? Or did he want to share his passion for fishing, proving that a personal passion for a hobby can provide a lifetime of pleasure? Write a brief analysis of the author's purpose, using details and information from the story to support your ideas.

Creative Writing

Reel It In Write a new ending to this story in which the narrator chooses to reel in the fish. Consider the following questions before you write. How will the action play out? How will Sheila react? How will the narrator feel about his decision when he looks back on it many years later? Exchange your writing with a classmate, and discuss how your endings are alike or different.

Extending Your Response

Literature Groups

Sentimental Survey Survey your group's opinion about the following question: Was the narrator's decision to cut the fish from the line romantic or foolish? Mark down each group member's opinion, then have each take a turn defending his or her opinion to the group. After all have had a chance to speak, survey the group again. Have any group members changed their minds? If so, why?

Performing

Her Side of the Story If Sheila were asked what happened on the date, what would she say? How would she say it? With a partner, write a dramatic monologue for Sheila that answers these questions. To help you choose gestures and an appropriate tone of voice, study Sheila's physical movements and dialogue in the story. Decide who will be the director and who will be the actor and then rehearse and perform the monologue for your classmates.

Interdisciplinary Activity

Biology: River Life From the story, you've learned that the largemouth bass is a freshwater fish living in rivers. What other types of fish and plant life thrive in rivers? How would you describe the river's food chain? Research the ecosystem of a river and present your findings to the class. Create visual aids to assist your presentation.

Reading Further

If you'd like to read more by W. D. Wetherell, you might enjoy these works:

Short Stories: "Volpi's Farewell," from the collection *The Man Who Loved Levittown,* tells of a father trying to understand his son.

"What Peter Saw," from the collection *Hyannis Boat and Other Stories,* tells about an important summer in the life of a twelve-year-old boy.

Essay: "Upland Stream," from the book of the same name, describes Wetherell's favorite New Hampshire creek.

Save your work for your portfolio.

Skill Minilessons

GRAMMAR AND LANGUAGE • Avoiding Double Comparisons

When comparing two things, either add *-er* to the modifier or place *more* before it. For example, *big* becomes *bigger;* and *delicious* becomes *more delicious.* When comparing three or more things, either add *-est* or *most: biggest* and *most delicious.* In general, add *-er* or *-est* to modifiers of one or two syllables, and use *more* and *most* before modifiers of three or more syllables.

A double comparison occurs when you use both comparing forms at the same time: *He was more stronger than his opponent.* Avoid making this mistake by using only one comparing form with each modifier.

PRACTICE On your paper, rewrite each sentence below to eliminate the double comparison.

1. The only creature more beautifuler than a largemouth bass was Sheila Mant.
2. I did my most impressivest tuck and a half for her.
3. Move more closer to the base if you're playing second.
4. It's more faster this way.
5. It was the most biggest bass I had ever hooked.

For more about comparative and superlative adjectives, see **Language Handbook,** p. R37.

READING AND THINKING • Evaluating

Evaluating means forming opinions and making judgments while you are reading—not just after you have finished. To evaluate, ask yourself whether what is happening makes sense to you and whether you agree with a character's decisions or actions. For example, when reading about how the narrator tries to impress Sheila Mant, you might ask yourself, "Is this a realistic reaction for a fourteen-year-old boy?" In this way, you are deciding whether the characters are believable and whether the author's writing is true to life—you are *evaluating.*

PRACTICE Write a brief evaluation for each action or decision below.

1. The narrator lies to Sheila, saying it's faster to go to Dixford by canoe.
2. The narrator brings his fishing pole on the date.
3. The narrator does not reveal that he has a bass on his fishing line.

For more about comprehension skills, see **Reading Handbook,** pp. R82–R94.

VOCABULARY • Analogies

An analogy is a comparison based on the relationships between things or ideas. To complete an analogy, decide what relationship exists between the first two things or ideas. Then apply that relationship to another pair of words and see if it is the same. For example, read the analogy below.

brave : courage :: inquisitive : curiosity

Brave people have *courage; inquisitive* people have *curiosity.*

For more about analogies, see **Communications Skills Handbook,** p. R77.

PRACTICE Choose the word that best completes each analogy below.

1. muscular : strength :: lithe :
   a. cleverness b. dishonesty c. flexibility
2. maternal : mother :: filial :
   a. child b. father c. friend
3. considerate : thoughtfulness :: dubious :
   a. doubts b. shyness c. fears
4. angrily : glare :: surreptitiously :
   a. stare b. peek c. gaze

Vo•cab•u•lar•y Skills

Using Context Clues

Anyone who reads will sometimes come across unfamiliar words. You can look them up in a dictionary, but that's not always convenient–or necessary. The help you need may be right on the page you're reading, in the form of **context clues.**

A word's "context" is the sentence or paragraph in which it appears. Often, the context contains clues, or information that can help you figure out the meaning of an unfamiliar word. There are five main types of context clues.

A. Julie's elation showed: we could see that she was very happy.

Here, the context implies a *definition* of the word.

B. The gold medalist erupted with elation. He shouted with delight; he wept with joy; he danced with happiness.

This context provides *examples* that imply the word's meaning.

C. Skiing gives me a feeling of elation, just as surfing gives me a feeling of bliss.

Through a *comparison,* this context implies that elation is similar to bliss.

D. Maurice went from misery to elation in an instant–a reversal that almost made him dizzy.

Here, a *contrast* implies that elation is the opposite of misery.

E. I could not hide my elation when I won the lottery.

This context mentions a *cause* (winning the lottery), which helps you to deduce that its *effect* (elation) means joy or happiness.

When context clues aren't enough, try using information you already have. For example, if you read that "Compact discs have made records obsolete," you can use what you know about musical recordings to infer that *obsolete* means "outdated" or "no longer useful."

EXERCISE

For each item below, use context clues to deduce the meaning of the underlined word. Write a brief definition or synonym for the word, and identify which type of context clue you used.

1. Because the narrator doesn't want Sheila to see his fishing equipment, he conceals it.
2. The narrator is a proficient fisher. He catches fish nearly every time he casts.
3. The narrator has a love for fishing, unlike Sheila's disdain for it.
4. Sheila is loath to enter the canoe, just as the narrator is extremely hesitant to cut the fish loose.
5. The narrator scoured the canoe, cleaning it until it gleamed.

MEDIA connection

Magazine Article

Has an older person's support or sacrifice ever helped you pursue a personal goal? In the article that follows, a successful athlete discovers the power of her mother's love and sacrifice.

Courage That Runs in the Family

by Barbara Jones—*Good Housekeeping*, May 1996

Two years ago, accepting the award for the Big East Player of the Year at a banquet in Hartford, Connecticut, basketball star Rebecca Lobo choked back tears. "This is for my mother," she said. "She's the real competitor." While 6' 4" Rebecca was scoring big points for the University of Connecticut, her mother, RuthAnn, was battling her own fierce opponent: breast cancer. Diagnosed in early December 1993, RuthAnn had waited several days—until after an especially important game—to break the news to Rebecca. "You take care of basketball," she told her, "and I'll take care of my health."

Her father taught Rebecca how to shoot hoops. But RuthAnn was the one who made her daughter's passion for sports possible.

[RuthAnn] dismisses any suggestion that she had some perfect formula for raising kids. Her toughest parenting challenge, she acknowledges, was handling her cancer.

Once she noticed the lump in her breast, things happened fast. A lumpectomy performed ten days after the disease was diagnosed and a mastectomy four days later were too late: the cancer had spread, and she needed extensive chemotherapy.

As her mother underwent aggressive chemotherapy, Rebecca found solace in basketball. Off the court, she couldn't make her mother well, but on the court, "I could put that ball in the basket," she says. Meanwhile, throughout three months of treatment, RuthAnn managed to attend all of Rebecca's home games.

RuthAnn's doctor says the chemotherapy worked: her prognosis is good. Rebecca's and RuthAnn's tandem battles are the subject of their poignant and funny memoir, *The Home Team*. RuthAnn says that writing the book has helped her to know Rebecca even better.

"You live with someone, you mother her, yet there's so much depth to her I'd never have uncovered had we not done this," RuthAnn says.

The collaboration was a revelation for Rebecca too. "I hadn't known how scared my mom was of the cancer," she says. "Instead of asking us for anything, she asked us to lean on her, which still amazes me. I wouldn't have wanted to have any other mother, that's for sure."

Analyzing Media

1. What do you find most remarkable about RuthAnn?
2. How would it feel to discover that the person who was your role model also looked up to you? Explain.

Before You Read

Sweet Potato Pie

Reading Focus

Sometimes people draw conclusions about others based on visual clues, such as their style of clothes or the kind of backpacks they carry.

List Ideas In your experience, what possessions suggest status or importance? What suggests a lack of it? List your items in a chart like the one shown.

High Status Items	Low Status Items

Setting a Purpose Read to see how two brothers view symbols of social status.

Building Background

The Time and Place

This story is set in New York City in the mid-1900s. The narrator also reflects on his childhood in the South.

Did You Know?

Sharecropping was a farming system widely practiced in the South in the years between the Civil War and World War II. Landowners allowed formerly enslaved people to live on and farm a portion of their land in exchange for half the crop. When the landowner supplied the farm equipment, work animals, and seed, sharecroppers could only keep about one-third of the crop for themselves, the sale of which provided barely enough income to pay for basic necessities. In the 1940s, mechanized cotton harvesters ended the need for sharecroppers, sending hundreds of thousands to seek work in cities.

Vocabulary Preview

collective (kə lek′ tiv) *adj.* having to do with a group of persons or things; common; shared; p. 213
antiquity (an tik′ wə tē) *n.* an ancient time or times; p. 214
ubiquitous (ū bik′ wə təs) *adj.* seeming to be everywhere at once; p. 214
futilely (fū′ til ē) *adv.* uselessly; vainly; hopelessly; p. 214
apex (ā′ peks) *n.* the highest point; climax; p. 216

Meet Eugenia Collier

"Because racism is not over, writing still needs to define who we are as well as be popular."

Eugenia Collier experienced racism firsthand, attending segregated schools before college. Collier obtained her doctorate in 1976 and has gone on to teach at many colleges and universities. She is also an award-winning author of stories, essays, poems, and articles. Of her career, the author remarked, "The fact of my blackness is the core and center of my creativity. . . . I discovered the richness, the diversity, the beauty of my black heritage. This discovery has meant . . . a lifetime commitment."

Eugenia Collier was born in 1928. This story was first published in 1972.

Sweet Potato Pie

Eugenia Collier

FROM UP HERE ON THE FOURTEENTH FLOOR, my brother Charley looks like an insect scurrying among other insects. A deep feeling of love surges through me. Despite the distance, he seems to feel it, for he turns and scans the upper windows, but failing to find me, continues on his way.

I watch him moving quickly—gingerly,[1] it seems to me—down Fifth Avenue and around the corner to his shabby taxicab. In a moment he will be heading back uptown.

I turn from the window and flop down on the bed, shoes and all. Perhaps because of what happened this afternoon or maybe just because I see Charley so seldom, my thoughts hover over him like hummingbirds. The cheerful, impersonal tidiness of this room is a world away from Charley's walk-up flat in Harlem[2] and a hundred worlds from the bare, noisy shanty where he and the rest of us spent what there was of childhood. I close my eyes, and side by side I see the Charley of my boyhood and the Charley of this afternoon, as clearly as if I were looking at a split TV screen. Another surge of love, seasoned with gratitude, wells up in me.

As far as I know, Charley never had any childhood at all. The oldest children of sharecroppers never do. Mama and Pa were shadowy figures whose voices I heard vaguely in the morning when sleep was shallow and whom I glimpsed as they left for the field before I was fully awake or as they trudged wearily into the house at night when my lids were irresistibly heavy.

They came into sharp focus only on special occasions. One such occasion was the day when the crops were in and the sharecroppers were paid. In our cabin there was so much excitement in the air that even I, the "baby," responded to it. For weeks we had been running out of things that we could neither grow nor get on credit. On the evening of that day we waited anxiously for our parents' return. Then we would cluster around the rough wooden table—I on Lil's lap or clinging to Charley's neck, little Alberta nervously tugging her plait,[3] Jamie crouched at Mama's elbow, like a panther about to spring, and all seven of us silent for once, waiting. Pa would place the money on the table—gently, for it was made from the sweat of their bodies and from their children's tears. Mama would count it out in little piles, her dark face stern and, I think now, beautiful. Not with the hollow beauty of well-modeled features but with the strong radiance of one who has suffered and never yielded.

"This for store bill," she would mutter, making a little pile. "This for c'llection. This for piece o'gingham . . ."[4] and so on,

1. *Gingerly* means "with caution; carefully."
2. *Harlem* is a section of New York City mainly inhabited by African Americans and Hispanics.

3. A *plait* (plāt) is a braid or pigtail.
4. *Gingham* (ging′ əm) is checked, striped, or plaid cotton fabric.

Field Workers. Ellis Wilson (1899–1977). Oil on Masonite, 29¾ x 34⅞ in. National Museum of American Art, Washington, DC.

Viewing the painting: How is your view of the narrator's family similar to or different from the family represented in the painting?

stretching the money as tight over our collective needs as Jamie's outgrown pants were stretched over my bottom. "Well, that's the crop." She would look up at Pa at last. "It'll do." Pa's face would relax, and a general grin flitted from child to child. We would survive, at least for the present.

The other time when my parents were solid entities was at church. On Sundays we would don our threadbare Sunday-go-to-meeting clothes and tramp, along with neighbors similarly attired, to the Tabernacle Baptist Church, the frail edifice of bare boards held together by God knows what, which was all that my parents ever knew of security and future promise.

Being the youngest and therefore the most likely to err, I was plopped between my father and my mother on the long wooden bench. They sat huge and eternal like twin mountains at my sides. I remember my

Vocabulary

collective (kə lek′ tiv) *adj.* having to do with a group of persons or things; common; shared father's still, black profile silhouetted against the sunny window, looking back into dark recesses of time, into some dim antiquity, like an ancient ceremonial mask. My mother's face, usually sternly set, changed with the varying nuances[5] of her emotion, its planes shifting, shaped by the soft highlights of the sanctuary, as she progressed from a subdued "amen" to a loud "Help me, Jesus" wrung from the depths of her gaunt frame.

My early memories of my parents are associated with special occasions. The contours of my everyday were shaped by Lil and Charley, the oldest children, who rode herd on the rest of us while Pa and Mama toiled in fields not their own. Not until years later did I realize that Lil and Charley were little more than children themselves.

Lil had the loudest, screechiest voice in the county. When she yelled, "Boy, you better git yourself in here!" you *got* yourself in there. It was Lil who caught and bathed us, Lil who fed us and sent us to school, Lil who punished us when we needed punishing and comforted us when we needed comforting. If her voice was loud, so was her laughter. When she laughed, everybody laughed. And when Lil sang, everybody listened.

Charley was taller than anybody in the world, including, I was certain, God. From his shoulders, where I spent considerable time in the earliest years, the world had a different perspective: I looked down at tops of heads rather than at the undersides of chins. As I grew older, Charley became more father than brother. Those days return in fragments of splintered memory: Charley's slender dark hands whittling a toy from a chunk of wood, his face thin and intense, brown as the loaves Lil baked when there was flour. Charley's quick fingers guiding a stick of charred kindling over a bit of scrap paper, making a wondrous picture take shape—Jamie's face or Alberta's rag doll or the spare figure of our bony brown dog. Charley's voice low and terrible in the dark, telling ghost stories so delightfully dreadful that later in the night the moan of the wind through the chinks in the wall sent us scurrying to the security of Charley's pallet, Charley's sleeping form.

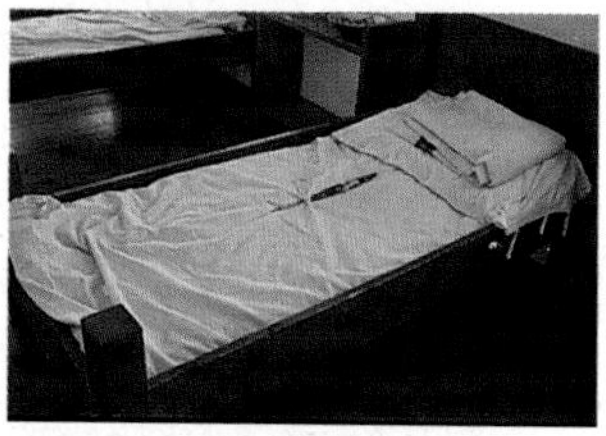

Did You Know?
A *pallet* is a crude bed or mattress, usually filled with straw.

Some memories are more than fragmentary. I can still feel the *whap* of the wet dish rag across my mouth. Somehow I developed a stutter, which Charley was determined to cure. Someone had told him that an effective cure was to slap the stutterer across the mouth with a sopping wet dish rag. Thereafter whenever I began, "Let's g-g-g--," *whap!* from nowhere would come the ubiquitous rag. Charley would always insist, "I don't want hurt you none, Buddy—" and *whap* again. I don't know when or why I stopped stuttering. But I stopped.

Already laid waste by poverty, we were easy prey for ignorance and superstition, which hunted us like hawks. We sought education feverishly—and, for most of us, futilely, for the sum total of our combined energies was required for mere brute survival.

5. A *nuance* (no͞o′ äns) is a slight shade of tone, expression, or meaning.

Vocabulary

antiquity (an tik′ wə tē) *n.* an ancient time or times
ubiquitous (ū bik′ wə təs) *adj.* seeming to be everywhere at once
futilely (fū′ til ē) *adv.* uselessly; vainly; hopelessly

Inevitably each child had to leave school and bear his share of the eternal burden.

Eventually the family's hopes for learning fastened on me, the youngest. I remember—I *think* I remember, for I could not have been more than five—one frigid day Pa, huddled on a rickety stool before the coal stove, took me on his knee and studied me gravely. I was a skinny little thing, they tell me, with large, solemn eyes.

"Well, boy," Pa said at last, "if you got to depend on your looks for what you get out'n this world, you just as well lay down right now." His hand was rough from the plow, but gentle as it touched my cheek. "Lucky for you, you got a *mind*. And that's something ain't everybody got. You go to school, boy, get yourself some learning. Make something out'n yourself. Ain't nothing you can't do if you got learning."

Charley was determined that I would break the chain of poverty, that I would "be somebody." As we worked our small vegetable garden in the sun or pulled a bucket of brackish[6] water from the well, Charley would tell me, "You ain gon be no poor farmer, Buddy. You gon be a teacher or maybe a doctor or a lawyer. One thing, bad as you is you ain gon be no preacher."

I loved school with a desperate passion, which became more intense when I began to realize what a monumental struggle it was for my parents and brothers and sisters to keep me there. The cramped, dingy classroom became a battleground where I was victorious. I stayed on top of my class. With glee I outread, out-figured, and out-spelled the country boys who mocked my poverty, calling me "the boy with eyes in back of his head"—the "eyes" being the perpetual holes in my hand-me-down pants.

As the years passed, the economic strain was eased enough to make it possible for me to go on to high school. There were fewer mouths to feed, for one thing: Alberta went North to find work at sixteen; Jamie died at twelve.

I finished high school at the head of my class. For Mama and Pa and each of my brothers and sisters, my success was a personal triumph. One by one they came to me the week before commencement bringing crumpled dollar bills and coins long hoarded, muttering, "Here, Buddy, put this on your gradiation clothes." My graduation suit was the first suit that was all my own.

On graduation night our cabin (less crowded now) was a frantic collage of frayed nerves. I thought Charley would drive me mad.

"Buddy, you ain pressed out them pants right . . . Can't you git a better shine on them shoes? . . . Lord, you done messed up that tie!"

Overwhelmed by the combination of Charley's nerves and my own, I finally exploded. "Man, cut it out!" Abruptly he stopped tugging at my tie, and I was afraid I had hurt his feelings. "It's okay, Charley. Look, you're strangling me. The tie's okay."

Charley relaxed a little and gave a rather sheepish chuckle. "Sure, Buddy." He gave my shoulder a rough joggle. "But you gotta look good. You *somebody*."

My valedictory address[7] was the usual idealistic, sentimental nonsense. I have forgotten what I said that night, but the sight of Mama and Pa and the rest is like a lithograph[8] burned on my memory; Lil, her round face made beautiful by her proud smile; Pa, his head held high, eyes loving and fierce; Mama radiant. Years later when her shriveled hands were finally still, my mind kept coming back to her as she

6. *Brackish* water tastes bad.

7. A *valedictory address* is a graduation speech, traditionally given by the class's highest-ranked student—the valedictorian.

8. A *lithograph* is a picture printed by a process in which part of a flat surface is treated to retain ink, and part is treated to repel it.

was now. I believe this moment was the apex of her entire life. All of them, even Alberta down from Baltimore—different now, but united with them in her pride. And Charley, on the end of the row, still somehow the protector of them all. Charley, looking as if he were in the presence of something sacred.

As I made my way through the carefully rehearsed speech it was as if part of me were standing outside watching the whole thing—their proud, work-weary faces, myself wearing the suit that was their combined strength and love and hope: Lil with her lovely, low-pitched voice, Charley with the hands of an artist, Pa and Mama with God knows what potential lost with their sweat in the fields. I realized in that moment that I wasn't necessarily the smartest—only the youngest.

And the luckiest. The war came along, and I exchanged three years of my life (including a fair amount of my blood and a great deal of pain) for the GI Bill[9] and a college education. Strange how time can slip by like water flowing through your fingers. One by one the changes came—the old house empty at last, the rest of us scattered; for me, marriage, graduate school, kids, a professorship, and by now a thickening waistline and thinning hair. My mind spins off the years, and I am back to this afternoon and today's Charley—still long and lean, still gentle-eyed, still my greatest fan, and still determined to keep me on the ball.

I didn't tell Charley I would be at a professional meeting in New York and would surely visit; he and Bea would have spent days in fixing up, and I would have had to be company. No, I would drop in on them, take them by surprise before they had a chance to stiffen up. I was anxious to see them—it had been so long. Yesterday and this morning were taken up with meetings in the posh Fifth Avenue hotel—a place we could not have dreamed in our boyhood. Late this afternoon I shook loose and headed for Harlem, hoping that Charley still came home for a few hours before his evening run. Leaving the glare and glitter of downtown, I entered the subway which lurks like the dark, inscrutable *id*[10] beneath the surface of the city. When I emerged, I was in Harlem.

Whenever I come to Harlem I feel somehow as if I were coming home—to some mythic ancestral home. The problems are real, the people are real—yet there is some mysterious epic[11] quality about Harlem, as if all Black people began and ended there, as if each had left something of himself. As if in Harlem the very heart of Blackness pulsed its beautiful tortured rhythms. Joining the throngs of people that saunter Lenox Avenue late afternoons, I headed for Charley's apartment. Along the way I savored the panorama of Harlem—women with shopping bags trudging wearily home; little kids flitting saucily through the crowd; groups of adolescent boys striding boldly along—some boisterous, some ominously silent; tables of merchandise spread on the sidewalks with hawkers singing their siren songs[12] of irresistible bargains; a blaring microphone sending forth waves of words to draw passersby into a restless bunch around a slender young man whose eyes have seen Truth; defeated men standing around on street corners or sitting on

9. The *G.I. Bill* of Rights provided educational and economic assistance to returning World War II soldiers.

10. In psychiatry, *id* is the part of the personality that is associated with the most natural, primitive, and (to most people) mysterious drives for pleasure and satisfaction.

11. Here, *epic* means "majestic" or "heroic."

12. In mythology, *siren songs* were sung by sea nymphs (who were part bird, part woman), and sailors who heard these irresistible songs were drawn to their destruction.

Vocabulary

apex (ā′ peks) *n.* the highest point; climax

Rooftops (No. 1, This is Harlem), 1942–43. Jacob Lawrence. Gouache on paper, 14⅜ x 21⅞ in. Hirshhorn Museum and Sculpture Garden, Washington, DC.

Viewing the art: **List three or four impressions about Harlem made by this scene. Does this picture fit Buddy's description of Harlem? Explain.**

steps, heads down, hands idle; posters announcing Garvey Day;[13] "Buy Black" stamped on pavements; store windows bright with things African; stores still boarded up, a livid[14] scar from last year's rioting. There was a terrible tension in the air; I thought of how quickly dry timber becomes a roaring fire from a single spark.

I mounted the steps of Charley's building—old and in need of paint, like all the rest—and pushed the button to his apartment. The graffiti on the dirty wall recorded the sexual fantasies of past visitors. Some of it was even a dialogue of sorts: Someone had scrawled, "Try Lola" and a telephone number, followed by a catalog of Lola's virtues. Someone else had written, "I tried Lola and she is a Dog." Charley's buzzer rang. I pushed open the door and mounted the urine-scented stairs.

"Well, do Jesus—it's Buddy!" roared Charley as I arrived on the third floor. "Bea! Bea! Come here, girl, it's Buddy!" And somehow I was simultaneously shaking Charley's hand, getting clapped on the back, and being buried in the fervor of Bea's gigantic hug. They swept me from the hall into their dim apartment.

"Lord, Buddy, what you doing here? Whyn't you tell me you was coming to New York?" His face was so lit up with pleasure that in spite of the inroads of time, he still looked like the Charley of years gone by, excited over a new litter of kittens.

"The place look a mess! Whyn't you let us know?" put in Bea, suddenly distressed.

"Looks fine to me, girl. And so do you!"

And she did. Bea is a fine-looking woman, plump and firm still, with rich brown skin and thick black hair.

"Mary, Lucy, look, Uncle Buddy's here!" Two neat little girls came shyly from the TV. Uncle Buddy was something of a celebrity in this house.

I hugged them heartily, much to their discomfort. "Charley, where you getting all these pretty women?"

We all sat in the warm kitchen, where Bea was preparing dinner. It felt good there. Beautiful odors mingled in the air. Charley sprawled in a chair near mine, his long arms and legs akimbo.[15] No longer shy, the tinier

13. *Garvey Day* is an unofficial holiday honoring Marcus Garvey (1887–1940), an African American leader in the 1920s.
14. *Livid* can mean both "angry" and "bruised."

15. *Akimbo* (ə kim′ bō) means "being in a bent, bowed, or arched position."

girl sat on my lap, while her sister darted here and there like a merry little water bug. Bea bustled about, managing to keep up with both the conversation and the cooking.

I told them about the conference I was attending and, knowing it would give them pleasure, I mentioned that I had addressed the group that morning. Charley's eyes glistened.

"You hear that, Bea?" he whispered. "Buddy done spoke in front of all them professors!"

"Sure I hear," Bea answered briskly, stirring something that was making an aromatic steam. "I bet he weren't even scared. I bet them professors learnt something, too."

We all chuckled. "Well anyway," I said, "I hope they did."

We talked about a hundred different things after that—Bea's job in the school cafeteria, my Jess and the kids, our scattered family.

"Seem like we don't git together no more, not since Mama and Pa passed on," said Charley sadly. "I ain't even got a Christmas card from Alberta for three-four year now."

"Well, ain't no two a y'all in the same city. An' everybody scratchin to make ends meet," Bea replied. "Ain't nobody got time to git together."

"Yeah, that's the way it goes, I guess," I said.

"But it sure is good to see you, Buddy. Say, look, Lil told me bout the cash you sent the children last winter when Jake was out of work all that time. She sure preciated it."

"Lord, man, as close as you and Lil stuck to me when I was a kid, I owed her that and more. Say, Bea, did I ever tell you about the time—" and we swung into the usual reminiscences.

They insisted that I stay for dinner. Persuading me was no hard job: fish fried golden, ham hocks and collard greens, corn bread—if I'd *tried* to leave, my feet wouldn't have taken me. It was good to sit there in Charley's kitchen, my coat and tie flung over a chair, surrounded by soul food and love.

"Say, Buddy, a couple months back I picked up a kid from your school."

"No stuff."

"I axed him did he know you. He say he was in your class last year."

"Did you get his name?"

"No, I didn't ax him that. Man, he told me you were the best teacher he had. He said you were one smart cat!"

"He told you that cause you're my brother."

"Your *brother*—I didn't tell him I was your brother. I said you was a old friend of mine."

I put my fork down and leaned over. "What you tell him *that* for?"

Charley explained patiently as he had explained things when I was a child and had missed an obvious truth. "I didn't want your students to know your brother wasn't nothing but a cab driver. You *somebody*."

"You're a nut," I said gently. "You should've told that kid the truth." I wanted to say, I'm proud of you, you've got more on the ball than most people I know, I wouldn't have been anything at all except for you. But he would have been embarrassed.

Bea brought in the dessert—homemade sweet potato pie! "Buddy, I must of knew you were coming! I just had a mind I wanted to make some sweet potato pie."

There's nothing in this world I like better than Bea's sweet potato pie! "Lord, girl, how you expect me to eat all that?"

The slice she put before me was outrageously big—and moist and covered with a light, golden crust—I ate it all.

"Bea, I'm gonna have to eat and run," I said at last.

Charley guffawed. "Much as you et, I don't see how you gonna *walk*, let alone *run*." He went out to get his cab from the garage several blocks away.

Bea was washing the tiny girl's face. "Wait a minute, Buddy, I'm gon give you the rest of that pie to take with you."

"Great!" I'd eaten all I could hold, but my *spirit* was still hungry for sweet potato pie.

Bea got out some waxed paper and wrapped up the rest of the pie. "That'll do you for a snack tonight." She slipped it into a brown paper bag.

I gave her a long good-bye hug. "Bea, I love you for a lot of things. Your cooking is one of them!" We had a last comfortable laugh together. I kissed the little girls and went outside to wait for Charley, holding the bag of pie reverently.

In a minute Charley's ancient cab limped to the curb. I plopped into the seat next to him, and we headed downtown. Soon we were assailed by the garish lights of New York on a sultry spring night. We chatted as Charley skillfully managed the heavy traffic. I looked at his long hands on the wheel and wondered what they could have done with artists' brushes.

We stopped a bit down the street from my hotel. I invited him in, but he said he had to get on with his evening run. But as I opened the door to get out, he commanded in the old familiar voice, "Buddy, you wait!"

For a moment I thought my fly was open or something. "What's wrong?"

"What's that you got there?"

I was bewildered. "That? You mean this bag? That's a piece of sweet potato pie Bea fixed for me."

"You ain't going through the lobby of no big hotel carrying no brown paper bag."

"Man, you *crazy!* Of course I'm going—Look, Bea fixed it for me—*That's my pie*—"

Charley's eyes were miserable. "Folks in that hotel don't go through the lobby carrying no brown paper bags. That's *country*. And you can't neither. You *somebody*, Buddy. You got to be *right*. Now, gimme that bag."

"I want that pie, Charley. I've got nothing to prove to anybody—"

I couldn't believe it. But there was no point in arguing. Foolish as it seemed to me, it was important to him.

"You got to look *right*, Buddy. Can't nobody look dignified carrying a brown paper bag."

So finally, thinking how tasty it would have been and how seldom I got a chance to eat anything that good, I handed over my bag of sweet potato pie. If it was that important to him—

I tried not to show my irritation. "Okay, man—take care now." I slammed the door harder than I had intended, walked rapidly to the hotel, and entered the brilliant, crowded lobby.

"That Charley!" I thought. Walking slower now, I crossed the carpeted lobby toward the elevator, still thinking of my lost snack. I had to admit that of all the herd of people who jostled each other in the lobby, not one was carrying a brown paper bag. Or anything but expensive attaché cases or slick packages from exclusive shops. I suppose we all operate according to the symbols that are meaningful to us, and to Charley a brown paper bag symbolizes the humble life he thought I had left. I was *somebody*.

Did You Know?
An *attaché* (at′ ə shā′) *case* is a slim briefcase.

I don't know what made me glance back, but I did. And suddenly the tears and laughter, toil and love of a lifetime burst around me like fireworks in a night sky.

For there, following a few steps behind, came Charley, proudly carrying a brown paper bag full of sweet potato pie.

Responding to Literature

Personal Response

What were your thoughts after you finished reading this story? Share them with a classmate.

Analyzing Literature

Recall

1. On what two occasions do the narrator's parents come into "sharp focus" as "solid entities"?
2. Who takes care of Buddy on a day-to-day basis when he is a boy?
3. What does Buddy accomplish that his parents and siblings do not?
4. Why doesn't the family get together anymore?
5. According to the narrator, what does the pie in the brown paper bag **symbolize** to Charley? (See Literary Terms Handbook, page R12.)

Interpret

6. Why, do you think, does Buddy have so few early memories of his parents?
7. How would you describe the relationship Buddy has with his siblings–especially Lil and Charley–as he is growing up? Use details from the story in your response.
8. What does Buddy mean when he thinks, ". . . I wasn't necessarily the smartest–only the youngest."
9. Are the members of this family close or have they become alienated from one another? Support your answer with details from the story.
10. In your opinion, why doesn't Charley mind carrying the paper bag?

Evaluate and Connect

11. In your opinion, what is the **theme** of this story? (See page R13.)
12. Charley withholds the truth about his identity from Buddy's former student. When Buddy learns this, he withholds the truth about his feelings for his brother. In your opinion, do you think Buddy and Charley should have been completely honest in each of these situations?
13. Evaluate the author's use of **dialect** in this story. (See Literary Terms Handbook, page R4.) When does she use it and why?
14. Would you recommend this story to a friend or family member? Why or why not?
15. **Theme Connections** Reread the story's final three paragraphs. Explain how the theme title "Looking Back" applies both literally and figuratively to this story.

Literary **ELEMENTS**

Tone

Tone is a reflection of the attitude a writer takes toward a subject. A writer's tone may be communicated through particular words and details that express particular emotions and that evoke an emotional response in the reader. For instance, a good-bye between members of a family could be expressed in a sad, formal, or angry manner. In "Sweet Potato Pie," however, the sentence "We had a last comfortable laugh together" conveys a warm, affectionate tone. To identify the tone of a literary work, it can be helpful to read the work aloud. Listen to how your voice sounds. The tone in your voice may reflect the tone of the work.

1. How would you describe the overall tone of "Sweet Potato Pie"? Make a list of words that come to mind.
2. Next, review the story, looking for the words or phrases that help to convey that tone. Make a list of at least five of them. Share your responses–and your lists–with a small group.

- See **Literary Terms Handbook,** p. R13.

Literature and Writing

Writing About Literature

Evaluating Characterization In "Sweet Potato Pie," does Eugenia Collier use direct or indirect characterization to bring the character of Charley to life? (See Literary Terms Handbook, pages R2–R3.) Does she use both techniques? Write an evaluation of Collier's methods of characterization, using details and examples from the story to support your ideas.

Personal Writing

Somebody Special Look over the chart you created for the Reading Focus on page 211 and think about what you read in the story. Do you think objects like the paper bag or the items in your chart should affect one's judgment of another person? In your opinion, what really makes somebody special? Write your thoughts in your journal.

Extending Your Response

Literature Groups

I Agree Near the end of the story Buddy says, "I want that pie, Charley. I've got nothing to prove to anybody. . . ." But Charley has insisted that the paper bag makes Buddy look bad, saying, "You *somebody,* Buddy. You got to be *right.*" Using evidence from the story, discuss what factors might have caused these brothers to think so differently. Then discuss the following questions: Whose opinion do you agree with, Buddy's or Charley's? Who holds more realistic views? Compare your conclusions with those of other groups.

Interdisciplinary Activity

Science/Health: A Sweet Treat Sweet potato pie is a healthful, sweet ending to a meal. Research the nutrients this kind of pie contains, and then give a report for your class about the way the body uses them. You may wish to bake a sweet potato pie to share—along with copies of the recipe—with your classmates.

Internet Connection

Focus on Harlem Working with a partner, use the Internet to find out more about the Harlem section of New York City—past and present. Let details from the story help guide your search. For instance, you might search for "Garvey Day," or discover which riots the narrator was referring to. Present your findings to the class.

Reading Further

If you're interested in reading more about strong family ties, you might enjoy these books:

Novels: *M.C. Higgins, the Great,* by Virginia Hamilton, is about a fifteen-year-old boy's fight to save his family's home from strip miners.

The Glory Field, by Walter Dean Myers, traces the struggles and triumphs of five generations of one family.

Oral History: *Spoonbread and Strawberry Wine: Recipes and Reminiscences of a Family,* by Norma Jean Darden and Carole Darden, celebrates one family's heritage through recipes, photos, and reminiscences.

Save your work for your portfolio.

Skill Minilessons

GRAMMAR AND LANGUAGE • Punctuating Dialogue

Dialogue is the conversation between characters in a literary work. Quotation marks are used to enclose the exact words spoken by a character. Each time the speaker changes, a new paragraph begins and a new set of quotation marks is used. Here is an example of dialogue from "Sweet Potato Pie."

"Say, Buddy, a couple months back I picked up a kid from your school."

"No stuff."

"I axed him did he know you. He say he was in your class last year."

"Did you get his name?"

PRACTICE Copy another example of dialogue from the story, omitting the quotation marks and the paragraph breaks. Exchange papers with a classmate. Using a colored pen or pencil and proofreading symbols, add quotation marks and paragraph breaks as needed. Check your work by comparing it with the dialogue in the story.

● For more about punctuating dialogue, see **Language Handbook,** p. R49.

READING AND THINKING • Questioning

Reading is an active process that engages your mind as well as your eyes. One way to read actively is to ask yourself questions as you read. For example, near the beginning of "Sweet Potato Pie," the narrator says, "Another surge of love, seasoned with gratitude, wells up in me." At this point, you might stop and ask yourself, "Why is he grateful?" Asking such questions–and predicting the answers–can help you read more actively and intelligently.

● For more about reading strategies, see **Reading Handbook,** pp. R78–R107.

PRACTICE Read the following passage from "Sweet Potato Pie." List three questions that it might raise.

> Perhaps because of what happened this afternoon or maybe just because I see Charley so seldom, my thoughts hover over him like hummingbirds. The cheerful, impersonal tidiness of this room is a world away from Charley's walk-up flat in Harlem and a hundred worlds from the bare, noisy shanty where he and the rest of us spent what there was of childhood.

APPLY The next time you read a short story, jot down a list of questions you have as you read. Also try predicting answers to some of those questions.

VOCABULARY • The Suffix *-ity*

You probably know that the adjective *antique* is a good synonym for *ancient.* But you may not be able to figure out what *antiquity* means unless you understand one fact: the suffix *-ity* means "state or condition." Like the suffix *-ness,* it turns adjectives into nouns. In "Sweet Potato Pie," Buddy remembers his father "looking back into dark recesses of time, into some dim *antiquity.* . . ." The word *antiquity,* then, means the same thing as *ancientness.*

PRACTICE For each word shown below, write a sentence that uses the word correctly.

1. artificiality
2. crudity
3. severity
4. confidentiality
5. negativity

● For more about adding suffixes, see **Language Handbook,** Spelling, pp. R55–R56.

Reading & Thinking Skills

Comparing and Contrasting

People compare and contrast all the time. Every time you read an advertisement, for example, phrases such as *as fast as* or *stronger than* invite you to think about how one thing is similar to or different from another thing. Comparing and contrasting provides the means to explore the distinctions between–and relationships among–people, things, and ideas.

Comparing and contrasting can also help you understand and interpret what you read. When you compare and contrast Charley's and Buddy's lives in "Sweet Potato Pie," you see that although they share the same parents and childhood memories, their adult lives are very different. Evaluating these similarities and differences can help you understand the brothers' present-day relationship.

To organize information as you read, it may be helpful to make a comparison frame such as the one on the right.

Categories	Subjects	
	Buddy	**Charley**
Childhood	• Low family income • Youngest child • Attends school • Tight-knit family • Like a son to Charley	• Low family income • Oldest child • Is not educated in school • Tight-knit family • Like a parent to Buddy
Adulthood	• Moderate to high income • College professor • Has wife, kids • Loves Charley and still is grateful for the love and support of his brother	• Low to moderate income • Cab driver • Has wife, kids • Looks up to Buddy–but still looks out for him in the old ways

● For more about reading strategies, see **Reading Handbook,** pp. R78–R107.

ACTIVITY

Read the following passage from "The Horned Toad" by Gerald Haslam, a story that appears later in this book. Then do the activity that follows.

> **"[Daddy] was a silent man, little given to emotional displays. It was difficult for him to show affection and I guess the openness of Mom's family made him uneasy. Daddy had no kin in California and rarely mentioned any in Texas. He couldn't seem to understand my mother's large, intimate family, their constant noisy concern for one another. . . .**
>
> **I heard her talking on the phone to my various aunts and uncles, usually in Spanish. . . . Daddy had warned her not to teach me that foreign tongue because it would hurt me in school, and she'd complied. . . ."**

Use a comparison frame to note the similarities and differences in the narrator's parents. Then write a paragraph comparing and contrasting the parents.

Before You Read

Rules of the Game

Reading Focus

One often hears of the "generation gap" that exists between people of different ages.

Quickwrite Write a definition for the term "generation gap" and give an example from your own experience to illustrate the term.

Setting a Purpose Read to learn how a generation gap affects a mother and daughter.

Building Background

The Time and Place

The narrator in this story reflects on her childhood in San Francisco's Chinatown in the 1950s and 1960s.

Did You Know?

Chess has been played for more than 500 years, making it one of the oldest known board games. Chess is a two-person game played on a board of light and dark squares. The object of the game is to checkmate, or capture, the opponent's king. Chess players, like athletes, work their way up through the ranks by winning first local, then regional, then national, then international tournaments, until finally reaching grand master status.

Vocabulary Preview

impart (im pärt′) *v.* to make known; tell; p. 225
relent (ri lent′) *v.* to become less harsh or strict; yield; p. 228
adversary (ad′ vər ser′ ē) *n.* an opponent or enemy; p. 229
obscure (əb skyoor′) *v.* to make difficult to understand; p. 229
benevolently (bə nev′ ə lənt lē) *adv.* kindly; p. 230
humility (hū mil′ ə tē) *n.* the quality of being humble or modest; p. 230
malodorous (mal ō′ dər əs) *adj.* bad-smelling; stinky; p. 232

Meet Amy Tan

When she was young, Amy Tan had a hard time relating to her mother. "We got into terrible battles by the time I reached my teens," says Tan. "It wasn't until my twenties that we began to get along. . . . Now we're very close." As a first-generation Chinese American, Tan had problems accepting her Chinese background. Writing about her cultural conflicts helped her understand her heritage. Her first work of fiction, *The Joy Luck Club*, was published in 1989 and became a best-seller. Now, says Tan, "I enjoy the freedom to write whatever I feel like writing."

Amy Tan was born in 1952.

RULES OF THE GAME

Amy Tan

I WAS SIX when my mother taught me the art of invisible strength. It was a strategy for winning arguments, respect from others, and eventually, though neither of us knew it at the time, chess games.

"Bite back your tongue," scolded my mother when I cried loudly, yanking her hand toward the store that sold bags of salted plums. At home, she said, "Wise guy, he not go against wind. In Chinese we say, Come from South, blow with wind—poom!—North will follow. Strongest wind cannot be seen."

The next week I bit back my tongue as we entered the store with the forbidden candies. When my mother finished her shopping, she quietly plucked a small bag of plums from the rack and put it on the counter with the rest of the items.

My mother imparted her daily truths so she could help my older brothers and me rise above our circumstances. We lived in San Francisco's Chinatown.[1] Like most of the other Chinese children who played in the back alleys of restaurants and curio shops, I didn't think we were poor. My bowl was always full, three five-course meals every day, beginning with a soup full of mysterious things I didn't want to know the names of.

We lived on Waverly Place, in a warm, clean, two-bedroom flat that sat above a small Chinese bakery specializing in steamed pastries and dim sum.[2] In the early morning, when the alley was still quiet, I could smell fragrant red beans as they were cooked down to a pasty sweetness. By daybreak, our flat was heavy with the odor of fried sesame balls and sweet curried chicken crescents. From my bed, I would listen as my father got ready for work, then locked the door behind him, one-two-three clicks.

At the end of our two-block alley was a small sandlot playground with swings and slides well-shined down the middle with use. The play area was bordered by wood-slat benches

1. *Chinatown* is a neighborhood or section of a city that is chiefly inhabited by Chinese people.

2. *Dim sum,* literally translated from the Chinese, means "dot-hearts," or "small treats that touch the heart." Dim sum foods are often bite-size dumplings, filled buns, or noodles.

Vocabulary
impart (im pärt′) *v.* to make known; tell

where old-country people sat cracking roasted watermelon seeds with their golden teeth and scattering the husks to an impatient gathering of gurgling pigeons. The best playground, however, was the dark alley itself. It was crammed with daily mysteries and adventures. My brothers and I would peer into the medicinal herb shop, watching Old Li dole out onto a stiff sheet of white paper the right amount of insect shells, saffron-colored[3] seeds, and pungent[4] leaves for his ailing customers. It was said that he once cured a woman dying of an ancestral curse that had eluded the best of American doctors. Next to the pharmacy was a printer who specialized in gold-embossed wedding invitations and festive red banners.

Farther down the street was Ping Yuen Fish Market. The front window displayed a tank crowded with doomed fish and turtles struggling to gain footing on the slimy green-tiled sides. A hand-written sign informed tourists, "Within this store, is all for food, not for pet." Inside, the butchers with their bloodstained white smocks deftly gutted the fish while customers cried out their orders and shouted, "Give me your freshest," to which the butchers always protested, "All are freshest." On less crowded market days, we would inspect the crates of live frogs and crabs which we were warned not to poke, boxes of dried cuttlefish, and row upon row

3. Anything *saffron-colored* is orange yellow.
4. Anything that is *pungent* has a sharp smell or taste.

Girl in San Francisco's Chinatown, 1992. Winson Trang. Acrylic on board, 8 x 10 in. Collection of the artist.

Viewing the painting: The girl in the painting stands apart from the street scene behind her. Finish reading the story and think about how she is like Meimei in the story.

Did You Know?
The *prawn* is a large shrimp.

of iced prawns, squid, and slippery fish. The sand dabs[5] made me shiver each time; their eyes lay on one flattened side and reminded me of my mother's story of a careless girl who ran into a crowded street and was crushed by a cab. "Was smash flat," reported my mother.

At the corner of the alley was Hong Sing's, a four-table café with a recessed stairwell in front that led to a door marked "Tradesmen." My brothers and I believed the bad people emerged from this door at night. Tourists never went to Hong Sing's, since the menu was printed only in Chinese. A Caucasian[6] man with a big camera once posed me and my playmates in front of the restaurant. He had us move to the side of the picture window so the photo would capture the roasted duck with its head dangling from a juice-covered rope. After he took the picture, I told him he should go into Hong Sing's and eat dinner. When he smiled and asked me what they served, I shouted, "Guts and duck's feet and octopus gizzards!" Then I ran off with my friends, shrieking with laughter as we scampered across the alley and hid in the entryway grotto of the China Gem Company, my heart pounding with hope that he would chase us.

My mother named me after the street that we lived on: Waverly Place Jong, my official name for important American documents. But my family called me Meimei,[7] "Little Sister." I was the youngest, the only daughter. Each morning before school, my mother would twist and yank on my thick black hair until she had formed two tightly wound pigtails. One day, as she struggled to weave a hard-toothed comb through my disobedient hair, I had a sly thought.

I asked her, "Ma, what is Chinese torture?" My mother shook her head. A bobby pin was wedged between her lips. She wetted her palm and smoothed the hair above my ear, then pushed the pin in so that it nicked sharply against my scalp.

"Who say this word?" she asked without a trace of knowing how wicked I was being. I shrugged my shoulders and said, "Some boy in my class said Chinese people do Chinese torture."

"Chinese people do many things," she said simply. "Chinese people do business, do medicine, do painting. Not lazy like American people. We do torture. Best torture."

My older brother Vincent was the one who actually got the chess set. We had gone to the annual Christmas party held at the First Chinese Baptist Church at the end of the alley. The missionary ladies had put together a Santa bag of gifts donated by members of another church. None of the gifts had names on them. There were separate sacks for boys and girls of different ages.

One of the Chinese parishioners had donned a Santa Claus costume and a stiff paper beard with cotton balls glued to it. I think the only children who thought he was the real thing were too young to know that Santa Claus was not Chinese. When my turn came up, the Santa man asked me how old I was. I thought it was a trick question; I was seven according to the American formula and eight by the Chinese calendar.[8] I said I was

5. The *sand dab* is a small, Pacific Coast flatfish related to the flounder.
6. *Caucasian* refers to the group of people who make up what is loosely known as the white race.
7. *Meimei* (mā′ mā)
8. By the *Chinese calendar,* the day on which a baby is born is counted as its first birthday. By this method, then, Meimei was one year old on the day she was born.

born on March 17, 1951. That seemed to satisfy him. He then solemnly asked if I had been a very, very good girl this year and did I believe in Jesus Christ and obey my parents. I knew the only answer to that. I nodded back with equal solemnity.

Having watched the other children opening their gifts, I already knew that the big gifts were not necessarily the nicest ones. One girl my age got a large coloring book of biblical characters, while a less greedy girl who selected a smaller box received a glass vial of lavender toilet water. The sound of the box was also important. A ten-year old boy had chosen a box that jangled when he shook it. It was a tin globe of the world with a slit for inserting money. He must have thought it was full of dimes and nickels, because when he saw that it had just ten pennies, his face fell with such undisguised disappointment that his mother slapped the side of his head and led him out of the church hall, apologizing to the crowd for her son who had such bad manners he couldn't appreciate such a fine gift.

As I peered into the sack, I quickly fingered the remaining presents, testing their weight, imagining what they contained. I chose a heavy, compact one that was wrapped in shiny silver foil and a red satin ribbon. It was a twelve-pack of Life Savers and I spent the rest of the party arranging and rearranging the candy tubes in the order of my favorites. My brother Winston chose wisely as well. His present turned out to be a box of intricate plastic parts; the instructions on the box proclaimed that when they were properly assembled he would have an authentic miniature replica of a World War II submarine.

Vincent got the chess set, which would have been a very decent present to get at a church Christmas party, except it was obviously used and, as we discovered later, it was missing a black pawn and a white knight. My mother graciously thanked the unknown benefactor,[9] saying, "Too good. Cost too much." At which point, an old lady with fine white, wispy hair nodded toward our family and said with a whistling whisper, "Merry, merry Christmas."

When we got home, my mother told Vincent to throw the chess set away. "She not want it. We not want it," she said, tossing her head stiffly to the side with a tight, proud smile. My brothers had deaf ears. They were already lining up the chess pieces and reading from the dog-eared instruction book.

I watched Vincent and Winston play during Christmas week. The chess board seemed to hold elaborate secrets waiting to be untangled. The chessmen were more powerful than Old Li's magic herbs that cured ancestral curses. And my brothers wore such serious faces that I was sure something was at stake that was greater than avoiding the tradesmen's door to Hong Sing's.

"Let me! Let me!" I begged between games when one brother or the other would sit back with a deep sigh of relief and victory, the other annoyed, unable to let go of the outcome. Vincent at first refused to let me play, but when I offered my Life Savers as replacements for the buttons that filled in for the missing pieces, he relented. He chose the flavors: wild cherry for the black pawn and peppermint for the white knight. Winner could eat both.

As our mother sprinkled flour and rolled out small doughy circles for the steamed dumplings that would be our dinner that night, Vincent explained the rules, pointing to each

9. A *benefactor* is someone who gives financial aid; here, it refers to the gift giver.

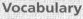

Vocabulary

relent (ri lent′) *v.* to become less harsh or strict; yield piece. "You have sixteen pieces and so do I. One king and queen, two bishops, two knights, two castles, and eight pawns. The pawns can only move forward one step, except on the first move. Then they can move two. But they can only take men by moving crossways like this, except in the beginning, when you can move ahead and take another pawn."

"Why?" I asked as I moved my pawn. "Why can't they move more steps?"

"Because they're pawns," he said.

"But why do they go crossways to take other men. Why aren't there any women and children?"

"Why is the sky blue? Why must you always ask stupid questions?" asked Vincent. "This is a game. These are the rules. I didn't make them up. See. Here. In the book." He jabbed a page with a pawn in his hand. "Pawn. P-A-W-N. Pawn. Read it yourself."

My mother patted the flour off her hands. "Let me see book," she said quietly. She scanned the pages quickly, not reading the foreign English symbols, seeming to search deliberately for nothing in particular.

"This American rules," she concluded at last. "Every time people come out from foreign country, must know rules. You not know, judge say, Too bad, go back. They not telling you why so you can use their way go forward. They say, Don't know why, you find out yourself. But they knowing all the time. Better you take it, find out why yourself." She tossed her head back with a satisfied smile.

I found out about all the whys later. I read the rules and looked up all the big words in a dictionary. I borrowed books from the Chinatown library. I studied each chess piece, trying to absorb the power each contained.

I learned about opening moves and why it's important to control the center early on; the shortest distance between two points is straight down the middle. I learned about the middle game and why tactics between two adversaries are like clashing ideas; the one who plays better has the clearest plans for both attacking and getting out of traps. I learned why it is essential in the endgame[10] to have foresight, a mathematical understanding of all possible moves, and patience; all weaknesses and advantages become evident to a strong adversary and are obscured to a tiring opponent. I discovered that for the whole game one must gather invisible strengths and see the endgame before the game begins.

I also found out why I should never reveal "why" to others. A little knowledge withheld is a great advantage one should store for future use. That is the power of chess. It is a game of secrets in which one must show and never tell.

I loved the secrets I found within the sixty-four black and white squares. I carefully drew a handmade chessboard and pinned it to the wall next to my bed, where at night I would stare for hours at imaginary battles. Soon I no longer lost any games or Life Savers, but I lost my adversaries. Winston and Vincent decided they were more interested in roaming the streets after school in their Hopalong Cassidy cowboy hats.

Did You Know?
Hopalong Cassidy is a fictional cowboy hero from early radio, movies, and TV.

10. When played at the expert level, a chess game has three parts—the *opening,* the *middle game,* and the *endgame*—each with its own tactics and strategies.

Vocabulary

adversary (ad′ vər ser′ ē) *n.* an opponent or enemy

obscure (əb skyoor′) *v.* to make difficult to understand

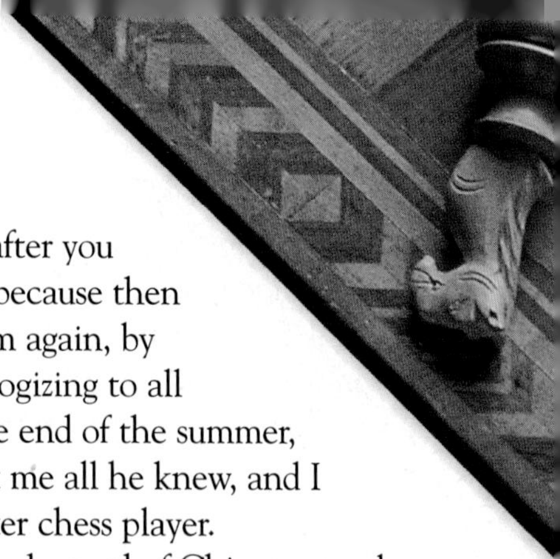

On a cold spring afternoon, while walking home from school, I detoured through the playground at the end of our alley. I saw a group of old men, two seated across a folding table playing a game of chess, others smoking pipes, eating peanuts, and watching. I ran home and grabbed Vincent's chess set, which was bound in a cardboard box with rubber bands. I also carefully selected two prized rolls of Life Savers. I came back to the park and approached a man who was observing the game.

"Want to play?" I asked him. His face widened with surprise and he grinned as he looked at the box under my arm.

"Little sister, been a long time since I play with dolls," he said, smiling benevolently. I quickly put the box down next to him on the bench and displayed my retort.[11]

Lau Po, as he allowed me to call him, turned out to be a much better player than my brothers. I lost many games and many Life Savers. But over the weeks, with each diminishing roll of candies, I added new secrets. Lau Po gave me the names. The Double Attack from the East and West Shores. Throwing Stones on the Drowning Man. The Sudden Meeting of the Clan. The Surprise from the Sleeping Guard. The Humble Servant Who Kills the King. Sand in the Eyes of Advancing Forces. A Double Killing Without Blood.

There were also the fine points of chess etiquette.[12] Keep captured men in neat rows, as well-tended prisoners. Never announce "Check" with vanity, lest someone with an unseen sword slit your throat. Never hurl pieces into the sandbox after you have lost a game, because then you must find them again, by yourself, after apologizing to all around you. By the end of the summer, Lau Po had taught me all he knew, and I had become a better chess player.

A small weekend crowd of Chinese people and tourists would gather as I played and defeated my opponents one by one. My mother would join the crowds during these outdoor exhibition games. She sat proudly on the bench, telling my admirers with proper Chinese humility, "Is luck."

A man who watched me play in the park suggested that my mother allow me to play in local chess tournaments. My mother smiled graciously, an answer that meant nothing. I desperately wanted to go, but I bit back my tongue. I knew she would not let me play among strangers. So as we walked home I said in a small voice that I didn't want to play in the local tournament. They would have American rules. If I lost, I would bring shame on my family.

"Is shame you fall down nobody push you," said my mother.

During my first tournament, my mother sat with me in the front row as I waited for my turn. I frequently bounced my legs to unstick them from the cold metal seat of the folding chair. When my name was called, I leapt up. My mother unwrapped something in her lap. It was her *chang*,[13] a small tablet of red jade which held the sun's fire. "Is luck," she whispered, and tucked it into my dress pocket. I turned to my opponent, a fifteen-year-old boy from Oakland. He looked at me, wrinkling his nose.

11. A *retort* (ri tôrt′) is a sharp, quick, witty reply.
12. *Chess etiquette* (et′ i kit) refers to the accepted practices or manners involved in playing chess.
13. A *chang* is a good luck charm.

Vocabulary

benevolently (bə nev′ ə lənt lē) *adv.* kindly

humility (hū mil′ ə tē) *n.* the quality of being humble or modest

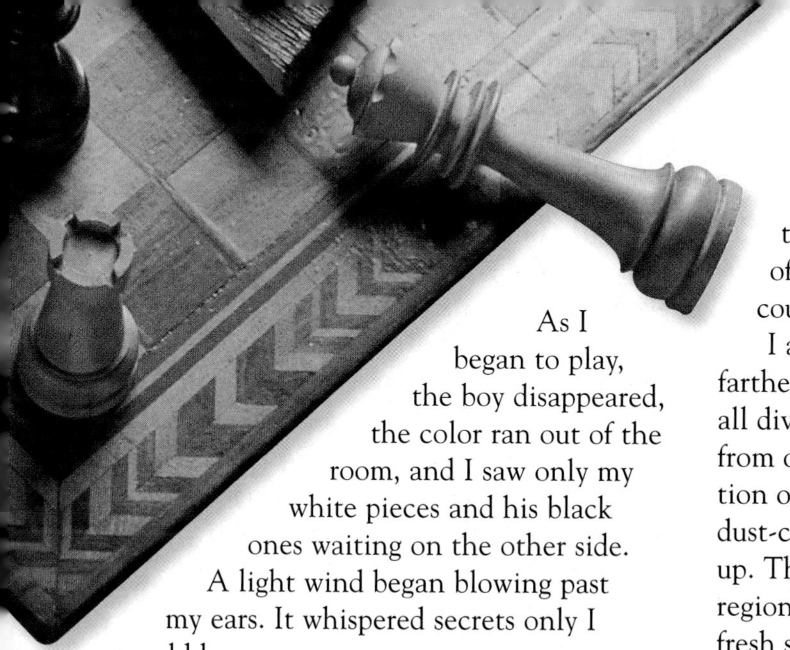

As I began to play, the boy disappeared, the color ran out of the room, and I saw only my white pieces and his black ones waiting on the other side. A light wind began blowing past my ears. It whispered secrets only I could hear.

"Blow from the South," it murmured. "The wind leaves no trail." I saw a clear path, the traps to avoid. The crowd rustled. "Shhh! Shhh!" said the corners of the room. The wind blew stronger. "Throw sand from the East to distract him." The knight came forward ready for the sacrifice. The wind hissed, louder and louder. "Blow, blow, blow. He cannot see. He is blind now. Make him lean away from the wind so he is easier to knock down."

"Check," I said, as the wind roared with laughter. The wind died down to little puffs, my own breath.

My mother placed my first trophy next to a new plastic chess set that the neighborhood Tao[14] society had given to me. As she wiped each piece with a soft cloth, she said, "Next time win more, lose less."

"Ma, it's not how many pieces you lose," I said. "Sometimes you need to lose pieces to get ahead."

"Better to lose less, see if you really need."

At the next tournament, I won again, but it was my mother who wore the triumphant grin.

"Lost eight piece this time. Last time was eleven. What I tell you? Better off lose less!" I was annoyed, but I couldn't say anything.

I attended more tournaments, each one farther away from home. I won all games, in all divisions. The Chinese bakery downstairs from our flat displayed my growing collection of trophies in its window, amidst the dust-covered cakes that were never picked up. The day after I won an important regional tournament, the window encased a fresh sheet cake with whipped-cream frosting and red script saying, "Congratulations, Waverly Jong, Chinatown Chess Champion." Soon after that, a flower shop, headstone engraver, and funeral parlor offered to sponsor me in national tournaments. That's when my mother decided I no longer had to do the dishes. Winston and Vincent had to do my chores.

"Why does she get to play and we do all the work," complained Vincent.

"Is new American rules," said my mother. "Meimei play, squeeze all her brains out for win chess. You play, worth squeeze towel."

By my ninth birthday, I was a national chess champion. I was still some 429 points away from grand-master status, but I was touted as the Great American Hope, a child prodigy[15] and a girl to boot. They ran a photo of me in *Life* magazine next to a quote in which Bobby Fischer said, "There will never be a woman

Did You Know?
Considered to be one of the greatest players in the history of chess, American *Bobby Fischer* (1943–) became the youngest international grand master by the age of fifteen.

14. *Tao* is short for *Taoism* (dou′ iz′ əm), one of the main religions of China. It is based on a belief in a harmony with nature and one's fellow human beings.

15. A *prodigy* (prod′ ə jē) is an extraordinarily gifted or talented person, especially a child.

grand master." "Your move, Bobby," said the caption.

The day they took the magazine picture I wore neatly plaited braids clipped with plastic barrettes trimmed with rhinestones. I was playing in a large high school auditorium that echoed with phlegmy coughs and the squeaky rubber knobs of chair legs sliding across freshly waxed wooden floors. Seated across from me was an American man, about the same age as Lau Po, maybe fifty. I remember that his sweaty brow seemed to weep at my every move. He wore a dark, malodorous suit. One of his pockets was stuffed with a great white kerchief on which he wiped his palm before sweeping his hand over the chosen chess piece with great flourish.

In my crisp pink-and-white dress with scratchy lace at the neck, one of two my mother had sewn for these special occasions, I would clasp my hands under my chin, the delicate points of my elbows poised lightly on the table in the manner my mother had shown me for posing for the press. I would swing my patent leather shoes back and forth like an impatient child riding on a school bus. Then I would pause, suck in my lips, twirl my chosen piece in midair as if undecided, and then firmly plant it in its new threatening place, with a triumphant smile thrown back at my opponent for good measure.

I no longer played in the alley of Waverly Place. I never visited the playground where the pigeons and old men gathered. I went to school, then directly home to learn new chess secrets, cleverly concealed advantages, more escape routes.

But I found it difficult to concentrate at home. My mother had a habit of standing over me while I plotted out my games. I think she thought of herself as my protective ally. Her lips would be sealed tight, and after each move I made, a soft "Hmmmmph" would escape from her nose.

"Ma, I can't practice when you stand there like that," I said one day. She retreated to the kitchen and made loud noises with the pots and pans. When the crashing stopped, I could see out of the corner of my eye that she was standing in the doorway. "Hmmmph!" Only this one came out of her tight throat.

My parents made many concessions to allow me to practice. One time I complained that the bedroom I shared was so noisy that I couldn't think. Thereafter, my brothers slept in a bed in the living room facing the street. I said I couldn't finish my rice; my head didn't work right when my stomach was too full. I left the table with half-finished bowls and nobody complained. But there was one duty I couldn't avoid. I had to accompany my mother on Saturday market days when I had no tournament to play. My mother would proudly walk with me, visiting many shops, buying very little. "This my daughter Waverly Jong," she said to whoever looked her way.

One day, after we left a shop I said under my breath, "I wish you wouldn't do that, telling everybody I'm your daughter." My mother stopped walking. Crowds of people with heavy bags pushed past us on the sidewalk, bumping into first one shoulder, then another.

"Aiii-ya. So shame be with mother?" She grasped my hand even tighter as she glared at me.

I looked down. "It's not that, it's just so obvious. It's just so embarrassing."

"Embarrass you be my daughter?" Her voice was cracking with anger.

"That's not what I meant. That's not what I said."

Vocabulary

malodorous (mal ō′ dər əs) *adj.* bad-smelling; stinky

"What you say?"

I knew it was a mistake to say anything more, but I heard my voice speaking. "Why do you have to use me to show off? If you want to show off, then why don't you learn to play chess."

My mother's eyes turned into dangerous black slits. She had no words for me, just sharp silence.

I felt the wind rushing around my hot ears. I jerked my hand out of my mother's tight grasp and spun around, knocking into an old woman. Her bag of groceries spilled to the ground.

"Aii-ya! Stupid girl!" my mother and the woman cried. Oranges and tin cans careened down the sidewalk. As my mother stooped to help the old woman pick up the escaping food, I took off.

I raced down the street, dashing between people, not looking back as my mother screamed shrilly, "Meimei! Meimei!" I fled down an alley, past dark curtained shops and merchants washing the grime off their windows. I sped into the sunlight, into a large street crowded with tourists examining trinkets and souvenirs. I ducked into another dark alley, down another street, up another alley. I ran until it hurt and I realized I had nowhere to go, that I was not running from anything. The alleys contained no escape routes.

My breath came out like angry smoke. It was cold. I sat down on an upturned plastic pail next to a stack of empty boxes, cupping my chin with my hands, thinking hard. I imagined my mother, first walking briskly down one street or another looking for me, then giving up and returning home to await my arrival. After two hours, I stood up on creaking legs and slowly walked home.

The alley was quiet and I could see the yellow lights shining from our flat like two tiger's eyes in the night. I climbed the sixteen steps to the door, advancing quietly up each so as not to make any warning sounds. I turned the knob; the door was locked. I heard a chair moving, quick steps, the locks turning—click! click! click!—and then the door opened.

"About time you got home," said Vincent. "Boy, are you in trouble."

He slid back to the dinner table. On a platter were the remains of a large fish, its fleshy head still connected to bones swimming upstream in vain escape. Standing there waiting for my punishment, I heard my mother speak in a dry voice.

"We not concerning this girl. This girl not have concerning for us."

Nobody looked at me. Bone chopsticks clinked against the insides of bowls being emptied into hungry mouths.

I walked into my room, closed the door, and lay down on my bed. The room was dark, the ceiling filled with shadows from the dinnertime lights of neighboring flats.

In my head, I saw a chessboard with sixty-four black and white squares. Opposite me was my opponent, two angry black slits. She wore a triumphant smile. "Strongest wind cannot be seen," she said.

Her black men advanced across the plane, slowly marching to each successive level as a single unit. My white pieces screamed as they scurried and fell off the board one by one. As her men drew closer to my edge, I felt myself growing light. I rose up into the air and flew out the window. Higher and higher, above the alley, over the tops of tiled roofs, where I was gathered up by the wind and pushed up toward the night sky until everything below me disappeared and I was alone.

I closed my eyes and pondered my next move.

Responding to Literature

Personal Response

With whom do you sympathize most at the end of the story, Meimei or her mother? Explain why.

Analyzing Literature

Recall

1. What useful life lesson did Meimei's mother teach her when she was six years old? How did she learn it?
2. When does Meimei first become interested in chess? Through what means does she learn to play the game?
3. As a first-generation Chinese immigrant, what challenges does the mother face? Explain her attitude toward "American rules."
4. What special treatment does Meimei receive in her home?
5. What **conflict** arises when the mother and daughter go shopping?

Interpret

6. Explain how Meimei applies her mother's strategy to "winning arguments, respect for others, and . . . chess games."
7. In your opinion, why does the narrator enjoy chess so much? Support your answer with evidence from the story.
8. How does Meimei trick her mother into letting her play in her first chess tournament? How does this scene reveal that she can "see the endgame before the game begins?"
9. How does the mother feel about her daughter's success? How can you tell?
10. What are Meimei and her mother *really* arguing about when they are shopping? Explain.

Evaluate and Connect

11. Do you think the mother is justified in being angry? Is Meimei? Support your opinion with examples from your own experience or with details from the story.
12. At the end of the story, Meimei considers her "next move." What move would you make if you were Meimei?
13. Think about your response to the Reading Focus on page 224. In what ways are Meimei and her mother victims of a "generation gap"?
14. How is Meimei's relationship with her mother like a game of chess?
15. How might you apply "the rules of the game" that are described in this story to your own life?

Literary ELEMENTS

Protagonist and Antagonist

The **protagonist** is the central character in a story and is often the person with whom readers easily identify. The **antagonist** is the person or force in society or nature that opposes the protagonist. The conflict between these two characters or forces is what drives the story.

1. Who is the protagonist and who is the antagonist in "Rules of the Game"? How do you know?
2. Is there another person or force working against the protagonist? Describe your impressions.
3. How does the protagonist grow or change during this story? How does the antagonist affect this growth?

- See **Literary Terms Handbook,** pp. R1 and R10.

Literary Criticism

Critic Gloria Shen says that in *The Joy Luck Club*, "the mothers are possessively trying to hold onto their daughters, and the daughters are battling to get away from their mothers." Write a paragraph explaining how this statement applies to Meimei and her mother in "Rules of the Game."

Literature and Writing

Writing About Literature

Appreciating Local Color Amy Tan's "Rules of the Game" is rich with local color, a writing device that uses specific details to recreate the language, customs, geography, and habits of a particular area. Look for passages in the story in which the streets and alleyways of San Francisco's Chinatown come alive for the reader. Then write a few paragraphs analyzing the effectiveness of the story's local color.

Creative Writing

Hometown Chess Champion Makes Good! As a reporter for a Chinatown newspaper, write a feature article about Meimei and her chess triumphs. In your article, be sure to include quotations from people who know her best and who have encouraged her success. To get ideas about what others might say, work with a partner to role-play interviews with Meimei's family members or Lau Po.

Extending Your Response

Literature Groups

Clarifying a Quotation In a different section of *The Joy Luck Club,* a character says that mothers and daughters "are like stairs, one step after another, going up and down, but all going the same way." Discuss this quotation in your group, and then consider how it might apply to the relationship between Meimei and her mother. Do you think the quotation could apply to fathers and sons?

Learning for Life

Playing for Real People learn a variety of skills from sports and games. For example, certain games teach one how to make quick decisions, whereas others teach the art of patience. Make a list of your favorite games and sports and name the skills that they have enabled you to develop. Share your list with a partner.

Internet Connection

Pawn on f2 Moves to f3 Use the Internet to learn more about the game of chess. See what you can uncover about the history of the game. How, for example, does today's game differ from the one played hundreds of years ago? What cultures are known to have played chess? You may also want to search for information about the rules of play and various strategies for the opening, the middle game, and the endgame.

Save your work for your portfolio.

Skill Minilesson

VOCABULARY • Prefixes and Suffixes

Malodorous may be an unfamiliar word, but when you break the word into its parts and examine each one, you'll be able to determine the word's meaning—without looking it up in the dictionary! *Malodorous* contains the familiar base word *odor. Mal-* is a common prefix that means "bad" (for example, *malfunction*). The common suffix *-ous* means "full of" (for example, *joyous*). So *malodorous* means "full of a bad smell" or "stinky."

PRACTICE Use what you know about the base words, prefixes, and suffixes in the words on the left to match each to its meaning on the right.

1. renumerate	a. already present
2. presuppose	b. to abuse
3. demonic	c. to count again
4. preexisting	d. of or like a devil
5. maltreat	e. to assume beforehand

Before You Read

The Child Is the Master

Reading Focus

"It doesn't matter whether you win or lose, it's how you play the game." This proverb is often given as advice by coaches, teachers, and parents.

Discuss Share your opinion of this saying with a small group of classmates.

Setting a Purpose Read to discover how Robert Horn plays the game.

Building Background

The Time and Place

In this essay, Robert Horn reminisces about a chess game he played in New York City in 1973, when he was sixteen years old.

Did You Know?

A prodigy is a person who shows exceptional talent at a very young age. For example, Wolfgang Amadeus Mozart performed in public when he was only six years old and wrote his first symphony at age nine. Opera singer Beverly Sills began her career at age three! Some prodigies remain in the limelight by excelling in their fields as adults, while others fade from public view.

Vocabulary Preview

avert (ə vurt′) *v.* to turn away or aside; p. 237
intimidate (in tim′ ə dāt′) *v.* to make timid or fearful; bully; p. 239
initiative (i nish′ ə tiv) *n.* the ability to lead or take the first step in an undertaking; p. 239
subtle (sut′ əl) *adj.* difficult to be perceived; not obvious; p. 240
reconcile (rek′ ən sīl′) *v.* make compatible or consistent; p. 240
ephemeral (i fem′ ər əl) *adj.* short-lived; temporary; passing quickly; p. 240

Meet Robert Horn

Robert Horn follows his passions, one of which is his concern about the struggle for democracy in Burma (also known as Myanmar). "I wish more Americans knew what was happening there and cared about it," he says. The democracy movement has been led by 1991 Nobel Peace Prize winner Aung San Suu Kyi, whom Horn counts among his heroes along with the late Pittsburgh Pirates baseball star and humanitarian Roberto Clemente. Horn moved to Southeast Asia after winning a Pulitzer Traveling Fellowship in 1993. He now lives and works as a journalist in Thailand.

Robert Horn was born in 1957 in New York City. This essay was first published in Sports Illustrated *in 1992.*

The Child Is the Master

Robert Horn

ON A COLD MARCH MORNING in 1973, Robert Donnelly climbed the sagging, rickety staircase that led to the Shelby Lyman Chess Institute in Greenwich Village.[1] The school was crowded. Cab drivers, college kids, beauticians, and bankers were battling it out over the boards. Bobby Fischer was the world champion, and now everyone wanted to learn chess. No one, however, wanted to lose to a five-year-old.

Chess master Bruce Pandolfini held Robert's tiny hand. As they walked between the tables, searching for an opponent to test the youngster's skill, the room fell silent except for the creaking of the wooden floor beneath their feet.

Players averted their eyes. Some suddenly remembered errands they had to run. All of them found a reason not to play the kid. They were as nervous as a pack of farmers when a gunslinger struts through town.

Then Pandolfini spotted me.

1. *Greenwich* (gren′ ich) *Village* is a neighborhood of New York City.

Vocabulary
avert (ə vurt′) *v.* to turn away or aside

Like Robert, I was one of Pandolfini's students. Unlike Robert, I showed little promise of achieving chess immortality. Nonetheless, I was obsessed with chess. So much so that my high school grades were plummeting. I was cracking the books, but the books were *Lasker's Manual of Chess* and *Practical Chess Endings*. The only lectures that held my interest were those delivered by Pandolfini.

Did You Know?
Granny glasses have small oval or round lenses and thin, wirelike metal frames. They became a fashion fad in the 1960s after *John Lennon*, one of the Beatles, began to wear them.

Other chess masters had offered to teach me for less money than I was paying Pandolfini, but I was devoted to Bruce. Bruce was cool. With his long, light-brown curls, hooked nose, granny glasses, and broad-brimmed black hats, he looked like a gangly John Lennon. He never got weird. And he never threw any chess-master tantrums.

At one time he was rated among the top 50 players in the U.S., but he had given up serious competition and dedicated himself to teaching. His speciality was young players and prodigies.

Pandolfini. His name had the ring of a sorcerer's,[2] and I imagined he conjured up his prodigies in the still, black hours of the night while poring over musty texts on alchemy and Alekhine.[3] Quietly he asked if I would play a game with Robert.

You think I wanted to lose to a five-year-old? Part of me, though, sympathized with the kid. Middle-aged players often avoided *me*. They assumed I was a young tiger. Their refusals were frequently accompanied by some cutting remark about my youth.

Pandolfini's eyes were pleading with me to accept. To please him I agreed to the game. But I was about to get crushed, and I knew it.

We went into an empty classroom, away from the other students. Pandolfini brought in a board, some pieces, and a score sheet. Then he sat on the side of the table, equidistant from Robert and me. "How are you, Robert?" I asked stiffly.

"O.K.," he said, staring at me suspiciously.

I was uncomfortable already. There was something surreal[4] and ridiculous about trying to talk to this five-year-old as though he was a five-year-old when he was about to blast me off the board.

His eyes rarely met mine. For all the encouragement Pandolfini had provided, Robert was alone in an odd and adult world. I gave him a smile. I was no bully. He didn't smile back.

Robert had drawn the white pieces. He wrapped his little hand around the head of his king's pawn and thrust it forward for his first move. Like two wary fighters pawing their way through the early rounds, we slid into a safe and standard Ruy Lopez opening.[5]

As we moved into the middle game, I was surprised to find that I was holding my own. I had been deliberate, cautious, and my position was strategically sound. But this was not my game. I prefer to attack savagely. Or even to scramble, slip, and dodge until my opponent is spent and prone for my kill. In such games brilliance and blunders abound, and the danger is exhilarating. Such games, however, require taking risks, and I was sure that at the first sign of my daring, Robert had a move waiting that would wallop me.

2. A *sorcerer* (sôr′ sər ər) is a wizard or magician.
3. *Alchemy* (al′ kə mē) is the chemistry of the Middle Ages, when people tried to turn base metals into gold. Alexander *Alekhine* was world chess champion for all but two years during the period 1927–1946.
4. *Surreal* means "having an odd, dreamlike quality."
5. A *Ruy Lopez* (ro͞o′ ē lō′ pez) *opening*, also called a Spanish opening, is a series of moves that beginners often learn first.

The Little Chess Master, 1992. Greg Spalenka. Mixed media on board, 9 x 15 in. Collection of the artist.

Viewing the art: What familiar elements appear in this artwork? Why do you think the artist, who created the work specifically for this essay, combined the elements this way?

Consequently, I was locked in a dry, balanced position. I was playing Robert's game. And as I watched him across the table, in his jumpsuit embroidered with little white bunnies, peering out at me from under his brown bangs, I knew I had been intimidated.

It was my move. I could continue to play it safe, push a pawn and hand the initiative back to Robert. Or I could be aggressive and try to seize the center—the chess equivalent of the high ground—with either my bishop or my knight.

The pawn, the bishop, or the knight. I considered long and hard. Eventually I eliminated the pawn from my plans. Meanwhile, masters were wandering in and out of the room to get a glimpse of the young wonder at work. Pandolfini was rubbing his chin and studying the position. He was doing his best to appear impartial, but it felt as if Robert and I were competing for his favor.

The bishop or the knight. Lines that seemed to lead to a win appeared and then evaporated like apparitions[6] meeting daylight. The bishop or the knight. The lady or the tiger.[7] My pondering was proving fruitless. Without conviction I sent my bishop crashing into Robert's center, and as we exchanged pieces, the crisp clacking of plastic colliding sheared the heavy silence.

I had blundered. When the smoke cleared, I was down a pawn. As Robert grabbed it with his little fingers and pulled it off the board, my confidence collapsed. Robert smiled at Pandolfini.

A pawn is a small advantage, but it is enough to win. I searched the board for a chance to retaliate. There was none. My only hope was to keep things complicated and pray that Robert would make a mistake.

I laid a trap for Robert on his kingside. Perhaps he wouldn't see it. Perhaps his mind would wander to thoughts of Captain Kangaroo. Robert kicked his buckled shoes in

6. *Apparitions* are ghosts.
7. This is a reference to the famous Frank R. Stockton story "The Lady, or the Tiger?" which appears on pages 45–50.

Vocabulary

intimidate (in tim′ ə dāt′) *v.* to make timid or fearful; bully

initiative (i nish′ ə tiv) *n.* the ability to lead or take the first step in an undertaking a staccato rhythm against his chair and nimbly danced around my snare.

I tried to lure him into a bad exchange on his queen side. Maybe I could fool him. Maybe he would be daydreaming about Big Bird.

Robert didn't fall for it. Instead, he launched his own attacks, and we battled on for another hour. Finally, on the 40th move, I could no longer prevent his extra pawn from reaching my end of the board and transforming itself into an all-powerful queen. I toppled over my king and surrendered.

Robert giggled. Pandolfini put his finger to his lips to signal Robert to stop. I let out a long, dejected sigh.

Anyone who says that chess is not a physical game ignores the subtle yet powerful connection between mind and body. My limbs were leaden, and a Jovian[8] gravity seemed to be pulling on my chest, draining me physically and emotionally. I was afraid to leave the classroom, believing I had been humiliated.

Pandolfini looked at me and smiled. "That," he said, "was an excellent game. Hard fought. Deep." Then he began to analyze the action, heaping praise on me for the things I had done well. As he did, my spirits began to lift, and as we analyzed Robert's moves, the concerns of my ego[9] dissolved, and I began to share in the wonder the masters felt in Robert's presence.

Still, I was left with troubling questions. I had valued chess as an intellectual pursuit. How could I reconcile that belief with this experience? Robert may have been ready for Fischer or Boris Spassky,[10] but he wasn't ready for Dostoyevsky or Camus.[11] Was his ability based on some cognitive[12] skill I would never possess to the same degree? I had a vision of myself dragged by the weight of my limitations, struggling for every yard on an uncertain road to the rank of master while Robert gleefully hopscotched ahead of me.

If that seems depressing, ultimately it was liberating. I had lost the game, but with it I also lost my illusions and ambitions. Stripped of that baggage, I rediscovered the pleasures of chess. I realized that, all along in our lessons, Pandolfini had been concerned less with my need to master chess than with making the beauty of the game accessible to me.

As for Robert, his brilliance was ephemeral. The rush of attention and acclaim, inevitably accompanied by the continual pressure to perform, became too much for him. By the age of 10 he was out of chess. Today he never plays. So when I go over our moves from so long ago, it's with a touch of sadness, knowing that, for all his talent, he doesn't love the game as much as I do.

8. *Jovian* (jō′ vē ən) refers to the planet Jupiter, which, because of its massive size, has enormous gravity.
9. Here, *ego* means "self-image or self-confidence."

10. Bobby *Fischer* and *Boris Spassky* are former world chess champions.
11. The works of Russian novelist Fyodor *Dostoyevsky* (dos′ tə yef′ skē) and French philosopher Albert *Camus* (ka mo͞o′) are commonly read in college literature classes.
12. *Cognitive* refers to the mental process of coming to know something, such as through reasoning or the senses.

Vocabulary

subtle (sut′ əl) *adj.* difficult to be perceived; not obvious
reconcile (rek′ ən sīl′) *v.* make compatible or consistent
ephemeral (i fem′ ər əl) *adj.* short-lived; temporary; passing quickly

Responding to Literature

Personal Response

What was your reaction to Robert Horn's attitude at the end of the essay? Share your response with a classmate.

Analyzing Literature

Recall and Interpret

1. Why doesn't Horn want to play chess with Robert Donnelly?
2. What style of chess game does Horn say he usually likes to play? Explain why he doesn't play that style in this game.
3. Why does Horn think Robert might fall for his traps? Describe the **irony** in what actually happens. (See page R7.)
4. What does each player do when the game ends? In your opinion, why does each player behave as he does?
5. What does Horn say about giving up his ambitions of becoming a chess master? Who does Horn think really won, and why?

Evaluate and Connect

6. How would you feel if you lost a competition to a child wearing a jumpsuit with white bunnies on it? Explain your answer.
7. In your opinion, does Horn make the reader feel his tension and anxiety? Use examples from the selection to support your opinion.
8. Would you like to have a teacher like Bruce Pandolfini? Why?
9. Think about the discussion you had in response to the Reading Focus on page 236. In your opinion, would the author agree with the saying?
10. **Theme Connections** Robert Horn wrote this essay years after the chess game was played. What does the essay suggest about the value of looking back at past events?

Literary ELEMENTS

Conclusion

Many personal narratives such as this one end with a **conclusion** that serves two main functions: providing a satisfying end to the piece and expressing the writer's thoughts and feelings about the experience. In other words, the conclusion tells what the experience meant to the writer.

1. Which paragraphs form the conclusion of "The Child Is the Master"?
2. How does the conclusion wrap up the loose ends of the narrative?
3. Summarize what this experience meant to Robert Horn.

- See **Literary Terms Handbook,** p. R3.

Extending Your Response

Literature Groups

Win or Lose Horn says that his teacher was concerned "with making the beauty of the game accessible to me." But he also thinks his teacher was impressed with Robert's chess playing. Do you think the teacher was more interested in making his students champions or in making them love the game? Share your opinions with your group.

Creative Writing

Once Upon a Time Rewrite Horn's personal narrative as a story for a children's magazine. Be sure to use realistic-sounding dialogue to help round out your characters. Also use language that children would understand. You might look at stories in children's magazines for ideas.

Save your work for your portfolio.

COMPARING *selections*

RULES OF THE GAME and The Child Is the Master

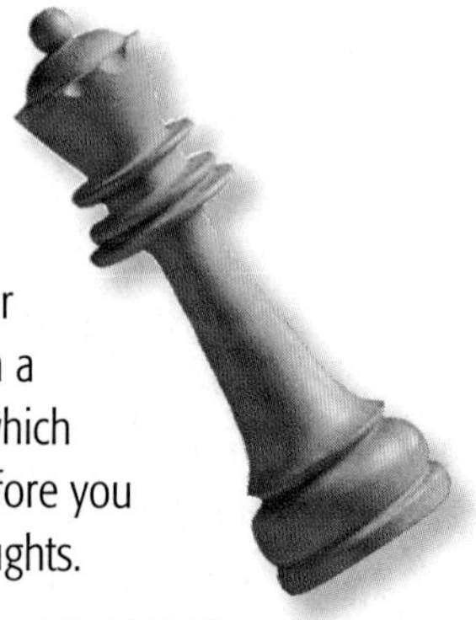

COMPARE PERSONALITIES

People's personalities affect not only how and why they play games, but whether they will continue to play as they grow older. Choose one narrator from these stories and put yourself in her or his shoes. Then team up with a classmate who has chosen the other narrator and role-play a meeting at which you discuss why you play chess and whether you will continue to play. Before you perform, create a chart like the one shown to help you organize your thoughts.

Questions to Consider	Meimei	Robert Horn
What is my personality like?		
Why do I play chess?		
What style do I like to play?		
Will I continue to play as I grow? Why or why not?		

COMPARE ADULTS

Compare and contrast Meimei's mother in "Rules of the Game" with Bruce Pandolfini in "The Child Is the Master." What is each adult trying to teach the young person in the selection? How would you describe Pandolfini's teaching style? Meimei's mother's teaching style? Who do you think is the more effective teacher? Explain.

COMPARE FACT AND FICTION

How much did you learn about the game of chess from these selections?

- In a small group, return to the selections and write down any information you find about how to play the game of chess.
- Next, search for library books on the game and surf the Internet for more information about the game.
- Record and organize the information you gather.
- How accurate were the two selections in giving information about chess? Share your findings with other groups.

LISTENING, SPEAKING, and VIEWING

Debating

The game of chess is a central aspect of the selections "Rules of the Game" and "The Child Is the Master." In chess, players consider the moves of their opponent and counter those moves with carefully planned strategies for both defense and offense.

When debating, one must also strategize against an opponent. In a debate, two people or teams argue for or against an idea. Each side takes turns presenting its case, then is given a chance to refute the other's arguments. The winner of the debate is the side that presents the most convincing argument. The checklist below can help you engage in a debate.

Gathering Information

- Choose a statement or question that has two clear sides.
- Take a position and gather facts, expert opinions, and examples to support your case.
- Organize your information in a logical manner.
- Anticipate your opponent's arguments and plan your rebuttal.
- Write key ideas and facts on note cards for easy reference during the debate.

Participating in a Debate

- Speak clearly and with expression. Don't rush.
- Stand straight, but be relaxed. Maintain eye contact with the judges and your audience. Use gestures to emphasize important points.
- Take notes during your opponent's presentation to help you remember the main arguments. Consider how you might counter them in your rebuttal.

ACTIVITIES

1. With your class, brainstorm a list of topics about which people have strong, differing opinions. Then choose a topic and a point of view and find a partner to take the opposing side. Research the topic and prepare a three-minute presentation of your case. Take turns giving presentations. Then, as a class, discuss effective rebuttals for the issues presented by each side.

2. Watch a television news program that regularly presents issues in a debate format. Take notes on what the speakers say and how they say it. Decide which speaker was the most effective, and share your decision with the class.

Before You Read

The Horned Toad

Reading Focus

What comes to mind when you hear the word "grandmother"?

Draw It! Draw a word web like the one shown. Write the word "grandmother" in the center circle and place any words, feelings, or ideas that you associate with "grandmother" in the other circles.

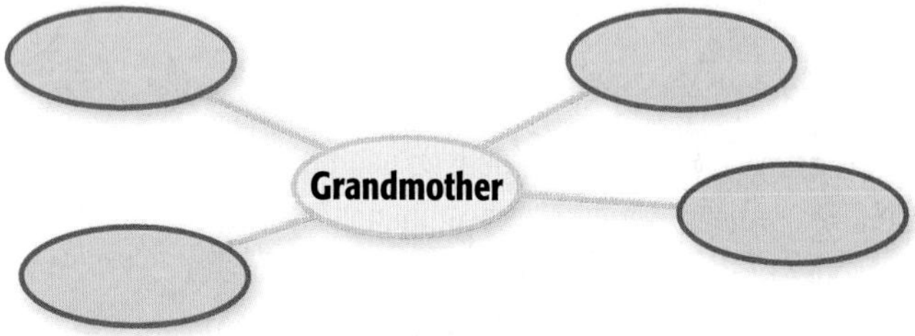

Setting a Purpose Read to learn about the narrator's relationship with his great-grandmother, whom he calls "Grandma."

Building Background

The Time and Place

This story takes place in the mid-1940s in Oildale, California.

Did You Know?

Named for its appearance, the horned toad is not a toad at all, but a small lizard. Ranging from 2½ to 4½ inches in length, horned toads have broad, flat bodies. The sharp spines resembling horns that protrude from their heads and the smaller, prickly spines along their backs help to protect them from predators. In addition, the animals can frighten oncoming predators by spurting tiny jets of blood from their eyes. Although horned toads are harmless creatures, this unusual defense mechanism has made them the object of many superstitions.

Vocabulary Preview

finality (fī nal′ ə tē) *n.* the state of being settled; decisiveness; p. 245
incongruously (in kong′ gro͞o′ əs lē) *adv.* in a way that does not fit; inappropriately; oddly; p. 246
millennium (mi len′ ē əm) *n.* one thousand years; *plural:* **millennia;** p. 246
periphery (pə rif′ ər ē) *n.* the surrounding area; outskirts; p. 246
incomprehensible (in′ kom pri hen′ sə bəl) *adj.* not understandable; p. 248

Meet Gerald Haslam

"I am more openly and proudly Hispanic than my pale skin and fair hair might suggest. . . ."

Award-winning author Gerald Haslam grew up in Oildale, California, in a mixed Anglo-Hispanic family. "'The Horned Toad' is fiction based on actual events. The boy is me, the grandmother my *abuelita* as I remember her." Haslam often focuses on California and the working-class people who live there. Yet his themes are universal. He has said, ". . . no matter what our color or sex, we have more uniting than separating us."

Gerald Haslam was born in 1937. This story was first published in New Arts Review *in 1983.*

The Horned Toad

Gerald Haslam

"Expectoran su sangre!"[1] exclaimed Great-grandma when I showed her the small horned toad I had removed from my breast pocket. I turned toward my mother, who translated: "They spit blood."

"De los ojos,"[2] Grandma added. "From their eyes," Mother explained, herself uncomfortable in the presence of the small beast.

I grinned, "Awwwwww."

But my great-grandmother did not smile. *"Son muy tóxicos,"*[3] she nodded with finality. Mother moved back an involuntary step, her hands suddenly busy at her breast. "Put that thing down," she ordered.

"His name's John," I said.

"Put John down and not in your pocket, either," my mother nearly shouted. "Those things are very poisonous. Didn't you understand what Grandma said?"

I shook my head.

"Well . . ." Mother looked from one of us to the other—spanning four generations of California, standing three feet apart—and said, "Of course you didn't. Please take him back where you got him, and be careful. We'll all feel better when you do." The tone of her voice told me that the discussion had ended, so I released the little reptile where I'd captured him.

During those years in Oildale,[4] the mid-1940s, I needed only to walk across the street to find a patch of virgin desert. Neighborhood kids called it simply "the vacant lot," less than an acre without houses or sidewalks. Not that we were desperate for desert then, since we could walk into its scorched skin a mere half-mile west, north, and east. To the south,

1. *Expectoran su sangre* (es pek tō′ rän soo̅ säng′ gre)
2. *De los ojos* (dā lōs ō′ hōs)
3. *Son muy tóxicos* (sōn mwē tok′ sē kōs) means "They are very poisonous."
4. *Oildale* is near Bakersfield in south central California. The climate is hot and dry, and deserts lie on the outskirts of town.

Vocabulary

finality (fī nal′ ə tē) *n.* the state of being settled; decisiveness incongruously, flowed the icy Kern River, fresh from the Sierras[5] and surrounded by riparian[6] forest.

Ours was rich soil formed by that same Kern River as it ground Sierra granite and turned it into coarse sand, then carried it down into the valley and deposited it over millennia along its many changes of channels. The ants that built miniature volcanoes on the vacant lot left piles of tiny stones with telltale markings of black on white. Deeper than ants could dig were pools of petroleum that led to many fortunes and lured men like my father from Texas. The dry hills to the east and north sprouted forests of wooden derricks.[7]

Despite the abundance of open land, plus the constant lure of the river where desolation and verdancy[8] met, most kids relied on the vacant lot as their primary playground. Even with its bullheads and stinging insects, we played everything from football to kick-the-can on it. The lot actually resembled my father's head, bare in the middle but full of growth around the edges: weeds, stickers, cactuses, and a few bushes. We played our games on its sandy center, and conducted such sports as ant fights and lizard hunts on its brushy periphery.

That spring, when I discovered the lone horned toad near the back of the lot, had been rough on my family. Earlier, there had been quiet, unpleasant tension between Mom and Daddy. He was a silent man, little given to emotional displays. It was difficult for him to show affection and I guess the openness of Mom's family made him uneasy. Daddy had no kin in California and rarely mentioned any in Texas. He couldn't seem to understand my mother's large, intimate family, their constant noisy concern for one another, and I think he was a little jealous of the time she gave everyone, maybe even me.

I heard her talking on the phone to my various aunts and uncles, usually in Spanish. Even though I couldn't understand—Daddy had warned her not to teach me that foreign tongue because it would hurt me in school, and she'd complied—I could sense the stress. I had been afraid they were going to divorce, since she only used Spanish to hide things from me. I'd confronted her with my suspicion, but she comforted me, saying, no, that was not the problem. They were merely deciding when it would be our turn to care for Grandma. I didn't really understand, although I was relieved.

I later learned that my great-grandmother —whom we simply called "Grandma"—had been moving from house to house within the family, trying to find a place she'd accept. She hated the city, and most of the aunts and uncles lived in Los Angeles. Our house in Oildale was much closer to the open country where she'd dwelled all her life. She had wanted to come to our place right away because she had raised my mother from a baby when my own grandmother died. But the old lady seemed unimpressed with Daddy, whom she called "*ese gringo.*"[9]

5. *The Sierras* refers to the Sierra Nevada mountains.
6. *Riparian* (ri pār′ ē ən) means "having to do with a river bank."
7. *Derricks* are the frames built to hold the machinery in drilling for oil.
8. Here, *desolation* means the state of being deserted or uninhabited, whereas *verdancy* is the state of being green and lush with vegetation.
9. A *gringo* is a non-Hispanic North American; the term is not usually used in a complimentary way. *Ese* (es′ ā) means simply "that."

Vocabulary

incongruously (in kong′ grōō′ əs lē) *adv.* in a way that does not fit; inappropriately; oddly
millennium (mi len′ ē əm) *n.* one thousand years; *plural:* **millennia**
periphery (pə rif′ ər ē) *n.* the surrounding area; outskirts

In truth, we had more room, and my dad made more money in the oil patch than almost anyone else in the family. Since my mother was the closest to Grandma, our place was the logical one for her, but Ese Gringo didn't see it that way, I guess, at least not at first. Finally, after much debate, he relented.

In any case, one windy afternoon, my Uncle Manuel and Aunt Toni drove up and deposited four-and-a-half feet of bewigged, bejeweled Spanish spitfire: a square, pale face topped by a tightly-curled black wig that hid a bald head—her hair having been lost to typhoid nearly sixty years before—her small white hands veined with rivers of blue. She walked with a prancing bounce that made her appear half her age, and she barked orders in Spanish from the moment she emerged from Manuel and Toni's car. Later, just before they left, I heard Uncle Manuel tell my dad, "Good luck, Charlie. That old lady's dynamite." Daddy only grunted.

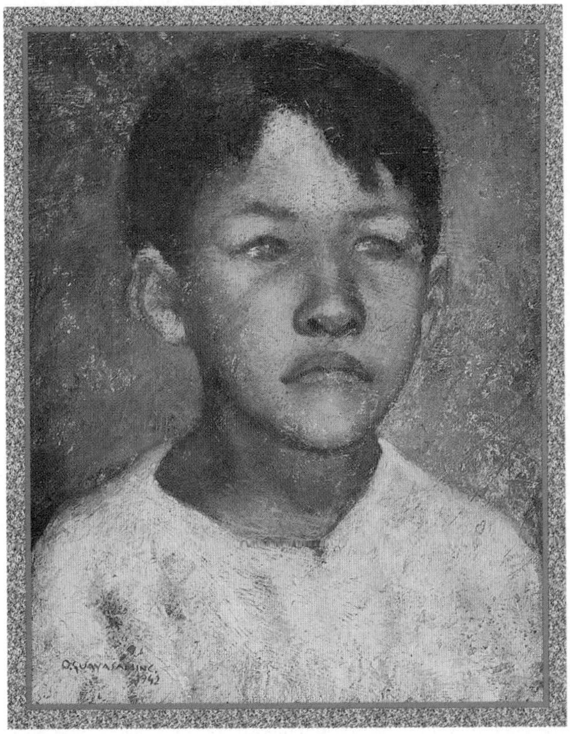

My Brother, 1942. Osvaldo Guayasamin. Oil on wood, 15⅞ x 12¾ in. Museum of Modern Art, New York.

Viewing the painting: How would you describe the expression of the boy in the painting? At what point in the story might the narrator have worn a similar expression?

She had been with us only two days when I tried to impress her with my horned toad. In fact, nothing I did seemed to impress her, and she referred to me as *el malcriado,*[10] causing my mother to shake her head. Mom explained to me that Grandma was just old and lonely for Grandpa and uncomfortable in town. Mom told me that Grandma had lived over half a century in the country, away from the noise, away from clutter, away from people. She refused to accompany my mother on shopping trips, or anywhere else. She even refused to climb into a car, and I wondered how Uncle Manuel had managed to load her up in order to bring her to us.

She disliked sidewalks and roads, dancing across them when she had to, then appearing to wipe her feet on earth or grass. Things too civilized simply did not please her. A brother of hers had been killed in the great San Francisco earthquake[11] and that had been the end of her tolerance of cities. Until my great-grandfather died, they lived on a small rancho near Arroyo Cantua, north of Coalinga.[12] Grandpa, who had come north from Sonora as a youth to work as a *vaquero,*[13] had bred horses and cattle, and cowboyed for other ranchers, scraping together enough of a living to raise eleven children.

He had been, until the time of his death, a lean, dark-skinned man with wide shoulders,

10. *El malcriado* (mal crē â′ dō) means "the rude fellow."
11. On April 18, 1906, the *San Francisco earthquake* damaged or destroyed much of the city and resulted in the deaths of 503 people.
12. The towns of *Arroyo Cantua* (a roi′ ō kän too̅′ ə) and *Coalinga* (kō′ ə lēng′ gə) are about a hundred miles northwest of Oildale.
13. A *vaquero* (və ke′ rō) is a cowboy.

Did You Know?
A *handlebar mustache* has long, curved ends and resembles the handlebars of a bicycle.

a large nose, and a sweeping handlebar mustache that was white when I knew him. His Indian blood darkened all his progeny[14] so that not even I was as fair-skinned as my great-grandmother, Ese Gringo for a father or not.

As it turned out, I didn't really understand very much about Grandma at all. She was old, of course, yet in many ways my parents treated her as though she were younger than me, walking her to the bathroom at night and bringing her presents from the store. In other ways—drinking wine at dinner, for example—she was granted adult privileges. Even Daddy didn't drink wine except on special occasions. After Grandma moved in, though, he began to occasionally join her for a glass, sometimes even sitting with her on the porch for a premeal sip.

She held court on our front porch, often gazing toward the desert hills east of us or across the street at kids playing on the lot. Occasionally, she would rise, cross the yard and sidewalk and street, skip over them, sometimes stumbling on the curb, and wipe her feet on the lot's sandy soil, then she would slowly circle the boundary between the open middle and the brushy sides, searching for something, it appeared. I never figured out what.

One afternoon I returned from school and saw Grandma perched on the porch as usual, so I started to walk around the house to avoid her sharp, mostly incomprehensible, tongue. She had already spotted me. "*¡Venga aquí!*"[15] she ordered, and I understood.

I approached the porch and noticed that Grandma was vigorously chewing something. She held a small white bag in one hand. Saying "*¿Qué deseas tomar?*" she withdrew a large orange gumdrop from the bag and began slowly chewing it in her toothless mouth, smacking loudly as she did so. I stood below her for a moment trying to remember the word for candy. Then it came to me: "*Dulce,*" I said.

Still chewing, Grandma replied, "*¿Mande?*"

Knowing she wanted a complete sentence, I again struggled, then came up with "*Deseo dulce.*"[16]

She measured me for a moment, before answering in nearly perfect English, "Oh, so you wan' some candy. Go to the store an' buy some."

I don't know if it was the shock of hearing her speak English for the first time, or the way she had denied me a piece of candy, but I suddenly felt tears warm my cheeks and I sprinted into the house and found Mom, who stood at the kitchen sink. "Grandma just talked English," I burst between light sobs.

"What's wrong?" she asked as she reached out to stroke my head.

"Grandma can talk English," I repeated.

"Of course she can," Mom answered. "What's wrong?"

I wasn't sure what was wrong, but after considering, I told Mom that Grandma had teased me. No sooner had I said that than the old woman appeared at the door and hiked her skirt. Attached to one of her petticoats by safety pins were several small tobacco sacks,

14. The father's *progeny* (proj′ ə nē) is all of his children or descendants, as a group.

15. *Venga aquí* (veng′ gə ə kē′) means "Come here."

16. *[Qué deseas . . . dulce]* In English, the conversation goes like this: "What would you like to have?" "Candy." "What did you say?" "I want candy."

Vocabulary
incomprehensible (in′ kom pri hen′ sə bəl) *adj.* not understandable

the white cloth kind that closed with yellow drawstrings. She carefully unhooked one and opened it, withdrawing a dollar, then handed the money to me. "*Para su dulce*," she said. Then, to my mother, she asked, "Why does he bawl like a motherless calf?"

"It's nothing," Mother replied.

"Do not weep, little one," the old lady comforted me, "Jesus and the Virgin[17] love you." She smiled and patted my head. To my mother she said as though just realizing it, "Your baby?"

Somehow that day changed everything. I wasn't afraid of my great-grandmother any longer and, once I began spending time with her on the porch, I realized that my father had also begun directing increased attention to the old woman. Almost every evening Ese Gringo was sharing wine with Grandma. They talked out there, but I never did hear a real two-way conversation between them. Usually Grandma rattled on and Daddy nodded. She'd chuckle and pat his hand and he might grin, even grunt a word or two, before she'd begin talking again. Once I saw my mother standing by the front window watching them together, a smile playing across her face.

No more did I sneak around the house to avoid Grandma after school. Instead, she waited for me and discussed my efforts in class gravely, telling Mother that I was a bright boy, "*muy inteligente*,"[18] and that I should be sent to the nuns who would train me. I would make a fine priest. When Ese Gringo heard that, he smiled and said, "He'd make a fair-to-middlin' Holy Roller[19] preacher, too." Even Mom had to chuckle, and my great-grandmother shook her finger at Ese Gringo. "Oh you debil, Sharlie!" she cackled.

Frequently, I would accompany Grandma to the lot where she would explain that no fodder could grow there. Poor pasture or not, the lot was at least unpaved, and Grandma greeted even the tiniest new cactus or flowering weed with joy. "Look how beautiful," she would croon. "In all this ugliness, it lives." Oildale was my home and it didn't look especially ugly to me, so I could only grin and wonder.

Because she liked the lot and things that grew there, I showed her the horned toad when I captured it a second time. I was determined to keep it, although I did not discuss my plans with anyone. I also wanted to hear more about the bloody eyes, so I thrust the small animal nearly into her face one afternoon. She did not flinch. "*Hola, señor sangre de ojos*," she said with a mischievous grin. "*¿Qué tal?*"[20] It took me a moment to catch on.

"You were kidding before," I accused.

"Of course," she acknowledged, still grinning.

"But why?"

"Because the little beast belongs with his own kind in his own place, not in your pocket. Give him his freedom, my son."

I had other plans for the horned toad, but I was clever enough not to cross Grandma. "Yes, Ma'am," I replied. That night I placed the reptile in a flower bed cornered by a brick wall Ese Gringo had built the previous summer. It was a spot rich with insects for the toad to eat, and the little wall, only a foot high, must have seemed massive to so squat an animal.

Nonetheless, the next morning, when I searched for the horned toad it was gone. I had no time to explore the yard for it, so I trudged off to school, my belly troubled. How could it

17. ***The Virgin*** refers to Mary, Jesus's mother.

18. ***Muy inteligente*** (mwē ēn te′ lē hen′ te) means "very intelligent."

19. ***Holy Roller*** is an uncomplimentary term referring to various Christian churches whose members express their spiritual enthusiasm by shouting, singing, and wildly moving their bodies.

20. ***[Hola, señor . . . ¿Qué tal?]*** Grandma is saying, "Hello, Mr. Bloody Eyes. How are you?"

Interior, 1969. Carel Victor Morlais Weight. Oil on canvas. Herbert Art Gallery, Bristol, England.

Viewing the art: With what characters in the story might you associate the two women in the picture?

have escaped? Classes meant little to me that day. I thought only of my lost pet—I had changed his name to Juan, the same as my great-grandfather—and where I might find him.

I shortened my conversation with Grandma that afternoon so I could search for Juan. "What do you seek?" the old woman asked me as I poked through flower beds beneath the porch. "Praying mantises,"[21] I improvised, and she merely nodded, surveying me. But I had eyes only for my lost pet, and I continued pushing through branches and brushing aside leaves. No luck.

Finally, I gave in and turned toward the lot. I found my horned toad nearly across the street, crushed. It had been heading for the miniature desert and had almost made it when an automobile's tire had run over it. One notion immediately swept me: if I had left it on its lot, it would still be alive. I stood rooted there in the street, tears slicking my cheeks, and a car honked its horn as it passed, the driver shouting at me.

Grandma joined me, and stroked my back. "The poor little beast," was all she said, then she bent slowly and scooped up what remained of the horned toad and led me out of the street. "We must return him to his own place," she explained, and we trooped, my eyes still clouded, toward the back of the vacant lot. Carefully, I dug a hole with a piece of wood. Grandma placed Juan in it and covered him. We said an Our Father and a Hail Mary,[22] then Grandma walked me back to the house. "Your little Juan is safe with God, my son," she comforted. We kept the horned toad's death a secret, and we visited his small grave frequently.

Grandma fell just before school ended and summer vacation began. As was her habit, she had walked alone to the vacant lot but this time, on her way back, she tripped over the curb and broke her hip. That following week, when Daddy brought her home from the hospital, she seemed to have shrunken. She sat hunched in a wheelchair on the porch, gazing with faded eyes toward the hills or at the lot, speaking rarely. She still sipped wine every evening with Daddy and even I could tell how concerned he was about her. It got to where he'd look in on her before leaving for work every morning and again at night before turning

21. *Praying mantises* are long, stick-like insects that hold their front legs in a position that makes them appear to be praying.

22. To say *an Our Father and a Hail Mary* is to recite the Lord's Prayer and a prayer to the Virgin Mary.

in. And if Daddy was home, Grandma always wanted him to push her chair when she needed moving, calling, "Sharlie!" until he arrived.

I was tugged from sleep on the night she died by voices drumming through the walls into darkness. I couldn't understand them, but was immediately frightened by the uncommon sounds of words in the night. I struggled from bed and walked into the living room just as Daddy closed the front door and a car pulled away.

Mom was sobbing softly on the couch and Daddy walked to her, stroked her head, then noticed me. "Come here, son," he gently ordered.

I walked to him and, uncharacteristically, he put an arm around me. "What's wrong?" I asked, near tears myself. Mom looked up, but before she could speak, Daddy said, "Grandma died." Then he sighed heavily and stood there with his arms around his weeping wife and son.

The next day my Uncle Manuel and Uncle Arnulfo, plus Aunt Chintia, arrived and over food they discussed with my mother where Grandma should be interred.[23] They argued that it would be too expensive to transport her body home and, besides, they could more easily visit her grave if she was buried in Bakersfield. "They have such a nice, manicured grounds at Greenlawn," Aunt Chintia pointed out. Just when it seemed they had agreed, I could remain silent no longer. "But Grandma has to go home," I burst. "She has to! It's the only thing she really wanted. We can't leave her in the city."

Uncle Arnulfo, who was on the edge, snapped to Mother that I belonged with the other children, not interrupting adult conversation. Mom quietly agreed, but I refused. My father walked into the room then. "What's wrong?" he asked.

"They're going to bury Grandma in Bakersfield, Daddy. Don't let 'em, please."

"Well, son . . ."

"When my horny toad got killed and she helped me to bury it, she said we had to return him to his place."

"Your horny toad?" Mother asked.

"He got squished and me and Grandma buried him in the lot. She said we had to take him back to his place. Honest she did."

No one spoke for a moment, then my father, Ese Gringo, who stood against the sink, responded: "That's right . . ." he paused, then added, "We'll bury her." I saw a weary smile cross my mother's face. "If she wanted to go back to the ranch then that's where we have to take her," Daddy said.

I hugged him and he, right in front of everyone, hugged back.

No one argued. It seemed, suddenly, as though they had all wanted to do exactly what I had begged for. Grown-ups baffled me. Late that week the entire family, hundreds it seemed, gathered at the little Catholic church in Coalinga for mass, then drove out to Arroyo Cantua and buried Grandma next to Grandpa. She rests there today.

My mother, father, and I drove back to Oildale that afternoon across the scorching westside desert, through sand and tumbleweeds and heat shivers. Quiet and sad, we knew we had done our best. Mom, who usually sat next to the door in the front seat, snuggled close to Daddy, and I heard her whisper to him, "Thank you, Charlie," as she kissed his cheek.

Daddy squeezed her, hesitated as if to clear his throat, then answered, "When you're family, you take care of your own."

23. *Interred* means "buried."

Responding to Literature

Personal Response
What memories did this story bring to mind?

Analyzing Literature

Recall

1. What causes the tension between the narrator's parents at the beginning of the story?
2. How does Grandma react when she first sees the horned toad?
3. Describe the vacant lot in which the children play.
4. What happens to the horned toad?
5. What does the boy urge his parents to do when Grandma dies?

Interpret

6. A **dynamic character** in a story is one who undergoes change as the plot unfolds. Explain why the narrator's father is a dynamic character.
7. How does the relationship between Grandma and the narrator change once the grandmother reveals that she can understand and speak English?
8. Why, do you think, does Grandma enjoy visiting the vacant lot?
9. Why might Grandma and the narrator have kept the horned toad's death and their visits to its grave a secret?
10. In your opinion, why does the narrator feel so strongly about his request to his parents?

Evaluate and Connect

11. Review your response to the Reading Focus on page 244. Do any of the words you wrote describe the narrator's great-grandmother? What other words could you add after reading this story?
12. Uncle Manuel says, "Good luck, Charlie. That old lady's dynamite." Do you think this metaphor accurately describes Grandma? Why or why not?
13. Explain the importance of the Spanish language to the grandmother, the mother, the father, and the narrator. Use details from the story to support your analysis.
14. At the beginning of the story, Grandma refers to the narrator's father as *"ese gringo,"* but by the end, she calls him "Sharlie." How does this change help to clarify their developing relationship?
15. How do you suppose the narrator feels as he rides home at the end of the story?

Literary ELEMENTS

Theme
The **theme** is the main idea or message of a work of literature. Some works have a **stated theme,** which the author expresses directly. Others have an **implied theme,** which the author reveals gradually through such other literary elements as plot, character, setting, point of view, or symbolism. Remember, the theme is not the subject of a story, but instead is an insight about life or human nature.

1. In your opinion, what is the main theme of "The Horned Toad"? Support your answer with details from the story.
2. Is the theme stated or implied? Explain your response.
3. Sometimes readers will discover more than one theme in a story. What other themes can you find in "The Horned Toad"?

- See **Literary Terms Handbook,** p. R13.

Literary Criticism

According to one critic, the character of the great-grandmother in "The Horned Toad" recalls the *curandera* (a spiritual healer in the Mexican American community). How does the great-grandmother function as a healer in the story? Discuss your response with a partner.

Literature and Writing

Writing About Literature

Review This story is called "The Horned Toad," but it is mostly a story about the relationship between the narrator and his great-grandmother. How do the scenes involving the horned toad help the reader gain insight about their relationship? What do you learn about the narrator and Grandma from these scenes? Do you see any parallels between the toad and one or more of the characters? Answer these questions in a critic's review of the story.

Personal Writing

Dear Mr. Haslam . . . If you could communicate directly with Gerald Haslam, the author of this story, what would you say? Write your questions and comments in a letter to him. You might like to actually send him your personal response to the story. Many contemporary authors have established Web sites on the Internet. Ask a librarian or a teacher to help you discover whether you can E-mail your message to a Web site devoted to Gerald Haslam and his works.

Extending Your Response

Literature Groups

Muy Importante In your opinion, which scene or passage was most important to this story? Have each member of your group choose a scene and then defend the choice to the rest of the group, giving reasons why it is the most significant part of the story. After hearing from all group members, decide together which of the scenes you discussed is truly most important. Make a sketch of the scene on a sheet of paper and write your reasons underneath it. Exchange papers with another group and discuss any differences in opinion that you find.

Interdisciplinary Activity

Geography: Hit the Road! Use a map of southern California to locate Oildale, Los Angeles, and Coalinga. You can find detailed maps at many Web sites on the Internet, or you may use a road atlas from the library. If the characters in this story were driving on today's roads, what major routes would Uncle Manuel and Aunt Toni take from Los Angeles to Oildale, and what routes would the family take from Oildale to Coalinga? About how many miles would each trip include? If the cars travel an average of fifty miles per hour, how long will each trip take?

Performing

If You Could Talk to Grandma With a partner, act out a scene between you and Grandma that takes place in the vacant lot. Imagine that you live near the vacant lot where the narrator's great-grandmother often walks. What questions might you ask her about her earlier life and experiences? What answers might she give you? Write a dialogue and then perform your scene for the class.

Reading Further

If you'd like to read other stories by Mexican American authors, you might enjoy these:

"Mother and Daughter," in the collection *Baseball in April* by Gary Soto, is about the struggles faced by a single-parent family.

"The Scholarship Jacket," by Marta Salinas, is about a girl who struggles to retain an award she won for being a good student. This story may be found in *Nosotras: Latina Literature Today,* edited by María del Carmen Boza, Beverly Silva, and Carmen Valle.

Save your work for your portfolio.

Skill Minilessons

GRAMMAR AND LANGUAGE • Using Participles

Participles are verb forms that are used as adjectives to modify nouns and pronouns (i.e., *barking* dog; *battered* suitcase). Present participles always end in *ing,* and past participles usually end in *ed* or *d.* Many adjectives commonly used in sentences are actually participles. When Haslam uses a participle like *prancing* to describe the bounce in Grandma's walk, he creates a vivid image of her movement.

- For more about participles, see **Language Handbook,** p. R40.

PRACTICE On your paper, identify the participle in each of these sentences. Then use the same participle in a sentence of your own.

1. The vacant lot had many stinging insects.
2. Grandpa had a sweeping handlebar mustache.
3. Grandma often spoke with a scolding voice.
4. The narrator found the crushed lizard in the street.

APPLY Review a piece of writing you did in response to this story. Find places where participles will improve your writing and insert them.

READING AND THINKING • Using Graphic Aids

One way to get the most out of a selection is by making and using a graphic aid. A plot diagram can help you understand the five stages in the development of a story: the *exposition,* the *rising action,* the *climax,* the *falling action,* and the *resolution.* A plot diagram may also help you stay on track when you're drafting a short story.

PRACTICE On your own paper, copy the plot diagram on page 3 and complete it with the five stages of "The Horned Toad."

APPLY The next time you write a short story, use a plot diagram to help you keep focused.

- For more about related reading strategies, see **Reading Handbook,** pp. R78–R107.

VOCABULARY • Prefixes Expressing Number

The combining form *mille-* means "one thousand," whereas *milli-* means "one thousandth." That's why a *millennium* is a period of a thousand years, but a *millisecond* is a really, really short time–one thousandth of a second! There is another combining form, *kilo-,* for words having to do with one thousand. A *kilogram* is one thousand grams; a *milligram* is one thousandth of a gram. Here are some prefixes that express numbers.

semi-	(half)	penta-	(five)
mono-	(one)	deca-	(ten)
bi-	(two)	poly-	(many, or more than one)

PRACTICE Use the list of prefixes to help you create words that answer the following questions.

1. If *monogamy* means "having one spouse," what word means "having more than one spouse"?
2. What word describes someone who is only half conscious?
3. If a *decathlon* is an athletic competition involving ten events, what word means a competition involving five events?
4. If a *millennial* event occurs every thousand years, what word describes one that occurs every two years?

MEDIA connection

Newspaper Column

As a guest columnist for a Utah newspaper, Lynn Zaritsky challenges readers to reevaluate their ideas about people with disabilities—and to think about the natural world in new ways.

Nature Is Not Preoccupied with "Imperfections"

by Lynn Zaritsky—*The Salt Lake Tribune*, July 12, 1998

As long as certain rules of Nature are followed, I find her to be a very welcoming and accepting companion.

If some friends and I were to take a trip to the Oregon coast, we would settle ourselves just the right distance from the ebbing tide, where the sand was neither too wet nor too dry, to make sand castles and sculptures. There would surely be one of us brave enough to sculpt a life-size dolphin, rising and arching with its impish smile, looking ready to instantly splash back into the sand-sea, drenching us all with glee.

The rest in our group would probably content ourselves with more modest sand castles, with their usual turrets and moats. As the tide returned, we would hurriedly take a few pictures of our masterpieces. Then we would watch the incoming ocean discover and devour our creations with equal joy: the sand castles, the dolphin, our footprints, my wheelchair tracks, now all part of the ocean.

The sea would not care that the dolphin was created by someone blind. There would be no aquatic comment about the fact that the sandcastle to my left was fashioned by someone who otherwise uses her hands to talk because she is deaf.

The giant redwoods just over the sand dunes would be equally welcoming. The red-headed young boy with us would attempt mightily to wrap his arms around the giant, mature trunk. In all its dignity and majesty, the tree would not even consider flinching, even if the boy's face pressing against the bark was totally scarred from an unmerciful fire, his nose now unrecognizable, his ears now shapeless.

I suppose, unlike some humans, Nature has learned to live with what we have labeled "imperfection." Trees permanently contort to accommodate perpetual winds. The wild iris that decides to grow in the midst of the bluebell patch is not ostracized. Bees don't lecture the dragonflies on purposeful motion and chide them for excessive off-task flitting around.

Nature invites everyone to smell her wild roses—people who walk, people who cannot; people who talk, people who talk with their hands, people who cannot talk at all; people who see nothing, people who only see that the rose is red, people who can see the minute blood-red veins coming out to nourish each petal; people who know what a rose is, people who do not; people who love, people who want to be loved.

The rose does not see canes or wheelchairs or braces; it does not hear that speech is slow or labored; it does not care if ears or sight or legs are missing. The rose just is. And when we smell the richness of the gift of the rose, we, too, just are.

Analyzing Media

1. What do you think was Lynn Zaritsky's purpose for writing this column?
2. What does Zaritsky imply about how people with disabilities are treated in human society?

Before You Read

The Scarlet Ibis

Reading Focus

Can you imagine what it would feel like to be embarrassed by or ashamed of someone you care about? How might it feel to know that a close friend or family member felt embarrassed around you?

Journal Write a journal entry exploring your thoughts about the questions above.

Setting a Purpose Read to learn how a young boy deals with his embarrassment about his brother.

Building Background

The Time and Place

The events in "The Scarlet Ibis" take place on a cotton farm in the deep South between 1912 and 1918–the year World War I ended.

Did You Know?

The scarlet ibis, a tropical bird with bright red feathers, breeds in large colonies in the swamps of northern South America. It can also occasionally be seen in Florida and on the Gulf coast of Texas and Louisiana. The bird has long, thin, red legs; a long, slender neck that can curve gracefully into an S-shape; a curved beak; and wing tips of glossy black. It can reach a total length of about twenty-three inches.

Meet James Hurst

James Hurst may have drawn inspiration for the setting of "The Scarlet Ibis" from his childhood home in North Carolina. Many of the lush flowers and plants he describes in the story grew on his farm. As a child, he even gained firsthand knowledge of hurricanes! This, no doubt, taught him about "tenacity," or courage and perseverance, which is one of the things he has said "The Scarlet Ibis" is all about. Although Hurst tried different careers—including opera singing—he spent most of his professional life as a banker in New York City, writing short stories and plays in his spare time.

James Hurst was born in 1922. Today he lives near his childhood home in North Carolina. This award-winning story was first published in the Atlantic Monthly *in July 1960.*

Vocabulary Preview

careen (kə rēn′) *v.* to tilt or sway while moving, as if out of control; p. 259

serene (sə rēn′) *adj.* calm; peaceful; undisturbed; p. 262

infallibility (in fal′ ə bil′ ə tē) *n.* the state of being incapable of making an error; p. 262

blighted (blīt′ əd) *adj.* damaged or spoiled; p. 264

doggedness (dô′ gid nəs) *n.* steady persistence; stubbornness; p. 264

reiterate (rē it′ ə rāt′) *v.* to say or do again; repeat; p. 265

precariously (pri kār′ ē əs lē) *adv.* dangerously; insecurely; p. 265

The Scarlet Ibis

James Hurst

It was in the clove[1] of seasons, summer was dead but autumn had not yet been born, that the ibis lit in the bleeding tree. The flower garden was stained with rotting brown magnolia petals and ironweeds grew rank[2] amid the purple phlox. The five o'clocks by the chimney still marked time, but the oriole nest in the elm was untenanted and rocked back and forth like an empty cradle. The last graveyard flowers were blooming, and their smell drifted across the cotton field and through every room of our house, speaking softly the names of our dead.

It's strange that all this is still so clear to me, now that that summer has long since fled and time has had its way. A grindstone stands where the bleeding tree stood, just outside the kitchen door, and now if an oriole sings in the elm, its song seems to die up in the leaves, a silvery dust. The flower garden is prim,[3] the house a gleaming white, and the pale fence across the yard stands straight and spruce. But sometimes (like right now), as I sit in the cool, green-draped parlor, the grindstone begins to turn, and time with all its changes is ground away—and I remember Doodle.

Doodle was just about the craziest brother a boy ever had. Of course, he wasn't a crazy crazy like old Miss Leedie, who was in love with President Wilson and wrote him a letter every day, but was a nice crazy, like someone you meet in your dreams. He was born when I was six and was, from the

1. Here, a *clove* is a separation or split between two things.
2. In this context, *rank* means "growing in vigorous, wild abundance."
3. Here, *prim* means "neat and trim."

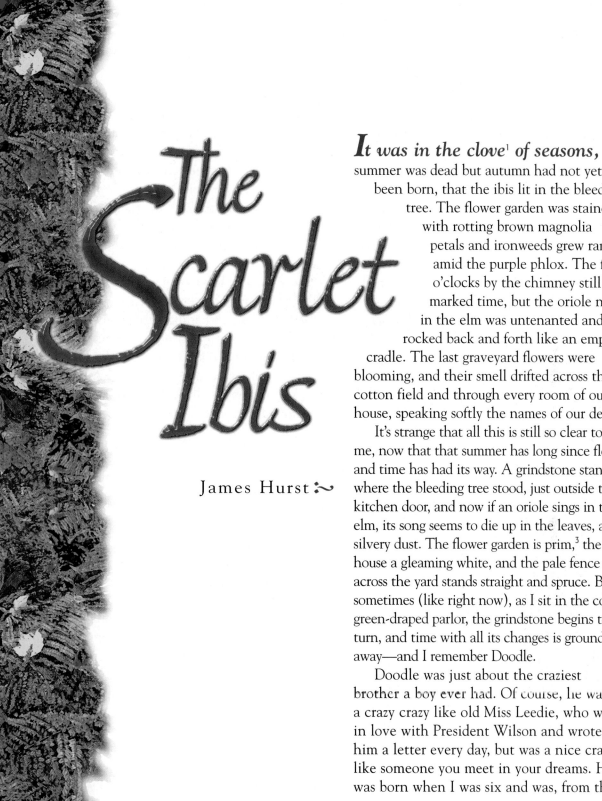

outset, a disappointment. He seemed all head, with a tiny body which was red and shriveled like an old man's. Everybody thought he was going to die—everybody except Aunt Nicey, who had delivered him. She said he would live because he was born in a caul[4] and cauls were made from Jesus' nightgown. Daddy had Mr. Heath, the carpenter, build a little mahogany coffin for him. But he didn't die, and when he was three months old Mama and Daddy decided they might as well name him. They named him William Armstrong, which was like tying a big tail on a small kite. Such a name sounds good only on a tombstone.

I thought myself pretty smart at many things, like holding my breath, running, jumping, or climbing the vines in Old Woman Swamp, and I wanted more than anything else someone to race to Horsehead Landing, someone to box with, and someone to perch with in the top fork of the great pine behind the barn, where across the fields and swamps you could see the sea. I wanted a brother. But Mama, crying, told me that even if William Armstrong lived, he would never do these things with me. He might not, she sobbed, even be "all there." He might, as long as he lived, lie on the rubber sheet in the center of the bed in the front bedroom where the white marquisette curtains billowed out in the afternoon sea breeze, rustling like palmetto fronds.

Did You Know?
Palmetto fronds are the large, divided leaves of the palmetto, a small, ornamental palm tree.

It was bad enough having an invalid brother, but having one who possibly was not all there was unbearable, so I began to make plans to kill him by smothering him with a pillow. However, one afternoon as I watched him, my head poked between the iron posts of the foot of the bed, he looked straight at me and grinned. I skipped through the rooms, down the echoing halls, shouting, "Mama, he smiled. He's all there! He's all there!" and he was.

When he was two, if you laid him on his stomach, he began to try to move himself, straining terribly. The doctor said that with his weak heart this strain would probably kill him, but it didn't. Trembling, he'd push himself up, turning first red, then a soft purple, and finally collapse back onto the bed like an old worn-out doll. I can still see Mama watching him, her hand pressed tight across her mouth, her eyes wide and unblinking. But he learned to crawl (it was his third winter), and we brought him out of the front bedroom, putting him on the rug before the fireplace. For the first time he became one of us.

As long as he lay all the time in bed, we called him William Armstrong, even though it was formal and sounded as if we were referring to one of our ancestors, but with his creeping around on the deerskin rug and beginning to talk, something had to be done about his name. It was I who renamed him. When he crawled, he crawled backwards, as if he were in reverse and couldn't change gears. If you called him, he'd turn around as if he were going in the other direction, then he'd back right up to you to be picked up. Crawling backward made him look like a doodlebug,[5] so I began to call him Doodle, and in time even Mama and Daddy thought it was a better name than William

4. The *caul* is a membrane, or layer of tissue, that sometimes clings to a baby's head at birth. It is thought by some to bring good luck and protection.

5. A *doodlebug* is the wormlike larva of the ant lion, which crawls backwards in order to dig a crater to trap ants and other insects.

Armstrong. Only Aunt Nicey disagreed. She said caul babies should be treated with special respect since they might turn out to be saints. Renaming my brother was perhaps the kindest thing I ever did for him, because nobody expects much from someone called Doodle.

Although Doodle learned to crawl, he showed no signs of walking, but he wasn't idle. He talked so much that we all quit listening to what he said. It was about this time that Daddy built him a go-cart and I had to pull him around. At first I just paraded him up and down the piazza,[6] but then he started crying to be taken out into the yard and it ended up by my having to lug him wherever I went. If I so much as picked up my cap, he'd start crying to go with me and Mama would call from wherever she was, "Take Doodle with you."

He was a burden in many ways. The doctor had said that he mustn't get too excited, too hot, too cold, or too tired and that he must always be treated gently. A long list of don'ts went with him, all of which I ignored once we got out of the house. To discourage his coming with me, I'd run with him across the ends of the cotton rows and careen him around corners on two wheels. Sometimes I accidentally turned him over, but he never told Mama. His skin was very sensitive, and he had to wear a big straw hat whenever he went out. When the going got rough and he had to cling to the sides of the go-cart, the hat slipped all the way down over his ears. He was a sight. Finally, I could see I was licked. Doodle was my brother and he was going to cling to me forever, no matter what I did, so I dragged him across the burning cotton field to share with him the only beauty I knew, Old Woman Swamp. I pulled the go-cart through the saw-tooth fern, down into the green dimness where the palmetto fronds whispered by the stream. I lifted him out and set him down in the soft rubber grass beside a tall pine. His eyes were round with wonder as he gazed about him, and his little hands began to stroke the rubber grass. Then he began to cry.

"For heaven's sake, what's the matter?" I asked, annoyed.

"It's so pretty," he said. "So pretty, pretty, pretty."

After that day Doodle and I often went down into Old Woman Swamp. I would gather wildflowers, wild violets, honeysuckle, yellow jasmine, snakeflowers, and water lilies, and with wire grass we'd weave them into necklaces and crowns. We'd bedeck ourselves with our handiwork and loll about thus beautified, beyond the touch of the everyday world. Then when the slanted rays of the sun burned orange in the tops of the pines, we'd drop our jewels into the stream and watch them float away toward the sea.

There is within me (and with sadness I have watched it in others) a knot of cruelty borne by the stream of love, much as our blood sometimes bears the seed of our destruction, and at times I was mean to Doodle. One day I took him up to the barn loft and showed him his casket, telling him how we all had believed he would die. It was covered with a film of Paris green[7] sprinkled to kill the rats, and screech owls had built a nest inside it.

Doodle studied the mahogany box for a long time, then said, "It's not mine."

"It is," I said. "And before I'll help you down from the loft, you're going to have to touch it."

6. A *piazza* (pē äz′ ə) is a large covered porch.

7. *Paris green* is a poisonous green powder formerly used as a pesticide.

Vocabulary

careen (kə rēn′) *v.* to tilt or sway while moving, as if out of control

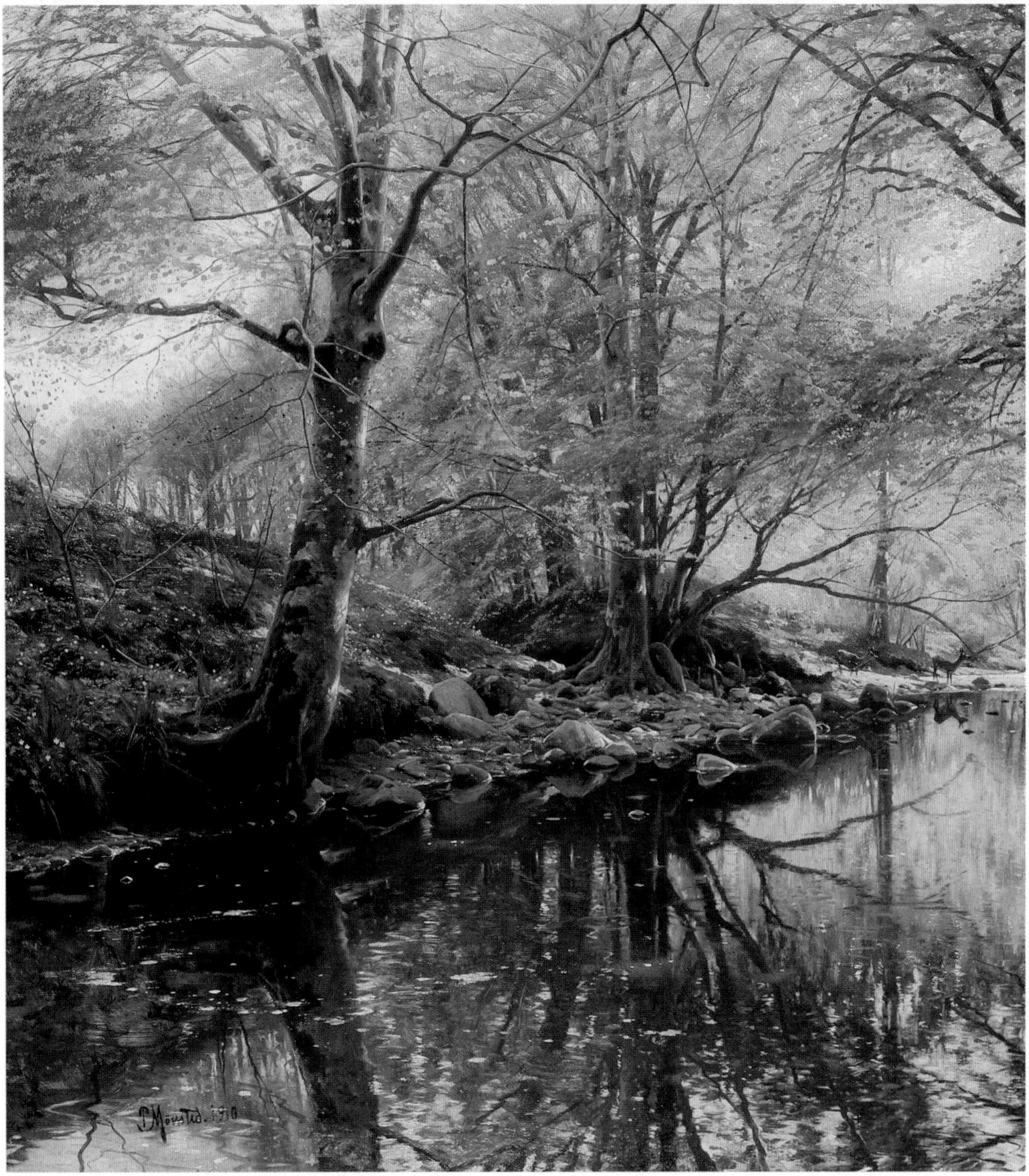

A Wooded River Landscape, 1910. Peder Monsted. Oil on canvas, 43.25 x 43.25 cm. Private collection.

Viewing the painting: If Brother had brought Doodle to a place like the one pictured, how might Doodle have reacted?

"I won't touch it," he said sullenly.

"Then I'll leave you here by yourself," I threatened, and made as if I were going down.

Doodle was frightened of being left. "Don't go leave me, Brother," he cried, and he leaned toward the coffin. His hand, trembling, reached out, and when he touched the casket he screamed. A screech owl flapped out of the box into our faces, scaring us and covering us with Paris green. Doodle was paralyzed, so I put him on my shoulder and carried him down the ladder, and even when we were outside in the bright sunshine, he clung to me, crying, "Don't leave me. Don't leave me."

When Doodle was five years old, I was embarrassed at having a brother of that age who couldn't walk, so I set out to teach him. We were down in Old Woman Swamp and it was spring and the sick-sweet smell of bay flowers hung everywhere like a mournful song. "I'm going to teach you to walk, Doodle," I said.

He was sitting comfortably on the soft grass, leaning back against the pine. "Why?" he asked.

I hadn't expected such an answer. "So I won't have to haul you around all the time."

"I can't walk, Brother," he said.

"Who says so?" I demanded.

"Mama, the doctor—everybody."

"Oh, you can walk," I said, and I took him by the arms and stood him up. He collapsed onto the grass like a half-empty flour sack. It was as if he had no bones in his little legs.

"Don't hurt me, Brother," he warned.

"Shut up. I'm not going to hurt you. I'm going to teach you to walk." I heaved him up again, and again he collapsed.

This time he did not lift his face up out of the rubber grass. "I just can't do it. Let's make honeysuckle wreaths."

"Oh yes you can, Doodle," I said. "All you got to do is try. Now come on," and I hauled him up once more.

It seemed so hopeless from the beginning that it's a miracle I didn't give up. But all of us must have something or someone to be proud of, and Doodle had become mine. I did not know then that pride is a wonderful, terrible thing, a seed that bears two vines, life and death. Every day that summer we went to the pine beside the stream of Old Woman Swamp, and I put him on his feet at least a hundred times each afternoon. Occasionally I too became discouraged because it didn't seem as if he was trying, and I would say, "Doodle, don't you *want* to learn to walk?"

He'd nod his head, and I'd say, "Well, if you don't keep trying, you'll never learn." Then I'd paint for him a picture of us as old men, white-haired, him with a long white beard and me still pulling him around in the go-cart. This never failed to make him try again.

Finally one day, after many weeks of practicing, he stood alone for a few seconds. When he fell, I grabbed him in my arms and hugged him, our laughter pealing through the swamp like a ringing bell. Now we knew it could be done. Hope no longer hid in the dark palmetto thicket but perched like a cardinal in the lacy toothbrush tree, brilliantly visible. "Yes, yes," I cried, and he cried it too, and the grass beneath us was soft and the smell of the swamp was sweet.

With success so imminent, we decided not to tell anyone until he could actually walk. Each day, barring rain, we sneaked into Old Woman Swamp, and by cotton-picking time Doodle was ready to show what he could do. He still wasn't able to walk far, but we could wait no longer. Keeping a nice secret is very hard to do, like holding your breath. We chose to reveal all on October eighth, Doodle's sixth birthday, and for weeks ahead we mooned around the house, promising everybody a most spectacular surprise. Aunt Nicey said that, after so much talk, if we produced anything less tremendous than the Resurrection,[8] she was going to be disappointed.

At breakfast on our chosen day, when Mama, Daddy, and Aunt Nicey were in the dining room, I brought Doodle to the door in the go-cart just as usual and had them turn their backs, making them cross their hearts and hope to die if they peeked. I helped Doodle up, and when he was standing alone I let them look. There wasn't a sound as

8. Here, the *Resurrection* refers to the Christian belief that Jesus rose from the dead after his burial.

Doodle walked slowly across the room and sat down at his place at the table. Then Mama began to cry and ran over to him, hugging him and kissing him. Daddy hugged him too, so I went to Aunt Nicey, who was thanks praying in the doorway, and began to waltz her around. We danced together quite well until she came down on my big toe with her brogans, hurting me so badly I thought I was crippled for life.

Did You Know?
Brogans are sturdy, ankle-high shoes.

Doodle told them it was I who had taught him to walk, so everyone wanted to hug me, and I began to cry.

"What are you crying for?" asked Daddy, but I couldn't answer. They did not know that I did it for myself; that pride, whose slave I was, spoke to me louder than all their voices, and that Doodle walked only because I was ashamed of having a crippled brother.

Within a few months Doodle had learned to walk well and his go-cart was put up in the barn loft (it's still there) beside his little mahogany coffin. Now, when we roamed off together, resting often, we never turned back until our destination had been reached, and to help pass the time, we took up lying. From the beginning Doodle was a terrible liar and he got me in the habit. Had anyone stopped to listen to us, we would have been sent off to Dix Hill.[9]

My lies were scary, involved, and usually pointless, but Doodle's were twice as crazy. People in his stories all had wings and flew wherever they wanted to go. His favorite lie was about a boy named Peter who had a pet peacock with a ten-foot tail. Peter wore a golden robe that glittered so brightly that when he walked through the sunflowers they turned away from the sun to face him. When Peter was ready to go to sleep, the peacock spread his magnificent tail, enfolding the boy gently like a closing go-to-sleep flower, burying him in the gloriously iridescent,[10] rustling vortex.[11] Yes, I must admit it. Doodle could beat me lying.

Doodle and I spent lots of time thinking about our future. We decided that when we were grown we'd live in Old Woman Swamp and pick dog-tongue for a living. Beside the stream, he planned, we'd build us a house of whispering leaves and the swamp birds would be our chickens. All day long (when we weren't gathering dog-tongue) we'd swing through the cypresses on the rope vines, and if it rained we'd huddle beneath an umbrella tree and play stickfrog. Mama and Daddy could come and live with us if they wanted to. He even came up with the idea that he could marry Mama and I could marry Daddy. Of course, I was old enough to know this wouldn't work out, but the picture he painted was so beautiful and serene that all I could do was whisper Yes, yes.

Once I had succeeded in teaching Doodle to walk, I began to believe in my own infallibility and I prepared a terrific development program for him, unknown to Mama and Daddy, of

9. *Dix Hill* refers to the state mental hospital in Raleigh, North Carolina.

10. The feathers are *iridescent,* or shimmering with rainbow colors.

11. A *vortex* is a whirling mass, like a whirlwind or whirlpool. Here, it is the wide funnel-shaped curve of the peacock's tail feathers.

Vocabulary

serene (sə rēn′) *adj.* calm; peaceful; undisturbed

infallibility (in fal′ ə bil′ ə tē) *n.* the state of being incapable of making an error course. I would teach him to run, to swim, to climb trees, and to fight. He, too, now believed in my infallibility, so we set the deadline for these accomplishments less than a year away, when, it had been decided, Doodle could start to school.

That winter we didn't make much progress, for I was in school and Doodle suffered from one bad cold after another. But when spring came, rich and warm, we raised our sights again. Success lay at the end of summer like a pot of gold, and our campaign got off to a good start. On hot days, Doodle and I went down to Horsehead Landing and I gave him swimming lessons or showed him how to row a boat. Sometimes we descended into the cool greenness of Old Woman Swamp and climbed the rope vines or boxed scientifically beneath the pine where he had learned to walk. Promise hung about us like the leaves, and wherever we looked, ferns unfurled and birds broke into song.

Young Fishermen in a Rowboat, 1909. Adam Emory Albright. Oil on canvas, 24 x 36 in. Private collection.
Viewing the painting: How does the mood of the painting reflect the mood of the boys' summer?

That summer, the summer of 1918, was blighted. In May and June there was no rain and the crops withered, curled up, then died under the thirsty sun. One morning in July a hurricane came out of the east, tipping over the oaks in the yard and splitting the limbs of the elm trees. That afternoon it roared back out of the west, blew the fallen oaks around, snapping their roots and tearing them out of the earth like a hawk at the entrails of a chicken. Cotton bolls were wrenched from the stalks and lay like green walnuts in the valleys between the rows, while the cornfield leaned over uniformly so that the tassels touched the ground. Doodle and I followed Daddy out into the cotton field, where he stood, shoulders sagging, surveying the ruin. When his chin sank down onto his chest, we were frightened, and Doodle slipped his hand into mine. Suddenly Daddy straightened his shoulders, raised a giant knuckly fist, and with a voice that seemed to rumble out of the earth itself began cursing heaven, hell, the weather, and the Republican Party.[12] Doodle and I, prodding each other and giggling, went back to the house, knowing that everything would be all right.

Did You Know?
A *boll* is the rounded seed pod of the cotton plant.

And during that summer, strange names were heard through the house: Château Thierry, Amiens, Soissons, and in her blessing at the supper table, Mama once said, "And bless the Pearsons, whose boy Joe was lost at Belleau Wood."[13]

So we came to that clove of seasons. School was only a few weeks away, and Doodle was far behind schedule. He could barely clear the ground when climbing up the rope vines and his swimming was certainly not passable. We decided to double our efforts, to make that last drive and reach our pot of gold. I made him swim until he turned blue and row until he couldn't lift an oar. Wherever we went, I purposely walked fast, and although he kept up, his face turned red and his eyes became glazed. Once, he could go no further, so he collapsed on the ground and began to cry.

"Aw, come on, Doodle," I urged. "You can do it. Do you want to be different from everybody else when you start school?"

"Does it make any difference?"

"It certainly does," I said. "Now, come on," and I helped him up.

As we slipped through dog days,[14] Doodle began to look feverish, and Mama felt his forehead, asking him if he felt ill. At night he didn't sleep well, and sometimes he had nightmares, crying out until I touched him and said, "Wake up, Doodle. Wake up."

It was Saturday noon, just a few days before school was to start. I should have already admitted defeat, but my pride wouldn't let me. The excitement of our program had now been gone for weeks, but still we kept on with a tired doggedness. It was too late to turn back, for we had both wandered too far into a net of expectations and had left no crumbs behind.

12. Daddy probably curses the *Republican Party* because he, like most Southerners at the time of the story, was a Democrat.

13. *Château-Thierry* (shä tō tye rē′), *Amiens* (am ē ənz′), *Soissons* (swä sōn′), and *Belleau* (bel ō′) *Wood* were the sites of famous battles in France near the end of World War I.

14. *Dog days* are the hot, humid days of July and August.

Vocabulary

blighted (blīt′ əd) *adj.* damaged or spoiled

doggedness (dô′ gid nəs) *n.* steady persistence; stubbornness

Daddy, Mama, Doodle, and I were seated at the dining-room table having lunch. It was a hot day, with all the windows and doors open in case a breeze should come. In the kitchen Aunt Nicey was humming softly. After a long silence, Daddy spoke. "It's so calm, I wouldn't be surprised if we had a storm this afternoon."

"I haven't heard a rain frog," said Mama, who believed in signs, as she served the bread around the table.

"I did," declared Doodle. "Down in the swamp."

"He didn't," I said contrarily.

"You did, eh?" said Daddy, ignoring my denial.

"I certainly did," Doodle reiterated, scowling at me over the top of his iced-tea glass, and we were quiet again.

Suddenly, from out in the yard, came a strange croaking noise. Doodle stopped eating, with a piece of bread poised ready for his mouth, his eyes popped round like two blue buttons. "What's that?" he whispered.

I jumped up, knocking over my chair, and had reached the door when Mama called, "Pick up the chair, sit down again, and say excuse me."

By the time I had done this, Doodle had excused himself and had slipped out into the yard. He was looking up into the bleeding tree. "It's a great big red bird!" he called.

The bird croaked loudly again, and Mama and Daddy came out into the yard. We shaded our eyes with our hands against the hazy glare of the sun and peered up through the still leaves. On the topmost branch a bird the size of a chicken, with scarlet feathers and long legs, was perched precariously. Its wings hung down loosely, and as we watched, a feather dropped away and floated slowly down through the green leaves.

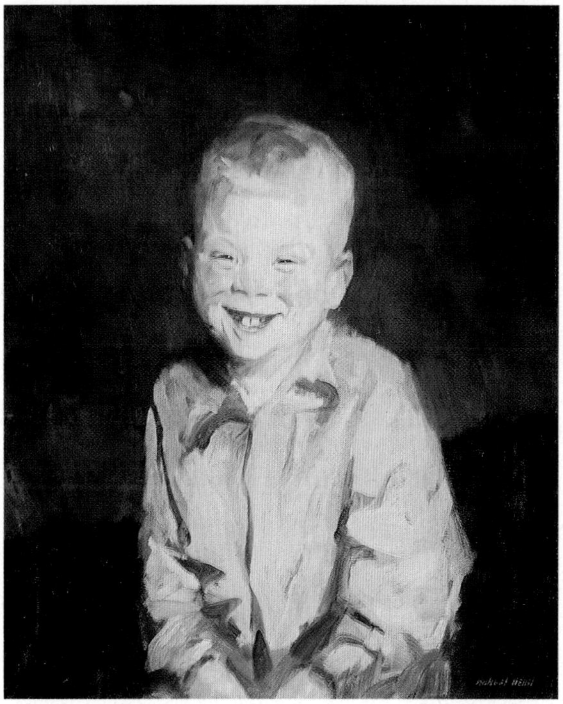

Jobie, the Laughing Boy, 1910. Robert Henri. Oil on canvas, 24 x 20 in. Private collection.

Viewing the painting: In what ways does the boy in the painting remind you of Doodle? In your opinion how does Doodle differ from the boy pictured?

"It's not even frightened of us," Mama said.

"It looks tired," Daddy added. "Or maybe sick."

Doodle's hands were clasped at his throat, and I had never seem him stand still so long. "What is it?" he asked.

Daddy shook his head. "I don't know, maybe it's—"

At that moment the bird began to flutter, but the wings were uncoordinated, and amid much flapping and a spray of flying feathers, it tumbled down, bumping through the limbs of the bleeding tree and landing at our feet with a thud. Its long, graceful neck jerked twice into an S, then straightened out, and the bird was still. A white veil came over the

Vocabulary

reiterate (rē it′ ə rāt′) *v.* to say or do again; repeat
precariously (pri kār′ ē əs lē) *adv.* dangerously; insecurely

eyes and the long white beak unhinged. Its legs were crossed and its clawlike feet were delicately curved at rest. Even death did not mar its grace, for it lay on the earth like a broken vase of red flowers, and we stood around it, awed by its exotic beauty.

"It's dead," Mama said.

"What is it?" Doodle repeated.

"Go bring me the bird book," said Daddy.

I ran into the house and brought back the bird book. As we watched, Daddy thumbed through its pages. "It's a scarlet ibis," he said, pointing to a picture. "It lives in the tropics—South America to Florida. A storm must have brought it here."

Sadly, we all looked back at the bird. A scarlet ibis! How many miles it had traveled to die like this, in *our* yard, beneath the bleeding tree.

"Let's finish lunch," Mama said, nudging us back toward the dining room.

"I'm not hungry," said Doodle, and he knelt down beside the ibis.

"We've got peach cobbler[15] for dessert," Mama tempted from the doorway.

Doodle remained kneeling. "I'm going to bury him."

"Don't you dare touch him," Mama warned. "There's no telling what disease he might have had."

"All right," said Doodle. "I won't."

Daddy, Mama, and I went back to the dining-room table, but we watched Doodle through the open door. He took out a piece of string from his pocket and, without touching the ibis, looped one end around its neck. Slowly, while singing softly *Shall We Gather at the River,* he carried the bird around to the front yard and dug a hole in the flower garden, next to the petunia bed. Now we were watching him through the front window, but he didn't know it. His awkwardness at digging the hole with a shovel whose handle was twice as long as he was made us laugh, and we covered our mouths with our hands so he wouldn't hear.

When Doodle came into the dining room, he found us seriously eating our cobbler. He was pale and lingered just inside the screen door. "Did you get the scarlet ibis buried?" asked Daddy.

Doodle didn't speak but nodded his head.

"Go wash your hands, and then you can have some peach cobbler," said Mama.

"I'm not hungry," he said.

"Dead birds is bad luck," said Aunt Nicey, poking her head from the kitchen door. "Specially *red* dead birds!"

As soon as I had finished eating, Doodle and I hurried off to Horsehead Landing. Time was short, and Doodle still had a long way to go if he was going to keep up with the other boys when he started school. The sun, gilded with the yellow cast of autumn, still burned fiercely, but the dark green woods through which we passed were shady and cool. When we reached the landing, Doodle said he was too tired to swim, so we got into a skiff and floated down the creek with the tide. Far off in the marsh a rail[16] was scolding, and over on the beach locusts were singing in the myrtle trees. Doodle did not speak and kept his head turned away, letting one hand trail limply in the water.

After we had drifted a long way, I put the oars in place and made Doodle row back against the tide. Black clouds began to gather in the southwest, and he kept watching them, trying to pull the oars a little faster. When we reached Horsehead Landing, lightning was playing across half the sky and thunder roared out, hiding even the sound of the sea. The sun disappeared and darkness descended,

15. ***Cobbler*** **is a deep-dish fruit pie with a thick top crust.**

16. **A *rail* is a small marsh bird.**

almost like night. Flocks of marsh crows flew by, heading inland to their roosting trees, and two egrets, squawking, arose from the oyster-rock shallows and careened away.

Doodle was both tired and frightened, and when he stepped from the skiff he collapsed onto the mud, sending an armada of fiddler crabs rustling off into the marsh grass. I helped him up, and as he wiped the mud off his trousers, he smiled at me ashamedly. He had failed and we both knew it, so we started back home, racing the storm. We never spoke (What are the words that can solder[17] cracked pride?), but I knew he was watching me, watching for a sign of mercy. The lightning was near now, and from fear he walked so close behind me he kept stepping on my heels. The faster I walked, the faster he walked, so I began to run. The rain was coming, roaring through the pines, and then, like a bursting Roman candle, a gum tree ahead of us was shattered by a bolt of lightning. When the deafening peal of thunder had died, and in the moment before the rain arrived, I heard Doodle, who had fallen behind, cry out, "Brother, Brother, don't leave me! Don't leave me!"

The knowledge that Doodle's and my plans had come to naught[18] was bitter, and that streak of cruelty within me awakened. I ran as fast as I could, leaving him far behind with a wall of rain dividing us. The drops stung my face like nettles, and the wind flared the wet glistening leaves of the bordering trees. Soon I could hear his voice no more.

I hadn't run too far before I became tired, and the flood of childish spite evanesced[19] as well. I stopped and waited for Doodle. The sound of rain was everywhere, but the wind had died and it fell straight down in parallel paths like ropes hanging from the sky. As I waited, I peered through the downpour, but no one came. Finally I went back and found him huddled beneath a red nightshade bush beside the road. He was sitting on the ground, his face buried in his arms, which were resting on his drawn-up knees. "Let's go, Doodle," I said.

He didn't answer, so I placed my hand on his forehead and lifted his head. Limply, he fell backwards onto the earth. He had been bleeding from the mouth, and his neck and the front of his shirt were stained a brilliant red.

"Doodle! Doodle!" I cried, shaking him, but there was no answer but the ropy rain. He lay very awkwardly, with his head thrown far back, making his vermilion[20] neck appear unusually long and slim. His little legs, bent sharply at the knees, had never before seemed so fragile, so thin.

I began to weep, and the tear-blurred vision in red before me looked very familiar. "Doodle!" I screamed above the pounding storm and threw my body to the earth above his. For a long long time, it seemed forever, I lay there crying, sheltering my fallen scarlet ibis from the heresy[21] of rain.

17. *Solder* (sod′ ər) means "to bond or repair."
18. *Naught* (nôt) means "nothing."
19. *Evanesced* (ev′ ə nest′) means "faded away; vanished."
20. *Vermilion* is a bright red or scarlet color.
21. *Heresy* (her′ ə sē) is an action or opinion contrary to what is generally considered right, true, or proper.

Responding to Literature

Personal Response
What are your thoughts about the relationship between the narrator and Doodle?

Analyzing Literature

Recall

1. Name two things Doodle accomplishes despite the doctor's predictions.
2. How is Brother both kind and cruel to Doodle?
3. Describe one of Doodle's "lies," or stories.
4. What is unusual about the scarlet ibis?
5. What happens to Doodle at the end of the story?

Interpret

6. What do Doodle's accomplishments reveal about his character?
7. Why does the narrator set such high goals for Doodle?
8. What do Doodle's lies tell you about his hopes and dreams?
9. How do both the fate of the ibis and Aunt Nicey's comment about it on page 266 serve as **foreshadowing?** Name another example of foreshadowing in the story. (See page R6.)
10. Do you think what happens to Doodle is Brother's fault?

Evaluate and Connect

11. Think about your response to the Reading Focus on page 256. How might Doodle have responded to the questions? How might the narrator have responded?
12. Doodle and Brother do not have much in common, yet they are inseparable. Do you find this believable? Tell why or why not.
13. In your opinion, why did Hurst set this story during World War I?
14. **Theme Connections** What reasons might the narrator have for "looking back" at the time he spent with Doodle?
15. Times have changed since 1912–1918, the short span of Doodle's life. How do you think his medical treatment might differ today from that available at the time?

Dismal Swamp in North Carolina.

Literary **ELEMENTS**

Figurative Language
Figurative language is language that is used for descriptive effect, often to imply ideas indirectly. In figurative language, words combine to express a meaning beyond the literal definition of each individual word. For example, when Hurst writes that naming the child William Armstrong was "like tying a big tail on a small kite," his meaning has little to do with actual kites. Rather, the author is using a comparison to suggest that the name William Armstrong was too big and heavy for the baby. Hurst uses two types of figurative language, similes and metaphors (comparisons of unlike things), to help make his writing more vivid and alive.

1. List three examples of figurative language in this story. For each of your examples, tell what the two things being compared have in common.
2. Reread the paragraphs in which your examples appear. How does Hurst's use of figurative language affect the meaning and tone of each passage?

- See **Literary Terms Handbook,** p. R5.

Literature and Writing

Writing About Literature

Examining Setting James Hurst once said that there were three characters in this story: the narrator, Doodle, and the setting. Why is the setting so important? Make a list of events that are influenced by different aspects of the setting–time, weather, vegetation, buildings. Then write several paragraphs explaining why the setting might be considered a "character" in the story.

Creative Writing

A Different Perspective Imagine that you are Doodle and you wish to tell your brother how you feel about his teaching you to walk. Write him a note in which you let him know how you felt before, during, and after you learned to walk. You may write about negative as well as positive feelings.

Extending Your Response

Literature Groups

Evaluating a Symbol A **symbol** is an object, person, place, or experience that represents something else. James Hurst has said that he chose the scarlet ibis as a symbol for Doodle. Discuss their similarities in appearance and in spirit. Consider Doodle's reaction to the bird and its death. Is the ibis a good symbol for Doodle? Why? Share your conclusions with other groups.

Learning for Life

Farm for Sale If you were a realtor hired to sell the farm on which this story takes place, how would you advertise it? Work with a partner to create a listing sheet for this property. Describe the farm's best features, including the beautiful flowers, working farmland, and scenic water.

Interdisciplinary Activity

Science: Swamped with Information This story contains a great deal of information about swamp life in the coastal southeastern United States. With a small group, list the different types of swamp life mentioned in the story–both plant and animal. Then, with the help of a CD-ROM encyclopedia or other reference sources, make a labeled drawing of a swamp ecosystem that includes some of the life forms from the story. You may wish to research one of the following real-life swamps in North Carolina, which may have served as a model for the swamp in this story: East Dismal, Wolf, Holly Shelter, or Green Swamp.

Save your work for your portfolio.

Skill Minilesson

VOCABULARY • Etymology

The etymology, or history, of some words is obvious. For example, if you've ever seen a dog that is eager to play, eat dinner, or go for a walk, you can imagine where the word *doggedness* comes from. The etymology of other words is less obvious. For example, the word *careen* comes from *carina,* the Latin word for *keel.* A keel is the strip along the bottom of a boat. If you tip a boat over, thereby turning the keel upwards, you keel the boat. This is why falling down, as in a faint, is called "keeling over." So, to *careen* is the same as to *keel,* that is, "to tilt or sway."

PRACTICE Use a dictionary to look up the etymologies of *exotic, precariously,* and *blighted.* (A word's etymology is usually given along with its definition.) Then, briefly explain something interesting or useful about the etymology of each word.

Writing Workshop

Narrative Writing: Short Story

If reading a short story can take you to another world, writing a short story makes you the captain of a globe-trotting vehicle. You can zoom into a character's mind, tour new kinds of conflicts and situations, or see how someone else would handle the problems you typically face. In the process, you may learn more about yourself and others. **Explore the life of a fictional character by writing a short story, using this workshop as your guide.**

- As you write your short story, refer to the **Writing Handbook,** pp. R58–R63.

EVALUATION RUBRIC
By the time you complete this Writing Workshop, you will have
- created one or more clearly defined characters
- told a story by developing a plot with conflict and rising action that leads to a climax
- presented a resolution to the conflict
- produced a short story that is free of errors in grammar, usage, and mechanics

The Writing Process

PREWRITING

PREWRITING TIP
Starting with your own experience is a good idea, but let your imagination take you beyond.

Explore ideas
The stories in this theme all involve looking back at events in a character's life. To find ideas for your story, look back at events in your life. If this search doesn't lead you to a story you want to tell, try using one of the following ideas as a starting point:

- characters in conflict, like the parent and child in Amy Tan's "Rules of the Game"
- a character your narrator admires, like Charley in Eugenia Collier's "Sweet Potato Pie"
- characters separated by generations or cultures, like the narrator and his great-grandmother in Gerald Haslam's "The Horned Toad"
- a memory that a character feels remorse about, as in James Hurst's "The Scarlet Ibis"

Consider your purpose
All stories are told for a reason. For example, a character may want to re-examine an act of cruelty in order to understand it better. To find out why you or your characters want to tell a particular story, keep asking yourself, "Why is this story being told now?" as you write. The answer will come to you in time.

Choose an audience
You can enter your story in a contest or send it to a magazine. You can share it with other writers in a writing workshop format, or you can circulate it among friends and family.

Explore story elements
All short stories contain certain basic elements. To figure out how you want these elements to work in your story, do some of the writing exercises on the next page. If it feels right, let one exercise blend into another. You may find your story taking shape before your eyes.

Characters	Describe your main characters using as many specific details as possible. For example, you might consider the clothes they wear, the music they listen to, or their attitudes about life.
Setting	Through the eyes of your main character, describe the setting–the time and place–for your story. Make this description reflect the character's personality or mood.
Plot	What problem or conflict is your character facing? Using dialogue where appropriate, write a scene in which this conflict is revealed.
Point of view	Will your story be told by a character, using the first-person point of view? Or will it be told in the third person by a narrator who knows everything? Rewrite your conflict-revealing scene using a different point of view.

STUDENT MODEL

CHARACTERS

The characters will be Felix and Chris, two brothers. Felix is my age. He's sort of an athlete and likes rap music, but lately he hasn't been liking anything very much. His brother is off at college and is estranged from the family, and Felix's dad was in a car accident two months ago and has been in a coma every since, so Felix is depressed, scared, and really lonely. Chris is more of a rebel type. He has shaggy, longish hair, wears dark, ripped up clothing, and likes alternative music. About a year ago he fought with his parents over the way he looks and acts, and since then he hasn't been in touch with anyone from home, including Felix.

Complete student model on p. R110.

Consider your story's form

The scenes in a story are often presented in the order in which they occur, leading to a climax. Sometimes, though, the narrator will interrupt this chronological order with flashbacks, or reflections on past incidents.

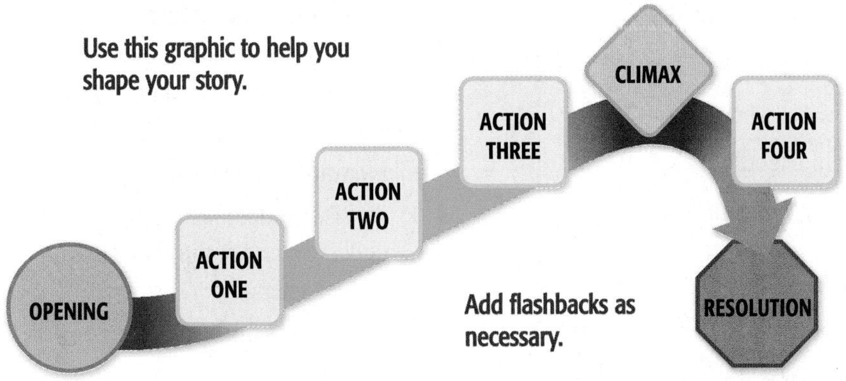

DRAFTING

DRAFTING TIP

Reread the writing you did at the prewriting stage and underline your favorite sentences. Choose one of these to use as the first sentence in your draft.

Start in the middle

If you're not sure how to begin your story or how to lead up to the main conflict, try starting your draft with the main conflict already underway. You might try opening with a conversation—or an argument—between two characters.

Write your draft

Instead of *telling* your readers what's happening in the story, use details and description to *show* them what's happening. These details might also provide you with more information about the characters and conflict. Drafting is a time to learn and explore. Writing about one thing may help you discover what you want to say next.

REVISING

REVISING TIP

Read the story to yourself aloud. If any passages sound confusing or awkward to you, put check marks beside them. Later, rework those passages to make them flow smoothly.

Test the audience reaction

Read your story to a friend. Then ask for his or her response, keeping it in mind as you make final changes to your manuscript.

Look back

After you finish your draft, set it aside for a few hours or days. Then read it again, using the **Rubric for Revising** as a guide for identifying ways to improve it.

STUDENT MODEL

Landing on ICU was like arriving on another planet.
^ We stepped out of the elevator and I saw
ominous
Chris's eyes were riveted straight ahead to the ^
sliding glass doors that welcome people to the
dreadful pain of
^ ICU. I suddenly turned to him and said, "Don't
move. I have to show you this." I went on to
explain how the entrance doors to ICU were
highly sensitive and designed to open at the
"But
slightest human approach. ^I ~~told him that I~~
can   " I said. At first,
~~could~~ beat the system. ^ Chris stood there
"what are you talking about" expression
wearing that ^ ~~silly grin of his~~, but then he
crossed his arms over his chest, cocked his
, for the first time that night, grinned.   "he said."
head, and ^ ~~smiled and said,~~ ^"OK, ^prove it."
¶

Complete student model on p. R110.

RUBRIC FOR REVISING

Your revised short story should have

- ☑ a plot that includes conflict and rising action that leads to a climax
- ☑ dialogue and details that help to advance the plot and reveal the thoughts, behavior, and appearance of one or more characters
- ☑ a consistent point of view
- ☑ details that describe the setting
- ☑ a conclusion that satisfactorily resolves the conflict

Your revised short story should be free of

- ☑ awkward, unnatural dialogue
- ☑ details that do not contribute to an understanding of the characters, plot, or setting
- ☑ errors in grammar, usage, and mechanics

EDITING/PROOFREADING

When you are satisfied with your story's content and style, proofread it to correct errors.

PROOFREADING TIP
Use the **Proofreading Checklist** on the inside back cover of this textbook as a guide for marking errors in your story.

Grammar Hint

Use punctuation marks to separate each part of a quotation from an interrupting phrase. Begin a new paragraph and use a new set of quotation marks when the speaker changes.

"I think so," I answered. "They say the machines are the only thing keeping him alive."

● For more about punctuation, see **Language Handbook,** p. R49.

STUDENT MODEL

```
Why did it take you so long to finally come
home, I asked? After I said it I realized I
didn't want the anser. Never mind. I'm just
glad you're here. I'm glad to be here, too,
Chris said.
```

Complete student model on p. R110.

Complete Student Model

For a complete version of the student model, see **Writing Workshop Models**, p. R110.

PUBLISHING/PRESENTING

Decide how you'll share your story with others. You might read it aloud to friends or make it into a small, handmade book called a chapbook. You can circulate your chapbook among friends or donate it to the school library.

PRESENTING TIP
If you read your story aloud, remember to speak slowly and loudly.

Reflecting

Write an evaluation of your story-writing experience. In it, discuss what you learned while writing and how you feel about your story. You might answer these questions: What was the hardest part? What was the most enjoyable part? What would you like to do differently the next time you write a story?

Save your work for your portfolio.

Unit Assessment

Personal Response

1. Which story in this unit did you find the most entertaining? Which story was the most thought-provoking? To which of the narrators could you most strongly relate? Why?
2. As a result of the work you did in this unit, what new ideas do you have about the following:
   - how to read a short story
   - how to work with other students in pairs or in groups
   - how to connect literature to your own life and interests

Analyzing Literature

Creating Your Own Theme The stories in this unit have been organized into three themes—"Matters of Life and Death," "Filling a Void," and "Looking Back." Choose at least five of the stories from this unit and organize them into a theme of your own choosing. Give a title to your theme, and then explain in writing how the selections you've chosen relate to your theme title and to each other.

Evaluate and Set Goals

Evaluate

1. What was your strongest contribution to group work as you moved through this unit?
2. What was the most challenging task you faced in this unit?
   - How did you approach the task?
   - Were you satisfied with the results?
   - What did you learn from the challenge?
3. If you could give a grade to the overall work you did in this unit, what would it be? Give at least two reasons for your assessment.

Set Goals

1. Think about the activities in this unit in which you feel you did your weakest work. How could you improve?
2. Choose a goal to work toward in the next unit to improve your performance.
3. Meet with your teacher to discuss your goal and the steps you will take to achieve it.
4. Plan a way to evaluate whether you have reached your goal.

Build Your Portfolio

Select Choose two pieces of work you did in this unit and include them in your portfolio. Use these questions to help you make your selection.
- Which are you most proud of?
- Which are the most creative?
- Which did you learn the most from?

Reflect Write some notes to accompany the pieces you selected. Use these questions to guide you.
- What do you like best about these pieces?
- What sets these pieces apart from the rest?
- What did you learn while creating them?
- What might you change if given the chance to do them over again?

Reading on Your Own

You might also be interested in the following books.

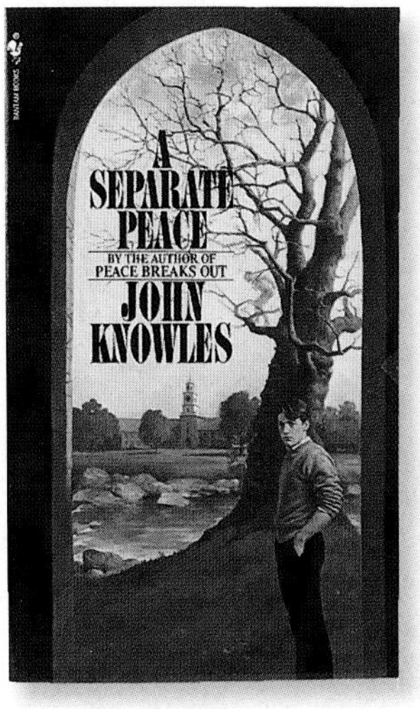

A Separate Peace
by John Knowles This celebrated novel is about the relationship between two boys at boarding school during World War II. One of the boys is a brilliant student, the other is a great athlete, and the tension between them leads to a tragedy that symbolizes the darkest forces of adolescence.

Great Expectations
by Charles Dickens
This popular novel is a mystery, a morality tale, and a coming-of-age story all rolled into one. The first-person narrator Pip falls into unrequited love and unexpected wealth as he makes his way from boyhood to adulthood.

Lord of the Flies
by William Golding When a group of boys becomes stranded on an uninhabited island, they must struggle for their lives. Two leaders emerge—one enthralled by savage ritual and the hunt for food, the other concerned with maintaining civility and seeking rescue—and the boys must choose sides in this frightening exploration of human nature.

A Place Where the Sea Remembers
by Sandra Benitez Through a series of intertwined stories, this novel explores the hopes, loves, failures, and relationships of the inhabitants of a small seaside village in Mexico. Their lives and dreams are guarded by Remedios, the village *curandera,* or healer.

Standardized Test Practice

Read the following passage. Then read each question on page 277. Decide which is the best answer to each question. Mark the letter for that answer on your paper.

A Small Fish in a Big Pond

Jenna Jacobs had been the most popular girl in the eighth grade class at Westwood Middle School. She had graduated first in her class and was ready for high school, both academically and socially. She had exceeded all of the goals she set for herself in middle school, and she was ready for new challenges in high school.

Unfortunately, high school was different from middle school. In the first week of school, Jenna went to tryouts for cheerleading. She was competing against very talented juniors and seniors, and she knew that making the squad would be difficult. After she completed her routine for the judges and senior captains, she sat down with the other girls and waited patiently. After two hours, the judges read off a list of names of the girls who were invited back for another tryout. Jenna's heart sank as the list ended without her name. She had failed to make the squad. Feeling awful, she walked home carrying her backpack full of the night's homework.

When she arrived home, she went upstairs to her room and began to work. She started with algebra and became more frustrated with each question she tried to answer. She had always been a good math student, but now she was struggling. She moved on to English and history, and was relieved to find that she didn't have any trouble with those subjects. Feeling better about what she had accomplished, she decided not to worry about math for the time being. Just then the phone rang and Jenna's mom called upstairs to her. Jenna reached over to her desk and answered it. It was Gina, her best friend, calling about the algebra homework.

"Hey, Jen. What's up? I was calling about math. Do you understand it?"

"No, not really. I just did as much as I could, but that's not saying much."

"Oh, I thought you could help me. You're so good in math."

"Well, it doesn't seem that way anymore. Sorry."

"That's all right. I'll figure it out, or just wait until tomorrow."

"Yeah, me too. See you tomorrow."

"Wait, Jen. I wanted to ask you something. How did tryouts go? I bet you were great."

"Not great enough. I didn't make the squad." Saying it out loud brought tears to Jenna's eyes.

"What? Jen, I can't believe it! How could they not take you?"

"I don't know. I have to go, my mom is calling me. See you tomorrow. Bye."

"But, Jen—" Gina heard only a dial tone, and was left staring at the phone.

The next day Jenna went to see Mrs. Biden about being on the school newspaper. Mrs. Biden wasn't as enthusiastic as Jenna was. "I'm sorry, but we have many writers for the paper already. I usually only have juniors and seniors on the staff, since so many of them want to participate. Come back and see me at the end of next year and we'll talk then." Jenna smiled weakly and left the room. "Why is high school so different?" she fumed.

Later in algebra class, Jenna saw Gina come in and waved for her to sit next to her. Gina came over and sat just as the bell rang, so she had no time to <u>interrogate</u> Jenna on why she had hung up on her so abruptly last night. Jenna devoted herself to figuring out the problems that had given her so much trouble the night before. By the end of class, she understood what she needed to do to get them right.

As she gathered her books at the end of class, Jenna decided she'd try one more time to fit in at her new high school, and look into joining the Homecoming Committee. She wasn't sure if she would succeed, but she knew she had to try. High school was just as her mom had said: "You will feel like a small fish in a big pond instead of a big fish in a small pond. The challenge is to become the best fish you can be."

---

1 Gina stared at the phone —

A when she heard her mother calling

B because Jenna was yelling

C as she tried to figure out why Jenna hung up on her

D because there was another call on the line

2 Which of the following is the best summary of this passage?

F A math whiz has a difficult time with history.

G Jenna tries to join the newspaper and finds that there is more to school than clubs.

H A new student comes to school and wins many friends.

J A freshman has a tough time fitting in but continues to try.

3 Which of the following best describes Jenna's mood at the beginning of the passage?

A Confident

B Frightened

C Melancholy

D Sarcastic

4 Jenna "fumed" after speaking with Mrs. Biden —

F because Mrs. Biden said something unkind about Gina

G because she had been frustrated in her attempts to succeed in high school

H in order to call attention to herself

J because she thought Mrs. Biden was being unfair to juniors

5 The main idea of the passage is that —

A some things are not as easy as you expect them to be

B high school is more difficult than middle school for everyone

C math is the most difficult subject in school

D cheerleading is a competitive sport

6 Based on the passage, what will Jenna probably do next?

F Go back to Mrs. Biden and complain

G Cry to her parents at home

H Continue to try to be involved in other activities

J Meet with the principal to discuss providing more opportunities for juniors

7 In the passage, the word <u>interrogate</u> means —

A tell stories to

B ask questions of

C be angry at

D confuse

STOP

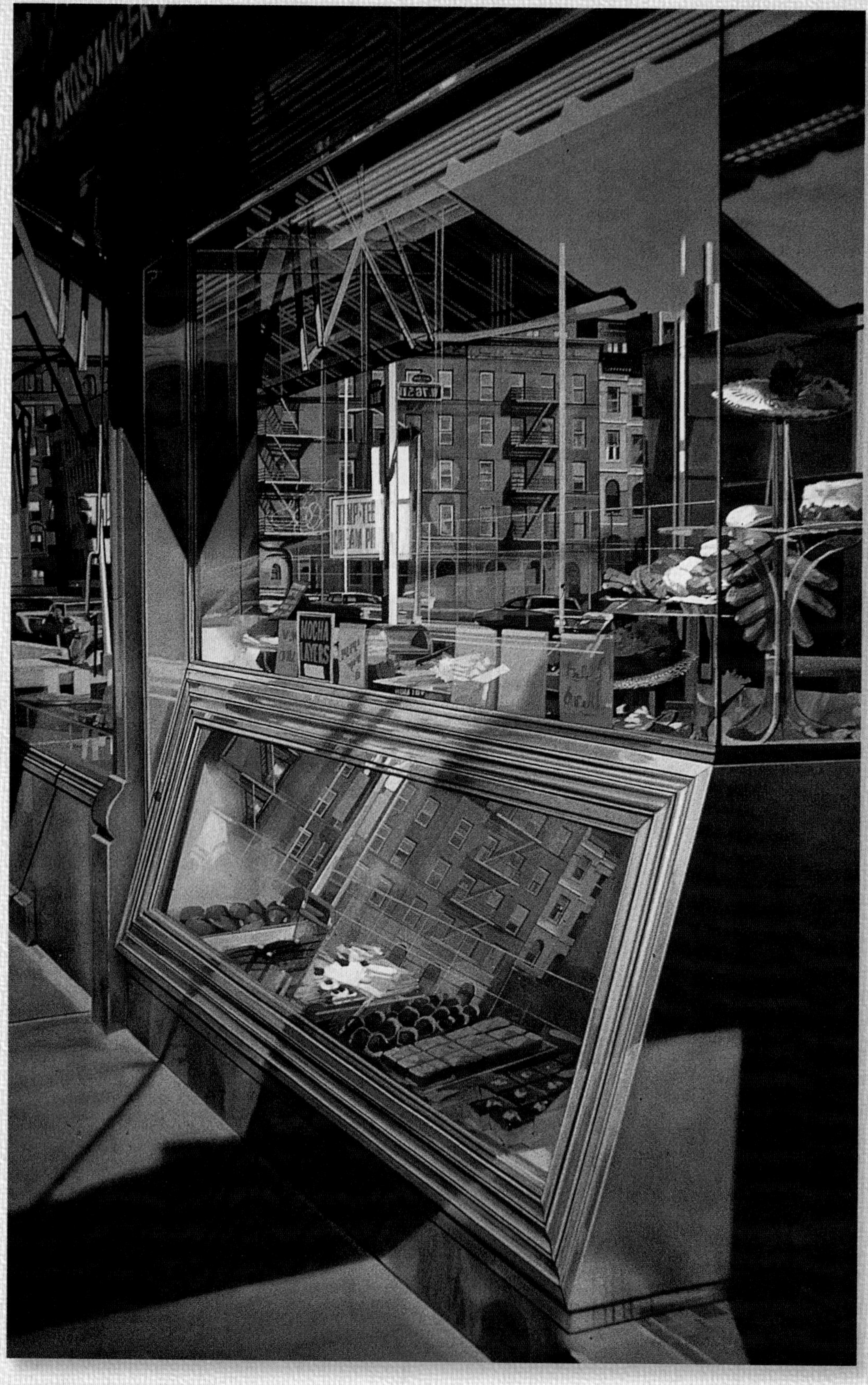

Grossinger's Bakery, 1972. Richard Estes. Oil on canvas. Private collection.

UNIT TWO

Nonfiction

"If fiction is a world, nonfiction is the world. In the end all writing is about the business of being human."

—William Sloane

Genre Focus

Nonfiction

Nonfiction is the broadest category of literature. Autobiographies, biographies, memoirs, letters, essays, speeches, and news articles are just a few of the many types of nonfiction writing. All these forms of prose concern real, rather than imaginary, subjects, and nonfiction writers present information they consider true. Like fiction, however, nonfiction writing can be creative.

Narrative Nonfiction

Some works of nonfiction tell a story, just as works of fiction do. Autobiographies, memoirs, biographies, and narrative essays are types of narrative nonfiction.

- In an **autobiography,** a writer tells his or her life story from the first-person point of view, using the pronoun *I*, and typically focuses on the most significant events that happened to him or her.
- In a **memoir,** a writer also uses the first-person point of view to relate events from his or her own life. Memoirs differ from autobiographies in that they typically focus on one period of a person's life. In a memoir, a writer will tend to emphasize his or her relationships with other people or the impact of significant historical events on his or her own life.
- In a **biography,** a writer uses the third-person point of view to write about the life of someone else.
- In a **narrative essay,** a writer may use either the first- or the third-person point of view to relate a true story in a short composition.

Because works of narrative nonfiction tell a story, they have many characteristics of fiction. For example, they may include such elements as setting, characters, theme, plot, and conflict. Their organization also may resemble that of fictional stories. An author may present events in **chronological order,** or the order in which they occurred. Or an author may use **flashback,** going back in time to present incidents that occurred before the beginning of the story.

Informative Nonfiction

Informative nonfiction includes essays, speeches, and articles that explain a topic or promote an opinion. Writers of informative nonfiction sometimes weave stories or personal anecdotes into their writing. Two major types of informative nonfiction are expository essays and persuasive essays.

- **Expository essays** explain a topic. Articles that explain the steps in a process, report the news, or analyze a work of literature are all examples of expository writing.
- **Persuasive essays** promote an opinion or a position. Advice columns, movie reviews, and editorials are all examples of persuasive writing.

Many expository and persuasive essays follow a general structure of lead, body, and conclusion.

- The **lead,** or introduction, captures the reader's attention and often includes a **thesis,** or statement of the essay's main idea.
- The **body** develops the main idea by providing **supporting details,** such as facts, reasons, quotations, statistics, sensory details, examples, observations, and personal experiences.
- The **conclusion** may restate the thesis or main idea, summarize the essay's main points, or leave the reader with something to think about. A persuasive essay may end with a call to action.

Analyzing Nonfiction

- When you analyze nonfiction, begin by identifying the type of work you are reading. By looking at the title and skimming the beginning, you can usually tell whether the work is an autobiography or a memoir, a biography, an essay, or another type of nonfiction writing.
- Identifying the author's purpose as you read may help you further classify the work. Does the author seek to entertain, to inform, or to persuade the reader? The answer will help you tell whether you are reading a narrative, an expository, or a persuasive essay.
- Once you identify the type of work you are reading, look for familiar elements. For example, look for short-story elements in a work of narrative nonfiction. Look for a thesis and supporting details in a work of informative nonfiction. Be aware, however, that a writer may combine various elements, and purposes, in a single work. For instance, you might read a humorous narrative essay that's not only entertaining but also persuasive and informative. Every piece of nonfiction writing is unique, so consider how each work is similar to as well as different from other writing of its kind.

Active Reading Model

Active Reading Strategies

Nonfiction

To get the most from reading nonfiction, active readers use strategies similar to those used in reading short stories. As an active reader, however, you must adapt the strategies to the particular type of nonfiction you are reading.

● For more about reading strategies, see **Reading Handbook,** pp. R78–R107.

PREDICT

Make educated guesses about what you are reading. Preview the topic and the type of nonfiction by making inferences from the title and by skimming the text. Also preview the work by reading the boldface titles or headlines and examining the photographs, artwork, graphics, or other visual elements. Make predictions before you begin to read the text and also as you read.

Ask yourself . . .

- What will this work be about?
- What supporting details might the writer use?
- What point will the writer make next?

CONNECT

Make connections with what you already know about a subject.

Ask yourself . . .

- What people and events in my own life are similar to those described here?
- What have I heard or read on this subject?
- How does the work add to or change my understanding of the subject?
- What connections can I make between this subject and other subjects I know about?

QUESTION

Question anything that you do not understand. Reread any part that confuses you. Read on to see if your questions are answered.

Ask yourself . . .

- What is the writer saying here?
- Why is the writer giving me this information?
- How does this concept relate to what I just read?

VISUALIZE Use details the writer gives you to form mental pictures. Try to see the steps in a process or the way something works.

Ask yourself . . .
- What do these people, places, and objects look like?
- How does this part fit together with the rest?

EVALUATE Make judgments about what you read.

Ask yourself . . .
- What does an action reveal about a person?
- Is this fact or opinion?
- Does this information support the thesis?
- Do I agree with the writer's opinions and interpretations?

REVIEW Pause often to think about what you have read.

Say to yourself . . .
- The writer's purpose is . . .
- The main idea is . . .
- The writer supports the thesis with these supporting details . . .
- The events described, in order, are . . .

RESPOND React to what you are reading. Take time to recognize the spontaneous thoughts and feelings you have about what the writer is saying. Identify what you like or dislike about the work.

Say to yourself . . .
- I'd like to ask the writer why . . .
- I think this idea is . . .
- That's interesting. I want to know more about . . .
- The people with whom I'd like to share this work include . . .

Applying the Strategies

Read the following excerpt from *Life on the Mississippi,* a memoir by Mark Twain, using the Active Reading Model in the margins. Then practice the strategies as you read another work of nonfiction.

Before You Read

from *Life on the Mississippi*

Reading Focus

Many people take snapshots of places they visit. How else could you remember sights, sounds, and events?

List Ideas As a class, brainstorm different ways to record memories and list your ideas on the chalkboard.

Setting a Purpose Read to enjoy some of Mark Twain's comments about his travels.

Building Background

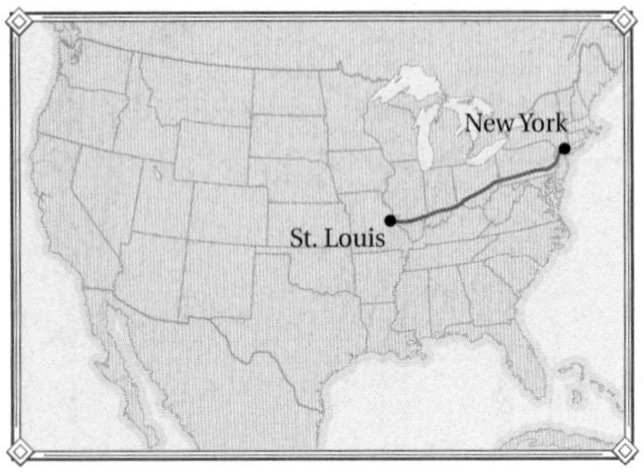

The Time and Place
In this excerpt, Mark Twain remembers his journey by rail from New York to St. Louis, Missouri, in the late 1880s.

Did You Know?
In the mid-1800s, steamboats provided the primary means of transporting cargo and people in the central United States. Cities grew rapidly along the banks of the Mississippi River as a result of river commerce. Before the end of the 1800s, however, the Civil War and the development of railroads put an end to the steamboat's dominance.

Vocabulary Preview

picturesque (pik′ chə resk′) *adj.* having pleasing visual qualities suitable for a picture; pretty; p. 285

ineffectual (in′ i fek′ cho͞o əl) *adj.* not producing a desired result or effect; p. 285

ostentatious (os′ tən tā′ shəs) *adj.* done with the intent of attracting notice; showy; p. 288

pompous (pom′ pəs) *adj.* showing an exaggerated sense of self-importance; p. 288

turbulent (tur′ byə lənt) *adj.* full of commotion, disorder, or violence; not calm or smooth; p. 288

wholesome (hōl′ səm) *adj.* promoting good health; healthful; p. 288

prodigious (prə dij′ əs) *adj.* extraordinary in size, number, or degree; enormous; p. 290

Meet Mark Twain

Samuel Clemens took his pen name, Mark Twain, from Mississippi riverboat slang. The phrase means "two fathoms deep," the shallowest depth at which boats can navigate the river. As a young man, Twain worked a number of different jobs. He was a printer, a steamboat captain, and a popular lecturer and humorist. He later became one of America's greatest writers, creating the immortal Huckleberry Finn and other enduring characters. Of his "call" to literature, he said, "It is nothing to be proud of, but it is my strongest suit . . . seriously scribbling to excite the *laughter* of God's creatures."

Mark Twain was born in 1835 and died in 1910. Life on the Mississippi *was first published in 1883.*

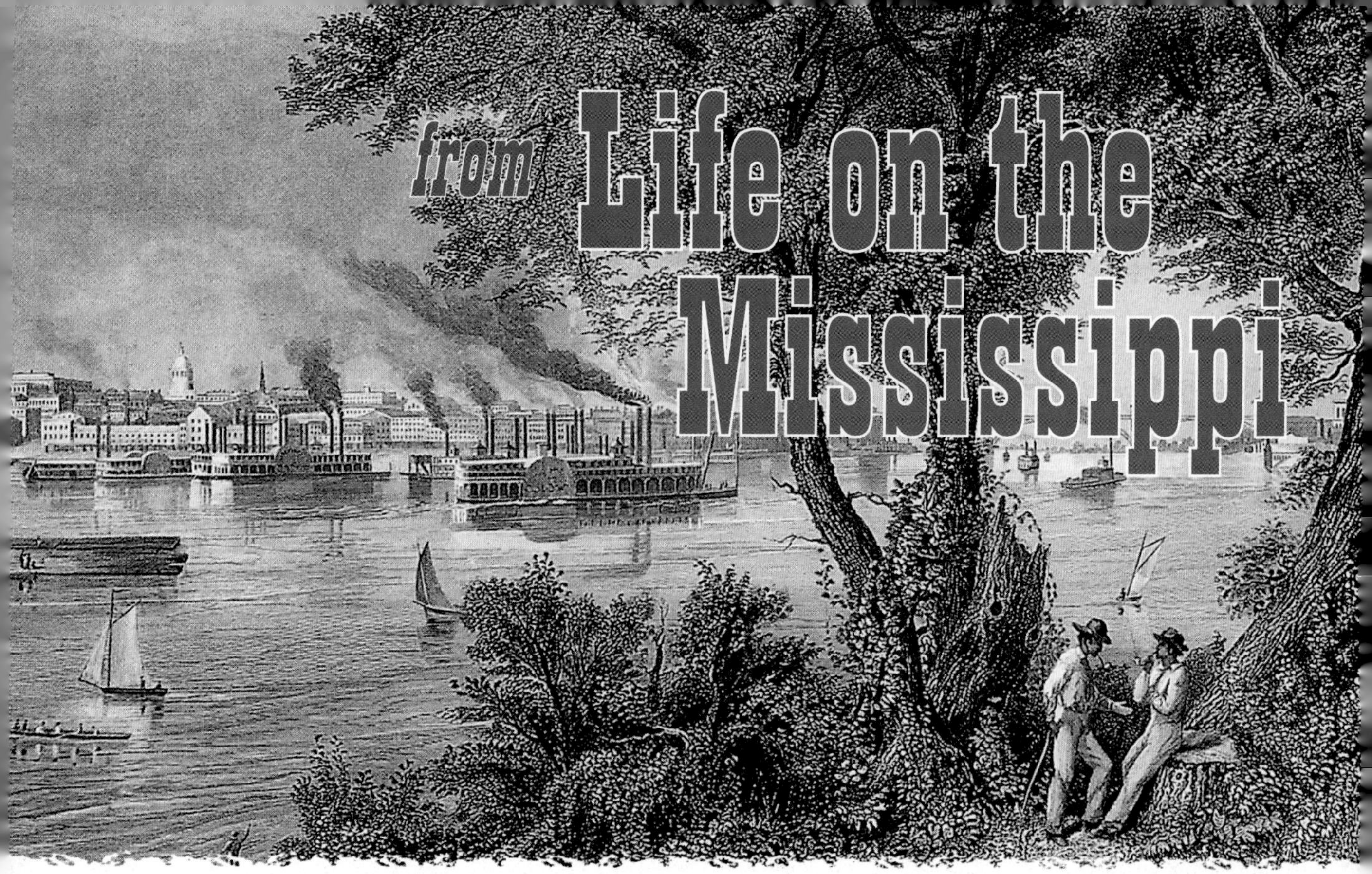

from Life on the Mississippi

Mark Twain

AFTER TWENTY-ONE YEARS' ABSENCE I felt a very strong desire to see the river again, and the steamboats, and such of the boys as might be left; so I resolved to go out there. I enlisted a poet for company, and a stenographer[1] to "take him down," and started westward about the middle of April.

Active Reading Model

As I proposed to make notes, with a view to printing, I took some thought as to methods of procedure. I reflected that if I were recognized, on the river, I should not be as free to go and come, talk, inquire, and spy around, as I should be if unknown; I remembered that it was the custom of steamboatmen in the old times to load up the confiding stranger with the most picturesque and admirable lies, and put the sophisticated friend off with dull and ineffectual facts: so I concluded that, from a business point of view, it would be an advantage to disguise our party with fictitious names. The idea

PREDICT

After reading the title and the first paragraph, what do you think the topic of this selection is? What type of non fiction is it?

1. A *stenographer* (stə nog′ rə fər) is a person hired to take dictation, quickly writing down what others say aloud.

Vocabulary

picturesque (pik′ chə resk′) *adj.* having pleasing visual qualities suitable for a picture; pretty

ineffectual (in′ i fek′ cho͞o əl) *adj.* not producing a desired result or effect

Active Reading Model

was certainly good, but it bred infinite bother; for although Smith, Jones, and Johnson are easy names to remember when there is no occasion to remember them, it is next to impossible to recollect them when they are wanted. How do criminals manage to keep a brand-new *alias* in mind? This is a great mystery. I was innocent; and yet was seldom able to lay my hand on my new name when it was needed; and it seemed to me that if I had had a crime on my conscience to further confuse me, I could never have kept the name by me at all.

We left per Pennsylvania Railroad, at 8 A.M. April 18.

> *Evening.*—Speaking of dress. Grace and picturesqueness drop gradually out of it as one travels away from New York.

I find that among my notes. It makes no difference which direction you take, the fact remains the same. Whether you move north, south, east, or west, no matter: you can get up in the morning and guess how far you have come, by noting what degree of grace and picturesqueness is by that time lacking in the costumes of the new passengers—I do not mean of the women alone, but of both sexes. It may be that *carriage*[2] is at the bottom of this thing; and I think it is; for there are plenty of ladies and gentlemen in the provincial cities whose garments are all made by the best tailors and dressmakers of New York; yet this has no perceptible effect upon the grand fact: the educated eye never mistakes those people for New-Yorkers. No, there is a godless grace and snap and style about a born and bred New-Yorker which mere clothing cannot effect.

CONNECT

In your experience, is it true that posture is more important than clothing when it comes to making a positive impression?

> *April 19.*—This morning struck into the region of full goatees—sometimes accompanied by a mustache, but only occasionally.

It was odd to come upon this thick crop of an obsolete and uncomely fashion; it was like running suddenly across a forgotten acquaintance whom you had supposed dead for a generation. The goatee extends over a wide extent of country, and is accompanied by an iron-clad belief in Adam, and the biblical history of creation, which has not suffered from the assaults of the scientists.[3]

EVALUATE

What is the author saying about people who wear goatees? What do these assumptions tell you about him?

Did You Know?
A *goatee* is a small, pointed chin beard (so named for its resemblance to a goat's beard). Twain says that this fashion is out-of-date *(obsolete)* and unattractive *(uncomely)*.

> *Afternoon.*—At the railway stations the loafers carry *both* hands in their breeches pockets; it was observable, heretofore that one hand was sometimes out-of-doors—here, never. This is an important fact in geography.

2. *Carriage* means "posture," or "a way of holding or carrying the head and body."
3. *Assaults of the scientists* refers to the theory of evolution by natural selection.

If the loafers determined the character of a country, it would be still more important, of course.

> Heretofore, all along, the station loafer has been often observed to scratch one shin with the other foot; here these remains of activity are wanting. This has an ominous look.

Active Reading Model

By and by we entered the tobacco-chewing region. Fifty years ago the tobacco-chewing region covered the Union. It is greatly restricted now.

QUESTION
What region of the country do you think the author is describing?

Next, boots began to appear. Not in strong force, however. Later—away down the Mississippi—they became the rule. They disappeared from other sections of the Union with the mud; no doubt they will disappear from the river villages, also, when proper pavements come in.

REVIEW
What is the author really saying about river village life?

We reached St. Louis at ten o'clock at night. At the counter of the hotel I tendered[4] a hurriedly invented fictitious name, with a miserable attempt at careless ease. The clerk paused, and inspected me in the compassionate way in which one inspects a respectable person who is found in doubtful circumstances; then he said:

"It's all right; I know what sort of room you want. Used to clerk at the St. James, in New York."

An unpromising beginning for a fraudulent career! We started to the supper-room, and met two other men whom I had known elsewhere. How odd and unfair it is: wicked impostors go around lecturing under my *nom de guerre*,[5] and nobody suspects them; but when an honest man attempts an imposture,[6] he is exposed at once.

QUESTION
Why does the author seem so frustrated?

One thing seemed plain: we must start down the river the next day, if people who could not be deceived were going to crop up at this rate: an unpalatable[7] disappointment, for we had hoped to have a week in St. Louis. The Southern was a good hotel, and we could have had a comfortable time there. It is large and well conducted, and its decorations do not make one cry, as do those of the vast Palmer House, in Chicago. True, the billiard-tables were of the Old Silurian Period, and the cues and balls of the Post-Pliocene; but there was refreshment in this, not discomfort; for there are rest and healing in the contemplation of antiquities.[8]

EVALUATE
Is the author being serious or humorous or both?

The most notable absence observable in the billiard-room was the absence of the river-man. If he was there, he had taken in his sign; he was in disguise.

---

4. Here, *tendered* means "presented; offered."
5. *Nom de guerre* (nôɴ də ger′) is French for "war name" and means "pseudonym or alias."
6. An *impostor* is someone who assumes the name or character of another person in order to deceive others; the effort to do this is an *imposture*.
7. *Unpalatable* means "not agreeable to the taste, mind, or feelings; unacceptable."
8. Twain finds comfort in the thoughtful study *(contemplation)* of objects from ancient times *(antiquities)*.

Active Reading Model

CONNECT

Do you know the names of people who work in stores in your community? What difference does such familiarity make?

RESPOND

What do you think of the author's sense of humor?

I saw there none of the swell airs and graces, and ostentatious displays of money, and pompous squanderings[9] of it, which used to distinguish the steamboat crowd from the dry-land crowd in the bygone days, in the thronged billiard-rooms of St. Louis. In those times the principal saloons were always populous with river-men; given fifty players present, thirty or thirty-five were likely to be from the river. But I suspected that the ranks were thin now, and the steamboatmen no longer an aristocracy. Why, in my time they used to call the "barkeep" Bill, or Joe, or Tom, and slap him on the shoulder; I watched for that. But none of these people did it. Manifestly,[10] a glory that once was had dissolved and vanished away in these twenty-one years.

When I went up to my room I found there the young man called Rogers, crying. Rogers was not his name; neither was Jones, Brown, Dexter, Ferguson, Bascom, nor Thompson; but he answered to either of these that a body found handy in an emergency; or to any other name, in fact, if he perceived that you meant him. He said:

"What is a person to do here when he wants a drink of water? drink this slush?"

"Can't you drink it?"

"I could if I had some other water to wash it with."

Here was a thing which had not changed; a score of years had not affected this water's brown complexion in the least; a score of centuries would succeed no better, perhaps. It comes out of the turbulent, bank-caving Missouri, and every tumblerful of it holds nearly an acre of land in solution. I got this fact from the bishop of the diocese. If you will let your glass stand half an hour, you can separate the land from the water as easy as Genesis; and then you will find them both good: the one good to eat, the other good to drink. The land is very nourishing, the water is thoroughly wholesome. The one appeases[11] hunger; the other, thirst. But the natives do not take them separately, but together, as nature mixed them. When they find an inch of mud in the bottom of a glass, they stir it up, and then take the draft as they would gruel.[12] It is difficult for a stranger to get used to this batter, but once used to it he will prefer it to water. This is really the case. It is good for steamboating, and good to drink; but it is worthless for all other purposes, except baptizing.

9. Here, *squanderings* refers to reckless or wasteful spending.
10. *Manifestly* means "obviously; clearly; evidently."
11. *Appeases* means "satisfies."
12. A *draft* is the amount taken in one swallow, and *gruel* is a thin porridge.

Vocabulary

ostentatious (os′ tən tā′ shəs) *adj.* done with the intent of attracting notice; showy
pompous (pom′ pəs) *adj.* showing an exaggerated sense of self-importance
turbulent (tur′ byə lənt) *adj.* full of commotion, disorder, or violence; not calm or smooth
wholesome (hōl′ səm) *adj.* promoting good health; healthful

Next morning we drove around town in the rain. The city seemed but little changed. It *was* greatly changed, but it did not seem so; because in St. Louis, as in London and Pittsburgh, you can't persuade a new thing to look new; the coal-smoke turns it into an antiquity the moment you take your hand off it. The place had just about doubled its size since I was a resident of it, and was now become a city of four hundred thousand inhabitants; still, in the solid business parts, it looked about as it had looked formerly. Yet I am sure there is not as much smoke in St. Louis now as there used to be. The smoke used to bank itself in a dense billowy black canopy over the town, and hide the sky from view. This shelter is very much thinner now; still, there is a sufficiency of smoke there, I think. I heard no complaint.

However, on the outskirts changes were apparent enough; notably in dwelling-house architecture. The fine new homes are noble and beautiful and modern. They stand by themselves, too, with green lawns around them; whereas the dwellings of a former day are packed together in blocks, and are all of one pattern, with windows all alike, set in an arched framework of twisted stone; a sort of house which was handsome enough when it was rarer.

There was another change—the Forest Park. This was new to me. It is beautiful and very extensive, and has the excellent merit of having been made mainly by nature. There are other parks, and fine ones, notably Tower Grove and the Botanical Gardens; for St. Louis interested herself to such improvements at an earlier day than did the most of our cities.

Active Reading Model

VISUALIZE

Pause and form a mental picture of smoke-filled St. Louis and its new suburbs.

Wooding-Up on the Mississippi, c. 1857–1907. Nathaniel Currier & James Merritt Ives. Hand-colored lithograph. Private collection.

Viewing the art: Look closely at this lithograph and read the title. Why might Twain be nostalgic for the steamboating way of life?

Active Reading Model

The first time I ever saw St. Louis I could have bought it for six million dollars, and it was the mistake of my life that I did not do it. It was bitter now to look abroad over this domed and steepled metropolis, this solid expanse of bricks and mortar stretching away on every hand into dim, measure-defying distances, and remember that I had allowed that opportunity to go by. Why I should have allowed it to go by seems, of course, foolish and inexplicable today, at a first glance; yet there were reasons at the time to justify this course. . . .

Mississippi steamboating was born about 1812; at the end of thirty years it had grown to mighty proportions; and in less than thirty more it was dead! A strangely short life for so majestic a creature. Of course it is not absolutely dead; neither is an octogenarian[13] who could once jump twenty-two feet on level ground; but as contrasted with what it was in its prime vigor, Mississippi steamboating may be called dead.

Did You Know?
A *keelboat* is a flat-bottomed riverboat that is rowed, towed, or poled, and used for carrying freight.

CONNECT
In more recent times, what has "killed" the railroads?

It killed the old-fashioned keel-boating, by reducing the freight trip to New Orleans to less than a week. The railroads have killed the steamboat passenger traffic by doing in two or three days what the steamboats consumed a week in doing: and the towing fleets have killed the through-freight traffic by dragging six or seven steamer-loads of stuff down the river at a time, at an expense so trivial that steamboat competition was out of the question.

Freight and passenger way traffic remains to the steamers. This is in the hands—along the two thousand miles of river between St. Paul and New Orleans—of two or three close corporations well fortified with capital; and by able and thoroughly businesslike management and system, these make a sufficiency of money out of what is left of the once prodigious steamboating industry. I suppose that St. Louis and New Orleans have not suffered materially[14] by the change, but alas for the wood-yard man!

REVIEW
In your opinion, what was the author's purpose in writing this section of *Life on the Mississippi*?

He used to fringe the river all the way; his close-ranked merchandise stretched from the one city to the other, along the banks, and he sold uncountable cords of it every year for cash on the nail; but all the scattering boats that are left burn coal now, and the seldomest spectacle on the Mississippi today is a wood-pile. Where now is the once wood-yard man?

13. An *octogenarian* is between eighty and ninety years old.
14. The cities have not suffered in an important, basic, or essential way *(materially)*.

Vocabulary
prodigious (prə dij′ əs) *adj.* extraordinary in size, number, or degree; enormous

Responding to Literature

Personal Response

What images from the selection linger in your mind? Sketch one of the images in your notebook.

Active Reading Response

Look back at the strategies described in the Active Reading Model notes on pages 285–290. Which strategy did you find most useful as you read?

Analyzing Literature

Recall

1. Name three observations Twain makes on his train ride to St. Louis.
2. Why does Twain say, ". . . it would be an advantage to disguise our party with fictitious names"? Is he able to deceive the hotel clerk?
3. What do you learn about the water in St. Louis?
4. What has changed in St. Louis since Twain was last there?
5. Summarize Twain's remarks in the last four paragraphs.

Interpret

6. What do Twain's remarks tell you about what he values?
7. In your opinion, does Twain like or dislike being recognized? Explain, using details from the selection to support your ideas.
8. Why might Twain use **hyperbole** in his description of the drinking water in St. Louis? (See Literary Terms Handbook, page R6.)
9. As Twain surveys "present-day" St. Louis, what changes seem to impress him most? Use details from the selection in your answer.
10. How does the writer's **tone** change between the beginning and the end of the selection? Use details from the selection to support your answer. (See Literary Terms Handbook, page R13.)

Evaluate and Connect

11. Think about your response to the Reading Focus on page 284. If Twain visited St. Louis today, what would he use to record his experiences?
12. In your opinion, does Twain succeed at capturing the changes that were taking place in the country in the 1800s? Explain your answer.
13. What are some of the important changes taking place around you today? Who is recording them and how?
14. In what way might contemporary readers find Twain's choice of details interesting or surprising? Explain.
15. Comedians often point out foolishness by focusing on small details. What comedian, in your view, is most like Mark Twain in this respect?

Literary ELEMENTS

Anecdote

An **anecdote** is a brief account of an interesting or amusing incident. An anecdote may be used as concrete evidence to support or explain an idea, or it may be used to entertain readers, revealing the writer's or another person's personality in the process. For instance, Twain's story about giving the hotel clerk a fake name is an example of an anecdote. It is an amusing story, but it also helps to reveal Twain's personality. Anecdotes are often humorous, and they help make writing lively and interesting.

1. What does the anecdote about Twain and the hotel clerk tell you about Twain's personality?
2. Why does Twain tell the anecdote about the young man crying in his room? Why doesn't he just give the facts about water in St. Louis?
3. What do the anecdotes in this selection have in common? Support your answer with evidence from the selection.

- See **Literary Terms Handbook,** p. R1.

Literature and Writing

Writing About Literature

Evaluate a Writer's Strategy Mark Twain once advised another writer to first get his facts straight and then do whatever he wanted with them. How does Twain use that strategy in this work? Find several examples and write a paragraph evaluating the effectiveness of Twain's strategy.

Personal Writing

Your Turn On your way home from school, jot down notes about the people and places you see along the way. Then write a short article that, like Twain's memoir, includes details to help readers get a feel for your journey. Try to include at least one anecdote in your article.

Extending Your Response

Literature Groups

Funny or Not? Mark Twain is considered one of America's foremost humorists. As a group, review the selection, looking for parts that the author meant to be funny. On the basis of your reading of this selection, do you think Twain is funny? Why or why not? Compare your group's conclusion with that of the other groups.

Interdisciplinary Activity

History: Full Steam Ahead Twain's love of the Mississippi steamboating era is evident in his description of it as "so majestic a creature." Investigate the steamboat era on the Mississippi River and the way of life it gave rise to. Find several anecdotes that paint a picture of the era and share them in an oral storytelling session in class.

Internet Connection

Meet Me in St. Louis Working with a partner, use the Internet to find out as much as you can about St. Louis–its history, population, parks, economy, weather, and any other interesting details you can uncover. Present your findings to the class as a travel poster about St. Louis.

Reading Further

You might enjoy these works by Mark Twain:

Novel: *The Tragedy of Pudd'nhead Wilson,* a reflection on racism and responsibility in the post–Civil War South.

Essays: *How to Tell a Story and Other Essays,* still brilliantly witty after more than one hundred years.

Save your work for your portfolio.

Skill Minilesson

VOCABULARY • Analogies

An analogy is a type of comparison that is based on the relationships between things or ideas. Some analogies feature words that have opposite meanings but that are not true antonyms.

insecure : confidence :: foolish : practicality

An insecure person lacks confidence; a foolish person lacks practicality. The paired words are not antonyms; they are not the same part of speech.

To finish an analogy, decide what relationship exists between the first two things or ideas. Then apply that relationship to another pair of words and see if it is the same.

PRACTICE Choose the word that best completes each analogy.

1. cruel : kindness :: pompous :
   a. meekness b. patience c. efficiency
2. dry : moisture :: turbulent :
   a. beauty b. motion c. calm
3. brief : duration :: ineffectual :
   a. doubts b. usefulness c. courage

For more on analogies, see **Communications Skills Handbook,** p. R77.

Theme 4 In the Face of Adversity

The philosopher Friedrich Nietzsche (frē′ drikH nē′ chə) *once said, "What does not destroy me, makes me strong." How does adversity, or hardship, affect you? In this theme, you will learn how a variety of people react to situations that challenge them physically, mentally, and emotionally.*

THEME PROJECTS

Performing

Stage a Talk Show Working with a small group, prepare to stage a talk show for your classmates about Nietzsche's statement.

1. Brainstorm ideas about how three writers from this theme might react to the statement. Why might each agree or disagree with it?
2. Discuss what experiences might have affected each writer's outlook on life.
3. Stage a talk show for the rest of your classmates. Group members should take the parts of host, guests, and studio audience.

Interdisciplinary Project

Music: Movie Soundtrack Imagine that one of the selections in this theme will be made into a movie, and you must compile a soundtrack to help set the scene and to convey the emotions of a particular situation.

1. Choose songs that would be appropriate as the opening and closing credits roll and that could be used as a bridge between scenes. Feel free to rewrite the lyrics for songs that musically capture the emotions you wish to evoke or compose original music and lyrics.
2. Make a list of selected songs, noting at which point in the movie each song will play.
3. Write a letter to the film's director that explains why your soundtrack will enhance the quality and effectiveness of the movie.

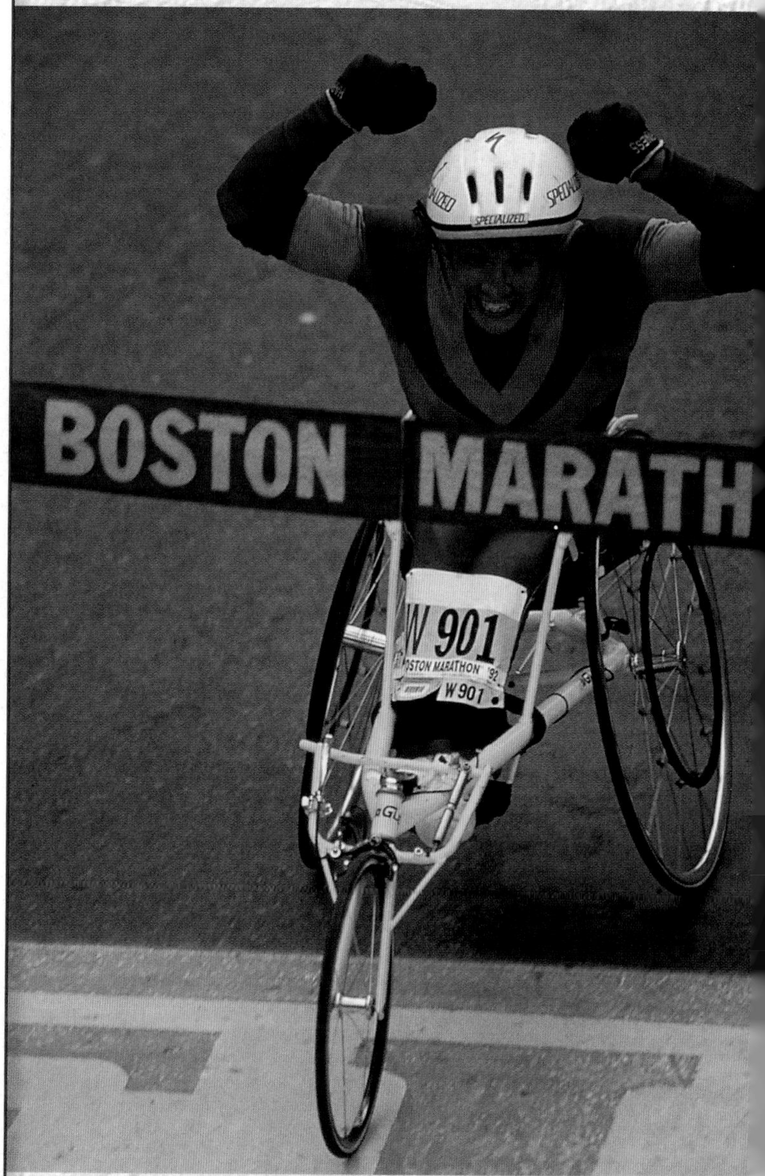

MEDIA connection

Magazine Article

Have you ever been inspired by the performance of a professional athlete? Some athletes have had to overcome tremendous obstacles to fulfill their dreams of reaching the top of their sport.

Pete Gray

by William C. Kashatus—*American History,* June 1995

On May 20, 1945, a crowd of thirty-six thousand packed Yankee Stadium to watch a doubleheader that pitted New York's finest against the defending American League champions, the St. Louis Browns. The Yankees, who had finished third the previous season, had something to prove that afternoon. Even though World War II had stripped their lineup of star players, their traditional Yankee pride inspired the belief that 1945 would be "their year."

Game one of the doubleheader got underway with the Browns' rookie outfielder, Pete Gray, leading off against former twenty-game winner "Spud" Chandler. After taking the first pitch, Gray lined a fastball into right field for the first hit of the game. During the rookie's second trip to the plate, Chandler challenged Gray with another fastball on the first pitch. Once again, the Brownie outfielder hit a line drive single into right field. Chandler responded like a mad bull, kicking the mound in frustration. By the end of the afternoon, Gray had reached base five times with four hits. He scored twice and knocked in two runs while fielding his positions flawlessly. The Browns swept the doubleheader, 10-1 and 5-2.

Any player would have been proud of that performance, but for the St. Louis rookie it was a dream come true. As a boy growing up in the coal region of Pennsylvania, Gray had committed himself to fulfilling that dream. More impressively, he managed it all with only one arm, having lost his right arm above the elbow in a truck accident at the age of six. A natural right-hander prior to the mishap, Gray learned to hit, catch, and throw with his left hand.

"The only thing I ever wanted to do as a kid was to play in Yankee Stadium," Gray, now in his eighties, recalls. "I had always been a big New York fan, and Babe Ruth was one of my childhood heroes." In fact, it was the Bambino's called shot against the Chicago Cubs in the 1932 World Series that inspired Gray. At age seventeen, Gray observed the famous round-tripper from Wrigley Field's bleachers. "After that called shot I said to myself, 'Pete, the whole trick is confidence in yourself. If you are sure you can do it, you will do it.' "

For the son of a Lithuanian immigrant coal miner, major-league baseball was an escape

from the difficult times and uncertain future experienced by his father. "When you have that kind of motivation," says Gray, "you tend to be hungrier than most other ballplayers." So while his father and brothers went to work in the mines, Pete Gray devoted himself to baseball.

"I'd spend hours just flipping up rocks and tin cans and hitting 'em with a club," says Gray. "But I had some trouble fielding the ball. I just couldn't figure out how to get rid of it after I made a catch." Eventually, however, Gray devised a way to catch the ball and shed his glove in one swift motion. "I'd catch the ball in my glove and stick it under the stub of my right arm. I'd sort of squeeze the ball out of my glove with my arm, allowing it to roll across my chest and drop right into my hand."

The one-armed sensation made things happen for himself through sheer determination. A visit to a tryout camp for the St. Louis Cardinals in the mid-1930s ended in a turn-down, as did an interview several years later with Connie Mack, the owner-manager of the Philadelphia Athletics. "Son," Mack told him, "I've got men with two arms who can't play this game." Gray's voice falters at the memory: "He never let me on the field to show him what I could do."

Gray finally got his chance in 1942 with the Three Rivers (Quebec) Club in the Canadian-American League. In only 42 games, the one-armed wonder collected 61 hits, 13 RBIs, and 31 runs scored—compiling a batting average of .381. His performance caught the attention of the Memphis Chicks of the Southern Association, who signed Gray in 1943. Gray was signed by the St. Louis Browns the following year.

For wounded war veterans, the one-armed outfielder—who asked no sympathy from anyone and competed on even terms with all rivals—became a heroic symbol on the home front. Gray's example gave these veterans hope that they, too, could succeed in whatever career they chose as long as they gave it their all. He delivered this message on playing fields as well as in veterans' hospitals where he spoke with amputees.

World War II and the effect of draft call-ups on the national pastime may have helped to make Pete Gray a major-league baseball player. But it also helped make him an authentic American hero.

Analyzing Media

1. What personal qualities helped Pete Gray succeed in fulfilling his dream?
2. What do you admire most about Pete Gray? Why?

Before You Read

from *Black Boy*

Reading Focus

What hobby, talent, or interest do you have that might lead to a satisfying career?

List Ideas Make a list of people you could go to for encouragement or advice about developing your talent. Next to each name, explain how he or she could help you.

Setting a Purpose Read to learn how a young boy finds support for his talent.

Building Background

The Time and Place
In this excerpt from *Black Boy,* Richard Wright recalls events that occurred in Jackson, Mississippi, in 1923.

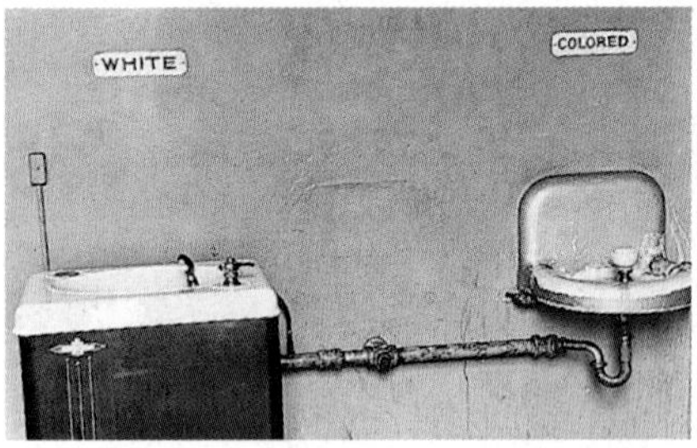

Did You Know?
In the post–Civil War South, many states passed unfair local laws to deny civil rights to African Americans. These were called "Jim Crow" laws, named after a black character in a song. Most of the laws required that blacks and whites use separate public facilities, including schools, washrooms, and drinking fountains. Some states also attempted to deny African Americans their right to vote by requiring them to pass unfair literacy tests that held blacks and whites to different standards. Supreme Court decisions in the 1950s and 1960s, as well as the Civil Rights Act of 1964, abolished these laws.

Vocabulary Preview

intuitive (in to͞o′ ə tiv) *adj.* rising from an impulse or natural tendency; instinctive; not learned; p. 297
conviction (kən vik′ shən) *n.* a firmly established opinion or belief; p. 297
naive (nä ēv′) *adj.* innocent; unsophisticated; p. 300
strive (strīv) *v.* to make an intense effort; p. 300
articulate (är tik′ yə lit) *adj.* able to express oneself well or effectively; p. 300
ultimate (ul′ tə mit) *adj.* most significant; highest or final; p. 300

Meet Richard Wright

Richard Wright's autobiography, *Black Boy,* tells of his childhood in the South, where he coped with both poverty and discrimination. At fifteen, Wright moved north, where he began writing stories, poems, and essays. In 1940 he published a highly praised novel, *Native Son.* In 1941 he received the Spingarn Medal, given by the NAACP for "the highest achievement by a black American." Despite these achievements, however, Wright suffered greatly from racism and in an effort to find a more tolerant society, Wright moved to Paris, France, where he lived from 1947 until his death.

Richard Wright was born in 1908 and died in 1960. Black Boy *was published in 1945.*

from Black Boy

Richard Wright

The eighth grade days flowed in their hungry path and I grew more conscious of myself; I sat in classes, bored, wondering, dreaming. One long dry afternoon I took out my composition book and told myself that I would write a story; it was sheer idleness that led me to it.

What would the story be about? It resolved itself into a plot about a villain who wanted a widow's home and I called it *The Voodoo of Hell's Half-Acre.* It was crudely atmospheric, emotional, intuitively psychological, and stemmed from pure feeling. I finished it in three days and then wondered what to do with it.

The local Negro newspaper! That's it . . . I sailed into the office and shoved my ragged composition book under the nose of the man who called himself the editor.

"What is that?" he asked.

"A story," I said.

"A news story?"

"No, fiction."

"All right. I'll read it," he said.

He pushed my composition book back on his desk and looked at me curiously, sucking at his pipe.

"But I want you to read it *now,*" I said.

He blinked. I had no idea how newspapers were run. I thought that one took a story to an editor and he sat down then and there and read it and said yes or no.

"I'll read this and let you know about it tomorrow," he said.

I was disappointed; I had taken time to write it and he seemed distant and uninterested.

"Give me the story," I said, reaching for it.

He turned from me, took up the book and read ten pages or more.

"Won't you come in tomorrow?" he asked. "I'll have it finished then."

I honestly relented.

"All right," I said. "I'll stop in tomorrow."

I left with the conviction that he would not read it. Now, where else could I take it after he had turned it down? The next afternoon, en route to my job, I stepped into the newspaper office.

"Where's my story?" I asked.

"It's in galleys," he said.

"What's that?" I asked; I did not know what galleys were.

"It's set up in type," he said. "We're publishing it."

"How much money will I get?" I asked, excited.

"We can't pay for manuscript," he said.

"But you sell your papers for money," I said with logic.

Vocabulary

intuitive (in tōō′ ə tiv) *adj.* rising from an impulse or natural tendency; instinctive; not learned

conviction (kən vik′ shən) *n.* a firmly established opinion or belief

"Yes, but we're young in business," he explained.

"But you're asking me to *give* you my story, but you don't *give* your papers away," I said.

He laughed.

"Look, you're just starting. This story will put your name before our readers. Now, that's something," he said.

"But if the story is good enough to sell to your readers, then you ought to give me some of the money you get from it," I insisted.

He laughed again and I sensed that I was amusing him.

"I'm going to offer you something more valuable than money," he said. "I'll give you a chance to learn to write."

I was pleased, but I still thought he was taking advantage of me.

"When will you publish my story?"

"I'm dividing it into three installments," he said. "The first installment appears this week. But the main thing is this: Will you get news for me on a space rate basis?"[1]

"I work mornings and evenings for three dollars a week," I said.

"Oh," he said. "Then you better keep that. But what are you doing this summer?"

"Nothing."

"Then come to see me before you take another job," he said. "And write some more stories."

A few days later my classmates came to me with baffled eyes, holding copies of the *Southern Register* in their hands.

"Did you really write that story?" they asked me.

"Yes."

"Why?"

"Because I wanted to."

"Where did you get it from?"

"I made it up."

"You didn't. You copied it out of a book."

"If I had, no one would publish it."

"But what are they publishing it for?"

"So people can read it."

"Who told you to do that?"

"Nobody."

"Then why did you do it?"

"Because I wanted to," I said again.

They were convinced that I had not told them the truth. We had never had any instruction in literary matters at school; the literature of the nation or the Negro had never been mentioned. My schoolmates could not understand why anyone would want to write a story; and, above all, they could not understand why I had called it *The Voodoo of Hell's Half-Acre*. The mood out of which a story was written was the most alien thing conceivable[2] to them. They looked at me with new eyes, and a distance, a suspiciousness came between us. If I had thought anything in writing the story, I had thought that perhaps it would make me more acceptable to them, and now it was cutting me off from them more completely than ever.

At home the effects were no less disturbing. Granny came into my room early one morning and sat on the edge of my bed.

"Richard, what is this you're putting in the papers?" she asked.

"A story," I said.

"About what?"

"It's just a story, granny."

"But they tell me it's been in three times."

"It's the same story. It's in three parts."

"But what is it about?" she insisted.

I hedged,[3] fearful of getting into a religious argument.

"It's just a story I made up," I said.

1. On a *space rate basis* means that payment would vary according to the length of each news article.

2. It was the strangest *(most alien)* idea imaginable *(conceivable)*.

3. Wright *hedged* when he avoided giving a direct answer or committing himself.

"Then it's a lie," she said.

"Oh, Christ," I said.

"You must get out of this house if you take the name of the Lord in vain," she said.

"Granny, please . . . I'm sorry," I pleaded. "But it's hard to tell you about the story. You see, granny, everybody knows that the story isn't true, but . . ."

"Then why write it?" she asked.

"Because people might want to read it."

"That's the Devil's work," she said and left.

My mother also was worried.

"Son, you ought to be more serious," she said. "You're growing up now and you won't be able to get jobs if you let people think that you're weak-minded. Suppose the superintendent of schools would ask you to teach here in Jackson, and he found out that you had been writing stories?"

I could not answer her.

"I'll be all right, mama," I said.

Uncle Tom, though surprised, was highly critical and contemptuous.[4] The story had no point, he said. And whoever heard of a story by the title of *The Voodoo of Hell's Half-Acre?* Aunt Addie said that it was a sin for anyone to use the word "hell" and that what was wrong with me was that I had nobody to guide me. She blamed the whole thing upon my upbringing.

In the end I was so angry that I refused to talk about the story. From no quarter,[5] with the exception of the Negro newspaper editor, had there come a single encouraging word. It was rumored that the principal wanted to know why I had used the word "hell." I felt that I had committed a crime. Had I been conscious of the full extent to which I was pushing against the current of my environment, I would have been frightened altogether out of my attempts at writing. But my reactions were

©John Wilson/Licensed by VAGA, New York, NY.

My Brother, 1942. John Wilson. Oil on panel, 12 x 10⅝ in. Smith College Museum of Art, Northampton, MA.

Viewing the painting: Compare and contrast your perception of this young man with your perception of Richard Wright.

4. *Contemptuous* means "scornful, lacking respect for something."
5. Here, *quarter* means "person, place, or group."

limited to the attitude of the people about me, and I did not speculate or generalize.[6]

I dreamed of going north and writing books, novels. The North symbolized to me all that I had not felt and seen; it had no relation whatever to what actually existed. Yet, by imagining a place where everything was possible, I kept hope alive in me. But where had I got this notion of doing something in the future, of going away from home and accomplishing something that would be recognized by others? I had, of course, read my Horatio Alger stories, my pulp stories, and I knew my Get-Rich-Quick Wallingford series[7] from cover to cover, though I had sense enough not to hope to get rich; even to my naive imagination that possibility was too remote. I knew that I lived in a country in which the aspirations of black people were limited, marked-off. Yet I felt that I had to go somewhere and do something to redeem[8] my being alive.

I was building up in me a dream which the entire educational system of the South had been rigged to stifle.[9] I was feeling the very thing that the state of Mississippi had spent millions of dollars to make sure that I would never feel; I was becoming aware of the thing that the Jim Crow laws had been drafted and passed to keep out of my consciousness; I was acting on impulses that southern senators in the nation's capital had striven to keep out of Negro life; I was beginning to dream the dreams that the state had said were wrong, that the schools had said were taboo.[10]

Had I been articulate about my ultimate aspirations, no doubt someone would have told me what I was bargaining for; but nobody seemed to know, and least of all did I. My classmates felt that I was doing something that was vaguely wrong, but they did not know how to express it. As the outside world grew more meaningful, I became more concerned, tense; and my classmates and my teachers would say: "Why do you ask so many questions?" Or: "Keep quiet."

I was in my fifteenth year; in terms of schooling I was far behind the average youth of the nation, but I did not know that. In me was shaping a yearning for a kind of consciousness, a mode[11] of being that the way of life about me had said could not be, must not be, and upon which the penalty of death had been placed. Somewhere in the dead of the southern night my life had switched onto the wrong track and, without my knowing it, the locomotive of my heart was rushing down a dangerously steep slope, heading for a collision, heedless of the warning red lights that blinked all about me, the sirens and the bells and the screams that filled the air.

6. Here, to *speculate* is to guess, and to *generalize* is to form a general opinion based on particular facts or instances.
7. *Horatio Alger stories, pulp stories,* and the *Wallingford series* are all works—some fictional and some claiming to be true—about people who achieved financial success through hard work or cleverness.
8. In this context, *redeem* means "to justify."
9. To *stifle* means "to smother."
10. *Taboo* means "prohibited or forbidden."
11. A *mode* is a manner or way.

Vocabulary

naive (nä ēv′) *adj.* innocent; unsophisticated
strive (strīv) *v.* to make an intense effort
articulate (är tik′ yə lit) *adj.* able to express oneself well or effectively
ultimate (ul′ tə mit) *adj.* most significant; highest or final

Responding to Literature

Personal Response

What words would you use to describe Richard Wright at fifteen?

Analyzing Literature

Recall

1. What reason does Wright give for writing his story?
2. Summarize the details of Wright's meeting with the newspaper editor.
3. How did Wright's classmates, family members, and school principal respond to his story?
4. What did Wright plan to do if he achieved his dream of going north?
5. What conclusions does Wright draw about the Jim Crow laws?

Interpret

6. Why might it have taken Wright only three days to finish his story?
7. What do Wright's words and actions at the newspaper office tell you about his personality?
8. In your opinion, why did Wright's classmates, family, and principal react as they did to his story? How were their reactions different from what he had hoped for?
9. Explain what Wright might have meant when he said, "The North symbolized to me all that I had not felt and seen; it had no relation whatever to what actually existed."
10. Why, in your opinion, was Wright "more concerned, tense" as he became more aware of his environment in the South?

Evaluate and Connect

11. **Theme Connections** What does Richard Wright do in the face of adversity? What does this reveal about him?
12. Review your response to the Reading Focus on page 296. What do you think would happen to your dreams if you received no support from your friends and family? Would a lack of support discourage you, or push you to achieve as it did Wright? Of what importance was the newspaper editor to Wright's success?
13. How might you react if a classmate's story were published in a newspaper? Would you react as Wright's classmates did? Explain.
14. Evaluate Wright's use of a **metaphor** in the last paragraph. (See Literary Terms Handbook, page R7.) Does the comparison help you understand his emotions and apprehension? Explain.
15. Would you like to read the rest of *Black Boy*? Why or why not?

Literary ELEMENTS

Autobiography

An **autobiography** is the story of a person's life, written by that person. Writers create autobiographies to share memories of events, people, and feelings that are important to them. Autobiographies can also give readers an idea of what society was like during the author's lifetime.

1. In your opinion, why did Wright choose to include this event in his autobiography?
2. What does this excerpt say about Southern society in the 1920s and its treatment of African Americans?
3. By looking back on events in their lives, writers often gain insight about themselves. What observations does Wright make about his own character and motivations?

- See **Literary Terms Handbook**, p. R2.

Literary Criticism

About Richard Wright's autobiography *Black Boy*, one critic writes, "Along with his accounts of mistreatment by whites, Wright describes the complicity of southern blacks in their own oppression." Do you think that this statement is true of the excerpt you have read? Share your ideas in a class discussion.

Literature and Writing

Writing About Literature

Analyzing Dialogue Much of this selection is made up of dialogue, or conversation. Rather than summarizing scenes and describing characters, Wright brings them to life by using dialogue. Choose a passage of dialogue that you think works well and analyze why it is effective. Tell what the dialogue reveals about the scene and the characters in it.

Creative Writing

Dear Readers When a newspaper or magazine publishes an article or story by a new writer, the editor may also publish a brief editorial explaining why he or she feels that readers will enjoy the work, or why he or she has confidence in the writer. As the newspaper editor, write an editorial introducing Richard Wright to his readers.

Extending Your Response

Literature Groups

Short but Sweet If you could use only one sentence to describe the main message of this excerpt, what would it be? Have each member of your group write a sentence in his or her notebook. Next, take turns reading your sentences aloud and discussing your ideas. Then, as a group, choose the best sentence, or create a new one that combines your ideas, and read it aloud to the class.

Interdisciplinary Activity

Social Studies: The Supreme Court The civil rights of African Americans have been enormously affected by historic Supreme Court decisions. In an encyclopedia or history book, read about these two cases: *Plessy v. Ferguson* (1896) and *Brown v. Board of Education of Topeka, Kansas* (1954). Use specific details from the Court's ruling in each case to explain how they affected civil rights.

Listening and Speaking

Book Review You are the host of a radio talk show called "Book Chat," for which you review books. Based on your reading of this excerpt from *Black Boy,* give an oral review. Using specific examples from the selection, discuss how writers can use their experiences to persuade readers to agree with a certain point of view.

Reading Further

The volume *First Fiction* contains the first published works of famous authors, including these short stories:

"To Hell with Dying," by Alice Walker, shows how a community supports an eccentric old man.

"Wunderkind," by Carson McCullers, tells about a dissatisfied teenage prodigy.

Save your work for your portfolio.

Skill Minilesson

VOCABULARY • Antonyms

What's an antonym for *down?* For *large? Up* and *small* probably come to mind rather quickly! But how quickly could you supply an antonym for *conviction?* Sometimes, finding an antonym requires a little more thought. For example, a conviction is not just a belief or opinion; it's a firm one—one based on a feeling of certainty. When you think about the precise meaning of *conviction,* you will realize that *doubt*—a belief or opinion based on a feeling of *un*certainty—is a good antonym.

PRACTICE Use your knowledge of the words in the left column to match each one to its antonym in the right column.

1. naive	a. allowed
2. ultimate	b. quit
3. strive	c. unimportant
4. intuitive	d. sophisticated
5. taboo	e. learned

MEDIA connection

Speech

Holocaust survivor Elie Wiesel was awarded the Nobel Peace Prize for his work advocating human rights and peace worldwide. Imagine what it might have been like to be in the audience as he delivered this speech.

Nobel Peace Prize Acceptance Speech

Elie Wiesel, December 10, 1986

Nobel Prize Medal

It is with a profound sense of humility that I accept the honor you have chosen to bestow upon me. I know: your choice transcends me. This both frightens and pleases me.

It frightens me because I wonder: do I have the right to represent the multitudes who have perished? Do I have the right to accept this great honor on their behalf? I do not. That would be presumptuous. No one may speak for the dead, no one may interpret their mutilated dreams and visions.

It pleases me because I may say that this honor belongs to all the survivors and their children, and through us, to the Jewish people with whose destiny I have always identified.

I remember: it happened yesterday or eternities ago. A young Jewish boy discovered the kingdom of night. I remember his bewilderment, I remember his anguish. It all happened so fast. The ghetto. The deportation. The sealed cattle car. The fiery altar upon which the history of our people and the future of mankind were meant to be sacrificed.

I remember: he asked his father: "Can this be true?" This is the twentieth century, not the Middle Ages. Who would allow such crimes to be committed? How could the world remain silent?

And now the boy is turning to me: "Tell me," he asks. "What have you done with my future? What have you done with your life?"

And I tell him that I have tried. That I have tried to keep memory alive, that I have tried to fight those who would forget. Because if we forget, we are guilty, we are accomplices. That is why I swore never to be silent whenever and wherever human beings endure suffering and humiliation. We must always take sides. Neutrality helps the oppressor, never the victim. Silence encourages the tormentor, never the tormented. Sometimes we must interfere. Action is the only remedy to indifference: the most insidious danger of all. One person of integrity can make a difference, a difference of life and death.

This is what I say to the young Jewish boy wondering what I have done with his years. It is in his name that I speak to you and that I express to you my deepest gratitude. No one is as capable of gratitude as one who has emerged from the kingdom of night. Every moment is a moment of grace, every hour an offering; not to share them would mean to betray them. Our lives no longer belong to us alone; they belong to all those who need us desperately.

Analyzing Media

1. Do you agree or disagree with Wiesel when he says, "Our lives no longer belong to us alone; they belong to all those who need us desperately"?
2. What purpose or purposes might Wiesel have had for delivering this speech?

Before You Read

from *Night*

Reading Focus

What do you know about the Holocaust—the killing of millions of Jews and other European civilians during World War II?

Discuss As a class, share your knowledge about what happened and generate a list of questions you'd like to know more about.

Setting a Purpose Read to share the author's horrors and anxieties in a concentration camp during the Holocaust.

Building Background

The Time and Place

The events in this excerpt from *Night,* Elie Wiesel's memoir, take place in 1944 inside a Nazi concentration camp in Poland.

Did You Know?

Adolf Hitler, founder of the Nazi party, became chancellor of Germany in 1933 and ruled as a dictator until 1945. Germany was in an economic depression when Hitler came to power, and the Jewish people were used as scapegoats for the country's many problems. Hitler began persecuting German Jews by taking away their citizenship and civil rights. After Germany invaded Poland in 1939 to start World War II, Jews from Germany and from each country Germany occupied—along with tens of thousands of others who opposed Hitler or were deemed "undesirable" by him—were imprisoned in forced-labor concentration camps. There they were overworked, starved, tortured, and sometimes killed outright. Several prison camps in Germany and Poland became "death camps," where the systematic extermination of Jews and others was carried out. Out of an estimated 8.3 million Jews living in German-occupied Europe after 1939, approximately 6 million were killed. About 6 million other people died at the hands of the Nazis.

Vocabulary Preview

emaciated (i mā′ shē āt′ əd) *adj.* extremely thin; p. 307
avidly (av′ id lē) *adv.* eagerly; enthusiastically; p. 307
meager (mē′ gər) *adj.* inadequate in amount or quantity; p. 308
din (din) *n.* loud, continuous noise; p. 309

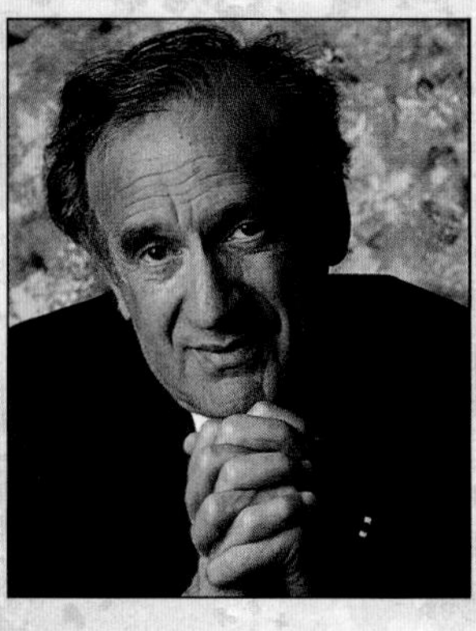

Meet Elie Wiesel

"For the dead and the living, we must bear witness."

At age fifteen, Romanian-born Elie Wiesel (el′ ē wē sel′) and his family were imprisoned in Auschwitz and Buchenwald, two of the most notorious death camps. Although Wiesel survived, most of his family perished. After the war, Wiesel lived and worked as a journalist in Paris before moving to the United States and becoming a citizen. He is a teacher, philosopher, and prolific writer of novels and nonfiction works about the Holocaust as well as about Jewish law, philosophy, and other subjects. Wiesel often speaks out against human rights violations in the world today.

Elie Wiesel was born in 1928. Night *was published in English in 1960.*

from NIGHT

Elie Wiesel
Translated by
Stella Rodway

The SS[1] gave us a fine New Year's gift.

We had just come back from work. As soon as we had passed through the door of the camp, we sensed something different in the air. Roll call did not take so long as usual. The evening soup was given out with great speed and swallowed down at once in anguish.[2]

I was no longer in the same block as my father. I had been transferred to another unit, the building one, where, twelve hours a day, I had to drag heavy blocks of stone about. The head of my new block was a German Jew, small of stature,[3] with piercing eyes. He told us that evening that no one would be allowed to go out after the evening soup. And soon a terrible word was circulating—selection.

We knew what that meant. An SS man would examine us. Whenever he found a weak one, a *musulman*[4] as we called them, he would write his number[5] down: good for the crematory.[6]

After soup, we gathered together between the beds. The veterans said:

"You're lucky to have been brought here so late. This camp is paradise today, compared with what it was like two years ago. Buna[7] was a real hell then. There was no water, no blankets, less soup and bread. At night we slept almost naked, and it was below thirty degrees. The corpses were collected in hundreds every day. The work was hard. Today, this is a little paradise. The Kapos[8] had orders to kill a certain number of prisoners every day. And every week—selection. A merciless selection. . . . Yes, you're lucky."

"Stop it! Be quiet!" I begged. "You can tell your stories tomorrow or on some other day."

They burst out laughing. They were not veterans for nothing.

"Are you scared? So were we scared. And there was plenty to be scared of in those days."

The old men stayed in their corner, dumb, motionless, haunted. Some were praying.

An hour's delay. In an hour, we should know the verdict—death or a reprieve.[9]

---

1. *SS* is the abbreviation of the German word *Schutzstaffel*, meaning "protection staff." At first, SS troops acted as Hitler's bodyguards. Later they were in charge of killing prisoners in countries conquered by Germany.
2. *Anguish* (ang′ gwish) means "extreme mental or physical suffering."
3. *Stature* (stach′ ər) means "height."
4. *Musulman* (moo′ sool män)
5. Upon imprisonment in the camps, all people were tattooed with a *number* on the left forearm. Guards would refer to each person by number instead of by name.
6. A *crematory* is a furnace used to burn bodies.
7. *Buna* (bo͞o′ nə) was a forced-labor camp in Poland near Auschwitz (oush′ vits).
8. *Kapos* (kä′ pōz) were themselves prisoners, serving as foremen of the prisoners' buildings or cell blocks.
9. *Reprieve* (ri prēv′) means "temporary relief or escape, as from danger or pain."

Anywhere in Europe 1933–45. Gertrude Jacobson. Acrylic and steel barbed wire on board, 34 x 44 x 4 in. Collection of Yad Vashem Museum of Art, Jerusalem.

Viewing the art: What do the title and the barbed wire contribute to the artist's message? How does this excerpt from *Night* convey what it might be like to be a person in this painting?

And my father? Suddenly I remembered him. How would he pass the selection? He had aged so much. . . .

The head of our block had never been outside concentration camps since 1933. He had already been through all the slaughterhouses, all the factories of death. At about nine o'clock, he took up his position in our midst:

"Achtung!"[10]

There was instant silence.

"Listen carefully to what I am going to say." (For the first time, I heard his voice quiver.) "In a few moments the selection will begin. You must get completely undressed. Then one by one you go before the SS doctors. I hope you will all succeed in getting through. But you must help your own chances. Before you go into the next room, move about in some way so that you give yourselves a little color. Don't walk slowly, run! Run as if the devil were after you! Don't look at the SS. Run, straight in front of you!"

He broke off for a moment, then added:

"And, the essential thing, don't be afraid!"

Here was a piece of advice we should have liked very much to be able to follow.

I got undressed, leaving my clothes on the bed. There was no danger of anyone stealing them this evening.

10. *Achtung* (äkh toong′) is German for "Attention!"

Tibi and Yossi, who had changed their unit at the same time as I had, came up to me and said:

"Let's keep together. We shall be stronger."

Yossi was murmuring something between his teeth. He must have been praying. I had never realized that Yossi was a believer. I had even always thought the reverse. Tibi was silent, very pale. All the prisoners in the block stood naked between the beds. This must be how one stands at the last judgment.[11]

"They're coming!"

There were three SS officers standing round the notorious Dr. Mengele,[12] who had received us at Birkenau.[13] The head of the block, with an attempt at a smile, asked us:

"Ready?"

Yes, we were ready. So were the SS doctors. Dr. Mengele was holding a list in his hand: our numbers. He made a sign to the head of the block: "We can begin!" As if this were a game!

The first to go by were the "officials" of the block: *Stubenaelteste*,[14] Kapos, foremen, all in perfect physical condition of course! Then came the ordinary prisoners' turn. Dr. Mengele took stock of them from head to foot. Every now and then, he wrote a number down. One single thought filled my mind: not to let my number be taken; not to show my left arm.

There were only Tibi and Yossi in front of me. They passed. I had time to notice that Mengele had not written their numbers down. Someone pushed me. It was my turn. I ran without looking back. My head was spinning: you're too thin, you're weak, you're too thin, you're good for the furnace. . . . The race seemed interminable.[15] I thought I had been running for years. . . . You're too thin, you're too weak. . . . At last I had arrived exhausted. When I regained my breath, I questioned Yossi and Tibi:

"Was I written down?"

"No," said Yossi. He added, smiling: "In any case, he couldn't have written you down, you were running too fast. . . ."

I began to laugh. I was glad. I would have liked to kiss him. At that moment, what did the others matter! I hadn't been written down.

Those whose numbers had been noted stood apart, abandoned by the whole world. Some were weeping in silence.

The SS officers went away. The head of the block appeared, his face reflecting the general weariness.

"Everything went off all right. Don't worry. Nothing is going to happen to anyone. To anyone."

Again he tried to smile. A poor, emaciated, dried-up Jew questioned him avidly in a trembling voice:

"But . . . but, *Blockaelteste*,[16] they did write me down!"

The head of the block let his anger break out. What! Did someone refuse to believe him!

"What's the matter now? Am I telling lies then? I tell you once and for all, nothing's

11. In some religions, the *last judgment* is God's final judgment of humankind, which is to occur on the day the world ends.
12. Infamous for his medical experiments on prisoners, *Dr. (Josef) Mengele* (meng′ ə lə) personally selected nearly half a million prisoners for death in the Auschwitz gas chambers.
13. *Birkenau* (bur′ kə nou) was the name of one large section of the Auschwitz camp.
14. *Stubenaelteste* (shtōō′ bən el′ tə stə), which translates as "elders of the rooms," refers to a rank of Kapos.
15. The race seemed *interminable*, as if it would never end.
16. *Blockaelteste* (blôk el′ tə stə), which translates as "elders of the buildings," refers to a higher rank of Kapos.

Vocabulary

emaciated (i mā′ shē āt′ əd) *adj.* extremely thin
avidly (av′ id lē) *adv.* eagerly; enthusiastically

going to happen to you! To anyone! You're wallowing in your own despair, you fool!"

The bell rang, a signal that the selection had been completed throughout the camp.

With all my might I began to run to Block 36. I met my father on the way. He came up to me:

"Well? So you passed?"

"Yes. And you?"

"Me too."

How we breathed again, now! My father had brought me a present—half a ration of bread obtained in exchange for a piece of rubber, found at the warehouse, which would do to sole a shoe.

The bell. Already we must separate, go to bed. Everything was regulated by the bell. It gave me orders, and I automatically obeyed them. I hated it. Whenever I dreamed of a better world, I could only imagine a universe with no bells.

Several days had elapsed. We no longer thought about the selection. We went to work as usual, loading heavy stones into railway wagons. Rations had become more meager: this was the only change.

We had risen before dawn, as on every day. We had received the black coffee, the ration of bread. We were about to set out for the yard as usual. The head of the block arrived, running.

"Silence for a moment. I have a list of numbers here. I'm going to read them to you. Those whose numbers I call won't be going to work this morning; they'll stay behind in the camp."

And, in a soft voice, he read out about ten numbers. We had understood. These were numbers chosen at the selection. Dr. Mengele had not forgotten.

The head of the block went toward his room. Ten prisoners surrounded him, hanging onto his clothes:

"Save us! You promised . . . ! We want to go to the yard. We're strong enough to work. We're good workers. We can . . . we will. . . ."

He tried to calm them, to reassure them about their fate, to explain to them that the fact that they were staying behind in the camp did not mean much, had no tragic significance.

"After all, I stay here myself every day," he added.

It was a somewhat feeble argument. He realized it, and without another word went and shut himself up in his room.

The bell had just rung.

"Form up!"

It scarcely mattered now that the work was hard. The essential thing was to be as far away as possible from the block, from the crucible[17] of death, from the center of hell.

I saw my father running toward me. I became frightened all of a sudden.

"What's the matter?"

Out of breath, he could hardly open his mouth.

"Me, too . . . me, too . . . ! They told me to stay behind in the camp."

They had written down his number without his being aware of it.

"What will happen?" I asked in anguish.

But it was he who tried to reassure me.

"It isn't certain yet. There's still a chance of escape. They're going to do another selection today . . . a decisive selection."

I was silent.

---

17. A *crucible* is a heat-resistant vessel for melting metals and ores. The word *crucible* is also used to describe a severe test or trial.

Vocabulary

meager (mē′ gər) *adj.* inadequate in amount or quantity

He felt that his time was short. He spoke quickly. He would have liked to say so many things. His speech grew confused; his voice choked. He knew that I would have to go in a few moments. He would have to stay behind alone, so very alone.

"Look, take this knife," he said to me. "I don't need it any longer. It might be useful to you. And take this spoon as well. Don't sell them. Quickly! Go on. Take what I'm giving you!"

The inheritance.

"Don't talk like that, Father." (I felt that I would break into sobs.) "I don't want you to say that. Keep the spoon and knife. You need them as much as I do. We shall see each other again this evening, after work."

He looked at me with his tired eyes, veiled with despair. He went on:

"I'm asking this of you. . . . Take them. Do as I ask, my son. We have no time. . . . Do as your father asks."

Our Kapo yelled that we should start. The unit set out toward the camp gate. Left, right! I bit my lips. My father had stayed by the block, leaning against the wall. Then he began to run, to catch up with us. Perhaps he had forgotten something he wanted to say to me. . . . But we were marching too quickly . . . Left, right!

We were already at the gate. They counted us, to the din of military music. We were outside.

The whole day, I wandered about as if sleep-walking. Now and then Tibi and Yossi would throw me a brotherly word. The Kapo, too, tried to reassure me. He had given me easier work today. I felt sick at heart. How well they were treating me! Like an orphan! I thought: even now, my father is still helping me.

I did not know myself what I wanted—for the day to pass quickly or not. I was afraid of finding myself alone that night. How good it would be to die here!

At last we began the return journey. How I longed for orders to run!

The military march. The gate.
The camp.

I ran to Block 36.

Were there still miracles on this earth? He was alive. He had escaped the second selection. He had been able to prove that he was still useful. . . . I gave him back his knife and spoon.

Vocabulary

din (din) *n.* loud, continuous noise

Holocaust/Outcry, 1973. Alfred Tibor. Cast bronze, height: 15 in. Collection of the artist.

Viewing the sculpture: Describe your immediate reaction to this sculpture. What connections do you see between the sculpture and this selection?

Responding to Literature

Personal Response

What would you like to say to Elie Wiesel if you could meet him? What questions might you ask? Write your response in your journal.

Analyzing Literature

Recall

1. To what does Wiesel refer when he says, "The SS gave us a fine New Year's gift"?
2. What advice did the head of Wiesel's block offer before the prisoners passed before the SS officers?
3. Why was the narrator's father told to stay behind in the camp?
4. Who are Tibi and Yossi?
5. What is the **resolution,** or final outcome, of this selection?

Interpret

6. Why is the first sentence of the selection an example of **verbal irony,** where someone says one thing and means another?
7. Why might the block leader have lied to the men who were selected, telling them nothing would happen to them?
8. Explain why Wiesel's father gives him the knife and spoon. What does this "inheritance" tell you about the state of their lives?
9. Of what importance might Tibi and Yossi be to Elie Wiesel and to his retelling of these events? Use details from the selection in your response.
10. Describe the range of emotions that Wiesel might have experienced on the day he was separated from his father.

Evaluate and Connect

11. Wiesel wrote, "Those whose numbers had been noted stood apart, abandoned by the whole world." Do you think this sentence effectively describes how these men might have been feeling? Explain.
12. If you were Elie Wiesel, what aspect of your experience in the camps would have been the most difficult to cope with?
13. Why might Wiesel have titled his memoir *Night*?
14. Think about your response to the Reading Focus on page 304. What have you learned by reading this selection? What difference does it make to hear about the Holocaust from one who lived through it?
15. **Theme Connections** How might Elie Wiesel complete the sentence, "In the face of adversity, one must . . ."? How would you complete it?

Literary ELEMENTS

Atmosphere

Atmosphere is the mood or emotional quality of a literary work. Atmosphere often is created by the writer's choice of words and details about the setting and people. For example, Wiesel says that in the camp, "Everything was regulated by the bell. It gave . . . orders. . . ." Imagine a place where the ringing of a bell determines your every move, and you can imagine a place where the atmosphere is tense and nerve-racking.

1. One of the prisoners ironically describes the camp as a "paradise." How is the atmosphere different from a paradise?
2. List the words and phrases from the selection that made the strongest impression on you. How do these words and phrases affect the atmosphere?

- See **Literary Terms Handbook,** p. R1.

Literary Criticism

One critic writes, "*Night* shows how what Wiesel calls the 'philosophy of the concentration camp' took over. That philosophy meant 'every man for himself, every man the enemy of the next man, for each lived at the other's expense.'" What evidence of this philosophy can you find in the excerpt from *Night*? What exceptions to it can you find? Discuss your ideas with classmates.

Literature and Writing

Writing About Literature

Describing Character What kind of man is the block leader, the German Jew who "had never been outside concentration camps since 1933"? Is he cold and heartless or kind and compassionate? Consider what might motivate him to act the way he does. Then write a brief description of the block leader, using details from the selection to support your ideas.

Creative Writing

Secret Letter Imagine that you are a concentration camp "veteran" and you've bribed an official to let you smuggle a letter out of the camp to your cousin in the United States. Write the letter, describing your environment—your living conditions and the people around you—and explaining how you manage to survive and whether or not you are hopeful about the future.

Extending Your Response

Literature Groups

Reading and Discussing a Poem Brazilian poet Paulo Leminski wrote the following short poem:

moon
did you shine like this
over auschwitz?

Take turns reading the poem aloud in your group, experimenting with the speed and tone of your reading, as well as with the emphasis you place on each word. Then discuss what sentiments you think the poet was trying to express. How would Elie Wiesel, the fifteen-year-old narrator of the selection, respond to this poem? Having survived the war, what might he say about the poem today? Share your conclusions with other groups.

Learning for Life

Making a Research Plan Genocide is the deliberate and systematic destruction of a racial, religious, ethnic, or political group. The Holocaust was neither the first nor the last genocide in modern history. What have you heard about Armenia in the 1920s, Cambodia in the 1970s, or Rwanda and Yugoslavia in the 1990s? Make a research plan for learning more about the Holocaust or another example of genocide in modern times. Your plan should include a list of sources—Internet sites; reference works; CD-ROMs; biographies; and works of literature, art, and music—that will help explain what happened and why.

Save your work for your portfolio.

Skill Minilesson

VOCABULARY • Connotation

The literal meaning of a word is called its *denotation.* A word may, however, have an unspoken or unwritten meaning associated with it. This meaning is called its *connotation.* For example, describing someone as *bony* means that the person's bones are evident. Describing someone as *emaciated,* however, suggests an abnormal thinness that appears to be the result of starvation. Several of the vocabulary words from the excerpt from *Night* have important connotations.

din suggests noise that does not let up, to the point of being maddening or deafening

meager suggests that more is not only desirable but badly needed

avidly suggests an eagerness that is deep and intense, maybe even desperate

PRACTICE Write a sentence for each word above that is consistent with that word's connotation. Writing additional sentences may help to set the context.

LISTENING, SPEAKING, and VIEWING

Making an Informative Speech

The power of a speech, such as Elie Wiesel's Nobel Prize acceptance speech, is that it can educate and inspire an audience: people in a room, a nation, or the world. When it's your turn to convey information to others in a speech, follow these steps.

Preparing

- Know your purpose, and try to sum it up in one sentence.
- Determine how much time you have to speak.
- Think about what kinds of information your audience will need or appreciate. Plan on defining unfamiliar terms or concepts.

Researching

- Gather facts, examples, and expert opinions. Your audience will believe you if your facts are well supported with evidence.
- Gather enough information to present the whole picture. Neglecting a major consideration will be obvious.

Drafting

- Use a numbered note card for each main point. Then put your cards in a sensible order.
- Carefully write an introduction that grabs your audience's attention, and a conclusion that reinforces or summarizes your main points.

Practicing

- Read the speech aloud to yourself and then to a few friends. Ask for their comments.
- Rehearse until you feel comfortable with your speech, but don't try to memorize it. If you do, you're more likely to rush through it during the actual delivery!

Delivering

- Stand straight and relaxed. Take a deep breath before you begin.
- Speak slowly and clearly, projecting your voice so that people sitting in the back of the room will hear you.
- Make eye contact with people in different parts of your audience.

ACTIVITY

Prepare a three-minute orientation speech for incoming freshmen based on your experience at school this year. Present your speech in class or to an audience of eighth-graders.

Before You Read

Only Daughter

Reading Focus

Does being a family's only daughter or son–or the eldest, middle, youngest, or only child–affect who a person is?

Discuss In a small group, discuss the effect of family structure on you or on other people you know. If you think there is an ideal family size or position in a family, explain what it might be and why.

Setting a Purpose Read to learn about how gender and family position affected the author.

Building Background

The Time and Place

Sandra Cisneros recalls events that occurred during her childhood in Chicago, during her years in college, and during a visit to her parents at Christmastime the year before this essay was written.

Did You Know?

- In this essay, the author remembers her father referring to his children as *"hijos"* (ē′ hōs). In Spanish, *hijos* means "sons," but it also means "children."
- When the author's father speaks directly to his daughter, he uses the feminine equivalent of the word *hijo,* which is *hija* (ē′ hä). He says *"mi'ja"* (mē′ hä), which is a shortening of *mi* and *hija,* meaning "my daughter."

Vocabulary Preview

anthology (an thol′ ə jē) *n.* a collection of written works, such as poems, stories, or essays, in a single book or set; p. 314

retrospect (ret′ rə spekt′) *n.* the act of looking back or thinking about the past; p. 314

embroider (em broi′ der) *v.* to make a story more interesting with imaginary details or exaggerations; p. 314

nostalgia (nos tal′ jə) *n.* a sentimental longing for what is past or far away; p. 315

fulfill (fool fil′) *v.* to measure up to, or satisfy; to bring to pass or make real; p. 315

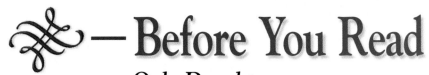

Meet Sandra Cisneros

Sandra Cisneros (sis nā′ rōs) says that coming from a Mexican American family gives her "two ways of looking at the world." It also gives her "twice as many words to pick from." Although Cisneros weaves Spanish words and phrases into her writing, she writes primarily in English. The stories she tells are about "poor families, brown families. People I knew and loved but never saw in the pages of the books I borrowed from the . . . library." Cisneros, who writes both fiction and poetry, won the American Book Award for her work of fiction, *The House on Mango Street.*

Sandra Cisneros was born in Chicago in 1954. This essay was first published in Glamour *magazine in 1990.*

ONLY

Once, several years ago, when I was just starting out my writing career, I was asked to write my own contributor's note for an anthology I was part of. I wrote: "I am the only daughter in a family of six sons. *That* explains everything."

Well, I've thought about that ever since, and yes, it explains a lot to me, but for the reader's sake I should have written: "I am the only daughter in a *Mexican* family of six sons." Or even: "I am the only daughter of a Mexican father and a Mexican-American mother." Or: "I am the only daughter of a working-class family of nine." All of these had everything to do with who I am today.

I was/am the only daughter and *only* a daughter. Being an only daughter in a family of six sons forced me by circumstance to spend a lot of time by myself because my brothers felt it beneath them to play with a *girl* in public. But that aloneness, that loneliness, was good for a would-be writer—it allowed me time to think and think, to imagine, to read and prepare myself.

Being only a daughter for my father meant my destiny would lead me to become someone's wife. That's what he believed. But when I was in the fifth grade and shared my plans for college with him, I was sure he understood. I remember my father saying, "*Qué bueno, mi'ja,*[1] that's good." That meant a lot to me, especially since my brothers thought the idea hilarious. What I didn't realize was that my father thought college was good for girls—good for finding a husband. After four years in college and two more in graduate school, and still no husband, my father shakes his head even now and says I wasted all that education.

In retrospect, I'm lucky my father believed daughters were meant for husbands. It meant it didn't matter if I majored in something silly like English. After all, I'd find a nice professional eventually, right? This allowed me the liberty to putter about embroidering my little poems and stories without my father interrupting with so much as a "What's that you're writing?"

But the truth is, I wanted him to interrupt. I wanted my father to understand what it was I was scribbling, to introduce me as "My only daughter, the writer." Not as "This is only my daughter. She teaches." *Es maestra*—teacher. Not even *profesora.*[2]

In a sense, everything I have ever written has been for him, to win his approval even though I know my father can't read English words, even though my father's only reading includes the brown-ink *Esto*[3] sports magazines from Mexico City and the bloody *¡Alarma!* magazines[4] that feature yet another sighting of

1. *Qué bueno, mi'ja* (kā bwā′ nō mē′ hä)

2. *Es maestra* (es mī äs′ trə); *profesora* (prō′ fes ō′ rə), means "professor."
3. *Esto* (es′ tō)
4. The *¡Alarma! magazines* feature exciting stories about famous people, strange events, and shocking crimes.

Vocabulary

anthology (an thol′ ə jē) *n.* a collection of written works, such as poems, stories, or essays, in a single book or set
retrospect (ret′ rə spekt′) *n.* the act of looking back or thinking about the past
embroider (em broi′ dər) *v.* to make a story more interesting with imaginary details or exaggerations

DAUGHTER

Sandra Cisneros

La Virgen de Guadalupe[5] on a tortilla or a wife's revenge on her philandering husband[6] by bashing his skull in with a *molcajete* (a kitchen mortar[7] made of volcanic rock). Or the *fotonovelas*,[8] the little picture paperbacks with tragedy and trauma erupting from the characters' mouths in bubbles.

My father represents, then, the public majority. A public who is disinterested in reading, and yet one whom I am writing about and for, and privately trying to woo.

When we were growing up in Chicago, we moved a lot because of my father. He suffered bouts of nostalgia. Then we'd have to let go our flat, store the furniture with mother's relatives, load the station wagon with baggage and bologna sandwiches and head south. To Mexico City.

Woman in Cordilleran Night, 1996. Maria Eugenia Terrazas. Watercolor, 70 x 70 cm. Kactus Foto, Santiago, Chile.

Viewing the painting: How does the artist's use of color and lines affect the mood of this painting? Compare and contrast this woman with the narrator in this selection.

We came back, of course. To yet another Chicago flat, another Chicago neighborhood, another Catholic school. Each time, my father would seek out the parish priest in order to get a tuition break, and complain or boast: "I have seven sons."

He meant *siete hijos*,[9] seven children, but he translated it as "sons." "I have seven sons." To anyone who would listen. The Sears Roebuck employee who sold us the washing machine. The short-order cook where my father ate his ham-and-eggs breakfasts. "I have seven sons." As if he deserved a medal from the state.

My papa. He didn't mean anything by that mistranslation, I'm sure. But somehow I could feel myself being erased. I'd tug my father's sleeve and whisper: "Not seven sons. Six! and *one daughter*."

When my oldest brother graduated from medical school, he fulfilled my father's dream that we study hard and use this—our heads, instead of this—our hands. Even now my father's hands are thick and yellow, stubbed by a history of hammer and nails and twine and coils and springs. "Use this," my father

5. *La Virgen de Guadalupe* (lä vēr′ hin dā gwä də loo′ pā), meaning "the Virgin of Guadalupe," is a name for Jesus' mother, Mary, the patron saint of Mexico.
6. A *philandering husband* is one who cheats on his wife.
7. A *molcajete* (mōl′ kə he′ tā), or *kitchen mortar,* is a thick bowl used to crush substances, such as dried spices, into powder.
8. *fotonovelas* (fō′ tō nō ve′ läs)
9. *Siete hijos* (sye′ tā ē′ hōs)

Vocabulary

nostalgia (nos tal′ jə) *n.* a sentimental longing for what is past or far away

fulfill (fool fil′) *v.* to measure up to, or satisfy; to bring to pass or make real

"I am the only daughter in a family of six sons. That explains everything."

said, tapping his head, "and not this," showing us those hands. He always looked tired when he said it.

Wasn't college an investment? And hadn't I spent all those years in college? And if I didn't marry, what was it all for? Why would anyone go to college and then choose to be poor? Especially someone who had always been poor.

Last year, after ten years of writing professionally, the financial rewards started to trickle in. My second National Endowment for the Arts[10] Fellowship. A guest professorship at the University of California, Berkeley. My book, which sold to a major New York publishing house.

At Christmas, I flew home to Chicago. The house was throbbing, same as always: hot *tamales*[11] and sweet *tamales* hissing in my mother's pressure cooker, and everybody—my mother, six brothers, wives, babies, aunts, cousins—talking too loud and at the same time, like in a Fellini[12] film, because that's just how we are.

I went upstairs to my father's room. One of my stories had just been translated into Spanish and published in an anthology of Chicano[13] writing, and I wanted to show it to him. Ever since he recovered from a stroke two years ago, my father likes to spend his leisure hours horizontally. And that's how I found him, watching a Pedro Infante movie on Galavision[14] and eating rice pudding.

There was a glass filmed with milk on the bedside table. There were several vials of pills and balled Kleenex. And on the floor, one black sock and a plastic urinal that I didn't want to look at but looked at anyway. Pedro Infante was about to burst into song, and my father was laughing.

I'm not sure if it was because my story was translated into Spanish, or because it was published in Mexico, or perhaps because the story dealt with Tepeyac, the *colonia*[15] my father was raised in and the house he grew up in, but at any rate, my father punched the mute button on his remote control and read my story.

I sat on the bed next to my father and waited. He read it very slowly. As if he were reading each line over and over. He laughed at all the right places and read lines he liked out loud. He pointed and asked questions: "Is this So-and-so?" "Yes," I said. He kept reading.

When he was finally finished, after what seemed like hours, my father looked up and asked: "Where can we get more copies of this for the relatives?"

Of all the wonderful things that happened to me last year, that was the most wonderful.

---

10. The *National Endowment for the Arts* is a U.S. government agency that awards money in the form of grants and fellowships to writers and other artists.
11. A *tamale* (tə mä′ lē) is a Mexican dish made of highly seasoned ground meat that is rolled in cornmeal dough, wrapped in corn husks, and steamed.
12. The movies of Italian director Federico *Fellini* (1920–1993) are often filled with strange characters and noisy, chaotic events.
13. *Chicano* (chi kä′ nō) means "Mexican American."
14. *Pedro Infante* (in fän′ tā) is a popular Mexican movie star who can occasionally be seen on *Galavision*, a Spanish-language, cable-TV channel.
15. *Tepeyac* (te pe yäk′) is a district *(colonia)* of Mexico City.

Responding to Literature

Personal Response

How did you react to the author's experience as a daughter?

Analyzing Literature

Recall and Interpret

1. Describe Sandra Cisneros's family. In your opinion, why does Cisneros write more about her father in this essay than about any other family member?
2. Explain how being the only daughter, and only a daughter, has proven to be both a positive and a negative experience for Cisneros.
3. What was the father's attitude toward a college education for his daughter? for his sons? Was Cisneros affected by her father's attitude? Explain why or why not, using details from the selection in your answer.
4. How does Cisneros react to her father's request for copies of her story? In your opinion, why does the father react differently to the story she gives him at Christmas than to all the other work she had done? What does his reaction predict for their future relationship?

Evaluate and Connect

5. By writing "My father represents . . . the public majority," what might Cisneros be saying about her father—and about society? Explain.
6. "I am the only daughter in a family of six sons. *That* explains everything." In what ways does the essay confirm Cisneros's statement? In what ways does the essay contradict it?
7. Cisneros says that she writes in order to win approval from her father. Whose approval do you try to win, and why is it important to you?
8. **Theme Connections** In your opinion, do all children face some adversity because of their family's expectations of them? Explain.

Literary **ELEMENTS**

Author's Purpose

An **author's purpose**, or reason for writing, may be to entertain, to persuade, to express opinions, or to inform. Sometimes an author may have more than one purpose for writing. For example, you may find parts of "Only Daughter" entertaining, but Cisneros also had something important to say about daughters and about the role of women in society.

1. In your opinion, what is Cisneros's purpose for writing? Explain.
2. This work was published in *Glamour* magazine, which is read almost exclusively by women, many of whom are young and single. How might this information help you understand the author's purpose?

- See **Literary Terms Handbook,** p. R2.

Extending Your Response

Personal Writing

Family Matters Think about your response to the Reading Focus on page 313. How does your position in your family affect you? Compare your experience with that of Cisneros. Write your thoughts in your journal.

Literature Groups

Would Dad Be Sad or Glad? As a group, decide what Cisneros's father's reactions to "Only Daughter" might be. Find places in the essay that might, for example, provoke him to smile, feel regret, ask questions, and so on. Share your conclusions with other groups.

Save your work for your portfolio.

Before You Read

Kipling and I

Reading Focus

What do you find comforting when times are hard? How have others assured you that things would work out for the best? What kinds of things do you tell yourself to help you keep going?

Sharing Ideas With your classmates, share your answers to the questions above.

Setting a Purpose Read to learn what inspires a young man facing difficult times.

Building Background

The Time and Place

The events in this selection take place in New York City in 1918, when the author was seventeen years old.

Did You Know?

Seeking better lives, thousands of immigrants from Europe, Puerto Rico, and other parts of the world came to live in New York City during the late 1800s and early 1900s. Most settled in the Lower East Side, where they lived in crowded tenement buildings–often without electricity, central heat, or running water. Many immigrants had difficulty finding jobs, and those who did were often paid extremely low wages and forced to work long hours in six- or seven-day work weeks. Eventually, labor unions were formed to protect the rights of workers, and laws guaranteed a minimum wage.

Vocabulary Preview

sage (sāj) *n.* a very wise person; p. 319

compendium (kəm pen′ dē əm) *n.* a complete summary of the most important information on a subject; p. 319

sonorous (sə nôr′ əs) *adj.* rich and full sounding; p. 320

innuendo (in′ ū en′ dō) *n.* an insinuation or hint suggesting something unfavorable; p. 320

paltry (pôl′ trē) *adj.* practically worthless; insignificant; p. 321

declaim (di klām′) *v.* to speak as though giving a speech in a loud, formal manner; p. 321

Meet Jesus Colon

Born in Puerto Rico, Jesus Colon (hā zo͞os′ kô lōn′) was sixteen years old when he stowed away on a ship bound for the United States. Arriving in New York City, he found work in factories, on the shipping docks, and in restaurants; he also attended night school. Colon eventually became a writer of short essays and newspaper columns. He devoted much of his adult life to helping workers fight against racism and social and political oppression.

Jesus Colon was born in 1901 and died in 1974. This selection appears in A Puerto Rican in New York and Other Sketches, *which was first published in 1961 and received an American Book Award in 1984.*

Kipling and I

Jesus Colon

SOMETIMES I PASS Debevoise Place at the corner of Willoughby Street . . . I look at the old wooden house, gray and ancient, the house where I used to live some forty years ago . . .

My room was on the second floor at the corner. On hot summer nights I would sit at the window reading by the electric light from the street lamp which was almost at a level with the windowsill.

It was nice to come home late during the winter, look for some scrap of old newspaper, some bits of wood and a few chunks of coal, and start a sparkling fire in the chunky four-legged coal stove. I would be rewarded with an intimate warmth as little by little the pigmy stove became alive puffing out its sides, hot and red, like the crimson cheeks of a Santa Claus.

My few books were in a soap box nailed to the wall. But my most prized possession in those days was a poem I had bought in a five-and-ten-cent store on Fulton Street. (I wonder what has become of these poems, maxims and sayings of wise men that they used to sell at the five-and-ten-cent stores?) The poem was printed on gold paper and mounted in a gilded frame[1] ready to be hung in a conspicuous place in the house. I bought one of those fancy silken picture cords finishing in a rosette[2] to match the color of the frame.

I was seventeen. This poem to me then seemed to summarize, in one poetical nutshell, the wisdom of all the sages that ever lived. It was what I was looking for, something to guide myself by, a way of life, a compendium of the wise, the true and the beautiful. All I had to do was to live according to the counsel of the poem and follow its instructions and I would be a perfect man—the useful, the good, the true human being. I was very happy that day, forty years ago.

---

1. A *gilded frame* is painted gold or covered with gold leaf (a very thin layer of gold).
2. A *rosette* is a rose-like ornament. In this case, it is in the middle of the picture cord and probably made from knotted threads of the cord.

Vocabulary

sage (sāj) *n.* a very wise person

compendium (kəm pen′ dē əm) *n.* a complete summary of the most important information on a subject

The poem had to have the most prominent place in the room. Where could I hang it? I decided that the best place for the poem was on the wall right by the entrance to the room. No one coming in and out would miss it. Perhaps someone would be interested enough to read it and drink the profound waters of its message. . . .

Every morning as I prepared to leave, I stood in front of the poem and read it over and over again, sometimes half a dozen times. I let the sonorous music of the verse carry me away. I brought with me a handwritten copy as I stepped out every morning looking for work, repeating verses and stanzas from memory until the whole poem came to be part of me. Other days my lips kept repeating a single verse of the poem at intervals throughout the day.

In the subways I loved to compete with the shrill noises of the many wheels below by chanting the lines of the poem. People stared at me moving my lips as though I were in a trance. I looked back with pity. They were not so fortunate as I who had as a guide to direct my life a great poem to make me wise, useful and happy.

And I chanted:

If you can keep your head when all about you
Are losing theirs and blaming it on you . . .

If you can wait and not be tired by waiting,
Or being lied about, don't deal in lies,
Or being hated don't give way to hating . . .

If you can make one heap of all your winnings;
And risk it on one turn of pitch-and-toss,
And lose, and start again at your beginnings . . .

"If—," by Kipling,[3] was the poem. At seventeen, my evening prayer and my first morning thought. I repeated it every day with the resolution to live up to the very last line of that poem.

I would visit the government employment office on Jay Street. The conversations among the Puerto Ricans on the large wooden benches in the employment office were always on the same subject. How to find a decent place to live. How they would not rent to Negroes or Puerto Ricans. How Negroes and Puerto Ricans were given the pink slips[4] first at work.

From the employment office I would call door to door at the piers, factories and storage houses in the streets under the Brooklyn and Manhattan bridges. "Sorry, nothing today." It seemed to me that that "today" was a continuation and combination of all the yesterdays, todays and tomorrows.

From the factories I would go to the restaurants, looking for a job as a porter[5] or dishwasher. At least I would eat and be warm in a kitchen.

"Sorry" . . . "Sorry" . . .

Sometimes I was hired at ten dollars a week, ten hours a day including Sundays and holidays. One day off during the week. My work was that of three men: dishwasher, porter, busboy. And to clear the sidewalk of snow and slush "when you have nothing else to do." I was to be appropriately humble and grateful not only to the owner but to everybody else in the place.

If I rebelled at insults or at a pointed innuendo or just the inhuman amount of work, I was unceremoniously[6] thrown out and told to come "next week for your pay." "Next

3. Rudyard *Kipling* (1865–1936) was an English writer who lived much of his life in India. *"If–,"* a poem that offers advice for personal success, is one of his better-known works.

4. A *pink slip* might say something like, "This is a notice of termination of employment for . . . ," but it means, "You're laid off," or "You're fired."

5. Here, a *porter* is a person who does routine cleaning.

6. *Unceremoniously* means "abruptly" or "rudely."

Vocabulary

sonorous (sə nôr′ əs) *adj.* rich and full sounding

innuendo (in′ ū en′ dō) *n.* an insinuation or hint suggesting something unfavorable week" meant weeks of calling for the paltry dollars owed me. The owners relished this "next week."

I clung to my poem as to a faith. Like a potent amulet,[7] my precious poem was clenched in the fist of my right hand inside my secondhand overcoat. Again and again I declaimed aloud a few precious lines when discouragement and disillusionment threatened to overwhelm me.

If you can force your heart and nerve and sinew
To serve your turn long after they are gone . . .

The weeks of unemployment and hard knocks turned into months. I continued to find two or three days of work here and there. And I continued to be thrown out when I rebelled at the ill treatment, overwork and insults. I kept pounding the streets looking for a place where they would treat me half decently, where my devotion to work and faith in Kipling's poem would be appreciated. I remember the worn-out shoes I bought in a secondhand store on Myrtle Avenue at the corner of Adams Street. The round holes in the soles that I tried to cover with pieces of carton were no match for the frigid knives of the unrelenting snow.

One night I returned late after a long day of looking for work. I was hungry. My room was dark and cold. I wanted to warm my numb body. I lit a match and began looking for some scraps of wood and a piece of paper to start a fire. I searched all over the floor. No wood, no paper. As I stood up, the glimmering flicker of the dying match was reflected in the glass surface of the framed poem. I unhooked the poem from the wall. I reflected for a minute, a minute that felt like an eternity. I took the frame apart, placing the square glass upon the small table. I tore the gold paper on which the poem was printed, threw its pieces inside the stove and, placing the small bits of wood from the frame on top of the paper, I lit it, adding soft and hard coal as the fire began to gain strength and brightness.

I watched how the lines of the poem withered into ashes inside the small stove.

7. An *amulet* is an object that is thought to bring good luck or to protect against evil. *Potent* means "strong and effective."

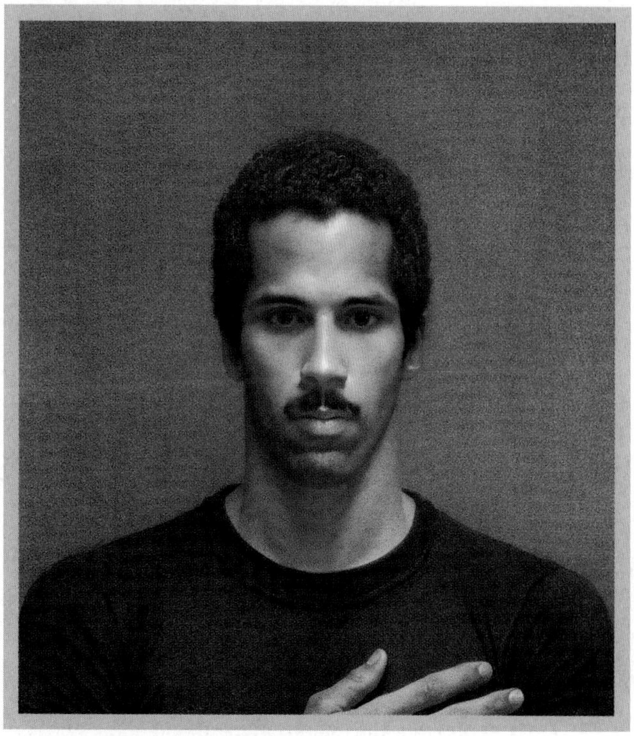

©Claudio Bravo/Licensed by VAGA, New York, NY.

Hombre, 1978. Claudio Bravo. Conte crayon on heavy paper, 20 x 18 in. Private collection.

Viewing the art: How would you compare this man to the narrator? What might his hand against his chest signify?

Vocabulary

paltry (pôl′ trē) *adj.* practically worthless; insignificant
declaim (di klām′) *v.* to speak as though giving a speech in a loud, formal manner

Responding to Literature

Personal Response

Were you surprised by what the narrator did at the end of the selection? Why or why not?

Analyzing Literature

Recall

1. Describe the room where Jesus Colon lived, and identify his most "prized possession."
2. What specific things did Colon do each day with his most "prized possession"?
3. How did the author spend most days, and why?
4. Describe the difficulties Colon experienced in the workplace.
5. What finally happened to Colon's most "prized possession"?

Interpret

6. Why might Colon have prized his favorite possession so highly?
7. Think about your discussion during the Reading Focus on page 318. What might Colon have said if he had been able to contribute to the conversation? Explain your response.
8. Who or what might be considered **antagonists** in this selection? Explain how each antagonist affected Colon. (See page R1.)
9. What character traits and moral convictions does Colon display that would account for his difficulty in keeping a job?
10. In your opinion, why did Colon choose to do what he did at the end of the selection?

Evaluate and Connect

11. How would you feel if you were Colon, and potential employers repeatedly said, "Sorry, nothing today"?
12. Reread the lines that Colon quotes from "If–." Why might Colon have felt that if he lived "according to the counsel of the poem," he would be "a perfect man–the useful, the good, the true human being"?
13. What advice might you have given to Jesus Colon, if you had been his neighbor or friend?
14. Reread the third paragraph and the last two paragraphs of the selection. How do you account for the shift in tone? Would the selection have been as effective without the third paragraph? Explain.
15. How might Colon have felt about his final action days later? How does he seem to feel about it now? Explain your reasoning.

Literary ELEMENTS

Memoir

A **memoir** is a type of nonfiction that presents the story of a person's life written by that person. A memoir is usually written from the first-person point of view and structured as a narrative. Unlike an autobiography that tells a person's entire life story, a memoir typically focuses on one period of a person's life, often emphasizing a person's thoughts and feelings, the person's relationships with significant people, or the person's experience of major events.

1. Explain why "Kipling and I" might be considered a memoir, and not an autobiography.
2. After reading this selection, what generalizations might you make about what life was like for immigrants living in New York City in 1918?

- See **Literary Terms Handbook,** p. R7.

Literary Criticism

In the *Dictionary of Hispanic Biography,* Jennifer Kramer says that Colon's writings "demonstrate that he could face [racial and class discrimination] with humor and dignity." In your journal, summarize Colon's ideas about race and class in "Kipling and I." Then tell whether you agree with Kramer's comment.

Literature and Writing

Writing About Literature

Character Sketch Based on details in the selection, make a list of Jesus Colon's character traits as a seventeen-year-old. Use the list as a starting point for a character sketch (a portrait in words) about Colon. Read your sketch aloud in a small group of classmates.

Creative Writing

Adding an Ending What do you think happens next? Does Colon's life take a turn for the better, or does his life continue to be full of hardship for some time to come? As Colon, write an epilogue, summarizing this period in your life and telling what happens next.

Extending Your Response

Literature Groups

Making the Conflict Real When Colon was unable to find wood and paper for a fire, he "unhooked the poem from the wall . . ." and "reflected for a minute, a minute that felt like an eternity." What was Colon thinking? What might he have said aloud if the poem could have heard him? What might the poem have said to keep Colon from setting it aflame? Find a partner within your group and role-play the conversation Colon and the poem might have had. Then share summaries of the conversations with the rest of the group. Did any poems convince Colon to choose a different course of action?

Learning for Life

Pay Scales In "Kipling and I," the author states that in a restaurant, he did the jobs of three men and earned ten dollars for working a six-day work week of sixty hours. If Colon were working full-time in a restaurant today, how many hours would he be expected to work? What jobs might he hold, and how would each be defined? How much would he earn? Find the answers by conducting interviews with several restaurant owners or by using newspaper or Internet job-search resources and classified ads.

Save your work for your portfolio.

Skill Minilesson

VOCABULARY • Analogies

An analogy is a comparison based on the relationships between things or ideas. Some analogies are of a type that could be called "defining characteristic." The characteristic given may not be the most important or most distinguishing one, but it is a necessary part of what makes the person, idea, or thing what it is. Study this example:

zebra : striped :: leopard : spotted

A zebra, by definition, is striped; a leopard, by definition, is spotted.

To complete an analogy, decide what relationship is represented by the first two words. Then apply that relationship to another pair of words.

For more about analogies, see **Communications Skills Handbook,** p. R77.

PRACTICE Complete each analogy. Which items have a defining characteristic?

1. whisper : quiet :: innuendo :
   a. short b. loud c. suggestive
2. scolding : critical :: maxim :
   a. motto b. brief c. alarming
3. dictator : powerful :: sage :
   a. strict b. wise c. old
4. trinket : paltry :: gem :
   a. round b. small c. valuable
5. blizzard : snowy :: tornado :
   a. violent b. cyclone c. tropical

Before You Read

Sympathy

Reading Focus

Frederick Douglass, a leader in the abolitionist and civil rights movements.

After the abolition of slavery in the United States, Frederick Douglass, who befriended Paul Laurence Dunbar and helped promote his career, wrote, "Though the colored man is no longer subject to be bought and sold, he is still surrounded by an adverse sentiment which fetters all his movements."

Quickwrite Write about how you think "adverse sentiment," or feelings against people, can "fetter," or chain, them.

Setting a Purpose Read to find out how the poet associates these feelings with those of a caged bird.

Building Background

Did You Know?

- Paul Laurence Dunbar's father escaped slavery, fled to Canada, and then returned to the United States to fight in the Civil War. After the war, he and his wife settled in Dayton, Ohio. Seven years later, their son was born.
- Despite early experience in journalism and publishing, Dunbar had great difficulty establishing a literary career, and had to work as an elevator operator to support himself. A break finally occurred when former classmate Orville Wright (who, with his brother, would later invent the airplane) helped him to find a publisher for his first volume of poems. His friend Frederick Douglass provided further help, as did author and literary critic William Dean Howells.
- Inspired by the poem you are about to read, award-winning African American author and poet Maya Angelou titled her first of five autobiographical books *I Know Why the Caged Bird Sings.* In this book, she shares experiences she had growing up in a racially segregated town in the South.

Meet Paul Laurence Dunbar

The only African American in his high school class, Paul Laurence Dunbar was class president, editor of the school newspaper, and president of the literary society. While still in school, he also edited an African American newspaper, the *Dayton Tattler*, and published poems in the *Dayton Herald*. As a young man, Dunbar wrote that his ambition was to "be able to interpret my own people through song and story, and to prove to the many that after all we are more human than African." Despite discrimination, Dunbar ultimately reached his ambition, publishing many highly acclaimed novels, poems, and short stories.

Paul Laurence Dunbar was born in 1872 and died in 1906.

Sympathy

Paul Laurence Dunbar

I know what the caged bird feels, alas!
When the sun is bright on the upland slopes;
When the wind stirs soft through the springing grass,
And the river flows like a stream of glass;
When the first bird sings and the first bud opes,
And the faint perfume from its chalice steals—
I know what the caged bird feels!

I know why the caged bird beats his wing
Till its blood is red on the cruel bars;
For he must fly back to his perch and cling
When he fain would be on the bough a-swing;
And a pain still throbs in the old, old scars
And they pulse again with a keener sting—
I know why he beats his wing!

I know why the caged bird sings, ah me,
When his wing is bruised and his bosom sore,—
When he beats his bars and he would be free;
It is not a carol of joy or glee,
But a prayer that he sends from his heart's deep core,
But a plea, that upward to Heaven he flings—
I know why the caged bird sings!

Responding to Literature

Personal Response

What feelings did you experience while you were reading this poem?

Analyzing Literature

Recall and Interpret

1. Does the speaker actually tell the reader what the caged bird feels? In your opinion, why or why not?
2. What images from nature does the speaker use in the first stanza? How do those images help the speaker–and you–to understand what the caged bird feels?
3. Why does the caged bird beat its wing? What do you think are the "old, old scars" in line 12, and why might they "pulse again with a keener sting"?
4. Why does the caged bird sing? What is the meaning of its song?
5. What can you infer about the speaker based on this poem?

Evaluate and Connect

6. Explain what you think is the **theme,** or central message, of this poem. How effective is the use of **personification** in conveying this theme? Explain, using details from the poem in your answer. (See Literary Terms Handbook, pages R13 and R9.)
7. Review the writing you did for the Reading Focus on page 324. How do your thoughts compare with the ideas expressed in the poem? What might you add to your response?
8. What kind of circumstances might lead a person to write a poem like "Sympathy" today?

Literary ELEMENTS

Rhyme

Rhyme is the repetition of similar or identical sounds at the ends of words that appear close to each other in a poem. **Internal rhyme** occurs within a line, while **end rhyme** occurs at the ends of lines. The use of certain rhymes can make the poem's message or tone seem playful or humorous. Or rhyme may produce a soothing, songlike, or serious effect. Rhyme may also suggest connections between certain words by calling attention to their shared sounds.

1. Review the end rhyme in the second and third stanzas. What connections exist between the words that rhyme?
2. What effect does the use of rhyme have in "Sympathy"?

- See **Literary Terms Handbook,** p. R10.

Extending Your Response

Literature Groups

What Does It Mean? In "Sympathy," Dunbar uses a captive bird and images from nature to send a message about what it is like to be less than fully free. But how does he do it? In your group, discuss what the cage, the bird, and the images from nature might represent. What does each of these symbols mean to you? Share your conclusions with other groups.

Creative Writing

The Song of a Bird Imagine that the song the caged bird sang had lyrics that humans could understand. Write the words of the caged bird's song. Reflect on the bird's past experience as well as on its hopes for the future.

Save your work for your portfolio.

COMPARING *selections*

Kipling and I **and** Sympathy

COMPARE **SITUATIONS**

Review Paul Laurence Dunbar's poem "Sympathy," and "Kipling and I," by Jesus Colon. Then discuss the following questions with a small group of classmates.

1. How might the dreams and disappointments of the young Jesus Colon be similar to those of the caged bird described in "Sympathy"?
2. How might the bird's physical environment be compared to Colon's?
3. In your opinion, how does racial discrimination affect the situations of Colon and the speaker in the poem?

COMPARE **ART'S EFFECTS**

With a partner, review Dunbar's poem and Colon's memoir. On the basis of these selections, what generalizations can you make about the functions literature and music serve in people's lives? What generalizations can you make about the benefits and limitations of these art forms? "Sympathy" suggests that the caged bird will continue to sing, but "Kipling and I" suggests that Colon will no longer recite his treasured poem. How do you account for this? Share your conclusions with the class.

COMPARE **ADAPTATIONS**

Imagine that "Kipling and I" has been adapted into a single episode of a television miniseries based on Colon's memoir, *A Puerto Rican in New York and Other Sketches*. The soundtrack of the miniseries includes the poem "Sympathy," which has been set to music and released on a CD single. Create a full-page magazine advertisement that will create interest in the miniseries and entice people to buy the CD. In your ad copy, be sure to tell your audience how each work perfectly complements the other. Include eye-catching visuals that connect the episode and the CD. You might use original art or pictures clipped from magazines or newspapers.

Before You Read

from *All God's Children Need Traveling Shoes*

Reading Focus

Where might you travel, what might you read, and whom might you interview to learn more about your ancestors?

Journal Write your answer in your journal. Also write about what connects you to the people who have come before you.

Setting a Purpose Read to learn about the author's experiences when she visits the land of her African ancestors.

Building Background

The Time and Place

This selection takes place in Ghana, Africa, in the early 1960s.

Did You Know?

- Maya Angelou spent four years living and working in Ghana, a nation that lies on the Atlantic coast of West Africa. Accra, its capital city, is a bustling seaport of approximately one million people.
- When fifteenth-century Portuguese explorers arrived in the region now known as Ghana, they found so much gold there that they named it the Gold Coast. This wealth drew other European powers, and the British ultimately made the Gold Coast a colony in the late 1800s. From the 1500s to the 1850s, the Gold Coast was a center of the international slave trade. In 1957 the nation attained its independence and renamed itself Ghana.

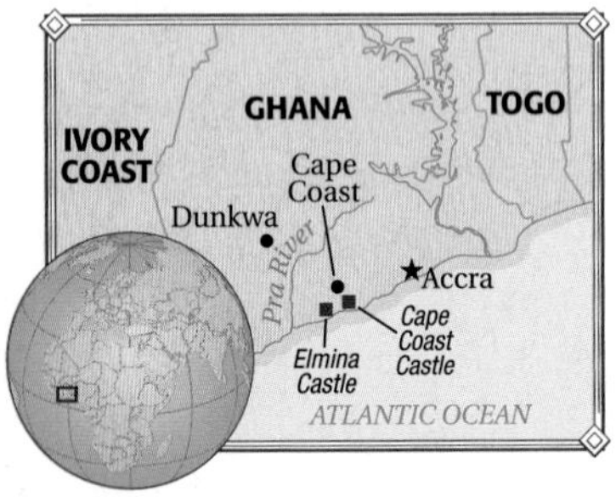

Vocabulary Preview

throng (thrông) *n.* a large number of people or things crowded together; p. 329

pang (pang) *n.* a sudden sharp feeling of pain or distress; p. 330

suffuse (sə fūz′) *v.* to spread through or over; p. 330

purging (pur′ jing) *n.* a removal of whatever is unclean or undesirable; cleansing; p. 330

impervious (im pur′ vē əs) *adj.* incapable of being passed through, affected, or disturbed; p. 331

sporadically (spə rad′ i kəl lē) *adv.* irregularly; occasionally; p. 333

reverberate (ri vur′ bə rāt′) *v.* to echo; resound; p. 334

Meet Maya Angelou

Born Marguerite Johnson in St. Louis, Missouri, Maya Angelou (mī′ yə an′ jə lō) had many careers before discovering her niche as an author and a poet. She has won several awards for her various achievements. Angelou spent much of her childhood in rural, racially segregated Stamps, Arkansas. She wrote eloquently about this and other periods of her life in a series of autobiographical books. Also considered a major U.S. poet, Angelou was selected by President Bill Clinton to write and read a poem at his first inaugural ceremony in January 1993.

Maya Angelou was born in 1928. This selection appears in her book All God's Children Need Traveling Shoes, *which was first published in 1986.*

from All God's Children Need Traveling Shoes

Maya Angelou

EACH MORNING Ghana's seven-and-one-half million people seemed to crowd at once into the capital city where the broad avenues as well as the unpaved rutted lanes became gorgeous with moving pageantry: bicycles, battered lorries, hand carts, American and European cars, chauffeur-driven limousines. People on foot struggled for right-of-way, white-collar workers wearing white knee-high socks brushed against market women balancing large baskets on their heads as they proudly swung their wide hips. Children, bright faces shining with palm oil, picked openings in the throng, and pretty young women in western clothes affected not to notice the attention they caused as they laughed together talking in the musical Twi language. Old men sat or stooped beside the road smoking homemade pipes and looking wise as old men have done eternally.

The too sweet aromas of flowers, the odors of freshly fried fish and stench from open sewers hung in my clothes and lay on my skin. Car horns blew, drums thumped. Loud radio music and the muddle of many languages shouted or murmured. I needed country quiet.

The Fiat was dependable, and I had a long weekend, money in my purse, and a working command of Fanti,[1] so I decided to travel into the bush. I bought roasted plantain stuffed with boiled peanuts, a quart of Club beer and headed my little car west. The stretch was a highway from Accra to Cape Coast,[2] filled with trucks and private cars passing from lane to lane with abandon. People hung out of windows of the crowded mammie lorries,[3] and I could hear singing and shouting when the drivers careened those antique vehicles up and down hills as if each was a little train out to prove it could.

1. *Fanti* (fan′ tē) is a dialect spoken by one of Ghana's many ethnic groups.
2. *Accra* is Ghana's capital and largest city; the town of *Cape Coast* is about 75 miles southwest of Accra.
3. *Mammie lorries* are small trucks or open-sided buses used for public transportation.

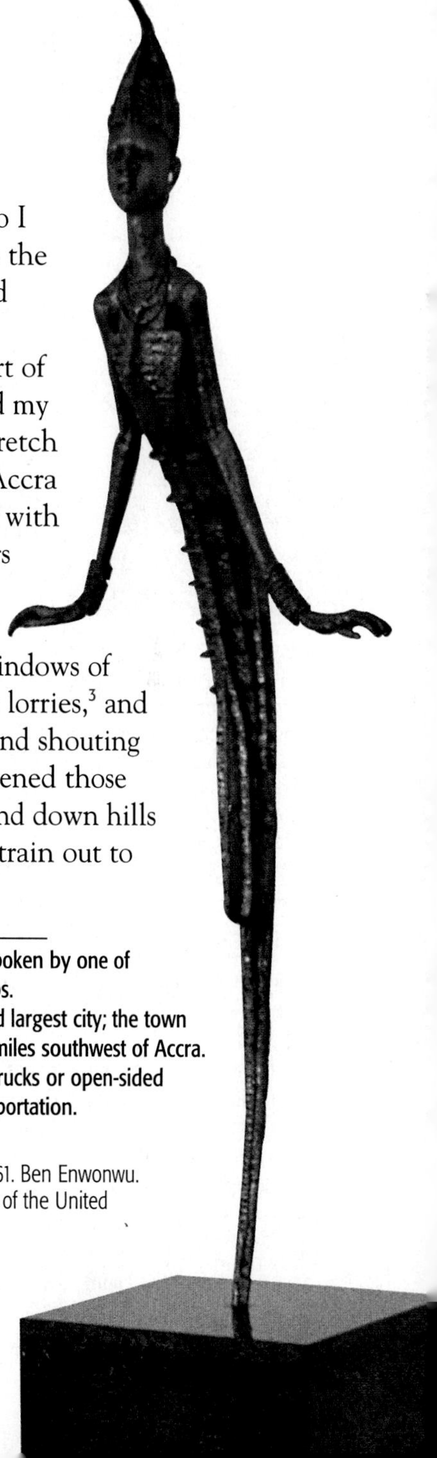

Anyanwu (The Awakening), 1961. Ben Enwonwu. Bronze, height: 82 in. Collection of the United Nations, New York.

Vocabulary

throng (thrông) *n.* a large number of people or things crowded together

I stopped in Cape Coast only for gas. Although many black Americans had headed for the town as soon as they touched ground in Ghana, I successfully avoided it for a year. Cape Coast Castle and the nearby Elmina Castle[4] had been holding forts for captured slaves. The captives had been imprisoned in dungeons beneath the massive buildings, and friends of mine who had felt called upon to make the trek reported that they felt the thick stone walls still echoed with old cries.

The palm tree–lined streets and fine white stone buildings did not tempt me to remain any longer than necessary. Once out of the town and again onto the tarred roads, I knew I had not made a clean escape. Despite my hurry, history had invaded my little car. Pangs of self-pity and a sorrow for my unknown relatives suffused me. Tears made the highway waver and were salty on my tongue.

Did You Know?
Found mostly in tropical Africa, *baobab* (bā′ ō bab′) *trees* have very broad trunks, thick branches, and large white flowers. They grow well on *savannahs,* which are open grasslands with scattered trees and shrubs.

What did they think and feel, my grandfathers, caught on those green savannas, under the baobab trees? How long did their families search for them? Did the dungeon wall feel chilly and its slickness strange to my grandmothers, who were used to the rush of air against bamboo huts and the sound of birds rattling their grass roofs?

I had to pull off the road. Just passing near Cape Coast Castle had plunged me back into the eternal melodrama.[5]

There would be no purging, I knew, unless I asked all the questions. Only then would the spirits understand that I was feeding them. It was a crumb, but it was all I had.

I allowed the shapes to come to my imagination: children passed tied together by ropes and chains, tears abashed, stumbling in dull exhaustion, then women, hair uncombed, bodies gritted with sand, and sagging in defeat. Men, muscles without memory, minds dimmed, plodding, leaving bloodied footprints in the dirt. The quiet was awful. None of them cried, or yelled, or bellowed. No moans came from them. They lived in a mute territory, dead to feeling and protest. These were the legions, sold by sisters, stolen by brothers, bought by strangers, enslaved by the greedy, and betrayed by history.

For a long time, I sat as in an open-air auditorium watching a troop of tragic players enter and exit the stage.

The visions faded as my tears ceased. Light returned and I started the car, turned off the main road, and headed for the interior. Using rutted track roads, and lanes a little larger than foot paths, I found the River Pra. The black water moving quietly, ringed with the tall trees, seemed enchanted. A fear of snakes kept me in the car, but I parked and watched the bright sun turn the water surface into a rippling cloth of lamé.[6] I passed

4. *Cape Coast Castle* and *Elmina Castle* are two slave-trade era fortifications. The castles' dungeons held thousands of captured men, women, and children in chains as they awaited export to North America as slaves. The United Nations has designated the buildings as World Heritage Monuments.

5. *[eternal melodrama]* Angelou compares the experience of slavery to a play that never fails to stir the emotions deeply.

6. *Lamé* (la mā′) is a fabric woven with metallic threads that give it a glittering appearance.

Vocabulary

pang (pang) *n.* a sudden sharp feeling of pain or distress

suffuse (sə fūz′) *v.* to spread through or over

purging (pur′ jing) *n.* a removal of whatever is unclean or undesirable; cleansing through villages which were little more than collections of thatch huts, with goats and small children wandering in the lanes. The noise of my car brought smiling adults out to wave at me.

In the late afternoon, I reached the thriving town that was my destination. A student whom I had met at Legon had spoken to me often of the gold-mining area, of Dunkwa, his birthplace. His reports had so glowed with the town's virtues, and I had chosen that spot for my first journey.

My skin color, features, and the Ghana cloth I wore made me look like any young Ghanaian[7] woman. I could pass if I didn't talk too much.

As usual, in the towns of Ghana, the streets were filled with vendors selling their wares of tinned pat milk, hot spicy Killi Willis (fried, ripe plantain chips), Pond's cold cream and antimosquito incense rings. Farmers were returning home, children returning from school. Young boys grinned at mincing[8] girls and always there were the market women, huge and impervious. I searched for a hotel sign in vain and as the day lengthened, I started to worry. I didn't have enough gas to get to Koforidua, a large town northeast of Dunkwa, where there would certainly be hotels, and I didn't have the address of my student's family. I parked the car a little out of the town center and stopped a woman carrying a bucket of water on her head and a baby on her back.

"Good day." I spoke in Fanti, and she responded. I continued, "I beg you, I am a stranger looking for a place to stay."

She repeated, "Stranger?" and laughed. "You are a stranger? No. No."

To many Africans only whites could be strangers. All Africans belonged somewhere, to some clan. All Akan-speaking[9] people belong to one of eight blood lines (Abosua) and one of eight spirit lines (Ntoro).

I said, "I am not from here."

For a second fear darted in her eyes. There was the possibility that I was a witch or some unhappy ghost from the country of the dead. I quickly said, "I am from Accra." She gave me a good smile. "Oh, one Accra. Without a home." She laughed. The Fanti word *Nkran*, for which the capitol was named, means the large ant that builds ten-foot-high domes of red clay and lives with millions of other ants.

"Come with me." She turned quickly, steadying the bucket on her head, and led me between two corrugated tin shacks. The baby bounced and slept on her back, secured by the large piece of cloth wrapped around her body. We passed a compound where women were pounding the dinner foo foo[10] in wooden bowls.

The woman shouted, "Look what I have found. One Nkran has no place to sleep tonight." The women laughed and asked, "One Nkran? I don't believe it."

"Are you taking it to the old man?"

"Of course."

"Sleep well, alone, Nkran, if you can." My guide stopped before a small house. She put the water on the ground and told me to wait while she entered the house. She returned immediately followed by a man who rubbed his eyes as if he had just been awakened.

7. *Ghanaian* (gä′ nə yən)

8. The *mincing* girls are trying to appear dainty and refined.

9. *Akan* (ä′ kän′) is the language spoken in southern Ghana; Fanti is a dialect of Akan.

10. *Foo foo* is a dough made from mashed yams, plantains, or other starchy fruits.

Vocabulary

impervious (im pur′ vē əs) *adj.* incapable of being passed through, affected, or disturbed

Ubi girl from Tai Region, 1972. Loïs Mailou Jones. Acrylic on canvas, 60 x 43¾ in. Museum of Fine Arts, Boston.

Viewing the painting: In your opinion, what does this painting say about the issue of identity, which Maya Angelou explores in this selection? Consider, for example, the painting's mix of images, shapes, and colors.

He walked close and peered hard at my face. "This is the Nkran?" The woman was adjusting the bucket on her head.

"Yes, Uncle. I have brought her." She looked at me, "Good-bye, Nkran. Sleep in peace. Uncle, I am going." The man said, "Go and come, child," and resumed studying my face. "You are not Ga." He was reading my features.

A few small children had collected around his knees. They could barely hold back their giggles as he interrogated me.

"Aflao?"[11]

I said, "No."

"Brong-ahafo?"

I said, "No. I am—." I meant to tell him the truth, but he said, "Don't tell me. I will soon know." He continued staring at me. "Speak more. I will know from your Fanti."

"Well, I have come from Accra and I need to rent a room for the night. I told that woman that I was a stranger . . ."

He laughed. "And you are. Now, I know. You are Bambara from Liberia. It is clear you are Bambara." He laughed again. "I always can tell. I am not easily fooled." He shook my hand. "Yes, we will find you a place for the night. Come." He touched a boy at his right. "Find Patience Aduah, and bring her to me."

11. Here and in the next few paragraphs, the man guesses at Angelou's ethnic group in the mistaken belief that she is a native West African.

The children laughed and all ran away as the man led me into the house. He pointed me to a seat in the neat little parlor and shouted, "Foriwa, we have a guest. Bring beer." A small black woman with an imperial air entered the room. Her knowing face told me that she had witnessed the scene in her front yard.

She spoke to her husband. "And, Kobina, did you find who the stranger was?" She walked to me. I stood and shook her hand. "Welcome, stranger." We both laughed. "Now don't tell me, Kobina, I have ears, also. Sit down, Sister, beer is coming. Let me hear you speak."

We sat facing each other while her husband stood over us smiling. "You, Foriwa, you will never get it."

I told her my story, adding a few more words I had recently learned. She laughed grandly. "She is Bambara. I could have told you when Abaa first brought her. See how tall she is? See her head? See her color? Men, huh. They only look at a woman's shape."

Two children brought beer and glasses to the man who poured and handed the glasses around. "Sister, I am Kobina Artey; this is my wife Foriwa and some of my children."

I introduced myself, but because they had taken such relish in detecting my tribal origin I couldn't tell them that they were wrong. Or, less admirably, at that moment I didn't want to remember that I was an American. For the first time since my arrival, I was very nearly home. Not a Ghanaian, but at least accepted as an African. The sensation was worth a lie.

Voices came to the house from the yard.

"Brother Kobina," "Uncle," "Auntie."

Foriwa opened the door to a group of people who entered speaking fast and looking at me.

"So this is the Bambara woman? The stranger?" They looked me over and talked with my hosts. I understood some of their conversation. They said that I was nice looking and old enough to have a little wisdom. They announced that my car was parked a few blocks away. Kobina told them that I would spend the night with the newlyweds, Patience and Kwame Duodu. Yes, they could see clearly that I was a Bambara.

"Give us the keys to your car, Sister; someone will bring your bag."

I gave up the keys and all resistance. I was either at home with friends, or I would die wishing that to be so.

Later, Patience, her husband, Kwame, and I sat out in the yard around a cooking fire near to their thatched house which was much smaller than the Artey bungalow. They explained that Kobina Artey was not a chief, but a member of the village council, and all small matters in that area of Dunkwa were taken to him. As Patience stirred the stew in the pot, which was balanced over the fire, children and women appeared sporadically out of the darkness carrying covered plates. Each time Patience thanked the bearers and directed them to the house, I felt the distance narrow between my past and present.

In the United States, during segregation, black American travelers, unable to stay in hotels restricted to white patrons, stopped at churches and told the black ministers or deacons of their predicaments. Church officials would select a home and then inform the unexpecting hosts of the decision. There was never a protest, but the new hosts relied on the generosity of their neighbors to help feed and even entertain their guests. After the travelers were settled, surreptitious knocks would sound on the back door.

In Stamps, Arkansas, I heard so often, "Sister Henderson, I know you've got guests. Here's a pan of biscuits."

Vocabulary

sporadically (spə rad′ i kəl lē) *adv.* irregularly; occasionally

"Sister Henderson, Mama sent a half a cake for your visitors."

"Sister Henderson, I made a lot of macaroni and cheese. Maybe this will help with your visitors."

My grandmother would whisper her thanks and finally when the family and guests sat down at the table, the offerings were so different and plentiful, it appeared that days had been spent preparing the meal.

Patience invited me inside, and when I saw the table I was confirmed in my earlier impression. Groundnut stew, garden egg stew, hot pepper soup, *kenke, kotomre,* fried plantain, *dukuno,* shrimp, fish cakes, and more, all crowded together on variously patterned plates.

In Arkansas, the guests would never suggest, although they knew better, that the host had not prepared every scrap of food, especially for them.

I said to Patience, "Oh, Sister, you went to such trouble."

She laughed, "It is nothing, Sister. We don't want our Bambara relative to think herself a stranger anymore. Come, let us wash and eat."

After dinner I followed Patience to the outdoor toilet, then they gave me a cot in a very small room.

In the morning I wrapped my cloth under my arms, sarong fashion, and walked with Patience to the bathhouse. We joined about twenty women in a walled enclosure that had no ceiling. The greetings were loud and cheerful as we soaped ourselves and poured buckets of water over our shoulders.

Patience introduced me. "This is our Bambara sister."

"She's a tall one all right. Welcome, Sister."

"I like her color."

"How many children, Sister?"

I apologized, "I only have one."

"One?"

"One?"

"One!" Shouts reverberated over the splashing water. I said, "One, but I'm trying."

They laughed. "Try hard, sister. Keep trying."

We ate leftovers from the last night feast and I said a sad good-bye to my hosts. The children walked me back to my car with the oldest boy carrying my bag. I couldn't offer money to my hosts, Arkansas had taught me that, but I gave change to the children. They bobbed and jumped and grinned.

"Good-bye, Bambara Auntie."

"Go and come, Auntie."

"Go and come."

I drove into Cape Coast before I thought of the gruesome castle and out of its environs before the ghosts of slavery caught me. Perhaps their attempts had been half-hearted. After all, in Dunkwa, although I let a lie speak for me, I had proved that one of their descendants, at least one, could just briefly return to Africa, and that despite cruel betrayals, bitter ocean voyages, and hurtful centuries, we were still recognizable.

Vocabulary

reverberate (ri vur′ bə rāt′) *v.* to echo; resound

Responding to Literature

Personal Response

Which emotion described in this selection could you relate to most?

Analyzing Literature

Recall

1. Describe what happened when Angelou pulled her car off the road after passing Cape Coast Castle.
2. Why did Angelou believe she could pass as "any young Ghanaian woman" in Dunkwa, as long as she "didn't talk too much"?
3. What nationality do Kobina and Foriwa think Angelou is? What reason does she offer for not correcting them?
4. Where did Angelou eat dinner? Who cooked the food?
5. What did Angelou feel that she had proved in Dunkwa?

Interpret

6. In your opinion, why did Angelou avoid Cape Coast? What questions might Cape Coast Castle raise for her?
7. Why might it have been so important to Angelou to be seen as a Ghanaian woman?
8. What unspoken reasons might Angelou have for not correcting her hosts when they misidentify her?
9. What special meaning does the plentiful dinner hold for Angelou?
10. Why did Angelou's time in Dunkwa quiet the "ghosts of slavery"?

Evaluate and Connect

11. Review your response to the Reading Focus on page 328. Compare and contrast it with what Maya Angelou might have said.
12. What effect does the discussion of Cape Coast Castle have on the **mood** of this selection? Why might Angelou have mentioned the castle both toward the beginning and at the ending of the selection?
13. If you had been Angelou, would you have corrected the mistake and revealed your true nationality? Why or why not?
14. Angelou has written, "The ache for home lives in all of us, the safe place where we can go as we are and not be questioned." What do you think she means? How might it apply to your own life?
15. Angelou found a parallel, or similarity, between the people of Stamps, Arkansas, and the people of Dunkwa. In your opinion, why might finding a parallel between the familiar and the unfamiliar help a stranger feel at ease in a new environment?

Literary ELEMENTS

Word Choice

Word choice is the selection of words to convey meaning, suggest attitude, and create images. Word choice is part of what makes a writer's style uniquely expressive. For example, Angelou writes, "despite *cruel* betrayals, *bitter* ocean voyages, and *hurtful* centuries, we were still recognizable." The repeated use of strong, negative adjectives emphasizes Angelou's grief over the plight of Africans who were captured and transported to North America as slaves.

Explain why you think Angelou chose each of the italicized words or phrases in the passages below. Try replacing the words or phrases with terms more common or general to see how the meaning is affected.

1. The *too sweet aromas* of flowers, the *odors* of freshly fried fish and *stench* from open sewers hung in my clothes.
2. I watched the bright sun turn the water surface *into a rippling cloth of lamé.*
3. For a second, fear *darted* in her eyes.

- See **Literary Terms Handbook,** p. R13.

Literature and Writing

Writing About Literature

Eloquent Thoughts, Clear Language Maya Angelou is often praised for expressing deep and eloquent thoughts in simple, clear language. For example: *These were the legions, sold by sisters, stolen by brothers, bought by strangers, enslaved by the greedy and betrayed by history.* This single sentence conveys the complex and numerous wrongs committed against those sold into slavery. Find another sentence in the selection that you feel is an example of eloquent thoughts expressed in clear language. Explain the sentence's meaning and analyze how it creates that meaning.

Creative Writing

Thank-you Letter Imagine that you are Maya Angelou, back in Accra after your trip. Write a letter to Kobina and Foriwa Artey or to Kwame and Patience Duodu, thanking them for their hospitality and filling them in on details of your life. Keep in mind as you write that they do not know your true identity. Decide how to deal with this fact, either correcting their assumptions or continuing the fiction.

Extending Your Response

Literature Groups

Should She Have Told the Truth? Review your answer to question 13 on page 335. Then, with a group, discuss whether Maya Angelou should have corrected the misconception about her nationality. What do you think she feared or felt shy about? What do you think would have happened if the people had found out that she was from the United States? How do you think her trip to Dunkwa would have changed, both in its actuality and in its impact upon her memory and life? Be sure to support your ideas with details in the selection, and share your conclusions with the class.

Performing

The Journey Home Many traditional African American spirituals, or folk hymns, were created by enslaved people as work songs. One of the most common themes was "going home," with "home" having a dual meaning: Africa and a heaven or a promised land to which one would go after death. Angelou has written that as she "went home" to the Africa of her ancestors, she thought of the words to familiar spirituals. With a group, research the words and music to one or more traditional spirituals. Decide whether you want to sing the song, play it on instruments, or present it as a choral reading. Then perform the spiritual for the rest of the class.

Internet Connection

Art Mirrors Life Much of Maya Angelou's writing is based on her own experiences. Use the Internet to learn more about her life and her writings. Find out what she has been doing recently and whether she has continued to write about her African roots. You might use a search engine to find sites dedicated to Angelou, or look up "online bookstores" to find out more about her publications.

Reading Further

You might also enjoy these poems by Maya Angelou:

"On the Pulse of the Morning," which appears in a collection titled *Poems,* is the poem that Angelou recited at the 1993 inaugural ceremony for President Bill Clinton.

"Equity," which appears in a collection titled *I Shall Not Be Moved,* expresses the human struggle to get along with others.

Save your work for your portfolio.

Skill Minilessons

GRAMMAR AND LANGUAGE • Possessive Pronouns

Possessive pronouns show ownership. They take the place of possessive nouns. *My, mine, your, yours, his, her, hers,* and *its* are singular possessive pronouns. *Our, ours, your, yours, their,* and *theirs* are plural possessive pronouns. When Angelou writes, "We sat facing each other while her husband stood over us smiling," she uses the possessive pronoun *her* to replace the possessive noun *the woman's.*

PRACTICE On your paper, write the possessive pronoun in each of the following sentences. Then write the noun that it replaces.

1. Market women balanced large baskets on their heads.
2. "Friends of mine," writes Angelou, "had felt called upon to make the trek."
3. Patience and I sat out in the yard behind her house.
4. I didn't actually lie to the villagers; the conclusion that I was from Bambara was theirs.
5. I drove into the city before I thought of the castle and out of its environs before the ghosts of slavery caught me.

● For more about possesive pronouns, see **Language Handbook,** p. R25.

READING AND THINKING • Reviewing

When you read nonfiction, it helps to pause every few paragraphs. At these points, you can summarize main ideas or events, or paraphrase what you've read by restating it simply in your own words. Useful sentence starters for reviewing are "So far . . ." and "In other words . . . ."

PRACTICE On your paper, write a paragraph that begins, "In other words . . . ." Complete the paragraph by paraphrasing this passage from the selection.

The palm tree–lined streets and fine white stone buildings did not tempt me to remain any longer than necessary.

Once out of town and again onto the tarred roads, I knew I had not made a clean escape. Despite my hurry, history had invaded my little car. Pangs of self-pity and a sorrow for my unknown relatives suffused me. Tears made the highway waver and were salty on my tongue.

APPLY Review the final paragraph of the selection. Use your own words to paraphrase Angelou's thoughts.

● For more about related reading strategies, see **Reading Handbook,** pp. R78–R107.

VOCABULARY • Shades of Meaning

Some synonyms have nearly identical meanings. Others do not. And even words that are very good synonyms often differ in small but important ways. For example, good synonyms for *pang* include *ache, twinge, distress, wrench, injury, pinch,* and *stitch.* Yet these words have slightly different meanings. A *pang* is sudden and sharp but not long-lasting (although it may recur). In certain situations, *pang* is the best word to use; in others, one of its synonyms would be much better. In some situations, a number of synonyms would work well, and the choice is a matter of personal preference.

PRACTICE In one sentence of each pair, the underlined word is used correctly. Write the letter of the sentence in which the underlined word is NOT a good choice, and suggest a preferable synonym.

1. a. A tree limb fell on his head, resulting in a serious <u>pang</u>.
   b. He loved her so much he could not think of losing her without feeling a <u>pang</u>.
2. a. The fragrance of flowers <u>suffused</u> the house.
   b. She shook her pen and <u>suffused</u> her shirt with blotches of ink.
3. a. A good roof is <u>impervious</u> to rain.
   b. An avalanche had made the mountain roads <u>impervious</u>.

Reading & Thinking Skills

Drawing Conclusions

Logical thinking sometimes allows you to draw conclusions. For example, in the selection from *All God's Children Need Traveling Shoes,* Maya Angelou concludes that at least one African descendant could return to the land of her ancestors and be recognized as belonging there. Angelou probably considered the following information before drawing her conclusion:

- The people of Dunkwa believe that she is African because her features, skin color, and dress make her look like any young Ghanaian woman.
- They vie with one another to determine the clan to which she belongs and are convinced that she is a Bambara woman.
- They address her as Sister Bambara and Auntie.
- They find lodging for her and provide her with a bountiful meal—just as people in her hometown of Stamps, Arkansas, used to do for travelers.

Like Maya Angelou, you must consider the evidence—any information that is available to you—before drawing a conclusion.

- For more about related comprehension skills, see **Reading Handbook,** pp. R78–R107.

EXERCISE

Read the following passage carefully, then do the exercise that follows.

> **LeRoi was doing calf stretches, warming up for the 400-meter dash, when he saw his brother enter the stands. For a moment, LeRoi's blood ran cold. Would he trip on the back stretch again? Would he face more ridicule? But then he was on his mark, crouching behind the starting line, and all his blood and muscle burned hot with the desire to run. For sixty-two seconds, that was all he knew, and he ran faster than he ever had before. He won cleanly. This time he wouldn't be called a loser, a failure, a family embarrassment.**
>
> **His teammates surrounded him, slapping him high fives. His coach jumped into the air waving a fist. And from the corner of his eye, LeRoi saw his older brother bounding down the bleacher stairs toward the field. When his brother approached the celebrating team, LeRoi looked straight at him, and then turned away in silence.**

Draw a conclusion about why LeRoi didn't speak to his brother. Make a list of the evidence you used to draw your conclusion.

Grammar Link

Making Sure Subjects and Verbs Agree

In every sentence, the subject tells who or what is doing an action, and the verb tells what action that person or thing is doing. Because the subject and verb work together, they must agree in number. That is, if the subject is singular, the verb must be singular. If the subject is plural, the verb must be plural.

Problem 1 A subject that is separated from the verb by an intervening prepositional phrase or other expression

A member of the village council helps her find lodging.
The children in the house bring beverages.
Many works written by this author are nonfiction.

Solution Make the verb agree with the subject. Remember that the number of the subject is never changed by an intervening expression. Be careful not to mistake the object of a preposition for the subject.

Problem 2 A subject that follows the verb

Beside the road sat the old men.
There are several children in the family.

Solution In an inverted sentence, look for the subject *after* the verb.

Problem 3 A compound subject that is joined by *and*

The family's hospitality and warmth are appreciated.
Macaroni and cheese was served to guests.

Solution If the parts of the compound subject do not belong to one unit or if they refer to different people or things, use a plural verb. If the parts of the compound subject belong to one unit or if both parts refer to the same person or thing, use a singular verb, as shown in the second example.

Problem 4 A compound subject that is joined by *or* or *nor*

Neither the old man nor his wife guessed her nationality correctly.
Either the mother or her children serve the guest.

Solution Make the verb agree with the subject that is closer to it.

For more about subject-verb agreement, see **Language Handbook,** p. R16.

EXERCISE

For each sentence, write the correct form of the verb.

1. Poems such as "Sympathy" (batters, batter) our hearts.
2. Neither the bird nor the speaker (know, knows) what it's like to be fully free.
3. The birds in the cage (beat, beats) their wings.
4. To the treetop (fly, flies) the wild birds.
5. Angelou, together with many other people, (understands, understand) Dunbar's message.

Before You Read

Field Trip

Reading Focus

When have you experienced an event that turned out differently than you expected?

Journal Write about an experience that stands out in your mind. Explain why it was so different from what you expected.

Setting a Purpose Read to learn about the author's recollections of events that turned out differently than she had expected.

Building Background

The Time and Place

In "Field Trip," the author recalls events from several times in her life. She implies that they happened in or near San Antonio, Texas.

Did You Know?

A commercial print shop is a place where written text and art are made into printed products such as business cards, stationery, brochures, posters, newspapers, magazines, and books. A print shop usually has many kinds of machinery–including darkroom equipment, printing presses, computers, photocopiers, and an electric paper cutter that can trim more than 500 sheets of paper with a single slice of its razor-sharp blade.

Vocabulary Preview

severance (sev′ ər əns) *n.* the act of cutting off or apart; p. 341
tediously (tē′ dē əs lē) *adv.* in a bored and tiresome manner; dully; p. 341
excruciating (iks kro͞o′ shē ā′ ting) *adj.* agonizing; intensely painful; p. 342
mortality (môr tal′ ə tē) *n.* the condition of being sure to die at some time; p. 342
parched (pärcht) *adj.* severely dry; p. 343
console (kən sōl′) *v.* to comfort or cheer someone experiencing sorrow or disappointment; p. 343

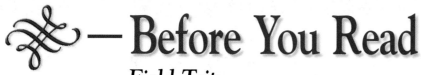

Meet Naomi Shihab Nye

Naomi Shihab Nye (shi′ häb nī) says her inspiration has always been "local life"—the voices of friends, neighbors, and people she meets on the street. Her work reflects her view that people around the world have much in common. A Palestinian American poet, teacher, essayist, and story writer, Nye spent most of her childhood in St. Louis, Missouri, then moved with her family to Jerusalem. She attended a year of high school in Jordan before her family moved back to the United States. Today she lives in San Antonio, Texas.

Naomi Shihab Nye was born in 1952. This essay was first published in The Houston Chronicle.

Field Trip

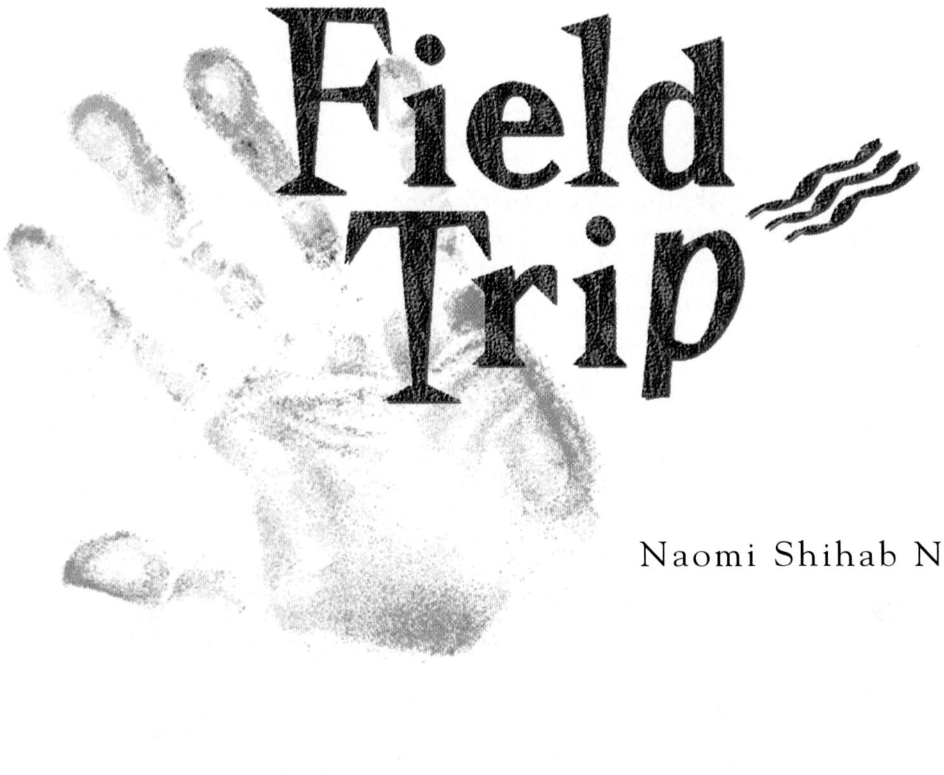

Naomi Shihab Nye

Only once did I ever take a large group of children on a field trip. I took a creative writing workshop to a printing office to see how pages were bound together to make books, and our cheerfully patient guide chopped her finger off with a giant paper cutter.

I had not prepared the children for experiences beyond typeface, camera-ready copy, collation.[1] Standing toward the back like a shepherd, I felt their happy little backs stiffen at the moment of severance. A collective gasp rose from their throats as a blot of blood grew outward in a rapid pool, staining all the pages. Cupping her wounded hand against her chest, the woman pressed through the crowd, not screaming, but mouthing silently, "Hospital. Now. Let's go."

The children stood motionless, suspended. The motion of the workers was like the flurry of feathers and wings when anyone steps too quickly into a chicken coop. People dialed, then asked one another why they were dialing. Couldn't they drive her to the hospital themselves? Someone at the emergency room said to place the severed finger on ice, and a man who, moments before, had been tediously pasting up layouts ran for ice.

One boy tugged my shirt and croaked, "The last thing she said was—you have to be very careful with this machine."

Someone dropped a ring of keys, and I immediately crawled around on the floor, reaching under a desk for them. It felt good to fall to my knees. For a second the stricken woman loomed above me, and I stuttered,

1. In the printing industry, a *typeface* is a style of letters to be printed. *Camera-ready copy* is text and art arranged on a page, ready to be photographed for printing. *Collation* is the process of sorting pages into the correct order, by hand or machine.

Vocabulary

severance (sev′ ər əns) *n.* the act of cutting off or apart

tediously (tē′ dē əs lē) *adv.* in a bored and tiresome manner; dully apologizing for having distracted her from business, but she was distracted by something else.

"Honey, look at that thing!" she said, staring into the cup of ice where the index finger now rested like a rare archival specimen.[2] "It's turning white! If that finger stays white, I don't want it on my body!"

We laughed long and hard and straight, and the children stared, amazed. Had we lost our senses? That she could joke at such a moment, as the big fans whirred and the collating machines paused over vast mountains of stacked paper . . . I wanted to sing her blackness, the sweet twist of her joy, to call out to those boys and girls, "This, my friends, is what words can do for you—make you laugh when your finger rests in a plastic cup!"

But she went quickly off into the day, and I shuffled an extremely silent group of budding writers back onto our bus. I wanted to say something promising recovery, or praising our guide's remarkable presence of mind, but my voice seemed lost among the seats. No one would look at me.

Later I heard how they went home and went straight to their rooms. Some had nightmares. A mother called my assistant to say, "What in the world happened on that field trip? Sarah came over today, and she and Molly climbed up on the bed and just sobbed."

At our next meeting we forgot poetry and made get-well cards. Or come-together-again cards. May the seam hold. May the two become one. They thought up all kinds of things. I had been calling the printing office to monitor her progress, and the reports sounded good. The students had been gathering stories: someone's farmer-uncle whose leg was severed in a cornfield but who lived to see it joined; someone's brother's toe.

I went to her home with a bundle of hopeful wishes tied in loops of pink ribbon. She was wearing a terry-cloth bathrobe and sitting in a comfortable chair, her hand hugely bandaged.

She shook her head. "I guess none of those cute kids will ever become printers now, will they? Gee, I hope they don't stop reading and writing! And to think of it happening in front of such an interested audience! Oh, I feel just terrible about it."

Reading their messages made her chuckle. I asked what the doctors had said about the finger turning black again. She said they thought it would, but it might be slightly paler than the rest of her hand. And it would be stiff, for a long time, maybe forever.

She missed being at work; vacations weren't much fun when they came this unexpectedly. The pain had been excruciating at first but was easing now, and wasn't modern medicine incredible, and would I please thank those kids for their flowers and hearts!

Once I'd dreamed of visiting every factory in town, the mattress factory, the hot sauce factory, the assembly line for cowboy boots, but I changed my mind. Now I took my workshops out onto the schoolyard, but no farther. I made them look for buttons and feathers, I made them describe the ways men and women stood as they waited for a bus.

By the time our workshops ended that summer, we felt more deeply bonded than other groups I'd known. Maybe our sense of mortality linked us, our shared vision of the fragility of body parts. One girl went on to

2. Archives (är′ kīvz) are a storage area, usually within a museum or a library, where documents or objects of historical or scientific interest are preserved. An *archival specimen*—such as a fossil or a rare book—is something kept in archives.

Vocabulary

excruciating (iks kroo̅′ shē ā′ ting) *adj.* agonizing; intensely painful

mortality (môr tal′ ə tē) *n.* the condition of being sure to die at some time become one of the best young writers in the city. I'd like to think her hands were blessed by our unexpected obsession with hands.

I continued to think about field trips in general. In San Antonio, school children are taken to the Hall of Horns, where legions[3] of exotic stuffed birds and beasts and fish stare back at them from glass habitats; to the missions, where the Indians' mounded bread ovens still rise from parched grass; and to the Alamo, where David Crockett's fork and fringed vest continue to reside. Here, we say, for your information, soak it up. See what you can learn.

Did You Know?
David (Davy) *Crockett*–pioneer, frontiersman, and Tennessee politician–became an American folk hero after being killed in 1836, while fighting to defend the Alamo against Mexican forces.

It was not always predictable. At the state mental hospital, my high school health teacher unwittingly herded us into a room of elderly women who'd recently had lobotomies,[4] just after telling us doctors didn't do that to people anymore.

On the day Robert Kennedy[5] was shot we found ourselves, numbed, staring at vats of creamy chocolate brew at the Judson Candy Factory. The air hung thickly around us. It didn't make much sense to consider all that work for something that wasn't even good for you. A worker joked that a few of his friends had ended up in those vats, and no one smiled.

As a child I finally grew brave enough to plot a camping trip years after my friends had first done it—to Camp Fiddlecreek for Girl Scouts. I'd postponed such an adventure because of a profound and unreasonable fear of spiders. I felt certain a giant spider would crawl into my bedroll and entangle itself in my hair the moment I got there. The zipper on the sleeping bag would stick, and I would die, die, die. Luckily I finally decided a life without courage might be worse than death, so I packed my greenest duds and headed to the hills.

The first night I confided my secret fear to the girl who slept next to me. She said she'd always been more scared of snakes than spiders. I said, "Snakes, phooey!"

The next day while we were hiking, a group of donkeys broke out of a nearby field, ran at us, knocked me down, and trampled me. My leg swelled with three large, hard lumps. I could not walk. I would have to be driven back to the city for X rays. My friend leaned over my bruised face, smoothing back my bangs and consoling me. "Donkeys! Can you believe it? Who could ever dream a donkey would be so mean?"

So began a lifetime of small discoveries linked by a common theme: the things we worry about are never the things that happen. And the things that happen are the things we never could have dreamed.

3. Here, *legions* means "huge numbers."
4. *Lobotomies* are surgical operations in which nerve connections in the brain are cut in an attempt to control inappropriate behavior of certain mentally ill patients.
5. *Robert Kennedy* was murdered while campaigning as a Democratic presidential candidate in 1968.

Vocabulary
parched (pärcht) *adj.* severely dry
console (kən sōl′) *v.* to comfort or cheer someone experiencing sorrow or disappointment

Responding to Literature

Personal Response

What part of this essay did you visualize or experience most vividly as you read?

Analyzing Literature

Recall

1. How do the people in the print shop react to the accident?
2. What does the print shop guide say before she goes to the hospital?
3. How do the children respond immediately after the incident and in the days that followed?
4. Name two unexpected things that happened to the author on other field trips or outings.
5. What conclusion does the author draw about field trips and, by extension, about life?

Interpret

6. What seems to be going on in the minds of the children, teacher, and coworkers at the moment of the accident?
7. How would you describe the injured woman's ability to handle the emergency? Why do you think she responds as she does?
8. Why might the children have shared stories of similar events? What purpose did their handcrafted cards serve?
9. Choose one of the field trips the author describes in the essay and explain why the events might be considered **ironic.** (See page R7.)
10. What might be the author's purpose for writing this essay?

Evaluate and Connect

11. How might you have reacted to the guide's accident if you had been a student or a chaperone on the field trip? What if you were the guide? Compare your reaction to the guide's reaction in the selection.
12. Do you think that field trips are a necessary or important part of education? Use your own experience to explain why or why not.
13. Reread what you wrote for the Reading Focus on page 340. What similarities and differences do you find between your experience and the author's? Does Nye's conclusion apply to your experience?
14. Do you find this essay to be funny, serious, or both? Use examples from the text to explain your response.
15. **Theme Connections** On the basis of this essay, what can people offer to those who are facing adversity?

Literary ELEMENTS

Thesis

A **thesis** is one or more sentences that state the central idea or purpose of an essay or other work of nonfiction. The thesis is often directly stated in the opening paragraph; however, it may appear later in the essay or in the conclusion.

1. What is Nye's thesis?
2. Where and when does Nye state her thesis? Why do you think she states it where she does?
3. How do Nye's examples support her thesis?

- See **Literary Terms Handbook,** p. R13.

Literary Criticism

Critic Mary Logue writes that "Nye often pulls gold from the ordinary" in her poems about ordinary daily life. Write a brief paragraph explaining whether you think Nye "pulls gold from the ordinary" in "Field Trip." Then share the paragraph with a partner.

Literature and Writing

Writing About Literature

Evaluating the Essay Did "Field Trip" successfully capture and hold your attention from beginning to end? If so, what was appealing about the work? If not, why? Write an evaluation of "Field Trip," explaining why the work was successful or how it could be revised so that it would be compelling from beginning to end.

Creative Writing

The Way I Saw It Imagine that you are the print shop guide who had the accident. Write a letter to a friend in which you relate what happened. What events do you remember? What did you see, think, and feel? Include your physical and emotional reactions to the event, to your pain, and to the people who were watching.

Extending Your Response

Literature Groups

Powerful Prose As a group, select three of the most interesting passages in this essay. List several reasons why you think each passage is particularly strong. Does it contain vivid verbs? descriptive language? gory details? Compare the passages you select–and your reasons for selecting them–with those of other groups.

Learning for Life

To the Rescue! Would you know how to help in an emergency? What's the proper treatment for a minor burn, a sprain, choking, or fainting? With a partner, use library resources, CD-ROMs, interviews, and the Internet to research a first-aid procedure of your choice. Demonstrate the procedure or explain it in an oral report.

Interdisciplinary Activity

Art: A Spectrum of Meaning If "Field Trip" were a painting, what colors would it be? Which parts of the essay would best be represented by warm colors, such as red or orange? Which parts would best be represented by cool colors, such as blue or green? Photocopy the essay and then, using colored pencils or markers and a color wheel for reference, shade or outline the passages with the appropriate color or colors. Finally, write a brief explanation of why the events or emotional content of each passage led you to select a particular color or colors.

Save your work for your portfolio.

Skill Minilesson

VOCABULARY • Analogies

An analogy is a type of comparison that is based on the relationships between things or ideas. One type of analogy features different degrees of intensity.

immense : large :: deafening : loud

Something *immense* is extremely *large;* something *deafening* is extremely *loud.*

To complete an analogy, decide what relationship is represented by the first two words. Then apply that relationship to another word pair and see if it is the same.

● For more about analogies, see **Communications Skills Handbook,** p. R77.

PRACTICE Choose the word that completes each analogy. Which ones represent degrees of intensity?

1. starving : hungry :: parched :
   a. sandy b. dry c. hot
2. scissors : severance :: ruler :
   a. inch b. length c. measurement
3. confine : release :: console :
   a. upset b. sympathize c. reveal
4. excellent : good :: excruciating :
   a. pleasant b. painful c. sharp

Writing Workshop

Narrative Writing:
Firsthand Account

Evaluation Rubric
By the time you complete this Writing Workshop, you will have
- described when, where, and why an event happened and who or what was involved
- presented events and specific, accurate details in a clear and logical order
- expressed your personal perceptions of the event
- presented a firsthand account that is free of errors in grammar, usage, and mechanics

You were there. You know what happened. You saw it happen. No one else would interpret it quite the way you do, and now you have a story to tell. **This workshop will help you write a firsthand account of something you actually experienced.** You may have participated in the event or events you describe, or you may only have observed them. In either case, your narrative will be told from your point of view, so you'll have the opportunity to communicate your unique perceptions and experiences in writing.

- As you write your account, refer to the **Writing Handbook,** pp. R58–R71.

The Writing Process

PREWRITING

PREWRITING TIP
Memories can fade fast, so jot down notes in a journal or notebook after any experience that you may want to re-create in writing.

Explore ideas
Any experience is a potential topic for your narrative. You can deliberately seek out an event to write about, such as a school football game. Or, you can write about a past occurrence, such as a time when you overcame adversity. To gather some ideas, see if you can recall

- an event that changed the course of your life, as in the excerpt from *Black Boy.*
- a period of uncertainty or of great fear, as in the excerpt from *Night.*
- something you did that brought you acceptance or recognition, as in "Only Daughter."
- an unexpected occurrence, as in "Field Trip."

Consider your purpose
Your goal in writing a firsthand account is to communicate your unique perceptions to a larger audience. In doing so, you allow others to see, feel, and understand an event as you did.

Choose an audience
Do you want to share your experience with others who may have experienced something similar? If so, you may want to focus your writing on your own personal response to the situation, or on what made your experience unique. If you want to introduce a situation to an audience for whom it would be unfamiliar, you may need to include details and explanations that you would omit for a different audience.

Make a plan

Use an event organizer like the one on this page to help you put the events of your firsthand account into the most effective order. First, write the events as they occur to you, using a separate block for each event. Use as many blocks as you need. Then, number the events in the order in which they'll appear in your final narrative. Or, if you wish, cut apart your graphic and arrange and rearrange the blocks until you find the best order for your account.

Once you've made a plan for the basic order of events, start gathering details that will make the scenes come alive for a reader. Ask yourself the following questions about each scene, then jot down your responses in the appropriate block.

- When, where, how, and why did the event happen?
- Who was involved?
- What did you see, smell, hear, taste, feel?

STUDENT MODEL

1 Waiting for the alarm The first day of high school. This year. Nervous. Hate being the new kid. Heard horror stories about upperclassmen and freshmen.	**5 Sitting down to lunch** Mortified that I had to sit alone. Ate bagel and iced tea. Hoped no one heard rumbling stomach. Noticed a girl with glasses and headgear eating alone.	**4 Walking into school** Heart pounding. Bigger than old school, but found homeroom. Sat silently while others talked about their summer. Classes seemed to run together.
2 Getting ready for school Could not decide what to wear. Felt unsure about what would be cool in the new school. Played it safe with T-shirt and jeans. Too nervous to eat.	**3 The ride to school** Mom tried to reassure me. Couldn't process what she was saying. Couldn't have handled a hug and kiss. Probably would have started crying.	**6 The end of lunch** Other freshmen sat down. Started talking. Realized everyone was a bit nervous, unsure. Began to relax knowing I wasn't the only one facing freshman fears.

Complete Student Model on p. R112.

DRAFTING

DRAFTING TIP

Because the smallest details can make the biggest impact, don't edit yourself as you write. Try to include everything you remember as you draft.

Begin writing

Refer to the event organizer you created and begin drafting anywhere, using a separate page or pages for the events in each block. If you prefer, draft the events in your narrative in their numbered order.

Convey emotion as you draft

In order to let readers know what it felt like to be there, spend a few minutes thinking about the atmosphere surrounding the events you're describing. Then let your pen flow or your fingers fly over the keyboard. Write about details in such a way that they help convey the mood of the event. Describe not only physical objects and actions, but also the emotions that you witnessed or experienced. Don't worry if your words come out in a disorganized rush. You can go back and smooth things out later.

STUDENT MODEL

I lay in bed staring at the ceiling, both anxiously waiting for my alarm to go off and dreading the sound. I had tossed and turned all night. My stomach was in knots. It was the first day of school. My family moved a month ago, and I was used to moving because we had three times already, but I still hated being the new kid. This time would be even worse than the others. Not only was I starting school where I didn't know anyone, but it was high school and I was a freshman. Double trouble. After all the stories I had heard about upperclassmen harassing freshmen, I was scared to death.

Complete Student Model on p. R112.

Strive for accuracy

Re-create your experience with specific, accurate details. Remember that you are writing nonfiction, a true story about an actual experience. You don't need to exaggerate the facts to make your description vivid. If you need to speculate about something, tell your reader. Don't pretend to know more than you do.

STUDENT MODEL

I waited in line for a bagel and iced tea. My stomach was growling because I hadn't eaten breakfast, and I hoped no one noticed. I felt paralyzed as I looked around for a place to sit, but I finally spotted an empty table by the windows. I sat alone and I studied the other kids. There was a girl with headgear and glasses who was also sitting alone. I felt bad for her and bad for myself.

Complete Student Model on p. R112.

REVISING

REVISING TIP

Use transitions to help readers follow the order of your narrative without getting lost. See the **Writing Skill** on page 382 for help using transitions.

Take another look

Set your draft aside for a while. When you're ready to revise, read it as though you hadn't lived through the events. Remember, your readers weren't there. Be sure that you haven't left out any information that will leave readers wondering. If you use vague, general words, your readers will fill in the details with impressions from their own experiences. To make sure they get the correct impression, use vivid, precise words. As you review your work, mark the places where you could make improvements, using the **Rubric for Revising** as a guide.

Read aloud your personal account

Try reading your draft to a friend. Then, together, go through the **Rubric for Revising** and brainstorm ways to further improve your draft.

RUBRIC FOR REVISING

Your revised firsthand account should have

- ☑ answers to the questions *Who? What? When? Where?* and *Why?*
- ☑ events and details that are presented in a logical and consistent order
- ☑ sensory words to describe sights, sounds, smells, and feelings
- ☑ your personal perceptions and opinions about the event
- ☑ specific and accurate details that make the event and your reaction to it vivid and believable

Your revised firsthand account should be free of

- ☑ gaps in the sequence of events
- ☑ confusing or irrelevant details
- ☑ errors in spelling, usage, and mechanics

STUDENT MODEL

I threw off my covers, crawled out of bed, and stumbled into the bathroom. Every outfit I ~~tried~~ put on ended up in a heap on my floor. I had to look my best on the first day, but I was ~~worried~~ paranoid that the clothes that were cool back home wouldn't be cool here. ~~I don't really like shopping for clothes anyway, my mom always has to make me.~~ Finally, I decided I couldn't go wrong with a T-shirt and jeans. My younger brother and sister ate their breakfast, but I was too nervous to eat. They had no idea ~~how I felt.~~ what it was like to stress over high school.

Complete Student Model on p. R112.

EDITING/PROOFREADING

PROOFREADING TIP

Use the **Proofreading Checklist** on the inside back cover of this book to help you review your writing and mark mistakes.

First, be sure that the content of your firsthand account is everything you want it to be. Then, reread it again slowly, checking for errors in grammar, usage, mechanics, and spelling.

Grammar Hint

Be sure that each pronoun refers clearly to a single antecedent.

VAGUE: *I lay awake in bed, staring first at my alarm clock and then at the ceiling, waiting for it to go off.*

CLEAR: *I lay awake in bed, staring first at my clock and then at the ceiling, waiting for the alarm to go off.*

● For more about pronouns, see **Language Handbook,** p. R19.

Complete Student Model

For a complete version of the model developed in this workshop, refer to **Writing Workshop Models**, p. R112.

STUDENT MODEL

Even though
The first outfit I tried on ended up in a heap on the floor, ~~and it~~ was my favorite one, it

Complete Student Model on p. R112.

PUBLISHING/PRESENTING

PRESENTING TIP

Add a photograph, drawing, diagram, or map if it will help the reader follow the course of events.

If you want to present your firsthand account to others, you could read it aloud or distribute photocopies. To share it with a larger audience, publish it in the student newspaper.

Reflecting

Now that you have completed your firsthand account, think about what you have learned about the writing process. In your journal, comment on which parts of the writing experience were most enjoyable for you and which were difficult. Also jot down notes explaining how you feel about your final product. Then set goals for your next piece of writing and jot them down in your journal. What would you like to do differently next time you write?

Save your work for your portfolio.

Theme 5 — Portraits

Every person, place, and thing has a particular essence, a combination of qualities that make him, her, or it unique. Artists and writers try to capture these essences with words or images by creating portraits. The selections in this theme portray animals who have impressed humans, humans who have changed history, and beings of all kinds who have affected the world around them.

THEME PROJECTS

Interdisciplinary Project

Art The word *portrait* refers to paintings, drawings, photographs, and sculpture as well as to descriptions created with words.

1. Identify the person or thing that is the subject of each portrait in this theme.
2. Using pencils, paints, clay, collage materials, or other media, create a visual representation of your three favorite subjects. Remember that a portrait should provide insight into a subject's essence.
3. Join with other students to create a portrait gallery in your classroom. Display your best portraits and invite other classes to view your work. Be prepared to discuss why the portraits capture the essence of each subject.

Performing

Trade Places When faced with identical situations, no two people will behave the same way.

1. Choose a favorite selection and imagine what would happen if the subject from another portrait entered the scene. Write a skit about what happens. Remember, the subject should keep his or her original essence while encountering a different set of obstacles or challenges in the new situation.
2. Perform your skit for the class.

Portrait of Eva Frederick, 1931. Frida Kahlo. Oil on canvas. Fundación Dolores Olmeda, Mexico City.

MEDIA connection

Book Excerpt

Fewer than one hundred years ago, women were not permitted by law to vote in an election. Today, that seems hard to imagine. Some absurd laws—such as the ones shown below—are still on the books!

It's the Law—But What Happens When It's Broken?

by Dick Hyman—from *The Trenton Pickle Ordinance and Other Bonehead Legislation*

- Barbers in Waterloo, Nebraska, are forbidden by law to eat onions between 7:00 A.M. and 7:00 P.M.
- It is Texas law that when two trains meet at a rail road crossing, each shall come to a full stop, and neither shall proceed until the other has gone.
- It is illegal in Salem, West Virginia, to leave your home or dwelling without having in mind a definite place to go.
- It is against the law to annoy squirrels in Topeka, Kansas.
- Toledo, Ohio, has an ordinance that prohibits throwing reptiles at another person.
- It is against the law for a monster to enter the corporate limits of Urbana, Illinois.
- In Owensboro, Kentucky, it is illegal for a woman to buy a new hat without her husband trying it on first.
- In Pocatello, Idaho, City Ordinance 1100 prohibits frowns, grimaces, scowls, threatening and lowering looks, and gloomy and depressed facial appearances generally, all of which reflect unfavorably upon the reputation of the city.
- In Hillsboro, Oregon, it is unlawful to allow a horse to ride around in the back seat of your car.
- In Racine, Wisconsin, it is illegal to wake a fireman when he is asleep.
- A Blue Earth, Minnesota, law declares that no child under the age of twelve may talk over the telephone unless accompanied by a parent.
- In Muskogee, Oklahoma, there is an old city ordinance that states that no baseball team shall be allowed to hit the ball over the fence or out of the ball park.
- In Santa Ana, California, it is unlawful to pass a fire truck while riding a bicycle.

Analyzing Media

1. Which law do you find most absurd? What are some possible reasons for the law?
2. In your opinion, what is the purpose of having laws? What might motivate a person to petition lawmakers to enact new laws–or repeal old ones?

Before You Read

The United States vs. *Susan B. Anthony*

Reading Focus

What stories have you heard about people fighting for their personal or political rights?

List Ideas With a partner, list several different approaches people might take to protest what they think are unfair rules or laws. Underline the methods that you think would have the greatest effect.

Setting a Purpose Read to learn how Susan B. Anthony challenged the legal system to achieve voting rights for women.

Building Background

The Time and Place

In this biography, Margaret Truman recounts what happened when Susan B. Anthony registered and voted in Rochester, New York, in the 1872 presidential election—nearly fifty years before women gained the right to vote.

Susan B. Anthony

Did You Know?

Intelligent, daring, and articulate, Susan B. Anthony (1820–1906) was a social reformer who became famous for her work in the woman suffrage movement. In 1878 Anthony proposed an amendment to the U.S. Constitution that would give women the right to vote. In 1920, fourteen years after her death, her proposal was ratified as the Nineteenth Amendment. In 1979 the U.S. government honored Anthony by placing her image on the one-dollar coin.

Vocabulary Preview

circuitous (sər kū′ ə təs) *adj.* roundabout; indirect; p. 354

incompetent (in kom′ pət ənt) *adj.* lacking ability, knowledge, or fitness; not capable; p. 356

disparity (dis par′ ə tē) *n.* inequality or difference; p. 356

vilify (vil′ ə fī′) *v.* to defame or malign someone with vicious and abusive statements; p. 358

prestigious (pres tē′ jəs) *adj.* having widely recognized importance and influence; p. 359

skeptic (skep′ tik) *n.* one who tends to be doubtful or suspicious; p. 361

Meet Margaret Truman

"Writing is the hardest and most exacting career I've ever had."

Margaret Truman worked in such challenging fields as singing, acting, and broadcasting before she became a writer. The daughter of President Harry S. Truman, Margaret Truman lived in the White House for seven years. She wrote about her unique life in her autobiography *Souvenir.* Although Truman primarily writes mystery novels set in Washington, D.C., she has also written best-selling biographies.

Margaret Truman was born in 1924. This selection was first published in Women of Courage *in 1976.*

The United States

Susan B. Anthony has never been one of my favorite characters. Stern-eyed and grim-lipped, she seemed utterly devoid[1] of warmth and humor and much too quick to dominate the women she worked with. I always thought her personality could be summed up in one word: battle-ax.[2] On top of that drawback, she was a fanatic. She joined the woman's suffrage movement in 1852, when she was thirty-two years old. From then until her death in 1906, she could think of little else.

The fanatics of one generation have a habit of turning into the heroes and heroines of the next, as Susan B. Anthony proved. And since I've been making a study of heroines, I decided to give Miss Anthony a second look. I have to report that my original assessment of her character was much too harsh.

Susan B. Anthony came to the woman's movement by a somewhat circuitous route. She was a reformer by inheritance as well as by temperament. Her parents were passionate supporters of abolition, temperance,[3] and woman's rights. They numbered among their friends some of the outstanding liberals of the nineteenth century, men like William Lloyd Garrison, Frederick Douglass, and Prudence Crandall's old ally, the Reverend Samuel J. May.

---

1. *Devoid* means "lacking."
2. *Battle-ax* is slang for a sharp-tongued, domineering woman.
3. Supporters of *abolition* sought to end slavery; supporters of *temperance* wanted to control or outlaw the use of alcoholic beverages.

Vocabulary

circuitous (sər kū′ ə təs) *adj.* roundabout; indirect

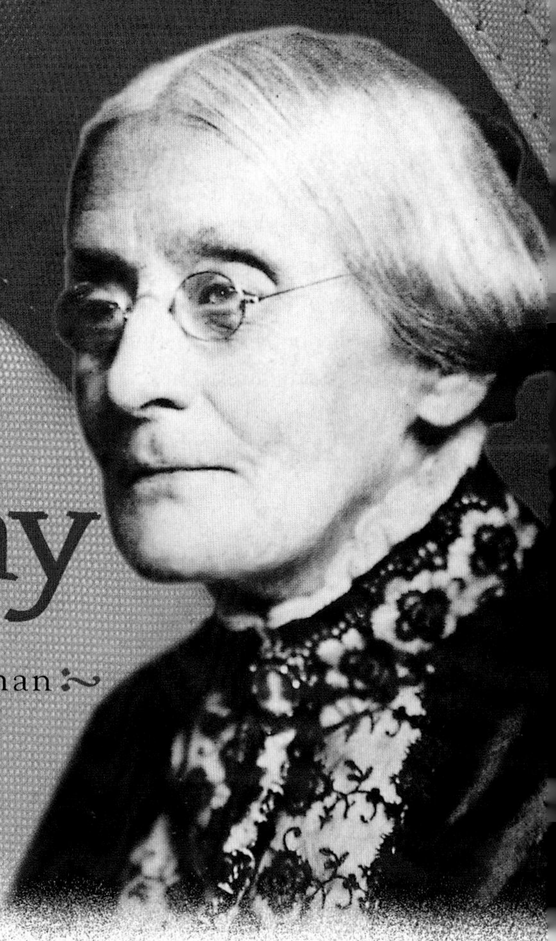

vs. Susan B. Anthony

Margaret Truman

Daniel Anthony had a succession of homes, a succession of jobs, and a succession of financial ups and downs. He began his career as a farmer in Adams, Massachusetts, but gave up farming to buy a cotton mill near Albany, New York. His business was wrecked by the panic of 1837,[4] and he bought another farm, this one a small plot of land just outside of Rochester, New York.

The collapse of the cotton mill left the Anthony family with a mountain of debts. Susan, by then in her late teens, became a teacher to help pay them off. After ten years in the classroom, she resigned and took over the management of her father's farm so Daniel Anthony could devote his attention to still another business venture—an insurance agency that eventually made him prosperous once more.

As I mentioned earlier, the instinct for reform had been bred into Susan since childhood. She was particularly concerned about temperance, and her work in that movement soon brought her in contact with Amelia Bloomer, who ran a temperance newspaper in Seneca Falls. Mrs. Bloomer introduced her to another temperance advocate, Elizabeth Cady Stanton, who was now pouring most of her energies into a campaign to give women the vote. Mrs. Stanton tried to enlist Susan's support in the suffrage movement, but Susan demurred.[5] She was too busy with temperance activities to have time for anything else.

4. *The panic of 1837* was a severe economic depression during which personal fortunes were lost and hundreds of banks and businesses failed.

5. When Susan *demurred* (di murd′), she hesitated to accept the proposal.

In 1852, Susan B. Anthony attended a rally in Albany where she was refused permission to speak because of her sex. The incident made her so angry that she withdrew from the regular temperance organization and set up a separate Woman's New York State Temperance Society with Elizabeth Cady Stanton as its president.

Not long after that, Susan went to a convention of the New York State Teachers' Association. More than two-thirds of the members were women, but the men ran the entire meeting, giving the speeches, voting on resolutions, and generally ignoring the women, who sat in an isolated bloc at the back of the room.

When a panel of male speakers began a lengthy debate on the topic: "Why the profession of a teacher is not as much respected as that of lawyer, doctor, or minister," Susan requested permission to state her opinion on the matter. After some discussion, the men agreed to let her be heard.

Susan offered a very simple answer to the question. "Do you not see," she said, "that so long as society says woman is incompetent to be a lawyer, minister, or doctor, but has ample ability to be a teacher, every man of you who chooses this profession tacitly[6] acknowledges that he has no more brains than a woman?"

She went on to say a few words about the disparity in the salaries of men and women teachers. It would be to the men's advantage to equalize them, she maintained, because their own incomes suffered when they had to compete with the cheap labor of women.

The speech left most of Susan's audience in a state of shock. A few men rushed over to congratulate her; the women remained silent. But she made at least one convert. A woman from Rochester pushed through a resolution affirming the right of women teachers to participate in all of the association's activities, including speaking at meetings, serving on committees, and holding office.

Susan B. Anthony's success with the teachers' association convinced her that discrimination against women should—and could—be overcome. Before long, she had become Elizabeth Cady Stanton's chief lieutenant in the woman's rights movement. Mrs. Stanton had young children at the time and was not free to travel extensively. She concentrated on writing letters and speeches, while Susan did most of the legwork. She proved to be a brilliant organizer and an indefatigable[7] lecturer, a master at circulating petitions, organizing conventions, and browbeating politicians.

All of the women who had the guts to demand the right to vote were cruelly criticized in the press, but Susan was invariably singled out as a special target. The fact that she was unmarried made her particularly vulnerable. This was declared proof positive that her crusade was simply the ranting of an embittered old maid.

The insulting newspaper articles and vicious cartoons must have bothered Susan. But she never let it show. She threw herself into her work. There was always a new speech to write, a new meeting to organize, a new petition to be drawn up and presented to a state legislature.

Susan B. Anthony was a stern and single-minded woman. Like most crusaders for causes—especially unpopular causes—she

6. *Tacitly* (tas′ it lē) means "in a way that is not expressed openly but is understood."

7. *Indefatigable* (in′ di fat′ ə gə bəl) means "untiring" or "incapable of being fatigued."

Vocabulary

incompetent (in kom′ pət ənt) *adj.* lacking ability, knowledge, or fitness; not capable

disparity (dis par′ ə tē) *n.* inequality or difference

had little time for fun and games. But I have a sneaky feeling that behind her severe manner and unremitting devotion to duty, she may actually have had a sense of humor. Let me tell you about my favorite episode in Susan B. Anthony's career, and perhaps you'll agree.

It began on Friday morning, November 1, 1872. Susan was reading the morning paper at her home in Rochester. There, at the top of the editorial page of the *Democrat and Chronicle*, was an exhortation[8] to the city's residents:

> Now register! Today and tomorrow are the only remaining opportunities. If you were not permitted to vote, you would fight for the right, undergo all privations for it, face death for it. You have it now at the cost of five minutes' time to be spent in seeking your place of registration and having your name entered. And yet, on election day, less than a week hence, hundreds of you are likely to lose your votes because you have not thought it worth while to give the five minutes. Today and tomorrow are your only opportunities. Register now!

Viewing the photograph: What details do you notice in this portrait of Elizabeth Cady Stanton (seated) and Susan B. Anthony?

Susan B. Anthony read the editorial again. Just as she thought, it said nothing about being addressed to men only. With a gleam in her eye, she put down the paper and summoned her sister Guelma, with whom she lived. The two women donned their hats and cloaks and went off to call on two other Anthony sisters who lived nearby. Together, the four women headed for the barber shop on West Street, where voters from the Eighth Ward were being registered.

For some time, Susan B. Anthony had been looking for an opportunity to test the Fourteenth Amendment to the Constitution as a weapon to win the vote for women. Adopted in 1870, the Amendment had been designed to protect the civil rights—especially the voting rights—of recently freed slaves. It stated that:

8. An *exhortation* (eg′ zôr tā′ shən) is a warning or urgent appeal.

> All persons born or naturalized in the United States, and subject to the jurisdiction thereof, are citizens of the United States and of the State wherein they reside. No State shall make or enforce any law which shall abridge the privileges or immunities of citizens of the United States, nor shall any State deprive any person of life, liberty, or property without due process of law, nor deny to any person within its jurisdiction the equal protection of the laws.

The Amendment did not say that "persons" meant only males, nor did it spell out "the privileges and immunities of citizens." Susan B. Anthony felt perfectly justified in concluding that the right to vote was among the privileges of citizenship and that it extended to women as well as men. I'm sure she must have also seen the humor of outwitting the supposedly superior males who wrote the Amendment.

It was bad enough for a bunch of women to barge into one sacred male precinct—the barber shop—but to insist on being admitted to another holy of holies—the voting booth—was absolutely outrageous. Moustaches twitched, throats were cleared, a whispered conference was held in the corner.

Susan had brought along a copy of the Fourteenth Amendment. She read it aloud, carefully pointing out to the men in charge of registration that the document failed to state that the privilege of voting extended only to males.

Only one man in the barber shop had the nerve to refuse the Anthony sisters the right to register. The rest buckled under Susan's determined oratory and allowed them to sign the huge, leather-bound voter registration book. If the men in the barber shop thought they were getting rid of a little band of crackpots the easy way, they were wrong. Susan urged all her followers in Rochester to register. The next day, a dozen women invaded the Eighth Ward barber shop, and another thirty-five appeared at registration sites elsewhere in the city. The *Democrat and Chronicle*, which had inadvertently prompted the registrations, expressed no editorial opinion on the phenomenon, but its rival, the *Union and Advertiser,* denounced the women.[9] If they were allowed to vote, the paper declared, the poll inspectors "should be prosecuted to the full extent of the law."

The following Tuesday, November 5, was Election Day. Most of the poll inspectors in Rochester had read the editorial in the *Union and Advertiser* and were too intimidated to allow any of the women who had registered to vote. Only in the Eighth Ward did the males weaken. Maybe the inspectors were *Democrat and Chronicle* readers, or perhaps they were more afraid of Susan B. Anthony than they were of the law. Whatever the reason, when Susan and her sisters showed up at the polls shortly after 7 A.M., there was only a minimum of fuss. A couple of inspectors were hesitant about letting the women vote, but when Susan assured them that she would pay all their legal expenses if they were prosecuted, the men relented, and one by one, the women took their ballots and stepped into the voting booth. There were no insults or sneers, no rude remarks. They marked their ballots, dropped them into the ballot box, and returned to their homes.

Susan B. Anthony's feat quickly became the talk of the country. She was applauded in some circles, vilified in others. But the

9. The first paper acted unintentionally *(inadvertently)* and then didn't comment on the extraordinary situation *(phenomenon).* However, the second paper openly condemned *(denounced)* the women.

Vocabulary

vilify (vil′ ə fī′) *v.* to defame or malign someone with vicious and abusive statements day of reckoning was not long in arriving. On November 28, Deputy U.S. Marshal E. J. Keeney appeared at her door with a warrant for her arrest. She had violated Section 19 of the Enforcement Act of the Fourteenth Amendment, which held that anyone who voted illegally was to be arrested and tried on criminal charges.

Susan B. Anthony was a great believer in planning ahead. The day after she registered, she decided to get a legal opinion on whether or not she should attempt to vote. A number of lawyers turned her away, but she finally found one who agreed to consider the case. He was Henry R. Selden, a former judge of the Court of Appeals, now a partner in one of Rochester's most prestigious law firms.

On the Monday before Election Day, Henry Selden informed his new client that he agreed with her interpretation of the Fourteenth Amendment and that in his opinion, she had every right to cast her ballot. The U.S. Commissioner of Elections in Rochester, William C. Storrs, did not concur.

E. J. Keeney, the marshal dispatched to arrest Susan B. Anthony, was not at all happy with his assignment. He nervously twirled his tall felt hat while waiting for her to come to the front door. When she finally appeared, he blushed and stammered, shifted uncomfortably from one foot to the other, and finally blurted out, "The Commissioner wishes to arrest you."

Susan couldn't help being amused at Keeney's embarrassment. "Is this your usual method of serving a warrant?" she asked calmly. With that, the marshal recovered his official dignity, presented her with the

Vocabulary
prestigious (pres tē′ jəs) *adj.* having widely recognized importance and influence

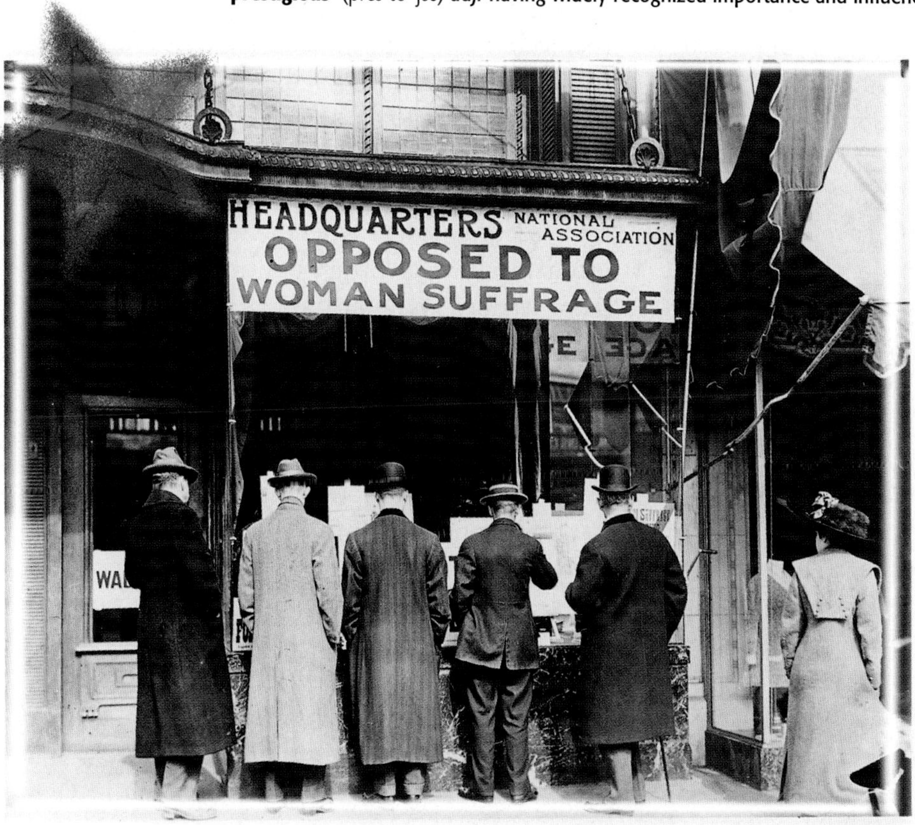

Viewing the photograph: What does this photograph capture about public sentiment for woman suffrage? What might the woman be thinking as she passes by these men?

warrant, and told her that he had come to escort her to the office of the Commissioner of Elections.

When Susan asked if she could change into a more suitable dress, the marshal saw his opportunity to escape. "Of course," he said, turning to leave. "Just come down to the Commissioner's office whenever you're ready."

"I'll do no such thing," Susan informed him curtly. "You were sent here to arrest me and take me to court. It's your duty to do so."

Keeney had no choice but to wait while his prisoner went upstairs and put on a more appropriate outfit. When she returned, she thrust out her wrists and said, "Don't you want to handcuff me, too?"

"I assure you, madam," Marshal Keeney stuttered, "it isn't at all necessary."

With the U.S. Marshal at her side, Susan was brought before the Federal Commissioner of Elections, William C. Storrs. Her arrest was recorded, and she was ordered to appear the next day for a hearing. It was conducted by U.S. District Attorney Richard Crowley and his assistant, John E. Pound.

Susan answered District Attorney Crowley's questions politely. She said that she thought the Fourteenth Amendment gave her the right to vote. She admitted that she had consulted an attorney on the question but said that she would have voted even if he had not advised her to do so. When Crowley asked if she had voted deliberately to test the law, she said, "Yes, sir. I have been determined for three years to vote the first time I happened to be at home for the required thirty days before an election."

The District Attorney's next step was to convene a grand jury to draw up a bill of indictment.[10] He and his assistant fell to wrangling over a suitable trial date. Susan interrupted them. "I have lecture dates that will take me to central Ohio," she said. "I won't be available until December 10."

"But you're supposed to be in custody until the hearing," Crowley informed her.

"Is that so?" said Susan coolly. "I didn't know that."

The District Attorney backed down without an argument and scheduled the grand jury session for December 23.

Sixteen women had voted in Rochester. All sixteen were arrested and taken before the grand jury, but Susan alone was brought to trial. The District Attorney had decided to single her out as a test case. The three poll inspectors who had allowed the women to vote were also arrested. The grand jury indicted them too, set bail at five hundred dollars each, and ordered their trial set for the summer term of the U.S. District Court.

Susan Anthony's case now involved nineteen other men and woman. All of them—including Susan—were liable to go to prison if they were found guilty and the judge was in a sentencing mood. Prison in the 1870s was a very unpleasant place. There were no minimum security setups where a benevolent government allowed corrupt politicians, crooked labor leaders, and political agitators to rest and rehabilitate, as we do today. Prison meant a cold cell, wretched food, the company of thieves and murderers.

For a while it looked as if Susan might be behind bars even before her trial. She refused to post a bond for her five-hundred-dollar bail. Henry Selden paid the money for her. "I could not see a lady I respected put in jail," he said.

It must be agonizing to sweat out the weeks before a trial. There is time to look ahead and brood about the possibility of an unfavorable verdict and time to look back, perhaps with regret, at the decision that placed you in the

10. A *grand jury* hears accusations in criminal cases. If its members decide that there is enough evidence for a trial, they issue an *indictment* (in dīt′ mənt), a formal charge against the accused.

hands of the law. But Susan B. Anthony had no regrets. Nor did she appear to have any anxieties about her trial. She had already proven her fortitude by devoting twenty years of her life to fighting for the right to vote. If she won her case, the struggle would be over. But even if she lost, Susan was not ready to give up the fight.

Some prospective defendants are too demoralized to do anything but sit around and worry. Not Susan B. Anthony. In the course of the next few months, she attended woman's rights conventions in Ohio, Illinois, and Indiana. She appeared before a session that was meeting in Albany to revise the New York State Constitution and tried to persuade them to include equal suffrage among its provisions. Then she went back to Rochester to cast her ballot again in the city elections on March 4, 1873.

Deputy Marshal Keeney appeared at the railroad every time she left Rochester. He reminded her that she was not supposed to leave the city while she was out on bail. Susan would smile, nod, and get on the train. Keeney never tried to stop her.

The summer term of the District Court opened in May. In mid-March, Susan launched a new lecture tour. Her topic: Is it a crime for a citizen of the United States to vote? The lecture centered on the U.S. Constitution, particularly the Fourteenth Amendment.

She spoke in every town in New York's Monroe County and drew surprisingly large audiences. When she polled the crowd at the end of each lecture, the majority invariably supported her. Even those who had been skeptics when they entered the hall usually changed their minds when they heard her arguments.

District Attorney Crowley soon decided that Susan was making it difficult for him to find an unprejudiced jury anywhere in the vicinity of Rochester. When he voiced his concern to Susan, she replied by asking him if he honestly believed that a jury could be prejudiced by having the Constitution of the United States read and explained to them.

Crowley became so exasperated that when the District Court opened on May 13, he requested a change of venue[11] from Rochester to Canandaigua[12] in adjacent Ontario County. The change forced a postponement of the trial until June 17. Susan promptly launched a whirlwind lecture tour of the villages around Canandaigua. She managed to cover twenty-one postal districts on her own, while her good friend and supporter, Matilda Joslyn Gage, covered the remaining sixteen.

The trial of *The United States* vs. *Susan B. Anthony* opened on the afternoon of June 17, 1873, with the tolling of the Canandaigua Courthouse bell. The presiding justice was Ward Hunt, a prim, pale man, who owed his judgeship to the good offices of Senator Roscoe Conkling, the Republican boss of New York State. Conkling was a fierce foe of woman suffrage, and Hunt, who had no wish to offend his powerful patron, had written his decision before the trial started.

District Attorney Crowley opened the arguments for the prosecution. They didn't make much sense at the time, and in retrospect, they sound nothing short of ridiculous. The District Attorney mentioned that Susan B. Anthony was a woman and therefore she had no right to vote. His principal witness was an inspector of elections for the

11. Normally, a jury must be called from, and the trial held in, the same *venue* (ven′ ū), or county or district, in which the crime was committed.
12. *Canandaigua:* (kan′ ən dā′ gwə)

Vocabulary
skeptic (skep′ tik) *n.* one who tends to be doubtful or suspicious

Viewing the political cartoon: What might Thomas Jefferson's ghost be thinking? What do you think was the artist's opinion of the woman suffrage movement? Why?

Eighth Ward, who swore that on November 5 he had seen Miss Anthony put her ballot in the ballot box. To back up his testimony, the inspector produced the voter registration book with Susan B. Anthony's signature in it.

Henry Selden's reply for the defense was equally simple. He contended that Susan Anthony had registered and voted in good faith, believing that it was her constitutional right to do so. When he attempted to call his client to the stand, however, District Attorney Crowley announced that she was not competent to testify in her own behalf. Judge Hunt agreed, and the only thing Henry Seldon could do was read excerpts from the testimony Susan had given at her previous hearings when presumably she was no less incompetent than she was right now.

Henry Selden tried to make up for this gross injustice by making his closing argument a dramatic, three-hour speech on behalf of woman suffrage. District Attorney Crowley replied with a two-hour rehash of the original charge.

By the afternoon of June 18, the case of *The United States* vs. *Susan B. Anthony* was ready to go to the jury. It was impossible to predict what their verdict might be, so Judge Hunt, determined to make it the verdict he and Roscoe Conkling wanted, took matters into his own hands. "Gentlemen of the jury," he said, "I direct that you find the defendant guilty."

Henry Selden leaped to his feet. "I object, your honor," he thundered. "The court has no power to direct the jury in a criminal case."

Judge Hunt ignored him. "Take the verdict, Mr. Clerk," he said.

The clerk of the court must have been another Conkling man. "Gentlemen of the jury," he intoned as if the whole proceeding was perfectly normal, "hearken to the verdict as the court hath recorded it. You say you find the defendant guilty of the offense charged. So say you all."

The twelve jurymen looked stunned. They had not even met to discuss the case, much less agree on a verdict. When Henry Selden asked if the clerk could at least poll the jury, Judge Hunt rapped his gavel sharply and declared, "That cannot be allowed. Gentlemen of the jury, you are discharged."

An enraged Henry Selden lost no time in introducing a motion for a new trial on the grounds that his client had been denied the right to a jury verdict. Judge Hunt denied the motion. He turned to Susan B. Anthony and said, "The prisoner will stand up. Has the prisoner anything to say why sentence shall not be pronounced?"

Thus far in the trial, Susan B. Anthony had remained silent. Now, she rose to her feet and said slowly, "Yes, your honor, I have many things to say."

Without further preliminaries, she launched into a scathing denunciation of Judge Hunt's conduct of her trial. ". . . In your ordered verdict of guilty," she said, "you have trampled underfoot every vital principle of our government. My natural rights, my civil rights, my political rights, are all alike ignored. Robbed of the fundamental privilege of citizenship, I am degraded from the status of a citizen to that of a subject; and not only myself individually, but all of my sex, are, by your honor's verdict, doomed to political subjection under this so-called Republican government."

Judge Hunt reached for his gavel, but Susan B. Anthony refused to be silenced.

"May it please your honor," she continued. "Your denial of my citizen's right to vote is the denial of my right to a trial by a jury of my peers as an offender against law, therefore, the denial of my sacred rights to life, liberty, property, and—"

"The court cannot allow the prisoner to go on," Judge Hunt cried out.

Susan ignored him and continued her impassioned tirade against the court. Hunt frantically rapped his gavel and ordered her to sit down and be quiet. But Susan, who must have been taking delight in his consternation,[13] kept on talking. She deplored the fact that she had been denied the right to a fair trial. Even if she had been given such a trial, she insisted, it would not have been by her peers. Jury, judges, and lawyers were not her equals, but her superiors, because they could vote and she could not. Susan was adamant[14] about the fact that she had been denied the justice guaranteed in the Constitution to every citizen of the United States.

Judge Hunt was sufficiently cowed[15] by now to try to defend himself. "The prisoner has been tried according to the established forms of law," he sputtered.

"Yes, your honor," retorted Susan, overlooking his blatant[16] lie, "but by forms of law all made by men, interpreted by men, administered by men, in favor of men, and against women; and hence your honor's ordered verdict of guilty, against a United States citizen for the exercise of that citizen's right to vote, simply because that citizen was a woman and not a man. But yesterday, the same manmade forms of law declared it a crime punishable with a one-thousand-dollar fine and six months imprisonment, for you, or me, or any of us, to give a cup of cold water, a crust of bread, or a night's shelter to a panting fugitive while he was tracking his way to Canada. And every man or woman in whose veins coursed a drop of human sympathy violated that wicked law, reckless of consequences, and was justified in so doing. As, then, the slaves who got their freedom must take it over, or under, or through the unjust forms of law, precisely so now must women, to get their right to a voice in this government, take it, and I have taken mine, and mean to take it at every opportunity."

Judge Hunt flailed his gavel and gave the by now futile order for the prisoner to sit down and be quiet. Susan kept right on talking.

13. *Consternation* (kon′ stər nā′ shən) is amazement or dismay that causes confusion or helplessness.

14. Anthony was totally firm and unyielding *(adamant)*.

15. *Cowed* means "intimidated."

16. *Blatant* (blāt′ ənt) means "very obvious."

"When I was brought before your honor for trial," she said, "I hoped for a broad and liberal interpretation of the Constitution and its recent Amendments. One that would declare all United States citizens under its protection. But failing to get this justice—failing, even, to get a trial by a jury *not* of my peers—I ask not leniency at your hands—but to take the full rigors[17] of the law."

With that Susan finally obeyed Judge Hunt's orders and sat down. Now he had to reverse himself and order her to stand up so he could impose sentence. As soon as he pronounced the sentence—a fine of one hundred dollars plus the costs of prosecuting the trial—Susan spoke up again. "May it please your honor," she said, "I shall never pay a dollar of your unjust penalty. All the stock in trade I possess is a ten-thousand-dollar debt, incurred by publishing my paper—*The Revolution*—four years ago, the sole object of which was to educate all women to do precisely as I have done, rebel against your manmade, unjust, unconstitutional forms of law, that tax, fine, imprison, and hang women, while they deny them the right of representation in the government; and I shall work on with might and main[18] to pay every dollar of that honest debt, but not a penny shall go to this unjust claim. And I shall earnestly and persistently continue to urge all women to the practical recognition of the old Revolutionary maxim, that 'Resistance to tyranny is obedience to God.'"

Judge Hunt must have had strict orders not only to see that the defendant was convicted, but to do everything he could to prevent the case from going on to a higher court. He allowed Susan to walk out of the courtroom without imposing a prison sentence in lieu of[19] her unpaid fine. If he had sent her to prison, she could have been released on a writ of habeas corpus[20] and would have had the right to appeal. As it was, the case was closed.

Although she was disappointed that her case would not go to the Supreme Court as she had originally hoped, Susan knew that she had struck an important blow for woman's suffrage. Henry Selden's arguments and her own speech at the end of the trial were widely publicized, and Judge Hunt's conduct of the trial stood as proof that women were treated unjustly before the law.

Susan did not forget the election inspectors who had allowed her to cast her ballot. The men were fined twenty-five dollars each and sent to jail when they refused to pay. In all, they spent about a week behind bars before Susan, through the influence of friends in Washington, obtained presidential pardons for each of them. In the meantime, her followers, who included some of the best cooks in Rochester, saw to it that the men were supplied with delicious hot meals and home-baked pies.

True to her promise, Susan paid the legal expenses for the three inspectors. With the help of contributions from sympathetic admirers, she paid the costs of her own trial. But she never paid that one-hundred-dollar fine. Susan B. Anthony was a woman of her word as well as a woman of courage.

17. Susan asked not for mercy *(leniency)* but for harshness in judgment *(rigors)*.
18. To work *with might and main* is to work with all one's strength and effort.
19. The expression *in lieu* (lo͞o) *of* means "in place of."
20. A *writ of habeas corpus* (hā′ bē əs kôr′ pəs) is a judge's order for a prisoner to be brought into court to establish whether he or she is being held legally.

Responding to Literature

Personal Response

Were you surprised by what happened to Anthony during her trial? Why or why not?

Analyzing Literature

Recall

1. What was Truman's first opinion of Susan B. Anthony, and how did her opinion change?
2. What personal experience spurred Anthony to work for women's rights?
3. Why did Anthony feel justified in registering to vote in 1872?
4. How did the press and the public react when Anthony and others registered and then voted? What did the poll inspectors do on election day in the Eighth Ward and elsewhere?
5. Summarize the conduct and results of Anthony's trial.

Interpret

6. In your opinion, what made Truman change her mind about Anthony?
7. Why do you suppose Anthony's speech at the teachers' convention "left most of [her] audience in a state of shock"?
8. What does Anthony's plan for voting reveal about her character?
9. How would you describe public opinion on woman suffrage in the late 1800s? Provide evidence to support your response.
10. How would you characterize Anthony's trial? Use details from the selection in your answer.

Evaluate and Connect

11. What new understanding of the woman suffrage movement did you gain from this selection?
12. Did any of Anthony's protest methods appear on the list you created for the Reading Focus on page 353? Which ones? If she were fighting to win the right to vote today, how might she conduct her campaign?
13. In your view, was Anthony's action during the election of 1872 a success or a failure? Explain.
14. What qualities, actions, and accomplishments does Truman use to **characterize** Susan B. Anthony as a "woman of courage"?
15. **Theme Connections** Based on this portrait, what is your opinion of Susan B. Anthony? Do you agree with Truman that Anthony was a fanatic but had a sense of humor? Why or why not?

Literary ELEMENTS

Biography

A **biography** is an account of a person's life written by someone other than the subject. Biographies can be short, like Truman's portrait of Susan B. Anthony, or they can be book length. They can even span several volumes. Some biographies focus on the admirable characteristics of their subjects, others present a balanced portrait, and still others paint a negative picture. While biographers may strive for accuracy, they usually have an attitude toward their subjects that affects their selection of facts and their interpretation of those facts.

1. How would you describe Truman's attitude toward Anthony and her actions?
2. How does Truman's attitude influence the details she selects for this essay on Anthony's life? Give examples to support your opinion.

- See **Literary Terms Handbook**, p. R2.

Literature and Writing

Writing About Literature

Analyzing Word Choice Margaret Truman's account of Susan B. Anthony's experiences is nonfiction, but it is still lively and personal. For example, Truman uses the word "battle-ax" to describe her initial impression of Anthony. Identify some of the other word choices that help enliven this biography. Explain how the words, phrases, or passages you choose enrich the biography and make it more interesting to read.

Personal Writing

Other Frontiers What is your opinion of the state of women's rights today? For example, consider the issues of women serving in military combat positions and equal pay for equal work. How can women effect change in their lives by exercising their right to vote? Write your thoughts in your journal.

Extending Your Response

Literature Groups

Assessing Personal Style Review the scene in which Susan B. Anthony is arrested by Deputy U.S. Marshal E. J. Keeney and the courtroom scene in which she is tried for voting in the election. With your group, discuss what is ironic—and amusing—about the arrest scene. What aspects of Anthony's personal style are revealed in that scene? Which of these are also revealed in her behavior in court? What impact does Anthony's personal style have on the men who are supposed to have authority over her? Share your conclusions in a class discussion.

Carrie Chapman Catt

Interdisciplinary Activity

History: Other Heroes Use library and Internet resources to research other prominent leaders in the women's rights movement, such as Carrie Chapman Catt, Virginia Minor, or Elizabeth Cady Stanton. Choose an individual whom you find especially inspiring. Give a class presentation about a noteworthy episode in the person's life. You might compare the person's experiences with those of Susan B. Anthony.

Listening and Speaking

Talk of the Town Consider what average women and men who lived in Anthony's day might have thought of her. With a small group, role-play a conversation between people who meet at a family gathering or at a public place, such as a lunch counter, drugstore, or school. Discuss what they have heard or read about Anthony's actions, arrest, and trial. Each group member might express a different point of view about Anthony, her goals, and her methods for achieving them.

Reading Further

If you enjoyed this biography, you might also like these other works:

Biographies: *Women of Courage,* by Margaret Truman, is a collection of biographies of twelve American women—including Susan B. Anthony—whom Truman considers heroes, including a freed slave and a first lady.

Harry S. Truman and *Bess W. Truman,* both by Margaret Truman, provide portraits of her famous parents.

Viewing: *Susan B. Anthony: Rebel for the Cause* examines the life and work of Susan B. Anthony.

Save your work for your portfolio.

Skill Minilessons

GRAMMAR AND LANGUAGE • Understanding Parallelism

Parallelism is the use of a series of words, phrases, or sentences that have similar grammatical form. Parallelism emphasizes the items that are arranged in these similar structures and helps to create unity in a piece of writing. Examples of parallelism, such as the one shown below, may be found throughout Margaret Truman's essay.

There was always a new speech to write, a new meeting to organize, a new petition to be drawn up and presented to a state legislature.

Notice that each phrase repeats the same structure: an adjective (here, it is always *new*) followed by a noun *(speech, meeting, petition)* followed by the infinitive form of a verb *(to write, to organize, to be drawn up and presented).*

PRACTICE Find another example of a sentence that includes parallelism in this selection and copy it on your paper. Then explain what grammatical elements in the sentence are parallel.

- For more about parallelism, see **Literary Terms Handbook,** p. R9.

READING AND THINKING • Main Ideas and Supporting Details

The opening paragraph of Truman's essay begins with a topic sentence that states the main idea: "Susan B. Anthony has never been one of my favorite characters." The rest of the sentences in the paragraph provide details that support this main idea. In reading nonfiction, you will find many paragraphs with this same structure. Being able to identify topic sentences and supporting details can help you to review material you have read and to write paraphrases and summaries.

PRACTICE On your paper, copy the fourth paragraph from "The United States *vs.* Susan B. Anthony," which begins, "Daniel Anthony had a succession. . . ." Underline the main idea of the paragraph and circle the supporting details.

APPLY Return to a piece of your own expository writing. In each paragraph, have you clearly stated a main idea and supported it with details? Revise your writing as necessary.

- For more about related reading strategies, see **Reading Handbook,** pp. R78–R107.

VOCABULARY • The Suffix *-fy*

If you were to *vilify* someone, you would make that person appear to be a villain, destroying his or her reputation. If you *glorify* someone, you make him or her seem glorious. To *magnify* a problem is to make it seem larger. To *clarify* a statement is to make it clear. As you can see, the suffix *-fy* means "to make."

- For more about suffixes, see **Language Handbook,** p. R55.

PRACTICE Use your understanding of the suffix *-fy* to determine the meaning of each underlined word. Then complete each sentence in a way that conveys the meaning of the word.

1. You would electrify a cabin if you . . .
2. A person might falsify a document by . . .
3. A school might diversify its curriculum by . . .
4. You can solidify water by . . .
5. A famous person who could be said to exemplify athletic skill is . . .

Technology Skills

E-mail: Communicating with Experts

Gathering information through research is an important skill not just for school but for life as well. For example, if you decide to buy some stereo equipment, reading through consumer publications may help you determine the best equipment for you. However, you may also get valuable information by asking an expert some questions about the equipment you are considering. Today, e-mail makes it easier than ever to find and communicate with experts on a wide variety of topics.

Before You Begin

With a partner discuss what makes a person an expert. Make a brief list of criteria you can use to determine someone's level of expertise in a particular area. Together, devise and write down your own definition for the word *expert*.

Finding Online Experts

A number of established Internet sites can help you locate experts. The chart below shows the Web addresses for four of these sites.

Expert Site	Web Address (URL)
Ask an Expert	http://www.askanexpert.com/askanexpert
The Ask an Expert Page	http://njnie.dl.stevens-tech.edu/curriculum/aska.html
AskA + Locator	http://www.vrd.org/locator/index.html
Homework Help	http://www.startribune.com/stonline/html/special/homework

You can also use a search engine to find other "Ask an Expert" sites. Try a keyword search for combinations such as e-mail + mentor, e-mail + expert, or ask + expert. Use the following checklist to help you evaluate the quality of any expert site you're considering using.

Checklist

- ☑ Is the site monitored?
- ☑ Are the experts screened?
- ☑ Do experts seem knowledgeable?
- ☑ Is there a central place to which users can direct questions?

Communicating with an Expert

Once you've located an expert on your topic, use your e-mail software to compose a message. State your questions as briefly and clearly as possible. If the expert site provides any guidelines for formatting messages, be sure to follow them.

Experts are busy people, so allow at least three days for a response. You should also be aware that some e-mail experts may not answer your questions directly. Rather, they may direct you to another site on the web where you can find the information you're seeking. In any case, always reply to the e-mail you receive, thanking the expert for his or her time.

TECHNOLOGY TIP

If an "ask an expert" site you use includes a list of FAQs (frequently asked questions), be sure to check the list first to see if your question has already been answered.

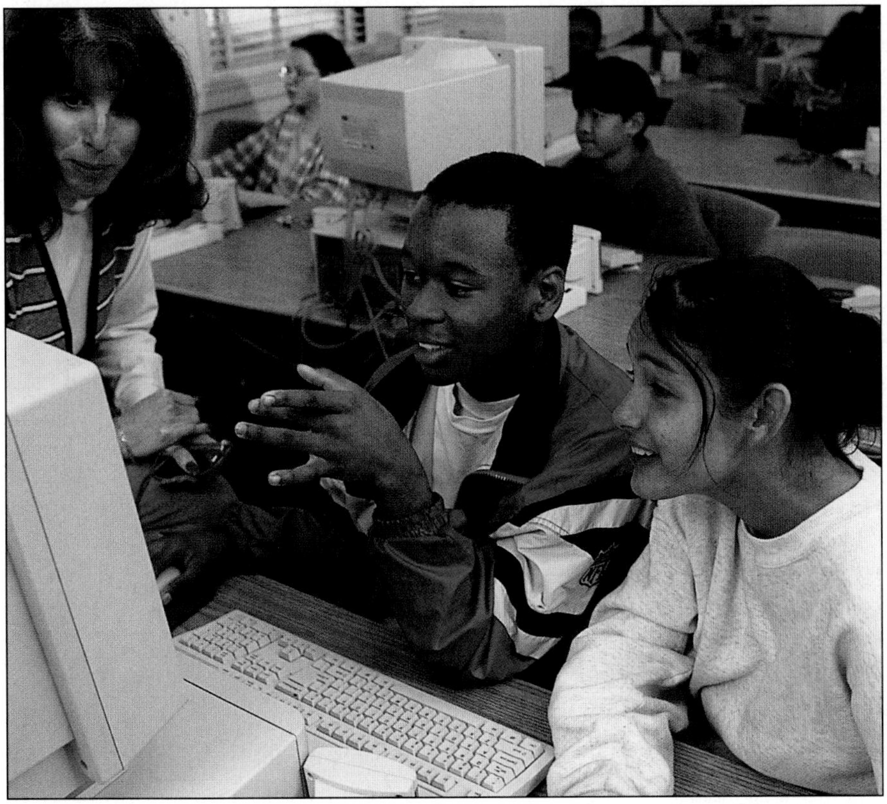

ACTIVITIES

1. Work with a partner to formulate two or three questions about the topic of one of the selections in this unit, such as Susan B. Anthony, wolves, or sunflowers. Find an e-mail expert and post your questions. Once you receive a response, look back through your definition of *expert*. Does the person with whom you've communicated fit that definition? Why or why not?

2 "Ask an Expert" sites come in handy when you need to do research for your own writing. Use e-mail experts to help gather information about the subject of the biographical essay you will write in the Writing Workshop at the end of this unit (pages 426–429).

Before You Read

from *Never Cry Wolf*

Reading Focus

What have you heard about wolves? What would you like to know about them?

Chart It! On your own paper, copy and complete a chart like the one shown below.

Wolves	
What I've Heard	What I Want to Know

Setting a Purpose Read to learn more about wolf behavior.

Building Background

The Time and Place

It is summer, on the sixth morning of Mowat's observation of a wolf habitat in the arctic wilderness of north central Canada.

Did You Know?

Once believed to be a fierce, destructive animal, the wolf is now known to be social, often gentle, harmless to humans unless threatened, and an important link in the ecosystem. Wolves live in packs, or family groups, that often include a female leader and a male leader (which mate for life), their pups, and other adult wolves who help take care of the pack and hunt. Wolves communicate with their voices and their bodies, sending messages not only by howling, barking, and growling but also by the position of the tail, lips, nose, and ears.

Apologetic

Happy

Warning

Vocabulary Preview

conundrum (kə nun′ drəm) *n.* a puzzling or difficult problem; p. 371
bevy (bev′ ē) *n.* a group; p. 371
stoicism (stō′ ə siz′ əm) *n.* the ability to remain calm and unemotional, especially in spite of pain or suffering; p. 372
harass (har′ əs) *v.* to bother or annoy repeatedly; p. 372
plaintive (plān′ tiv) *adj.* expressing sorrow; mournful; sad; p. 372
vulnerable (vul′ nər ə bəl) *adj.* easily hurt or damaged; p. 373
somnolence (som′ nə ləns) *n.* sleepiness; drowsiness; p. 373

Meet Farley Mowat

Farley Mowat has always lived as far north as possible in Canada. As an official biologist for the Canadian government, he was sent to study wildlife in the "Barrens," or Barren Lands, an arctic region of treeless plains, low hills, and lakes, west of Hudson Bay. In addition to writing nonfiction about the animals and people of the arctic, Mowat writes adventure novels and stories set in Canada. He has won numerous literary awards for his work. Mowat says he especially likes writing for young adults, whom he considers to be most "natural" and "unspoiled."

Farley Mowat was born in 1921 in Ontario, Canada. Never Cry Wolf *was first published in 1963.*

from

Never Cry Wolf

Farley Mowat

DURING MY EARLY VISIT TO THE DEN I had seen *three* adult wolves; and during the first few days of observing the den I had again glimpsed the odd-wolf-out several times. He posed a major conundrum, for while I could accept the idea of a contented domestic group consisting of mated male and female and a bevy of pups, I had not yet progressed far enough into the wolf world to be able to explain, or to accept, the apparent existence of an eternal triangle.

Vocabulary

conundrum (kə nun′ drəm) *n.* a puzzling or difficult problem

bevy (bev′ ē) *n.* a group

Whoever the third wolf was, he was definitely a character. He was smaller than George, not so lithe[1] and vigorous, and with a gray overcast to his otherwise white coat. He became "Uncle Albert" to me after the first time I saw him with the pups.

The sixth morning of my vigil had dawned bright and sunny, and Angeline and the pups took advantage of the good weather. Hardly was the sun risen (at three A.M.) when they all left the den and adjourned to a nearby sandy knoll. Here the pups worked over their mother with an enthusiasm which would certainly have driven any human female into hysterics. They were hungry; but they were also full to the ears with hellery.[2] Two of them did their best to chew off Angeline's tail, worrying it and fighting over it until I thought I could actually see her fur flying like spindrift;[3] while the other two did what they could to remove her ears.

Angeline stood it with noble stoicism for about an hour and then, sadly disheveled,[4] she attempted to protect herself by sitting on her tail and tucking her mauled head down between her legs. This was a fruitless effort. The pups went for her feet, one to each paw, and I was treated to the spectacle of the demon killer of the wilds trying desperately to cover her paws, her tail, and her head at one and the same instant.

Eventually she gave it up. Harassed beyond endurance she leaped away from her brood and raced to the top of a high sand ridge behind the den. The four pups rolled cheerfully off in pursuit, but before they could reach her she gave vent[5] to a most peculiar cry.

The whole question of wolf communications was to intrigue me more and more as time went on, but on this occasion I was still laboring under the delusion[6] that complex communications among animals other than man did not exist. I could make nothing definite of Angeline's high-pitched and yearning whine-cum-howl.[7] I did, however, detect a plaintive quality in it which made my sympathies go out to her.

I was not alone. Within seconds of her *cri-de-coeur*,[8] and before the mob of pups could reach her, a savior appeared.

It was the third wolf. He had been sleeping in a bed hollowed in the sand at the southern end of the esker[9] where it dipped down to disappear beneath the waters of the bay. I had not known he was there until I saw his head come up. He jumped to his feet,

1. *Lithe* (līth) means "flexible, limber."
2. Here, *hellery* is mischief.
3. The spray blown up from waves is called *spindrift.*
4. *Disheveled* (di shev′ əld) means "untidy" or "rumpled."
5. *Gave vent* means "let out" or "let off."
6. Here, *delusion* means "false belief."
7. The Latin preposition *cum* (koom) means "together with."
8. The French phrase *cri-de-coeur* (krēt kœr′) translates as "cry of the heart" and means "a heartfelt plea for sympathy or help."
9. An *esker* is a narrow ridge, or mound, of sand and gravel.

Vocabulary

stoicism (stō′ ə siz′ əm) *n.* the ability to remain calm and unemotional, especially in spite of pain or suffering

harass (har′ əs) *v.* to bother or annoy repeatedly

plaintive (plān′ tiv) *adj.* expressing sorrow; mournful; sad

shook himself, and trotted straight toward the den—intercepting the pups as they prepared to scale the last slope to reach their mother.

I watched, fascinated, as he used his shoulder to bowl the leading pup over on its back and send it skidding down the lower slope toward the den. Having broken the charge, he then nipped another pup lightly on its fat behind; then he shepherded the lot of them back to what I later came to recognize as the playground area.

I hesitate to put human words into a wolf's mouth, but the effect of what followed was crystal clear. "If it's a workout you kids want," he might have said, "then I'm your wolf!"

And so he was. For the next hour he played with the pups with as much energy as if he were still one himself. The games were varied, but many of them were quite recognizable. Tag was the standby, and Albert was always "it." Leaping, rolling and weaving amongst the pups, he never left the area of the nursery knoll, while at the same time leading the youngsters on such a chase that they eventually gave up.

Albert looked them over for a moment and then, after a quick glance toward the crest where Angeline was now lying in a state of peaceful relaxation, he flung himself in among the tired pups, sprawled on his back, and invited mayhem. They were game. One by one they roused and went into battle. They were really roused this time, and no holds were barred—by them, at any rate.

Some of them tried to choke the life out of Albert, although their small teeth, sharp as they were, could never have penetrated his heavy ruff.[10] One of them, in an excess of infantile sadism,[11] turned its back on him and pawed a shower of sand into his face. The others took to leaping as high into the air as their bowed little legs would propel them; coming down with a satisfying thump on Albert's vulnerable belly. In between jumps they tried to chew the life out of whatever vulnerable parts came to tooth.

I began to wonder how much he could stand. Evidently he could stand a lot, for not until the pups were totally exhausted and had collapsed into complete somnolence did he get to his feet, careful not to step on the small, sprawled forms, and disengage himself. Even then he did not return to the comfort of his own bed (which he had undoubtedly earned after a night of hard hunting) but settled himself instead on the edge of the nursery knoll, where he began wolf-napping, taking a quick look at the pups every few minutes to make sure they were still safely near at hand.

His true relationship to the rest of the family was still uncertain; but as far as I was concerned he had become, and would remain, "good old Uncle Albert."

10. A wolf's *ruff* is the longer hair that forms a sort of wide collar around its neck.
11. *Sadism* (sā′ diz′əm) is the practice of getting pleasure from causing pain to another. Here, it is *infantile* (in′ fən tīl′) in that it is done in childlike playfulness.

Vocabulary

vulnerable (vul′ nər ə bəl) *adj.* easily hurt or damaged
somnolence (som′ nə ləns) *n.* sleepiness; drowsiness

MEDIA connection

Newspaper Article

"Sunflowers are pure, undistilled summer," says writer Dennis Rodkin. "It's those big yellow and black flower heads that captivate us most." And as you'll read, they have a fascinating history as well.

Sunflowers Are as American as They Come

by Dennis Rodkin—*Chicago Tribune*, August 10, 1997

You've probably heard of the War of the Roses, but what about the Skirmish of the Sunflowers?

It seems that in 1969 an Iowa legislator tried to convince his colleagues that feral sunflowers were causing too much trouble in the state's crop fields and ought to be officially declared noxious weeds. That declaration would have prompted Iowa's county weed commissioners to launch all-out sunflower eradication programs.

Trouble was, Iowa lies near Kansas, where the sunflower has been the state flower since 1903. When legislators there got wind of the plan sprouting in Iowa, they retaliated by hatching a scheme to brand the eastern goldfinch, Iowa's state bird, a public nuisance in Kansas.

Both states eventually backed down, but not before a dissenting Iowa legislator asked his colleagues, "Have you no love of beauty in your souls?"

"Sunflowers are the American flower," says Diane Morey Sitton, the Texan who wrote *Sunflowers: Growing, Cooking and Crafting with the Sunniest of Plants*. "They're very sturdy and resilient."

Historically, various American Indian tribes used sunflowers for everything from ceremonial decorations to a cure for rattlesnake bites to bread. The Cochiti used the juice of fresh-cut sunflower stems as a poultice left to dry on top of a wound and harden into a bandage. A Paiute tribe made a flour out of roasted sunflower seeds, while Apaches ground the seeds on metates. The Iroquois used the oil from sunflower seeds to season their food and as a base for skin paints.

Sitton suggests that gardeners who grow sunflowers for the seeds protect the harvest from hungry birds, squirrels, and other animals. Cover seed-heads with mesh bags, pantyhose, cheesecloth, or any other permeable material, she says.

That way you'll prevent having to wage your own local sunflower battle.

Analyzing Media

1. What did you learn about sunflowers that you didn't know before? What details did you find most interesting?
2. Did this article successfully capture and hold your attention from the beginning to the end? Why or why not?

Literature and Writing

Writing About Literature

Examining Point of View Farley Mowat writes from the **third-person limited point of view.** He describes what he sees and tells readers that he's making a guess when he interprets wolf behavior. Look for instances where Mowat himself becomes a character in his narrative. Then write an explanation of how his point of view affects what you learn about the wolf family.

Creative Writing

Through the Eyes of Wolves If you were George, Angeline, and Uncle Albert, you would certainly know that Mowat was watching you. Write a "conversation" the wolves might have about this stranger who has watched them constantly for six days. Include their questions, speculations, and conclusions, based on their awareness of Mowat's appearance, actions, smells, and sounds.

Extending Your Response

Literature Groups

If You Were He How do you think it might have felt to be Farley Mowat, living in arctic isolation? In your group, discuss the pros and cons of such an assignment. Also discuss the impact that a lack of human companionship might have had on Mowat, using examples from the text to support your ideas. For example, why might he have named the wolves George, Angeline, and Albert? Share your conclusions with the rest of the class.

Interdisciplinary Activity

Science: Call of the Wild One of the fascinating things about wolves, as Mowat observes, is their use of specific howls, growls, barks, and body language to communicate. Use library and Internet resources to research wolf language. You may want to look for audiocassettes, such as *The Language and Music of the Wolves* by Robert Redford, and books, such as *Of Wolves and Men* by Barry Lopez. Share your findings with the class in an oral report.

Save your work for your portfolio.

Skill Minilesson

VOCABULARY • Analogies

An analogy is a type of comparison that is based on the relationships between things or ideas. Some analogies are based on part-to-whole relationships.

flower : bouquet :: fish : school

One flower can be part of a bouquet; one fish can be part of a school. This analogy may also be expressed in reverse: bouquet : flower :: school : fish.

To finish an analogy, decide what relationship exists between the first two things or ideas. Then apply that relationship to another pair of words.

For more about analogies, see **Communications Skills Handbook,** p. R77.

PRACTICE Choose the word that best completes each analogy. Which analogy is based on a part-to-whole relationship?

1. sleeplessness : alert :: somnolence :
   a. awake b. sleepy c. somber
2. individual : bevy :: horse :
   a. rider b. herd c. stallion
3. fearless : vulture :: vulnerable :
   a. bear b. mother c. baby
4. temptation : resist :: conundrum :
   a. solve b. notice c. choose

MEDIA connection

Newspaper Article

"Sunflowers are pure, undistilled summer," says writer Dennis Rodkin. "It's those big yellow and black flower heads that captivate us most." And as you'll read, they have a fascinating history as well.

Sunflowers Are as American as They Come

by Dennis Rodkin—*Chicago Tribune*, August 10, 1997

You've probably heard of the War of the Roses, but what about the Skirmish of the Sunflowers?

It seems that in 1969 an Iowa legislator tried to convince his colleagues that feral sunflowers were causing too much trouble in the state's crop fields and ought to be officially declared noxious weeds. That declaration would have prompted Iowa's county weed commissioners to launch all-out sunflower eradication programs.

Trouble was, Iowa lies near Kansas, where the sunflower has been the state flower since 1903. When legislators there got wind of the plan sprouting in Iowa, they retaliated by hatching a scheme to brand the eastern goldfinch, Iowa's state bird, a public nuisance in Kansas.

Both states eventually backed down, but not before a dissenting Iowa legislator asked his colleagues, "Have you no love of beauty in your souls?"

"Sunflowers are the American flower," says Diane Morey Sitton, the Texan who wrote *Sunflowers: Growing, Cooking and Crafting with the Sunniest of Plants*. "They're very sturdy and resilient."

Historically, various American Indian tribes used sunflowers for everything from ceremonial decorations to a cure for rattlesnake bites to bread. The Cochiti used the juice of fresh-cut sunflower stems as a poultice left to dry on top of a wound and harden into a bandage. A Paiute tribe made a flour out of roasted sunflower seeds, while Apaches ground the seeds on metates. The Iroquois used the oil from sunflower seeds to season their food and as a base for skin paints.

Sitton suggests that gardeners who grow sunflowers for the seeds protect the harvest from hungry birds, squirrels, and other animals. Cover seed-heads with mesh bags, pantyhose, cheesecloth, or any other permeable material, she says.

That way you'll prevent having to wage your own local sunflower battle.

Analyzing Media

1. What did you learn about sunflowers that you didn't know before? What details did you find most interesting?
2. Did this article successfully capture and hold your attention from the beginning to the end? Why or why not?

Before You Read

Walking

Reading Focus

Luther Standing Bear, a Lakota chief and author, wrote, "The world was a library and its books were the stones, leaves, grass, brooks, and the birds and animals that shared, alike with us, the storms and blessings of earth. We learned to do what only the student of nature ever learns, and that was to feel beauty."

Quickwrite What do you think people can learn from nature? What have you learned? Take a few minutes to jot down your thoughts.

Setting a Purpose Read to discover what this author learns from nature.

Building Background

The Time and Place

This contemporary essay was inspired by a walk the author took many times, throughout the seasons of the year, on a country road.

Did You Know?

Known for its showy yellow blossoms, the sunflower may grow up to fifteen feet tall. Its flower head may reach a diameter of more than one foot and produce thousands of seeds. The flower head actually consists of many small, tubular flowers growing closely together, all fringed by large yellow petals. Wild sunflowers grow in meadows, on hillsides, and in gullies along roads and highways throughout the United States.

Vocabulary Preview

elemental (el′ ə ment′ əl) *adj.* of or like the forces of nature; ancient and powerful; p. 379

diverse (di vurs′) *adj.* markedly different; varied; p. 379

evade (i vād′) *v.* to escape or avoid, often by cleverness; p. 379

communal (kə mūn′ əl) *adj.* belonging to a community, society, or group; common; shared; p. 379

audible (ô′ də bəl) *adj.* capable of being heard; loud enough to be heard; p. 380

Meet Linda Hogan

"We want to live as if there is no other place, as if we will always be here. We want to live with devotion to . . . the universe of life."

Inspired by her Chickasaw heritage, Linda Hogan holds a deep belief in the sacredness of all living things. An award-winning poet, novelist, playwright, and essayist, Hogan writes eloquently about the beauty of the natural world and the need to respect and preserve the environment.

Linda Hogan was born in Denver, Colorado, in 1947. This selection appears in her collection of essays Dwellings: A Spiritual History of the Living World, *which was published in 1995.*

Walking

Linda Hogan

IT BEGAN IN DARK and underground weather, a slow hunger moving toward light. It grew in a dry gulley beside the road where I live, a place where entire hillsides are sometimes yellow, windblown tides of sunflower plants. But this plant was different. It was alone and larger than the countless others that had established their lives farther up the hill. This one was a traveler, a settler, and like a dream beginning in conflict, it grew where the land had been disturbed.

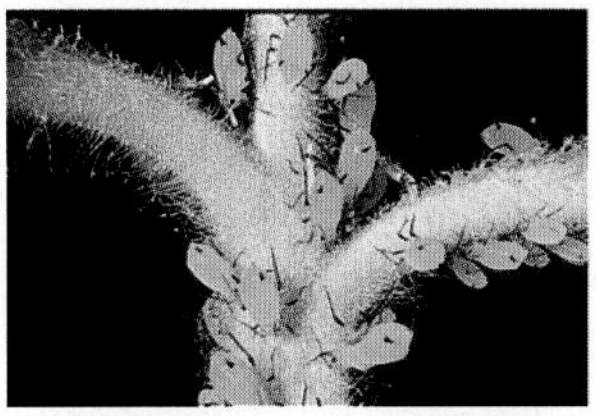

Did You Know?
Aphids (ā′ fidz) are small insects that live by sucking juices from plants. They are often cared for by ants, which obtain a honeylike substance from them.

I saw it first in early summer. It was a green and sleeping bud, raising itself toward the sun. Ants worked around the unopened bloom, gathering aphids and sap. A few days later, it was a tender young flower, soft and new, with a pale green center and a troop of silver-gray insects climbing up and down the stalk. Over the summer this sunflower grew into a plant of incredible beauty, turning its face daily toward the sun in the most subtle of ways, the black center of it dark and alive with a deep blue light, as if flint had sparked an elemental fire there, in community with rain, mineral, mountain air, and sand.

As summer changed from green to yellow there were new visitors daily, the lace-winged insects, the bees whose legs were fat with pollen, and grasshoppers with their clattering wings and desperate hunger. There were other lives I missed, those too small or hidden to see. It was as if this plant with its host of lives was a society, one in which moment by moment, depending on light and moisture, there was great and diverse change.

There were changes in the next larger world around the plant as well. One day I rounded a bend in the road to find the disturbing sight of a dead horse, black and still against a hillside, eyes rolled back. Another day I was nearly lifted by a wind and sandstorm so fierce and hot that I had to wait for it to pass before I could return home. On this day the faded dry petals of the sunflower were swept across the land. That was when the birds arrived to carry the new seeds to another future.

In this one plant, in one summer season, a drama of need and survival took place. Hungers were filled. Insects coupled. There was escape, exhaustion, and death. Lives touched down a moment and were gone.

I was an outsider. I only watched. I never learned the sunflower's golden language or the tongues[1] of its citizens. I had a small understanding, nothing more than a shallow observation of the flower, insects, and birds. But they knew what to do, how to live. An old voice from somewhere, gene or cell, told the plant how to evade the pull of gravity and find its way upward, how to open. It was instinct, intuition, necessity. A certain knowing directed the seed-bearing birds on paths to ancestral homelands they had never seen. They believed it. They followed.

There are other summons and calls, some even more mysterious than those commandments to birds or those survival journeys of insects. In bamboo plants, for instance, with their thin green canopy of light and golden stalks that creak in the wind. Once a century, all of a certain kind of bamboo flower on the same day. Neither the plants' location, in Malaysia or in a greenhouse in Minnesota, nor their age or size make a difference. They flower. Some current of an inner language passes among them, through space and separation, in ways we cannot explain in our language. They are all, somehow, one plant, each with a share of communal knowledge.

1. Here, *tongues* means languages.

Vocabulary

elemental (el′ ə ment′ əl) *adj.* of or like the forces of nature; ancient and powerful
diverse (di vurs′) *adj.* markedly different; varied
evade (i vād′) *v.* to escape or avoid, often by cleverness
communal (kə mūn′ əl) *adj.* belonging to a community, society, or group; common; shared

Walking

John Hay, in *The Immortal Wilderness*, has written: "There are occasions when you can hear the mysterious language of the Earth, in water, or coming through the trees, emanating[2] from the mosses, seeping through the undercurrents of the soil, but you have to be willing to wait and receive."

Sometimes I hear it talking. The light of the sunflower was one language, but there are others more audible. Once, in the redwood forest, I heard a beat, something like a drum or heart coming from the ground and trees and wind. That underground current stirred a kind of knowing inside me, a kinship and longing, a dream barely remembered that disappeared back to the body. Another time, there was the booming voice of an ocean storm thundering from far out at sea, telling about what lived in the distance, about the rough water that would arrive, wave after wave revealing the disturbance at center.

Sunflowers in the Field, 1989. Eric Eisenberger. Oil on canvas, 26¼ x 36 in. Private collection.

Viewing the painting: Do you think that you and Linda Hogan would have the same reaction if you were both standing in this field of sunflowers? Why or why not?

Tonight I walk. I am watching the sky. I think of the people who came before me and how they knew the placement of stars in the sky, watched the moving sun long and hard enough to witness how a certain angle of light touched a stone only once a year. Without written records, they knew the gods of every night, the small, fine details of the world around them and of immensity above them.

Walking, I can almost hear the redwoods beating. And the oceans are above me here, rolling clouds, heavy and dark, considering snow. On the dry, red road, I pass the place of the sunflower, that dark and secret location where creation took place. I wonder if it will return this summer, if it will multiply and move up to the other stand of flowers in a territorial struggle.

It's winter and there is smoke from the fires. The square, lighted windows of houses are fogging over. It is a world of elemental attention, of all things working together, listening to what speaks in the blood. Whichever road I follow, I walk in the land of many gods, and they love and eat one another. Walking, I am listening to a deeper way. Suddenly all my ancestors are behind me. Be still, they say. Watch and listen. You are the result of the love of thousands.

2. *Emanating* means "coming, issuing, or flowing from."

Vocabulary

audible (ô′ də bəl) *adj.* capable of being heard; loud enough to be heard

Responding to Literature

Personal Response

What images or ideas from this essay linger in your mind? Why?

Analyzing Literature

Recall and Interpret

1. Name three things that impress Hogan about the sunflower she sees along her walk. What do these things suggest about Hogan herself?
2. What point does Hogan emphasize by including the **anecdote** about bamboo plants? (See Literary Terms Handbook, page R1.)
3. What examples does Hogan give of "languages" in nature? Use details from the selection to explain whether people can understand those languages.
4. Reread the last paragraph of the essay. In your own words, explain what the author is saying.

Evaluate and Connect

5. Review your response to the Reading Focus on page 377. Compare and contrast your thoughts about the "lessons" of nature with those of the author.
6. Reread the fourth paragraph of the essay. Then explain how each thing Hogan witnesses connects to the themes of life and death, the future and the past.
7. In your opinion, why does Hogan think of her ancestors as she walks?
8. Have you ever had an experience in which you felt especially attuned to the natural world? Describe the experience.

Literary ELEMENTS

Description

A **description** is a carefully detailed portrayal of a person, place, thing, or event. Description appeals to the senses, helping readers to see, hear, smell, taste, or feel the subject. "Walking" is an example of a descriptive essay. Using vivid and precise adjectives, nouns, and verbs, the author has painted a detailed word portrait of the unique world of a sunflower plant.

1. In Hogan's essay, find two descriptions of nature that appeal to the sense of sight and two that appeal to the sense of hearing.
2. What attitude toward her subject does the author reveal in these descriptions? Explain your answer.

- See **Literary Terms Handbook,** p. R4.

Extending Your Response

Literature Groups

On the Outside Looking In Why does Hogan say she is "an outsider" after watching the sunflower all summer long? In what ways are people part of the natural world, and in what ways do people stand outside it? Discuss these questions with your group and share your conclusions in a class discussion.

Creative Writing

One Striking Image **Haiku** is a Japanese form of poetry that has three unrhymed lines of five, seven, and five syllables (see pages 498 and R6). Using descriptive details from Hogan's essay as inspiration, write a haiku about a sunflower.

Save your work for your portfolio.

Writing Skills

Using Transitions

Reading good writing is easy when the writer's ideas are logically linked from sentence to sentence and paragraph to paragraph. To ensure a clear, logical flow of ideas, writers use **transitions**–words and phrases that imply relationships between ideas. Notice how Linda Hogan uses transitions in the following paragraph from "Walking."

> **"I saw it first in early summer. It was a green and sleeping bud, raising itself toward the sun. Ants worked around the unopened bloom, gathering aphids and sap. A few days later, it was a tender young flower, soft and new, with a pale green center and a troop of silver-gray insects climbing up and down the stalk. Over the summer this sunflower grew into a plant of incredible beauty. . . ."**

Hogan is describing changes that take place over time, so she uses transitions to clarify the order of events and make her ideas flow smoothly–*first, a few days later, over the summer.*

The transitions you use in your writing will depend on your topic and purpose. The chart below shows some transition words and phrases that imply different relationships.

Relationships	Transitions
Time	first, when, until, before, later, finally, afterward, meanwhile, then, soon, simultaneously, after, next
Location	above, below, here, underneath, inside, beside, nearby, next to, around, in the distance, up, over, through, behind
Importance	first, second, mainly, primarily, last, most important, least important, best, worst
Cause and Effect	as a result, because, consequently, therefore, then
Comparison	similarly, like, just as, also, in comparison with, in the same way
Contrast	but, even so, yet, however, in contrast, on the other hand, unlike, on the contrary, instead

EXERCISES

1. Write a paragraph describing the childhood of someone you know or admire. Decide how you want to organize the details about this person's childhood, and use at least three transitions to link your ideas.
2. Look for a newspaper or magazine article that uses at least three transitions. Circle these words and phrases. Then note beside each one what kind of relationship the transition is indicating.

Grammar Link

Making Sure Pronouns and Antecedents Agree

Pronouns have important work to do–substituting for nouns. Without them, sentences such as this would result: "Susan B. Anthony was arrested because Susan B. Anthony behaved consistently with Susan B. Anthony's belief that Susan B. Anthony should be allowed to vote."

Every pronoun refers back to a noun or another pronoun, called its *antecedent.* The pronoun must agree with its antecedent in number, gender, and person.

Problem 1 A singular antecedent that can be either male or female
Imagine how a person would feel if he were denied the right to vote.
Although using *he* alone is traditional, using *he or she* is preferable.

Solution A Reword the sentence to use *he or she, him or her,* and so on.
Imagine how a person would feel if he or she were denied the right to vote.

Solution B Reword the sentence; make the antecedent and the pronoun plural.
Imagine how people would feel if they were denied the right to vote.

Problem 2 A second-person pronoun that refers to a third-person antecedent
Judges should remember that you cannot direct a jury's decision.

Solution Use the appropriate third-person pronoun.
Judges should remember that they cannot direct a jury's decision.

Problem 3 A singular indefinite pronoun as an antecedent
Each of the suffragists made their own contributions.
Each, everyone, either, neither, one, and several other pronouns are singular and therefore require singular personal pronouns.

Solution A Change the pronoun to agree with its antecedent.
Each of the suffragists made her own contributions.

Solution B Change the antecedent to one that agrees with the pronoun.
The suffragists made their own contributions.

For more about pronouns, see **Language Handbook,** pp. R19–R20.

EXERCISE

Revise each sentence to solve problems in pronoun-antecedent use.

1. Every nonfiction writer hopes his topic will interest readers.
2. Each of the forest creatures were hiding from the storm.
3. People will miss nature's miracles, if you forget to look closely.
4. Any walker may discover life and death in her environment.
5. Studying a sunflower, others too might feel like outsiders, since you can't be part of a blossom.

MEDIA connection

Newspaper Article

How do you train a green horse—one that is wild or young? As you will read, times have changed, and so have people's understanding of the best way to treat a horse.

"Horse Whisperer" Takes a Different Tack in Training

by Dawn Hobbs—*Los Angeles Times*, January 12, 1998

SOMIS—The next step for Charley, a 9-year-old quarter horse–thoroughbred mix, was death.

He was so out-of-control—constantly rearing and bucking—that his new owner, Gail Eneriz of Camarillo, feared he would seriously hurt someone. One trainer urged her to sell the horse.

"And when he didn't sell, she had me convinced that I should send him to the killers," she said.

As a last-ditch effort, Eneriz met with Somis trainer Jim Frazier on the recommendation of a friend. Rather than use force, the traditional means for training horses, Frazier communicates through verbal and nonverbal signals.

He is part of a movement that has emerged in recent years called "horse whispering." Its practitioners believe in cultivating a partnership with the horse.

"It's a gentler way of training," said Mary Jo Lord, director of the horsemanship program at Cal Lutheran University. "You're not yelling or being aggressive toward the horse."

The trainers do not literally whisper to the horse. "Whispering just means using a softer, quieter technique," Lord said. "The key word is patience."

Traditionally, horses have been trained through negative reinforcement—a jerk on the bridle, a kick in the belly, or a slap with reins or a fist.

"Horse whispering," by contrast, relies on hand gestures and other body language, along with words, to communicate with the horse.

For instance, Lord teaches her students to work their horses in a small pen to keep their attention. "Walking toward the horse slows the animal down, and holding up a hand stops the horse," Lord said.

"A lot of people think there is something mystical about it, but there isn't," she said. "It's truly common sense. If you're kind to the horse, the horse will respond better."

"We're in an era now when the horse industry is beginning to move away from breaking horses," Frazier said. "The philosophy is not to make a horse do things, but to get a horse to want to do things."

Although trainers for some time have been moving away from beating horses into submission, the gentler technique has only recently come to the attention of many people outside the field, through Nicholas Evans' book "The Horse Whisperer" and Robert Redford's movie of the same name.

"This will be the system everyone will be using in the future, more and more so, without a doubt," Frazier said.

Analyzing Media

1. Why might it be important for a horse trainer to "get a horse to want to do things"?
2. How might the principles of horse whispering–patience, communication, and sensitivity–be applied in daily life?

Before You Read

from *West with the Night*

Reading Focus

Have you, or has someone you know or have read about, ever ridden a powerful, spirited, willful horse?

Freewrite Imagine yourself in the saddle! What feelings might you have? Excitement? Fear? Spend a few minutes writing about what is going through your head as you climb onto a horse and begin your ride.

Setting a Purpose Read to learn about a g experience with a powerful horse.

Building Background

The Time and Place

The events in this selection occurred around 1912 in Njoro (ən jôr ō), a village in British East Africa (now Kenya).

Did You Know?

- In the late 1880s, the British began to colonize eastern Africa. Attracted by its fertile land, British settlers established large farms or ranches where they grew coffee or tea, and raised cattle, sheep, or horses.
- A thoroughbred horse is a special type of saddle horse bred chiefly for racing. Because thoroughbreds are valued for such inherited qualities as speed and stamina, their pedigree, or record of parentage, is carefully recorded.

Vocabulary Preview

concede (kən sēd′) *v.* to allow or grant, as a right or privilege; p. 387

indulgence (in dul′ jəns) *n.* something granted or given; favor; privilege; p. 387

whim (hwim) *n.* a sudden notion or fanciful idea; p. 387

unprovoked (un′ prə vōkt′) *adj.* not incited or stirred to action (by something); p. 389

remorse (ri môrs′) *n.* a deep, painful feeling of guilt or sorrow for wrongdoing; p. 389

saunter (sôn′ tər) *n.* a slow, relaxed walk; stroll; p. 389

Meet Beryl Markham

"... Africa was the breath and life of my childhood."

At the age of four, Beryl Markham went with her British parents to Africa, where her father bred racehorses. Markham became an expert horse trainer by the age of seventeen. As an adult, she took up flying, transporting mail, passengers, and supplies in an open-cockpit plane above the rugged terrain of East Africa. In 1936 Markham gained world fame as the first pilot to fly solo from England to North America—crash-landing in Nova Scotia, Canada! *West with the Night* is an account of her adventures.

Beryl Markham was born in 1902 and died in 1986. West with the Night *was first published in 1942.*

from *West with the Night*

Beryl Markham

TO AN EAGLE OR TO AN OWL or to a rabbit, man must seem a masterful and yet a forlorn animal; he has but two friends. In his almost universal unpopularity he points out, with pride, that these two are the dog and the horse. He believes, with an innocence peculiar to himself, that they are equally proud of this alleged confraternity.[1] He says, "Look at my two noble friends—they are dumb, but they are loyal." I have for years suspected that they are only tolerant.

Suspecting it, I have nevertheless depended on this tolerance all my life, and if I were, even now, without either a dog or a horse in my keeping, I should feel I had lost contact with the earth. I should be as concerned as a Buddhist monk having lost contact with Nirvana.[2]

1. *Alleged* means "so-called; stated without proof"; a *confraternity* is a brotherhood.
2. In Buddhism, *Nirvana* is the state of perfect contentment and freedom from care and pain.

Horses in particular have been as much a part of my life as past birthdays. I remember them more clearly. There is no phase of my childhood I cannot recall by remembering a horse I owned then, or one my father owned, or one I knew. They were not all gentle and kind. They were not all alike. With some my father won races and with some he lost. His black-and-yellow colors[3] have swept past the post from Nairobi to Peru, to Durban. Some horses he brought thousands of miles from England just for breeding.

Camciscan[4] was one of these.

When he came to Njoro, I was a straw-haired girl with lanky legs and he was a stallion bred out of a stud book thick as a tome[5]—and partly out of fire. The impression of his coming and of the first weeks that followed are clear in my mind.

But sometimes I wonder how it seemed to him.

He arrived in the early morning, descending the ramp from the noisy little train with the slow step of a royal exile. He held his head above the heads of those who led him, and smelled the alien earth and the thin air of the Highlands. It was not a smell that he knew.

There was a star of white on his forehead; his nostrils were wide and showed crimson like the lacquered nostrils of a Chinese dragon. He was tall, deep in girth, slender-chested, on strong legs clean as marble.

He was not chestnut; he was neither brown nor sorrel.[6] He stood uncertainly against the foreign background—a rangy bay stallion[7] swathed in sunlight and in a sheen of reddish gold.

He knew that this was freedom again. He knew that the darkness and the terrifying movement of the ship that strained his legs and bruised his body against walls too close together were gone now.

The net of leather rested on his head in those same places, and the long lines that he had learned to follow hung from the thing in his mouth that could not be bitten. But these he was used to. He could breathe, and he could feel the spring of the earth under his hooves. He could shake his body, and he could see that there was distance here, and a breadth of land into which he fitted. He opened his nostrils and smelled the heat and the emptiness of Africa and filled his lungs and let the rush of air go out of them again in a low, undulant[8] murmur.

He knew men. In the three quick years of his life he had seen more of them than of his own kind. He understood that men were to serve him and that, in exchange, he was to concede them the indulgence of minor whims. They got upon his back and most often he let them stay. They rubbed his body and did things to his hooves, none of which was really unpleasant. He judged them by their smells and by the way they touched him. He did not like a hand with a tremor, or a hand that was hard, or one that moved

3. *Colors* refers to a jockey's racing jacket and cap; their colors and pattern identify the horse's owner.
4. *Camciscan* (kam sis′ kən)
5. A *stud book* is a register that lists a horse's ancestors to prove that it is a thoroughbred; a *tome* is any very large or thick book.
6. *Sorrel* is brownish-orange to light brown.
7. This male horse kept for breeding *(stallion)* is reddish-brown with black legs, mane, and tail *(bay)* and long-limbed and long-bodied *(rangy)*.
8. *Undulant* means "rising and falling in waves."

Vocabulary

concede (kən sēd′) *v.* to allow or grant, as a right or privilege
indulgence (in dul′ jəns) *n.* something granted or given; favor; privilege
whim (hwim) *n.* a sudden notion or fanciful idea

too quickly. He did not trust the smell of a man that had nothing of the earth in it nor any sweat in it. Men's voices were bad, but there were some not too loud that came to his ears slowly, without insistence, and these he could bear.

A white man came up to him now and walked around him. Other men, all of them very black—as black as his own mane—stood in a circle and watched the first man. The stallion was used to this. It was always the same, and it made him impatient. It made him bend the sleek bow of his neck and jab at the earth with his hooves.

The white man put a hand on the stallion's shoulder and said a word that he knew because it was an old word and almost all men said it when they touched him or when they saw him.

The white man said, "So you are Camciscan," and the black men repeated, more slowly, "Camciscan," one after another. And a girl, who was white too, with straw-colored hair and legs like a colt's, said "Camciscan" several times.

The girl seemed foolishly happy saying it. She came close to him and said it again and he thought her smell was good enough, but he saw that she was familiar in her manner and he blew a little snort into her straw-colored hair to warn her, but she only laughed. She was attended by a dog, ugly with scars, who never left her heels.

After a little while the girl tugged gently on the lines Camciscan had learned to follow, and so he followed.

The black men, the white girl, the scarred dog, and the bay stallion walked along a dirt road while the white man rode far ahead in a buggy.

Camciscan looked neither to one side nor another. He saw nothing but the road before him. He walked as if he were completely alone, like an abdicated king.[9] He felt alone. The country smelled unused and clean, and the smells of the black men and the white girl were not outside of his understanding. But still he was alone and he felt some pride in that, as he always had.

He found the farm large and to his liking. It harbored many other horses in long rows of stables, but his box was separate from theirs.

He remembered the old routine of food and saddle and workout and rest, but he did not remember ever being attended before by a girl with straw-colored hair and legs that were too long, like a colt's. He did not mind, but the girl was too familiar. She walked into his stall as if they had been old friends, and he had no need of friends.

He depended upon her for certain things, but, in turn, she got on his back in the morning and they went to a valley bigger than any he had ever seen, or sometimes up the side of a certain hill that was very high, and then they came back again.

In time he found himself getting used to the girl, but he would not let it be more than that. He could feel that she was trying to break through the loneliness that he lived by, and he remembered the reasons there were to mistrust men. He could not see that she was any different, but he felt that she was, and that disturbed him.

In the early morning she would come to his stable, slip his head-collar on and remove his heavy rug. She would smooth him down with a cloth and brush his black mane and his tail. She would clean the urine from his floor, and separate the good bedding from that spoiled with manure. She did these things with care. She did them with a kind of intimate knowledge of his needs and

9. An *abdicated king* is one who has given up his throne and the right to rule.

with a scarcely hidden sense of possession which he felt—and resented.

He was by Spearmint out of Camlarge, and the blood flowed arrogantly in arrogant[10] veins.

Mornings came when Camciscan waited for the girl with his ears and with his eyes, because he had learned the sound of her bare feet on the ground that was still unsoftened by any sun, and he could distinguish the tangle of straw-colored hair among other things. But when she was in his stable, he retreated to a far corner and stood watching her work.

He sometimes felt the urge to move closer to her, but the loneliness of which he was so proud never permitted this. Instead, the urge turned often to anger which was, to himself, as unreasonable as the unprovoked anger of another might have been. He did not understand this anger; when it had passed, he would tremble as if he had caught the scent of something evil.

The girl vaulted to his back one morning, as she always did when they went to the hill or the valley, and the anger surged suddenly through his body like a quick pain. He threw her from him so that she fell against the root of a tree and lay there with blood running through the straw-colored hair. Her legs that were too long, like a colt's, did not move even when the white man and the black men carried her away.

Afterward, Camciscan trembled and sweated in his box and let his mistrust of the men who tried to feed him boil into hate. For seven mornings the girl did not return.

When she did return, he moved again to the farthest corner and watched her work, or stood still as death while she lifted his feet, one by one, and cleaned them with a hard tool that never hurt. He was a Thoroughbred stallion and he knew nothing of remorse. He knew that there were things that made him tremble and things that filled him with anger. He did not know, always, what these things were.

He did not know what the thing was that made him tremble on the morning he saw the chestnut filly, or how it happened that there was suddenly a voice in his throat that came to his own ears unfamiliar and distant, startling him. He saw his dignity slip away like a blanket fallen from his back, and pride that had never before deserted him was in an instant shamefully vanished.

He saw the filly, smooth, young, and with a saunter in her pose, standing in an open field, under the care of four black men. Unaccountably, he had been led to this field, and unaccountably he strained against restraint toward this filly.

Camciscan called to her in a tone as unfamiliar to him as it was to her, but there must have been danger in it. It was a new sound that he did not know himself. He went toward her, holding his head high, lifting his clean legs, and the filly broke from the kicking-straps that held her and fled, screaming, in a voice as urgent as his own.

For the first time in his life he would have exchanged the loneliness he lived by for something else, but his willingness had gained him only the humility of rejection and disdain. He could understand this, but not more than this. He returned to his

10. Camciscan's father is named *Spearmint,* and his mother is named *Camlarge; arrogant* means "exaggerating one's own worth or importance in an overbearing manner."

Vocabulary

unprovoked (un′ prə vōkt′) *adj.* not incited or stirred to action (by something)
remorse (ri môrs′) *n.* a deep, painful feeling of guilt or sorrow for wrongdoing
saunter (sôn′ tər) *n.* a slow, relaxed walk; stroll

stable, not trembling. He returned walking with careful steps, each as even as another.

When the girl came as she always did and kneaded the new dead hairs from his bright coat with supple fingers and ran the soft body-brush over him, he turned his head and watched her, accepting the soothing stroke of her hand, but he knew that the old anger was in him again. It had welled up in his heart until now it burst and made him whirl round and catch her slender back with his teeth, biting until the brush dropped from her hand, flinging her bodily against the far wall of the box. She lay there huddled in the trampled bedding for a long time, and he stood over her, trembling, not touching her with any of his feet. He would not touch her. He would have killed any living creature that touched her then, but he did not know why this was so.

After a while the girl moved and then crawled out of the box and he pawed through the bedding to the earthen floor, tossing his head up and down, letting the anger run out of him.

But the girl was there again, in the stable, the next day. She cleaned it as she had cleaned it each other day and her touch on his body was the same, except there was a new firmness in it, and Camciscan knew, without knowing, that his strength, his anger, and his loneliness at last were challenged.

Nothing about the morning ride was different. The black men worked with the other horses and about the stables in their usual positions, with their usual movements. The large tree against which he had thrown the girl was still there making the same little pond of shade, bees criss-crossed the unresisting air like golden bullets, birds sang or just dipped in and out of the sky. Camciscan knew that the morning was slow with peacefulness. But he also knew that this thing would happen; he knew that his anger would come and would be met by the girl's anger.

By then he understood, in his own way, that the girl loved him. Also he understood now why it was that when she had lain hurt in his box, he could not trample her with his hooves, nor allow any other living thing to touch her—and the reason for this frightened him.

They came to a level spot on the green hill and he stopped suddenly with sweat stinging his blood-bay neck and his blood-bay flanks. He stopped because this was the place.

The girl on his back spoke to him, but he did not move. He felt the anger again, and he did not move. For the first time her heels struck against his ribs, sharply, and he was motionless. He felt her hand relax the lines that held his head so that he was almost free. But she did not speak; she rapped him again with her heels, roughly, so that it hurt, and he whirled, baring his teeth, and tried to sink them into her leg.

The girl struck his muzzle with a whip, hard and without mercy, but he was startled by the act more than by the pain. The alchemy[11] of his pride transformed the pain to anger that blinded him. He bit at her again and she struck again making the whip burn against his flesh. He whirled until their world was a cone of yellow dust, but she clung to his back, weightless, and lashed at him in tireless rhythm.

He reared upward, cutting the dust cloud with his hooves. Plunging, he kicked at her legs and felt the thin whip bite at his quarters, time after time, until they glowed with pain.

He knew that his bulk could crush her. He knew that if he reared high enough, he would fall backward, and this terrified him. But he was neither mastered by the girl nor by his

11. *Alchemy* (al′ kə mē) is a power or process that transforms one thing into another.

terror. He reared until the ground fell away before him, and he saw only the sky, through bulging eyes, and inch by inch he went over, feeling the whip on his head, between his ears, against his neck. He began to fall, and the terror returned, and he fell.

When he knew that the girl was not caught under his weight, his anger left him as quickly as the wind had whisked the dust away. This was not reason, but it was so.

He got up, churning the air awkwardly, and the girl stood, watching him, still holding the lines and the whip, her straw-colored hair matted with dust.

She came to him and touched the hurt places on his body and stroked his neck and his throat and the place between his eyes.

In a little time she vaulted again to his back and they went on along the familiar road, slowly, with no sound but the sound of his hooves.

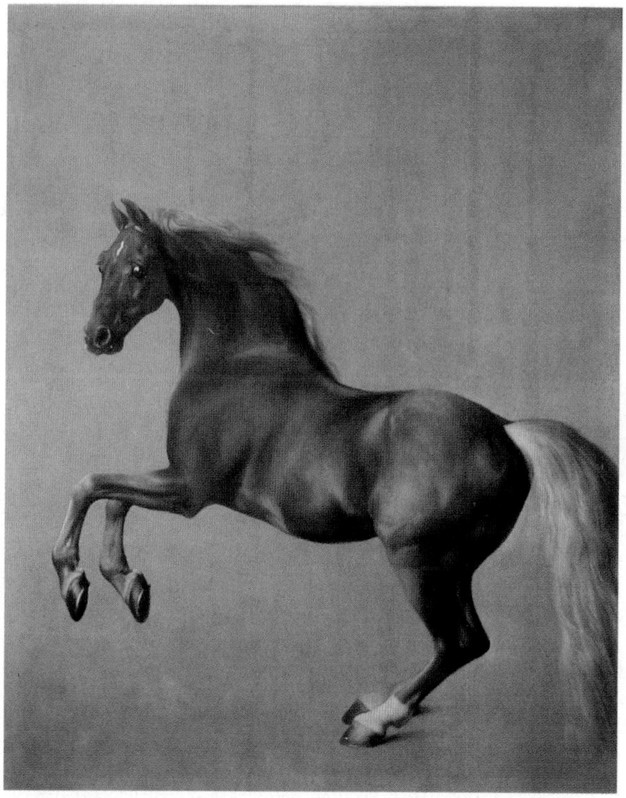

Whistlejacket, 1762. George Stubbs. Oil on canvas. Kenwood House, Hampstead, London.

Viewing the painting: How does this horse compare with Camciscan? How would it feel to approach this horse?

Camciscan remained Camciscan. In relation to himself, nothing changed, nothing was different. If there were horses on the farm that whinnied at the approach of certain men or forsook their peculiar nobility for the common gifts of common creatures, he was not one.

He held a heritage of arrogance, and he cherished it. If he had yielded once to a will as stubborn as his own, even this had left no bruise upon his spirit. The girl had triumphed—but in so small a thing.

He still stood in the far corner of his stable each morning while she worked. Sometimes he still trembled, and once in the late evening when there was a storm outside and a nervous wind, she came and lay down in the clean bedding under his manger. He watched her while there was light, but when that failed, and she must surely have been asleep, he stepped closer, lowering his head a little, breathing warmly through widened nostrils, and sniffed at her.

She did not move, and he did not. For a moment he ruffled her hair with his soft muzzle. And then he lifted his head as high as he had ever held it and stood, with the girl at his feet, all through the storm. It did not seem a strong storm.

When morning came, she got up and looked at him and spoke to him. But he was in the farthest corner, where he always was, staring, not at her, but at the dawn, and at the warm clouds of his breath against the cold.

Responding to Literature

Personal Response

What do you think of the relationship between the girl and the horse?

Analyzing Literature

Recall

1. Who is Camciscan and why does he come to Njoro?
2. How does Camciscan feel about people? What does he like about them, and what does he dislike?
3. What happens to the girl when Camciscan becomes angry on their ride, and on another day, when she is grooming him in the stall?
4. Summarize what happens when Camciscan sees the chestnut filly.
5. How does Camciscan behave in the stable during the storm?

Interpret

6. Why might Camciscan be compared to a "royal exile" and an "abdicated king"?
7. Using details from the text, explain why Camciscan might feel the way he does about people.
8. In your opinion, did Camciscan want to injure the girl? Explain.
9. What impact does Camciscan's meeting with the filly have on him?
10. In your opinion, why did the girl enter Camciscan's stall during the storm and sleep there during the night? On the basis of Camciscan's behavior toward the girl, what do you predict will be their future relationship?

Evaluate and Connect

11. The narrator says that Camciscan is proud of his loneliness. What does this mean? Under what circumstances might anyone–including Camciscan–feel that way?
12. Review your response to the Reading Focus on page 385. Compare and contrast your thoughts and feelings with those of the girl.
13. Do you like Camciscan? Is he a good horse or a bad horse, or is he something in between? Explain your answers.
14. Markham uses **repetition** to describe herself in this selection, often referring to her "straw-colored hair" and "legs like a colt's." Why might she have wanted to emphasize this description of herself, using these words to call attention to her hair and legs?
15. Markham suspects that dogs and horses are "only tolerant" of humans. Does her tale of Camciscan effectively support that idea? Explain.

Literary ELEMENTS

Parallelism

Parallelism is the use of a series of words, phrases, or sentences that have similar grammatical form. Parallelism helps to make writing rhythmic and memorable, thereby heightening its emotional effect. For example, Markham begins this chapter with three prepositional phrases, each beginning with *to:* "To an eagle or to an owl or to a rabbit, man must seem a masterful and yet a forlorn animal. . . ." By structuring her sentence this way, Markham emphasizes the perspective that she imagines these animals share.

1. Review the story and find two other examples of parallelism. Identify what grammatical forms, or parts of speech, are being repeated.
2. Explain the effect of each example of parallelism you find and tell what concept you think Markham was trying to emphasize.

- See **Literary Terms Handbook,** p. R9.

Literature and Writing

Writing About Literature

Analyzing Point of View Why do you think Markham uses **third-person limited point of view** for all but the first six paragraphs of the chapter? Write an analysis, explaining what impact the point of view has on the information Markham is able to convey. For example, what image of herself does Markham communicate in each section of the story? What image do you get of the horse?

Creative Writing

Horse for Sale Imagine that you are Beryl Markham and that your father has told you Camciscan must be sold. Create a magazine advertisement announcing the sale of Camciscan. Your ad copy should emphasize those qualities and characteristics that would appeal to a potential buyer. You may wish to include a painting or drawing of Camciscan to heighten interest.

Extending Your Response

Literature Groups

Analyzing Personalities Compare and contrast the personalities of Camciscan and the girl. What traits, emotions, and types of behavior do the girl and the horse share and not share? What does each learn from–and learn to accept about–the other? Discuss these questions in your group and share your conclusions with the class.

Learning for Life

Letter of Application Beryl Markham became a professional horse trainer at a time when this work was reserved for men. Imagine that you are Beryl Markham and write a letter of application to a thoroughbred horse owner applying for a job as a trainer. State your horse-training qualifications, using your experience with Camciscan as evidence of your skills. Persuade the owner to hire you!

Reading Further

You might like these works by or about Beryl Markham:

Autobiography: *The Splendid Outcast* is based on Markham's childhood in Africa.

Biography: *Beryl Markham: Never Turn Back* is by Catherine Gourley.

Save your work for your portfolio.

Skill Minilesson

VOCABULARY • **Parts of Speech**

Understanding parts of speech is useful in vocabulary study. Some words are spelled and pronounced the same way, whether they are verbs or nouns. For example, *saunter* is both a noun, meaning "a slow, relaxed walk," and a verb, meaning "to walk in a relaxed way." However, most words must be modified, or changed, when they are to be used as different parts of speech. For example, *concede* is a verb; the noun related to it is the word *concession.*

PRACTICE Use your knowledge of the vocabulary words in the selection to figure out the meanings of the underlined words below. For each word, write its part of speech and a synonym or definition.

1. Her message was remorseful.
2. It was a whimsical film.
3. Do not provoke me.
4. They were indulgent parents.

Before You Read

Of Dry Goods and Black Bow Ties

Reading Focus

In your opinion, what does it mean to be successful?

Journal In your journal, write down what accomplishments, personal traits, or possessions might be marks of successfulness.

Setting a Purpose Read to learn about what success and failure mean to an immigrant in the United States.

Building Background

The Time and Place

The selection's main events begin and end in Berkeley, California, sometime after the mid-1940s. The author also recalls events that happened between 1880 and 1929 in Seattle, Portland, and San Francisco.

Did You Know?

- During a few days in October 1929, a panic triggered widespread selling of stocks on the New York Stock Exchange. The result was a drastic drop in the dollar value of investments, which meant lost savings for individuals and ruin for banks and businesses. The Great Crash, as it is called, sparked the beginning of the Depression era, a ten-year period of severe economic hardship.
- Before supermarkets became widespread in the late 1940s and early 1950s, people purchased fabric, clothing, canned or packaged foods, and other nonperishable merchandise in "dry goods" stores.

Vocabulary Preview

expediency (iks pē′ dē ən sē) *n.* a means of achieving a particular goal; the quality of being appropriate to the end in view; p. 396

confidant (kon′ fə dant′) *n.* a person to whom secrets are entrusted; p. 396

imposing (im pō′ zing) *adj.* impressive in appearance or manner; p. 397

exhilarated (ig zil′ ə rāt′ əd) *adj.* cheerful, lively, or excited; p. 398

irreverent (i rev′ ər ənt) *adj.* showing a lack of proper respect; p. 399

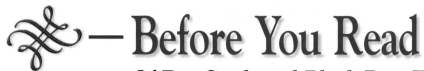

Meet Yoshiko Uchida

"I hope the young people who read [my] books will dare to have big dreams."

Yoshiko Uchida (yō shē′ kō o͞o chē′ dä) was born and raised in California. During World War II, she and her family were among the thousands of Japanese Americans who were imprisoned in "relocation centers," or internment camps. After the war, Uchida became an award-winning author of twenty-eight books. Uchida said she hoped her books would inspire readers not only to appreciate Asian American life and history, but above all, to "celebrate our common humanity."

Yoshiko Uchida was born in 1921 and died in 1992. This essay, based on her own life, was published in 1979.

Of Dry Goods and Black Bow Ties

Yoshiko Uchida

Long after reaching the age of sixty, when my father was persuaded at last to wear a conservative four-in-hand tie,[1] it was not because of his family's urging, but because Mr. Shimada[2] (I shall call him that) had died. Until then, for some forty years, my father had always worn a plain black bow tie, a formality which was required on his first job in America and which he had continued to observe as faithfully as his father before him had worn his samurai[3] sword.

My father came to America in 1906 when he was not yet twenty-one. Sailing from Japan on a small six-thousand-ton ship which was buffeted all the way by rough seas, he landed in Seattle on a bleak January day. He revived himself with the first solid meal he had enjoyed in many days, and then allowed himself one day of rest to restore his sagging spirits. Early on the second morning, wearing a stiff new bowler,[4] he went to see Mr. Shozo Shimada to whom he carried a letter of introduction.

At that time, Shozo Shimada was Seattle's most successful Japanese business man. He owned a chain of dry goods stores which extended not only from Vancouver to Portland, but to cities in Japan as well. He had come to America in 1880, penniless but enterprising, and sought work as a laborer. It wasn't long, however, before he saw the

---

1. A *four-in-hand tie* is a man's necktie that is tied in a slip knot with the ends hanging down vertically.
2. *Shimada* (shē mä′ dä)
3. In feudal Japan, the sword-carrying *samurai* (sam′ oo rī′) were an aristocratic class of warriors who valued honor above life itself.
4. A *bowler* is a hard, round hat with a narrow, curled brim.

futility of trying to compete with American laborers whose bodies were twice his in muscle and bulk. He knew he would never go far as a laborer, but he did possess another skill that could give him a start toward better things. He knew how to sew. It was a matter of expediency over masculine pride. He set aside his shovel, bought a second-hand sewing machine, and hung a dressmaker's sign in his window. He was in business.

In those days, there were some Japanese women in Seattle who had neither homes nor families nor sewing machines, and were delighted to find a friendly Japanese person to do some sewing for them. They flocked to Mr. Shimada with bolts of cloth, elated to discover a dressmaker who could speak their native tongue and, although a male, sew western-styled dresses for them.

Mr. Shimada acquainted himself with the fine points of turning a seam, fitting sleeves, and coping with the slippery folds of satin, and soon the women ordered enough dresses to keep him thriving and able to establish a healthy bank account. He became a trusted friend and confidant to many of them and soon they began to bring him what money they earned for safekeeping.

"Keep our money for us, Shimada-san,"[5] they urged, refusing to go to American banks whose tellers spoke in a language they could not understand.

At first the money accumulated slowly and Mr. Shimada used a pair of old socks as a repository,[6] stuffing them into a far corner of his drawer beneath his union suits.[7] But after a time, Mr. Shimada's private bank began to overflow and he soon found it necessary to replenish his supply of socks.

He went to a small dry goods store downtown, and as he glanced about at the buttons, threads, needles and laces, it occurred to him that he owed it to the women to invest their savings in a business venture with more future than the dark recesses of his bureau drawer. That night he called a group of them together.

"Think, ladies," he began. "What are the two basic needs of the Japanese living in Seattle? Clothes to wear and food to eat," he answered himself. "Is that not right? Every man must buy a shirt to put on his back and pickles and rice for his stomach."

The women marveled at Mr. Shimada's cleverness as he spread before them his fine plans for a Japanese dry goods store that would not only carry everything available in an American dry goods store, but Japanese foodstuff as well. That was the beginning of the first Shimada Dry Goods Store on State Street.

By the time my father appeared, Mr. Shimada had long since abandoned his sewing machine and was well on his way to becoming a business tycoon.[8] Although he had opened cautiously with such stock items as ginghams, flannel, handkerchiefs, socks, shirts, overalls, umbrellas, and ladies' silk and cotton stockings, he now carried tins of salt, rice crackers, bottles of soy sauce, vinegar, ginger root, fish-paste cakes, bean paste, Japanese pickles, dried mushrooms, salt fish,

5. According to Japanese custom, the suffix *-san* (sän) is added after a person's name to express respect.
6. A *repository* is a place or object in which something may be stored for safekeeping.
7. One-piece undergarments that combine shirt with long pants are called *union suits.*
8. A *tycoon* is a wealthy, powerful businessman.

Vocabulary

expediency (iks pē′ dē ən sē) *n.* a means of achieving a particular goal; the quality of being appropriate to the end in view

confidant (kon′ fə dant′) *n.* a person to whom secrets are entrusted

Viewing the photograph: How might this 1903 dry goods store in Sacramento, California, compare with Mr. Shimada's store?

red beans, and just about every item of canned food that could be shipped from Japan. In addition, his was the first Japanese store to install a U.S. Post Office Station, and he therefore flew an American flag in front of the large sign that bore the name of his shop.

When my father first saw the big American flag fluttering in front of Mr. Shimada's shop, he was overcome with admiration and awe. He expected that Mr. Shozo Shimada would be the finest of Americanized Japanese gentlemen, and when he met him, he was not disappointed.

Although Mr. Shimada was not very tall, he gave the illusion of height because of his erect carriage. He wore a spotless black alpaca[9] suit, an immaculate[10] white shirt, and a white collar so stiff it might have overcome a lesser man. He also wore a black bow tie, black shoes that buttoned up the side and a gold watch whose thick chain looped grandly on his vest. He was probably in his fifties then, a ruddy-faced man whose hair, already turning white, was parted carefully in the center. He was an imposing figure to confront a young man fresh from Japan with scarcely a future to look forward to. My father bowed, summoned as much dignity as he could muster, and presented the letter of introduction he carried to him.

Mr. Shimada was quick to sense his need. "Do you know anything about bookkeeping?" he inquired.

"I intend to go to night school to learn this very skill," my father answered.

Mr. Shimada could assess a man's qualities in a very few minutes. He looked my father straight in the eye and said, "Consider yourself hired." Then he added, "I have a few basic rules. My employees must at all times wear a clean white shirt and a black bow tie. They must answer the telephone promptly with the

9. *Alpaca* (al pak′ ə) is the fleece of the alpaca, a South American mammal related to the llama.
10. *Immaculate* (i mak′ yə lit) means "perfectly clean; spotless."

Vocabulary
imposing (im pō′ zing) *adj.* impressive in appearance or manner

words, 'Good morning or good afternoon, Shimada's Dry Goods,' and they must always treat each customer with respect. It never hurts to be polite," he said thoughtfully. "One never knows when one might be indebted to even the lowliest of beggars."

My father was impressed with these modest words from a man of such success. He accepted them with a sense of mission and from that day was committed to white shirts and black bow ties, and treated every customer, no matter how humble, with respect and courtesy. When, in later years, he had his own home, he never failed to answer the phone before it could ring twice if at all possible.

My father worked with Mr. Shimada for ten years, becoming first the buyer for his Seattle store and later, manager of the Portland branch. During this time Mr. Shimada continued on a course of exhilarated expansion. He established two Japanese banks in Seattle, bought a fifteen-room house outside the dreary confines of the Japanese community and dressed his wife and daughter in velvets and ostrich feathers. When his daughter became eighteen, he sent her to study in Paris, and the party he gave on the eve of her departure, with musicians, as well as caterers to serve roast turkey, venison, baked ham and champagne, seemed to verify rumors that he had become one of the first Japanese millionaires of America.

In spite of his phenomenal success, however, Mr. Shimada never forgot his early friends nor lost any of his generosity, and this, ironically enough, was his undoing. Many of the women for whom he had once sewn dresses were now well established, and they came to him requesting loans with which they and their husbands might open grocery stores and laundries and shoe repair shops. Mr. Shimada helped them all and never demanded any collateral.[11] He operated his banks on faith and trust and gave no thought to such common prudence as maintaining a reserve.[12]

When my father was called to a new position with a large Japanese firm in San Francisco, Mr. Shimada came down to Portland to extend personally his good wishes. He took Father to a Chinese dinner and told him over the peanut duck and chow mein that he would like always to be considered a friend.

"If I can ever be of assistance to you," he said, "don't ever hesitate to call." And with a firm shake of the hand, he wished my father well.

That was in 1916. My father wrote regularly to Mr. Shimada telling him of his new job, of his bride, and later, of his two children. Mr. Shimada did not write often, but each Christmas he sent a box of Oregon apples and pears, and at New Year's a slab of heavy white rice paste from his Seattle shop.

In 1929 the letters and gifts stopped coming and Father learned from friends in Seattle that both of Mr. Shimada's banks had failed. He immediately dispatched a letter to Mr. Shimada, but it was returned unopened. The next news he had was that Mr. Shimada had had to sell all of his shops. My father was now manager of the San Francisco branch of his firm. He wrote once more asking Mr. Shimada if there was anything he could do to help. The letter did not come back, but there was no reply, and my father did not write again. After all, how do you offer help to the head of a fallen empire?

11. A moneylender sometimes requires a borrower to provide *collateral:* something of equivalent value offered or promised as proof that a loan will be repaid.
12. A bank maintains a *reserve* of uninvested funds to meet possible demands or emergencies (such as a drop in the value of its invested funds).

Vocabulary
exhilarated (ig zil′ ə rāt′ əd) *adj.* cheerful, lively, or excited

Did You Know?
A *morning coat* is a man's jacket for formal daytime wear, traditionally worn with striped trousers and a top hat.

It seemed almost irreverent.

It was many years later that Mr. Shimada appeared one night at our home in Berkeley. In the dim light of the front porch my mother was startled to see an elderly gentleman wearing striped pants, a morning coat, and a shabby black hat. In his hand he carried a small black satchel. When she invited him inside, she saw that the morning coat was faded, and his shoes badly in need of a shine.

"I am Shimada," he announced with a courtly bow, and it was my mother who felt inadequate to the occasion. She hurriedly pulled off her apron and went to call my father. When he heard who was in the living room, he put on his coat and tie before going out to greet his old friend.

Mr. Shimada spoke to them about Father's friends in Seattle and about his daughter who was now married and living in Denver. He spoke of a typhoon that had recently swept over Japan, and he drank the tea my mother served and ate a piece of her chocolate cake. Only then did he open his black satchel.

"I thought your girls might enjoy these books," he said, as he drew out a brochure describing *The Book of Knowledge*.

"Fourteen volumes that will tell them of the wonders of this world." He spread his arms in a magnificent gesture that recalled his eloquence of the past. "I wish I could give them to your children as a personal gift," he added softly.

Without asking the price of the set, my father wrote a check for one hundred dollars and gave it Mr. Shimada.

Mr. Shimada glanced at the check and said, "You have given me fifty dollars too much." He seemed troubled for only a moment, however, and quickly added, "Ah, the balance is for a deposit, is it? Very well, yours will be the first deposit in my next bank."

"Is your home still in Seattle then?" Father asked cautiously.

"I am living there, yes," Mr. Shimada answered.

And then, suddenly overcome with memories of the past, he spoke in a voice so low he could scarcely be heard.

"I paid back every cent," he murmured. "It took ten years, but I paid it back. All of it. I owe nothing."

"You are a true gentleman, Shimada-san," Father said. "You always will be." Then he pointed to the black tie he wore, saying, "You see, I am still one of the Shimada men."

That was the last time my father saw Shozo Shimada. Some time later he heard that he had returned to Japan as penniless as the day he set out for America.

It wasn't until the Christmas after we heard of Mr. Shimada's death that I ventured to give my father a silk four-in-hand tie. It was charcoal gray and flecked with threads of silver. My father looked at it for a long time before he tried it on, and then fingering it gently, he said, "Well, perhaps it is time now that I put away my black bow ties."

Vocabulary
irreverent (i rev′ ər ənt) *adj.* showing a lack of proper respect

Responding to Literature

Personal Response

In your journal, describe your reaction to what happened to Mr. Shimada.

Analyzing Literature

Recall

1. What skill enabled Mr. Shimada to establish himself in business?
2. Why were the Japanese Americans in Mr. Shimada's neighborhood so eager to entrust him with their savings?
3. Summarize what happened to Mr. Shimada and his businesses after the stock market crashed.
4. Compare Mr. Shimada's appearance in his dry goods store and on his visit to the author's father in Berkeley.
5. When did the author's father decide that it was time to put away his black bow ties?

Interpret

6. In your opinion, why might Mr. Shimada have considered his first business plan to be "a matter of expediency over masculine pride"?
7. When Mr. Shimada invests his customers' money in a dry goods store, do you think he is being generous or selfish? Explain.
8. Why does Mr. Shimada's generosity prove to be his "undoing"?
9. Early on, Mr. Shimada states, "One never knows when one might be indebted to even the lowliest of beggars." How is this an example of **foreshadowing?** (See Literary Terms Handbook, page R6.)
10. Why might the author's father have continued to wear black bow ties even after he no longer worked for Mr. Shimada?

Evaluate and Connect

11. "I paid back every cent," [Mr. Shimada] murmured. . . . I owe nothing." Do you think people today are as careful about paying their debts? Why or why not?
12. Would you want to work for a boss like Mr. Shimada? Explain.
13. Which personality trait do you think is more important to Mr. Shimada, generosity or pride? Explain your answer.
14. In your opinion, was Mr. Shimada a clever or a naive businessman? Use evidence from the story to support your answer.
15. What might black bow ties have **symbolized** to Mr. Shimada? By comparison, what does a necktie symbolize to you–at work, at school, and in other situations? (See Literary Terms Handbook, page R12.)

Literary ELEMENTS

Title

The **title,** or name, of a work of literature is sometimes linked to the work's central theme or to the traits of a major character. The link may be subtle or obvious. Often, writers attempt to select for their titles catchy, intriguing words and phrases to spark their readers' curiosity and interest.

1. In your opinion, why did Uchida give her essay the title "Of Dry Goods and Black Bow Ties"?
2. Do you think the title is effective? Explain.
3. If Uchida had invited you to think of a good title for this selection, what would you have suggested?

- See **Literary Terms Handbook,** p. R13.

Literary Criticism

According to one critic, many of Uchida's books "reflect her interests not only in Japan but also in her Japanese American heritage." With your classmates, discuss what can be learned from this story about Japanese American culture during the early 1900s.

Literature and Writing

Writing About Literature

A Summary Most of this selection focuses upon the experiences of Mr. Shimada. However, it also conveys information about Uchida's father and about what life was like for Japanese immigrants to the United States near the turn of the nineteenth century. Write a few paragraphs summarizing what you have learned about these topics. Be sure to include specific references to the selection.

Personal Writing

You're the Boss Mr. Shimada had definite rules that he expected his employees to follow. Imagine that you have a customer-oriented business. What rules would you expect your employees to follow? Write them in your notebook. After each rule, add a brief explanation of why you think the rule is important. Read your rules to some classmates, and invite them to guess your reasons.

Extending Your Response

Literature Groups

Examining a Paradox A **paradox** is an idea that includes two parts, both of which are true but seem to contradict each other (see Literary Terms Handbook, page R9). With your group, discuss these paradoxes regarding Mr. Shimada:

- He appeared to be tall, but he was not very tall.
- He was a success and a failure.

You may wish to review the selection and your response to the Reading Focus on page 394 before discussing each paradox. Then, identify facts that support the "truth" within each paradox and vote on which part of the paradox seems more true than the other. Share the results of your vote with the class.

Interdisciplinary Activity

Mathematics: Graphing Life Events How would you plot the events in the lives of the author's father and Mr. Shimada on a graph? First, decide what shape might best represent each man's life. For example, might life be represented by a zigzag line, with many ups and downs? Is a straight timeline appropriate? Would a circle work to represent one man's life? Could you create a bar graph to compare time periods in each man's life? Work with a partner to make a chronological list of important events and periods in each man's life. Then plot those events on a circle graph, line graph, timeline, bar graph, or another type of graphic aid.

Learning for Life

Spend and Save Suppose that you are a copywriter hired by Mr. Shimada to write an advertisement that encourages customers to shop at his stores and invest at his banks. Ask yourself: What information might persuade potential customers of Mr. Shimada to buy his goods and trust his banks? As you plan and write, remember that while advertisements may "stretch" the truth to persuade people to buy or invest, they must also communicate respect for the business and for the customer.

Reading Further

If you'd like to read more by Yoshiko Uchida, you might enjoy these works:

Memoir: *The Invisible Thread,* a compelling personal memoir about Uchida's experiences at Topaz, a Japanese internment camp in the Utah desert, during World War II.

Fiction: *Journey to Topaz,* a novel about the evacuation of a Japanese American family from their home in California after the attack on Pearl Harbor.

Folktales: *The Sea of Gold and Other Tales from Japan,* traditional Japanese tales adapted by Uchida.

Save your work for your portfolio.

Skill Minilessons

GRAMMAR AND LANGUAGE • Who vs. Whom

The pronoun *who* is used as the subject of a question *(**Who** is at the door?)* or as the subject of a dependent clause *(I see **who** is at the door.)* The pronoun *whom* is used as the object of the verb in a question *(**Whom** did Mr. Shimada hire?)*, the object of a verb in a dependent clause *(Mr. Shimada, **whom** I admired, was a great man)*, or as the object of a preposition *(For **whom** did you make this gift?)*.

PRACTICE On your paper, write the pronoun that correctly completes each sentence.

1. It was Mr. Shimada (who, whom) hired my father.
2. I know the women for (who, whom) he made clothes.
3. (Who, Whom) did Father recommend?
4. (Who, Whom) dropped by in a shabby coat?
5. From (who, whom) did Mr. Shimada request a loan?

For more about using *who* and *whom,* see **Language Handbook,** p. R36.

READING AND THINKING • Analyzing Details

Writers often give hints about a person or character by using vivid details and precise adjectives to describe the individual's actions, words, and physical appearance. Readers may then draw conclusions about the individual's personality or values on the basis of those details. This sentence from the selection describes Mr. Shimada's appearance.

He wore a spotless black alpaca suit, an immaculate white shirt, and a white collar so stiff it might have overcome a lesser man.

From this you may conclude that Mr. Shimada was a proud man who paid careful attention to his attire.

PRACTICE In the selection, find examples of sentences rich with descriptive details from which a reader can draw conclusions. Draw a conclusion from each one. Challenge a partner to find evidence to support each of your conclusions.

For more about related comprehension skills, see **Reading Handbook,** pp. R82–R94.

VOCABULARY • Synonyms

A **synonym** is a word that shares the same or almost the same definition of another word. For example, since one definition of *irony* is "something that is the opposite of what is expected," the words *unexpectedly* and *ironically* may be considered synonyms. But remember that synonyms may also have different shades of meaning. For example, *ironic* events are always unexpected, but not all *unexpected* events are ironic. If you are walking on the sidewalk, and a flowerpot falls on your head, that event occurs *unexpectedly* but not *ironically.* But if you are walking on the sidewalk close to the building because it seems safest there, then the flowerpot's descent onto your head does occur *ironically.*

PRACTICE Each pair of synonyms below includes a vocabulary word from "Of Dry Goods and Black Bow Ties." Briefly explain how each vocabulary word differs in meaning from its given synonym. Use a dictionary as necessary.

1. imposing; big
2. confidant; buddy
3. exhilarated; merry
4. irreverent; rude
5. expedient; appropriate

INTERDISCIPLINARY COMMUNICATIONS CONNECTION

Body Language Across Cultures

In "Of Dry Goods and Black Bow Ties," Yoshiko Uchida writes that her father and Mr. Shimada bow when they meet. If these men were fully "Americanized," they might shake hands instead. People from different cultures use different *body language*—or gestures, postures, facial expressions, and eye contact—to communicate nonverbally. Understanding the body language of other cultures can prevent a great deal of misunderstanding.

For example, crossing the legs so that the sole of one shoe faces another person is an insult in Saudi Arabia. The sole is considered the lowest part of the body because it steps in dirt.

Also, different cultures have different customs regarding touching and eye contact. In some Middle Eastern countries, males often hold hands while walking along the street, but any public display of affection between males and females is considered unacceptable. When they greet each other, Middle Eastern men may embrace and kiss cheeks as well as shake hands. In conversation, they maintain strong eye contact. Just the opposite is true in Japan, where physical contact is generally avoided and looking into another's eyes for a long time is considered rude.

Therefore, a man visiting Saudi Arabia should not be surprised if his host takes his hand to guide him down a street. Nor should he be offended in Japan if an acquaintance fails to maintain eye contact in a conversation.

Different cultures also have different ideas about personal space. In normal social situations, people in the United States stand about an arm's length apart while conversing. The Japanese keep farther apart, while Latin Americans and Middle Easterners stand much closer together—almost toe-to-toe. In fact, Latin Americans describe the behavior of an American and a Latin American conversing as the "conversational tango." The American, startled by the Latin American's practice of standing close to speak, steps backward. The Latin American moves closer. The American steps backward . . . and on it goes, until the American is backed into a corner.

Learning about body language is useful both in travel and in international relations. And in a multicultural society like that of the United States, it can also be helpful in everyday life.

Activity

Plan a trip to a country of your choice and research the customs and taboos of body language in that culture. Look in guidebooks for tourists and business travelers to find this information. Prepare a list of tips for travelers to the country and present your findings to the class.

Before You Read

A Christmas Memory

Reading Focus

What personal qualities do you value in a best friend?

List and Rate Ideas Jot down the qualities you value. Then rate each one by assigning it a number, with number one being the most important.

Setting a Purpose Read to find out about an unusual best friend the author had as a child.

Building Background

The Time and Place

The author recalls a Christmas season in rural Alabama in the early 1930s.

Did You Know?

- Many homes in rural areas did not yet have electricity or indoor plumbing in the early 1930s. Some homes were still heated by fireplaces and lit by candles and oil lanterns, and cooking was done on large wood- or coal-burning stoves or on gas ranges.
- Long a traditional Christmas dessert, fruitcake is a heavy cake made with candied or dried fruits, nuts, spices, and often a liquor, such as whiskey, sherry, or rum. Fruitcakes may be made three to four weeks before the holidays, which allows time for the flavors to blend and mellow.

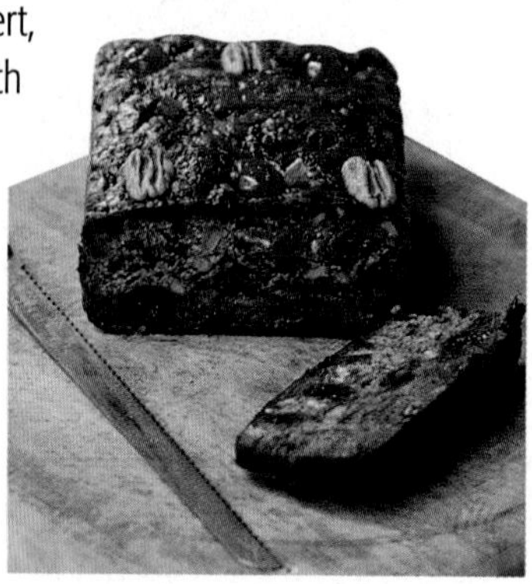

Vocabulary Preview

inaugurate (in ô′ gyə rāt′) *v.* to make a formal beginning; p. 406
conspiracy (kən spir′ ə sē) *n.* the act of secretly planning together; p. 408
potent (pōt′ ənt) *adj.* having or exercising force, power, authority, or effectiveness; strong and powerful; p. 410
muse (mūz) *v.* to think or reflect, especially in an idle, dreamy manner; p. 411
cavort (kə vôrt′) *v.* to run and jump around playfully; p. 414

Meet Truman Capote

When Truman Capote published his first novel before he was twenty-five, critics expressed amazement that anyone so young could write so well. During a lonely and difficult childhood, Capote spent many hours writing stories. He won his first literary prize at age ten. For part of his childhood, Capote lived in rural Alabama with a family of adult cousins. Miss Sook Faulk, a cousin who was already in her sixties, became his closest childhood friend. In 1967 Capote won an Emmy Award for his television adaptation of "A Christmas Memory," which was inspired by Sook Faulk.

Truman Capote was born in New Orleans in 1924 and died in 1984. This memoir was first published in 1956.

A Christmas Memory

Truman Capote

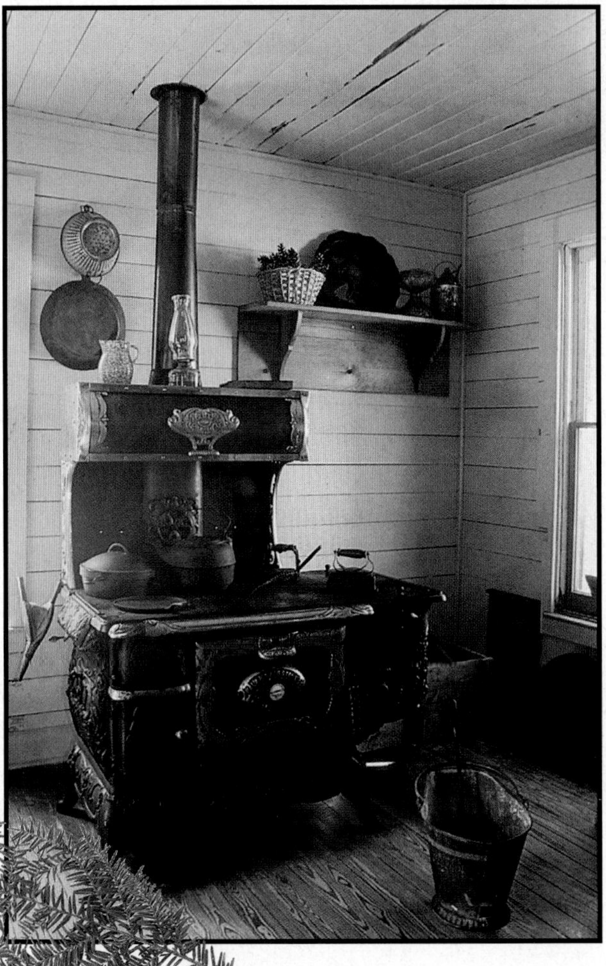

Imagine a morning in late November. A coming of winter morning more than twenty years ago. Consider the kitchen of a spreading old house in a country town. A great black stove is its main feature; but there is also a big round table and a fireplace with two rocking chairs placed in front of it. Just today the fireplace commenced its seasonal roar.

A woman with shorn white hair is standing at the kitchen window. She is wearing tennis shoes and a shapeless gray sweater over a summery calico dress. She is small and sprightly, like a bantam hen; but, due to a long youthful illness, her shoulders are pitifully hunched. Her face is remarkable—not unlike Lincoln's, craggy like that, and tinted by sun and wind; but it is delicate too, finely boned, and her eyes are sherry-colored and timid. "Oh my," she exclaims, her breath smoking the windowpane, "it's fruitcake weather!"

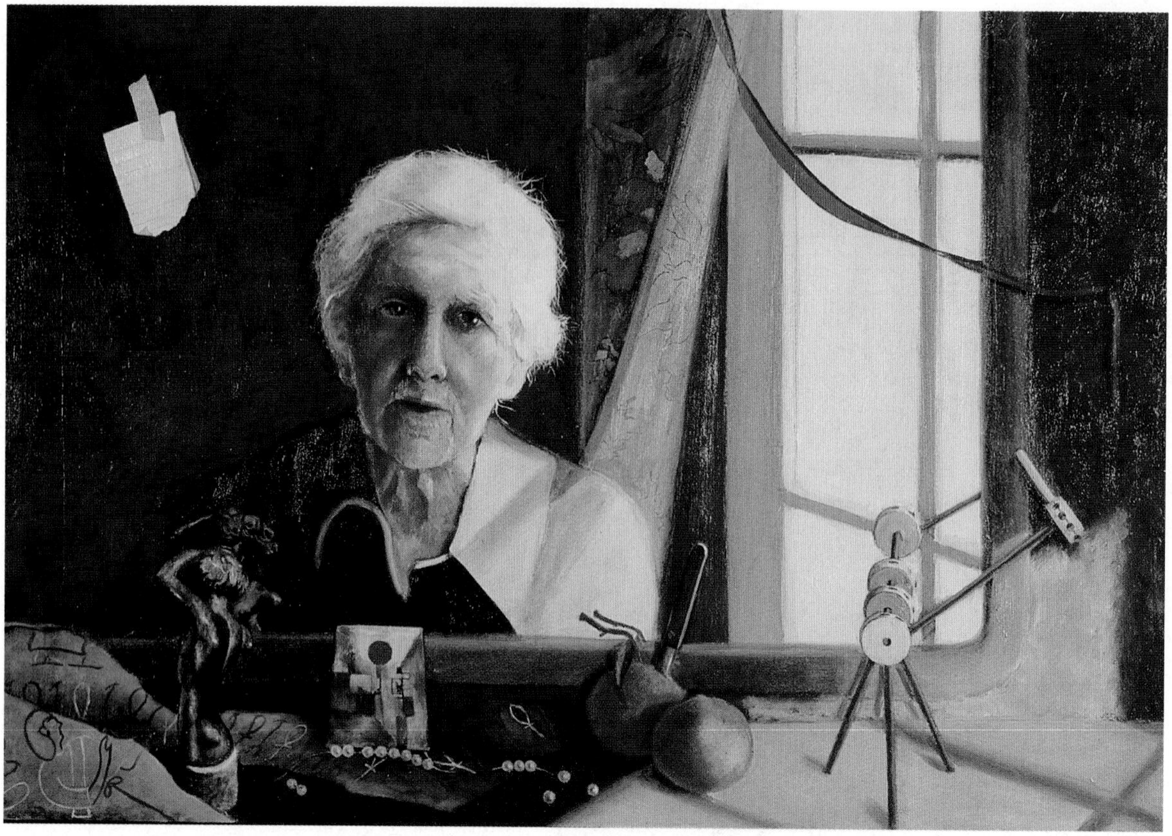

Apostrophe, 1989. G. G. Kopilak. Oil on canvas, 24 x 36 in. Private collection.
Viewing the painting: What might this woman have in common with Buddy's friend?

The person to whom she is speaking is myself. I am seven; she is sixty-something. We are cousins, very distant ones, and we have lived together—well, as long as I can remember. Other people inhabit the house, relatives; and though they have power over us, and frequently make us cry, we are not, on the whole, too much aware of them. We are each other's best friend. She calls me Buddy, in memory of a boy who was formerly her best friend. The other Buddy died in the 1880s, when she was still a child. She is still a child.

"I knew it before I got out of bed," she says, turning away from the window with a purposeful excitement in her eyes. "The courthouse bell sounded so cold and clear. And there were no birds singing; they've gone to warmer country, yes indeed. Oh, Buddy, stop stuffing biscuit and fetch our buggy. Help me find my hat. We've thirty cakes to bake."

It's always the same: a morning arrives in November, and my friend, as though officially inaugurating the Christmas time of year that exhilarates her imagination and fuels the blaze of her heart, announces: "It's fruitcake weather! Fetch our buggy. Help me find my hat."

The hat is found, a straw cartwheel corsaged with velvet roses out-of-doors has faded: it once belonged to a more fashionable relative. Together, we guide our buggy, a

Vocabulary
inaugurate (in ô′ gyə rāt′) *v.* to make a formal beginning

dilapidated baby carriage, out to the garden and into a grove of pecan trees. The buggy is mine; that is, it was bought for me when I was born. It is made of wicker, rather unraveled, and the wheels wobble like a drunkard's legs. But it is a faithful object; springtimes, we take it to the woods and fill it with flowers, herbs, wild fern for our porch pots; in the summer, we pile it with picnic paraphernalia[1] and sugar-cane fishing poles and roll it down to the edge of a creek; it has its winter uses, too: as a truck for hauling firewood from the yard to the kitchen, as a warm bed for Queenie, our tough little orange and white rat terrier who has survived distemper[2] and two rattlesnake bites. Queenie is trotting beside it now.

Three hours later we are back in the kitchen hulling a heaping buggyload of windfall pecans. Our backs hurt from gathering them: how hard they were to find (the main crop having been shaken off the trees and sold by the orchard's owners, who are not us) among the concealing leaves, the frosted, deceiving grass. Caarackle! A cheery crunch, scraps of miniature thunder sound as the shells collapse and the golden mound of sweet oily ivory meat mounts in the milk-glass bowl. Queenie begs to taste, and now and again my friend sneaks her a mite, though insisting we deprive ourselves. "We mustn't, Buddy. If we start, we won't stop. And there's scarcely enough as there is. For thirty cakes." The kitchen is growing dark. Dusk turns the window into a mirror: our reflections mingle with the rising moon as we work by the fireside in the firelight. At last, when the moon is quite high, we toss the final hull into the fire and, with joined sighs, watch it catch flame. The buggy is empty, the bowl is brimful.

We eat our supper (cold biscuits, bacon, blackberry jam) and discuss tomorrow. Tomorrow the kind of work I like best begins: buying. Cherries and citron, ginger and vanilla and canned Hawaiian pineapple, rinds and raisins and walnuts and whiskey and oh, so much flour, butter, so many eggs, spices, flavorings: why, we'll need a pony to pull the buggy home.

Did You Know?
Citron is a large, thick-skinned, lemonlike fruit.

But before these purchases can be made, there is the question of money. Neither of us has any. Except for skinflint sums[3] persons in the house occasionally provide (a dime is considered very big money); or what we earn ourselves from various activities: holding rummage sales, selling buckets of hand-picked blackberries, jars of home-made jam and apple jelly and peach preserves, rounding up flowers for funerals and weddings. Once we won seventy-ninth prize, five dollars, in a national football contest. Not that we know a fool thing about football. It's just that we enter any contest we hear about: at the moment our hopes are centered on the fifty-thousand-dollar Grand Prize being offered to name a new brand of coffee (we suggested "A.M."; and, after some hesitation, for my friend thought it perhaps sacrilegious,[4] the slogan "A.M.! Amen!"). To tell the truth, our only *really* profitable enterprise was the Fun and Freak Museum we conducted in a back-yard woodshed two summers ago. The Fun

1. *Paraphernalia* (par′ ə fər nāl′ yə) means "equipment," or "things used in a particular activity."
2. Dogs (and some other mammals) can contract *distemper,* a highly contagious and sometimes fatal disease caused by a virus.
3. The relatives are stingy and miserly when they give only *skinflint sums.*
4. *Sacrilegious* (sak′ rə lij′ əs) means "showing disrespect for something sacred or cherished."

Did You Know?
A device that projects two images, either overlapping or in quick succession so that one fades into the other, is a *stereopticon* (ster′ ē op′ ti kən).

was a stereopticon with slide views of Washington and New York lent us by a relative who had been to those places (she was furious when she discovered why we'd borrowed it); the Freak was a three-legged biddy chicken hatched by one of our own hens. Everybody hereabouts wanted to see that biddy: we charged grownups a nickel, kids two cents. And took in a good twenty dollars before the museum shut down due to the decease[5] of the main attraction.

But one way and another we do each year accumulate Christmas savings, a Fruitcake Fund. These moneys we keep hidden in an ancient bead purse under a loose board under the floor under a chamber pot[6] under my friend's bed. The purse is seldom removed from this safe location except to make a deposit, or, as happens every Saturday, a withdrawal; for on Saturdays I am allowed ten cents to go to the picture show. My friend has never been to a picture show, nor does she intend to: "I'd rather hear you tell the story, Buddy. That way I can imagine it more. Besides, a person my age shouldn't squander their eyes. When the Lord comes, let me see Him clear." In addition to never having seen a movie, she has never: eaten in a restaurant, traveled more than five miles from home, received or sent a telegram, read anything except funny papers and the Bible, worn cosmetics, cursed, wished someone harm, told a lie on purpose, let a hungry dog go hungry. Here are a few things she has done, does do: killed with a hoe the biggest rattlesnake ever seen in this county (sixteen rattles), dip snuff (secretly), tame hummingbirds (just try it) till they balance on her finger, tell ghost stories (we both believe in ghosts) so tingling they chill you in July, talk to herself, take walks in the rain, grow the prettiest japonicas in town, know the recipe for every sort of old-time Indian cure, including a magical wart-remover.

Did You Know?
Japonicas (jə pon′ i kəz) are shrubs in the rose family, bearing bright red, pink, or white flowers.

Now, with supper finished, we retire to the room in a faraway part of the house where my friend sleeps in a scrap-quilt-covered iron bed painted rose pink, her favorite color. Silently, wallowing in the pleasures of conspiracy, we take the bead purse from its secret place and spill its contents on the scrap quilt. Dollar bills, tightly rolled and green as May buds. Somber fifty-cent pieces, heavy enough to weight a dead man's eyes.[7] Lovely dimes, the liveliest coin, the one that really jingles. Nickels and quarters, worn smooth as creek pebbles. But mostly a hateful heap of bitter-odored pennies. Last summer others in the house contracted to pay us a penny for every twenty-five flies we killed. Oh, the carnage[8] of August: the flies that flew to heaven! Yet it was not work in which we took pride. And, as we sit counting pennies, it is as though we were back tabulating dead flies. Neither of us has a head for

5. *Decease* means "death."
6. A *chamber pot* is a portable container used as a toilet.
7. The phrase *heavy enough to weight a dead man's eyes* refers to the custom of placing coins on the eyelids of a corpse to keep them closed.
8. *Carnage* is a great and bloody slaughter.

Vocabulary
conspiracy (kən spir′ ə sē) *n.* the act of secretly planning together

figures; we count slowly, lose track, start again. According to her calculations, we have $12.73. According to mine, exactly $13. "I do hope you're wrong, Buddy. We can't mess around with thirteen. The cakes will fall. Or put somebody in the cemetery. Why, I wouldn't dream of getting out of bed on the thirteenth." This is true: she always spends thirteenths in bed. So, to be on the safe side, we subtract a penny and toss it out the window.

Of the ingredients that go into our fruitcakes, whiskey is the most expensive, as well as the hardest to obtain: State laws forbid its sale.[9] But everybody knows you can buy a bottle from Mr. Haha Jones. And the next day, having completed our more prosaic[10] shopping, we set out for Mr. Haha's business address, a "sinful" (to quote public opinion) fish-fry and dancing café down by the river. We've been there before, and on the same errand; but in previous years our dealings have been with Haha's wife, an iodine-dark Indian woman with brassy peroxided hair and a dead-tired disposition. Actually, we've never laid eyes on her husband, though we've heard that he's an Indian too. A giant with razor scars across his cheeks. They call him Haha because he's so gloomy, a man who never laughs. As we approach his café (a large log cabin festooned inside and out with chains of garish-gay[11] naked light bulbs and standing by the river's muddy edge under the shade of river trees where moss drifts through the branches like gray mist) our steps slow down. Even Queenie stops prancing and sticks close by. People have been murdered in Haha's café. Cut to pieces. Hit on the head. There's a case coming up in court next month. Naturally these goings-on happen at night when the colored lights cast crazy patterns and the Victrola wails. In the daytime Haha's is shabby and deserted. I knock at the door, Queenie barks, my friend calls: "Mrs. Haha, ma'am? Anyone to home?"

Footsteps. The door opens. Our hearts overturn. It's Mr. Haha Jones himself! And he *is* a giant; he *does* have scars; he *doesn't* smile. No, he glowers at us through Satan-tilted eyes and demands to know: "What you want with Haha?"

For a moment we are too paralyzed to tell. Presently my friend half-finds her voice, a whispery voice at best: "If you please, Mr. Haha, we'd like a quart of your finest whiskey."

His eyes tilt more. Would you believe it? Haha is smiling! Laughing, too. "Which one of you is a drinkin' man?"

"It's for making fruitcakes, Mr. Haha. Cooking."

This sobers him. He frowns. "That's no way to waste good whiskey." Nevertheless, he retreats into the shadowed café and seconds later appears carrying a bottle of daisy-yellow unlabeled liquor. He demonstrates its sparkle in the sunlight and says: "Two dollars."

We pay him with nickels and dimes and pennies. Suddenly, jangling the coins in his hand like a fistful of dice, his face softens. "Tell you what," he proposes, pouring the money back into our bead purse, "just send me one of them fruitcakes instead."

"Well," my friend remarks on our way home, "there's a lovely man. We'll put an extra cup of raisins in *his* cake."

The black stove, stoked with coal and firewood, glows like a lighted pumpkin. Eggbeaters whirl, spoons spin round in bowls of butter and sugar, vanilla sweetens the air, ginger

Did You Know?
Victrola is the trademark name of an early record player.

9. *[State laws forbid its sale.]* From 1920 to 1933, federal law prohibited the manufacture, sale, and consumption of alcoholic beverages.
10. *Prosaic* (prō zā′ ik) means "ordinary" or "commonplace."
11. To be *festooned* is to have decorations that hang in loops or curves. Here, the *garish-gay* lights are bright and gaudy.

spices it; melting, nose-tingling odors saturate the kitchen, suffuse the house, drift out to the world on puffs of chimney smoke. In four days our work is done. Thirty-one cakes, dampened with whiskey, bask on window sills and shelves.

Who are they for?

Friends. Not necessarily neighbor friends: indeed, the larger share is intended for persons we've met maybe once, perhaps not at all. People who've struck our fancy. Like President Roosevelt. Like the Reverend and Mrs. J. C. Lucey, Baptist missionaries to Borneo who lectured here last winter. Or the little knife grinder who comes through town twice a year. Or Abner Packer, the driver of the six o'clock bus from Mobile, who exchanges waves with us every day as he passes in a dust-cloud whoosh. Or the young Wistons, a California couple whose car one afternoon broke down outside the house and who spent a pleasant hour chatting with us on the porch (young Mr. Wiston snapped our picture, the only one we've ever had taken). Is it because my friend is shy with everyone *except* strangers that these strangers, and merest acquaintances, seem to us our truest friends? I think yes. Also, the scrapbooks we keep of thank-you's on White House stationery, time-to-time communications from California and Borneo, the knife grinder's penny post cards, make us feel connected to eventful worlds beyond the kitchen with its view of a sky that stops.

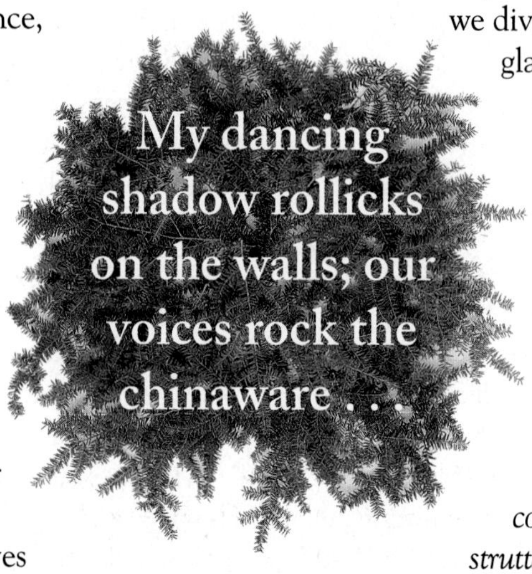
My dancing shadow rollicks on the walls; our voices rock the chinaware . . .

Now a nude December fig branch grates against the window. The kitchen is empty, the cakes are gone; yesterday we carted the last of them to the post office, where the cost of stamps turned our purse inside out. We're broke. That rather depresses me, but my friend insists on celebrating—with two inches of whiskey left in Haha's bottle. Queenie has a spoonful in a bowl of coffee (she likes her coffee chicory-flavored and strong). The rest we divide between a pair of jelly glasses. We're both quite awed at the prospect of drinking straight whiskey; the taste of it brings screwed-up expressions and sour shudders. But by and by we begin to sing, the two of us singing different songs simultaneously. I don't know the words to mine, just: *Come on along, come on along, to the dark-town strutters' ball.* But I can dance: that's what I mean to be, a tap-dancer in the movies. My dancing shadow rollicks[12] on the walls; our voices rock the chinaware; we giggle: as if unseen hands were tickling us. Queenie rolls on her back, her paws plow the air, something like a grin stretches her black lips. Inside myself, I feel warm and sparky as those crumbling logs, carefree as the wind in the chimney. My friend waltzes round the stove, the hem of her poor calico skirt pinched between her fingers as though it were a party dress: *Show me the way to go home*, she sings, her tennis shoes squeaking on the floor. *Show me the way to go home.*

Enter: two relatives. Very angry. Potent with eyes that scold, tongues that scald.

12. *Rollick* means "to play in a carefree, happy way."

Vocabulary

potent (pōt′ ənt) *adj.* having or exercising force, power, authority, or effectiveness; strong and powerful

Listen to what they have to say, the words tumbling together into a wrathful tune: "A child of seven! whiskey on his breath! are you out of your mind? feeding a child of seven! must be loony! road to ruination! remember Cousin Kate? Uncle Charlie? Uncle Charlie's brother-in-law? shame! scandal! humiliation! kneel, pray, beg the Lord!"

Queenie sneaks under the stove. My friend gazes at her shoes, her chin quivers, she lifts her skirt and blows her nose and runs to her room. Long after the town has gone to sleep and the house is silent except for the chimings of clocks and the sputter of fading fires, she is weeping into a pillow already as wet as a widow's handkerchief.

"Don't cry," I say, sitting at the bottom of her bed and shivering despite my flannel nightgown that smells of last winter's cough syrup, "don't cry," I beg, teasing her toes, tickling her feet, "you're too old for that."

"It's because," she hiccups, "I *am* too old. Old and funny."

"Not funny. Fun. More fun than anybody. Listen. If you don't stop crying you'll be so tired tomorrow we can't go cut a tree."

She straightens up. Queenie jumps on the bed (where Queenie is not allowed) to lick her cheeks. "I know where we'll find real pretty trees, Buddy. And holly, too. With berries big as your eyes. It's way off in the woods. Farther than we've ever been. Papa used to bring us Christmas trees from there: carry them on his shoulder. That's fifty years ago. Well, now: I can't wait for morning."

Morning. Frozen rime[13] lusters the grass; the sun, round as an orange and orange as hot-weather moons, balances on the horizon, burnishes[14] the silvered winter woods. A wild turkey calls. A renegade hog[15] grunts in the undergrowth. Soon, by the edge of knee-deep, rapid-running water, we have to abandon the buggy. Queenie wades the stream first, paddles across barking complaints at the swiftness of the current, the pneumonia-making coldness of it. We follow, holding our shoes and equipment (a hatchet, a burlap sack) above our heads. A mile more: of chastising thorns, burs and briers that catch at our clothes; of rusty pine needles brilliant with gaudy fungus and molted feathers. Here, there, a flash, a flutter, an ecstasy of shrillings remind us that not all the birds have flown south. Always, the path unwinds through lemony sun pools and pitch-black vine tunnels. Another creek to cross: a disturbed armada of speckled trout froths the water round us, and frogs the size of plates practice belly flops; beaver workmen are building a dam. On the farther shore, Queenie shakes herself and trembles. My friend shivers, too: not with cold but enthusiasm. One of her hat's ragged roses sheds a petal as she lifts her head and inhales the pine-heavy air. "We're almost there; can you smell it, Buddy?" she says, as though we were approaching an ocean.

And, indeed, it is a kind of ocean. Scented acres of holiday trees, prickly-leafed holly. Red berries shiny as Chinese bells: black crows swoop upon them screaming. Having stuffed our burlap sacks with enough greenery and crimson to garland a dozen windows, we set about choosing a tree. "It should be," muses my friend, "twice as tall as a boy. So a boy can't steal the

13. The white coating formed on a surface by frost is called *rime.*

14. *Burnishes* means "polishes."

15. A *renegade hog* is one that has escaped its pen and run away.

Vocabulary

muse (mūz) *v.* to think or reflect, especially in an idle, dreamy manner star." The one we pick is twice as tall as me. A brave handsome brute that survives thirty hatchet strokes before it keels with a creaking rending cry. Lugging it like a kill, we commence the long trek out. Every few yards we abandon the struggle, sit down and pant. But we have the strength of triumphant huntsmen; that and the tree's virile, icy perfume revive us, goad us on. Many compliments accompany our sunset return along the red clay road to town; but my friend is sly and noncommittal[16] when passers-by praise the treasure perched in our buggy: what a fine tree and where did it come from? "Yonderways," she murmurs vaguely. Once a car stops and the rich mill owner's lazy wife leans out and whines: "Giveya two-bits cash for that ol tree." Ordinarily my friend is afraid of saying no; but on this occasion she promptly shakes her head: "We wouldn't take a dollar." The mill owner's wife persists. "A dollar, my foot! Fifty cents. That's my last offer. Goodness, woman, you can get another one." In answer, my friend gently reflects: "I doubt it. There's never two of anything."

Home: Queenie slumps by the fire and sleeps till tomorrow, snoring loud as a human.

Did You Know?
An *ermine* (ur′ min) is a weasel with a black-tipped tail. In the winter, its brown fur usually changes to white. This winter fur is used for women's coats, often with black tails inserted at intervals for decorative effect.

A trunk in the attic contains: a shoebox of ermine tails (off the opera cape of a curious lady who once rented a room in the house), coils of frazzled tinsel gone gold with age, one silver star, a brief rope of dilapidated, undoubtedly dangerous candy-like light bulbs. Excellent decorations, as far as they go, which isn't far enough: my friend wants our tree to blaze "like a Baptist window," droop with weighty snows of ornament. But we can't afford the made-in-Japan splendors at the five-and-dime. So we do what we've always done: sit for days at the kitchen table with scissors and crayons and stacks of colored paper. I make sketches and my friend cuts them out: lots of cats, fish too (because they're easy to draw), some apples, some watermelons, a few winged angels devised from saved-up sheets of Hershey-bar tin foil. We use safety pins to attach these creations to the tree; as a final touch, we sprinkle the branches with shredded cotton (picked in August for this purpose). My friend, surveying the effect, clasps her hands together. "Now honest, Buddy. Doesn't it look good enough to eat?" Queenie tries to eat an angel.

After weaving and ribboning holly wreaths for all the front windows, our next project is the fashioning of family gifts. Tie-dye scarves for the ladies, for the men a home-brewed lemon and licorice and aspirin syrup to be taken "at the first Symptoms of a Cold and after Hunting." But when it comes time for making each other's gift, my friend and I separate to work secretly. I would like to buy her a pearl-handled knife, a radio, a whole pound of chocolate-covered cherries (we tasted some once, and she always swears: "I could live on them, Buddy, Lord yes I could—and that's not taking His name in vain"). Instead, I am building her a kite. She would like to give me a bicycle (she's said so on several million occasions: "If only I could, Buddy. It's bad enough in life to do without something *you* want; but confound it, what gets my goat is not being able to give somebody something you want *them* to have. Only one of these days I will, Buddy. Locate you a bike. Don't ask how. Steal it, maybe"). Instead, I'm fairly certain that she is building me a kite—the same as last year, and the year before: the year before that we

16. Here, *noncommittal* means "not revealing thoughts, feelings, or other information."

exchanged slingshots. All of which is fine by me. For we are champion kite-fliers who study the wind like sailors; my friend, more accomplished than I, can get a kite aloft when there isn't enough breeze to carry clouds.

Christmas Eve afternoon we scrape together a nickel and go to the butcher's to buy Queenie's traditional gift, a good gnawable beef bone. The bone, wrapped in funny paper, is placed high in the tree near the silver star. Queenie knows it's there. She squats at the foot of the tree staring up in a trance of greed: when bedtime arrives she refuses to budge. Her excitement is equaled by my

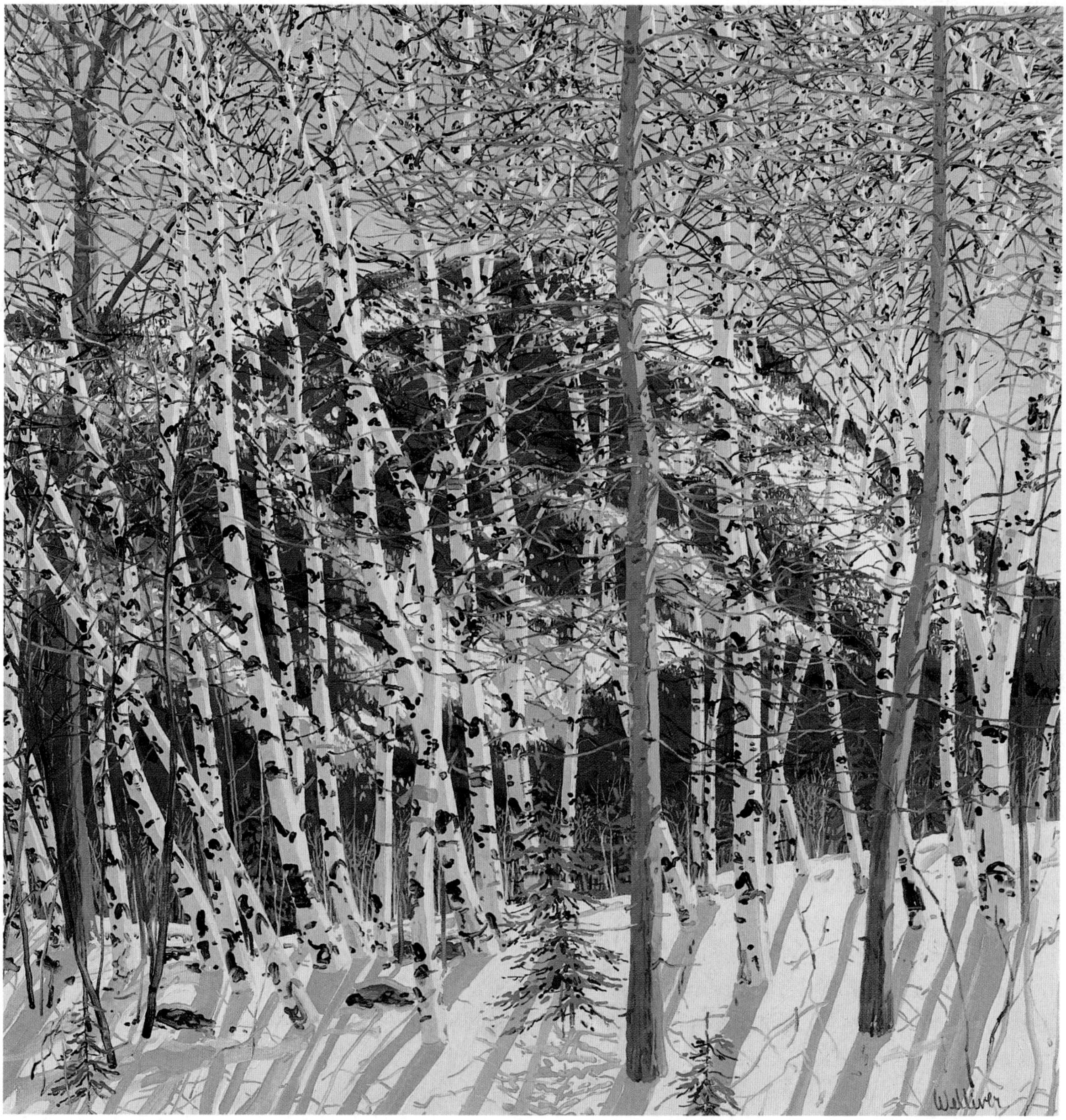

The Birches, 1977. Neil Welliver. Oil on canvas, 60 x 60 in. The Metropolitan Museum of Art, New York.

Viewing the painting: What does this painting add to your enjoyment of "A Christmas Memory"?

own. I kick the covers and turn my pillow as though it were a scorching summer's night. Somewhere a rooster crows: falsely, for the sun is still on the other side of the world.

"Buddy, are you awake?" It is my friend, calling from her room, which is next to mine; and an instant later she is sitting on my bed holding a candle. "Well, I can't sleep a hoot," she declares. "My mind's jumping like a jack rabbit. Buddy, do you think Mrs. Roosevelt will serve our cake at dinner?" We huddle in the bed, and she squeezes my hand I-love-you. "Seems like your hand used to be so much smaller. I guess I hate to see you grow up. When you're grown up, will we still be friends?" I say always. "But I feel so bad, Buddy. I wanted so bad to give you a bike. I tried to sell my cameo Papa gave me. Buddy"—she hesitates, as though embarrassed—"I made you another kite." Then I confess that I made her one, too; and we laugh. The candle burns too short to hold. Out it goes, exposing the starlight, the stars spinning at the window like a visible caroling that slowly, slowly daybreak silences. Possibly we doze; but the beginnings of dawn splash us like cold water; we're up, wide-eyed and wandering while we wait for others to waken. Quite deliberately my friend drops a kettle on the kitchen floor. I tap-dance in front of closed doors. One by one the household emerges, looking as though they'd like to kill us both; but it's Christmas, so they can't. First, a gorgeous breakfast: just everything you can imagine—from flapjacks and fried squirrel to hominy grits and honey-in-the-comb. Which puts everyone in a good humor except my friend and me. Frankly, we're so impatient to get at the presents we can't eat a mouthful.

Did You Know?
A *cameo* (kam′ ē ō′) is a piece of jewelry made from a precious or semiprecious stone that is carved in layers to produce a raised design, usually a woman's profile.

Well, I'm disappointed. Who wouldn't be? With socks, a Sunday school shirt, some handkerchiefs, a hand-me-down sweater and a year's subscription to a religious magazine for children. *The Little Shepherd.* It makes me boil. It really does.

My friend has a better haul. A sack of Satsumas, that's her best present. She is proudest, however, of a white wool shawl knitted by her married sister. But she *says* her favorite gift is the kite I built her. And it *is* very beautiful; though not as beautiful as the one she made me, which is blue and scattered with gold and green Good Conduct stars; moreover, my name is painted on it, "Buddy."

Did You Know?
Satsumas are seedless tangerines native to Japan but now grown in parts of the United States and Mexico.

"Buddy, the wind is blowing."

The wind is blowing, and nothing will do till we've run to a pasture below the house where Queenie has scooted to bury her bone (and where, a winter hence, Queenie will be buried, too). There, plunging through the healthy waist-high grass, we unreel our kites, feel them twitching at the string like sky fish as they swim into the wind. Satisfied, sun-warmed, we sprawl in the grass and peel Satsumas and watch our kites cavort. Soon I forget the socks and hand-me-down sweater. I'm as happy as if we'd already won the fifty-thousand-dollar Grand Prize in that coffee-naming contest.

Vocabulary
cavort (kə vôrt′) *v.* to run and jump around playfully

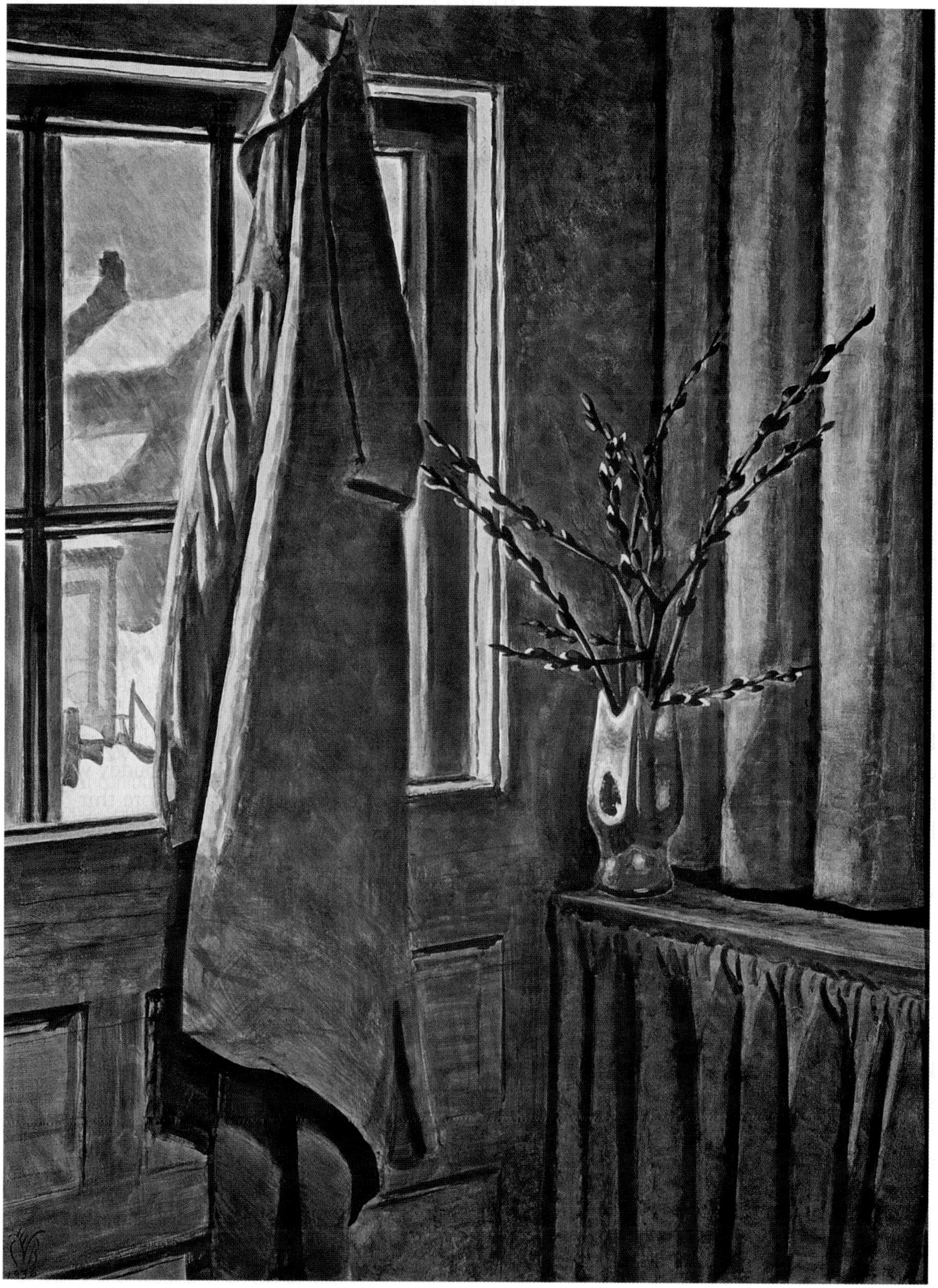

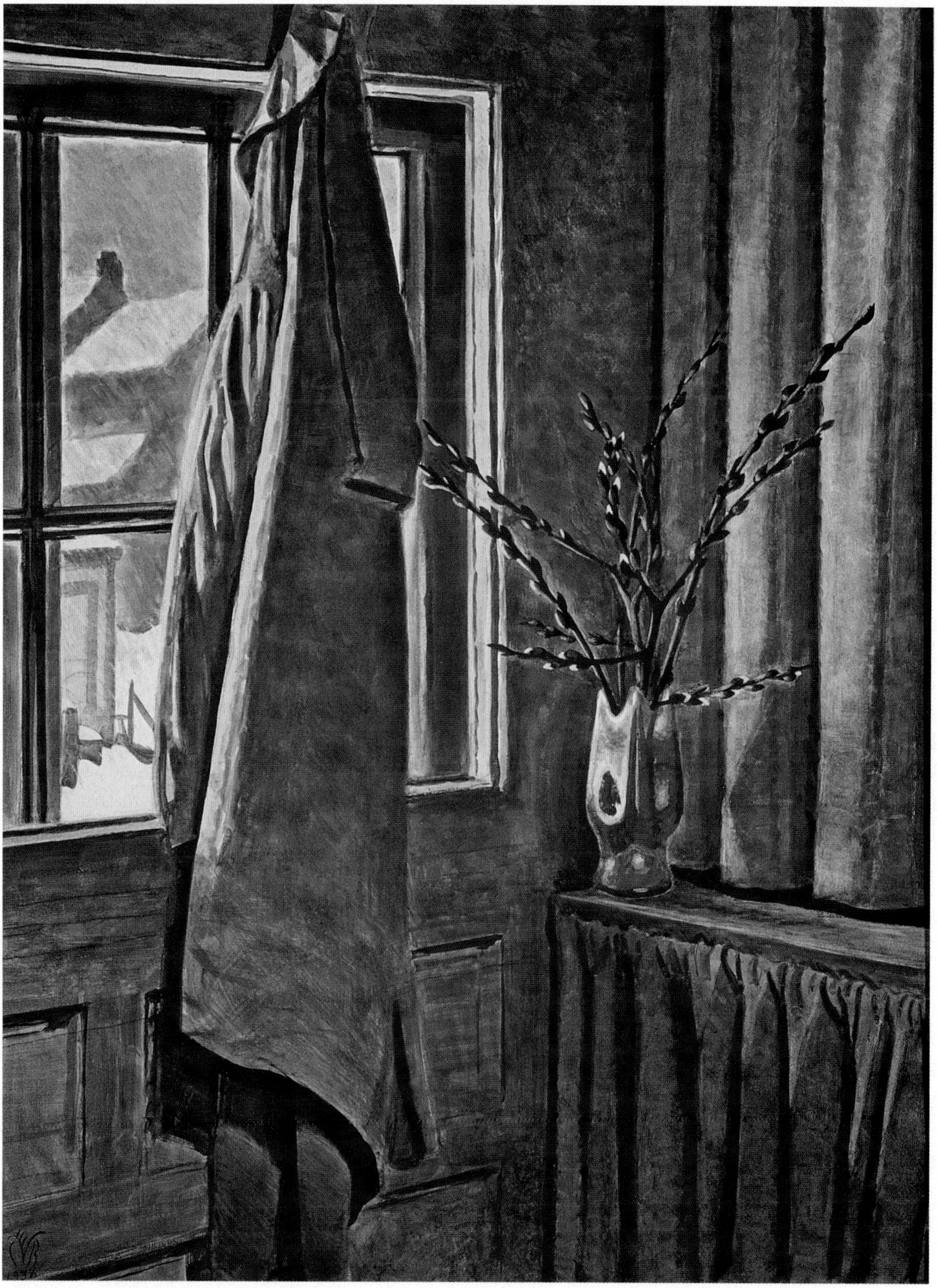

Pussy Willows, 1936. Charles Burchfield. Watercolor on paper, 32 15/16 x 25 1/4 in. Munson-Williams-Proctor Institute Museum of Art, Utica, NY.

Viewing the painting: Finish reading this story. How might this painting reflect the mood of the ending?

"My, how foolish I am!" my friend cries, suddenly alert, like a woman remembering too late she has biscuits in the oven. "You know what I've always thought?" she asks in a tone of discovery, and not smiling at me but a point beyond. "I've always thought a body would have to be sick and dying before they saw the Lord. And I imagined that when He came it would be like looking at the Baptist window: pretty as colored glass with the sun pouring through, such a shine you don't know it's getting dark. And it's been a comfort: to think of that shine taking away all the spooky feeling. But I'll wager it never happens. I'll wager at the very end a body realizes the Lord has already shown Himself. That things as they are"—her hand circles in a gesture that gathers clouds and kites and grass and Queenie pawing earth over her bone—"just what they've always seen, was seeing Him. As for me, I could leave the world with today in my eyes."

This is our last Christmas together.

Life separates us. Those who Know Best decide that I belong in a military school. And so follows a miserable succession of bugle-blowing prisons, grim reveille-ridden[17] summer camps. I have a new home too. But it doesn't count. Home is where my friend is, and there I never go.

Home is
where my friend
is, and there
I never go.

And there she remains, puttering around the kitchen. Alone with Queenie. Then alone. ("Buddy dear," she writes in her wild hard-to-read script, "yesterday Jim Macy's horse kicked Queenie bad. Be thankful she didn't feel much. I wrapped her in a Fine Linen sheet and rode her in the buggy down to Simpson's pasture where she can be with all her Bones . . .") For a few Novembers she continues to bake her fruitcakes single-handed; not as many, but some: and, of course, she always sends me "the best of the batch." Also, in every letter she encloses a dime wadded in toilet paper: "See a picture show and write me the story." But gradually in her letters she tends to confuse me with her other friend, the Buddy who died in the 1880s; more and more thirteenths are not the only days she stays in bed: a morning arrives in November, a leafless birdless coming of winter morning, when she cannot rouse herself to exclaim: "Oh my, it's fruitcake weather!"

And when that happens, I know it. A message saying so merely confirms a piece of news some secret vein had already received, severing from me an irreplaceable part of myself, letting it loose like a kite on a broken string. That is why, walking across a school campus on this particular December morning, I keep searching the sky. As if I expected to see, rather like hearts, a lost pair of kites hurrying toward heaven.

17. *Reveille* (rev′ ə lē) is the signal, usually played on a bugle, used to call soldiers to roll-call formation in the morning.

Responding to Literature

Personal Response

How did you react to the end of the selection?

Analyzing Literature

Recall

1. What project do Buddy and his friend undertake each November? What does the project entail? Who benefits from their efforts?
2. Why does Buddy's friend run to her room and cry in bed for a long time? What does Buddy do to comfort her?
3. What gift does Buddy's friend tell him "on several million occasions" that she'd like to give?
4. What gifts do Buddy and his friend give each other? What do they do after all the gifts have been opened?
5. What leads to the permanent separation of Buddy and his friend?

Interpret

6. In your opinion, why is the project so special to Buddy and his friend?
7. What kind of relationship seems to exist between the relatives in the house and Buddy and his friend? Explain.
8. The friend says, "It's bad enough in life to do without something *you* want; but confound it, what gets my goat is not being able to give somebody something you want *them* to have." Why might this gift be so important to her?
9. Summarize and interpret the friend's speech on page 416 that begins "My, how foolish I am!" and ends "I could leave the world with today in my eyes." Then explain why "today" might be so special to her.
10. Of what might the kites at the end of the selection be a **symbol?** (See Literary Terms Handbook, page R12.)

Evaluate and Connect

11. **Theme Connections** In your opinion, is this portrait of a friendship realistic and believable? Explain why or why not.
12. Why might Capote's relatives have sent him away to school, separating him from his friend? What do you think of their decision?
13. What lessons about life and about friendship might young Capote have learned from his friend?
14. What might Capote have wanted his audience to come away thinking or feeling after reading "A Christmas Memory"?
15. What makes the friend so special to Buddy? How might Buddy have responded to the Reading Focus on page 404? Compare his list with yours.

Literary ELEMENTS

Alliteration

Alliteration is the repetition of sounds, most often consonant sounds, at the beginnings of words. Writers often use alliteration to lend a musical quality to phrases and sentences. This line from "A Christmas Memory" contains alliteration: ". . . we're up, wide-eyed and wandering while we wait for others to waken."

1. Find three more examples of alliteration in the selection and copy them on your paper. Underline the repeated sounds in each example.
2. On your paper, complete each phrase with one or more words to make the phrase an example of alliteration.
   a. a purse full of ______
   b. a ______ wind
   c. fruitcakes for ______

- See **Literary Terms Handbook,** p. R1.

Literary Criticism

Critic William L. Nance calls "A Christmas Memory" "one of [Capote's] best and most satisfying works because it places the feelings he can dramatize most powerfully in the setting which is best suited to them." Discuss this quotation with your class. What feelings are dramatized most powerfully? What is the connection between these feelings and the setting?

Literature and Writing

Writing About Literature

A Review Do you find "A Christmas Memory" to be overly sentimental, or do you find it to be emotionally stirring and powerful? Do you think others would enjoy this memoir or do you think they would be disappointed? Why? Write a review of "A Christmas Memory" for a school newspaper. Be sure to include information about Capote's writing style, along with examples and details from the story to support your point of view.

Personal Writing

What Makes a Friend Unique? Buddy cites a number of things his friend has never done and then lists some remarkable things she *has* done and continues to do. What do such lists reveal about Buddy's friend–and about what Buddy finds significant? Answer this question in your journal. Then make similar lists about a special friend of yours. Reflect on what the items in your lists reveal not only about your friend but also about you.

Extending Your Response

Literature Groups

The Essence of Childhood In describing his friend, Buddy says that she is "still a child." What does Buddy mean by this statement? In what ways is his friend childlike? Is this a positive or a negative trait to Buddy? to you? What childlike qualities, if any, would you like to retain into adulthood? Jot down your responses to these questions and discuss them in your group. Make a chart that shows which childlike qualities are desirable in adulthood and which are undesirable.

Learning For Life

Thank You! One of the joys associated with sending fruitcakes was the pile of thank-you notes that Buddy and his friend received. Some were formal notes, written on White House stationery; others were quite informal, written on postcards. Working in a small group, compose several short thank-you notes to Buddy and his friend, varying the style to fit the different writers. Be sure to include a thank-you note from Mr. Haha Jones!

Interdisciplinary Activity

Art: Capturing the Mood Make a collage that captures the mood of "A Christmas Memory." You might put together family photographs, found objects, pieces of your own original artwork, or images cut from magazines or newspapers. Your final product should reflect the scenes you found most memorable in the selection as well as the overall mood of the work. Display your collage in the classroom, and allow others to respond to it and ask you questions about the choices you made.

Reading Further

You might also enjoy the following works:

Memoirs: *The Thanksgiving Visitor* and *One Christmas* are both about Capote's childhood in the South.

Viewing: *Breakfast at Tiffany's,* based on a novel by Capote, is a comic movie about the adventures of a small-town girl in New York City.

The Grass Harp, another film based on a novel by Capote, is about an orphaned boy and two old ladies who one day move into a tree house.

Save your work for your portfolio.

Skill Minilessons

GRAMMAR AND LANGUAGE • Using Appositives

An **appositive** is a noun or pronoun that is placed next to another noun or pronoun to identify, define, or give additional information about it. An **appositive phrase** is an appositive plus the words that modify it. For example:

"Together, we guide our buggy, a *dilapidated baby carriage,* out to the garden and into a grove of pecan trees."

Here, *baby carriage* defines the word *buggy. Dilapidated* gives additional information about its appearance.

● For more about appositives, see **Language Handbook,** p. R37.

PRACTICE Combine each pair of sentences by changing the second sentence into an appositive phrase.

1. We ate our supper at six. It was biscuits and bacon.
2. The kitchen was filled with spicy odors. It was our fruitcake workroom.
3. We opened the museum last summer. It was our greatest money-making project.
4. Mr. Haha Jones runs a café down by the river. He is a man who never laughs.

READING AND THINKING • Drawing Conclusions

You can draw conclusions about characters by noting how they are described, what they say and do, and how other characters respond to them. In "A Christmas Memory," Capote refers to adult relatives as "Those who Know Best." From that sarcastic description, readers might conclude that Capote finds these people distant and domineering.

PRACTICE On your paper, draw a conclusion about each character named in parentheses.

1. Buddy says that his friend has never been more than five miles from home. (Buddy; his friend)
2. Buddy says that his friend can tame hummingbirds "till they balance on her finger." (Buddy; his friend)
3. Mr. Haha Jones gives Buddy and his friend the whiskey without charging them. (Haha Jones)
4. Buddy says that his friend is shy with everyone *except* strangers. (Buddy's friend)

● For more about related comprehension skills, see **Reading Handbook,** pp. R82–R94.

VOCABULARY • Analogies

An analogy is a type of comparison that is based on the relationships between things or ideas. Some analogies are based on the manner, or way, in which something is done. Here is an example:

stow away : travel :: eavesdrop : listen

To *stow away* is to travel secretively; to *eavesdrop* is to listen secretively. When you come across an analogy in which the first two words are close in meaning, think of an adjective or adverb that defines the relationship between them. Then see if the same adjective or adverb also works to identify the relationship between another pair of words.

PRACTICE Choose the pair of words that best completes each analogy.

1. cavort : move ::
   - a. fight : box
   - b. challenge : dare
   - c. smile : grin
   - d. sip : drink
   - e. roughhouse : wrestle
2. muse : think ::
   - a. stroll : walk
   - b. laugh : joke
   - c. compliment : flatter
   - d. concentrate : study
   - e. entertain : amuse

● For more about analogies, see **Communications Skills Handbook,** p. R77.

Before You Read

Tía Chucha

Reading Focus

Do you know anyone who has a strikingly unique personality? Who's the funniest, zaniest, or most adventuresome person you have ever met?

Freewrite Jot down a description of the person, including details that convey how this person is unique. Then tell how you respond to this person, or how it feels to be with him or her.

Setting a Purpose Read to see how the speaker in this poem responds to a zany relative.

Building Background

Did You Know?

- Author Luis J. Rodriguez has said, "We all have the capabilities of great art and poetry. It's a matter of tapping into that creative reservoir we contain as human beings. Once tapped, this reservoir is inexhaustible. Skills and technique can always be learned." As the founder of Tía Chucha Press, Rodriguez has helped publish the work of emerging poets.
- *Tía* (tē′ ə) is the Spanish word for "aunt." In traditional Hispanic culture, strong ties exist among extended family members, which include grandparents, aunts, uncles, and cousins, as well as parents and children.

Meet Luis J. Rodriguez

Growing up as a gang member in Los Angeles, Luis J. Rodriguez saw twenty-five of his childhood friends die as the victims of gang violence. He credits a caring counselor and his own growing interest in writing as the forces that enabled him to escape the brutality of gang life. An award-winning poet, author, and journalist, Rodriguez has dedicated himself to helping and guiding young people who, like himself, come from disadvantaged backgrounds. He has developed and led writing workshops in schools, housing projects, migrant labor communities, homeless shelters, and prisons.

Luis J. Rodriguez was born in 1954. This poem appears in his collection of poems The Concrete River, *which was published in 1991.*

Evening Serenade. Konstantin Korovin (1861–1939). Oil on canvas. Private collection.

TÍA CHUCHA

Luis J. Rodriguez

Every few years
Tía Chucha would visit the family
in a tornado of song
and open us up
as if we were an overripe avocado.
She was a dumpy, black-haired
creature of upheaval,
who often came unannounced
with a bag of presents
including home-made perfumes and
colognes
that smelled something like
rotting fish
on a hot day at the tuna cannery.

They said she was crazy.
Oh sure, she once ran out naked
to catch the postman
with a letter that didn't belong to us.
I mean, she had this annoying habit
of boarding city buses
and singing at the top of her voice
(one bus driver even refused to go on
until she got off).
But crazy?

To me, she was the wisp°
of the wind's freedom,
a music-maker
who once tried to teach me guitar
but ended up singing
and singing,
me listening,
and her singing
until I put the instrument down
and watched the clock
click the lesson time away.

I didn't learn guitar,
but I learned something
about her craving
for the new, the unbroken
. . . so she could break it.
Periodically she banished°
herself from the family
and was the better for it.

I secretly admired Tía Chucha.
She was always quick with a story,
another "*Pepito*" joke,
or a hand-written lyric°
that she would produce
regardless of the occasion.

She was a despot°
of desire;
uncontainable
as a splash of water
on a varnished table.

I wanted to remove
the layers
of unnatural seeing
the way Tía Chucha beheld
the world, with first eyes,
like an infant
who can discern°
the elixir°
within milk.

I wanted to be
one of the prizes
she stuffed into
her rumpled bag.

24 A *wisp* is a fleeting trace or a hint of something.
40 *Banished* means "forced to leave" or "exiled."

46 *Lyric* may refer to a poem or to the words of a song.
49 A *despot* is a tyrant, a ruler with absolute power.
60 Here, *discern* means "detect."
61 An *elixir* is a substance believed to maintain life or a medicine with the power to cure all ills.

Responding to Literature

Personal Response

What is your reaction to the character of Tía Chucha? Share your response with your classmates.

Analyzing Literature

Recall and Interpret

1. Describe Tía Chucha's appearance and behavior. Why did people say she was "crazy"?
2. How does the speaker in the poem view Tía Chucha? Why might the speaker's reaction to her be different from that of other people?
3. What activity did the speaker and Tía Chucha once try to do together? In what ways was the activity a failure, and in what ways was it a success?
4. Reread lines 54–66. In your own words, state the two things that the speaker wanted to do and why the speaker wanted to do them.

Evaluate and Connect

5. Review the writing you did for the Reading Focus on page 420. How does your response to the person you described compare with the speaker's response to Tía Chucha?
6. If Tía Chucha were your aunt, would you look forward to her visits? Why or why not?
7. The speaker says that Tía Chucha banished herself from the family from time to time and was "better for it." Based on your own observations and experiences, why might this be so?
8. Explain the meaning of the **image** "uncontainable as a splash of water on a varnished table." Do you feel that this is an effective image for describing Tía Chucha? Explain why or why not. (See page R6.)

Literary ELEMENTS

Metaphor

A **metaphor** is a type of figurative language used to compare or equate two seemingly unlike things. Look at this example from the poem: *"Tía Chucha would visit the family / in a tornado of song."* Although a tornado and a song are very different, Rodriguez's metaphor conveys the force and power of Tía Chucha's singing.

1. Explain the following metaphors:
   - "To me, she was the wisp/of the wind's freedom"
   - "She was a despot/of desire"
2. Why do you think Rodriguez used metaphors in his portrait of Tía Chucha? What do they add to your understanding of her character?

- See **Literary Terms Handbook,** p. R7.

Extending Your Response

Literature Groups

The Value of Eccentricity Tía Chucha is an eccentric, a person whose behavior is unconventional. What can we learn from people like her? Discuss this question in your group. Then work together to create a cartoon of Tía Chucha that expresses your ideas about the value of eccentricity. Share your cartoon with the rest of the class.

Creative Writing

A Tía Chucha Fest The speaker in the poem says that Tía Chucha always had a story or a joke to tell or a "hand-written lyric." Put yourself into the character of Tía Chucha. Write a story or a joke that she might tell or a song she might sing. Have a Tía Chucha Fest in class and share your stories, jokes, and songs.

Save your work for your portfolio.

COMPARING *selections*

A Christmas Memory and TÍA CHUCHA

COMPARE **RESPONSES**

In their own distinct ways, Capote and Rodriguez each paint a portrait of a unique and memorable woman. In a small group, discuss your responses to the two selections. Which selection do you prefer? Why? What image or event from each selection stands out in your mind? Which woman would you most enjoy spending a day with? Why? Would these women befriend each other? Why or why not?

COMPARE **CHARACTERS**

Write a paragraph in which you compare and contrast the friend in "A Christmas Memory" with Tía Chucha in "Tía Chucha." Use a Venn diagram like the one shown below to organize your thoughts. Consider the following points in your comparison:

- physical characteristics
- attitudes and behaviors
- the types of gifts each gives
- other adults' reactions to each woman
- the feelings about each woman that the narrator or speaker reveals

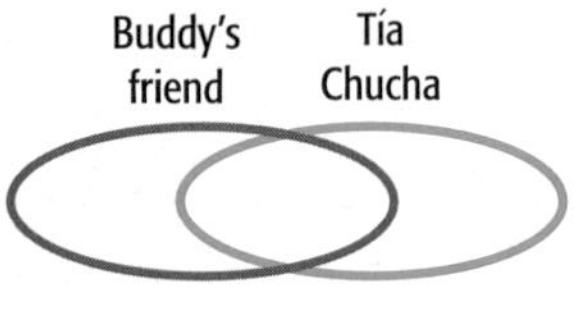

COMPARE **LESSONS**

What do Buddy in "A Christmas Memory" and the speaker in "Tía Chucha" learn from their unusual relatives? How are their lives enriched?

1. Imagine both Buddy and the speaker in the poem as adults. What would they say about the importance of these women in their lives?
2. Work with two partners to role-play an interview with Buddy and the speaker in "Tía Chucha," in which they discuss what they learned from their relatives and how these lessons have affected their lives.
3. To prepare for the interview, brainstorm a short list of questions and responses. Include specific incidents and details from the selections as part of your responses.
4. Practice your interview, and then present it to the class.

Vo•cab•u•lar•y Skills

Dictionary Skills: Pronunciation

Dictionaries show pronunciation by "respelling" each word with a system that combines letters and symbols. For example, the pronunciation of the word *gauge* is respelled as (gāj). The first *g* has the "hard" *g* sound, as in *go,* which is represented by *g.* The second *g* has the "soft" *g* sound, the same sound as *j,* so it is written as *j.* Another consonant that can be pronounced two ways is *c.* Depending on which sound *c* has in a word, it can be represented by the letter *s* or the letter *k.* Therefore, *cyclone* is respelled as (sī′ klōn).

Some vowel sounds are indicated by symbols. A straight line above a vowel indicates that the vowel sound is "long." (Long vowels "say their own name.") A vowel without any symbol has the "short" sound. The chart below shows other pronunciation symbols.

Symbol	Pronunciation
ä	an **ah** sound, as in **car**
ô	an **aw** sound, as in **coffee** and **law**
oo	the vowel sound in **wood**
o͞o	the vowel sound in **fool**
oi	the vowel sound in **toy**
ou	an **ow** sound, as in **cow** and **out**
ə	the vowel sound in the second syllable of **pencil** and **lemon**
th	**th** as in **thin** and **both**
t̲h̲	**th** as in **this**
zh	the sound made by the **s** in **treasure**

An accent mark follows each syllable that must be stressed, or emphasized, for correct pronunciation. If there is more than one accent mark for a word, the heavier, or darker, one shows which syllable receives the most emphasis.

EXERCISE

Use the pronunciation given for each word to answer the question that follows it.

1. stoicism (stō′ ə siz′ əm) Does the first syllable of *stoicism* rhyme with *toe, toy,* or *two?*
2. saunter (sôn′ tər) Does the first syllable of *saunter* rhyme with *pant, haunt,* or *won't?*
3. circuitous (sər kū′ ə təs) Is the second syllable of *circuitous* pronounced like *cue, cute,* or *cut?*
4. plaintive (plān′ tiv) Is the first syllable of *plaintive* pronounced like *plant, play,* or *plane?*

Writing Workshop

Expository Writing: Biographical Essay

Written from the third-person point of view, a biographical essay tells the story of someone's life. It does more than explain what happened to someone, however. A biographical essay explains why something happened or why the person made certain choices–and how those events or choices affected the course of a person's life. **In this workshop, you will write a biographical essay that shows the impact that personal choices or significant events have made on someone else's life.**

- As you write your biographical essay, refer to the **Writing Handbook**, pp. R58–R71.

EVALUATION RUBRIC

By the time you complete this Writing Workshop, you will have
- shown the impact that specific events or choices have had on your subject's life
- written a thesis that clearly states your main idea about the subject
- elaborated your thesis with details, information, and anecdotes
- organized information logically
- presented a biographical essay that is free of errors in grammar, usage, and mechanics

The Writing Process

PREWRITING

PREWRITING TIP

Brainstorming with a friend is a great way to come up with a list of good subjects for your biographical essay.

Choose a subject and begin developing goals

An interesting biography starts with a subject you find interesting, so choose someone you think will be fun to write about. Choosing a subject may lead you to develop some goals to pursue as you learn more about the person. For example, if you choose a person with an interesting job, your goal may be to learn more about his or her career path. Think not only about who you would like to write about; also consider why you find that person a good subject for your essay and what you want to learn about him or her.

Consider your approach

You have a number of options for how to approach your subject and focus your biographical essay. Would any of the approaches of the selections in this theme fit your subject and goals?

- Consider focusing on a single defining moment in a person's life, as Margaret Truman does in "The United States vs. Susan B. Anthony."
- Consider basing the essay entirely on your observations of the subject, as Capote does in "A Christmas Memory" and Mowat does in the excerpt from *Never Cry Wolf.*
- Consider putting yourself into the mind of your subject, as Beryl Markham does in the excerpt from *West with the Night.*
- Consider focusing on the effect that the subject had on you or on people close to you, as Yoshiko Uchida does in "Of Dry Goods and Black Bow Ties."

Consider your audience

Decide whether you want to write for young children, people your own age, or adults. You will need to adjust your vocabulary according to the reading level of your audience.

Gather information

One of the best ways to gather information for a biographical essay is to conduct interviews with your subject or with others who know your subject extremely well. Make a list of questions in advance that will lead your interviewee to talk about areas of specific interest, but keep an open mind; he or she may tell you fascinating stories that will take your essay in a different direction. If you're writing about someone from history, you will need to conduct library research.

Make a plan

Before you begin writing, think about how you'll organize your biographical essay. Having a plan early on can help you find a focus and determine which material to include in your draft. The most common organizational techniques for biographies are cause and effect, chronological order, and order of importance. Your content may allow you to combine more than one of these techniques. By using a graphic organizer like the one shown in the Student Model here, you can combine cause and effect with chronological order.

STUDENT MODEL

In my introduction, I'll talk about how Heather never lets hard times get her down. The main idea will be that even after her massive skiing accident, she had such a good attitude and worked so hard that she ended up being an even better athlete than she was before. Then, using chronological order in the body of the essay, I'll explain the details of Heather's accident and her road to recovery. I'll conclude by describing Heather's ultimate triumph.

Complete Student Model on p. R113.

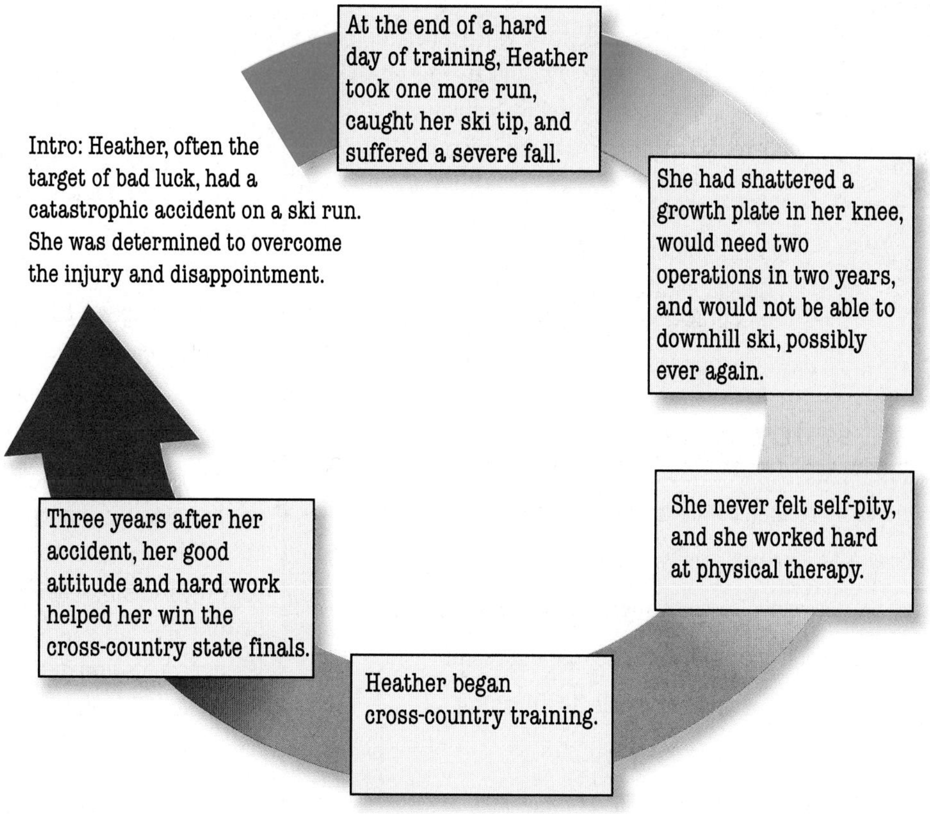

At the end of a hard day of training, Heather took one more run, caught her ski tip, and suffered a severe fall.
Intro: Heather, often the target of bad luck, had a catastrophic accident on a ski run. She was determined to overcome the injury and disappointment.
She had shattered a growth plate in her knee, would need two operations in two years, and would not be able to downhill ski, possibly ever again.
She never felt self-pity, and she worked hard at physical therapy.
Heather began cross-country training.
Three years after her accident, her good attitude and hard work helped her win the cross-country state finals.

DRAFTING

DRAFTING TIP

Use transitions to show how events are related and the order in which they occur. To help you decide which transitions to use, see the Writing Skill "Using Transitions" on page 382.

Write a thesis statement

A thesis statement is one or two sentences that state the main idea of your essay. A thesis statement can help focus your writing, since almost everything you discuss in the body of your paper should explain or give evidence in support of it. Because it's so important, spend time composing your thesis statement.

STUDENT MODEL

Heather had been challenged by many obstacles in her life, but her positive attitude and perseverance enabled her to succeed in spite of—or perhaps even because of—these hardships.

Complete Student Model on p. R113.

Draft your essay

Follow your plan as you write, but feel free to make changes to your plan if you uncover new material you would like to include or if you decide to steer your writing in a different direction. You can double-check your organization when you revise.

REVISING

REVISING TIP

Read a short biography written by someone else while you let your work "rest."

Evaluate your work

Set your work aside for a while. Then, before you revise, just *read* your work. Don't make changes. Just read. After that, read it again slowly. Using the **Rubric for Revising** to guide you, mark the weak spots that you want to strengthen. Then make the revisions.

Have a writing conference

Work with a revision partner and read your biographical essays aloud to each other. Use the **Rubric for Revising** to offer suggestions for improving each other's work.

STUDENT MODEL

Heather had to be rushed to the hospital. ~~The doctor who examined her was not gentle.~~ She learned that she had ~~messed up~~ shattered the growth plate in her knee. Doctors informed her that she would need two major operations during the course of the next two years. During that time, ~~S~~she wouldn't be able to do anything athletic.

Complete Student Model on p. R113.

RUBRIC FOR REVISING

Your revised biographical essay should have

- ☑ an attention-getting introduction that includes a clearly stated thesis
- ☑ details, anecdotes, and information that elaborate the thesis
- ☑ transitions that show how events are related
- ☑ a conclusion that reinforces the thesis

Your revised biographical essay should be free of

- ☑ anecdotes and details that don't relate to the thesis
- ☑ errors in grammar, usage, and mechanics

EDITING/PROOFREADING

Content comes first, so continue revising and rewriting sections as necessary until your biographical essay says what you want it to say. Then edit it painstakingly for errors in grammar, usage, mechanics, and spelling.

PROOFREADING TIP

Use the **Proofreading Checklist** on the inside back cover of this book to help you mark errors that will be distracting to your readers.

Grammar Hint

When two or more events happen at the same time, be sure to use the same verb tense to describe each event.

INCORRECT: *The ski team called it quits, but Heather wants one more run.*

CORRECT: *The ski team called it quits, but Heather wanted one more run.*

- For more about verb tense, see **Language Handbook,** p. R22.

STUDENT MODEL

She ~~sees~~ saw the finish line in the near distance, and was the first one to cross it. She was greeted by the well-earned aplause of hundreds of freinds.

Complete Student Model on p. R113.

Complete Student Model

For a complete version of the model developed in this workshop, refer to **Writing Workshop Models**, p. R113.

PUBLISHING/PRESENTING

If you wrote about a person from your community, your local newspaper may be interested in publishing your biographical essay. If you wrote for a younger audience, you may want to illustrate your work and present it to the library of a grade school or middle school.

PRESENTING TIP

A time line makes a good addition to a biography. Include historical and personal events

Reflecting

Now that you have examined someone else's life, think about how it would feel to be the subject of a biography. What would you want your biographer to understand about you? Write about those things in your journal. Then jot an honest assessment of your work's strengths and weaknesses. Plan to use the strengths in your next piece of writing.

Save your work for your portfolio.

Unit Assessment

Personal Response

1. Which of the readings in this unit could you relate to most? Which of the readings taught you the most about something you didn't already know?
2. As a result of the work you have done in this unit, what new ideas do you have about the following:
   - how to get the most out of your reading
   - how to classify the type of material you are reading
   - how to work in groups with your classmates

Analyzing Literature

Classifying Nonfiction Write a few paragraphs defining the terms *narrative nonfiction* and *informative nonfiction.* Use specific examples from the readings in this unit to support and elaborate on your definitions. (For help in identifying these types of writing, see pages 280–281.) You may draw all your examples from just two selections, or you may use examples from several works.

As part of your analysis, focus on the differences between these types of writing by contrasting things like content, author's purpose, and writing style. Remember, however, that any individual piece of nonfiction can contain both narrative and informative elements.

Evaluate and Set Goals

Evaluate

1. What was your strongest contribution to the class as you worked through this unit?
2. What was the most difficult task you were asked to do in this unit?
   - How did you approach the task?
   - What was the result?
3. How would you assess your work in this unit, using the following scale? Give at least two reasons for your assessment.
   4 = outstanding **3** = good **2** = fair **1** = weak

Set Goals

1. Choose a goal to work toward in the next unit. It could involve reading, writing, speaking, working in a group, or whatever you feel you need to concentrate on.
2. Discuss your goal with your teacher.
3. Write down the steps you will take to help you achieve the goal.
4. Plan checkpoints to help you monitor your progress.

Build Your Portfolio

Select Choose two of the pieces of work you did in this unit, and include them in your portfolio. Use these questions to help you choose.

- Which do you consider your best work?
- Which "stretched" you the most?
- Which did you learn the most from?
- Which did you most enjoy working on?

Reflect Write some notes to accompany the pieces you selected. Use these questions to guide you.

- What do you like best about the piece?
- What did you learn from the process of creating it?
- What might you do differently if you were beginning this piece again?

Reading on Your Own

You might also be interested in the following books.

The House on Mango Street

by Sandra Cisneros Sandra Cisneros uses her childhood experience as a subject in both her fiction and her nonfiction writing. This novel tells the story of Esperanza, a Mexican American girl, who lives, as Cisneros did, in a Spanish-speaking community in Chicago. Esperanza's hopes, joys, and fears are explored in a series of short vignettes.

Sojourner Truth: Ain't I a Woman?

by Patricia C. McKissack and Fredrick L. McKissack

This page-turning biography explores the dramatic life of a woman who was born into slavery and eventually gained her freedom. After struggling to keep her family together under extremely difficult conditions, Sojourner Truth became an eloquent spokesperson for the abolitionist cause and greatly influenced the politics of her day.

Last Chance to See

by Douglas Adams and Mark Carwardine

A best-selling author and a well-known zoologist team up to travel the world looking for endangered species. Adams and Carwardine recount their adventures with humor and flair, even while describing the heartbreaking plight of the exotic animals they encounter.

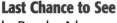

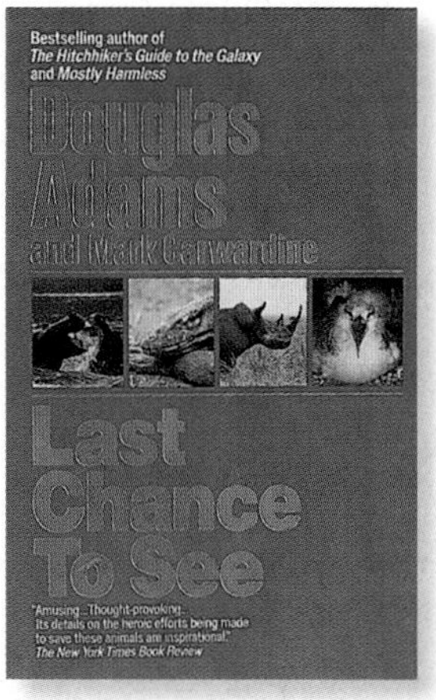

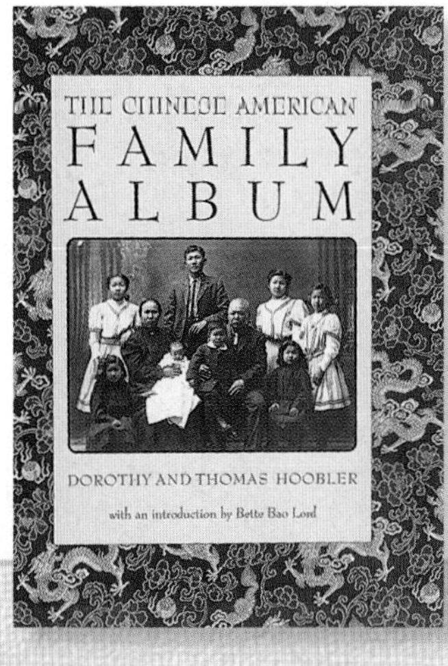

The Chinese American Family Album

by Dorothy and Thomas Hoobler In order to tell the story of Chinese immigration to the United States, the Hooblers gather photographs, letters, journals, and other firsthand accounts from the people who made the trip from one country to the other. Life in China, the conditions of the journey, and the challenges of the new world are all explained in personal, intimate detail.

Standardized Test Practice

Read the following passage. Then read each question on page 433. Decide which is the best answer to each question. Mark the letter for that answer on your paper.

What Is Troop 597 Trying to Do?

Dear Neighbor,

Every October, the members of Willimet County Scout Troop 597 choose an activity to raise money for a local charity. Last year we were pleased to present a check for $3,578 to the town library for restorations and groundskeeping. Troop 597 raised the money by holding a car wash in the library parking lot every Saturday in the month of October. It was great fun, and the money helped keep our library beautiful!

This year I am the Chairman of Troop 597's October Charity Drive. The proceeds of our activities will benefit the Willimet Community Center on Dodd Street. To raise money, we are holding a recycling drive, and you can help!

As you may know, our state laws require a 5-cent deposit on all bottles and aluminum cans sold at local stores. When a bottle or can is emptied, it may be redeemed at the local recycling center for the nickel deposit. However, many people don't do this. Many bottles and cans that could be redeemed may be found along our highways and in our parks, causing a litter problem and preventing the reuse of our natural resources. Many people throw their "empties" out with the common trash, another waste of money and a further environmental hazard.

Help us to help the environment and our Community Center all at once. Troop 597 will set up a collection stall in the Community Center parking lot from October 1st–31st. Please stop by between the hours of 6:00 P.M. and 8:00 P.M. weekdays to drop off any empty bottles or cans you would like to donate to our cause. Please be sure to thoroughly rinse your cans and bottles and put them in paper or plastic bags. In addition, Troop 597 will lead volunteer clean-up crews to key sites across town to collect discarded containers for recycling. If you would like to join us, the crews will meet in the Community Center parking lot every Saturday in October at 9:00 A.M.

On behalf of Troop 597, I'd like to thank you in advance for whatever efforts you can make on behalf of this worthy campaign. Whether you donate a few bags of old cans or a few hours of your time, we're sure you'll agree that Willimet County will greatly benefit from this drive. Troop 597's motto has always been "Together We Can Do More." Thank you for helping us all participate in building a better tomorrow.

Yours,

David Benzefengo, Troop 597

1 David's purpose for writing this letter is primarily to —

A ask the community for its support in the scout troop's fund-raising activities

B explain why members of his scout troop will take up space in the Community Center parking lot during the month of October

C try to get more boys to join the scout troop

D request that people not park in the Community Center parking lot on Saturday mornings

2 Which of the following is a concerned member of the community most likely to do after reading David's letter?

F Buy fewer bottles and cans at local stores

G Discard more bottles and cans in local parks and along highways

H Drop off empty bottles and cans at the Community Center parking lot

J Go to the library to find out more about fund-raising drives

3 The writer probably thinks that people who throw their empty cans and bottles in the parks are —

A helpful and concerned

B careless and wasteful

C uninformed about state laws

D likely to volunteer for a clean-up crew

4 The writer attempts to show that this year's October Charity Drive will not only raise money for the Community Center but also —

F allow the scouts to earn a merit badge

G help restore and maintain buildings on Dodd Street

H convince the local government to increase the 5-cent deposit on bottles and aluminum cans

J help clean up local highways and parks

5 The main idea of David's letter is that the scout troop —

A is angry because they have to pick up littered bottles and cans from local parks and highways

B wants the public to send donation checks to the Community Center

C hopes that the public will support its fund-raiser by dropping off bottles and cans or by working on a clean-up crew

D is concerned that this year's fund-raiser may not raise as much money as last year's fund-raiser

6 According to David's letter, people who want to donate cans and bottles to the scout troop's fund-raiser should —

F leave the cans and bottles along highways or in local parks

G contact the town library for further instruction

H rinse the cans and bottles and bring them to the Community Center

J put them out with the common trash pick-up

STOP

"Poetry is an echo, asking a shadow to dance."

—Carl Sandburg

Equivalents #20: Days Remembered, Days to Come, 1996. Anne Banas. Oil on canvas, 36 x 78 in. Gallery Contemporanea, Jacksonville, FL.

UNIT THREE

Poetry

Genre Focus

Poetry

According to Nicaraguan poet Daisy Zamora, poetry is "a way of feeling life." But how does poetry help us "feel" life? Poetry captures intense experiences or creative perceptions of the world in a musical language. If prose is like talking, poetry is like singing. Understanding the basic elements of poetry outlined on these pages is necessary to analyzing the poems you read and hear—and to "feeling life" in them.

● For more on elements of poetry, see **Literary Terms Handbook,** pp. R1–R13.

ELEMENTS OF POETRY

MODELS

Speaker

Every poem has a **speaker,** or voice, that talks to the reader. Like a narrator in prose, the speaker is not necessarily the poet. It can also be a fictional person, an animal, or even a thing.

> But believe me, son.
> I want to be what I used to be
> when I was like you.
>
> [speaker is a father]
>
> *from "Once Upon a Time" by Gabriel Okara*

Lines and Stanzas

A **line** is a word or row of words that may or may not form a complete sentence. A **stanza** is a group of lines forming a unit. The stanzas in a poem are separated by a space.

> Open it. — line
>
> Go ahead, it won't bite.
> Well . . . maybe a little.
>
> [stanza]
>
> *from "The First Book" by Rita Dove*

Rhythm and Meter

Rhythm is the pattern of sound created by the arrangement of stressed and unstressed syllables in a line. Rhythm can be regular or irregular. **Meter** is a regular pattern of stressed and unstressed syllables, which sets the overall rhythm of certain poems. Typically, stressed syllables are marked with (´) and unstressed syllables with (˘).

> Mán ănd bóy stŏod chéerĭng bý,
> Ănd hóme wĕ broúght yŏu shóuldĕr-hígh.
>
> *from "To an Athlete Dying Young" by A. E. Housman*

Rhyme

Rhyme is the repetition of the same stressed vowel sound and any succeeding sounds in two or more words.

- **Internal rhyme** occurs within a line of poetry.
- **End rhyme** occurs at the ends of lines.
- **Rhyme scheme,** the pattern of the end rhymes, may be designated by assigning a different letter of the alphabet to each new rhyme.

The golden brooch my mother wore — a
She left behind for me to wear; — b
I have no thing I treasure more: — a
Yet, it is something I could spare. — b

from "The Courage That My Mother Had" by Edna St. Vincent Millay

Other Sound Devices

- **Alliteration** is the repetition of consonant sounds at the beginnings of words.
- **Assonance** is the repetition of vowel sounds within a line of poetry.
- **Onomatopoeia** is the use of a word or phrase, such as "hiss" or "buzz," that imitates or suggests the sound of what it describes.

In the steamer is the trout
seasoned with slivers of ginger — alliteration

from "Eating Together" by Li-Young Lee

And the stars never rise but I
see the bright eyes — assonance

from "Annabel Lee" by Edgar Allan Poe

Imagery

Imagery is descriptive language that appeals to the senses–sight, sound, touch, taste, or smell. Some images appeal to more than one sense.

Her knotted hands showing slow
blue rivers / jerked nervously through
cornbread frying

from "Yonosa House" by R. T. Smith

Figures of Speech

A **figure of speech** is a word or expression that is not meant to be read literally.

- A **simile** is a figure of speech using a word such as *like* or *as* to compare seemingly unlike things.
- A **metaphor** also compares or equates seemingly unlike things, but does not use *like* or *as.*
- **Personification** attributes human characteristics to an animal, object, or idea.

Does it stink like rotten meat? — simile

from "Harlem" by Langston Hughes

the moon is a white sliver — metaphor

from "I Am Singing Now" by Luci Tapahonso

A Spider sewed at Night — personification

from "A Spider sewed at Night" by Emily Dickinson

TYPES OF POETRY

There are many types of poetry, and many poems fit within more than one category. **Narrative poetry** is verse that tells a story. **Lyric poetry** expresses the personal thoughts and feelings of the speaker. **Dramatic poetry** usually has one or more characters who speak to other characters, to themselves, or to the reader.

Active Reading Model

Active Reading Strategies

Poetry

To get the most from a poem, you have to be receptive and alert. As the poet W. S. Merwin advises readers, "You've got to stop what you're doing, what you're thinking, and what you're expecting and just be there for the poem for however long it takes." Use the following strategies to help you *experience* a poem.

● For more about related reading strategies, see **Reading Handbook,** pp. R78–R107.

LISTEN

Read a poem aloud, listening to the way it sounds. Take a breath when you come to a punctuation mark or a natural pause, which may or may not come at the end of a line.

Ask yourself . . .

- What kind of rhythm does this poem have? Is it slow, fast, regular, irregular?
- How does the rhythm or rhyme of the poem affect its mood? How do such elements affect *me?*
- What sound devices does the poet use? How do these sound devices affect me–and the mood of the poem?

IMAGINE

Many poems contain sensory images. Try to imagine the sights, sounds, smells, tastes, and sense of touch that the poem evokes.

Ask yourself . . .

- How does this scene or subject look?
- How would this sound, smell, taste, or feel?

RESPOND

Respond to the poem by thinking about your spontaneous thoughts and feelings.

Say to yourself . . .

- This poem makes me think . . .
- This poem reminds me of . . .
- I feel like this poem is . . .
- Wow! That was beautiful (funny . . .)

QUESTION Ask yourself questions to help you understand and interpret the poem. Jot down or mentally note questions you can't answer.

Ask yourself . . .

- Do I understand what I've read?
- What is this poem about?
- What story or situation does the poem relate?
- What does this image mean or represent? Why does the poet use figurative language in this way?

CLARIFY Clarify the poem by putting it in your own words. Summarize what the poem is about. Think about what it might mean on a deeper level.

Say to yourself . . .

- This stanza is basically saying . . .
- These lines can be restated as . . .
- This image seems to be a symbol for . . .

INTERPRET Read the poem several times, and then focus on its meaning one stanza at a time. Discuss the poem with others if you wish. Explain what the speaker or the poet is saying.

Ask yourself . . .

- How does the title contribute to the meaning of the poem?
- Might the poem have more than one meaning? What else might it mean?
- What is the poem's theme, or message, about life or human nature?

Applying the Strategies

1. Read the next poem, "The Charge of the Light Brigade," using the Active Reading Model in the margins.
2. Choose a poem you have not read, and practice using all of these strategies.

Before You Read

The Charge of the Light Brigade

Reading Focus

What kinds of actions do you consider heroic?

Quickwrite Jot down a list of your ideas. Briefly note why you consider each action heroic.

Setting a Purpose Read to find out about an action that the poet considered heroic.

Building Background

Did You Know?

The Crimean (krī mē′ ən) War (1853–1856) pitted the allied forces of Great Britain, France, Turkey, and Sardinia against Russia. Fought largely on the Crimean Peninsula in what is now Ukraine, the war began after Russia tried to expand into the Black Sea region by invading Turkish territory.

At the Battle of Balaklava on October 25, 1854, a brigade, or unit, of British troops on horseback made a suicidal assault on some entrenched Russian artillery. More than 600 men charged into battle. With cannons firing at them from three sides, nearly 250 men were quickly killed or wounded.

Compounding the disaster was the realization that the charge resulted from confused orders. Lord Raglan, the British commander-in-chief, had wanted to stop isolated Russian soldiers from removing guns from Turkish artillery posts the Russians had captured. However, his orders did not specify which artillery posts to attack: "Lord Raglan wishes the cavalry to advance rapidly to the front, and try to prevent the enemy carrying away the guns." The messenger, Captain Louis Nolan, misinterpreted the orders and identified the entrenched Russian artillery as the target. After Raglan saw that his orders had been mistaken, he sent messengers to stop the charge, but it was too late. Captain Nolan, who botched the orders, was killed early in the charge.

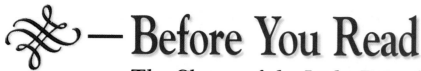

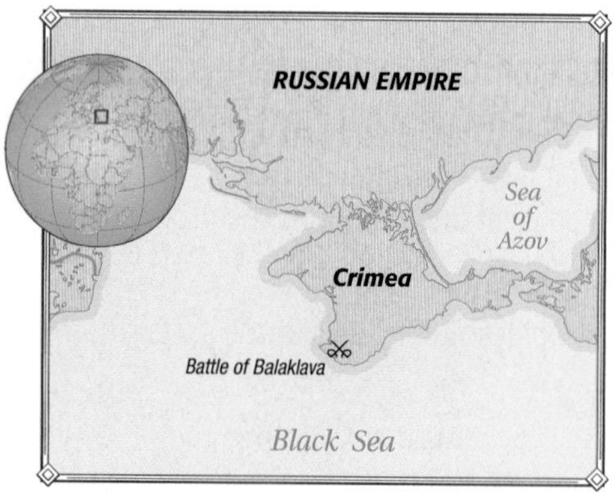

Meet Alfred, Lord Tennyson

An immensely popular writer during his lifetime, Alfred, Lord Tennyson followed William Wordsworth as the poet laureate of Great Britain. Tennyson, the literary spokesperson of his nation at the time of the Battle of Balaklava, commemorated the bungled charge in verse after reading about it in the newspaper. A large, gruff man who dressed in a cloak and broad-brimmed hat, Tennyson made a striking impression on people. Considered by many to be the greatest poet of Victorian Britain, he accepted the title of baron and a seat in the House of Lords in 1884.

Alfred, Lord Tennyson was born in 1809 and died in 1892. This poem was first published on December 9, 1854.

Scotland Forever, 1881. Lady Butler (Elizabeth Southerden Thompson). Oil on canvas, 101.6 x 194.3 cm. Leeds City Art Gallery, England.

The Charge of the Light Brigade

Alfred, Lord Tennyson

Half a league,° half a league,
Half a league onward,
All in the valley of Death
Rode the six hundred.
"Forward the Light Brigade!°
Charge for the guns!" he said.
Into the valley of Death
Rode the six hundred.

Active Reading Model

LISTEN

What does the strong, predictable rhythm remind you of?

1 A full *league* is a distance of about 3 miles (4.8 kilometers).

5 *[Light Brigade]* This British cavalry unit was called "light" because the men were armed only with swords.

Active Reading Model

RESPOND

What is your impression of these soldiers?

IMAGINE

Imagine the sight and sound of the cannons firing on the riders from three sides. Smell and taste the smoke from the cannon fire.

"Forward, the Light Brigade!"
Was there a man dismay'd?
Not tho' the soldier knew
 Some one had blunder'd.
Theirs not to make reply,
Theirs not to reason why,
Theirs but to do and die.
Into the valley of Death
 Rode the six hundred.

Cannon to right of them,
Cannon to left of them,
Cannon in front of them
 Volley'd° and thunder'd;
Storm'd at with shot and shell,
Boldly they rode and well,
Into the jaws of Death,
Into the mouth of hell
 Rode the six hundred.

---

21 In this context, *volley* refers to the firing of many cannons at once or in rapid succession.

Flash'd all their sabers° bare,
Flash'd as they turn'd in air
Sabring the gunners there,
Charging an army, while
All the world wonder'd.
Plunged in the battery-smoke
Right thro' the line they broke;
Cossack° and Russian
Reel'd from the saber-stroke
Shatter'd and sunder'd.°
Then they rode back, but not,
Not the six hundred.

Cannon to right of them,
Cannon to left of them,
Cannon behind them
Volley'd and thunder'd;
Storm'd at with shot and shell,
While horse and hero fell,
They that had fought so well
Came thro' the jaws of Death,
Back from the mouth of hell,
All that was left of them,
Left of six hundred.

When can their glory fade?
O the wild charge they made!
All the world wonder'd.
Honor the charge they made!
Honor the Light Brigade,
Noble six hundred!

---

27 *Sabers* (sā' bərz) are swords.

34 The *Cossacks* are a people of southern Russia, but they are not Russian by culture. Cossack men were famous as horsemen in the Russian cavalry.

36 *Sunder'd* means "wrenched apart; severed."

Active Reading Model

QUESTION

What is happening in lines 27–28?

INTERPRET

What effect did the charge have on the brigade?

CLARIFY

Who and what does the speaker say should be honored?

Balaclava, 1876. Lady Butler (Elizabeth Southerden Thompson). Oil on canvas, 101.6 x 194.3 cm. Manchester City Art Galleries, England.

Responding to Literature

Personal Response

How did you react to the description of the charge in the poem? Explain your answer.

Active Reading Response

Look back at the strategies described in the Active Reading Model notes on pages 438–439. Which strategy did you use most often as you read?

Analyzing Literature

Recall and Interpret

1. Summarize the events described in the poem.
2. Why do the men of the Light Brigade charge when they know the order is a mistake?
3. What weapons are used by the Light Brigade and by the enemy?
4. In your opinion, why doesn't the speaker reveal the identity of the person who orders the brigade to go forward?
5. What is meant by the phrase "All the world wonder'd"?
6. What does the speaker want readers of this poem to do? Why might this be so important to him?

Evaluate and Connect

7. In your opinion, what is most memorable about this poem? Why might the poem remain popular nearly 150 years after it was written?
8. Look back over the notes you made for the Reading Focus on page 440. How do your notions of heroism compare with those expressed by the speaker in this poem? Do you consider the soldiers of the Light Brigade heroes? Explain.
9. The Crimean War was the first war in which newspaper reporters and photographers covered battles at the front. How might the media treat a bungled military action today? Why?
10. Tennyson uses repetition throughout the poem. What effect does the repetition have? Use examples in your answer.
11. Identify two examples of **personification** in this poem. What effect or effects does the personification have? (See Literary Terms Handbook, page R9.)
12. If a close relative of yours had died in this battle, would you feel better about the sacrifice he made after reading this poem? Why or why not?

Literary **ELEMENTS**

Meter

Meter is a regular pattern of stressed and unstressed syllables that sets the overall rhythm of certain poems. The basic unit of meter is the **foot.** Each type of foot has a unique pattern of stressed and unstressed syllables. Read "The Charge of the Light Brigade" aloud, and note where the natural accents, or stresses, fall. Stressed syllables are marked with (ʹ), and unstressed syllables are marked with (˘). The feet and meter are marked in the passage below. Vertical lines separate the feet.

Háłf ă leăgue, | hálf ă leăgue,
Hálf ă leăgue | ónwărd

1. How does the rhythm of the lines above reflect the action in the poem?
2. Copy the first three lines of the third stanza on your paper and mark the stressed and unstressed syllables. What happens to the rhythm if you add the word *the* before the words *right, left,* and *front?*
3. How does the orderly meter reinforce the theme of the poem?

- See **Literary Terms Handbook,** p. R8.

Literature and Writing

Writing About Literature

Analyzing Imagery Read the poem again, and pay close attention to the battle imagery. How would you describe the imagery in this poem? Is it vividly realistic or "literary"? down to earth or glorified? How does the imagery fit with the theme of the poem? In a few paragraphs, analyze the poem's imagery and how it helps convey the poem's theme. Give specific examples from the poem to support your analysis.

Creative Writing

Telling It Like It Is Imagine that, as a newspaper reporter on the front lines of battle, you have the opportunity to interview a British survivor of the charge as well as a member of the Russian army. With a partner, brainstorm for questions you would ask the soldiers and the answers you might receive. Then write the questions and answers in their final form. You may find inspiration by looking at the paintings on pages 441 to 443 and imagining that you are there.

Extending Your Response

Literature Groups

Do and Die! With your group, discuss the meaning of these famous lines: "Theirs not to make reply, / Theirs not to reason why, / Theirs but to do and die." Do you agree with the sentiment expressed in these lines? Might being in the military affect how one views these lines? Share your ideas and be ready to support your opinions. Also feel free to challenge other members in your group. Share a summary of the discussion with your classmates.

Internet Connection

Poetry on the Web Look for information about "The Charge of the Light Brigade" and Alfred, Lord Tennyson on the Internet. Use what you find to create an illustrated pamphlet about this famous war poem and its author.

Performing

Honor the Charge Honor the Light Brigade by performing a dramatic reading of Tennyson's poem for your classmates or at a student assembly. Try to bring this exciting battle to life for your audience. Rehearse by reading the poem aloud to yourself, experimenting with the rhythm of the poem and with the tone, volume, and pitch of your voice.

Reading Further

You might also like to read these works by Alfred, Lord Tennyson:

Poems: *The Complete Poetical Works of Tennyson* includes "The Eagle," which contains vivid imagery of an eagle; "Crossing the Bar" is a meditation on death; and "Break, Break, Break" is a lyric poem expressing the speaker's feelings after the loss of a loved one.

Idylls of the King, a series of twelve narrative poems, tells the story of King Arthur and his knights of the Round Table.

Save your work for your portfolio.

Scotland Forever, 1881 (detail).

INTERDISCIPLINARY HISTORY CONNECTION

Fighting Against the Odds

Immortalized in Alfred, Lord Tennyson's famous poem, the charge of the Light Brigade is remembered as one of the bravest, and most tragically useless, cavalry charges in British military history. U.S. history includes infamous battle engagements of its own, in which soldiers faced heavy odds in deadly confrontations.

- When Texas fought for its independence from Mexico, 189 men defended the Alamo, a mission in San Antonio. For thirteen days a force of about 4,000 Mexican soldiers held the mission under siege. Using rifles as clubs after they ran out of ammunition, the Texans finally succumbed on March 6, 1836. Their deaths led to the famous slogan "Remember the Alamo!"—a rallying cry that spurred Texans on to victory in the war.

The battle of the Alamo.

- In the Civil War, Confederate general Robert E. Lee faced overwhelming odds in fighting against the North, which had twice the manpower of the South and thirty times the arms-making capacity. Still, in the first years of the war, Lee's army seemed nearly invincible. Lee's fortunes changed, however, in the biggest battle of the war—the Battle of Gettysburg. At Gettysburg, Pennsylvania, about 75,000 Southern soldiers fought for three days against about 93,000 Northern soldiers. On the third day of the battle, July 3, 1863, Lee ordered Major General George E. Pickett to launch an attack with about 15,000 men directly into the middle of the Northern lines. Pickett's men marched across an open field and up Cemetery Ridge as they were raked by enemy fire. Those few who reached the top of the ridge were shot or captured. The rest retreated under fire, leaving about 7,000 dead. After the battle, Lee's army escaped to Virginia, having suffered nearly 23,000 casualties.

Activity

Find out more about one of the battles mentioned here, or investigate another battle fought against great odds, such as the attack on the Gallipoli Peninsula in World War I, the invasion of Iwo Jima, or the landing of troops at Omaha Beach on D-Day during World War II. Write a brief summary of the challenges and outcome of the battle.

Theme 6 Life Lessons

Perhaps the most important thing life teaches us is that there is always more to learn. Every experience brings a new lesson. The selections in this theme explore the wisdom gained from some of life's greatest teachers—love, family, death, and nature. What lessons about life have you gleaned from recent experience?

THEME PROJECTS

Listening and Speaking

Gather Lessons In most cases, the longer someone has lived, the more he or she has learned about life.

1. Choose four or five of your favorite poems in this theme, and share them with someone much older than yourself.
2. Ask that person to use one poem as a springboard to his or her own memories. Ask him or her to describe an experience the poem brings to mind and to share what was learned as a result. Be sure to take notes or tape-record the conversation.
3. In an oral presentation for your classmates, read the poem your subject focused on and the story he or she shared.

Interdisciplinary Project

Science Both scientists and poets have a keen desire to learn about life's mysteries.

1. As you read the poems in this theme, think about which ones might interest a scientist.
2. Choose a poem that deals with phenomena also explored by science, and make a list of scientific questions that the poem brings to mind. Then conduct research to find the answers to one or more of the questions.
3. Make a poster that presents the poem, the questions, and the scientific explanations.

The Family, 1962. Marisol (Escobar). Painted wood and other materials in three sections, 82½ x 65½ x 15½ in. The Museum of Modern Art, New York.

Before You Read

The Black Snake and *The Meadow Mouse*

Reading Focus

Do you consider yourself an animal lover, or are you indifferent to animals?

Sharing Ideas With a small group, share your thoughts about animals and your reactions to them. Consider whether you feel about wild animals as you do about domestic ones. For example, do you react to reptiles and rodents in the same way that you react to cats and dogs?

Setting a Purpose Read to learn how some people can be affected by encounters with wild animals.

Building Background

Did You Know?

- Of the 2,400 to 2,700 snake species alive today, only about ten percent are extremely dangerous to people, and only a few of these—including coral snakes, rattlesnakes, and water moccasins—live in North America. Most snakes, by helping to control rodent and insect populations, benefit humans. Snakes have much more reason to fear people—their worst enemies—than people have to fear them.
- Many ancient and modern cultures have considered snakes to be valuable or even sacred. One symbol of medicine depicts two "healing" snakes entwined around a staff. The Aztecs worshiped the feathered serpent god Quetzalcoatl. In Arizona, Hopi people still perform the snake dance. This is a ceremony in which dancers carry live snakes in their mouths and then release them in all directions to deliver to the gods the people's pleas for rain.

- The most common rodents in North America are meadow voles, also called meadow mice. Voles are similar to mice, but they have short tails, blunt snouts, small eyes and ears, and short limbs. They are somewhat larger than house mice, and they have shaggier fur. Because voles have enormous appetites, they sometimes cause great damage to crops and trees. Their natural predators include cats, foxes, coyotes, weasels, hawks, owls, snakes, and skunks.

Meet Mary Oliver

Mary Oliver writes often about the natural world in simple language filled with vibrant images. To write creatively, Oliver says, she needs "a place apart—to pace, to chew pencils, to scribble and erase and scribble again." Her "scribbling" has produced many books of poetry and has won for her the Pulitzer Prize and the National Book Award.

Mary Oliver was born in 1935 in Cleveland, Ohio.

Meet Theodore Roethke

"I have a genuine love of nature," Theodore Roethke (ret′ kē) once wrote. "I can sense the moods of nature almost instinctively." Roethke was a college professor, tennis teacher, and poet. Roethke, one of the most distinguished U.S. poets of the mid-twentieth century, won the Pulitzer Prize and two National Book Awards.

Theodore Roethke was born in Saginaw, Michigan, in 1908 and died in 1963 on Bainbridge Island, Washington.

The Black Snake

Mary Oliver

The Lurking Place, 1985. Ismael Frigerio. Tempera and acrylic on burlap, 92 x 120 in. Collection of the artist.

When the black snake
flashed onto the morning road,
and the truck could not swerve—
death, that is how it happens.

Now he lies looped and useless
as an old bicycle tire.
I stop the car
and carry him into the bushes.

He is as cool and gleaming
as a braided whip, he is as beautiful and quiet
as a dead brother.
I leave him under the leaves

and drive on, thinking
about *death:* its suddenness,
its terrible weight,
its certain coming. Yet under

reason burns a brighter fire, which the bones
have always preferred.
It is the story of endless good fortune.
It says to oblivion:° not me!

It is the light at the center of every cell.
It is what sent the snake coiling and flowing forward
happily all spring through the green leaves before
he came to the road.

---

20 *Oblivion* is the state of being entirely forgotten.

The Meadow Mouse

Theodore Roethke

Wendell Minor. Collection of the artist.

Viewing the art: Does this mouse capture your sympathies the way the meadow mouse captured the sympathies of the speaker? Explain why or why not.

1

In a shoe box stuffed in an old nylon stocking
Sleeps the baby mouse I found in the meadow,
Where he trembled and shook beneath a stick
Till I caught him up by the tail and brought him in,
Cradled in my hand,
A little quaker, the whole body of him trembling,
His absurd whiskers sticking out like a cartoon-mouse,
His feet like small leaves,
Little lizard-feet,
Whitish and spread wide when he tried to struggle away,
Wriggling like a minuscule° puppy.

Now he's eaten his three kinds of cheese and drunk from his bottle-
cap watering-trough—
So much he just lies in one corner,
His tail curled under him, his belly big
As his head; his bat-like ears
Twitching, tilting toward the least sound.

Do I imagine he no longer trembles
When I come close to him?
He seems no longer to tremble.

2

But this morning the shoe-box house on the back porch is empty.
Where has he gone, my meadow mouse,
My thumb of a child that nuzzled in my palm?—
To run under the hawk's wing,
Under the eye of the great owl watching from the elm-tree,
To live by courtesy of the shrike,° the snake, the tom-cat.

I think of the nestling fallen into the deep grass,
The turtle gasping in the dusty rubble of the highway,
The paralytic stunned in the tub, and the water rising,—
All things innocent, hapless,° forsaken.

---

11 Something that is *minuscule* (min′ əs kūl′) is very, very small.
25 Sometimes called a butcherbird, a *shrike* is a bird that feeds on small animals.
29 To be *hapless* is to be unlucky or unfortunate.

Responding to Literature

Personal Response

What went through your mind as you finished reading each poem?

Analyzing Literature

The Black Snake

Recall and Interpret

1. At the start of the poem, where is the black snake and what has happened to it? How does the speaker react to it?
2. To what things does the speaker compare the snake? What do these comparisons suggest about the speaker's view of the snake?
3. What does the snake's fate make the speaker think about?
4. What might the speaker mean when she says, "Yet under / reason burns a brighter fire, which the bones / have always preferred"?
5. What do you suppose is "the light at the center of every cell"? Explain.

Evaluate and Connect

6. On the whole, would you call this poem cheerful or depressing, serious or playful? Explain, using details from the poem to support your answer.
7. Think about your response to the Reading Focus on page 448. If you had discovered the snake, how would your reactions compare with the speaker's? Which, if any, of your usual attitudes about snakes changed as you read the poem? Explain.

The Meadow Mouse

Recall and Interpret

8. What does the speaker do after finding the meadow mouse?
9. What does the speaker's action suggest about his personality and values?
10. How does the mouse behave at the beginning of the poem, and how does the speaker interpret the mouse's behavior after it has been fed?
11. What is the speaker afraid of in the second part of the poem? In your opinion, why is he so affected by what has happened?

Evaluate and Connect

12. In lines 21–22, the speaker calls the mouse "my meadow mouse, / My thumb of a child." In your opinion, is the speaker reasonable or misguided to think of the mouse as his own? Explain.
13. What is the **theme,** or perception about life or human nature, of this poem? Consider what happens in section 2 and what this event causes the speaker to think about.
14. Have you ever had a pet that ran away, or can you imagine that happening? Compare your feelings with the ones the speaker probably experienced.
15. **Theme Connections** What lessons about life might "The Black Snake" and "The Meadow Mouse" offer you? Explain.

Literary ELEMENTS

Simile and Metaphor

Writers often use comparisons to help readers experience things in new ways. A **simile** is a figure of speech using a word such as *like* or *as* to compare seemingly unlike things. For example, Theodore Roethke says the mouse's feet are "like small leaves." A **metaphor** is also a form of figurative language that compares or equates seemingly unlike things. A metaphor, which does not use *like* or *as,* suggests the comparison rather than stating it directly. For example, still describing the mouse's feet, Roethke calls them "little lizard-feet."

1. What three similes does Mary Oliver use in the second and third stanzas of her poem? What does each simile suggest about the snake? How could Oliver have stated the same ideas by using metaphors?
2. How do these similes help you see the snake in a new way? What do the comparisons tell you about the speaker and about what is important to her?
3. Roethke describes the mouse as "my thumb of a child that nuzzled in my palm." What images does this metaphor bring to mind?

- See **Literary Terms Handbook,** pp. R11 and R7.

Literature and Writing

Writing About Literature

Sunday Supplement Write an analysis of Oliver's or Roethke's poem for the literary supplement of a newspaper or for your school literary magazine. Identify the setting and theme of the poem, and explain the poet's attitude toward the subject. Be sure to use plenty of details and examples from the poem in your analysis.

Creative Writing

Poet Pen Pal Write a letter to Roethke or Oliver, giving your response to the poem you have read. You might also share your response to the Reading Focus on page 448 or tell about a personal experience similar to the one described by the poet. Then exchange letters with a classmate, and imagine that you are the poet as you write a response.

Extending Your Response

Literature Groups

On a Slow News Day Imagine that you and the members of your group work for a small cable access television station, and you are asked to produce a special report on what actually happened to the snake and the meadow mouse. Draft a list of questions to ask the speakers of each poem, framing them in the style of a police investigation into an accident or a disappearance. Then role-play the two interviews. Find out what happened and why.

Interdisciplinary Activity

Music: Sing Out Use your responses to the poems as the basis for song lyrics about an animal. Try to communicate images and life lessons that you associate with the animal. Match your lyrics to a familiar tune, and then, working solo or with a small group, make a recording of your song. Play your song for the class.

Internet Connection

Save the Animals The speakers in both poems recognize the vulnerability of animals. What is being done in your community, county, or state to protect wildlife? Working with a partner, use the Internet and other resources to find out what is being done near you and how citizens can get involved. Make Web site bookmarks, take notes, and report your findings to the class. You might also create a Web page for your community with links to other pertinent sites.

Save your work for your portfolio.

Reading & Thinking Skills

Monitoring Comprehension

Have you ever sung along to a song, even though you didn't understand all the words? In the same way, it's possible to read a poem without understanding it. To truly understand a poem, you will need to read it more than once, **monitoring your comprehension** as you go. Suppose you are reading the last stanza of Theodore Roethke's "The Meadow Mouse."

> "I think of the nestling fallen into the deep grass,
> The turtle gasping in the dusty rubble of the highway,
> The paralytic stunned in the tub, and the water rising,—
> All things innocent, hapless, forsaken."

You might use the following strategies to monitor your comprehension:

- **Read the stanza slowly and then read it again.**
- **Use a dictionary to look up the meanings of any unfamiliar words.**
- **Paraphrase the lines.** That is, put the lines in your own words.
- **Make connections with other parts of the poem.** For example, ask yourself why the poet might have repeated a word or an image.
- **Ask yourself questions.** What questions do you have about a line, a stanza, or the entire poem? You might list them and discuss them with a classmate.

● For information on related comprehension skills, see **Reading Handbook,** pp. R78–R107.

EXERCISES

Use the list of strategies above to monitor your comprehension of the following poem by John Haines, "Trees Are People and the People Are Trees."

> And there in the crowded commons
> three hundred striding people,
> gesturing, eating the air,
> halted around us, suddenly quiet.
>
> They sprouted leaves and cones,
> they wore strange bark for clothing,
> and gently lifted their arms.

1. List three questions you could ask about the poem to monitor your comprehension of it.
2. Write a short paragraph in which you explain the meaning of this poem to someone else.

MEDIA connection

Newspaper Article

Do you ever feel frustrated by what society and tradition say you can and cannot do? It's not easy to break down barriers and stereotypes, but as you'll read in the article that follows, it *is* possible!

Getting Her Kicks In: Butler's Earning Fame for Skill, Not Gender

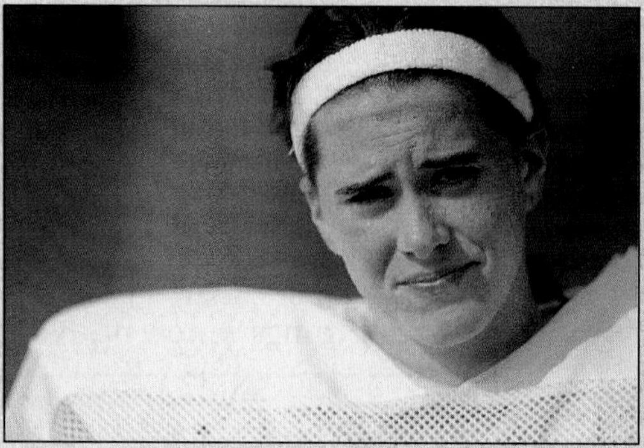

by Michael Lee—*The Atlanta Journal and Constitution*, August 21, 1997

Enough with the girl stuff, already. Yes, Riverdale High School junior place-kicker Tonya Butler is the only girl on the Raiders' football team. And yes, she likes to wear dresses and shops regularly. And yes, she loves teddy bears: She owns 53.

Just let the novelty die right there, OK?

Butler can kick.

"I don't want people to say, 'Hey, look. There's a girl. Let's get entertained,'" Butler said. "When it comes to football, I want to be seen as a good kicker. That's all."

Last year, the 16-year-old junior [hit] 7 of 8 field goals and 28 of 31 extra points. She also earned all-state honorable mention honors in Class AAA, the state's second-largest classification.

"I know people get caught up that she's a girl," Riverdale head coach George Spencer said. "I'll admit, I'm old school. I used to say, 'They don't let girls play this sport.' I had to stop saying that."

And for the first time since playing football, Butler finally has a boyfriend who's supportive of her exploits—Riverdale senior tight end and punter Joey Wilson.

"It's different having your boyfriend on the team," Butler said. "I guess it was intimidating for most guys—a girl playing football. It's always been a guy ego thing."

Not so for Wilson.

"I really don't think about it," Wilson said. "It was easy to keep my eye on her. I know where she is when I'm at football practice."

Spencer said their relationship doesn't cause any distractions. "They take a business approach with it," the coach said.

Every now and then, someone does joke about it.

"We kid with him sometimes that she can kick better than him," Spencer said. Cool. Wilson said it's no question who has the better foot: "I can't kick."

Butler dresses in the coach's office, which has such perks as a couch and a TV. "It's got cable, too," she brags.

And she's finally over the embarrassment of wearing shoulder pads and a helmet. "I felt out of place big time," Butler said.

As much as she'd like to be seen as a player on the field, off the field, Butler is a girl.

"What, [Spencer] has me listed at 135?" Butler asked. "I work hard to stay at 130. Girls have to be small. Guys have to be big."

Analyzing Media

1. Why does Tonya Butler want people to overlook her gender when they watch her play football?
2. Were you surprised by Butler's final remark? Why or why not?

Before You Read

I Was a Skinny Tomboy Kid and *Purchase*

Reading Focus

What activities do you enjoy? Why do you like them so much?

Chart It! Do you feel good about yourself when you're doing things you enjoy? What do these activities say about your personality? Complete a chart like the one shown below, listing the activities you like most and the personal qualities you associate with them.

Activities	Qualities

Building Background

Did You Know?

Bessie Coleman (1893–1926). First African American woman pilot.

- In many societies and during different times in history, girls and women have been expected to fulfill certain roles and behave in certain ways. Traditional female roles–wife, mother, homemaker, housekeeper, babysitter, nurse–have fostered nurturing, cooperative behavior. Often, the assigned "female" roles and behavior have been enforced by law as well as by custom. For example, until well into the twentieth century, girls and women in the United States were not expected to seek the same education, professions, wages, and legal rights as men. They were not to vote; they were not to take part in competitive sports; they were not to be aggressive, loud, or argumentative; and they were certainly not to wear jeans!
- The English language itself reveals that our society's gender-based values are even older than our country. In the 1400s, the word *tomboy* meant "a rude, boisterous, or forward boy"; by the late 1500s, it meant "a bold or immodest woman." Modern British and U.S. definitions of *tomboy*–"a wild romping girl who behaves like a boy"; "a girl who enjoys those activities and interests that are usually considered to be preferred by boys"–continue to imply that there are distinct codes of female behavior, and that girls' interests should be different from those of boys.

Meet Alma Luz Villanueva

"Writing takes all your courage," says Alma Luz Villanueva, "to stand by your work and see it through to publication—courage and luck and discipline, discipline, discipline." Villanueva, a prolific author and American Book Award winner, has all of these. Her poetry, stories, and novels often explore the experiences of Mexican American girls and women trying to be themselves.

Alma Luz Villanueva was born in 1944 in Santa Barbara, California.

Meet Naomi Long Madgett

Naomi Long Madgett had trouble getting her first book of poetry published, but "I was determined to keep writing in my voice," she says. To help other African American writers, she founded Lotus Press, Inc. In 1993 she received an American Book Award for her work as an editor and publisher.

Naomi Long Madgett was born in Norfolk, Virginia, in 1923.

I Was a Skinny Tomboy Kid

Alma Luz Villanueva

I was a skinny tomboy kid
who walked down the streets
with my fists clenched into
tight balls.
I knew all the roofs
and back yard fences,
I liked traveling that way
sometimes
not touching
the sidewalks
for blocks and blocks
it made
me feel

victorious
somehow
over the streets.
I liked to fly
from roof
to roof
the gravel
falling
away
beneath my feet,
I liked
the edge
of almost
not making it.

And the freedom
of riding
my bike
to the ocean
and smelling it
long before
I could see it,
and I traveled disguised
as a boy
(I thought)
in an old army jacket
carrying my
fishing tackle
to the piers, and
bumming bait
and a couple of cokes
and catching crabs
sometimes and
selling them
to some Chinese guys
and I'd give
the fish away,
I didn't like fish
I just liked to fish—
and I vowed
to never
grow up
to be a woman
and be helpless
like my mother,
but then I didn't realize
the kind of guts
it often took
for her to just keep
standing
where she was.

I grew like a thin, stubborn weed
watering myself whatever way I could
believing in my own myth
transforming my reality
and creating a
legendary/self
every once in a while
late at night
in the deep
darkness of my sleep
I wake
with a tenseness
in my arms
and I follow
it from my elbow to
my wrist
and realize
my fists are tightly clenched
and the streets come grinning
and I forget who I'm protecting
and I coil up
in a self/mothering fashion
and tell myself
it's o.k.

Purchase

Naomi Long Madgett

I like the smell of new clothes,
The novel° aroma of challenge.
This dress has no past
Linked with regretful memories
To taint° it,
Only a future as hopeful
As my own.
I can say of an old garment
Laid away in a trunk:
"This lace I wore on that day when. . . ."
But I prefer the new scent
Of a garment unworn,
Untainted like the new self
That I become
When I first wear it.

---

2 Here, ***novel*** **means "new."**
5 **To *taint* something is to spoil or contaminate it.**

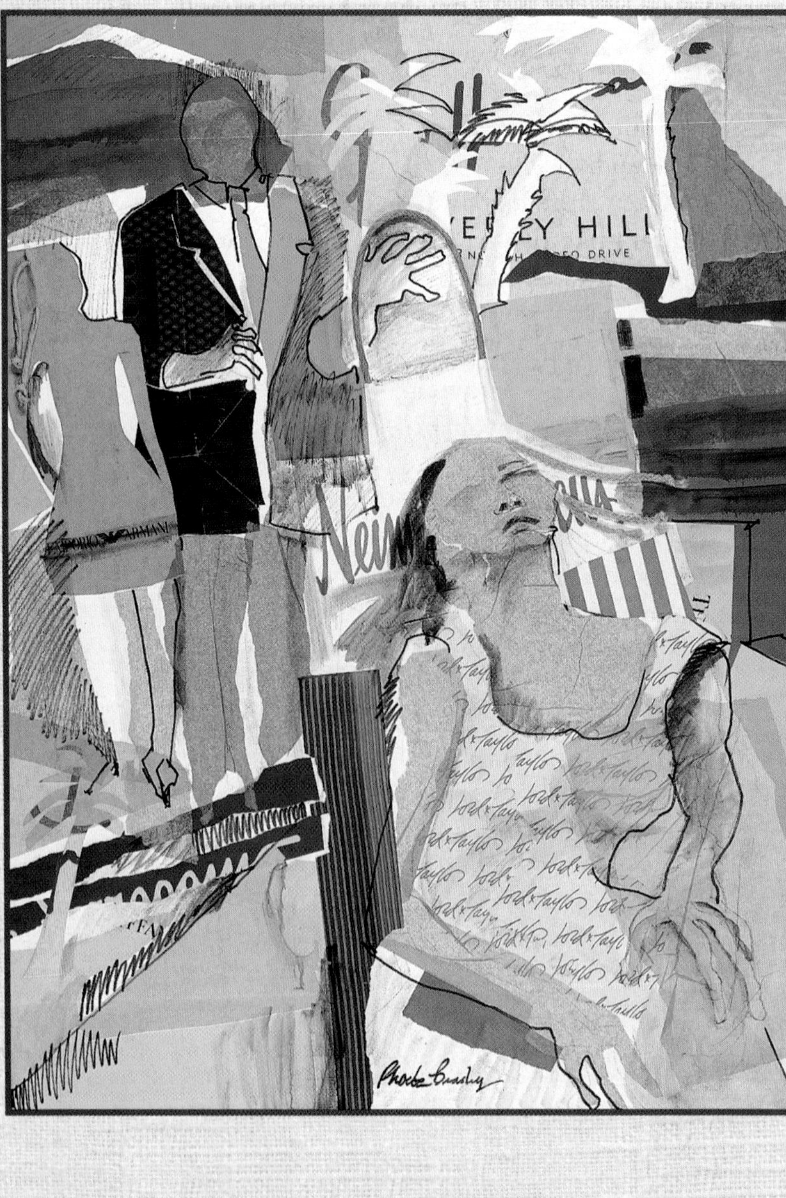

Between Paradise and Rodeo Drive, 1994. Phoebe Beasley. Mixed media collage, 40 x 30 in. Private collection.

Viewing the art: What connections can you make between this image and the ideas expressed in the poem?

Responding to Literature

Personal Response

Which of the two speakers would you like to meet more, and why?

Analyzing Literature

I Was a Skinny Tomboy Kid

Recall and Interpret

1. Describe the speaker's childhood appearance and activities. How did her looks and actions give her pleasure?
2. What were the speaker's childhood thoughts about her mother? How and why might they have changed?
3. The speaker mentions "believing in my own myth," "transforming my reality," and "creating a legendary self." In your opinion, what might she mean by each of these phrases?
4. What line marks the shift from past to present? How has the speaker's childhood affected her later life? What does she tell herself, and why?

Evaluate and Connect

5. Does the speaker's childhood behavior seem familiar to you, or does it seem unusual? Explain your answer.
6. The speaker says, "I grew like a thin, stubborn weed / watering myself whatever way I could." Explain the **simile:** how is her growth like that of a thin, stubborn weed? How did she nourish herself? Given the poem's setting, do you think this simile is effective? Explain.
7. Why might the speaker have felt the need to disguise herself when she went fishing? Do you think girls would need this disguise today? Explain.
8. In your opinion, does the speaker refer to herself as "a skinny tomboy kid" with pride, or does she do so with a sense of guilt or shame? Explain.

Purchase

Recall and Interpret

9. Why does the speaker like new clothes? Explain what they mean to her.
10. What might the speaker mean by "the novel aroma of challenge"?
11. What effect does an old garment have on the speaker? Explain.
12. Would you say the speaker prefers to think about the past or anticipate the future? What details from the poem support your answer?

Evaluate and Connect

13. The speaker emphasizes the "smell," "aroma," and "scent" of new clothes. What does this appeal to the sense of smell add to your experience of the poem?
14. Do you think a regretful memory can spoil a moment in the present? Explain.
15. How do you feel when you first put on new clothes? Why do you think new clothes have this effect on you?

Literary ELEMENTS

Speaker

Just as all prose works have a narrator, all poems have a **speaker,** or voice, that talks to the reader. The speaker is not necessarily the poet. It can also be a fictional or real person, an animal, or even a thing. The speaker's words communicate a particular tone or attitude toward the subject of the poem. For example, the speaker in "I Was a Skinny Tomboy Kid" is a woman whose tone is one of self-acceptance.

1. What words and details tell you that the speakers of both poems are women?
2. Identify several words or phrases in "I Was a Skinny Tomboy Kid" that reveal a tone of self-acceptance.
3. What words and phrases in "Purchase" suggest that the speaker has a positive attitude?

- See **Literary Terms Handbook,** p. R12.

Literature and Writing

Writing About Literature

Analyzing Theme Both poems concern the theme of identity, and the forces—both internal and external—that help to shape it. Write a brief analysis explaining how this theme applies to "I Was a Skinny Tomboy Kid" and "Purchase."

Personal Writing

Who Are You? Review your response to the Reading Focus on page 455. Use it to draw a cartoon strip or series of pictures of yourself doing the things that you enjoy most. Write thought bubbles or captions for each picture that explain how it feels to engage in such an activity. If you want, share your work with a partner or a small group.

Extending Your Response

Literature Groups

Debating the Issue Do you think that the speakers of these poems express universal thoughts and feelings, or thoughts and feelings that only girls and women can relate to? Debate the question, backing up your opinions with details from the poems and from your experience. Share your conclusions with other groups.

Listening and Speaking

Other Voices Many songs are essentially poems set to music. Find and listen to a popular song (folk, rock, blues, or other) that is about a person becoming who he or she wants to be. If possible, share the song with the class, and discuss what the words and music seem to reveal about the "speaker" of the lyrics.

Learning for Life

What Are the Rules? When the speaker in "I Was a Skinny Tomboy Kid" walked down the street with her fists clenched, disguised as a boy, she may have felt as if she were breaking some rules of conduct for being a girl. Make a list of the rules of conduct boys are expected to follow and a list of rules girls are expected to follow. Share your lists with a partner, and discuss which rules are toughest to obey.

Reading Further

If you'd like to read more by Alma Luz Villanueva and Naomi Long Madgett, you might enjoy these poems:

"A Poet's Job" can be found in *Bloodroot* by Alma Luz Villanueva.

"November" and "Reply" can be found in *Remembrances of Spring* by Naomi Long Madgett.

Save your work for your portfolio.

Vo•cab•u•lar•y Skills

Word Roots

The most basic part of a word is called its "root." For example, the root of *novel* (a word that is used in the poem "Purchase") is *nov,* meaning "new." This root is used in *renovate* ("to make like new"), *novelty* ("something new"), and *novice* ("a beginner"). All of these words share a common root, *nov,* and they all have to do with the idea of newness.

Some roots, like *nov,* can only be used as part of another word. Other roots are whole words that can stand alone. In "I Was a Skinny Tomboy Kid," for example, the speaker says she is "transforming [her] reality." The root of *transforming* is *form,* a word meaning "shape; appearance; state of existence." Other word parts may be added to the root form to create such words as *reform, conform,* and *formula*. The charts below list some common roots.

Root	Meaning	Example
corp	body	corpse
dict	speak	predict
duc	lead	educate
form	form, shape	uniform
init	beginning	initial

Root	Meaning	Example
mem	mindful	memory
min	small	minor
mort	death	immortal
nat	born	native
vac	empty	vacant

EXERCISE

Use the information in the charts above to help you complete each of the following sentences.

1. Poets who describe the formative experiences of their youth write about things that
   a. molded them. b. frightened them. c. inspired them.
2. In "The Meadow Mouse," the baby mouse vacated the shoe box when he
   a. slept in it. b. lived in it. c. left it.
3. The innate characteristic that Oliver describes in "The Black Snake" is one that
   a. exists naturally. b. is dangerous. c. is acquired over time.
4. To say that both "The Black Snake" and "The Meadow Mouse" deal with the idea of mortality is to say that both are concerned with
   a. nature. b. death. c. innocence.
5. According to the poem "Purchase," some old garments are mementos; that is, they are
   a. rags. b. as good as new. c. reminders of the past.

Before You Read

Desmet, Idaho, March 1969 and *The Funeral*

Reading Focus

Have you ever attended a wake, funeral, or memorial service or watched one on television?

Journal In your journal, describe the event and something it made you think about. If you have never experienced such an event, describe what might go through your mind if you were to do so.

Setting a Purpose Read to learn about the thoughts that went through the minds of two people at their fathers' funerals.

Building Background

Did You Know?

- Desmet is the community that grew up around the Catholic church and mission school on the Coeur d'Alene (cur dä len′) reservation in northern Idaho. Poet Janet Campbell Hale's father attended the mission school around 1904, when he was twelve years old. In those days, following the "Indian wars" of the late 1800s, the U.S. government and Christian churches tried to educate Native Americans to become "mainstream" Americans. Like other children attending the mission school, Hale's father was taught English, reading, and writing, and was punished if he spoke his own language. But when Hale revisited the school after her father's death, things had changed. The school was now operated by the tribe, and students' courses included Coeur d'Alene language and history.
- A traditional wake is a constant watch kept over a person who has died, lasting from one to three days and nights before burial. Historically, the wake had one purpose: to make sure the dead person was really dead—so that he or she wouldn't be buried alive by mistake! In modern American wakes, friends and relatives gather to pay their respects to the person who has died and to the bereaved family. The underlying social purpose of the wake is to allow people to adjust together to the change that the death has brought to their family and to their community.
- At a funeral in the United States, pallbearers hold a coffin by its handles and carry it to the gravesite.

Meet Janet Campbell Hale

"How I wished I, too, had known [my father's mother], had listened to her stories, had understood the language," Janet Campbell Hale wrote. Hale never learned the Coeur d'Alene language because she was schooled in English and as an older child had moved away from the reservation in Idaho. Today, Hale's poetry, stories, and essays focus on Native American experience.

Janet Campbell Hale was born in 1947.

Meet Gordon Parks

As a boy growing up in the small town of Fort Scott, Kansas, Gordon Parks felt fettered by poverty and racism. But equipped with perseverance, "curiosity and a great [ambition] to achieve," Parks distinguished himself as a photographer, photojournalist, writer, musician, and film director. Although he never went to college, he has been awarded thirty honorary doctorate degrees.

Gordon Parks was born in 1912.

Desmet, Idaho, March 1969

Janet Campbell Hale

At my father's wake,
The old people
Knew me,
Though I
Knew them not,
And spoke to me
In our tribe's
Ancient tongue,°
Ignoring
The fact
That I
Don't speak
The language,
And so
I listened
As if I understood
What it was all about,
And,
Oh,
How it
Stirred me
To hear again
That strange,
Softly
Flowing
Native tongue,
So
Familiar to
My childhood ear.

8 In this context, *tongue* means language.

The Funeral

Gordon Parks

After many snows I was home again.
Time had whittled down to mere hills
The great mountains of my childhood.
Raging rivers I once swam trickled now
like gentle streams.
And the wide road curving on to China or
Kansas City or perhaps Calcutta,
Had withered to a crooked path of dust
Ending abruptly at the county burying ground.
Only the giant who was my father
remained the same.
A hundred strong men strained beneath his coffin
When they bore him to his grave.

Responding to Literature

Personal Response

Which lines or images from each of these poems seem most important or powerful to you? In your journal, explain what effect they have on you.

Analyzing Literature

Desmet, Idaho, March 1969

Recall and Interpret

1. What happened at the wake that strongly affected the speaker?
2. Explain how the "old people" could know the speaker, although she did not know them. How well do you suppose they knew her?
3. Why might the "old people" have talked to the speaker in a language she couldn't understand or speak?
4. In your opinion, how does the speaker feel about hearing the tribe's "ancient" or "native" language? Which details from the poem give you these impressions?

Evaluate and Connect

5. How might it feel to be addressed in a language you couldn't understand? Explain.
6. Describe the **mood** of this poem. What words and phrases from the poem help to establish this mood? (See Literary Terms Handbook, page R8.)

The Funeral

Recall and Interpret

7. How long has it been since the speaker was home, and why has he returned?
8. How has his home changed since the speaker was last there? How does the speaker account for such changes?
9. Why might a "crooked path" appear to a child as a "wide road curving on to China or / Kansas City or perhaps Calcutta"? In your opinion, what does this image suggest about the kind of child the speaker was?

Evaluate and Connect

10. What has "remained the same" for the speaker? In your opinion, what does this say about the kind of relationship the speaker had with his father?
11. Why might a child think of a parent as a "giant"?
12. What person–someone you know personally or someone you know about–might you describe as a "giant"? Explain what qualities the person has that would cause you to think of him or her that way.

Literary Criticism

Reviewer Louise Giles says that Gordon Parks's novel *The Learning Tree* was written "with rueful reminiscence, even humor. It is an unassuming and thoroughly conventional book, but it has freshness, sincerity, and charm." Write a letter to Giles explaining whether her statement also has validity when applied to Parks's poem "The Funeral."

Literary ELEMENTS

Hyperbole

Hyperbole is a type of figurative language in which great exaggeration is used for emphasis or humorous effect. For example, in "The Funeral," hyperbole is used to emphasize the way in which the speaker idolizes his father. The father is a "giant," and "A hundred strong men strained beneath his coffin."

1. Find another example of hyperbole in "The Funeral."
2. Do you think that hyperbole is used effectively in this poem? Explain your answer.

- See **Literary Terms Handbook,** p. R6.

Literature and Writing

Writing About Literature

Analyzing Theme The passage of time–and the changes it brings–could be said to be a theme of both poems. Write one or more paragraphs about each poem, analyzing the importance of this theme. Be sure to include in your analysis details from the poems–specific words and lines that relate to the passage of time and its effects.

Personal Writing

Come Along Imagine that you are a friend of the speaker in "Desmet, Idaho, March 1969" or "The Funeral," and that you went with her or him to the wake or funeral. Write an explanation of how your emotions differed from those of the speaker. The journal entry you wrote for the Reading Focus on page 462 might provide a springboard to writing.

Extending Your Response

Literature Groups

First or Second Language? In your group, reflect on the importance of continuing to speak the language of your parents, grandparents, or more distant ancestors. What might you gain from knowing the language of your original culture if it were different from English? What might you lack if you couldn't speak your ancestors' language? Share your opinions and reasons with other groups.

Performing

Message in Movement Janet Campbell Hale and Gordon Parks both chose poetry as an art form to communicate something about their experience at a solemn time. Imagine that you are a mime or a dancer, and create a pantomime or modern dance to express the same message as one of the poems. If you choose the dance, select some recorded music, or have a partner provide music or drumming, to accompany you. After practicing your performance, share it with the class.

Interdisciplinary Activity

Mathematics: Dead Reckoning Carrying a coffin, or pallbearing, has its own mathematics. With a partner, estimate the combined weight of a 150-pound coffin and that of a 187-pound man. If there are six pallbearers at the man's funeral, what will be each pallbearer's share of the load? If, as in the poem "The Funeral," there were one hundred pallbearers with fifty on each side, how long would the coffin have to be for each pallbearer to have twelve inches of space? Make up other morbid math problems and exchange them with other pairs.

Reading Further

You might enjoy these nonfiction works by Janet Campbell Hale and Gordon Parks:

Bloodlines: Odyssey of a Native American Daughter, by Janet Campbell Hale, is a collection of eight essays about Hale's family history.

Voices in the Mirror is an autobiography by Gordon Parks.

Save your work for your portfolio.

Before You Read

The Space and *who are you,little i*

Reading Focus

Have you ever looked out a window or at a landscape and taken comfort from what you saw? If you have not, imagine what such a comforting scene would look and sound like.

Picture It! Draw a picture of a comforting place you know or imagine, or photocopy or download a picture that represents something similar. Imagine yourself within the picture, and write a caption that tells what you see and hear.

Setting a Purpose Read to learn about the special scenes that two poets remember.

Building Background

Did You Know?

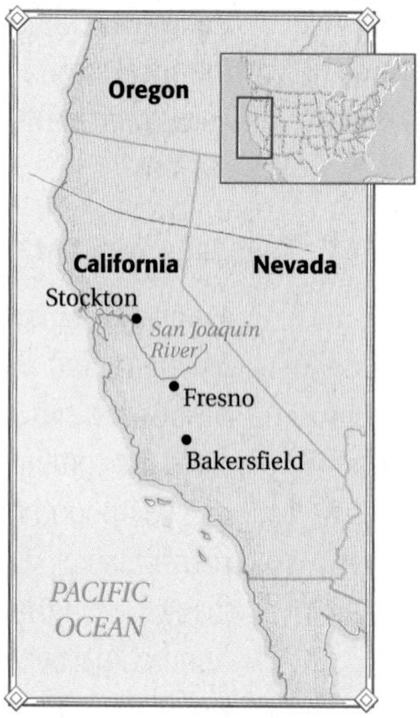

- In his preface to a poetry collection, Gary Soto writes, "My pulse was timed to the heart of this valley." Soto refers to the San Joaquin Valley, a place that inspired his first poetry collection, *The Elements of San Joaquin,* and continues to inspire his works of poetry, fiction, and nonfiction. The San Joaquin Valley is the southern portion of California's Central Valley, extending from Stockton to Bakersfield. With its warm weather, flat terrain, and rich topsoil washed down from the mountains, this region produces abundant fruits, vegetables, and grains. The harvesting of these crops provides work for large numbers of migrant farm laborers, many of whom are Mexican American.
- Unconventional spacing, punctuation, and capitalization–or the lack thereof–are hallmarks of E. E. Cummings's writing style, and they have won the poet both praise and criticism. Cummings also has been known to weave slang, jazzy rhythms, and invented words into his poems. Many of his poems are thought to be joyous celebrations.

Meet Gary Soto

Having worked as a day laborer and lived in a Chicano barrio (a Mexican American, low-income neighborhood), Gary Soto has known poverty too well. He remembers that his family was "poor as sparrows picking at the free fruits of the valley." But through his poetry, fiction, and nonfiction essays, Soto has become a creative spokesperson for the Mexican American experience. He lives and teaches in Berkeley, California.

Gary Soto was born in Fresno, California, in 1952.

Meet E. E. Cummings

Edward Estlin Cummings was a poet, prose writer, playwright, and painter. E. E. Cummings served in an ambulance corps in France during World War I. He lived in Paris and New York City during the 1920s and 1930s.

E. E. Cummings was born in Cambridge, Massachusetts, in 1894, and died in 1962.

The Space

Gary Soto

West of town,
Near Hermosa's° well,
I sleep sometimes—
In a hammock of course—
Among avocado trees,
Cane, spider-grass,
The hatchet-faced *chula,*°
The banana's umbrella
Of leaves.
It is here
In the spiny brush
Where cocks gabble,
Where the javelina°
Lies on its side
Like an overturned high-heel.
I say it is enough
To be where the smells
Of creatures
Braid like rope
And to know if
The grasses rustle
It is only
A lizard passing.
It is enough, brother,
Listening to a bird coo
A leash° of parables,°
Keeping an eye
On the moon,
The space
Between cork trees
Where the sun first appears.

2 *Hermosa* (är mō´ sə).

7 Here, the *chula* (chōō´ lə) is a type of cactus. Note that the word in Mexican Spanish also means "cute"—and suggests the opposite of Soto's "hatchet-faced" image.

13 An animal resembling a small pig, the *javelina* (hä´ və lē´ nə), or peccary, lives in parts of the southwestern United States, and in Central and South America.

26 Here, *leash* means "a set of three." *Parables* are brief stories intended to illustrate a truth or moral lesson.

who are you,little i

E. E. Cummings

who are you,little i

(five or six years old)
peering from some high

window;at the gold

of november sunset

(and feeling:that if day
has to become night

this is a beautiful way)

Responding to Literature

Personal Response

Which of these two poems do you like better? Explain your choice to a partner.

Analyzing Literature

The Space

Recall and Interpret

1. Where does the speaker sometimes sleep? Why might he choose to sleep there?
2. Why might the speaker say "of course" at the end of line four? How does this line affect your perception of the speaker?
3. Compare line 16 with line 24. What might the speaker mean by "it is enough"? What reasons could he have for repeating himself, and why might the two lines differ slightly?
4. List three examples of **simile** or **metaphor** in the poem, and tell what they have in common. What might these images reveal about the speaker or his experience? (See Literary Terms Handbook, pages R11 and R7.)
5. What do you think "the space" is? In your opinion, why did Soto give his poem this title? In your answer, consider the many possible meanings of the word.

Evaluate and Connect

6. Do you like this speaker? Why or why not? Think about what the poem's details say about what he might be like and what is important to him.
7. Is there a "space"–in nature or somewhere else–that is "enough" for you? Explain.

who are you,little i

Recall and Interpret

8. What do you think this poem is about? Use details from the poem to support your answer.
9. Explain the **pun** in the name "little i." (See Literary Terms Handbook, page R10.)
10. What does the speaker remember doing as a young child? Why do you think this event was so memorable?
11. How would you describe the **mood** of this poem? Use words or phrases from the poem to support your answer.

Evaluate and Connect

12. In your opinion, how does the speaker feel as the day–and the year–nears an end? How do you feel at those times?
13. Look at the way Cummings uses **rhyme** in this poem. Why might he have chosen not to rhyme "sunset" and "night"?
14. In your opinion, would a five- or six-year-old have the "feeling" attributed to the child at the end of the poem? Why and by whom might that feeling have been added?
15. How does Cummings's use of lowercase letters and unconventional punctuation affect your understanding of the poem? Explain.

Literary ELEMENTS

Imagery

Imagery is the "word pictures" that writers use to re-create vivid experiences and evoke an emotional response in readers. In creating effective imagery, writers use descriptions that appeal to the senses–sight, sound, touch, taste, or smell. In "The Space," for example, "the smells / Of creatures / Braid like rope." This image helps readers experience the mingling of odors in the setting that is described.

1. Find two other examples of imagery in "The Space." Tell what senses they appeal to and explain how the imagery helps you experience the poem's setting.
2. Find an example of imagery in "who are you,little i." Tell what senses the image appeals to and explain how this image helps bring the poem to life.

- See **Literary Terms Handbook,** p. R6.

Literature and Writing

Writing About Literature

Making Connections In your opinion, how are these two poems alike and different? For example, how do the speakers compare in age? What is the theme of each poem? Make a list of comparisons and contrasts. Write a paragraph to explain why these poems might be paired.

Creative Writing

One Style or the Other Write a poem about a sunset or about the special place you thought about for the Reading Focus on page 466. Try to imitate the style of Cummings or Soto as you write. Share copies of your poem with others or include it in a class poetry collection.

Extending Your Response

Literature Groups

Travel Poster With your group, create a travel poster that would lure tourists to the destination described in "The Space." Together, brainstorm a list of information that tourists will need to know about, such as possible accommodations and things to do in this place. Some students may focus on the poster's text; others may focus on artistically depicting the setting Soto describes. Try to convey the special appeal the place has for the speaker. Display your poster on a bulletin board.

Listening and Speaking

Poetry Reading Working with a partner, plan to read each of these poems before an audience. Experiment with different ways of communicating the poems' rhythm, rhyme, and mood. Then present your readings to the class. Listen to several students' oral presentations and discuss the difference between reading the poems and hearing them read aloud.

Interdisciplinary Activity

Science: Sunset's Glow In "who are you,little i," Cummings writes about the glow of a November sunset. Investigate the atmospheric conditions that produce a beautiful sunset. What causes sunsets to display more beautiful and varied colors in one location than in another? What effect do pollutants have on sunset colors? Why might the color look gold one evening and pink and purple the next? Share your findings with the class.

Reading Further

You might enjoy these works by Gary Soto and E. E. Cummings:

Memoir: *Living Up the Street,* by Gary Soto, is an award-winning collection of prose essays about growing up in a barrio in Fresno.

Poems: "in Just–" and "anyone lived in a pretty how town" can be found in *Complete Poems* by E. E. Cummings.

Save your work for your portfolio.

MEDIA connection

Song

In 1991 singer-songwriter Eric Clapton's four-year-old son fell to his death from the forty-ninth-floor window of a New York City apartment building. Clapton co-wrote "Tears in Heaven" in memory of the boy. The song won a Grammy Award for best song of 1992.

Tears in Heaven

by Eric Clapton and Will Jennings

© 1991 EC Music Limited (PRS) and Blue Sky Rider Songs (BMI)

Would you know my name if I saw you in heaven?
Would it be the same if I saw you in heaven?
I must be strong and carry on 'cause I know I don't belong here in heaven.

Would you hold my hand if I saw you in heaven?
Would you help me stand if I saw you in heaven?
I'll find my way through night and day 'cause I know I just can't stay here
in heaven.

Time can bring you down, time can bend your knees.
Time can break the heart, have you beggin' "please," beggin' "please."
Beyond the door there's peace, I'm sure.
And I know there'll be no more tears in heaven.

Would you know my name if I saw you in
heaven?
Would you be the same if I saw you in heaven?
I must be strong and carry on 'cause I know
I don't belong here in heaven.
'Cause I know I don't belong here in heaven.

Analyzing Media

1. How does knowing that this song was written by the father of a little boy who died affect your reading of it?
2. Explain whether you find this song to be optimistic or pessimistic. How else could you describe this song?

Before You Read

"Good Night, Willie Lee, I'll See You in the Morning" and The Reading

Reading Focus

Civility means "politeness." Sometimes people choose to be civil when, in truth, they do not feel like it. Have you ever felt forced into civility? Have you ever decided to be civil as a kindness?

Journal In your journal, describe a time that you acted civilly even though you didn't want to. Explain the situation and how you felt about what happened.

Setting a Purpose Read "Good Night, Willie Lee, I'll See You in the Morning" to learn about an unusual instance of civility.

Building Background

Did You Know?

- Alice Walker's parents were poor Georgia sharecroppers who raised a family of eight children. Walker and her father, whose name was Willie Lee, were often at odds. For a long time, the two of them did not even speak to each other. What Walker regrets most about their relationship is that "it did not improve until after his death."

  In an essay titled "Father," Walker writes that Willie Lee "was one of the leading supporters of the local one-room black school, and according to everyone who knew him then, including my older brothers and sister, believed in education above all else. Years later, when I knew him, he seemed fearful of both education and politics and disappointed and resentful as well. . . . Education merely seemed to make his children more critical of him."

  In addition to writing essays and poems about him, Walker has drawn on her father's experience in her novels. She states, "Though it is more difficult to write about my father than about my mother . . . it is equally liberating. Partly this is because writing about people helps us understand them, and understanding them helps us understand ourselves."
- "When I was young, I used to read my poems to my mother and father," says Gabriel Gbadamosi. He explains that as he did so, his parents would be "couched," or sitting on the sofa. Gbadamosi says the word *couched* in his poem "The Reading" is also a play on the word *coached,* since his parents were like coaches to him.

Meet Alice Walker

"The black woman is one of America's greatest heroes. . . . Not enough credit has been given to the black woman, who has been oppressed beyond recognition." With these words Alice Walker sums up an important theme in her novels, short stories, and poems: Despite all that black women have suffered, they still triumph. Walker herself has triumphed, winning many awards and honors.

Alice Walker was born in Eatonton, Georgia, in 1944.

Meet Gabriel Gbadamosi

The British son of an Irish mother and a Nigerian father, Gabriel Gbadamosi (bäd ə mō′ zē) says he speaks "with my father's voice in my mother's tongue." An award-winning playwright as well as a poet, Gbadamosi lives in South London and travels extensively.

Gabriel Gbadamosi was born in 1961 in South London, England.

"Good Night, Willie Lee, I'll See You in the Morning"

Alice Walker

Looking down into my father's
dead face
for the last time
my mother said without
tears, without smiles
without regrets
but with *civility*
"Good night, Willie Lee, I'll see you
in the morning."

And it was then I knew that the healing
of all our wounds
is forgiveness
that permits a promise
of our return
at the end.

The Reading

Gabriel Gbadamosi

In memory of my parents

I'm doing it again—
reading my father my new poems
in a trance-struck
adolescent voice.

Only this time
they're about my mother—
no-longer with him,
couched° in her cold repose.°

She peers over
the charmed boundary
from her corner
of our triangle,

to wonder am I alright
(her son, the poet)
and to squeeze my father's hand
so I don't notice.

8 *Couched* can mean either "lying down" or "hidden, as if in waiting." *Repose* can refer to rest and relaxation, peacefulness, sleep, or death.

Responding to Literature

Personal Response
What questions would you like to ask the speakers of these poems?

Analyzing Literature

"Good Night, Willie Lee, I'll See You in the Morning"

Recall and Interpret

1. Explain what happens in this poem and where the events might be taking place.
2. The mother speaks "without / tears, without smiles / without regrets." In your opinion, what does the absence of these things convey?
3. What might be going through the mother's mind as she says, "Good night, Willie Lee, I'll see you / in the morning"? Why might she say "good night" rather than "good-bye," and what might "morning" refer to?
4. **Theme Connections** What life lesson does the speaker learn from her mother's words to her husband? Explain how lines 10–15 support your interpretation.

Evaluate and Connect

5. Describe your reaction to the mother's words. What does her statement make you think or feel about her?
6. What kind of relationship do you imagine the speaker's mother had with her husband? What kind of relationship do you imagine the speaker had with her father? Give evidence from the poem to support your answers.
7. Describe a situation in your life in which forgiveness was–or could have been–a healing force.

The Reading

Recall and Interpret

8. How would you describe the speaker? Explain why he might read to his father "in a trance-struck / adolescent voice."
9. What has happened to the speaker's mother? Use details from the poem to explain how the speaker thinks of her and how she influences his life.
10. What emotion or thought does the speaker's mother convey by squeezing her husband's hand? Why, do you think, is the speaker not supposed to notice?

Evaluate and Connect

11. What impression do you get of the speaker's relationship with his parents? Use details from the poem in your answer.
12. Why might the speaker refer to his family as a "triangle"? Explain what it can feel like to be in a triangle of family or friends.
13. Do you think "The Reading" is a good **title** for this poem? Tell why or why not.
14. How might loved ones who have died still influence a person's life?

Literary ELEMENTS

Tone

Tone is the attitude toward a subject that is expressed by the author or speaker. Tone may be communicated through particular words and details that express emotions and that evoke an emotional response in the reader. For example, word choice or phrasing may seem to convey humor, sarcasm, respect, dread, or playfulness. In Alice Walker's poem, the speaker's tone at first seems matter-of-fact, but toward the end of the poem, as she reflects on what she has learned, her tone might be described as thoughtful, tender, or optimistic. Reading a poem aloud may help you "hear" the tone.

1. What adjectives besides *civil* might you use to describe the tone of the mother as she says "good night" to her husband?
2. How would you describe the tone of "The Reading"?

- See **Literary Terms Handbook,** p. R13.

Literature and Writing

Writing About Literature

Comparing Relationships How are the husband-wife and the parent-child relationships similar and different in the two poems? Choose one kind of relationship, and write a paragraph or two comparing Walker's handling of it with Gbadamosi's. Support your insights with evidence from the poems.

Personal Writing

Virtual Vision How do you envision the mother in "The Reading"? In your journal, describe in detail what you picture when you read lines 7–16. You might also sketch a picture of the mother in your journal. Show how you think of her in relation to other members of her family.

Extending Your Response

Literature Groups

Stage a Meeting What if the mothers in these poems met? What if the speakers did? With a small group, imagine a meeting of one of the pairs. Decide what they might say to each other. Then stage a meeting for the rest of the class. You might use your response to the Reading Focus on page 471 to help you decide the extent to which civility would play a role in the meeting.

Interdisciplinary Activity

Psychology: Dealing with Death One of the greatest struggles in a person's life—and potentially one of the greatest learning experiences—is dealing with the death of a loved one. Elisabeth Kübler-Ross is a world-renowned psychiatrist who has devoted her life to helping people deal with death. Research her teachings about death and prepare an oral or written summary of them.

Learning for Life

Advice Column Imagine that you write an advice column and you receive a letter from a person grieving over someone's death. Your correspondent is upset because the person died before a problem in their relationship could be resolved. Write a column consoling the person and advising others who have this common problem. Model your message on the lesson in Walker's poem.

Reading Further

You might enjoy these poems by Alice Walker and Gabriel Gbadamosi:

"Women," "Burial," and "Forgiveness," in Alice Walker's *Her Blue Body Everything We Know.*

"Death of the Polar Explorers," by Gabriel Gbadamosi, in *The Heinemann Book of African Poetry in English.*

Save your work for your portfolio.

Writing Skills

Using Formal and Informal Language

If you were explaining a class project to the principal of your school, you probably would use sentences that were respectful in tone and grammatically correct. In other words, you would use **formal language.** If you were describing last night's game to a friend, you might use slang and incomplete sentences to relate what you saw. In that case, you would use **informal language.** You decide whether to use formal or informal language in writing too. Read the letters below to see how writers use formal or informal language to suit their purpose and their audience.

> **Dear Mr. Gbadamosi,**
>
> **I am writing to offer my condolences for the death of your mother. I was fortunate to have Mrs. Gbadamosi as my seventh-grade teacher, and her high standards and unflagging support have inspired my endeavors ever since. My thoughts are with you during this difficult time.**
>
> **Gabe,**
>
> **I hear you got a poetry reading at the Bolivar Library. Way to go! You'll bring down the house, right? Sorry I can't be there to hear you read. Let's hang out when I get back to town.**

In the first letter, the writer is expressing sympathy to someone she doesn't know. Serious words, such as *condolences* and *endeavors,* are in keeping with the gravity of the situation. Complete sentences and precise phrasing establish a tone of respectful distance and courtesy.

On the other hand, the second letter is written to a friend who has something to celebrate. Here, the writer uses simple vocabulary and includes slang expressions such as *bring down the house* and *hang out.* The letter includes incomplete sentences, such as *Way to go!,* and a rhetorical question–*right?,* which give the writing a conversational tone.

When deciding whether to use formal or informal language in your writing, consider your purpose and your audience. Do you want to write as you might speak to that person or group? Would informal language help you to establish an intimate connection with an audience you don't know? Or would formal language be more effective and appropriate? Experiment with vocabulary and sentence structure until you find the degree of formality that fits your purpose.

EXERCISE

Imagine that both the principal of the high school and an eighth grader from your neighborhood have asked you for advice about how to ease the transition from eighth grade to ninth. Write a separate letter to each of them. Use formal and informal language appropriately.

Before You Read

The World Is Not a Pleasant Place to Be and *Suavidades/Serenity*

Reading Focus

The British poet William Wordsworth wrote, "There is a comfort in the strength of love; t'will make a thing endurable which else would overset the brain, or break the heart."

Sharing Ideas Discuss this quotation with a small group. What kind of love might he have been referring to? The love of a family member? of a pet? of a boyfriend or girlfriend? How might that love "make a thing endurable"?

Setting a Purpose Read to discover what two other poets have to say about the importance of love and companionship in life.

Building Background

Did You Know?

- The U.S. writer Nikki Giovanni first became a prominent poet in the black literary movement of the 1960s. Many of her early poems focus on social and political issues, including black pride and black solidarity. In her later poetry, she has turned increasingly to such personal subjects as family, love, and loneliness. "The World Is Not a Pleasant Place to Be" appears in the book of poems *My House,* which was first published in 1972. Giovanni has often emphasized the importance of family love in her life. An often-quoted line from her poem "Nikki-Rosa" is "Black love is Black wealth."
- The Chilean poet Gabriela Mistral once declared, "I have written as one who speaks in solitude, for I have lived very much in solitude, in every place." Mistral obviously felt her aloneness keenly, even though she spent much of her life surrounded by people. She never married or bore children of her own, and yet she had a great love for children and a great respect for motherhood, which many of her poems express. Mistral was a much-loved teacher and was called "the poet of motherhood by adoption" in the citation for her Nobel Prize for Literature in 1945. It was for children that she wrote a series of "cradle songs," or lullabies, including "Serenity."

Celebration of Life, 1986. Phillip Joe King, MD. Swedish Medical Center, Seattle, WA.

Meet Nikki Giovanni

Nikki Giovanni has traveled throughout the United States and Europe, giving poetry readings and lectures that attract large, enthusiastic crowds. Asked why she kept up a grueling schedule of poetry readings, Giovanni replied, "Because . . . some people who've never gotten what they asked for . . . ask for you, that you would make them feel better or help them understand. . . . love is the word."

Nikki Giovanni was born in Tennessee in 1943.

Meet Gabriela Mistral

Born Lucila Godoy Alcayaga, Gabriela Mistral was the first Latin American woman to win the Nobel Prize for Literature. Even so, she placed more importance on her career as a teacher than on her writing. As an international diplomat, she became an advocate for the poor.

Gabriela Mistral was born in 1889 in Chile and died in 1957 in New York.

The World Is Not a Pleasant Place to Be

Nikki Giovanni

the world is not a pleasant place
to be without
someone to hold and be held by

a river would stop
its flow if only
a stream were there
to receive it

an ocean would never laugh
if clouds weren't there
to kiss her tears

the world is not
a pleasant place to be without
someone

Seated Figure, 1979.
Elizabeth Catlett. Mahogany,
22 x 13½ x 15¾ in.
Collection of the artist.

©Elizabeth Catlett/Licensed by
VAGA, New York, NY

Suavidades

Gabriela Mistral

Cuando yo te estoy cantando,
en la Tierra acaba el mal:
todo es dulce por tus sienes:
la barranca, el espinar.

Cuando yo te estoy cantando,
se me acaba la crueldad:
suaves son, como tus párpados,
¡la leona y el chacal!

Serenity

Gabriela Mistral
Translated by Doris Dana

When I am singing to you,
on earth all evil ends:
as smooth as your forehead
are the gulch and the bramble.

When I am singing to you,
for me all cruel things end:
as gentle as your eyelids,
the lion with the jackal.

Responding to Literature

Personal Response

Which of your friends, relatives, or acquaintances would you like to have read these poems? Why?

Analyzing Literature

The World Is Not a Pleasant Place to Be

Recall and Interpret

1. According to this poem, what makes the world "not pleasant"?
2. The speaker uses two examples from the natural world to make her point. Put each of these examples in your own words, and tell how each connects to the main idea expressed in the first and last stanzas.
3. Do you imagine the speaker as being "without someone"? Why or why not?

Evaluate and Connect

4. In your opinion, why did Giovanni repeat the first stanza in the last stanza but leave out the last few words? What is the effect?
5. How does the third stanza express a scientific fact in a poetic way? In your opinion, why does the poet make a connection between laughter and tears in this stanza?
6. Do you agree with the sentiment expressed in this poem? Does it apply to your life? Why or why not?
7. What other title would you give this poem?

Suavidades/ Serenity

Recall and Interpret

8. For the speaker in this poem, what is the source of serenity?
9. How are the stanzas of this poem alike? How are they different?
10. In your own words, explain the speaker's message in the first two lines of each stanza.
11. How would you describe the speaker and the "you" in this poem? How old might each be? What might be the relationship between them?

Evaluate and Connect

12. What is the effect of **repetition** in this poem? (See Literary Terms Handbook, page R10.)
13. Look again at the quotation in the Reading Focus on page 476. How might Wordsworth have responded to Mistral's poem?
14. On what occasion(s) might you have experienced feelings similar to those expressed by the speaker in the poem? Explain.

Literary Criticism

According to one critic, the poetry of Nikki Giovanni "is conversational and strongly influenced by contemporary rhythm and blues music." Write a one-paragraph analysis of "The World Is Not a Pleasant Place to Be" in which you consider how certain literary devices contribute to the poem's conversational and musical qualities.

Literary ELEMENTS

Personification

Personification is a figure of speech in which an animal, object, or idea is given human qualities or characteristics. In "The World Is Not a Pleasant Place to Be," Giovanni speaks of an ocean laughing and a cloud kissing the ocean's tears: laughing, kissing, and crying are all human actions. She also gives the river the human characteristic of being able to control its own actions.

1. What is the effect of Giovanni's use of personification?
2. How does the use of personification emphasize the speaker's loneliness?

- See **Literary Terms Handbook,** p. R9.

Literature and Writing

Writing About Literature

Comparing Imagery Both of these poems express the need for human relationships. In a few paragraphs, compare the imagery in the two poems and explain which poem conveys its theme most vividly to you.

Creative Writing

A Lyric Poem Think about an experience you had that came to mind as you read these poems. Use these thoughts as a springboard to write a short lyric poem about the need for human closeness and companionship in life.

Extending Your Response

Literature Groups

Solo vs. Social In both poems, the speaker expresses dependence on human relationships to escape unpleasantness and cruelty. Do all people thrive on social contact, or is living on one's own best for some people? Spend some time on your own thinking about this question–and about how Nikki Giovanni and Gabriela Mistral might answer it–and jot down your thoughts in your journal. Then meet with your group to compare ideas.

Learning for Life

Print Advertisement Because many poems are pithy and poignant, they are sometimes used in advertising. In your group, choose an excerpt from one of these poems to be used in a magazine advertisement for UNICEF, a United Nations organization that aids poor children and that Gabriela Mistral helped found. Create the advertisement, combining the excerpt with photos or other illustrations, and display it in class.

Interdisciplinary Activity

Music: A Common Refrain Solitude and companionship, comfort and grief, love and abandonment–all are common subjects for musicians as well as artists and writers. Look for contemporary songs, as well as songs from earlier decades, that express the same feelings expressed in "The World Is Not a Pleasant Place to Be" and "Serenity." Bring in recordings of these songs and share them with your class.

Reading Further

You might enjoy these poems by Nikki Giovanni and Gabriela Mistral:

"Nikki-Rosa," by Nikki Giovanni, may be found in *Ego Tripping and Other Poems for Young People.*

"Close to Me" and "Night" are in *Selected Poems by Gabriela Mistral,* translated by Langston Hughes.

Save your work for your portfolio.

Before You Read

Defining the Grateful Gesture and *My Mother Combs My Hair*

Reading Focus

There is a song that begins, "Parents are people, people with children." What do these lyrics suggest to you?

Map It! Make a word web with the phrase "Parents are people" in the center. Jot down your associations, thoughts, and reactions, and connect them to that phrase.

Setting a Purpose Read these two poems to share in the reactions the speakers have to their mothers.

Building Background

Did You Know?

- The childhood home of the mother in "Defining the Grateful Gesture" is Puerto Rico, a small, resource-poor island that has long suffered the effects of overpopulation. Its population density is more than one thousand people per square mile. By comparison, the average for the United States is about seventy people per square mile. By U.S. standards, Puerto Rico has a high rate of unemployment and poverty. But the situation today is much better than it was in the past. In the 1940s, a self-help program called "Operation Bootstrap" was launched to promote social welfare and stimulate economic growth by developing manufacturing and service industries. Tourism in particular grew tremendously. The program helped ease much of the dire poverty on the island.
- In traditional East Indian households, the senior male is considered the head of the family, and the women are subservient to the men. Marriages are typically arranged by family elders. As part of a marriage agreement, the woman's family provides a *dowry,* a payment in money or property, to the husband. Throughout their married lives, wives are expected to obey their husbands.

Meet Yvonne Sapia

Yvonne Sapia says that her poetry is an attempt "to understand what is happening to all of us in a world we have become too busy to observe significantly." Sapia has written an award-winning volume of poetry, *Valentino's Hair.* Her novel of the same name won praise for its "well-chosen details of Puerto Rican life."

Yvonne Sapia was born in 1946 in New York City.

Meet Chitra Banerjee Divakaruni

Chitra Banerjee Divakaruni (dē′ vä kä ro͞o′ nē) is an award-winning poet, novelist, and short-story writer. She is also the president of an organization that aids South Asian women. Like a heroine in one of her novels, Divakaruni says, "I too have lived in the diametrically opposed worlds of India and America. I too have taken on a new identity in a new land."

Chitra Banerjee Divakaruni was born in Calcutta, India, in 1956.

Defining the Grateful Gesture

Yvonne Sapia

According to our mother,
when she was a child
what was placed before her
for dinner was not a feast,
but she would eat it
to gain back the strength
taken from her by long hot days
of working in her mother's house
and helping her father make
candy in the family kitchen.
No idle passenger
Traveling through life was she.

And that's why she resolved
to tell stories about
the appreciation for satisfied hunger.
When we would sit down
for our evening meal
of arroz con pollo°
or frijoles negros con plátanos°
she would expect us
to be reverent to the sources
of our undeserved nourishment
and to strike a thankful pose
before each lift of the fork
or swirl of the spoon.

For the dishes she prepared,
we were ungrateful,
she would say, and repeat
her archetypal° tale about the Pérez
brothers who stumbled over themselves
with health in her girlhood town
of Ponce,° looking like ripe mangoes,
their cheeks rosed despite poverty.

My mother would then tell us about
the day
she saw Mrs. Pérez searching
the neighborhood garbage,
picking out with a missionary's care
the edible potato peels, the plantain
skins,
the shafts of old celery to take
home to her muchachos°
who required more food
than she could afford.

Although my brothers and I
never quite mastered the ritual
of obedience our mother craved,
and as supplicants° failed
to feed her with our worthiness,
we'd sit like solemn loaves of bread,
sighing over the white plates
with a sense of realization, or relief,
guilty about possessing appetite.

---

18 *Arroz con pollo* (ä rōs′ kōn pō′ yō) is Spanish for "rice with chicken."

19 *Frijoles negros con plátanos* (frē hō′ les neg′ rōs kōn plä′ tä nōs) are black beans with plantains (plant′ əns). Plantain is a banana-like fruit that is starchy and eaten cooked.

29 If a thing is *archetypal* (är′ kə tī′ pəl), it serves as an ideal example or perfect model.

32 *Ponce* (pōn′ sā) is a city in Puerto Rico.

40 *Muchachos* (mo͞o chä′ chōs) means "boys."

46 People who beg or make humble requests are *supplicants.*

Woman Dressing Her Hair, 18th century India. Private collection.

My Mother Combs My Hair

Chitra Banerjee Divakaruni

The room is full
of the scent of crushed hibiscus,°
my mother's breath.
Our positions are of childhood,
I kneeling on the floor,
she crosslegged
on the chair behind.
She works the comb
through permed strands
rough as dry seaweed.
I can read regret in her fingers
untangling snarls,
rubbing red *jabakusum*° oil
into brittle ends.

When she was my age,
her hair reached her knees,
fell in a thick black rush
beyond the edges
of old photographs. In one,
my father has daringly
covered her hand with his
and made her smile.
At their marriage, she told me,
because of her hair
he did not ask for a dowry.

This afternoon I wait
for the old comments,
how you've ruined your hair,
this plait's like a lizard's tail,
or, *if you don't take better care*
of it, you'll never get married.
But the braiding is done,
each strand
in its neat place, shining,
the comb put away.

I turn to her, to the gray
snaking in at the temples,
the cracks growing
at the edges of her eyes
since father left.
We hold the silence
tight between us
like a live wire,
like a strip of gold
torn from a wedding brocade.

---

2 *Hibiscus* (hī bis′ kəs) is a showy red flower that grows in India and other tropical climates.

13 *Jabakusum* is the brand name of expensive scented oil from the hibiscus flower that is sometimes rubbed into the hair of both men and women, mainly in northern India.

Responding to Literature

Personal Response

Which lines from each poem do you find most memorable? Share your responses with a partner.

Analyzing Literature

Defining the Grateful Gesture

Recall and Interpret

1. How would you describe the childhood of the mother in this poem? How does her experience differ from that of her children? Use details from the poem in your answer.
2. What might the speaker mean when she describes her mother with these words: "No idle passenger / Traveling through life was she"? What might the description imply about the speaker and her brothers and about the mother's impression of them?
3. In your opinion, what effect does the mother intend her stories to have?
4. How would you describe the effect the mother's stories actually have on her children?

Evaluate and Connect

5. In your opinion, does the poet create a believable portrait of a mother and her children? If so, how does she do it? If not, what is missing or wrong?
6. Whose point of view do you relate to more, the mother's or the speaker's? Why?
7. Do you think it is worthwhile for parents to try to teach their children to appreciate what they have? Why or why not? What is a good way to teach someone to be grateful?

My Mother Combs My Hair

Recall and Interpret

8. How would you describe the speaker in this poem? You might consider her age, where she might live, and whether she is single or married.
9. How does the speaker's hair compare with the hair of her mother at the same age?
10. Why has the daughter's hair been a source of conflict between the daughter and mother?
11. What changes does the daughter notice in her mother, and why have these changes occurred?

Evaluate and Connect

12. Look back at the word web you created for the Reading Focus on page 480. What associations, thoughts, or reactions connect with a **theme** of this poem? Explain.
13. Do you think the mother and the speaker can relate to each other? Why are they both silent after the braid is complete? Support your answers with details from the poem.
14. **Theme Connections** What lesson about life does the daughter learn from her mother? Is this the lesson her mother had hoped to teach her? Explain.
15. Name one tradition or attitude–perhaps toward grooming or dress–that has been handed down to you by a parent or other relative. How have you lived by that tradition or departed from it?

Literary ELEMENTS

Symbol

A **symbol** is any object, person, place, or experience that represents something else, usually something abstract. For example, in "My Mother Combs My Hair," long black hair is a symbol of Indian tradition; it is seen as a hallmark of feminine beauty.

1. The daughter's perming of her hair in "My Mother Combs My Hair" is a symbolic act. What might it symbolize?
2. What might food or the act of eating symbolize in "Defining the Grateful Gesture"?

- See **Literary Terms Handbook,** p. R12.

Literature and Writing

Writing About Literature

Comparing Characters How are the mothers in these two poems similar and different? How are the speakers' reactions to them similar and different? Write at least one paragraph in answer to each question. Give evidence from the poems to support your answers.

Personal Writing

Connecting Your Experience In one sense, both poems concern parents' desires for their children to look, behave, and feel certain ways. Do you and your parents or guardians face struggles similar to the ones described by the speakers? Answer this question in your journal, making connections between your experience and that of one of the speakers.

Extending Your Response

Literature Groups

Imagery and Meaning In your group, discuss the meaning of the last complete sentence in each of the two poems. What do these sentences convey? How do the poets use imagery to convey their meanings? Give evidence from each poem to support your interpretations, and share your responses with the rest of the class.

Learning for Life

Change: A Fact of Life Interview two sets of parents and their children to discover how things have changed for the younger generation. Find out what things the children have that the parents did not and what things the parents enjoyed that have been lost to their children. For example, the parents may have enjoyed safer neighborhoods. You might also ask what each generation does not understand about the other. Report your findings to the class.

Interdisciplinary Activity

Social Studies: Making a Collage With a partner, create a collage of words and images that suggest the cultural situations and the family relationships explored in these two selections. Conduct research if necessary into the cultures of India and Puerto Rico. Your collage may depict characters, scenes, or objects as well as suggest moods or feelings. Display your collage in your classroom.

Reading Further

If you'd like to read other poems by Yvonne Sapia and Chitra Banerjee Divakaruni, you might look for these:

"Childhood," by Chitra Banerjee Divakaruni, depicts a nightmarish memory of a place in India; it may be found in the anthology *The Open Boat.*

"The Figure at the Door" and "Visiting Esperanza," by Yvonne Sapia, explore childhood memories; they may be found in the collection *Valentino's Hair.*

Save your work for your portfolio.

Writing Workshop

Persuasive Writing: Advice Essay

Once you've learned a lesson from your life experience, you may want to pass on your new knowledge to others. Everybody needs a little advice sometimes, so you're likely to find an audience for what you want to share. **In this workshop, you will write a persuasive advice essay, offering help to others who might benefit from your experience.**

- As you write your advice essay, refer to the **Writing Handbook,** pp. R58–R71.

EVALUATION RUBRIC
By the time you complete this Writing Workshop, you will have
- written an introduction that includes a clear statement of the problem
- stated advice in a clear, convincing way
- supported your advice with reasons, facts, and personal experience
- concluded with a persuasive restatement of the advice
- presented an advice essay that is free of errors in grammar, usage, and mechanics

The Writing Process

PREWRITING

PREWRITING TIP
Study how advice columns in newspapers and magazines present and organize the advice they offer.

Explore ideas

Base your advice essay on the lessons life has taught you. Have you learned how to deal with peer pressure or how to manage your time? If you have trouble coming up with ideas, consider what suggestions you could give to others about

- how to be appreciative, as the speaker is in "The Space"
- how to understand why your parents or other relatives act the way they do, as each speaker does in "Defining the Grateful Gesture" and "My Mother Combs My Hair"
- how to find meaning in the death of a loved one, as each speaker does in "Good Night, Willie Lee, I'll See You in the Morning" and "The Reading"
- how to get a fresh start, as the speaker does in "Purchase"
- how to combat loneliness, as the speaker does in "The World Is Not a Pleasant Place to Be"

Keep your purpose and audience in mind

Your ultimate purpose is to persuade readers to follow your advice. To achieve this goal, you must state your advice clearly and show that it is reasonable. Remember that your audience doesn't know what you know. Try to anticipate your readers' questions so you can address them in your writing. See the Writing Skill "Using Formal and Informal Language" on page 475 for tips on how to adjust your language to suit your audience and purpose.

Make a plan

Be clear. Be firm. Be personal. You'll persuade your readers if you present your advice in a clear, orderly way and if you seem confident about your suggestions. Readers also need to sense that there's a real person behind the essay.

Organize your advice within the basic essay structure: introduction, body, and conclusion. Some of the issues you may want to address in each section are shown below.

		STUDENT MODEL
Introduction	Focus on your readers' needs: • What problem will you help readers avoid? • What lesson are you going to pass along? • What benefit will readers gain? • What are your qualifications?	• Disagreements between parents and children • How to get along with family • Learning how to understand the other person's point of view • I've had problems with my parents, and now things are better.
Body	State your advice: • What, exactly, should readers do? Convince readers that your advice is good: • What reason do you have for giving it? • What facts support your reason? • What personal experiences support it?	• Wait until anger subsides after an argument. Then sit down and listen to the other person's reasons. He or she should listen to yours. You are on the road to understanding and compromise. • It allows for family harmony, or at least open communication. • My relationship with my family is much better now than it was a year ago. • We used this technique when making decisions about everything from what cereal to buy to whether to get a scanner.
Conclusion	Persuade readers to follow your advice: • Restate why advice will benefit readers.	• I know from my own experience that a little understanding can go a long way.

Complete Student Model on p. R114.

Use this graphic to help you visualize the structure of your advice essay.

Introduction		**Body**		**Conclusion**
Position statement	→	Supported by reasons, facts, and experiences	→	Reinforcement of your position statement

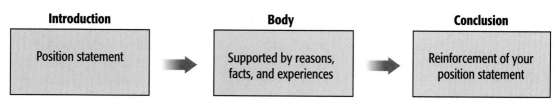

DRAFTING

DRAFTING TIP

As you draft, picture a friend who could use your advice. This will help you adopt a concerned, personal tone.

Is your argument sound?

In any persuasive writing, a sound argument combines a worthwhile position with solid support. Your advice essay is no different. As you draft, keep the following questions in mind: Has the advice you're giving actually worked for you? Can you reasonably expect it to work for your readers? Are there pitfalls or potential problems that readers should know about? Are special skills required?

Next, provide evidence to show that your advice will benefit others. Evidence generally includes facts, statistics, and expert opinions, but personal experience may provide the strongest, most convincing support in an advice essay.

Write your draft

As you write, work from your plan and keep your audience and overall purpose in mind. Remember, however, that this is only a first draft, and you'll be able to revise and refine your writing once you get your ideas down on paper. The world will see the work when you're ready to let it be seen—after you've polished it.

STUDENT MODEL

After my parents and I first had our discussion on why we felt as we did, we understood each other a lot better. I started to think more carefully about what I asked for, and my parents were more willing to talk to me about what I wanted instead of just calling me selfish or greedy. Then we felt better when we reached a compromise on an issue. Most importantly, understanding each other helped us get along better on a daily basis.

Complete Student Model on p. R114.

REVISING

REVISING TIP

Effective persuasion appeals to reason and emotion. Strengthen the emotional appeal by using forceful language, including active verbs.

Don't overlook the possibility that your plan might need revising. Your essay might benefit from reordering.

Take another look

Before you begin revising, shift from the writer's role to the reader's role. Approach your essay as if you were an advice-column reader. Jot down your reactions in the margins. Then shift back into the writer's role and revise.

Read your persuasive advice essay aloud

Read your essay aloud to someone who fits the description of your target audience. When you have finished reading, ask your listener whether he or she would follow your advice. If the listener would not, ask what would persuade him or her. Use the listener's responses and the **Rubric for Revising** to help you revise your essay and make it more persuasive.

Rubric for Revising

Your revised advice essay should have

- ☑ an introduction that clearly states the problem
- ☑ an explanation of why you are qualified to give advice on the problem
- ☑ strong, persuasive language and arguments designed to appeal to your audience
- ☑ reasons, facts, and personal experiences that support your advice
- ☑ a conclusion that persuasively restates your advice

Your revised advice essay should be free of

- ☑ dry, impersonal language
- ☑ confusing, conflicting, or unrealistic advice
- ☑ errors in grammar, usage, and mechanics

STUDENT MODEL

~~As you probably know,~~ parents and teenagers often have trouble getting along, and for a long time, my parents and I were no exception. Things have been a lot better ~~for~~ between us this year, though. The reason ~~why~~ is that we've each learned to try to understand where the other one is coming from, which makes it easier to compromise. ~~You should do what we do, just try to get along by talking it out and stuff like that. Figure out~~ I advise any parents and kids who are fighting to try our approach: Identify the reasons that the other person feels the way ~~they do and take~~ he or she does, take those into account ~~before you try to tackle the problem.~~ and then search for common ground.

Complete Student Model on p. R114.

EDITING/PROOFREADING

Shift into the editor's role and make corrections in grammar, usage, mechanics, and spelling. The **Proofreading Checklist** on the inside back cover of this textbook can help you mark these final adjustments. When you feel your essay is ready to show to a reader whose opinion you respect, then you know your writing is finished. Your job as writer is done.

PROOFREADING TIP

Remember that long introductory phrases should be set off from the rest of the sentence by a comma.

Grammar Hint

Keep prepositional phrases close to the word or words they modify. Misplaced modifiers may seem to modify the wrong word or phrase. Move them to make the meaning clear.

MISPLACED: *I started to think more carefully about what I asked my parents to buy after this conversation.*

CLEAR: *After this conversation, I started to think more carefully about what I asked my parents to buy.*

- For more about misplaced modifiers, see **Language Handbook,** p. R24.

STUDENT MODEL

However;
~~But~~ here's where we turned the corner: my parents asked me to sit down with them. a few days later, They asked me for the first time in a caulm and serious way why I wanted the things that I did.

Complete Student Model on p. R114.

Complete Student Model

For a complete version of the student model, see **Writing Workshop Models**, p. R114.

PUBLISHING/PRESENTING

PRESENTING TIP

If you're working on a computer, you might want to format your essay so that it looks as if it's been published in a newspaper. Divide the text into columns, add a headline or title, and separate sections with boldface heads.

If your school newspaper doesn't have an advice column, why not use your essay to start one? If you do so, consider opening the column with a letter from an imaginary reader asking for advice on the topic of your essay. You might also create an attention-getting headline for your column, and invent a persona for yourself, an advice-giving character with a catchy name. At the head of your column, include an illustrated self-portrait.

You could also gather classmates' essays into an advice booklet. Each person's advice-giving character could be featured here too. Give the booklet an appropriate title, such as "A Little Free Advice," and make it available to other students in your school.

Reflecting

Spend some time thinking about your process of writing an advice essay. What motivated you to choose the topic you did? Why did you feel it was important to advise others on this issue? What was easiest–and hardest–about writing an advice essay? Then decide whether you want to include your advice essay in your portfolio, and consider how you might use your personal experience and the techniques of persuasion in other writing.

Save your work for your portfolio.

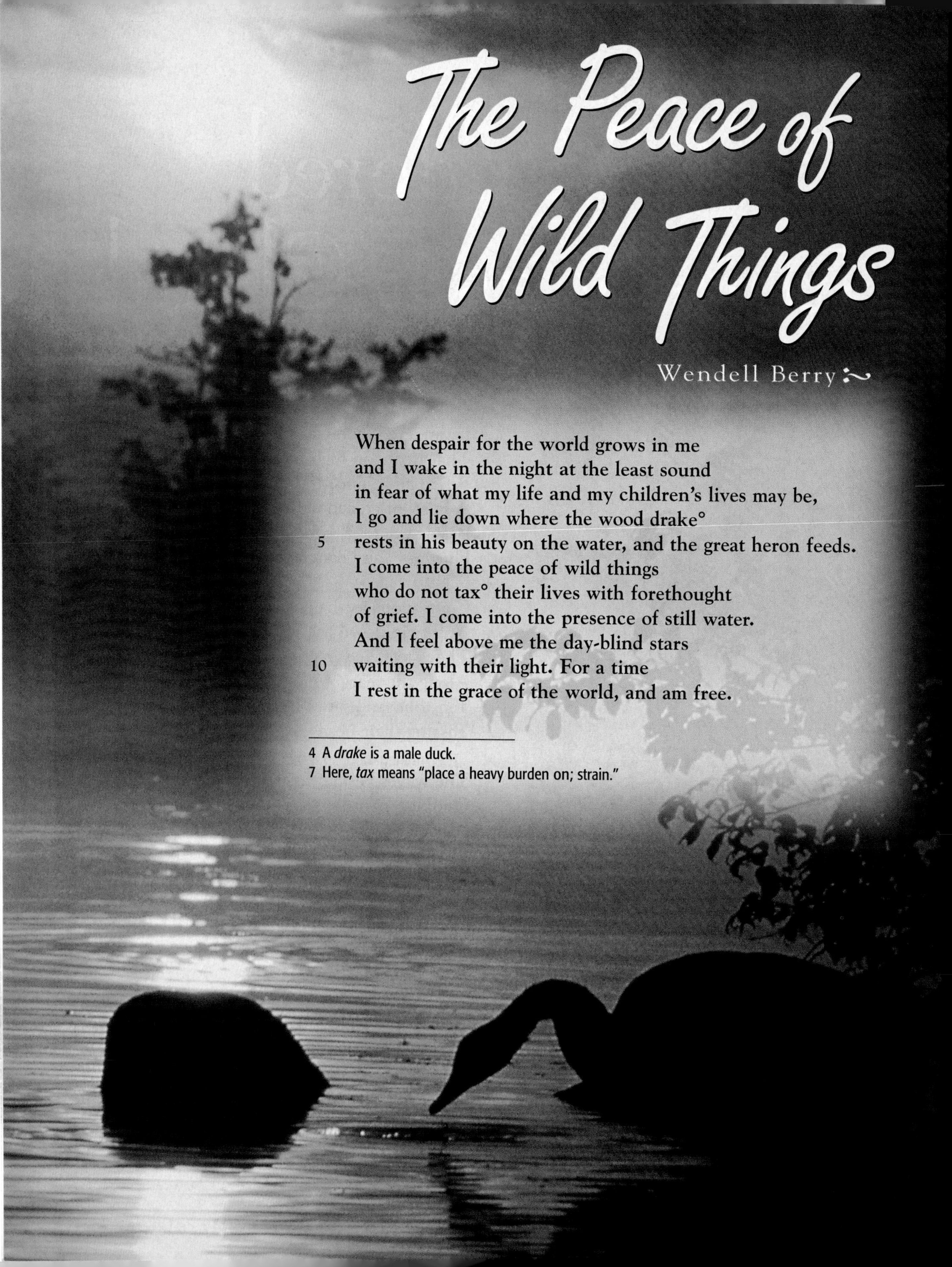

Theme 7 Expressions

Love lost or won, awe of natural beauty, delight from a new sight or sound—these types of emotions are often too big to stay bottled up inside a person. They need to be shared through writing, movement, or song. The authors in this theme use poetry to express their feelings about life's wonders and joys, trials and tribulations. What's your favorite way to express yourself?

THEME PROJECTS

Internet Project

Teen Expression Today, many people use the World Wide Web as a forum for expression.

1. Using terms such as "teen 'zines" or "teen pages," conduct an Internet search for Web pages built by people your age.
2. Look through your search results to see how teens use the World Wide Web to express themselves on subjects covered by the poems in this theme.
3. Make a list of the best Web sites you find. Describe each site, provide its address, and explain how it relates to a poem in the theme. Share your list with the class.

Performing

Switching Mediums Use drama, movement, and sound to convey the feelings that a poem expresses through language.

1. With a small group, look through the theme and select the poem that you like best.
2. Identify the feelings expressed by the poem. Then decide how you can use performance to communicate those feelings.
3. As you rehearse your performance, experiment with music, motion, or dialogue to express the feelings conveyed in the poem.
4. Perform for the class. Afterwards, ask your audience how the emotions you conveyed compared with those conveyed by the original poem.

Before You Read

The Secret and *My Poetry/Mi Poesía*

Reading Focus

What are different forms of communication that people can use to express themselves?

List Ideas List as many answers as you can, including verbal and nonverbal forms of communication. Share your list with classmates and compile a master list with everyone's ideas.

Setting a Purpose Read to see how poetry can be a form of communication with the power to change people's lives.

Building Background

Did You Know?

Since ancient times, people around the world have enjoyed and respected poetry as a special form of communication. In times and places where many people have not known how to read, the memorizing, reciting, and teaching of poetry has offered a way to pass along knowledge and ideas from one generation to another. Today poetry remains a popular art form. By reading, writing, and reciting poetry, combining it with visual arts, music, and drama, and even "publishing" it on the World Wide Web, people of all ages continue to demonstrate their delight in poetic expression.

In the 1950s, poets belonging to the beat movement began reciting their works in coffeehouses. The practice continues today.

Meet Denise Levertov

According to one biographer, Denise Levertov grew up "surrounded by books and people talking about them." One of the most respected poets of her generation, Levertov wrote on personal, spiritual, political, and nature themes. She published more than thirty books of poetry, essays, and translations.

Denise Levertov was born in 1923 in England and died in 1997 in Seattle.

Meet María Herrera-Sobek

María Herrera-Sobek grew up listening to her grandmother tell stories. "Poetry really haunted me," Herrera-Sobek says. Her interest in the civil rights movement and César Chávez's work with the United Farm Workers led her to the field of Latin American studies and Hispanic languages and literature. Today Herrera-Sobek writes and teaches at the University of California.

María Herrera-Sobek was born in 1942 in Mexico.

The Secret

Denise Levertov

Two girls discover
the secret of life
in a sudden line of
poetry.

I who don't know the
secret wrote
the line. They
told me

(through a third person)
they had found it
but not what it was
not even

what line it was. No doubt
by now, more than a week
later, they have forgotten
the secret,

the line, the name of
the poem. I love them
for finding what
I can't find,

and for loving me
for the line I wrote,
and for forgetting it
so that

a thousand times, till death
finds them, they may
discover it again, in other
lines

in other
happenings. And for
wanting to know it,
for

assuming there is
such a secret, yes,
for that
most of all.

My Poetry

My poetry
follows me
between tin cans
between chiles and tomatoes
apples and peaches
brooms and garbage
that on another day
were my only song.

My poetry
bursts out between cries
of children
and husbands hurt
by the explosion
of a pen
that bleeds
and leaves
gutted worms
on the pages.

My poetry
assaults me
among the rivers of embraces
I receive
from impatient lovers
in desperate competition
with my pen.

Mi Poesía

Mi poesía
me persigue
entre botes de hojalata,
entre chiles y tomates,
manzanas y duraznos,
escobas y basura
que otro día
eran mi única canción.

Mi poesía
surge entre chillidos
de niños
y esposos lastimados
por la explosión
de pluma
que sangra
y deja
gusanos destripados
en las páginas.

Mi poesía
me asalta
entre ríos de caricias
que recibo
de impacientes amantes
en desesperada competencia
con mi pluma.

María Herrera-Sobek

Responding to Literature

Personal Response

Which poem do you like more, and why? Record your answers in your journal.

Analyzing Literature

The Secret

Recall and Interpret

1. Where and by whom has the secret of life been discovered? What seems **ironic** about the discovery? (See Literary Terms Handbook, page R7.)
2. What does the speaker assume has happened a week after the discovery? Why might she think this way?
3. How does the speaker feel about the two girls, and why?
4. What seems to please the speaker most of all? Use details from the poem to explain.

Evaluate and Connect

5. What might it mean to discover the secret of life in a line of poetry? In your opinion, why does the poet use the word "sudden" in line 3?
6. Do you think there is a "secret of life"? If you think it exists, explain what it is or where a person might look for it. If you think it doesn't exist, explain your reasons.
7. If you were a poet, what relationship–if any–might you hope or expect to have with your readers?

My Poetry / Mi Poesía

Recall and Interpret

8. What is your interpretation of the first stanza? Describe what the speaker's "only song" on "another day" might have been.
9. What does the second verse imply about the speaker's poetry? What details give you this impression?
10. Who or what seems to be "in desperate competition" with the speaker's pen? What does this suggest about the speaker's life and the role of poetry in it?
11. What conclusions can you draw about the quality of the speaker's life? What conflicts–and joys–does she seem to experience every day?

Evaluate and Connect

12. What type of **figurative language** does the speaker use to describe her poetry in all three stanzas? Why do you suppose she uses this literary device?
13. How might the speaker in this poem have responded to the Reading Focus on page 492? Besides poetry, what forms of personal expression might be high on her list?
14. In your opinion, is the speaker's relationship to her work unusual? What other people can you think of who are passionate about their work or hobbies?
15. Even if you don't know Spanish, how does seeing the poem in Spanish as well as English affect your thinking about it? Explain.

Literary ELEMENTS

Free Verse

Free verse is poetry that has no fixed pattern of meter, rhyme, line length, or stanza arrangement. When writing free verse, a poet is free to vary these poetic elements to emphasize an idea or create a tone. In writing free verse, a poet may choose to use repetition or similar grammatical structures to emphasize and unify the ideas in the poem.

1. Why might free verse be an appropriate form for expressing a person's thoughts and feelings?
2. Identify examples of parallel grammar in "My Poetry." What does parallel grammar add to the poem?
3. In "The Secret," how is free verse like ordinary speech? How is it different?

- See **Literary Terms Handbook,** p. R6.

Literature and Writing

Writing About Literature

Writing Definitions Many poets have tried to define poetry. William Wordsworth, for instance, called it "the spontaneous overflow of powerful feelings." Write definitions of poetry that you think Levertov and Herrera-Sobek might have written. Then, explain your definitions, supporting your ideas with evidence from each of the poems.

Personal Writing

As You Like It The speakers in these poems have a passion for writing poetry. What fuels your enthusiasm? Creeping through cyberspace? Fast dancing? Playing the lute? In your journal, explain what activity inspires you, and why. Try to include vivid details or comparisons that creatively communicate your passion.

Extending Your Response

Literature Groups

Comparing Themes In 1791 the Chinese poet Yüan Mei wrote "Expression of Feelings, VII":

> Only be willing to search for poetry, and there will be poetry:
> My soul, a tiny speck, is my tutor.
> Evening sun and fragrant grass are common things,
> But, with understanding, they can become glorious verse.

With your group, discuss Yüan Mei's poem. Compare and contrast its theme with the themes of "My Poetry" and "The Secret." For example, what does each poem say about the relationship between the poet and poetry? Where would each poet say the inspiration for poetry comes from? Share your conclusions with other groups.

Interdisciplinary Activity

Art: Silent Poems Paintings have sometimes been called "silent poems," and poems have been called "word pictures." In a library book, a magazine, on the World Wide Web, or in this textbook, find a painting that you think powerfully communicates a feeling or experience. Then share the work with the class, explaining what and how it communicates through images rather than words. If you want, write a poem that communicates the painting's message and display both in your classroom.

Performing

Poetry Reading Practice reading aloud one of these poems until you can read it comfortably and expressively. Let the punctuation guide your pauses and stops. Use inflection and rhythm in your voice to convey your understanding of the speaker's identity and intention. Then take your turn in a class poetry reading.

Save your work for your portfolio.

Grammar Link

Misplaced or Dangling Modifiers

A word or phrase that makes specific the meaning of another word or phrase is called a **modifier.** The position of a modifier in a sentence is extremely important. If the modifier is not near the word or phrase it modifies, the meaning of the sentence will be either unclear or incorrect. For example, "Fangs gleaming, Marcy stared in terror at the mountain lion" means that Marcy has a threatening set of teeth. In this example, "Fangs gleaming" is called a *misplaced modifier;* it's in the wrong place. A *dangling modifier* is meant to modify a word or phrase that is not present in the sentence. Such a modifier "dangles."

Problem 1 A misplaced modifier
I took a backpack on the plane stuffed with my favorite books of poetry.
[The wrong noun is modified.]

Solution Move the misplaced modifier as close as possible to the word or words it modifies.
I took a backpack stuffed with my favorite books of poetry on the plane.

Problem 2 The misplaced adverb *only*
Vicki only plays basketball in the winter. [The meaning is unclear. In winter, is Vicki the sole person who plays basketball? Or, is winter the only season in which Vicki plays basketball? Or, does Vicki play no other sports in the winter?]

Solution Place *only* immediately in front of the word or phrase it modifies.
Vicki plays only basketball in the winter.

Problem 3 A dangling modifier
Waiting nervously for the poetry quiz, a surprise fire drill was called.
[The sentence contains no word for the modifier to modify logically.]

Solution Rewrite the sentence, adding a noun to which the dangling phrase clearly refers. Often you will have to add other words to the sentence.
Waiting nervously for the poetry quiz, my classmates and I were relieved when a surprise fire drill was called.

• For more on misplaced or dangling modifiers, see **Language Handbook,** p. R24.

EXERCISE

Rewrite each sentence to correct the misplaced or dangling modifier.

1. Noticing the teacher's look, the student's giggle faded.
2. The teacher told her class to read the poems in a strict tone of voice.
3. She turned and looked at a giggling student with a steely gaze.
4. That student only cared about clothes, jokes, and parties.
5. Walking quickly to the chalkboard, the titles were written in large letters.

Before You Read

Haiku

Reading Focus

Think of a beautiful, inspiring, surprising, or thought-provoking moment you have experienced in nature. What single image comes to mind?

Map It! In the center of a word web, name the experience. Then, jot down precise nouns, adjectives, and verbs to describe it.

Setting a Purpose
Read to learn how four poets have used a unique poetic form, haiku, to capture a special moment in nature.

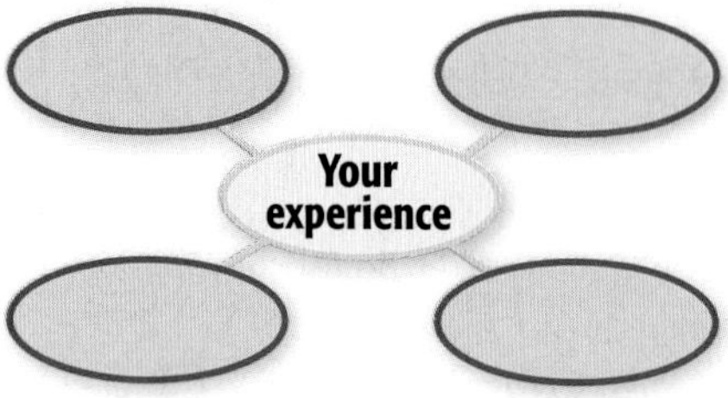

Building Background

Did You Know?

- The purpose of a haiku—a traditionally untitled, unrhymed, seventeen-syllable poem—is to capture a flash of insight that occurs during a solitary observation of nature. Since nature may change suddenly, the poet's challenge in writing a haiku is to record a fleeting moment in language that is quick and precise.
- Traditional haiku include one *kigo,* or "season word," to suggest the season associated with the moment in the poem. Season words do not simply name the seasons; they may be associated with astronomy, climate, geography, animals, plants, and even human events. For example, the term *kare-hasu,* meaning "withered lotus flower," is a season word associated with winter. *Koromo-gae,* meaning "changing clothes," implies summer. When haiku are translated from Japanese into English (or are written in English), the season word must be carefully implied.

Matsushima no Tsubone, 1875. Yoshitoshi Taiso. Woodblock print, 14¼ x 9½ in. Private collection.

Meet Matsuo Bashō

Matsuo Bashō is revered as one of Japan's great masters of haiku poetry. In the seventeenth century, he traveled on foot through parts of Japan, recording his observations in haiku.

Matsuo Bashō was born in 1644 and died in 1694.

Meet Chiyo

When she was eighteen, Kaga no Chiyo's poetry was admired by a well-known disciple of Bashō, who helped to make her famous in Japan. Later, after becoming a nun, she was known as Chiyo Ni (the Nun Chiyo).

Chiyo was born in 1703 and died in 1775.

Meet Paula Yup

Chinese American poet Paula Yup spent two years in Japan studying Japanese language and literature. In addition to writing poetry, she translates Japanese poems into English.

Paula Yup was born in 1957.

Meet Katy Peake

Catherine Anne ("Katy") Peake was a poet, artist, author of children's stories, photographer, and social activist from Santa Barbara, California.

Katy Peake was born in 1917 and died in 1995.

Haiku

The old pond;
A frog jumps in:
Sound of water.

Matsuo Bashō
Translated by Robert Hass

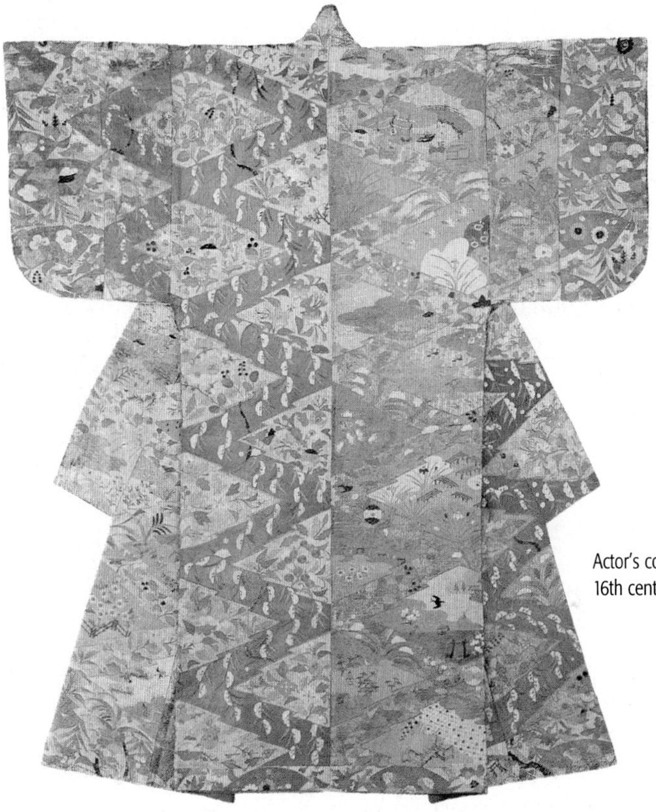

Actor's costume. Japan, 16th century.

a clear sheet of sky
calligraphy of blackbirds
written and erased

Katy Peake

A morning glory
Twined round the bucket:
I will ask my neighbor for water.

Chiyo
Translated by Yasuko Horioka

Peace

I spy butterfly
In quietly still waters
living for today.

Paula Yup

Responding to Literature

Personal Response

Which of the haiku gives you the clearest image of a specific moment in time in a natural setting? In your journal, describe what you see.

Analyzing Literature

Recall and Interpret

1. Describe what sights and sounds might have inspired Bashō to write this haiku.
2. If you had been at the pond with Bashō, what else might your senses have perceived?
3. Based on the poem, name at least two reasons why Chiyo might have noticed the morning glory.
4. Why, do you think, does Chiyo decide to go to her neighbor for water?
5. Where might Paula Yup have been standing when she saw the butterfly?
6. How do you suppose the appearance of the water compares with that of the butterfly? Why might Yup think that the butterfly is "living for today"?
7. Describe the image expressed in Katy Peake's haiku.

Evaluate and Connect

8. Reread Bashō's haiku. In which season do you think this moment took place? Explain your opinion.
9. The speaker in most traditional Japanese haiku does not often appear on the scene as "I." Do you think Chiyo's break with tradition makes the haiku more effective or less effective? Explain.
10. Explain how Paula Yup's poem is both similar to and different from traditional Japanese haiku.
11. What does the title "Peace" add to the meaning of Yup's haiku?
12. Explain the importance of the **metaphors,** or comparisons that do not use *like* or *as,* in Katy Peake's haiku. (See Literary Terms Handbook, page R7.) What does each metaphor help you to visualize?

Literary **ELEMENTS**

Haiku

The traditional Japanese **haiku** is an unrhymed poem that contains exactly seventeen syllables, arranged in three lines of five, seven, and five syllables each. However, when poems written in Japanese are translated into another language, this pattern is often lost.

Haiku often include a "cutting," or separation, that signals a contrast or change of some kind. In English, the "cutting" is usually marked with punctuation such as a colon or dash. For example, in Bashō's haiku, the translator has used a colon as a cutting device to separate the poet's impressions of the pond before and after the frog jumps in.

1. Identify another use of punctuation to mark a "cutting" in one of the haiku. Describe any contrast you notice in the poem's images or the poet's mood.
2. Katy Peake and Paula Yup have both written haiku without adding colons or dashes to mark a contrast. Is there a contrast in either or both of these modern haiku? Explain.

- See **Literary Terms Handbook,** p. R6.

Literature and Writing

Writing About Literature

Focus on Genre As an art form, the haiku has sometimes been compared to the photograph, which can capture a fleeting moment in black and white or vivid color. Do you think this is an appropriate comparison? Write two or three paragraphs in which you explain your opinion and support it with reasons and examples from the haiku you have read.

Creative Writing

Haiku by You Refer back to your response to the Reading Focus on page 498. Use your notes to write a haiku in three lines of five, seven, and five syllables each. Make sure you include a "cutting" and at least one detail that suggests a certain season. Using this verse form, see how much you can communicate about the experience you remember.

Extending Your Response

Literature Groups

Season Words Reread the Building Background section of page 498 about Japanese *kigo,* or "season words," for use in haiku. What season words can you find in the haiku you read? In your group, discuss how these words help to set the season in the haiku. Then identify other words in English or in your native language that may be used in a haiku to indicate a season. Work together to create a list of words associated with the seasons for each of the following categories: animals and insects, astronomy, climate, geography, human events, and plants. For example, for animals, you might include "mosquito" (summer). Then work together to write haiku that include one season word. Share your poems and season word lists with other groups.

Like haiku, bonsai, or the growing and training of miniature trees in containers, is a traditional Japanese art still practiced today.

Interdisciplinary Activity

Art: Illustrate the Moment Draw or paint an illustration to accompany an original haiku or one of the haiku you have just studied. Use your artwork to convey how you "see" the haiku's main image. Be sure to incorporate the words of the haiku into your illustration.

Internet Connection

International Haiku More than five thousand haiku magazines are published in modern Japan, and haiku is popular in many other countries as well. Using an Internet search engine, find out more facts about haiku and the people who experiment with this ancient literary form. You can easily find haiku studies, forums, writing tips, and information regarding worldwide competitions for poets of all ages.

Reading Further

If you would like to read more haiku, you might enjoy these collections:

Bashō's Narrow Road: Spring and Autumn Passages, translated by Hiroaki Sato, is an English-language version of Bashō's most famous work, *Narrow Road to the Interior.*

A Haiku Menagerie, by Stephen Addiss with Fumiko and Akira Yamamoto, features haiku and paintings whose subjects are animals.

Save your work for your portfolio.

MEDIA connection

Comic Strip

Expressing your feelings of affection for someone can be tricky—especially when you're not sure how the person will respond. Valentine's Day poses a dilemma for people who are confused about whether to show their feelings.

FOXTROT ©1992 Bill Amend. Reprinted with permission of UNIVERSAL PRESS SYNDICATE. All rights reserved.

FOXTROT ©1992 Bill Amend. Reprinted with permission of UNIVERSAL PRESS SYNDICATE. All rights reserved.

FOXTROT ©1992 Bill Amend. Reprinted with permission of UNIVERSAL PRESS SYNDICATE. All rights reserved.

Analyzing Media

1. What lesson about life and love is Paige struggling to learn?
2. What role can parents play in helping their children learn about love? What role can friends play?

Before You Read

A Red, Red Rose and *I Am Offering This Poem*

Reading Focus

What is love?

Quickwrite In your journal, write your personal definition of love. Also describe what kinds of love there are. Are some types of love fleeting, while others are enduring? Explain.

Setting a Purpose Read to see how the feeling of deep and abiding love can be expressed in poetry.

Building Background

Mayan clay figures, A.D. c. 700–1000, Campeche, Mexico.

Did You Know?

- Because it is such a basic and universal experience, romantic love has been the subject of artwork, songs, and poems for centuries. Finding ways to express love is a basic part of courtship. People commonly offer poems, play romantic music, and exchange gifts.
- "A Red, Red Rose" is a love song that Robert Burns pieced together from various Scottish folk songs. He composed it to the tune of "Major Graham," a song from *Oswald's Companion Book,* published in the mid-1700s. From the time of his youth, Burns took a great interest in Scottish folk songs. He both wrote original songs and collected and expanded upon existing songs. If he liked a tune that had no words—and felt it was worth preserving—he wrote lyrics for it. And for many tunes that had lyrics, he improved upon the words.
- Jimmy Santiago Baca credits a love of poetry and books with helping to save his life. Abandoned by his parents as a child and raised first by a grandparent and then in an orphanage, Baca became a runaway, got into trouble with the law, and ended up in prison at the age of eighteen. But he turned his life around after he began writing poetry. Today, this award-winning poet of Chicano and Apache descent lives with his wife and sons on a small farm near Albuquerque, New Mexico.

Meet Robert Burns

If you've ever sung "Auld Lang Syne" on New Year's Eve, then you know one of Robert Burns's famous works. Burns is considered the national poet of Scotland. Born into a poor farming family, he was sometimes called the "ploughman poet." His works have been translated into about fifty languages, and they have never been out of print since 1786.

Robert Burns was born in 1759 and died in 1796.

Meet Jimmy Santiago Baca

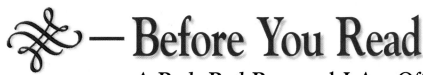

Jimmy Santiago Baca learned to read and write in prison so that he could leave something behind when he died. "I wanted to tell the world I had been here," he said. His first break came when he sent a poem to a magazine whose editor, poet Denise Levertov, published it. His semiautobiographical book of verse, *Martin and Meditations on the South Valley*, won an American Book Award in 1988.

Jimmy Santiago Baca was born in 1952 in Santa Fe, New Mexico.

A Red, Red Rose

Robert Burns

I

O, my love is like a red, red rose,
That's newly sprung in June.
O, my love is like the melody,
That's sweetly play'd in tune.

II

As fair art thou, my bonny lass,°
So deep in love am I,
And I will love thee still, my dear,
Till a' the seas gang dry.°

III

Till a' the seas gang dry, my dear,
And the rocks melt wi' the sun!
And I will love thee still, my dear,
While the sands o' life shall run.

IV

And fare thee weel,° my only love,
And fare thee weel a while!
And I will come again, my love,
Tho' it were ten thousand mile!

---

5 *Bonny lass* means "pretty young woman" or "sweetheart."
8 *[Till a' the seas gang dry]* This line, in Standard English, is "Until all the seas go dry."
13 *Weel* means "well."

I Am Offering This Poem

Jimmy Santiago Baca

Outline Weave Blanket, c. 1880–1890. Navajo. Wool, 89 x 53 in. Lowe Art Museum at the University of Miami, FL.

I am offering this poem to you,
since I have nothing else to give.
Keep it like a warm coat
when winter comes to cover you,
or like a pair of thick socks
the cold cannot bite through,

I love you,

I have nothing else to give you,
so it is a pot full of yellow corn
to warm your belly in winter,
it is a scarf for your head, to wear
over your hair, to tie up around your face,

I love you,

Keep it, treasure this as you would
if you were lost, needing direction,
in the wilderness life becomes when mature;
and in the corner of your drawer,
tucked away like a cabin or hogan°
in dense trees, come knocking,
and I will answer, give you directions,
and let you warm yourself by this fire,
rest by this fire, and make you feel safe,

I love you,

It's all I have to give,
and all anyone needs to live,
and to go on living inside,
when the world outside
no longer cares if you live or die;
remember,
I love you.

---

18 A *hogan* is a traditional Navajo dwelling.

Responding to Literature

Personal Response

If these poems had been written for you, which one would you rather receive? Why?

Analyzing Literature

A Red, Red Rose

Recall and Interpret

1. To what two things does the speaker compare his love in the first verse? When the speaker says "my love," do you think he refers to the person he loves or to his own feeling of love? Explain.
2. What does the speaker promise in the second and third verses? What **imagery** does he use in this promise, and why do you think he uses this language?
3. Summarize and explain what the speaker is saying in the last verse.

Evaluate and Connect

4. Describe the pattern of **end rhyme** in this song. Why do you think Burns used rhyme in this way, and what is its effect? (See Literary Terms Handbook, pages R10–R11.)
5. What examples of **repetition** do you find in this song? What effect does this repetition have on the sound of the song? (See Literary Terms Handbook, page R10.)
6. Do you exaggerate the way Burns does when describing your feelings about an issue or about someone you know? Why might a person do such a thing?
7. Theme Connections Do you find the expression of love in this song convincing? Why or why not?

I Am Offering This Poem

Recall and Interpret

8. Who do you think is the "you" in this poem? Explain.
9. What **similes** and **metaphors** does the speaker use in the first two stanzas? What do these comparisons have in common?
10. Explain how the poem–and the speaker–are to be used like a compass through life. Use details from the third stanza in your answer.
11. According to the speaker, what is the most basic human need? How can having this need satisfied help a person to "go on living inside"?

Evaluate and Connect

12. Do you agree with the sentiment expressed in the last stanza of this poem? Why or why not?
13. Theme Connections Besides expressing his own feelings for one person, what else is the speaker in this poem expressing?
14. Look back at the writing you did for the Reading Focus on page 503. In your opinion, what kind of love are Burns and Baca writing about in these poems? How does your definition of love compare with that of the poets?

Literary ELEMENTS

Lyric Poetry

Poetry that expresses a speaker's personal thoughts and feelings is called **lyric poetry.** This broad category covers many poetic types and styles, including free verse and rhymed poetry. Most lyric poems are short and musical, and in fact, lyric poems were originally sung. The musical quality may come from the poem's rhythm, rhyme, or repetition.

1. Why would both "A Red, Red Rose" and "I Am Offering This Poem" be considered lyric poems?
2. Compare and contrast the musical qualities of the two poems.

- See **Literary Terms Handbook,** p. R7.

Literature and Writing

Writing About Literature

Comparing Sensory Details Both poets use a variety of sensory details in these poems. What senses do these images appeal to? Which poet more effectively uses sensory details to convey the feeling of being in love? Write a few paragraphs comparing the use of sensory details in "A Red, Red Rose" and "I Am Offering This Poem."

Creative Writing

Parody A **parody** is a literary or musical work that imitates the style of some other work in a satirical or humorous way. (See page R9.) Choose one of these poems and write a parody of it. You might apply the poet's style to another subject, or make up silly comparisons and use them in a love poem.

Extending Your Response

Literature Groups

A Critic's Viewpoint One Burns critic has written that "A Red, Red Rose" captures the "combination of swagger and tender protectiveness so characteristic of the male in love." Reread the poem. In your group, discuss what evidence you find to support the critic's viewpoint. Do you agree with the critic? Do you find a similar tone in "I Am Offering This Poem"? Use examples from the poem to explain your answer when you share your ideas with the rest of the class.

Learning for Life

Learning Skills Both Burns and Baca discovered that language has the power to change people's lives, and they learned to use it to transform their own. What would you most like to learn to do, and how might learning it change your life? Research a subject or skill you would like to learn. Then create a flow chart that explains the process you would follow to learn the necessary basics.

Internet Connection

Big Man on the Net Hundreds of Robert Burns fan clubs exist throughout the world, and thousands of Burns sites are on the Internet. Use any search engine to find out what types of Web sites exist and the kinds of information they have. See if you can find and listen to a musical version of "A Red, Red Rose." Report to the class on why the poet still has so many fans.

Reading Further

You might also enjoy these works by Robert Burns and Jimmy Santiago Baca:

Folk Songs: "Comin Thro' the Rye" and "Green Grow the Rashes, O," are love songs by Robert Burns.

Poems: "Old Man," "Wishes," and "Since You've Come," by Jimmy Santiago Baca, are lyric poems about everyday life; they appear in his collection *Black Mesa Poems.*

Save your work for your portfolio.

Before You Read

Rain in My Heart and *Pain—has an Element of Blank—*

Reading Focus

Think of a time when you felt pain. Was it physical pain or emotional pain? What was the experience like?

Sketch It! Create a drawing, either realistic or abstract, that captures the feeling of the pain you experienced.

Setting a Purpose Read to see how two poets describe the feeling of pain.

Building Background

Did You Know?

- Edgar Lee Masters suffered many disappointments in love during his life, but he kept looking for a woman who could ease his lifelong loneliness. In his autobiography, *Across Spoon River,* he wrote, "Lovers who pass from our lives are more pathetic than the dead, for departed lovers are those who are buried alive. They are somewhere yet in the world, reminding us of hopes that failed, of dreams that were misled."
- Emily Dickinson's poetry is full of unusual capitalization and lots of dashes. The capitalization puts extra emphasis on certain words. The dashes serve as interrupters, breaking up text, slowing the reader down, and usually adding emphasis. For example, the first line of the poem you will read, "Pain–has an Element of Blank–" (which is used as the title because Dickinson seldom titled her poems), contains two dashes. The first adds emphasis to the word *Pain* and invites the reader to pause slightly. The second sets off the complete predicate "has an Element of Blank" and invites the reader to pause again. Although just a few of Dickinson's poems were published during her lifetime, editors, who perhaps thought her work a bit strange, often changed them and eliminated the very things that made her poems unique–such as these dashes.

Meet Edgar Lee Masters

Affairs of the heart were an important topic in Edgar Lee Masters's poetry, reflecting their importance in his life. He wrote novels, an autobiography, a biography of Abraham Lincoln, and some twenty books of poetry. However, only one book, *Spoon River Anthology*, brought him great fame and remains famous to this day.

Edgar Lee Masters was born in Garnett, Kansas, in 1869 and died in 1950.

Meet Emily Dickinson

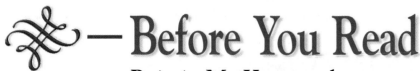

"If I feel physically as if the top of my head were taken off, I know that is poetry," wrote Emily Dickinson. To the outside world, Dickinson lived a lonely, eccentric life. She stayed inside her home, typically wore white clothing, and wrote her poems on little scraps of paper which she tucked along with her pencil in an apron pocket. Then she stashed the poems in bureau drawers, where nearly eighteen hundred were discovered after her death.

Emily Dickinson was born in 1830 and died in 1886 in Amherst, Massachusetts.

Rain in My Heart

Edgar Lee Masters

There is a quiet in my heart
Like one who rests from days of pain.
Outside, the sparrows on the roof
Are chirping in the dripping rain.

Rain in my heart; rain on the roof;
And memory sleeps beneath the gray
And windless sky and brings no dreams
Of any well remembered day.

I would not have the heavens fair,
Nor golden clouds, nor breezes mild,
But days like this, until my heart
To loss of you is reconciled.°

I would not see you. Every hope
To know you as you were has ranged.°
I, who am altered, would not find
The face I loved so greatly changed.

---

12 In this context, *reconciled* means "caused to accept something unpleasant."
14 Here, *ranged* means "wandered; roamed."

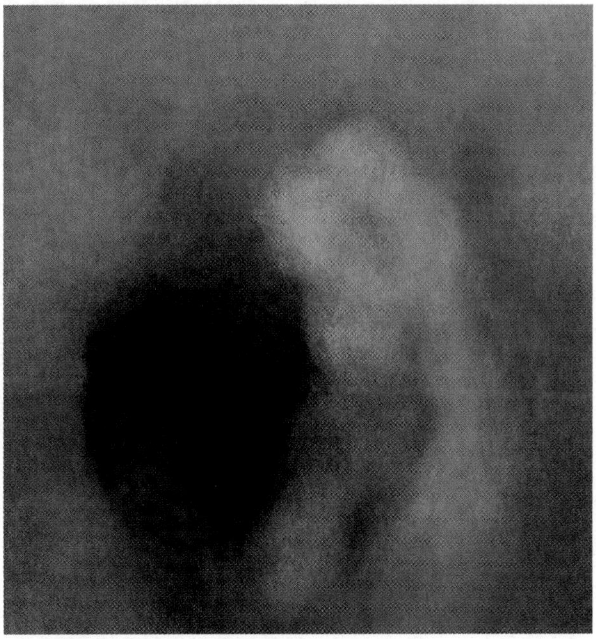

In Three's, 1985. Rebecca Purdum. Oil on canvas, 82¾ x 80½ in. Private collection.

Viewing the painting: What connections do you see between this painting and the poems on this page?

Pain—has an Element of Blank—

Emily Dickinson

Pain—has an Element of Blank—
It cannot recollect
When it begun—or if there were
A time when it was not—

It has no Future—but itself—
Its Infinite contain
Its Past—enlightened to perceive
New Periods—of Pain.

Responding to Literature

Personal Response

What do either or both of these poems make you wonder about? Record your ideas in your journal.

Analyzing Literature

Rain in My Heart

Recall and Interpret

1. What **simile** does the speaker use in the first stanza to describe what is in his heart? What does this tell you about his emotional state and about what he's been through?
2. Why might the speaker notice the chirping sparrows?
3. In your opinion, what is the "rain" in the speaker's "heart"? What might be the cause of it?
4. According to the speaker, what is memory doing? Does the speaker currently remember happy times? What future role might memory play in the speaker's healing process?
5. In your opinion, who is the "you" in the last two stanzas, and what does the speaker think about him or her? Explain, using details from the poem in your answer.

Evaluate and Connect

6. How would you describe the **mood** of this poem? What words or phrases from the poem contribute to the mood? (See Literary Terms Handbook, page R8.)
7. Do you think this poem effectively captures the feelings of a person who has lost love? Why or why not?

Pain—has an Element of Blank—

Recall and Interpret

8. What might the speaker mean by "an Element of Blank"?
9. According to the poem, what can pain do, and what can't it do? What does pain have, and what doesn't it have? What does this suggest about the speaker's experience of pain?
10. What do you think is meant by "Its Infinite contain / Its Past"?

Evaluate and Connect

11. What words does Dickinson capitalize in the poem? Why might she have chosen these words to capitalize?
12. How would you rate this poem as a definition of pain? Explain the reason for your rating.
13. Did you find it easy or difficult to relate to this description of pain? Why?
14. Look at the drawing you made for the Reading Focus on page 508. If you were to pair your drawing with one of these two poems, which one would you choose, and why?

Literary ELEMENTS

Rhythm

Rhythm is the pattern of beats created by the arrangement of stressed and unstressed syllables in a poem. This pattern can be regular, as it is in these lines from "Rain in My Heart":

> There is a quiet in my heart
> Like one who rests from days of pain.

Notice the four pairs of an unstressed syllable followed by a stressed syllable. This even, regular rhythm helps move the poem along. Sometimes, however, a poet may interrupt a rhythm pattern. Notice the change in pattern in another line from "Rain in My Heart":

> Rain in my heart; rain on the roof

The change in rhythm slows the reader down and emphasizes this key line, adding to its significance.

1. In what other lines of "Rain in My Heart" does the rhythm vary from the first example? What is the effect?
2. Copy the poem "Pain–has an Element of Blank–" on your paper. Mark the stressed and unstressed syllables. How would you describe the rhythm of the poem?

- See **Literary Terms Handbook,** p. R11.

Literature and Writing

Writing About Literature

Summarizing and Responding On separate pieces of paper, write a brief summary of these poems, using your own words to explain each poem's message. Imagine how Dickinson and Masters would react to each other's poem. What words of comfort might they offer each other? Beneath each summary, write your answers to these questions from the point of view of the other poet.

Creative Writing

Getting the Scoop Imagine that the speaker in "Rain in My Heart" is a famous movie star or singer. Write an interview between this person and a popular radio or television talk-show host. Get the scoop about the relationship referred to in this poem. You will need to invent the details, but be sure that you stay true to the poem's message and mood.

Extending Your Response

Literature Groups

Sorting It Out With your group, decide which poem you'd like to discuss. Then, brainstorm ideas about what the last stanza might mean. Analyze each line, and then connect the stanza's meaning to the rest of the poem. Share your interpretations with the class.

Interdisciplinary Activity

Biology: The Transmission of Pain Using the Internet, reference books, or interviews with medical professionals, research how pain is transmitted in the human body. Make a poster or diagram that helps to explain the process, and use it in an oral presentation of your findings.

Reading Further

You might also enjoy these works by or about Edgar Lee Masters and Emily Dickinson:

Poetry: "Hare Drummer," "Lucinda Matlock," and "Aaron Hatfield," by Edgar Lee Masters, appear in the *Spoon River Anthology.*

Final Harvest, by Emily Dickinson, is a collection of more than five hundred poems.

Viewing: *The Belle of Amherst* is an adaptation of a well-known biographical play about Dickinson.

Save your work for your portfolio.

MEDIA connection

Web Site

You need them desperately, you use them ceaselessly, but how well do you know your feet? As the lowest part of the human body, feet tend to get overlooked, but there's a lot to learn about them.

Foot Facts

Address: www.apma.org

AMERICAN PODIATRIC MEDICAL ASSOCIATION

1. Seventy-five percent of Americans will experience foot health problems of varying degrees of severity at one time or another in their lives.
2. The foot is an intricate structure containing 26 bones. Thirty-three joints, 107 ligaments, 19 muscles, and tendons hold the structure together and allow it to move in a variety of ways.
3. The 52 bones in your feet make up about one quarter of all the bones in your body.
4. Women have about four times as many foot problems as men; lifelong patterns of wearing high heels often are the culprit.
5. The American Podiatric Medical Association says the average person takes 8,000 to 10,000 steps a day, covering several miles. These steps add up to about 115,000 miles in a lifetime—more than four times the circumference of the globe.
6. There are times when you're walking that the pressure on your feet exceeds your body weight, and when you're running, it can be three or four times your weight.
7. Shopping for shoes is best done in the afternoon. Your feet tend to swell a little during the day, and it's best to buy shoes to fit them then. Have your feet measured every time you purchase shoes, and do it while you're standing. When you try on shoes, try them on both feet; many people have one foot larger than the other, and it's best to fit the larger one.
8. Trim your toenails straight across with clippers specially designed for the purpose. Leave them slightly longer than the tips of your toes.
9. Walking is the best exercise for your feet. It also contributes to your general health by improving circulation, contributing to weight control, and promoting all-around well being.
10. Your feet mirror your general health. Such conditions as arthritis, diabetes, and nerve and circulatory disorders can show their initial symptoms in the feet—so foot ailments can be your first sign of more serious medical problems.

Analyzing Media

1. After reading the above facts, what advice would you offer someone about buying and wearing shoes? What other advice might you offer to someone who wanted healthy feet?
2. To what can you compare your feet? Use the facts above to invent several metaphors to describe the role feet play in a person's life.

Before You Read

To the Foot from Its Child

Reading Focus

Picture the hands and feet of a young child. Contrast their appearance with that of the hands and feet of an elderly person.

List Ideas What factors, other than the natural aging process, might cause the differences you see? Jot down your ideas.

Setting a Purpose Read to learn how a poet views the impact one's life journey can have on the feet.

Building Background

Did You Know?

- Pablo Neruda has been called the Pablo Picasso of poetry because his poems, like Picasso's paintings, cover such a wide range of styles, techniques, and themes. Also like Picasso's paintings, Neruda's writing is often categorized into distinct periods. Neruda wrote lyric love poems, political poems, surrealistic poems, realistic poems, epic poems, and highly personal poems. "To the Foot from Its Child" appears in *Extravagaria,* a collection of Neruda's poems published in 1958. This collection was written during what Neruda called his "autumnal" period, in which he wrote highly personal, lyric poetry. At this stage in his life, Neruda lived at Isla Negra, his retreat along Chile's Pacific coast.
- Personification is a figure of speech in which an animal, object, or idea is given human qualities or characteristics. Often the object gains the ability to think and feel as though it were human. As you read this poem, pay attention to Neruda's use of personification.

Blind Old Man and Boy, 1903. Pablo Picasso (from his Blue Period). Oil on canvas, 125 x 92 cm. Pushkin Museum of Fine Arts, Moscow.

Meet Pablo Neruda

Pablo Neruda was born in a small farming town in southern Chile and given the name Neftalí Ricardo Reyes Basoalto. He first published his poems under pseudonyms because his father, a railway worker, objected to his son becoming a poet. At the age of sixteen, the young poet began to use the pen name Pablo Neruda, which he later legally adopted. By the age of twenty, Neruda was already considered one of the world's most promising young poets. Like many other Latin American writers, Neruda became deeply involved in the political life of his country. Neruda was awarded the Nobel Prize for Literature in 1971.

Pablo Neruda was born in 1904 in Parral, Chile, and died in 1973.

Foot, 1894. Pablo Picasso. Charcoal and conte crayon on paper, 33.2 x 49.7 cm. Museo Picasso, Barcelona, Spain.

To the Foot from Its Child

Pablo Neruda

The child's foot is not yet aware it's a foot,
and wants to be a butterfly or an apple.

But later, stones and glass shards,°
streets, ladders,
and the paths in the rough earth
go on teaching the foot it cannot fly,
cannot be a fruit swollen on the branch.
Then, the child's foot
was defeated, fell
in the battle,
was a prisoner
condemned to live in a shoe.

Bit by bit, in that dark
it grew to know the world in its own way,
out of touch with its fellow, enclosed,
feeling out life like a blind man.

These soft nails
of quartz, bunched together,
grew hard, and changed themselves
into opaque° substance, hard as horn,
and the tiny, petaled toes of the child
grew bunched and out of trim,
took on the form of eyeless reptiles
with triangular heads, like worms.
Later, they grew calloused
and were covered
with the faint volcanoes of death,
a coarsening hard to accept.

But this blind thing walked
without respite,° never stopping
for hour after hour,
the one foot, the other,
now the man's,
now the woman's,
up above,
down below,
through fields, mines,
markets and ministries,
backward,
far afield, inward,
forward,
this foot toiled in its shoe,
scarcely taking time
to bare itself in love or sleep;
it walked, they walked,
until the whole man chose to stop.

And then it descended
to earth, and knew nothing,
for there, everything everywhere
was dark.
It did not know it had ceased to be
a foot,
or if they were burying it so that it
might fly,
or so that it might become
an apple.

---

3 *Shards* are broken, sharp-edged fragments.

20 An *opaque* (ō pāk′) substance is dull-looking and does not let light pass through.

30 A *respite* (res′ pit) is a short time of rest or relief from work or unpleasantness.

Responding to Literature

Personal Response

What do you find most surprising about this poem? Write your response in your journal.

Analyzing Literature

Recall and Interpret

1. Why might the child's foot be "not yet aware it's a foot"?
2. What does the child's foot want to be? Why might the foot want to be these things?
3. The foot became "a prisoner / condemned to live in a shoe." In your opinion, is the man to whom the foot belongs also a prisoner, or is he free? Use details from the poem to support your answer.
4. How does the foot change over time? In your opinion, what causes these changes, and what do the changes represent?
5. What does the foot continue to do, despite its many changes?
6. Lines 46–49 describe what events?
7. How are lines 50–53 like the first two lines of the poem? What does this similarity suggest to you about Neruda's view of the life cycle?

Evaluate and Connect

8. How does Neruda create **rhythm** in lines 29–46? What does the rhythm remind you of? (See Literary Terms Handbook, page R11.)
9. **Theme Connections** Would you say that this poem expresses an optimistic or pessimistic view of life? Explain, giving evidence from the poem to support your answer.
10. How is your view of the human life cycle similar to or different from the view expressed in this poem?
11. According to the poem, what factors, other than the natural aging process, caused the child's foot to change? How do these factors compare with those that appear in your response to the Reading Focus on page 513?
12. What do you find most intriguing about this poem?

Literary Criticism

Critic Fernando Alegria says the following about one of Neruda's poems: "Complex in structure and meaning, this work [presents a] vision of the earth in which existence is viewed as a continuous process of decay and despair." Write a one-page essay in which you either support or contest this quotation as it relates to "To the Foot from Its Child."

Literary ELEMENTS

Structure

The **structure** of a poem is created through the organization of its images, ideas, words, and lines. Poets build structure into their poems in several ways. They may use rhythm and rhyme to connect ideas. They may use repetition to emphasize main ideas or images. And they may use stanzas, or groups of lines, to separate the poem into distinct parts, in much the same way paragraphs separate the ideas in an essay. Each stanza within a poem may serve a different purpose. For example, one stanza could describe a problem, one stanza could explore solutions, and one stanza could recreate a time before the problem existed.

1. How would you describe the structure of "To the Foot from Its Child"?
2. In your opinion, what is the purpose of each of the poem's six stanzas?
3. How does Neruda use transitional words and phrases to show the structure and organization of the poem's main ideas?

- See **Literary Terms Handbook**, p. R12.

Literature and Writing

Writing About Literature

A Critical Review Write a critical review in which you analyze and evaluate Neruda's ability to compare and contrast an individual's hopes, dreams, and imagination with the sober reality of an individual's daily life. Support your analysis with specific lines and images from the poem.

Personal Writing

A Foot's Eye View In what new ways might you think about your feet after reading this poem? How would you describe the life of *your* foot? If you could talk directly to your feet—and they could respond—what would you say to each other? Write a personal note from you to your feet, telling them what you most want them to know. Then write a note of response from your feet's point of view.

Extending Your Response

Literature Groups

Memorable Lines Have two members of your group each read the poem aloud, while the others read along silently. Then, take turns naming particularly interesting or memorable lines. Discuss each of the lines as a group, sharing ideas about what the line might mean and about what the image brings to mind. Choose a representative to summarize your discussion for the whole class.

Learning for Life

Notes from the Doctor Suppose that you were the podiatrist (foot doctor) of the poem's human character from infancy until death. Research the medical facts about such common foot conditions as calluses, bunions, bone spurs, sweaty feet and foot odor, and hardening of the toenails. Then write a summary of your medical observations and treatment of the person's feet during various stages of life. Your summary should incorporate details from the poem and from your research.

Performing

This Is Your Life Picture a specific human character for this poem and imagine him at various stages of life. With a small group of classmates, make up details about the man's appearance, relationships, occupation, home, and lifestyle. Then, stage a television show in which people from the man's past appear as guests, telling stories about his life. For example, the man's mother might describe what he was like as a boy, taking off his socks every chance he had. Choose one group member to act as the man, one to act as a host, and others to be the guests.

Reading Further

For more by or about Pablo Neruda, you might enjoy these works:

Poems: "We Are Many," about self-identity; "Too Many Names," about the unity of life; and "Lazybones," about contentment, all appear in the collection titled *Extravagaria.*

Viewing: *Il Postino* (The Postman) is an Italian film about Pablo Neruda's friendship with a postman and how he helps the postman to woo a woman with poetry.

Save your work for your portfolio.

Technology Skills

Multimedia: Presenting Poetry

As you already know, text is simply words on a page. You normally read text from left to right, top to bottom. Multimedia authoring software such as HyperStudio allows you to manipulate words and graphics to communicate in ways that go beyond traditional linear ideas. Writers can incorporate such multimedia features as hot links and buttons to permit *readers* to participate in the authoring process. As a multimedia author, you lay all the groundwork, but your readers choose what directions their paths will take.

Navigating a Multimedia Authoring Program

Take a few minutes to familiarize yourself with some important features you will find in such typical authoring programs as HyperCard or HyperStudio.

SELECTED FEATURES OF MULTIMEDIA AUTHORING PROGRAMS

Features	Functions
Cards	Each "page" you create with a multimedia authoring program is called a card. A card can contain text, graphics, sound, movies, and links to other cards.
Stacks	A series of related cards is called a stack. A multimedia project can consist of a single stack or several stacks that have been linked together.
Text tools	Text tools enable users to write on a card.
Paint tools	Paint tools enable users to draw on a card.
Art/sound directories	Art and sound directories contain predrawn backgrounds, clip art, and photos–or prerecorded music and sounds–that can be imported into your cards.
Buttons	Buttons are the tools that tell the multimedia authoring program to perform an action. A button can take a reader to another card, start a movie, play a recorded message, and more.

Presenting Poetry in Multimedia

Readers bring their own thoughts and experiences to a poem. You can share your own ideas about a poem with other readers. With a multimedia authoring program, you can present a poem and include your own analysis and interpretation of it. You can also present other information about the poem and its author.

Create a multimedia stack that will become your presentation of "The Charge of the Light Brigade" by Alfred, Lord Tennyson.

1. In a small group, open the multimedia authoring program on your computer.
2. Select **New Stack** from the **File** menu. (See Figure 1.) Name it "Light Brigade." The blank screen is your first card.

TECHNOLOGY TIP

You can add color to the background of your cards by clicking on one of the paint tools from the **Tools** palette and selecting a color from the **Colors** menu.

3. Make the first card a Title and Author card by typing in the names of the poem and the poet.

4. Add buttons to link this card to other cards by selecting **Add a Button…** under the **Objects** menu. (See Figure 2.)

5. To make additional cards select **New Card** from the **Edit** menu. (See Figure 3.) Create cards for the text of the poem, background to the poem, and a brief biography of the author. For example, from the Title and Author card you could arrange for the readers to choose from three buttons that take them to a brief biography of Tennyson, the first stanza of the poem, or a recorded reading of the poem. (See Figure 4.)

6. Your completed stack should include at least fifteen cards. If you have the necessary hardware and software to include sounds and images, add some of them to your stack. For example, you could include music or sound effects, a photo of the author, or even artwork of a nineteenth-century cavalry charge.

7. When you've completed your poetry project, save it on a disk or on the shared drive of your Local Area Network.

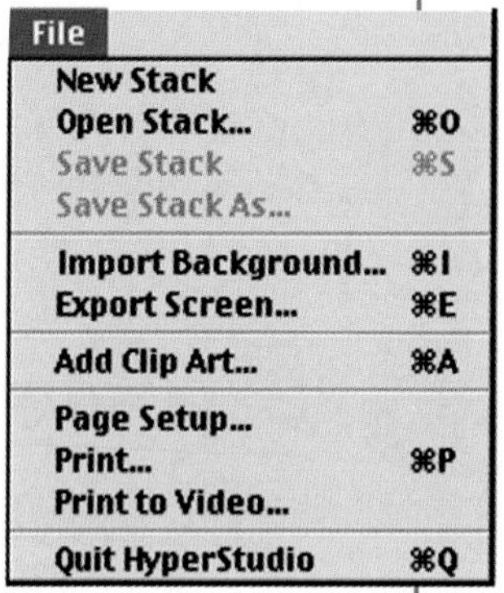

Figure 1

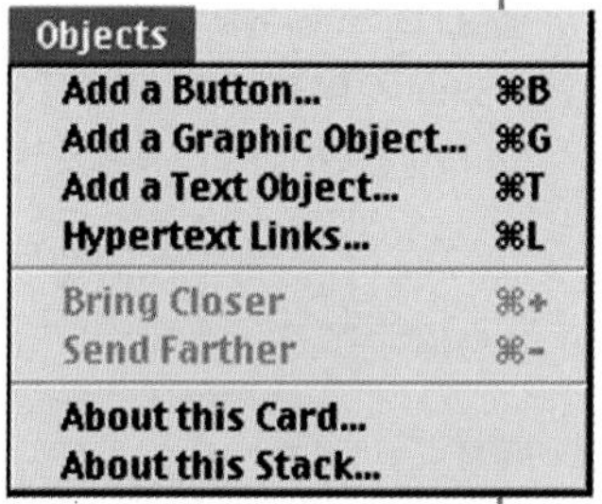

Figure 2

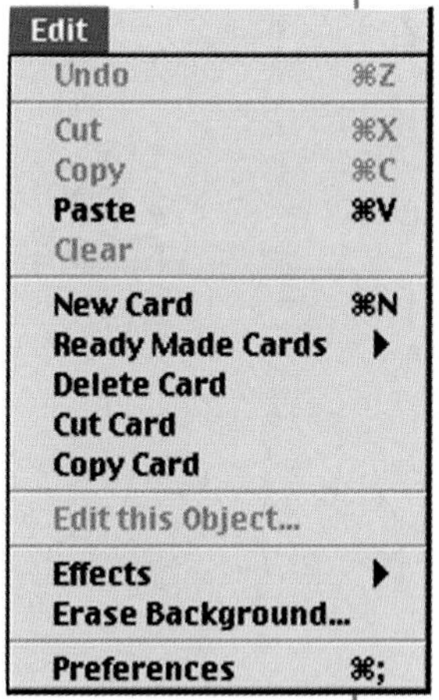

Figure 3

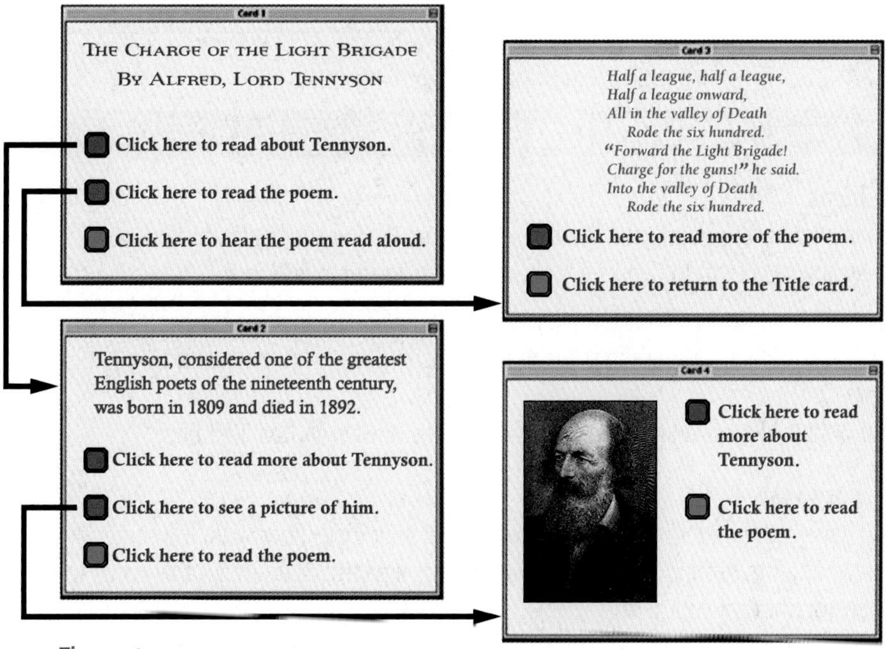

Figure 4

ACTIVITIES

1. Create a stack, presenting a poem of your choosing.

2. Link the stack you make for your poem with the stacks made by your fellow students to create a class multimedia poetry anthology. Include a title card for your anthology and a table of contents card with links to the poems.

Writing Workshop

Expository Writing:
Extended Definition

What's in a word? Dictionaries may give basic definitions, but sometimes not much more. An extended definition can explore a word in all its many aspects, from the philosophical to the personal, from the metaphoric to the scientific. **In this workshop, you will write an expository essay that combines formal and personal definitions of a word or term.**

- As you write your extended definition, refer to the **Writing Handbook,** pp. R58–R71.

EVALUATION RUBRIC
By the time you complete this Writing Workshop, you will have
- written an introduction that identifies the word or term to be defined
- classified the word or term into a general category
- provided a formal definition of the word or term as well as personal examples and descriptions of it
- compared and contrasted uses of the word or term
- presented an extended definition that is free of errors in grammar, usage, and mechanics

The Writing Process

PREWRITING

PREWRITING TIP
Explore a few terms before choosing one for your topic.

Explore ideas
Some poems in this theme may be thought of as personal definitions of common words. Before deciding on a term to define, ask yourself the following questions.

- Do you want to describe an art form, as María Herrera-Sobek does in "My Poetry"?
- Do you want to define a sensation, as Emily Dickinson does in "Pain—has an Element of Blank—"?
- Do you want to discuss an emotion, as Robert Burns does in "A Red, Red Rose"?

Make a word web
Once you have chosen a term, use a word web to get your ideas flowing. In the center of the web, write your term. Around it, write down any words, images, or examples that come to mind when you think of your term.

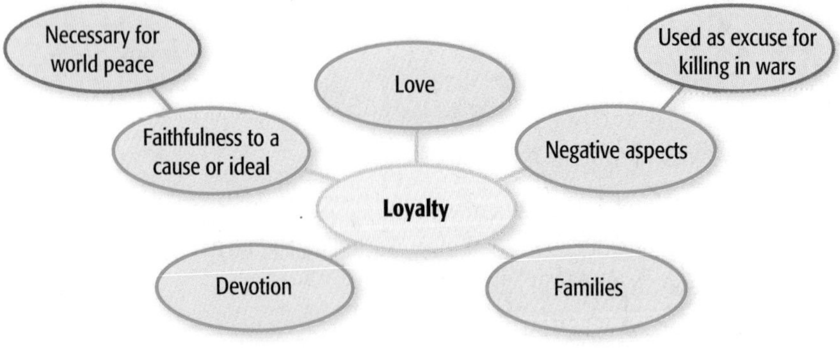

Consider your audience and purpose

With whom would you like to share your writing? Think about who might benefit from understanding your term the way you do. Your purpose is to help your audience fully understand what the term means to you. To accomplish this goal, you will need to **classify** the term, **give examples** of it, and **compare** it to other things.

Make a plan

Plan an introduction, body, and conclusion. In the body, use at least one paragraph for each method of defining. Here's how one student used a chart and information from her word web to plan her paper.

STUDENT MODEL

Classifying	• Put the term in its general category. What *kind* of thing is it? Is your term a feeling? a place? an action? an adjective?	loyalty is a feeling and a set of behaviors
	• Then, use contrast to show how it is different from other terms in that category.	contrast with affection, which is just an emotion, and gallantry, which is just an action; broken friendships; divorces
	• Name some subtopics or synonyms, and explain them.	love; trust; devotion; reliability
Giving examples	• To help explain your topic, give at least two examples of it.	family loyalty; friendship; team loyalty; marriage
Comparing	• Compare the term with something familiar to your readers. Figurative language—such as metaphors, similes, and analogies—can help you make comparisons.	loyalty is like an intense devotion to someone; loyalty is sweetness and romance

Complete Student Model on p. R115.

DRAFTING

DRAFTING TIP

Neatness doesn't count in a draft (as long as *you* can read it). If new ideas come to you, squeeze them in between lines, in the margins, or at the top or bottom of your page.

Write your draft

With your plan beside you, write your draft. Refer to your plan, but don't let it restrict you. Don't spend too much time trying to find the right word or form the perfect sentence. You can improve everything in the revision stage.

From the formal to the personal

You might begin your essay by stating a formal definition of your term. Formal language and organization are appropriate here. As you move from classifying your term to explaining it and comparing it, you may want to shift from the formal definition to a more personal one.

It would be appropriate to shift the tone from formal to informal too. In fact, the shift in tone will alert readers to the shift in the style of definition. At any stage in the process, you can use parallel structure to help make your writing clear. See the Writing Skill "Using Parallelism" on page 607 for advice.

STUDENT MODEL

(FORMAL DEFINITION) Loyalty is a faithfulness that one feels and displays toward a person, cause, government, or duty. Loyalty is both a feeling and a set of behaviors.

(PERSONAL DEFINITION) One type of loyalty is found between people. There's a sweet feeling of certainty when you know that you'll stick by someone no matter what. My family members all feel that kind of loyalty toward each other, and it goes beyond just liking or loving each other. We can fight with each other, ignore each other, and get sick of each other, but there's never any doubt that we'd be there if someone needed it. The loyalty I get from my family is like a security blanket that I know will keep me safe wherever I go.

Complete Student Model on p. R115.

Check in with yourself as you draft

Stop and ask yourself how the writing process is going. If you feel as if you are losing interest in your topic, try approaching it from a different angle. Return to your word web and add items of particular interest to you. If you feel as if you have nothing to say, your topic may be too narrow. Try choosing a similar but more general term to help you expand your thinking—and your writing.

REVISING

Take another look

When the draft seems complete, set it aside. Then, collect some additional information. Try to find a poem on the subject, check a reference book, or ask someone else to define the term you've chosen. Reconsider the draft in the light of your new knowledge.

Have a writing conference

Work with a group of students to help one another with revision. Make sure that each student participating in the conference has a copy of the **Rubric for Revising.** Take turns reading your extended definitions aloud. When you are a listener, use the **Rubric for Revising** to guide your comments. When you are a reader, take notes on the comments that the listeners make. Refer to the notes as you revise, but use your own judgment when deciding whether to make changes.

REVISING TIP

You may find that the addition of an anecdote, or story, that illustrates your term will enliven your writing, making it more interesting for others to read.

RUBRIC FOR REVISING

Your revised extended definition should have

- ☑ an introduction that identifies the word or term to be defined
- ☑ body paragraphs that classify the word or term, give examples of the word or term, and compare the word or term to something else
- ☑ vivid imagery that captures the audience's attention and helps clarify your definition
- ☑ a conclusion that summarizes your overall definition

Your revised extended definition should be free of

- ☑ confusing comparisons
- ☑ cliches and overused imagery that do not help to illuminate the meaning of the word or term
- ☑ errors in grammar, usage, and mechanics

STUDENT MODEL

~~But~~ However I want to think more about when loyalty works. Because loyalty is a feeling ~~and actions~~ as well as a set of behaviors, you can really trust someone who is loyal to you. A loyal person won't claim to feel one way but act another way. ~~He or she will put his or her money where his or her mouth is.~~ Loyal people sincerely connect what they say with what they do. The unswerving support that comes from loyalty can occasionally cause problems if ~~it~~ the sentiment is misdirected, but without loyalty, ~~we~~ the human race would be a scared ~~and~~ lonely vulnerable species.

Complete Student Model on p. R115.

EDITING/PROOFREADING

PROOFREADING TIP

Use the **Proofreading Checklist** on the inside back cover of this textbook to help you correct errors.

When you have defined your topic completely enough for a reader to understand it as you do, check for errors in grammar, usage, mechanics, and spelling.

Grammar Hint

Place the adverb *only* immediately before the word or phrase that it modifies. A misplaced *only* may make your meaning unclear.

UNCLEAR: *People only can understand emotions by experiencing them.*

MEANING 1: *People can understand emotions only by experiencing them.*

MEANING 2: *Only people can understand emotions by experiencing them.*

For more about the adverb *only*, see **Language Handbook**, p. R24.

Complete Student Model

For a complete version of the student model, see **Writing Workshop Models**, p. R115.

STUDENT MODEL

```
                     from            d
Loyalty is different than affection, or gallantry.
                        e
Loyalty only involvs both emotion and action.
```

Complete Student Model on p. R115.

PUBLISHING/PRESENTING

PRESENTING TIP

If you present your definition aloud, begin by inviting a few audience members to give their personal definitions of your word.

For a group presentation, you can combine your definitions to create and publish a group dictionary. Add illustrations and donate the dictionary to the school library. If your definition falls within the area of interest of a friend or relative, include it in a letter and invite comments.

Reflecting

Now that you have written an extended definition, how would you define *extended definition*? How would you classify it? What examples would you give? What would you compare it to? Also think about how you can use defining techniques in other kinds of expository writing.

Save your work for your portfolio.

Theme 8 Inspirations

What is it that makes you try harder, reach higher, or believe in something larger than yourself? Perhaps the history of your family has taught you inner strength, or the vastness of an ocean view has expanded the reaches of your imagination. Maybe the love of someone else has helped you to believe in yourself. The poems in this theme explore these and other sources of inspiration.

THEME PROJECTS

Listening and Speaking

Document Difference The same source may inspire people in different ways.

1. With a small group, identify the sources of inspiration for each poet in this theme.
2. Interview people to find out how they feel about these sources. If they are inspired by them, ask why. If they are indifferent to them, ask what sorts of things they do find inspiring. You may want to tape record or videotape people's responses.
3. Present your interview results to your classmates. Then discuss the most common sources of inspiration and those that are most unique.

Interdisciplinary Project

Art Athletes, students, and businesspeople often use visual and verbal reminders to help them stay focused on their inspiration.

1. Using lines from the poems in this theme or from a book such as *Bartlett's Familiar Quotations,* choose three inspirational passages.
2. Then find photographs in magazines or newspapers—or create artwork of your own—that reflects the meaning behind the quotations. Combine the words and the images to make a poster for each passage.

Before You Read

I Wandered Lonely as a Cloud and *The Peace of Wild Things*

Reading Focus

Think about an experience you have had whose full meaning or significance did not really "hit" you until much later.

Journal In your journal, briefly describe what happened. What benefit do you gain from thinking about it after the fact?

Setting a Purpose Read to find out about a kind of experience that continues to have meaning long after it first occurred.

Building Background

Did You Know?

- For most of his life, William Wordsworth lived in the Lake District of northern England, a region famous for its scenic mountains, hills, and lake-strewn valleys. An avid student of nature, Wordsworth explored the region during many long walks. The experience that inspired "I Wandered Lonely as a Cloud" occurred on a walk that Wordsworth took in the Lake District countryside on April 15, 1802, with his beloved sister and companion, Dorothy. Wordsworth's sister was also moved by the experience, and she recorded it in her journal. Today, thousands of tourists flock each year to the picturesque Lake District, which was made into a national park in 1951.

England's Lake District

- As a nature writer, Wendell Berry is often compared to William Wordsworth and Henry David Thoreau. An avid outdoorsman, Berry is a native of Kentucky, and after living in New York and California for a time, he returned to his native state to live, farm, and write. In returning to Kentucky, Berry wished to become rooted in a particular place and to live in harmony with his surroundings.

Meet William Wordsworth

William Wordsworth started writing early in life, completing his first significant poem when he was seventeen. Most poets of his day saw nature as something wild and forbidding, but Wordsworth was inspired by the natural landscape. For years, critics and reviewers attacked his work, but by the end of his life, he had gained fame and fortune for his poetry. Today he's considered one of the greatest British poets.

William Wordsworth was born in England in 1770 and died in 1850.

Meet Wendell Berry

Writer and organic farmer Wendell Berry firmly believes in the importance of sustaining local community life and small farms. In his poetry, novels, and essays, Berry promotes the message that respect and appreciation for nature is essential to human life.

Wendell Berry was born in Kentucky in 1934.

I Wandered Lonely as a Cloud

William Wordsworth

I wandered lonely as a cloud
That floats on high o'er vales and hills,
When all at once I saw a crowd,
A host, of golden daffodils;
Beside the lake, beneath the trees,
Fluttering and dancing in the breeze.

Continuous as the stars that shine
And twinkle on the milky way,
They stretched in never-ending line
Along the margin of a bay:
Ten thousand saw I at a glance,
Tossing their heads in sprightly° dance.

The waves beside them danced; but they
Outdid the sparkling waves in glee:
A poet could not but be gay,
In such a jocund° company:
I gazed—and gazed—but little thought
What wealth the show to me had brought:

For oft,° when on my couch I lie
In vacant or in pensive mood,
They flash upon that inward eye
Which is the bliss of solitude;
And then my heart with pleasure fills,
And dances with the daffodils.

12 *Sprightly* (sprīt′ lē) means "lighthearted" or "merry."
16 *Jocund* (jok′ ənd) means "cheerful and carefree."
19 *Oft* is an old, poetic form of "often."

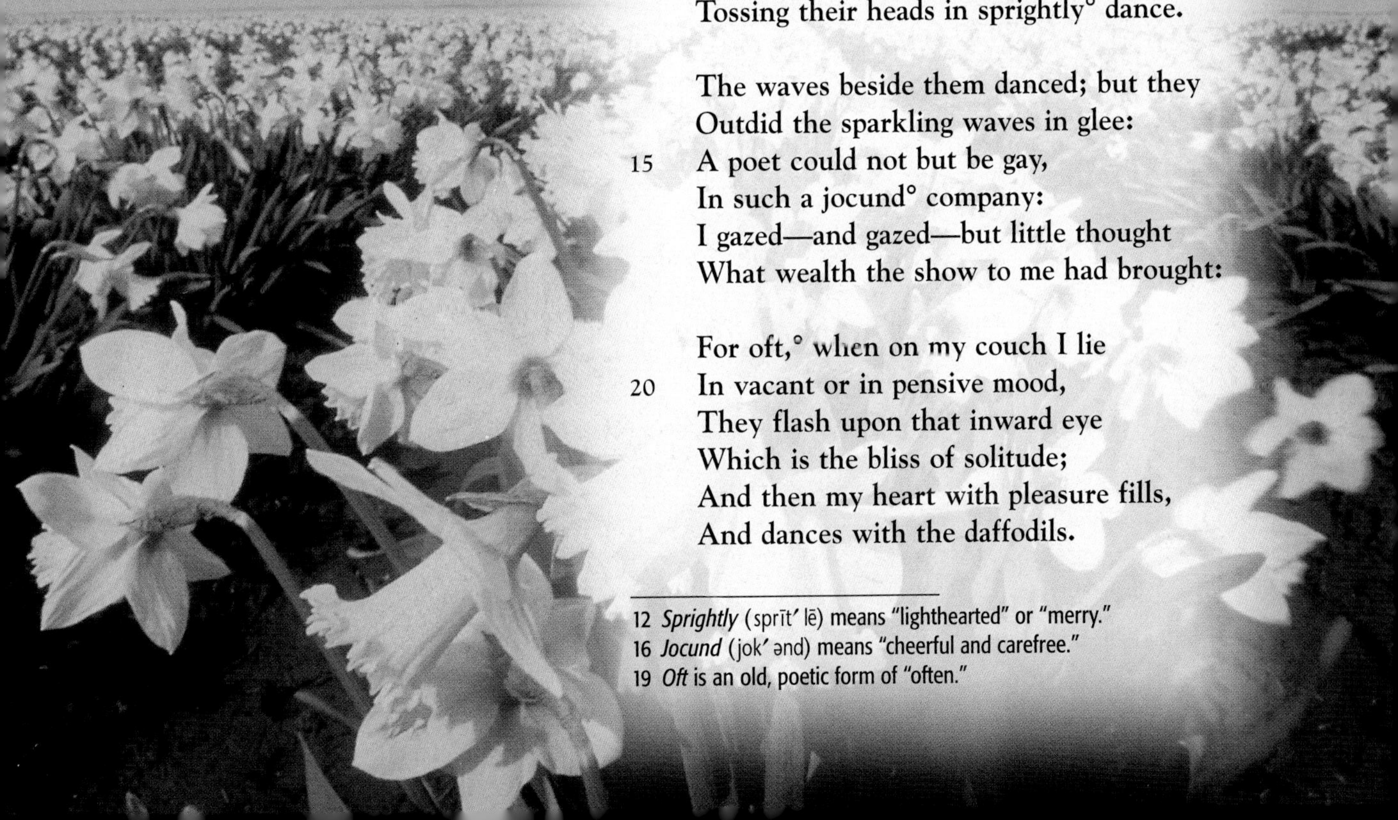

The Peace of Wild Things

Wendell Berry

When despair for the world grows in me
and I wake in the night at the least sound
in fear of what my life and my children's lives may be,
I go and lie down where the wood drake°
rests in his beauty on the water, and the great heron feeds.
I come into the peace of wild things
who do not tax° their lives with forethought
of grief. I come into the presence of still water.
And I feel above me the day-blind stars
waiting with their light. For a time
I rest in the grace of the world, and am free.

4 A *drake* is a male duck.
7 Here, *tax* means "place a heavy burden on; strain."

Responding to Literature

Personal Response

Which lines from these poems did you find most memorable, powerful, or surprising? Share your response with a partner.

Analyzing Literature

I Wandered Lonely as a Cloud

Recall and Interpret

1. In your own words, describe the scene that the speaker sees. Why does the speaker find the sight so special?
2. What is the "wealth" that the sight brings to the speaker? In your opinion, why does the speaker experience that "wealth" after the fact, rather than in the moment of his vision?
3. Explain what the speaker means by the "inward eye" in line 21.
4. What does Wordsworth's use of **personification** suggest about his response to the scene? (See Literary Terms Handbook, page R9.)

Evaluate and Connect

5. "I Wandered Lonely as a Cloud" is considered by many to be one of Wordsworth's most memorable poems. What do you think makes it so?
6. What would make you incredibly happy to look at or remember?
7. Review your writing for the Reading Focus on page 526. How is your experience similar to or different from Wordsworth's experience?

The Peace of Wild Things

Recall and Interpret

8. What words would you use to describe the speaker's frame of mind in lines 1–3? What might have caused him to feel this way?
9. What does the speaker do when in this frame of mind? What does this suggest about his personal values or philosophy of life?
10. What is it that people do that "wild things" do not?
11. What might the speaker mean when he says, "For a time / I rest in the grace of the world, and am free"?

Evaluate and Connect

12. What do you think of the way the speaker frees himself from worry and anxiety? What do you do when you're feeling stressed?
13. A current trend in travel is the eco-vacation, or eco-tour, during which people journey to remote places to see unusual geography and wildlife. Based on your reading of this poem, what might account for the popularity of such vacations?
14. What importance does nature have in your life? How does its importance in your life compare with its importance for Wendell Berry?

Literary ELEMENTS

Theme

Often an insight about life or human nature, **theme** is the main idea or message of a work of literature. A poem may have a **stated theme,** which is expressed directly and explicitly, or an **implied theme,** which is not stated directly but is revealed through imagery and figures of speech. In "I Wandered Lonely as a Cloud," Wordsworth directly states that the sight of the host of daffodils is a treasure, because it brings him intense pleasure whenever he remembers it. Readers may uncover one or more themes in any literary work, depending on their interpretations of it.

1. In your opinion, what is the theme of "The Peace of Wild Things"?
2. Is the theme stated or implied? Explain.

- See **Literary Terms Handbook,** p. R13.

Literature and Writing

Writing About Literature

Comparing Imagery and Mood Imagery is descriptive language that appeals to the senses. In a paragraph or two, compare the imagery in "I Wandered Lonely as a Cloud" with that of "The Peace of Wild Things." How does the imagery help create a different mood in each poem? To accompany your writing, create a drawing or painting that conveys the imagery and mood of each poem.

Creative Writing

Nature's Healing Power Imagine that you are a psychologist who believes in the curative power of nature. Make up a chart listing five or more worries, stresses, or fears that your patients suffer. For each problem, write a "prescription" that suggests a benefit to be gained from different experiences in the natural world.

Extending Your Response

Literature Groups

Rate the Wordsworths Dorothy Wordsworth wrote this description of the daffodils she spotted while walking with her brother: "[We] saw that there was a long belt of them along the shore, about the breadth of a country turnpike road. I never saw daffodils so beautiful. They grew among the mossy stones about and about them; some rested their heads upon these stones as on a pillow for weariness; and the rest tossed and reeled and danced, and seemed as if they verily laughed with the wind, that blew upon them over the lake; they looked so gay, ever glancing, ever changing." Using specific details from each account, debate within your group which writer, Dorothy or her brother, has given (1) the more accurate, (2) the more vivid, (3) the more poetic, and (4) the more meaningful description of the same experience. Discuss your evaluations with the rest of the class.

Listening and Speaking

A "Berry" Great Poet Prepare and perform a monologue in which you assume the role of Wendell Berry reflecting on Wordsworth's poem. Tell what you think about the poem, how it might have influenced you, and what attitudes about nature you and Wordsworth share. Allow your classmates time to respond and ask questions.

Reading Further

You might enjoy these works by William Wordsworth and Wendell Berry:

Poetry: *The Essential Wordsworth* includes the best of the poet's works.

Essays: *The Unforeseen Wilderness,* by Wendell Berry, is a collection of essays on Kentucky's Red River Gorge and on experiencing the wilderness.

Save your work for your portfolio.

LISTENING, SPEAKING, and VIEWING

Oral Interpretation of a Poem

Have you noticed that two people's readings of the same poem can sound completely different? Since people's experiences are unique, they often have different interpretations of what they read. Oral interpretation of a poem gives readers a chance to share their impressions. It also offers listeners new insights on a poem's tone or meaning.

In preparing an oral interpretation of a poem, you might find these suggestions helpful:

- Read the poem silently to yourself and consider who the speaker might be. Do you "hear" the voice of the poet, of an unidentified person, or of a character? What is this person's mood? What tone of voice would the person use if he or she were saying the poem aloud? Through oral interpretation, you will use your own voice to represent the speaker.
- As you read the poem silently, pay attention to your feelings, ideas, and questions. List any unfamiliar terms and look them up. Make notes on passages that are especially powerful or puzzling. Try to decide how the poet has used rhyme, rhythm, and other sound devices, as well as imagery and figurative language, to affect your responses. You may want to emphasize those techniques in your reading.
- Look for clues that will help you read the poem fluently, in an easy and flowing manner. Punctuation marks such as periods, semicolons, commas, or dashes may suggest where to pause for breath. Remember that you may need to read through the ends of lines, even lines that rhyme, to reach a proper place to pause.
- Practice reading or reciting the poem aloud. Experiment with different speeds, volumes, and other ways of using your voice to get the results you want. Practice again and again until you are satisfied that your oral interpretation of the poem clearly expresses your understanding of it.

ACTIVITY

Select a poem to interpret orally. It could be "The Peace of Wild Things," "I Wandered Lonely as a Cloud," or another poem you would like to spend some time thinking about. Practice reading or reciting it, following the suggestions above. Then share it with a group. You may want to make and distribute copies of the poem before you begin your oral interpretation. After everyone in your group has presented an oral interpretation of a poem, compare and discuss your understanding of each other's interpretations.

Before You Read

A Noiseless Patient Spider and *Wanderer*

Reading Focus

Have you ever seen a bird play with a stick or a feather, or watched two squirrels engaged in a game of chase?

Sketch It! Draw a quick sketch of a wild animal that you've seen or read about engaged in an activity that seems familiar–almost human. Then jot down a few notes about the ways in which animals and people are alike and different.

Setting a Purpose Read to discover the connections that two poets make between animal behavior and human emotion.

Building Background

Did You Know?

- Spiders are well known for spinning sticky silk webs in which they trap their prey. And although all species of spiders spin silk, not all use the silk to make webs. Spiders also use it to build nests, to quickly escape from enemies, and to move from place to place, spinning silk threads behind themselves everywhere they go. Spiders are so dependent on their silk that they could not live without it.
- Geese are water birds that are closely related to ducks and swans–and between the two in size. Although their webbed feet make them good swimmers, they are as comfortable on land as they are in the water. As young adults, geese will choose their mates and then remain paired for life. Geese are migratory birds, flying south in fall and north in spring. They often fly in V-shaped formations, and they always travel along the same routes, called flyways. Some scientists believe the V formation enables the geese to stay together, following one leader. Others believe that the birds at the front of the V create air currents that make flying easier for the birds in back. Geese are graceful flyers and have remarkable endurance, sometimes flying more than a thousand miles without resting. With their loud honking cries, the migrating geese signal a change in the seasons for those who watch them from below.

Meet Walt Whitman

When Walt Whitman first published *Leaves of Grass*, a poetry collection that broke with tradition both in form and content, reviewers panned it, calling the poet a lunatic and a beast. But in his later years, Whitman's genius was acknowledged, and his home became a mecca for visiting writers. *Leaves of Grass*, which includes "A Noiseless Patient Spider," is today considered one of the most important works of American literature.

Walt Whitman was born in 1819 in New York. He died in 1892.

Meet Joan Fallert

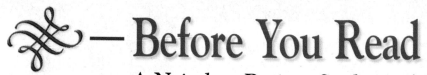

Joan Fallert was raised by a mother who loved and quoted poetry. As a result, Fallert claims, "I have had a love affair with language for as long as I can remember." Birds are a particular source of inspiration to Fallert, who feels a special bond with water birds because "they're comfortable on the ground, in the air, and in the water."

Joan Fallert was born in 1925 in New York.

A Noiseless Patient Spider

Walt Whitman

A noiseless patient spider,
I mark'd where on a little promontory° it stood isolated,
Mark'd how to explore the vacant vast surrounding,
It launch'd forth filament,° filament, filament, out of itself,
Ever unreeling them, ever tirelessly speeding them.

And you O my soul where you stand,
Surrounded, detached, in measureless oceans of space,
Ceaselessly musing,° venturing, throwing, seeking the spheres°
   to connect them,
Till the bridge you will need be form'd, till the ductile°
   anchor hold,
Till the gossamer° thread you fling catch somewhere, O my soul.

---

2 A *promontory* is a high ridge of rock or land, jutting out into a body of water.

4 Here, *filament* refers to the thin thread of a spider's silk.

8 *Musing* (mū′ zing) is thinking or meditating. The phrase *seeking the spheres* means something like "seeking the truth about the heavens."

9 Something that's *ductile* (dukt′ əl) is easily molded or shaped.

10 Here, *gossamer* means "light, delicate, filmy."

Wanderer

Joan Fallert

Calling
each to each, each
lifts and the great V drives
a wedge in the late autumn sky.
Snow Geese

flying
south, south to feed
and nest, ride the thermals°
mile after guileless° mile without
resting.

Coupled
for life they fly,
fly sometimes past midnight
into day, bills opening and
closing

slightly,
ceaselessly, necks
straight, eyes clear, opened wide,
fly toward the place they know they must
go to

and I
with no place to
be drawn to of my own
watch, listen for a heartland to
call me,

call me
back in the chill
air to somewhere which can
make my pulse pound, powerful as
wing beat

heading
for the sweet ground
on which the wild goose knows
it will be able to set down
at last.

---

8 *Thermals* are rising currents of warm air.
9 *Guileless* (gīl′ lis) means "innocent; naive."

Active Reading and Critical Thinking

Responding to Literature

Personal Response

What image in each poem do you find most memorable? Why? Note your responses in your journal.

Analyzing Literature

A Noiseless Patient Spider

Recall and Interpret

1. Where is the spider, and what is it doing? What might be the purpose of the spider's actions?
2. What adjectives and adverbs does the speaker use to describe the spider and its actions? Why do you suppose he chose these words to describe the spider?
3. In your opinion, why does the speaker address the second stanza to his soul, rather than simply using "I" to refer to himself?
4. How is the predicament of the speaker's soul like that of the spider? Use details from the poem in your answer.
5. In your opinion, what does the speaker seek? How might he feel once he finds what he's looking for?

Evaluate and Connect

6. How would you describe the speaker's attitude toward the spider? Compare and contrast his attitude with your own ideas about spiders. Explain whether your ideas about spiders have changed after reading the poem.
7. Explain how "A Noiseless Patient Spider" might reflect Whitman's response to the Reading Focus on page 532.
8. **Theme Connections** In what way is the spider an inspiration to the speaker?

Wanderer

Recall and Interpret

9. What kind of bird does the speaker describe in the first four stanzas? What are the birds doing and why?
10. What other details do you learn from this poem about the lives of these birds? Use details from the poem in your answer.
11. How would you describe the speaker? What can you infer about the circumstances of her life?
12. What feelings or yearnings do the birds evoke in the speaker?

Evaluate and Connect

13. In the sixth stanza, the speaker compares a pounding pulse with a powerful wingbeat. Do you think this is an effective comparison? Why or why not?
14. In your experience, why might people yearn for a "heartland," or a place that "calls" to them? What connotations does the word *heartland* have?

Literary ELEMENTS

Cinquain

A **cinquain** is a five-line poem or stanza that follows a specific pattern. In a cinquain, each line contains a specific number of syllables: the first line has two syllables, the next line has four, then six, then eight, and finally two again. American poet Adelaide Crapsey (1878–1914), who was influenced by haiku and other Japanese verse forms, developed this poetic form. Each stanza of the poem "Wanderer" is a cinquain.

1. The stanzas in "Wanderer" have a similar shape. How does this shape fit the subject of the poem?
2. Each stanza has a rhythm that builds and then falls with the length of the lines. What does this rhythm suggest to you?

- See **Literary Terms Handbook,** p. R3.

Literature and Writing

Writing About Literature

Comparing Speakers With a partner, discuss the similarities you see between the speakers of the two poems. What inspires them? What longings does each person have? Write a few paragraphs, comparing the two speakers. Be sure to use details from both poems to support your analysis.

Creative Writing

Animal Language What if the spider or a snow goose could talk directly to the speaker in each poem? What advice or counsel could each animal offer to the speaker? How might the speaker respond? Write a dialogue—serious or silly—that captures the conversation.

Extending Your Response

Literature Groups

Sharing Interpretations Reread the two poems aloud in your group. Then, work together to define the central problem that each speaker faces and brainstorm a list of possible solutions. What comforting advice can you offer each speaker? Share your conclusions with the rest of the class.

Interdisciplinary Activity

Biology: Spider Silk and Bird Navigation Investigate one of the following subjects: how spiders spin and use silk or how birds find their way on migratory flights. Use your findings to create a poster display explaining your subject.

Learning for Life

Job Description Many people turn their love of animals and wildlife into a career. For example, they may become park rangers, veterinarians, zoologists, or dog trainers. Using the Internet, interviews, and print sources, investigate the range of jobs that deal with animals and wildlife. Find out what workers do, what training or education they need, and what they can expect to earn. Use what you discover to create a chart about careers in this field.

Reading Further

You might also enjoy reading the poems in these collections:

Selected Poems and Prose, by Walt Whitman, includes some of Whitman's most famous poems.

Shared Sightings, edited by Sheila Golburgh Johnson, is an anthology of bird poems that includes Joan Fallert's "Wanderer."

Save your work for your portfolio.

MEDIA connection

Magazine Article

Have you ever forgotten the name of a person you just met or the answer to a question that you had just reviewed? Here is some practical information on memory—how it works and how you can improve it.

How to Remember When You're Always Forgetting

by Dianne Hales—*Ladies Home Journal*, August 1995

FACTS ABOUT MEMORY

1. Memory is a process—and it isn't always exact. Memory is an invisible process. As we create or recall a memory, we activate electrical impulses that travel along a network of brain cells and cause chemical interactions. Some experts believe that because of subtle alterations in these interactions over time, an individual's recall of events can change.

2. It takes concentration to make a memory. To insert the information into long-term memory, you need to focus on it exclusively for a minimum of eight seconds.

3. Forgetting happens fast. Facts are most likely to slip from our memories when they are fresh.

4. Training can improve anyone's memory. Different people have different abilities to remember, just as they have various types of intelligence. Virtually all memory skills can be improved with a little bit of effort.

TYPES OF MEMORY

There are several ways that the brain stores information: *Working* or *"short-term" memory* is the equivalent of a mental blackboard. It's the place we scribble a phone number or post a reminder to pick up a quart of milk. *Long-term memory* is the mind's equivalent of a computer's hard disk. Facts are stored in the *semantic memory*, which can be harder to access as we age. Experiences (last year's vacation, for example) are stored in the *episodic memory*. Behaviors that are repeated often (driving, typing) become a part of *procedural memory*, the most enduring type.

TRICKS TO MAKE IT STICK

Names: When you meet someone, say his name aloud as soon as you can. Then, look closely at him and repeat his name silently to yourself ten times.

Numbers: Break long numbers down into meaningful chunks. For instance, a checking-account number, 1048630, will be more memorable if you think of it as 10:48 (time for a coffee break) and 6:30 (dinnertime).

Shopping lists: Visualize your house and imagine a giant version of each item in various rooms: A huge egg in the kitchen, a big loaf of bread in the bedroom. When shopping, mentally scan your house to recall your list.

Analyzing Media

1. Which of these strategies seems the most helpful to you? Explain.
2. Describe some other methods you have used or heard about that can help people remember things they should not forget.

Before You Read

Remember and *You Will Forget*

Reading Focus

Imagine that you are a grandparent, speaking to your grandchild. What would you urge the child to appreciate and remember about your family, your surroundings, your values, and your cultural heritage?

Quickwrite Jot down all the ideas that come to mind.

Setting a Purpose Read to see how poetry may be used to communicate the importance of remembering one's family heritage and community values.

Building Background

Did You Know?

- From earliest times, Native American cultures have believed in a deep spiritual connection between humans, animals, and forces of nature. Such values as respect–for the past, for social traditions, and for the various processes of all life–are deeply embedded in the Native American cultural heritage.
- Archeological discoveries of primitive tools indicate that humans existed as early as the Stone Age in what is now the African nation of Zimbabwe. By A.D. 800, productive farming and mining cultures existed there. However, Portuguese and other Europeans, who were eager to profit from the land's wealth of gold and other important minerals, began to settle in the area during the 1500s. During the nineteenth century, Great Britain imposed colonial rule. Most Europeans settled in the cities, and most of the native black majority (94 percent of the population) lived in poverty in rural farming areas. For more than a hundred years, the white minority controlled the government. After a long struggle, the colony gained its independence, established democratic reforms, and became the free nation of Zimbabwe in April 1980.

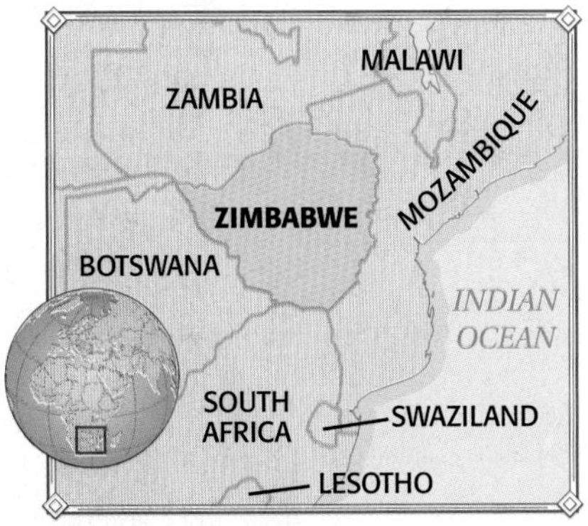

Meet Joy Harjo

Hailed as one of the most powerful Native American voices of her generation, Joy Harjo is a member of the Muskogee tribe of the Creek Nation. Harjo has written a screenplay, television documentary narration, song lyrics, and several volumes of poetry. She has received awards from the National Endowment for the Arts and the Poetry Society of America. Harjo currently teaches English at the University of New Mexico.

Joy Harjo was born in Tulsa, Oklahoma, in 1951.

Meet Chenjerai Hove

Chenjerai Hove (chen′ jə rī hō′ vā) has written both poems and novels to celebrate the cultural heritage of Africa. He currently works as a cultural journalist in Harare, the capital of Zimbabwe. His work has earned several awards, including the Zimbabwean Publishers/ Writers Literary Award and the Noma Award.

Chenjerai Hove was born in Zimbabwe in 1956.

Remember

Joy Harjo

Remember the sky that you were born under,
know each of the star's stories.
Remember the moon, know who she is.
Remember the sun's birth at dawn, that is the
strongest point of time. Remember sundown
and the giving away to night.
Remember your birth, how your mother struggled
to give you form and breath. You are evidence of
her life, and her mother's, and hers.
Remember your father. He is your life, also.
Remember the earth whose skin you are:
red earth, black earth, yellow earth, white earth
brown earth, we are earth.
Remember the plants, trees, animal life who all have their
tribes, their families, their histories, too. Talk to them,
listen to them. They are alive poems.
Remember the wind. Remember her voice. She knows the
origin of this universe.
Remember you are all people and all people
are you.
Remember you are this universe and this
universe is you.
Remember all is in motion, is growing, is you.
Remember language comes from this.
Remember the dance language is, that life is.
Remember.

In the Wind. Tim Nicola. Utah alabaster, height: 19 in. Artistic Gallery, Santa Fe.

You Will Forget

Chenjerai Hove

If you stay in comfort too long
you will not know
the weight of a water pot
on the bald head of the village woman

You will forget
the weight of three bundles of thatch
grass
on the sinewy° neck of the woman
whose baby cries on her back
for a blade of grass in its eyes

Sure, if you stay in comfort too long
you will not know the pain
of childbirth without a nurse in white

You will forget
the thirst, the cracked dusty lips
of the woman in the valley
on her way to the headman° who
isn't there

You will forget
the pouring pain of a thorn prick
with a load on the head.
If you stay in comfort too long

You will forget
the wailing in the valley
of women losing a husband in the mines

You will forget
the rough handshake of coarse palms
full of teary sorrow at the funeral.

If you stay in comfort too long
You will not hear
the shrieky voice of old warriors sing
the songs of fresh stored battlefields.

You will forget
the unfeeling bare feet
gripping the warm soil turned by the
plough

You will forget
the voice of the season talking to the
oxen.

7 *Sinewy* (sin′ ū ē) means "physically strong; muscular."
16 A *headman* is a chief or tribal leader.

Responding to Literature

Personal Response

What questions would you like to ask the speakers of these poems?

Analyzing Literature

Remember

Recall and Interpret

1. Give five examples of elements in nature and in the universe that the speaker urges readers to remember. Why might she want readers to remember these things?
2. How does the speaker describe dawn? Why might she describe dawn this way?
3. How does the speaker suggest the connectedness of life on earth?
4. According to the speaker, what is language and where does it come from? What do lines 23–25 mean to you?

Evaluate and Connect

5. The speaker urges readers to remember that all plants and animals "have their / tribes, their families, their histories, too." Does this concept of nature strike a chord of truth in you? Explain why or why not.
6. How would you describe the **mood** of this poem? What words or phrases from the poem contribute to the mood? (See Literary Terms Handbook, page R8.)
7. In your own words, paraphrase the speaker's statements in lines 19–23. In what ways might you be all of the things that the speaker says you are?

You Will Forget

Recall and Interpret

8. Whom does the speaker seem to be addressing? Explain your opinion.
9. How might the speaker define "comfort"? Why do you suppose "staying in comfort too long" would lead someone to forget the things the speaker describes?
10. How might the speaker define "pain"? Which feeling does the speaker seem to value more highly, comfort or pain? Explain, using details from the poem in your answer.
11. What type of **figurative language** does the speaker use in the last stanza? (See Literary Terms Handbook, page R5.) Explain the meaning of the image, and tell whether you think it ends the poem on an upbeat or a depressing note.

Evaluate and Connect

12. Which of the five senses does each stanza appeal to? What is the overall effect of these strong sensory images?
13. What aspects of the speaker's culture seem to be most important to him? In your opinion, is it possible to share his values, even if you aren't from his culture? Explain.
14. Based on the poem's subject matter, how do you think the poet might predict the future lifestyle of his people? How might you predict it? Explain.

Literary ELEMENTS

Repetition

In poetry, **repetition** is the recurrence of sounds, words, phrases, lines, or stanzas. A poet may use repetition to emphasize an idea or to lend a feeling of unity and continuity to a poem. When a line or stanza is repeated in a poem, it is sometimes called a refrain.

1. Identify an important example of repetition in Harjo's poem. In your opinion, what effect or effects does the poet achieve by using repetition?
2. Identify two examples of repetition in Hove's poem. In your opinion, what ideas does the poet emphasize through this repetition?

- See **Literary Terms Handbook,** p. R10.

Literature and Writing

Writing About Literature

Analyzing Titles and Themes Do the titles of these poems mean the same thing or do they appear to be opposite in meaning? What is the difference between an imperative command ("Remember") and a warning ("You Will Forget")? Write an analysis of each title, explaining how it relates to the theme of its poem. Then, explain how the themes of the two poems are similar and different.

Personal Writing

Don't Forget Look back at the writing you did for the Reading Focus on page 539. In your journal, make notes of any additional things that the poems of Harjo and Hove have convinced you are important to remember. Then write a letter to your imaginary grandchild, explaining what the child should not forget.

Extending Your Response

Literature Groups

Views on Cultural Preservation Both poets are concerned with cultural preservation. With your group, discuss the similarities and differences between their points of view as expressed in the two poems. Then discuss the following questions in terms of how you, as well as each poet, might answer them: What factors may lead to the loss of culture? What steps should people take to preserve their culture? Be sure to support your ideas with details from both poems. Share your conclusions with the rest of your class.

Interdisciplinary Activity

Art: Create a Collage Reread "Remember" and "You Will Forget," and choose your favorite poem. What images from the poem stand out in your mind? Make a collage to illustrate the poem by arranging and pasting together pictures from magazines or newspapers, images you have drawn or painted, fragments of printed text, and words in your own handwriting. Add your collage to a class anthology.

Listening and Speaking

Choral Reading With a group, select one poem for a choral reading. Experiment with different ways of reading the poem aloud. For example, you might try reading the poem in unison. Or, going around in a circle, take turns reading the poem aloud one line or group of lines at a time. Try to increase your fluency, or ease of reading, each time through the poem. A cassette recorder may be useful: record your practice readings, play them back, and evaluate the results. When you're satisfied with your reading, present it to the class.

Save your work for your portfolio.

MEDIA connection

Art Exhibition Catalogue

Do you know someone who weaves or quilts? As you'll read, family traditions and cultural identity may be passed on by teaching such crafts and skills to younger generations.

from Woven by the Grandmothers

Nineteenth-Century Navajo Textiles from the National Museum of the American Indian

edited by Eulalie H. Bonar

Dedication

For the Navajo people, especially Navajo weavers.

We take great pride in our rugs. We still weave as our great-great-grandmothers, and perhaps our great-great-grandfathers, did more than one hundred years ago. The tradition of Navajo weaving lies in the process of weaving. That has not changed much from the time the first blankets were made. The materials may change, the designs may change, the colors may change, but our techniques, values, and weaving customs remain the same.

Our mothers and fathers encourage us to continue to weave as they have and as our great-great-grandmothers have; they say it is a way of survival. It's the Navajo way. Navajo weaving is part of our religion, oral history, language, and *k'é* (family structure).

Plate 7

Plate 7

Bi ni ghá dzi itł' ó ni, (sarape poncho), 1825–60.
Handspun wool and raveled yarn,
172.2 × 132.6 cm.

I believe very strongly that we need to educate our young people about this early period of weaving in Navajo life. Rugs like this speak volumes. They can give our children a sense of pride, and the kind of self-respect they need to face the two worlds we live in.

—*Kalley Keams*

For all we know, weaving may be the central core in perpetuating Navajo culture.

—*Wesley Thomas*

Analyzing Media

1. What might Kalley Keams mean by "the two worlds we [Navajo] live in"?
2. How else can young people learn about their cultural heritage?

Before You Read

Lineage and *Where Are Those Songs?*

Reading Focus

What older person in your family or community do you most admire, and why?

Sharing Ideas Share your answer to the question above with a partner or small group. You may want to share an experience that reveals why the person is important to you or what you have learned from him or her.

Setting a Purpose Read to find out how two poets are inspired by their ancestors.

Building Background

Did You Know?

- According to Kenyan-born poet Micere Githae Mugo (mi she′ rā gi′ thī moo̅ gō′), Africa has a long and great tradition of verbal art called *orature,* which consists of stories, songs, and poems that have been passed on from generation to generation. Mugo celebrates this tradition and the women who have helped pass it on in "Where Are Those Songs?" Mugo says she nearly lost this tradition after attending British colonial schools where "we were supposed to erase our own traditions." Quoting the African proverb "everyone has got a voice," Mugo explains that in their songs, Africans tell their own stories in their own words and pass along their traditions.
- Whenever she reads the poem "Where Are Those Songs," Mugo tries to involve her audience. She says the poem contains songs, as well as some deliberate pauses. The critical point in the poem is the question "What do you remember?" Mugo always becomes silent at this moment in the reading, as her audience struggles with the painful realization of all that has been lost. The mother's command to sing, along with the constant, deliberate repetition in the poem, emphasizes how important it is that people not forget their own songs. Even if the old songs have been lost, Mugo says, people should pass along their own, new traditions.

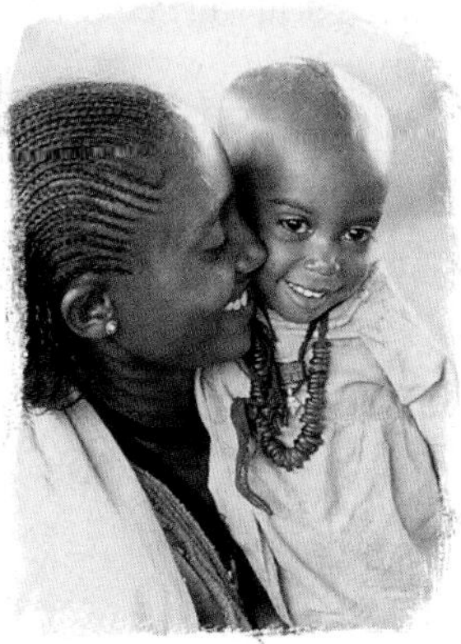

Meet Margaret Walker

Here lies Margaret Walker / Poet and Dreamer / She tried to make her life / a Poem. This is the epitaph that Margaret Walker wrote for herself. Among the most important influences on her poetry were her mother's music, her father's advice and sermons, the Bible, and her nearly life-long residence in the South. In fact, Walker said the South is "the subject and source of all my poetry."

Margaret Walker was born in Alabama in 1915 and died in 1998.

Meet Micere Githae Mugo

"The first slave to escape captivity was he/she who learned to read and write," says Micere Githae Mugo. A firm believer in the power of literacy, Mugo devotes her life to teaching and to writing. She has taught in several African universities and recently in the African American Studies department at Syracuse University in New York.

Micere Githae Mugo was born in Kenya in 1942.

Africa, 1995. Elizabeth Barakah Hodges. Acrylic on canvas, 25 x 18 in. Private collection.

Lineage

Margaret Walker

My grandmothers were strong.
They followed plows and bent to toil.
They moved through fields sowing seed.
They touched earth and grain grew.
They were full of sturdiness and singing.
My grandmothers were strong.

My grandmothers are full of memories
Smelling of soap and onions and wet clay
With veins rolling roughly over quick hands
They have many clean words to say.
My grandmothers were strong.
Why am I not as they?

Where Are Those Songs?

Micere Githae Mugo

Where are those songs
my mother and yours
always sang
fitting rhythms
to the whole
vast span of life?

What was it again
they sang
  harvesting maize, threshing millet,°
    storing the grain . . .

What did they sing
bathing us, rocking us to sleep . . .
and the one they sang
stirring the pot
(swallowed in parts by choking smoke)?

What was it
the woods echoed
as in long file
my mother and yours and all the women
    on our ridge
beat out the rhythms
  trudging gaily
  as they carried
  piles of wood
  through those forests
  miles from home

What song was it?

And the row of bending women
hoeing our fields
to what beat
did they
break the stubborn ground
as they weeded
our *shambas?*°

What did they sing
at the ceremonies
  child-birth
  child-naming
  second birth
  initiation. . . ?
how did they trill the *ngemi*°
what was
the warriors' song?
how did the wedding song go?
sing me
the funeral song.
What do you remember?

continued on next page

9 *Millet* is a wheatlike grain.

32 The word *shamba* can refer to a garden, farm, or plantation.

39 To *trill* is to sing or play a high-pitched sound that rapidly alternates between two notes, like the songs of some birds. *Ngemi* (n′ gem′ ē).

Sing
I have forgotten
my mother's song
my children
will never know.
This I remember:
Mother always said
sing child sing
make a song
and sing
beat out your own rhythms
the rhythms of your life
but make the song soulful
and make life
sing

Sing daughter sing
around you are
uncountable tunes
some sung
others unsung
sing them
to your rhythms
observe
listen
absorb
soak yourself
bathe
in the stream of life
and then sing
sing
simple songs
for the people
for all to hear
and learn
and sing
with you

To Market, 1954. Ellis Wilson. Oil with turpentine on panel, 22⅜ x 28$^{13}/_{16}$ in. North Carolina Museum of Art, Raleigh.

Viewing the painting: In what ways does this painting reflect the traditions described in "Where Are Those Songs?"

Responding to Literature

Personal Response

What reactions do these poems evoke in you? Share your reactions with your classmates.

Analyzing Literature

Lineage

Recall and Interpret

1. In the first stanza, what does the speaker say her grandmothers did? What do these details suggest to you about the grandmothers?
2. In your opinion, who are the grandmothers? How would you describe the speaker's attitude toward them? What details from the poem reveal this attitude?
3. What might the speaker mean by "They have many clean words to say"?
4. In your opinion, why might the speaker describe herself as different from her grandmothers? In what ways might she be different?

Evaluate and Connect

5. What does the **title** of the poem mean? Why might Walker have chosen this title?
6. How might the speaker define *strength?* Give evidence from the poem to support your opinion.
7. Think about the conversation you had for the Reading Focus on page 545. In what ways were your reasons for admiring an older person similar to or different from the speaker's reasons?

Where Are Those Songs?

Recall and Interpret

8. Make a list of all the times when the women who are recalled in this poem sing their songs. What role does singing play in their lives?
9. What do you know about the lifestyle of the women described in lines 1–45? How might those women perceive their lives? Give evidence from the poem in your answer.
10. What advice does the speaker's mother give in lines 52–60? Why do you suppose she gives this advice to her daughter?
11. In the last stanza, what is the daughter told about singing? Why might this be important?

Evaluate and Connect

12. The title poses a question. How might the speaker answer it? How would you answer it?
13. **Theme Connections** What do you like most about this poem? What is inspirational about its message?
14. If someone gave you the advice to "beat out your own rhythms" and to "make life sing," how would you carry out that advice in your own life?
15. What role does music and singing play in your life?

Literary ELEMENTS

Sound Devices

Poetry often contains such sound devices as alliteration and assonance. **Alliteration** is the repetition of sounds, most often consonant sounds, at the beginnings of words. Margaret Walker uses alliteration when she writes "grain grew." **Assonance** is the repetition of vowel sounds. In "Where Are Those Songs?" you can hear assonance in the repetition of the long *o* in "swallowed in parts by choking smoke." Poets often use these sound devices to emphasize certain words and underscore their meaning, to create or enhance rhythm, and to add a musical quality to their work.

1. Copy the following phrases on your paper: "followed plows," "rolling roughly," and "sing at the ceremonies." Tell whether each is an example of alliteration or assonance and underline the sounds that are repeated.
2. Find one additional example of alliteration and assonance in each poem.
3. Explain what the use of sound devices contributes to the overall effect of "Where Are Those Songs?"

- See **Literary Terms Handbook,** pp. R1 and R12.

Literature and Writing

Writing About Literature

Comparing Speakers How are the speakers in these two poems alike? How are they different? Think about their subjects and how close or distant each speaker seems to be from her subject. Consider also the speakers' attitudes toward their own lives. Then write one or more paragraphs, comparing and contrasting the speakers.

Personal Writing

Keeping and Creating Traditions In your journal, jot down a list of traditions that you value and would like to pass on to future children. Note why these traditions are meaningful to you. Then make another list of traditions you would like to start and tell why.

Extending Your Response

Literature Groups

A Father's Advice Walker has said that her father advised her to include three elements in every poem: "pictures or images; music or rhythm; and meaning." In a small group, decide whether Walker followed her father's advice when she wrote "Lineage." Support your answer as much as possible with details from the poem. Then share your response with other groups.

Internet Connection

From Plowshares to Web Sites Both of these poems depict African or African American women who, in Margaret Walker's words, were "full of sturdiness and singing." Today you can encounter descendants of these women on the Internet whose *work* is singing. Look for Web sites devoted to your favorite female African or African American recording artists, such as Whitney Houston, Valerie Wellington, Queen Latifah, or Ella Fitzgerald. Make a list of your favorite sites and share them with your classmates.

Listening and Speaking

Songs and Voices With a small group, prepare a reading of "Where Are Those Songs?" Plan to have some lines read by one reader, and others read in unison. Consider adding background music or sound effects. Practice your reading and experiment with the pace. Then perform your reading for the class.

Save your work for your portfolio.

Writing Workshop

Creative Writing: Narrative Poem

A narrative poem, such as "The Charge of the Light Brigade," is a poem that tells a story. Although the story is told in lines and stanzas–and may include figurative language, imagery, rhythm, or rhyme–it still includes such elements of fiction as setting, characters, and plot.

In this workshop, you will write a narrative poem, telling a story about something that is important to you.

- As you write your narrative poem, refer to the **Writing Handbook,** pp. R58–R71.

EVALUATION RUBRIC

By the time you complete this Writing Workshop, you will have

- told a story in verse, developing a plot with several events that lead to a climax
- included one or more clearly defined characters
- described the setting of the narrative
- used sensory images, sound devices, and figurative language to enrich the narrative
- presented a narrative poem that is free of unintentional errors in grammar, usage, and mechanics

The Writing Process

PREWRITING

PREWRITING TIP

Browsing through your journal is a good way to find topic ideas for your narrative poem.

Explore ideas

The poets in this theme have been inspired by their culture and family history and by the natural world. You may want to focus your poem on a moment of inspiration in your own life. Think back, and jot down some notes about what you remember about such moments. Perhaps you remember

- witnessing an act of bravery, generosity, or skill.
- encountering an animal that seemed to embody a positive character trait.
- traveling to a place that inspired you to think about your home in a new way.

Consider your purpose and audience

Think of your narrative poem as a journey: The lines of the poem represent a pathway, leading readers through your story from beginning to end. The audience for your poem could be anyone. Your goal is to make sure that your poem leads readers where you want them to go. Remember that you're writing about an experience that will be unfamiliar to others; make sure you provide enough information for them to follow the story.

Make a plan

Your narrative poem will have many of the same elements as a short story. As you begin planning your poem, write a synopsis, or summary, of the story as a guide. Then, to avoid leaving confusing gaps, identify the key parts of your narrative before you begin to write.

STUDENT MODEL

Synopsis	What will happen in the poem?	The speaker is Korean American. He fights going to visit Korea, then feels both strange and at home there. He misses his American food, friends, and life, but gradually accepts and learns to appreciate his parents' homeland. When he returns to the U.S., he feels both foreign and at home.
Setting	Where does the story take place? What will create atmosphere?	primarily in Korea sights, smells, and new foods
Characters	What people are important to the narrative? What other people are involved?	the speaker (me) my parents my Korean relatives Korean strangers I come in contact with
Plot	What four or five events tell the heart of the story?	parents announce a one-month visit to Korea and I explode with anger; we go to Korea; I cling to American music and food, but am surrounded by everything Korean; my father teaches me about the city and my mother introduces me to Korean food; we return to New Jersey where I feel both foreign and at home, as I did in Korea

Complete Student Model on p. R116.

Use graphic organizers to help you gather and organize ideas. You may want to plot the events of your narrative poem on a story map like the one on page 3. Or, make a word web like this one to help you gather the sensory details you will use to make the story of your poem real for an audience.

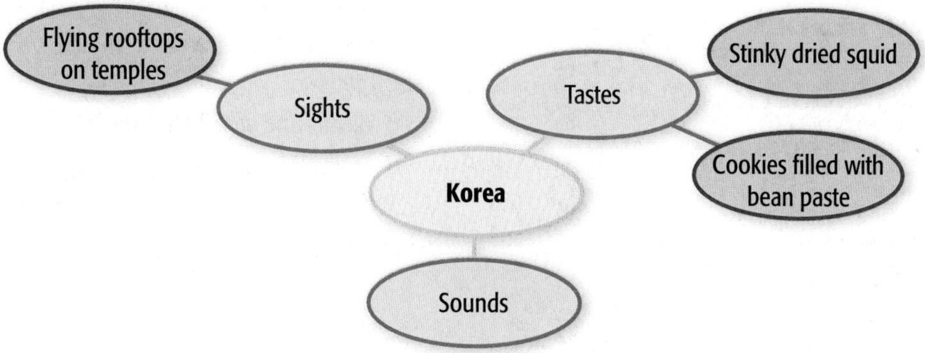

DRAFTING

DRAFTING TIP

Read phrases and lines aloud as you draft to see how well their sound fits their sense.

Write your draft

Stay flexible as you draft, and don't censor any ideas. Feel free to stray from your plan if the writing process takes you in new directions. Also, don't feel that you must complete your draft before you begin to revise. Often poets rethink and revise lines while they are drafting.

Enrich the story with images

Present the action in brief moments of narrative, writing each one as a phrase or sentence on a line of its own. Leave space between each line. Then, bring the action to life by filling in the spaces with imagery and sensory details. Using vivid verbs also will strengthen your poem.

STUDENT MODEL

I see a giant container full of dried squid:
Hateful morsels, so chewy, so salty, so pungent.
My parents' favorite snack
Makes my lip curl and leaves me craving
crackers.

Complete Student Model on p. R116.

REVISING

REVISING TIP

Use rhythm or rhyme to strengthen the pace of your poem.

Read the draft of your narrative poem and identify the strongest images. Do you want to expand them at this time? As you revise, be sure that the action flows smoothly from beginning to end. Use the **Rubric for Revising** to guide your work.

Read your narrative poem aloud

Read your poem to a writing partner. Ask your partner to listen for places where you can improve your use of imagery or where there seem to be gaps in the logical flow of details.

RUBRIC FOR REVISING

Your revised narrative poem should have

- ☑ clearly defined characters and a plot that leads to a climax
- ☑ sensory images that evoke the setting and set mood
- ☑ sound devices and figurative language that effectively enhance the story
- ☑ appropriate transitions and enough information so that readers can follow the story

Your revised narrative poem should be free of

- ☑ clichés and vague statements
- ☑ errors in grammar, usage, and mechanics

STUDENT MODEL

After I turn thirteen, my parents tell me:
come summer, we are going to korea for a month.
"My ~~I want to stay~~ home, is here!" I yell.
I blow up ~~run~~ to my room like a storm. ~~and slam the door~~.

Complete Student Model on p. R116.

EDITING/PROOFREADING

Poets sometimes ignore traditional rules of grammar, usage, and mechanics to make a specific point or to create a certain tone in their work. If you choose to do so, you will still need to check over your work to make sure you haven't included unintentional errors that could confuse your readers.

PROOFREADING TIP

Use the **Proofreading Checklist** on the inside back cover of this textbook to help you mark mistakes.

Grammar Hint

In poetry as in prose, subjects and verbs that belong together need to agree in number. If the subject is singular, the verb must be singular. If the subject is plural, as in the example below, the verb must be plural.

INCORRECT: *The young girls at the hotel wears white gloves.*
CORRECT: *The young girls at the hotel wear white gloves.*

- For more about subject-verb agreement, see **Language Handbook,** pp. R16–R19.

STUDENT MODEL

```
My parents speaks a native tongue
that is different.
```

Complete Student Model on p. R116.

Complete Student Model

For a complete version of the student model, see **Writing Workshop Models**, p. R116.

PUBLISHING/PRESENTING

If you want to submit your poem for publication, reference books in your local library will give you the addresses and submission requirements for journals around the country. You might also hold a poetry festival. Have each presenter tell the story behind the story—what inspired the poem and how an understanding of the experience developed during the course of writing the poem.

PRESENTING TIP

Make a class audio anthology. Have each classmate choose appropriate background music for his or her poem and make a recording of the poetry readings.

Reflecting

In what ways did writing the narrative poem change your understanding of your experience or of a special moment of inspiration? What parts of the writing process came easily to you, and what parts were more difficult? Jot down some notes in your journal, and think about how you can apply the lessons you learned to your next piece of writing.

Save your work for your portfolio.

Unit Assessment

Personal Response

1. Which of the poems in this unit would you like to read again? Explain your reasons.
2. As a result of the work you did in this unit, what new ideas do you have about the following:
   - how to discover meaning in a poem
   - how to talk about a poem's imagery, theme, structure, rhythm, and symbols
   - how to set and reach goals in your writing

Analyzing Literature

Compare Favorite Poems Choose your favorite poems from this unit. (Select at least two, but not more than four.) What draws you to them?

- Are you intrigued by the subjects of the poems?
- Do you especially like the poets' style?
- Does the rhythm of the poems draw you in?
- Are you captivated by the poets' word choice or use of imagery?

Compare each poem's elements with those of the others, identifying differences as well as similarities. Then explain what features attract you to the poems.

Evaluate and Set Goals

Evaluate

1. In this unit you probably had to read, write, speak publicly, and work with others. Which of your skills improved the most?
2. Think about the problems you faced in this unit.
   - How did you solve them when you worked alone?
   - How did you solve them when you worked with a group?
   - How might the solutions you found help you meet future challenges?
3. How would you assess your work in this unit, using the following scale? Give at least two reasons for your assessment.
   4 = outstanding **3** = good **2** = fair **1** = weak

Set Goals

1. With your teacher, decide what goal you would like to work toward in the next unit.
2. Write the goal down in your journal. Underneath it, explain your reasons for setting that particular goal and list three steps you will take to achieve it.
3. Schedule checkpoints to monitor your progress.

Build Your Portfolio

Select Choose two of the pieces of writing you did in this unit and include them in your portfolio. Use these questions to help you choose.

- Which work shows the most original ideas?
- Which work contains your best writing?
- Which work did you most enjoy writing?
- Which work did you spend the most time writing, revising, and polishing?

Reflect Write some notes to accompany each of the pieces you selected. Use these questions to guide you.

- What do you like best about the piece?
- What did you learn from the process of creating it?
- How could the piece be improved?
- What problems did you encounter while writing? How did you solve them?

Reading on Your Own

You might also be interested in the following books.

Fallen Angels
by Walter Dean Myers When seventeen-year-old Perry's college plans fall through, he enlists in the army and fights in the Vietnam War. Perry faces both racism and death, but he also manages to find friendship and virtue through his experiences.

This Same Sky: A Collection of Poems from Around the World
selected by Naomi Shihab Nye
Nearly every culture has a poetic tradition, and all over the world, poets share similar subjects: childhood, family, and the beauty of the natural world. This collection of 129 poets from 68 countries celebrates both the diversity of their origins and the similarity of their feelings and aspirations.

Earth Always Endures: Native American Poems
selected by Neil Philip Whether in the death song of a Cheyenne warrior or in an Apache prayer for happiness, this collection of traditional Native American chants, prayers, and songs vibrates with a sense of the sacred. The historic photographs included in this volume contribute to the book's appeal, making past eras come alive.

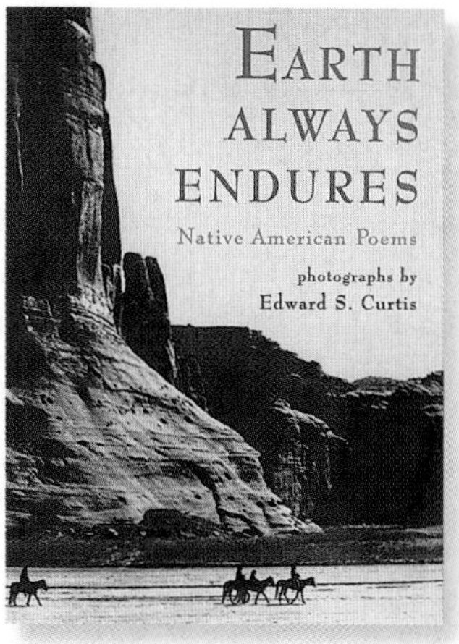

Poems for Life: Famous People Select Their Favorite Poem and Say Why It Inspires Them
compiled by the Grade V Classes from The Nightingale-Bamford School Determined to raise money for a good cause, a group of students in New York City mailed letters to a host of famous people. "We were wondering if you would like to send us a copy of your favorite poem with an explanation of why you chose it," they wrote. Fifty renowned writers, musicians, politicians, actors, and television personalities responded, and the result is this fascinating collection.

Standardized Test Practice

Read the passage and choose the word or group of words that belongs in each space. Mark the letter for that answer on your paper.

> Many scientists __(1)__ that about 245 million years ago, all the continents __(2)__ joined together in a single landmass called Pangaea. Over time, the one continent __(3)__ into two, and eventually it became all the separate landmasses we know today. The scientific theory of how the continents move is called plate tectonics. The "plates" are pieces of the Earth's crust that __(4)__ push against each other, moving and shifting. __(5)__ for the theory of plate tectonics can be found both in fossil remains and in the way certain species are distributed across continents that have an ocean between __(6)__.

1. **A** thinks
   B has thought
   C are thinking
   D think

2. **F** was
   G were
   H is
   J are

3. **A** break
   B broke
   C breaking
   D will break

4. **F** constant
   G constantly
   H more constant
   J most constant

5. **A** Supporting
   B Supportive
   C Support
   D Supported

6. **F** them
   G it
   H their
   J you

Read the passage and decide which type of error, if any, appears in each underlined section. Mark the letter for your answer on your paper.

When the Roosevelt's entered the White House, (7) the nation was worn down from the Great Depression. Eleanor Roosevelt led crusades to boost the national morale and inspire the revitalization of American culture. She planed work groups for young women, (8) supported the National Youth Administration, and fought to ensure equal wages for both sexes. She started projects to employ artists of all types to energize domestic culture. An outspoken advocate of civil rights, Eleanor fought to bring African American leaders and issues to the forefront of the public interest. (9) Her commitment to racial equality extended to other groups as well. Because of her efforts, health care and education on native american reservations became an issue in Washington. (10)

In the midst of the second world war, Eleanor Roosevelt became a diplomat (11) to the thousands of American troops stationed overseas. She flew a remarkable number of miles (12) attempting to boost the spirits of the armed forces.

7 A Spelling error
B Capitalization error
C Punctuation error
D No error

8 F Spelling error
G Capitalization error
H Punctuation error
J No error

9 A Spelling error
B Capitalization error
C Punctuation error
D No error

10 F Spelling error
G Capitalization error
H Punctuation error
J No error

11 A Spelling error
B Capitalization error
C Punctuation error
D No error

12 F Spelling error
G Capitalization error
H Punctuation error
J No error

STOP

Comedia dell'Arte, 1991. André Rouillard. Acrylic on canvas, 73 x 100 cm. Private collection.

UNIT FOUR

Drama

"'Tis plain, in real life, from youth to age,
All wear their masks. Here only on the stage,
You see us as we are; here trust your eyes,
Our wish to please cannot be mere disguise."

—Hannah Cowley

Genre Focus

Drama

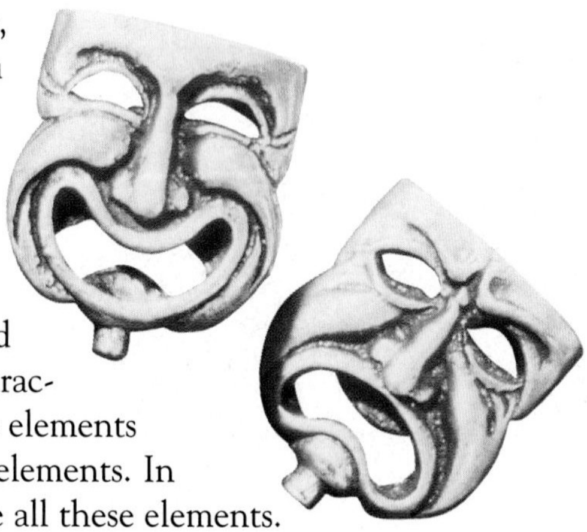

What is your favorite television drama series, and why do you like to watch it? Perhaps you identify strongly with one of the characters. Maybe the plots are intriguing, or you find the dialogue funny. You'll find these elements—and others—in the dramas you *read* as well.

A **drama,** which is written to be performed by actors in front of an audience, is a story told mainly through the speech and actions of characters. Whereas drama includes many of the same elements as other narratives, it also has its own unique elements. In order to analyze works of drama, you'll examine all these elements.

Because drama is meant to be performed, actors, directors, and readers need to be able to visualize what is happening in the play. Consequently, playwrights include **stage directions** interspersed among the lines of the script. Stage directions are typically printed in italics and enclosed in brackets or parentheses to stand out clearly from the dialogue. The directions explain how characters should look, speak, move, and behave. They also might specify details of the setting and scenery, such as lighting, props, and sound effects. Several of the models below are stage directions from *The Miracle Worker* by William Gibson.

ELEMENTS OF DRAMA

Characters

The cast of characters is listed at the beginning of a play. Sometimes the cast list includes a brief description of one or more characters. In other cases (as in *The Miracle Worker,* for example), the playwright may briefly describe a character when he or she first appears in the play. You also learn about characters through their actions and through their words.

MODEL: *The Miracle Worker*

[*Inside, three adults in the bedroom are grouped around a crib, in lamplight. They have been through a long vigil, and it shows in their tired bearing and disarranged clothing. One is a young gentlewoman with a sweet girlish face,* KATE KELLER*; the second is an elderly* DOCTOR*, stethoscope at neck, thermometer in fingers; the third is a hearty gentleman in his forties with chin whiskers,* CAPTAIN ARTHUR KELLER.]

Setting

Typically, the setting is identified at the beginning of the play, after the cast of characters. Additional details about the setting may appear throughout the play, often at the beginning of acts and scenes.

> **TIME:** *The 1880s.*
> **PLACE:** *In and around the Keller homestead in Tuscumbia, Alabama; also, briefly, the Perkins Institution for the Blind, in Boston.*

Plot

As in other narratives, the plot of a drama is the series of related events in which a problem, or conflict, is explored and then solved. The conflict may be a struggle between people, between ideas, or between other forces.

> *The Miracle Worker* relates how teacher Annie Sullivan comes to the Keller household to teach sign language to the young blind, deaf, and mute Helen Keller. Sullivan comes into conflict with both Helen and her family but perseveres until she succeeds in teaching Helen to communicate.

Dialogue

The text of a play consists largely of dialogue, or conversation between the characters. Most of the plot and characterization in a play is revealed through the dialogue.

> **KATE.** Language.
>
> [*She shakes her head.*]
>
> *We* can't get through to teach her to sit still. You *are* young, despite your years, to have such—confidence. Do you, inside?
>
> [ANNIE *studies her face; she likes her, too.*]
>
> **ANNIE.** No, to tell you the truth I'm as shaky inside as a baby's rattle!

Acts and Scenes

Just as books are divided into chapters, plays are divided into acts and scenes, which indicate a change in location or the passage of time.

> **ACT 2**
>
> *It is evening. The only room visible in the* KELLER *house is* ANNIE*'s, where by lamplight* ANNIE *in a shawl is at a desk writing a letter . . .*

Active Reading Strategies

Drama

A key to reading and understanding a play is to use the stage directions and the dialogue to help you "see" the play in your mind. The following strategies in particular will help you mentally direct, perform, and react to a work of drama.

- For more about these and other related reading strategies, see **Reading Handbook**, pp. R78–R94.

VISUALIZE As you read, picture the elements the playwright describes. Let yourself imagine what other physical details might look like.

Ask yourself . . .

- How does this scene look? Have I ever seen a place like this?
- What might this character look like?
- How might this character dress, walk, talk, and gesture?

LISTEN While a playwright may provide clues for how a line should be delivered, most often this decision will be left to the actor, director, or reader. Therefore, as you read, imagine how each character says his or her lines. If possible, read the lines aloud.

Say to yourself . . .

- What is the character feeling at this moment, and how might that emotion be conveyed in the way he or she delivers the line?
- What tone of voice should the character use?
- Which words should the character emphasize?

QUESTION Note the questions you have as you read. The answers to your questions may become clear as you read on.

Ask yourself . . .

- Do I understand what is happening here?
- Why did the character say or do this?
- What does the character mean by this?

CONNECT Draw parallels between the play and your own life.

Think to yourself . . .
- Whom does this character remind me of?
- When did something similar happen to me?
- How would I respond in this situation?

PREDICT Use stage directions and clues in the dialogue to guess what is going to happen next.

Think to yourself . . .
- What is this character likely to do next?
- What will other characters do when they find out . . . ?
- How will this conflict be resolved?

INTERPRET Think about the characters, what they do, and what happens to them. Assess why the characters act as they do and what their actions mean.

Say to yourself . . .
- What kind of personality does this character have?
- What effects do the characters have on one another?
- What ideas about life or human nature is the playwright conveying?

RESPOND React to the play. Consider your spontaneous thoughts and feelings.

Say to yourself . . .
- How does this make me feel?
- What's interesting about this is . . .
- I like this character because . . .

Applying the Strategies

1. Read *The Inspector-General,* using the Active Reading Model notes in the margins.
2. Choose another play, and practice using all of these strategies. Use stick-on notes to annotate the play, or write notes on a separate piece of paper.

Before You Read

The Inspector-General

Reading Focus

Writer Zora Neale Hurston once said, "People are prone to build a statue of the kind of person that it pleases them to be."

Sharing Ideas Do you agree with Hurston's view that people are prone to self-deception? What kinds of things do you think people tend to deceive themselves about? In a small group, brainstorm a list of common self-deceptions.

Setting a Purpose Read to see how a character is confronted with his self-deception.

Building Background

The Time and Place

The events in this play take place in Russia during the 1800s.

Did You Know?

- In the 1800s, Russia was headed by monarchs called *czars* (zärz), who had absolute rule over the country. Ministers, provincial governors, and governors-general carried out the policies and decisions of the czars. Many average Russian citizens of the time regarded government officials as incompetent, arrogant, and often corrupt.

Czar Alexander III

- Anton Chekhov felt that the aim of literature is "truth, unconditional and honest." He even proposed that writers should eliminate their stories' beginnings and endings because they were most likely to lie in those parts. "The artist is not meant to be a judge of his characters and what they say; his only job is to be an impartial witness," he said.
- *The Inspector-General* is a one-act play adapted from Chekhov's short story "An Awl in a Sack," written in 1885. The title of the story comes from a Russian saying: "You can't hide an awl in a sack." Since an awl is a sharp tool that would poke through a sack, the saying may be interpreted this way: "You can't hide the obvious."

Meet Anton Chekhov

While in medical school, Anton Chekhov earned money to support his family by writing humorous stories and sketches. During this time, he also developed tuberculosis, a deadly lung disease. As his writing became more serious and his literary reputation grew, he struggled against the illness. He bought a small estate near Moscow, where he wrote many short stories and plays, but eventually his health forced him to move farther south. He died at the age of forty-four. In the last decade of his brief life, he focused on longer dramas and created his four most famous plays: *The Sea Gull*, *Uncle Vanya*, *The Three Sisters*, and *The Cherry Orchard*.

Anton Chekhov was born in 1860 in Taganrog, Russia. He died in 1904.

The Inspector-General

Anton Chekhov

Adapted by Michael Frayn

[The curtain goes up to reveal falling snow and a cart facing away from us. Enter a STORYTELLER. *As he, or she, begins to read the story, the* TRAVELER *enters. He is a middle-aged man of entirely urban appearance, wearing dark glasses, and a long overcoat with its collar turned up. He is carrying a modest traveling bag. He climbs onto the cart and sits facing us.]*

STORYTELLER. The Inspector-General. In deepest incognito,[1] first by express train, then along cart tracks and back roads, Pyotr Pavlovich Posudin[2] was hastening towards the little town of N, to which he had been summoned by an anonymous letter. "I'll take them by surprise," he thought to himself. "I'll come down on them like a thunderbolt out of the blue. I can just imagine their faces when they hear who I am . . ."

[Enter the DRIVER, *a peasant bundled up in old sacks against the weather. He climbs up onto the cart, so that he is sitting with his back to us, and the cart begins to trundle[3] slowly away from us along a potholed country road.]*

And when he'd thought to himself for long enough, he fell into conversation with the driver of the cart. What did he talk about? About himself, of course.

[Exit the STORYTELLER.*]*

TRAVELER. I gather you've got a new Inspector-General in these parts.

DRIVER. True enough.

TRAVELER. Know anything about him?

[The DRIVER *turns around in his seat and looks at the* TRAVELER, *who inconspicuously turns his coat collar up a little higher.]*

DRIVER. Know anything about him? Of course we do! We know everything about all of them up there! Every last little clerk—we know the color of his

Active Reading Model

VISUALIZE

Picture the striking difference in appearance between the driver and the traveler.

INTERPRET

Note the storyteller's description of the traveler's actions. What do his remarks indicate about the traveler's personality?

1. *Incognito* (in′ kōg nē′ tō) means the state of being hidden under a false appearance so as to be unknown.
2. *Pyotr Pavlovich Posudin* (pyō′ tr päv lō′ vēch pō sōō′ dēn)
3. To *trundle* is to roll along on wheels.

Active Reading Model

PREDICT

Do you think the Inspector-General's disguise will be revealed? How?

LISTEN

In what tone of voice do you imagine the driver speaking? Is he very demonstrative, or simply matter-of-fact? Take clues from his manner of speech.

QUESTION

Do you think the driver knows who his passenger is?

hair and the size of his boots! Know about the top man? That's why they've sent him here, so we know about him!

[*The* DRIVER *turns back to the front, and the* TRAVELER *permits himself a slight smile.*]

TRAVELER. So, what do you reckon? Any good, is he?

[*The* DRIVER *turns around and considers this.*]

DRIVER. Oh, yes, he's a good one, this one.

TRAVELER. Really?

DRIVER. Did one good thing straight off.

TRAVELER. What was that?

DRIVER. He got rid of the last one. Holy terror he was! Hear him coming five miles off! Say he's going to this little town. Somewhere like we're going, say. He'd let all the world know about it a month before. So now he's on his way, say, and it's like thunder and lightning coming down the road. They're all jumping in front of him, they're all jumping behind him, they're all jumping either side of him. And when he gets where he's going he has a good sleep, he has a good eat and drink—and then he starts. Stamps his feet, shouts his head off. Then he has another good sleep, and off he goes.

TRAVELER. But the new one's not like that?

DRIVER. Oh, no, the new one goes everywhere on the quiet, like. Creeps around like a cat. Don't want no one to see him, don't want no one to know who he is. Say he's going to this town down the road here. Someone there sent him a letter on the sly,[4] let's say. "Things going on here you should know about." Something of that kind. Well, now, he creeps out of his office, so none of them up there see him go. He hops on a train just like anyone else, just like you or me. Then when he gets off he don't go jumping into a cab or nothing fancy. Oh, no. An ordinary horse and cart will do for him! He wraps himself up from head to toe, so you can't see his face, and he wheezes away like an old dog so no one can recognize his voice.

TRAVELER. Wheezes? That's not wheezing! That's the way he talks! So I gather.

DRIVER. Oh, is it? But the tales they tell about him. You'd laugh till you burst your tripes![5]

TRAVELER. [*Sourly.*] I'm sure I should.

DRIVER. Drinks, mind!

TRAVELER. [*Startled.*] Drinks?

4. The expression *on the sly* means "secretly" or "sneakily."
5. The expression *burst your tripes* is similar to "split your sides" or "bust your gut." *Tripe* usually refers to the walls lining the stomachs of cows or sheep.

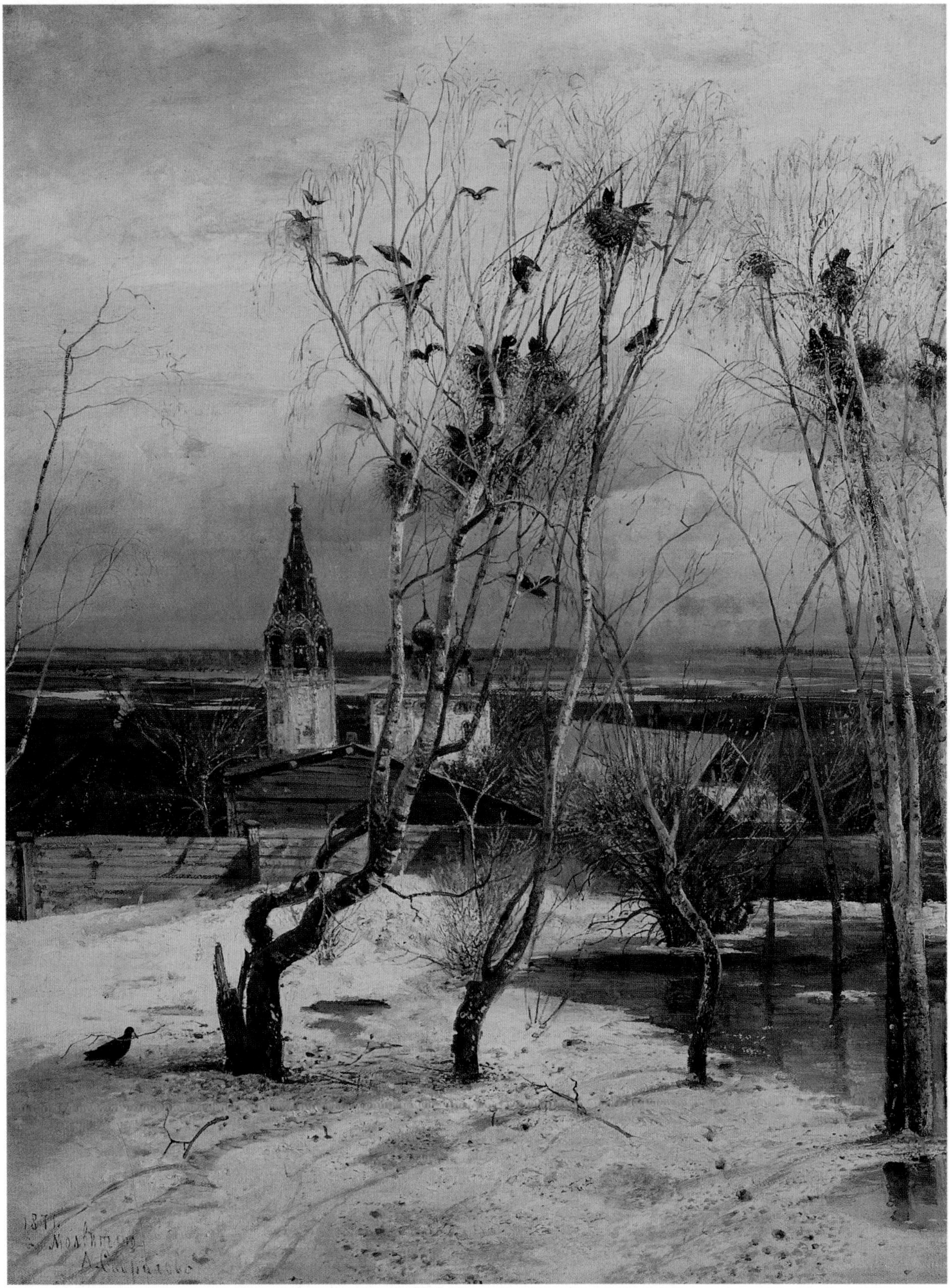

The Rooks Have Returned, 1871. Alexei Savrasov. Tretyakov Gallery, Moscow.

Viewing the painting: What kind of scenic backdrop would be appropriate for a stage production of *The Inspector-General*? Would it look like this painting? Explain why or why not.

Active Reading Model

DRIVER. Oh, like a hole in the ground. Famous for it.

TRAVELER. He's never touched a drop! I mean, from what I've heard.

DRIVER. Oh, not in public, no. Goes to some great ball—"No thank you, not for me." Oh, no, he puts it away at home! Wakes up in the morning, rubs his eyes, and the first thing he does, he shouts, "Vodka!" So in runs his valet[6] with a glass. "And another!" says he. Fixed himself up a tube behind his desk, he has. Leans down, takes a pull on it, no one the wiser.

TRAVELER. [*Offended.*] How do you know all this, may I ask?

CONNECT

How do people learn about the private lives of public officials today?

DRIVER. Can't hide it from the servants, can you? The valet and the coachman have got tongues in their heads. Then again, he's on the road, say, going about his business—and he keeps the bottle in his little bag. [*The TRAVELER discreetly pushes his traveling bag out of the DRIVER's sight.*] It's the same with his women.

TRAVELER. [*Startled.*] His women?

DRIVER. Oh, he's a devil for the women, this one! Ten of them, he's got!

TRAVELER. Ten? That's absolute nonsense! I mean . . . surely . . . ?

DRIVER. He's got two of them living in the house! One of them, they say she's the housekeeper—that's Nastasya Ivanovna.[7] The other one—what's her name, now? Forget my own name next . . . Ludmila Semyonovna[8]—she's supposed to be some sort of clerk. But Nastasya—she's the top one. Whatever she wants she's only to say and he does it. Runs circles around him, she does, like a fox around his tail. She's the one who wears the trousers.[9] The people aren't half so frightened of him as what they are of her. Now, Number Three, she lives on Kachalnaya[10] Street. Public scandal, that one, because her husband's niece by his first wife—she's Number Four . . . !

RESPOND

Can you imagine the traveler's discomfort?

TRAVELER. Yes, yes, quite, quite . . . But at least he's good at his job, you say?

DRIVER. Oh, he's a blessing from heaven, I'll grant him that.

TRAVELER. Very cunning—you were saying.

DRIVER. Oh, he creeps around all right.

TRAVELER. And then he pounces, yes? I should think some people must get the surprise of their life, mustn't they?

PREDICT

How do you think this play will end? Why?

DRIVER. No, no—let's be fair, now. Give him his due. He don't make no trouble.

TRAVELER. No, I mean, if no one knows he's coming . . .

DRIVER. Oh, that's what *he* thinks! Oh, Lord bless you—*we* all know!

TRAVELER. You know?

---

6. A man's male servant is called a *valet* (val′ it) or (val′ ā).
7. *Nastasya Ivanovna* (näs täs′ yə ē vän ōv′ nə)
8. *Ludmila Semyonovna* (lo͞od mēl′ ə sem yən ōv′ nə)
9. A woman who *wears the trousers* is thought to be in charge.
10. *Kachalnaya* (kä chəl näy′ ə)

Active Reading Model

DRIVER. Oh, some gentleman gets off the train at the station back there with his greatcoat up to his eyebrows and says, "No, I don't want a cab, thank you, I don't want nothing fancy, just an ordinary horse and cart for me"—well, we'd put two and two together, wouldn't we! Say it was you, now, creeping along down the road here. The lads would be down there in a cab by now! By the time you got there the whole town would be as regular as clockwork! And you'd think to yourself, "Oh, look at that! As clean as a whistle! And they didn't know I was coming!" No, that's why he's such a blessing after the other one. This one believes it!

INTERPRET
In your opinion, what is the driver communicating to the traveler here?

TRAVELER. Oh, I see.

DRIVER. What, you thought we wouldn't know him? Why, we've got the electric telegraph these days! Take today, now. I'm going past the station back there this morning, and the fellow who runs the buffet[11] comes out like a bolt of lightning. Arms full of baskets and bottles. "Where are you off to?" I say. "Doing drinks and refreshments for the Inspector-General!" he says, and he jumps into a post chaise[12] and goes flying off down the road here. So there's the old Inspector-General, all muffled up like a roll of carpet, going secretly along in a cart somewhere—and when he gets there, nothing to be seen but vodka and cold salmon!

TRAVELER. [*Shouts.*] Right—turn around, then, damn you!

DRIVER. [*To the horse.*] Whoa, boy! Whoa! [*To the* TRAVELER.] Oh, so what's this, then? Don't want to go running into the Inspector-General, is that it?

[*The* TRAVELER *gestures impatiently to the* DRIVER *to turn the cart around.*]

[*To the horse.*] Back we go, then, boy. Home we go.

[*The* DRIVER *turns the cart around, and the* TRAVELER *tips back his head and takes a swig from his traveling bag.*]

Though if I know the old devil, he's like as not turned around and gone home again himself.

INTERPRET
What larger point might Chekhov be making in this short drama?

[*Blackout.*]

11. At a *buffet* (bə fā′), dishes of food are laid out on a table so that people can serve themselves.
12. A *post chaise* (shāz) is a four-wheeled, horse-drawn carriage used to carry mail and passengers from station to station.

Active Reading Model

Active Reading and Critical Thinking

Responding to Literature

Personal Response

Do you find this play funny? Why or why not?

Analyzing Literature

Recall and Interpret

1. Who is the traveler and what is his job? Where is he headed and why?
2. What does the traveler hope to learn by questioning the driver? In the end, what does he actually learn?
3. How do the driver and the traveler differ in their views about what makes a good inspector?
4. Who does the driver think the traveler is? How do you know? Support your answer with details from the play.
5. What does the traveler do at the end of the play and why?

Evaluate and Connect

6. What kind of man does the Inspector-General first imagine himself to be? What kind of man is he really? How does his self-deception compare with the kinds you listed during the Reading Focus on page 566?
7. **Dramatic irony** occurs when the audience has important information that characters in a literary work do not have. How does Chekhov use dramatic irony in this play? What is the effect of its use?
8. What adjectives would you use to characterize the driver? Give details from the play to support your ideas.
9. What does this play suggest about the relationship between ordinary people and government officials in Russia during the 1800s?
10. How are the foibles of the government officials in the play similar to foibles of government officials today? How are they different?

Literary ELEMENTS

Satire

Satire is a form of writing that ridicules people, practices, or institutions in order to reveal their failings. In *The Inspector-General,* for example, Chekhov pokes fun at certain government officials of his time. Satires vary in tone from mild amusement to boiling anger. They often aim to make people think critically about the subject at hand, but they can also be written for pure entertainment.

1. What flaws of the Inspector-General does Chekhov expose?
2. What lessons might a government official learn from this play?

- See **Literary Terms Handbook,** p. R11.

Extending Your Response

Literature Groups

Live and Learn With your group, discuss the different ways the traveler could have reacted to the driver's comments. Which way do you think would have shown the most character? How might the driver's comments affect the traveler's future behavior? Do you think he would behave differently if he were to encounter the same situation again in a year? Share your ideas with the class.

Writing About Literature

Less Is More "Conciseness is the sister of talent," wrote Chekhov, who believed in paring down a work to its essentials. Write one or more paragraphs explaining how this play reflects that belief. Include examples that show how Chekhov was able to convey a lot of information in a few words or sentences.

Save your work for your portfolio.

Theme 9 The Power of Love

A mother can gain the strength of five men if she must defend her child from danger. A suitor can function for days without sleep if it will bring him closer to his sweetheart. Such is the power of love. In this theme, you will read about love that is strong enough to overcome hatred, transform prejudice, and shatter the will to live.

THEME PROJECTS

Performing

Modern Love Create a modern version of one scene from *Romeo and Juliet*; then videotape it.

1. With a small group, decide which scene you're going to bring into the modern age. How will you update the scene? Will you alter the language? the music? the situation?
2. Divide group members into actors, directors, and videographers. Rehearse the scene a few times, then record it.
3. Screen your scene for the class.

Interdisciplinary Project

Biology: Animal Instinct Do animals have their own version of love and marriage?

1. Identify a mammal, bird, or fish that bonds with a partner for life.
2. Use the Internet, encyclopedias, and science books to research the animal's courtship behavior. How do the partners deal with each other's death or absence? In what ways is their behavior similar to or different from Romeo and Juliet's?
3. Present your findings in a poster or give an oral report for your classmates.

Sanctuary. Daniel Nevins (b. 1963). Oil, acrylic, and collage on wood, 51 x 39 in. Private collection.

Literature FOCUS

Understanding Shakespeare and Elizabethan Drama

It's a summer afternoon in London, England. People from all classes of Elizabethan society are going to the suburb of Southwark to see a play. Gentlemen and ladies pay steep fares to cross the River Thames by ferry. Others—including market women, laborers, soldiers, and students—walk across London Bridge. Passing taverns, vendors, and seedy places of entertainment, they come to a large round building—the Globe Theatre. A fanfare of trumpets signals that the performance will soon begin. Because a black flag flies over the theater, everyone knows that today's play is a tragedy. The play-goers take their seats, except for those "groundlings" who stand in an open yard around the stage. The actors are about to perform a play based on an old story that remains a great favorite: **The Tragedy of Romeo and Juliet.**

The Age of Shakespeare

Most Elizabethans would have been surprised to learn that their age became best known for its theater. They considered drama a lower form of literature than poetry. In their eyes, no mere playwright could compare with the celebrated poet Edmund Spenser. Who would have expected William Shakespeare's fame to one day surpass that of the queen herself?

Part of the English Renaissance (1485–1660) is called the Elizabethan Age after Queen Elizabeth I, who reigned from 1558 to 1603. Elizabeth was a shrewd and charismatic ruler. She managed to control the religious conflict that tore England apart under previous monarchs, and her skillful diplomacy helped protect the nation from foreign enemies. The economy grew rapidly, fueled by trade and a flourishing textile industry. London, the center of English commerce and government, was on its way to becoming the largest city in Europe.

However, not everyone thrived under Elizabeth's rule. English women enjoyed greater social and economic freedom than women in most other European countries, but they still had limited rights. The vast majority of English people were commoners who, unlike the wealthier, educated classes, often suffered from poor diet and crowded living conditions. Rich and poor alike were vulnerable to outbreaks of bubonic plague. In 1564, the year of Shakespeare's birth, the plague

The original Globe Theatre as it might have looked in 1599.

Cutaway view of the Globe Theater. Drawing by David Gentleman.

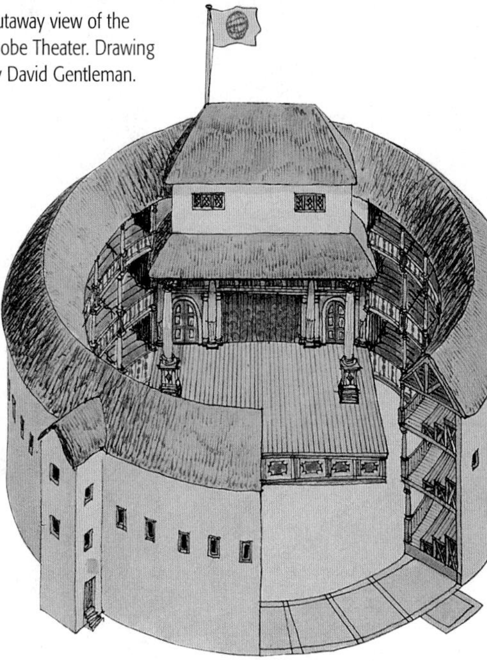

killed nearly a third of the people in his hometown.

Following Queen Elizabeth's death in 1603, her cousin King James of Scotland assumed the English throne. Like his predecessor, James was a great supporter of the arts and literature. He became the direct patron of Shakespeare's theater company, renaming it the King's Men and thus confirming its status as England's foremost theater company.

The Rise of Prestigious Playhouses

Shakespeare was fortunate to begin his career late in the 1500s, when English theater was undergoing profound changes. Professional actors had been performing in England for hundreds of years, but their positions were insecure. They traveled from town to town, setting up makeshift stages in public halls, marketplaces, and the courtyards of inns. Often they met hostility from local authorities who feared that crowds of playgoers might cause disturbances.

Actor James Burbage built England's first permanent playhouse in 1576. Other open-air theaters sprang up over the next few decades. They were all located in the suburbs rather than in London, which had strict laws governing entertainment. Shakespeare's company, the Lord Chamberlain's Men, built their own playhouse, the Globe, in 1599. This roughly circular building had three levels of covered galleries. A platform stage about forty feet wide projected out into the open yard, where people who paid a pence, or a penny, could stand and watch the play. Admission to the gallery benches cost twopence. Wealthy people paid sixpence to sit in a "lords' room" directly over the stage. In all, the Globe could accommodate about three thousand spectators. Toward the end of Shakespeare's career, his company acquired a fully enclosed theater in London for the winter season.

Theatrical Conventions

At the Globe and similar theaters, all performances took place in the afternoon because there was no artificial lighting. The stage was mostly bare. Instead of relying on scenery, Shakespeare used language to create illusions of a setting. For example, his long descriptions of the moon are more than just beautiful writing—they reminded Elizabethan audiences that the characters were meeting at night.

Boys had an important function in Elizabethan theater. Because it was considered immoral for women to appear onstage, boy actors played the female roles. They used wigs, costumes, and their voices to create this illusion.

Shakespeare's Life

Few authors have proven as timeless as William Shakespeare. Nearly four centuries after his death, his plays are still performed around the world, and he continues to inspire writers, filmmakers, and other artists. Unfortunately, however, there are no biographical portraits of

Shakespeare from his own time. Most information about his life comes from public records and comments by his contemporaries.

Shakespeare was born in 1564 in Stratford-upon-Avon, a market town about one hundred miles from London. His father was a glove maker, tradesman, and bailiff (the equivalent of a mayor). His mother came from a prosperous farming family. Because of his family's status, Shakespeare almost certainly attended the town's excellent grammar school, where he would have learned Latin and read classical literature. At eighteen, he married Anne Hathaway. The couple had a daughter, Susanna, in 1583, and twins, Judith and Hamnet, in 1585. Hamnet, Shakespeare's only son, died at age eleven.

Sometime between 1585 and the early 1590s, Shakespeare moved to London to pursue a career in theater. He worked as an actor and playwright, quickly gaining attention for his comedies and historical plays. By 1594 he had joined the Lord Chamberlain's Men, which remained his theatrical home for the rest of his career. Shakespeare made substantial earnings not from the sale of his plays, but from his share in the company's profits and his investments in its theater buildings. He bought a large estate for his family in Stratford, although he himself spent much of the year in London.

Shakespeare began spending more time in Stratford around 1610 and eventually retired there. He died in 1616. Seven years later, a group of friends published a collected edition of his works known as the *First Folio*. The volume played a crucial role in preserving his plays for future generations.

Reading Shakespeare

Shakespeare wrote thirty-seven plays, including such tragic masterpieces as *Hamlet*, *Othello*, *Macbeth*, and *King Lear*, in addition to *Romeo and Juliet*. The richness and complexity of Shakespeare's writing make his plays rewarding to read as well as to see and hear. However, the English language has changed since Elizabethan times, and some modern readers are intimidated by Shakespeare's language and style. The following suggestions may help you better understand and enjoy *Romeo and Juliet*.

William Shakespeare, 1564–1616.

- Some of the words in the play are no longer used today, and some others have changed in meaning. The side notes in this book will help you translate such words.
- Most of the play is written in **blank verse.** This verse form consists of unrhymed lines of iambic pentameter, a rhythm pattern with five units, or feet, each of which has an unstressed syllable followed by a stressed syllable (see Literary Terms Handbook, page R2). To create such a pattern, Shakespeare commonly placed words in an unusual order within a sentence. He also frequently divided a line of poetry between two speakers. In such cases, the second character's first line is indented to begin where the preceding character's line ends.
- Shakespeare's writing is full of figurative language and wordplay. You might find a single metaphor or simile extended throughout an entire speech. Other speeches contain a number of metaphors and similes packed together. *Romeo and Juliet* also contains many puns, or plays on

the different meanings of a word or on the similar meaning or sound of different words.

Romeo and Juliet

Despite its sad ending, *Romeo and Juliet* is an entertaining play, full of bawdy humor, swordplay, vivid characters, and passionate love scenes. Unlike Shakespeare's other tragic heroes, the main characters do not possess great power or ability. Their situation is also ordinary: young lovers coming into conflict with parental authority. What distinguishes them is the passion they feel for each other and the way they express it. The play features some of Shakespeare's most memorable poetry.

Shakespeare probably wrote *Romeo and Juliet* in 1595. Following an Elizabethan practice, he borrowed the story from other writers. His main source was the *Tragical History of Romeus and Juliet* (1562), a narrative poem by Arthur Brooke that was based on an ancient tale. Shakespeare departed from Brooke's version in several ways. He fleshed out some of the characters, including the Nurse, Benvolio, and Mercutio. Juliet's age dropped from sixteen to thirteen. Instead of taking place over several months, the action occurs within a single week, giving the play a breathless pace.

Scene from Franco Zeffirelli's 1968 film version of *Romeo and Juliet.*

Like Brooke's poem, Shakespeare's play opens with a sonnet, a fourteen-line poem of rhymed iambic pentameter. When Romeo and Juliet first encounter each other, their dialogue completes another sonnet. During the early 1590s, sonnets were a fad in England; poets created long series of sonnets on the subject of love. Shakespeare used the stereotypes and conventional attitudes of love poetry to develop the romantic mood of *Romeo and Juliet*. He also poked fun at these stereotypes and attitudes, especially in Mercutio's witty dialogue. The play offers a sophisticated view of passionate love—both sympathetic and critical.

Romeo and Juliet was popular with Elizabethan audiences, and its popularity continues through today. Several film versions have been made, and the play has inspired ballets, symphonies, an opera, and the musical *West Side Story*.

Famous Lines

As you read *Romeo and Juliet,* you may recognize some often quoted phrases and lines:

- But soft! What light through yonder window breaks? / It is the East, and Juliet is the sun! (act 2, scene 2, 2–3)
- O Romeo, Romeo! Wherefore art thou Romeo? (act 2, scene 2, 33)
- What's in a name? That which we call a rose / By any other word would smell as sweet. (act 2, scene 2, 43–44)
- Good night, good night! Parting is such sweet sorrow (act 2, scene 2, 184)

ACTIVITY

Look for examples of similes and metaphors as you read *Romeo and Juliet*. Think about how figurative language might have helped Shakespeare's audiences to imagine the action taking place on a bare stage.

MEDIA connection

Newspaper Article

The story of Romeo and Juliet continues to inspire young lovers to travel hundreds and thousands of miles to Verona, Italy, the setting of Shakespeare's play.

Tale of Doomed Lovers Pulls Romantic to Verona

***Orange County* [Calif.] *Register*, March 10, 1996**

Verona, Italy—They entwine in each other's arms, pressed against the cold stone wall, kissing softly. Or walk, hand-in-hand, gazing at the high stone balcony above the cool, leafy courtyard.

Two by two they come to the yellow brick house on Verona's Via Cappello, savoring a pilgrimage of love that's drawn them from Rome or London, Tokyo or Los Angeles.

Here Juliet stood on the balcony, calling out to her forbidden love lingering in the shadows.

"O Romeo, Romeo! Wherefore art thou Romeo?" Or so Shakespeare wrote in *Romeo and Juliet*.

"It is not a true story, not completely; everybody in Verona knows this," says Alessandra Marianelli, hotel receptionist who is in her 20s. "But what does it matter? It is a beautiful, sad story. And it has meant good luck and good money for Verona."

The intertwining of medieval history, Renaissance writing, and modern marketing have made Verona among Italy's most popular cities for foreign visitors.

A lovely city on the Adige River about 200 miles west of Venice, Verona boasts some of Europe's best-preserved Roman ruins and Romanesque architecture.

But it is a pair of star-crossed teens who may or may not have lived here 700 years ago that remains the city's top drawing card.

In Verona, tourism officials have laid out a walking tour of sites believed to be connected with the star-crossed lovers. The most popular is the 13th-century house that the city says tradition claims is the home of Juliet.

The quiet inner courtyard is often full of lovers. Visitors climb narrow stairs to the balcony for a kiss. Others look over their shoulders for police before pulling out thick marking pens to scribble "Pietro + Anna" or "Kiki loves Farrell forever" on any surface.

"They say it is a legend, but I choose to believe it is true," said Sonia Cipriani, 26, a tourist from Rome. "They lived. And they died for love."

Analyzing Media

1. Why might people want to believe that the story of Romeo and Juliet is true?
2. Would you like to visit Verona? Why or why not?

Before You Read

The Tragedy of Romeo and Juliet

Reading Focus

Think of a few times when an adult made demands that you considered difficult. What happened? How did you respond?

Chart It! Describe the situations and your responses in a chart similar to the one shown here.

Demand made by adult	Why difficult	What happened

Setting a Purpose Read to discover the tragic results of a demand that a youth finds impossible to obey.

Building Background

The Time and Place
The events in this play take place during the summer in Verona and Mantua, two cities in northern Italy, in the 1300s.

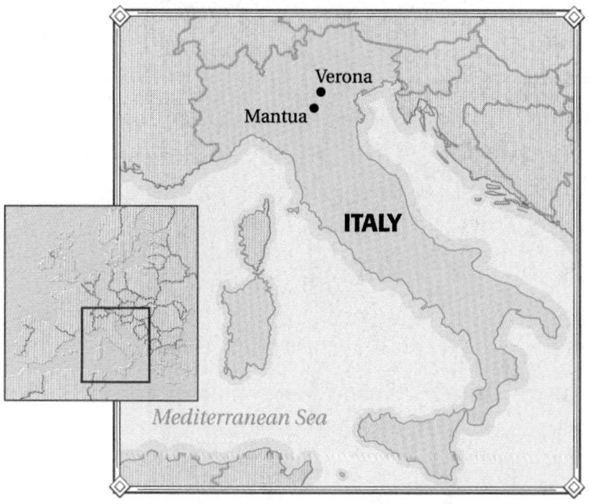

Did You Know?
Parents and Marriage Many of Shakespeare's plays revolve around the complications of courtship and marriage. In *Romeo and Juliet,* parents are the biggest obstacle to the couple's marriage. During the Renaissance, young people needed permission from their parents or guardians to get married. Parents commonly arranged marriages for their children, especially in upper-class households. Arranged marriages customarily required the bride's consent, however. Girls could legally get married at age twelve, but they were usually fifteen or sixteen when they married. Juliet, at age thirteen, would have been considered a young bride.

The Influence of Astrology Romeo Montague (mon′ tə gū) and Juliet Capulet (kap′ yə lət) are described as "a pair of star-cross'd lovers" in the play's *prologue,* or introduction. This description suggests that their tragic downfall was influenced by the position of the stars and planets at their birth. Belief in astrology was widespread in Elizabethan England. In fact, physicians often studied their patients' horoscopes before deciding on a diagnosis and treatment.

Family Feuds Romeo and Juliet come from two distinguished families who are embroiled in a bitter feud. In northern Italy during the Renaissance (1300s to 1600s), such feuds between families were common. Italian families were extended to include brothers, sisters, aunts, uncles, nieces, nephews, cousins, and even servants. All these members of a family might become involved in a *vendetta,* a feud between two families often initially caused by a killing and then perpetuated by acts of revenge.

The Tragedy of Romeo and Juliet

William Shakespeare

Juliet on the Balcony. Illumination from text *The Tragedy of Romeo and Juliet,* 1920. Sangorski and Sutcliffe, binders, calligraphers, and illuminators. Private collection.

CHARACTERS

The Montagues

LORD MONTAGUE: wealthy nobleman of Verona and enemy to Lord Capulet

LADY MONTAGUE: his wife

ROMEO: their son

BENVOLIO: Lord Montague's nephew, Romeo's cousin and friend

BALTHASAR: Romeo's servant

ABRAM: a servant

The Capulets

LORD CAPULET: wealthy nobleman of Verona and enemy to Lord Montague

LADY CAPULET: his wife

JULIET: their daughter, who is thirteen years old

TYBALT: Lady Capulet's nephew, Juliet's cousin

OLD MAN: elderly relative of the family

NURSE: servant who has cared for Juliet since infancy

PETER: the Nurse's servant

SAMPSON: servant

GREGORY: servant

Others

CHORUS: actor who speaks directly to the audience to introduce the play

PRINCE ESCALUS: ruler of Verona

COUNT PARIS: relative of the Prince and suitor to Juliet

MERCUTIO: relative of the Prince and Romeo's friend

FRIAR LAWRENCE: Catholic priest of the order of Franciscans and a pharmacist

APOTHECARY: pharmacist in Mantua

FRIAR JOHN: Franciscan priest

PAGE: servant to Paris

OFFICERS AND CITIZENS OF VERONA, RELATIVES OF BOTH FAMILIES, MASKERS, OFFICERS, GUARDS, WATCHMEN, SERVANTS, AND ATTENDANTS

SETTING

SCENE: *Italy—the cities of Verona and Mantua. The fourteenth century.*

Act 1

Prologue

CHORUS.° Two households, both alike in dignity,°
In fair Verona, where we lay our scene,
From ancient grudge break to new mutiny,°
Where civil blood makes civil hands unclean.°
From forth the fatal° loins of these two foes
A pair of star-cross'd° lovers take their life;
Whose misadventur'd° piteous overthrows°
Doth with their death bury their parents' strife.
The fearful passage of their death-mark'd love,
And the continuance of their parents' rage,
Which, but° their children's end, nought could remove,
Is now the two hours' traffic of our stage;°
The which if you with patient ears attend,
What here shall miss, our toil shall strive to mend.°

[The CHORUS *exits.]*

1 **Chorus:** Elizabethan dramatists sometimes used a figure known as the chorus to comment on a play's action and describe events not shown on stage. In this prologue, or introduction, the chorus explains what the play is about. **dignity:** social status.

3 **mutiny** (mū′ tə nē): violence.

4 **civil blood . . . unclean:** citizens soil their hands with each other's blood.

5 **fatal:** ill-fated.

6 **star-cross'd:** doomed because of the positions of the planets when they were born.

7 **misadventur'd:** unfortunate. **overthrows:** ruin.

11 **but:** except for.

12 **two hours' . . . stage:** subject of our play.

14 **What here . . . mend:** We will try to clarify in our performance whatever is unclear in this prologue.

SCENE 1. Early morning. A public square in Verona.

*[*SAMPSON *and* GREGORY*, servants of the Capulets, enter. Because of the feud between the powerful Capulet and Montague families, they are armed with swords and bucklers, or small shields.]*

SAMPSON. Gregory, on my word, we'll not carry coals.°

GREGORY. No, for then we should be colliers.°

SAMPSON. I mean, and we be in choler, we'll draw.°

GREGORY. Ay, while you live, draw your neck out of collar.°

SAMPSON. I strike quickly,° being mov'd.°

GREGORY. But thou art not quickly° mov'd to strike.

SAMPSON. A dog of the house of Montague moves me.

GREGORY. To move is to stir, and to be valiant is to stand. Therefore, if thou art mov'd, thou run'st away.

SAMPSON. A dog of that house shall move me to stand. I will take the wall° of any man or maid of Montague's.

GREGORY. That shows thee a weak slave, for the weakest goes to the wall.°

SAMPSON. 'Tis true, and therefore women, being the weaker vessels, are ever thrust to the wall;° therefore I will push Montague's men from the wall, and thrust his maids to the wall.

1 **carry coals:** put up with insults (an Elizabethan expression).

2 **colliers** (kol′ yərz): coal vendors.

3 **and . . . draw:** if we are angry, or **in choler** (kol′ ər), we will draw our swords.

4 **collar:** the hangman's noose. (Gregory extends the pun with *collier* and *choler.*)

5 **quickly:** vigorously. **mov'd:** roused.

6 **quickly:** speedily.

11 **take the wall:** walk on the side of the path closest to the walls of houses. (Since this was the cleaner side, Sampson is asserting his superiority over any of the Montague servants.)

12–13 **weakest . . . wall:** the weakest are pushed to the rear.

15 **thrust to the wall:** assaulted.

Detail from *Camera degli Sposi (The Wedding Chamber),* 1474. Andrea Mantegna. Fresco. Palazzo Ducale, Mantua, Italy.

Viewing the painting: What details in this fresco help you visualize what life was like in northern Italy in the 14th and 15th centuries?

GREGORY. The quarrel is between our masters and us their men.

SAMPSON. 'Tis all one.° I will show myself a tyrant. When I have fought with the men, I will be civil with the maids; I will cut off their heads.

GREGORY. The heads of the maids?

SAMPSON. Ay, the heads of the maids, or their maidenheads, take it in what sense thou wilt.

GREGORY. They must take it in sense° that feel it.

SAMPSON. Me they shall feel while I am able to stand, and 'tis known I am a pretty piece of flesh.

GREGORY. 'Tis well thou art not fish; if thou hadst, thou hadst been poor-John.° Draw thy tool,° here comes two of the house of Montagues.

[*ABRAM and BALTHASAR, servants of the Montagues, enter.*]

SAMPSON. My naked weapon is out. Quarrel! I will back thee.

GREGORY. How? Turn thy back and run?

SAMPSON. Fear me not.

GREGORY. No, marry.° I fear thee!

SAMPSON. Let us take the law of our sides; let them begin.°

19 **one:** the same.

25 Gregory plays on two meanings of **sense,** "feeling" and "meaning."

29 **poor-John:** salted fish (considered a poor man's dish). **tool:** sword.

34 **marry:** by the Virgin Mary (a mild oath similar to *indeed*).

35 **Let us . . . begin:** Sampson wants to let them begin the fight so that he and Gregory can claim to have fought in self-defense.

GREGORY. I will frown as I pass by, and let them take it as they list.°

SAMPSON. Nay, as they dare. I will bite my thumb° at them, which is disgrace to them if they bear it.

ABRAM. Do you bite your thumb at us, sir?

SAMPSON. I do bite my thumb, sir.

ABRAM. Do you bite your thumb at us, sir?

SAMPSON. [*Aside to* GREGORY.] Is the law of our side if I say ay?

GREGORY. [*Aside to* SAMPSON.] No.

SAMPSON. No, sir, I do not bite my thumb at you, sir; but I bite my thumb, sir.

GREGORY. Do you quarrel, sir?

ABRAM. Quarrel, sir? No, sir.

SAMPSON. But if you do, sir, I am for you.° I serve as good a man as you.

ABRAM. No better?

SAMPSON. Well, sir.

[*Enter* BENVOLIO, LORD MONTAGUE*'s nephew.*]

GREGORY. Say "better." Here comes one of my master's kinsmen.

SAMPSON. Yes, better, sir.

ABRAM. You lie.

SAMPSON. Draw, if you be men. Gregory, remember thy washing° blow.

[*They fight.*]

BENVOLIO. Part, fools!
Put up your swords. You know not what you do. [*Beats down their swords.*]

[TYBALT, LADY CAPULET*'s nephew, enters with his sword drawn. He speaks first to* BENVOLIO.]

TYBALT. What, art thou drawn among these heartless hinds?°
Turn thee, Benvolio; look upon thy death.

BENVOLIO. I do but keep the peace. Put up thy sword,
Or manage it to part these men with me.

TYBALT. What, drawn, and talk of peace? I hate the word
As I hate hell, all Montagues, and thee.
Have at thee, coward!

37 **list:** please.

38 **bite my thumb:** an insulting gesture.

49 **I am for you:** I accept your challenge.

58 **washing:** slashing.

61 **heartless hinds:** cowardly servants. Tybalt, assuming that Benvolio is involved in the servants' quarrel, challenges him to fight someone of his own rank.

[*BENVOLIO and TYBALT fight as men of both families enter and join the brawl. Then an OFFICER of the town and several CITIZENS enter. They carry clubs, battle-axes (bills), and spears (partisans).*]

CITIZENS. Clubs, bills and partisans! Strike! Beat them down!
Down with the Capulets! Down with the Montagues!

[*LORD CAPULET, in his dressing gown, and LADY CAPULET enter.*]

CAPULET. What noise is this? Give me my long sword, ho!

LADY CAPULET. A crutch, a crutch! Why call you for a sword?

CAPULET. My sword, I say! Old Montague is come
And flourishes his blade in spite° of me.

[*LORD MONTAGUE and LADY MONTAGUE enter. LADY MONTAGUE tries to hold back her husband.*]

MONTAGUE. Thou villain Capulet!—Hold me not; let me go.

LADY MONTAGUE. Thou shalt not stir one foot to seek a foe.

[*PRINCE ESCALUS enters with his TRAIN.*]

PRINCE. Rebellious subjects, enemies to peace,
Profaners of this neighbor-stained steel°—
Will they not hear? What, ho! You men, you beasts,
That quench the fire of your pernicious° rage
With purple fountains issuing from your veins!
On pain of torture, from those bloody hands
Throw your mistemper'd° weapons to the ground
And hear the sentence of your moved° prince.
Three civil brawls, bred of an airy word
By thee, old Capulet, and Montague,
Have thrice disturb'd the quiet of our streets
And made Verona's ancient citizens
Cast by their grave beseeming ornaments°
To wield old partisans, in hands as old,
Cank'red with peace,° to part your cank'red hate.°
If ever you disturb our streets again,
Your lives shall pay the forfeit of the peace.°
For this time all the rest depart away.
You, Capulet, shall go along with me;
And, Montague, come you this afternoon,
To know our farther pleasure in this case,
To old Freetown, our common judgment place.
Once more, on pain of death, all men depart.

[*Everyone leaves except MONTAGUE, LADY MONTAGUE, and their nephew BENVOLIO.*]

73 **spite:** defiance.

77 **Profaners . . . steel:** Those who disrespect the law by staining their weapons with neighbors' blood.

79 **pernicious** (pər nish′ əs): deadly.

82 **mistemper'd:** "poorly made" or "put to bad use."

83 **moved:** angry.

88 **Cast by . . . ornaments:** put aside the dignified clothing appropriate for their age.

90 **Cank'red with peace:** rusty from disuse. **cank'red hate:** dangerous feud.

92 **Your lives . . . peace:** You will pay with your lives for disturbing the peace.

MONTAGUE. Who set this ancient quarrel new abroach?°
Speak, nephew, were you by when it began?

BENVOLIO. Here were the servants of your adversary
And yours, close fighting ere I did approach.
I drew to part them. In the instant came
The fiery Tybalt, with his sword prepar'd;
Which, as he breath'd° defiance to my ears,
He swung about his head and cut the winds,
Who, nothing hurt withal,° hiss'd him in scorn.
While we were interchanging thrusts and blows,
Came more and more, and fought on part and part,°
Till the Prince came, who parted either part.

LADY MONTAGUE. O, where is Romeo? Saw you him today?
Right glad I am he was not at this fray.

BENVOLIO. Madam, an hour before the worship'd sun
Peer'd forth° the golden window of the east,
A troubl'd mind drive° me to walk abroad;
Where, underneath the grove of sycamore
That westward rooteth from° this city side,
So early walking did I see your son.
Towards him I made, but he was ware° of me
And stole into the covert of the wood.°
I, measuring his affections,° by my own,
Which then most sought where most might not be found,°
Being one too many by my weary self,
Pursued my humor not pursuing his,°
And gladly shunn'd who gladly fled from me.

MONTAGUE. Many a morning hath he there been seen,
With tears augmenting the fresh morning's dew,
Adding to clouds more clouds with his deep sighs;
But all so soon as the all-cheering sun
Should in the farthest east begin to draw
The shady curtains from Aurora's° bed,
Away from light steals home my heavy° son
And private in his chamber pens himself,
Shuts up his windows, locks fair daylight out,
And makes himself an artificial night.
Black and portentous must this humor prove
Unless good counsel may the cause remove.°

BENVOLIO. My noble uncle, do you know the cause?

MONTAGUE. I neither know it nor can learn of him.

99 **Who . . . abroach:** Who reopened this old feud?

105 **breath'd:** uttered.

107 **nothing hurt withal:** not hurt by this.

109 **Came more . . . part:** More and more men arrived and fought on one side or the other.

114 **forth:** out from.

115 **drive:** drove.

117 **westward rooteth from:** grows to the west of.

119 **ware:** aware.

120 **covert of the wood:** concealment of the forest.

121 **affections:** feelings.

122 **most sought . . . found:** wanted to find a solitary place.

124 **Pursued my . . . his:** followed my own mood **(humor)** by not following him.

131 **Aurora** (ə rôr′ ə): the goddess of the dawn in classical mythology.

132 **heavy:** sad.

136–137 **Black and . . . remove:** Montague fears that this mood will lead to trouble if allowed to continue.

BENVOLIO. Have you importun'd° him by any means?

MONTAGUE. Both by myself and many other friends;
But he, his own affections' counselor,
Is to himself—I will not say how true°—
But to himself so secret and so close,°
So far from sounding and discovery,°
As is the bud bit with an envious worm
Ere he can spread his sweet leaves to the air
Or dedicate his beauty to the sun.°
Could we but learn from whence his sorrows grow,
We would as willingly give cure as know.

[*ROMEO enters. He appears distracted and does not notice the others on stage.*]

BENVOLIO. See where he comes. So please you step aside;
I'll know his grievance, or be much denied.

MONTAGUE. I would thou wert so happy by thy stay
To hear true shrift.° Come, madam, let's away.

[*MONTAGUE and LADY MONTAGUE leave.*]

BENVOLIO. Good morrow,° cousin.

ROMEO. Is the day so young?

BENVOLIO. But new° struck nine.

ROMEO. Ay me! Sad hours seem long.
Was that my father that went hence so fast?

BENVOLIO. It was. What sadness lengthens Romeo's hours?

ROMEO. Not having that which having makes them short.

BENVOLIO. In love?

ROMEO. Out—

BENVOLIO. Of love?

ROMEO. Out of her favor where I am in love.

BENVOLIO. Alas that love, so gentle in his view,
Should be so tyrannous and rough in proof!°

ROMEO. Alas that love, whose view is muffled still,
Should without eyes see pathways to his will!°
Where shall we dine? O me! What fray was here?°
Yet tell me not, for I have heard it all.
Here's much to do with hate, but more with love.
Why then, O brawling love, O loving hate,
O any thing, of nothing first create!°
O heavy lightness, serious vanity,

140 **importun'd:** questioned.

143 **how true:** how trustworthy (a counselor Romeo is to himself).

144 **close:** secretive, reticent.

145 **far from . . . discovery:** unwilling to let others question and come to understand him.

146–148 **As is the bud . . . the sun:** Montague compares Romeo to a bud that is destroyed by a malicious caterpillar before it can open its petals.

153–154 **I would . . . shrift:** I hope that by waiting (for Romeo) you will be lucky enough to hear a true confession.

155 **morrow:** morning.

156 **But new:** only just.

164–165 **love . . . proof:** love appears so gentle but proves to be a rough tyrant.

166–167 **Alas that . . . will:** Romeo regrets that love, although blind, is still able to hit its target. (Cupid, the god of love, is often portrayed wearing a blindfold.)

168 **What fray was here:** Romeo only now notices blood or some other sign of the fighting.

172 **of nothing first create:** Romeo refers to the idea that God created the universe from nothing.

Misshapen chaos of well-seeming forms,
Feather of lead, bright smoke, cold fire, sick health,
Still-waking sleep, that is not what it is!°
This love feel I, that feel no love in this.°
Dost thou not laugh?

BENVOLIO. No, coz,° I rather weep.

ROMEO. Good heart, at what?

BENVOLIO. At thy good heart's oppression.

ROMEO. Why, such is love's transgression.
Griefs of mine own lie heavy in my breast,
Which thou wilt propagate, to have it press'd
With more of thine.° This love that thou hast shown

170–176 **Here's much . . . it is:** Romeo says that the feud involves love (of fighting and devotion to family) as well as hatred. He then suggests the paradoxical nature of love.

177 **that feel no love in this:** who feels no happiness from this sort of love.

178 **coz:** cousin. (Any relative might be addressed as cousin.)

182–183 **Which thou . . . thine:** Your concern over my grief only increases the burden of my sorrow.

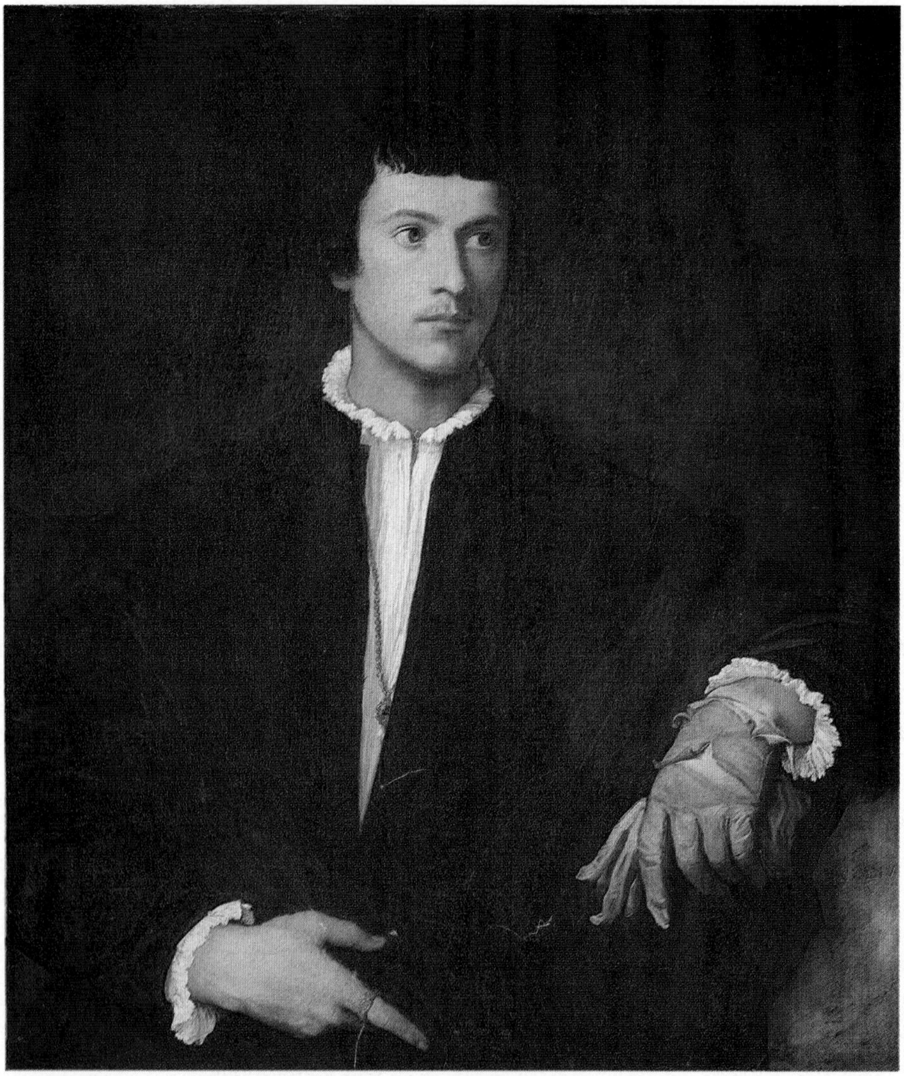

Portrait of a Man, 1523. Titian (Tiziano Vecellio). Oil on canvas, 100 x 89 cm. Louvre Museum, Paris.

Viewing the painting: In what ways does the young man in the painting remind you of Romeo?

Doth add more grief to too much of mine own.
Love is a smoke made with the fume of sighs;
Being purg'd,° a fire sparkling in lovers' eyes;
Being vex'd, a sea nourish'd with loving tears.
What is it else? A madness most discreet,°
A choking gall,° and a preserving sweet.
Farewell, my coz.

BENVOLIO. Soft!° I will go along.
And if you leave me so, you do me wrong.

ROMEO. Tut! I have lost myself; I am not here;
This is not Romeo, he's some other where.

BENVOLIO. Tell me in sadness,° who is that you love?

ROMEO. What, shall I groan and tell thee?

BENVOLIO. Groan? Why, no;
But sadly tell me who.

ROMEO. Bid a sick man in sadness make his will.
A word ill urg'd to one that is so ill!
In sadness, cousin, I do love a woman.

BENVOLIO. I aim'd so near when I suppos'd you lov'd.

ROMEO. A right good markman. And she's fair I love.

BENVOLIO. A right fair mark,° fair coz, is soonest hit.

ROMEO. Well, in that hit you miss. She'll not be hit
With Cupid's arrow. She hath Dian's wit,°
And, in strong proof° of chastity well arm'd,
From Love's weak childish bow she lives uncharm'd.
She will not stay the siege of loving terms,°
Nor bide° th' encounter of assailing eyes,
Nor ope her lap to saint-seducing gold.°
O, she is rich in beauty; only poor
That, when she dies, with beauty dies her store.°

BENVOLIO. Then she hath sworn that she will still° live chaste?

ROMEO. She hath, and in that sparing makes huge waste;
For beauty starv'd with her severity
Cuts beauty off from all posterity.°
She is too fair,° too wise, wisely too fair,
To merit bliss° by making me despair.
She hath forsworn to° love, and in that vow
Do I live dead that live to tell it now.

BENVOLIO. Be ruled by me; forget to think of her.

186 **Being purg'd:** when the smoke has cleared.

188 **discreet:** discriminating.

189 **gall:** bitterness.

190 **Soft:** Wait a minute!

194 **in sadness:** seriously.

202 **right fair mark:** easily seen target.

204 **Dian's wit:** the cleverness of Diana, Roman goddess of chastity.

205 **proof:** armor.

207 **stay . . . terms:** submit to courtship.

208 **bide:** tolerate.

209 **Nor ope . . . gold:** Nor can she be seduced by expensive gifts.

211 **when she . . . store:** When she dies, all her wealth will die with her beauty (because she will have no children to inherit her beauty).

212 **still:** always.

213–215 **In that sparing . . . posterity:** Romeo says that her thriftiness is really wasteful, because no children will be born to perpetuate her beauty.

216 **fair:** "beautiful" or "just."

217 **To merit bliss:** to win heavenly bliss.

218 **forsworn to:** sworn not to.

ROMEO. O, teach me how I should forget to think!

BENVOLIO. By giving liberty unto thine eyes.
Examine other beauties.

ROMEO. 'Tis the way
To call hers, exquisite, in question more.°
These happy° masks° that kiss fair ladies' brows,
Being black puts us in mind they hide the fair.
He that is strucken blind cannot forget
The precious treasure of his eyesight lost.
Show me a mistress that is passing° fair:
What doth her beauty serve but as a note
Where I may read who pass'd° that passing fair?
Farewell. Thou canst not teach me to forget.

BENVOLIO. I'll pay that doctrine, or else die in debt.°

[*They exit.*]

223–224 **'Tis . . . more:** Examining other women will only make me dwell more upon her exquisite beauty.

225 **happy:** fortunate. **masks:** worn by fashionable Elizabethan women to protect fair complexions from the sun.

229 **passing:** surpassingly.

231 **pass'd:** surpassed.

233 **I'll pay . . . debt:** I'll teach you to forget, or never give up trying until I die.

SCENE 2. Later that afternoon. A street near CAPULET's house in Verona.

[*CAPULET enters with COUNT PARIS, a young relative of the PRINCE, and with a SERVANT.*]

CAPULET. But Montague is bound as well as I,
In penalty alike; and 'tis not hard, I think,
For men so old as we to keep the peace.

PARIS. Of honorable reckoning° are you both,
And pity 'tis you liv'd at odds so long.
But now, my lord, what say you to my suit?

CAPULET. But saying o'er what I have said before:
My child is yet a stranger in the world,
She hath not seen the change of fourteen years;
Let two more summers wither in their pride
Ere we may think her ripe to be a bride.

PARIS. Younger than she are happy mothers made.

CAPULET. And too soon marr'd are those so early made.
Earth hath swallowed all my hopes but she;°
She is the hopeful lady of my earth.°
But woo her, gentle Paris, get her heart;
My will to her consent is but a part.
And she agreed within her scope of choice
Lies my consent and fair according voice.°
This night I hold an old accustom'd° feast,
Whereto I have invited many a guest,

4 **reckoning:** reputation.

14 **Earth hath . . . she:** She is my only surviving child.

15 **She is . . . earth:** "She will inherit all my property," or "she is the woman in whom all my hopes lie."

18–19 **And she . . . voice:** As long as she chooses appropriately, I will let her marry whomever she chooses.

20 **old accustom'd:** long established.

Such as I love; and you among the store,
One more, most welcome, makes my number more.
At my poor house look to behold this night
Earth-treading stars° that make dark heaven light.
Such comfort as do lusty young men feel
When well-apparel'd April on the heel
Of limping Winter treads, even such delight
Among fresh fennel buds shall you this night
Inherit at my house.° Hear all, all see,
And like her most whose merit most shall be;
Which, on more view of many, mine, being one,
May stand in number, though in reck'ning none.°
Come, go with me.

[*CAPULET speaks to his SERVANT and hands him a piece of paper that contains the names of the people he is inviting to his party.*]

Go, sirrah,° trudge about
Through fair Verona; find those persons out
Whose names are written there, and to them say
My house and welcome on their pleasure stay.°

[*CAPULET and PARIS exit. The SERVANT, who cannot read, looks at the paper.*]

SERVANT. Find them out whose names are written here! It is written that the shoemaker should meddle with his yard and the tailor with his last, the fisher with his pencil and the painter with his nets; but I am sent to find those persons whose names are here writ, and can never find what names the writing person hath here writ.° I must to the learned. In good time!°

[*ROMEO and BENVOLIO enter, still talking about ROMEO's unhappiness in love.*]

BENVOLIO. Tut, man, one fire burns out another's burning;
One pain is less'ned by another's anguish;
Turn giddy, and be holp by backward turning,°
One desperate grief cures with another's languish.
Take thou some new infection to thy eye,
And the rank poison of the old will die.

ROMEO. Your plantan° leaf is excellent for that.

BENVOLIO. For what, I pray thee?

ROMEO. For your broken° shin.

BENVOLIO. Why, Romeo, art thou mad?

25 **Earth-treading stars:** young women.

26–30 **Such comfort . . . house:** Tonight the pleasure you will take at my house is like the joy that young men feel when spring replaces winter.

30–33 **Hear all . . . none:** Capulet suggests that after Paris has compared Juliet to the others, she may strike him as merely one woman among many, not worth special consideration.

34 **sirrah** (sir′ ə): a term of address used when speaking to someone inferior in rank.

37 **stay:** wait.

38–43 **Find them . . . writ:** The illiterate servant means to say that people should stick to what they know how to do, but he comically mixes up the types of workers and their tools.

43 **In good time:** Just in time! (He sees men who appear to be educated.)

47 **Turn giddy . . . turning:** Become dizzy, and be helped by turning in the opposite direction.

51 **plantan:** plantain (a type of leaf used to stop bleeding).

52 **broken:** scraped.

ROMEO. Not mad, but bound more than a madman is;
Shut up in prison, kept without my food,
Whipt and tormented and—God-den,° good fellow.

SERVANT. God gi'° god-den. I pray, sir, can you read?

ROMEO. Ay, mine own fortune in my misery.

SERVANT. Perhaps you have learn'd it without book.
But, I pray, can you read anything you see?

ROMEO. Ay, if I know the letters and the language.

SERVANT. Ye say honestly. Rest you merry.°

ROMEO. Stay, fellow; I can read. [*He reads.*]
"Signior Martino and his wife and daughters; County°
Anselm and his beauteous sisters; the lady widow of Vitruvio; Signior Placentio and his lovely nieces; Mercutio and his brother Valentine; mine uncle Capulet, his wife and daughters; my fair niece Rosaline; Livia; Signior Valentio and his cousin Tybalt; Lucio and the lively Helena."
A fair assembly. Whither should they come?

SERVANT. Up.

ROMEO. Whither? To supper?

SERVANT. To our house.

ROMEO. Whose house?

SERVANT. My master's.

ROMEO. Indeed I should have ask'd thee that before.

SERVANT. Now I'll tell you without asking. My master is the great
rich Capulet; and if you be not of the house of Montagues,
I pray come and crush a cup° of wine. Rest you merry.

[*The* SERVANT *exits.*]

BENVOLIO. At this same ancient° feast of Capulet's
Sups the fair Rosaline whom thou so loves;
With all the admired beauties of Verona.
Go thither,° and with unattainted° eye
Compare her face with some that I shall show,
And I will make thee think thy swan a crow.

ROMEO. When the devout religion of mine eye
Maintains such falsehood, then turn tears to fires;
And these, who, often drown'd, could never die,
Transparent heretics,° be burnt for liars!°
One fairer than my love? The all-seeing sun
Ne'er saw her match since first the world begun.

56 **God-den:** good afternoon; good evening.

57 **God gi':** God give you.

62 **Rest you merry:** The servant misunderstands Romeo's reply and bids him farewell.

64 **County:** Count.

79 **crush a cup:** have a drink.

80 **ancient:** traditional.

83 **thither:** there. **unattainted:** impartial.

86–89 **When the . . . liars:** Romeo says that if he accepted such a falsehood, his tearful eyes would be heretics for having broken faith with Rosaline, and he would wish the tears turned to fire so that his eyes could be burned like heretics.

89 **heretics:** People who maintain a religious belief contrary to accepted doctrine.

BENVOLIO. Tut! you saw her fair, none else being by,
Herself pois'd° with herself in either eye;
But in that crystal scales° let there be weigh'd
Your lady's love against some other maid
That I will show you shining at this feast,
And she shall scant show well that now seems best.

ROMEO. I'll go along, no such sight to be shown,
But to rejoice in splendor of mine own.°

[*They exit.*]

93 **pois'd:** weighed; compared.

94 **crystal scales:** That is, Romeo's eyes.

99 **in splendor of mine own:** in the splendor of my own lady (Rosaline).

SCENE 3. Later that evening, before the party. A room in CAPULET's house.

[*LADY CAPULET and the Capulets' NURSE enter.*]

LADY CAPULET. Nurse, where's my daughter? Call her forth to me.

NURSE. Now by my maidenhead at twelve year old,
I bade her come. What, lamb! What, ladybird!
God forbid! Where's this girl? What, Juliet!

[*JULIET enters.*]

JULIET. How now? Who calls?

NURSE. Your mother.

JULIET. Madam, I am here.
What is your will?

LADY CAPULET. This is the matter—Nurse, give leave° awhile;
We must talk in secret. Nurse, come back again.
I have rememb'red me; thou's hear our counsel.°
Thou knowest my daughter's of a pretty age.

NURSE. Faith, I can tell her age unto an hour.

LADY CAPULET. She's not fourteen.

NURSE. I'll lay fourteen of my teeth—
And yet, to my teen° be it spoken, I have but four—
She's not fourteen. How long is it now
To Lammastide?°

LADY CAPULET. A fortnight and odd days.°

NURSE. Even or odd, of all days in the year,
Come Lammas Eve at night shall she be fourteen.
Susan and she (God rest all Christian souls!)
Were of an age.° Well, Susan is with God;
She was too good for me. But, as I said,
On Lammas Eve at night shall she be fourteen;
That shall she, marry;° I remember it well.

7 **give leave:** leave us alone.

9 **thou's hear our counsel:** You shall hear our conversation.

13 **teen:** sorrow.

15 **Lammastide:** August 1, a religious feast day. **A fortnight and odd days:** two weeks plus a few days.

19 **of an age:** the same age. (The Nurse's daughter, now dead, was born around the same time as Juliet.)

22 **marry:** indeed.

'Tis since the earthquake now eleven years;
And she was wean'd—I shall never forget it—
Of all the days of the year, upon that day;
For I had then laid wormwood° to my dug,°
Sitting in the sun under the dove-house wall.
My lord and you were then at Mantua—
Nay, I do bear a brain°—but as I said,
When it did taste the wormwood on the nipple
Of my dug and felt it bitter, pretty fool,
To see it teachy° and fall out wi' th' dug!
Shake, quoth the dove-house;° 'twas no need, I trow,
To bid me trudge.°
And since that time it is eleven years,
For then she could stand high-lone;° nay, by th' rood,°
She could have run and waddled all about;
For even the day before, she broke her brow,
And then my husband—God be with his soul!
'A° was a merry man—took up the child.
"Yea," quoth he, "dost thou fall upon thy face?
Thou wilt fall backward when thou hast more wit,°
Wilt thou not, Jule?" and by my holidam,°
The pretty wretch left crying and said, "Ay."
To see now how a jest shall come about!
I warrant, and I should live a thousand years,
I never should forget it: "Wilt thou not, Jule?" quoth he;
And, pretty fool, it stinted° and said, "Ay."

LADY CAPULET. Enough of this, I pray thee hold thy peace.

NURSE. Yes, madam, yet I cannot choose but laugh
To think it should leave crying and say, "Ay."
And yet I warrant it had upon it brow
A bump as big as a young cock'rel's stone—
A perilous knock—and it cried bitterly.
"Yea," quoth my husband, "fall'st upon thy face?
Thou wilt fall backward when thou comest to age,
Wilt thou not, Jule?" It stinted and said, "Ay."

JULIET. And stint thou too, I pray thee, nurse, say I.

NURSE. Peace, I have done. God mark thee to his grace!
Thou wast the prettiest babe that e'er I nurs'd.
And I might live to see thee married once,
I have my wish.

LADY CAPULET. Marry, that "marry" is the very theme
I came to talk of. Tell me, daughter Juliet,
How stands your dispositions to be married?

26 **wormwood:** a bitter oil from the leaves of a plant. **dug:** breast.

29 **I do bear a brain:** My mind is still sharp.

32 **teachy:** tetchy; irritably or peevishly sensitive.

33 **Shake . . . dove-house:** The dove-house began to shake from the earthquake.

33–34 **'twas . . . trudge:** I didn't need any urging to get away.

36 **high-lone:** upright without support. **rood:** cross.

40 **'A:** he.

42 **wit:** knowledge.

43 **by my holidam:** by my holiness (an oath).

48 **stinted:** stopped.

JULIET. It is an honor that I dream not of.

NURSE. An honor! were not I thine only nurse,
I would say thou hadst suck'd wisdom from thy teat.

LADY CAPULET. Well, think of marriage now. Younger than you,
Here in Verona, ladies of esteem,
Are made already mothers. By my count,
I was your mother much upon these years°
That you are now a maid. Thus then in brief:
The valiant Paris seeks you for his love.

NURSE. A man, young lady! Lady, such a man
As all the world—Why, he's a man of wax.°

LADY CAPULET. Verona's summer hath not such a flower.

NURSE. Nay, he's a flower, in faith—a very flower.

LADY CAPULET. What say you? Can you love the gentleman?
This night you shall behold him at our feast.
Read o'er the volume° of young Paris' face,
And find delight writ there with beauty's pen;
Examine every married lineament,°
And see how one another lends content;
And what obscur'd in this fair volume lies
Find written in the margent° of his eyes.
This precious book of love, this unbound lover,
To beautify him only lacks a cover.°
The fish lives in the sea, and 'tis much pride
For fair without the fair within to hide.°
That book in many's eyes doth share the glory,
That in gold clasps locks in the golden story;
So shall you share all that he doth possess,
By having him making yourself no less.

NURSE. No less! nay, bigger: women grow° by men.

LADY CAPULET. Speak briefly, can you like of Paris' love?

JULIET. I'll look to like, if looking liking move;
But no more deep will I endart mine eye
Than your consent gives strength to make it fly.°

[A *SERVANT enters.*]

SERVINGMAN. Madam, the guests are come, supper served up, you call'd, my young lady ask'd for, the nurse curs'd° in the pantry, and everything in extremity. I must hence to wait. I beseech you follow straight.°

[*The SERVANT exits.*]

72 **much upon these years:** at about the same age.

76 **man of wax:** a model man, as perfect as a wax statue.

81 **volume:** book. (This metaphor is extended in lines 82–92.)

83 **every married lineament** (lin′ ē ə mənt): all the harmonious features of his face.

86 **margent** (mär′ jənt): margin (which, like the marginal notes in a book, reveal whatever is not clear in the rest of his face).

88 **cover:** binding (that is, a wife).

89–90 **The fish . . . hide:** The fair sea is made even more beautiful by the fair fish hiding within it.

95 **grow:** become pregnant.

97–99 **I'll look . . . fly:** I am prepared to look favorably on him, if looking can persuade me, but I won't give him encouraging glances beyond your approval.

101 **curs'd:** The Nurse is cursed because she is not helping.

103 **straight:** immediately.

LADY CAPULET. We follow thee. Juliet, the County stays.°

NURSE. Go, girl, seek happy nights to happy days.

[*They exit.*]

SCENE 4. Later that night. A street in Verona.

[*ROMEO enters with his friends MERCUTIO and BENVOLIO. They are on their way to CAPULET's party; they wear masks to conceal their identities because ROMEO and BENVOLIO are Montagues. Several other MASKERS and TORCHBEARERS accompany them.*]

ROMEO. What, shall this speech be spoke for our excuse?
Or shall we on without apology?°

BENVOLIO. The date is out of such prolixity:°
We'll have no Cupid hoodwink'd° with a scarf,
Bearing a Tartar's painted bow of lath,°
Scaring the ladies like a crow-keeper,°
Nor no without-book prologue,° faintly spoke
After the prompter, for our entrance;
But let them measure us by what they will,
We'll measure them a measure° and be gone.

ROMEO. Give me a torch. I am not for this ambling.
Being but heavy,° I will bear the light.

MERCUTIO. Nay, gentle Romeo, we must have you dance.

ROMEO. Not I, believe me. You have dancing shoes
With nimble soles; I have a soul of lead
So stakes me to the ground I cannot move.

MERCUTIO. You are a lover. Borrow Cupid's wings
And soar with them above a common bound.°

ROMEO. I am too sore enpierced with his shaft°
To soar with his light feathers; and so bound
I cannot bound a pitch° above dull woe.
Under love's heavy burden do I sink.

MERCUTIO. And, to sink in it, should you burden love—
Too great oppression for a tender thing.

ROMEO. Is love a tender thing? It is too rough,
Too rude, too boist'rous and it pricks like thorn.

MERCUTIO. If love be rough with you, be rough with love.
Prick love for pricking, and you beat love down.
Give me a case° to put my visage° in. [*Puts on a mask.*]
A visor° for a visor! What care I

104 **the County stays:** Count Paris is waiting.

1–2 **What, shall . . . apology:** Maskers would arrive uninvited to a festival or celebration and expect hospitality. Romeo wonders if they should deliver a customary speech greeting the host and apologizing for their intrusion.

3 **The date . . . prolixity:** Such wordiness is out of fashion.

4 **hoodwink'd:** blindfolded.

5 **Tartar's . . . lath:** a short bow made of thin wood.

6 **crow-keeper:** scarecrow holding a bow.

7 **without-book prologue:** memorized speech.

10 **measure them a measure:** stay for a dance.

12 **heavy:** sad.

18 **bound:** leap (in a dance).

19 **enpierced . . . shaft:** wounded with Cupid's arrow.

21 **a pitch:** any height.

29 **case:** cover. **visage:** face.

30 **visor:** mask.

What curious eye doth quote° deformities?
Here are the beetle brows° shall blush for me.

BENVOLIO. Come, knock and enter; and no sooner in
But every man betake him to his legs.°

ROMEO. A torch for me! Let wantons light of heart
Tickle the senseless rushes° with their heels;
For I am proverb'd with a grandsire phrase,°
I'll be a candleholder° and look on;
The game was ne'er so fair, and I am done.

MERCUTIO. Tut, dun's the mouse,° the constable's own word.
If thou art Dun, we'll draw thee from the mire
Of this sir-reverence° love, wherein thou stickest
Up to the ears. Come, we burn daylight,° ho!

31 **quote:** make note of.

32 **beetle brows:** bushy eyebrows.

34 **betake . . . legs:** begin to dance.

36 **rushes:** straw floor covering.

37 **proverb'd . . . phrase:** guided by an old saying.

38 **candleholder:** spectator. The proverb advises leaving a gambling table when you are ahead.

40 **dun's the mouse:** an expression meaning, "Keep quiet and hidden." (Mercutio plays off the word *done* with *dun,* meaning "dark.")

42 **sir-reverence:** an apologetic expression used to introduce something thought indecent (but Mercutio ironically uses it to introduce the word *love*).

43 **burn daylight:** waste time.

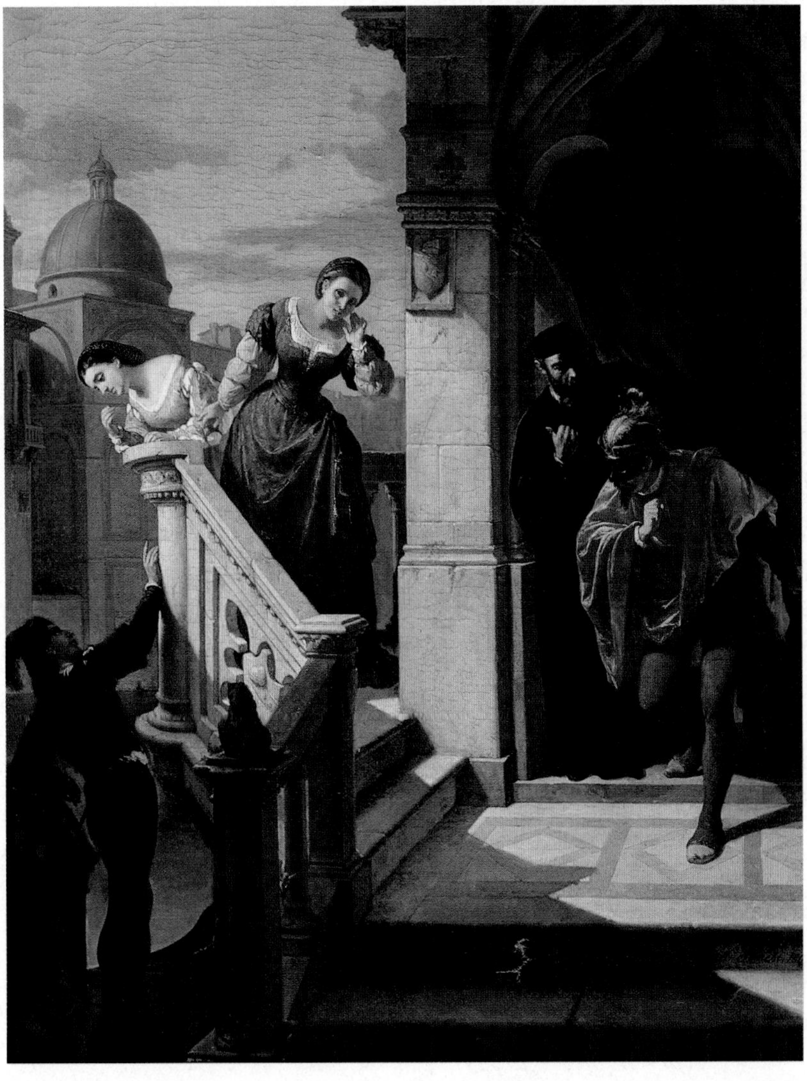

Venetian Intrigue, 1862. Niccolo Sanesi. Oil on canvas, 99 x 77.5 cm. Private collection.

Viewing the painting: How might the scene in the painting reflect the action in this portion of *Romeo and Juliet*?

ROMEO. Nay, that's not so.

MERCUTIO. I mean, sir, in delay
We waste our lights in vain, like lights by day!
Take our good meaning, for our judgment sits
Five times in that ere once in our five wits.°

ROMEO. And we mean well in going to this mask,
But 'tis no wit to go.

MERCUTIO. Why, may one ask?

ROMEO. I dreamt a dream tonight.°

MERCUTIO. And so did I.

ROMEO. Well, what was yours?

MERCUTIO. That dreamers often lie.

ROMEO. In bed asleep, while they do dream things true.

[*As* ROMEO *speaks with his friends, the* MASKERS *and* TORCHBEARERS *march about the stage.* MERCUTIO *continues trying to cheer* ROMEO.]

MERCUTIO. O, then I see Queen Mab° hath been with you.
She is the fairies' midwife,° and she comes
In shape no bigger than an agate stone°
On the forefinger of an alderman,
Drawn with a team of little atomi°
Over men's noses as they lie asleep;
Her chariot is an empty hazelnut,
Made by the joiner° squirrel or old grub,
Time out o' mind the fairies' coachmakers.
Her wagon spokes made of long spinners'° legs,
The cover, of the wings of grasshoppers;
Her traces,° of the smallest spider web;
Her collars, of the moonshine's wat'ry beams;
Her whip, of cricket's bone; the lash, of film;°
Her wagoner,° a small gray-coated gnat,
Not half so big as a round little worm
Pricked from the lazy finger of a maid;°
And in this state° she gallops night by night
Through lovers' brains, and then they dream of love;
O'er courtiers' knees, that dream on curtsies straight;°
O'er lawyers' fingers, who straight dream on fees;
O'er ladies' lips, who straight on kisses dream,
Which oft the angry Mab with blisters plagues,
Because their breath with sweetmeats° tainted are.
Sometime she gallops o'er a courtier's nose,

46–47 **Take our . . . wits:** Accept our intended **(good)** meaning, for true understanding is five times as likely to be found there as in cleverness.

50 **tonight:** last night.

53 **Queen Mab:** queen of the fairies.

54 **fairies' midwife:** the fairy who helps sleepers give birth to dreams.

55 **agate stone:** gem set in a ring.

57 **little atomi:** tiny creatures.

60 **joiner:** carpenter.

62 **spinners':** spiders'.

64 **traces:** harnesses.

66 **film:** cobweb.

67 **wagoner:** driver.

68–69 **worm . . . maid:** Worms were said to grow in the fingers of lazy maids.

70 **state:** majestic style.

72 **that dream . . . straight:** who immediately dream of respectful bows.

76 **sweetmeats:** sweets.

And then dreams he of smelling out a suit;°
And sometime comes she with a tithe pig's° tail
Tickling a parson's nose as 'a lies asleep,
Then he dreams of another benefice.°
Sometime she driveth o'er a soldier's neck,
And then dreams he of cutting foreign throats,
Of breaches, ambuscadoes,° Spanish blades,
Of healths° five fathom deep; and then anon°
Drums in his ear, at which he starts and wakes,
And being thus frighted, swears a prayer or two
And sleeps again. This is that very Mab
That plats° the manes of horses in the night,
And bakes the elf-locks° in foul sluttish hairs,
Which, once untangled, much misfortune bodes.
This is the hag, when maids lie on their backs,
That presses them and learns them first to bear,
Making them women of good carriage.
This is she—

ROMEO. Peace, peace Mercutio, peace!
Thou talk'st of nothing.

MERCUTIO. True, I talk of dreams;
Which are the children of an idle brain,
Begot of nothing but vain fantasy;
Which is as thin of substance as the air,
And more inconstant° than the wind, who woos
Even now the frozen bosom of the north
And, being anger'd, puffs away from thence,
Turning his side to the dew-dropping south.

BENVOLIO. This wind you talk of blows us from ourselves.
Supper is done, and we shall come too late.

ROMEO. I fear, too early; for my mind misgives
Some consequence yet hanging in the stars
Shall bitterly begin his fearful date
With this night's revels and expire the term
Of a despised life, clos'd in my breast,
By some vile forfeit of untimely death.°
But He that hath the steerage of my course
Direct my sail! On, lusty gentlemen!

BENVOLIO. Strike, drum.

[*They march about the stage and exit.*]

78 **smelling out a suit:** having someone pay him for his influence with the king.

79 **tithe** (tīth) **pig:** a pig that a parishioner gives to a parson as a customary contribution to the church.

81 **benefice** (ben′ ə fis): church appointment with an assured income.

84 **ambuscadoes** (am′ bus kä′ dōz): ambushes.

85 **healths:** drinking toasts. **anon:** at once.

89 **plats:** tangles.

90 **elf-locks:** hair that is matted from lack of grooming.

100 **inconstant:** fickle, changing.

106–111 **I fear . . . death:** Romeo says that he has a premonition that some event **(consequence)** being worked out by fate will occur at the festivities and lead to his premature death, like a loan that comes due early.

SCENE 5. Immediately following the previous scene. A hall in CAPULET's house.

[*SERVANTS enter carrying napkins. They are clearing away the tables from dinner and making the hall ready for dancing.*]

FIRST SERVINGMAN. Where's Potpan, that he helps not to take away?° He shift a trencher!° He scrape a trencher!

SECOND SERVINGMAN. When good manners° shall lie all in one or two men's hands, and they unwash'd too, 'tis a foul thing.

FIRST SERVINGMAN. Away with the join-stools,° remove the court cupboard,° look to the plate.° Good thou, save me a piece of marchpane,° and, as thou loves me, let the porter let in Susan Grindstone and Nell. Anthony, and Potpan!

[*ANTHONY and POTPAN enter. SECOND SERVANT exits.*]

ANTHONY. Ay, boy, ready.

FIRST SERVINGMAN. You are look'd for and call'd for, ask'd for and sought for, in the great chamber.

POTPAN. We cannot be here and there too. Cheerly, boys! Be brisk awhile, and the longer liver take all.°

[*The SERVANTS retire to the back. CAPULET enters with LADY CAPULET, JULIET, TYBALT, and other CAPULETS, the NURSE, and all the GUESTS. The MASKERS join the group.*]

CAPULET. Welcome, gentlemen! Ladies that have their toes
Unplagu'd with corns will walk a bout° with you.
Ah, my mistresses, which of you all
Will now deny to dance? She that makes dainty,°
She I'll swear hath corns. Am I come near ye now?°

[*CAPULET notices the MASKERS and speaks to them.*]

Welcome, gentlemen! I have seen the day
That I have worn a visor and could tell
A whispering tale in a fair lady's ear,
Such as would please. 'Tis gone, 'tis gone, 'tis gone.
You are welcome, gentlemen! Come, musicians, play.

[*Music plays, and the GUESTS dance.*]

A hall, a hall! Give room!° And foot it, girls.
More light, you knaves, and turn the tables up,
And quench the fire; the room is grown too hot.
Ah, sirrah, this unlook'd-for sport° comes well.
Nay, sit; nay, sit, good cousin Capulet;
For you and I are past our dancing days.

1–2 take away: clean up after dinner.

2 trencher: wooden platter.

3 manners: a pun on the Latin root for "hands."

5 join-stools: sturdy stools made by a joiner, or carpenter.

6 court cupboard: cabinet that holds linen, silver, and china. **plate:** silverware.

7 marchpane: marzipan, a sweet made of sugar and almonds.

13 the longer . . . all: The one who outlives the rest of us takes everything.

15 walk a bout: dance.

17 makes dainty: coyly hesitates.

18 Am I . . . now: Have I struck close to home?

24 A hall . . . room: Clear the hall and make room for dancing!

27 unlook'd-for sport: unexpected entertainment (referring to the arrival of the maskers).

How long is't now since last yourself and I
Were in a mask?

SECOND CAPULET. By'r Lady, thirty years.

CAPULET. What, man? 'Tis not so much, 'tis not so much;
'Tis since the nuptial° of Lucentio,
Come Pentecost° as quickly as it will,
Some five-and-twenty years, and then we mask'd.

SECOND CAPULET. 'Tis more, 'tis more. His son is elder, sir;
His son is thirty.

CAPULET. Will you tell me that?
His son was but a ward° two years ago.

[*ROMEO has been watching JULIET and stops a SERVANT to ask about her.*]

ROMEO. [*To a SERVINGMAN.*] What lady's that which doth enrich the hand
Of yonder knight?

SERVINGMAN. I know not, sir.

ROMEO. O, she doth teach the torches to burn bright!
It seems she hangs upon the cheek of night
As a rich jewel in an Ethiop's ear—
Beauty too rich for use, for earth too dear!
So shows° a snowy dove trooping with crows
As yonder lady o'er her fellows shows.
The measure done, I'll watch her place of stand°
And, touching hers, make blessed my rude° hand.
Did my heart love till now? Forswear° it, sight!
For I ne'er saw true beauty till this night.

TYBALT. This, by his voice, should be a Montague.
Fetch me my rapier,° boy. What! Dares the slave
Come hither, cover'd with an antic face,°
To fleer and scorn at our solemnity?°
Now, by the stock and honor of my kin,
To strike him dead I hold it not a sin.

CAPULET. Why, how now, kinsman? Wherefore° storm you so?

TYBALT. Uncle, this is a Montague, our foe,
A villain, that is hither come in spite
To scorn at our solemnity this night.

CAPULET. Young Romeo is it?

TYBALT. 'Tis he, that villain Romeo.

33 **nuptial** (nup′ shəl): wedding.

34 **Pentecost** (pen′ tə kôst): seventh Sunday after Easter.

38 **but a ward:** only a minor (under twenty-one).

46 **shows:** appears.

48 **The measure . . . stand:** After this dance I will see where she goes to stand.

49 **rude:** "rough" or "unmannerly."

50 **Forswear:** deny.

53 **rapier** (rā′ pē ər): sword.

54 **antic face:** grotesque mask.

55 **fleer . . . solemnity:** mock our celebration.

58 **Wherefore:** why.

CAPULET. Content thee, gentle coz,° let him alone.
'A bears him like a portly gentleman,°
And, to say truth, Verona brags of him
To be a virtuous and well-govern'd youth.
I would not for the wealth of all this town
Here in my house do him disparagement.°
Therefore be patient; take no note of him.
It is my will, the which if thou respect,
Show a fair presence and put off these frowns,
An ill-beseeming semblance° for a feast.

TYBALT. It fits when such a villain is a guest.
I'll not endure him.

CAPULET. He shall be endured.
What, goodman boy! I say he shall. Go to!°
Am I the master here, or you? Go to!
You'll not endure him, God shall mend my soul!°
You'll make a mutiny among my guests!
You will set cock-a-hoop!° You'll be the man!

TYBALT. Why, uncle, 'tis a shame.

CAPULET. Go to, go to!
You are a saucy boy. Is't so, indeed?
This trick may chance to scathe you.° I know what.
You must contrary me! Marry, 'tis time—
Well said, my hearts°—You are a princox°—go!
Be quiet, or—More light, more light!—For shame!
I'll make you quiet. What!—Cheerly, my hearts!

TYBALT. Patience perforce° with willful choler° meeting
Makes my flesh tremble in their different greeting.°
I will withdraw; but this intrusion shall,
Now seeming sweet, convert to bitt'rest gall.

[Trembling with anger, TYBALT *exits. At the same time,* ROMEO *walks over to* JULIET *and speaks to her.]*

ROMEO. If I profane with my unworthiest hand
This holy shrine,° the gentle sin is this:
My lips, two blushing pilgrims, ready stand
To smooth that rough touch with a tender kiss.

JULIET. Good pilgrim, you do wrong your hand too much,
Which mannerly devotion shows in this;
For saints° have hands that pilgrims' hands do touch,
And palm to palm is holy palmers'° kiss.

ROMEO. Have not saints lips, and holy palmers too?

63 **Content . . . coz:** Be calm, noble cousin.

64 **'A bears . . . gentleman:** He bears himself like a well-mannered gentleman.

68 **do him disparagement:** insult him.

72 **ill-beseeming semblance:** inappropriate appearance.

75 **Go to:** an expression of impatience. Capulet rebukes Tybalt by calling him a boy and using a term of address **(goodman)** appropriate for someone below the rank of gentleman.

77 **God . . . soul:** God save me!

79 **set cock-a-hoop:** abandon all restraint.

82 **This trick . . . you:** This mischief may come to harm you.

84 **Well said, my hearts:** Well done, my friends (addressed to the dancers). **princox:** conceited youngster.

87 **Patience perforce:** enforced restraint. **choler** (kol′ ər): anger.

88 **different greeting:** opposition.

92 **holy shrine:** referring to Juliet's hand, which Romeo has taken.

97 **saints:** statues of saints.

98 **palmers:** pilgrims who visited the Holy Sepulcher in Jerusalem. (The term is derived from their practice of wearing palm leaves as a sign of devotion.)

The Ball Scene from Romeo and Juliet, 1882. Sir Frank Dicksee. Gouache, en grisaille. Private collection.

Viewing the painting: What does this painting suggest about Romeo and Juliet at the ball? Consider their body language, facial expressions, and relationship to the rest of the people at the ball.

JULIET. Ay, pilgrim, lips that they must use in pray'r.

ROMEO. O, then, dear saint, let lips do what hands do!
They pray; grant thou, lest faith turn to despair.

JULIET. Saints do not move, though grant for prayers' sake.°

ROMEO. Then move not while my prayer's effect I take.
Thus from my lips, by thine my sin is purg'd.

[*He kisses her.*]

JULIET. Then have my lips the sin that they have took.

ROMEO. Sin from my lips? O trespass sweetly urg'd!°
Give me my sin again.

[*He kisses her again.*]

JULIET. You kiss by th' book.°

[*The* NURSE *joins* JULIET.]

NURSE. Madam, your mother craves a word with you.

[JULIET *goes to speak with her mother.*]

ROMEO. What is her mother?

NURSE. Marry, bachelor,°
Her mother is the lady of the house,
And a good lady, and a wise and virtuous.
I nurs'd her daughter that you talk'd withal.°
I tell you, he that can lay hold of her
Shall have the chinks.°

ROMEO. Is she a Capulet?
O dear account! My life is my foe's debt.°

BENVOLIO. Away, be gone; the sport is at the best.°

ROMEO. Ay, so I fear; the more is my unrest.

CAPULET. Nay, gentlemen, prepare not to be gone;
We have a trifling foolish banquet towards.°
[*They whisper in his ear.*]
Is it e'en so?° Why then, I thank you all.
I thank you, honest gentlemen. Good night.
More torches here! Come on then; let's to bed.
Ah, sirrah, by my fay,° it waxes° late;
I'll to my rest.

[JULIET *returns to the* NURSE *as everyone else starts to leave.* JULIET *disguises her interest in* ROMEO *by asking about other men first.*]

JULIET. Come hither, nurse. What is yond gentleman?

NURSE. The son and heir of old Tiberio.

103 **Saints . . . sake:** Statues of saints cannot move, although saints may help people if they are moved by prayer.

107 **urg'd:** argued.

108 **kiss by th' book:** "kiss as if you've studied books of etiquette" or "use poetry and rhetoric to gain kisses from me."

110 **bachelor:** young man.

113 **withal:** with.

115 **the chinks:** plenty of money.

116 **O dear . . . debt:** O costly transaction! My life now belongs to my enemy.

117 **the sport is at the best:** The fun has already reached its peak.

120 **banquet towards:** light refreshment in preparation.

121 **Is it e'en so:** Do you insist (on leaving)?

124 **fay:** faith. **waxes:** grows.

JULIET. What's he that now is going out of door?

NURSE. Marry, that, I think, be young Petruchio.

JULIET. What's he that follows here, that would not dance?

NURSE. I know not.

JULIET. Go ask his name.

[*The* NURSE *goes to ask* ROMEO*'s name.*]

—If he be married,
My grave is like to be my wedding bed.

[*The* NURSE *returns.*]

NURSE. His name is Romeo, and a Montague,
The only son of your great enemy.

JULIET. My only love, sprung from my only hate!
Too early seen unknown, and known too late!
Prodigious° birth of love it is to me
That I must love a loathed enemy.

NURSE. What's this? What's this?

JULIET. A rhyme I learnt even now
Of one I danc'd withal.

[*Someone calls from another room, "Juliet."*]

NURSE. Anon,° anon!
Come, let's away; the strangers all are gone.

[*They exit.*]

138 **Prodigious** (prə dij′ əs): unnatural and ominous.

141 **Anon:** at once.

Responding to Literature

Personal Response

What are your thoughts about the first encounter between Romeo and Juliet?

Analyzing Act 1

Recall and Interpret

1. What causes members of the Capulet and Montague households to fight in the streets of Verona? What might the quarrel reveal about Verona's society?
2. Why is Romeo depressed at the beginning of the play? How would you characterize Benvolio's attitude toward Romeo?
3. What does Paris seek from Capulet? From his response to Paris, what do you infer about the kind of father Capulet is?
4. How does Benvolio propose to cure Romeo of his lovesickness? Does Romeo appear to have much experience with women? Give reasons for your answer.
5. Describe the circumstances that lead to Romeo meeting Juliet. What seems to be the basis for their attraction to each other?

Evaluate and Connect

6. The feud in *Romeo and Juliet* is between two families. What kinds of feuds are you familiar with? What are the causes?
7. Which character do you like the most so far? Which one do you like the least? Explain your responses.
8. Which example of **figurative language** in act 1 stands out most in your mind? Why? (See Literary Terms Handbook, page R5.)
9. What is your impression of Mercutio? Do you think he is a good influence on Romeo? Explain.
10. How would you feel about being asked to marry at age thirteen? Why?

Literary ELEMENTS

Foil

A **foil** is a character who provides a strong contrast to another character. Writers may use a foil to emphasize another character's distinctive traits or to make a character look better by comparison. For example, Mercutio's bawdiness and cynical views about love contrast with Romeo's idealism and innocence.

1. Which character serves as a foil to Lady Capulet? Explain the contrast between the two characters.
2. Which character serves as a foil to Tybalt? What does the contrast between the two characters tell you about each of them?

- See **Literary Terms Handbook**, p. R6.

Extending Your Response

Creative Writing

Rating Romeo Imagine that Juliet speaks to Rosaline after the party. Write a scene in which they discuss Romeo and what they think of him. Feel free to make up details, but make sure that your dialogue for Juliet is consistent with her character in the play. Base Rosaline's dialogue on Romeo's descriptions of her attitude toward him.

Learning for Life

Combating Feuds In *Romeo and Juliet,* civil peace and order in Verona is repeatedly disrupted by conflicts between the Capulet and Montague families. With a partner, create a proposal for ending this feud. Refer to details and incidents from act 1 in your proposal. When you are finished, present your proposal to the class.

Save your work for your portfolio.

Writing Skills

Using Parallelism

Have you ever heard the line "I came, I saw, I conquered"? That famous quotation is attributed to Julius Caesar, a real-life ruler who is also the subject of one of Shakespeare's plays. The line's **parallelism**–the like structures of sentence parts with like meanings–creates a catchy rhythm. Writers use parallelism to emphasize ideas and to give their writing a sense of unity. In the paragraph below, notice how one student uses parallelism in explaining the action in act 1 of *Romeo and Juliet.*

> **When we first meet Romeo, he is sighing, whining, and complaining about his lost love, Rosaline. When we first meet Juliet, she seems like a content and dutiful daughter. At the Capulets' party, Romeo plans to look at Rosaline, whom he loves, but who does not love him. Juliet plans to look at Paris, whom she does not love, but who loves her. Neither Romeo nor Juliet has any plans about the other at this point. By the end of the party, though, things have changed. Romeo and Juliet have met each other, forgotten all others, and found true love.**

- In the first sentence, the writer creates parallelism by using a series of participles to describe the main character: *Romeo is sighing, whining, and complaining.*
- In the middle of the paragraph, the writer creates parallelism by using two similarly constructed sentences: *At the Capulets' party, Romeo plans to look at Rosaline, whom he loves, but who does not love him. Juliet plans to look at Paris, whom she does not love, but who loves her.*
- In the last sentence of the paragraph, the writer creates parallelism by using a series of grammatically similar phrases: *Romeo and Juliet have met each other, forgotten all others, and found true love.*

EXERCISES

1. Write a paragraph in which you compare and contrast two people you know, using parallelism to emphasize similarities and differences and to help unify your writing.
2. Finish each series below with a sentence element that will create parallelism.
   a. At the class reunion, people were eating, dancing, and ______ .
   b. I skipped lunch, worked through study hall, and ______ .
   c. I phoned, I faxed, and ______ , but you never answered me.

Act 2

Prologue

[*The* CHORUS *enters and addresses the audience*.]

CHORUS. Now old desire° doth in his deathbed lie,
And young affection gapes° to be his heir;
That fair° for which love groan'd for and would die,
With tender Juliet match'd, is now not fair.
Now Romeo is belov'd and loves again,°
Alike bewitched by the charm of looks;
But to his foe suppos'd he must complain,°
And she steal love's sweet bait from fearful hooks.
Being held a foe, he may not have access
To breathe such vows as lovers use° to swear,
And she as much in love, her means much less
To meet her new beloved anywhere;
But passion lends them power, time means, to meet,
Temp'ring extremities with extreme sweet.°

[*The* CHORUS *exits*.]

1 **old desire:** Romeo's love for Rosaline.

2 **young affection gapes:** new love is eager.

3 **fair:** beautiful one (Rosaline).

5 **is belov'd . . . again:** is loved and loves in return.

7 **to his foe . . . complain:** he must express his love to a supposed enemy.

10 **use:** are accustomed.

14 **Temp'ring . . . sweet:** mixing difficulties with great delights.

SCENE 1. Later the same night. Outside the wall that surrounds CAPULET's orchard.

[ROMEO *enters. He is walking alone after the party*.]

ROMEO. Can I go forward when my heart is here?
Turn back, dull earth,° and find thy center° out.

[BENVOLIO *and* MERCUTIO *enter; they are looking for* ROMEO. *Because he wishes to remain near* JULIET *and because he prefers to be alone,* ROMEO *avoids his friends and climbs the wall into* CAPULET*'s orchard*.]

BENVOLIO. Romeo! My cousin Romeo! Romeo!

MERCUTIO. He is wise
And, on my life, hath stol'n him home to bed.

BENVOLIO. He ran this way and leapt this orchard wall.
Call, good Mercutio.

MERCUTIO. Nay, I'll conjure° too.
Romeo! Humors! Madman! Passion! Lover!
Appear thou in the likeness of a sigh;
Speak but one rhyme, and I am satisfied!
Cry but "Ay me!" pronounce but "love" and "dove."
Speak to my gossip Venus one fair word,
One nickname for her purblind° son and heir,

2 **dull earth:** Romeo's body. **center:** heart (that is, Juliet).

6 **conjure** (kon′ jər): summon a spirit. (In the conjuring that follows, Mercutio mocks Romeo's lovesickness.)

12 **purblind:** completely blind.

Young Abraham Cupid, he that shot so trim
When King Cophetua lov'd the beggar-maid!°
He heareth not, he stirreth not, he moveth not;
The ape is dead,° and I must conjure him.
I conjure thee by Rosaline's bright eyes,
By her high forehead and her scarlet lip,
By her fine foot, straight leg, and quivering thigh,
And the demesnes° that there adjacent lie,
That in thy likeness thou appear to us!

BENVOLIO. And if he hear thee, thou wilt anger him.

MERCUTIO. This cannot anger him; 'twould anger him
To raise a spirit in his mistress' circle,
Of some strange nature, letting it there stand
Till she had laid it and conjur'd it down.°
That were° some spite. My invocation
Is fair and honest:° in his mistress' name,
I conjure only but to raise up him.

BENVOLIO. Come, he hath hid himself among these trees
To be consorted with° the humorous° night.
Blind is his love and best befits the dark.

MERCUTIO. If love be blind, love cannot hit the mark.
Now will he sit under a medlar tree,
And wish his mistress were that kind of fruit
As maids call medlars, when they laugh alone.
O, Romeo, that she were, O that she were
An open-arse, thou a pop'rin pear!
Romeo, good night. I'll to my truckle bed;°
This field bed° is too cold for me to sleep.
Come, shall we go?

BENVOLIO. Go then, for 'tis in vain
To seek him here that means not to be found.

[*They exit.*]

13–14 Young . . . beggar-maid: Mercutio refers to an old ballad about a king who falls in love with a beggar maid after being wounded by Cupid's arrow.

16 The ape is dead: Romeo is playing dead, like a trained ape.

20 demesnes (di mānz′): regions.

23–26 This . . . down: Mercutio says that his conjuring would anger Romeo only if it led to someone else sleeping with Rosaline.

27 were: would be.

28 honest: honorable.

31 consorted with: in the company of. **humorous:** damp.

39 truckle bed: a small rollaway bed for a child or servant.

40 field bed: portable bed used by soldiers during a campaign.

SCENE 2. Immediately following the previous scene. CAPULET's orchard.

[*ROMEO, alone, comments on MERCUTIO's joking.*]

ROMEO. He jests at scars that never felt a wound.

[*JULIET enters at a window above and stands on a balcony. She does not know that ROMEO is nearby.*]

But soft!° What light through yonder window breaks?
It is the East, and Juliet is the sun!

2 soft: wait!

Arise, fair sun, and kill the envious moon,
Who is already sick and pale with grief
That thou her maid art far more fair than she.
Be not her maid, since she is envious.
Her vestal livery is but sick and green,
And none but fools do wear it. Cast it off.°
It is my lady! O, it is my love!
O, that she knew she were!
She speaks, yet she says nothing. What of that?
Her eye discourses; I will answer it.
I am too bold; 'tis not to me she speaks.
Two of the fairest stars in all the heaven,
Having some business, do entreat her eyes
To twinkle in their spheres till they return.
What if her eyes were there, they in her head?
The brightness of her cheek would shame those stars
As daylight doth a lamp; her eyes in heaven
Would through the airy region stream so bright°
That birds would sing and think it were not night.
See how she leans her cheek upon her hand!
O, that I were a glove upon that hand,
That I might touch that cheek!

JULIET. Ay me!

ROMEO. [*Aside.*] She speaks.
O, speak again, bright angel, for thou art
As glorious to this night, being o'er my head,
As is a winged messenger of heaven
Unto the white-upturned wond'ring eyes
Of mortals that fall back to gaze on him
When he bestrides the lazy puffing clouds
And sails upon the bosom of the air.

JULIET. O Romeo, Romeo! Wherefore art thou Romeo?°
Deny thy father and refuse thy name;
Or, if thou wilt not, be but sworn my love,
And I'll no longer be a Capulet.

ROMEO. [*Aside.*] Shall I hear more, or shall I speak at this?

JULIET. 'Tis but thy name that is my enemy.
Thou art thyself, though not° a Montague.
What's Montague? It is nor hand, nor foot,°
Nor arm, nor face, nor any other part
Belonging to a man. O, be some other name!
What's in a name? That which we call a rose

4–9 **Arise . . . off:** The moon is associated with Diana, Roman goddess of chastity. Romeo urges Juliet to cast off the virginal uniform **(vestal livery)** she wears as one of the moon's maids, since the moon is envious of her beauty.

21 **stream so bright:** shine so brightly.

33 **Wherefore . . . Romeo:** Why are you Romeo (a Montague)?

39 **though not:** even if you were not.

40 **nor hand, nor foot:** neither hand nor foot.

By any other word would smell as sweet.
So Romeo would, were he not Romeo call'd,
Retain that dear perfection which he owes°
Without that title. Romeo, doff° thy name;
And for thy name, which is no part of thee,
Take all myself.

[ROMEO *speaks aloud so that* JULIET *can hear him for the first time*.]

ROMEO. I take thee at thy word.
Call me but love, and I'll be new baptiz'd;°
Henceforth I never will be Romeo.

46 **owes:** owns.

47 **doff:** remove.

50 **Call . . . baptiz'd:** Romeo says that if she only calls him her love, he will take ***love*** for his new name (as infants are given their Christian names when they are baptized).

The Soul of the Rose, 1908. John William Waterhouse. Oil on canvas, 33¼ x 22½ in. Private collection.

Viewing the painting: What does the action of the woman in the painting suggest about her mood? In what way might her mood resemble that of Juliet in this scene?

JULIET. What man art thou, that, thus bescreen'd° in night,
So stumblest on my counsel?°

ROMEO. By a name
I know not how to tell thee who I am.
My name, dear saint, is hateful to myself
Because it is an enemy to thee.
Had I it written, I would tear the word.

JULIET. My ears have yet not drunk a hundred words
Of thy tongue's uttering, yet I know the sound.
Art thou not Romeo, and a Montague?

ROMEO. Neither, fair maid, if either thee dislike.

JULIET. How camest thou hither, tell me, and wherefore?
The orchard walls are high and hard to climb,
And the place death, considering who thou art,
If any of my kinsmen find thee here.

ROMEO. With love's light wings did I o'erperch° these walls;
For stony limits cannot hold love out,
And what love can do, that dares love attempt.
Therefore thy kinsmen are no stop° to me.

JULIET. If they do see thee, they will murder thee.

ROMEO. Alack, there lies more peril in thine eye
Than twenty of their swords! Look thou but sweet,
And I am proof against° their enmity.

JULIET. I would not for the world they saw thee here.

ROMEO. I have night's cloak to hide me from their eyes;
And but° thou love me, let them find me here.
My life were better ended by their hate
Than death prorogued,° wanting of° thy love.

JULIET. By whose direction foundst thou out this place?

ROMEO. By love, that first did prompt me to inquire.
He lent me counsel,° and I lent him eyes.
I am no pilot; yet, wert thou as far
As that vast shore wash'd with the farthest sea,
I should adventure° for such merchandise.

JULIET. Thou knowest the mask of night is on my face;
Else would a maiden blush bepaint my cheek
For that which thou hast heard me speak tonight.
Fain would I dwell on form°—fain, fain deny
What I have spoke; but farewell compliment!°

52 **bescreen'd:** hidden.

53 **counsel:** secret thoughts.

66 **o'erperch:** fly over.

69 **stop:** obstacle.

73 **proof against:** protected from.

76 **but:** unless.

78 **prorogued** (prō rōgd'): postponed. **wanting of:** lacking.

81 **counsel:** advice.

84 **adventure:** risk a journey.

88 **Fain . . . form:** Gladly would I show concern for decorum.

89 **compliment:** formal manners.

Dost thou love me? I know thou wilt say "Ay";
And I will take thy word. Yet, if thou swear'st,
Thou mayst prove false. At lovers' perjuries,
They say Jove° laughs. O gentle Romeo,
If thou dost love, pronounce it faithfully.
Or if thou thinkest I am too quickly won,
I'll frown and be perverse and say thee nay,
So thou wilt woo;° but else,° not for the world.
In truth, fair Montague, I am too fond,°
And therefore thou mayst think my behavior light;°
But trust me, gentleman, I'll prove more true
Than those that have more coying to be strange.°
I should have been more strange, I must confess,
But that thou overheard'st, ere I was ware,°
My truelove passion. Therefore pardon me,
And not impute this yielding° to light love,
Which the dark night hath so discovered.°

ROMEO. Lady, by yonder blessed moon I vow,
That tips with silver all these fruit-tree tops—

JULIET. O, swear not by the moon, th' inconstant moon,
That monthly changes in her circle orb,
Lest that thy love prove likewise variable.

ROMEO. What shall I swear by?

JULIET. Do not swear at all;
Or if thou wilt, swear by thy gracious self,
Which is the god of my idolatry,°
And I'll believe thee.

ROMEO. If my heart's dear love—

JULIET. Well, do not swear. Although I joy in thee,
I have no joy of this contract° tonight.
It is too rash, too unadvis'd, too sudden;
Too like the lightning, which doth cease to be
Ere one can say it lightens. Sweet, good night!
This bud of love, by summer's ripening breath,
May prove a beauteous flow'r when next we meet.
Good night, good night! As sweet repose and rest
Come to thy heart as that within my breast!

ROMEO. O, wilt thou leave me so unsatisfied?

JULIET. What satisfaction canst thou have tonight?

ROMEO. Th' exchange of thy love's faithful vow for mine.

93 **Jove:** the most powerful god in Roman mythology.

97 **So thou wilt woo:** so you will have to woo me. **else:** otherwise.

98 **fond:** loving, infatuated.

99 **light:** frivolous, unmaidenly.

101 **coying to be strange:** ability to appear distant.

103 **ere I was ware:** before I was aware (of your presence).

105 **not impute this yielding:** do not attribute this giving in so easily.

106 **discovered:** revealed.

114 **idolatry** (ī dol′ ə trē): blind devotion.

117 **contract:** exchange of vows.

JULIET. I gave thee mine before thou didst request it;
And yet I would it were to give again.°

ROMEO. Wouldst thou withdraw it? For what purpose, love?

JULIET. But to be frank° and give it thee again.
And yet I wish but for the thing I have.
My bounty is as boundless as the sea,
My love as deep; the more I give to thee,
The more I have, for both are infinite. [*The* NURSE *calls from within the house.*]
I hear some noise within. Dear love, adieu!
Anon,° good nurse! Sweet Montague, be true.
Stay but a little, I will come again.

[*JULIET goes into the house.*]

ROMEO. O blessed, blessed night! I am afeard,
Being in night, all this is but a dream,
Too flattering-sweet to be substantial.°

[*JULIET reappears on the balcony.*]

JULIET. Three words, dear Romeo, and good night indeed.
If that thy bent° of love be honorable,
Thy purpose marriage, send me word tomorrow,
By one that I'll procure° to come to thee,
Where and what time thou wilt perform the rite;°
And all my fortunes at thy foot I'll lay
And follow thee my lord throughout the world.

NURSE. [*She calls from within the house.*] Madam!

JULIET. [*To the* NURSE.] I come anon. [*To* ROMEO.]—But if thou meanest not well,
I do beseech° thee—

NURSE. [*From within again.*] Madam!

JULIET. [*To the* NURSE.] By and by° I come.—
[*To* ROMEO.] To cease thy strife° and leave me to my grief.
Tomorrow will I send.

ROMEO. So thrive my soul—

JULIET. A thousand times good night!

[*JULIET goes into the house.*]

ROMEO. A thousand times the worse, to want° thy light!
Love goes toward love as schoolboys from their books;
But love from love, toward school with heavy looks.

[*JULIET returns to the balcony.*]

129 **I would . . . again:** I wish I had it back.

131 **frank:** generous.

137 **Anon:** right away.

141 **substantial:** real.

143 **bent:** intention.

145 **procure** (prə kyoor′): obtain.

146 **rite:** marriage ceremony.

151 **beseech** (bi sēch′): beg. **By and by:** in a moment.

152 **strife:** efforts.

155 **want:** be deprived of.

JULIET. Hist! Romeo, hist! O for a falc'ner's voice To lure this tassel gentle back again!° Bondage is hoarse and may not speak aloud.° Else would I tear the cave where Echo° lies And make her airy tongue more hoarse than mine With repetition of my Romeo's name. Romeo!

ROMEO. It is my soul that calls upon my name. How silver-sweet sound lovers' tongues by night, Like softest music to attending ears!

JULIET. Romeo!

ROMEO.

My niesse?°

IULIET.

160

165

170

175

180

185

What o'clock tomorrow

Shall I send to thee?

ROMEO.

By the hour of nine.

JULIET. I will not fail. 'Tis twenty year till then. I have forgot why I did call thee back.

ROMEO. Let me stand here till thou remember it.

JULIET. I shall forget, to have thee still stand there, Rememb'ring how I love thy company.

ROMEO. And I'll still stay, to have thee still forget, Forgetting any other home but this.

JULIET. 'Tis almost morning. I would have thee gone— And yet no farther than a wanton's bird. That lets it hop a little from his hand. Like a poor prisoner in his twisted gyves.° And with a silken thread plucks it back again, So loving-jealous of his liberty.

ROMEO. I would I were thy bird.

IULIET. Sweet, so would I. Yet I should kill thee with much cherishing. Good night, good night! Parting is such sweet sorrow That I shall say good night till it be morrow.

[JULIET goes into the house.]

ROMEO. Sleep dwell upon thine eyes, peace in thy breast! Would I were sleep and peace, so sweet to rest! Hence will I to my ghostly sire's close cell. His help to crave and my dear hap to tell.

[ROMEO exits to find the FRIAR.]

158–159 Hist! . . . again: Juliet refers to the special call that a falcon master (falc'ner) uses to lure back a male falcon (tassel gentle).

160 Bondage . . . aloud: Juliet compares being under her family's control to hoarseness, since it prevents her from speaking loudly.

161 Echo: a wood nymph in classical mythology. After being rejected in love, she retired to a cave and wasted away until only her voice was left.

167 niesse (nē es'): a young hawk ready to leave the nest.

177 wanton's: spoiled child's.

179 gyves (jīvz): shackles.

188 ghostly sire's: spiritual advisor's. close cell: small private room. 189 hap: good fortune.

SCENE 3. Early the next morning. FRIAR LAWRENCE's cell.

[*FRIAR LAWRENCE, ROMEO's spiritual advisor, enters alone carrying a basket full of herbs.*]

FRIAR. The gray-ey'd morn smiles on the frowning night,
Check'ring the eastern clouds with streaks of light;
And flecked° darkness like a drunkard reels
From forth day's path and Titan's fiery wheels.°
Now, ere the sun advance his burning eye
The day to cheer and night's dank dew to dry,
I must upfill this osier cage° of ours
With baleful° weeds and precious-juiced flowers.
The earth that's nature's mother is her tomb;
What is her burying grave, that is her womb;
And from her womb children of divers° kind
We sucking on her natural bosom find:
Many for many virtues° excellent,
None but for some,° and yet all different.
O, mickle° is the powerful grace° that lies
In plants, herbs, stones, and their true qualities;
For naught° so vile that on the earth doth live
But to the earth some special good doth give;
Nor aught so good but, strained from that fair use,°
Revolts from true birth, stumbling on abuse.°
Virtue itself turns vice, being misapplied,
And vice sometime by action dignified.

[*ROMEO enters. The FRIAR does not see him and continues speaking until ROMEO interrupts him.*]

Within the infant rind° of this weak flower
Poison hath residence and medicine power;°
For this, being smelt, with that part cheers each part;
Being tasted, stays all senses with the heart.°
Two such opposed kings encamp them still
In man as well as herbs—grace and rude will;°
And where the worser is predominant,
Full soon the canker° death eats up that plant.

ROMEO. Good morrow, father.

FRIAR. *Benedicite!*°
What early tongue so sweet saluteth me?
Young son, it argues a distempered head°
So soon to bid good morrow to thy bed.
Care keeps his watch in every old man's eye,
And where care lodges, sleep will never lie;

3 **flecked:** spotted.

4 **From . . . wheels:** out of the path of the sun god (who was said to drive a fiery chariot across the sky).

7 **upfill this osier cage:** fill up this willow basket.

8 **baleful:** harmful.

11 **divers** (dī′ vərz): varied.

13 **virtues:** healing properties.

14 **None but for some:** None that isn't good for some use.

15 **mickle:** great. **grace:** divine goodness.

17 **naught** (nôt): there is nothing.

19 **strained from that fair use:** diverted from its proper use.

20 **Revolts . . . abuse:** rebels against its natural state and becomes harmful.

23 **infant rind:** tender skin.

24 **Poison . . . power:** there dwells poison and medicinal power.

25–26 **For this . . . heart:** When the flower is smelled, it stimulates every part of the body, but when tasted it causes the heart to stop beating.

27–28 **Two such . . . will:** Two such opposing qualities are always present in man as well as in herbs–goodness and a tendency toward violence.

30 **canker:** cankerworm, a larva that feeds on buds.

31 ***Benedicite*** (ben′ ə dis′ ə tē): God bless you!

33 **argues a distempered head:** suggests a disturbed mind.

But where unbruised youth with unstuff'd brain
Doth couch° his limbs, there golden sleep doth reign.
Therefore thy earliness doth me assure
Thou art uprous'd with some distemp'rature;°
Or if not so, then here I hit it right—
Our Romeo hath not been in bed tonight.

ROMEO. That last is true. The sweeter rest was mine.

FRIAR. God pardon sin! Wast thou with Rosaline?

ROMEO. With Rosaline, my ghostly father? No.
I have forgot that name and that name's woe.

FRIAR. That's my good son! But where hast thou been then?

ROMEO. I'll tell thee ere thou ask it me again.
I have been feasting with mine enemy,
Where on a sudden one hath wounded° me
That's by me wounded. Both our remedies
Within thy help and holy physic° lies.
I bear no hatred, blessed man, for, lo,
My intercession° likewise steads° my foe.

FRIAR. Be plain, good son, and homely in thy drift.
Riddling confession finds but riddling shrift.°

38 **couch:** lay down.

40 **uprous'd . . . distemp'rature:** awakened by some emotional or mental disturbance.

50 **wounded:** That is, wounded with Cupid's arrow.

52 **physic:** medicine; healing power.

54 **intercession:** petition. **steads:** benefits.

55–56 **Be plain . . . shrift:** Speak plainly and directly. A confusing confession only leads to confusing forgiveness.

Studies of the Heads of Two Men, 1517. Raphael (Raffaello Sanzio). Chalk on gray paper. Ashmolean Museum, Oxford, England.

Viewing the drawing: What attitudes and emotions are conveyed by the facial expressions and hand gestures of these men? What parallels can you draw between these men and Romeo and the Friar?

ROMEO. Then plainly know my heart's dear love is set
On the fair daughter of rich Capulet;
As mine on hers, so hers is set on mine,
And all combin'd,° save what thou must combine
By holy marriage. When and where and how
We met, we wooed, and made exchange of vow,
I'll tell thee as we pass; but this I pray,
That thou consent to marry us today.

FRIAR. Holy Saint Francis! What a change is here!
Is Rosaline, that thou didst love so dear,
So soon forsaken? Young men's love then lies
Not truly in their hearts, but in their eyes.
Jesu Maria! What a deal of brine°
Hath washed thy sallow° cheeks for Rosaline!
How much salt water thrown away in waste
To season love, that of it doth not taste!
The sun not yet thy sighs from heaven clears,
Thy old groans yet ringing in mine ancient ears.
Lo, here upon thy cheek the stain doth sit
Of an old tear that is not wash'd off yet.
If e'er thou wast thyself, and these woes thine,
Thou and these woes were all for Rosaline.
And art thou chang'd? Pronounce this sentence° then:
Women may fall when there's no strength in men.°

ROMEO. Thou chidst° me oft for loving Rosaline.

FRIAR. For doting, not for loving, pupil mine.

ROMEO. And badst me° bury love.

FRIAR. Not in a grave
To lay one in, another out to have.

ROMEO. I pray thee chide me not. Her I love now
Doth grace for grace and love for love allow.°
The other did not so.

FRIAR. O, she knew well
Thy love did read by rote, that could not spell.°
But come, young waverer, come go with me.
In one respect I'll thy assistant be;
For this alliance may so happy prove
To turn your households' rancor to pure love.

ROMEO. O, let us hence! I stand° on sudden haste.

FRIAR. Wisely and slow. They stumble that run fast.

[*They exit.*]

60 **all combin'd:** We are completely united.

69 **brine:** salt water (tears).

70 **sallow:** sickly yellow.

79 **sentence:** saying; general truth.

80 **Women . . . men:** Women can be expected to be unfaithful when men are so fickle.

81 **chidst** (chīdst): scolded.

83 **badst** (bādst) **me:** urged me to.

85–86 **Her I love . . . allow:** I love her because she gives back or exchanges favor for favor and love for love.

88 **read . . . spell:** read by memorizing words, without understanding their meaning.

93 **stand:** insist.

SCENE 4. Approximately nine o'clock in the morning, the time at which JULIET was to send a messenger to ROMEO. A street in Verona.

[*BENVOLIO and MERCUTIO enter; they are still concerned about ROMEO's disappearance the night before.*]

MERCUTIO. Where the devil should this Romeo be?
Came he not home tonight?

BENVOLIO. Not to his father's. I spoke with his man.

MERCUTIO. Why, that same pale hardhearted wench, that Rosaline,
Torments him so that he will sure run mad.

BENVOLIO. Tybalt, the kinsman to old Capulet,
Hath sent a letter to his father's house.

MERCUTIO. A challenge, on my life.

BENVOLIO. Romeo will answer it.°

MERCUTIO. Any man that can write may answer a letter.

BENVOLIO. Nay, he will answer the letter's master, how he dares, being dared.

MERCUTIO. Alas, poor Romeo, he is already dead: stabbed with a white wench's black eye; run through the ear with a love song; the very pin° of his heart cleft with the blind bow-boy's butt-shaft;° and is he a man to encounter Tybalt?

BENVOLIO. Why, what is Tybalt?

MERCUTIO. More than Prince of Cats.° O, he's the courageous captain of compliments.° He fights as you sing prick-song,° keeps time, distance, and proportion;° he rests his minim rests,° one, two, and the third in your bosom: the very butcher of a silk button, a duelist, a duelist! A gentleman of the very first house,° of the first and second cause.° Ah, the immortal *passado!*° The *punto reverso!*° The *hay!*°

BENVOLIO. The what?

MERCUTIO. The pox of such antic, lisping, affecting phantasimes, these new tuners of accent! "By Jesu, a very good blade! a very tall man! a very good whore!" Why, is not this a lamentable thing, grand-sire, that we should be thus afflicted with these strange flies, these fashion-mongers, these pardon-me's who stand so much on the new form, that they cannot sit at ease on the old bench? O, their bones, their bones!°

[*ROMEO enters. He seems much happier than he was at the beginning of the play.*]

10 **answer it:** accept the challenge to a duel.

16 **pin:** peg in the center of an archery target.

16–17 **blind . . . shaft:** Cupid's blunt practice arrow.

19 **Prince of Cats:** a pun on Tybalt's name. In a popular fable, the Prince of Cats was called Tybert.

20 **captain of compliments:** master of all the formal rules of dueling. **prick-song:** from printed music (as opposed to the less accurate singing from memory).

21 **proportion:** rhythm.

21–22 **minim rests:** shortest possible musical pauses.

23–24 **very first house:** best fencing school.

24 **cause:** excuse for challenging a man to a duel.

25 ***passado*** (pə sä′ dō): forward sword thrust. ***punto reverso*** (poon′ tō rə ver′ sō): back-handed thrust. ***hay:*** a fencing term signaling a hit.

27–33 **The pox . . . bones:** Mercutio mimics an old traditionalist complaining about the younger fencers who use new-fangled and foreign terminology.

BENVOLIO. Here comes Romeo! Here comes Romeo!

MERCUTIO. Without his roe,° like a dried herring: O flesh, flesh, how art thou fishified! Now is he for the numbers° that Petrarch° flow'd in. Laura° to his lady was a kitchen wench (marry, she had a better love to berhyme her), Dido a dowdy, Cleopatra a gipsy, Helen and Hero hildings and harlots, Thisby a gray eye or so, but not to the purpose.° Signior Romeo, *bonjour!* there's a French salutation to your French slop!° You gave us the counterfeit° fairly last night.

ROMEO. Good morrow to you both. What counterfeit did I give you?

MERCUTIO. The slip, sir, the slip. Can you not conceive?°

ROMEO. Pardon, good Mercutio. My business was great, and in such a case as mine a man may strain courtesy.

MERCUTIO. That's as much as to say, such a case as yours constrains a man to bow in the hams.

ROMEO. Meaning to cur'sy.°

MERCUTIO. Thou hast most kindly hit it.°

ROMEO. A most courteous exposition.

MERCUTIO. Nay, I am the very pink° of courtesy.

ROMEO. Pink for flower.

MERCUTIO. Right.

ROMEO. Why then is my pump° well flower'd.°

MERCUTIO. Sure wit! Follow me this jest now, till thou hast worn out thy pump, that when the single sole of it is worn, the jest may remain, after the wearing, soly singular.

ROMEO. O single-sol'd jest, soly singular for the singleness!°

MERCUTIO. Come between us, good Benvolio, my wits faints.

ROMEO. Swits and spurs,° swits and spurs, or I'll cry a match.°

MERCUTIO. Nay, if our wits run the wild-goose chase,° I am done; for thou hast more of the wild goose° in one of thy wits than, I am sure, I have in my whole five. Was I with you° there for the goose?°

ROMEO. Thou wast never with me for any thing when thou wast not there for the goose.

MERCUTIO. I will bite thee by the ear for that jest.

ROMEO. Nay, good goose, bite not.

35 **roe:** fish eggs. Mercutio makes a pun on Romeo's name (without "Ro" he is all sighs—"meo" or "oh me!").

36 **numbers:** verses; poems.

37 **Petrarch** (pē′ trärk): an influential Italian poet who composed love sonnets to his chaste love, **Laura.**

37–40 **Laura . . . purpose:** Mercutio refers to famous women from classical mythology and ancient history. He suggests these women are good-for-nothings **(hildings)** and not worth mentioning **(to the purpose)** in Romeo's eyes.

41–42 **French slop:** loose breeches, or pants. **counterfeit:** A counterfeit coin was called a *slip,* a word that also means "escape."

45 **conceive:** understand (my pun).

50 **cur'sy:** curtsy, a slight lowering of the body with bending of the knees, usually done by women.

51 **most kindly hit it:** put it most graciously.

53 **pink:** perfection.

54–56 **Pink . . . flower'd:** Romeo plays on two other meanings of *pink:* "flower" and "decorative perforations," which might be found on a shoe **(pump).**

57–60 **Sure . . . singleness:** Mercutio and Romeo play on the words **sole** ("solitary" or "bottom of a shoe"), **soly** ("only" or "uniquely"), **single-sol'd** ("shoddy"), **singular** ("unique"), and **singleness** ("silliness").

62 **Swits and spurs:** spur on your horse (keep going). **cry a match:** claim victory.

63 **wild-goose chase:** a game of "follow the leader" on horseback.

64 **goose:** fool.

66 **with you:** even with you. **for the goose:** to chase women.

MERCUTIO. Thy wit is a very bitter sweeting, it is a most sharp sauce.

ROMEO. And is it not then well serv'd in to a sweet goose?°

MERCUTIO. O, here's a wit of cheverel,° that stretches from an inch narrow to an ell° broad!

ROMEO. I stretch it out for that word "broad,"° which, added to the goose, proves thee far and wide a broad goose.

MERCUTIO. Why, is not this better now than groaning for love? Now art thou sociable, now art thou Romeo; now art thou what thou art, by art as well as by nature, for this drivelling love is like a great natural that runs lolling up and down to hide his bable in a hole.°

BENVOLIO. Stop there, stop there.

MERCUTIO. Thou desirest me to stop in my tale against the hair.

BENVOLIO. Thou wouldst else have made thy tale large.

MERCUTIO. O, thou art deceiv'd; I would have made it short, for I was come to the whole depth of my tale and meant indeed to occupy the argument no longer.

ROMEO. Here's goodly gear!°

[*The* NURSE *enters with* PETER, *a servant.*]

A sail,° a sail!

MERCUTIO. Two, two! A shirt and a smock.°

NURSE. Peter!

PETER. Anon.

NURSE. My fan, Peter.

MERCUTIO. Good Peter, to hide her face; for her fan's the fairer face.

NURSE. God ye° good morrow, gentlemen.

MERCUTIO. God ye good den,° fair gentlewoman.

NURSE. Is it good den?

MERCUTIO. 'Tis no less, I tell ye, for the bawdy hand of the dial is now upon the prick° of noon.

NURSE. Out upon you, what a man are you?

ROMEO. One, gentlewoman, that God hath made, himself to mar.°

NURSE. By my troth, it is well said; "for himself to mar," quoth 'a! Gentlemen, can any of you tell me where I may find the young Romeo?

73 **is it not . . . goose:** doesn't my wit (a sharp sauce) go well with you (its sweet victim).

74 **cheverel** (shev′ ər el′): kid leather (which stretches easily).

75 **ell:** forty-five inches.

76 **broad:** "obvious" or "indecent."

79–82 **Now art . . . hole:** Mercutio compares love to a drooling idiot **(natural)** running around with his fool's wand **(bable),** a stick with an inflated bladder, or balloon, on one end.

89 **goodly gear:** fine stuff (an inappropriate reference to the Nurse's appearance or outfit that is meant to be funny).

90 **A sail:** an expression used when a sailor sees another ship.

91 **A shirt and a smock:** a man and a woman.

97 **God ye:** God give you.

98 **good den:** good afternoon.

101 **prick:** mark on a clock.

102–104 **Out upon. . . mar:** The Nurse indignantly asks Mercutio what sort of a man he is. Romeo responds that Mercutio was made in God's image but marred by himself.

ROMEO. I can tell you; but young Romeo will be older when you have found him than he was when you sought him. I am the youngest of that name, for fault of a worse.°

NURSE. You say well.

MERCUTIO. Yea, is the worst well? Very well took, i' faith! Wisely, wisely.

NURSE. If you be he, sir, I desire some confidence with you.

BENVOLIO. She will indite him to some supper.°

MERCUTIO. A bawd, a bawd, a bawd! So ho!°

ROMEO. What hast thou found?

MERCUTIO. No hare, sir, unless a hare, sir, in a lenten pie, that is something stale and hoar° ere it be spent.°
[*MERCUTIO walks by them and sings.*]

An old hare hoar,
And an old hare hoar,
Is very good meat in Lent;
But a hare that is hoar
Is too much for a score,
When it hoars ere it be spent

Romeo, will you come to your father's? We'll to dinner thither.

ROMEO. I will follow you.

MERCUTIO. Farewell, ancient lady. Farewell. [*Singing.*] "lady, lady, lady."

[*BENVOLIO and MERCUTIO exit.*]

NURSE. I pray you, sir, what saucy merchant° was this that was so full of his ropery?°

ROMEO. A gentleman, nurse, that loves to hear himself talk and will speak more in a minute than he will stand to° in a month.

NURSE. And 'a° speak anything against me, I'll take him down, and 'a were lustier than he is, and twenty such Jacks; and if I cannot, I'll find those that shall. Scurvy knave, I am none of his flirt-gills,° I am none of his skains-mates.° [*She turns to PETER, her man.*] And thou must stand by too and suffer every knave to use me at his pleasure!

PETER. I saw no man use you at his pleasure; if I had, my weapon should quickly have been out. I warrant you, I dare draw as soon as another man, if I see occasion in a good quarrel, and the law on my side.

110 **fault of a worse:** Romeo plays on the expression "for want of a better." **fault:** lack.

114–115 **If you . . . supper:** Benvolio deliberately misuses **indite** to mean "invite" as a way of mocking the Nurse's use of **confidence** to mean "private conversation."

116 **So ho:** The cry a hunter makes upon spotting prey.

118–119 **No hare . . . spent:** Mercutio compares the Nurse to meat hidden in a pie for Lent (when it is forbidden to eat meat) and kept long after it has become stale and moldy.

119 **hoar:** gray or white from age.

131 **saucy merchant:** rude fellow.

132 **ropery:** lewd jesting.

134 **stand to:** carry out.

135 **And 'a:** if he.

138 **flirt-gills:** loose women. **skains-mates:** cutthroats' companions.

A Capriccio with Figures Conversing Under an Archway, a Courtyard Beyond. Francesco Guardi (1712–1793). Oil on canvas, 24.2 x 17.7 cm. Private collection.

Viewing the painting: How does the scene depicted in this painting resemble your impression of the setting of act 2, scene 4?

NURSE. Now, afore God, I am so vex'd that every part about me quivers. Scurvy Knave! Pray you, sir, a word; and, as I told you, my young lady bid me inquire you out. What she bid me say, I will keep to myself; but first let me tell ye, if ye should lead her in a fool's paradise, as they say, it were a very gross kind of behavior, as they say; for the gentlewoman is young; and therefore, if you should deal double with her, truly it were an ill thing to be off'red to any gentlewoman, and very weak° dealing.

ROMEO. Nurse, commend me° to thy lady and mistress. I protest° unto thee—

NURSE. Good heart, and i' faith I will tell her as much. Lord, Lord, she will be a joyful woman.

ROMEO. What wilt thou tell her, nurse? Thou dost not mark° me.

153 **weak:** contemptible.

154 **commend me:** send my regards.

155 **protest:** swear.

159 **mark:** pay attention to.

NURSE. I will tell her, sir, that you do protest, which, as I take it, is a gentlemanlike offer.

ROMEO. Bid her devise
Some means to come to shrift° this afternoon;
And there she shall at Friar Lawrence' cell
Be shriv'd° and married. Here is for thy pains.

[*He puts money into her hand.*]

NURSE. No, truly, sir; not a penny.

ROMEO. Go to! I say you shall.

NURSE. This afternoon, sir? Well, she shall be there.

ROMEO. And stay, good nurse, behind the abbey wall.
Within this hour my man shall be with thee
And bring thee cords made like a tackled stair,°
Which to the high topgallant° of my joy
Must be my convoy° in the secret night.
Farewell. Be trusty, and I'll quit thy pains.°
Farewell. Commend me to thy mistress.

NURSE. Now God in heaven bless thee! Hark you, sir.

ROMEO. What say'st thou, my dear nurse?

NURSE. Is your man secret? Did you ne'er hear say,
"Two may keep counsel, putting one away?"°

ROMEO. Warrant thee my man's as true as steel.

NURSE. Well, sir, my mistress is the sweetest lady. Lord, Lord! When 'twas a little prating° thing—O, there is a nobleman in town, one Paris, that would fain lay knife aboard;° but she, good soul, had as lieve° see a toad, a very toad, as see him. I anger her sometimes, and tell her that Paris is the properer man; but I'll warrant you, when I say so, she looks as pale as any clout in the versal world.° Doth not rosemary and Romeo begin both with a letter?°

ROMEO. Ay, nurse; what of that? Both with an *R*.

NURSE. Ah, mocker! That's the dog's name.° *R* is for the—No; I know it begins with some other letter; and she hath the prettiest sententious° of it, of you and rosemary, that it would do you good to hear it.

ROMEO. Commend me to thy lady.

NURSE. Ay, a thousand times. [*ROMEO exits.*] Peter!

PETER. Anon.

NURSE. Before, and apace.°

[*PETER exits, followed by the NURSE.*]

161 **shrift:** confession.

163 **shriv'd:** forgiven of her sins.

169 **tackled stair:** rope ladder.

170 **topgallant:** a platform atop a ship's mast.

171 **convoy:** means of conveyance.

172 **quit thy pains:** reward your trouble.

177 **Two . . . away:** A secret can't be kept by more than one person.

180 **prating:** chattering.

181 **lay knife aboard:** claim her for himself.

182 **had as lieve** (lēv): would as willingly.

185 **any clout in the versal world:** any cloth in the whole world.

186 **a letter:** the same letter.

188 **dog's name:** The letter *R* sounds like a dog's growl.

190 **sententious** (sen ten′ shəs): The Nurse means to say *sentences,* or "pithy sayings."

195 **Before, and apace:** Go before me, and hurry.

SCENE 5. Later that day. CAPULET's orchard.

[JULIET, waiting for the NURSE to return from the meeting with ROMEO, paces impatiently.]

JULIET. The clock struck nine when I did send the nurse;
In half an hour she promised to return.
Perchance she cannot meet him. That's not so.
O, she is lame! Love's heralds should be thoughts,
Which ten times faster glides than the sun's beams
Driving back shadows over low'ring° hills.
Therefore do nimble-pinion'd doves draw Love,°
And therefore hath the wind-swift Cupid wings.
Now is the sun upon the highmost hill
Of this day's journey, and from nine till twelve
Is three long hours; yet she is not come.
Had she affections and warm youthful blood,
She would be as swift in motion as a ball;
My words would bandy° her to my sweet love,
And his to me.
But old folks, many feign as they were dead—
Unwieldy, slow, heavy and pale as lead.

[The NURSE enters, with PETER.]

O God, she comes! O honey nurse, what news?
Hast thou met with him? Send thy man away.

NURSE. Peter, stay at the gate. *[PETER exits.]*

JULIET. Now, good sweet nurse—O Lord, why lookest thou sad?
Though news be sad, yet tell them merrily;
If good, thou shamest the music of sweet news
By playing it to me with so sour a face.

NURSE. I am aweary, give me leave° awhile.
Fie, how my bones ache! What a jaunce° have I!

JULIET. I would thou hadst my bones, and I thy news.
Nay, come, I pray thee speak. Good, good nurse, speak.

NURSE. Jesu, what haste! Can you not stay awhile?
Do you not see that I am out of breath?

JULIET. How art thou out of breath when thou hast breath
To say to me that thou art out of breath?
The excuse that thou dost make in this delay
Is longer than the tale thou dost excuse.
Is thy news good or bad? Answer to that.
Say either, and I'll stay the circumstance.°
Let me be satisfied, is't good or bad?

6 **low'ring:** dark, threatening.

7 **Therefore . . . Love:** Venus, the goddess of love, was often portrayed riding a chariot drawn by nimble-winged **(nimble-pinion'd)** doves.

14 **bandy:** toss back and forth.

25 **give me leave:** let me alone.

26 **jaunce** (jôns): rough walk.

36 **stay the circumstance:** wait for the details.

NURSE. Well, you have made a simple° choice; you know not how to choose a man. Romeo? No, not he. Though his face be better than any man's, yet his leg excels all men's; and for a hand and a foot, and a body, though they be not to be talk'd on,° yet they are past compare. He is not the flower of courtesy, but, I'll warrant him, as gentle as a lamb. Go thy ways,° wench; serve God. What, have you din'd at home?

JULIET. No, no. But all this did I know before.
What says he of our marriage? What of that?

NURSE. Lord, how my head aches! What a head have I!
It beats as it would fall in twenty pieces.
My back a t'other side—ah, my back, my back!
Beshrew° your heart for sending me about
To catch my death with jauncing up and down!

38 **simple:** foolish.

41–42 **not to be talk'd on:** not worth mentioning.

43–44 **Go thy ways:** off you go.

50 **Beshrew:** curse.

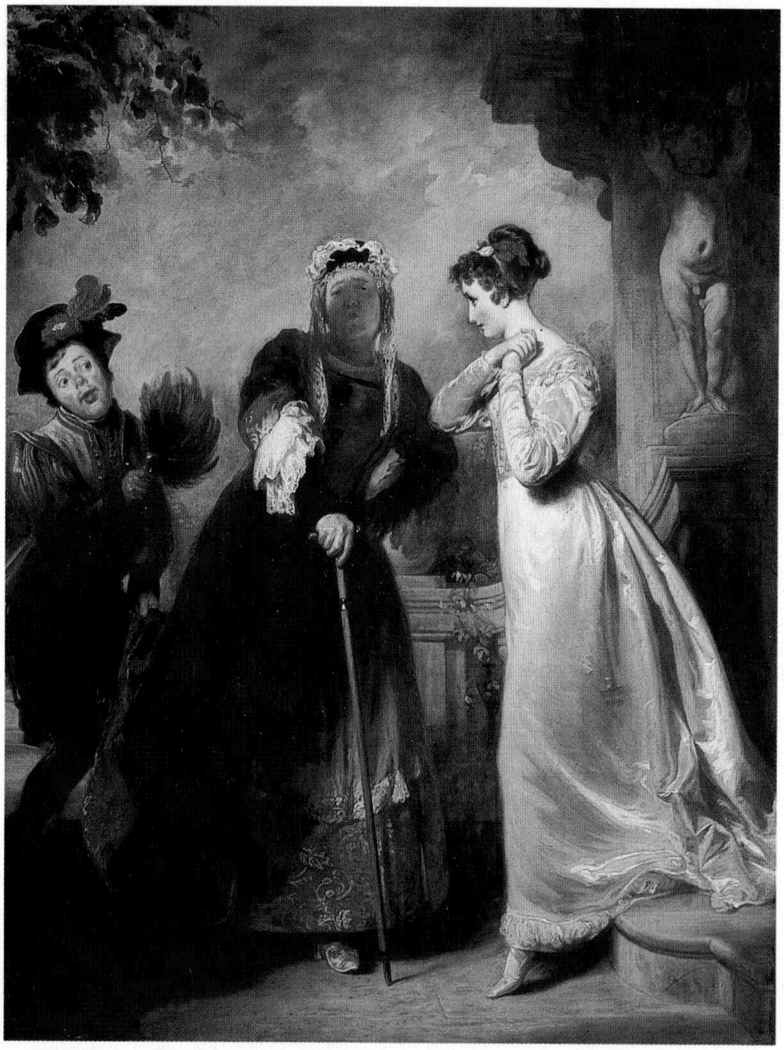

Juliet and the Nurse, exhibited 1827. Henry P. Briggs. Oil on canvas. Tate Gallery, London.

Viewing the painting: Which lines in this scene might the artist have had in mind in creating this painting?

JULIET. I'faith, I am sorry that thou art not well.
Sweet, sweet, sweet nurse, tell me, what says my love?

NURSE. Your love says, like an honest° gentleman,
And a courteous, and a kind, and a handsome,
And, I warrant, a virtuous— Where is your mother?

JULIET. Where is my mother? Why, she is within.
Where should she be? How oddly thou repliest!
"Your love says, like an honest gentleman,
'Where is your mother?'"

NURSE. O God's Lady dear!
Are you so hot?° Marry come up, I trow.°
Is this the poultice for my aching bones?
Henceforward do your messages yourself.

JULIET. Here's such a coil!° Come, what says Romeo?

NURSE. Have you got leave to go to shrift today?

JULIET. I have.

NURSE. Then hie you hence° to Friar Lawrence' cell;
There stays a husband to make you a wife.
Now comes the wanton° blood up in your cheeks:
They'll be in scarlet straight° at any news.
Hie you to church; I must another way,
To fetch a ladder, by the which your love
Must climb a bird's nest soon when it is dark.
I am the drudge, and toil in your delight;
But you shall bear the burthen soon at night.
Go; I'll to dinner; hie you to the cell.

JULIET. Hie to high fortune! Honest nurse, farewell.

[*They exit in separate directions.*]

54 **honest:** honorable.

61 **hot:** impatient. **Marry . . . trow:** Come on now, I declare.

64 **coil:** fuss.

67 **hie you hence:** hurry from here.

69 **wanton** (wont′ ən): unrestrained.

70 **They'll . . . straight:** They will turn red immediately.

SCENE 6. Later that afternoon. FRIAR LAWRENCE's cell.

[*ROMEO and FRIAR LAWRENCE are waiting for JULIET so that the wedding can take place.*]

FRIAR. So smile the heavens upon this holy act
That after hours with sorrow chide us not!°

ROMEO. Amen, amen! But come what sorrow can,
It cannot countervail the exchange of joy°
That one short minute gives me in her sight.
Do thou but close our hands with holy words,
Then love-devouring death do what he dare—
It is enough I may but call her mine.

2 **That after . . . not:** and not punish us for it later.

4 **countervail the exchange of joy:** outweigh the joy I receive.

FRIAR. These violent delights have violent ends
And, in their triumph die, like fire and powder,
Which, as they kiss, consume.° The sweetest honey
Is loathsome in his own deliciousness
And in the taste confounds the appetite.°
Therefore love moderately: long love doth so;
Too swift arrives as tardy as too slow.

[*JULIET enters.*]

Here comes the lady. O, so light a foot
Will ne'er wear out the everlasting flint.°
A lover may bestride the gossamers°
That idles in the wanton° summer air,
And yet not fall; so light is vanity.°

JULIET. Good even to my ghostly confessor.

FRIAR. Romeo shall thank thee, daughter, for us both.

JULIET. As much to° him, else is his thanks too much.

ROMEO. Ah, Juliet, if the measure of thy joy
Be heap'd like mine, and that thy skill be more
To blazon it,° then sweeten with thy breath
This neighbor air, and let rich music's tongue
Unfold the imagin'd happiness that both
Receive in either by this dear encounter.

JULIET. Conceit, more rich in matter than in words,
Brags of his substance, not of ornament.°
They are but beggars that can count their worth;
But my true love is grown to such excess
I cannot sum up sum of° half my wealth.

FRIAR. Come, come with me, and we will make short work;
For, by your leaves, you shall not stay alone
Till Holy Church incorporate two in one.

[*They exit to perform the wedding ceremony.*]

9–11 **These violent . . . consume:** Like lighted gunpowder, these extreme joys destroy themselves as they reach their high point.

12–13 **Is loathsome . . . appetite:** becomes cloying and destroys our appetite for it.

16–17 **Here . . . flint:** In observing Juliet's light footsteps, the Friar alludes to a saying that small drops of water can wear away stones.

18 **bestride the gossamers:** walk on the cobwebs.

19 **wanton:** Here, it means "playful."

20 **vanity:** the temporary pleasures of this world.

23 **As much to:** the same to.

25–26 **that thy . . . blazon it:** if you are better able to proclaim it.

30–31 **Conceit . . . ornament:** True understanding does not need to be elaborated in words.

34 **sum up sum of:** add up the total of.

Responding to Literature

Personal Response

Do you approve of Romeo and Juliet's quick actions? Why or why not?

Analyzing Act 2

Recall and Interpret

1. Why does Mercutio make fun of Romeo after they leave the party? Explain the **irony** in this incident. (See Literary Terms Handbook, page R7.)
2. How does Romeo find out that Juliet shares his feelings? What does Juliet seem most concerned about in the balcony scene?
3. Who has sent a challenge to Romeo and why? What is Mercutio's opinion of Romeo's challenger?
4. How do Romeo and Juliet carry out their plan to marry? Why do they want to act so quickly?

Evaluate and Connect

5. **Theme Connections** What do you think of Friar Lawrence's reaction to Romeo's declaration of love for Juliet? Do you think he acts responsibly by agreeing to marry them? Why or why not?
6. Who seems more mature to you, Romeo or Juliet? Why?
7. What is your opinion of the way Mercutio treats the Nurse? Have you ever witnessed a teenager making fun of an older person? Do you think the reason for the teasing was the same as Mercutio's? Explain.
8. Compare Friar Lawrence and the Nurse. How are their roles in the play similar?

Literary ELEMENTS

Pun

A **pun** is a humorous play on different meanings of a word or on words that sound alike but have different meanings. Shakespeare includes many puns in *Romeo and Juliet.* For example, when Benvolio says that Romeo will answer Tybalt's challenge in scene 4, Mercutio responds, "Any man that can write may answer a letter." His pun plays on two meanings of *answer:* "accept a challenge to duel" and "reply in writing."

1. Find a pun in act 2, scene 4 of *Romeo and Juliet* that plays on different meanings of a word.
2. Find a pun in act 1, scene 1 that plays on words that sound alike but have different meanings.

- See **Literary Terms Handbook,** p. R10.

Extending Your Response

Literature Groups

Passionate Poetry *Romeo and Juliet* is thought to contain some of the finest love poetry ever written. The dialogue in the balcony scene has been quoted and parodied in hundreds of literary works. Select your favorite lines and share them with your group. Then discuss why this poetry might be so memorable. Consider such literary elements as imagery and figurative language as well as the dramatic setting of the poetry.

Personal Writing

Love and Laughter How does the play's humor affect your feelings about Romeo and Juliet? Do the comical scenes make it difficult for you to take these young lovers seriously? Does the humor increase your interest in the love scenes? Describe your responses in your journal.

Save your work for your portfolio.

MEDIA connection

Comic Strip

Have you ever misquoted a song? What happens when the famous bard Shakespeare himself is misquoted?

Mutts

by Patrick McDonnell

Printed by permission. MUTTS ©1998 Patrick McDonnell. Distributed by King Features Syndicate. All rights reserved.

Analyzing Media

1. In what ways does the cartoonist parody Shakespeare's famous balcony scene? What other cartoon character can you imagine starring in a parody of this scene?
2. Do you find this comic strip humorous? Why or why not?

INTERDISCIPLINARY CONNECTION

THE ARTS

Music and Dance in the 1500s

When Romeo and his friends crash the Capulets' party, they find music, dancing, and the love of Romeo's life. If you were to crash a party during Shakespeare's time, what sights and sounds might you experience? You would probably recognize the sounds of some musical instruments, including the drum, the flute, and the harp. Other instruments might be less familiar to you. These include

- the lute, a stringed instrument that looks like a guitar with a pear-shaped body
- the viol, a stringed instrument that resembles a violin but has a more delicate tone
- the clavichord, a keyboard instrument that was a forerunner of the piano and was usually played solo
- the harpsichord, a keyboard instrument that sounds similar to a lute and was played both solo and in groups

At social events in the homes of the nobility, couples danced to the music of the lute, viol, and keyboard instruments. Typically, court dances of the period were grouped in pairs—the first dance being slow and stately, the second more lively. When a new fast dance called *la volta* was introduced from Italy, many lords and ladies of northern Europe were scandalized. This dance featured a leap into the air by the woman, assisted by her partner. Some people in polite society considered this jump highly improper for a lady. King Louis XIII of France banned the dance from his court. *La volta* became very popular in England, however, and even Queen Elizabeth I performed the dance.

Wealthy people weren't the only ones dancing, though. Dance numbers were also arranged for widespread use, and music of all sorts was so popular that even some barbershops made lutes available for customers to play.

Activity

Choose one popular musical instrument of the Renaissance and find out more about it by researching library sources and the Internet. Look for information on the instrument's distinctive features, how it is played, how it sounds, and whether it is played today. Then prepare a report of your findings. Be sure to cite your sources completely so that anyone who might be interested in more information can find it.

Act 3

SCENE 1. The same afternoon. A street in Verona.

[*BENVOLIO and MERCUTIO enter with some of their SERVANTS.*]

BENVOLIO. I pray thee, good Mercutio, let's retire.
The day is hot, the Capels° are abroad,
And, if we meet, we shall not 'scape a brawl,
For now, these hot days, is the mad blood stirring.

MERCUTIO. Thou art like one of these fellows that, when he enters the confines of a tavern, claps me his sword upon the table and says, "God send me no need of thee!" and by the operation of the second cup draws him on the drawer,° when indeed there is no need.

BENVOLIO. Am I like such a fellow?

MERCUTIO. Come, come, thou art as hot a Jack° in thy mood as any in Italy; and as soon mov'd to be moody, and as soon moody to be mov'd.°

BENVOLIO. And what to?

MERCUTIO. Nay, and° there were two such, we should have none shortly, for one would kill the other. Thou! Why, thou wilt quarrel with a man that hath a hair more or a hair less in his beard than thou hast. Thou wilt quarrel with a man for cracking nuts, having no other reason but because thou hast hazel eyes. What eye but such an eye would spy out such a quarrel? Thy head is as full of quarrels as an egg is full of meat;° and yet thy head hath been beaten as addle° as an egg for quarreling. Thou hast quarreled with a man for coughing in the street, because he hath wakened thy dog that hath lain asleep in the sun. Didst thou not fall out with a tailor for wearing his new doublet° before Easter? With another for tying his new shoes with old riband?° And yet thou wilt tutor me from quarreling!°

BENVOLIO. And I were so apt to quarrel as thou art, any man should buy the fee simple of my life for an hour and a quarter.°

MERCUTIO. The fee simple? O simple!°

[*TYBALT, JULIET's cousin, enters with other CAPULETS. He has not been able to find ROMEO since sending him a challenge earlier that day.*]

BENVOLIO. By my head, here comes the Capulets.

MERCUTIO. By my heel, I care not.

2 **Capels:** Capulets.

7–8 **by the . . . drawer:** when the second cup has had its effect, draws his sword on the waiter.

11 **Jack:** fellow.

12–13 **and as soon mov'd . . . mov'd:** as easily provoked to be angry as you are angry at being provoked.

15 **and:** if.

22 **meat:** food. **addle:** confused; rotten.

26 **doublet:** jacket. (New fashions were traditionally not supposed to be worn before Easter.)

27 **riband:** ribbon.

28 **tutor me from quarreling:** teach me not to quarrel.

30 **buy . . . quarter:** buy complete ownership of my life for a fraction of its value (since I wouldn't live long).

31 **O simple:** Oh, how stupid!

TYBALT. [*To his companions.*] Follow me close, for I will speak to them. [*To* BENVOLIO *and* MERCUTIO.] Gentlemen, good-den. A word with one of you.

MERCUTIO. And but one word with one of us? Couple it with something; make it a word and a blow.

TYBALT. You shall find me apt enough to that, sir, and you will give me occasion.

MERCUTIO. Could you not take some occasion without giving?

TYBALT. Mercutio, thou consortest with Romeo.

MERCUTIO. Consort? What, dost thou make us minstrels?° And thou make minstrels of us, look to hear nothing but discords. [*He places his hand on the hilt of his sword.*] Here's my fiddlestick;° here's that shall make you dance. 'Zounds,° consort!

BENVOLIO. We talk here in the public haunt of men.
Either withdraw unto some private place,
Or reason coldly of your grievances,
Or else depart. Here all eyes gaze on us.

MERCUTIO. Men's eyes were made to look, and let them gaze.
I will not budge for no man's pleasure, I.

[ROMEO *enters. He is calm and happy after his secret marriage to* JULIET.]

TYBALT. Well, peace be with you, sir. Here comes my man.°

MERCUTIO. But I'll be hang'd, sir, if he wear your livery.°
Marry, go before to field,° he'll be your follower!°
Your worship in that sense may call him man.

TYBALT. Romeo, the love I bear thee can afford
No better term than this: thou art a villain.

ROMEO. Tybalt, the reason that I have to love thee
Doth much excuse the appertaining rage°
To such a greeting. Villain am I none.
Therefore farewell. I see thou knowest me not.

TYBALT. Boy, this shall not excuse the injuries
That thou hast done me; therefore turn and draw.

ROMEO. I do protest I never injured thee,
But love thee better than thou canst devise°
Till thou shalt know the reason of my love;
And so, good Capulet, which name I tender°
As dearly as mine own, be satisfied.

MERCUTIO. O calm, dishonorable, vile submission!
Alla stoccata° carries it away.

42–43 **Mercutio . . . minstrels:** Mercutio plays on the word *consort,* which can refer to a group of musicians **(minstrels)**. Here, **consortest** means "keep company."

46 **fiddlestick:** violin bow. **'Zounds:** an exclamation of surprise or anger.

54 **my man:** the man I am looking for.

55 **But . . . livery:** Mercutio then plays on another meaning of *my man,* which is "servant," declaring that Romeo shall never wear the servant's uniform **(livery)** of Tybalt's household.

56 **field:** dueling field. **follower:** servant (but Mercutio means that Romeo will follow him to fight).

61 **the appertaining rage:** the appropriate angry response.

67 **devise:** imagine.

69 **tender:** value.

72 ***Alla stoccata:*** (ä′ lä stə kä′ tə) Italian fencing term that means "at the thrust." Mercutio may be using this as a contemptuous nickname for Tybalt, or he may mean that his sword thrust will erase Romeo's "vile submission."

[MERCUTIO, *upset at* TYBALT*'s insults and at* ROMEO*'s refusal to fight, draws his sword.*]

Tybalt, you ratcatcher, will you walk?°

TYBALT. What wouldst thou have with me?

MERCUTIO. Good King of Cats, nothing but one of your nine lives. That I mean to make bold withal,° and, as you shall use me hereafter, dry-beat the rest of the eight.° Will you pluck your sword out of his pilcher° by the ears?° Make haste, lest mine be about your ears ere it be out.

TYBALT. I am for you. [TYBALT *draws his sword.*]

ROMEO. Gentle Mercutio, put thy rapier up.

73 **walk:** withdraw (to fight).

76 **make bold withal:** take.

76–77 **as you shall . . . eight:** According to how you treat me from now on, I will either spare your other lives or thrash them.

78 **pilcher:** scabbard, sheath. **by the ears:** as one would pull out a coward from hiding.

Rival Factions from Romeo & Juliet, 1882. Sir Frank Dicksee. Gouache, en grisaille. Private collection.
Viewing the painting: Does this painting fit your image of the fight scene? Why or why not?

MERCUTIO. Come sir, your *passado!*°

[*MERCUTIO and TYBALT fight. ROMEO, trying to stop the fight, turns to BENVOLIO for help.*]

ROMEO. Draw, Benvolio; beat down their weapons.
Gentlemen, for shame! Forbear this outrage!
Tybalt, Mercutio, the Prince expressly hath
Forbid this bandying in Verona streets.
Hold, Tybalt! Good Mercutio!

[*ROMEO, trying to separate the two men, steps between them and blocks MERCUTIO's sword arm. At that moment TYBALT thrusts his sword under ROMEO's arm and stabs MERCUTIO. TYBALT flees with his followers.*]

MERCUTIO. I am hurt.
A plague a' both houses!° I am sped.°
Is he gone and hath nothing?

BENVOLIO. What, art thou hurt?

MERCUTIO. Ay, ay, a scratch, a scratch. Marry, 'tis enough.
Where is my page? Go, villain, fetch a surgeon.

[*The PAGE, a servant, exits.*]

ROMEO. Courage, man. The hurt cannot be much.

MERCUTIO. No, 'tis not so deep as a well, nor so wide as a church door; but 'tis enough, 'twill serve. Ask for me tomorrow, and you shall find me a grave° man. I am pepper'd,° I warrant, for this world. A plague a' both your houses! 'Zounds, a dog, a rat, a mouse, a cat, to scratch a man to death! A braggart, a rogue, a villain, that fights by the book of arithmetic!° Why the devil came you between us? I was hurt under your arm.

ROMEO. I thought all for the best.

MERCUTIO. Help me into some house, Benvolio.
Or I shall faint. A plague a' both your houses!
They have made worms' meat of me. I have it,
And soundly too. Your houses!

[*MERCUTIO exits, supported by BENVOLIO and his men.*]

ROMEO. This gentleman, the Prince's near ally,°
My very friend, hath got this mortal hurt
In my behalf—my reputation stain'd
With Tybalt's slander—Tybalt, that an hour
Hath been my cousin. O sweet Juliet,
Thy beauty hath made me effeminate
And in my temper soft'ned valor's steel!°

82 ***passado:*** Italian fencing term meaning "pass" or "lunge."

88 **a' both houses:** on the Montagues and Capulets. **sped:** done for.

95 **grave:** "serious" or "dead." **pepper'd:** finished.

98 **book of arithmetic:** fencing manual.

105 **near ally:** close relative.

111 **in my . . . steel:** softened the courage in my character.

[*BENVOLIO returns.*]

BENVOLIO. O Romeo, Romeo, brave Mercutio is dead!
That gallant spirit hath aspir'd° the clouds,
Which too untimely here did scorn the earth.

ROMEO. This day's black fate on moe days doth depend;°
This but begins the woe others must end.

[*TYBALT returns.*]

BENVOLIO. Here comes the furious Tybalt back again.

ROMEO. He gone in triumph, and Mercutio slain?
Away to heaven, respective lenity,°
And fire-ey'd fury be my conduct° now!
Now, Tybalt, take the "villain" back again
That late thou gavest me; for Mercutio's soul
Is but a little way above our heads,
Staying for thine to keep him company.
Either thou or I, or both, must go with him.

TYBALT. Thou, wretched boy, that didst consort him here,
Shalt with him hence.

ROMEO. This shall determine that.

[*ROMEO draws his sword; TYBALT draws his in response. They fight until ROMEO stabs TYBALT, who falls.*]

BENVOLIO. Romeo, away, be gone!
The citizens are up, and Tybalt slain.
Stand not amazed. The Prince will doom thee death
If thou art taken. Hence, be gone, away!

ROMEO. O, I am fortune's fool!

BENVOLIO. Why dost thou stay?

[*ROMEO flees just before a group of angry CITIZENS enters.*]

CITIZEN. Which way ran he that kill'd Mercutio?
Tybalt, that murderer, which way ran he?

BENVOLIO. There lies that Tybalt.

CITIZEN. Up, sir, go with me.
I charge thee in the Prince's name obey.

[*PRINCE ESCALUS, LORD MONTAGUE, LADY MONTAGUE, LORD CAPULET, and LADY CAPULET enter with various followers.*]

PRINCE. Where are the vile beginners of this fray?

BENVOLIO. O noble Prince, I can discover° all
The unlucky manage° of this fatal brawl.

113 **aspir'd** (əs pīrd′): risen to.

115 **This day's . . . depend:** Today's fatal event will darken future days.

119 **respective lenity** (len′ə tē): careful leniency.

120 **conduct:** guide.

138 **discover:** disclose.

139 **manage:** course.

There lies the man, slain by young Romeo,
That slew thy kinsman, brave Mercutio.

LADY CAPULET. Tybalt, my cousin! O my brother's child!
O Prince! O husband! O, the blood is spill'd
Of my dear kinsman! Prince, as thou art true,
For blood of ours shed blood of Montague.
O cousin, cousin!

PRINCE. Benvolio, who began this bloody fray?

BENVOLIO. Tybalt, here slain, whom Romeo's hand did slay.
Romeo, that spoke him fair, bid him bethink
How nice the quarrel was, and urg'd withal
Your high displeasure.° All this—uttered
With gentle breath, calm look, knees humbly bowed—
Could not take truce with the unruly spleen
Of Tybalt deaf to peace, but that he tilts°
With piercing steel at bold Mercutio's breast;
Who, all as hot,° turns deadly point to point,
And, with a martial scorn, with one hand beats
Cold death aside and with the other sends
It back to Tybalt, whose dexterity
Retorts it.° Romeo he cries aloud,
"Hold, friends! Friends, part!" and swifter than his tongue,
His agile arm beats down their fatal points,
And 'twixt them rushes; underneath whose arm
An envious° thrust from Tybalt hit the life
Of stout Mercutio, and then Tybalt fled;
But by and by comes back to Romeo,
Who had but newly entertain'd revenge,
And to't they go like lightning; for, ere I
Could draw to part them, was stout Tybalt slain;
And, as he fell, did Romeo turn and fly.
This is the truth, or let Benvolio die.

LADY CAPULET. He is a kinsman to the Montague;
Affection makes him false, he speaks not true.
Some twenty of them fought in this black strife,
And all those twenty could but kill one life.
I beg for justice, which thou, Prince, must give.
Romeo slew Tybalt; Romeo must not live.

PRINCE. Romeo slew him; he slew Mercutio.
Who now the price of his dear blood doth owe?

MONTAGUE. Not Romeo, Prince; he was Mercutio's friend;
His fault concludes but what the law should end,
The life of Tybalt.°

149–151 Romeo . . . displeasure: Romeo, who spoke courteously to him, asked him to consider how trivial the quarrel was, and also argued that it would greatly displease you.

154 tilts: points.

156 all as hot: just as angry.

157–160 And, with . . . Retorts it: This description suggests that both Mercutio and Tybalt ward off the other's jabs with a dagger held in one hand and return **(Retorts)** the jabs with a sword held in the other hand.

164 envious (en′ vē əs): hateful.

181–182 His fault . . . Tybalt: His only offense was that he killed Tybalt, which the law should have done anyway.

PRINCE. And for that offense
Immediately we do exile him hence.
I have an interest in your heart's proceeding,
My blood° for your rude brawls doth lie a-bleeding;
But I'll amerce° you with so strong a fine
That you shall all repent the loss of mine.
I will be deaf to pleading and excuses;
Nor tears nor prayers shall purchase out abuses.°
Therefore use none. Let Romeo hence in haste,
Else, when he is found, that hour is his last.
Bear hence this body and attend our will.°
Mercy but murders, pardoning those that kill.

[*They all exit.*]

185 **blood:** relative.

186 **amerce** (ə murs′): penalize.

189 **purchase out abuses:** buy forgiveness for crimes.

192 **attend our will:** obey my wishes.

SCENE 2. Later that day. CAPULET's orchard.

[*JULIET, unaware of what has happened, waits impatiently for the night so that she can see ROMEO again.*]

JULIET. Gallop apace, you fiery-footed steeds,
Towards Phoebus' lodging! Such a wagoner
As Phaëton would whip you to the west
And bring in cloudy night immediately.°
Spread thy close° curtain, love-performing night,
That th' runaway's eyes may wink,° and Romeo
Leap to these arms untalk'd of and unseen!
Lovers can see to do their amorous rites
By their own beauties, or, if love be blind,
It best agrees with night. Come, civil° night,
Thou sober-suited matron all in black,
And learn me how to lose a winning match,
Play'd for a pair of stainless maidenhoods.
Hood my unmann'd blood, bating in my cheeks,
With thy black mantle; till strange love grows bold,
Think true love acted simple modesty.°
Come, night, come, Romeo, come, thou day in night,
For thou wilt lie upon the wings of night,
Whiter than new snow upon a raven's back.
Come, gentle night; come, loving, black-brow'd night;
Give me my Romeo; and, when I shall die,
Take him and cut him out in little stars,
And he will make the face of heaven so fine
That all the world will be in love with night
And pay no worship to the garish sun.
O, I have bought the mansion of a love,

1–4 **Gallop . . . immediately:** Juliet urges the horses that drive **Phoebus** (fē′ bus) the sun god's chariot across the sky to hurry home. **Phaëton** (fā′ ət ən), a son of the sun god, was known for recklessly driving the chariot.

5 **close:** concealing.

6 **That . . . wink:** so that the eyes of wandering observers may close.

10 **civil:** solemn.

14–16 **Hood . . . modesty:** Falconers would place a hood on an untamed **(unmanned)** falcon to prevent it from fluttering **(bating)** its wings. Juliet asks the night to conceal her blushing until she overcomes her innocent modesty.

Juliet, 1896. Phillip Hermogenes Calderon. From the text *The Graphic Gallery of Shakespeare's Heroines.* 8 x 10 in. The Folger Shakespeare Library, Washington, DC.

Viewing the painting: Why might the artist have depicted Juliet in this pose?

But not possess'd it, and though I am sold,
Not yet enjoy'd. So tedious is this day
As is the night before some festival
To an impatient child that hath new robes
And may not wear them. O, here comes my nurse,

[*The* NURSE *enters carrying a rope ladder.*]

And she brings news; and every tongue that speaks
But Romeo's name speaks heavenly eloquence.
Now, nurse, what news? What hast thou there, the cords
That Romeo bid thee fetch?

NURSE. Ay, ay, the cords.

[*She throws down the ladder.*]

JULIET. Ay me! What news? Why dost thou wring thy hands?

NURSE. Ah, weraday!° He's dead, he's dead, he's dead!
We are undone, lady, we are undone!
Alack the day! He's gone, he's kill'd, he's dead!

JULIET. Can heaven be so envious?

NURSE. Romeo can,
Though heaven cannot. O Romeo, Romeo!
Who ever would have thought it? Romeo!

JULIET. What devil art thou that dost torment me thus?
This torture should be roar'd in dismal hell.
Hath Romeo slain himself? Say thou but ay,
And that bare vowel *I* shall poison more
Than the death-darting eye of cockatrice.°
I am not I, if there be such an ay,
Or those eyes shut, that makes thee answer ay.
If he be slain, say ay, or if not, no.
Brief sounds determine my weal° or woe.

NURSE. I saw the wound, I saw it with mine eyes,
(God save the mark!)° here on his manly breast.
A piteous corse, a bloody piteous corse;°
Pale, pale as ashes, all bedaub'd in blood,
All in gore-blood. I sounded° at the sight.

JULIET. O, break, my heart! Poor bankrout,° break at once!
To prison, eyes; ne'er look on liberty!
Vile earth, to earth resign;° end motion here,
And thou and Romeo press one heavy bier!°

NURSE. O Tybalt, Tybalt, the best friend I had!
O courteous Tybalt! Honest gentleman!
That ever I should live to see thee dead!

37 **weraday:** welladay (alas!).

47 **cockatrice** (kok′ə tris′): a mythical serpent that was thought to kill with a glance.

51 **weal:** happiness.

53 **God save the mark:** an expression uttered to ward off bad luck when something unpleasant is mentioned.

54 **corse:** corpse.

56 **sounded:** swooned, fainted.

57 **bankrout:** bankrupt (because it has lost everything it values).

59 **Vile earth, to earth resign:** Miserable body, give yourself back to the earth.

60 **bier** (bēr): a platform on which corpses are displayed before burial.

JULIET. What storm is this that blows so contrary?
Is Romeo slaught'red, and is Tybalt dead?
My dearest cousin, and my dearer lord?
Then, dreadful trumpet, sound the general doom!
For who is living, if those two are gone?

NURSE. Tybalt is gone, and Romeo banished;
Romeo that kill'd him, he is banished.

JULIET. O God! Did Romeo's hand shed Tybalt's blood?

NURSE. It did, it did! Alas the day, it did!

JULIET. O serpent heart, hid with a flow'ring face!°
Did ever dragon keep° so fair a cave?
Beautiful tyrant! fiend angelical!
Dove-feather'd raven! wolvish ravening lamb!
Despised substance of divinest show!°
Just opposite to what thou justly seem'st,
A damned saint, an honorable villain!
O nature, what hadst thou to do in hell
When thou didst bower° the spirit of a fiend
In mortal paradise of such sweet flesh?
Was ever book containing such vile matter
So fairly bound? O, that deceit should dwell
In such a gorgeous palace!

NURSE. There's no trust,
No faith, no honesty in men; all perjur'd,
All forsworn, all naught,° all dissemblers.°
Ah, where's my man? Give me some aqua vitae.°
These griefs, these woes, these sorrows make me old.
Shame come to Romeo!

JULIET. Blister'd be thy tongue
For such a wish! He was not born to shame.
Upon his brow shame is asham'd to sit;
For 'tis a throne where honor may be crown'd
Sole monarch of the universal earth.
O, what a beast was I to chide at him!

NURSE. Will you speak well of him that kill'd your cousin?

JULIET. Shall I speak ill of him that is my husband?
Ah, poor my lord, what tongue shall smooth° thy name
When I, thy three-hours wife, have mangled it?
But wherefore, villain, didst thou kill my cousin?
That villain cousin would have kill'd my husband.
Back, foolish tears, back to your native spring!

73 **hid with a flow'ring face:** hidden by a flower-like face. (Similar images throughout this speech express Juliet's shock that evil can dwell within one she finds so attractive.)

74 **keep:** guard.

77 **show:** appearance.

81 **bower:** enclose, conceal.

87 **naught:** wicked. **dissemblers:** liars.

88 **aqua vitae** (ak′ wə vī′ tē): brandy.

98 **smooth:** speak well of.

Your tributary drops° belong to woe,
Which you, mistaking, offer up to joy.
My husband lives, that Tybalt would have slain;
And Tybalt's dead, that would have slain my husband.
All this is comfort; wherefore weep I then?
Some word there was, worser than Tybalt's death,
That murd'red me. I would forget it fain;°
But O, it presses to my memory
Like damned guilty deeds to sinners' minds!
"Tybalt is dead, and Romeo—banished."
That "banished," that one word "banished,"
Hath slain ten thousand Tybalts. Tybalt's death
Was woe enough, if it had ended there;
Or, if sour woe delights in fellowship
And needly will be rank'd with° other griefs,
Why followed not, when she said "Tybalt's dead,"

103 **Your tributary drops:** the drops you have contributed.

109 **fain:** gladly.

117 **needly . . . with:** must be accompanied by.

Juliet and Her Nurse, 1836. Joseph Mallord William Turner. Oil on canvas, 23 x 30.5 cm. Private collection.

Viewing the painting: Turner depicted Juliet and the Nurse in the lower right corner of this painting. How might this scene help you understand Juliet's dismay at Romeo's banishment?

Thy father, or thy mother, nay, or both,
Which modern lamentation might have moved?°
But with a rearward° following Tybalt's death,
"Romeo is banished"—to speak that word
Is father, mother, Tybalt, Romeo, Juliet,
All slain, all dead. "Romeo is banished"—
There is no end, no limit, measure, bound,
In that word's death; no words can that woe sound.°
Where is my father and my mother, nurse?

NURSE. Weeping and wailing over Tybalt's corse.
Will you go to them? I will bring you thither.

JULIET. Wash they his wounds with tears? Mine shall be spent,
When theirs are dry, for Romeo's banishment.
Take up those cords. Poor ropes, you are beguil'd,°
Both you and I, for Romeo is exil'd.
He made you for a highway to my bed,
But I, a maid, die maiden-widowed.
Come, cords, come, nurse, I'll to my wedding-bed,
And death, not Romeo, take my maidenhead!

NURSE. Hie to your chamber. I'll find Romeo
To comfort you. I wot° well where he is.
Hark ye, your Romeo will be here at night.
I'll to him; he is hid at Lawrence' cell.

JULIET. O, find him! Give this ring to my true knight
And bid him come to take his last farewell.

[*They exit.*]

SCENE 3. Later. FRIAR LAWRENCE's cell.

[*FRIAR LAWRENCE enters and notices that ROMEO is hiding in the room.*]

FRIAR. Romeo, come forth; come forth, thou fearful man.
Affliction is enamor'd of thy parts,°
And thou art wedded to calamity.

[*ROMEO steps forward.*]

ROMEO. Father, what news? What is the Prince's doom?°
What sorrow craves acquaintance at my hand
That I yet know not?

FRIAR. Too familiar
Is my dear son with such sour company.
I bring thee tidings of the Prince's doom.

ROMEO. What less than doomsday° is the Prince's doom?

120 modern . . . moved: might have roused ordinary grief.

121 rearward: rear guard.

126 no words can that woe sound: no words can express the depth of that misery.

132 beguil'd: cheated.

139 wot: know.

2 Affliction . . . parts: Misfortune has fallen in love with your attractive qualities.

4 doom: judgment.

9 doomsday: my death.

FRIAR. A gentler judgment vanish'd° from his lips—
Not body's death, but body's banishment.

ROMEO. Ha, banishment? Be merciful, say "death";
For exile hath more terror in his look,
Much more than death. Do not say "banishment."

FRIAR. Here from Verona art thou banished.
Be patient, for the world is broad and wide.

ROMEO. There is no world without° Verona walls,
But purgatory, torture, hell itself.
Hence "banished" is banish'd from the world,
And world's exile is death. Then "banished"
Is death misterm'd. Calling death "banished,"
Thou cut'st my head off with a golden ax
And smilest upon the stroke that murders me.

FRIAR. O deadly sin! O rude unthankfulness!
Thy fault our law calls death;° but the kind Prince,
Taking thy part, hath rush'd° aside the law,
And turn'd that black word "death" to "banishment."
This is dear° mercy, and thou seest it not.

ROMEO. 'Tis torture, and not mercy. Heaven is here,
Where Juliet lives; and every cat and dog
And little mouse, every unworthy thing,
Live here in heaven and may look on her;
But Romeo may not. More validity,°
More honorable state, more courtship lives
In carrion flies than Romeo. They may seize
On the white wonder of dear Juliet's hand
And steal immortal blessing from her lips.
Who, even in pure and vestal° modesty,
Still° blush, as thinking their own kisses sin;°
But Romeo may not, he is banished.
Flies may do this but I from this must fly;
They are free men, but I am banished.
And sayest thou yet that exile is not death?
Hadst thou no poison mix'd, no sharp-ground knife,
No sudden mean° of death, though ne'er so mean,°
But "banished" to kill me—"banished"?
O friar, the damned use that word in hell;
Howling attends it! How hast thou the heart,
Being a divine, a ghostly confessor,
A sin-absolver, and my friend profess'd,
To mangle me with that word "banished"?

10 **vanish'd:** escaped.

17 **without:** outside.

25 **our law calls death:** is punishable by death.

26 **rush'd:** brushed.

28 **dear:** uncommon.

33 **validity:** value.

38 **vestal** (vest′ əl): virginal.

39 **Still:** always. **thinking . . . sin:** believing it is sinful for them to touch when her mouth closes.

45 **mean:** means. **mean:** lowly.

FRIAR. Thou fond° mad man, hear me a little speak.

ROMEO. O, thou wilt speak again of banishment.

FRIAR. I'll give thee armor to keep off that word;
Adversity's sweet milk, philosophy,
To comfort thee, though thou art banished.

ROMEO. Yet "banished"? Hang up° philosophy!
Unless philosophy can make a Juliet,
Displant° a town, reverse a prince's doom,
It helps not, it prevails not. Talk no more.

FRIAR. O, then I see that madmen have no ears.

ROMEO. How should they, when that wise men have no eyes?

FRIAR. Let me dispute with thee of thy estate.°

ROMEO. Thou canst not speak of that thou dost not feel.
Wert thou as young as I, Juliet thy love,
An hour but married, Tybalt murdered,
Doting like me,° and like me banished,
Then mightst thou speak, then mightst thou tear thy hair,
And fall upon the ground, as I do now,

[*ROMEO throws himself on the floor.*]

Taking the measure of an unmade grave.°

[*There is a knock at the door to the cell.*]

FRIAR. Arise, one knocks. Good Romeo, hide thyself.

ROMEO. Not I; unless the breath of heartsick groans
Mistlike infold me° from the search of eyes.

[*Another knock.*]

FRIAR. Hark, how they knock! Who's there? Romeo, arise;
Thou wilt be taken.—Stay° awhile!—Stand up;

[*The knocking continues more loudly than before.*]

Run to my study.—By and by!°—God's will,
What simpleness° is this.—I come, I come!

[*There is a very loud knock. The FRIAR goes to the door.*]

Who knocks so hard? Whence come you? What's your will?

NURSE. Let me come in, and you shall know my errand.
I come from Lady Juliet.

FRIAR. Welcome then.

[*The NURSE enters.*]

NURSE. O holy friar, O, tell me, holy friar,
Where is my lady's lord, where's Romeo?

52 **fond:** foolish.

57 **Hang up:** forget about.

59 **Displant:** transplant.

63 **dispute . . . estate:** discuss your situation with you.

67 **Doting like me:** as obsessively in love as I am.

69–70 **And fall . . . grave:** Romeo makes his gesture of throwing himself to the ground even more melodramatic by suggesting that he is seeing how large a grave he will need.

73 **Mistlike infold me:** forms a mist to hide me.

75 **Stay:** wait.

76 **By and by:** in a moment. The Friar interrupts his pleading with Romeo to address the person knocking at the door.

77 **simpleness:** foolishness.

FRIAR. There on the ground, with his own tears made drunk.

NURSE. O, he is even in my mistress' case,°
Just in her case! O woeful sympathy!
Piteous predicament! Even so lies she,
Blubb'ring and weeping, weeping and blubb'ring.
Stand up, stand up! Stand, and you be a man.
For Juliet's sake, for her sake, rise and stand!
Why should you fall into so deep an O?°

ROMEO. [*He rises.*] Nurse—

NURSE. Ah sir, ah sir! Death's the end of all.

ROMEO. Spakest thou of Juliet? How is it with her?
Doth not she think me an old° murderer,
Now I have stain'd the childhood of our joy
With blood removed but little from her own?
Where is she? And how doth she! And what says
My conceal'd lady° to our cancel'd° love?

NURSE. O, she says nothing, sir, but weeps and weeps;
And now falls on her bed, and then starts up,
And Tybalt calls; and then on Romeo cries,
And then down falls again.

ROMEO. As if that name,
Shot from the deadly level of a gun,
Did murder her; as that name's cursed hand
Murder'd her kinsman. O, tell me, friar, tell me,
In what vile part of this anatomy
Doth my name lodge? Tell me, that I may sack°
The hateful mansion.

[*ROMEO takes out his dagger and offers to stab himself. The NURSE snatches the dagger away.*]

FRIAR. Hold thy desperate hand.
Art thou a man? Thy form cries out thou art;
Thy tears are womanish, thy wild acts denote
The unreasonable fury of a beast.
Unseemly woman in a seeming man,
And ill-beseeming beast in seeming both,°
Thou hast amaz'd me. By my holy order,
I thought thy disposition better temper'd.
Hast thou slain Tybalt? Wilt thou slay thyself?
And slay thy lady that in thy life lives,
By doing damned hate upon thyself?
Why railest thou on° thy birth? the heaven and earth?

84 **even in my mistress' case:** exactly in Juliet's condition.

90 **so deep an O:** so heavy a cry of grief.

94 **old:** hardened.

98 **conceal'd lady:** secret bride. **cancel'd:** nullified.

107 **sack:** plunder.

110–113 **Thy tears . . . both:** The Friar scolds Romeo for grieving like a woman and expressing fury inappropriate **(ill-beseeming)** even for a beast.

119 **Why railest thou on:** why do you complain bitterly about.

Since birth,° and heaven,° and earth,° all three do meet
In thee at once, which thou at once wouldst lose.
Fie, fie, thou shamest thy shape, thy love, thy wit,
Which like a usurer abound'st in all,
And usest none in that true use indeed
Which should bedeck thy shape, thy love, thy wit.°
Thy noble shape is but a form of wax,
Digressing from the valor of a man;°
Thy dear love sworn but hollow perjury,
Killing that love which thou hast vow'd to cherish;
Thy wit, that ornament to shape and love,
Misshapen in the conduct° of them both,
Like powder in a skilless soldier's flask,
Is set afire by thine own ignorance,
And thou dismemb'red with thine own defense.°
What, rouse thee, man! Thy Juliet is alive,
For whose dear sake thou wast but lately dead.°
There art thou happy. Tybalt would kill thee,
But thou slewest Tybalt. There art thou happy.
The law, that threat'ned death, becomes thy friend
And turns it to exile. There art thou happy.
A pack of blessings light° upon thy back;
Happiness courts thee in her best array;°
But, like a mishaved° and sullen wench,
Thou pouts upon thy fortune and thy love.
Take heed, take heed, for such die miserable.
Go get thee to thy love, as was decreed,
Ascend her chamber, hence and comfort her.
But look thou stay not till the watch be set,°
For then thou canst not pass to Mantua,
Where thou shalt live till we can find a time
To blaze° your marriage, reconcile your friends,
Beg pardon of the Prince, and call thee back
With twenty hundred thousand times more joy
Than thou went'st forth in lamentation.°
Go before, nurse. Commend me to thy lady,
And bid her hasten all the house to bed,
Which heavy sorrow makes them apt unto.°
Romeo is coming.

NURSE. O Lord, I could have stay'd here all the night
To hear good counsel. O, what learning is!
My lord, I'll tell my lady you will come.

ROMEO. Do so, and bid my sweet prepare to chide.°

120 **birth:** family origin. **heaven:** soul. **earth:** body.

122–125 **thou shamest . . . thy wit:** Like a moneylender who misuses his wealth, you are misusing the appearance **(shape)**, love, and intelligence **(wit)** you've been blessed with.

126–127 **Thy noble . . . man:** You are nothing but a waxwork figure, straying from a real man's courage.

131 **Misshapen in the conduct:** badly flawed in the guidance.

132–134 **Like powder . . . defense:** Just as a clumsy soldier might accidentally set off his container of gunpowder, you have ignored good reason and let yourself be blown apart by your intelligence, which should have been your defense.

136 **but lately dead:** only just now declaring yourself dead.

141 **light:** alight, set down lightly.

142 **array** (ə rā′): outfit.

143 **mishaved:** misbehaved.

148 **look . . . set:** See that you don't remain with her until the watchmen go on duty at the city gates.

151 **blaze:** make public.

154 **lamentation:** sorrowful outcry.

157 **apt unto:** inclined to.

162 **prepare to chide:** to be ready to scold.

[*The* NURSE *begins to exit but turns again to* ROMEO *handing him a ring.*]

NURSE. Here, sir, a ring she bid me give you, sir.
Hie you,° make haste, for it grows very late.

ROMEO. How well my comfort is reviv'd by this!

[*NURSE exits.*]

FRIAR. Go hence; good night; and here stands all your state:°
Either be gone before the watch be set,
Or by the break of day disguis'd from hence.
Sojourn in Mantua. I'll find out your man,
And he shall signify from time to time
Every good hap to you that chances here.°
Give me thy hand. 'Tis late. Farewell; good night.

ROMEO. But that a joy past joy calls out on me,
It were a grief so brief to part with thee.
Farewell.

[ROMEO *and* FRIAR LAWRENCE *clasp hands and then exit in opposite directions.*]

164 **Hie you:** hurry.

166 **here . . . state:** this is your situation.

169–171 **Sojourn . . . here:** The Friar asks Romeo to stay temporarily **(sojourn)** in **Mantua,** a city near Verona. He will send Romeo's servant there occasionally to bring news of favorable events.

SCENE 4. Late that night. A room in CAPULET's house.

[*PARIS, LORD CAPULET, and LADY CAPULET enter.*]

CAPULET. Things have fall'n out, sir, so unluckily
That we have had no time to move° our daughter.
Look you, she lov'd her kinsman Tybalt dearly,
And so did I. Well, we were born to die.
'Tis very late; she'll not come down tonight.
I promise you, but for your company,
I would have been abed an hour ago.

PARIS. These times of woe afford no times to woo.
Madam, good night. Commend me to your daughter.

LADY. I will, and know her mind early tomorrow;
Tonight she's mewed up to her heaviness.°

CAPULET. Sir Paris, I will make a desperate tender°
Of my child's love. I think she will be rul'd
In all respects by me; nay more, I doubt it not.
Wife, go you to her ere you go to bed;
Acquaint her here of my son Paris' love
And bid her (mark you me?) on Wednesday next—
But soft! What day is this?

PARIS. Monday, my lord.

2 **move:** persuade.

11 **mewed up to her heaviness:** confined to her sadness. (Hawks were housed in structures called *mews.*)

12 **desperate tender:** bold offer.

CAPULET. Monday! Ha, ha! Well, Wednesday is too soon.
A'° Thursday let it be—a' Thursday, tell her,
She shall be married to this noble earl.
Will you be ready? Do you like this haste?
We'll keep no great ado°—a friend or two;
For hark you, Tybalt being slain so late,
It may be thought we held him carelessly,°
Being our kinsman, if we revel much.
Therefore we'll have some half a dozen friends,
And there an end. But what say you to Thursday?

PARIS. My lord, I would that Thursday were tomorrow.

CAPULET. Well, get you gone. A' Thursday be it then.
[*To his wife.*] Go you to Juliet ere you go to bed;
Prepare her, wife, against° this wedding day.
Farewell, my lord.—Light to my chamber, ho!
Afore me,° it is so very late that we
May call it early by and by. Good night.

[*They exit.*]

20 **A':** on.

23 **keep no great ado:** not make a big fuss.

25 **held him carelessly:** had little regard for him.

32 **against:** for.

34 **Afore me:** indeed.

SCENE 5. Later that night, just before daybreak. CAPULET's orchard and, above, JULIET's room and balcony.

[*ROMEO and JULIET are on the balcony. The rope ladder hangs down from the balcony into the garden.*]

JULIET. Wilt thou be gone? It is not yet near day.
It was the nightingale, and not the lark,
That pierc'd the fearful hollow of thine ear.
Nightly she sings on yond pomegranate tree.
Believe me, love, it was the nightingale.

ROMEO. It was the lark, the herald of the morn;
No nightingale. Look, love, what envious streaks
Do lace the severing° clouds in yonder east.
Night's candles° are burnt out, and jocund° day
Stands tiptoe on the misty mountaintops.
I must be gone and live, or stay and die.

JULIET. Yond light is not daylight; I know it, I.
It is some meteor° that the sun exhal'd
To be to thee this night a torchbearer
And light thee on thy way to Mantua.
Therefore stay yet; thou need'st not to be gone.

ROMEO. Let me be ta'en, let me be put to death.
I am content, so thou wilt have it so.

8 **severing:** dispersing.

9 **Night's candles:** the stars. **jocund** (jok′ ənd): cheerful.

13 **meteor:** thought to be gasses that the sun ignited.

I'll say yon gray is not the morning's eye,°
'Tis but the pale reflex° of Cynthia's brow;°
Nor that is not the lark whose notes do beat
The vaulty heaven so high above our heads.
I have more care to stay than will to go.
Come, death, and welcome! Juliet wills it so.
How is't, my soul! Let's talk; it is not day.

JULIET. It is, it is! Hie hence, be gone, away!
It is the lark that sings so out of tune,
Straining harsh discords and unpleasing sharps.°
Some say the lark makes sweet division;°
This doth not so, for she divideth us.
Some say the lark and loathed toad change° eyes;
O, now I would they had chang'd voices too,
Since arm from arm that voice doth us affray,°
Hunting thee hence with hunt's-up° to the day.
O, now be gone! More light and light it grows.

ROMEO. More light and light—more dark and dark our woes.

[The NURSE enters JULIET's room.]

NURSE. Madam!

JULIET. Nurse?

NURSE. Your lady mother is coming to your chamber.
The day is broke; be wary, look about.

[She exits.]

JULIET. Then, window, let day in, and let life out.

ROMEO. Farewell, farewell! One kiss, and I'll descend.

[They kiss. Then ROMEO climbs down the rope ladder to the garden below.]

JULIET. Art thou gone so, love, lord, ay husband, friend?
I must hear from thee every day in the hour,
For in a minute there are many days.
O, by this count I shall be much in years
Ere I again behold my Romeo!

ROMEO. Farewell!
I will omit no opportunity
That may convey my greetings, love, to thee.

JULIET. O, think'st thou we shall ever meet again?

ROMEO. I doubt it not; and all these woes shall serve
For sweet discourses° in our times to come.

19 **morning's eye:** sunrise.

20 **reflex:** reflection. **Cynthia's brow:** the forehead of Cynthia, the moon goddess.

28 **Straining . . . sharps:** singing harsh sounds and unpleasant high notes.

29 **division:** melody.

31 **change:** exchange. (The lark has a beautiful body and ugly eyes, while the toad has an ugly body and beautiful eyes.)

33 **affray:** frighten.

34 **hunt's-up:** a morning song to awaken hunters.

53 **discourses:** conversations.

Romeo and Juliet, 18th century. John Francis Rigaud. Oil on canvas. Agnew & Sons, London.

Viewing the painting: What words would you use to describe the emotions conveyed by Romeo, Juliet, and the Nurse in this painting?

JULIET. O God, I have an ill-divining soul!°
Methinks I see thee, now thou art so low,
As one dead in the bottom of a tomb.
Either my eyesight fails, or thou lookest pale.

ROMEO. And trust me, love, in my eye so do you.
Dry° sorrow drinks our blood. Adieu, adieu!

[*ROMEO leaves.*]

JULIET. O Fortune, Fortune! All men call thee fickle.
If thou art fickle, what dost thou with him
That is renown'd for faith?° Be fickle, Fortune,
For then I hope thou wilt not keep him long
But send him back.

[*LADY CAPULET enters JULIET's room.*]

LADY CAPULET. Ho, daughter! Are you up?

JULIET. Who is't that calls? It is my lady mother.
Is she not down° so late, or up so early?
What unaccustom'd cause procures her hither?°

[*JULIET returns to her room from the balcony.*]

LADY CAPULET. Why, how now, Juliet?

JULIET. Madam, I am not well.

LADY CAPULET. Evermore weeping for your cousin's death?
What, wilt thou wash him from his grave with tears?
And if thou couldst, thou couldst not make him live.
Therefore have done. Some grief shows much of love;
But much of grief shows still some want of wit.°

JULIET. Yet let me weep for such a feeling loss.

LADY CAPULET. So shall you feel the loss, but not the friend°
Which you weep for.

JULIET. Feeling so the loss,
I cannot choose but ever weep the friend.

LADY CAPULET. Well, girl, thou weep'st not so much for his death
As that the villain lives which slaughter'd him.

JULIET. What villain, madam?

LADY CAPULET. That same villain Romeo.

JULIET. [*Aside.*] Villain and he be many miles asunder.°—
[*To LADY CAPULET.*] God pardon him! I do, with all my heart;
And yet no man like he doth grieve my heart.

LADY CAPULET. That is because the traitor murderer lives.

54 **ill-divining soul:** soul that foresees misfortune.

59 **Dry:** thirsty. (Romeo refers to a belief that each sigh draws a drop of blood from the heart.)

61–62 **If thou . . . faith:** If you are unfaithful, why are you involved with a man known for his faithfulness?

66 **down:** going to bed.

67 **What . . . hither:** What unusual reason brings her here?

73 **shows . . . wit:** always shows lack of judgment.

75 **friend:** "cousin" or "lover."

81 **asunder:** apart.

JULIET. Ay, madam, from the reach of these my hands.
Would none but I might venge my cousin's death!

LADY CAPULET. We will have vengeance for it, fear thou not.
Then weep no more. I'll send to one in Mantua,
Where that same banish'd runagate° doth live,
Shall give him such an unaccustom'd dram°
That he shall soon keep Tybalt company;
And then I hope thou wilt be satisfied.

JULIET. Indeed I never shall be satisfied
With Romeo till I behold him—dead°—
Is my poor heart so for a kinsman vex'd.
Madam, if you could find out but a man
To bear a poison, I would temper° it;
That Romeo should, upon receipt thereof,
Soon sleep in quiet. O, how my heart abhors
To hear him nam'd and cannot come to him,
To wreak° the love I bore my cousin
Upon his body that hath slaughter'd him!

LADY CAPULET. Find thou the means, and I'll find such a man.
But now I'll tell thee joyful tidings, girl.

JULIET. And joy comes well in such a needy time.
What are they, beseech your ladyship?

LADY CAPULET. Well, well, thou hast a careful° father, child;
One who, to put thee from thy heaviness,°
Hath sorted out° a sudden day of joy
That thou expects not nor I look'd not for.

JULIET. Madam, in happy time! What day is that?

LADY CAPULET. Marry, my child, early next Thursday morn
The gallant, young, and noble gentleman,
The County Paris, at Saint Peter's Church,
Shall happily make thee there a joyful bride.

JULIET. Now by Saint Peter's Church, and Peter too,
He shall not make me there a joyful bride!
I wonder at this haste, that I must wed
Ere he that should be husband comes to woo.
I pray you tell my lord and father, madam,
I will not marry yet; and when I do, I swear
It shall be Romeo, whom you know I hate,
Rather than Paris. These are news indeed!

LADY CAPULET. Here comes your father. Tell him so yourself,
And see how he will take it at your hands.

89 **runagate:** renegade; runaway.

90 **unaccustom'd dram:** unexpected dose (of poison).

94 Here, as elsewhere in this dialogue, Juliet communicates one thing to her mother and something else to the audience. The word ***dead*** can be understood to complete this line ("till I behold him dead") or to begin the next line ("Dead is my poor heart").

97 **temper:** "mix" or "dilute."

101 **wreak** (rēk): "avenge" or "express."

107 **careful:** considerate.

108 **put . . . heaviness:** remove you from sorrow.

109 **sorted out:** chosen.

[*CAPULET and the NURSE enter.*]

CAPULET. When the sun sets the earth doth drizzle dew,
But for the sunset of my brother's son
It rains downright.
How now? A conduit,° girl? What, still in tears?
Evermore show'ring? In one little body
Thou counterfeits° a bark,° a sea, a wind:
For still thy eyes, which I may call the sea,
Do ebb and flow with tears; the bark thy body is,
Sailing in this salt flood; the winds, thy sighs,
Who, raging with thy tears and they with them,
Without a sudden calm will overset°
Thy tempest-tossed body. How now, wife?
Have you delivered to her our decree?

LADY CAPULET. Ay, sir; but she will none, she gives you thanks.
I would the fool were married to her grave!

CAPULET. Soft! Take me with you, take me with you,° wife.
How? Will she none? Doth she not give us thanks?
Is she not proud? Doth she not count her blest,
Unworthy as she is, that we have wrought°
So worthy a gentleman to be her bride?°

JULIET. Not proud you have, but thankful that you have.
Proud can I never be of what I hate,
But thankful even for hate that is meant love.

CAPULET. How, how, how, how, chopp'd-logic?° What is this?
"Proud"—and "I thank you"—and "I thank you not"—
And yet "not proud"? Mistress minion° you,
Thank me no thankings, nor proud me no prouds,
But fettle your fine joints 'gainst° Thursday next
To go with Paris to Saint Peter's Church,
Or I will drag thee on a hurdle° thither.
Out, you green-sickness carrion!° Out, you baggage!°
You tallow-face!°

LADY CAPULET. [*To CAPULET.*] Fie, fie! What, are you mad?

JULIET. [*She kneels before her father.*] Good father, I beseech you on my knees,
Hear me with patience but to speak a word.

CAPULET. Hang thee, young baggage! Disobedient wretch!
I tell thee what—get thee to church a' Thursday
Or never after look me in the face.
Speak not, reply not, do not answer me!

129 **conduit** (kon′ do͞o it): fountain.

131 **counterfeits:** resemble. **bark:** small sailing vessel.

136 **overset:** upset, capsize.

141 **Soft! . . . you:** Wait, let me understand you.

144 **wrought** (rôt): arranged for.

145 **bride:** bridegroom.

149 **chopp'd-logic:** clever but false argument.

151 **Mistress minion:** spoiled miss.

153 **fettle your fine joints 'gainst:** prepare your fine limbs for.

155 **hurdle:** a sled used to bring prisoners to their executions.

156 **green-sickness carrion:** anemic flesh. **baggage:** shameless girl.

157 **tallow-face:** pale face.

My fingers itch. Wife, we scarce thought us blest
That God had lent us but this only child;
But now I see this one is one too much,
And that we have a curse in having her.
Out on her, hilding!°

NURSE. God in heaven bless her!
You are to blame, my lord, to rate° her so.

CAPULET. And why, my Lady Wisdom? Hold your tongue,
Good Prudence. Smatter with your gossips, go!°

NURSE. I speak no treason.°

CAPULET. O, God-i-god-en!°

NURSE. May not one speak?

CAPULET. Peace, you mumbling fool!
Utter your gravity° o'er a gossip's bowl,°
For here we need it not.

LADY CAPULET. You are too hot.

CAPULET. God's bread! It makes me mad. Day, night; work, play;
Alone, in company; still my care hath been
To have her match'd; and having now provided
A gentleman of noble parentage,
Of fair demesnes,° youthful, and nobly lien'd,°
Stuff'd, as they say, with honorable parts,°
Proportion'd as one's thought would wish a man—
And then to have a wretched puling° fool,
A whining mammet,° in her fortune's tender,°
To answer, "I'll not wed, I cannot love;
I am too young, I pray you pardon me"!
But, and° you will not wed, I'll pardon you!°
Graze where you will, you shall not house with me.
Look to't, think on't; I do not use° to jest.
Thursday is near; lay hand on heart, advise:°
And you be mine, I'll give you to my friend;
And you be not, hang, beg, starve, die in the streets,
For, by my soul, I'll ne'er acknowledge thee,
Nor what is mine shall never do thee good.°
Trust to't. Bethink you. I'll not be forsworn.°

[*CAPULET exits. JULIET rises and speaks to her mother.*]

JULIET. Is there no pity sitting in the clouds
That sees into the bottom of my grief?
O sweet my mother, cast me not away!

168 **hilding:** worthless person.

169 **rate:** scold angrily.

171 **Smatter with your gossips, go:** Go chatter with your old pals.

172 **treason:** disloyalty. **God-i-god-en:** God give you good evening (used here as a mild oath).

174 **gravity:** wisdom. **gossip's bowl:** cup of hot punch.

180 **demesnes** (di mānz′): property. **lien'd:** descended.

181 **parts:** qualities.

183 **puling** (pūl′ ing): whimpering.

184 **mammet:** puppet. **in her fortune's tender:** when good fortune is offered her.

187 **and:** if. **pardon you:** excuse you (from this house).

189 **I do not use:** it isn't my custom.

190 **advise:** consider.

193–194 **I'll ne'er . . . good:** Capulet threatens to disown Juliet and cut off any family support.

195 **be forsworn:** break my vow.

Delay this marriage for a month, a week;
Or if you do not, make the bridal bed
In that dim monument where Tybalt lies.

LADY CAPULET. Talk not to me, for I'll not speak a word.
Do as thou wilt, for I have done with thee.

[*LADY CAPULET exits.*]

JULIET. O God!—O nurse, how shall this be prevented?
My husband is on earth, my faith in heaven.°
How shall that faith return again to earth
Unless that husband send it me from heaven
By leaving earth?° Comfort me, counsel me.
Alack, alack, that heaven should practice stratagems°
Upon so soft a subject as myself!
What say'st thou? Hast thou not a word of joy?
Some comfort, nurse.

NURSE. Faith, here it is.
Romeo is banished; and all the world to nothing
That he dares ne'er come back to challenge you;°
Or if he do, it needs must be by stealth.
Then, since the case so stands as now it doth,
I think it best you married with the County.
O, he's a lovely gentleman!
Romeo's a dishclout to him.° An eagle, madam,
Hath not so green, so quick, so fair an eye
As Paris hath. Beshrew° my very heart,
I think you are happy in this second match,
For it excels your first; or if it did not,
Your first is dead—or 'twere as good he were
As living here and you no use of him.

JULIET. Speak'st thou from thy heart?

NURSE. And from my soul too; else beshrew them both.

JULIET. Amen!

NURSE. What?

JULIET. Well, thou has comforted me marvelous much.
Go in; and tell my lady I am gone,
Having displeas'd my father, to Lawrence' cell,
To make confession and to be absolv'd.°

NURSE. Marry, I will; and this is wisely done.

[*The NURSE exits to find LADY CAPULET.*]

205 **my faith in heaven:** my marriage vow is recorded in heaven.

206–208 **How . . . earth:** How can I be free to pledge myself again unless by Romeo's death?

209 **stratagems** (strat′ ə jəmz): tricks.

213–214 **all the world . . . you:** The odds are greatly against his ever coming back to claim you.

219 **dishclout to him:** dish cloth compared to him.

221 **Beshrew** (bi shro͞o′): curse (used in mild oaths).

233 **absolv'd:** forgiven.

The Pained Heart, 1868. Arthur Hughes. Oil on canvas, 94 x 109.9 cm. The Maas Gallery, London.

Viewing the painting: What connections do you see between the title of this painting and the action of the play in this scene?

JULIET. Ancient damnation!° O most wicked fiend!
Is it more sin to wish me thus forsworn,
Or to dispraise my lord with that same tongue
Which she hath prais'd him with above compare
So many thousand times? Go, counselor!
Thou and my bosom henceforth shall be twain.°
I'll to the friar to know his remedy.
If all else fail, myself have power to die.

[*JULIET exits.*]

235 **Ancient damnation:** wicked old woman.

240 **Thou and . . . twain:** From now on I'll keep my secrets from you.

Responding to Literature

Personal Response

What would you do if you were Juliet?

Analyzing Act 3

Recall and Interpret

1. How does Romeo respond to Tybalt's challenge? Why does Mercutio decide to fight in Romeo's place?
2. How does Romeo accidentally help cause Mercutio's death? How do you interpret Romeo's description of himself as "fortune's fool"?
3. In scene 3, what plan for the future does the Friar propose to Romeo?
4. What does Capulet demand of Juliet? Does his treatment of her surprise you? Why or why not?
5. What solution does the Nurse offer to Juliet's predicament? How does Juliet's relationship with the Nurse change during this act?
6. What excuse does Juliet use to leave her house? How would you describe her state of mind at this point?

Evaluate and Connect

7. How does the **mood** of the play change during act 3? (See Literary Terms Handbook, page R8.)
8. Do you agree with the Prince's decision to banish Romeo? Explain.
9. What different viewpoints of love and marriage are presented in the play so far? What is your viewpoint?
10. The prologue of the play reveals its ending. What effect do you imagine this information has on readers and theater audiences during acts 1–3?

Literary ELEMENTS

Soliloquy and Aside

A **soliloquy** is a speech delivered by a character who is alone onstage. An **aside** is a comment made by a character that is heard by the audience or another character but is not heard by the other characters onstage. Both of these theatrical devices are used frequently in Elizabethan drama to provide information to the audience and to reveal the private thoughts of characters.

1. Find a soliloquy in act 3. What thoughts or feelings does it reveal?
2. Find an aside in act 3. What information does it provide to the audience?

- See **Literary Terms Handbook,** pp. R12 and R1.

Extending Your Response

Writing About Literature

Analyzing Characterization Choose a character from act 3, and write an analysis of the methods Shakespeare uses to develop the character. What do you learn from the character's own words and actions? How is your impression of the character influenced by the comments of other characters? Use specific examples from the play to illustrate Shakespeare's methods of characterization.

Performing

Act It Out With a partner or in a small group, choose a scene or portion of a scene from act 3 to perform for the class. Rehearse the scene together, and discuss different ways of delivering the dialogue to express the intended emotions. Be sure to consider pitch, tone of voice, posture, and eye contact.

Save your work for your portfolio.

Grammar Link

Incorrect Verb Tense or Form

The "tenses" of a verb are the forms that help to show time. For regular verbs, the past tense and past participle forms are created by adding *-ed* or *-d* to the base form of the verb. For example, both the past and past participle forms of *love* are *loved.* The past and past participle forms of irregular verbs are created in a variety of ways. For example, the past form of *begin* is *began;* the past participle form is *begun.*

Problem 1 An improperly formed irregular verb
Romeo and Juliet falled deeply in love.

Solution The past and past participle forms of irregular verbs are formed in some way other than by adding *-ed.* Memorize or look up the correct past or past participle form of an irregular verb.
Romeo and Juliet fell deeply in love.

Problem 2 Confusion between the past form and the past participle
Romeo asks what light has broke through the window.

Solution The past participle form of an irregular verb may be different from the past form. Use the past participle form of a verb when the auxiliary, or "helping," verb *have* is used.
Romeo asks what light has broken through the window.

Problem 3 Improper use of the past participle
Romeo and Juliet seen each other at a party.

Solution A The past participle form of an irregular verb cannot stand alone. Add the auxiliary verb *have* to the past participle to form a complete verb.
Romeo and Juliet had seen each other at a party.

Solution B Replace the past participle with the past form of the verb.
Romeo and Juliet saw each other at a party.

For more about verb tense, see **Language Handbook,** pp. R22–R23.

EXERCISE

Rewrite each sentence correctly, using either the past or past participle form of the verb.

1. The families' feud had went on for a long time. (Use the past participle form.)
2. One night, Capulet gived a ball. (Use the past form.)
3. Romeo seen Juliet there. (Use the past form.)
4. Before he knew it, she had stole his heart. (Use the past participle form.)
5. She drived all other thoughts from his mind. (Use the past form.)

Act 4

SCENE 1. Later that morning. FRIAR LAWRENCE's cell.

[*FRIAR LAWRENCE and PARIS enter. PARIS has just explained to the confused FRIAR that he will marry JULIET.*]

FRIAR. On Thursday, sir? The time is very short.

PARIS. My father° Capulet will have it so,
And I am nothing slow to slack his haste.°

FRIAR. You say you do not know the lady's mind.
Uneven is the course;° I like it not.

PARIS. Immoderately she weeps for Tybalt's death,
And therefore have I little talk'd of love;
For Venus smiles not in a house of tears.
Now, sir, her father counts it dangerous
That she do give her sorrow so much sway,
And in his wisdom hastes our marriage
To stop the inundation of her tears,
Which, too much minded° by herself alone,
May be put from her by society.
Now do you know the reason of this haste.

FRIAR. [*Aside.*] I would I knew not why it should be slowed.—
Look, sir, here comes the lady toward my cell.

[*JULIET enters. Surprised to see PARIS there, she pretends to be in good spirits.*]

PARIS. Happily met, my lady and my wife!

JULIET. That may be, sir, when I may be a wife.

PARIS. That "may be" must be, love, on Thursday next.

JULIET. What must be shall be.

FRIAR. That's a certain text.°

PARIS. Come you to make confession to this father?

JULIET. To answer that, I should confess to you.

PARIS. Do not deny to him that you love me.

JULIET. I will confess to you that I love him.

PARIS. So will ye, I am sure, that you love me.

JULIET. If I do so, it will be of more price,°
Being spoke behind your back, than to your face.

PARIS. Poor soul, thy face is much abus'd with tears.

JULIET. The tears have got small victory by that,
For it was bad enough before their spite.°

2 **father:** father-in-law.

3 **I am . . . haste:** I will not delay him.

5 **Uneven is the course:** The plan is irregular.

13 **minded:** brooded over.

21 **That's a certain text:** That's an indisputable saying.

27 **price:** value.

31 **it was . . . spite:** my face was bad enough before the tears marred it.

PARIS. Thou wrong'st it more than tears with that report.

JULIET. That is no slander, sir, which is a truth;
And what I spake, I spake it to my face.°

PARIS. Thy face is mine, and thou hast sland'red it.

JULIET. It may be so, for it is not mine own.°
[*To* FRIAR LAWRENCE.] Are you at leisure, holy father, now,
Or shall I come to you at evening mass?

FRIAR. My leisure serves me, pensive° daughter, now.
[*To* PARIS.] My lord, we must entreat the time alone.

PARIS. God shield I should disturb devotion!
Juliet, on Thursday early will I rouse ye.
Till then, adieu, and keep this holy kiss.

[*PARIS exits.*]

JULIET. O, shut the door, and when thou hast done so,
Come weep with me—past hope, past cure, past help!

FRIAR. O Juliet, I already know thy grief;
It strains me past the compass of my wits.°
I hear thou must, and nothing may prorogue° it,
On Thursday next be married to this County.

JULIET. Tell me not, friar, that thou hearest of this,
Unless thou tell me how I may prevent it.
If in thy wisdom thou canst give no help,
Do thou but call my resolution wise
And with this knife I'll help it presently.°
God join'd my heart and Romeo's, thou our hands;
And ere this hand, by thee to Romeo's seal'd,
Shall be the label to another deed,°
Or my true heart with treacherous revolt
Turn to another, this shall slay them both.
Therefore, out of thy long-experienc'd time,
Give me some present counsel;° or, behold,
'Twixt my extremes and me this bloody knife
Shall play the umpire, arbitrating that
Which the commission of thy years and art
Could to no issue of true honor bring.°
Be not so long to speak. I long to die
If what thou speak'st speak not of remedy.

FRIAR. Hold, daughter. I do spy a kind of hope,
Which craves° as desperate an execution°
As that is desperate which we would prevent.

34 **to my face:** openly (not behind my back).

36 **It may . . . own:** Juliet's reply suggests that her face belongs to Romeo or that she is presenting a false face to Paris.

39 **pensive** (pen′ siv): thoughtful; sad.

47 **strains me past the compass of my wits:** forces me beyond the limits of my understanding.

48 **prorogue** (prō rōg′): postpone.

53–54 **Do thou . . . presently:** Juliet asks the Friar to approve of her resolution to kill herself, a mortal sin.

57 **be the . . . deed:** confirm another marriage.

61 **present counsel:** immediate advice.

62–65 **'Twixt my . . . bring:** Juliet threatens that her knife will settle the dispute between herself and her great difficulties, which the Friar's wisdom and learning could not bring to an honorable outcome.

69 **craves:** requires. **execution:** act.

Friar Lawrence and Juliet, exhibited 1874. John Pettie. Oil on canvas, 110.5 x 76.5 cm. Royal Shakespeare Theatre Collection, Stratford-upon-Avon, England.

Viewing the painting: Does this portrayal of Friar Lawrence match your own image of him? Why or why not?

If, rather than to marry County Paris,
Thou hast the strength of will to slay thyself,
Then is it likely thou wilt undertake
A thing like death to chide away this shame,
That cop'st with death himself to scape from it;°
And, if thou darest, I'll give thee remedy.

JULIET. O, bid me leap, rather than marry Paris,
From off the battlements of any tower,
Or walk in thievish ways,° or bid me lurk
Where serpents are; chain me with roaring bears,
Or hide me nightly in a charnel house,°
O'ercover'd quite with dead men's rattling bones,
With reeky shanks° and yellow chapless° skulls;
Or bid me go into a new-made grave
And hide me with a dead man in his shroud—
Things that, to hear them told, have made me tremble—
And I will do it without fear or doubt,
To live an unstain'd wife to my sweet love.

FRIAR. Hold, then. Go home, be merry, give consent
To marry Paris. Wednesday is tomorrow.
Tomorrow night look that thou lie alone;
Let not the nurse lie with thee in thy chamber.
Take thou this vial, being then in bed,
And this distilling liquor° drink thou off;
When presently through all thy veins shall run
A cold and drowsy humor;° for no pulse
Shall keep his native progress,° but surcease;°
No warmth, no breath, shall testify thou livest;
The roses in thy lips and cheeks shall fade
To wanny ashes,° thy eyes' windows° fall
Like death when he shuts up the day of life;
Each part, depriv'd of supple government,°
Shall, stiff and stark and cold, appear like death;
And in this borrowed likeness of shrunk death
Thou shalt continue two-and-forty hours,
And then awake as from a pleasant sleep.
Now, when the bridegroom in the morning comes
To rouse thee from thy bed, there art thou dead.
Then, as the manner of our country is,
In thy best robes uncovered on the bier
Thou shalt be borne to that same ancient vault
Where all the kindred of the Capulets lie.
In the meantime, against° thou shalt awake,

71–75 If, rather . . . from it: The Friar says that since Juliet is willing to face **(cop'st)** death itself to avoid the shame of marrying Paris, then she probably would go through something similar to death to achieve the same result.

79 in thievish ways: on roads where thieves lurk.

81 charnel (chärn′ əl) **house:** a vault where skulls and bones were stored.

83 reeky shanks: foul-smelling limbs. **chapless:** jawless.

94 distilling liquor: liquid medicine that permeates the body.

96 cold and drowsy humor: a fluid that will make your body cold and put you to sleep.

97 his native progress: its natural movement. **surcease:** stop.

100 To wanny ashes: to the paleness of ashes. **eyes' windows:** eyelids.

102 supple government: the ability to move.

113 against: in preparation for when.

Shall Romeo by my letters know our drift;°
And hither shall he come; and he and I
Will watch thy waking, and that very night
Shall Romeo bear thee hence to Mantua.
And this shall free thee from this present shame,
If no inconstant toy° nor womanish fear
Abate thy valor° in the acting it.

[*JULIET takes the vial.*]

JULIET. Give me, give me! O, tell not me of fear!

FRIAR. Hold! Get you gone, be strong and prosperous°
In this resolve. I'll send a friar with speed
To Mantua, with my letters to thy lord.

JULIET. Love give me strength, and strength shall help afford.°
Farewell, dear father.

[*They exit.*]

114 **drift:** intentions.

119 **inconstant toy:** whim.

120 **Abate thy valor:** lessen your courage.

122 **prosperous:** successful.

125 **afford:** carry out.

SCENE 2. Later that day. A hall in CAPULET's house.

[*LORD CAPULET, LADY CAPULET, and the NURSE enter with several SERVANTS. They are making arrangements for the wedding that will be held in just two days.*]

CAPULET. So many guests invite as here are writ.

[*CAPULET hands a SERVANT a guest list, and the SERVANT exits to invite the wedding guests.*]

Sirrah, go hire me twenty cunning° cooks.

SERVINGMAN. You shall have none ill, sir; for I'll try° if they
can lick their fingers.

CAPULET. How canst thou try them so?

SERVINGMAN. Marry, sir, 'tis an ill cook that cannot lick his
own fingers.° Therefore he that cannot lick his fingers goes
not with me.

[*The second SERVANT exits to hire more cooks.*]

CAPULET. Go begone.
We shall be much unfurnish'd° for this time.
What, is my daughter gone to Friar Lawrence?

NURSE. Ay, forsooth.°

CAPULET. Well, he may chance to do some good on her.
A peevish self-will'd harlotry it is.°

[*JULIET enters, returning from FRIAR LAWRENCE's cell.*]

NURSE. See where she comes from shrift with merry look.

2 **cunning:** skilled.

3 **try:** test.

6–7 **'tis an ill . . . fingers:** a proverbial expression for cooks who lack faith in their cooking.

10 **unfurnish'd:** unprepared.

12 **forsooth:** in truth.

14 **A peevish . . . is:** She is a quarrelsome, stubborn good-for-nothing.

CAPULET. How now, my headstrong? Where have you been gadding?

JULIET. Where I have learnt me to repent the sin
Of disobedient opposition
To you and your behests,° and am enjoin'd°
By holy Lawrence to fall prostrate° here
To beg your pardon.

[*She kneels before her father.*]

Pardon, I beseech you!
Henceforward I am ever rul'd by you.

CAPULET. Send for the County. Go tell him of this.
I'll have this knot knit up tomorrow morning.°

JULIET. I met the youthful lord at Lawrence' cell
And gave him what becomed° love I might,
Not stepping o'er the bounds of modesty.

CAPULET. Why, I am glad on't. This is well. Stand up.

[*JULIET rises.*]

This is as't should be. Let me see the County.
Ay, marry, go, I say, and fetch him hither.
Now, afore God, this reverend holy friar,
All our whole city is much bound° to him.

JULIET. Nurse, will you go with me into my closet°
To help me sort such needful ornaments°
As you think fit to furnish me tomorrow?

LADY CAPULET. No, not till Thursday. There is time enough.

CAPULET. Go, nurse, go with her. We'll to church tomorrow.

[*JULIET and the NURSE exit.*]

LADY CAPULET. We shall be short in our provision.
'Tis now near night.

CAPULET. Tush, I will stir about,
And all things shall be well, I warrant thee, wife.
Go thou to Juliet, help to deck up her.°
I'll not to bed tonight; let me alone.
I'll play the housewife for this once. What, ho!
They are all forth; well, I will walk myself°
To County Paris, to prepare up him
Against tomorrow. My heart is wondrous light,
Since this same wayward girl is so reclaim'd.

[*CAPULET and LADY CAPULET exit.*]

19 **behests** (bi hests′): requests. **enjoin'd:** directed.

20 **fall prostrate:** kneel down in humility.

23–24 **Send for . . . morning:** Juliet's apparent change of heart moves Capulet to change the wedding day to Wednesday.

26 **becomed:** becoming; proper.

32 **bound:** indebted.

33 **closet:** private room.

34 **sort such needful ornaments:** select the necessary clothing.

41 **deck up her:** dress her.

43–44 **I'll play . . . walk myself:** Capulet calls for a servant but realizes that he has already sent them all on errands.

SCENE 3. The evening of the same day, the night before the wedding. JULIET's room.

[*JULIET and the NURSE have been preparing JULIET's clothing for the wedding.*]

JULIET. Ay, those attires are best; but, gentle nurse,
I pray thee leave me to myself tonight;
For I have need of many orisons°
To move the heavens to smile upon my state,
Which, well thou knowest, is cross° and full of sin.

[*LADY CAPULET enters.*]

LADY CAPULET. What, are you busy, ho? Need you my help?

JULIET. No, madam; we have cull'd° such necessaries
As are behoveful for our state° tomorrow.
So please you, let me now be left alone,
And let the nurse this night sit up with you;
For I am sure you have your hands full all
In this so sudden business.

LADY CAPULET. Good night.
Get thee to bed, and rest; for thou hast need.

[*LADY CAPULET and the NURSE exit.*]

JULIET. Farewell! God knows when we shall meet again.
I have a faint cold fear thrills through my veins
That almost freezes up the heat of life.
I'll call them back again to comfort me.
Nurse!—What should she do here?
My dismal scene I needs must act alone.
Come, vial.
What if this mixture do not work at all?
Shall I be married then tomorrow morning?
No, no! This shall forbid it. Lie thou there.

[*She places a dagger beside the bed.*]

What if it be a poison which the friar
Subtly hath minist'red to have me dead,
Lest in this marriage he should be dishonor'd
Because he married me before to Romeo?
I fear it is; and yet methinks it should not,
For he hath still been tried° a holy man.
How if, when I am laid into the tomb,
I wake before the time that Romeo
Come to redeem° me? There's a fearful point!
Shall I not then be stifled in the vault,
To whose foul mouth no healthsome air breathes in,

3 **orisons** (ôr′i zənz): prayers.

5 **cross:** wrong; perverse.

7 **cull'd:** selected.

8 **behoveful for our state:** appropriate for our ceremony.

29 **still been tried:** always proven to be.

32 **redeem:** rescue.

And there die strangled ere my Romeo comes?
Or, if I live, is it not very like°
The horrible conceit° of death and night,
Together with the terror of the place—
As in a vault, an ancient receptacle
Where for this many hundred years the bones
Of all my buried ancestors are pack'd;
Where bloody Tybalt, yet but green in earth,°
Lies fest'ring° in his shroud; where, as they say,
At some hours in the night spirits resort°—
Alack, alack, is it not like that I,
So early waking—what with loathsome smells,
And shrieks like mandrakes° torn out of the earth,
That living mortals, hearing them, run mad—
O, if I wake, shall I not be distraught,°
Environed° with all these hideous fears,
And madly play with my forefathers' joints,
And pluck the mangled Tybalt from his shroud,
And, in this rage, with some great kinsman's bone
As with a club dash out my desp'rate brains?
O, look! Methinks I see my cousin's ghost
Seeking out Romeo, that did spit° his body
Upon a rapier's point. Stay,° Tybalt, stay!
Romeo, Romeo, Romeo! Here's drink—I drink to thee.

[*JULIET drinks the contents of the vial and falls onto her bed, which is surrounded with curtains.*]

36 **like:** likely.

37 **conceit:** thought.

42 **green in earth:** newly buried.

43 **fest'ring:** decaying.

44 **resort:** gather.

47 **mandrakes:** plants with thick forked roots. (Many people in Shakespeare's time believed that mandrakes shrieked when pulled up and that anyone who heard the sound would become insane.)

49 **distraught** (dis trôt′): crazed.

50 **Environed:** surrounded.

56 **spit:** impale.

57 **Stay:** Remain where you are.

SCENE 4. During the night. A hall in CAPULET's house.

[*Preparations for the wedding continue.* LADY CAPULET *and the* NURSE *enter.*]

LADY CAPULET. Hold, take these keys and fetch more spices, nurse.

NURSE. They call for dates and quinces° in the pastry.°

[*LORD CAPULET enters.*]

CAPULET. Come, stir, stir, stir! The second cock hath crowed,
The curfew bell° hath rung, 'tis three o'clock.
Look to the bak'd meats, good Angelica;
Spare not for cost.

NURSE. Go, you cotquean,° go,
Get you to bed! Faith, you'll be sick tomorrow
For this night's watching.°

CAPULET. No, not a whit. What, I have watch'd ere now
All night for lesser cause, and ne'er been sick.

2 **quinces** (kwin′ səz): a golden, apple-shaped fruit. **pastry:** place where baking is done.

4 **curfew bell:** rung in the morning at daybreak as well as in the evening.

6 **cotquean** (kät′ kwēn): a man who does housework.

8 **watching:** staying awake.

Story of Alatiel Tavoli (detail), 15th century. Master of Jarves Cassoni. Tempera on panel. Museo Correr, Venice.

Viewing the painting: How might Juliet react if she were to see the preparations for her wedding? How might Paris react?

LADY CAPULET. Ay, you have been a mouse hunt° in your time;
But I will watch you from such watching now.

[*LADY CAPULET and the NURSE exit.*]

CAPULET. A jealous hood,° a jealous hood!

[*Several SERVANTS enter with spits, logs, and baskets for preparing the wedding feast.*]

Now, fellow, what is there?

FIRST FELLOW. Things for the cook, sir; but I know not what.

CAPULET. Make haste, make haste.

[*One SERVANT exits.*]

Sirrah, fetch drier logs.
Call Peter; he will show thee where they are.

SECOND FELLOW. I have a head, sir, that will find out logs
And never trouble Peter for the matter.

11 **mouse hunt:** woman chaser.

13 **jealous hood:** "jealousy" or "jealous woman."

CAPULET. Mass,° and well said; a merry whoreson,° ha!
Thou shalt be loggerhead.°

[The SERVANTS *exit.]*

Good faith, 'tis day.
The County will be here with music straight,°
For so he said he would.

[Music plays from offstage. PARIS *is outside the house with musicians.]*

I hear him near.
Nurse! Wife! What, ho! What, nurse, I say!

[The NURSE *enters.]*

Go waken Juliet; go and trim her up.
I'll go and chat with Paris. Hie, make haste,
Make haste! The bridegroom he is come already:
Make haste, I say.

[They exit.]

20 **Mass:** by the mass (a mild oath). **whoreson** (hōr′ sən): rascal.

21 **loggerhead:** blockhead.

22 **straight:** immediately.

SCENE 5. Immediately after the previous scene. JULIET's room.

*[*JULIET *is behind the curtain that surrounds her bed. The* NURSE *enters.]*

NURSE. Mistress! What, mistress! Juliet! Fast,° I warrant her, she.
Why, lamb! Why, lady! Fie, you slugabed.
Why, love, I say! Madam; Sweetheart! Why, bride!
What, not a word? You take your pennyworths° now;
Sleep for a week, for the next night, I warrant,
The County Paris hath set up his rest°
That you shall rest but little, God forgive me!
Marry and amen! How sound is she asleep!
I needs must wake her. Madam, madam, madam!
Ay, let the County take you° in your bed,
He'll fright you up, i' faith. Will it not be?

[The NURSE *pulls open the bed curtain.]*

What, dress'd, and in your clothes, and down again?°
I must needs wake you. Lady! Lady! Lady!
Alas, alas! Help, help! My lady's dead!
O weraday that ever I was born!
Some aqua vitae, ho! My lord! My lady!

*[*LADY CAPULET *enters.]*

LADY CAPULET. What noise is here?

NURSE. O lamentable day!

LADY CAPULET. What is the matter?

NURSE. Look, look! O heavy day!

1 **Fast:** fast asleep.

4 **pennyworths:** small amounts (of rest).

6 **set up his rest:** resolved.

10 **take you:** catch you.

12 **down again:** gone back to bed.

LADY CAPULET. O me, O me! My child, my only life!
Revive, look up, or I will die with thee!
Help, help! Call help.

[*LORD CAPULET enters.*]

CAPULET. For shame, bring Juliet forth; her lord is come.

NURSE. She's dead, deceas'd; she's dead, alack the day!

LADY CAPULET. Alack the day, she's dead, she's dead, she's dead!

CAPULET. Ha! Let me see her. Out alas! She's cold,
Her blood is settled, and her joints are stiff;
Life and these lips have long been separated.
Death lies on her like an untimely frost
Upon the sweetest flower of all the field.

NURSE. O lamentable day!

LADY CAPULET. O woeful time!

CAPULET. Death, that hath ta'en her hence to make me wail,
Ties up my tongue and will not let me speak.

[*FRIAR LAWRENCE and PARIS enter.*]

FRIAR. Come, is the bride ready to go to church?

CAPULET. Ready to go, but never to return.
O son, the night before thy wedding day
Hath Death lain with thy wife. There she lies,
Flower as she was, deflowered by him.
Death is my son-in-law, Death is my heir;
My daughter he hath wedded. I will die
And leave him all. Life, living, all is Death's.

PARIS. Have I thought long to see this morning's face,
And doth it give me such a sight as this?

LADY CAPULET. Accurs'd, unhappy, wretched, hateful day!
Most miserable hour that e'er time saw
In lasting labor of his pilgrimage!
But one, poor one, one poor and loving child,
But one thing to rejoice and solace° in,
And cruel Death hath catch'd it from my sight.

NURSE. O woe! O woeful, woeful, woeful day!
Most lamentable day, most woeful day
That ever ever I did yet behold!
O day, O day, O day! O hateful day!
Never was seen so black a day as this.
O woeful day! O woeful day!

47 **solace** (sol′ is): take comfort.

PARIS. Beguil'd,° divorced, wronged, spited, slain!
Most detestable Death, by thee beguil'd,
By cruel, cruel thee quite overthrown.
O love! O life!—not life, but love in death!

CAPULET. Despis'd, distressed, hated, martyr'd, kill'd!
Uncomfortable° time, why cam'st thou now
To murder, murder our solemnity?°
O child, O child! My soul, and not my child!
Dead art thou—alack, my child is dead,
And with my child my joys are buried!

FRIAR. Peace, ho, for shame! Confusion's cure lives not
In these confusions.° Heaven and yourself
Had part° in this fair maid—now heaven hath all,
And all the better is it for the maid.
Your part° in her you could not keep from death,
But heaven keeps his part in eternal life.

55 **Beguil'd** (bi gīld′): cheated.

60 **Uncomfortable:** bringing no comfort.

61 **solemnity** (sə lem′ nə tē): celebration.

65–66 **Confusion's . . . confusions:** The healing of this calamity does not lie in your uncontrolled outbursts.

67 **Had part:** shared.

69 **Your part:** that is, Juliet's mortal self.

The Feigned Death of Juliet, c. 1856–1858. Frederick Leighton. Oil on canvas, 44 x 68½ in. Art Gallery of South Australia, Adelaide.

Viewing the painting: In your opinion, do the emotions portrayed in the painting reflect the emotions of this scene? Explain.

The most you sought was her promotion,°
For 'twas your heaven she should be advanc'd;°
And weep ye now, seeing she is advanc'd
Above the clouds, as high as heaven itself?
O, in this love, you love your child so ill
That you run mad, seeing that she is well.°
She's not well married that lives married long,
But she's best married that dies married young.
Dry up your tears and stick your rosemary°
On this fair corse, and, as the custom is,
And in her best array bear her to church;
For though fond nature bids us all lament,
Yet nature's tears are reason's merriment.°

CAPULET. All things that we ordained festival°
Turn from their office° to black funeral—
Our instruments to melancholy bells,
Our wedding cheer to a sad burial feast;
Our solemn hymns to sullen dirges° change;
Our bridal flowers serve for a buried corse;
And all things change them to the contrary.

FRIAR. Sir, go you in; and, madam, go with him;
And go, Sir Paris. Everyone prepare
To follow this fair corse unto her grave.
The heavens do low'r° upon you for some ill;°
Move them no more by crossing their high will.

[*They all cast rosemary leaves on* JULIET. *All but the* NURSE *and the* MUSICIANS *exit.*]

FIRST MUSICIAN. Faith, we may put up our pipes and be gone.

NURSE. Honest good fellows, ah, put up, put up,
For well you know this is a pitiful case.°

[NURSE *exits.*]

FIRST MUSICIAN. Ay, by my troth, the case° may be amended.°

[PETER *enters.*]

PETER. Musicians, O musicians, "Heart's ease,"° "Heart's ease"! O, and you will have me live, play "Heart's ease."

FIRST MUSICIAN. Why "Heart's ease"?

PETER. O musicians, because my heart itself plays "My heart is full." O, play me some merry dump° to comfort me.

FIRST MUSICIAN. Not a dump we, 'tis no time to play now.

PETER. You will not then?

71 promotion: social advancement (from marrying Paris).

72 For 'twas . . . advanc'd: For the greatest joy you could imagine was to see her elevated to a higher station in life.

76 well: in heaven.

79 rosemary: an herb used in funerals as a symbol of remembrance.

82–83 For though . . . merriment: Although foolish human nature commands us to grieve, reason finds cause for rejoicing (because Juliet is in heaven).

84 ordained festival: ordered for festive purposes.

85 office: function.

88 sullen dirges (dur′ jəz): gloomy funeral music.

94 low'r: frown. **ill:** sin.

98 case: situation.

99 the case: my instrument's case. **amended:** repaired. (This may be a pun, or the First Musician might have misunderstood the Nurse.)

100 "Heart's ease": a popular song.

104 dump: sad tune.

FIRST MUSICIAN. No.

PETER. I will then give it you soundly.°

FIRST MUSICIAN. What will you give us?

PETER. No money, on my faith, but the gleek;° I will give you the minstrel.°

FIRST MUSICIAN. Then will I give you the serving-creature.

PETER. Then will I lay the serving-creature's dagger on your pate.° I will carry° no crotchets,° I'll *re*° you, I'll *fa*° you. Do you note° me?

FIRST MUSICIAN. And you *re* us and *fa* us, you note us.

SECOND MUSICIAN. Pray you put up your dagger, and put out° your wit.

PETER. Then have at you with my wit! I will drybeat° you with an iron wit, and put up my iron dagger. Answer me like men:

When griping° griefs the heart doth wound,
And doleful dumps the mind oppress,
Then music with her silver sound"—

why "silver sound"? Why "music with her silver sound"? What say you, Simon Catling?°

FIRST MUSICIAN. Marry, sir, because silver hath a sweet sound.

PETER. Pretty! What say you, Hugh Rebeck?°

SECOND MUSICIAN. I say, "silver sound," because musicians sound° for silver.

PETER. Pretty too! What say you, James Soundpost?°

THIRD MUSICIAN. Faith, I know not what to say.

PETER. O, I cry you mercy, you are the singer;° I will say for you; it is "music with her silver sound," because musicians have no gold for sounding:

"Then music with her silver sound
With speedy help doth lend redress."

[*PETER exits.*]

FIRST MUSICIAN. What a pestilent knave is this same!

SECOND MUSICIAN. Hang him, Jack! Come, we'll in here, tarry for the mourners, and stay° dinner.

[*MUSICIANS exit.*]

108 **give it you soundly:** let you have it thoroughly.

110–111 **gleek:** insulting jest. **give you the minstrel:** call you a minstrel (an insult).

114 **pate:** head. **carry:** put up with. **crotchets** (kroch′ itz): "whims" or "quarter notes in music." ***Re*** and ***fa*** are musical notes, which Peter uses threateningly.

115 **note:** understand.

117 **put out:** display.

119 **drybeat:** thrash.

121 **griping:** distressing. (Peter is reciting lines from a poem.)

125 **Catling** (kat′ ling): a lute string.

127 **Rebeck** (rē′ bek): a three-stringed fiddle.

129 **sound:** play.

130 **Soundpost:** a small peg beneath the bridge of a stringed instrument.

132 **you are the singer:** that is, you can only sing, not say.

139 **stay:** wait for.

Responding to Literature

Personal Response

What do you think of Friar Lawrence's plan and its consequences?

Analyzing Act 4

Recall and Interpret

1. Whom does Juliet meet when she goes to see Friar Lawrence? How does she behave in this encounter?
2. What plan does the Friar suggest to Juliet? Why does he suggest this plan?
3. What does Capulet decide when Juliet agrees to marry Paris? Why do you think he makes this decision? How might this decision cause problems for Juliet?
4. What does Juliet fear most about carrying out the Friar's plan? What does her resolve to go ahead with the plan indicate about her?
5. How does Capulet respond after Juliet's body is found? Do you think he regrets his earlier harshness toward her? Why or why not?

Evaluate and Connect

6. Do you think the Friar's plan is realistic? Why or why not?
7. Look back at Juliet's soliloquy in act 4, scene 3, lines 14–58. What does the **imagery** in this passage contribute to the drama of the play? Explain your response. (See Literary Terms Handbook, page R7.)
8. What would you have done if you had been in Juliet's situation? Explain.

Literary ELEMENTS

Comic Relief

Comic relief occurs when a short, funny episode interrupts an otherwise serious or tragic work. Such an episode can serve a variety of functions. For example, it may break the tension after a particularly intense scene, it may provide a bitterly humorous twist on the work's theme, or it may emphasize an unfolding tragedy.

1. Look at the ending of act 4, scene 3, and at the beginning of scene 4. Find the lines that create comic relief. Write them down, and describe what function the relief serves.
2. Find another incidence of comic relief in act 4. Describe this scene and the relief it provides.

- See **Literary Terms Handbook,** p. R3.

Extending Your Response

Interdisciplinary Activity

Social Studies: With This Ring . . . Use library resources, CD-ROMs, and the Internet to find out more about marriage laws and customs during the Renaissance. Answer questions such as the following: How did parents choose spouses for their children? Was love considered an important basis for marriage? Who could perform the marriage ceremony? Use your findings to prepare and present an oral report.

Creative Writing

Dear Diary Imagine that you are either Friar Lawrence or the Nurse—characters who have been entrusted with the secret of Romeo and Juliet's marriage. Write a diary entry about the events in act 4. Discuss the young lovers' dilemma, the advice you have offered, and your hopes and fears about their future. Include specific details from the play in your diary entry.

Save your work for your portfolio.

LISTENING, SPEAKING, and VIEWING

Readers Theater

In Shakespeare's day, plays were performed without scenery or artificial lighting. Although some plays are still performed simply today, many modern theatrical productions have complicated sets, elaborate lighting, and highly technical special effects. All this costs a great deal of money, which means that putting on a play is a gamble. In other words, it better be good.

No matter how sophisticated a production, a quality script is still essential to the success of a play. But how do playwrights know whether their dialogue will captivate an audience? How do actors learn to deliver their lines effectively? One way is by participating in **readers theater.** Using their voices and facial expressions to convey emotion, actors read their lines from a script instead of speaking them from memory. The players may sit in a semicircle of chairs in front of an audience, or they may walk through the stage directions, using body language to help make the words come alive.

Readers theater helps playwrights, directors, and cast members judge how well a new play is shaping up. Performing in readers theater is useful for students of theater as well. It gives them an opportunity to take on the role of a character and to learn about the dramatic arts, without going through the lengthy preparations necessary for a full-fledged play.

Tips for a Readers Theater Performer

- Read the script silently several times. Make sure you understand the characters and their relationships with one another.
- Practice reading your lines aloud. Make sure you understand–and can pronounce–each word. Stage directions often provide clues to the way that certain lines should be delivered.
- Try to actually *feel* what your character feels. Then use the tone and pitch of your voice to express your unique interpretation of the script.
- With your readers theater group, analyze the scene. What's happening? What kinds of emotions are being displayed? Then decide whether you want to stand in front of your audience, or whether you'd rather sit in chairs, and rehearse that way.

ACTIVITY

With a small group, choose a favorite scene from *Romeo and Juliet* and give a readers theater performance of it. Decide who will play what role, and rehearse the scene, referring to the **Tips for a Readers Theater Performer** listed above. After a rehearsal or two, perform your scene for the class.

Act 5

SCENE 1. The next day. A street in Mantua, the city where ROMEO lives in exile.

[ROMEO *enters; he is waiting for his servant,* BALTHASAR, *to return from Verona with news of* JULIET.]

ROMEO. If I may trust the flattering truth of sleep,
My dreams presage,° some joyful news at hand.
My bosom's lord° sits lightly in his throne,
And all this day an unaccustom'd spirit
Lifts me above the ground with cheerful thoughts.
I dreamt my lady came and found me dead
(Strange dream that gives a dead man leave to think!)
And breath'd such life with kisses in my lips
That I reviv'd and was an emperor.
Ah me! How sweet is love itself possess'd,
When but love's shadows° are so rich in joy!

[ROMEO's *servant,* BALTHASAR, *enters.*]

News from Verona! How now, Balthasar?
Dost thou not bring me letters from the friar?
How doth my lady? Is my father well?
How fares my Juliet? That I ask again,
For nothing can be ill if she be well.

BALTHASAR. Then she is well, and nothing can be ill.
Her body sleeps in Capel's monument,°
And her immortal part with angels lives.
I saw her laid low in her kindred's vault
And presently took post° to tell it you.
O, pardon me for bringing these ill news,
Since you did leave it for my office,° sir.

ROMEO. Is it e'en so? Then I defy you, stars!
Thou knowest my lodging. Get me ink and paper
And hire post horses. I will hence° tonight.

BALTHASAR. I do beseech you, sir, have patience.
Your looks are pale and wild and do import
Some misadventure.°

ROMEO. Tush, thou art deceiv'd.
Leave me and do the thing I bid thee do.
Hast thou no letters to me from the friar?

BALTHASAR. No, my good lord.

ROMEO. No matter. Get thee gone.
And hire those horses. I'll be with thee straight.

2 **presage** (pres′ ij): predict.

3 **bosom's lord:** heart.

11 **but love's shadows:** only dreams of love.

18 **Capel's monument:** the Capulet tomb.

21 **presently took post:** immediately set out on post horses.

23 **office:** duty.

26 **hence:** leave here.

28–29 **and do . . . misadventure:** suggest that some misfortune will occur.

[*BALTHASAR exits. ROMEO, grief stricken, begins to walk aimlessly.*]

Well, Juliet, I will lie with thee tonight.
Let's see for means. O mischief, thou art swift
To enter in the thoughts of desperate men!
I do remember an apothecary,°
And hereabouts 'a dwells, which late I noted
In tatt'red weeds,° with overwhelming° brows,
Culling of simples.° Meager were his looks,
Sharp misery had worn him to the bones;
And in his needy shop a tortoise hung,
An alligator stuff'd, and other skins
Of ill-shap'd fishes; and about his shelves
A beggarly account° of empty boxes,
Green earthen pots, bladders, and musty seeds.
Remnants of packthread,° and old cakes of roses°
Were thinly scattered, to make up a show.
Noting this penury,° to myself I said,
"An' if a man did need a poison now
Whose sale is present death° in Mantua,
Here lives a caitiff° wretch would sell it him."
O, this same thought did but forerun my need,
And this same needy man must sell it me.
As I remember, this should be the house.
Being holiday, the beggar's shop is shut.
What, ho! Apothecary!

[*APOTHECARY enters.*]

APOTHECARY. Who calls so loud?

ROMEO. Come hither, man. I see that thou art poor.
Hold, there is forty ducats.° Let me have
A dram of poison, such soon-speeding gear°
As will disperse itself through all the veins
That the life-weary taker may fall dead.
And that the trunk° may be discharg'd of breath
As violently as hasty powder fir'd
Doth hurry from the fatal cannon's womb.

APOTHECARY. Such mortal° drugs I have; but Mantua's law
Is death to any he that utters° them.

ROMEO. Art thou so bare and full of wretchedness
And fearest to die? Famine is in thy cheeks,
Need and oppression starveth in thy eyes,
Contempt and beggary hangs upon thy back:
The world is not thy friend, nor the world's law;

37 **apothecary** (ə poth′ə ker′ ē): one who prepares and sells drugs.

39 **tatt'red weeds:** torn clothing. **overwhelming:** overhanging.

40 **Culling of simples:** sorting medicinal herbs.

45 **beggarly account:** small number.

47 **packthread:** twine for tying packages. **cakes of roses:** rose petals pressed into cakes and used for perfume.

49 **penury** (pen′ yər ē): poverty.

51 **Whose sale . . . death:** the sale of which is punishable by immediate execution.

52 **caitiff** (kā′ tif): miserable.

59 **ducats** (duk′ ətz): gold coins.

60 **soon-speeding gear:** fast-working stuff.

63 **trunk:** body.

66 **mortal:** deadly.

67 **any he that utters:** any man who dispenses.

The world affords no law to make thee rich;
Then be not poor, but break it and take this.

APOTHECARY. My poverty but not my will consents.

ROMEO. I pay thy poverty and not thy will.

APOTHECARY. Put this in any liquid thing you will
And drink it off, and if you had the strength
Of twenty men, it would dispatch you straight.

ROMEO. There is thy gold—worse poison to men's souls,
Doing more murder in this loathsome world,
Than these poor compounds that thou mayst not sell.
I sell thee poison; thou hast sold me none.
Farewell. Buy food and get thyself in flesh.

[*APOTHECARY exits.*]

Come, cordial° and not poison, go with me
To Juliet's grave; for there must I use thee.

[*ROMEO exits.*]

85 **cordial** (kôr′ jəl): tonic, restoring drink.

SCENE 2. The same afternoon. FRIAR LAWRENCE's cell in Verona.

[*FRIAR JOHN enters. Sent by FRIAR LAWRENCE to Mantua with a letter for ROMEO, he has just returned.*]

JOHN. Holy Franciscan friar, brother, ho!

[*FRIAR LAWRENCE enters.*]

LAWRENCE. This same should be the voice of Friar John.
Welcome from Mantua. What says Romeo?
Or, if his mind be writ,° give me his letter.

JOHN. Going to find a barefoot brother° out,
One of our order, to associate° me
Here in this city visiting the sick,
And finding him, the searchers° of the town,
Suspecting that we both were in a house
Where the infectious pestilence° did reign,
Seal'd up the doors, and would not let us forth,
So that my speed to Mantua there was stay'd.°

LAWRENCE. Who bare° my letter, then, to Romeo?

JOHN. I could not send it—here it is again—
Nor get a messenger to bring it thee,
So fearful were they of infection.

LAWRENCE. Unhappy fortune! By my brotherhood,
The letter was not nice, but full of charge,°
Of dear import;° and the neglecting it

4 **if his mind be writ:** if his message is written.

5 **barefoot brother:** Franciscan friar.

6 **associate:** accompany.

8 **searchers:** health officials who searched houses for victims of the plague and quarantined, or isolated, them.

10 **infectious pestilence:** plague.

12 **stay'd:** stopped.

13 **bare:** bore; carried.

18 **not nice, but full of charge:** not trivial, but full of importance.

19 **dear import:** serious consequence.

May do much danger. Friar John, go hence,
Get me an iron crow° and bring it straight
Unto my cell.

JOHN. Brother, I'll go and bring it thee.

[*FRIAR JOHN exits.*]

LAWRENCE. Now must I to the monument alone.
Within this three hours will fair Juliet wake.
She will beshrew° me much that Romeo
Hath had no notice of these accidents,°
But I will write again to Mantua,
And keep her at my cell till Romeo come—
Poor living corse, clos'd in a dead man's tomb!

[*He exits.*]

21 **crow:** crowbar.

25 **beshrew:** blame; scold.

26 **accidents:** occurrences.

SCENE 3. Late that night. The churchyard that contains the Capulets' tomb.

[*PARIS enters with his PAGE who carries a torch and flowers.*]

PARIS. Give me thy torch, boy. Hence, and stand aloof.
Yet put it out, for I would not be seen.
Under yond yew trees lay thee all along,°
Holding thy ear close to the hollow ground.
So shall no foot upon the churchyard tread
(Being loose, unfirm, with digging up of graves)
But thou shalt hear it. Whistle then to me,
As signal that thou hearest something approach.
Give me those flowers. Do as I bid thee, go.

PAGE. [*Aside.*] I am almost afraid to stand alone
Here in the churchyard; yet I will adventure.°

[*The PAGE retires to a watching place while PARIS sprinkles the tomb with flowers.*]

PARIS. Sweet flower, with flowers thy bridal bed I strew
(O woe! thy canopy is dust and stones)
Which with sweet° water nightly I will dew;°
Or, wanting that, with tears distill'd by moans.
The obsequies° that I for thee will keep
Nightly shall be to strew thy grave and weep.

[*The PAGE whistles, his signal that someone is coming.*]

The boy gives warning something doth approach.
What cursed foot wanders this way tonight
To cross° my obsequies and true love's rite?
What, with a torch? Muffle° me, night, awhile.

3 **lay thee all along:** lie flat on the ground.

11 **adventure:** risk it.

14 **sweet:** perfumed. **dew:** sprinkle.

16 **obsequies** (ob′ sə kwēz): funeral rites.

20 **cross:** interrupt.

21 **Muffle:** hide.

[*PARIS hides as ROMEO and BALTHASAR enter.*]

ROMEO. Give me that mattock° and the wrenching iron.°
Hold, take this letter. Early in the morning
See thou deliver it to my lord and father.
Give me the light. Upon thy life I charge° thee,
Whate'er thou hearest or seest, stand all aloof
And do not interrupt me in my course.
Why I descend into this bed of death
Is partly to behold my lady's face,
But chiefly to take thence from her dead finger
A precious ring—a ring that I must use
In dear employment.° Therefore hence, be gone.
But if thou, jealous,° dost return to pry
In what I farther shall intend to do,
By heaven, I will tear thee joint by joint
And strew this hungry churchyard with thy limbs.
The time and my intents are savage-wild,
More fierce and more inexorable far°
Than empty° tigers or the roaring sea.

BALTHASAR. I will be gone, sir, and not trouble ye.

ROMEO. So shalt thou show me friendship. Take thou that.

[*He hands BALTHASAR money.*]

Live, and be prosperous; and farewell, good fellow.

BALTHASAR. [*Aside.*] For all this same, I'll hide me hereabout.
His looks I fear, and his intents I doubt.

[*BALTHASAR hides.*]

ROMEO. Thou detestable maw,° thou womb of death,
Gorg'd° with the dearest morsel of the earth,
Thus I enforce thy rotten jaws to open,
And in despite° I'll cram thee with more food.

[*As ROMEO forces open the tomb, PARIS watches from his hiding place.*]

PARIS. This is that banish'd haughty Montague
That murd'red my love's cousin—with which grief
It is supposed the fair creature died—
And here is come to do some villainous shame
To the dead bodies. I will apprehend° him.

[*PARIS comes forward and speaks to ROMEO.*]

Stop thy unhallowed° toil, vile Montague!
Can vengeance be pursued further than death?
Condemned villain, I do apprehend thee.
Obey, and go with me; for thou must die.

22 **mattock** (mat′ək): pickaxe. **wrenching iron:** crowbar.

25 **charge:** command.

32 **In dear employment:** for an important purpose.

33 **jealous:** suspicious.

38 **More . . . far:** far more fierce and determined.

39 **empty:** hungry.

45 **maw:** the mouth, jaws, or stomach of a flesh-eating animal.

46 **Gorg'd** (gôrjd): stuffed.

48 **in despite:** to spite you.

53 **apprehend:** arrest.

54 **unhallowed:** unholy.

ROMEO. I must indeed; and therefore came I hither.
Good gentle youth, tempt not a desp'rate man.
Fly hence and leave me. Think upon these gone;
Let them affright thee. I beseech thee, youth,
Put not another sin upon my head
By urging me to fury. O, be gone!
By heaven, I love thee better than myself,
For I come hither arm'd against myself.
Stay not, be gone. Live, and hereafter say
A madman's mercy bid thee run away.

PARIS. I do defy thy conjurations.°
And apprehend thee for a felon here.

ROMEO. Wilt thou provoke me? Then have at thee, boy!

[*They draw swords and fight.*]

68 **conjurations:** appeals.

Romeo Slaying Paris at the Bier of Juliet, 1809. Henry Fuseli. Folger Shakespeare Library, Washington, DC.

Viewing the painting: Why might only the figure of Juliet seem to radiate light? What does that tell you about Juliet's importance in this scene?

PAGE. O Lord, they fight! I will go call the watch.

[*The* PAGE *runs off to call the* WATCHMEN. PARIS *is wounded and falls.*]

PARIS. O, I am slain! If thou be merciful,
Open the tomb, lay me with Juliet.

[PARIS *dies.*]

ROMEO. In faith, I will. Let me peruse° this face.
Mercutio's kinsman, noble County Paris!
What said my man when my betossed° soul
Did not attend° him as we rode? I think
He told me Paris should have married Juliet.
Said he not so, or did I dream it so?
Or am I mad, hearing him talk of Juliet,
To think it was so? O, give me thy hand,
One writ with me in sour misfortune's book!

74 **peruse** (pə ro͞oz′): examine.

76 **betossed:** upset.

77 **attend:** pay attention to.

Juliet's Chamber from Romeo & Juliet, 1882. Sir Frank Dicksee. Gouache, en grisaille. 31.1 x 43.9 cm. Private collection.

Viewing the painting: In your opinion, does the artist capture the mood of this scene? Why or why not? What details in the painting contribute to the mood?

I'll bury thee in a triumphant grave.
A grave? O, no, a lanthorn,° slaught'red youth,
For here lies Juliet, and her beauty makes
This vault a feasting presence,° full of light.
Death, lie thou there, by a dead man interr'd.

[*ROMEO carries PARIS into the tomb and lays him there. Then he walks to JULIET's body.*]

How oft when men are at the point of death
Have they been merry! Which their keepers call
A lightning before death.° O, how may I
Call this a lightning? O my love, my wife!
Death, that hath suck'd the honey of thy breath,
Hath had no power yet upon thy beauty.
Thou art not conquer'd. Beauty's ensign° yet
Is crimson in thy lips and in thy cheeks,
And death's pale flag is not advanced there.
Tybalt, liest thou there in thy bloody sheet?
O, what more favor can I do to thee
Than with that hand that cut thy youth in twain
To sunder his that was° thine enemy?
Forgive me, cousin! Ah, dear Juliet,
Why art thou yet so fair? Shall I believe
That unsubstantial° Death is amorous,°
And that the lean abhorred monster keeps
Thee here in dark to be his paramour?°
For fear of that I still will stay with thee
And never from his pallet° of dim night
Depart again. Here, here will I remain
With worms that are thy chambermaids. O, here
Will I set up my everlasting rest
And shake the yoke of inauspicious stars°
From this world-wearied flesh. Eyes, look your last!
Arms, take your last embrace! And, lips, O you
The doors of breath, seal with a righteous kiss
A dateless° bargain to engrossing death!°
Come, bitter conduct; come, unsavory guide!
Thou desperate pilot, now at once run on
The dashing rocks thy seasick weary bark!°
Here's to my love!

[*He takes out the poison and drinks it.*]

O true apothecary!
Thy drugs are quick. Thus with a kiss I die.

84 **lanthorn** (lan′ tərn): a dome with windows that let sunlight into a church or palace.

86 **feasting presence:** a hall lit brightly for celebration.

90 **lightning before death:** a proverbial phrase based on the idea that people's spirits revive just before death.

94 **ensign** (en′ sīn): flag.

100 **sunder his that was:** cut off the youth of the man who was.

103 **unsubstantial:** without a body. **amorous:** in love.

105 **paramour** (par′ ə moor′): mistress.

107 **pallet:** bed.

111 **inauspicious** (in′ ôs pish′ əs) **stars:** ill fate.

115 **dateless:** eternal. **engrossing death:** death who buys up everything.

116–118 **Come . . . bark:** Romeo addresses the poison as a guide **(conduct)** who, like a navigator that runs a ship **(bark)** into the rocks, will lead him to destruction.

[*ROMEO kisses JULIET and falls. Outside the tomb, FRIAR LAWRENCE enters the churchyard carrying a lantern, crowbar, and spade.*]

FRIAR. Saint Francis be my speed! How oft tonight
Have my old feet stumbled at graves! Who's there?

[*BALTHASAR steps out from his hiding place.*]

BALTHASAR. Here's one, a friend, and one that knows you well.

FRIAR. Bliss be upon you! Tell me, good my friend,
What torch is yond that vainly lends his light
To grubs° and eyeless skulls? As I discern,°
It burneth in the Capels' monument.

126 **grubs:** worms. **discern:** make out.

BALTHASAR. It doth so, holy sir; and there's my master,
One that you love.

FRIAR. Who is it?

BALTHASAR. Romeo.

FRIAR. How long hath he been there?

BALTHASAR. Full half an hour.

FRIAR. Go with me to the vault.

BALTHASAR. I dare not, sir.
My master knows not but I am gone hence,
And fearfully° did menace me with death
If I did stay to look on his intents.

133 **fearfully:** fearsomely.

FRIAR. Stay then; I'll go alone. Fear comes upon me.
O, much I fear some ill unthrifty° thing.

136 **unthrifty:** unfortunate.

BALTHASAR. As I did sleep under this yew tree here,
I dreamt my master and another fought,
And that my master slew him.

FRIAR. Romeo!
Alack, alack, what blood is this which stains
The stony entrance of this sepulcher?
What mean these masterless and gory swords
To lie discolor'd by this place of peace?

[*He enters the tomb.*]

Romeo! O, pale! Who else? What, Paris too?
And steep'd in blood? Ah, what an unkind hour
Is guilty of this lamentable chance!°
The lady stirs.

146 **chance:** event.

[*JULIET wakes.*]

Romeo and Juliet: The Tomb Scene, exhibited 1790. Joseph Wright of Derby. Oil on canvas, 177.8 x 241 cm. Derby Museum & Art Gallery, England.

Viewing the painting: How would you describe what Juliet is feeling at this moment?

JULIET. O comfortable friar! Where is my lord?
I do remember well where I should be,
And there I am. Where is my Romeo?

FRIAR. I hear some noise. Lady, come from that nest
Of death, contagion, and unnatural sleep.
A greater power than we can contradict
Hath thwarted our intents.° Come, come away.
Thy husband in thy bosom there lies dead;
And Paris too. Come, I'll dispose of thee
Among a sisterhood of holy nuns.
Stay not to question, for the watch is coming.
Come, go, good Juliet. I dare no longer stay.

JULIET. Go, get thee hence, for I will not away.

[*Hearing the approaching* WATCHMAN, FRIAR LAWRENCE *hurries off*.]

What's here? A cup, clos'd in my true love's hand?

154 **thwarted our intents:** ruined our plans.

Poison, I see, hath been his timeless° end.
O churl!° Drunk all, and left no friendly drop
To help me after? I will kiss thy lips.
Haply° some poison yet doth hang on them
To make me die with a restorative.°

[*She kisses* ROMEO*'s lips*.]

Thy lips are warm!

CHIEF WATCHMAN. [*He calls from off stage.*]
Lead, boy. Which way?

JULIET. Yea, noise? Then I'll be brief. O happy dagger!

[*She snatches* ROMEO*'s dagger.*]

This is thy sheath; there rust, and let me die.

[*She stabs herself, falls, and dies.* PARIS' PAGE *enters the churchyard with a troop of* WATCHMEN.]

PAGE. This is the place. There, where the torch doth burn.

CHIEF WATCHMAN. The ground is bloody. Search about the churchyard.
Go, some of you; whoe'er you find attach.°

[*Some of the* WATCHMEN *exit to search the churchyard. The remainder of the* WATCHMEN, *with the* PAGE, *enter the tomb.*]

Pitiful sight! Here lies the County slain;
And Juliet bleeding, warm, and newly dead,
Who here hath lain this two days buried.
Go, tell the Prince; run to the Capulets;
Raise up the Montagues; some others search.

[*Other* WATCHMEN *exit.*]

We see the ground° whereon these woes do lie,
But the true ground of all these piteous woes
We cannot without circumstance descry.°

[*Some* WATCHMEN *return with* BALTHASAR.]

SECOND WATCHMAN. Here's Romeo's man. We found him in the churchyard.

CHIEF WATCHMAN. Hold him in safety till the Prince come hither.

[*Another* WATCHMAN *returns with* FRIAR LAWRENCE.]

THIRD WATCHMAN. Here is a friar that trembles, sighs, and weeps.
We took this mattock and this spade from him
As he was coming from this churchyard's side.

CHIEF WATCHMAN. A great suspicion! Stay the friar too.

162 **timeless:** untimely.

163 **churl:** miser.

165 **Haply:** perhaps.

166 **restorative:** a medicine or other substance that restores health or consciousness. (However, Juliet wants the kiss to restore her to Romeo by killing her.)

173 **attach:** arrest.

179 **ground:** cause.

181 **without circumstance descry** (di skrī): understand without more information.

[*PRINCE ESCALUS enters with his ATTENDANTS*.]

PRINCE. What misadventure is so early up,
That calls our person from our morning rest?

[*LORD CAPULET and LADY CAPULET enter with others*.]

CAPULET. What should it be, that is so shriek'd abroad?

LADY CAPULET. O, the people in the street cry "Romeo,"
Some "Juliet," and some "Paris"; and all run
With open outcry toward our monument.

PRINCE. What fear is this which startles in your ears?

CHIEF WATCHMAN. Sovereign,

[*He calls them to the entrance of the tomb*.]

here lies the County Paris slain;
And Romeo dead; and Juliet, dead before,
Warm and new kill'd.

PRINCE. Search, seek, and know how this foul murder comes.

CHIEF WATCHMAN. Here is a friar, and slaughter'd Romeo's man,
With instruments upon them fit to open
These dead men's tombs.

CAPULET. O heavens! O wife, look how our daughter bleeds!
This dagger hath mista'en,° for, lo, his house°
Is empty on the back of Montague,
And it missheathed in my daughter's bosom!

LADY CAPULET. O me, this sight of death is as a bell
That warns° my old age to a sepulcher.

[*LORD MONTAGUE enters with others. The PRINCE calls them to the entrance of the tomb*.]

PRINCE. Come, Montague; for thou art early up
To see thy son and heir now early down.

MONTAGUE. Alas, my liege,° my wife is dead tonight!
Grief of my son's exile hath stopp'd her breath.
What further woe conspires against mine age?

PRINCE. Look, and thou shalt see.

MONTAGUE. O thou untaught!° What manners is in this,
To press before thy father to a grave?

PRINCE. Seal up the mouth of outrage° for a while,
Till we can clear these ambiguities°
And know their spring,° their head, their true descent;
And then will I be general of your woes°

203 **mista'en:** missed its proper target. **his house:** its sheath.

207 **warns:** summons; calls.

210 **liege** (lēj): lord.

214 **untaught:** one who is unschooled in manners.

216 **Seal up the mouth of outrage:** hold off your emotional outcry.

217 **ambiguities:** mysteries.

218 **spring:** source.

219 **general of your woes:** chief mourner.

And lead you even to death. Meantime forbear,
And let mischance be slave to patience.°
Bring forth the parties of suspicion.

FRIAR. I am the greatest,° able to do least,
Yet most suspected, as the time and place
Doth make against me, of this direful murder;
And here I stand, both to impeach and purge°
Myself condemned and myself excus'd.

PRINCE. Then say at once what thou dost know in this.

FRIAR. I will be brief, for my short date of breath°
Is not so long as is a tedious tale.
Romeo, there dead, was husband to that Juliet;
And she, there dead, that's Romeo's faithful wife.
I married them; and their stol'n marriage day
Was Tybalt's doomsday, whose untimely death
Banish'd the new-made bridegroom from this city;
For whom, and not for Tybalt, Juliet pin'd.
You, to remove that siege of grief from her,
Betroth'd and would have married her perforce°
To County Paris. Then comes she to me
And with wild looks bid me devise some mean
To rid her from this second marriage,
Or in my cell there would she kill herself.
Then gave I her (so tutor'd by my art)°
A sleeping potion; which so took effect
As I intended, for it wrought on her
The form of death. Meantime I writ to Romeo
That he should hither come as this° dire night
To help to take her from her borrowed° grave,
Being the time the potion's force should cease.
But he which bore my letter, Friar John,
Was stayed by accident,° and yesternight
Return'd my letter back. Then all alone
At the prefixed hour of her waking
Came I to take her from her kindred's vault;
Meaning to keep her closely° at my cell
Till I conveniently could send to Romeo.
But when I came, some minute ere the time
Of her awakening, here untimely lay
The noble Paris and true Romeo dead.
She wakes; and I entreated her come forth
And bear this work of heaven with patience;

221 **let mischance be slave to patience:** let your response to misfortune be governed by restraint.

223 **greatest:** most suspect.

226 **impeach and purge:** blame and clear from blame.

229 **date of breath:** time I have left to live.

238 **perforce:** forcibly.

243 **so tutor'd by my art:** which I learned to do from my studies.

247 **as this:** this.

248 **borrowed:** temporary.

251 **stayed by accident:** prevented from going by circumstances.

255 **closely:** secretly.

But then a noise did scare me from the tomb,
And she, too desperate, would not go with me,
But, as it seems, did violence on herself.
All this I know, and to the marriage
Her nurse is privy;° and if aught in this
Miscarried by my fault, let my old life
Be sacrific'd some hour before his time
Unto the rigor of severest law.

PRINCE. We still° have known thee for a holy man.
Where's Romeo's man? What can he say to this?

BALTHASAR. I brought my master news of Juliet's death;
And then in post he came from Mantua
To this same place, to this same monument.
This letter he early bid me give his father,
And threat'ned me with death, going in the vault,
If I departed not and left him there.

PRINCE. Give me the letter. I will look on it.

[*BALTHASAR hands the letter to the PRINCE.*]

Where is the County's page that rais'd the watch?
Sirrah, what made your master in this place?°

PAGE. He came with flowers to strew his lady's grave;
And bid me stand aloof, and so I did.
Anon° comes one with light to ope the tomb;
And by and by my master drew on him;
And then I ran away to call the watch.

PRINCE. [*He is reading ROMEO's letter.*] This letter doth make good the friar's words,
Their course of love, the tidings of her death;
And here he writes that he did buy a poison
Of a poor pothecary and therewithal°
Came to this vault to die and lie with Juliet.
Where be these enemies? Capulet, Montague,
See what a scourge is laid upon your hate,
That heaven finds means to kill your joys with love.
And I, for winking at your discords too,
Have lost a brace of kinsmen.° All are punish'd.

CAPULET. O brother Montague, give me thy hand.
This is my daughter's jointure,° for no more
Can I demand.

MONTAGUE. But I can give thee more;
For I will raise her statue in pure gold,

266 **is privy:** shares the secret.

270 **still:** always.

280 **what . . . place:** What was your master doing here?

283 **Anon:** shortly.

289 **therewithal:** with this.

295 **brace of kinsmen:** pair of relatives (Mercutio and Paris).

297 **jointure** (join′chər): marriage settlement.

That whiles Verona by that name is known,
There shall no figure at such rate° be set
As that of true and faithful Juliet.

CAPULET. As rich shall Romeo's by his lady's lie—
Poor sacrifices of our enmity!

PRINCE. A glooming° peace this morning with it brings.
The sun for sorrow will not show his head.
Go hence, to have more talk of these sad things;
Some shall be pardon'd, and some punished;
For never was a story of more woe
Than this of Juliet and her Romeo.

[*Everyone exits.*]

301 **rate:** value.

305 **glooming:** cloudy; gloomy.

The Reconciliation of the Montagues and Capulets Over the Dead Bodies of Romeo and Juliet, 1853–1855. Frederick Leighton. Oil on canvas, 70 x 91 in. Agnes Scott College, Decatur, GA.

Viewing the painting: What do you suppose the Friar is thinking? What would you be thinking?

Responding to Literature

Personal Response

What is your reaction to the end of the play?

Analyzing Act 5

Recall

1. While in Mantua, what does Romeo learn about Juliet? How does he learn the news?
2. What is Romeo's plan? What preparations does he make in Mantua?
3. What prevents Romeo from finding out the truth about Juliet?
4. Summarize what happens at the tomb.
5. As a result of the deaths, what do Capulet, Montague, and the Prince say they will do?

Interpret

6. Why do you think Romeo isn't surprised by the news he hears in Mantua about Juliet? Why doesn't he ask questions?
7. In your opinion, why does Romeo choose such a drastic course of action? What does his decision indicate about his frame of mind?
8. Do you think Friar Lawrence understands the gravity of Friar John's inability to reach Romeo? How do you know?
9. What does Friar Lawrence's action at the tomb indicate about his character?
10. How do the deaths of Romeo, Juliet, and Paris affect the way the Capulets and Montagues feel about their feud?

Evaluate and Connect

11. Compare and contrast Shakespeare's characterization of Paris and Romeo. Tell whether each is a **flat** or a **round character** (see Literary Terms Handbook, page R2).
12. **Theme Connections** Do Romeo and Juliet have the kind of love you would like to have sometime in your life? Explain your answer.
13. Review the chart you made for the Reading Focus on page 579, and compare one of your situations with that of Romeo and Juliet. What are some positive ways of responding to difficult demands made by adults?
14. Which characters, if any, do you think deserve punishment at the end of the play? Did Romeo and Juliet get what they deserved? Explain.
15. In your opinion, are the characters' words and actions at the end of the play realistic? Why or why not? Do you think it matters if they are realistic or not? Explain.

Literary ELEMENTS

Tragedy

A **tragedy** is a play in which a main character, called the tragic hero, suffers a downfall. The downfall may result from outside forces or from a weakness within the character—a **tragic flaw.** *Romeo and Juliet* is an unusual tragedy because it has two tragic heroes.

1. Does Romeo have a tragic flaw? Does Juliet? If so, what?
2. Do you think that Romeo and Juliet are destroyed by fate, by their own character flaws, by the flaws of others, or by a combination of factors? Explain your answer.

- See **Literary Terms Handbook,** p. R13.

Romeo and Juliet (detail).

Literature and Writing

Writing About Literature

Review Write a review stating your opinion of *Romeo and Juliet.* Include a brief plot summary, discuss the play's major themes, and describe its strengths and weaknesses as you see them. Use quotes from the play and references to specific scenes to support your analysis. Then, using the Internet or periodical indexes, find a professional review of the play and compare it to the one you've written.

Creative Writing

Shakespearean Insults The Montagues and Capulets carry on their feud partly through verbal dueling–hurling insults at one another. Scan the play for examples of Shakespeare's skill at creating sizzling slurs. Make two lists–one of adjectives and one of nouns used in these insults. Then combine words from the two lists to create ten original barbs of your own.

Extending Your Response

Literature Groups

Meathead Award *Romeo and Juliet* features many characters who act foolishly. In your group, make a list of the characters who act foolishly, and rank the characters from most to least foolish. Use your list to complete a chart like the one shown. As a group, decide which character's foolishness was most responsible for the tragic outcome of the play. Compare your decision with that of other groups in the class.

Character	Foolish action	Results

Listening and Speaking

Special Report from Verona The mysterious deaths in the Capulet tomb affect the entire city of Verona. Imagine that you are a radio reporter who follows the Prince to the tomb. Create and present a news broadcast about this tragic event, using sensory details to describe the scene. Provide background information on the victims, and inform listeners about the results of the Prince's investigation.

Internet Connection

The Bard on the Web What resources does the Internet offer on Shakespeare and his works? Investigate, and use what you find to create a guide to Internet resources on Shakespeare.

Reading Further

If you liked this play, you might also enjoy these other works by William Shakespeare on the theme of love:

Plays: *A Midsummer Night's Dream,* a play about love and magic in ancient Athens; *Much Ado About Nothing,* two unlikely lovers come together when a villain threatens the happiness of their friends; *Twelfth Night,* mistaken identity, a shipwreck, disguise, and chance meetings all play a role in this romantic comedy.

Poems: "Shall I compare thee to a summer's day?" and "Let me not to the marriage of true minds," in *The Complete Works of Shakespeare,* two well-known love sonnets.

Viewing: Two film versions of *Romeo and Juliet,* a 1968 version directed by Franco Zeffirelli, and a 1996 version directed by Baz Luhrmann.

Literary Criticism

Critic Susan Snyder observes, "For Shakespeare, tragedy is usually a matter of both character and circumstance, a fatal interaction of man and moment. But in [*Romeo and Juliet*], although the central characters have their weaknesses, their destruction does not really stem from these weaknesses." With your classmates, debate the truth of Snyder's opinion. Assign someone in your group the task of taking notes during the debate. Use those notes to create a summary of the issues raised in the debate and share the summary with the class.

Save your work for your portfolio.

Skill Minilessons

GRAMMAR AND LANGUAGE • Subordinating Conjunctions

A **subordinating conjunction** joins two unequal clauses. The clause introduced by a subordinating conjunction is called "subordinate" because it cannot stand by itself as a complete sentence. In the following example from *Romeo and Juliet,* the word *although* is a subordinating conjunction.

Well, do not swear. Although I joy in thee,
I have no joy of this contract tonight.

When a subordinate clause appears at the beginning of a sentence, a comma separates it from the main clause.

- For more about subordinating conjunctions, see **Language Handbook,** p. R39.

PRACTICE On your paper, identify the subordinating conjunction in each sentence below.

1. Romeo learned of Juliet's love when he overheard her speaking at her balcony.
2. While Romeo visited Friar Lawrence, a letter from Tybalt arrived at the Montague's house.
3. As Mercutio and Benvolio talked in the street, Tybalt approached them.
4. Romeo went to Mantua because he was banished from Verona.
5. Because Friar Lawrence's messenger was delayed, Romeo believed that Juliet was dead.

READING AND THINKING • Context Clues

When you read a work of literature, you can often figure out the meaning of a difficult passage by looking in the surrounding text for context clues such as definitions, synonyms, antonyms, examples, comparisons, or descriptive phrases. In the following lines from *Romeo and Juliet,* the word *adding* is a context clue for the meaning of *augmenting.* The words are synonyms.

Many a morning hath he there been seen,
With tears augmenting the fresh morning's dew,
Adding to clouds more clouds with his deep sighs;

The verb *augment* means "to make greater in size, extent, or quantity."

PRACTICE Write your own definition for each underlined word in the passages below. Then identify the context clues you used to determine each word's meaning.

1. For this alliance may so happy prove
   To turn your households' rancor to pure love.
2. Most detestable Death, by thee beguil'd,
   By cruel, cruel thee quite overthrown.
3. Our instruments to melancholy bells,
   Our wedding cheer to a sad burial feast;

- For more about context clues, see **Reading Handbook,** p. R78.

VOCABULARY • Prefixes and Suffixes

Prefixes and **suffixes** are syllables added to root words to change their meaning. A prefix is added to the beginning of a root word; a suffix to the end. The word *inauspicious,* for example, has both a prefix and a suffix. The prefix *in-* means "not," the suffix *-ous* means "full of," and the root word *auspice* means "omen or sign." *Auspicious* means "full of good signs" or "favorable." *Inauspicious* means "not favorable."

Like *in-,* the prefix *un-* means "not." The prefix *mis-* means "bad," or "wrong."

PRACTICE Identify the prefix or suffix in each word below. Then write a definition for the word.

1. unsavory
2. portentous
3. misadventure
4. tedious

Before You Read

Counting the Beats

Reading Focus

Put your hand over your heart, close your eyes, and listen to and feel your heartbeat for a few minutes.

List Ideas What does a heartbeat make you think of? What associations do you have with it? List your thoughts and associations in your journal.

Setting a Purpose Read to hear how the poet connects feelings of love to the rhythmic beating of a heart.

Building Background

Did You Know?

- Although Robert Graves also wrote novels and nonfiction, he considered himself primarily a poet. Critics regard his love poems as among the finest written in the twentieth century. In Graves's life, as well as in his poetry, romantic love was vitally important. He regarded the women he loved as muses who inspired his poetry, and he believed that the "main theme of poetry is, properly, the relations of man and woman." The poem "Counting the Beats" first appeared in *Poems and Satires,* which was published in 1951, while Graves was living on the island of Majorca in Spain, his home for most of his adult life.
- The critic Michael Kirkham states that the power of "Counting the Beats" lies in "its maintenance of a tension between conflicting awareness . . . of love and death." According to Kirkham, Graves creates this tension through "plainness in diction," "spareness of detail," and the "rhythms and the stanza form, which enact, generally speaking, a nervous, jerky expansion followed by a sudden contraction of feeling."

Meet Robert Graves

Robert Graves decided at the age of fifteen to become a poet. Pestered by bullies at an English boarding school called Charterhouse, Graves took refuge in writing poetry. At the suggestion of a friend, he also took up boxing, which he found more effective in warding off his tormentors. He later tested his physical skills through mountain climbing. While still a teenager, Graves was sent to France to fight in World War I, an experience that he said "permanently changed [his] outlook on life." Graves was haunted by death after one-third of his generation at school died in the war. In some of his poems, Graves envisioned himself as a lone survivor living among ghosts.

Robert Graves was born in 1895 in Wimbledon, England, and died in 1985 on the island of Majorca in Spain.

Counting the Beats

Robert Graves

Untitled, 1996. Janet Atkinson. Acrylic on board. Collection of the artist.

You, love, and I,
(He whispers) you and I,
And if no more than only you and I
What care you or I?

Counting the beats,
Counting the slow heart beats,
The bleeding to death of time in slow heart beats,
Wakeful they lie.

Cloudless day,
Night, and a cloudless day,
Yet the huge storm will burst upon their heads one day
From a bitter sky.

Where shall we be,
(She whispers) where shall we be,
When death strikes home, O where then shall we be
Who were you and I?

Not there but here,
(He whispers) only here,
As we are, here, together, now and here,
Always you and I.

Counting the beats,
Counting the slow heart beats,
The bleeding to death of time in slow heart beats,
Wakeful they lie.

Responding to Literature

Personal Response

Which lines from this poem do you find most powerful? Why?

Analyzing Literature

Recall and Interpret

1. Identify the three voices you can hear in this poem, and tell which stanzas are spoken by which voice.
2. What can you infer about "he" and "she" and about their situation?
3. In the third stanza, what might the "huge storm" refer to? In your opinion, what does the speaker mean by a "bitter sky"?
4. Express in your own words what the man asks in the first stanza and what the woman asks in the fourth stanza.
5. What do you think the heartbeats in the second and last stanzas represent or **symbolize?** (See Literary Terms Handbook, page R12.)

Evaluate and Connect

6. **Theme Connections** What message does this poem convey about the nature of romantic love?
7. Look back at the list you made for the Reading Focus on page 694. How do your associations with heartbeats compare with those of the speaker in this poem?
8. How might the knowledge of death affect one's view of life and love?
9. How has the prevalence of divorce affected your views of romantic love and marriage?
10. Reread the critic's comments in the Building Background section of page 694. Do you agree with the critic's analysis? If not, explain why. If so, identify examples in the poem of the elements the critic cites.

Literary ELEMENTS

Mood

The **mood** of a work of literature is its emotional quality or atmosphere. In poetry, the choice of words, the length of lines, the rhythm, and other elements all contribute to creating a certain mood. "Counting the Beats" has a serious, even grave, mood. One critic noted that Robert Graves "relies on the snowball repetition of key phrases to reinforce the effect of mounting panic in each stanza."

1. Identify phrases or lines that contribute to a feeling of "mounting panic" in this poem.
2. How does the rhythm of the poem contribute to its mood?

- See **Literary Terms Handbook,** p. R8.

Extending Your Response

Literature Groups

Debating the Poet's Word In a foreword to a 1966 edition of *Collected Poems,* which includes "Counting the Beats," Graves declares: "My main theme was always the practical impossibility, transcended only by a belief in miracle, of absolute love continuing between man and woman." In your group, discuss how this quotation applies to the poem "Counting the Beats." Share your conclusions with the rest of the class.

Creative Writing

Descriptive Sketch Close your eyes and imagine the man and the woman in this poem. What do these people look like? What might make this couple special to one another and to other people they might know? How did they meet and fall in love? Write a descriptive sketch of the couple.

Save your work for your portfolio.

Critical Thinking

COMPARING *selections*

Romeo and Juliet and Counting the Beats

COMPARE **THEMES**

Both *Romeo and Juliet* and "Counting the Beats" concern the subjects of love and death. With a group of classmates, answer the following questions as you compare and contrast the messages about love and death that the two works convey.

1. What is similar about the themes of the two works?
2. How do the themes differ?
3. In your opinion, which work conveys its theme or themes most effectively? Why do you think so?

The Ball Scene from Romeo and Juliet (detail).

COMPARE **ATTITUDES**

How do your friends' and classmates' attitudes about romantic love compare with the attitudes portrayed in these two selections? How do the attitudes of older people compare?

- Working with a partner, write five to ten statements that describe the attitudes that Romeo, Juliet, and the voices in "Counting the Beats" have toward romantic love.
- Use the statements as the basis of a survey. Circulate the survey among students in your age group, and also among teachers, parents, or other adults in your community. Have each person indicate whether he or she agrees or disagrees with each statement.
- Compile the results and draw some conclusions. Share your results and conclusions with the rest of the class.

COMPARE **LINES**

Both of these selections contain powerful and memorable lines of poetry. Scan both selections and make a list of the lines that you find the most powerful. Use the lines to create a collage of words and images on the theme of romantic love.

Technology Skills

Word Processing: Publishing Your Own 'Zine

'Zines began as publications written by high school and college students who didn't care for the mass-market magazines in their libraries and bookstores. Today's versions use word processing or desktop publishing software and laser printers, and they appear in both paper and digital forms.

Starting Out

Skim some current magazines published for students your age. Are the articles and illustrations useful or engaging? What aspects of these magazines do you like, and what would you change? What stories or interviews would you like to see? Imagine the appearance and content of the perfect 'zine—the articles, the features, the design, and the feeling the reader gets from the publication. In your journal, describe your ideal 'zine.

Reviewing the Toolbar

Before you start, go over the features of your word processing software that can help you create a unique look and feel for your 'zine. Most word processing programs have some or all of the features described in the chart below. All of these features are available through pull-down menus, but the toolbar makes them more convenient. If you have trouble finding any of them, click on the **Help** feature and find the topic in the index.

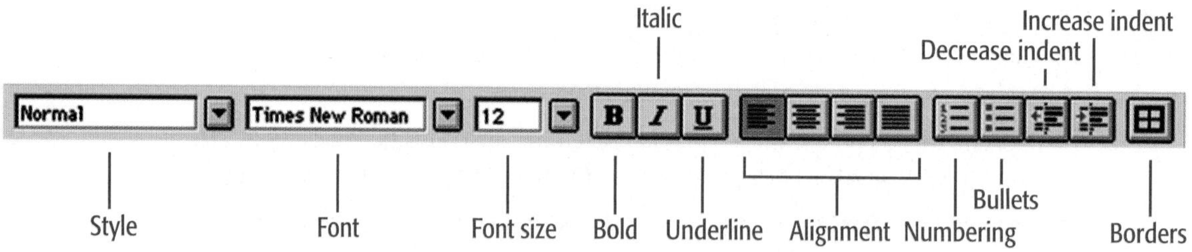

Publishing Tools	Function
Style	Formats to preset styles of typography
Font/Font size	Chooses a typeface/Controls type size
Bold, italic, underline	Emphasizes characters, words
Alignment	Aligns text at left, center, or right, or aligns left and right
Numbering	Selected paragraphs become a numbered list
Bullets	Selected paragraphs become a bulleted list
Increase indent	Increases the size of an indentation
Decrease indent	Decreases the size of an indentation

The following tools may or may not appear as icons on a toolbar, but your word processing software will include most or all of them.

- **Drawing** allows you to draw and color lines and simple shapes.
- **Insert table** sets up a table format into which you can insert text.
- **Columns** allows you to change the number of columns on a page.
- **Borders** adds various kinds of borders around text or graphics.
- **Spell-check** checks the spelling of every word in a document.
- **Grammar-check** checks for a variety of grammar and usage problems.

TECHNOLOGY TIP
Find out if your word processor has templates that will help you get started in designing the cover and pages of your 'zine. You can start with a template and make adjustments to it based on your own ideas about what looks good.

Creating a 'Zine

1. Decide on your 'zine's title and the topics you want to write about.
   - What audience will you target?
   - Will you include fiction as well as articles?
   - What sorts of illustrations will you use?
   - How many pages will you want to fill?
2. Design a cover page for your 'zine. Include the title, a related image or graphic, the date of the issue, and your name.
3. Now write and design the text of your 'zine. Include whatever you like: poetry, opinions, interviews, graphics, lyrics, ideas. You can include writing you did earlier in the school year if it's suitable for your 'zine.
4. Put your 'zine's first version aside for a few days, and then come back to it with a fresh eye. Take another look at what you've produced. Are you satisfied with it? Can you improve it further? Play around with the presentation and the content, and alter your 'zine to bring it even closer to your ideal.
5. Consider letting friends or relatives look at your 'zine-in-progress to tell you whether you have accomplished what you set out to do. Ask for lots of advice; if you don't agree with it, you don't have to accept it.
6. Print out a copy of your 'zine and share it with your teacher. Get her or his opinion and make appropriate changes.

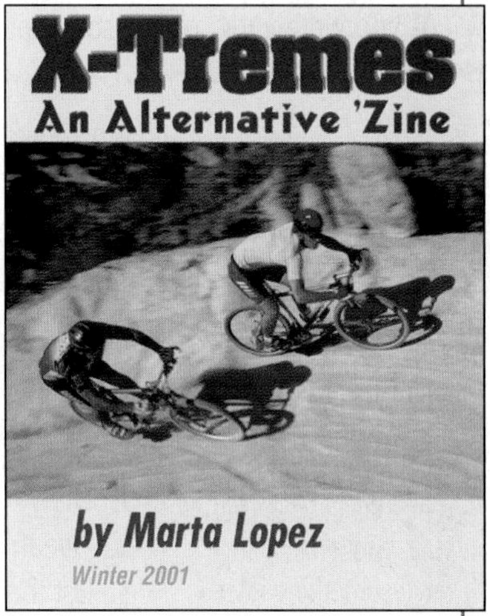

ACTIVITIES

1. In a small group, decide what kinds of material you want to publish. Then create a 'zine for your class. You can include material from students' individual 'zines as well as new material. Print enough copies for your class.
2. Create a movie review 'zine with a small group of classmates. Interview friends about recent movies and review recent videocassettes and DVDs as well as current films. You might even interview the movie critic of a local newspaper.
3. Ask a teacher in another class if you can do a content-related 'zine for extra credit.

Writing Workshop

Expository Writing:
Comparison-Contrast Essay

EVALUATION RUBRIC
By the time you complete this Writing Workshop, you will have
- clearly stated your main idea in a thesis statement
- presented comparisons and contrasts between two characters in a logical, consistent order
- supported each comparison and contrast with evidence from the literature
- concluded by restating your thesis and demonstrating how it has been proven
- presented a comparison-contrast essay that is free of errors in grammar, usage, and mechanics

We recognize that all people are basically alike, but we also recognize that each person is unique. Our similarities make us human. Our differences make us individuals. The same is true for characters in literature. Because our responses to characters often depend on the similarities and differences between them, comparing and contrasting characters can help us understand the way we react to them. **In this workshop, you will write an essay comparing and contrasting two characters in a work of literature.**

- As you write your comparison-contrast essay, refer to the **Writing Handbook,** pp. R58–R71.

The Writing Process

PREWRITING

PREWRITING TIP
When deciding which characters to compare, choose the ones who inspire the strongest reactions in you. That way, you're likely to have something interesting to write about.

Explore ideas

A Venn diagram like the one shown below can help you explore similarities and differences between two characters. To set up a Venn diagram, follow these steps:

1. Draw two intersecting circles.
2. Title the circles with the names of the subjects to be compared.
3. List the subjects' similarities in the space where the circles intersect.
4. List the subjects' differences in the nonintersecting spaces.

The Venn diagram below was created to compare Romeo and Mercutio, two characters from *Romeo and Juliet.*

STUDENT MODEL

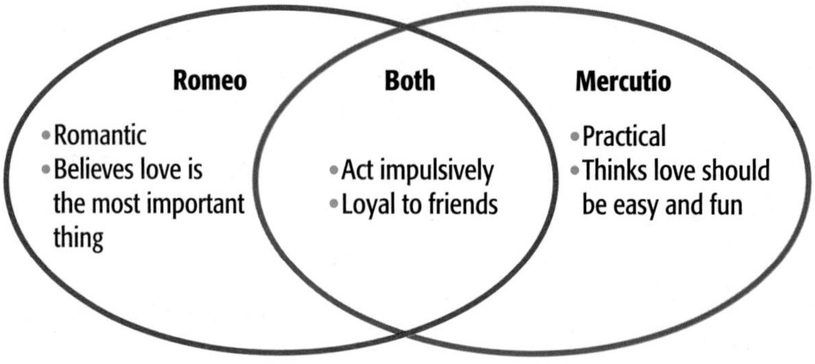

Keep your audience and purpose in mind

The amount of background information you need to provide in your essay will depend on whether your audience is familiar with the work you're discussing. No matter how much background you supply, remember that your purpose is to use details to show how two characters are alike and different.

Make a plan

Your essay should contain the basic elements of introduction, body, and conclusion. In the introduction, present a thesis that states the main point or set of ideas you will explore in your essay. You might even include a thesis statement that tells how the similarities or differences between the characters affect the literary work as a whole. In the body, compare and contrast the same features, or characteristics, of each of your subjects. In the conclusion, you may want to restate your thesis, emphasizing the most important points of similarity and difference between the characters.

The outlines below show two different methods of organizing the body of your comparison-contrast essay. Note that you may substitute the specific features that will be compared to suit your particular subjects.

Outline by Subject

A. *Character 1*
   1. *Attitude*
   2. *Behavior*
   3. *Importance to theme*

B. *Character 2*
   1. *Attitude*
   2. *Behavior*
   3. *Importance to theme*

Outline by Feature

A. *Attitude*
   1. *Character 1*
   2. *Character 2*

B. *Behavior*
   1. *Character 1*
   2. *Character 2*

C. *Importance to theme*
   1. *Character 1*
   2. *Character 2*

DRAFTING

DRAFTING TIP

Whenever you cite a quotation from a work of literature, make sure you note the page number if you are quoting a story or novel, or the act, scene, and line number if you are quoting a play. Include this information in parentheses after the quotation.

Be considerate of your readers

Help your reader to see the similarities and differences that you see. You can do this in three ways:

- **Consistent organization** Make sure that your writing reflects a clear, logical plan. If you're organizing by subject, address the traits of each subject in the same order. If you're organizing by feature, be sure that you always treat the two characters in the same sequence in each paragraph.
- **Transitions and relational terms** When shifting your discussion from one subject to another, use transitions such as these: *but, in the same way, however, like, on the other hand, similarly.* State your comparisons directly. Use terms or phrases that clearly state the relationships between the subjects you're comparing, such as *unlike Romeo* or *in contrast to Mercutio.*
- **Parallel structure** Use parallel structures to help make comparisons and contrasts clear. See the Writing Skill "Using Parallelism" on page 607 for help with this technique.

Write your draft

While you're writing, remind yourself that the draft does not have to be perfect or even close to perfect. You will be able to revise and reorganize later. The draft is just a start.

STUDENT MODEL

Romeo and Mercutio have very different ideas of romantic love. Love is Romeo's entire motivation and the main source of both his happiness and his suffering. In the beginning of the play, before Romeo meets Juliet, he tells Mercutio about his lovesickness over his relationship with Rosaline: "Under love's heavy burden do I sink" (1.4.22). He's really upset and can't stand to eat, or joke around, or dance, or anything. Romeo describes the emotional pain of love by saying, "Is love a tender thing? It is too rough,/Too rude, too boist'rous and it pricks like thorn" (1.4.25-26). In contrast, Mercutio has a more practical attitude toward love and dating. Mercutio offers Romeo sensible advice: "If love be rough with you, be rough with love" (1.4.27). In matters of romance, Mercutio does not believe in playing the helpless victim. He is more light-hearted and fun-loving than Romeo.

Complete Student Model on p. R117.

REVISING

REVISING TIP
Use marking pens in contrasting colors to highlight your comments on the two characters. Check for parallel phrasing.

Take another look

Put your essay aside and refresh your thinking about the characters by reviewing the literary work in which they appear. Then return to your draft, and use the **Rubric for Revising** to help you strengthen your essay.

Have a writing conference

Work with another writer to find places in your essay that would benefit from revision. Take turns reading your work aloud or share a copy of your draft. Then respond to each other's work, focusing on the points of comparison you have made. Together, discuss ways that the comparisons can be strengthened or clarified. Use the **Rubric for Revising** as a guide to your discussion. When you make your revisions, take your partner's suggestions into consideration, but remember that the work is your own.

RUBRIC FOR REVISING

Your revised comparison-contrast essay should have
- ☑ an introduction that identifies the characters you will be writing about and the work of literature in which they appear
- ☑ a clear, strong thesis
- ☑ a consistent organization with paragraphs that focus on a single character or feature
- ☑ comparisons clearly presented in parallel structure
- ☑ evidence that supports and elaborates the comparisons
- ☑ transitions and relational terms that make the comparisons clear
- ☑ a conclusion that restates the thesis and demonstrates how it has been proven

Your revised comparison-contrast essay should be free of
- ☑ awkward transitions from one paragraph to the next
- ☑ dull, flat, or uninteresting passages
- ☑ errors in grammar, usage, and mechanics

STUDENT MODEL

Romeo and Mercutio, however, do ~~The two characters~~ share similar views, ~~though,~~ about the powerful bond of love and loyalty between friends and family. In act 3, scene 1, the strength of their friendship is put to the test. ~~when~~ Tybalt challenges Romeo to a duel, but Romeo refuses to fight him. Mercutio, seeing Romeo's refusal to fight as a threat to Romeo's reputation, feels compelled to save Romeo's honor and fights Tybalt in Romeo's place. As Romeo tries to stop the duel, Tybalt stabs and kills Mercutio. Romeo then rises to defend Mercutio's honor by slaying Tybalt. This scene shows how both Romeo and Mercutio are willing to sacrifice ~~give up~~ their lives for the sake of friendship.

Complete Student Model on p. R117.

EDITING/PROOFREADING

PROOFREADING TIP

Use the **Proofreading Checklist** on the inside back cover of this book to help you mark errors.

Even the best ideas may seem weak if they are marred by errors in grammar, usage, mechanics, and spelling. When the content of your essay is what you want it to be, edit your work carefully to find and correct errors.

Grammar Hint

Eliminate dangling modifiers. A dangling modifier does not logically seem to modify any word in its sentence. Rewrite the sentence, adding a word or phrase to which the modifier clearly refers.

UNCLEAR: ***Overcome with sadness, the party didn't sound fun.***
CLEAR: ***Overcome with sadness, Romeo didn't think the party sounded fun.***

For more about dangling modifiers, see **Language Handbook,** p. R24.

STUDENT MODEL

Having married Juliet in secret, [Romeo experiences] a new feeling of happiness. ~~results~~

Complete Student Model on p. R117.

Complete Student Model

For a complete version of the model developed in this workshop, refer to **Writing Workshop Models**, p. R117.

PUBLISHING/PRESENTING

PRESENTING TIP

You may want to add a chart showing the points of comparison and contrast between the characters.

For a presentation to the class, use the chalkboard as you discuss your essay. Write each of your main points on the board as you come to them. During your conclusion, return to each point and review it. To reach a wider audience, look for an Internet discussion group devoted to the work in which your characters appear.

Reflecting

Having examined the similarities and differences between two characters, think about how comparing and contrasting might help you better understand your reactions to the real people you meet. Also think about how you can incorporate comparison and contrast into other kinds of writing you do.

Save your work for your portfolio.

Theme 10 The Mysteries of Life

Every day you see and hear thousands of things—words, whispers, colors, shapes, shadows. How does your mind make sense of all these sights and sounds? Understanding is a mysterious process. In this theme, you will meet someone who—despite being isolated from the hearing and seeing world—learns to solve some of life's mysteries.

THEME PROJECTS

Listening and Speaking

Signing American Sign Language allows people to talk with gestures.

1. With a partner, write a short skit in which one of you meets Helen Keller.
2. Using an American Sign Language dictionary, translate your skit into sign language. ASL dictionaries are available on the Internet and on CD-ROM, as well as in book form.
3. Decide who will play Helen. Then practice the skit and perform it for the class. Have someone speak the lines as you sign.

Interdisciplinary Project

Art Make a mobile depicting the important people and objects in Helen Keller's life.

1. As you read the selections, note the important people and objects in Helen's life.
2. Draw or paint these people and objects on heavy paper or posterboard, and cut them out.
3. Using string, drinking straws, and a coat hanger, construct your mobile. Organize the drawings based on their level of importance to Helen, the order in which she encountered them, or some other criteria.
4. Explain your mobile to your class.

The Sense of Smell, 1987. Jack Beal. Oil on canvas, 65¾ x 48 in. The George Adams Gallery, New York.

MEDIA connection

Magazine Article

To communicate with players spread out across the field, baseball coaches and managers have developed a sign language all their own. But what happens when their opponents can translate?

Sign Language: The Game Within the Game of Baseball

by Tim Kurkjian—*Sports Illustrated,* July 28, 1997

There's no place for a manager to hide in the visitor's dugout at Chicago's Comiskey Park. That is by design. So when the Minnesota Twins play there, two of their coaches are responsible for creating a human shield near manager Tom Kelly so he can be seen only by his third base coach, his hitter and his catcher. When the Texas Rangers play at Comiskey, the Rangers form a similar barrier around their manager. These teams are trying to thwart the ancient baseball practice of stealing signs—a practice admired by some as the epitome of heads-up baseball and reviled by others as one of the lowest forms of cheating in the game.

Stealing signs has been going on in baseball for more than 100 years, but it's more complicated today than ever because managers are taking greater control of the game and thus sending more signals. For example, most managers call every pitchout, pickoff attempt, step off and hold. Each of those calls requires a sign that goes from the bench to the catcher to the pitcher.

Teams go to elaborate lengths to protect their signs. The third base coach will go through his usual gyrations, touching every part of his body, but the signs mean nothing unless he uses an indicator—say, tapping his belt. There's also a wipe-off sign, meaning the signs will be flashed, but they are to be ignored if, say, the third base coach tugs on his ear. If a manager suspects an opponent is stealing his signs he might tell his leadoff hitter, "If you get on, we're going to give you the hit-and-run sign. Ignore it."

No matter how hard teams work to perfect their signaling system or crack the enemy's code, there's always the chance something will get lost in the translation. Orioles pitching coach Ray Miller tells a story about Marlins skipper Jim Leyland managing in the early 80s. Leyland gave a player named Kirby Farrell the bunt sign three times, and Farrell missed it each time. Finally, Leyland cupped his hands and from the dugout yelled, "Bunt!" Farrell cupped his hands and yelled back, "What?"

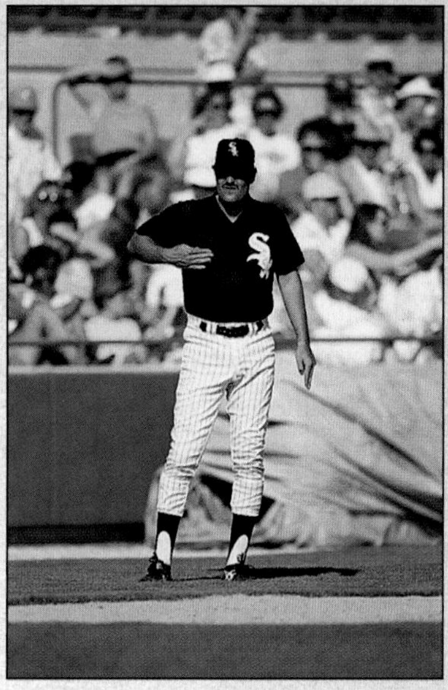

Analyzing Media

1. In your opinion, what is the cleverest aspect of baseball signs mentioned in this article?
2. Do you think stealing signs is to be admired or reviled? Explain.

Before You Read

The Miracle Worker, Act 1

Reading Focus

How would you define the word *miracle?* If a person could be said to "work miracles," what would he or she be capable of doing?

Journal Explore your answers to these questions in your journal.

Setting a Purpose Read to learn how Annie Sullivan "worked miracles" for Helen Keller and her family.

Building Background

The Time and Place

Most of the play's events occur during the 1880s at the Keller family home in Tuscumbia, Alabama.

Did You Know?

Annie Sullivan survived a difficult, often traumatic childhood. She was born in Massachusetts in 1866 to impoverished Irish immigrants. At the age of five, she began to go blind. Three years later, her mother died, leaving her and her siblings with a father who could not or would not support his children. When Annie was about ten, she and her beloved brother Jimmie were sent to live at the state poorhouse in Tewksbury. This asylum cared for some 940 residents of all ages–many suffering from mental illness or contagious diseases–in dangerously unhealthful conditions. After just a few months there, Jimmie died. Annie endured the place for nearly six years, until she drew the attention of state investigators to her plight and was sent to the Perkins Institution for the Blind in Boston. There she excelled as a student and graduated with honors.

Vocabulary Preview

unkempt (un kempt′) *adj.* untidy; uncombed; messy; p. 711
vivacious (vi vā′ shəs) *adj.* full of life; lively; p. 711
inarticulate (in′ är tik′ yə lit) *adj.* not clearly expressed or pronounced; unclear; p. 716
obstinate (ob′ stə nit) *adj.* stubborn; difficult to persuade; p. 716
precocious (pri kō′ shəs) *adj.* displaying maturity at an unusually early age; p. 717
irately (ī rāt′ lē) *adv.* in an enraged manner; angrily; p. 722
simultaneously (sī′ məl tā′ nē əs lē) *adv.* at the same time; p. 725
contemplate (kon′ təm plāt′) *v.* to give intense attention to; consider carefully; p. 725
oblivious (ə bliv′ ē əs) *adj.* unaware; not noticing; p. 733

Meet William Gibson

William Gibson completed only two years of college before dropping out to pursue a writing career. At first, he taught piano to supplement his income, but eventually he earned fame and fortune as an author—particularly as the playwright of *The Miracle Worker.* He once said that this play was his "love letter" to Annie Sullivan. Originally written as a television drama, it was rewritten for the stage and for film. The income Gibson earned from its success enabled him to found the Berkshire Theater Festival in Stockbridge, Massachusetts.

William Gibson was born in 1914. The stage version of The Miracle Worker *was first performed in 1959.*

The Miracle Worker

William Gibson

THE PLAYING SPACE is divided into two areas by a more or less diagonal line, which runs from downstage right to upstage left.

THE AREA behind this diagonal is on platforms and represents the Keller house; inside we see, down right, a family room, and up center, elevated, a bedroom. On stage level near center, outside a porch, there is a water pump.

THE OTHER AREA, in front of the diagonal, is neutral ground; it accommodates various places as designated at various times—the yard before the Keller home, the Perkins Institution for the Blind, the garden house, and so forth.

THE CONVENTION OF THE STAGING[1] is one of cutting through time and place, and its essential qualities are fluidity and spatial counterpoint. To this end, the less set there is, the better; in a literal set, the fluidity will seem merely episodic. The stage therefore should be free, airy, unencumbered by walls. Apart from certain practical items—such as the pump, a window to climb out of, doors to be locked—locales should be only skeletal suggestions, and the movement from one to another should be accomplishable by little more than lights.

1. Here, the *convention of the staging* is the general plan for using the stage set and lighting.

In the 1959 Broadway production of *The Miracle Worker,* Annie Sullivan was played by Anne Bancroft and Helen Keller was played by Patty Duke. The same award-winning actresses later starred in the movie production of William Gibson's play. The images on pages 708–778 are from either the stage or movie production.

CHARACTERS

A DOCTOR	MARTHA	ANAGNOS	VINEY
KATE	PERCY	ANNIE SULLIVAN	A SERVANT
KELLER	AUNT EV	BLIND GIRLS	OFFSTAGE VOICES
HELEN	JAMES		

SETTING

TIME: *The 1880s.*

PLACE: *In and around the Keller homestead in Tuscumbia, Alabama; also, briefly, the Perkins Institution for the Blind, in Boston.*

ACT 1

[It is night over the KELLER *homestead. Inside, three adults in the bedroom are grouped around a crib, in lamplight. They have been through a long vigil, and it shows in their tired bearing and disarranged clothing. One is a young gentlewoman with a sweet girlish face,* KATE KELLER*; the second is an elderly* DOCTOR*, stethoscope at neck, thermometer in fingers; the third is a hearty gentleman in his forties with chin whiskers,* CAPTAIN ARTHUR KELLER*.]*

DOCTOR. She'll live.

KATE. Thank God.

[The DOCTOR *leaves them together over the crib, packs his bag.]*

DOCTOR. You're a pair of lucky parents. I can tell you now, I thought she wouldn't.

KELLER. Nonsense, the child's a Keller, she has the constitution of a goat. She'll outlive us all.

DOCTOR. [*Amiably.*] Yes, especially if some of you Kellers don't get a night's sleep. I mean you, Mrs. Keller.

KELLER. You hear, Katie?

KATE. I hear.

KELLER. [*Indulgent.*] I've brought up two of them, but this is my wife's first, she isn't battle-scarred yet.

KATE. Doctor, don't be merely considerate, will my girl be all right?

DOCTOR. Oh, by morning she'll be knocking down Captain Keller's fences again.

KATE. And isn't there anything we should do?

KELLER. [*Jovial.*] Put up stronger fencing, ha?

DOCTOR. Just let her get well, she knows how to do it better than we do.

[He is packed, ready to leave.]

Main thing is the fever's gone, these things come and go in infants, never know why. Call it acute congestion of the stomach and brain.

KELLER. I'll see you to your buggy, Doctor.

DOCTOR. I've never seen a baby with more vitality, that's the truth.

[He beams a good night at the baby and KATE*, and* KELLER *leads him downstairs with a lamp. They go down the porch steps, and across the yard, where the* DOCTOR *goes off left;* KELLER *stands with the lamp aloft.* KATE *meanwhile is bent lovingly over the crib, which emits a bleat; her finger is playful with the baby's face.]*

KATE. Hush. Don't you cry now, you've been trouble enough. Call it acute congestion, indeed, I don't see what's so cute about a congestion, just because it's yours. We'll have your father run an editorial in his paper, the wonders of modern medicine, they don't know what they're curing even when they cure it. Men, men and their battle scars, we women will have to—

[But she breaks off, puzzled, moves her finger before the baby's eyes.]

Will have to—Helen?

[Now she moves her hand, quickly.]

Helen.

[She snaps her fingers at the baby's eyes twice, and her hand falters; after a moment she calls out, loudly.]

Captain. Captain, will you come—

[But she stares at the baby, and her next call is directly at her ears.]

Captain!

[And now, still staring, KATE *screams.* KELLER *in the yard hears it, and runs with the lamp*

back to the house. KATE *screams again, her look intent on the baby and terrible.* KELLER *hurries in and up.*]

KELLER. Katie? What's wrong?

KATE. Look.

[*She makes a pass with her hand in the crib, at the baby's eyes.*]

KELLER. What, Katie? She's well, she needs only time to—

KATE. She can't see. Look at her eyes.

[*She takes the lamp from him, moves it before the child's face.*]

She can't *see!*

KELLER. [*Hoarsely.*] Helen.

KATE. Or hear. When I screamed she didn't blink. Not an eyelash—

KELLER. Helen. Helen!

KATE. She can't *hear* you!

KELLER. *Helen!*

[*His face has something like fury in it, crying the child's name;* KATE *almost fainting presses her knuckles to her mouth, to stop her own cry.*

The room dims out quickly.

Time, in the form of a slow tune of distant belfry chimes which approaches in a crescendo and then fades, passes; the light comes up again on a day five years later, on three kneeling children and an old dog outside around the pump.

The dog is a setter named BELLE, *and she is sleeping. Two of the children are Negroes,* MARTHA *and* PERCY. *The third child is* HELEN, *six and a half years old, quite unkempt, in body a vivacious little person with a fine head, attractive, but noticeably blind, one eye larger and protruding; her gestures are abrupt, insistent, lacking in human restraint, and her face never smiles. She is flanked by the other two, in a litter of paper-doll cutouts, and while they speak* HELEN*'s hands thrust at their faces in turn, feeling baffledly at the movements of their lips.*]

MARTHA. [*Snipping.*] First I'm gonna cut off this doctor's legs, one, two, now then—

PERCY. Why you cuttin' off that doctor's legs?

MARTHA. I'm gonna give him a operation. Now I'm gonna cut off his arms, one, two. Now I'm gonna fix up—

[*She pushes* HELEN*'s hand away from her mouth.*]

You stop that.

PERCY. Cut off his stomach, that's a good operation.

MARTHA. No, I'm gonna cut off his head first, he got a bad cold.

PERCY. Ain't gonna be much of that doctor left to fix up, time you finish all them opera—

[*But* HELEN *is poking her fingers inside his mouth, to feel his tongue; he bites at them, annoyed, and she jerks them away.* HELEN *now fingers her own lips, moving them in imitation, but soundlessly.*]

MARTHA. What you do, bite her hand?

PERCY. That's how I do, she keep pokin' her fingers in my mouth, I just bite 'em off.

MARTHA. What she tryin' do now?

PERCY. She tryin' *talk.* She gonna get mad. Looka her tryin' talk.

[HELEN *is scowling, the lips under her fingertips moving in ghostly silence, growing more and more frantic, until in a bizarre rage she bites at her own fingers. This sends* PERCY *off into laughter, but alarms* MARTHA.]

Vocabulary

unkempt (un kempt′) *adj.* untidy; uncombed; messy
vivacious (vi vā′ shəs) *adj.* full of life; lively

MARTHA. Hey, you stop now.

[She pulls HELEN'S *hand down.]*

You just sit quiet and—

[But at once HELEN *topples* MARTHA *on her back, knees pinning her shoulders down, and grabs the scissors.* MARTHA *screams.* PERCY *darts to the bell string on the porch, yanks it, and the bell rings.*

Inside, the lights have been gradually coming up on the main room, where we see the family informally gathered, talking, but in pantomime: KATE *sits darning socks near a cradle, occasionally rocking it;* CAPTAIN KELLER *in spectacles is working over newspaper pages at a table; a benign*[2] *visitor in a hat,* AUNT EV, *is sharing the sewing basket, putting the finishing touches on a big shapeless doll made out of towels; an indolent*[3] *young man,* JAMES KELLER, *is at the window watching the children.*

With the ring of the bell, KATE *is instantly on her feet and out the door onto the porch, to take in the scene; now we see what these five years have done to her, the girlish playfulness is gone, she is a woman steeled in grief.]*

KATE. *[For the thousandth time.]* Helen.

[She is down the steps at once to them, seizing HELEN'S *wrists and lifting her off* MARTHA; MARTHA *runs off in tears and screams for momma, with* PERCY *after her.]*

Let me have those scissors.

[Meanwhile the family inside is alerted, AUNT EV *joining* JAMES *at the window;* CAPTAIN KELLER *resumes work.]*

JAMES. *[Blandly.]* She only dug Martha's eyes out. Almost dug. It's always almost, no point worrying till it happens, is there?

[They gaze out, while KATE *reaches for the scissors in* HELEN'S *hand. But* HELEN *pulls the scissors back, they struggle for them a moment, then* KATE *gives up, lets* HELEN *keep them. She tries to draw* HELEN *into the house.* HELEN *jerks away.* KATE *next goes down on her knees, takes* HELEN'S *hands gently, and using the scissors like a doll, makes* HELEN *caress and cradle them; she points* HELEN'S *finger housewards.* HELEN'S *whole body now becomes eager; she surrenders the scissors,* KATE *turns her toward the door and gives her a little push.* HELEN *scrambles up and toward the house, and* KATE *rising follows her.]*

AUNT EV. How does she stand it? Why haven't you seen this Baltimore man? It's not a thing you can let go on and on, like the weather.

JAMES. The weather here doesn't ask permission of me, Aunt Ev. Speak to my father.

AUNT EV. Arthur. Something ought to be done for that child.

KELLER. A refreshing suggestion. What?

*[*KATE *entering turns* HELEN *to* AUNT EV, *who gives her the towel doll.]*

AUNT EV. Why, this very famous oculist[4] in Baltimore I wrote you about, what was his name?

KATE. Dr. Chisholm.

AUNT EV. Yes, I heard lots of cases of blindness people thought couldn't be cured he's cured, he just does wonders. Why don't you write to him?

KELLER. I've stopped believing in wonders.

KATE. *[Rocks the cradle.]* I think the Captain will write to him soon. Won't you, Captain?

KELLER. No.

JAMES. *[Lightly.]* Good money after bad, or bad after good. Or bad after bad—

2. ***Benign*** (bi nīn′) means "kind and gentle."
3. ***Indolent*** (ind′ əl ənt) means "habitually lazy."

4. An ***oculist*** (ok′ yə list) is an ophthalmologist, or eye doctor.

AUNT EV. Well, if it's just a question of money, Arthur, now you're marshal you have this Yankee money. Might as well—

KELLER. Not money. The child's been to specialists all over Alabama and Tennessee, if I thought it would do good I'd have her to every fool doctor in the country.

KATE. I think the Captain will write to him soon.

KELLER. Katie. How many times can you let them break your heart?

KATE. Any number of times.

[*HELEN meanwhile sits on the floor to explore the doll with her fingers, and her hand pauses over the face: this is no face, a blank area of towel, and it troubles her. Her hand searches for features, and taps questioningly for eyes, but no one notices. She then yanks at her AUNT's dress, and taps again vigorously for eyes.*]

AUNT EV. What, child?

[*Obviously not hearing, HELEN commences to go around, from person to person, tapping for eyes, but no one attends or understands.*]

KATE. [*No break.*] As long as there's the least chance. For her to see. Or hear, or—

KELLER. There isn't. Now I must finish here.

KATE. I think, with your permission, Captain, I'd like to write.

KELLER. I said no, Katie.

AUNT EV. Why, writing does no harm, Arthur, only a little bitty letter. To see if he can help her.

KELLER. He can't.

KATE. We won't know that to be a fact, Captain, until after you write.

KELLER. [*Rising, emphatic.*] Katie, he can't.

[*He collects his papers.*]

JAMES. [*Facetiously.*] Father stands up, that makes it a fact.

KELLER. You be quiet! I'm badgered enough here by females without your impudence.

[*JAMES shuts up, makes himself scarce. HELEN now is groping among things on KELLER's desk, and paws his papers to the floor. KELLER is exasperated.*]

Katie.

[*KATE quickly turns HELEN away, and retrieves the papers.*]

I might as well try to work in a henyard as in this house—

JAMES. [*Placating.*] You really ought to put her away, Father.

KATE. [*Staring up.*] What?

JAMES. Some asylum. It's the kindest thing.

AUNT EV. Why, she's your sister, James, not a nobody—

JAMES. Half sister, and half-mentally defective, she can't even keep herself clean. It's not pleasant to see her about all the time.

KATE. Do you dare? Complain of what you *can* see?

KELLER. [*Very annoyed.*] This discussion is at an end! I'll thank you not to broach it again, Ev.

[*Silence descends at once. HELEN gropes her way with the doll, and KELLER turns back for a final word, explosive.*]

I've done as much as I can bear, I can't give my whole life to it! The house is at sixes and sevens[5] from morning till night over the child, it's time some attention was paid to Mildred here instead!

KATE. [*Gently dry.*] You'll wake her up, Captain.

KELLER. I want some peace in the house, I don't care how, but one way we won't have it

5. *At sixes and sevens* is an expression that means "in a state of complete confusion."

is by rushing up and down the country every time someone hears of a new quack. I'm as sensible to this affliction as anyone else, it hurts me to look at the girl.

KATE. It was not our affliction I meant you to write about, Captain.

[HELEN is back at AUNT EV, fingering her dress, and yanks two buttons from it.]

AUNT EV. Helen! My buttons.

[HELEN pushes the buttons into the doll's face. KATE now sees, comes swiftly to kneel, lifts HELEN's hand to her own eyes in question.]

KATE. Eyes?

[HELEN nods energetically.]

She wants the doll to have eyes.

[Another kind of silence now, while KATE takes pins and buttons from the sewing basket and attaches them to the doll as eyes. KELLER stands, caught, and watches morosely.[6] AUNT EV blinks, and conceals her emotion by inspecting her dress.]

AUNT EV. My goodness me, I'm not decent.

KATE. She doesn't know better, Aunt Ev. I'll sew them on again.

JAMES. Never learn with everyone letting her do anything she takes it into her mind to—

KELLER. You be quiet!

JAMES. What did I say now?

KELLER. You talk too much.

JAMES. I was agreeing with you!

KELLER. Whatever it was. Deprived child, the least she can have are the little things she wants.

[JAMES, very wounded, stalks out of the room onto the porch; he remains here, sulking.]

AUNT EV. *[Indulgently.]* It's worth a couple of buttons, Kate, look.

[HELEN now has the doll with eyes, and cannot contain herself for joy; she rocks the doll, pats it vigorously, kisses it.]

This child has more sense than all these men Kellers, if there's ever any way to reach that mind of hers.

[But HELEN suddenly has come upon the cradle, and unhesitatingly overturns it; the swaddled baby tumbles out, and CAPTAIN KELLER barely manages to dive and catch it in time.]

KELLER. *Helen!*

[All are in commotion, the baby screams, but HELEN unperturbed is laying her doll in its place. KATE on her knees pulls her hands off the cradle, wringing them; HELEN is bewildered.]

KATE. Helen, Helen, you're not to do such things, how can I make you understand—

KELLER. *[Hoarsely.]* Katie.

KATE. How can I get it into your head, my darling, my poor—

KELLER. Katie, some way of teaching her an iota of discipline has to be—

KATE. *[Flaring.]* How can you discipline an afflicted child? Is it her fault?

[HELEN's fingers have fluttered to her MOTHER's lips, vainly trying to comprehend their movements.]

KELLER. I didn't say it was her fault.

KATE. Then whose? I don't know what to do! How can I teach her, beat her—until she's black and blue?

KELLER. It's not safe to let her run around loose. Now there must be a way of confining her, somehow, so she can't—

KATE. Where, in a cage? She's a growing child, she has to use her limbs!

KELLER. Answer me one thing, is it fair to Mildred here?

6. Here, *morosely* means "in a bad-tempered, gloomy mood."

KATE. [*Inexorably.*][7] Are you willing to put her away?

[*Now* HELEN's *face darkens in the same rage as at herself earlier, and her hand strikes at* KATE's *lips.* KATE *catches her hand again, and* HELEN *begins to kick, struggle, twist.*]

KELLER. Now what?

KATE. She wants to talk, like—*be* like you and me.

[*She holds* HELEN *struggling until we hear from the child her first sound so far, an inarticulate weird noise in her throat such as an animal in a trap might make; and* KATE *releases her. The second she is free* HELEN *blunders away, collides violently with a chair, falls, and sits weeping.* KATE *comes to her, embraces, caresses, soothes her, and buries her own face in her hair, until she can control her voice.*]

Every day she slips further away. And I don't know how to call her back.

AUNT EV. Oh, I've a mind to take her up to Baltimore myself. If that doctor can't help her, maybe he'll know who can.

KELLER. [*Presently, heavily.*] I'll write the man, Katie.

[*He stands with the baby in his clasp, staring at* HELEN's *head, hanging down on* KATE's *arm.*

The lights dim out, except the one on KATE *and* HELEN. *In the twilight,* JAMES, AUNT EV, *and* KELLER *move off slowly, formally, in separate directions;* KATE *with* HELEN *in her arms remains, motionless, in an image which overlaps into the next scene and fades only when it is well under way.*

Without pause, from the dark down left we hear a man's voice with a Greek accent speaking:]

ANAGNOS. —who could do nothing for the girl, of course. It was Dr. Bell[8] who thought she might somehow be taught. I have written the family only that a suitable governess, Miss Annie Sullivan, has been found here in Boston—

[*The lights begin to come up, down left, on a long table and chair. The table contains equipment for teaching the blind by touch—a small replica of the human skeleton, stuffed animals, models of flowers and plants, piles of books. The chair contains a girl of 20,* ANNIE SULLIVAN, *with a face which in repose is grave and rather obstinate, and when active is impudent, combative, twinkling with all the life that is lacking in* HELEN's, *and handsome; there is a crude vitality to her. Her suitcase is at her knee.* ANAGNOS, *a stocky bearded man, comes into the light only towards the end of his speech.*]

ANAGNOS. —and will come. It will no doubt be difficult for you there, Annie. But it has been difficult for you at our school too, hm? Gratifying, yes, when you came to us and could not spell your name, to accomplish so much here in a few years, but always an Irish battle. For independence.

[*He studies* ANNIE, *humorously; she does not open her eyes.*]

This is my last time to counsel you, Annie, and you do lack some—by some I mean *all*—what, tact or talent to bend. To others. And what has saved you on more than one

7. *[Inexorably]* Kate responds in a relentless manner; she is persistent, unable to be persuaded by her husband.

8. *Dr.* (Alexander Graham) *Bell,* the inventor of the telephone, took a personal interest in education for the deaf, including that of Helen Keller. His wife was deaf.

Vocabulary

inarticulate (in′ är tik′ yə lit) *adj.* not clearly expressed or pronounced; unclear
obstinate (ob′ stə nit) *adj.* stubborn; difficult to persuade

occasion here at Perkins is that there was nowhere to expel you to. Your eyes hurt?

ANNIE. My ears, Mr. Anagnos.

[*And now she has opened her eyes; they are inflamed, vague, slightly crossed, clouded by the granular growth of trachoma,*[9] *and she often keeps them closed to shut out the pain of light.*]

ANAGNOS. [*Severely.*] Nowhere but back to Tewksbury, where children learn to be saucy. Annie, I know how dreadful it was there, but that battle is dead and done with, why not let it stay buried?

ANNIE. [*Cheerily.*] I think God must owe me a resurrection.[10]

ANAGNOS. [*A bit shocked.*] What?

ANNIE. [*Taps her brow.*] Well, He keeps digging up that battle!

ANAGNOS. That is not a proper thing to say, Annie. It is what I mean.

ANNIE. [*Meekly.*] Yes. But I know what I'm like, what's this child like?

ANAGNOS. Like?

ANNIE. Well— Bright or dull, to start off.

ANAGNOS. No one knows. And if she is dull, you have no patience with this?

ANNIE. Oh, in grownups you have to, Mr. Anagnos. I mean in children it just seems a little—precocious, can I use that word?

ANAGNOS. Only if you can spell it.

9. Annie's eyes are *inflamed*—or swollen, red, and irritated—by *trachoma* (trə kō′ mə), a contagious bacterial infection that makes the eyelids and eyeballs grainy *(granular)*. Trachoma results in blindness if left untreated.

10. *Resurrection* is a miraculous return to life after death. In this context, Annie refers to some sort of new beginning. Her meaning will be clearer when she repeats this sentence in act 3.

ANNIE. Premature. So I hope at least she's a bright one.

ANAGNOS. Deaf, blind, mute—who knows? She is like a little safe, locked, that no one can open. Perhaps there is a treasure inside.

ANNIE. Maybe it's empty, too?

ANAGNOS. Possible. I should warn you, she is much given to tantrums.

ANNIE. Means something is inside. Well, so am I, if I believe all I hear. Maybe you should warn *them*.

ANAGNOS. [*Frowns.*] Annie. I wrote them no word of your history. You will find yourself among strangers now, who know nothing of it.

ANNIE. Well, we'll keep them in a state of blessed ignorance.

ANAGNOS. Perhaps *you* should tell it?

ANNIE. [*Bristling.*] Why? I have enough trouble with people who don't know.

ANAGNOS. So they will understand. When you have trouble.

ANNIE. The only time I have trouble is when I'm right.

[*But she is amused at herself, as is* ANAGNOS.]

Is it my fault it's so often? I won't give them trouble, Mr. Anagnos, I'll be so ladylike they won't notice I've come.

ANAGNOS. Annie, be—humble. It is not as if you have so many offers to pick and choose. You will need their affection, working with this child.

ANNIE. [*Humorously.*] I hope I won't need their pity.

ANAGNOS. Oh, we can all use some pity.

[*Crisply.*]

So. You are no longer our pupil, we throw you

Vocabulary

precocious (pri kō′ shəs) *adj.* displaying maturity at an unusually early age into the world, a teacher. *If* the child can be taught. No one expects you to work miracles, even for twenty-five dollars a month. Now, in this envelope a loan, for the railroad, which you will repay me when you have a bank account. But in this box, a gift. With our love.

[*ANNIE opens the small box he extends, and sees a garnet ring. She looks up, blinking, and down.*]

I think other friends are ready to say good-bye.

[*He moves as though to open doors.*]

ANNIE. Mr. Anagnos.

[*Her voice is trembling.*]

Dear Mr. Anagnos, I—

[*But she swallows over getting the ring on her finger, and cannot continue until she finds a woebegone*[11] *joke.*]

Well, what should I say, I'm an ignorant opinionated girl, and everything I am I owe to you?

ANAGNOS. [*Smiles.*] That is only half true, Annie.

ANNIE. Which half? I crawled in here like a drowned rat, I thought I died when Jimmie died, that I'd never again—come alive. Well, you say with love so easy, and I haven't *loved* a soul since and I never will, I suppose, but this place gave me more than my eyes back. Or taught me how to spell, which I'll never learn anyway, but with all the fights and the trouble I've been here it taught me what help is, and how to live again, and I don't want to say good-bye. Don't open the door, I'm crying.

ANAGNOS. [*Gently.*] They will not see.

[*He moves again as though opening doors, and in comes a group of girls, 8-year-olds to 17-year-olds; as they walk we see they are blind. ANAGNOS shepherds them in with a hand.*]

A CHILD. Annie?

ANNIE. [*Her voice cheerful.*] Here, Beatrice.

[*As soon as they locate her voice they throng joyfully to her, speaking all at once; ANNIE is down on her knees to the smallest, and the following are the more intelligible fragments in the general hubbub.*]

CHILDREN. There's a present. We brought you a going-away present, Annie!

ANNIE. Oh, now you shouldn't have—

CHILDREN. We did, we did, where's the present?

SMALLEST CHILD. [*Mournfully.*] Don't go, Annie, away.

CHILDREN. Alice has it. Alice! Where's Alice? Here I am! Where? Here!

[*An arm is aloft out of the group, waving a present; ANNIE reaches for it.*]

ANNIE. I have it. I have it, everybody, should I open it?

CHILDREN. Open it! Everyone be quiet! Do, Annie! She's opening it. Ssh!

[*A settling of silence while ANNIE unwraps it. The present is a pair of smoked glasses, and she stands still.*]

Is it open, Annie?

ANNIE. It's open.

CHILDREN. It's for your eyes, Annie. Put them on, Annie! 'Cause Mrs. Hopkins said your eyes hurt since the operation. And she said you're going where the sun is *fierce.*

ANNIE. I'm putting them on now.

SMALLEST CHILD. [*Mournfully.*] Don't go, Annie, where the sun is fierce.

CHILDREN. Do they fit all right?

ANNIE. Oh, they fit just fine.

CHILDREN. Did you put them on? Are they pretty, Annie?

11. Here, *woebegone* is used literally, to mean "sorrow-be-gone," or "humorous." It usually means "sad" or "forlorn."

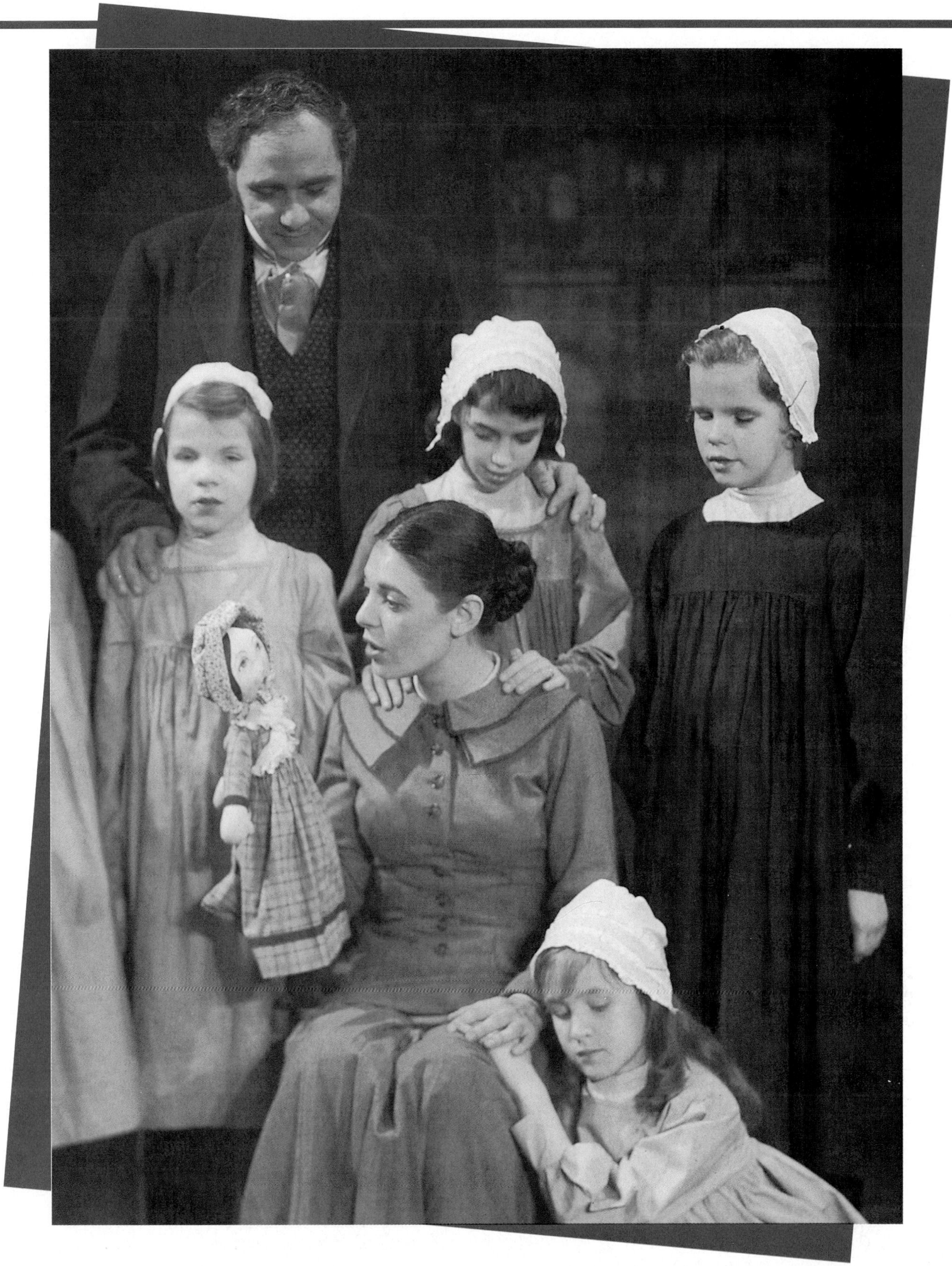

ANNIE. Oh, my eyes feel hundreds of percent better already, and pretty, why, do you know how I look in them? Splendiloquent.[12] Like a racehorse!

CHILDREN. [*Delighted.*] There's another present! Beatrice! We have a present for Helen, too! Give it to her, Beatrice. Here, Annie!

[*This present is an elegant doll, with movable eyelids and a momma sound.*]

It's for Helen. And we took up a collection to buy it. And Laura dressed it.

ANNIE. It's beautiful!

CHILDREN. So don't forget, you be sure to give it to Helen from us, Annie!

ANNIE. I promise it will be the first thing I give her. If I don't keep it for myself, that is, you know I can't be trusted with dolls!

SMALLEST CHILD. [*Mournfully.*] Don't go, Annie, to her.

ANNIE. [*Her arm around her.*] Sarah, dear. I don't *want* to go.

SMALLEST CHILD. Then why are you going?

ANNIE. [*Gently.*] Because I'm a big girl now, and big girls have to earn a living. It's the only way I can. But if you don't smile for me first, what I'll just have to do is—

[*She pauses, inviting it.*]

SMALLEST CHILD. What?

ANNIE. Put *you* in my suitcase, instead of this doll. And take *you* to Helen in Alabama!

[*This strikes the children as very funny, and they begin to laugh and tease the smallest child, who after a moment does smile for* ANNIE.]

ANAGNOS. [*Then.*] Come, children. We must get the trunk into the carriage and Annie into her train, or no one will go to Alabama. Come, come.

[*He shepherds them out and* ANNIE *is left alone on her knees with the doll in her lap. She reaches for her suitcase, and by a subtle change in the color of the light, we go with her thoughts into another time. We hear a boy's voice whispering; perhaps we see shadowy intimations*[13] *of these speakers in the background.*]

BOY'S VOICE. Where we goin', Annie?

ANNIE. [*In dread.*] Jimmie.

BOY'S VOICE. Where we goin'?

ANNIE. I said—I'm takin' care of you—

BOY'S VOICE. Forever and ever?

MAN'S VOICE. [*Impersonal.*] Annie Sullivan, aged nine, virtually blind. James Sullivan, aged seven—What's the matter with your leg, Sonny?

ANNIE. Forever and ever.

MAN'S VOICE. Can't he walk without that crutch?

[ANNIE *shakes her head, and does not stop shaking it.*]

Girl goes to the women's ward. Boy to the men's.

BOY'S VOICE. [*In terror.*] Annie! Annie, don't let them take me—Annie!

ANAGNOS. [*Offstage.*] Annie! Annie?

[*But this voice is real, in the present, and* ANNIE *comes up out of her horror, clearing her head with a final shake; the lights begin to pick out* KATE *in the* KELLER *house, as* ANNIE *in a bright tone calls back.*]

ANNIE. Coming!

[*This word catches* KATE, *who stands half turned and attentive to it, almost as though hearing it. Meanwhile* ANNIE *turns and hurries out, lugging the suitcase.*]

12. *Splendiloquent* is an invented word, possibly a combination of *splendid* and *eloquent.*

13. *Intimations* are hints or indications.

The room dims out; the sound of railroad wheels begins from off left, and maintains itself in a constant rhythm underneath the following scene; the remaining lights have come up on the KELLER *homestead.* JAMES *is lounging on the porch, waiting. In the upper bedroom which is to be* ANNIE'S, HELEN *is alone, puzzledly exploring, fingering and smelling things, the curtains, empty drawers in the bureau, water in the pitcher by the washbasin, fresh towels on the bedstead. Downstairs in the family room* KATE *turning to a mirror hastily adjusts her bonnet, watched by a Negro servant in an apron,* VINEY.]

VINEY. Let Mr. Jimmie go by hisself, you been pokin' that garden all day, you ought to rest your feet.

KATE. I can't wait to see her, Viney.

VINEY. Maybe she ain't gone be on this train neither.

KATE. Maybe she is.

VINEY. And maybe she ain't.

KATE. And maybe she is. Where's Helen?

VINEY. She upstairs, smellin' around. She know somethin' funny's goin' on.

KATE. Let her have her supper as soon as Mildred's in bed, and tell Captain Keller when he comes that we'll be delayed tonight.

VINEY. Again.

KATE. I don't think we need say *again*. Simply delayed will do.

[*She runs upstairs to* ANNIE'S *room,* VINEY *speaking after her.*]

VINEY. I mean that's what he gone say. "What, again?"

[VINEY *works at setting the table. Upstairs* KATE *stands in the doorway, watching* HELEN'S *groping explorations.*]

KATE. Yes, we're expecting someone. Someone for my Helen.

[HELEN *happens upon her skirt, clutches her leg;* KATE *in a tired dismay kneels to tidy her hair and soiled pinafore.*]

Oh, dear, this was clean not an hour ago.

[HELEN *feels her bonnet, shakes her head darkly, and tugs to get it off.* KATE *retains it with one hand, diverts* HELEN *by opening her other hand under her nose.*]

Here. For while I'm gone.

[HELEN *sniffs, reaches, and pops something into her mouth, while* KATE *speaks a bit guiltily.*]

I don't think one peppermint drop will spoil your supper.

[*She gives* HELEN *a quick kiss, evades her hands, and hurries downstairs again. Meanwhile* CAPTAIN KELLER *has entered the yard from around the rear of the house, newspaper under arm, cleaning off and munching on some radishes; he sees* JAMES *lounging at the porch post.*]

KELLER. Jimmie?

JAMES. [*Unmoving.*] Sir?

KELLER. [*Eyes him.*] You don't look dressed for anything useful, boy.

JAMES. I'm not. It's for Miss Sullivan.

KELLER. Needn't keep holding up that porch, we have wooden posts for that. I asked you to see that those strawberry plants were moved this evening.

JAMES. I'm moving your—Mrs. Keller, instead. To the station.

KELLER. [*Heavily.*] Mrs. Keller. Must you always speak of her as though you haven't met the lady?

[KATE *comes out on the porch, and* JAMES *inclines his head.*]

JAMES. [*Ironic.*] Mother.

[*He starts off the porch, but sidesteps* KELLER'S *glare like a blow.*]

I said mother!

KATE. Captain.

KELLER. Evening, my dear.

KATE. We're off to meet the train, Captain. Supper will be a trifle delayed tonight.

KELLER. What, again?

KATE. [*Backing out.*] With your permission, Captain?

[*And they are gone.* KELLER *watches them offstage, morosely.*

Upstairs HELEN *meanwhile has groped for her mother, touched her cheek in a meaningful gesture, waited, touched her cheek, waited, then found the open door, and made her way down. Now she comes into the family room, touches her cheek again;* VINEY *regards her.*]

VINEY. What you want, honey, your momma?

[HELEN *touches her cheek again.* VINEY *goes to the sideboard, gets a tea-cake, gives it into* HELEN*'s hand;* HELEN *pops it into her mouth.*]

Guess one little tea-cake ain't gone ruin your appetite.

[*She turns* HELEN *toward the door.* HELEN *wanders out onto the porch, as* KELLER *comes up the steps. Her hands encounter him, and she touches her cheek again, waits.*]

KELLER. She's gone.

[*He is awkward with her; when he puts his hand on her head, she pulls away.* KELLER *stands regarding her, heavily.*]

She's gone, my son and I don't get along, you don't know I'm your father, no one likes me, and supper's delayed.

[HELEN *touches her cheek, waits.* KELLER *fishes in his pocket.*]

Here. I brought you some stick candy, one nibble of sweets can't do any harm.

[*He gives her a large stick candy;* HELEN *falls to it.* VINEY *peers out the window.*]

VINEY. [*Reproachfully.*] Cap'n Keller, now how'm I gone get her to eat her supper you fill her up with that trash?

KELLER. [*Roars.*] Tend to your work!

[VINEY *beats a rapid retreat.* KELLER *thinks better of it, and tries to get the candy away from* HELEN, *but* HELEN *hangs on to it; and when* KELLER *pulls, she gives his leg a kick.* KELLER *hops about,* HELEN *takes refuge with the candy down behind the pump, and* KELLER *then irately flings his newspaper on the porch floor, stamps into the house past* VINEY *and disappears.*

The lights half dim on the homestead, where VINEY *and* HELEN *going about their business soon find their way off. Meanwhile, the railroad sounds off left have mounted in a crescendo to a climax typical of a depot at arrival time, the lights come up on stage left, and we see a suggestion of a station. Here* ANNIE *in her smoked glasses and disarrayed by travel is waiting with her suitcase, while* JAMES *walks to meet her; she has a battered paper-bound book, which is a Perkins report,*[14] *under her arm.*]

JAMES. [*Coolly.*] Miss Sullivan?

ANNIE. [*Cheerily.*] Here! At last, I've been on trains so many days I thought they must be backing up every time I dozed off—

JAMES. I'm James Keller.

ANNIE. James?

[*The name stops her.*]

I had a brother Jimmie. Are you Helen's?

14. The *Perkins report* Annie carries was written by Dr. Samuel G. Howe, founder of the Perkins Institution for the Blind in Boston. It describes his work in the 1830s, teaching a young deaf, blind, and mute woman (Laura Bridgman) to communicate.

Vocabulary

irately (ī rāt′ lē) *adv.* in an enraged manner; angrily

JAMES. I'm only half a brother. You're to be her governess?

ANNIE. [*Lightly.*] Well. Try!

JAMES. [*Eying her.*] You look like half a governess.

[*KATE enters. ANNIE stands moveless, while JAMES takes her suitcase. KATE's gaze on her is doubtful, troubled.*]

Mrs. Keller, Miss Sullivan.

[*KATE takes her hand.*]

KATE. [*Simply.*] We've met every train for two days.

[*ANNIE looks at KATE's face, and her good humor comes back.*]

ANNIE. I changed trains every time they stopped, the man who sold me that ticket ought to be tied to the tracks—

JAMES. You have a trunk, Miss Sullivan?

ANNIE. Yes.

[*She passes JAMES a claim check, and he bears the suitcase out behind them. ANNIE holds the battered book. KATE is studying her face, and ANNIE returns the gaze; this is a mutual appraisal, southern gentlewoman and working-class Irish girl, and ANNIE is not quite comfortable under it.*]

You didn't bring Helen, I was hoping you would.

KATE. No, she's home.

[*A pause. ANNIE tries to make ladylike small talk, though her energy now and then erupts; she catches herself up whenever she hears it.*]

ANNIE. You—live far from town, Mrs. Keller?

KATE. Only a mile.

ANNIE. Well. I suppose I can wait one more mile. But don't be surprised if I get out to push the horse!

KATE. Helen's waiting for you, too. There's been such a bustle in the house, she expects something, heaven knows what.

[*Now she voices part of her doubt, not as such, but* ANNIE *understands it.*]

I expected—a desiccated spinster.[15] You're very young.

ANNIE. [*Resolutely.*] Oh, you should have seen me when I left Boston. I got much older on this trip.

KATE. I mean, to teach anyone as difficult as Helen.

ANNIE. *I* mean to try. They can't put you in jail for trying!

KATE. Is it possible, even? To teach a deaf-blind child *half* of what an ordinary child learns—has that ever been done?

ANNIE. Half?

KATE. A tenth.

ANNIE. [*Reluctantly.*] No.

[KATE'*s face loses its remaining hope, still appraising her youth.*]

Dr. Howe did wonders, but—an ordinary child? No, never. But then I thought when I was going over his reports—

[*She indicates the one in her hand.*]

—he never treated them like ordinary children. More like—eggs everyone was afraid would break.

KATE. [*A pause.*] May I ask how old you are?

ANNIE. Well, I'm not in my teens, you know! I'm twenty.

KATE. All of twenty.

[ANNIE *takes the bull by the horns, valiantly.*]

ANNIE. Mrs. Keller, don't lose heart just because I'm not on my last legs. I have three big advantages over Dr. Howe that money couldn't buy for you. One is his work behind me, I've read every word he wrote about it and he wasn't exactly what you'd call a man of few words. Another is to *be* young, why, I've got energy to do anything. The third is, I've been blind.

[*But it costs her something to say this.*]

KATE. [*Quietly.*] Advantages.

ANNIE. [*Wry.*] Well, some have the luck of the Irish, some do not.

[KATE *smiles; she likes her.*]

KATE. What will you try to teach her first?

ANNIE. First, last, and—in between, language.

KATE. Language.

ANNIE. Language is to the mind more than light is to the eye. Dr. Howe said that.

KATE. Language.

[*She shakes her head.*]

We can't get through to teach her to sit still. You *are* young, despite your years, to have such—confidence. Do you, inside?

[ANNIE *studies her face; she likes her, too.*]

ANNIE. No, to tell you the truth I'm as shaky inside as a baby's rattle!

[*They smile at each other, and* KATE *pats her hand.*]

KATE. Don't be.

[JAMES *returns to usher them off.*]

We'll do all we can to help, and to make you feel at home. Don't think of us as strangers, Miss Annie.

ANNIE. [*Cheerily.*] Oh, strangers aren't so strange to me. I've known them all my life!

[KATE *smiles again,* ANNIE *smiles back, and they precede* JAMES *offstage.*

15. *Desiccated* (des′ i kāt′ əd) means "dried up," and a *spinster* is an older woman who has never been married.

The lights dim on them, having simultaneously risen full on the house; VINEY *has already entered the family room, taken a water pitcher, and come out and down to the pump. She pumps real water. As she looks offstage, we hear the clop of hoofs, a carriage stopping, and voices.*]

VINEY. Cap'n Keller! Cap'n Keller, they comin'!

[*She goes back into the house, as* KELLER *comes out on the porch to gaze.*]

She sure 'nuff came, Cap'n.

[KELLER *descends, and crosses toward the carriage; this conversation begins offstage and moves on.*]

KELLER. [*Very courtly.*] Welcome to Ivy Green, Miss Sullivan. I take it you are Miss Sullivan—

KATE. My husband, Miss Annie, Captain Keller.

ANNIE. [*Her best behavior.*] Captain, how do you do.

KELLER. A pleasure to see you, at last. I trust you had an agreeable journey?

ANNIE. Oh, I had several! When did this country get so big?

JAMES. Where would you like the trunk, father?

KELLER. Where Miss Sullivan can get at it, I imagine.

ANNIE. Yes, please. Where's Helen?

KELLER. In the hall, Jimmie—

KATE. We've put you in the upstairs corner room, Miss Annie, if there's any breeze at all this summer, you'll feel it—

[*In the house the setter* BELLE *flees into the family room, pursued by* HELEN *with groping hands; the dog doubles back out the same door, and* HELEN *still groping for her makes her way out to the porch; she is messy, her hair tumbled, her pinafore now ripped, her shoelaces untied.* KELLER *acquires the suitcase, and* ANNIE *gets her hands on it too, though still endeavoring to live up to the general air of propertied manners.*]

KELLER. And the suitcase—

ANNIE. [*Pleasantly.*] I'll take the suitcase, thanks.

KELLER. Not at all, I have it, Miss Sullivan.

ANNIE. I'd like it.

KELLER. [*Gallantly.*] I couldn't think of it, Miss Sullivan. You'll find in the south we—

ANNIE. Let me.

KELLER. —view women as the flowers of civiliza—

ANNIE. [*Impatiently.*] I've got something in it for Helen!

[*She tugs it free;* KELLER *stares.*]

Thank you. When do I see her?

KATE. There. There is Helen.

[ANNIE *turns, and sees* HELEN *on the porch. A moment of silence. Then* ANNIE *begins across the yard to her, lugging her suitcase.*]

KELLER. [*Sotto voce.*][16] Katie—

[KATE *silences him with a hand on his arm. When* ANNIE *finally reaches the porch steps she stops, contemplating* HELEN *for a last moment before entering her world. Then she drops the suitcase on the porch with intentional heaviness,* HELEN *starts with the jar,*

16. The Italian phrase *sotto voce* (sot′ ō vō′ chē) means "in a low voice or soft tones, so as not to be overheard."

Vocabulary

simultaneously (sī′ məl tā′ nē əs lē) *adv.* at the same time

contemplate (kon′ təm plāt′) *v.* to give intense attention to; consider carefully *and comes to grope over it.* ANNIE *puts forth her hand, and touches* HELEN*'s.* HELEN *at once grasps it, and commences to explore it, like reading a face. She moves her hand on to* ANNIE*'s forearm, and dress; and* ANNIE *brings her face within reach of* HELEN*'s fingers, which travel over it, quite without timidity, until they encounter and push aside the smoked glasses.* ANNIE*'s gaze is grave, unpitying, very attentive. She puts her hands on* HELEN*'s arms, but* HELEN *at once pulls away, and they confront each other with a distance between. Then* HELEN *returns to the suitcase, tries to open it, cannot.* ANNIE *points* HELEN*'s hand overhead.* HELEN *pulls away, tries to open the suitcase again;* ANNIE *points her hand overhead again.* HELEN *points overhead, a question, and* ANNIE*, drawing* HELEN*'s hand to her own face, nods.* HELEN *now begins tugging the suitcase toward the door, when* ANNIE *tries to take it from her, she fights her off and backs through the doorway with it.* ANNIE *stands a moment, then follows her in, and together they get the suitcase up the steps into* ANNIE*'s room.*]

KATE. Well?

KELLER. She's very rough, Katie.

KATE. I like her, Captain.

KELLER. Certainly rear a peculiar kind of young woman in the north. How old is she?

KATE. [*Vaguely.*] Ohh— Well, she's not in her teens, you know.

KELLER. She's only a child. What's her family like, shipping her off alone this far?

KATE. I couldn't learn. She's very close-mouthed about some things.

KELLER. Why does she wear those glasses? I like to see a person's eyes when I talk to—

KATE. For the sun. She was blind.

KELLER. Blind.

KATE. She's had nine operations on her eyes. One just before she left.

KELLER. Blind, good heavens, do they expect one blind child to teach another? Has she experience at least, how long did she teach there?

KATE. She was a pupil.

KELLER. [*Heavily.*] Katie, Katie. This is her first position?

KATE. [*Bright voice.*] She was valedictorian[17]—

KELLER. Here's a houseful of grown-ups can't cope with the child, how can an inexperienced half-blind Yankee schoolgirl manage her?

[*JAMES moves in with the trunk on his shoulder.*]

JAMES. [*Easily.*] Great improvement. Now we have two of them to look after.

KELLER. You look after those strawberry plants!

[*JAMES stops with the trunk. KELLER turns from him without another word, and marches off.*]

JAMES. Nothing I say is right.

KATE. Why say anything?

[*She calls.*]

Don't be long, Captain, we'll have supper right away—

[*She goes into the house, and through the rear door of the family room. JAMES trudges in with the trunk, takes it up the steps to ANNIE's room, and sets it down outside the door. The lights elsewhere dim somewhat.*

Meanwhile, inside, ANNIE has given HELEN a key; while ANNIE removes her bonnet, HELEN unlocks and opens the suitcase. The first thing she pulls out is a voluminous shawl. She fingers it until she perceives what it is; then she wraps it around her, and acquiring ANNIE's bonnet and smoked glasses as well, dons the lot: the shawl swamps her, and the bonnet settles down upon the glasses, but she stands before a mirror cocking her head to one side, then to the other, in a mockery of adult action. ANNIE is amused, and talks to her as one might to a kitten, with no trace of company manners.]

ANNIE. All the trouble I went to and that's how I look?

[*HELEN then comes back to the suitcase, gropes for more, lifts out a pair of female drawers.*]

Oh, no. Not the drawers!

[*But HELEN discarding them comes to the elegant doll. Her fingers explore its features, and when she raises it and finds its eyes open and close, she is at first startled, then delighted. She picks it up, taps its head vigorously, taps her own chest, and nods questioningly. ANNIE takes her finger, points it to the doll, points it to HELEN, and touching it to her own face, also nods. HELEN sits back on her heels, clasps the doll to herself, and rocks it. ANNIE studies her, still in bonnet and smoked glasses like a caricature[18] of herself, and addresses her humorously.*]

All right, Miss O'Sullivan. Let's begin with doll.

[*She takes HELEN's hand; in her palm ANNIE's forefinger points, thumb holding her other fingers clenched.*]

17. A *valedictorian* is usually the highest-ranked student, who delivers the farewell speech to his or her graduating class.

18. *[caricature]* Helen looks like a comic imitation of Annie.

D.

[Her thumb next holds all her fingers clenched, touching HELEN*'s palm.]*

O.

[Her thumb and forefinger extend.]

L.

[Same contact repeated.]

L.

[She puts HELEN*'s hand to the doll.]*

Doll.

JAMES. You spell pretty well.

*[*ANNIE *in one hurried move gets the drawers swiftly back into the suitcase, the lid banged shut, and her head turned, to see* JAMES *leaning in the doorway.]*

Finding out if she's ticklish? She is.

*[*ANNIE *regards him stonily, but* HELEN *after a scowling moment tugs at her hand again, imperious.* ANNIE *repeats the letters, and* HELEN *interrupts her fingers in the middle, feeling each of them, puzzled.* ANNIE *touches* HELEN*'s hand to the doll, and begins spelling into it again.]*

JAMES. What is it, a game?

ANNIE. *[Curtly.]* An alphabet.

JAMES. Alphabet?

ANNIE. For the deaf.

*[*HELEN *now repeats the finger movements in air, exactly, her head cocked to her own hand, and* ANNIE*'s eyes suddenly gleam.]*

Ho. How *bright* she is!

JAMES. You think she knows what she's doing?

[He takes HELEN*'s hand, to throw a meaningless gesture into it; she repeats this one too.]*

She imitates everything, she's a monkey.

ANNIE. *[Very pleased.]* Yes, she's a bright little monkey, all right.

[She takes the doll from HELEN*, and reaches for her hand;* HELEN *instantly grabs the doll back.* ANNIE *takes it again, and* HELEN*'s hand next, but* HELEN *is incensed now; when* ANNIE *draws her hand to her face to shake her head no, then tries to spell to her,* HELEN *slaps at* ANNIE*'s face.* ANNIE *grasps* HELEN *by both arms, and swings her into a chair, holding her pinned there, kicking, while glasses, doll, bonnet fly in various directions.* JAMES *laughs.]*

JAMES. She wants her doll back.

ANNIE. When she spells it.

JAMES. Spell, she doesn't know the thing has a name, even.

ANNIE. Of course not, who expects her to, now? All I want is her fingers to learn the letters.

JAMES. Won't mean anything to her.

*[*ANNIE *gives him a look. She then tries to form* HELEN*'s fingers into the letters, but* HELEN *swings a haymaker*[19] *instead, which* ANNIE *barely ducks, at once pinning her down again.]*

Doesn't like that alphabet, Miss Sullivan. You invent it yourself?

*[*HELEN *is now in a rage, fighting tooth and nail to get out of the chair, and* ANNIE *answers while struggling and dodging her kicks.]*

ANNIE. Spanish monks under a—vow of silence. Which I wish *you'd* take!

[And suddenly releasing HELEN*'s hands, she comes and shuts the door in* JAMES*'s face.* HELEN *drops to the floor, groping around for the doll.* ANNIE *looks around desperately, sees her purse on the bed, rummages in it, and comes up with a battered piece of cake wrapped in newspaper; with her foot she*

19. A *haymaker* is a powerful blow or punch.

moves the doll deftly out of the way of HELEN's groping, and going on her knee she lets HELEN smell the cake. When HELEN grabs for it, ANNIE removes the cake and spells quickly into the reaching hand.]

Cake. From Washington up north, it's the best I can do.

[*HELEN's hand waits, baffled. ANNIE repeats it.*]

C, a, k, e. Do what my fingers do, never mind what it means.

[*She touches the cake briefly to HELEN's nose, pats her hand, presents her own hand. HELEN spells the letters rapidly back. ANNIE pats her hand enthusiastically, and gives her the cake; HELEN crams it into her mouth with both hands. ANNIE watches her, with humor.*]

Get it down fast, maybe I'll steal that back too. Now.

[*She takes the doll, touches it to HELEN's nose, and spells again into her hand.*]

D, o, l, l. Think it over.

[*HELEN thinks it over, while ANNIE presents her own hand. Then HELEN spells three letters. ANNIE waits a second, then completes the word for HELEN in her palm.*]

L.

[She hands over the doll, and HELEN *gets a good grip on its leg.]*

Imitate now, understand later. End of the first les—

[She never finishes, because HELEN *swings the doll with a furious energy, it hits* ANNIE *squarely in the face, and she falls back with a cry of pain, her knuckles up to her mouth.* HELEN *waits, tensed for further combat. When* ANNIE *lowers her knuckles she looks at blood on them; she works her lips, gets to her feet, finds the mirror, and bares her teeth at herself. Now she is furious herself.]*

You little wretch, no one's taught you *any* manners? I'll—

[But rounding from the mirror she sees the door slam, HELEN *and the doll are on the outside, and* HELEN *is turning the key in the lock.* ANNIE *darts over, to pull the knob, the door is locked fast. She yanks it again.]*

Helen! Helen, let me out of—

[She bats her brow at the folly of speaking, but JAMES*, now downstairs, hears her and turns to see* HELEN *with the key and doll groping her way down the steps;* JAMES *takes in the whole situation, makes a move to intercept* HELEN*, but then changes his mind, lets her pass, and amusedly follows her out onto the porch. Upstairs* ANNIE *meanwhile rattles the knob, kneels, peers through the keyhole, gets up. She goes to the window, looks down, frowns.* JAMES *from the yard sings gaily up to her:]*

JAMES.

Buffalo girl, are you coming out tonight,
Coming out tonight,
Coming out—

[He drifts back into the house. ANNIE *takes a handkerchief, nurses her mouth, stands in the middle of the room, staring at door and window in turn, and so catches sight of herself in the mirror, her cheek scratched, her hair dishevelled, her handkerchief bloody, her face disgusted with herself. She addresses the mirror, with some irony.]*

ANNIE. Don't worry. They'll find you, you're not lost. Only out of place.

[But she coughs, spits something into her palm, and stares at it, outraged.]

And toothless.

[She winces.]

Oo! It hurts.

[She pours some water into the basin, dips the handkerchief, and presses it to her mouth. Standing there, bent over the basin in pain—with the rest of the set dim and unreal, and the lights upon her taking on the subtle color of the past—she hears again, as do we, the faraway voices, and slowly she lifts her head to them; the boy's voice is the same, the others are cracked old crones[20] in a nightmare, and perhaps we see their shadows.]

BOY'S VOICE. It hurts. Annie, it hurts.

FIRST CRONE'S VOICE. Keep that brat shut up, can't you, girlie, how's a body to get any sleep in this damn ward?

BOY'S VOICE. It hurts. It hurts.

SECOND CRONE'S VOICE. Shut up, you!

BOY'S VOICE. Annie, when are we goin' home? You promised!

ANNIE. Jimmie—

BOY'S VOICE. Forever and ever, you said forever—

*[*ANNIE *drops the handkerchief, averts to the window, and is arrested there by the next cry.]*

Annie? Annie, you there? Annie! It *hurts!*

THIRD CRONE'S VOICE. Grab him, he's fallin'!

BOY'S VOICE. *Annie!*

---

20. *Cracked old crones* are crazy old women.

DOCTOR'S VOICE. [*A pause, slowly.*] Little girl. Little girl, I must tell you your brother will be going on a—

[*But* ANNIE *claps her hands to her ears, to shut this out, there is instant silence.*

As the lights bring the other areas in again, JAMES *goes to the steps to listen for any sound from upstairs.* KELLER *re-entering from left crosses toward the house; he passes* HELEN *en route to her retreat under the pump.* KATE *re-enters the rear door of the family room, with flowers for the table.*]

KATE. Supper is ready, Jimmie, will you call your father?

JAMES. Certainly.

[*But he calls up the stairs, for* ANNIE*'s benefit:*]

Father! Supper!

KELLER. [*At the door.*] No need to shout, I've been cooling my heels for an hour. Sit down.

JAMES. Certainly.

KELLER. Viney!

[VINEY *backs in with a roast, while they get settled around the table.*]

VINEY. Yes, Cap'n, right here.

KATE. Mildred went directly to sleep, Viney?

VINEY. Oh yes, that babe's a angel.

KATE. And Helen had a good supper?

VINEY. [*Vaguely.*] I dunno, Miss Kate, somehow she didn't have much of a appetite tonight—

KATE. [*A bit guilty.*] Oh. Dear.

KELLER. [*Hastily.*] Well, now. Couldn't say the same for my part, I'm famished. Katie, your plate.

KATE. [*Looking.*] But where is Miss Annie?

[*A silence.*]

JAMES. [*Pleasantly.*] In her room.

KELLER. In her room? Doesn't she know hot food must be eaten hot? Go bring her down at once, Jimmie.

JAMES. [*Rises.*] Certainly. I'll get a ladder.

KELLER. [*Stares.*] What?

JAMES. I'll need a ladder. Shouldn't take me long.

KATE. [*Stares.*] What shouldn't take you—

KELLER. Jimmie, do as I say! Go upstairs at once and tell Miss Sullivan supper is getting cold—

JAMES. She's locked in her room.

KELLER. Locked in her—

KATE. What on earth are you—

JAMES. Helen locked her in and made off with the key.

KATE. [*Rising.*] And you sit here and say nothing?

JAMES. Well, everyone's been telling me not to say anything.

[*He goes serenely out and across the yard, whistling.* KELLER *thrusting up from his chair makes for the stairs.*]

KATE. Viney, look out in back for Helen. See if she has that key.

VINEY. Yes, Miss Kate.

[VINEY *goes out the rear door.*]

KELLER. [*Calling down.*] She's out by the pump!

[KATE *goes out on the porch after* HELEN*, while* KELLER *knocks on* ANNIE*'s door, then rattles the knob, imperiously.*]

Miss Sullivan! Are you in there?

ANNIE. Oh, I'm in here, all right.

KELLER. Is there no key on your side?

ANNIE. [*With some asperity.*] Well, if there was a key in here, *I* wouldn't be in here. Helen took it, the only thing on my side is me.

KELLER. Miss Sullivan. I—

[*He tries, but cannot hold it back.*]

Not in the house ten minutes, I don't see *how* you managed it!

[*He stomps downstairs again, while* ANNIE *mutters to herself.*]

ANNIE. And even I'm not on my side.

KELLER. [*Roaring.*] Viney!

VINEY. [*Reappearing.*] Yes, Cap'n?

KELLER. Put that meat back in the oven!

[VINEY *bears the roast off again, while* KELLER *strides out onto the porch.* KATE *is with* HELEN *at the pump, opening her hands.*]

KATE. She has no key.

KELLER. Nonsense, she must have the key. Have you searched in her pockets?

KATE. Yes. She doesn't have it.

KELLER. Katie, she must have the key.

KATE. Would you prefer to search her yourself, Captain?

KELLER. No, I would not prefer to search her! She almost took my kneecap off this evening, when I tried merely to—

[JAMES *reappears carrying a long ladder, with* PERCY *running after him to be in on things.*]

Take that ladder back!

JAMES. Certainly.

[*He turns around with it.* MARTHA *comes skipping around the upstage corner of the house to be in on things, accompanied by the setter* BELLE.]

KATE. She could have hidden the key.

KELLER. Where?

KATE. Anywhere. Under a stone. In the flower beds. In the grass—

KELLER. Well, I can't plow up the entire grounds to find a missing key! Jimmie!

JAMES. Sir?

KELLER. Bring me a ladder!

JAMES. Certainly.

[VINEY *comes around the downstage side of the house to be in on things; she has* MILDRED *over her shoulder, bleating.* KELLER *places the ladder against* ANNIE*'s window and mounts.* ANNIE *meanwhile is running about making herself presentable, washing the blood off her mouth, straightening her clothes, tidying her hair. Another Negro servant enters to gaze in wonder, increasing the gathering ring of spectators.*]

KATE. [*Sharply.*] What is Mildred doing up?

VINEY. Cap'n woke her, ma'am, all that hollerin'.

KELLER. Miss Sullivan!

[ANNIE *comes to the window, with as much air of gracious normality as she can manage;* KELLER *is at the window.*]

ANNIE. [*Brightly.*] Yes, Captain Keller?

KELLER. Come out!

ANNIE. I don't see how I can. There isn't room.

KELLER. I intend to carry you. Climb onto my shoulder and hold tight.

ANNIE. Oh, no. It's—very chivalrous[21] of you, but I'd really prefer to—

KELLER. Miss Sullivan, follow instructions! I will not have you also tumbling out of our windows.

[ANNIE *obeys, with some misgivings.*][22]

I hope this is not a sample of what we may expect from you. In the way of simplifying the work of looking after Helen.

ANNIE. Captain Keller, I'm perfectly able to go down a ladder under my own—

---

21. Here, *chivalrous* means behaving in a gallant or heroic manner, showing gentlemanly courage, strength, and honor.
22. *Misgivings* are feelings of doubt, distrust, or anxiety.

KELLER. I doubt it, Miss Sullivan. Simply hold onto my neck.

[*He begins down with her, while the spectators stand in a wide and somewhat awe-stricken circle, watching.* KELLER *half-misses a rung, and* ANNIE *grabs at his whiskers.*]

My *neck*, Miss Sullivan!

ANNIE. I'm sorry to inconvenience you this way—

KELLER. No inconvenience, other than having that door taken down and the lock replaced, if we fail to find that key.

ANNIE. Oh, I'll look everywhere for it.

KELLER. Thank you. Do not look in any rooms that can be locked. There.

[*He stands her on the ground.* JAMES *applauds.*]

ANNIE. Thank you very much.

[*She smooths her skirt, looking as composed and ladylike as possible.* KELLER *stares around at the spectators.*]

KELLER. Go, go, back to your work. What are you looking at here? There's nothing here to look at.

[*They break up, move off.*]

Now would it be possible for us to have supper, like other people?

[*He marches into the house.*]

KATE. Viney, serve supper. I'll put Mildred to sleep.

[*They all go in.* JAMES *is the last to leave, murmuring to* ANNIE *with a gesture.*]

JAMES. Might as well leave the l, a, d, d, e, r, hm?

[ANNIE *ignores him, looking at* HELEN; JAMES *goes in too. Imperceptibly the lights commence to narrow down.* ANNIE *and* HELEN *are now alone in the yard,* HELEN *seated at the pump, where she has been oblivious to it all, a battered little savage, playing with the doll in a picture of innocent contentment.* ANNIE *comes near, leans against the house, and taking off her smoked glasses, studies her, not without awe. Presently* HELEN *rises, gropes around to see if anyone is present;* ANNIE *evades her hand, and when* HELEN *is satisfied she is alone, the key suddenly protrudes out of her mouth. She takes it in her fingers, stands thinking, gropes to the pump, lifts a loose board, drops the key into the well, and hugs herself gleefully.* ANNIE *stares. But after a moment she shakes her head to herself, she cannot keep the smile from her lips.*]

ANNIE. You *devil*.

[*Her tone is one of great respect, humor, and acceptance of challenge.*]

You think I'm so easily gotten rid of? You have a thing or two to learn, first. I have nothing else to do.

[*She goes up the steps to the porch, but turns for a final word, almost of warning.*]

And nowhere to go.

[*And presently she moves into the house to the others, as the lights dim down and out, except for the small circle upon* HELEN *solitary at the pump, which ends the act.*]

Vocabulary
oblivious (ə bliv′ ē əs) *adj.* unaware; not noticing

Responding to Literature

Personal Response

What are your early impressions of James, Kate, Captain Keller, Helen, and Annie? Jot down your thoughts in your journal.

Analyzing Act 1

Recall and Interpret

1. How and when does Helen Keller's family first discover that she can neither hear nor see?
2. How do Helen's parents, half-brother, and aunt treat her? Support your answer with details from the play.
3. What does act 1 reveal about Annie Sullivan's life prior to her work with Helen? What impact do you predict her early experience will have on her ability to teach Helen and to get along with the Kellers?
4. How does each of the Kellers react to Annie when she first arrives? In your opinion, why does each react that way?
5. Describe Annie's attitude toward the Keller family and toward her job, using details from the play in your answer.

Evaluate and Connect

6. In your opinion, is Annie Sullivan qualified for this job? Explain.
7. Will Annie measure her own success with Helen in the same way that Helen's family will measure it? Explain.
8. What conclusions can you draw about Captain Keller's relationship with his wife and with his son?
9. At this point in the play, what advice would you like to give to James, Mr. Keller, or Mrs. Keller?
10. Evaluate Gibson's job of **exposition.** That is, how effectively has he introduced the setting, the situation, and the characters in act 1?

Literary ELEMENTS

Stage Directions

Typically printed in italics and enclosed in brackets, **stage directions** explain how characters should look, speak, move, and behave. They also specify details of the setting and scenery, such as lighting, props, and sound effects. In *The Miracle Worker,* stage directions also indicate how the stage is divided, how each area is set (with or without simple platforms and props), and how the lighting is used to suggest changes in time and place.

1. Reread the stage directions at the beginning of the play. In your own words, describe Gibson's plan for using the stage.
2. Explain how Gibson uses lighting to indicate shifts in time and place. Use examples from act 1 in your answer.

- See **Literary Terms Handbook,** p. R12.

Extending Your Response

Interdisciplinary Activity

Art: Setting the Stage Using William Gibson's stage directions at the beginning of the play, work with a partner to draw a stage set. Show how each part of the stage might be used, and indicate which parts should change. Write a caption that explains how the set accommodates changes in both time and place.

Writing About Literature

Characterization Write a **thesis statement** that conveys an important aspect of Annie's personality. Back up your thesis by writing two or three paragraphs that include examples of things that Annie says, does, or thinks that reveal this aspect of her personality.

Save your work for your portfolio.

Skill Minilesson

VOCABULARY • **The Latin Roots *vit* and *viv***

Six-and-a-half-year-old Helen cannot see and cannot hear, but, as the play tells us, she is a *vivacious* little girl. The root of *vivacious* is *viv,* which comes from the Latin word *vivo,* meaning "live." A related word is *vita,* meaning "life." Words with the root *viv* or *vit* have to do with life. For example, a *vivacious* person is full of life, and *vitamins* are necessary for life.

PRACTICE Use what you know about the roots *vit* and *viv* to answer each question.

1. Is a *vivid* imagination limited or active?
2. Name one of the human body's *vital* organs.
3. Is a person with great *vitality* very smart, very energetic, or very rich?
4. Does a neighborhood tend to be *revitalized* when people move into it or move out of it?
5. Who is most likely to *revive* someone—a teacher, a judge, or a member of an ambulance crew?

Before You Read

The Miracle Worker, Act 2

Building Background

Did You Know?

- In one part of act 2, Captain Keller and his son, James, debate military leaders, battles, and tactics of the Civil War, which raged from 1861 to 1865—more than twenty years before the time of the play. The war pitted North against South. After the North won and slavery had been abolished, many Southerners, including Captain Keller, were bitter. The South lay in ruins; wealth had been lost; and hundreds of thousands of men had been seriously wounded or killed.
- Captain Keller served with the Confederate army defending Vicksburg, a stronghold on the Mississippi, against a Union campaign that lasted fourteen months. Two of the military leaders to whom James and his father refer in conversation are General Ulysses S. Grant (later, president of the United States), who led the Union forces to victory at Vicksburg, and Confederate general "Stonewall" Jackson (killed during the war). Both were known for their skillful military tactics and their unwillingness to give up.

Vocabulary Preview

impassively (im pas′ iv lē) *adv.* in a way that shows no feeling; unemotionally; p. 736

temperance (tem′ pər əns) *n.* self-restraint or self-discipline in any kind of behavior; p. 736

impaired (im pārd′) *adj.* damaged; weakened; p. 737

ominous (om′ ə nəs) *adj.* threatening; indicating harm or evil to come; p. 738

deferential (def′ ə ren′ shəl) *adj.* respectful; p.738

relinquish (ri ling′ kwish) *v.* to give up or surrender (something); p. 746

compassion (kəm pash′ ən) *n.* sympathy for another person's suffering or misfortune, combined with a desire to help; p. 753

ACT 2

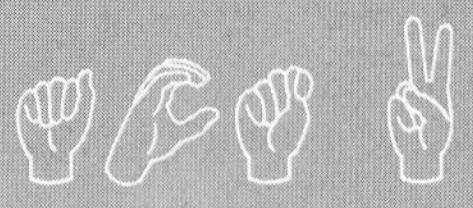

[*It is evening. The only room visible in the* KELLER *house is* ANNIE*'s, where by lamplight* ANNIE *in a shawl is at a desk writing a letter; at her bureau* HELEN *in her customary unkempt state is tucking her doll in the bottom drawer as a cradle, the contents of which she has dumped out, creating as usual a fine disorder.*

ANNIE *mutters each word as she writes her letter, slowly, her eyes close to and almost touching the page, to follow with difficulty her penwork.*]

ANNIE. ". . . and, nobody, here, has, attempted, to, control, her. The, greatest, problem, I, have, is, how, to, discipline, her, without, breaking, her, spirit."

[*Resolute voice.*]

"But, I, shall, insist, on, reasonable, obedience, from, the, start—"

[*At which point* HELEN*, groping about on the desk, knocks over the inkwell.* ANNIE *jumps up, rescues her letter, rights the inkwell, grabs a towel to stem the spillage, and then wipes at* HELEN*'s hands;* HELEN *as always pulls free, but not until* ANNIE *first gets three letters into her palm.*]

Ink.

[HELEN *is enough interested in and puzzled by this spelling that she proffers her hand again; so* ANNIE *spells and impassively dunks it back in the spillage.*]

Ink. It has a name.

[*She wipes the hand clean, and leads* HELEN *to her bureau, where she looks for something to engage her. She finds a sewing card, with needle and thread, and going to her knees, shows* HELEN*'s hand how to connect one row of holes.*]

Down. Under. Up. And be careful of the needle—

[HELEN *gets it, and* ANNIE *rises.*]

Fine. You keep out of the ink and perhaps I can keep out of—the soup.

[*She returns to the desk, tidies it, and resumes writing her letter, bent close to the page.*]

"These, blots, are, her, handiwork. I—"

[*She is interrupted by a gasp:* HELEN *has stuck her finger, and sits sucking at it, darkly. Then with vengeful resolve she seizes her doll, and is about to dash its brains out on the floor when* ANNIE *diving catches it in one hand, which she at once shakes with hopping pain but otherwise ignores, patiently.*]

All right, let's try temperance.

[*Taking the doll, she kneels, goes through the motion of knocking its head on the floor, spells into* HELEN*'s hand:*]

Bad, girl.

[*She lets* HELEN *feel the grieved expression on her face.* HELEN *imitates it. Next she makes* HELEN *caress the doll and kiss the hurt spot and hold it gently in her arms, then spells into her hand:*]

Good, girl.

[*She lets* HELEN *feel the smile on her face.* HELEN *sits with a scowl, which suddenly clears; she pats the doll, kisses it, wreathes her face in a large artificial smile, and bears the doll to the washstand, where she carefully sits it.* ANNIE *watches, pleased.*]

Very good girl—

Vocabulary

impassively (im pas′ iv lē) *adv.* in a way that shows no feeling; unemotionally
temperance (tem′ pər əns) *n.* self-restraint or self-discipline in any kind of behavior

[*Whereupon* HELEN *elevates the pitcher and dashes it on the floor instead.* ANNIE *leaps to her feet, and stands inarticulate;* HELEN *calmly gropes back to sit to the sewing card and needle.*

ANNIE *manages to achieve self-control. She picks up a fragment or two of the pitcher, sees* HELEN *is puzzling over the card, and resolutely kneels to demonstrate it again. She spells into* HELEN*'s hand.*

KATE *meanwhile coming around the corner with folded sheets on her arm, halts at the doorway and watches them for a moment in silence; she is moved, but level.*]

KATE. [*Presently.*] What are you saying to her?

[ANNIE *glancing up is a bit embarrassed, and rises from the spelling, to find her company manners.*]

ANNIE. Oh, I was just making conversation. Saying it was a sewing card.

KATE. But does that—

[*She imitates with her fingers.*]

—mean that to her?

ANNIE. No. No, she won't know what spelling is till she knows what a word is.

KATE. Yet you keep spelling to her. Why?

ANNIE. [*Cheerily.*] I like to hear myself talk!

KATE. The Captain says it's like spelling to the fence post.

ANNIE. [*A pause.*] Does he, now.

KATE. Is it?

ANNIE. No, it's how I watch you talk to Mildred.

KATE. Mildred.

ANNIE. Any baby. Gibberish, grown-up gibberish, baby-talk gibberish, do they understand one word of it to start? Somehow they begin to. If they hear it, I'm letting Helen hear it.

KATE. Other children are not—impaired.

ANNIE. Ho, there's nothing impaired in that head, it works like a mousetrap!

KATE. [*Smiles.*] But after a child hears how many words, Miss Annie, a million?

ANNIE. I guess no mother's ever minded enough to count.

[*She drops her eyes to spell into* HELEN*'s hand, again indicating the card;* HELEN *spells back, and* ANNIE *is amused.*]

KATE. [*Too quickly.*] What did she spell?

ANNIE. I spelled card. She spelled cake!

[*She takes in* KATE*'s quickness, and shakes her head, gently.*]

No, it's only a finger-game to her, Mrs. Keller. What she has to learn first is that things have names.

KATE. And when will she learn?

ANNIE. Maybe after a million and one words.

[*They hold each other's gaze;* KATE *then speaks quietly.*]

KATE. I should like to learn those letters, Miss Annie.

ANNIE. [*Pleased.*] I'll teach you tomorrow morning. That makes only half a million each!

KATE. [*Then.*] It's her bedtime.

[ANNIE *reaches for the sewing card,* HELEN *objects,* ANNIE *insists, and* HELEN *gets rid of* ANNIE*'s hand by jabbing it with the needle.* ANNIE *gasps, and moves to grip* HELEN*'s wrist; but* KATE *intervenes with a proffered*[23]

23. To *intervene* is to come between, and *proffered* means "offered."

Vocabulary

impaired (im pārd′) *adj.* damaged; weakened

sweet, and HELEN *drops the card, crams the sweet into her mouth, and scrambles up to search her mother's hands for more.* ANNIE *nurses her wound, staring after the sweet.*]

I'm sorry, Miss Annie.

ANNIE. [*Indignantly.*] Why does she get a reward? For stabbing me?

KATE. Well—

[*Then, tiredly.*]

We catch our flies with honey, I'm afraid. We haven't the heart for much else, and so many times she simply cannot be compelled.

ANNIE. [Ominous.] Yes. I'm the same way myself.

[KATE *smiles, and leads* HELEN *off around the corner.* ANNIE *alone in her room picks up things and in the act of removing* HELEN*'s doll gives way to unmannerly temptation: she throttles it. She drops it on her bed, and stands pondering. Then she turns back, sits decisively, and writes again, as the lights dim on her.*]

[*Grimly.*] "The, more, I, think, the, more, certain, I, am, that, obedience, is, the, gateway, through, which, knowledge, enters, the, mind, of, the, child—"

[*On the word "obedience" a shaft of sunlight hits the water pump outside, while* ANNIE*'s voice ends in the dark, followed by a distant cockcrow; daylight comes up over another corner of the sky, with* VINEY*'s voice heard at once.*]

VINEY. Breakfast ready!

[VINEY *comes down into the sunlight beam, and pumps a pitcherful of water. While the pitcher is brimming we hear conversation from the dark; the light grows to the family room of the house where all are either entering or already seated at breakfast, with* KELLER *and* JAMES *arguing the war.*[24] HELEN *is wandering around the table to explore the contents of the other plates. When* ANNIE *is in her chair, she watches* HELEN. VINEY *re-enters, sets the pitcher on the table;* KATE *lifts the almost empty biscuit plate with an inquiring look,* VINEY *nods and bears it off back, neither of them interrupting the men.* ANNIE *meanwhile sits with fork quiet, watching* HELEN, *who at her mother's plate pokes her hand among some scrambled eggs.* KATE *catches* ANNIE*'s eyes on her, smiles with a wry gesture.* HELEN *moves on to* JAMES*'s plate, the male talk continuing,* JAMES *deferential and* KELLER *overriding.*]

JAMES. —no, but shouldn't we give the devil his due, father? The fact is we lost the South two years earlier when he outthought us behind Vicksburg.

KELLER. Outthought is a peculiar word for a butcher.

JAMES. Harness maker, wasn't he?

KELLER. I said butcher, his only virtue as a soldier was numbers and he led them to slaughter with no more regard than for so many sheep.

JAMES. But even if in that sense he was a butcher, the fact is he—

KELLER. And a drunken one, half the war.

JAMES. Agreed, father. If his own people said he was I can't argue he—

KELLER. Well, what is it you find to admire in such a man, Jimmie, the butchery or the drunkenness?

24. ***[arguing the war]*** James and Captain Keller are debating the events and outcome of the Civil War. Here, they focus on General Ulysses S. Grant, leader of the Union army.

Vocabulary

ominous (om′ ə nəs) *adj.* threatening; indicating harm or evil to come

deferential (def′ ə ren′ shəl) *adj.* respectful

JAMES. Neither, father, only the fact that he beat us.

KELLER. He didn't.

JAMES. Is it your contention[25] we won the war, sir?

KELLER. He didn't beat us at Vicksburg. We lost Vicksburg because Pemberton gave Bragg five thousand of his cavalry and Loring, whom I knew personally for a nincompoop before you were born, marched away from Champion's Hill with enough men to have held them, we lost Vicksburg by stupidity verging on treason.

JAMES. I would have said we lost Vicksburg because Grant was one thing no Yankee general was before him—

KELLER. Drunk? I doubt it.

JAMES. Obstinate.

KELLER. Obstinate. Could any of them compare even in that with old Stonewall?[26] If he'd been there we would still have Vicksburg.

JAMES. Well, the butcher simply wouldn't give up, he tried four ways of getting around Vicksburg and on the fifth try he got around. Anyone else would have pulled north and—

KELLER. He wouldn't have got around if we'd had a Southerner in command, instead of a half-breed Yankee traitor like Pemberton—

[*While this background talk is in progress,* HELEN *is working around the table, ultimately toward* ANNIE*'s plate. She messes with her hands in* JAMES*'s plate, then in* KELLER*'s, both men taking it so for granted they hardly notice. Then* HELEN *comes groping with soiled hands past her own plate, to* ANNIE*'s; her hand goes to it, and* ANNIE*, who has been waiting, deliberately lifts and removes her hand.* HELEN *gropes again,* ANNIE *firmly pins her by the wrist, and removes her hand from the table.* HELEN *thrusts her hands again,* ANNIE *catches them, and* HELEN *begins to flail and make noises; the interruption brings* KELLER*'s gaze upon them.*]

What's the matter there?

KATE. Miss Annie. You see, she's accustomed to helping herself from our plates to anything she—

ANNIE. [*Evenly.*] Yes, but *I'm* not accustomed to it.

KELLER. No, of course not. Viney!

KATE. Give her something, Jimmie, to quiet her.

JAMES. [*Blandly.*] But her table manners are the best she has. Well.

[*He pokes across with a chunk of bacon at* HELEN*'s hand, which* ANNIE *releases; but* HELEN *knocks the bacon away and stubbornly thrusts at* ANNIE*'s plate,* ANNIE *grips her wrists again, the struggle mounts.*]

KELLER. Let her this time, Miss Sullivan, it's the only way we get any adult conversation. If my son's half merits that description.

[*He rises.*]

I'll get you another plate.

ANNIE. [*Gripping* HELEN.] I have a plate, thank you.

KATE. [*Calling.*] Viney! I'm afraid what Captain Keller says is only too true, she'll persist in this until she gets her own way.

KELLER. [*At the door.*] Viney, bring Miss Sullivan another plate—

ANNIE. [*Stonily.*] I have a plate, nothing's wrong with the *plate*, I intend to keep it.

25. A *contention* is a point or belief expressed in an argument or debate.

26. Confederate general Thomas J. *"Stonewall"* Jackson got his nickname after commanding his soldiers to hold their ground, blocking the advance of the Union army at Manassas (Bull Run), Virginia.

[Silence for a moment, except for HELEN's *noises as she struggles to get loose; the* KELLERS *are a bit nonplussed,*[27] *and* ANNIE *is too darkly intent on* HELEN's *manners to have any thoughts now of her own.]*

JAMES. Ha. You see why they took Vicksburg?

KELLER. *[Uncertainly.]* Miss Sullivan. One plate or another is hardly a matter to struggle with a deprived child about.

ANNIE. Oh, I'd sooner have a more—

*[*HELEN *begins to kick,* ANNIE *moves her ankles to the opposite side of the chair.]*

—heroic issue myself, I—

KELLER. No, I really must insist you—

*[*HELEN *bangs her toe on the chair and sinks to the floor, crying with rage and feigned*[28] *injury;* ANNIE *keeps hold of her wrists, gazing down, while* KATE *rises.]*

Now she's hurt herself.

ANNIE. *[Grimly.]* No, she hasn't.

KELLER. Will you please let her hands go?

KATE. Miss Annie, you don't know the child well enough yet, she'll keep—

ANNIE. I know an ordinary tantrum well enough, when I see one, and a badly spoiled child—

27. Being ***nonplussed*** (non plust′), the Kellers are bewildered and at a loss for what to say or do.

28. Helen's injury is faked, or ***feigned*** (fānd).

JAMES. Hear, hear.

KELLER. [*Very annoyed.*] Miss Sullivan! You would have more understanding of your pupil if you had some pity in you. Now kindly do as I—

ANNIE. Pity?

[*She releases* HELEN *to turn equally annoyed on* KELLER *across the table; instantly* HELEN *scrambles up and dives at* ANNIE*'s plate. This time* ANNIE *intercepts her by pouncing on her wrists like a hawk, and her temper boils.*]

For this *tyrant?*[29] The whole house turns on her whims, is there anything she wants she doesn't get? I'll tell you what I pity, that the sun won't rise and set for her all her life, and every day you're telling her it will, what good will your pity do her when you're under the strawberries, Captain Keller?

KELLER. [*Outraged.*] Kate, for the love of heaven will you—

KATE. Miss Annie, please, I don't think it serves to lose our—

ANNIE. It does you good, that's all. It's less trouble to feel sorry for her than to teach her anything better, isn't it?

KELLER. I fail to see where you have taught her anything yet, Miss Sullivan!

ANNIE. I'll begin this minute, if you'll leave the room, Captain Keller!

KELLER. [*Astonished.*] Leave the—

ANNIE. Everyone, please.

[*She struggles with* HELEN, *while* KELLER *endeavors to control his voice.*]

KELLER. Miss Sullivan, you are here only as a paid teacher. Nothing more, and not to lecture—

ANNIE. I can't *un*teach her six years of pity if you can't stand up to one tantrum! Old Stonewall, indeed. Mrs. Keller, you promised me help.

KATE. Indeed I did, we truly want to—

ANNIE. Then leave me alone with her. Now!

KELLER. [*In a wrath.*] Katie, will you come outside with me? At once, please.

[*He marches to the front door.* KATE *and* JAMES *follow him. Simultaneously* ANNIE *releases* HELEN*'s wrists, and the child again sinks to the floor, kicking and crying her weird noises;* ANNIE *steps over her to meet* VINEY *coming in the rear doorway with biscuits and a clean plate, surprised at the general commotion.*]

VINEY. Heaven sakes—

ANNIE. Out, please.

[*She backs* VINEY *out with one hand, closes the door on her astonished mouth, locks it, and removes the key.* KELLER *meanwhile snatches his hat from a rack, and* KATE *follows him down the porch steps.* JAMES *lingers in the doorway to address* ANNIE *across the room with a bow.*]

JAMES. If it takes all summer,[30] general.

[ANNIE *comes over to his door in turn, removing her glasses grimly; as* KELLER *outside begins speaking,* ANNIE *closes the door on* JAMES, *locks it, removes the key, and turns with her back against the door to stare ominously at* HELEN, *kicking on the floor.*

JAMES *takes his hat from the rack, and going down the porch steps joins* KATE *and* KELLER *talking in the yard,* KELLER *in a sputter of ire.*]

KELLER. This girl, this—cub of a girl—*presumes!* I tell you, I'm of half a mind to ship her back to Boston before the week is out. You can inform her so from me!

KATE. [*Eyebrows up.*] I, Captain?

---

29. A *tyrant* (tī′ rənt) is a selfish, unjust ruler whose use of power creates hardship for others.

30. James is borrowing a phrase from General Grant, who, following a series of disastrous battles, said, "I propose to fight it out . . . *if it takes all summer.*"

KELLER. She's a *hireling!* Now I want it clear, unless there's an apology and complete change of manner she goes back on the next train! Will you make that quite clear?

KATE. Where will you be, Captain, while I am making it quite—

KELLER. At the office!

[*He begins off left, finds his napkin still in his irate hand, is uncertain with it, dabs his lips with dignity, gets rid of it in a toss to* JAMES, *and marches off.* JAMES *turns to eye* KATE.]

JAMES. Will you?

[KATE's *mouth is set, and* JAMES *studies it lightly.*]

I thought what she said was exceptionally intelligent. I've been saying it for years.

KATE. [*Not without scorn.*] To his face?

[*She comes to relieve him of the white napkin, but reverts again with it.*]

Or will you take it, Jimmie? As a flag?

[JAMES *stalks out, much offended, and* KATE *turning stares across the yard at the house; the lights narrowing down to the following pantomime in the family room leave her motionless in the dark.*

ANNIE *meanwhile has begun by slapping both keys down on a shelf out of* HELEN's *reach; she returns to the table, upstage.* HELEN's *kicking has subsided, and when from the floor her hand finds* ANNIE's *chair empty she pauses.* ANNIE *clears the table of* KATE's, JAMES's, *and* KELLER's *plates; she gets back to her own across the table just in time to slide it deftly away from* HELEN's *pouncing hand. She lifts the hand and moves it to* HELEN's *plate, and after an instant's exploration,* HELEN *sits again on the floor and drums her heels.* ANNIE *comes around the table and resumes her chair. When* HELEN *feels her skirt again, she ceases kicking, waits for whatever is to come, renews some kicking, waits again.* ANNIE *retrieving her plate takes up a forkful of food, stops it halfway to her mouth, gazes at it devoid of appetite, and half-lowers it; but after a look at* HELEN *she sighs, dips the forkful toward* HELEN *in a for-your-sake toast, and puts it in her own mouth to chew, not without an effort.*

HELEN *now gets hold of the chair leg, and half-succeeds in pulling the chair out from under her.* ANNIE *bangs it down with her rear, heavily, and sits with all her weight.* HELEN's *next attempt to topple it is unavailing, so her fingers dive in a pinch at* ANNIE's *flank.* ANNIE *in the middle of her mouthful almost loses it with startle, and she slaps down her fork to round on* HELEN. *The child comes up with curiosity to feel what* ANNIE *is doing, so* ANNIE *resumes eating, letting* HELEN's *hand follow the movement of her fork to her mouth; whereupon* HELEN *at once reaches into* ANNIE's *plate.* ANNIE *firmly removes her hand to her own plate.* HELEN *in reply pinches* ANNIE's *thigh, a good mean pinchful that makes* ANNIE *jump.* ANNIE *sets the fork down, and sits with her mouth tight.* HELEN *digs another pinch into her thigh, and this time* ANNIE *slaps her hand smartly away;* HELEN *retaliates with a roundhouse fist*[31] *that catches* ANNIE *on the ear, and* ANNIE's *hand leaps at once in a forceful slap across* HELEN's *cheek;* HELEN *is the startled one now.* ANNIE's *hand in compunction*[32] *falters to her own face, but when* HELEN *hits at her again,* ANNIE *deliberately slaps her again.* HELEN *lifts her fist irresolute for another roundhouse,* ANNIE *lifts her hand resolute for another slap, and they freeze in this posture, while* HELEN *mulls it over. She thinks better of it, drops her fist, and giving* ANNIE *a wide berth, gropes around to her*

31. Helen gets even *(retaliates)* with a *roundhouse fist*—a punch delivered with a wide, swinging arm movement.
32. *Compunction* means "uneasiness caused by guilt; regret."

MOTHER's chair, to find it empty; she blunders her way along the table upstage, and encountering the empty chairs and missing plates, she looks bewildered; she gropes back to her MOTHER's chair, again touches her cheek and indicates the chair, and waits for the world to answer.

ANNIE now reaches over to spell into her hand, but HELEN yanks it away; she gropes to the front door, tries the knob, and finds the door locked, with no key. She gropes to the rear door, and finds it locked, with no key. She commences to bang on it. ANNIE rises, crosses, takes her wrists, draws her resisting back to the table, seats her, and releases her hands upon her plate; as ANNIE herself begins to sit, HELEN writhes out of her chair, runs to the front door, and tugs and kicks at it. ANNIE rises again, crosses, draws her by one wrist back to the table, seats her, and sits; HELEN escapes back to the door, knocking over her MOTHER's chair en route. ANNIE rises again in pursuit, and this time lifts HELEN bodily from behind and bears her kicking to her chair. She deposits her, and once more turns to sit. HELEN scrambles out, but as she passes ANNIE catches her up again from behind and deposits her in the chair; HELEN scrambles out on the other side, for the rear door, but ANNIE at her heels catches her up and deposits her again in the chair. She stands behind it. HELEN scrambles out to her right, and the instant her feet hit the floor ANNIE lifts and deposits her back; she scrambles out to her left, and is at once lifted and deposited back. She tries right again and is deposited back, and tries left again and is deposited back, and now feints[33] *ANNIE to the right but is off to her left, and is promptly deposited back. She sits a moment, and then starts straight over the tabletop, dishware notwithstanding; ANNIE hauls her in and deposits her back, with her plate spilling in her lap, and she melts to the floor and crawls under the table, laborious among its legs and chairs; but ANNIE is swift around the table and waiting on the other side when she surfaces, immediately bearing her aloft; HELEN clutches at JAMES's chair for anchorage, but it comes with her, and halfway back she abandons it to the floor. ANNIE deposits her in her chair, and waits. HELEN sits tensed motionless. Then she tentatively puts out her left foot and hand, ANNIE interposes her own hand, and at the contact HELEN jerks hers in. She tries her right foot, ANNIE blocks it with her own, and HELEN jerks hers in. Finally, leaning back, she slumps down in her chair, in a sullen biding.*

ANNIE backs off a step, and watches; HELEN offers no move. ANNIE takes a deep breath. Both of them and the room are in considerable disorder, two chairs down and the table a mess, but ANNIE makes no effort to tidy it; she only sits on her own chair, and lets her energy refill. Then she takes up knife and fork, and resolutely addresses her food. HELEN's hand comes out to explore, and seeing it ANNIE sits without moving; the child's hand goes over her hand and fork, pauses—ANNIE still does not move—and withdraws. Presently it moves for her own plate, slaps about for it, and stops, thwarted.[34] *At this, ANNIE again rises, recovers HELEN's plate from the floor and a handful of scattered food from the deranged tablecloth, drops it on the plate, and pushes the plate into contact with HELEN's fist. Neither of them now moves for a pregnant moment*[35]*—until HELEN suddenly takes a grab of food and wolfs it down. ANNIE permits herself the humor of a minor bow and warming of her hands together; she wanders off a step or two, watching. HELEN cleans up the plate.*

After a glower of indecision, she holds the empty plate out for more. ANNIE accepts it, and crossing to the removed plates, spoons food from them onto it; she stands debating the spoon, tapping it a few times on HELEN's plate; and when she returns with the plate she brings the spoon, too. She puts the spoon first into HELEN's hand, then sets the plate down. HELEN discarding the spoon reaches with her hand, and ANNIE stops it by the wrist; she replaces the spoon in it. HELEN impatiently discards it again, and again ANNIE stops her hand, to replace the spoon in it. This time HELEN throws the spoon on the floor. ANNIE after considering it lifts HELEN bodily out of the chair, and in a wrestling match on the floor closes her fingers upon the spoon, and returns her with it to the chair. HELEN again throws the spoon on the floor. ANNIE lifts her out of the chair again; but in the struggle over the spoon HELEN with ANNIE on her back sends her sliding over her head; HELEN flees back to her chair and scrambles into it. When ANNIE comes after her she clutches it for dear life; ANNIE pries one hand loose, then the other, then the first again, then the other again, and then lifts HELEN by the waist, chair and all, and shakes the chair loose. HELEN wrestles to get free, but ANNIE pins her to the floor, closes her fingers upon the spoon, and lifts her kicking under one arm; with her other hand she gets the chair in place again, and plunks HELEN back on it. When she releases her hand, HELEN throws the spoon at her.

33. ***[feints]*** **Helen tries to mislead Annie with a deceptive movement.**
34. **To be *thwarted* (thwôr′ təd) is to be prevented from doing or achieving something.**
35. **Here, a *pregnant moment* is one filled with importance, meaning, or suspense.**

ANNIE now removes the plate of food. HELEN grabbing finds it missing, and commences to bang with her fists on the table. ANNIE collects a fistful of spoons and descends with them and the plate on HELEN; she lets her smell the plate, at which HELEN ceases banging, and ANNIE puts the plate down and a spoon in HELEN's hand. HELEN throws it on the floor. ANNIE puts another spoon in her hand. HELEN throws it on the floor. ANNIE puts another spoon in her hand. HELEN throws it on the floor. When ANNIE comes to her last spoon she sits next to HELEN, and gripping the spoon in HELEN's hand compels her to take food in it up to her mouth. HELEN sits with lips shut. ANNIE waits a stolid[36] *moment, then lowers HELEN's hand. She tries again; HELEN's lips remain shut. ANNIE waits, lowers HELEN's hand. She tries again; this time HELEN suddenly opens her mouth and accepts the food. ANNIE lowers the spoon with a sigh of relief, and HELEN spews the mouthful out at her face. ANNIE sits a moment with eyes closed, then takes the pitcher and dashes its water into HELEN's face, who gasps astonished. ANNIE with HELEN's hand takes up another spoonful, and shoves it into her open mouth. HELEN swallows involuntarily, and while she is catching her breath ANNIE forces her palm open, throws four swift letters into it, then another four, and bows toward her with devastating pleasantness.]*

36. *Stolid* means "unemotional."

ANNIE. Good girl.

[ANNIE lifts HELEN's hand to feel her face nodding; HELEN grabs a fistful of her hair, and yanks. The pain brings ANNIE to her knees, and HELEN pummels her; they roll under the table, and the lights commence to dim out on them.

Simultaneously the light at left has been rising, slowly, so slowly that it seems at first we only imagine what is intimated in the yard: a few ghostlike figures, in silence, motionless, waiting. Now the distant belfry chimes commence to toll the hour, also very slowly, almost—it is twelve—interminably;[37] *the sense is that of a long time passing. We can identify the figures before the twelfth stroke, all facing the house in a kind of watch:* KATE *is standing exactly as before, but now with the baby* MILDRED *sleeping in her arms, and placed here and there, unmoving, are* AUNT EV *in her hat with a hanky to her nose, and the two Negro children,* PERCY *and* MARTHA *with necks outstretched eagerly, and* VINEY *with a knotted kerchief on her head and a feather duster in her hand.*

The chimes cease, and there is silence. For a long moment none of the group moves.]

VINEY. [*Presently.*] What am I gone do, Miss Kate? It's noontime, dinner's comin', I didn't get them breakfast dishes out of there yet.

[KATE *says nothing, stares at the house.* MARTHA *shifts* HELEN*'s doll in her clutch, and it plaintively says momma.*]

KATE. [*Presently.*] You run along, Martha.

[AUNT EV *blows her nose.*]

AUNT EV. [*Wretchedly.*] I can't wait out here a minute longer, Kate, why, this could go on all afternoon, too.

KATE. I'll tell the captain you called.

VINEY. [*To the children.*] You hear what Miss Kate say? Never you mind what's going on here.

[*Still no one moves.*]

You run along tend your own bizness.

[*Finally* VINEY *turns on the children with the feather duster.*]

Shoo!

[*The two children divide before her. She chases them off.* AUNT EV *comes to* KATE, *on her dignity.*]

AUNT EV. Say what you like, Kate, but that child is a *Keller.*

[*She opens her parasol, preparatory to leaving.*]

I needn't remind you that all the Kellers are cousins to General Robert E. Lee.[38] I don't know *who* that girl is.

[*She waits; but* KATE *staring at the house is without response.*]

The only Sullivan I've heard of—from Boston too, and I'd think twice before locking her up with that kind—is that man John L.[39]

[*And* AUNT EV *departs, with head high. Presently* VINEY *comes to* KATE, *her arms out for the baby.*]

VINEY. You give me her, Miss Kate, I'll sneak her in back, to her crib.

[*But* KATE *is moveless, until* VINEY *starts to take the baby;* KATE *looks down at her before relinquishing her.*]

KATE. [*Slowly.*] This child never gives me a minute's worry.

VINEY. Oh yes, this one's the angel of the family, no question bout *that.*

---

37. The chiming seems to go on endlessly *(interminably)* before the clock finally reaches twelve.

38. *General Robert E. Lee* commanded the Confederate Army of Northern Virginia during the Civil War. To Aunt Ev, among others, he was a model of Southern chivalry and good manners.

39. From 1882 to 1892, *John L. Sullivan* was the world champion in heavyweight boxing.

Vocabulary

relinquish (ri ling′ kwish) *v.* to give up or surrender (something)

[She begins off rear with the baby, heading around the house; and KATE *now turns her back on it, her hand to her eyes. At this moment there is the slamming of a door, and when* KATE *wheels* HELEN *is blundering down the porch steps into the light, like a ruined bat out of hell.* VINEY *halts, and* KATE *runs in;* HELEN *collides with her mother's knees, and reels off and back to clutch them as her savior.* ANNIE *with smoked glasses in hand stands on the porch, also much undone, looking as though she had indeed just taken Vicksburg.* KATE *taking in* HELEN*'s ravaged state becomes steely in her gaze up at* ANNIE.*]*

KATE. What happened?

*[*ANNIE *meets* KATE*'s gaze, and gives a factual report, too exhausted for anything but a flat voice.]*

ANNIE. She ate from her own plate.

[She thinks a moment.]

She ate with a spoon. Herself.

*[*KATE *frowns, uncertain with thought, and glances down at* HELEN.*]*

And she folded her napkin.

*[*KATE*'s gaze now wavers, from* HELEN *to* ANNIE, *and back.]*

KATE. *[Softly.]* Folded—her napkin?

ANNIE. The room's a wreck, but her napkin is folded.

[She pauses, then:]

I'll be in my room, Mrs. Keller.

[She moves to re-enter the house; but she stops at VINEY*'s voice.]*

VINEY. *[Cheery.]* Don't be long, Miss Annie. Dinner be ready right away!

*[*VINEY *carries* MILDRED *around the back of the house.* ANNIE *stands unmoving, takes a deep breath, stares over her shoulder at* KATE *and* HELEN, *then inclines her head graciously, and goes with a slight stagger into the house. The lights in her room above steal up in readiness for her.*

KATE *remains alone with* HELEN *in the yard, standing protectively over her, in a kind of wonder.]*

KATE. *[Slowly.]* Folded her napkin.

[She contemplates the wild head in her thighs, and moves her fingertips over it, with such a tenderness, and something like a fear of its strangeness, that her own eyes close; she whispers, bending to it:]

My Helen—folded her napkin—

[And still erect, with only her head in surrender, KATE *for the first time that we see loses her protracted[40] war with grief; but she will not let a sound escape her, only the grimace[41] of tears comes, and sobs that shake her in a grip of silence. But* HELEN *feels them, and her hand comes up in its own wondering, to interrogate her mother's face, until* KATE *buries her lips in the child's palm.*

Upstairs, ANNIE *enters her room, closes the door, and stands back against it; the lights, growing on her with their special color, commence to fade on* KATE *and* HELEN. *Then* ANNIE *goes wearily to her suitcase, and lifts it to take it toward the bed. But it knocks an object to the floor, and she turns back to regard it. A new voice comes in a cultured murmur, hesitant as with the effort of remembering a text:]*

MAN'S VOICE. This—soul—

*[*ANNIE *puts the suitcase down, and kneels to the object: it is the battered Perkins report, and she stands with it in her hand, letting memory try to speak:]*

40. Something that is *protracted* goes on for a long time.
41. A *grimace* (grim′ is) is a twisted facial expression, usually caused by pain or displeasure.

This—blind, deaf, mute—woman—[42]

[*ANNIE sits on her bed, opens the book, and finding the passage, brings it up an inch from her eyes to read, her face and lips following the overheard words, the voice quite factual now:*]

Can nothing be done to disinter[43] this human soul? The whole neighborhood would rush to save this woman if she were buried alive by the caving in of a pit, and labor with zeal until she were dug out. Now if there were one who had as much patience as zeal, he might awaken her to a consciousness of her immortal—

[*When the boy's voice comes, ANNIE closes her eyes, in pain.*]

BOY'S VOICE. Annie? Annie, you there?

ANNIE. Hush.

BOY'S VOICE. Annie, what's that noise?

[*ANNIE tries not to answer; her own voice is drawn out of her, unwilling.*]

ANNIE. Just a cot, Jimmie.

BOY'S VOICE. Where they pushin' it?

ANNIE. To the deadhouse.

BOY'S VOICE. Annie. Does it hurt, to be dead?

[*ANNIE escapes by opening her eyes, her hand works restlessly over her cheek; she retreats into the book again, but the cracked old crones interrupt, whispering. ANNIE slowly lowers the book.*]

FIRST CRONE'S VOICE. There is schools.

SECOND CRONE'S VOICE. There is schools outside—

THIRD CRONE'S VOICE. —schools where they teach blind ones, worse'n you—

FIRST CRONE'S VOICE. To read—

SECOND CRONE'S VOICE. To read and write—

THIRD CRONE'S VOICE. There is schools outside where they—

FIRST CRONE'S VOICE. There is schools—

[*Silence. ANNIE sits with her eyes shining, her hand almost in a caress over the book. Then:*]

BOY'S VOICE. You ain't goin' to school, are you, Annie?

ANNIE. [*Whispering.*] When I grow up.

BOY'S VOICE. You ain't either, Annie. You're goin' to stay here take care of me.

ANNIE. I'm goin' to school when I grow up.

BOY'S VOICE. You said we'll be together, forever and ever and ever—

ANNIE. [*Fierce.*] I'm goin' to school when I grow up!

DOCTOR'S VOICE. [*Slowly.*] Little girl. Little girl, I must tell you. Your brother will be going on a journey, soon.

[*ANNIE sits rigid, in silence. Then the boy's voice pierces it, a shriek of terror.*]

BOY'S VOICE. *Annie!*

[*It goes into ANNIE like a sword, she doubles onto it; the book falls to the floor. It takes her a racked moment to find herself and what she was engaged in here; when she sees the suitcase she remembers, and lifts it once again toward the bed. But the voices are with her, as she halts with suitcase in hand.*]

FIRST CRONE'S VOICE. Good-bye, Annie.

DOCTOR'S VOICE. Write me when you learn how.

SECOND CRONE'S VOICE. Don't tell anyone you came from here. Don't tell anyone—

THIRD CRONE'S VOICE. Yeah, don't tell anyone you came from—

FIRST CRONE'S VOICE. Yeah, don't tell anyone—

SECOND CRONE'S VOICE. Don't tell any—

42. *[This–blind, deaf, mute–woman]* Annie is remembering a passage from the Perkins report in which Dr. Howe explains why it is worthwhile to try to teach a deaf-blind person (in this case, his pupil, Laura Bridgman) to communicate.
43. *To disinter* means "to dig up, unbury, or bring to light."

[*The echoing voices fade. After a moment* ANNIE *lays the suitcase on the bed; and the last voice comes faintly, from far away.*]

BOY'S VOICE. Annie. It hurts, to be dead. Forever.

[ANNIE *falls to her knees by the bed, stifling her mouth in it. When at last she rolls blindly away from it, her palm comes down on the open report; she opens her eyes, regards it dully, and then, still on her knees, takes in the print.*]

MAN'S VOICE. [*Factual.*] —might awaken her to a consciousness of her immortal nature. The chance is small indeed; but with a smaller chance they would have dug desperately for her in the pit; and is the life of the soul of less import than that of the body?

[ANNIE *gets to her feet. She drops the book on the bed, and pauses over her suitcase; after a moment she unclasps and opens it. Standing before it, she comes to her decision; she at once turns to the bureau, and taking her things out of its drawers, commences to throw them into the open suitcase.*

In the darkness down left a hand strikes a match, and lights a hanging oil lamp. It is KELLER*'s hand, and his voice accompanies it, very angry; the lights rising here before they fade on* ANNIE *show* KELLER *and* KATE *inside a suggestion of a garden house, with a bay-window seat towards center and a door at back.*]

KELLER. Katie, I will not *have* it! Now you did not see when that girl after supper tonight went to look for Helen in her room

KATE. No.

KELLER. The child practically climbed out of her window to escape from her! What kind of teacher *is* she? I thought I had seen her at her worst this morning, shouting at me, but I come home to find the entire house disorganized by her—Helen won't stay one second in the same room, won't come to the table with her, won't let herself be bathed or undressed or put to bed by her, or even by Viney now, and the end result is that *you* have to do more for the child than before we hired this girl's services! From the moment she stepped off the train she's been nothing but a burden, incompetent, impertinent, ineffectual, immodest[44]—

KATE. She folded her napkin, Captain.

KELLER. What?

KATE. Not ineffectual. Helen did fold her napkin.

KELLER. What in heaven's name is so extraordinary about folding a napkin?

KATE. [*With some humor.*] Well. It's more than you did, Captain.

KELLER. Katie. I did not bring you all the way out here to the garden house to be frivolous.[45] Now, how does Miss Sullivan propose to teach a deaf-blind pupil who won't let her even touch her?

KATE. [*A pause.*] I don't know.

KELLER. The fact is, today she scuttled any chance she ever had of getting along with the child. If you can see any point or purpose to her staying on here longer, it's more than—

KATE. What do you wish me to do?

KELLER. I want you to give her notice.

KATE. I can't.

KELLER. Then if you won't, I must. I simply will not—

[*He is interrupted by a knock at the back door.* KELLER *after a glance at* KATE *moves to open the door;* ANNIE *in her smoked glasses is standing outside.* KELLER *contemplates her, heavily.*]

Miss Sullivan.

44. Keller thinks Annie is unable to do the job *(incompetent),* boldly rude *(impertinent),* unable to produce results *(ineffectual),* and brashly self-confident *(immodest).*

45. Here, *frivolous* means "silly."

ANNIE. Captain Keller.

[She is nervous, keyed up to seizing the bull by the horns again, and she assumes a cheeriness which is not unshaky.]

Viney said I'd find you both over here in the garden house. I thought we should—have a talk?

KELLER. *[Reluctantly.]* Yes, I— Well, come in.

[ANNIE enters, and is interested in this room; she rounds on her heel, anxiously, studying it. KELLER turns the matter over to KATE, sotto voce.]

Katie.

KATE. *[Turning it back, courteously.]* Captain.

[KELLER clears his throat, makes ready.]

KELLER. I, ah—wanted first to make my position clear to Mrs. Keller, in private. I have decided I—am not satisfied—in fact, am deeply dissatisfied—with the manner in which—

ANNIE. *[Intent.]* Excuse me, is this little house ever in use?

KELLER. *[With patience.]* In the hunting season. If you will give me your attention, Miss Sullivan.

[ANNIE turns her smoked glasses upon him; they hold his unwilling stare.]

I have tried to make allowances for you because you come from a part of the country where people are—women, I should say—come from who—well, for whom—

[It begins to elude him.]

—allowances must—be made. I have decided, nevertheless, to—that is, decided I—

[Vexedly.]

Miss Sullivan, I find it difficult to talk through those glasses.

ANNIE. *[Eagerly, removing them.]* Oh, of course.

KELLER. *[Dourly.]* Why do you wear them, the sun has been down for an hour.

ANNIE. *[Pleasantly, at the lamp.]* Any kind of light hurts my eyes.

[A silence; KELLER ponders her, heavily.]

KELLER. Put them on. Miss Sullivan, I have decided to—give you another chance.

ANNIE. *[Cheerfully.]* To do what?

KELLER. To—remain in our employ.

[ANNIE's eyes widen.]

But on two conditions. I am not accustomed to rudeness in servants or women, and that is the first. If you are to stay, there must be a radical change of manner.

ANNIE. *[A pause.]* Whose?

KELLER. *[Exploding.]* Yours, young lady, isn't it obvious? And the second is that you persuade me there's the slightest hope of your teaching a child who flees from you now like the plague, to anyone else she can find in this house.

ANNIE. *[A pause.]* There isn't.

[KATE stops sewing, and fixes her eyes upon ANNIE.]

KATE. What, Miss Annie?

ANNIE. It's hopeless here. I can't teach a child who runs away.

KELLER. *[Nonplussed.]* Then—do I understand you—propose—

ANNIE. Well, if we all agree it's hopeless, the next question is what—

KATE. Miss Annie.

[She is leaning toward ANNIE, in deadly earnest; it commands both ANNIE and KELLER.]

I am not agreed. I think perhaps you—underestimate Helen.

ANNIE. I think everybody else here does.

KATE. She did fold her napkin. She learns, she learns, do you know she began talking when she was six months old? She could say "water." Not really—"wahwah." "Wahwah," but she meant water, she knew what it meant, and only six months old, I never saw a child so—bright, or outgoing—

[*Her voice is unsteady, but she gets it level.*]

It's still in her, somewhere, isn't it? You should have seen her before her illness, such a good-tempered child—

ANNIE. [*Agreeably.*] She's changed.

[*A pause,* KATE *not letting her eyes go; her appeal at last is unconditional, and very quiet.*]

KATE. Miss Annie, put up with it. And with us.

KELLER. Us!

KATE. Please? Like the lost lamb in the parable, I love her all the more.

ANNIE. Mrs. Keller, I don't think Helen's worst handicap is deafness or blindness. I think it's your love. And pity.

KELLER. Now what does that mean?

ANNIE. All of you here are so sorry for her you've kept her—like a pet, why, even a dog you housebreak. No wonder she won't let me come near her. It's useless for me to try to teach her language or anything else here. I might as well—

KATE. [*Cuts in.*] Miss Annie, before you came we spoke of putting her in an asylum.

[ANNIE *turns back to regard her. A pause.*]

ANNIE. What kind of asylum?

KELLER. For mental defectives.

KATE. I visited there. I can't tell you what I saw, people like—animals, with—*rats*, in the halls, and—

[*She shakes her head on her vision.*]

What else are we to do, if you give up?

ANNIE. Give up?

KATE. You said it was hopeless.

ANNIE. Here. Give up, why, I only today saw what has to be done, to begin!

[*She glances from* KATE *to* KELLER, *who stare, waiting; and she makes it as plain and simple as her nervousness permits.*]

I—want complete charge of her.

KELLER. You already have that. It has resulted in—

ANNIE. No, I mean day and night. She has to be dependent on me.

KATE. For what?

ANNIE. Everything. The food she eats, the clothes she wears, fresh—

[*She is amused at herself, though very serious.*]

—air, yes, the air she breathes, whatever her body needs is a—primer,[46] to teach her out of. It's the only way, the one who lets her have it should be her teacher.

[*She considers them in turn; they digest it,* KELLER *frowning,* KATE *perplexed.*]

Not anyone who *loves* her, you have so many feelings they fall over each other like feet, you won't use your chances and you won't let me.

KATE. But if she runs from you—*to* us—

ANNIE. Yes, that's the point. I'll have to live with her somewhere else.

KELLER. What!

ANNIE. Till she learns to depend on and listen to me.

KATE. [*Not without alarm.*] For how long?

ANNIE. As long as it takes.

[*A pause. She takes a breath.*]

I packed half my things already.

---

46. A *primer* (prim′ ər) is a book for teaching children to read, or any simple book that provides basic information on a subject.

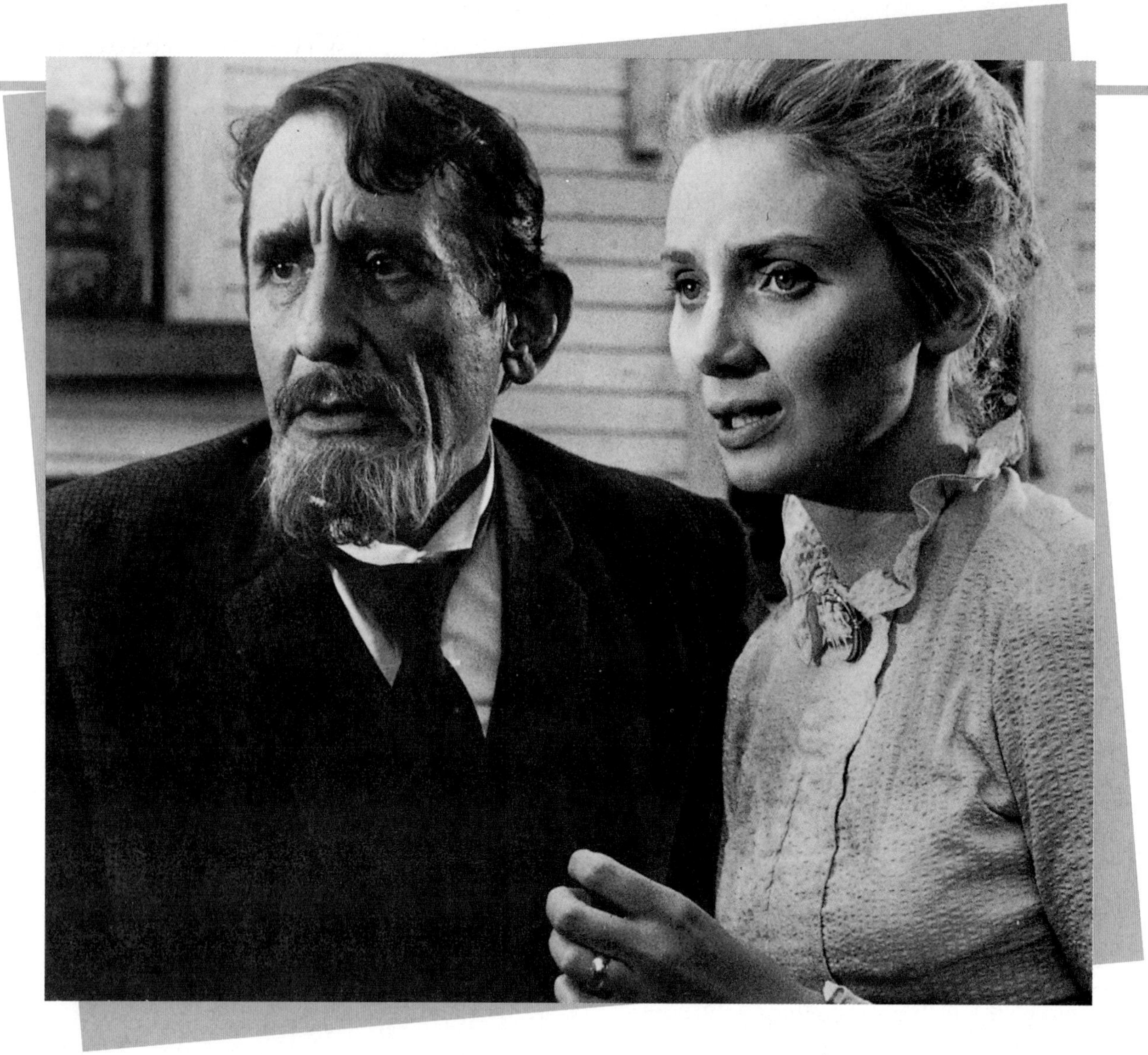

KELLER. Miss—Sullivan!

[But when ANNIE attends upon him he is speechless, and she is merely earnest.]

ANNIE. Captain Keller, it meets both your conditions. It's the one way I can get back in touch with Helen, and I don't see how I can be rude to you again if you're not around to interfere with me.

KELLER. *[Red-faced.]* And what is your intention if I say no? Pack the other half, for home, and abandon your charge to—to—

ANNIE. The asylum?

[She waits, appraises KELLER's glare and KATE's uncertainty, and decides to use her weapons.]

I grew up in such an asylum. The state almshouse.[47]

[KATE's head comes up on this, and KELLER stares hard; ANNIE's tone is cheerful enough, albeit level as gunfire.]

Rats—why, my brother Jimmie and I used to play with the rats because we didn't have toys. Maybe you'd like to know what Helen will find there, not on visiting days? One ward was full of the—old women, crippled, blind, most of them dying, but even if what

47. An *almshouse* (ämz′ hous′) is a poorhouse, or home for the poor; here, Annie refers to the one she lived in at Tewksbury, Massachusetts.

they had was catching there was nowhere else to move them, and that's where they put us. There were younger ones across the hall, prostitutes mostly, with T.B., and epileptic fits, and a couple of the kind who—keep after other girls, especially young ones, and some insane. Some just had the D.T.'s.[48] The youngest were in another ward to have babies they didn't want, they started at thirteen, fourteen. They'd leave afterwards, but the babies stayed and we played with them, too, though a lot of them had—sores all over from diseases you're not supposed to talk about, but not many of them lived. The first year we had eighty, seventy died. The room Jimmie and I played in was the deadhouse, where they kept the bodies till they could dig—

KATE. [*Closes her eyes.*] Oh, my dear—

ANNIE. —the graves.

[*She is immune to* KATE*'s* compassion.]

No, it made me strong. But I don't think you need send Helen there. She's strong enough.

[*She waits again; but when neither offers her a word, she simply concludes.*]

No, I have no conditions, Captain Keller.

KATE. [*Not looking up.*] Miss Annie.

ANNIE. Yes.

KATE. [*A pause.*] Where would you—take Helen?

ANNIE. Ohh—

[*Brightly.*]

Italy?

48. *D.T.'s* is short for "delirium tremens," a temporary mental disturbance that is usually caused by excessive drinking of alcohol.

KELLER. [*Wheeling.*] What?

ANNIE. Can't have everything, how would this garden house do? Furnish it, bring Helen here after a long ride so she won't recognize it, and you can see her every day. If she doesn't know. Well?

KATE. [*A sigh of relief.*] Is that all?

ANNIE. That's all.

KATE. Captain.

[KELLER *turns his head; and* KATE*'s request is quiet but firm.*]

With your permission?

KELLER. [*Teeth in cigar.*] Why must she depend on you for the food she eats?

ANNIE. [*A pause.*] I want control of it.

KELLER. Why?

ANNIE. It's a way to reach her.

KELLER. [*Stares.*] You intend to *starve* her into letting you touch her?

ANNIE. She won't starve, she'll learn. All's fair in love and war, Captain Keller, you never cut supplies?

KELLER. This is hardly a war!

ANNIE. Well, it's not love. A siege is a siege.

KELLER. [*Heavily.*] Miss Sullivan. Do you *like* the child?

ANNIE. [*Straight in his eyes.*] Do you?

[*A long pause.*]

KATE. You could have a servant here—

ANNIE. [*Amused.*] I'll have enough work without looking after a servant! But that boy Percy could sleep here, run errands—

KATE. [*Also amused.*] We can let Percy sleep here, I think, Captain?

Vocabulary

compassion (kəm pash′ ən) *n.* sympathy for another person's suffering or misfortune, combined with a desire to help

ANNIE. [*Eagerly.*] And some old furniture, all our own—

KATE. [*Also eager.*] Captain? Do you think that walnut bedstead in the barn would be too—

KELLER. I have not yet consented to Percy! Or to the house, or to the proposal! Or to Miss Sullivan's—staying on when I—

[*But he erupts in an irate surrender.*]

Very well, I consent to everything!

[*He shakes the cigar at* ANNIE.]

For two weeks. I'll give you two weeks in this place, and it will be a miracle if you get the child to tolerate you.

KATE. Two weeks? Miss Annie, can you accomplish anything in two weeks?

KELLER. Anything or not, two weeks, then the child comes back to us. Make up your mind, Miss Sullivan, yes or no?

ANNIE. Two weeks. For only one miracle?

[*She nods at him, nervously.*]

I'll get her to tolerate me.

[KELLER *marches out, and slams the door.* KATE *on her feet regards* ANNIE, *who is facing the door.*]

KATE. [*Then.*] You can't think as little of love as you said.

[ANNIE *glances questioning.*]

Or you wouldn't stay.

ANNIE. [*A pause.*] I didn't come here for love. I came for money!

[KATE *shakes her head to this, with a smile; after a moment she extends her open hand.* ANNIE *looks at it, but when she puts hers out it is not to shake hands, it is to set her fist in* KATE*'s palm.*]

KATE. [*Puzzled.*] Hm?

ANNIE. A. It's the first of many. Twenty-six!

[KATE *squeezes her fist, squeezes it hard, and hastens out after* KELLER. ANNIE *stands as the door closes behind her, her manner so apprehensive*[49] *that finally she slaps her brow, holds it, sighs, and, with her eyes closed, crosses herself for luck.*

The lights dim into a cool silhouette scene around her, the lamp paling out, and now, in formal entrances, persons appear around ANNIE *with furniture for the room:* PERCY *crosses the stage with a rocking chair and waits;* MARTHA *from another direction bears in a stool,* VINEY *bears in a small table, and the other Negro servant rolls in a bed partway from left; and* ANNIE, *opening her eyes to put her glasses back on, sees them. She turns around in the room once, and goes into action, pointing out locations for each article; the servants place them and leave, and* ANNIE *then darts around, interchanging them. In the midst of this—while* PERCY *and* MARTHA *reappear with a tray of food and a chair, respectively—*JAMES *comes down from the house with* ANNIE*'s suitcase, and stands viewing the room and her quizzically;* ANNIE *halts abruptly under his eyes, embarrassed, then seizes the suitcase from his hand, explaining herself brightly.*]

ANNIE. I always wanted to live in a doll's house!

[*She sets the suitcase out of the way, and continues;* VINEY *at left appears to position a rod with drapes for a doorway, and the other servant at center pushes in a wheelbarrow loaded with a couple of boxes of* HELEN*'s toys and clothes.* ANNIE *helps lift them into the room, and the servant pushes the wheelbarrow off. In none of this is any heed taken of the imaginary walls of the garden house, the furniture is moved in from every side and itself defines the walls.*

ANNIE *now drags the box of toys into center, props up the doll conspicuously on top; with the people melted away, except for* JAMES, *all*

49. To be *apprehensive* is to be anxious or fearful of what may happen.

is again still. The lights turn again without pause, rising warmer.]

JAMES. You don't let go of things easily, do you? How will you—win her hand now, in this place?

ANNIE. [*Curtly.*] Do I know? I lost my temper, and here we are!

JAMES. [*Lightly.*] No touching, no teaching. Of course, you *are* bigger—

ANNIE. I'm not counting on force, I'm counting on her. That little imp is dying to know.

JAMES. Know what?

ANNIE. Anything. Any and every crumb in God's creation. I'll have to use that appetite too.

[*She gives the room a final survey, straightens the bed, arranges the curtains.*]

JAMES. [*A pause.*] Maybe she'll teach you.

ANNIE. Of course.

JAMES. That she isn't. That there's such a thing as—dullness of heart. Acceptance. And letting go. Sooner or later we all give up, don't we?

ANNIE. Maybe you all do. It's my idea of the original sin.

JAMES. What is?

ANNIE. [*Witheringly.*] Giving up.

JAMES. [*Nettled.*] You won't open her. Why can't you let her be? Have some—pity on her, for being what she is—

ANNIE. If I'd ever once thought like that, I'd be dead!

JAMES. [*Pleasantly.*] You will be. Why trouble?

[*ANNIE turns to glare at him; he is mocking.*]

Or will you teach me?

[*And with a bow, he drifts off.*

Now in the distance there comes the clopping of hoofs, drawing near, and nearer, up to the door; and they halt. ANNIE wheels to face the door. When it opens this time, the KELLERS—KATE in traveling bonnet, KELLER also hatted—are standing there with HELEN between them; she is in a cloak. KATE gently cues her into the room. HELEN comes in groping, baffled, but interested in the new surroundings; ANNIE evades her exploring hand, her gaze not leaving the child.]

ANNIE. Does she know where she is?

KATE. [*Shakes her head.*] We rode her out in the country for two hours.

KELLER. For all she knows, she could be in another town—

[*HELEN stumbles over the box on the floor and in it discovers her doll and other battered toys, is pleased, sits to them, then becomes puzzled and suddenly very wary. She scrambles up and back to her mother's thighs, but ANNIE steps in, and it is hers that HELEN embraces. HELEN recoils, gropes, and touches her cheek instantly.*]

KATE. That's her sign for me.

ANNIE. I know.

[*HELEN waits, then recommences her groping, more urgently. KATE stands indecisive, and takes an abrupt step toward her, but ANNIE's hand is a barrier.*]

In two weeks.

KATE. Miss Annie, I— Please be good to her. These two weeks, try to be very good to her—

ANNIE. I will.

[*KATE, turning then, hurries out. The KELLERS cross back of the main house.*

ANNIE closes the door. HELEN starts at the door jar, and rushes it. ANNIE holds her off. HELEN kicks her, breaks free, and careens around the room like an imprisoned bird, colliding with furniture, groping wildly, repeatedly touching her cheek in a growing panic.

When she has covered the room, she commences her weird screaming. ANNIE *moves to comfort her, but her touch sends* HELEN *into a paroxysm*[50] *of rage: she tears away, falls over her box of toys, flings its contents in handfuls in* ANNIE*'s direction, flings the box too, reels to her feet, rips curtains from the window, bangs and kicks at the door, sweeps objects off the mantelpiece and shelf, a little tornado incarnate,*[51] *all destruction, until she comes upon her doll and, in the act of hurling it, freezes. Then she clutches it to herself, and in exhaustion sinks sobbing to the floor.* ANNIE *stands contemplating her, in some awe.*]

Two weeks.

[*She shakes her head, not without a touch of disgusted bewilderment.*]

What did I get into now?

[*The lights have been dimming throughout, and the garden house is lit only by moonlight now, with* ANNIE *lost in the patches of dark.*

KATE, *now hatless and coatless, enters the family room by the rear door, carrying a lamp.* KELLER, *also hatless, wanders simultaneously around the back of the main house to where* JAMES *has been waiting, in the rising moonlight, on the porch.*]

KELLER. I can't understand it. I had every intention of dismissing that girl, not setting her up like an empress.

JAMES. Yes, what's her secret, sir?

KELLER. Secret?

JAMES. [*Pleasantly.*] That enables her to get anything she wants out of you? When I can't.

[JAMES *turns to go into the house, but* KELLER *grasps his wrist, twisting him half to his knees.* KATE *comes from the porch.*]

KELLER. [*Angrily.*] She does *not* get anything she—

JAMES. [*In pain.*] Don't—don't—

KATE. Captain.

KELLER. He's afraid.

[*He throws* JAMES *away from him, with contempt.*]

What *does* he want out of me?

JAMES. [*An outcry.*] My God, don't you know?

[*He gazes from* KELLER *to* KATE.]

Everything you forgot, when you forgot my mother.

KELLER. What!

[JAMES *wheels into the house.* KELLER *takes a stride to the porch, to roar after him.*]

One thing that girl's secret is not, she doesn't fire one shot and disappear!

[KATE *stands rigid, and* KELLER *comes back to her.*]

Katie. Don't mind what he—

KATE. Captain, *I* am proud of you.

KELLER. For what?

KATE. For letting this girl have what she needs.

KELLER. Why can't my son be? He can't bear me, you'd think I treat him as hard as this girl does Helen—

[*He breaks off, as it dawns in him.*]

KATE. [*Gently.*] Perhaps you do.

KELLER. But he has to learn some respect!

KATE. [*A pause, wryly.*] *Do* you like the child?

[*She turns again to the porch, but pauses, reluctant.*]

How empty the house is, tonight.

[*After a moment she continues on it.* KELLER *stands moveless, as the moonlight dies on him.*

50. A *paroxysm* (par′ ək siz′ əm) is a sudden outburst or fit.
51. *Incarnate* (in kär′ nit) means "in human form."

The distant belfry chimes toll, two o'clock, and with them, a moment later, comes the boy's voice on the wind, in a whisper:]

BOY'S VOICE. Annie. Annie.

[In her patch of dark ANNIE, *now in her nightgown, hurls a cup into a corner as though it were her grief, getting rid of its taste through her teeth.]*

ANNIE. No! No pity, I won't have it.

[She comes to HELEN, *prone on the floor.]*

On either of us.

[She goes to her knees, but when she touches HELEN*'s hand the child starts up awake, recoils, and scrambles away from her under the bed.* ANNIE *stares after her. She strikes her palm on the floor, with passion.]*

I *will* touch you!

[She gets to her feet, and paces in a kind of anger around the bed, her hand in her hair, and confronting HELEN *at each turn.]*

How, how? How do I—

*[*ANNIE *stops. Then she calls out urgently, loudly.]*

Percy! Percy!

[She moves swiftly to the drapes, at left.]

Percy, wake up!

*[*PERCY*'s voice comes in a thick sleepy mumble, unintelligible.]*

Get out of bed and come in here, I need you.

*[*ANNIE *darts away, finds and strikes a match, and touches it to the hanging lamp; the lights come up dimly in the room, and* PERCY *stands bare to the waist in torn overalls between the drapes, with eyes closed, swaying.* ANNIE *goes to him, pats his cheeks vigorously.]*

Percy. You awake?

PERCY. No'm.

ANNIE. How would you like to play a nice game?

PERCY. Whah?

ANNIE. With Helen. She's under the bed. Touch her hand.

[She kneels PERCY *down at the bed, thrusting his hand under it to contact* HELEN*'s;* HELEN *emits an animal sound and crawls to the opposite side, but commences sniffing.* ANNIE *rounds the bed with* PERCY *and thrusts his hand again at* HELEN*; this time* HELEN *clutches it, sniffs in recognition, and comes scrambling out after* PERCY*, to hug him with delight.* PERCY *alarmed struggles, and* HELEN*'s fingers go to his mouth.]*

PERCY. Lemme go. Lemme go—

*[*HELEN *fingers her own lips, as before, moving them in dumb imitation.]*

She tryin' talk. She gonna hit me—

ANNIE. *[Grimly.]* She *can* talk. If she only knew, I'll show you how. She makes letters.

[She opens PERCY*'s other hand, and spells into it:]*

This one is C. C.

[She hits his palm with it a couple of times, her eyes upon HELEN *across him;* HELEN *gropes to feel what* PERCY*'s hand is doing, and when she encounters* ANNIE*'s she falls back from them.]*

She's mad at me now, though, she won't play. But she knows lots of letters. Here's another, A. C, a. C, a.

[But she is watching HELEN, *who comes groping, consumed with curiosity;* ANNIE *makes the letters in* PERCY*'s hand, and* HELEN *pokes to question what they are up to. Then* HELEN *snatches* PERCY*'s other hand, and quickly spells four letters into it.* ANNIE *follows them aloud.]*

C, a, k, e! She spells cake, she gets cake.

[She is swiftly over to the tray of food, to fetch cake and a jug of milk.]

She doesn't know yet it means this. Isn't it funny she knows how to spell it and doesn't *know* she knows?

[*She breaks the cake in two pieces, and extends one to each;* HELEN *rolls away from her offer.*]

Well, if she won't play it with me, I'll play it with you. Would you like to learn one she doesn't know?

PERCY. No'm.

[*But* ANNIE *seizes his wrist, and spells to him.*]

ANNIE. M, i, l, k. M is this. I, that's an easy one, just the little finger. L is this—

[*And* HELEN *comes back with her hand, to feel the new word.* ANNIE *brushes her away, and continues spelling aloud to* PERCY. HELEN*'s hand comes back again, and tries to get in;* ANNIE *brushes it away again.* HELEN*'s hand insists, and* ANNIE *puts it away rudely.*]

No, why should I talk to you? I'm teaching Percy a new word. L. K is this—

[HELEN now yanks their hands apart; she butts PERCY away, and thrusts her palm out insistently. ANNIE's eyes are bright, with glee.]

Ho, you're *jealous*, are you!

[HELEN's hand waits, intractably[52] *waits.]*

All *right*.

[ANNIE spells into it, milk; and HELEN after a moment spells it back to ANNIE. ANNIE takes her hand, with her whole face shining. She gives a great sigh.]

Good! So I'm finally back to where I can touch you, hm? Touch and go! No love lost, but here we go.

[She puts the jug of milk into HELEN's hand and squeezes PERCY's shoulder.]

You can go to bed now, you've earned your sleep. Thank you.

[PERCY stumbling up weaves his way out through the drapes. HELEN finishes drinking, and holds the jug out, for ANNIE; when ANNIE takes it, HELEN crawls onto the bed, and makes for sleep. ANNIE stands, looks down at her.]

Now all I have to teach you is—one word. Everything.

[She sets the jug down. On the floor now ANNIE spies the doll, stoops to pick it up, and with it dangling in her hand, turns off the lamp. A shaft of moonlight is left on HELEN in the bed, and a second shaft on the rocking chair; and ANNIE, after putting off her smoked glasses, sits in the rocker with the doll. She is rather happy, and dangles the doll on her knee, and it makes its momma sound. ANNIE whispers to it in mock solicitude.]

Hush, little baby. Don't—say a word—

[She lays it against her shoulder, and begins rocking with it, patting its diminutive behind; she talks the lullaby to it, humorously at first.]

Momma's gonna buy you—a mockingbird:
If that—mockingbird don't sing—

[The rhythm of the rocking takes her into the tune, softly, and more tenderly.]

Momma's gonna buy you a diamond ring:
If that diamond ring turns to brass—

[A third shaft of moonlight outside now rises to pick out JAMES at the main house, with one foot on the porch step; he turns his body, as if hearing the song.]

Momma's gonna buy you a looking-glass:
If that looking-glass gets broke—

[In the family room a fourth shaft picks out KELLER seated at the table, in thought; and he, too, lifts his head, as if hearing.]

Momma's gonna buy you a billy goat:
If that billy goat won't pull—

[The fifth shaft is upstairs in ANNIE's room, and picks out KATE, pacing there; and she halts, turning her head, too, as if hearing.]

Momma's gonna buy you a cart and bull:
If that cart and bull turns over,
Momma's gonna buy you a dog named
Rover;
If that dog named Rover won't bark—

[With the shafts of moonlight on HELEN, and JAMES, and KELLER, and KATE, all moveless, and ANNIE rocking the doll, the curtain ends the act.]

52. Helen's hand waits *intractably,* or stubbornly.

Responding to Literature

Personal Response

In act 2, which characters do you sympathize with most, and why? Discuss your judgments with a partner.

Analyzing Act 2

Recall and Interpret

1. What is Annie's theory about how children learn language? Explain how this theory affects Annie's approach to teaching Helen.
2. According to Annie, what mistakes have the Kellers been making with Helen? Why does Captain Keller react to Annie the way he does?
3. What does the episode at the breakfast table reveal about Annie and about Helen? Use details from the play to support your answers.
4. Why does Annie ask for Percy's help at the end of the act? How does this episode show that Annie understands Helen's personality?

Evaluate and Connect

5. Annie writes, "obedience is the gateway through which knowledge enters the mind of the child." In your opinion, is she right? Why might obedience be so important to Annie?
6. What purpose do **flashbacks** serve in this play? Consider how flashbacks contribute to your understanding of Annie's character.
7. Do you think Annie makes the right decision in telling the Kellers about her past? How could the decision be seen as a desperate measure? How could it be seen as a way to draw closer to the Kellers? Explain.
8. In your opinion, why are references to the Civil War included in act 2? What do they add to the play?

Literary ELEMENTS

Protagonist and Antagonist

The **protagonist** is the central character in a play with whom audience members often sympathize or identify. The **antagonist** is a character or force in society or nature that opposes the protagonist. The conflict between the characters or forces is what drives the plot.

1. Who is the protagonist in this play?
2. Identify two people who might be considered antagonists in the play. Explain.
3. Why might society in the 1880s be considered an antagonist in this play? Consider women's roles as well as the use of asylums for the poor and the mentally and physically challenged.

- See **Literary Terms Handbook,** pp. R10 and R1.

Extending Your Response

Literature Groups

Family Fare Helen may be learning to communicate—but is the rest of her family? With your group, analyze the Kellers' typical ways of interacting. Which characters conflict when they speak to one another, and why? Whose efforts at communication do you admire or sympathize with? Do you predict that the members of this family will learn to communicate so that everyone will understand? Support your opinions with details from the play.

Creative Writing

If It Were You Imagine that you are Helen, alone with Annie at the breakfast table. What do you experience through your senses of touch, taste, and smell? Write down your stream of sensations, thoughts, and feelings during this scene. You may want to experiment with using single words, sentence fragments, and unconventional punctuation to express yourself.

Save your work for your portfolio.

Skill Minilesson

VOCABULARY • The Prefix *com-*

The prefix *com-* means "with" or "together." For example, when Annie tells Kate that she and Jimmie had only one place to play—in the deadhouse—Kate feels *compassion.* One meaning of the base word *passion* is "suffering," so *compassion* means "suffering with." But the prefix *com-* blends with whatever it touches. While its meaning stays the same, its last letter changes if the prefix joins a root or base word beginning with certain letters of the alphabet. The variations of *com-* are *co-, col-, con-,* and *cor-.*

PRACTICE Match each word listed on the left with its definition on the right.

1. coexist	a. to gather together or put together
2. confront	b. to work with another person
3. compile	c. to come face to face with
4. collaborate	d. to live together or alongside
5. condescend	e. to go down to the same level (as something or someone)

Before You Read

The Miracle Worker, Act 3

Building Background

Did You Know?

- The manual alphabet that Annie Sullivan teaches Helen Keller is a sign-language system that she had learned at the Perkins Institution for the Blind so that she could talk to Laura Bridgman. The first deaf, blind, and mute person to be successfully educated in the United States, Bridgman assisted teachers at the Perkins Institution.
- Dr. Samuel Gridley Howe, the founder of Perkins, was Laura Bridgman's teacher in the 1830s. He pasted labels with raised lettering onto a variety of objects and taught Bridgman to feel the letters with her fingers until she sensed that the labels were different. Then he taught her to match each label with the object it named. One day, Bridgman realized that she could use signs of her own to express thoughts. Howe said that at that moment, Bridgman's whole face "lighted up" with excitement.

Vocabulary Preview

wistful (wist′ fəl) *adj.* sadly longing; yearning; p. 764

ruefully (ro͞o′ fəl lē) *adv.* regretfully; p. 770

bountiful (boun′ ti fəl) *adj.* overflowing with generosity; p. 773

aversion (ə vur′ zhən) *n.* definite dislike combined with a desire to avoid whatever is disliked; p. 774

genially (jēn′ yəl lē) *adv.* in a friendly way; pleasantly and cheerfully; p. 774

trepidation (trep′ ə dā′ shən) *n.* a feeling of nervous expectation; anxiety; p. 775

mediate (mē′ dē āt′) *v.* to settle a dispute between persons or sides by acting as a go-between; p. 775

transfixed (trans fikst′) *adj.* made motionless, as from awe or fear; p. 775

ACT 3

[The stage is totally dark, until we see ANNIE *and* HELEN *silhouetted on the bed in the garden house.* ANNIE*'s voice is audible, very patient, and worn; it has been saying this for a long time.]*

ANNIE. Water, Helen. This is water. W, a, t, e, r. It has a *name.*

[A silence. Then:]

Egg, e, g, g. It has a *name,* the name stands for the thing. Oh, it's so simple, simple as birth, to explain.

[The lights have commenced to rise, not on the garden house but on the homestead. Then:]

Helen, Helen, the chick *has* to come out of its shell, sometime. You come out, too.

[In the bedroom upstairs, we see VINEY *unhurriedly washing the window, dusting, turning the mattress, readying the room for use again; then in the family room a diminished group at one end of the table—*KATE, KELLER, JAMES*—finishing up a quiet breakfast; then outside, down right, the other Negro servant on his knees, assisted by* MARTHA, *working with a trowel around a new trellis and wheelbarrow. The scene is one of everyday calm, and all are oblivious to* ANNIE*'s voice.]*

There's only one way out, for you, and it's language. To learn that your fingers can talk. And say anything, anything you can name. This is mug. Mug, m, u, g. Helen, it has a *name.* It—has—a—*name*—

*[*KATE *rises from the table.]*

KELLER. *[Gently.]* You haven't eaten, Katie.

KATE. *[Smiles, shakes her head.]* I haven't the appetite. I'm too—restless, I can't sit to it.

KELLER. You should eat, my dear. It will be a long day, waiting.

JAMES. *[Lightly.]* But it's been a short two weeks. I never thought life could be so—noiseless, went much too quickly for me.

*[*KATE *and* KELLER *gaze at him, in silence.* JAMES *becomes uncomfortable.]*

ANNIE. C, a, r, d. Card. C, a—

JAMES. Well, the house has been practically normal, hasn't it?

KELLER. *[Harshly.]* Jimmie.

JAMES. Is it wrong to enjoy a quiet breakfast, after five years? And you two even seem to enjoy each other—

KELLER. It could be even more noiseless, Jimmie, without your tongue running every minute. Haven't you enough feeling to imagine what Katie has been undergoing, ever since—

*[*KATE *stops him, with her hand on his arm.]*

KATE. Captain.

[To JAMES.*]*

It's true. The two weeks have been normal, quiet, all you say. But not short. Interminable.

[She rises, and wanders out; she pauses on the porch steps, gazing toward the garden house.]

ANNIE. *[Fading.]* W, a, t, e, r. But it means *this.* W, a, t, e, r. *This.* W, a, t—

JAMES. I only meant that Miss Sullivan is a boon. Of contention,[53] though, it seems.

KELLER. *[Heavily.]* If and when you're a parent, Jimmie, you will understand what separation means. A mother loses a—protector.

JAMES. *[Baffled.]* Hm?

---

53. A *boon* is a gift or blessing, and *contention,* here, is an argument or quarrel. James is making a pun on the expression "bone of contention," which refers to the subject of an argument. The pun implies that Annie has helped the Kellers but is also a source of family conflict.

KELLER. You'll learn, we don't just keep our children safe. They keep us safe.

[*He rises, with his empty coffee cup and saucer.*]

There are of course all kinds of separation, Katie has lived with one kind for five years. And another is disappointment. In a child.

[*He goes with the cup out the rear door.* JAMES *sits for a long moment of stillness. In the garden house the lights commence to come up;* ANNIE, *haggard at the table, is writing a letter, her face again almost in contact with the stationery;* HELEN, *apart on the stool, and for the first time as clean and neat as a button, is quietly crocheting an endless chain of wool, which snakes all around the room.*]

ANNIE. "I, feel, every, day, more, and, more, in—"

[*She pauses, and turns the pages of a dictionary open before her; her finger descends the words to a full stop. She elevates her eyebrows, then copies the word.*]

"—adequate."

[*In the main house* JAMES *pushes up, and goes to the front doorway, after* KATE.]

JAMES. Kate?

[KATE *turns her glance.* JAMES *is rather weary.*]

I'm sorry. Open my mouth, like that fairy tale, frogs jump out.

KATE. No. It has been better. For everyone.

[*She starts away, up center.*]

ANNIE. [*Writing.*] "If, only, there, were, someone, to, help, me, I, need, a, teacher, as, much, as, Helen—"

JAMES. Kate.

[KATE *halts, waits.*]

What does he want from me?

KATE. That's not the question. Stand up to the world, Jimmie, that comes first.

JAMES. [*A pause, wryly.*] But the world is him.

KATE. Yes. And no one can do it for you.

JAMES. Kate.

[*His voice is humble.*]

At least we— Could you—be my friend?

KATE. I am.

[KATE *turns to wander, up back of the garden house.* ANNIE*'s murmur comes at once; the lights begin to die on the main house.*]

ANNIE. "—my, mind, is, undisciplined, full, of, skips, and, jumps, and—"

[*She halts, rereads, frowns.*]

Hm.

[ANNIE *puts her nose again in the dictionary, flips back to an earlier page, and fingers down the words;* KATE *presently comes down toward the bay window with a trayful of food.*]

Disinter—disinterested—disjoin—dis—

[*She backtracks, indignant.*]

Disinterested, disjoin— Where's disipline?

[*She goes a page or two back, searching with her finger, muttering.*]

What a dictionary, have to know how to spell it before you can look up how to spell it, disciple, *discipline!* Diskipline.

[*She corrects the word in her letter.*]

Undisciplined.

[*But her eyes are bothering her, she closes them in exhaustion and gently fingers the eyelids.* KATE *watches her through the window.*]

KATE. What are you doing to your eyes?

[ANNIE *glances around; she puts her smoked glasses on, and gets up to come over, assuming a cheerful energy.*]

ANNIE. It's worse on my vanity! I'm learning to spell. It's like a surprise party, the most unexpected characters turn up.

KATE. You're not to overwork your eyes, Miss Annie.

ANNIE. Well.

[She takes the tray, sets it on her chair, and carries chair and tray to HELEN.*]*

Whatever I spell to Helen I'd better spell right.

KATE. *[Almost wistful.]* How—serene she is.

ANNIE. She learned this stitch yesterday. Now I can't get her to stop!

[She disentangles one foot from the wool chain, and sets the chair before HELEN. HELEN *at its contact with her knee feels the plate, promptly sets her crocheting down, and tucks the napkin in at her neck, but* ANNIE *withholds the spoon; when* HELEN *finds it missing, she folds her hands in her lap, and quietly waits.* ANNIE *twinkles at* KATE *with mock devoutness.*[54]*]*

Such a little lady, she'd sooner starve than eat with her fingers.

[She gives HELEN *the spoon, and* HELEN *begins to eat, neatly.]*

KATE. You've taught her so much, these two weeks. I would never have—

ANNIE. Not enough.

[She is suddenly gloomy, shakes her head.]

Obedience isn't enough. Well, she learned two nouns this morning, key and water, brings her up to eighteen nouns and three verbs.

KATE. *[Hesitant.]* But—not—

ANNIE. No. Not that they mean things. It's still a finger-game, no meaning.

[She turns to KATE, *abruptly.]*

Mrs. Keller—

[But she defers it; she comes back, to sit in the bay and lift her hand.]

Shall we play our finger-game?

KATE. How will she learn it?

ANNIE. It will come.

[She spells a word; KATE *does not respond.]*

KATE. How?

ANNIE. *[A pause.]* How does a bird learn to fly?

[She spells again.]

We're born to use words, like wings, it has to come.

KATE. How?

ANNIE. *[Another pause, wearily.]* All right. I don't know how.

[She pushes up her glasses, to rub her eyes.]

I've done everything I could think of. Whatever she's learned here—keeping herself clean, knitting, stringing beads, meals, setting-up exercises each morning, we climb trees, hunt eggs, yesterday a chick was born in her hands—all of it I spell, everything we do, we never stop spelling. I go to bed with—writer's cramp from talking so much!

KATE. I worry about you, Miss Annie. You must rest.

ANNIE. Now? She spells back in her *sleep,* her fingers make letters when she doesn't know! In her bones those five fingers know, that hand aches to—speak out, and something in her mind is asleep, how do I—nudge that awake? That's the one question.

KATE. With no answer.

ANNIE. *[Long pause.]* Except keep at it. Like this.

54. Here, *mock devoutness* is feigned, or pretended, sincerity.

Vocabulary
wistful (wist′ fəl) *adj.* sadly longing; yearning

[*She again begins spelling—I, need—and KATE's brows gather, following the words.*]

KATE. More—time?

[*She glances at ANNIE, who looks her in the eyes, silent.*]

Here?

ANNIE. Spell it.

[*KATE spells a word—no—shaking her head; ANNIE spells two words—why, not—back, with an impatient question in her eyes; and KATE moves her head in pain to answer it.*]

KATE. Because I can't—

ANNIE. Spell it! If she ever learns, you'll have a lot to tell each other, start now.

[*KATE painstakingly spells in air. In the midst of this the rear door opens, and KELLER enters with the setter BELLE in tow.*]

KELLER. Miss Sullivan? On my way to the office, I brought Helen a playmate—

ANNIE. Outside please, Captain Keller.

KELLER. My dear child, the two weeks are up today, surely you don't object to—

ANNIE. [*Rising.*] They're not up till six o'clock.

KELLER. [*Indulgent.*] Oh, now. What difference can a fraction of one day—

ANNIE. An agreement is an agreement. Now you've been very good, I'm sure you can keep it up for a few more hours.

[*She escorts KELLER by the arm over the threshold; he obeys, leaving BELLE.*]

KELLER. Miss Sullivan, you are a tyrant.

ANNIE. Likewise, I'm sure. You can stand there, and close the door if she comes.

KATE. I don't think you know how eager we are to have her back in our arms—

ANNIE. I do know, it's my main worry.

KELLER. It's like expecting a new child in the house. Well, she *is*, so—composed, so—

[*Gently.*]

Attractive. You've done wonders for her, Miss Sullivan.

ANNIE. [*Not a question.*] Have I.

KELLER. If there's anything you want from us in repayment tell us, it will be a privilege to—

ANNIE. I just told Mrs. Keller. I want more time.

KATE. Miss Annie—

ANNIE. Another week.

[*HELEN lifts her head, and begins to sniff.*]

KELLER. We miss the child. *I* miss her, I'm glad to say, that's a different debt I owe you—

ANNIE. Pay it to Helen. Give *her* another week.

KATE. [*Gently.*] Doesn't she miss us?

KELLER. Of course she does. What a wrench[55] this unexplainable—exile must be to her, can you say it's not?

ANNIE. No. But I—

[*HELEN is off the stool, to grope about the room; when she encounters BELLE, she throws her arms around the dog's neck in delight.*]

KATE. Doesn't she need affection too, Miss Annie?

ANNIE. [*Wavering.*] She—never shows me she needs it, she won't have any—caressing or—

KATE. But you're not her mother.

KELLER. And what would another week accomplish? We are more than satisfied, you've done more than we ever thought possible, taught her constructive—

ANNIE. I can't promise anything. All I can—

55. Keller uses *wrench* to mean a feeling of anguish, distress, or pain.

KELLER. [*No break.*] —things to do, to behave like—even look like—a human child, so manageable, contented, cleaner, more—

ANNIE. [*Withering.*] Cleaner.

KELLER. Well. We say cleanliness is next to godliness, Miss—

ANNIE. Cleanliness is next to nothing, she has to learn that everything has its name! That words can be her *eyes*, to everything in the world outside her, and inside too, what is she without words? With them she can think, have ideas, be reached, there's not a thought or fact in the world that can't be hers. You publish a newspaper, Captain Keller, do I have to tell you what words are? And she has them already—

KELLER. Miss Sullivan.

ANNIE. —eighteen nouns and three verbs, they're in her fingers now, I need only time to push *one* of them into her mind! One, and everything under the sun will follow. Don't you see what she's learned here is only clearing the way for that? I can't risk her unlearning it, give me more time alone with her, another week to—

KELLER. Look.

[*He points, and* ANNIE *turns.* HELEN *is playing with* BELLE*'s claws; she makes letters with her fingers, shows them to* BELLE*, waits with her palm, then manipulates the dog's claws.*]

What is she spelling?

[*A silence.*]

KATE. Water?

[ANNIE *nods.*]

KELLER. Teaching a dog to spell.

[*A pause.*]

The dog doesn't know what she means, any more than she knows what you mean, Miss Sullivan. I think you ask too much, of her and yourself. God may not have meant Helen to have the—eyes you speak of.

ANNIE. [*Toneless.*] I mean her to.

KELLER. [*Curiously.*] What is it to you?

[ANNIE*'s head comes slowly up.*]

You make us see how we indulge her for our sake. Is the opposite true, for you?

ANNIE. [*Then.*] Half a week?

KELLER. An agreement *is* an agreement.

ANNIE. Mrs. Keller?

KATE. [*Simply.*] I want her back.

[*A wait;* ANNIE *then lets her hands drop in surrender, and nods.*]

KELLER. I'll send Viney over to help you pack.

ANNIE. Not until six o'clock. I have her till six o'clock.

KELLER. [*Consenting.*] Six o'clock. Come, Katie.

[KATE *leaving the window joins him around back, while* KELLER *closes the door; they are shut out.*

Only the garden house is daylit now, and the light on it is narrowing down. ANNIE *stands watching* HELEN *work* BELLE*'s claws. Then she settles beside them on her knees, and stops* HELEN*'s hand.*]

ANNIE. [*Gently.*] No.

[*She shakes her head, with* HELEN*'s hand to her face, then spells.*]

Dog. D, o, g. Dog.

[*She touches* HELEN*'s hand to* BELLE. HELEN *dutifully pats the dog's head, and resumes spelling to its paw.*]

Not water.

[ANNIE *rolls to her feet, brings a tumbler of water back from the tray, and kneels with it, to seize* HELEN*'s hand and spell.*]

Here. Water. *Water.*

[*She thrusts* HELEN*'s hand into the tumbler.* HELEN *lifts her hand out dripping, wipes it daintily on* BELLE*'s hide, and taking the tumbler from* ANNIE, *endeavors to thrust* BELLE*'s paw into it.* ANNIE *sits watching, wearily.*]

I don't know how to tell you. Not a soul in the world knows how to tell you. Helen, Helen.

[*She bends in compassion to touch her lips to* HELEN*'s temple, and instantly* HELEN *pauses, her hands off the dog, her head slightly averted. The lights are still narrowing, and* BELLE *slinks off. After a moment* ANNIE *sits back.*]

Yes, what's it to me? They're satisfied. Give them back their child and dog, both housebroken, everyone's satisfied. But me, and you.

[HELEN*'s hand comes out into the light, groping.*]

Reach. *Reach!*

[ANNIE *extending her own hand grips* HELEN*'s; the two hands are clasped, tense in the light, the rest of the room changing in shadow.*]

I wanted to teach you—oh, everything the earth is full of, Helen, everything on it that's ours for a wink and it's gone, and what we are on it, the—light we bring to it and leave behind in—words, why, you can see five thousand years back in a light of words, everything we feel, think, know—and share, in words, so not a soul is in darkness, or done with, even in the grave. And I know, I *know,* one word and I can—put the world in your hand—and whatever it is to me, I won't take less! How, how, how do I tell you that *this*—

[*She spells.*]

—means a *word,* and the word means this *thing,* wool?

[*She thrusts the wool at* HELEN*'s hand;* HELEN *sits, puzzled.* ANNIE *puts the crocheting aside.*]

Or this—s, t, o, o, l—means this *thing,* stool?

[*She claps* HELEN*'s palm to the stool.* HELEN *waits, uncomprehending.* ANNIE *snatches up her napkin, spells:*]

Napkin!

[*She forces it on* HELEN*'s hand, waits, discards it, lifts a fold of the child's dress, spells:*]

Dress!

[*She lets it drop, spells:*]

F, a, c, e, face!

[*She draws* HELEN*'s hand to her cheek, and pressing it there, staring into the child's responseless eyes, hears the distant belfry begin to toll, slowly: one, two, three, four, five, six.*

On the third stroke the lights stealing in around the garden house show us figures waiting: VINEY, *the other servant,* MARTHA, PERCY *at the drapes, and* JAMES *on the dim porch.* ANNIE *and* HELEN *remain, frozen. The chimes die away. Silently* PERCY *moves the drape-rod back out of sight;* VINEY *steps into the room—not using the door—and unmakes the bed; the other servant brings the wheelbarrow over, leaves it handy, rolls the bed off;* VINEY *puts the bed linens on top of a waiting boxful of* HELEN*'s toys, and loads the box on the wheelbarrow;* MARTHA *and* PERCY *take out the chairs, with the trayful, then the table; and* JAMES, *coming down and into the room, lifts* ANNIE*'s suitcase from its corner.* VINEY *and the other servant load the remaining odds and ends on the wheelbarrow, and the servant wheels it off.* VINEY *and the children departing leave only* JAMES *in the room with* ANNIE *and* HELEN. JAMES *studies the two of them, without mockery, and then, quietly going to the door and opening it, bears the suitcase out, and housewards. He leaves the door open.*

KATE *steps into the doorway, and stands.* ANNIE *lifting her gaze from* HELEN *sees her; she takes* HELEN*'s hand from her cheek, and* *returns it to the child's own, stroking it there twice, in her mother-sign, before spelling slowly into it:*]

M, o, t, h, e, r. Mother.

[*HELEN with her hand free strokes her cheek, suddenly forlorn. ANNIE takes her hand again.*]

M, o, t, h—

[*But KATE is trembling with such impatience that her voice breaks from her, harsh.*]

KATE. Let her *come!*

[*ANNIE lifts HELEN to her feet, with a turn, and gives her a little push. Now HELEN begins groping, sensing something, trembling herself; and KATE falling one step in onto her knees clasps her, kissing her. HELEN clutches her, tight as she can. KATE is inarticulate, choked, repeating HELEN's name again and again. She wheels with her in her arms, to stumble away out the doorway; ANNIE stands unmoving, while KATE in a blind walk carries HELEN like a baby behind the main house, out of view.*

ANNIE is now alone on the stage. She turns, gazing around at the stripped room, bidding it silently farewell, impassively, like a defeated general on the deserted battlefield. All that remains is a stand with a basin of water; and here ANNIE takes up an eyecup, bathes each of her eyes, empties the eyecup, drops it in her purse, and tiredly locates her smoked glasses on the floor. The lights alter subtly; in the act of putting on her glasses ANNIE hears something that stops her, with head lifted. We hear it too, the voices out of the past, including her own now, in a whisper:]

BOY'S VOICE. You said we'd be together, forever— You promised, forever and—*Annie!*

ANAGNOS'S VOICE. But that battle is dead and done with, why not let it stay buried?

ANNIE'S VOICE. [*Whispering.*] I think God must owe me a resurrection.

ANAGNOS'S VOICE. What?

[*A pause, and ANNIE answers it herself, heavily.*]

ANNIE. And I owe God one.

BOY'S VOICE. Forever and ever—

[*ANNIE shakes her head.*]

—forever, and ever, and—

[*ANNIE covers her ears.*]

—forever, and ever, and ever—

[*It pursues ANNIE; she flees to snatch up her purse, wheels to the doorway, and KELLER is standing in it. The lights have lost their special color.*]

KELLER. Miss—Annie.

[*He has an envelope in his fingers.*]

I've been waiting to give you this.

ANNIE. [*After a breath.*] What?

KELLER. Your first month's salary.

[*He puts it in her hand.*]

With many more to come, I trust. It doesn't express what we feel, it doesn't pay our debt. For what you've done.

ANNIE. What have I done?

KELLER. Taken a wild thing, and given us back a child.

ANNIE. [*Presently.*] I taught her one thing, no. Don't do this, don't do that—

KELLER. It's more than all of us could, in all the years we—

ANNIE. I wanted to teach her what language is. I wanted to teach her yes.

KELLER. You will have time.

ANNIE. I don't know how. I know without it to do nothing but obey is—no gift, obedience without understanding is a—blindness, too. Is that all I've wished on her?

KELLER. [*Gently.*] No, no—

ANNIE. Maybe. I don't know what else to do. Simply go on, keep doing what I've done, and have—faith that inside she's—That inside it's waiting. Like water, underground. All I can do is keep on.

KELLER. It's enough. For us.

ANNIE. You can help, Captain Keller.

KELLER. How?

ANNIE. Even learning no has been at a cost. Of much trouble and pain. Don't undo it.

KELLER. Why should we wish to—

ANNIE. [*Abruptly.*] The world isn't an easy place for anyone, I don't want her just to obey but to let her have her way in everything is a lie, to *her*, I can't—

[*Her eyes fill, it takes her by surprise, and she laughs through it.*]

And I don't even love her, she's not my child! Well. You've got to stand between that lie and her.

KELLER. We'll try.

ANNIE. Because *I* will. As long as you let me stay, that's one promise I'll keep.

KELLER. Agreed. We've learned something too, I hope.

[*A pause.*]

Won't you come now, to supper?

ANNIE. Yes.

[*She wags the envelope, ruefully.*]

Why doesn't God pay His debts each month?

KELLER. I beg your pardon?

ANNIE. Nothing. I used to wonder how I could—

[*The lights are fading on them, simultaneously rising on the family room of the main house, where* VINEY *is polishing glassware at the table set for dinner.*]

—earn a living.

KELLER. Oh, you do.

ANNIE. I really do. Now the question is, can I survive it!

[KELLER *smiles, offers his arm.*]

KELLER. May I?

[ANNIE *takes it, and the lights lose them as he escorts her out.*

Now in the family room the rear door opens, and HELEN *steps in. She stands a moment, then sniffs in one deep grateful breath, and her hands go out vigorously to familiar things, over the door panels, and to the chairs around the table, and over the silverware on the table, until she meets* VINEY; *she pats her flank approvingly.*]

VINEY. Oh, we glad to have you back too, prob'ly.

[HELEN *hurries groping to the front door, opens and closes it, removes its key, opens and closes it again to be sure it is unlocked, gropes back to the rear door and repeats the procedure, removing its key and hugging herself gleefully.*

AUNT EV *is next in by the rear door, with a relish tray; she bends to kiss* HELEN*'s cheek.* HELEN *finds* KATE *behind her, and thrusts the keys at her.*]

KATE. What? Oh.

[*To* EV.]

Keys.

[*She pockets them, lets* HELEN *feel them.*]

Yes, *I'll* keep the keys. I think we've had enough of locked doors, too.

Vocabulary

ruefully (ro͞o′ fəl lē) *adv.* regretfully

[JAMES, having earlier put ANNIE's suitcase inside her door upstairs and taken himself out of view around the corner, now reappears and comes down the stairs as ANNIE and KELLER mount the porch steps. Following them into the family room, he pats ANNIE's hair in passing, rather to her surprise.]

JAMES. Evening, general.

[He takes his own chair opposite.

VINEY bears the empty water pitcher out to the porch. The remaining suggestion of garden house is gone now, and the water pump is unobstructed; VINEY pumps water into the pitcher.

KATE surveying the table breaks the silence.]

KATE. Will you say grace, Jimmie?

[They bow their heads, except for HELEN, who palms her empty plate and then reaches to be sure her mother is there. JAMES considers a moment, glances across at ANNIE, lowers his head again, and obliges.]

JAMES. *[Lightly.]* And Jacob was left alone, and wrestled with an angel until the breaking of the day; and the hollow of Jacob's thigh was out of joint, as he wrestled with him; and the angel said, Let me go, for the day breaketh. And Jacob said, I will not let thee go, except thou bless me. Amen.[56]

[ANNIE has lifted her eyes suspiciously at JAMES, who winks expressionlessly and inclines his head to HELEN.]

Oh, you angel.

[The others lift their faces; VINEY returns with the pitcher, setting it down near KATE, then goes out the rear door; and ANNIE puts a napkin around HELEN.]

AUNT EV. That's a very strange grace, James.

KELLER. Will you start the muffins, Ev?

56. *[And Jacob was . . . Amen]* In reciting these Bible verses, James slyly compares Jacob's struggle with the angel to Annie's struggle with Helen.

JAMES. It's from the Good Book, isn't it?

AUNT EV. *[Passing a plate.]* Well, of course it is. Didn't you know?

JAMES. Yes, I knew.

KELLER. *[Serving.]* Ham, Miss Annie?

ANNIE. Please.

AUNT EV. Then why ask?

JAMES. I meant it *is* from the Good Book, and therefore a fitting grace.

AUNT EV. Well. I don't know about *that.*

KATE. *[With the pitcher.]* Miss Annie?

ANNIE. Thank you.

AUNT EV. There's an awful *lot* of things in the Good Book that I wouldn't care to hear just before eating.

[When ANNIE reaches for the pitcher, HELEN removes her napkin and drops it to the floor. ANNIE is filling HELEN's glass when she notices it; she considers HELEN's bland expression a moment, then bends, retrieves it, and tucks it around HELEN's neck again.]

JAMES. Well, fitting in the sense that Jacob's thigh was out of joint, and so is this piggie's.

AUNT EV. I declare, James—

KATE. Pickles, Aunt Ev?

AUNT EV. Oh, I should say so, you know my opinion of your pickles—

KATE. This is the end of them, I'm afraid. I didn't put up nearly enough last summer, this year I intend to—

[She interrupts herself, seeing HELEN deliberately lift off her napkin and drop it again to the floor. She bends to retrieve it, but ANNIE stops her arm.]

KELLER. *[Not noticing.]* Reverend looked in at the office today to complain his hens have stopped laying. Poor fellow, *he* was out of joint, all he could—

[*He stops too, to frown down the table at* KATE, HELEN, *and* ANNIE *in turn, all suspended in mid-motion.*]

JAMES. [*Not noticing.*] I've always suspected those hens.

AUNT EV. Of what?

JAMES. I think they're Papist.[57] Has he tried—

[*He stops, too, following* KELLER's *eyes.* ANNIE *now stops to pick the napkin up.*]

AUNT EV. James, now you're pulling my—lower extremity, the first thing you know we'll be—

[*She stops, too, hearing herself in the silence.* ANNIE, *with everyone now watching, for the third time puts the napkin on* HELEN. HELEN *yanks it off, and throws it down.* ANNIE *rises, lifts* HELEN's *plate, and bears it away.* HELEN, *feeling it gone, slides down and commences to kick up under the table; the dishes jump.* ANNIE *contemplates this for a moment, then coming back takes* HELEN's *wrists firmly and swings her off the chair.* HELEN *struggling gets one hand free, and catches at her mother's skirt; when* KATE *takes her by the shoulders,* HELEN *hangs quiet.*]

KATE. Miss Annie.

ANNIE. No.

KATE. [*A pause.*] It's a very special day.

57. *Papist* (pā′ pist) refers to the pope or to Roman Catholicism. James suggests that Catholic hens won't lay eggs for a Protestant preacher.

ANNIE. [*Grimly.*] It will be, when I give in to that.

[*She tries to disengage* HELEN*'s hand;* KATE *lays hers on* ANNIE*'s.*]

KATE. Please. I've hardly had a chance to welcome her home—

ANNIE. Captain Keller.

KELLER. [*Embarrassed.*] Oh. Katie, we—had a little talk, Miss Annie feels that if we indulge Helen in these—

AUNT EV. But what's the child done?

ANNIE. She's learned not to throw things on the floor and kick. It took us the best part of two weeks and—

AUNT EV. But only a napkin, it's not as if it were breakable!

ANNIE. And everything she's learned *is?* Mrs. Keller, I don't think we should—play tug-of-war for her, either give her to me or you keep her from kicking.

KATE. What do you wish to do?

ANNIE. Let me take her from the table.

AUNT EV. Oh, let her stay, my goodness, she's only a child, she doesn't have to wear a napkin if she doesn't want to her first evening—

ANNIE. [*Level.*] And ask outsiders not to interfere.

AUNT EV. [*Astonished.*] Out—outsi— I'm the child's *aunt!*

KATE. [*Distressed.*] Will once hurt so much, Miss Annie? I've—made all Helen's favorite foods, tonight.

[*A pause.*]

KELLER. [*Gently.*] It's a homecoming party, Miss Annie.

[ANNIE *after a moment releases* HELEN. *But she cannot accept it, at her own chair she shakes her head and turns back, intent on* KATE.]

ANNIE. She's testing you. You realize?

JAMES. [*To* ANNIE.] She's testing you.

KELLER. Jimmie, be quiet.

[JAMES *sits, tense.*]

Now she's home, naturally she—

ANNIE. And wants to see what will happen. At your hands. I said it was my main worry, is this what you promised me not half an hour ago?

KELLER. [*Reasonably.*] But she's *not* kicking, now—

ANNIE. And not learning not to. Mrs. Keller, teaching her is bound to be painful, to everyone. I know it hurts to watch, but she'll live up to just what you demand of her, and no more.

JAMES. [*Palely.*] She's testing *you.*

KELLER. [*Testily.*] Jimmie.

JAMES. I have an opinion, I think I should—

KELLER. No one's interested in hearing your opinion.

ANNIE. *I'm* interested, of course she's testing me. Let me keep her to what she's learned and she'll go on learning from me. Take her out of my hands and it all comes apart.

[KATE *closes her eyes, digesting it;* ANNIE *sits again, with a brief comment for her.*]

Be bountiful, it's at her expense.

[*She turns to* JAMES, *flatly.*]

Please pass me more of—her favorite foods.

[*Then* KATE *lifts* HELEN*'s hand, and turning her toward* ANNIE, *surrenders her;* HELEN *makes for her own chair.*]

Vocabulary

bountiful (boun′ ti fəl) *adj.* overflowing with generosity

KATE. [*Low.*] Take her, Miss Annie.

ANNIE. [*Then.*] Thank you.

[*But the moment* ANNIE *rising reaches for her hand,* HELEN *begins to fight and kick, clutching to the tablecloth, and uttering laments.* ANNIE *again tries to loosen her hand, and* KELLER *rises.*]

KELLER. [*Tolerant.*] I'm afraid you're the difficulty, Miss Annie. Now I'll keep her to what she's learned, you're quite right there—

[*He takes* HELEN*'s hands from* ANNIE*, pats them;* HELEN *quiets down.*]

—but I don't see that we need send her from the table, after all, she's the guest of honor. Bring her plate back.

ANNIE. If she was a seeing child, none of you would tolerate one—

KELLER. Well, she's not, I think some compromise is called for. Bring her plate, please.

[ANNIE*'s jaw sets, but she restores the plate, while* KELLER *fastens the napkin around* HELEN*'s neck; she permits it.*]

There. It's not unnatural, most of us take some aversion to our teachers, and occasionally another hand can smooth things out.

[*He puts a fork in* HELEN*'s hand;* HELEN *takes it. Genially:*]

Now. Shall we start all over?

[*He goes back around the table, and sits.* ANNIE *stands watching.* HELEN *is motionless, thinking things through, until with a wicked glee she deliberately flings the fork on the floor. After another moment she plunges her hand into her food, and crams a fistful into her mouth.*]

JAMES. [*Wearily.*] I think we've started all over—

[KELLER *shoots a glare at him, as* HELEN *plunges her other hand into* ANNIE*'s plate.* ANNIE *at once moves in, to grasp her wrist, and* HELEN *flinging out a hand encounters the pitcher; she swings with it at* ANNIE*;* ANNIE *falling back blocks it with an elbow, but the water flies over her dress.* ANNIE *gets her breath, then snatches the pitcher away in one hand, hoists* HELEN *up bodily under the other arm, and starts to carry her out, kicking.* KELLER *stands.*]

ANNIE. [*Savagely polite.*] Don't get up!

KELLER. Where are you going?

ANNIE. Don't smooth anything else out for me, don't interfere in any way! I treat her like a seeing child because I *ask* her to see, I *expect* her to see, don't undo what I do!

KELLER. Where are you taking her?

ANNIE. To make her fill this pitcher again!

[*She thrusts out with* HELEN *under her arm, but* HELEN *escapes up the stairs and* ANNIE *runs after her.* KELLER *stands rigid.* AUNT EV *is astounded.*]

AUNT EV. You let her speak to you like that, Arthur? A creature who *works* for you?

KELLER. [*Angrily.*] No. I don't.

[*He is starting after* ANNIE *when* JAMES*, on his feet with shaky resolve, interposes his chair between them in* KELLER*'s path.*]

JAMES. Let her go.

KELLER. What!

JAMES. [*A swallow.*] I said—let her go. She's right.

[KELLER *glares at the chair and him.* JAMES *takes a deep breath, then headlong:*]

She's right, Kate's right, I'm right, and

Vocabulary

aversion (ə vur′ zhən) *n.* definite dislike combined with a desire to avoid whatever is disliked
genially (jēn′ yəl lē) *adv.* in a friendly way; pleasantly and cheerfully

you're wrong. If you drive her away from here it will be over my dead—chair, has it never occurred to you that on one occasion you might be consummately wrong?[58]

[KELLER's stare is unbelieving, even a little fascinated. KATE rises in trepidation, to mediate.]

KATE. Captain.

[KELLER stops her with his raised hand; his eyes stay on JAMES's pale face, for a long hold. When he finally finds his voice, it is gruff.]

KELLER. Sit down, everyone.

[He sits. KATE sits. JAMES holds onto his chair. KELLER speaks mildly.]

Please sit down, Jimmie.

[JAMES sits, and a moveless silence prevails; KELLER's eyes do not leave him.

ANNIE has pulled HELEN downstairs again by one hand, the pitcher in her other hand, down the porch steps, and across the yard to the pump. She puts HELEN's hand on the pump handle, grimly.]

ANNIE. All right. Pump.

[HELEN touches her cheek, waits uncertainly.]

No, she's not here. Pump!

[She forces HELEN's hand to work the handle, then lets go. And HELEN obeys. She pumps till the water comes, then ANNIE puts the pitcher in her other hand and guides it under the spout, and the water tumbling half into and half around the pitcher douses HELEN's hand. ANNIE takes over the handle to keep water coming, and does automatically what she has done so many times before, spells into HELEN's free palm:]

Water. W, a, t, e, r. *Water.* It has a—*name*—

[And now the miracle happens. HELEN drops the pitcher on the slab under the spout, it shatters. She stands transfixed. ANNIE freezes on the pump handle: there is a change in the sundown light, and with it a change in HELEN's face, some light coming into it we have never seen there, some struggle in the depths behind it; and her lips tremble, trying to remember something the muscles around them once knew, till at last it finds its way out, painfully, a baby sound buried under the debris of years of dumbness.]

HELEN. Wah. Wah.

[And again, with great effort.]

Wah. Wah.

[HELEN plunges her hand into the dwindling water, spells into her own palm. Then she gropes frantically, ANNIE reaches for her hand, and HELEN spells into ANNIE's hand.]

ANNIE. *[Whispering.]* Yes.

[HELEN spells into it again.]

Yes!

[HELEN grabs at the handle, pumps for more water, plunges her hand into its spurt and grabs ANNIE's to spell it again.]

Yes! Oh, my dear—

[She falls to her knees to clasp HELEN's hand, but HELEN pulls it free, stands almost bewildered, then drops to the ground, pats it swiftly, holds up her palm, imperious.[59] ANNIE spells into it:]

58. To be *consummately* (kən sum′ it lē) *wrong* is to be absolutely and completely wrong.

59. Here, *imperious* (im pēr′ ē əs) means "urgent, pressing."

Vocabulary

trepidation (trep′ ə dā′ shən) *n.* a feeling of nervous expectation; anxiety

mediate (mē′ dē āt′) *v.* to settle a dispute between persons or sides by acting as a go-between

transfixed (trans fikst′) *adj.* made motionless, as from awe or fear

Ground.

[*HELEN spells it back.*]

Yes!

[*HELEN whirls to the pump, pats it, holds up her palm, and ANNIE spells into it.*]

Pump.

[*HELEN spells it back.*]

Yes! Yes!

[*Now HELEN is in such an excitement she is possessed, wild, trembling, cannot be still, turns, runs, falls on the porch steps, claps it, reaches out her palm, and ANNIE is at it instantly to spell:*]

Step.

[*HELEN has no time to spell back now, she whirls groping, to touch anything, encounters the trellis, shakes it, thrusts out her palm, and ANNIE while spelling to her cries wildly at the house.*]

Trellis. Mrs. Keller! Mrs. *Keller!*

[*Inside, KATE starts to her feet. HELEN scrambles back onto the porch, groping, and finds the bell string, tugs it; the bell rings, the distant chimes begin tolling the hour, all the bells in town seem to break into speech while HELEN reaches out and ANNIE spells feverishly into her hand. KATE hurries out, with KELLER after her; AUNT EV is on her feet, to peer out the window; only JAMES remains at the table, and with a napkin wipes his damp brow. From up right and left the servants—VINEY, the two Negro children, the other servant—run in, and stand watching from a distance as HELEN, ringing the bell, with her other hand encounters her mother's skirt; when she throws a hand out, ANNIE spells into it:*]

Mother.

[*KELLER now seizes HELEN's hand, she touches him, gestures a hand, and ANNIE again spells:*]

Papa— She *knows!*

[*KATE and KELLER go to their knees, stammering, clutching HELEN to them, and ANNIE steps unsteadily back to watch the threesome, HELEN spelling wildly into KATE's hand, then into KELLER's, KATE spelling back into HELEN's; they cannot keep their hands off her, and rock her in their clasp.*

Then HELEN gropes, feels nothing, turns all around, pulls free, and comes with both hands groping, to find ANNIE. She encounters ANNIE's thighs, ANNIE kneels to her, HELEN's hand pats ANNIE's cheek impatiently, points a finger, and waits; and ANNIE spells into it:]

Teacher.

[*HELEN spells it back, slowly; ANNIE nods.*]

Teacher.

[*She holds HELEN's hand to her cheek. Presently HELEN withdraws it, not jerkily, only with reserve, and retreats a step. She stands thinking it over, then turns again and stumbles back to her parents. They try to embrace her, but she has something else in mind, it is to get the keys, and she hits KATE's pocket until KATE digs them out for her.*

ANNIE with her own load of emotion has retreated, her back turned, toward the pump, to sit; KATE moves to HELEN, touches her hand questioningly, and HELEN spells a word to her. KATE comprehends it, their first act of verbal communication, and she can hardly utter the word aloud, in wonder, gratitude, and deprivation; it is a moment in which she simultaneously finds and loses a child.]

KATE. Teacher?

[*ANNIE turns; and KATE, facing HELEN in her direction by the shoulders, holds her back, holds her back, and then relinquishes her. HELEN feels her way across the yard, rather shyly, and when her moving hands touch ANNIE's skirt she stops. Then she holds out the keys and places them in ANNIE's hand. For a moment neither of them moves. Then HELEN slides into ANNIE's arms, and lifting away her smoked glasses, kisses her on the cheek. ANNIE gathers her in.*

KATE torn both ways turns from this, gestures the servants off, and makes her way into the house, on KELLER's arm. The servants go, in separate directions.

The lights are half down now, except over the pump. ANNIE and HELEN are here, alone in the yard. ANNIE has found HELEN's hand, almost without knowing it, and she spells slowly into it, her voice unsteady, whispering:]

ANNIE. I, love, Helen.

[*She clutches the child to her, tight this time, not spelling, whispering into her hair.*]

Forever, and—

[*She stops. The lights over the pump are taking on the color of the past, and it brings ANNIE's head up, her eyes opening, in fear; and as slowly as though drawn she rises, to listen, with her hand on HELEN's shoulders. She waits, waits, listening with ears and eyes both, slowly here, slowly there: and hears only silence. There are no voices. The color passes on, and when her eyes come back to HELEN she can breathe the end of her phrase without fear:*]

—ever.

[In the family room KATE *has stood over the table, staring at* HELEN*'s plate, with* KELLER *at her shoulder; now* JAMES *takes a step to move her chair in, and* KATE *sits, with head erect, and* KELLER *inclines his head to* JAMES*; so it is* AUNT EV*, hesitant, and rather humble, who moves to the door.*

Outside HELEN *tugs at* ANNIE*'s hand, and* ANNIE *comes with it.* HELEN *pulls her toward the house; and hand in hand, they cross the yard, and ascend the porch steps, in the rising lights, to where* AUNT EV *is holding the door open for them.*

The curtain ends the play.]

Responding to Literature

Personal Response

When you think of this play in the future, what will you remember most? Share your ideas with a classmate.

Analyzing Act 3

Recall

1. Describe your impressions of Helen at the beginning of act 3.
2. Why won't Annie let Helen go with her parents when they arrive to pick her up?
3. Describe the final flashback Annie experiences as she gets ready to leave the garden house.
4. Summarize the events that lead up to Annie's return with Helen to the water pump.
5. What "miracle" occurs at the end of the play?

Interpret

6. How do you account for the changes in Helen that are evident at the beginning of act 3?
7. Is Annie as proud of Helen's progress as the Kellers are? Explain.
8. In your opinion, why is Annie haunted by a memory as she leaves the garden house and Helen returns to her parents?
9. Early in act 3, Kate encourages James to "stand up to the world." What effect does this advice have on him?
10. What emotional miracle does Annie experience at the end of the play? In your opinion, why does this happen?

Evaluate and Connect

11. Compare and contrast the breakfast scene in act 2 with the dinner scene in act 3. What, if anything, has each of the characters learned?
12. Why is the relationship between James and his father so strained? Do you think the relationship has the potential to improve? Explain.
13. Locate several instances in the play where light and darkness are used as **symbols.** Explain.
14. Twice during the play, Annie says that God owes her a resurrection, or a rebirth. In the end, do you think she feels that the debt has been paid? Explain.
15. Review your response to the Reading Focus on page 707. What would Captain and Mrs. Keller have written about miracles and miracle workers—before and after the events of this play?

Literary ELEMENTS

Dynamic and Static Characters

A **dynamic character** changes or develops in the course of a play or story. This change may result from a conflict or a newfound understanding of him- or herself or others. A **static character,** on the other hand, is one who remains the same from beginning to end.

1. Are Annie and Helen static or dynamic characters? Explain your answer, using evidence from the play.
2. Who else might be regarded as a dynamic character in this play, and why?
3. In your opinion, which character or characters remain static?

- See **Literary Terms Handbook,** p. R2.

Literary Criticism

Critic Stephen C. Coy says, "If trying to teach Helen is the ultimate test of Annie's native wit, guile, stamina, and sense of humor, then her confrontations with the captain are the test of her integrity and her faith in her methods." With a partner, discuss whether you agree with Coy's opinion. Be sure to support your ideas with details from the play.

Literature and Writing

Writing About Literature

Analyzing Plot Like novels and short stories, dramas have plots. Map the plot of this drama by identifying the exposition; the rising action, including the conflicts; the climax; and the resolution. Then, in two or three paragraphs, explain how the plot not only keeps the viewer or reader involved in the drama but also brings about a satisfying close.

Personal Writing

Solving the Mystery How does this play fit the theme "The Mysteries of Life"? Think about the kinds of questions each of the characters might have had at the outset of the play, as Helen grew into a little girl no one understood, and at the end of the play. What mysteries were solved for this family, and what mysteries still exist for them–and for you? Write your thoughts in your journal.

Extending Your Response

Literature Groups

Causes and Effects Why did the "miracle" occur? Did Annie Sullivan "work" it by persevering, or by teaching Helen obedience? Did it come about because of things Annie and Helen experienced in common? Was it the result of Helen's own will? With a group, identify probable causes of the "miracle." Then rank them in order of importance. Share your ideas with another group.

Learning for Life

Job Evaluation How well did Annie Sullivan do her job? Work with a partner to write a job evaluation for her. Begin by listing various criteria for evaluation, such as attitude, knowledge, creativity, and communication skills. Then come up with an evaluation scale, using adjectives (from "poor" to "excellent") or numbers (1–5). Rate Annie's job performance in each category. Then write a short summary of your evaluation.

Listening and Speaking

Signs and Sense With a partner, learn the manual sign language for the deaf-blind that Annie Sullivan taught to Helen Keller. Then take turns spelling words into each others' hands. With eyes closed or blindfolded, the person "reading" the signs should try to identify each letter, say it aloud, and then pronounce the word the letters spell. You may also want to research and learn how to sign familiar phrases and share them with classmates.

Reading Further

If you'd like to learn more about Annie Sullivan and Helen Keller, you might enjoy these works:

Biography: *Helen and Teacher,* by Joseph P. Lash, is a biography that relates the life stories of both Keller and Sullivan, emphasizing their remarkable relationship.

Viewing: *The Miracle Worker* is an MGM/UA home video starring Anne Bancroft and Patty Duke.

Save your work for your portfolio.

Sign Language Alphabet

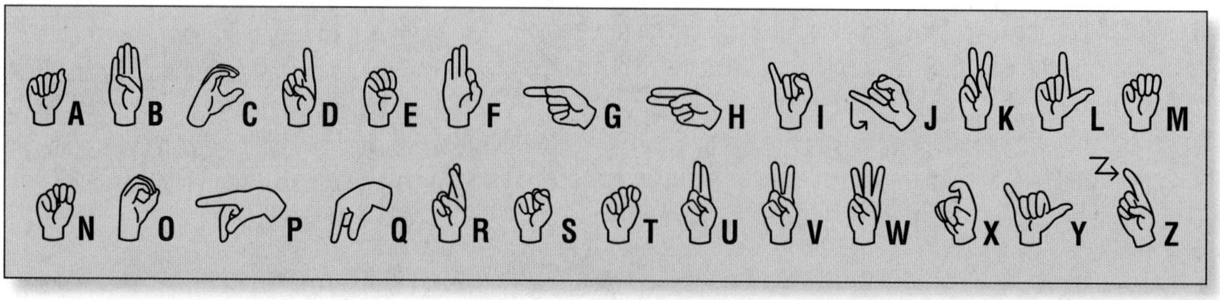

Skill Minilessons

GRAMMAR AND LANGUAGE • Using Commas

Use a comma to set off words of direct address, whether at the beginning, the middle, or the end of a sentence.

Miss Sullivan, you are a tyrant.

I didn't know, my friend, that you could be so strict!

Would you please release Helen's wrists, Annie?

Also use a comma to set off *yes* and *no* and mild interjections when they begin a sentence, as in this example from the play: "Oh, strangers aren't so strange to me."

PRACTICE On your own paper, rewrite the following sentences, adding commas as necessary.

1. Well I hope Helen's behavior improves.
2. Don't go Annie until I tell you to.
3. Yes we're expecting the teacher.
4. Helen please slide the key under the door.
5. No Captain she's not here.

APPLY Find five examples in the play of commas used in direct address or after mild interjections.

● For more about commas and direct address, see **Language Handbook,** pp. R47–R48.

READING AND THINKING • Visualizing

When you read a play, you must visualize the action and the set. Pay attention to stage directions and ask yourself questions such as these: How does this scene look? Who is in this scene? Where are the characters in relation to one another and to their surroundings?

PRACTICE On your paper, describe everything you can visualize as you read this segment from act 1.

AUNT EV. Helen! My buttons.

[*HELEN pushes the buttons into the doll's face. KATE now sees, comes swiftly to kneel, lifts HELEN's hand to her own eyes in question.*]

KATE. Eyes?

[*HELEN nods energetically.*]

She wants the doll to have eyes.

[*Another kind of silence now, while KATE takes pins and buttons from the sewing basket and attaches them to the doll as eyes. KELLER stands, caught, and watches morosely. AUNT EV blinks, and conceals her emotion by inspecting her dress.*]

● For more about visualizing, see **Reading Handbook,** p. R84.

VOCABULARY • Analogies

An **analogy** is a type of comparison that is based on a relationship between things or ideas. To complete an analogy, you must know more than just the meanings of the words. You must be able to figure out what relationship exists between the first pair of words and describe it in a clear and specific way. Describing the relationship allows you to try different answer choices until you have found the one that makes the second relationship like the first.

● For more on analogies, see **Communications Skills Handbook,** p. R77.

PRACTICE The analogies below involve several different types of relationships. Choose the word that best completes each analogy.

1. shudder : aversion :: laugh :
   a. sound b. sadness c. amusement
2. chat : genially :: whisper :
   a. quietly b. cheerfully c. fearfully
3. sleepiness : yawn :: trepidation :
   a. tremble b. grin c. applaud
4. kind : cruel :: bountiful :
   a. slow b. confident c. stingy

Before You Read

from *The Story of My Life*

Reading Focus

Think about a time when you had a sudden realization—a moment when you felt as if you finally understood something about yourself or about a subject you had been studying.

Quickwrite Write what you remember about such a moment—or about how it would feel to suddenly understand a concept you have been struggling to learn. Once you grasped such a concept, what would change for you?

Setting a Purpose Read to learn how Helen Keller felt when she was first led to connect words with things and ideas.

Building Background

The Time and Place

In this excerpt from her autobiography, Helen Keller recalls events that occurred in the late 1880s in Tuscumbia, Alabama.

Did You Know?

In 1902 Helen Keller first published *The Story of My Life* as a series of five articles in the *Ladies' Home Journal.* Anne Sullivan and John Macy, a young editor and writer whom Sullivan later married, assisted Keller in the painstaking writing process. Keller used a braille machine to make notes for herself. Then, on a manual typewriter, she typed the first drafts, describing events in her life in no special order. Sullivan and Macy helped her put the material in chronological order. They pointed out "gaps," and she dictated transitions and revisions. A copy of the final manuscript was created in braille, for Helen to read and approve.

Vocabulary Preview

languor (lang′ gər) *n.* a lack of spirit, interest, energy, or activity; mental or physical fatigue; p. 783

traverse (trə vurs′) *v.* to pass across or through; p. 786

symmetrical (si met′ ri kəl) *adj.* exactly agreeing in size, form, and arrangement on both sides of something; p. 786

verbatim (vər bā′ tim) *adv.* word for word; in exactly the same words; p. 787

augment (ôg ment′) *v.* to become greater; increase; grow; p. 787

Meet Helen Keller

"Life is either a daring adventure, or nothing."

When Helen Keller was nineteen months old, she was left deaf and blind by a serious illness. By the time she was eight, she had learned to write by hand on paper and to read and write in braille. When she was ten, she began learning speech. After only seven lessons, she said with her voice, "I am not dumb now." Keller read, wrote letters, kept a journal, and constantly worked to increase her vocabulary. She even "talked" in her sleep—spelling words using the manual alphabet. Keller spent much of her life writing and lecturing to raise people's awareness of the needs and abilities of the blind, deaf, and deaf-blind.

Helen Keller was born in 1880 and died in 1968. The Story of My Life *was published in 1903.*

from *The Story of My Life*

Helen Keller

Helen Keller at work on a braille typewriter.

THE MOST IMPORTANT DAY I remember in all my life is the one on which my teacher, Anne Mansfield Sullivan, came to me. I am filled with wonder when I consider the immeasurable contrasts between the two lives which it connects. It was the third of March, 1887, three months before I was seven years old.

On the afternoon of that eventful day, I stood on the porch, dumb, expectant. I guessed vaguely from my mother's signs and from the hurrying to and fro in the house that something unusual was about to happen, so I went to the door and waited on the steps. The afternoon sun penetrated the mass of honeysuckle that covered the porch, and fell on my upturned face. My fingers lingered almost unconsciously on the familiar leaves and blossoms which had just come forth to greet the sweet southern spring. I did not know what the future held of marvel or surprise for me. Anger and bitterness had preyed upon me continually for weeks and a deep languor had succeeded this passionate struggle.

Have you ever been at sea in a dense fog, when it seemed as if a tangible white darkness shut you in, and the great ship, tense and

Vocabulary

languor (lang′ gər) *n.* a lack of spirit, interest, energy, or activity; mental or physical fatigue anxious, groped her way toward the shore with plummet and sounding-line,[1] and you waited with beating heart for something to happen? I was like that ship before my education began, only I was without compass or sounding-line, and had no way of knowing how near the harbor was. "Light! give me light!" was the wordless cry of my soul, and the light of love shone on me in that very hour.

I felt approaching footsteps. I stretched out my hand as I supposed to my mother. Someone took it, and I was caught up and held close in the arms of her who had come to reveal all things to me, and, more than all things else, to love me.

The morning after my teacher came she led me into her room and gave me a doll. The little blind children at the Perkins Institution had sent it and Laura Bridgman[2] had dressed it; but I did not know this until afterward. When I had played with it a little while, Miss Sullivan slowly spelled into my hand the word "d-o-l-l." I was at once interested in this finger play and tried to imitate it. When I finally succeeded in making the letters correctly I was flushed with childish pleasure and pride. Running downstairs to my mother I held up my hand and made the letters for doll. I did not know that I was spelling a word or even that words existed; I was simply making my fingers go in monkeylike imitation. In the days that followed I learned to spell in this uncomprehending[3] way a great many words, among them *pin*, *hat*, *cup*, and a few verbs like *sit*, *stand*, and *walk*. But my teacher had been with me several weeks before I understood that everything has a name.

One day, while I was playing with my new doll, Miss Sullivan put my big rag doll into my lap also, spelled "d-o-l-l," and tried to make me understand that "d-o-l-l" applied to both. Earlier in the day we had had a tussle over the words "m-u-g" and "w-a-t-e-r." Miss Sullivan had tried to impress it upon me that "m-u-g" is *mug* and that "w-a-t-e-r" is *water*, but I persisted in confounding[4] the two. In despair she had dropped the subject for the time, only to renew it at the first opportunity. I became impatient at her repeated attempts and, seizing the new doll, I dashed it upon the floor. I was keenly delighted when I felt the fragments of the broken doll at my feet. Neither sorrow nor regret followed my passionate outburst. I had not loved the doll. In the still, dark world in which I lived there was no strong sentiment or tenderness. I felt my teacher sweep the fragments to one side of the hearth, and I had a sense of satisfaction that the cause of my discomfort was removed. She brought me my hat, and I knew I was going out into the warm sunshine. This thought, if a wordless sensation may be called a thought, made me hop and skip with pleasure.

We walked down the path to the wellhouse, attracted by the fragrance of the honeysuckle with which it was covered. Some one was drawing water and my teacher placed my hand under the spout. As the cool stream gushed over one hand she spelled into the other the word *water*, first slowly, then rapidly. I stood still, my whole attention fixed upon the motions of her fingers. Suddenly I felt a misty consciousness as of something forgotten—a thrill of returning thought; and somehow the mystery of language was revealed to me. I knew then that "w-a-t-e-r" meant the wonderful cool something that was

1. *[plummet and sounding-line]* This device is used to measure the depth of water. A line of rope or cord is marked at intervals and has a weight, or *plummet,* at one end.
2. *Laura Bridgman* (1829–1889), a student of Dr. Samuel G. Howe of the Perkins Institution for the Blind, was the first deaf, blind, and mute person to be successfully educated in the United States.
3. *Uncomprehending* means "without understanding."
4. Here, *confounding* means "confusing; mixing up," or "failing to understand the difference between."

Helen Keller reading braille.

flowing over my hand. That living word awakened my soul, gave it light, hope, joy, set it free! There were barriers still, it is true, but barriers that could in time be swept away.

I left the well-house eager to learn. Everything had a name, and each name gave birth to a new thought. As we returned to the house every object which I touched seemed to quiver with life. That was because I saw everything with the strange, new sight that had come to me. On entering the door I remembered the doll I had broken. I felt my way to the hearth and picked up the pieces. I tried vainly to put them together. Then my eyes filled with tears; for I realized what I had done, and for the first time I felt repentance and sorrow.

I learned a great many new words that day. I do not remember what they all were; but I do know that *mother, father, sister, teacher* were among them—words that were to make the world blossom for me, "like Aaron's rod,[5] with flowers." It would have been difficult to find a happier child than I was as I lay in my crib at the close of that eventful day and lived over the joys it had brought me, and for the first time longed for a new day to come. . . .

I had now the key to all language, and I was eager to learn to use it. Children who hear acquire language without any particular effort; the words that fall from others' lips they catch on the wing, as it were, delightedly, while the little deaf child must trap them by a slow and often painful process. But whatever the process, the result is

5. In the Bible, *Aaron's rod,* a wooden walking stick, miraculously blossoms and bears almonds.

wonderful. Gradually from naming an object we advance step by step until we have traversed the vast distance between our first stammered syllable and the sweep of thought in a line of Shakespeare.

At first, when my teacher told me about a new thing I asked very few questions. My ideas were vague, and my vocabulary was inadequate; but as my knowledge of things grew, and I learned more and more words, my field of inquiry broadened, and I would return again and again to the same subject, eager for further information. Sometimes a new word revived an image that some earlier experience had engraved on my brain.

> *I thought it strange that my teacher could not show me love.*

I remember the morning that I first asked the meaning of the word, "love." This was before I knew many words. I had found a few early violets in the garden and brought them to my teacher. She tried to kiss me: but at that time I did not like to have anyone kiss me except my mother. Miss Sullivan put her arm gently round me and spelled into my hand, "I love Helen."

"What is love?" I asked.

She drew me closer to her and said, "It is here," pointing to my heart, whose beats I was conscious of for the first time. Her words puzzled me very much because I did not then understand anything unless I touched it.

I smelled the violets in her hand and asked, half in words, half in signs, a question which meant, "Is love the sweetness of flowers?"

"No," said my teacher.

Again I thought. The warm sun was shining on us.

"Is this not love?" I asked, pointing in the direction from which the heat came. "Is this not love?"

It seemed to me that there could be nothing more beautiful than the sun, whose warmth makes all things grow. But Miss Sullivan shook her head, and I was greatly puzzled and disappointed. I thought it strange that my teacher could not show me love.

A day or two afterward I was stringing beads of different sizes in symmetrical groups—two large beads, three small ones, and so on. I had made many mistakes, and Miss Sullivan had pointed them out again and again with gentle patience. Finally I noticed a very obvious error in the sequence and for an instant I concentrated my attention on the lesson and tried to think how I should have arranged the beads. Miss Sullivan touched my forehead and spelled with decided emphasis, "Think."

In a flash I knew that the word was the name of the process that was going on in my head. This was my first conscious perception of an abstract[6] idea.

For a long time I was still—I was not thinking of the beads in my lap, but trying to find a meaning for "love" in the light of this

6. *Abstract* means "not concrete; unlike any specific example or thing."

Vocabulary

traverse (trə vurs′) *v.* to pass across or through

symmetrical (si met′ ri kəl) *adj.* exactly agreeing in size, form, and arrangement on both sides of something new idea. The sun had been under a cloud all day, and there had been brief showers; but suddenly the sun broke forth in all its southern splendor.

Again I asked my teacher, "Is this not love?"

"Love is something like the clouds that were in the sky before the sun came out," she replied. Then in simpler words than these, which at that time I could not have understood, she explained: "You cannot touch the clouds, you know; but you feel the rain and know how glad the flowers and the thirsty earth are to have it after a hot day. You cannot touch love either; but you feel the sweetness that it pours into everything. Without love you would not be happy or want to play."

The beautiful truth burst upon my mind—I felt that there were invisible lines stretched between my spirit and the spirits of others.

From the beginning of my education Miss Sullivan made it a practice to speak to me as she would speak to any hearing child; the only difference was that she spelled the sentences into my hand instead of speaking them. If I did not know the words and idioms[7] necessary to express my thoughts she supplied them, even suggesting conversation when I was unable to keep up my end of the dialogue.

This process was continued for several years; for the deaf child does not learn in a month, or even in two or three years, the numberless idioms and expressions used in the simplest daily intercourse.[8] The little hearing child learns these from constant repetition and imitation. The conversation he hears in his home stimulates his mind and suggests topics and calls forth the spontaneous[9] expression of his own thoughts. This natural exchange of ideas is denied to the deaf child. My teacher, realizing this, determined to supply the kinds of stimulus[10] I lacked. This she did by repeating to me as far as possible, verbatim, what she heard, and by showing me how I could take part in the conversation. But it was a long time before I ventured to take the initiative, and still longer before I could find something appropriate to say at the right time.

The deaf and the blind find it very difficult to acquire the amenities of conversation.[11] How much more this difficulty must be augmented in the case of those who are both deaf and blind! They cannot distinguish the tone of the voice or, without assistance, go up and down the gamut[12] of tones that give significance to words; nor can they watch the expression of the speaker's face, and a look is often the very soul of what one says.

7. *Idioms* (id′ ē əmz) are expressions that have a meaning different from the literal meaning of the words. Examples are "She's on the ball," "My stomach is in knots," and "The test is a piece of cake."

8. *Intercourse* is the exchange of thoughts, ideas, and feelings through conversation or other communication.

9. *Spontaneous* means "arising from a natural impulse or cause; unplanned."

10. A *stimulus* is something that causes a response.

11. By *amenities of conversation* Keller means those things besides words, such as tone of voice or facial expression, that help communicate meaning.

12. Here, *gamut* means the "entire series" or "entire range" of possible tones or sounds.

Vocabulary

verbatim (vər bā′ tim) *adv.* word for word; in exactly the same words

augment (ôg ment′) *v.* to become greater; increase; grow

Responding to Literature

Personal Response

After reading this selection, what questions would you like to ask Helen Keller? List them in your journal.

Analyzing Literature

Recall and Interpret

1. How does Keller describe her state of mind just before Sullivan arrived? What do you suppose she means when she says that the wordless cry of her soul was "Light! give me light!"
2. What is the first word Keller both learns to spell and truly understand? What changes inside Helen when "the mystery of language [is] revealed" to her?
3. Why was it difficult for Keller to understand the word *love*? How is she finally able to reach an understanding?
4. How does Sullivan help Keller acquire language and develop conversational skills? What do you perceive is the difference between the two?

Evaluate and Connect

5. How and why was Helen Keller's process of learning language different from that of a hearing child?
6. Compare and contrast the ideas in your response to the Reading Focus on page 782 with the ones Keller expresses in this selection.
7. Who in today's world might be "left behind" as Keller herself was almost left behind? Who might be their Annie Sullivans?
8. **Theme Connections** What examples of life's mysteries do you find in this excerpt from Keller's autobiography?

Literary ELEMENTS

Analogy

An **analogy** is a comparison of two things that are alike in some way. An extended analogy is lengthened by elaboration to explain something abstract or unfamiliar. For example, to show her readers what it means to be deaf, blind, and without language, Keller draws an analogy in the third paragraph between herself and a ship in a dense fog.

1. Keller says that she was "without compass or sounding-line." What do these details imply about her experience?
2. What does Keller mean when she says that she "had no way of knowing how near the harbor was"?

- See **Literary Terms Handbook,** p. R1.

Extending Your Response

Literature Groups

Sights and Sounds Helen Keller once stood atop a skyscraper in New York City and said she could visualize Manhattan. "All sight is of the soul," she believed. Someone else once said that Keller was lucky to have been spared the vision of ugly sights in the world and the hearing of terrible sounds. What do you think of these opinions? How might Keller have responded to the latter one? Discuss and debate these opinions with your group, and share your conclusions with other groups.

Writing About Literature

Descriptive Details Nonfiction can be vividly descriptive, and in this work, Keller takes pains at the beginning to provide details about surroundings that she could neither see nor hear. In your opinion, why might she have included these details? Do they describe some types of sensory impressions more than others? Answer these questions in a well-developed paragraph.

Save your work for your portfolio.

COMPARING selections

The Miracle Worker and from The Story of My Life

COMPARE AUDIENCES AND PURPOSES

Although both of these works focus on the same period in Keller's life, they differ in purpose. Each author wrote with a different audience in mind. With a small group, discuss the following questions:

1. What might Gibson's purpose be? How might it differ from Keller's?
2. Who do you suppose is Gibson's intended audience?
3. Who might Keller's intended audience be? How might the expectations of these audiences differ?

COMPARE AUTHORS' CHALLENGES

Whether a writer hopes to bring a story to life on the stage or in the pages of an autobiography, the finished work must hold the interest of viewers or readers. In three or more paragraphs, explore the challenges each writer faced. Consider the following questions:

- In your opinion, might the unusual nature of Keller's life experience have made her job harder or easier than the job of the average autobiographer?
- Does it seem easier to write about your own life or about someone else's life? If you were a celebrity, how would you answer this question?

COMPARE INFORMATION

Prepare a review of these two works and present it in an oral report to the class. Your purpose is to recommend one or the other, or both equally, as a source of information about Helen Keller. You might use a graphic organizer like the one below to evaluate the types of information each source offers on various topics.

Information about	*The Miracle Worker*	*The Story of My Life*
blindness		
Anne Sullivan		
Helen Keller's family		
acquiring language		

MEDIA connection

Magazine Article

Unconditional love is a powerful and mysterious force. It can help people overcome personal difficulties—some say it can even work miracles. Read to learn what it does for a physically challenged boy.

The Boy Who Talked With Dolphins

by Paula McDonald—*Reader's Digest,* April 1996

Jeff Siegel was born hyperactive, partially deaf and lacking normal coordination. Since he couldn't hear words clearly, he developed a severe speech impediment that made it almost impossible for others to understand him.

On the first day of kindergarten, Jeff climbed over the schoolyard fence and ran home. His mother hauled him back to school and forced him to apologize to the teacher. As the mispronounced and barely intelligible words were dragged out of him, he became instant prey for his classmates. To fend off the hostile world, Jeff kept to isolated corners of the playground and hid in his room at home, dreaming of a place where he could be accepted.

When Jeff was nine, he went with his fourth-grade class to Los Angeles's Marineland. At the dolphin show, he was electrified by the energy and exuberant friendliness of the beautiful animals. They seemed to smile directly at him, something that happened rarely

in his life. The boy sat transfixed, overwhelmed with emotion and a longing to stay. . . .

Seventh grade was unfolding as the worst year of Jeff's life—until the day his father took him to Sea World in San Diego. The minute the boy saw the dolphins, the same rush of joy welled up in him. He stayed rooted to the spot as the sleek mammals glided past.

Jeff worked to earn money for an annual pass to Marineland. The outgoing dolphins quickly became the friends Jeff had never had, and he began to live from visit to visit.

Even when there were summer crowds of 500 around the pool, the gregarious creatures recognized their friend and swam to him wherever he wiggled his hand in the water.

Today, Jeff is a full-time dolphin trainer at Marine Animal Productions in Gulfport, Mississippi, where he organizes programs for schools.

"I'm completely fulfilled," he says. "The dolphins did so much for me when I was a child. They gave me unconditional love. When I think about what I owe the dolphins. . . ." His voice trails off momentarily, and he smiles. "They gave me life. I owe them everything."

Analyzing Media

1. Explain what Jeff might mean when he says that the dolphins gave him life.
2. Have you ever loved an animal or another person "unconditionally"? Have you ever felt loved in that way? Describe what either of these experiences might feel like.

Grammar Link

Missing or Misplaced Possessive Apostrophes

Apostrophes are most often used to show possession. To make a word possessive, either add an apostrophe or an apostrophe and *-s.*

Problem 1 Singular, possessive nouns
James name is the same as Annies brothers.

Solution To make a singular noun possessive, add an apostrophe and *-s.*
James's name is the same as Annie's brother's.

Problem 2 Plural nouns ending in *-s*
During the Kellers breakfast, Helen explores all the plates contents.

Solution If a plural noun ends in *-s,* make it possessive by adding only an apostrophe.
During the Kellers' breakfast, Helen explores all the plates' contents.

Problem 3 Plural nouns not ending in *-s*
Annie gives Helen a doll that is the childrens gift to her.

Solution If a plural noun does not end in *-s,* add an apostrophe and *-s.*
Annie gives Helen a doll that is the children's gift to her.

Problem 4 Pronouns
Annie realizes that everyones behavior must change, including hers.

Solution Form the possessive of an indefinite pronoun by adding an apostrophe and *-s.* Apostrophes are not used in possessive pronouns, such as *hers.*
Annie realizes that everyone's behavior must change, including hers.

For more about using apostrophes, see **Language Handbook,** p. R25.

EXERCISE

If the sentence is correct, write *C* on your paper. If the sentence is incorrect, rewrite it to correct any errors.

1. Helens parent's concern for her prompted them to hire a teacher.
2. The teachers' goal was to contact the childs mind through the sense of touch.
3. Annies approach was different from the Kellers's.
4. The success that followed several weeks' hard work was hers and Helen's.
5. This success changed peoples ideas about disabled childrens's abilities.

Vo•cab•u•lar•y Skills

Idioms

An **idiom** is a word or phrase that has a special meaning different from its standard or dictionary meaning. For example, the statement "It serves her right" means that the punishment or negative result someone received was deserved. In many cases, idioms are not confusing because they are a common, familiar part of everyday speech. However, someone who has never heard a particular idiom might wonder what it means.

When you come across a phrase that does not immediately make sense, it might be an idiom. Thinking about what the words ordinarily mean can help you understand the idiom. For example, these idioms are fairly easy to figure out:

blow hot and cold	be inconsistent
put one's best foot forward	try to make a good impression
down in the mouth	depressed looking

Context clues can also help you interpret an unfamiliar idiom. The context may not reveal the specific meaning of the idiom, but it will almost always give you a general sense of what the idiom means.

> **"I've done as much as I can bear! I can't give my whole life to it! The house is <u>at sixes and sevens</u> from morning till night over the child . . ."**

Captain Keller is upset when he speaks these lines. The idiom's specific meaning, "in a state of complete confusion," is not completely clear, yet it is obvious that being "at sixes and sevens" is not a good condition to be in.

EXERCISES

Think about what is suggested by the ordinary meanings of the underlined words, use context clues, or do both to figure out what each idiom means. Then write a short definition or phrase that could be substituted for the idiom.

1. Annie <u>makes no bones about</u> her belief that the Kellers' pity has harmed Helen.
2. Annie insists that Helen learn table manners. The excuse that Helen is "deprived" <u>cuts no ice with</u> her.
3. Helen <u>sets her face against</u> using a spoon, but Annie continues to insist.
4. Once, when Helen misbehaves, Captain Keller says that "another hand can smooth things out." Helen's resulting behavior proves that his statement was <u>wide of the mark.</u>
5. Helen's realization that things have names <u>paves the way</u> for a lifetime of learning.

Writing Skills

Combining Sentences

Have you ever tried to listen to someone who speaks only in a monotone, never raising or lowering his or her voice? If so, you've probably noticed that your mind wanders and your eyelids droop! In writing, the equivalent to speaking in one tone of voice is to use only short, choppy sentences. You can prevent your writing from becoming dull by using **sentence combining**–combining some short sentences into longer ones to improve their rhythm and flow. Notice how sentence combining improves the writing below.

Before Sentences Are Combined

Captain Keller had a problem. He loved his daughter, Helen. Helen was blind and deaf. No one could communicate with her. Helen was undisciplined.

After Sentences Are Combined

Captain Keller had a problem. He loved his deaf and blind daughter, Helen, but because no one could communicate with her, she was undisciplined.

Try these strategies to combine sentences:

- Use a conjunction (*or, and,* or *but*) and a comma to join sentences that express related ideas of equal importance.
  Separate: *Helen ate from other people's plates. She threw tantrums when things didn't go her way.*
  Combined: *Helen ate from other people's plates, and she threw tantrums when things didn't go her way.*
- Add key words or phrases from one sentence to another sentence.
  Separate: *He loved his daughter Helen. Helen was blind and deaf.*
  Combined: *He loved his deaf and blind daughter, Helen.*
- Combine sentences using *who, which,* or *that* to eliminate repetition in related sentences.
  Separate: *Mrs. Keller hired Annie Sullivan. Annie Sullivan had been blind as a child.*
  Combined: *Mrs. Keller hired Annie Sullivan, who had been blind as a child.*
- Combine sentences using subordinating conjunctions, such as *because, although, unless,* and *after,* when you combine two sentences of unequal importance.
  Separate: *Mrs. Keller allowed this to occur. She felt sorry for her daughter.*
  Combined: *Mrs. Keller allowed this to occur because she felt sorry for her daughter.*

EXERCISE

Combine the following pairs of sentences.

1. Annie wanted to remove Helen from the house. She wanted to get Helen away from her mother.
2. Helen threw her fork on the floor. Helen threw her food on the floor.
3. Captain Keller was a stern man. He had served in the military.

Writing Workshop

Business Writing:
Problem/Solution Report

Because Helen Keller was blind and deaf, her family believed that they would never be able to communicate with her. Annie Sullivan managed to find a solution to this problem. Like all good problem-solvers, she was inventive, persistent, and flexible. Do you have those qualities?
In this workshop, you'll put them to the test when you write a report summarizing a problem and a possible solution.

- As you write your report, refer to the **Writing Handbook,** pp. R58–R71.

EVALUATION RUBRIC
By the time you complete this Writing Workshop, you will have
- written an introduction that states a problem and shows that it is worth considering
- identified the causes of the problem
- described a solution and explained how the solution can be implemented
- concluded with a summary of the problem/solution
- presented a problem/solution report that is free of errors in grammar, usage, and mechanics

The Writing Process

PREWRITING

PREWRITING TIP
In your journal, list circumstances that make you want to complain. Identify the problems behind those circumstances.

Explore ideas
What problem would you like to solve? The strategies below can help you generate ideas.

- Talk with family members about household problems to solve.
- Check a local newspaper for stories that suggest community problems to solve.
- Talk with classmates and teachers to identify school problems to solve.

In order to solve a problem, you must be able to state it clearly and to identify where the problem originates. First, narrow the scope of your problem to make it as specific as possible. Then think about what causes the problem. Remember, problems usually have more than one cause. They may have several separate causes, or they may result from a chain reaction of causes. Use the graphic organizers below to help you visualize the cause or causes of your problem.

Several Separate Causes

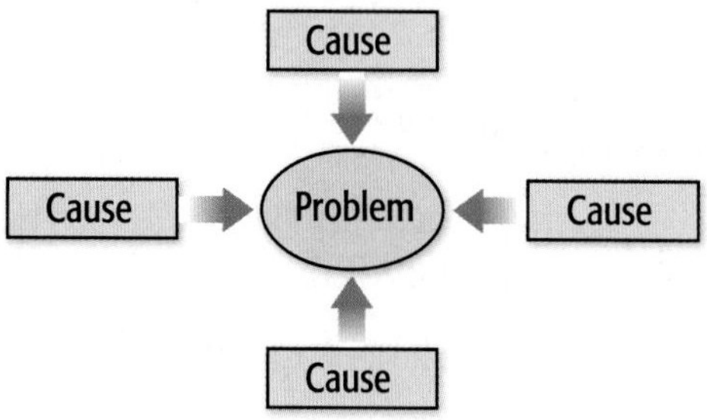

Chain Reaction of Causes

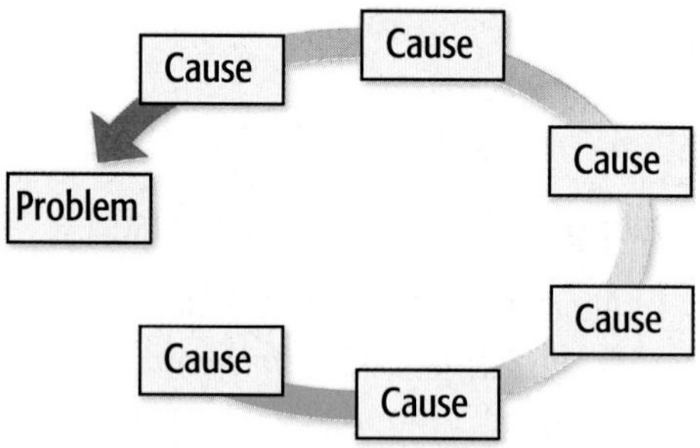

Next, brainstorm a list of possible solutions. Compare the advantages, disadvantages, and practicality of each possible solution. Which solution best addresses the causes you've identified?

Choose an audience and consider your purpose

The obvious audience is people who face the problem you've chosen. If you want to write for people who don't know that the problem exists, you will have to convince them that it does. Your *prewriting* purpose is to find a solution to the problem. Your *writing* purpose is to present the problem and solution in summary form, as briefly and concisely as you can.

Make a plan

Once you've identified a problem and a solution, you're ready to plan your report. It should include the basic elements of introduction, body, and conclusion.

		STUDENT MODEL
Introduction	Briefly state the problem and show that it is worth considering. An anecdote can help illustrate and clarify the problem.	—for six weeks of the year, our driveway is a bog —the car gets stuck in the mud —we can't put in a basketball hoop
Body	Plan two parts for the body of your report. In the first part, describe the problem and explain its causes. Your explanation should follow your own reasoning in identifying the cause or causes of the problem.	—Our dirt driveway is impassable in the spring —cause: when snow melts on the steep slope behind our house, the water rushes under the back wall of the house and settles in the driveway, saturating the dirt
	In the second part of the body, describe the solution. Show how changing or eliminating a cause results in the reduction or elimination of the problem.	—channel water away from driveway —dig a ditch and properly line with drain tiles to accommodate water flow —top the tiles with gravel to further encourage proper water routing —result: a dry driveway that can be paved
Conclusion	In the conclusion, provide a summary that gives the gist of the report in a few sentences. In many business reports, this section is labeled *SUMMARY.*	—if we reroute the water by digging a ditch, we'll solve the muddy driveway problem. We'll also be able to pave it. If our changes affect the drainage on other properties, we'll help our neighbors reroute their water also.

Complete Student Model on p. R118.

DRAFTING

DRAFTING TIP

See the Writing Skill "Using Transitions" on page 382 for advice on how to use transitions to make your reasoning clear.

Cause-effect relationships

At this stage, show every step of your reasoning. Explain exactly how the causes relate to the problem. Then show how your proposed solution addresses those causes. This will enable your readers to follow your thinking. You can edit down any lengthy explanations later.

Write your draft

Let your draft flow. If you're not sure you've landed on exactly the right solution, keep refining your ideas in writing. You will have ample opportunity to revise and simplify later.

STUDENT MODEL

The reason our driveway turns to mush in the spring is that we have steep hills right behind our house. When the winter snow melts, the water rushes toward lower ground. Our driveway is on lower ground, and the driveway gets so muddy, you can't use it for anything.

Complete Student Model on p. R118.

REVISING

REVISING TIP

Start by rereading your conclusion. As you go back through the rest of the report, make sure everything in it supports your final statements.

Evaluate your work

Review your thinking about the problem and solution. Then go through your report and eliminate any unnecessary information. Use the **Rubric for Revising** to guide your revision.

Talk it over

Read your draft to someone, and discuss the problem and the proposed solution. Ask your listener for a frank reaction to your solution. Then go through the **Rubric for Revising** together, and use the responses as guidelines when you revise.

RUBRIC FOR REVISING

Your revised problem/solution report should have

- ☑ an introduction that clearly states a problem and shows its importance
- ☑ anecdotes, examples, and explanations that illustrate the problem and its causes
- ☑ a proposal for a solution and a clear explanation of how the solution can be implemented
- ☑ clear, logical transitions
- ☑ a conclusion that summarizes the problem/solution and calls for action

Your revised problem/solution report should be free of

- ☑ illogical or confusing reasoning
- ☑ errors in grammar, usage, and mechanics

STUDENT MODEL

Of course if we rerout^e the water, it might cause problems for our neighbors. ^Gravity pulls water to lower ground, and ~~T~~their yard is lower than ours ~~is~~. If our new drainage system causes any problems for other families, we ~~could~~ ^should help them set up their own drainage systems ^as well.

Complete Student Model on p. R118.

EDITING/PROOFREADING

When your report is clear, concise, and complete, edit it to be sure that there are no errors in spelling, punctuation, grammar, or usage. Use the **Proofreading Checklist** on the inside back cover of this textbook to help you mark mistakes.

TECHNOLOGY TIP

If you use the spell-check function on your computer, keep a dictionary close at hand to check those words for which spell-check has no suggestions.

Grammar Hint

Do not use an apostrophe to form the possessive of *it*. Be sure to use an apostrophe to form the contraction of *it is*.

INCORRECT: *To solve the problem, its necessary to dig a ditch and line it's bottom and sides with drain tiles.*

CORRECT: *To solve the problem, it's necessary to dig a ditch and line its bottom and sides with drain tiles.*

For more about *its* and *it's*, see **Language Handbook**, pp. R25–R26.

STUDENT MODEL

```
The hill is right behind our house and its covered
with snow all Winter. When the snow melt in the
spring, it's run-off must be redirected.
```

Complete Student Model on p. R118.

Complete Student Model

For a complete version of the student model, see **Writing Workshop Models**, p. R118.

PUBLISHING/PRESENTING

You could compile the essays of the entire class into a booklet, giving it a title that indicates its content, such as *How to Solve (Almost) Any Problem.* Or, if your topic is of interest to the community at large, you could include your ideas in a letter to the editor of a local newspaper.

PRESENTING TIP

Graphics, such as diagrams, may help to make the details of your solution clearer.

Reflecting

It has been said that describing a problem accurately is 90 percent of its solution. Based on your experience writing this essay, do you think that this statement is correct? Reread your report and decide how you can put your problem-solving skills to use in other aspects of your life.

Save your work for your portfolio.

Unit Assessment

Personal Response

1. Thinking back on the plays in this unit, which role would you most like to perform? Give reasons for your answer.
2. As a result of the work you did in this unit, what new ideas do you have about the following:
   - how to glean information from stage directions
   - how to visualize characters, setting, and action
   - how to interpret a deeper meaning behind characters' words and actions
   - how to perform in front of others

Analyzing Literature

Evaluating the Plays Review the plays in this unit. In your opinion, what aspects of each play are most effective? Consider such literary elements as character, plot, conflict, dialogue, and theme. On the basis of your analysis, tell which play you prefer and why.

Although you are stating your opinion, remember to support any statements you make with specific information and examples from the plays.

Evaluate and Set Goals

Evaluate

1. Which two of your accomplishments in this unit make you feel most proud? What skills did these accomplishments require?
2. Consider a challenge that you faced in each of the following areas. How did you meet the challenge?
   - reading
   - writing
   - public speaking
   - working with others
3. How would you assess your work in this unit, using the following scale? Give at least two reasons for your assessment.
   4 = outstanding 3 = good 2 = fair 1 = weak

Set Goals

1. With your teacher, decide what goal you would like to work toward in the next unit.
2. Write the goal down in your journal. Explore your reasons for setting that goal. Then list steps that you can take in order to reach it.
3. Schedule checkpoints to monitor your progress.

Build Your Portfolio

Select Choose two of the pieces of writing you did in this unit and include them in your portfolio. Consider including pieces that

- contain your best writing
- take a creative approach to the topic
- demonstrate logical thought
- provided you with the biggest challenge

Reflect Consider the following questions, then write a short response to include with each piece.

- What changes did you make between the first draft and the final version?
- What was your purpose in writing the piece?
- How is this piece an improvement over previous work?
- What would you do differently next time?

Reading on Your Own

You might also be interested in the following books.

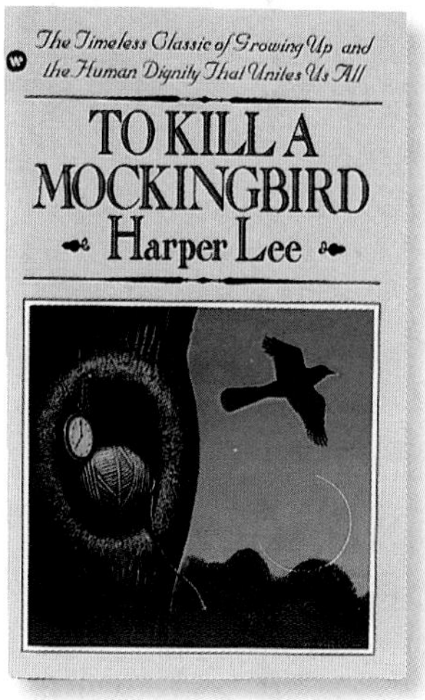

To Kill a Mockingbird
by Harper Lee One of the most beloved characters in modern American literature, Scout Finch is a bold, smart, and funny little girl growing up in a small Alabama town in the 1930s. When her father, a brilliant lawyer, agrees to defend an African American in court, many people react with anger. In the controversy that follows, Scout learns about justice as her father and his defendant embark on a life-or-death struggle against racial prejudice.

Our Town
by Thornton Wilder
In Grover's Corners, New Hampshire, at the turn of the nineteenth century, two neighbor children fall in love and grow into adulthood. Each of the play's acts takes place at a different point in the characters' lives, providing snapshots of life and death in a small town. Generations of readers have been moved by this Pulitzer Prize–winning play, which includes one of the most famous last acts in American theater.

Plays of America from American Folklore for Young Actors
by L. E. McCullough The ten plays in this collection draw on subjects ranging from Native American myths to traditional European, African, and Asian stories and include pioneer-era heroes as well as recent cultural figures such as Elvis Presley. Each play includes historical notes and tips on staging.

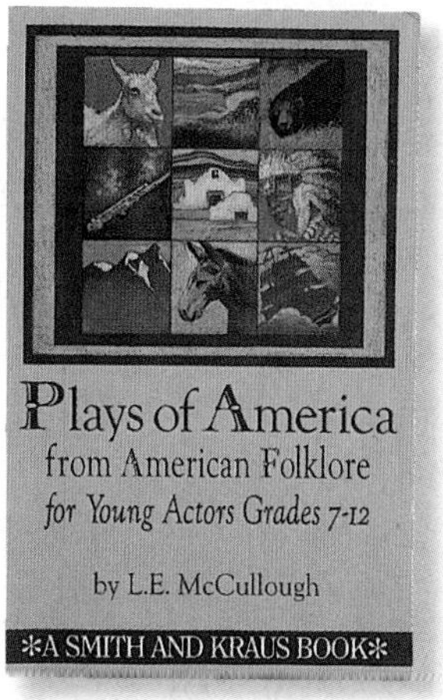

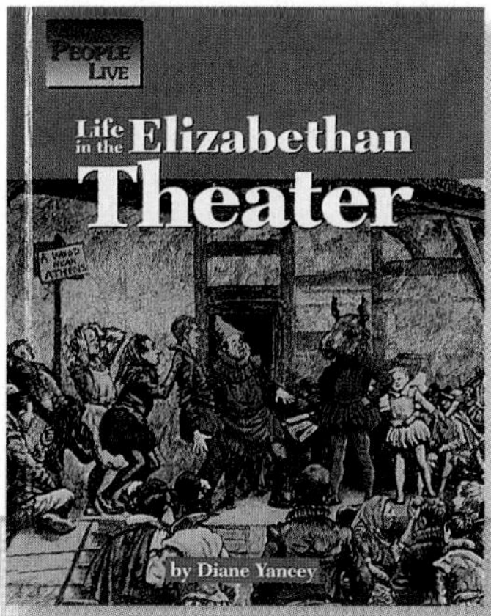

Life in the Elizabethan Theater
by Diane Yancey Actors have not always been glamorous stars and respected professionals. In fact, in the past they were considered little more than vagabonds. It wasn't until Shakespeare's time that their lowly status began to change, and they gained admittance to Queen Elizabeth's court. This book provides fascinating details of what life was like for those involved with the English theater during the sixteenth and seventeenth centuries.

Standardized Test Practice

Read the following passage. Then read each question on page 801. Decide which is the best answer to each question. Mark the letter for that answer on your paper.

What Does Roberta Learn About Herself?

Roberta took a huge breath and began to speak. "The quality of mercy is not strained," she said. "It droppeth as the gentle rain from heaven upon those beneath. It is twice blessed. It blesseth him that gives and him that takes . . ."

On the stage, the rest of the cast stood silently. They were listening as they had never listened before. Roberta had never really perfected this speech in rehearsal. But now, on opening night, with the theater filled to capacity with an eager audience, the words seemed to flow effortlessly from her. Her voice hummed with a power she had never before experienced.

Yikes, she thought in a fleeting moment. *What am I doing in front of all these people?*

Roberta had never acted a day in her life before this show. In fact, she hated being in front of other people. Her classmates teased her that she was the shyest girl at Wichita High School. Roberta had never thought she was good enough at anything to attract much attention. She stayed mostly to herself, making few friends. She did her homework well and had excellent grades, but she always thought that something was missing.

When the Drama Club announced its auditions for Shakespeare's *The Merchant of Venice*, everyone wondered who would play Portia, the strong-willed character who is smart enough to dupe an entire courtroom into believing that she is a master lawyer. It was a famous role, one of Shakespeare's best, and it would certainly require the talents of an excellent actress.

Roberta remembered the evening she looked up from her textbook to see her mother standing in the doorway to her room. "When did you say your audition appointment for the play was?" her mother asked.

Roberta frowned. "I didn't. What audition appointment?"

Her mother smiled. "The one you should make so you can win that role. I can't think of anyone else better suited to play it. Remember all the plays you used to act out for us?"

Roberta blushed and looked down at her book. "I'm not interested."

Her mother wouldn't let the matter drop. "Oh, I think you are. I think you know you can do it. You're just a little scared. Everyone gets scared. The trick is to look past the fear to find the love of what you're doing underneath."

Roberta looked up to protest, but her mother had gone.

So she had made the appointment with the head of the Drama Club. She had read the play and found herself excited by the idea of speaking such rich words, electric with poetry and meaning. In secret she practiced Portia's part, memorizing the lines by repeating them over and over again until they stuck. It wasn't hard; she loved every minute of it. Every time she spoke the words again, she found a new interpretation of what she was saying, as if Shakespeare had written Portia on many levels, some of them for Roberta alone.

The audition had been nerve-racking with all those people watching. Whenever she felt her fear begin to overwhelm her, she thought about the words the Bard had written and the fear disappeared. She performed two of Portia's famous speeches for the auditors. When she had finished, she stood alone before them, blushing as they stared silently at her. The head of the Drama Club finally cleared his throat and told her the part was hers.

The rest was history. Now she was Portia, a powerful actress in a classic play, capturing an audience's attention completely. The other actors stood dumbfounded, entranced by her voice and the explosive life she had suddenly found in the old lines of text. They were waiting for her to speak again. Roberta tossed them a sly smile before opening her mouth and continuing.

1 Which of the following is a FACT found in the passage?

- A Roberta was the most talented member of the drama club.
- B Roberta was too scared to play the role of Portia as well as another student might have.
- C Roberta's mother encouraged her to try out for the role of Portia in the play.
- D Without a talented actress like Roberta, the play would have been boring.

2 The word dupe in this passage means —

- F trick
- G persuade
- H force
- J ask

3 From the passage, you can tell that Roberta is most likely to —

- A become nervous and forget her lines
- B continue to pursue her newfound love of acting
- C make friends with the head of the Drama Club
- D cause the other actors to forget their lines

4 What helped Roberta to overcome her fear as she tried out for the part in the play?

- F her love of Shakespeare's writing
- G the elegant costumes she would be allowed to wear in the play
- H her desire to make friends with the members of the Drama Club
- J encouragement from her mother

5 Which of the following best summarizes this passage?

- A Roberta decides that being involved with the Drama Club is more important than earning excellent grades.
- B The Drama Club is saved at the last minute when Roberta agrees to play the role of Portia.
- C Roberta overcomes her fear of public speaking and finds a new love for drama.
- D Roberta's mother urges her to join the Drama Club in order to make friends.

6 In this passage the word dumbfounded means —

- F satisfied
- G angered
- H disappointed
- J amazed

STOP

The Return of Ulysses, 1976. Romare Bearden. Serigraph, 18½ x 22½ in. National Museum of American Art, Washington, DC.

UNIT FIVE

Epic

*"It is good to have
an end to journey toward;
but it is the journey that matters
in the end."*

—Ursula K. LeGuin

Theme 11

Journeys

pages 807–897

Literature FOCUS

Homer and the Epic

The banquet is over and the fire has collapsed to a bed of embers. Amid bursts of laughter and boisterous conversation, serving maids clear the remains of bread and meat from the long wooden table. A dog prowls among the seats in search of scraps, and a bird drops from the rafters to snatch a crust on the floor.

From his place at the head of the table, the lord of the hall signals to a man holding a stringed instrument and sitting apart from the others. Taking his cue, the musician stands up and plucks a few notes close to his ear while the guests shift their attention and slowly cease their talk. Then he begins to sing. Chanting rhythmically, occasionally touching the strings of his lyre, he sings of gods, heroes, and monsters; of love, war, travel, death, and homecoming. A stillness settles upon the hall; even the dog, now motionless on the hearth, falls under the spell. The singer of tales is working his magic.

Since the earliest forms of civilization, people have been curious about the past. Who made us? we wonder. How did we get here? Who were the heroes of the old days? What can we learn from our ancestors? Today we reach for a history book, switch on the TV, or summon instant information to the computer screen. But electronic technology—and even books—have been available only in the relatively recent past. Throughout most of human history—for the thousands of years before the invention of writing—people stored knowledge in their minds and passed information down to future generations orally, relating it over and over again.

Not everyone, of course, was equally talented at remembering and repeating the tales of long ago. But in every society there were individuals with a gift for storytelling. In ancient Greece, these artists composed poems and chanted them to a musical accompaniment. In this way, classic Greek tales, told as poetry, were kept alive and constantly re-created, until some were recorded in writing. Of the few poets from ancient Greece whose names we still know today, one of the greatest was a man known simply as Homer.

Homer and His Times

There are lingering uncertainties about who Homer was and what part of Greece he was from. What we do know for certain is that his works include two of the earliest surviving epic poems: the *Iliad* and the *Odyssey*.

A book illustration depicts Homer reciting one of his epic poems.

Hercules fighting Cerberus, the monstrous three-headed dog that guards the entrance to Hades. 530–525 B.C. Terra-cotta. Louvre Museum, Paris.

Although the precise dates are uncertain, most experts believe that Homer composed and recited his poems before the eighth century B.C.: that is, over 2,700 years ago, before the year 700 B.C. This was the period when speakers of Greek were developing an alphabet and learning the benefits of recording things on a kind of paper called papyrus. It was a time when Greece was emerging from an age of illiteracy and political confusion. Yet, in those days, people were still accustomed to hearing, rather than reading, their literature.

Subjects and Sources

Homer's poetic tales describe famous people and events from history as well as from legends, myths, and folktales—characters and events that people had been describing for centuries. What Homer added to these portraits, facts, and fictions included his insights into human experience, his imaginative plots, and his expert storytelling style.

Homer's audience was fascinated by tales of the Mycenaean era of 500 years earlier: it seemed like a golden age. Through the mists of time, everything back then seemed bigger or greater. People said the huge stones of ruined Mycenaean walls had been toppled by a race of giants, known as the Cyclopes. People thought palaces had been grander and cities larger in those days; that men had been braver, women more alluring, and monsters more terrifying. Those were the days, they thought, when people struggled against impossible odds with extraordinary—even superhuman—courage, brains, and strength.

The tales of Homer and his fellow poets suggest that they were as fascinated by Mycenaean heroes as their audiences were. Sometimes their heroes triumphed; sometimes they came crashing magnificently down. But whether a hero won or lost, the tale as a whole uplifted the human spirit. Hearing about the lives of heroes made audiences feel inspired.

Homer's repertoire probably included hundreds of tales by the time he was a mature artist. Audiences would call for certain ones—the "action-adventure" stories of the day—again and again: the legends of Theseus and of Jason, the twelve labors of Hercules, and the many love affairs of Zeus. But Homer's audiences weren't, like modern ones, accustomed to action and adventure stories on television. They believed the stories were true.

Homer's Compositions

How did Homer compose his poems? In some ways, he was like a jazz musician who starts with a well-known tune and plays different variations of it every time he performs. Just as a musician plays to a steady rhythm, so Homer had a steady rhythm in his words. The Greek singers recited their poems so that long syllables and short syllables alternated in a regular pattern.

Composing poetry in front of an audience without hesitating or "drawing a blank" may sound like an impossible task, but the fact that

Homer performed to a rhythm simplified the job. It meant that certain phrases worked better than others because they would fit rhythmically into a line of poetry. So Homer used them again and again. When describing people or things, he often used verbal "formulas." For example, he repeatedly refers to the goddess Athena as "gray-eyed Athena," and mentions Dawn's "fingertips of rose."

Homer would also recycle longer passages of description. These passages often concerned routine actions, such as a character's way of entering a room, putting on his armor, going to bed, or saying good-bye to his host.

His use of repetition helped both Homer and his audience. The poet did not have to memorize or make up every word. Most of his story was a little different each time it was told, but the repeated phrases remained like handles for the poet to grip. Homer's audience looked forward to these repetitions, as listeners look forward to the repeated chorus of a song.

Epic Poetry

Homer's most famous compositions, the *Iliad* and the *Odyssey*, have been read for centuries as **epic poems.** Since Homer's day, epic poetry has been considered a genre, or type of literature, just as nonfiction, fiction, and drama are genres.

The epic poem has the following main characteristics:

- It is a long narrative poem.
- The speaker is a narrator, telling a story.
- The theme or subject of the tale is important.
- The setting is huge. It may be a sea, a region, the world, or a universe.
- There is a main character, who is, or is capable of being, a hero.
- The action includes extraordinary or superhuman deeds. Typically, the epic hero has a goal and has embarked upon a long journey. In this journey, he struggles with natural and supernatural obstacles and antagonists—gods, monsters, and other humans—which test his bravery, wits, and battle skills.
- Gods or supernatural beings take a part, or an interest, in the action.
- The purpose of an epic poem is not only to entertain, but to teach and inspire the listener or reader with examples of how people can strive and succeed against great odds.

Epic Narration

An epic poem is narrated in predictable ways:

- In an invocation, the poet-narrator starts the poem by stating the tale's subject and asking for poetic inspiration from a guiding spirit.
- The narrator begins telling the tale in the "middle of things," describing what is happening after certain important events have already occurred.
- The narrative includes speeches by principal characters—including gods and antagonists of the epic hero—which reveal their personalities.
- The narrative's tone and style are formal rather than conversational.
- The use of figurative language makes the narrative vivid and exciting for listeners and readers.

The epic you are about to read, the *Odyssey*, is a celebration of the human spirit and of ordinary life. It is for this timeless appeal to our common humanity that the *Odyssey* is still read and enjoyed nearly three thousand years after its creation.

ACTIVITY

As you read the *Odyssey,* identify the elements of epic poetry and epic narration listed on this page.

Theme 11 Journeys

Is there a place you dream of traveling to? What wonderful things do you hope to find there? What obstacles do you expect to encounter along the way? In this theme, you'll meet a man who journeys through lands and seas of mythical proportions to get to that most elusive destination of all—home. You'll also meet a woman who represents another side of travel—learning how to plan and wait.

THEME PROJECTS

Performing

This Is Your Life What if Odysseus was invited to be the special guest on a TV show that focused on the guest's past life?

1. With a group, choose which characters from Odysseus's past you want to reintroduce to him.
2. Think about how Odysseus might react to surprise visits from the characters you have chosen. Then decide who will play those characters, who will play Odysseus, and who will play the show's host.
3. Stage the TV show. Have the host introduce each character by telling what role he or she played in Odysseus's life. Then let the characters talk with Odysseus, sharing opinions about what happened.

Internet Connection

Ancient References References to the *Odyssey* appear widely in today's culture. In what ways do these modern references connect to the ancient poem?

1. Search the Internet for businesses or other ventures that use the word *Odyssey* in their names or titles.
2. Choose three or four organizations whose goals or services relate to Homer's poem.
3. Design a brochure for the organizations you've chosen. Use quotations from the *Odyssey* to highlight the connections between each organization and the poem.

Land of the Odyssey, 1901.
Emilie Mediz-Pelikian. Oil on canvas, 61¼ x 72¼ in. Private collection.

MEDIA connection

Magazine Article

Can you imagine anyone setting out on an epic adventure these days? Read about one man who sailed as far as anyone can sail.

Bill Pinkney's Commitment to Sailing

***New Choices*, May 1994**

When Bill Pinkney sailed into Boston Harbor after a 27,000-mile solo journey around the earth, thousands of students were waiting to greet him. His first words were for those children: "The whole idea of this trip was to show you one thing. No matter who you are, or where you come from, or what anybody tells you, you and your dream are important—*and doable*."

The kids cheered him on, just as they had for the past two years. As Pinkney had navigated the world's five southernmost capes on the 47-foot *Commitment*, he'd sent back radio messages, "video postcards," and math and science problems to classrooms in Boston and Chicago.

Pinkney says he "wanted a great adventure" ever since the 7th grade, when he read an inspirational book about a boy who went to sea alone.

"But until I was 50, I didn't realize that great adventures don't just happen," he says. "You have to *make* them happen.

"The sea doesn't care what your economic status is, your religion, your nationality, your sex," Pinkney says. "It doesn't care what you think. It cares about one thing: 'I am the sea. If you come out here, you better be prepared to deal with me.'" For him, preparation meant spending several years procuring corporate sponsorship and private donations for the boat, navigational equipment and supplies.

Once under sail, he experienced countless highs and lows from Boston to Bermuda to Brazil and onward.

Storms along the way bashed the boat for days at a time. It was especially treacherous on the final leg of his journey around Cape Horn. As he drew near the tip of South America, he was in danger of being blown into the surrounding islands. His navigational electronics had gone out. The sails were down because winds were blowing 55 to 60 miles an hour, and the seas were 30 feet tall.

After spending 48 hours at the helm, he finally rounded Cape Horn. All smiles, he recorded some hilarious video footage, playing triumphant Olympic music, blowing party favors and popping a cork to toast his survival. "It's dumb," he said to the camera, "but you only do it once in your lifetime!"

Analyzing Media

1. What seems to be the most important aspect of sailing around the world for Bill Pinkney?
2. Describe an adventure you'd like to undertake.

Before You Read

from the *Odyssey, Part 1*

Reading Focus

Have you—or has someone you know—ever faced a challenge in sports, in school, or in your personal life that seemed nearly impossible to meet?

Quickwrite Describe how you or your acquaintance met this challenge. Was the outcome successful?

Setting a Purpose Read to learn about the extraordinary challenges faced by Odysseus, a hero of epic proportions.

Building Background

The Time and Place

The *Odyssey* describes the wanderings of the Greek general Odysseus on his return from the city of Troy in what is now northwest Turkey to his home island of Ithaca (ith′ ə kə), off the west coast of Greece. The events take place shortly before the year 1200 B.C.

Did You Know?

The events in another one of Homer's epic poems, the *Iliad,* take place during the Trojan War, which was well known to Homer's audience. This great siege, which the poet claimed lasted ten years, ended with the destruction of the city of Troy by a huge Greek army. The mastermind behind the army's success was a Greek general known for his bravery, but even more for his cunning: Odysseus, hero of the *Odyssey.* The *Odyssey* is about Odysseus's trip home after the war.

Vocabulary Preview

plunder (plun′ dər) *v.* to take (property) by force, especially in warfare; p. 813

valor (val′ ər) *n.* great courage, especially in battle; p. 813

formidable (fôr′ mi də bəl) *adj.* causing fear, dread, awe, or admiration as a result of size, strength, power, or some other impressive quality; p. 815

guile (gīl) *n.* slyness; craftiness; skillful deception; p. 815

ponderous (pon′ dər əs) *adj.* having great weight or bulk; heavy; p. 820

profusion (prə fū′ zhən) *n.* plentiful amount; abundance; p. 821

Meet Homer

Legend has it that Homer was a blind man who lived on the rocky Greek island of Chios, but like all legends, it is hard to prove. No one has found any convincing evidence to indicate who Homer was, where he lived, or whether he was actually blind. Most scholars agree, however, that he was active before the year 700 B.C. Although he was one of the greatest poets of the ancient world, he composed his works orally and recited or sang them aloud. Like most people in his day, Homer could probably neither read nor write.

Homer lived in Greece or Asia Minor (modern Turkey) probably before the eighth century B.C. No one knows when the Odyssey *was first written down, but it may have been as many as 200 years after Homer's death.*

from the Odyssey

Homer

Translated by Robert Fitzgerald

PRINCIPAL CHARACTERS IN THE *ODYSSEY*

HUMANS

AGAMEMNON (ag′ ə mem′ non)**:** king and leader of Greek forces during the Trojan war

ALCINOUS (al sin′ ō əs)**:** king of the Phaeacians and person to whom Odysseus relates his story

AMPHINOMUS (am fin′ ə məs)**:** one of Penelope's suitors

ANTINOUS (an tin′ ō əs)**:** rudest of Penelope's suitors

EUMAEUS (yoo mē′ əs)**:** Odysseus's loyal swineherd

EURYCLEIA (yoo′ ri klē′ ə)**:** Odysseus's faithful old nurse

EURYLOCHUS (yoo ril′ ə kəs)**:** one of Odysseus's crew

EURYMACHUS (yoo rim′ ə kəs)**:** one of Penelope's suitors

EURYNOME (yoo rin′ ə mē)**:** Penelope's housekeeper

LAERTES (lā ur′ tēz)**:** Odysseus's father

MARON (mār′ on)**:** priest of Apollo who gives Odysseus a gift of powerful wine

ODYSSEUS (ō dis′ ē əs)**:** king of Ithaca and hero of the Trojan war

PENELOPE (pə nel′ ə pē)**:** Odysseus's wife

PERIMEDES (per′ i mē′ dēz)**:** one of Odysseus's crew

TELEMACHUS (tə lem′ ə kəs)**:** Odysseus and Penelope's son

TIRESIAS (tī rē′ sē əs)**:** blind prophet from the underworld

GODS AND IMMORTALS

APOLLO (ə pol′ ō)**:** god of sunlight, music, poetry, medicine, law, and the tending of flocks and herds

ATHENA (ə thē′ nə)**:** daughter of Zeus and goddess of wisdom, skills, and warfare who helps her chosen heroes

CALYPSO (kə lip′ sō)**:** immortal sea nymph who held Odysseus captive for many years

CHARYBDIS (kə rib′ dis)**:** dangerous whirlpool personified as a female monster

CIRCE (sur′ sē)**:** enchantress who lives on the island of Aeaea

CYCLOPES (sī′ klō pēz)**:** race of one-eyed giants; an individual member of the race is a **CYCLOPS** (sī′ klops)

HELIOS (hē′ lē os′)**:** god of the sun; another name for Apollo

LOTUS (lō′ təs) **EATERS:** inhabitants of a land visited by Odysseus and his crew

POLYPHEMUS (pol′ i fē′ məs)**:** a Cyclops and son of Poseidon

POSEIDON (pə sīd′ ən)**:** god of the sea and earthquakes

SCYLLA (sil′ ə)**:** six-headed female sea monster

SIRENS (sī′ rənz)**:** sea nymphs who sing songs that lure men to their death

ZEUS (zo͞os)**:** king of the gods

Part 1

An Invocation

Poets in Homer's day believed that the gods inspired their storytelling and singing. According to custom, Homer begins his performance with an invocation, calling upon the Muse, the goddess of epic poetry, for help and inspiration. The invocation serves a second purpose: to capture the audience's attention with highlights of heroic adventures that the poet will later describe in detail.

Sing in me, Muse, and through me tell the story
of that man skilled in all ways of contending,°
the wanderer, harried° for years on end,
after he plundered the stronghold
on the proud height of Troy.

He saw the townlands
and learned the minds of many distant men,
and weathered° many bitter nights and days
in his deep heart at sea, while he fought only
to save his life, to bring his shipmates home.
But not by will nor valor could he save them,
for their own recklessness destroyed them all—
children and fools, they killed and feasted on
the cattle of Lord Helios,° the Sun,
and he who moves all day through heaven
took from their eyes the dawn of their return.

Of these adventures, Muse, daughter of Zeus,°
tell us in our time, lift the great song again.
Begin when all the rest who left behind them
headlong death in battle or at sea
had long ago returned, while he alone still hungered
for home and wife. Her ladyship Calypso°
clung to him in her sea-hollowed caves—
a nymph,° immortal° and most beautiful,
who craved him for her own.

And when long years and seasons

Vocabulary

plunder (plun′ dər) *v.* to take (property) by force, especially in warfare
valor (val′ ər) *n.* great courage, especially in battle

2 **contending:** fighting or dealing with difficulty.

3 **harried:** constantly tormented or troubled.

8 **weathered:** got through safely; survived.

14 **Helios** (hē′ lē os′): the god of the sun.

17 **Zeus** (zo͞os): The most powerful of the gods, Zeus is the father of countless major and minor gods.

22 **Calypso** (kə lip′ sō)

24 **nymph:** a young, beautiful spirit, or minor goddess, representing the divine power of a place or of something in nature, such as a tree, cave, or body of water. **immortal:** living forever; eternal.

wheeling brought around that point of time
ordained° for him to make his passage homeward,
trials and dangers, even so, attended him
even in Ithaca, near those he loved.
Yet all the gods had pitied Lord Odysseus,
all but Poseidon, raging cold and rough°
against the brave king° till he came ashore
at last on his own land.

28 **ordained:** set or determined by an authority—in this case, fate or the gods.

31–33 **Odysseus** (ō dis′ ē əs) . . . **the brave king:** Odysseus is the king of Ithaca.

32 **Poseidon** (pə sīd′ ən), **raging cold and rough:** Poseidon, brother of Zeus, governs the oceans as well as earthquakes. In the next section, you will find clues to his anger at Odysseus.

New Coasts and Poseidon's Son

The gods are worried. Nearly ten years have passed since the end of the war against Troy, but one of the greatest Greek generals has not yet returned home. Odysseus has encountered a series of disasters on his voyage and is now the prisoner of a nymph named Calypso. He has also angered Poseidon, who has prevented him from returning to his wife, Penelope (pə nel′ ə pē)*, and his son, Telemachus* (tə lem′ ə kəs)*, on the island of Ithaca. But Poseidon is visiting Africa, and the other gods agree to act behind his back.*

The poet now tells of Odysseus, who is miserable after seven years on his island prison. Calypso loves her handsome captive and will not let him go, but she is forced to reconsider her position when she receives a strongly worded order from Mount Olympus. Giving in, Calypso helps Odysseus make a raft, and he thankfully departs. But he does not have smooth sailing. Poseidon, returning from Africa, spots his old enemy at sea and shipwrecks him in an instant with a fierce storm.

Zeus's daughter Athena intervenes. She casts Odysseus, naked and near death, ashore on the island of Phaeacia (fē ā′ shə)*. There a beautiful princess discovers him and takes him home to the palace of her father, King Alcinous* (al sin′ ō əs)*. The Phaeacians treat Odysseus as a noble guest and urge him to reveal his identity. At last he relents and uncertainly begins to tell his gripping story.*

"What shall I
say first? What shall I keep until the end?
The gods have tried° me in a thousand ways.
But first my name: let that be known to you,
and if I pull away from pitiless death,
friendship will bind us, though my land lies far.

I am Laertes'° son, Odysseus.
Men hold° me

3 **tried:** tested.

7 **Laertes** (lā ur′ tēz)

8 **hold:** regard; consider.

formidable for guile in peace and war:
this fame has gone abroad to the sky's rim.
My home is on the peaked sea-mark of Ithaca
under Mount Neion's° wind-blown robe of leaves,
in sight of other islands—Dulichium,°
Same,° wooded Zacynthus°—Ithaca
being most lofty in that coastal sea,
and northwest, while the rest lie east and south.
A rocky isle, but good for a boy's training;
I shall not see on earth a place more dear,
though I have been detained long by Calypso,
loveliest among goddesses, who held me
in her smooth caves, to be her heart's delight,
as Circe of Aeaea, the enchantress,°
desired me, and detained me in her hall.
But in my heart I never gave consent.
Where shall a man find sweetness to surpass
his own home and his parents? In far lands
he shall not, though he find a house of gold.

What of my sailing, then, from Troy?
What of those years
of rough adventure, weathered under Zeus?"°

12 **Neion** (nē′ on)

13 **Dulichium** (do͞o lik′ ē əm)

14 **Same** (sā′ mē). **Zacynthus** (zə sin′ thəs)

22 **Circe** (sur′ sē) . . . **the enchantress:** Circe is a goddess capable of enchanting, or working magic upon, men. **Aeaea** (ē ē′ ə) is her island.

30 **weathered under Zeus:** Odysseus uses words craftily. Here, he appears to give respectful credit to Zeus for getting him safely through danger; but he also is making a pun on the word *weathered.* Zeus governs the heavens and the weather, and is well known for sending people storms, lightning, and thunder when he is displeased.

Odysseus relates his first adventure. He and his fleet of twelve ships attacked and plundered the coastal settlement of the Cicones (si kō′ nēz). *The raid was a success, but the overconfident men became drunk and mutinous (unresponsive to Odysseus's orders to retreat). The Cicones's army surprised Odysseus and his men at dawn, and drove them back to sea with heavy losses.*

"I might have made it safely home, that time,
but as I came round Malea° the current
took me out to sea, and from the north
a fresh gale drove me on, past Cythera.°
Nine days I drifted on the teeming sea
before dangerous high winds. Upon the tenth
we came to the coastline of the Lotus Eaters,
who live upon that flower. We landed there

32 **Malea** (mə lē′ ə)

34 **Cythera** (sith′ ə rə)

Vocabulary

formidable (fôr′ mi də bəl) *adj.* causing fear, dread, awe, or admiration as a result of size, strength, power, or some other impressive quality

guile (gīl) *n.* slyness; craftiness; skillful deception

An Egyptian Lotus Plant, 1834.
Unattributed woodcut.
Private collection.

Viewing the art: What connection can you make between the appearance of the lotus plant and its effect on Odysseus's men?

to take on water. All ships' companies
mustered° alongside for the mid-day meal.
Then I sent out two picked men and a runner
to learn what race of men that land sustained.°
They fell in, soon enough, with Lotus Eaters,
who showed no will to do us harm, only
offering the sweet Lotus to our friends—
but those who ate this honeyed plant, the Lotus,
never cared to report, nor to return:
they longed to stay forever, browsing on
that native bloom, forgetful of their homeland.
I drove them, all three wailing, to the ships,
tied them down under their rowing benches,
and called the rest: 'All hands aboard;
come, clear the beach and no one taste
the Lotus, or you lose your hope of home.'
Filing in to their places by the rowlocks
my oarsmen dipped their long oars in the surf,
and we moved out again on our sea faring.

In the next land we found were Cyclopes,°
giants, louts,° without a law to bless them.
In ignorance leaving the fruitage of the earth in mystery
to the immortal gods, they neither plow
nor sow by hand, nor till the ground, though grain—
wild wheat and barley—grows untended, and
wine-grapes, in clusters, ripen in heaven's rain.
Cyclopes have no muster and no meeting,

40 **mustered:** gathered together.

42 **sustained:** kept alive; supported.

58 **Cyclopes** (sī klō′ pēz): a race of one-eyed giants.

59 **louts:** stupid beings.

no consultation or old tribal ways,
but each one dwells in his own mountain cave
dealing out rough justice to wife and child,
indifferent to what the others do."

Just offshore from the land of the Cyclopes is a deserted island with a fine natural harbor. Odysseus and his men spend two comfortable nights there. On the second day, overcome by curiosity, Odysseus sails with one ship and a crew to the mainland. He wants to see just what sort of creatures these Cyclopes are.

"As we rowed on, and nearer to the mainland,
at one end of the bay, we saw a cavern
yawning above the water, screened with laurel,°
and many rams and goats about the place
inside a sheepfold°—made from slabs of stone
earthfast between tall trunks of pine and rugged
towering oak trees.
A prodigious° man
slept in this cave alone, and took his flocks
to graze afield—remote from all companions,
knowing none but savage ways, a brute
so huge, he seemed no man at all of those
who eat good wheaten bread; but he seemed rather
a shaggy mountain reared in solitude.
We beached there, and I told the crew
to stand by and keep watch over the ship;
as for myself I took my twelve best fighters
and went ahead. I had a goatskin full
of that sweet liquor that Euanthes' son,
Maron, had given me. He kept Apollo's
holy grove at Ismarus;° for kindness
we showed him there, and showed his wife and child,
he gave me seven shining golden talents°
perfectly formed, a solid silver winebowl,
and then this liquor—twelve two-handled jars
of brandy, pure and fiery. Not a slave
in Maron's household knew this drink; only
he, his wife and the storeroom mistress knew;
and they would put one cupful—ruby-colored,
honey-smooth—in twenty more of water,
but still the sweet scent hovered like a fume
over the winebowl. No man turned away
when cups of this came round.

72 screened with laurel: partly hidden behind laurel trees.

74 sheepfold: an enclosure, or pen, for holding sheep.

77 prodigious: huge; enormous.

88–90 Euanthes' (yoo an′ thēz) **son, . . . Ismarus** (iz mār′ əs): In ancient Greece, worshippers of certain gods built shrines to them, surrounded by woods, or "groves," that were considered sacred sanctuaries. Priests oversaw the planting and tending of the groves. **Maron** (mār′ on) is a priest of **Apollo** (ə pol′ ō), an important god associated with music, medicine, law, and the tending of flocks and herds.

92 talents: bars of gold used as money in ancient Greece.

A wineskin full
I brought along, and victuals° in a bag,
for in my bones I knew some towering brute
would be upon us soon—all outward power,
a wild man, ignorant of civility.°

We climbed, then, briskly to the cave. But Cyclops°
had gone afield, to pasture his fat sheep,
so we looked round at everything inside:
a drying rack that sagged with cheeses, pens
crowded with lambs and kids, each in its class:
firstlings apart from middlings, and the 'dewdrops,'
or newborn lambkins, penned apart from both.°
And vessels full of whey° were brimming there—
bowls of earthenware and pails for milking.
My men came pressing round me, pleading:

'Why not
take these cheeses, get them stowed, come back,
throw open all the pens, and make a run for it?
We'll drive the kids and lambs aboard. We say
put out again on good salt water!'

Ah,
how sound° that was! Yet I refused. I wished
to see the caveman, what he had to offer—
no pretty sight, it turned out, for my friends.
We lit a fire, burnt an offering,°
and took some cheese to eat; then sat in silence
around the embers, waiting. When he came
he had a load of dry boughs on his shoulder
to stoke his fire at suppertime. He dumped it
with a great crash into that hollow cave,
and we all scattered fast to the far wall.
Then over the broad cavern floor he ushered
the ewes he meant to milk. He left his rams
and he-goats in the yard outside, and swung
high overhead a slab of solid rock
to close the cave. Two dozen four-wheeled wagons,
with heaving wagon teams, could not have stirred
the tonnage of that rock from where he wedged it
over the doorsill. Next he took his seat
and milked his bleating ewes. A practiced job

104 victuals (vit′ əls): food

107 civility: polite and courteous behavior.

108 Cyclops (sī′ klops): Note the different spelling and pronunciation of this reference to a single one-eyed giant.

111–114 pens . . . both: The lambs are grouped by age.

115 whey: the watery part of milk that separates from the curd, or solid part, during the cheese-making process.

124 sound: sensible.

127 burnt an offering: The men burned some food as a gift to the gods in the hope of winning their support.

he made of it, giving each ewe her suckling;
thickened his milk, then, into curds and whey,
sieved out the curds to drip in withy baskets,°
and poured the whey to stand in bowls
cooling until he drank it for his supper.
When all these chores were done, he poked the fire,
heaping on brushwood. In the glare he saw us.

144–145 thickened . . . baskets: The milk is curdled **(thickened)** by adding fig juice, and the whey is drained off through wicker **(withy)** baskets.

'Strangers,' he said, 'who are you? And where from?
What brings you here by sea ways—a fair traffic?
Or are you wandering rogues, who cast your lives
like dice, and ravage other folk by sea?'°

151–153 What brings . . . by sea: What brings you here from the sea—honest trade? Or are you wandering scoundrels who carelessly risk your lives and steal from others?

We felt a pressure on our hearts, in dread
of that deep rumble and that mighty man.
But all the same I spoke up in reply:

'We are from Troy, Achaeans,° blown off course
by shifting gales on the Great South Sea;
homeward bound, but taking routes and ways
uncommon; so the will of Zeus would have it.
We served under Agamemnon, son of Atreus°—
the whole world knows what city
he laid waste, what armies he destroyed.
It was our luck to come here; here we stand,
beholden for your help, or any gifts
you give—as custom is to honor strangers.
We would entreat you, great Sir, have a care
for the gods' courtesy; Zeus will avenge
the unoffending guest.'°

157 Achaeans (ə kē′ əns): Greeks.

161 Agamemnon (ag′ ə mem′ non), **son of Atreus** (ā′ trē əs): king of Argos, in southern Greece, who led the war against Troy.

167–169 We would . . . guest: Odysseus earnestly asks or begs **(entreat)** for the Cyclops's hospitality and warns him that Zeus punishes anyone who mistreats a harmless guest.

He answered this
from his brute chest, unmoved:

'You are a ninny,°
or else you come from the other end of nowhere,
telling me, mind the gods! We Cyclopes
care not a whistle for your thundering Zeus
or all the gods in bliss; we have more force by far.
I would not let you go for fear of Zeus—
you or your friends—unless I had a whim to.
Tell me, where was it, now, you left your ship—
around the point, or down the shore, I wonder?'

172 ninny: fool.

He thought he'd find out, but I saw through this,
and answered with a ready lie:

'My ship?
Poseidon Lord, who sets the earth a-tremble,
broke it up on the rocks at your land's end.
A wind from seaward served him, drove us there.
We are survivors, these good men and I.'

Neither reply nor pity came from him,
but in one stride he clutched at my companions
and caught two in his hands like squirming puppies
to beat their brains out, spattering the floor.
Then he dismembered them and made his meal,
gaping and crunching like a mountain lion—
everything: innards, flesh, and marrow bones.
We cried aloud, lifting our hands to Zeus,
powerless, looking on at this, appalled;°
but Cyclops went on filling up his belly
with manflesh and great gulps of whey,
then lay down like a mast among his sheep.
My heart beat high now at the chance of action,
and drawing the sharp sword from my hip I went
along his flank to stab him where the midriff
holds the liver. I had touched the spot
when sudden fear stayed me: if I killed him
we perished there as well, for we could never
move his ponderous doorway slab aside.
So we were left to groan and wait for morning.

When the young Dawn with fingertips of rose
lit up the world, the Cyclops built a fire
and milked his handsome ewes, all in due order,
putting the sucklings to the mothers. Then,
his chores being all dispatched,° he caught
another brace° of men to make his breakfast,
and whisked away his great door slab
to let his sheep go through—but he, behind,
reset the stone as one would cap a quiver.°
There was a din of whistling as the Cyclops
rounded his flock to higher ground, then stillness.

196 appalled: horrified; shocked; terrified.

212 dispatched: finished.

213 brace: pair.

216 cap a quiver: put the cap on a case for holding arrows.

Vocabulary

ponderous (pon′ dər əs) *adj.* having great weight or bulk; heavy

And now I pondered how to hurt him worst,
if but Athena° granted what I prayed for.
Here are the means I thought would serve my turn:

a club, or staff, lay there along the fold—
an olive tree, felled green and left to season
for Cyclops' hand. And it was like a mast
a lugger of twenty oars, broad in the beam—
a deep-sea-going craft—might carry:°
so long, so big around, it seemed. Now I
chopped out a six foot section of this pole
and set it down before my men, who scraped it;
and when they had it smooth, I hewed° again
to make a stake with pointed end. I held this
in the fire's heart and turned it, toughening it,
then hid it, well back in the cavern, under
one of the dung piles in profusion there.
Now came the time to toss for it: who ventured
along with me? whose hand could bear to thrust
and grind that spike in Cyclops' eye, when mild
sleep had mastered him? As luck would have it,
the men I would have chosen won the toss—
four strong men, and I made five as captain.

At evening came the shepherd with his flock,
his woolly flock. The rams as well, this time,
entered the cave: by some sheep-herding whim—
or a god's bidding—none were left outside.
He hefted his great boulder into place
and sat him down to milk the bleating ewes
in proper order, put the lambs to suck,
and swiftly ran through all his evening chores.
Then he caught two more men and feasted on them.
My moment was at hand, and I went forward
holding an ivy bowl of my dark drink,°
looking up, saying:

'Cyclops, try some wine.
Here's liquor to wash down your scraps of men.
Taste it, and see the kind of drink we carried

Vocabulary
profusion (prə fū′ zhən) *n.* plentiful amount; abundance

220 **Athena:** Odysseus prays for the support of Athena, his patron goddess who guides and protects him. Among other things, Athena is a warrior goddess who directly helps her chosen heroes.

221–226 **Here are . . . carry:** Odysseus spies the trunk of an olive tree, which the Cyclops cut down **(felled)** when the wood was green and left to dry **(season)** before carving it into a club or staff. Odysseus compares its size to that of a mast on a seafaring ship **(lugger)** that is wide in the middle **(broad in the beam).**

230 **hewed:** chopped or hacked.

251 **dark drink:** This is the liquor Odysseus described in lines 94–102.

under our planks. I meant it for an offering
if you would help us home. But you are mad,
unbearable, a bloody monster! After this,
will any other traveler come to see you?'

He seized and drained the bowl, and it went down
so fiery and smooth he called for more:

'Give me another, thank you kindly. Tell me,
how are you called? I'll make a gift will please you.
Even Cyclopes know the wine-grapes grow
out of grassland and loam in heaven's rain,
but here's a bit of nectar and ambrosia!'°

Three bowls I brought him, and he poured them down.
I saw the fuddle and flush° cover over him,
then I sang out in cordial tones:

'Cyclops,
you ask my honorable name? Remember
the gift you promised me, and I shall tell you.
My name is Nohbdy: mother, father, and friends,
everyone calls me Nohbdy.'

And he said:
'Nohbdy's my meat, then, after I eat his friends.
Others come first. There's a noble gift, now.'

Even as he spoke, he reeled and tumbled backward,
his great head lolling to one side; and sleep
took him like any creature. Drunk, hiccuping,
he dribbled streams of liquor and bits of men.

Now, by the gods, I drove my big hand spike
deep in the embers, charring it again,
and cheered my men along with battle talk
to keep their courage up: no quitting now.
The pike of olive,° green though it had been,
reddened and glowed as if about to catch.
I drew it from the coals and my four fellows
gave me a hand, lugging it near the Cyclops
as more than natural force nerved them; straight
forward they sprinted, lifted it, and rammed it
deep in his crater eye, and I leaned on it

266 nectar and ambrosia: the foods of the gods, causing immortality. The Cyclops suggests that any wine is a gift from heaven, but this one is like the gods' own drink.

268 fuddle and flush: the confused mental state and reddish complexion caused by drinking alcohol.

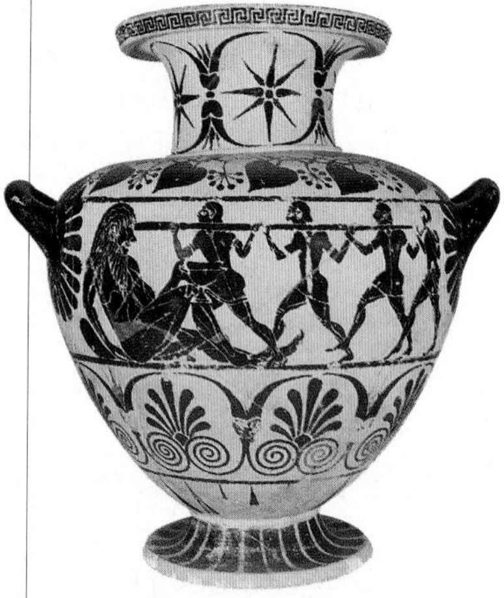

The Blinding of Polyphemus. Greek hydra. Museo Nazionale di Villa Giulia, Rome.

286 pike of olive: the sharpened stake made from the olive tree.

turning it as a shipwright turns a drill
in planking, having men below to swing
the two-handled strap that spins it in the groove.
So with our brand° we bored that great eye socket
while blood ran out around the red hot bar.
Eyelid and lash were seared; the pierced ball
hissed broiling, and the roots popped.

296 brand: the piece of burning hot wood.

In a smithy
one sees a white-hot axehead or an adze°
plunged and wrung in a cold tub, screeching steam—
the way they make soft iron hale° and hard—:
just so that eyeball hissed around the spike.
The Cyclops bellowed and the rock roared round him,
and we fell back in fear. Clawing his face
he tugged the bloody spike out of his eye,
threw it away, and his wild hands went groping;
then he set up a howl for Cyclopes
who lived in caves on windy peaks nearby.
Some heard him; and they came by divers° ways
to clump around outside and call:

301 adze: an axlike tool with a curved blade.

303 hale: strong.

311 divers: several different; various.

'What ails you,
Polyphemus?° Why do you cry so sore
in the starry night? You will not let us sleep.
Sure no man's driving off your flock? No man
has tricked you, ruined you?'

314 Polyphemus (pol′ i fē′ məs): the blinded Cyclops's name.

Out of the cave
the mammoth Polyphemus roared in answer:

'Nohbdy, Nohbdy's tricked me, Nohbdy's ruined me!'

To this rough shout they made a sage° reply:

321 sage: wise.

'Ah well, if nobody has played you foul
there in your lonely bed, we are no use in pain
given by great Zeus. Let it be your father,
Poseidon Lord, to whom you pray.'

So saying
they trailed away. And I was filled with laughter
to see how like a charm the name deceived them.
Now Cyclops, wheezing as the pain came on him,

fumbled to wrench away the great doorstone
and squatted in the breach° with arms thrown wide
for any silly beast or man who bolted°—
hoping somehow I might be such a fool.
But I kept thinking how to win the game:
death sat there huge; how could we slip away?
I drew on all my wits, and ran through tactics,
reasoning as a man will for dear life,
until a trick came—and it pleased me well.
The Cyclops' rams were handsome, fat, with heavy
fleeces, a dark violet.
Three abreast
I tied them silently together, twining
cords of willow from the ogre's° bed;
then slung a man under each middle one
to ride there safely, shielded left and right.
So three sheep could convey each man. I took
the woolliest ram, the choicest of the flock,
and hung myself under his kinky belly,
pulled up tight, with fingers twisted deep
in sheepskin ringlets for an iron grip.
So, breathing hard, we waited until morning.

When Dawn spread out her fingertips of rose
the rams began to stir, moving for pasture,
and peals of bleating echoed round the pens
where dams with udders full called for a milking.
Blinded, and sick with pain from his head wound,
the master stroked each ram, then let it pass,
but my men riding on the pectoral fleece°
the giant's blind hands blundering never found.
Last of them all my ram, the leader, came,
weighted by wool and me with my meditations.
The Cyclops patted him, and then he said:

'Sweet cousin ram, why lag behind the rest
in the night cave? You never linger so,
but graze before them all, and go afar
to crop sweet grass, and take your stately way
leading along the streams, until at evening
you run to be the first one in the fold.
Why, now, so far behind? Can you be grieving
over your Master's eye? That carrion° rogue
and his accurst companions burnt it out

331 **breach:** a gap or opening.

332 **bolted:** broke away.

343 **ogre:** monster; fearsome giant.

358 **pectoral fleece:** the wool on the rams' chests.

370 **carrion:** rotten, filthy.

Odysseus. Jacob Jordaens (1593–1678). Oil on canvas, 61 x 97 cm. Pushkin Museum, Moscow.

Viewing the painting: Imagine that you are the man beneath the ram on the left. What is going through your mind? What might the Cyclops be thinking and feeling in this scene?

when he had conquered all my wits with wine.
Nohbdy will not get out alive, I swear.
Oh, had you brain and voice to tell
where he may be now, dodging all my fury!
Bashed by this hand and bashed on this rock wall
his brains would strew the floor, and I should have
rest from the outrage Nohbdy worked upon me.'

He sent us into the open, then. Close by,
I dropped and rolled clear of the ram's belly,
going this way and that to untie the men.
With many glances back, we rounded up
his fat, stiff-legged sheep to take aboard,
and drove them down to where the good ship lay.
We saw, as we came near, our fellows' faces
shining; then we saw them turn to grief
tallying those who had not fled from death.
I hushed them, jerking head and eyebrows up,
and in a low voice told them: 'Load this herd;
move fast, and put the ship's head toward the breakers.'°
They all pitched in at loading, then embarked°
and struck their oars into the sea. Far out,
as far off shore as shouted words would carry,
I sent a few back to the adversary:

'O Cyclops! Would you feast on my companions?
Puny, am I, in a Caveman's hands?
How do you like the beating that we gave you,
you damned cannibal? Eater of guests
under your roof! Zeus and the gods have paid you!'°

390 put . . . breakers: turn the ship around, toward the open sea.

391 embarked: got on board.

395–399 O Cyclops! . . . you: In his boasting, Odysseus assumes that the gods have favored him. Why might there be danger in such boasts and assumptions?

The blind thing in his doubled fury broke
a hilltop in his hands and heaved it after us.
Ahead of our black prow it struck and sank
whelmed in a spuming geyser, a giant wave
that washed the ship stern foremost back to shore.
I got the longest boathook out and stood
fending us off, with furious nods to all
to put their backs into a racing stroke—
row, row, or perish. So the long oars bent
kicking the foam sternward, making head
until we drew away, and twice as far.°
Now when I cupped my hands I heard the crew
in low voices protesting:

'Godsake, Captain!
Why bait the beast again? Let him alone!'
'That tidal wave he made on the first throw
all but beached us.'

'All but stove us in!'

'Give him our bearing with your trumpeting,
he'll get the range and lob a boulder.'°

'Aye
He'll smash our timbers and our heads together!'

402–410 Ahead . . . twice as far: The sinking hilltop creates a wave at the ship's front end **(prow)** that washes the boat backwards **(stern foremost)** to the shore.

415–419 That tidal . . . boulder: The men complain, reasonably enough, that Polyphemus nearly smashed the ship **(All but stove us in)** and that Odysseus's shouting will give away their position **(bearing)**.

Polyphemus Attacking Sailors in Their Boat, 1855. Alexandre Gabriel Decamps. Oil on canvas, 98 x 145 cm. Musée des Beaux-Arts, Rouen, France.

Viewing the painting: How does this painting reinforce the sense of urgency conveyed by the description of Odysseus's escape?

I would not heed them in my glorying spirit,
but let my anger flare and yelled:

'Cyclops,
if ever mortal man inquire
how you were put to shame and blinded, tell him
Odysseus, raider of cities, took your eye:
Laertes' son, whose home's on Ithaca!'

At this he gave a mighty sob and rumbled:

'Now comes the weird° upon me, spoken of old.
A wizard, grand and wondrous, lived here—Telemus,°
a son of Eurymus;° great length of days
he had in wizardry among the Cyclopes,
and these things he foretold for time to come:
my great eye lost, and at Odysseus' hands.
Always I had in mind some giant, armed
in giant force, would come against me here.
But this, but you—small, pitiful and twiggy—
you put me down with wine, you blinded me.
Come back, Odysseus, and I'll treat you well,
praying the god of earthquake° to befriend you—
his son I am, for he by his avowal
fathered me, and, if he will, he may
heal me of this black wound—he and no other
of all the happy gods or mortal men.'

Few words I shouted in reply to him:

'If I could take your life I would and take
your time away, and hurl you down to hell!
The god of earthquake could not heal you there!'

At this he stretched his hands out in his darkness
toward the sky of stars, and prayed Poseidon:

'O hear me, lord, blue girdler of the islands,
if I am thine indeed, and thou art father:
grant that Odysseus, raider of cities, never
see his home: Laertes' son, I mean,
who kept his hall on Ithaca. Should destiny
intend that he shall see his roof again

430 **the weird:** the strange fate.

431 **Telemus** (tel′ ə məs)

432 **Eurymus** (yoo ri′ məs)

441 **god of earthquake:** Poseidon

among his family in his father land,
far be that day, and dark the years between.
Let him lose all companions, and return
under strange sail to bitter days at home.'°

In these words he prayed, and the god heard him.
Now he laid hands upon a bigger stone
and wheeled around, titanic for the cast,°
to let it fly in the black-prowed vessel's track.
But it fell short, just aft° the steering oar,
and whelming seas rose giant above the stone
to bear us onward toward the island.°

There
as we ran in we saw the squadron waiting,
the trim° ships drawn up side by side, and all
our troubled friends who waited, looking seaward.
We beached her, grinding keel in the soft sand,
and waded in, ourselves, on the sandy beach.
Then we unloaded all the Cyclops' flock
to make division, share and share alike,
only my fighters voted that my ram,
the prize of all, should go to me. I slew him
by the seaside and burnt his long thighbones
to Zeus beyond the stormcloud, Cronus'° son,
who rules the world. But Zeus disdained° my offering;
destruction for my ships he had in store
and death for those who sailed them, my companions.
Now all day long until the sun went down
we made our feast on mutton and sweet wine,
till after sunset in the gathering dark
we went to sleep above the wash of ripples.

When the young Dawn with fingertips of rose
touched the world, I roused the men, gave orders
to man the ships, cast off the mooring lines;
and filing in to sit beside the rowlocks
oarsmen in line dipped oars in the gray sea.
So we moved out, sad in the vast offing,°
having our precious lives, but not our friends."

452–461 O hear . . . home: In ancient cultures, curses were neither made nor taken lightly. Homer's audience would have believed in their power. In his curse upon Odysseus, Polyphemus begs Poseidon to make his enemy suffer, using every detail he knows about Odysseus to make sure the god's punishment will be directed toward the right person.

464 titanic for the cast: drawing upon his great size and strength in preparation for the throw.

466 aft: behind.

468 the island: the deserted island where the other eleven ships and their crews have remained while Odysseus and his handpicked men explored the Cyclops's mainland.

471 trim: in good condition and ready to sail.

480 Cronus (krō′ nəs): Heaven and Earth, the first gods, had been dethroned by their son Cronus, who was in turn overthrown by his son Zeus.

481 disdained: rejected.

493 vast offing: the visible expanse of open sea.

Responding to Literature

Personal Response

Which images from part 1 do you remember best? Jot them down.

Analyzing Part 1

Recall and Interpret

1. What happens to the men who go ashore in the land of the Lotus Eaters? Why might Odysseus be so opposed to the eating of lotus?
2. Why might Odysseus have commented on the Cyclopes's way of life before relating his adventure in their land?
3. Summarize the events that occur after Odysseus and his men become trapped inside the Cyclops's cave. What personality traits does Odysseus reveal in leading his men to safety?
4. Describe the character of the Cyclops, using evidence from the selection in your answer. What is **ironic** about his speech in lines 363–378?
5. Describe an instance of Odysseus acting against the advice of his men. In your opinion, why doesn't Odysseus listen to them?

Evaluate and Connect

6. Does Odysseus's longing to return to Ithaca seem true to life? Explain. What would you miss most if you were away from home?
7. The Cyclops loses his sight as well as his rams. Do you feel sorry for him? In your opinion, does Homer? Explain your answers.
8. What do you think of Odysseus's decision to taunt the Cyclops from his ship? Would you have done the same? Why or why not?
9. Who would you say is responsible for the loss of life in part 1? Explain your response.
10. The invocation reveals what happens to Odysseus and his men. Does having this information affect your reading of the *Odyssey*? Explain.

Literary ELEMENTS

Epic Simile

A simile is an expression that uses *like* or *as* to compare two seemingly unlike things. For example, Homer writes that the Cyclops "caught two [men] in his hands like squirming puppies" and ate them, "gaping and crunching like a mountain lion." An **epic simile,** also called a Homeric simile, extends a comparison with elaborate descriptive details that can fill several lines of verse.

1. The scene describing the blinding of the Cyclops on pages 822–823 contains two epic similes. Identify the lines of each simile and tell what is being compared.
2. In your opinion, why might Homer have used more than one extended simile to describe this event?

- See **Literary Terms Handbook,** p. R5.

Extending Your Response

Literature Groups

Evaluating a Hero's Actions With your group, discuss Odysseus's actions as a leader: When does he make mistakes, and when does he act wisely? Categorize your group's responses by making a list of "good moves" and "bad moves." For each "bad move," decide on another course of action that might have had a better result. Share your lists and new scenarios with other groups.

Creative Writing

Behind His Back Imagine that you and a partner are sailors on Odysseus's journey, discussing the events that occurred in the land of the Cyclopes. Pass a piece of paper back and forth, as each of you writes lines for one of the sailors. Read your "conversation" to the class.

Save your work for your portfolio.

Writing Skills

Using Evidence

How do you know that Odysseus *really* stabbed the Cyclops in the eye? You don't. The *Odyssey* is a work of fiction, so it doesn't have to be proved true. If you're writing nonfiction, however, you will need to support your statements with evidence, such as facts and reliable opinions. Notice how one writer uses evidence to support a claim.

> **The Long March was one of the most incredible journeys in history. It took place in China in 1934 and 1935 as the communist Red Army escaped from the Nationalist army by walking west and north for over a year. "The journey," wrote one journalist, "took them across some of the world's most difficult trails, unfit for wheeled traffic, and across the high snow mountains and the great rivers of Asia." Of some 90,000 people who began the march, more than half died along the way. Altogether, the survivors traveled about 6,000 miles.**

The writer claims that the Long March was an incredible journey. Why should you believe her? She provides evidence in the form of **facts**—statements, statistics, observations, or examples that can be verified, or proved true. Facts in the passage above include the number of marchers and the number of miles they walked.

Make sure that you evaluate the evidence you gather to support your ideas. Before you assume that a fact provides sufficient evidence, evaluate it by asking these questions:

- Is it accurate? Can it be verified in several **credible, reliable** sources?
- Is it **up-to-date?** Might recent discoveries have made the information obsolete?
- Is it **relevant?** Does it clearly serve the purpose you intended?

Sometimes you can use **opinions** as evidence. The value of an opinion depends on the qualifications of the person stating it. Evaluate an opinion by asking these questions:

- Is the person giving the opinion **qualified,** having specific knowledge of the subject?
- What is the **motive** of the person giving the opinion? Is he or she **biased,** having something to gain by supporting one viewpoint?

EXERCISES

1. Imagine that you are writing a report about what it is like to drive from Houston to Mexico City. List two types of facts and a reasonable opinion you could use as evidence.
2. Read a story in a magazine or newspaper, and list the facts and opinions used as evidence. Then evaluate the text based on the criteria above.

LISTENING, SPEAKING, and VIEWING

Conducting an Interview

Suppose you want to know what it would be like to live aboard a ship the way Odysseus did. One of the best ways to find out is to interview someone who has had the experience, because talking to the right person can provide you with the kind of vivid, personal information unavailable elsewhere. The following tips can help you conduct a successful interview.

Before the Interview

- Contact your subject. Explain why you want to talk to him or her, and request an interview. Arrange to meet at a time and place convenient to the interviewee.
- Prepare for the interview. Collect information about your interviewee and about the topic you wish to discuss.
- Make up a list of questions that cannot be answered with a simple yes or no. Try questions that start with "Tell me about . . ." or "How did you . . ."

During the Interview

- Request permission to take notes or to tape-record the conversation. Begin with friendly, open-ended questions to help you both relax.
- Ask the questions you have prepared. Refer to your notes if you must, but try to maintain eye contact. Listen carefully. If you don't understand something or if you want additional information, ask follow-up questions.

After the Interview

- If you took notes, rewrite them neatly, and include any additional impressions. If you recorded the interview, transcribe, or make a written copy of, the taped conversation. Make sure that you copy statements accurately.
- Be sure to document the first and last name of your interviewee, the date of the interview, and contact information in case you need to reach the person later.

ACTIVITIES

1. Using the guidelines above, interview someone about a subject of your choice. Transcribe and edit the interview so that all the questions and answers pertain to your focus. Then share the interview with someone else.

2. Watch an interview on television. On the basis of what you see, what additional tips might you add to those above? Share your ideas with the class.

Before You Read

from the *Odyssey, Part 2*

Building Background

Did You Know?

- To the ancient Greeks, the gods were a common yet important part of everyday life. People believed in deities who were supernatural and immortal—that is, they had magical powers and lived forever—but who sometimes behaved and looked like human beings. The gods quarreled with each other, had love affairs, sulked, and celebrated.
- Many of the gods were believed to live on Mount Olympus, the highest mountain on the Greek peninsula. Others supposedly lived in the underworld or in the heavens. The Olympians—gods on Olympus—saw everything that happened below, and occasionally paid visits in disguise to help a favorite mortal or mislead an enemy.
- Some gods had more power than others. Some were associated with abstract ideas, such as wisdom, while others were associated with particular activities, such as warfare. Some were said to have power over natural forces, while others were linked to planets or heavenly bodies.
- For the ancient Greeks, belief in interfering gods was a way of explaining disaster or good luck. A storm sweeps across the Mediterranean Sea and sinks a ship. Why? Perhaps because Zeus is angry, or has made a promise to another god that he will inflict punishment. Although the gods were thought to influence, help, test, or punish people, they did not run people's lives. Deciding how to be and what to do were the true challenges of life—and these were left up to the individual.

Zeus rides in a golden chariot drawn by eagles, his hand full of thunderbolts. Illustration by P. Palagi.

Vocabulary Preview

shun (shun) *v.* to keep away from; avoid; p. 834

ardor (är′ dər) *n.* passion; intensity of emotion; enthusiasm; p. 835

dwindle (dwind′ əl) *v.* to gradually lessen; diminish; p. 835

tumult (to͞o′ məlt) *n.* commotion; uproar; p. 836

peril (per′ əl) *n.* danger; risk; something that may cause injury or destruction; p. 836

quest (kwest) *v.* to seek; search or pursue in order to find something or achieve a goal; p. 838

shroud (shroud) *v.* to cover, as with a veil or burial cloth; conceal; p. 840

supplication (sup′ lə kā′ shən) *n.* earnest or humble request or prayer; p. 841

insidious (in sid′ ē əs) *adj.* slyly treacherous or deceitful; scheming; p. 841

adorn (ə dôrn′) *v.* to decorate; add beauty, honor, or distinction to; p. 841

restitution (res′ tə to͞o′ shən) *n.* compensation for something that has been lost, damaged, or taken away; p. 843

contentious (kən ten′ shəs) *adj.* quarrelsome; argumentative; p. 845

Part 2

Sea Perils and Defeat

Odysseus and his men traveled to the floating islands of Aeolus (ē′ ə ləs), *god of the winds, who then gave Odysseus a bag containing all of the unfavorable winds. With only the good west wind behind them, Odysseus and his crew made rapid progress. Odysseus fell asleep when Ithaca was in sight, but his men, believing that Odysseus was not sharing valuable treasures with them, opened the bag. Instantly, the winds rushed out, blowing them back to Aeolus, who refused to help them a second time.*

After several days back at sea, they reached the land of the Laestrygonians, monstrous cannibals. Only Odysseus's ship and crew escaped destruction.

Next stop: a thickly forested island. When Odysseus sent half of his remaining men to explore the interior, only a single breathless survivor returned. He told Odysseus that the goddess Circe had lured the rest of the men to her house with food and wine and then turned them into pigs. Odysseus rescued them, forcing Circe to restore his men to their original forms with a magical herb provided by the messenger god Hermes (hur′ mēz).

Before Circe allowed Odysseus to leave a year later, he had to journey to the land of the dead. There he learned from the blind prophet, Tiresias (tī rē′ sē əs), *that he would eventually return home, but that he must not injure the cattle of the sun god Helios. Upon Odysseus's return from the land of the dead, Circe repeated this warning and described the dangers that Odysseus would encounter. First, he'd meet the sirens, who lure sailors to their deaths with a beautiful song; then, the many-headed Scylla, who lurks in a cave on a high cliff above a ship-devouring whirlpool named Charybdis. She instructed him to steer toward Scylla and not try to fight back.*

Odysseus continues telling his host about his adventures.

"As Circe spoke, Dawn mounted her golden throne,
and on the first rays Circe left me, taking
her way like a great goddess up the island.
I made straight for the ship, roused up the men
to get aboard and cast off at the stern.
They scrambled to their places by the rowlocks
and all in line dipped oars in the gray sea.

Circe and the Swine.

Viewing the art: What do you find comical about this image? What is serious about it?

But soon an off-shore breeze blew to our liking—
a canvas-bellying breeze, a lusty shipmate
sent by the singing nymph with sunbright hair.°
So we made fast the braces,° and we rested,
letting the wind and steersman work the ship.
The crew being now silent before me, I
addressed them, sore at heart:

'Dear friends,
more than one man, or two, should know those things
Circe foresaw for us and shared with me,
so let me tell her forecast: then we die
with our eyes open, if we are going to die,
or know what death we baffle if we can. Sirens
weaving a haunting song over the sea
we are to shun, she said, and their green shore
all sweet with clover; yet she urged that I
alone should listen to their song. Therefore
you are to tie me up, tight as a splint,

8–10 But soon . . . hair: The goddess Calypso has sent the breeze.

11 made fast the braces: tied down the ropes used to maneuver the sails.

Vocabulary

shun (shun) *v.* to keep away from; avoid

erect along the mast, lashed to the mast,
and if I shout and beg to be untied,
take more turns of the rope to muffle me.'

I rather dwelt on this part of the forecast,
while our good ship made time, bound outward down
the wind for the strange island of Sirens.
Then all at once the wind fell, and a calm
came over all the sea, as though some power
lulled the swell.
The crew were on their feet
briskly, to furl the sail, and stow it; then,
each in place, they poised the smooth oar blades
and sent the white foam scudding° by. I carved
a massive cake of beeswax into bits
and rolled them in my hands until they softened—
no long task, for a burning heat came down
from Helios, lord of high noon. Going forward
I carried wax along the line, and laid it
thick on their ears. They tied me up, then, plumb
amidships,° back to the mast, lashed to the mast,
and took themselves again to rowing. Soon,
as we came smartly° within hailing distance,°
the two Sirens, noting our fast ship
off their point, made ready, and they sang. . . .

The lovely voices in ardor appealing over the water
made me crave to listen, and I tried to say
'Untie me!' to the crew, jerking my brows;
but they bent steady to the oars. Then Perimedes°
got to his feet, he and Eurylochus,°
and passed more line about, to hold me still.
So all rowed on, until the Sirens
dropped under the sea rim,° and their singing
dwindled away.
My faithful company
rested on their oars now, peeling off
the wax that I had laid thick on their ears;
then set me free.
But scarcely had that island

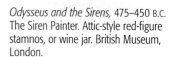

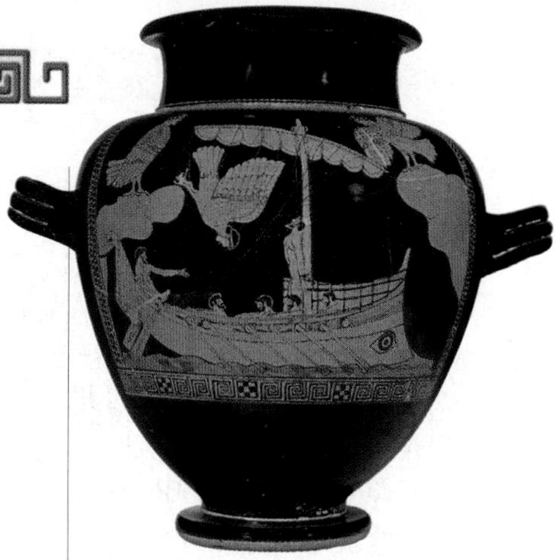

Odysseus and the Sirens, 475–450 B.C. The Siren Painter. Attic-style red-figure stamnos, or wine jar. British Museum, London.

38 **scudding:** moving swiftly.

44–45 **plumb amidships:** at the exact center of the ship.

47 **smartly:** proudly; insultingly. **hailing distance:** earshot.

53 **Perimedes** (per′ i mē′ dēz)

54 **Eurylochus** (yoo ril′ ə kəs)

57 **sea rim:** horizon.

Vocabulary

ardor (är′ dər) *n.* passion; intensity of emotion; enthusiasm
dwindle (dwind′ əl) *v.* to gradually lessen; diminish

faded in blue air than I saw smoke
and white water, with sound of waves in tumult—
a sound the men heard, and it terrified them.
Oars flew from their hands; the blades went knocking
wild alongside till the ship lost way,
with no oarblades to drive her through the water.

Well, I walked up and down from bow to stern,
trying to put heart into them, standing over
every oarsman, saying gently,

'Friends,
have we never been in danger before this?
More fearsome, is it now, than when the Cyclops
penned us in his cave? What power he had!
Did I not keep my nerve, and use my wits
to find a way out for us?

Now I say
by hook or crook this peril too shall be
something that we remember.

Heads up, lads!
We must obey the orders as I give them.
Get the oarshafts in your hands, and lay back
hard on your benches; hit these breaking seas.
Zeus help us pull away before we founder.
You at the tiller, listen, and take in
all that I say—the rudders are your duty;
keep her out of the combers and the smoke;
steer for that headland; watch the drift, or we
fetch up in the smother, and you drown us.'

That was all, and it brought them round to action.
But as I sent them on toward Scylla,° I
told them nothing, as they could do nothing.
They would have dropped their oars again, in panic,
to roll for cover under the decking. Circe's
bidding against arms had slipped my mind,
so I tied on my cuirass° and took up
two heavy spears, then made my way along
to the foredeck—thinking to see her first from there,

93 Scylla (sil′ ə): an immortal monster with twelve tentacled arms, six heads, and three rows of teeth in each of her six mouths.

98 cuirass: armor.

Vocabulary

tumult (to͞o′ məlt) *n.* commotion; uproar
peril (per′ əl) *n.* danger; risk; something that may cause injury or destruction

Scylla and Charybdis, from the Ulysses Cycle, 1560. Alessandro Allori. Fresco. Banca Toscana, Florence, Italy.

Viewing the art: How does the artist's depiction of this scene in the *Odyssey* compare with what you envision as you read? Does the image effectively convey the powerlessness of Odysseus's men?

the monster of the gray rock, harboring
torment for my friends. I strained my eyes
upon that cliffside veiled in cloud, but nowhere
could I catch sight of her.
                                        And all this time,
in travail,° sobbing, gaining on the current,
we rowed into the strait—Scylla to port
and on our starboard beam Charybdis, dire
gorge of the salt sea tide. By heaven! when she
vomited, all the sea was like a cauldron
seething over intense fire, when the mixture
suddenly heaves and rises.
                                        The shot spume
soared to the landside heights, and fell like rain.°

But when she swallowed the sea water down
we saw the funnel of the maelstrom,° heard
the rock bellowing all around, and dark

106 **travail:** exhausting, painful labor.

107–114 **we rowed . . . rain:** The ship enters a narrow channel **(strait)** between Scylla on the left and **Charybdis** (kə rib′ dis) on the right. Rising and falling with the surge of tidal currents, the whirlpool sucks water down her dreadful throat **(dire gorge),** then spews it into the air as a geyser.

116 **maelstrom:** violent whirlpool.

sand raged on the bottom far below.
My men all blanched° against the gloom, our eyes
were fixed upon that yawning mouth in fear
of being devoured.
Then Scylla made her strike,
whisking six of my best men from the ship.
I happened to glance aft at ship and oarsmen
and caught sight of their arms and legs, dangling
high overhead. Voices came down to me
in anguish, calling my name for the last time.

A man surfcasting on a point of rock
for bass or mackerel, whipping his long rod
to drop the sinker and the bait far out,
will hook a fish and rip it from the surface
to dangle wriggling through the air:
so these
were borne aloft in spasms° toward the cliff.

She ate them as they shrieked there, in her den,
in the dire grapple,° reaching still for me—
and deathly pity ran me through
at that sight—far the worst I ever suffered,
questing the passes of the strange sea.
We rowed on.
The Rocks were now behind; Charybdis, too,
and Scylla dropped astern.
Then we were coasting
the noble island of the god, where grazed
those cattle with wide brows, and bounteous flocks
of Helios, lord of noon, who rides high heaven.

From the black ship, far still at sea, I heard
the lowing of the cattle winding home
and sheep bleating; and heard, too, in my heart
the words of blind Tiresias of Thebes
and Circe of Aeaea: both forbade me
the island of the world's delight, the Sun.
So I spoke out in gloom to my companions:

119 blanched: turned pale.

134 borne aloft in spasms: carried high while struggling furiously.

136 dire grapple: desperate struggle.

Vocabulary

quest (kwest) *v.* to seek; search or pursue in order to find something or achieve a goal

'Shipmates, grieving and weary though you are,
listen: I had forewarning from Tiresias
and Circe, too; both told me I must shun
this island of the Sun, the world's delight.
Nothing but fatal trouble shall we find here.
Pull away, then, and put the land astern.'
That strained them to the breaking point, and, cursing,
Eurylochus cried out in bitterness:

'Are you flesh and blood, Odysseus, to endure
more than a man can? Do you never tire?
God, look at you, iron is what you're made of.
Here we all are, half dead with weariness,
falling asleep over the oars, and you
say "No landing"—no firm island earth
where we could make a quiet supper. No:
pull out to sea, you say, with night upon us—
just as before, but wandering now, and lost.
Sudden storms can rise at night and swamp
ships without a trace.
                                        Where is your shelter
if some stiff gale blows up from south or west—
the winds that break up shipping every time
when seamen flout° the lord gods' will? I say
do as the hour demands and go ashore
before black night comes down.
                                        We'll make our supper
alongside, and at dawn put out to sea.'

Now when the rest said 'Aye' to this, I saw
the power of destiny devising ill.
Sharply I answered, without hesitation:

'Eurylochus, they are with you to a man.
I am alone, outmatched.
                                        Let this whole company
swear me a great oath: Any herd of cattle
or flock of sheep here found shall go unharmed;
no one shall slaughter out of wantonness°
ram or heifer; all shall be content
with what the goddess Circe put aboard.'

They fell at once to swearing as I ordered,
and when the round of oaths had ceased, we found

176 flout: defy; ignore; scoff at.

189 wantonness: recklessness or lack of restraint.

a halfmoon bay to beach and moor the ship in,
with a fresh spring nearby. All hands ashore
went about skillfully getting up a meal.
Then, after thirst and hunger, those besiegers,
were turned away, they mourned for their companions
plucked from the ship by Scylla and devoured,
and sleep came soft upon them as they mourned.

In the small hours of the third watch, when stars
that shone out in the first dusk of evening
had gone down to their setting, a giant wind
blew from heaven, and clouds driven by Zeus
shrouded land and sea in a night of storm;
so, just as Dawn with fingertips of rose
touched the windy world, we dragged our ship
to cover in a grotto, a sea cave
where nymphs had chairs of rock and sanded floors.
I mustered all the crew and said:

'Old shipmates,
our stores are in the ship's hold, food and drink;
the cattle here are not for our provision,
or we pay dearly for it.

Fierce the god is
who cherishes these heifers and these sheep:
Helios; and no man avoids his eye.'

To this my fighters nodded. Yes. But now
we had a month of onshore gales, blowing
day in, day out—south winds, or south by east.
As long as bread and good red wine remained
to keep the men up, and appease their craving,
they would not touch the cattle. But in the end,
when all the barley in the ship was gone,
hunger drove them to scour the wild shore
with angling hooks, for fishes and sea fowl,
whatever fell into their hands; and lean days
wore their bellies thin.

The storms continued.
So one day I withdrew to the interior

Vocabulary

shroud (shroud) *v.* to cover, as with a veil or burial cloth; conceal to pray the gods in solitude, for hope that one might show me some way of salvation. Slipping away, I struck across the island to a sheltered spot, out of the driving gale. I washed my hands there, and made supplication 235 to the gods who own Olympus, all the gods but they, for answer, only closed my eyes under slow drops of sleep.

Now on the shore Eurylochus

made his insidious plea: 240

245

250

255

260

265

'Comrades,' he said,

'You've gone through everything; listen to what I say. All deaths are hateful to us, mortal wretches, but famine is the most pitiful, the worst end that a man can come to.

Will you fight it?

for sacrifice to the gods who own the sky; and once at home, in the old country of Ithaca, if ever that day comes we'll build a costly temple and adorn it with every beauty for the Lord of Noon. But if he flares up over his heifers lost, wishing our ship destroyed, and if the gods make cause with him, why, then I say: Better open your lungs to a big sea once for all than waste to skin and bones on a lonely island!'

Come, we'll cut out the noblest of these cattle

Thus Eurylochus; and they murmured 'Aye!' trooping away at once to round up heifers. Now, that day tranquil cattle with broad brows were grazing near, and soon the men drew up around their chosen beasts in ceremony. They plucked the leaves that shone on a tall oak having no barley meal—to strew the victims,° performed the prayers and ritual, knifed the kine° and flaved° each carcass, cutting thighbones free to wrap in double folds of fat. These offerings,

263-264 They ... victims: Usually, in preparing a burnt offering, fruit or grain was spread over and around the animal's carcass.

265 kine: cattle.

266 flayed: stripped off the skin of.

Vocabulary

supplication (sup' la kā' shan) n. earnest or humble request or prayer insidious (in sid' ē əs) adj. slyly treacherous or deceitful; scheming adorn (a dôrn') v. to decorate; add beauty, honor, or distinction to

The Companions of Ulysses Slaying the Cattle of the Sun God Helios, 16th century. Pellegrino Tibaldi. Fresco. Palazzo Poggi, Bologna, Italy.

Viewing the art: **What does the facial expression and body language of the man in the lower left corner of the painting suggest to you? Consider the warning Odysseus has given his crew.**

with strips of meat, were laid upon the fire.
Then, as they had no wine, they made libation°
with clear spring water, broiling the entrails° first;
and when the bones were burnt and tripes° shared,
they spitted° the carved meat.
Just then my slumber
left me in a rush, my eyes opened,
and I went down the seaward path. No sooner
had I caught sight of our black hull, than savory
odors of burnt fat eddied° around me;
grief took hold of me, and I cried aloud:

'O Father Zeus and gods in bliss forever,
you made me sleep away this day of mischief!
O cruel drowsing, in the evil hour!
Here they sat, and a great work they contrived.'°

269 **libation:** a ritual pouring of wine or another liquid as part of an offering.

270–271 **entrails, tripes:** internal organs.

272 **spitted:** threaded pieces onto a spit, or rod, for roasting over a fire.

276 **eddied:** swirled.

281 **contrived:** schemed; plotted.

Lampetia° in her long gown meanwhile
had borne swift word to the Overlord of Noon:

'They have killed your kine.'

And the Lord Helios
burst into angry speech amid the immortals:

'O Father Zeus and gods in bliss forever,
punish Odysseus' men! So overweening,°
now they have killed my peaceful kine, my joy
at morning when I climbed the sky of stars,
and evening, when I bore westward from heaven.
Restitution or penalty they shall pay—
and pay in full—or I go down forever
to light the dead men in the underworld.'°

Then Zeus who drives the stormcloud made reply:

'Peace, Helios: shine on among the gods,
shine over mortals in the fields of grain.
Let me throw down one white-hot bolt, and make
splinters of their ship in the winedark sea.'°

—Calypso later told me of this exchange,
as she declared that Hermes° had told her.
Well, when I reached the sea cave and the ship,
I faced each man, and had it out;° but where
could any remedy be found? There was none.
The silken beeves° of Helios were dead.
The gods, moreover, made queer signs appear:
cowhides began to crawl, and beef, both raw
and roasted, lowed like kine upon the spits.

Now six full days my gallant crew could feast
upon the prime beef they had marked for slaughter
from Helios' herd; and Zeus, the son of Cronus,
added one fine morning.

All the gales
had ceased, blown out, and with an offshore breeze

282 Lampetia (lam pē′ shə): a guardian of the island and animals. Her father is Helios; her mother is a human woman.

288 overweening: arrogant; self-important; not humble enough.

292–294 Restitution . . . underworld: Helios threatens to abandon the sky and shine, instead, on the land of the dead if the gods don't punish Odysseus's men.

296–299 Peace . . . winedark sea: Zeus coolly silences Helios, offering to set matters straight with a single thunderbolt.

301 Hermes (hur′ mēz): the messenger god.

303 I faced each man, and had it out: Odysseus confronts each crewman.

305 beeves: cattle.

Vocabulary

restitution (res′ tə to͞o′ shən) *n.* **compensation for something that has been lost, damaged, or taken away**

we launched again stepping° the mast and sail,
to make for the open sea. Astern of us
the island coastline faded, and no land
showed anywhere, but only sea and heaven,
when Zeus Cronion° piled a thunderhead
above the ship, while gloom spread on the ocean.
We held our course, but briefly. Then the squall
struck whining from the west, with gale force, breaking
both forestays,° and the mast came toppling aft
along the ship's length, so the running rigging°
showered into the bilge.°
On the afterdeck
the mast had hit the steersman a slant blow
bashing the skull in, knocking him overside,
as the brave soul fled the body, like a diver.
With crack on crack of thunder, Zeus let fly
a bolt against the ship, a direct hit,
so that she bucked, in reeking fumes of sulphur,
and all the men were flung into the sea.
They came up 'round the wreck, bobbing awhile
like petrels° on the waves.
No more seafaring
homeward for these, no sweet day of return;
the god had turned his face from them.
I clambered
fore and aft my hulk until a comber
split her, keel from ribs, and the big timber
floated free; the mast, too, broke away.
A backstay floated dangling from it, stout
rawhide rope, and I used this for lashing
mast and keel together. These I straddled,
riding the frightful storm.°
Nor had I yet
seen the worst of it: for now the west wind
dropped, and a southeast gale came on—one more
twist of the knife—taking me north again,
straight for Charybdis. All that night I drifted,
and in the sunrise, sure enough, I lay
off Scylla mountain and Charybdis deep.
There, as the whirlpool drank the tide, a billow°
tossed me, and I sprang for the great fig tree,
catching on like a bat under a bough.
Nowhere had I to stand, no way of climbing,

315 **stepping:** fixing into position.

319 **Cronion:** a name that identifies Zeus as Cronus's son.

323 **forestays:** the ropes that support the main mast.

324 **running rigging:** the ropes that support all masts and sails.

325 **bilge:** the lowest interior part of a ship.

335 **petrels:** sea birds.

339–346 **I clambered . . . storm:** Before the ship is broken in two by a long breaking wave **(comber),** Odysseus scrambles from front to back **(fore and aft);** afterwards, he grabs a mast rope **(backstay)** and pieces together a crude raft.

354 **billow:** a great, swelling wave.

the root and bole° being far below, and far
above my head the branches and their leaves,
massed, overshadowing Charybdis pool.
But I clung grimly, thinking my mast and keel
would come back to the surface when she spouted.
And ah! how long, with what desire, I waited!
till, at the twilight hour, when one who hears
and judges pleas in the marketplace all day
between contentious men, goes home to supper,
the long poles at last reared from the sea.

Now I let go with hands and feet, plunging
straight into the foam beside the timbers,
pulled astride, and rowed hard with my hands
to pass by Scylla. Never could I have passed her
had not the Father of gods and men, this time,
kept me from her eyes. Once through the strait,
nine days I drifted in the open sea
before I made shore, buoyed up by the gods,
upon Ogygia° Isle. The dangerous nymph
Calypso lives and sings there, in her beauty,
and she received me, loved me.

But why tell
the same tale that I told last night in hall
to you and to your lady?° Those adventures
made a long evening, and I do not hold
with° tiresome repetition of a story."

358 **bole:** trunk.

376 **Ogygia** (ō gij′ yə)

379–381 **But why . . . lady:** Still speaking to Alcinous, King of Phaeacia, and his daughter, Odysseus now winds up his story.

382–383 **hold with:** approve of; have patience for.

Scylla. 5th century B.C. Melos, Greece. Terra-cotta relief. British Museum, London.

Vocabulary

contentious (kən ten′ shəs) *adj.* quarrelsome; argumentative

Responding to Literature

Personal Response

Is Odysseus very lucky, very unlucky, or something else? Explain.

Analyzing Part 2

Recall

1. How does Odysseus protect his men from the song of the sirens? How do his men protect him?
2. How does Odysseus help his men overcome their fear as the ship approaches Scylla and Charybdis?
3. How does Eurylochus persuade Odysseus to stop at Helios?
4. Why do Odysseus and his men stay longer than planned on the island of Helios? What is the result of the delay?
5. What agreement do Zeus and Helios make?

Interpret

6. In your opinion, why does the weather in the vicinity of the sirens change suddenly? What might be the intended effect of the change?
7. Odysseus says, "But as I sent them on toward Scylla, I / told them nothing, as they could do nothing." What does he mean? In your opinion, is Odysseus being thoughtful or deceitful in this scene? Explain.
8. Explain how Odysseus's statement, "Eurylochus, they are with you to a man. / I am alone, outmatched," is an example of **foreshadowing.**
9. Explain why Eurylochus was a more persuasive leader on the island of Helios than Odysseus was.
10. In your opinion, is Zeus or Odysseus responsible for Odysseus's survival? Support your answer with details from the selection.

Evaluate and Connect

11. What do the adventures Odysseus recounts in part 2 teach about temptation and human nature?
12. How would you describe the relationship Odysseus has with his men? What, if anything, might Odysseus have done to improve it?
13. Would Eurylochus's argument (lines 241–257) have persuaded you to kill the cattle of Helios? Explain.
14. Do you think that the people of Homer's time understood the *Odyssey* differently than you do? Refer to the Background on page 832 as you develop your answer.
15. **Theme Connections** Which circumstances of Odysseus's journey so far might happen on real-life journeys? Explain.

Literary ELEMENTS

Personification

Personification is a figure of speech in which an animal, force of nature, idea, or an inanimate object is given human qualities or characteristics. Homer frequently uses personification to describe events in the natural world and to create vivid images that would capture the imagination of his audience. For example, dawn, the rising of the sun, is repeatedly personified in the *Odyssey* as "the young Dawn with fingertips of rose." Dawn is also treated royally, as Odysseus says, "Dawn mounted her golden throne."

1. Reread the description of Charybdis on page 837. What natural phenomenon is Homer actually describing? What words does he use to personify it? Why, do you suppose, does he choose to describe Charybdis in this way?
2. Find and explain another example of personification in the *Odyssey.*

- See **Literary Terms Handbook,** p. R9.

Literary Criticism

Critic Mark Van Doren says, "The greatness of Odysseus is where the Cyclops cannot see it, in his wit." Write a brief persuasive essay in which you use evidence from the text either to argue Van Doren's position or to refute it.

Literature and Writing

Writing About Literature

Analyzing Details Review Odysseus's encounters with the sirens, Scylla and Charybdis, Helios's cattle, and Zeus's wrath. List the details that are most important in each episode. Then write a paragraph explaining how the descriptive details in the episode make the action more vivid or exciting.

Creative Writing

What If? What if some of the sailors had removed the wax from their ears? What if the ship had steered toward Charybdis? What if Odysseus hadn't fallen asleep on the island of Helios? What if . . . ? Rewrite a scene from part 2 using the vivid style of Homer to describe something that might have happened differently.

Extending Your Response

Literature Groups

Critiquing Leadership With your group, weigh Odysseus's effectiveness as a leader. What are his strongest and weakest leadership qualities? How do these strengths and weaknesses play out in a crisis? Discuss whether or not you would trust Odysseus to lead you through a difficult situation. Then discuss how you would lead a group through a challenge. Share your decisions with the class.

Interdisciplinary Activity

Art: Cover Design This part of the *Odyssey* contains some of the poem's most famous scenes. Choose a scene and use it to illustrate a jacket for the book. Be sure to leave room for the title and author in your design.

Learning for Life

Memo from the Chief Imagine that the Greek gods work in a big corporate office, full of cubicles and computers. Compose a formal memo from Zeus to the other gods, describing Helios's grievance and explaining the action he took to remedy the situation.

Save your work for your portfolio.

Skill Minilesson

VOCABULARY • Unlocking Meaning

Whenever you learn a new word, you also learn its base word or its word root, as well as any prefix or suffix it may contain. Understanding these parts in turn helps you to understand unfamiliar words that contain some of the same parts. For example, *profusion* means "abundance." If you come across the word *profuse,* you might notice how similar it is to *profusion.* The context of the word might tell you that *profuse* is an adjective, and then you could figure out that it means "abundant."

PRACTICE Use what you know about the vocabulary words in parentheses to complete the sentences.

1. (supplication) A supplicant might be most likely to
   a. kneel. b. yawn. c. scowl.
2. (valor) A valorous hero is one who is
   a. vigorous. b. brave. c. handsome.
3. (adorn) An example of an adornment is a
   a. blush. b. ring. c. bruise.
4. (contentious) When a sailor contends that the captain knows best, he
   a. suggests. b. argues. c. hints.

Before You Read

Siren Song

Reading Focus

In Homer's *Odyssey,* Odysseus has to be tied to the ship's mast to resist the song of the sirens. What kind of song could be so irresistible?

Sharing Ideas With a partner, discuss what aspects of a song—such as the music, the message, or the performance—might make it irresistible to its listeners. Jot down a summary of your ideas.

Setting a Purpose Read to learn what one poet thinks would be an irresistible song.

Building Background

Did You Know?

- In ancient Greek mythology, a siren is a sea creature—half woman and half bird—who sings an irresistible song that lures men to their death. In the *Odyssey,* Homer refers to two sirens, but later classical authors describe a musical trio who supposedly lived on an island near Sicily. In some accounts, the sirens were princesses who changed themselves into birds to look for their friend Persephone (per sef′ ə nē), who had been abducted by the god of the underworld. In other stories, they were the daughters of a sea or river god.

Siren ornament from the rim of a cauldron. 7th century B.C. Bronze. Museum of Fine Art, Boston.

- The mythologies of many cultures contain various versions of the sirens, including creatures that are half woman and half fish as well as ones that are half woman and half snake. Stories of sirens and references to them have appeared in literature through the ages, including the present day. Today, the word *siren* may be used to refer to a beautiful, seductive woman.

Meet Margaret Atwood

"I became a poet at the age of sixteen. I did not intend to do it. It was not my fault."

Poet and novelist Margaret Atwood says that her first poem popped into her head as she was walking home from high school. Having spent a large part of her childhood in the Canadian wilderness aided her development as a poet. With "no theatres, movies, parades, or very functional radios," she had plenty of time for meditation and reading. She produced her first award-winning book of poems, *The Circle Game,* while still in her twenties. She has also written a number of novels, including *The Handmaid's Tale.*

Margaret Atwood was born in Ottawa, Ontario, in 1939.

The Song of the Sirens. Stuart Davis (flourished 1893–1917). Mallett & Sons Antiques Ltd., London.

Siren Song

Margaret Atwood

This is the one song everyone
would like to learn: the song
that is irresistible:

the song that forces men
to leap overboard in squadrons°
even though they see the beached skulls

the song nobody knows
because anyone who has heard it
is dead, and the others can't remember.

Shall I tell you the secret
and if I do, will you get me
out of this bird suit?

I don't enjoy it here
squatting on this island
looking picturesque° and mythical

with these two feathery maniacs,
I don't enjoy singing
this trio, fatal and valuable.

I will tell the secret to you,
to you, only to you.
Come closer. This song

is a cry for help: Help me!
Only you, only you can,
you are unique°

at last. Alas
it is a boring song
but it works every time.

5 Here, *squadrons* (skwod′ rənz) means "large numbers."

15 Something that is *picturesque* (pik′ chə resk′) may be suggestive of a painted scene, or it may appear striking or interesting in an unusual way.

24 *Unique* means "one of a kind."

Responding to Literature

Personal Response

Did any images in this poem amuse you? Explain your response to a partner.

Analyzing Literature

Recall and Interpret

1. In your opinion, who is the speaker in the poem and to whom do you think she is speaking?
2. Why might the "siren song" be "the one song everyone / would like to learn"? Describe the song's power.
3. What trade does the speaker want to make with the reader in stanza four? What reasons does the speaker then give for making this trade?
4. In your opinion, does the speaker have a secret, and if so, what is it?

Evaluate and Connect

5. In your opinion, how does the speaker really feel about her intended audience? Explain, using details from the poem in your answer.
6. Why do you think this siren song, as the speaker describes it, would be alluring to someone?
7. What techniques does Atwood use to draw in the reader and sustain the reader's attention?
8. Think about the ways women attract men today in movies, television commercials, and other media. Do they use the siren's "secret"? Discuss examples.

Literary ELEMENTS

Tone

Tone is the attitude taken by the author or speaker toward the subject of a work. Tone may be communicated through particular words and details that express emotions and that evoke an emotional response in the reader. Various readers have described the tone of "Siren Song" as comic, sinister, and sarcastic.

1. How would *you* describe the tone of "Siren Song"?
2. What words or phrases in the poem create this tone?

- See **Literary Terms Handbook,** p. R13.

Extending Your Response

Listening and Speaking

Tuning In With your partner, review the notes you made for the Reading Focus on page 848. Work together to compose the lyrics for your own "Siren Song." Set the lyrics to a familiar tune, and then perform it for your class. If you wish, tape-record the song and then play it back.

Personal Writing

Uniquely Yours The speaker in "Siren Song" thinks that her intended audience can be lured with the suggestion that he is unique. Would you like to be considered unique and irresistible in some way? If so, in what way? If not, why? Describe your response in your journal.

Save your work for your portfolio.

COMPARING *selections*

from the Odyssey Part 2 **and** Siren Song

COMPARE **SIRENS**

Margaret Atwood's poem "Siren Song" contains **allusions,** or references, to the sirens in Homer's *Odyssey,* yet important differences exist between her version of the creatures and his.

1. In a small group, discuss the similarities and differences between the sirens depicted in each poem. You may want to use a Venn diagram like the one shown to record your ideas.
2. Identify the reasons behind the differences. What might Atwood be trying to accomplish by creating sirens that differ from Homer's?

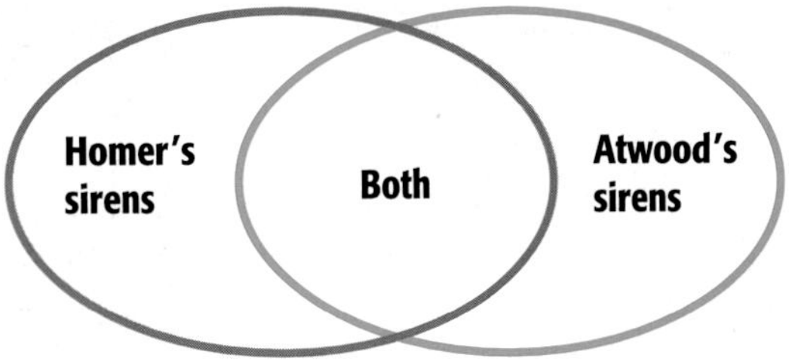

COMPARE **SONGS**

With a partner, compare the song sung by Homer's sirens with the one sung by Atwood's.

- What lyrics do you imagine each group of sirens sings? What melody might each group sing? What instruments might each group play?
- On the basis of your speculations, comment on the similarities and differences between each song's appeal.

COMPARE **SAILORS**

Compare the reaction of Odysseus and his men to that of the man being addressed in "Siren Song." What accounts for the differences? You might consider the point of view of the author, the appeal of the sirens' song, and the personalities of the sailors. Then speculate about whether Atwood's sailor would have behaved differently if he had heard a warning from Circe beforehand.

Before You Read

from the *Odyssey, Part 3*

Building Background

Did You Know?

- While facts about Homer himself are not available, a great deal is known about the role of poets and the stories they sang or recited in the days before writing. From this information, it may be possible to infer some things about Homer's training. Like other oral poets, he probably spent years learning his art. The demand for master poets grew as their reputation spread, and as a student, Homer probably traveled from city to city with his teacher, listening and learning the secrets of the trade.
- Although they were rarely aristocrats by birth, poet-singers were often treated royally by patrons who valued the entertainment they could provide at great occasions. Sometimes their fame could be a disadvantage. It is said that unscrupulous nobles in Greece had their favorite singers blinded so that they would be compelled to perform for them for the rest of their lives.

Homer sings a poem to sailors.

Vocabulary Preview

cower (kou′ ər) *v.* to crouch or shrink back, as in fear or shame; p. 853

impudence (im′ pyə dəns) *n.* speech or behavior that is aggressively forward or rude; p. 858

mortified (môr′ tə fīd′) *adj.* deeply embarrassed, shamed, or humiliated; p. 859

rebuke (ri būk′) *v.* to scold sharply; criticize; p. 859

guise (gīz) *n.* outward appearance; false appearance; p. 859

renowned (ri nound′) *adj.* famous; widely known; p. 861

commandeer (kom′ ən dēr′) *v.* to seize by force or threats; p. 862

justification (jus′ tə fə kā′ shən) *n.* a reason for an action that shows it to be just, right, or reasonable; p. 863

omen (ō′ mən) *n.* a sign or event thought to foretell good or bad fortune; forewarning; p. 865

contemptible (kən temp′ tə bəl) *adj.* deserving of scorn; disgraceful; p. 865

Part 3

Father and Son

The kindly Phaeacians load Odysseus with gifts and take him home, leaving him fast asleep on the shores of Ithaca. On their return journey, Poseidon turns their ship into a lump of stone for daring to assist Odysseus.

Odysseus is disoriented after twenty years away from home, but the goddess Athena meets him and tells him what happened: during his long absence, a number of young men from Ithaca and neighboring islands have moved into Odysseus's great house. Thinking Odysseus is dead, the suitors, as they are called, eat his food, drink his wine, and insist that Odysseus's wife Penelope choose one of them as her husband. Penelope, who still loves Odysseus and prays for his safe return, has put off a decision as long as she can, but the situation has become very tense.

Athena disguises Odysseus as an old beggar and promises to help him. She tells him to seek shelter with a swineherd named Eumaeus (yoo mē′ əs). *Meanwhile, Odysseus's son, Telemachus* (tə lem′ ə kəs), *who had set out on a journey to discover the fate of his father, escapes an ambush planned by the suitors and secretly lands on Ithaca. Following Athena's instructions, he also goes to Eumaeus's hut. While the loyal swineherd is informing Penelope of her son's return, Athena appears to the disguised Odysseus.*

Statue of Athena, 340–330 B.C. Bronze. National Archaeological Museum, Athens.

From the air
she walked, taking the form of a tall woman,
handsome and clever at her craft, and stood
beyond the gate in plain sight of Odysseus,
unseen, though, by Telemachus, unguessed,
for not to everyone will gods appear.°
Odysseus noticed her; so did the dogs,
who cowered whimpering away from her. She only
nodded, signing to him with her brows,
a sign he recognized. Crossing the yard,
he passed out through the gate in the stockade
to face the goddess. There she said to him:

1–6 From . . . appear: Athena's "craft" includes the ability to disguise herself or others and to make herself visible or invisible. She has already made Odysseus appear to be an old beggar. Now she makes herself visible to Odysseus and, at the same time, invisible to his son **Telemachus.**

Vocabulary

cower (kou′ər) *v.* to crouch or shrink back, as in fear or shame

"Son of Laertes and the gods of old,
Odysseus, master of land ways and sea ways,
dissemble° to your son no longer now.
The time has come: tell him how you together
will bring doom on the suitors in the town.
I shall not be far distant then, for I
myself desire battle."

Saying no more,
she tipped her golden wand upon the man,
making his cloak pure white, and the knit tunic
fresh around him. Lithe and young she made him,
ruddy° with sun, his jawline clean, the beard
no longer gray upon his chin. And she
withdrew when she had done.

Then Lord Odysseus
reappeared—and his son was thunderstruck.°
Fear in his eyes, he looked down and away
as though it were a god, and whispered:

"Stranger,
you are no longer what you were just now!
Your cloak is new; even your skin! You are
one of the gods who rule the sweep of heaven!
Be kind to us, we'll make you fair oblation°
and gifts of hammered gold. Have mercy on us!"

The noble and enduring man replied:

"No god. Why take me for a god? No, no.
I am that father whom your boyhood lacked
and suffered pain for lack of. I am he."

Held back too long, the tears ran down his cheeks
as he embraced his son.

Only Telemachus,
uncomprehending,° wild
with incredulity,° cried out:

"You cannot
be my father Odysseus! Meddling spirits
conceived this trick to twist the knife in me!°
No man of woman born could work these wonders

15 **dissemble:** pretend.

24 **ruddy:** tanned.

28 **thunderstruck:** astonished. The word is carefully chosen for its additional association with the works of one of the gods (Zeus).

35 **make you fair oblation:** offer you good sacrifices and proper worship.

44 **uncomprehending:** not understanding.

45 **incredulity:** disbelief.

47–48 **Meddling . . . me:** Telemachus assumes that interfering gods **(Meddling spirits)** thought up **(conceived)** this astonishing transformation to intensify his pain **(twist the knife)** over his father's long absence and possible death.

by his own craft, unless a god came into it
with ease to turn him young or old at will.
I swear you were in rags and old,
and here you stand like one of the immortals!"°

Odysseus brought his ranging mind to bear°
and said:

"This is not princely, to be swept
away by wonder at your father's presence.
No other Odysseus will ever come,
for he and I are one, the same; his bitter
fortune and his wanderings are mine.
Twenty years gone, and I am back again
on my own island.

As for my change of skin,
that is a charm Athena, Hope of Soldiers,°
uses as she will; she has the knack
to make me seem a beggar man sometimes
and sometimes young, with finer clothes about me.
It is no hard thing for the gods of heaven
to glorify a man or bring him low."°

When he had spoken, down he sat.

Then, throwing
his arms around this marvel of a father
Telemachus began to weep. Salt tears
rose from the wells of longing in both men,
and cries burst from both as keen and fluttering
as those of the great taloned hawk,
whose nestlings farmers take before they fly.
So helplessly they cried, pouring out tears,
and might have gone on weeping so till sundown,
had not Telemachus said:

"Dear father! Tell me
what kind of vessel put you here ashore
on Ithaca? Your sailors, who were they?
I doubt you made it, walking on the sea!"

Then said Odysseus, who had borne the barren sea:°

53 **the immortals:** a common reference to the gods, who never die.

54 **Odysseus . . . bear:** Odysseus focuses his thoughts.

64 **Hope of Soldiers:** When she chooses to be, Athena is a fierce battle-goddess, defending Greece—and favored Greeks—from outside enemies.

68–69 **It is . . . low:** It isn't difficult for the gods to make a man appear great or humble.

85 **borne the barren sea:** endured the hardships of the sea.

Penelope and Her Handmaidens, 1920. A. F. Gorguet. Illustration from text *L'illustration.* Private collection.

Viewing the art: What does this image add to your understanding of Penelope and of what life has been like at Odysseus's great house during his absence?

"Only plain truth shall I tell you, child.
Great seafarers, the Phaeacians, gave me passage
as they give other wanderers. By night
over the open ocean, while I slept,
they brought me in their cutter,° set me down
on Ithaca, with gifts of bronze and gold
and stores of woven things. By the gods' will
these lie all hidden in a cave. I came
to this wild place, directed by Athena,
so that we might lay plans to kill our enemies.
Count up the suitors for me, let me know
what men at arms are there, how many men.
I must put all my mind to it, to see
if we two by ourselves can take them on
or if we should look round for help."

90 cutter: a single-masted sailboat.

The Beggar at the Manor

The next morning Telemachus returns home and tells Penelope about his travels but not about his father's homecoming. Odysseus, disguised again as a beggar, also returns to his own house. No one recognizes him except his faithful old dog, which lifts up its head, wags its tail, and dies. In the great hall, Telemachus permits the "beggar" to ask for food. The suitors give him bread and meat, as is the custom, but one of their leaders, a man named Antinous (an tin′ ō əs), *is particularly insulting. He refuses to offer any food, and while Odysseus is talking, he angrily interrupts.*

But here Antinous broke in, shouting:

"God!
What evil wind blew in this pest?
Get over,
stand in the passage! Nudge my table, will you?
Egyptian whips are sweet
to what you'll come to here, you nosing rat,
making your pitch to everyone!
These men have bread to throw away on you
because it is not theirs. Who cares? Who spares
another's food, when he has more than plenty?"

With guile Odysseus drew away,° then said:

12 With guile . . . away: Odysseus is slyly provoking Antinous.

"A pity that you have more looks than heart.
You'd grudge a pinch of salt from your own larder
to your own handy man. You sit here, fat
on others' meat, and cannot bring yourself
to rummage out a crust of bread for me!"

Then anger made Antinous' heart beat hard,
and, glowering° under his brows, he answered:

"Now!
You think you'll shuffle off and get away
after that impudence? Oh, no you don't!"

The stool he let fly hit the man's right shoulder
on the packed muscle under the shoulder blade—
like solid rock, for all the effect one saw.
Odysseus only shook his head, containing
thoughts of bloody work,° as he walked on,
then sat, and dropped his loaded bag again
upon the door sill. Facing the whole crowd
he said, and eyed them all:

"One word only,
my lords, and suitors of the famous queen.
One thing I have to say.
There is no pain, no burden for the heart
when blows come to a man, and he defending
his own cattle—his own cows and lambs.
Here it was otherwise. Antinous
hit me for being driven on by hunger—
how many bitter seas men cross for hunger!
If beggars interest the gods, if there are Furies
pent in the dark to avenge a poor man's wrong, then may
Antinous meet his death before his wedding day!"°

Then said Eupeithes'° son, Antinous:

"Enough.
Eat and be quiet where you are, or shamble elsewhere,
unless you want these lads to stop your mouth

19 glowering: scowling; looking at angrily.

26–27 containing thoughts of bloody work: keeping murderous thoughts under control. Odysseus imagines killing Antinous, but holds his temper.

34–42 There is . . . wedding day: A man isn't really hurt, the beggar says, when he is injured defending his property; but when he is attacked for being hungry, that's another matter. Odysseus's curse upon Antinous calls upon the **Furies**–three female spirits who punish wrongdoers–to bring about his death.

43 Eupeithes (yoo pē′ thēz)

Vocabulary

impudence (im′ pyə dəns) *n.* speech or behavior that is aggressively forward or rude

pulling you by the heels, or hands and feet,
over the whole floor, till your back is peeled!"

But now the rest were mortified, and someone
spoke from the crowd of young bucks to rebuke him:

"A poor show, that—hitting this famished tramp—
bad business, if he happened to be a god.
You know they go in foreign guise, the gods do,
looking like strangers, turning up
in towns and settlements to keep an eye
on manners, good or bad."

But at this notion
Antinous only shrugged.

Telemachus,
after the blow his father bore, sat still
without a tear, though his heart felt the blow.
Slowly he shook his head from side to side,
containing murderous thoughts.

Penelope
on the higher level of her room had heard
the blow, and knew who gave it. Now she murmured:

"Would god you could be hit yourself, Antinous—
hit by Apollo's bowshot!"°

And Eurynome°
her housekeeper, put in:

"He and no other?
If all we pray for came to pass, not one
would live till dawn!"

Her gentle mistress said:
"Oh, Nan, they are a bad lot; they intend
ruin for all of us; but Antinous
appears a blacker-hearted hound than any.

68 Apollo's bowshot: Among other things, Apollo is the archer god and the god of truth. His sacred silver bow can kill literally with an arrow, and figuratively with the truth.

69 Eurynome (yoo rin′ ə mē)

Vocabulary

mortified (môr′ tə fīd′) *adj.* deeply embarrassed, shamed, or humiliated
rebuke (ri būk′) *v.* to scold sharply; criticize
guise (gīz) *n.* outward appearance; false appearance

Here is a poor man come, a wanderer,
driven by want to beg his bread, and everyone
in hall gave bits, to cram his bag—only
Antinous threw a stool, and banged his shoulder!"

So she described it, sitting in her chamber
among her maids—while her true lord was eating.
Then she called in the forester and said:

"Go to that man on my behalf, Eumaeus,°
and send him here, so I can greet and question him.
Abroad in the great world, he may have heard
rumors about Odysseus—may have known him!"

85 Eumaeus (yoo mē′ əs)

Lively action continues in the great hall, where another beggar attempts to bully Odysseus. Antinous mockingly arranges a boxing match between the two, which Odysseus wins. Telemachus orders the disorderly crowd to leave for the evening. Surprised by his authority, the suitors obey, giving Odysseus and Telemachus time to remove all weapons from the hall as part of their preparation for battle. Then Odysseus goes to meet his wife for the first time in nearly twenty years.

Carefully Penelope began:
"Friend, let me ask you first of all:
who are you, where do you come from, of what nation
and parents were you born?"

And he replied:
"My lady, never a man in the wide world
should have a fault to find with you. Your name
has gone out under heaven like the sweet
honor of some god-fearing king, who rules
in equity° over the strong: his black lands bear
both wheat and barley, fruit trees laden bright,
new lambs at lambing time—and the deep sea
gives great hauls of fish by his good strategy,
so that his folk fare well.

O my dear lady,
this being so, let it suffice° to ask me
of other matters—not my blood, my homeland.
Do not enforce me to recall my pain.
My heart is sore; but I must not be found
sitting in tears here, in another's house:

98 equity: fairness and justice.

104 suffice: be enough.

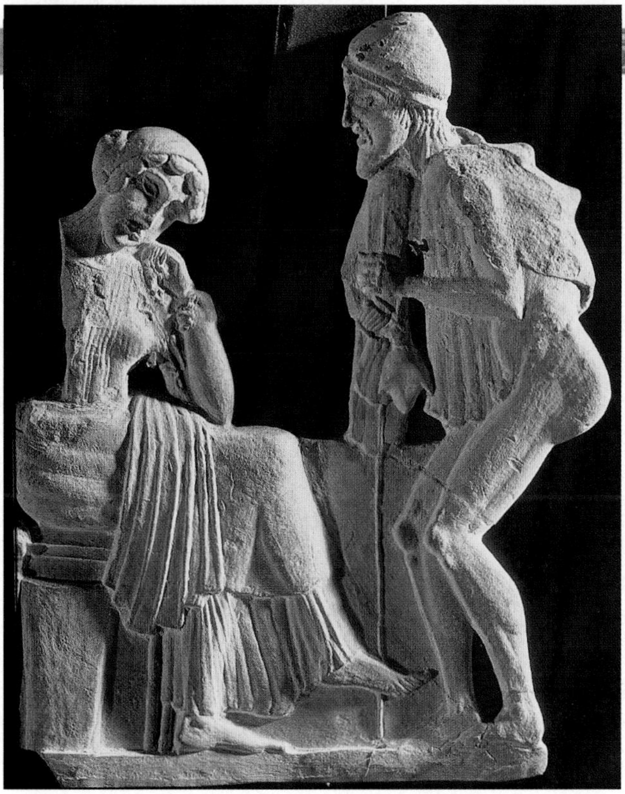

Odysseus Reunited with Penelope. Terra-cotta relief. Louvre Museum, Paris.

it is not well forever to be grieving.
One of the maids might say—or you might think—
I had got maudlin° over cups of wine."

And Penelope replied:

"Stranger, my looks,
my face, my carriage,° were soon lost or faded
when the Achaeans crossed the sea to Troy,
Odysseus my lord among the rest.
If he returned, if he were here to care for me,
I might be happily renowned!
But grief instead heaven sent me—years of pain.
Sons of the noblest families on the islands,
Dulichium, Same, wooded Zacynthus,
with native Ithacans, are here to court me,
against my wish; and they consume this house.
Can I give proper heed to guest or suppliant°
or herald° on the realm's affairs?

How could I?
wasted with longing for Odysseus, while here
they press for marriage.

111 **maudlin:** excessively and foolishly emotional.

114 **carriage:** manner of moving or holding the head and body.

124 **suppliant** (sup′ lē ənt): one who humbly begs or requests something.

125 **herald:** court messenger.

Vocabulary
renowned (ri nound′) *adj.* famous; widely known

Ruses° served my turn
to draw the time out—first a close-grained web
I had the happy thought to set up weaving
on my big loom in hall. I said, that day:
'Young men—my suitors, now my lord is dead,
let me finish my weaving before I marry,
or else my thread will have been spun in vain.
It is a shroud I weave for Lord Laertes°
when cold Death comes to lay him on his bier.°
The country wives would hold me in dishonor
if he, with all his fortune, lay unshrouded.'
I reached their hearts that way, and they agreed.
So every day I wove on the great loom,
but every night by torchlight I unwove it;
and so for three years I deceived the Achaeans.
But when the seasons brought a fourth year on,
as long months waned,° and the long days were spent,
through impudent folly in the slinking maids
they caught me—clamored up to me at night;°
I had no choice then but to finish it.
And now, as matters stand at last,
I have no strength left to evade a marriage,
cannot find any further way; my parents
urge it upon me, and my son
will not stand by while they eat up his property.
He comprehends it, being a man full grown,
able to oversee the kind of house
Zeus would endow° with honor.

129 Ruses: tricks; schemes.

136 It is . . . Laertes: Penelope has claimed to be weaving a burial cloth **(shroud)** for Odysseus's father.

137 bier: a platform on which a corpse or coffin is placed before burial.

145 waned: drew to an end.

146–147 through . . . night: After outwitting the suitors for more than three years, Penelope is finally betrayed by some of her own sneaky **(slinking)** maids, who crept into her room at night and caught her in the act of undoing her weaving.

156 endow: provide or equip.

The Test of the Bow

Resigned to ending the suitors' reign over her home, Penelope cries herself to sleep that night, dreaming of the husband she believes is lost forever. The next day the suitors return to the hall, more unruly than ever. Penelope appears, carrying the huge bow that belongs to Odysseus. Her maids follow, bearing twelve iron ax heads. Penelope has a proposition for the suitors.

"My lords, hear me:
suitors indeed, you commandeered this house
to feast and drink in, day and night, my husband

Vocabulary
commandeer (kom′ ən dēr′) *v.* to seize by force or threats

being long gone, long out of mind. You found
no justification for yourselves—none
except your lust to marry me. Stand up, then:
we now declare a contest for that prize.
Here is my lord Odysseus' hunting bow.
Bend and string it if you can. Who sends an arrow
through iron axe-helve sockets, twelve in line?°
I join my life with his, and leave this place, my home,
my rich and beautiful bridal house, forever
to be remembered, though I dream it only."

9–10 Bend . . . line: The challenge has two parts: First, a suitor must bend and string the heavy bow—a task requiring strength and skill. Second, he must shoot an arrow through the narrow holes of twelve ax-heads set in a row.

One by one the suitors try to string the bow, and all fail. Only Antinous delays his attempt. In the meantime, Odysseus steps outside with the swineherd Eumaeus and Philoetius (fi loi′ tē əs)*, another faithful herdsman, and reveals his identity to them. Odysseus returns to the hall and asks to try his hand at stringing the bow. Antinous sneers at this idea, but Penelope and Telemachus both insist he proceed. Telemachus orders the women to leave, Philoetius locks the gates of the hall, and Eumaeus presents to Odysseus the great bow he has not held for twenty years.*

And Odysseus took his time,
turning the bow, tapping it, every inch,
for borings that termites might have made
while the master of the weapon was abroad.
The suitors were now watching him, and some
jested among themselves:

"A bow lover!"

"Dealer in old bows!"

"Maybe he has one like it
at home!"

"Or has an itch to make one for himself."

"See how he handles it, the sly old buzzard!"°

And one disdainful suitor added this:

14–25 And Odysseus . . . old buzzard: As Odysseus examines the old bow for termite holes **(borings)** that might have weakened the wood since he last used it, the suitors take the chance to make fun of the "beggar."

Vocabulary

justification (jus′ tə fə kā′ shən) *n.* a reason for an action that shows it to be just, right, or reasonable

"May his fortune grow an inch for every inch he bends it!"

But the man skilled in all ways of contending,
satisfied by the great bow's look and heft,°
like a musician, like a harper, when
with quiet hand upon his instrument
he draws between his thumb and forefinger
a sweet new string upon a peg: so effortlessly
Odysseus in one motion strung the bow.
Then slid his right hand down the cord and plucked it,

29 **heft:** weight.

Odysseus Competes with the Suitors (detail). 5th century B.C., Greek. Attic red-figured skyphos. Staatliche Museum, Antikensammlung, Berlin, Germany.

Viewing the art: What do you suppose Odysseus is thinking as he takes aim?

so the taut gut° vibrating hummed and sang
a swallow's note.
In the hushed hall it smote° the suitors
and all their faces changed. Then Zeus thundered
overhead, one loud crack for a sign.
And Odysseus laughed within him that the son
of crooked-minded Cronus had flung that omen down.°
He picked one ready arrow from his table
where it lay bare: the rest were waiting still
in the quiver for the young men's turn to come.°
He nocked it,° let it rest across the handgrip,
and drew the string and grooved butt of the arrow,
aiming from where he sat upon the stool.
Now flashed
arrow from twanging bow clean as a whistle
through every socket ring, and grazed° not one,
to thud with heavy brazen head° beyond.

Then quietly
Odysseus said:

"Telemachus, the stranger
you welcomed in your hall has not disgraced you.
I did not miss, neither did I take all day
stringing the bow. My hand and eye are sound,
not so contemptible as the young men say.
The hour has come to cook their lordships' mutton°—
supper by daylight. Other amusements later,
with song and harping that adorn a feast."

He dropped his eyes and nodded, and the prince
Telemachus, true son of King Odysseus,
belted his sword on, clapped hand to his spear,
and with a clink and glitter of keen bronze
stood by his chair, in the forefront near his father.

36 **taut gut:** tightly drawn bowstring (made of animal "gut" or intestine).

38 **smote:** struck, as though from a hard blow; affected suddenly with a powerful and unexpected feeling, such as fear.

39–42 **Then Zeus . . . down:** Odysseus recognizes the crack of thunder as a sign that Zeus is on his side.

44–45 **the rest . . . come:** The remaining arrows will be used by the contestants who follow Odysseus.

46 **nocked it:** fitted the nock, or notched end, of the arrow into the string.

51 **grazed:** touched.

52 **brazen head:** brass arrowhead.

60 **cook their lordships' mutton:** literally, cook their sheep meat. But Odysseus is using a phrase that Telemachus can take metaphorically, like the phrase *cook their goose* ("get even").

Vocabulary

omen (ō′ mən) *n.* a sign or event thought to foretell good or bad fortune; forewarning

contemptible (kən temp′ tə bəl) *adj.* deserving of scorn; disgraceful

Responding to Literature

Personal Response

Did any aspects of Odysseus's behavior surprise you in part 3? Explain, telling what you might have done if you were in his place.

Analyzing Part 3

Recall and Interpret

1. What role does Athena play in reuniting Odysseus with his son, Telemachus? Give two reasons why Telemachus might have had trouble identifying his father.
2. In the first 85 lines of "The Beggar at the Manor," find at least two examples of **foreshadowing** that the suitors will be punished.
3. Why does Penelope summon Odysseus? What is **ironic** about her interview with him? What does his restraint say about his character?
4. What is "the test of the bow"? In your opinion, is this a fair test? Explain your answer.

Evaluate and Connect

5. In your opinion, is the recognition scene between Telemachus and Odysseus true-to-life? Explain why or why not.
6. Describe how Homer establishes Antinous as Odysseus's principal **antagonist** among the suitors. (See Literary Terms Handbook, page R1.)
7. What do you think of Antinous's behavior toward the "beggar"? Do people treat each other this way today? Explain.
8. Paraphrase lines 28–37 of "The Test of the Bow." Why do you suppose Homer uses an **epic simile** to describe this moment? (See page R5.)

Literary **ELEMENTS**

Characterization

Characterization is the method a writer uses to reveal a character's personality. In **indirect characterization,** a character's personality is revealed through the character's words, thoughts, or actions or through those of other characters. In **direct characterization,** direct statements are made about a character's personality.

1. What methods of characterization does Homer use to reveal Penelope's personality? Support your ideas with examples.
2. For another character in part 3, find an action, a line or two of dialogue, or another clue to characterization. Tell what this evidence suggests about the character's personality.

- See **Literary Terms Handbook,** p. R2.

Extending Your Response

Literature Groups

Assessing Options Odysseus is planning to make the suitors pay for their behavior—but do they all deserve the same fate? What do you predict will happen? What do you want to happen? Discuss these questions in your group. Then discuss the advantages and disadvantages of two opposite courses of action available to Odysseus and Telemachus. Call one "Let 'em have it" and the other "Let's be reasonable." Vote on which course of action you prefer. Share your results with the class.

Personal Writing

A Sweet Reunion Reread "Father and Son" from part 3. Then imagine that you are either Odysseus or Telemachus. Write in your journal what you were thinking and feeling when you became reunited with your loved one. Remember that it's been twenty years since the two have seen each other and that Telemachus was just a little boy when his father left home.

Save your work for your portfolio.

Vo•cab•u•lar•y Skills

Understanding Homophones

Homophones (hom′ ə fōnz) are words that sound the same but have different spellings. The word comes from the Latin *homo,* meaning "same," and *phone,* meaning "sound." You'll confuse your readers if you use an incorrect homophone in your writing.

Some homophones differ greatly in meaning but only slightly in spelling. These are the ones that cause the most problems. For example, you must memorize that *stationary* means "unmoving" and *stationery* means "writing paper." To keep the spellings of *principal* and *principle* clear in your mind, remember that "the *principal* (of your school) is your *pal.*"

Recognizing the difference between a pronoun and contraction can be especially tricky, and you need to think about these homophones very carefully. Remember that *it's* is a shortened form for *it is* and not the possessive form of the pronoun *it.* The same is true for *who's* and *whose,* and *your* and *you're.*

Although computers allow you to write and correct work easily, homophones present a problem if you rely on a computer program to check spelling. Such a program can tell you that *thier* is misspelled. It cannot, however, tell you that you used *their* when you should have used *there. There* are some things for which people cannot rely on *their* computers!

EXERCISE

If the underlined word is the correct one to use, write *Correct.* If it is a homophone for the correct word, write the word that should have been used. Use your dictionary if you're not sure which word is correct.

The *Odyssey* is a rip-roaring tail (1). In the coarse (2) of his journey, Odysseus guides his ship threw (3) straights (4) and across stormy waters. On his route (5) homeward, he listens to the pleas (6) of his men as monsters seas (7), mall (8), and slay (9) them. Tied to the ship's massed (10), he hears the Sirens' call. He consults prophets (11) and he praise (12) to the gods, who constantly medal (13) in human affairs, often in response to their own miner (14) jealousies about each other. His life is very hard, but perhaps Penelope's is harder. For twenty years, she must play the roll (15) of faithful wife without even knowing if Odysseus is alive or dead.

Reading & Thinking Skills

Identifying Main Ideas and Supporting Details

Whether you are reading a piece of expository writing or an epic poem, you will probably encounter a good deal of description and detail. One way to increase your comprehension of heavily detailed material is to identify the main idea of individual passages. How might you identify the main idea in the following passage from the *Odyssey*?

> **"But in the end,**
> **when all the barley in the ship was gone,**
> **hunger drove them to scour the wild shore**
> **with angling hooks, for fishes and sea fowl,**
> **whatever fell into their hands; and lean days**
> **wore their bellies thin."**

Identify the supporting details: facts, statistics, sensory details, incidents, or examples. Next, ask yourself what main idea these details support. Main ideas appear in one of two ways.

- The main idea may be **directly stated** in a topic sentence at the beginning, middle, or end of a paragraph. Directly stated main ideas are often found in expository writing.
- The main idea may be **indirectly stated,** or implied. This occurs when the supporting details are strongly linked by a common idea.

In the above passage, the main idea–that the men are growing thin from inadequate nourishment–is directly stated.

- For more about related comprehension skills, see **Reading Handbook,** pp. R82–R94.

EXERCISE

Read the following passage about Homer, then answer the questions that follow.

> **Homer would commonly recycle whole passages of poetry. These typically involved routine actions. How a character enters a room, puts on his armor, goes to bed, or says good-bye to his host may be expressed in exactly the same way several times throughout a poem. It has been estimated that about one-third of the *Odyssey* and the *Iliad* consists of repeated lines!**

1. What is the main idea of this passage? Is it stated directly or implied?
2. What details from the passage support the main idea?

Before You Read

from the *Odyssey, Part 4*

Building Background

Did You Know?

Although Homer probably composed the *Odyssey* between 750 and 700 B.C., the epic is set during the Mycenaean period, which is a much earlier time in Greek history. Archaeological research has discovered that during the 400-year era from about 1600 B.C. to 1200 B.C., a remarkable civilization grew up around the city of Mycenae. This culture built massive palaces and forts. On a smaller scale, its skilled artisans created exquisitely decorated tools, including weapons and drinking vessels in bronze and silver. There was a form of writing.

But the Mycenaean culture came tumbling down swiftly and mysteriously. By about 1100 B.C., its palaces were in ruins, its artists were scattered, and the secret of its writing had been lost (it was rediscovered three thousand years later, after World War II). The brilliance of Greece entered a dark age from which it did not return until the age of Homer. In part 4, as in much of the *Odyssey,* Homer offers his audience glimpses of the government, social classes, customs, architecture, and values of Mycenaean culture, which he collected from the myths and legends that had been passed on orally from that time. To Homer's generations, his works were history, the only connection to the glorious past.

Gold funerary mask from Mycenae, c. 1600–1200 B.C.

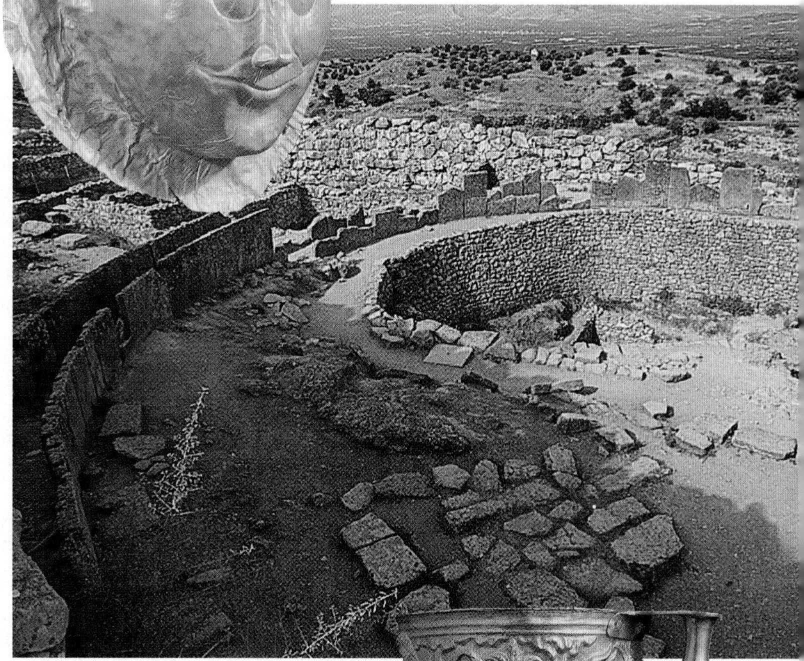

Ruins of a grave circle in Mycenae, c. 1200 B.C.

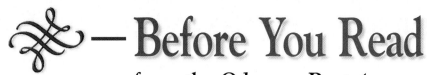

Mycenaean gold cup, c. 1500 B.C.

Vocabulary Preview

wily (wī′ lē) *adj.* tricky or sly; crafty; p. 870

revelry (rev′ əl rē) *n.* noisy festivity; merrymaking; p. 870

jostle (jos′ əl) *v.* to bump, push, or shove roughly, as with elbows in a crowd; p. 870

implacable (im plak′ ə bəl) *adj.* impossible to satisfy or soothe; unyielding; p. 872

deflect (di flekt′) *v.* to cause to go off course; turn aside; p. 872

revulsion (ri vul′shən) *n.* intense dislike, disgust, or horror; p. 872

lavish (lav′ ish) *v.* to give generously; provide in abundance; p. 877

aloof (ə lo͞of′) *adj.* emotionally distant; uninvolved; disinterested; standoffish; p. 878

tremulous (trem′ yə ləs) *adj.* characterized by trembling; shaky; p. 879

Part 4

Death in the Great Hall

Now shrugging off his rags the wiliest fighter of the islands
leapt and stood on the broad door sill, his own bow in his hand.
He poured out at his feet a rain of arrows from the quiver
and spoke to the crowd:

"So much for that. Your clean-cut game is over.
Now watch me hit a target that no man has hit before,
if I can make this shot. Help me, Apollo."

He drew to his fist the cruel head of an arrow for Antinous
just as the young man leaned to lift his beautiful drinking cup,
embossed,° two-handled, golden: the cup was in his fingers:
the wine was even at his lips: and did he dream of death?
How could he? In that revelry amid his throng of friends
who would imagine a single foe—though a strong foe indeed—
could dare to bring death's pain on him and darkness on his eyes?
Odysseus' arrow hit him under the chin
and punched up to the feathers° through his throat.

Backward and down he went, letting the winecup fall
from his shocked hand. Like pipes his nostrils jetted
crimson runnels,° a river of mortal red,
and one last kick upset his table
knocking the bread and meat to soak in dusty blood.
Now as they craned to see their champion where he lay
the suitors jostled in uproar down the hall,
everyone on his feet. Wildly they turned and scanned
the walls in the long room for arms; but not a shield,
not a good ashen spear was there for a man to take and throw.°
All they could do was yell in outrage at Odysseus:

"Foul! to shoot at a man! That was your last shot!"

"Your own throat will be slit for this!"

10 embossed: decorated with designs that are slightly raised from the surface.

16 punched up to the feathers: The arrow goes clear through the throat so that only the arrow's feathers remain visible in front.

19 runnels: streams.

24–26 Wildly . . . throw: Odysseus and Telemachus had removed all weapons and armor from the room on the previous night.

Vocabulary

wily (wī′ lē) *adj.* tricky or sly; crafty
revelry (rev′ əl rē) *n.* noisy festivity; merrymaking
jostle (jos′ əl) *v.* to bump, push, or shove roughly, as with elbows in a crowd

"Our finest lad is down!
You killed the best on Ithaca."

"Buzzards will tear your eyes out!"

For they imagined as they wished—that it was a wild shot,
an unintended killing—fools, not to comprehend
they were already in the grip of death.°
But glaring under his brows Odysseus answered:

"You yellow dogs, you thought I'd never make it
home from the land of Troy. You took my house to plunder,
twisted my maids to serve your beds. You dared
bid for my wife while I was still alive.
Contempt was all you had for the gods who rule wide heaven,
contempt for what men say of you hereafter.
Your last hour has come. You die in blood."

As they all took this in, sickly green fear
pulled at their entrails, and their eyes flickered
looking for some hatch or hideaway from death.
Eurymachus alone could speak. He said:

"If you are Odysseus of Ithaca come back,
all that you say these men have done is true.
Rash actions, many here, more in the countryside.
But here he lies, the man who caused them all.
Antinous was the ringleader, he whipped us on°
to do these things. He cared less for a marriage
than for the power Cronion° has denied him
as king of Ithaca. For that
he tried to trap your son and would have killed him.
He is dead now and has his portion.° Spare
your own people. As for ourselves, we'll make
restitution of wine and meat consumed,
and add, each one, a tithe° of twenty oxen
with gifts of bronze and gold to warm your heart.
Meanwhile we cannot blame you for your anger."

Odysseus glowered under his black brows
and said:

"Not for the whole treasure of your fathers,
all you enjoy, lands, flocks, or any gold

33–35 For they . . . death: The suitors still don't realize that their opponent is Odysseus, and that he has killed Antinous intentionally.

52 whipped us on: encouraged us; drove us.

54 Cronion: Zeus.

57 his portion: what he deserved; what fate had in store for him.

60 tithe (tīth): payment; tax.

put up by others, would I hold my hand.
There will be killing till the score is paid.
You forced yourselves upon this house. Fight your way out,
or run for it, if you think you'll escape death.
I doubt one man of you skins by."°

They felt their knees fail, and their hearts—but heard
Eurymachus for the last time rallying them.

"Friends," he said, "the man is implacable.
Now that he's got his hands on bow and quiver
he'll shoot from the big door stone there
until he kills us to the last man.
Fight, I say,
let's remember the joy of it. Swords out!
Hold up your tables to deflect his arrows.
After me, everyone: rush him where he stands.
If we can budge him from the door, if we can pass
into the town, we'll call out men to chase him.
This fellow with his bow will shoot no more."

He drew his own sword as he spoke, a broadsword of fine bronze,
honed like a razor on either edge. Then crying hoarse and loud
he hurled himself at Odysseus. But the kingly man let fly
an arrow at that instant, and the quivering feathered butt°
sprang to the nipple of his breast as the barb° stuck in his liver.
The bright broadsword clanged down. He lurched and fell aside,
pitching across his table. His cup, his bread and meat,
were spilt and scattered far and wide, and his head slammed
on the ground.
Revulsion, anguish in his heart, with both feet kicking out,
he downed his chair, while the shrouding wave of mist° closed
on his eyes.

Amphinomus° now came running at Odysseus,
broadsword naked in his hand. He thought to make
the great soldier give way at the door.
But with a spear throw from behind Telemachus hit him
between the shoulders, and the lancehead drove

71 **skins by:** gets out alive.

88 **butt:** end.

89 **barb:** arrowhead; point.

94 **shrouding wave of mist:** death.

95 **Amphinomus** (am fin′ ə məs)

Vocabulary

implacable (im plak′ ə bəl) *adj.* impossible to satisfy or soothe; unyielding
deflect (di flekt′) *v.* to cause to go off course; turn aside
revulsion (ri vul′ shən) *n.* intense dislike, disgust, or horror

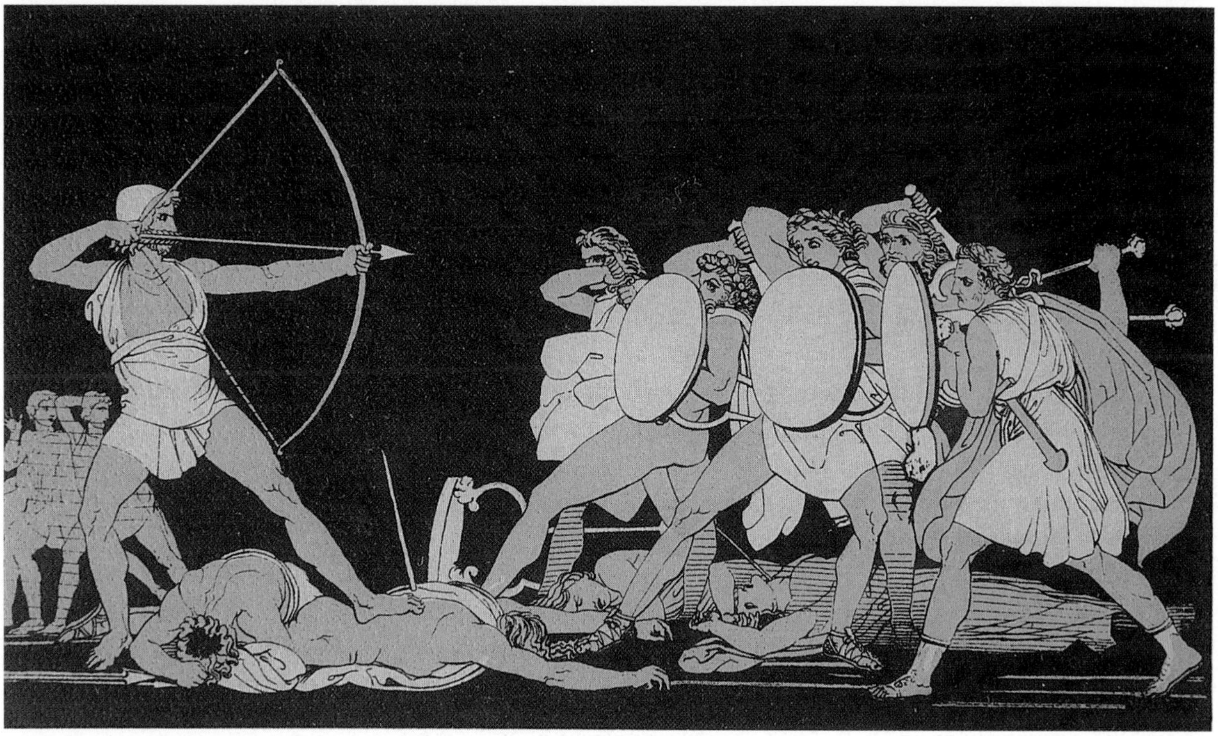

Odysseus Slaying the Suitors.
Viewing the art: What does this image suggest to you about Odysseus's standing among other men?

clear through his chest. He left his feet and fell
forward, thudding, forehead against the ground.
Telemachus swerved around him, leaving the long dark spear
planted in Amphinomus. If he paused to yank it out
someone might jump him from behind or cut him down with a sword
at the moment he bent over. So he ran—ran from the tables
to his father's side and halted, panting, saying:

"Father let me bring you a shield and spear,
a pair of spears, a helmet.
I can arm on the run myself; I'll give
outfits to Eumaeus and this cowherd.
Better to have equipment."

Said Odysseus:

"Run then, while I hold them off with arrows
as long as the arrows last. When all are gone
if I'm alone they can dislodge° me."

115 **dislodge:** force back; kill.

Quick
upon his father's word Telemachus
ran to the room where spears and armor lay.
He caught up four light shields, four pairs of spears,
four helms of war high-plumed with flowing manes,°
and ran back, loaded down, to his father's side.
He was the first to pull a helmet on
and slide his bare arm in a buckler strap.°
The servants armed themselves, and all three took their stand
beside the master of battle.°
While he had arrows
he aimed and shot, and every shot brought down
one of his huddling enemies.
But when all barbs had flown from the bowman's fist,
he leaned his bow in the bright entry way
beside the door, and armed: a four-ply shield
hard on his shoulder, and a crested helm,
horsetailed, nodding stormy upon his head,
then took his tough and bronze-shod spears.

120 **helms . . . manes:** war helmets decorated from front to back with a crest or ridge of long feathers resembling horses' manes.

123 **slide . . . strap:** The Greeks' small, round shield **(buckler)** had a strap in back through which the warrior slid his arm.

125 **master of battle:** Odysseus.

Odysseus and Telemachus, along with their two allies, cut down all the suitors. Athena also makes an appearance, rallying their spirits and ensuring that none of her favorites is injured. Finally the great hall is quiet.

In blood and dust
he saw that crowd all fallen, many and many slain.

Think of a catch that fishermen haul in to a halfmoon bay
in a fine-meshed net from the whitecaps of the sea:
how all are poured out on the sand, in throes for° the salt sea,
twitching their cold lives away in Helios' fiery air:
so lay the suitors heaped on one another.

139 **in throes for:** in pain or struggle to return to.

The Trunk of the Olive Tree

Penelope's old nurse hurries upstairs to tell her mistress that Odysseus has returned and that all the suitors are dead. Penelope is amazed but refuses to admit that the stranger could be her husband. Instead, she believes that he must be a god.

The old nurse sighed:

"How queer, the way you talk!

Here he is, large as life, by his own fire,
and you deny he ever will get home!
Child, you always were mistrustful!
But there is one sure mark that I can tell you:
that scar left by the boar's tusk long ago.
I recognized it when I bathed his feet
and would have told you, but he stopped my mouth,
forbade me, in his craftiness.
Come down,
I stake my life on it, he's here!
Let me die in agony if I lie!"

Penelope said:

"Nurse dear, though you have your wits about you,
still it is hard not to be taken in
by the immortals. Let us join my son, though,
and see the dead and that strange one who killed them."
She turned then to descend the stair, her heart
in tumult. Had she better keep her distance
and question him, her husband? Should she run
up to him, take his hands, kiss him now?°
Crossing the door sill she sat down at once
in firelight, against the nearest wall,
across the room from the lord Odysseus.
There
leaning against a pillar, sat the man
and never lifted up his eyes, but only waited
for what his wife would say when she had seen him.
And she, for a long time, sat deathly still
in wonderment—for sometimes as she gazed
she found him—yes, clearly—like her husband,
but sometimes blood and rags were all she saw.°
Telemachus' voice came to her ears:

"Mother,
cruel mother, do you feel nothing,
drawing yourself apart this way from Father?
Will you not sit with him and talk and question him?
What other woman could remain so cold?
Who shuns her lord, and he come back to her
from wars and wandering, after twenty years?
Your heart is hard as flint and never changes!"

19–22 She turned . . . now: Penelope's thoughts reveal that she is not so uncertain of "that strange one" as she has let on.

33 blood . . . saw: Odysseus is again disguised as the old beggar.

Penelope answered:

"I am stunned, child.
I cannot speak to him. I cannot question him.
I cannot keep my eyes upon his face.
If really he is Odysseus, truly home,
beyond all doubt we two shall know each other
better than you or anyone. There are
secret signs we know, we two."°

A smile
came now to the lips of the patient hero, Odysseus,
who turned to Telemachus and said:

"Peace: let your mother test me at her leisure.
Before long she will see and know me best.
These tatters, dirt—all that I'm caked with now—
make her look hard at me and doubt me still.
As to this massacre, we must see the end.
Whoever kills one citizen, you know,
and has no force of armed men at his back,
had better take himself abroad by night
and leave his kin. Well, we cut down the flower of Ithaca,
the mainstay of the town. Consider that."°

Telemachus replied respectfully:

"Dear Father,
enough that you yourself study the danger,
foresighted in combat as you are,
they say you have no rival.

We three stand
ready to follow you and fight. I say
for what our strength avails,° we have the courage."

And the great tactician,° Odysseus, answered:

"Good.
Here is our best maneuver, as I see it:
bathe, you three,° and put fresh clothing on,
order the women to adorn themselves,
and let our admirable harper choose a tune
for dancing, some lighthearted air, and strum it.

50 secret . . . two: Eurynome has already said that she recognized Odysseus's scar; but Penelope is thinking of signs that are a secret strictly between her and Odysseus.

58–63 As to . . . Consider that: Odysseus warns that the "massacre" will have consequences, since the suitors were the most promising young men of Ithaca. (A ship's main mast is steadied by ropes called *mainstays.*) He suggests that he may be forced to flee at night—leaving his family again.

71 avails: is worth; helps.

72 tactician: one skilled in forming and carrying out (military) tactics or plans.

75 you three: Telemachus, Eumaeus, and Philoetius.

Anyone going by, or any neighbor,
will think it is a wedding feast he hears.
These deaths must not be cried about the town
till we can slip away to our own woods. We'll see
what weapon, then, Zeus puts into our hands."°

They listened attentively, and did his bidding,
bathed and dressed afresh; and all the maids
adorned themselves. Then Phemius° the harper
took his polished shell° and plucked the strings,
moving the company to desire
for singing, for the sway and beat of dancing,
until they made the manor hall resound
with gaiety of men and grace of women.
Anyone passing on the road would say:

"Married at last, I see—the queen so many courted.
Sly, cattish wife! She would not keep—not she!—
the lord's estate until he came."

So travelers'
thoughts might run—but no one guessed the truth.
Greathearted Odysseus, home at last,
was being bathed now by Eurynome
and rubbed with golden oil, and clothed again
in a fresh tunic and a cloak. Athena
lent him beauty, head to foot. She made him
taller, and massive, too, with crisping hair
in curls like petals of wild hyacinth
but all red-golden. Think of gold infused
on silver by a craftsman, whose fine art
Hephaestus° taught him, or Athena:° one
whose work moves to delight: just so she lavished
beauty over Odysseus' head and shoulders.
He sat then in the same chair by the pillar,
facing his silent wife, and said:

"Strange woman,
the immortals of Olympus made you hard,
harder than any. Who else in the world

Vocabulary
lavish (lav′ ish) *v.* to give generously; provide in abundance

74–83 Here . . . hands: Odysseus's plan is this: First, stall for time by making people think that Penelope's wedding feast is in progress. Then escape to the woods, and trust in Zeus.

86 Phemius (fē′ mē əs)

87 polished shell: harp.

Youth Singing and Playing the Kithara, c. 490 B.C. Terra-cotta, height: 16⅜ in. The Metropolitan Museum of Art, New York.

107 Hephaestus (hi fes′ təs): the god of fire and metalworking. **Athena:** in addition to all her other roles, she was the goddess of arts and crafts.

would keep aloof as you do from her husband
if he returned to her from years of trouble,
cast on his own land in the twentieth year?°

Nurse, make up a bed for me to sleep on.
Her heart is iron in her breast."

Penelope
spoke to Odysseus now. She said:

"Strange man,
if man you are . . . This is no pride on my part
nor scorn for you—not even wonder, merely.
I know so well how you—how he—appeared
boarding the ship for Troy. But all the same . . .

Make up his bed for him, Eurycleia.°
Place it outside the bedchamber my lord
built with his own hands. Pile the big bed
with fleeces, rugs, and sheets of purest linen."°

With this she tried him to the breaking point,
and he turned on her in a flash raging:

"Woman, by heaven you've stung me now!
Who dared to move my bed?
No builder had the skill for that—unless
a god came down to turn the trick. No mortal
in his best days could budge it with a crowbar.
There is our pact and pledge, our secret sign,
built into that bed—my handiwork
and no one else's!

An old trunk of olive
grew like a pillar on the building plot,
and I laid out our bedroom round that tree,
lined up the stone walls, built the walls and roof,
gave it a doorway and smooth-fitting doors.
Then I lopped off the silvery leaves and branches,
hewed and shaped that stump from the roots up
into a bedpost, drilled it, let it serve

112–117 Strange . . . year: Finally, after all his other battles have been won, Odysseus must win back his wife. Now he questions and criticizes her with uncharacteristic directness.

127 Eurycleia (yoo′ ri klē′ ə)

127–130 Make up . . . linen: Sounding sweetly hospitable, Penelope now tests the man who says he is her husband. She proposes that her maid move Odysseus's big bed out of the bedchamber and make it up.

Vocabulary

aloof (ə lo͞of′) *adj.* emotionally distant; uninvolved; disinterested; standoffish as model for the rest. I planed them all, inlaid them all with silver, gold and ivory, 150 and stretched a bed between—a pliant web of oxhide thongs dyed crimson.

There's our sign!

I know no more. Could someone else's hand have sawn that trunk and dragged the frame away?"° 155

> Their secret! as she heard it told, her knees grew tremulous and weak, her heart failed her. With eyes brimming tears she ran to him, throwing her arms around his neck, and kissed him, murmuring:

> > "Do not rage at me, Odysseus!

No one ever matched your caution! Think what difficulty the gods gave: they denied us life together in our prime and flowering years, kept us from crossing into age together. Forgive me, don't be angry. I could not welcome you with love on sight! I armed myself

long ago against the frauds of men, impostors who might come—and all those many whose underhanded ways bring evil on! . . .

But here and now, what sign could be so clear as this of our own bed? No other man has ever laid eyes on it—

only my own slave, Actoris,° that my father sent with me as a gift—she kept our door.

You make my stiff heart know that I am yours."

Now from his breast into his eyes the ache of longing mounted, and he wept at last, his dear wife, clear and faithful, in his arms,

longed for 180

160

165

170

175

185

as the sunwarmed earth is longed for by a swimmer spent in rough water where his ship went down under Poseidon's blows, gale winds and tons of sea. Few men can keep alive through a big surf to crawl, clotted with brine, on kindly beaches

133-155 Woman, ... away: The original bed could not be moved. One bedpost was a tree trunk rooted in the ground, a secret known only by Penelope, a servant, and Odysseus, who built the bed with his own hands. Furious and hurt, Odvsseus thinks Penelope has allowed someone to saw the bed frame from

174 Actoris (ak tôr' is)

Vocabulary

tremulous (trem' yə ləs) adj. characterized by trembling; shaky

in joy, in joy, knowing the abyss behind:°
and so she too rejoiced, her gaze upon her husband,
her white arms round him pressed as though forever.

181–186 a swimmer . . . behind: Odysseus is compared to someone who swims to shore after a shipwreck. Coated with sea salt **(clotted with brine)**, he rejoices that his wife is in his arms and his hellish experience **(the abyss)** is over.

The next day, Odysseus is reunited with his father, Laertes, as news of the death of the suitors passes through town. Families go to Odysseus's manor to gather the bodies for burial. There, Antinous's father rallies the families to avenge the deaths of their sons and brothers. As battle begins, however, Athena appears and calls the island to peace.

Odysseus Returns to Penelope. Isaac Taylor. Engraving. Private collection.

Viewing the art: What can you tell about the relationship between Penelope and Odysseus? How does this engraving enhance your understanding?

Responding to Literature

Personal Response

How did you respond to the way in which Odysseus dealt with the suitors?

Analyzing Part 4

Recall

1. Describe the death of Antinous.
2. How does Eurymachus attempt to avert bloodshed? How does Odysseus respond?
3. What role does Telemachus play in the fight against the suitors?
4. What evidence do the nurse and Telemachus provide to convince Penelope that the stranger is Odysseus? How does she respond?
5. In the end, what convinces Penelope that her husband has returned?

Interpret

6. In your opinion, why does Odysseus choose Antinous as his first victim? Why do the suitors react to Antinous's death as they do?
7. Review Eurymachus's speech on page 871, lines 48–62. Why might he have thought that these words could persuade Odysseus to choose another course of action? Why does Odysseus refuse to give in?
8. How does Telemachus prove that he can think and act like his father?
9. Penelope faces this dilemma after the suitors are killed: "Had she better keep her distance / and question him, her husband? Should she run / up to him, take his hands, kiss him now?" What are her choices? Why might she be unclear about what to do?
10. Explain why Penelope's test of Odysseus's identity brings him "to the breaking point." Of all his challenges, why might this be the toughest?

Evaluate and Connect

11. Do you believe that Odysseus's desire for revenge is common in society today? Explain.
12. Reread your response to the Reading Focus on page 809. How does your experience, or that of your acquaintance, compare with that of Odysseus?
13. Give one or more reasons why the **epic simile** on pages 879–880, lines 177–188, is particularly appropriate.
14. From the way he describes Penelope, would you say that Homer's attitude toward women seems old-fashioned or modern? Explain.
15. What is your response to the ending of part 4? Are happy endings ever true-to-life? Explain.

Literary ELEMENTS

Climax

In a story or epic narrative, the **climax** is the moment when the events of the plot reach an emotional high point and the action takes a new turn. Very often this is also the moment of greatest interest or excitement for the reader. In a long work such as the *Odyssey,* there may be more than one climax. Odysseus's encounter with Polyphemus, for example, is a self-contained tale within the epic—and the moment when Odysseus blinds the Cyclops is its climax.

1. What is the climax of "Death in the Great Hall"? What is the climax of "The Trunk of the Olive Tree"?
2. Which of these climaxes could be considered the climax of the epic as a whole? Explain your answer.

- See **Literary Terms Handbook,** p. R3.

Literary Criticism

"Homer possessed an exceptionally powerful and imaginative visual sense," writes Michael Grant, "which prompted Voltaire to define him as a 'sublime painter.'" How does Homer use sensory details and descriptive language to paint vivid visual images in the *Odyssey*? Write a brief essay, analyzing the work's visual elements. Support your ideas with specific references to the text.

Literature and Writing

Writing About Literature

Analyzing Character Reread the section in which Odysseus's identity is revealed to Penelope. Why doesn't Penelope immediately accept her long-lost husband? What does her hesitation say about her character and about her twenty-year ordeal? In a few paragraphs, explain why Penelope acts the way she does and explore how her reaction affects your own response to this part of the *Odyssey.*

Creative Writing

The End Several authors have written works describing Odysseus's life after his return home. What might *you* include in a sequel to Homer's tale? Does Odysseus remain settled with his wife and son–or do the gods, or adventure, lead him elsewhere? Write an imaginative account of Odysseus's life and death after his odyssey. Be sure to include at least one epic simile!

Extending Your Response

Literature Groups

Defining a Hero With a group, decide whether or not Odysseus is a hero. Come to a consensus about what a hero is and whether a hero can have any flaws or weaknesses. Discuss Odysseus's specific actions, qualities, or decisions. Then explain to the class why you do or do not think Odysseus is a hero.

Internet Connection

Traveling in Time After twenty years away, Odysseus found things had changed on the island of Ithaca. What would he discover there today? Generate some researchable questions about modern-day Ithaca, and use the Internet to find the answers. Present your findings in a report that includes a list of works cited.

The island of Ithaca.

Interdisciplinary Activity

Art: Movie Poster Design a poster advertising a movie version of the *Odyssey.* Draw, paint, and use collage to create eye-catching images that you think represent the spirit, events, and characters (including gods and monsters) of Homer's epic poem. Include a few lines of catchy description or excerpts from rave reviews to attract potential viewers. You might even include a cast of well-known actors who fit the principal roles.

Reading Further

If you enjoyed these excerpts from the *Odyssey,* you might enjoy reading the complete poem, available in several translations. You might also enjoy these epic poems:

The *Iliad,* Homer's tale of gods and men at the siege of Troy. Meet Odysseus before he begins his journey home.

Beowulf, written in Old English by an unknown author, tells of the adventures of another epic hero during the Middle Ages.

Save your work for your portfolio.

Skill Minilessons

GRAMMAR AND LANGUAGE • Compound Adjectives

Sometimes writers find it pleasing to shorten and simplify a descriptive passage by connecting two words with a hyphen and using them as an adjective before a noun. For example, instead of "a net with fine mesh," this translation of the *Odyssey* says "a fine-meshed net." Likewise, the phrase "caves hollowed by the sea" has become "sea-hollowed caves." "Fine-meshed" and "sea-hollowed" are called compound adjectives.

PRACTICE Rewrite the following phrases so that they contain compound adjectives:

1. strap with two handles
2. sheep with stiff legs
3. thunderbolt that is white with heat
4. bow that is made well

For more about punctuation of compound adjectives, see **Language Handbook,** p. R51.

READING AND THINKING • Recognizing Cause and Effect

Writers often try to show their readers why things happen as they do. The ancient Greeks believed that gods caused many of life's mysteries: thunder, war, particular storms at sea. How a person behaved mattered too. Good and bad actions led to rewards and punishments. The *Odyssey* is full of examples of cause and effect.

For more on comprehension strategies, see **Reading Handbook,** p. R86.

PRACTICE Decide whether each event listed below is a cause, an effect, or both. If the event is a cause, write down one effect, and vice versa. If it is both, include a cause and an effect.

1. Odysseus suffers a series of misfortunes at sea.
2. Odysseus's men kill the cattle of Helios.
3. Each night Penelope unravels the shroud she is weaving.
4. Antinous throws a stool at Odysseus.

VOCABULARY • Etymology

It is not always obvious how the history of a word is tied to its present-day meaning. *Aloof,* for example, comes from the Dutch *a-*, meaning "toward," and *loef,* meaning "windward," so *aloof* literally means "to turn into the wind." A sailor would turn a ship into the wind to keep it away from the shore. To behave in an *aloof* fashion is very much like "steering clear of" other people.

Here are the etymologies of four other vocabulary words from the *Odyssey:*

- *comprehend:* from the Latin *com-*, "with," and *prehendere,* "to seize"
- *commandeer:* from the French *commander,* "to command"
- *implacable:* from the Latin *in-*, "not," and *placare,* "to make peaceful"
- lavish: from the French lavache, "a torrent of rain," which is from the Latin lavare, "to wash"

PRACTICE Use the etymologies to answer the questions below.

1. If a criminal is *apprehended,* is that person suspected, arrested, or convicted?
2. Which example of forcefully "taking" could be described as *commandeering*–mugging or hijacking?
3. Would you be most likely to *placate* a baby by rocking it, waking it, or tickling it?
4. Which word might be more likely to share a history with *lavish–lavatory* or *lavender?*

MEDIA connection

Song

When people who love each other are separated—by death, war, or irreconcilable differences, for example—the healing process can take years and years.

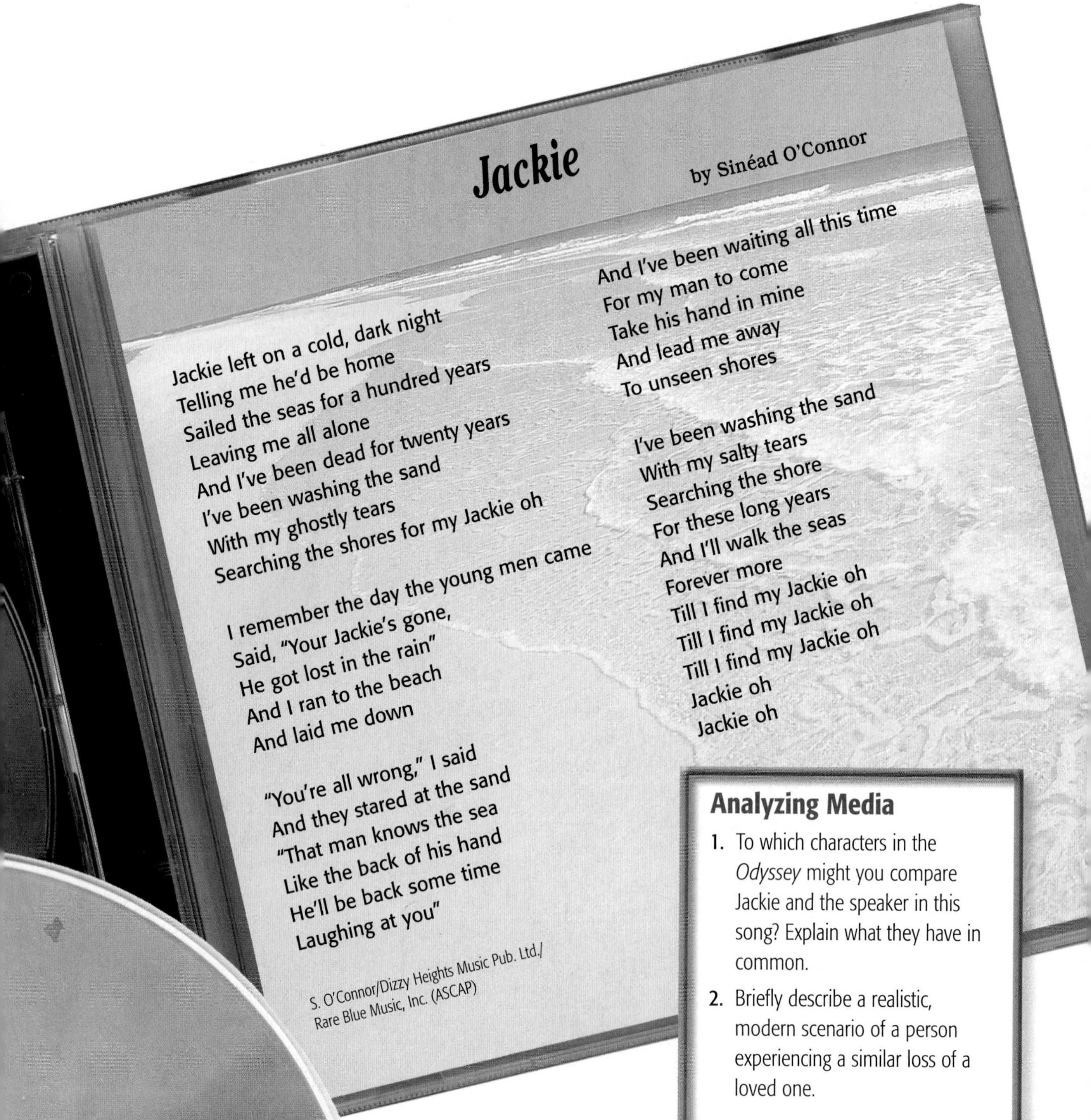

Jackie
by Sinéad O'Connor
Jackie left on a cold, dark night
Telling me he'd be home
Sailed the seas for a hundred years
Leaving me all alone
And I've been dead for twenty years
I've been washing the sand
With my ghostly tears
Searching the shores for my Jackie oh
I remember the day the young men came
Said, "Your Jackie's gone,
He got lost in the rain"
And I ran to the beach
And laid me down
"You're all wrong," I said
And they stared at the sand
"That man knows the sea
Like the back of his hand
He'll be back some time
Laughing at you"
And I've been waiting all this time
For my man to come
Take his hand in mine
And lead me away
To unseen shores
I've been washing the sand
With my salty tears
Searching the shore
For these long years
And I'll walk the seas
Forever more
Till I find my Jackie oh
Till I find my Jackie oh
Till I find my Jackie oh
Jackie oh
Jackie oh
S. O'Connor/Dizzy Heights Music Pub. Ltd./
Rare Blue Music, Inc. (ASCAP)

Analyzing Media

1. To which characters in the *Odyssey* might you compare Jackie and the speaker in this song? Explain what they have in common.
2. Briefly describe a realistic, modern scenario of a person experiencing a similar loss of a loved one.

Grammar Link

Missing Commas with Nonessential Elements

In writing, commas can represent the subtle pauses you would use if you were speaking. Read these examples and note how commas can change the meaning in a sentence.

- Maria claimed Fernando was the best center fielder.
- Maria, claimed Fernando, was the best center fielder.

The commas in the second sentence change the best center fielder from Fernando to Maria.

A sentence is made up of a number of elements–words, phrases, clauses–some of which are essential to the meaning of the sentence. Elements that are *not* essential to the meaning of the sentence must be set off with commas. In the second sentence above, for example, *claimed Fernando* is nonessential.

Essential: The man who has the starring role in Homer's tale is Odysseus.

The underlined section could not be left out of the sentence. The point of the sentence is that this man is the main character, so those words are essential to the meaning.

Nonessential: The oarsman, who was screaming in terror, was consumed by Scylla.

The underlined section gives "extra" information. Omitting it would not change the meaning of the sentence. Therefore, the information is nonessential and must be set off with commas.

If you are not sure whether information is essential or nonessential, try saying the sentence aloud. If it sounds right with pauses where the commas might go, put them in. If not, leave them out.

Problem Missing commas with a nonessential element
The Cyclops hungry and brutal consumed several men.

Solution Set off a nonessential element with commas
The Cyclops, hungry and brutal, consumed several men.

- For more information about commas with nonessential elements, see **Language Handbook,** pp. R26–R27.

EXERCISE

Rewrite incorrect sentences, adding necessary commas. If the sentence is correct, write *Correct.*

1. The men's brave leader Odysseus came up with a plan.
2. The men waited until the Cyclops sleepy with wine was helpless.
3. Driving a spike into the Cyclops's eye of course blinded him.
4. Only the Cyclopes who lived nearby could hear the screams of rage and pain.
5. Odysseus laughing heard the Cyclops say that nobody had tricked him.

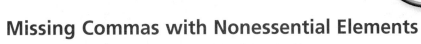

Technology Skills

Using Scanners and Photo Editing Software

Scanners take photographs and other images and digitize them for your computer. Once the images become objects your computer recognizes, you can manipulate them in a variety of ways. With a scanner and photo editing software, you can create a background for your Web site out of a photograph of autumn leaves, import public-domain images into your word processing documents, and turn a pencil sketch into a digitized image you can add to your e-mail messages.

Scanners

Scanners vary greatly, from small, handheld devices to large, print-shop-quality drum models. The type typically found in homes and classrooms is the flatbed scanner, a machine with a smooth glass bed that's usually large enough to scan an 8½-by-11-inch image. Often these scanners come bundled with photo editing software.

Your classroom may also have a handheld scanner with a smaller scan head. Such models are less expensive than their flatbed counterparts, and they are extremely portable. Unfortunately, they sometimes produce less accurate images because of a weaker light source. If you use a handheld scanner, images can be improved somewhat with photo editing software.

Scanners can also scan text. With the aid of optical character recognition (OCR) software, you can insert scanned text into a word processing document. For example, if you wanted to quote the text of a long poem in a report you're writing, you could scan the poem with the OCR software, and then insert it into your report. Once a piece of text is in your document, you can edit it, change its typeface, or manipulate it in any other way your word processing program allows. Remember, however, that you may not alter the wording of copyrighted material.

Photo editing software was used to create this composite image.

TECHNOLOGY TIP

Scanning resolution is measured in dpi (dots per inch). The more dots per inch, the better the quality. On a computer monitor, the dots are called pixels. The maximum resolution on most monitors is 72 pixels per inch. However, printers can exceed that resolution. Inexpensive 600 dpi black-and-white laser printers are fairly common. If you intend to print an image, scan it to the resolution of your printer.

Photo Editing Software

Photo editing software does exactly what the name implies: it revises and corrects digitized photographs and other graphic images. Most editing packages allow you to improve images that may be over- or underexposed, change the size of an image, increase or decrease contrast, eliminate flaws in the original, change color quality, enhance the focus, make a composite image from two or more images, and add interesting special effects.

Original photo

Retouched photo

When using scanners and photo editing software, keep the following points in mind:

1. **It is illegal to scan money, postage stamps, and identification documents such as drivers' licenses.**
2. **If you scan photographs or text from copyrighted documents, secure permission before using the material. Many of the images you can download from Web sites are not public-domain images. That means that it is illegal to use them in a printed document or on your Web site without securing permission from the copyright holder.**
3. **If you include scanned images or text in an academic report, be sure to cite your sources.**

ACTIVITIES

1. Scan several images to accompany your work for the Writing Workshop in this unit. For each, explain why the picture complements what you've written. Be sure to cite the source of each image.
2. Experiment with the filters and other special effects included with your photo editing software. See how a scanned image takes on new life by changing the appearance of the texture and other elements of the piece.

Before You Read

An Ancient Gesture and *Ithaca*

Reading Focus

In all your reading of literature, what character, setting, or event has inspired you the most?

Journal In your journal, describe the person, place, or event from literature that you find most inspiring, and explain your choice.

Setting a Purpose Read to discover what kind of inspiration these poets have found in Homer's classic epic the *Odyssey.*

Building Background

- The *Odyssey* relates the adventures of the Greek hero Odysseus, who spends twenty years trying to return home to Ithaca after the Trojan War. The characters, places, and events in the *Odyssey* have inspired countless writers of later times, who have elaborated on these and other aspects of this ancient Greek epic. Many of the characters and settings in the *Odyssey* have become part of the storehouse of common symbols in Western culture. Odysseus, for example, is a symbol of the courageous, determined adventurer. He and other characters from the *Odyssey* are frequently referred to in other works of literature and in other forms of art.
- In the *Odyssey,* Odysseus's wife, Penelope, remains faithful during his long absence even though she is not sure whether he will ever return. When many suitors come to court her, she devises a trick to hold them at bay. She says that she will decide on a marriage partner after she has woven a shroud, or burial garment, for her father-in-law. By day she weaves, and each night she unravels her work.

Penelope, c. 1865.
Kate Faulkner. Painted earthenware. Fitzwilliam Museum, Cambridge, UK.

Meet Edna St. Vincent Millay

Through her poetry and life, Edna St. Vincent Millay came to represent the rebellious, independent, youthful spirit of the 1920s. Like Penelope in the *Odyssey*, Millay held off many suitors, preferring her independence and writing career to marriage and domestic life. At age thirty-one, however, she married a man who supported her dedication to her writing and who assumed all domestic responsibilities to give her time to write.

Edna St. Vincent Millay was born in Rockland, Maine, in 1892. She died in 1950.

Meet C. P. Cavafy

Greek poet C. P. Cavafy (kə vä′fē) published few poems and received little literary acclaim during his lifetime. Today, however, he is regarded as the finest Greek poet of the 1900s. Much of Cavafy's poetry reflects his interest in ancient Greek and Roman culture.

C. P. Cavafy was born in Alexandria, Egypt, in 1863. He died in 1933.

An Ancient Gesture

Edna St. Vincent Millay

Self Portrait at Table, 1893. Käthe Kollwitz. Etching and aquatint, 178 x 128 mm. National Gallery of Art, Washington, DC.

I thought, as I wiped my eyes on the corner of my apron:
Penelope did this too.
And more than once: you can't keep weaving all day
And undoing it all through the night;
Your arms get tired, and the back of your neck gets tight;
And along towards morning, when you think it will never be light,
And your husband has been gone, and you don't know where, for years,
Suddenly you burst into tears;
There is simply nothing else to do.

And I thought, as I wiped my eyes on the corner of my apron:
This is an ancient gesture, authentic, antique,
In the very best tradition, classic, Greek;
Ulysses° did this too.
But only as a gesture,—a gesture which implied
To the assembled throng that he was much too moved to speak.
He learned it from Penelope . . .
Penelope, who really cried.

---

13 *Ulysses* (ū lis' ēz) was the Roman name for the Greek hero Odysseus.

Ithaca

C. P. Cavafy

Translated by Rae Dalven

When you start on your journey to Ithaca,
then pray that the road is long,
full of adventure, full of knowledge.
Do not fear the Lestrygonians
and the Cyclopes and the angry Poseidon.°
You will never meet such as these on your path,
if your thoughts remain lofty, if a fine
emotion touches your body and your spirit.
You will never meet the Lestrygonians,
the Cyclopes and the fierce Poseidon,
if you do not carry them within your soul,
if your soul does not raise them up before you.

Then pray that the road is long.
That the summer mornings are many,
that you will enter ports seen for the first time
with such pleasure, with such joy!
Stop at Phoenician markets,
and purchase fine merchandise,
mother-of-pearl and corals, amber and ebony,
and pleasurable perfumes of all kinds,
buy as many pleasurable perfumes as you can;
visit hosts of Egyptian cities,
to learn and learn from those who have knowledge.

Always keep Ithaca fixed in your mind.
To arrive there is your ultimate goal.
But do not hurry the voyage at all.
It is better to let it last for long years;
and even to anchor at the isle when you are old,
rich with all that you have gained on the way,
not expecting that Ithaca will offer you riches.

Ithaca has given you the beautiful voyage.
Without her you would never have taken the road.
But she has nothing more to give you.

And if you find her poor, Ithaca has not defrauded you.
With the great wisdom you have gained, with so much experience,
you must surely have understood by then what Ithacas mean.

4–5 Do not . . . Poseidon: After his misadventure with the one-eyed giants called **Cyclopes** (sī klō′ pēz), Odysseus had a disastrous encounter with the **Lestrygonians** (les′ tri gō′ nē ənz). These gigantic cannibals destroyed all the ships except the one Odysseus himself was in. **Poseidon** (pə sīd′ ən) was the Greek god of the sea, who became angry with Odysseus for blinding his son, the Cyclops Polyphemus, and tried to keep Odysseus from returning home.

Responding to Literature

Personal Response

Which of these two poems do you prefer? Explain why in your journal.

Analyzing Literature

An Ancient Gesture

Recall and Interpret

1. In the first stanza, what is the speaker doing and thinking about? How would you describe her emotional state?
2. A gesture is a movement that expresses an idea or sentiment. What "ancient gesture" does the speaker refer to in the second stanza, and what idea or feeling do you think it is meant to express?
3. According to the speaker, how is the gesture different for Ulysses than it is for Penelope? In your opinion, what does the speaker imply when she says that Penelope is the one "who really cried"?

Evaluate and Connect

4. Why might the speaker describe her gesture as "ancient," "antique," and "classic"? What impact does this description have on your understanding of the speaker's contemporary situation and her attitude toward it?
5. What does this poem imply about a difference between the lives of men and women? Do you agree with that message? Why or why not?

Ithaca

Recall and Interpret

6. What advice does the speaker give in the first three stanzas about the journey to Ithaca? That is, what should one pray for or keep in mind along the way?
7. Under what conditions does the speaker say one need not fear the Lestrygonians, Cyclopes, and Poseidon? What might these characters be **symbols** of?
8. What are your thoughts about "what Ithacas mean" in the last line? Explain what importance the last two stanzas have to the overall meaning of the poem.
9. **Theme Connections** In the last two stanzas, what does the speaker say is Ithaca's gift? What do Ithaca and the journey to Ithaca symbolize in this poem?

Evaluate and Connect

10. How would you describe the speaker? What can you infer about what he finds most important in life?
11. To what senses does this poem appeal? What effect do these sensory images have on your understanding of the speaker's message?
12. Who might find the speaker's advice most valuable? Do you agree with the advice? Why or why not?

Literary ELEMENTS

Allusion

An **allusion** is a reference in a work of literature to a character, place, or situation from another work of literature, music, or art, or from history. Allusions to classical literature, to the Bible, and to William Shakespeare's works are especially common. Both "An Ancient Gesture" and "Ithaca" contain allusions to characters, places, and events in the *Odyssey.* Allusion is a powerful literary device because it can evoke associations in the mind of a reader.

1. Make a chart in which you list all the allusions in "An Ancient Gesture" and "Ithaca," and briefly describe what each allusion symbolizes or evokes.
2. Choose one of the poems, and describe how the poem gains power from its allusions to classical literature.

- See **Literary Terms Handbook,** p. R1.

Literature and Writing

Writing About Literature

Compare and Contrast Themes What attitudes about life and about human nature do these two poems convey? How are the attitudes similar or different? In a paragraph or two, compare and contrast the **themes** of the two poems.

Personal Writing

Creating a Personal Symbol Review the journal writing you did for the Reading Focus on page 888 about the most inspiring person, place, or event you have discovered in literature. Using either "An Ancient Gesture" or "Ithaca" as a model, write a poem that turns this character, setting, or event into a personal **symbol,** or one that has special meaning for you.

Extending Your Response

Literature Groups

Value of the Classics? Humorist Mark Twain defined a classic as "something everybody wants to have read and nobody wants to read." With your group, discuss whether Edna St. Vincent Millay and C. P. Cavafy might have agreed or disagreed with Twain. Consider these poets' references to the *Odyssey* as you formulate your opinion. Then discuss whether or not you agree with Twain. What relevance, if any, do the classics have to life today? Share your group's opinions with the rest of the class.

Performing

Dramatize the Gesture Imagine that you are the speaker in "An Ancient Gesture." What is it that you want others to know about your life and hardships you have endured? Write and perform a monologue, answering this question for your classmates. Remember to include "the ancient gesture" and other body language to communicate your thoughts and feelings.

Learning for Life

Life Itinerary The poem "Ithaca" urges readers to make an adventure out of the journey of life. Create an itinerary for your life, describing the places you'd like to visit and the experiences you'd like to have. You might choose to display your information graphically on a "lifeline"—a timeline that shows what experiences you'd like to have at specific times in your life.

Save your work for your portfolio.

INTERDISCIPLINARY GEOGRAPHY CONNECTION

Sites of the *Odyssey*

Did Homer have real places in mind when he plotted Odysseus's fantastic voyage? Or did he create imaginary settings? People have been pondering these questions since ancient times. Over the centuries, many scholars have tried to show that Odysseus did follow a real geographical route. Some theorists think he sailed as far away as Iceland. Others think he simply circled the island of Sicily. However, many of Homer's geographical descriptions are hazy, confusing, or even contradictory.

Even so, at least two of the places mentioned in the Odyssey definitely exist—the locations where Odysseus begins and ends his journey. Archaeological excavations on the northwest coast of Turkey have uncovered what scholars believe to be the site of ancient Troy, the place from which Odysseus began his journey home. Ithaca, his destination, is an island off the west coast of Greece.

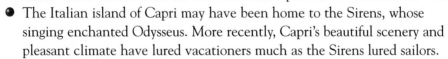

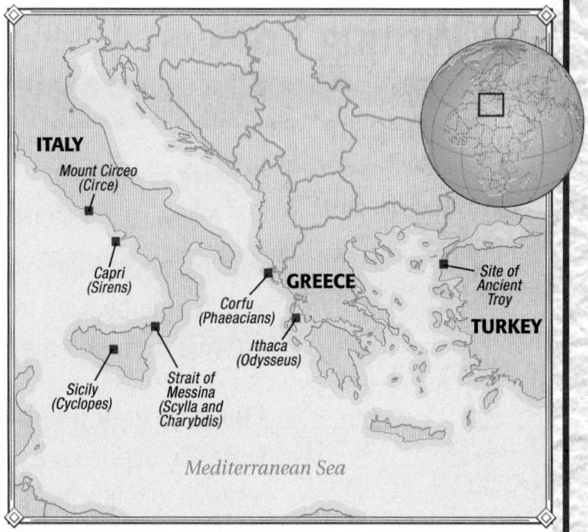

Although the fantastic characters in the *Odyssey* are mythical, their homes are often associated with the real places listed below.

- The Strait of Messina is associated with the sea monsters Scylla and Charybdis. The rocks and currents in this narrow passageway between the island of Sicily and southern Italy make ship travel quite perilous.
- Mount Circeo, located on the west coast of Italy, is said to be the home of the witch Circe. The mountain looks like an island when viewed from the sea. A national park there is named for Circe.
- The Italian island of Capri may have been home to the Sirens, whose singing enchanted Odysseus. More recently, Capri's beautiful scenery and pleasant climate have lured vacationers much as the Sirens lured sailors.
- Sicily, an island off the coast of Italy, is commonly believed to have been the home of the Cyclops. Modern-day visitors to the island are shown the rocks that he is said to have hurled at Odysseus's ship.
- On the Greek island of Corfu, which is identified as the home of the Phaeacians, tourists can view the cove where Odysseus supposedly came ashore after being shipwrecked.

Activity

Choose one of the *Odyssey* sites shown on the map. Do further research on what the site is like today. Create a travel brochure describing the place.

Writing Workshop

Expository Writing: Research Report

Conducting research is a little like taking a trip in uncharted territory. You begin with curiosity, follow an unfamiliar path through the library and World Wide Web, and end up with a hard-earned discovery. A research paper documents that discovery by compiling and ordering facts and opinions from the sources that you have explored. **In this workshop, you will write a research report on a famous journey.**

- As you write your report, refer to the **Writing Handbook,** pp. R58–R71.

EVALUATION RUBRIC

By the time you complete this Writing Workshop, you will have

- written an introduction that presents your main idea in a thesis statement
- supported your thesis with facts, details, and quotations from a variety of sources
- cited sources correctly
- effectively organized the information you have gathered
- concluded with a summary of the main points and restatement of the thesis
- presented a research report that is free of errors in grammar, usage, and mechanics

The Writing Process

PREWRITING

PREWRITING TIP

With a partner, brainstorm a list of famous journeys.

Explore ideas

The following questions may give you some ideas to pursue in your research.

- What was the longest journey a person ever made? Where did it lead?
- What journeys led to places where people had never been before?
- What journeys were people forced to take?

Choose a topic and narrow its focus

Once you decide on a journey or a type of journey to focus on, do some preliminary research to refine and shape your topic into a manageable size. If your topic is too narrow, you won't be able to find enough information on it. If your topic is too broad, you'll be overwhelmed with data, and your report may be too general–or too disorganized–as a result. This chart shows examples of topics that are too broad, too narrow, and just the right size.

Choosing a Topic		
Too Broad	**Too Narrow**	**Just Right**
Journeys of Native Americans	Quatie Ross's journey along the Trail of Tears	Cherokee journey along the Trail of Tears

Consider your purpose

Your purpose will be to provide information about the journey clearly and concisely, supporting your main idea with statistics and other facts, as well as with the opinions of experts.

Consider your audience

By the time you finish your research, you will probably know more about your topic than your readers do. Keep your readers' needs in mind, and adjust your level of detail accordingly.

Gather information

Begin by generating four or five research questions, each focusing on one aspect of the topic you've chosen. As the student has done in the model shown, ask *what, why, how,* and *where.* Then look for answers to your questions in books and magazines and on reliable Web sites. Library indexes and databases can make your search easier. Depending on your topic, you may want to use primary sources, such as letters, diaries, and interviews, as well as secondary sources, in your report. Be sure to allocate several days of your writing process to conducting research and locating adequate sources of information.

STUDENT MODEL

- Where is the Trail of Tears, and why does it bear this name?
- Why were the Cherokee forced to make this journey?
- What conditions did they face along the way?
- How did Cherokee culture change as a result?

Complete Student Model on p. R119.

Take notes

As you study your sources, write down useful information on index cards. Be sure to keep track of your sources as you go. You will need to know your sources when you compile a bibliography or a list of works cited at the end of your report. See the Writing Handbook, pages R65–R66, for help with these steps in the research process.

Make an outline

Once you've gathered your information, you need to decide how to organize it. Do you want to present it chronologically, in order of importance, or according to cause and effect? A working outline can allow you to experiment with different methods. The writer of the model outline used chronological order.

STUDENT MODEL

The Trail of Tears

I. Background
   A. Cherokee life in their homeland
   B. White settlers' demand for more land
   C. Ratification of the Treaty of Echota
II. Forced relocation
   A. Rounding up the Cherokee
   B. March to Oklahoma
III. Effect on Cherokee life
   A. Life in Oklahoma
   B. Life for Cherokee who escaped the roundup

Complete Student Model on p. R119.

DRAFTING

Develop a thesis statement

Before you begin drafting, develop a thesis statement–one or two sentences that clearly express the central idea you will focus on, or prove, in your report. Your thesis may convey your point of view on your topic, and it may also signal the overall organization of the report. Drawing conclusions on the basis of your research can help you develop your thesis.

DRAFTING TIP

See "Using Evidence" on page 830 for help with supporting your claims.

Write your draft

As you draft, use your outline as a guide. If you realize you need to gather more information, don't worry. Make a list of additional questions and research them. You can incorporate your findings as you revise.

Carefully craft your introduction

You may want to compose your introduction as you begin your draft, or you may want to write it after your first draft is complete. No matter when you write it, your introduction should include your thesis statement and capture a reader's attention. Any of the following techniques can help you hook your reader.

- Make your reader comfortable with your topic by summarizing it, referring to the main headings on your outline.
- Arouse your reader's curiosity by posing an interesting question that your report will answer.
- Entertain your reader by describing an unusual fact or anecdote about your topic.

STUDENT MODEL

> Why would one group of people forcibly remove another group from their homeland? Could the relocated group ever recover from such a move? These questions must occur to anyone on first hearing about the Trail of Tears. In 1838 Cherokee living in Georgia were rounded up by federal troops and forced to walk eight hundred miles westward to an assigned section of Oklahoma.

Complete Student Model on p. R119.

REVISING

REVISING TIP

Don't include every fact you find. Use only those that relate to your thesis.

TECHNOLOGY TIP

Investigate software programs that can help you format your list of works cited.

Evaluate your work

Read your introduction and then your conclusion, and make sure that they support each other. If they don't, you will need to revise them–and the report in between–so that they do. Use the **Rubric for Revising** to guide your revision. Then refer to the Writing Handbook, pages R68–R69, for help in citing the sources of quotations and information in the body of your report and for help with formatting your list of works cited.

Hold a writing conference

Exchange reports with a partner. Then use the **Rubric for Revising** to offer suggestions for improving each other's work.

STUDENT MODEL

> The army ~~went into~~ invaded homes and pulled people from the fields. ~~Most people were farmers then.~~ Thousands of Cherokee were put into stockades to wait for the long march west. ~~Someone~~ Reverend James who visited the stockades wrote, "many Cherokees, who a few days ago were in comfortable circumstances, are now victims of abject poverty . . . . It is a work of war in a time of peace." (Fremon 78).

Complete Student Model on p. R119.

RUBRIC FOR REVISING

Your revised research report should have
- ☑ an introduction that presents your main idea in a thesis statement
- ☑ body paragraphs that support your main points with facts, details, and quotations from a variety of sources
- ☑ a consistent organizational structure that helps the audience to follow the ideas
- ☑ a conclusion that summarizes your main points and restates the thesis

Your revised research report should be free of
- ☑ plagiarism–the presentation of other people's ideas or words as your own
- ☑ details that do not support the thesis
- ☑ errors in grammar, usage, and mechanics

EDITING/PROOFREADING

When you are satisfied that what you have written will interest and inform readers, give your paper one final proofreading. Besides checking spelling, punctuation, and usage, make sure that you have cited your sources correctly.

PROOFREADING TIP

Use the **Proofreading Checklist** on the inside back cover of this textbook to help you mark errors.

Grammar Hint

Use an apostrophe and an *-s* to form the possessive of a singular noun, even if it ends in *-s*.

INCORRECT: ***John Ross' appeal to President Van Buren seemed to gain the Cherokee people two more years on their land.***

CORRECT: ***John Ross's appeal to President Van Buren seemed to gain the Cherokee people two more years on their land.***

- For more on punctuating possessives, see **Language Handbook**, p. R50.

STUDENT MODEL

The inaugural address' [s] call for relocating eastern Native Americans reflected the wishes of many white settlers.

Complete Student Model on p. R119.

Complete Student Model

For a complete version of the model developed in this workshop, refer to **Writing Workshop Models**, p. R119.

PUBLISHING/PRESENTING

Many professional scholars and researchers share their findings by writing articles or books. In addition to showing your paper to your teacher, you may want to give a copy to the school library so that others can benefit from the information you have gathered.

PRESENTING TIP

Include a cover sheet that states the title of your report, your name, your class, and the date.

Reflecting

Why is it worthwhile for others to learn about the journey that you have just researched? How might the knowledge you gained on your topic affect your understanding of other places, other people, or other periods in history? Explore these questions in your journal or learning log. Then write a few tips to keep in mind when you work on your next research project.

Save your work for your portfolio.

Unit Assessment

Personal Response

1. Which section of the *Odyssey* did you find most exciting? Which did you find most moving? Give reasons for your answer.
2. As a result of the work you did in this unit, what new ideas do you have about the following:
   - how to read long passages of verse
   - how to appreciate and understand epic similes
   - how to identify and discuss literary themes
   - how to make connections between the past and the present

Analyzing Literature

Categorize Challenges Not all of the obstacles Odysseus faced on his long journey home were equally difficult to overcome. Which obstacle do you think presented him with the greatest challenge? Using details from the selection, explain your reasoning. You may want to compare the incident you choose with others from Odysseus's journey. You may also want to identify the internal and external factors that contributed to the difficulty.

Evaluate and Set Goals

Evaluate

1. How did your understanding of the *Odyssey* develop over the course of this unit? In what ways did that development affect your reading? In what ways did it affect your writing?
2. What was your greatest contribution to a group project? What was the most important benefit you received from working in a group?
3. How would you assess your work in this unit, using the following scale? Give at least two reasons for your assessment.
   4 = outstanding **3** = good **2** = fair **1** = weak

Set Goals

1. Look back on your work for this unit and identify a weakness.
2. With your teacher, discuss ways to strengthen that weakness. Decide on a goal that will help you to do so.
3. Write down the weakness and the goal in your journal.
4. Monitor your progress by scheduling checkpoints with yourself and with your teacher.

Build Your Portfolio

Select Choose two pieces of writing you did in this unit and include them in your portfolio. Use the following questions to guide your selection.

- Which piece was more interesting to write?
- Which piece demonstrates a creative use of language?
- Which piece would you most like to share with someone else?
- Which piece is the product of the deepest thought?

Reflect Include a short written response with each selected piece. Your notes may address the following:

- the ways in which you incorporated the comments of others
- the ways in which past writing experiences contributed to this one
- what you learned by writing the piece
- your changing feelings about the piece

Reading on Your Own

You might be interested in the following books.

Picture Bride
by Yoshiko Uchida
In 1917, Hana Omiya leaves her native Japan and sails to San Francisco to marry a man she has never met. Living with a stranger in a new country isn't easy, and when Japanese citizens are interned during World War II, Hana's troubles increase.

Mythology
by Edith Hamilton Zeus and Odysseus, Cupid and Psyche, Hercules and the Titans—these and other Greek gods and heroes have inspired, frightened, enlightened, and entertained generations of readers around the world. This classic book presents many of the Greek myths that are an important part of Western culture.

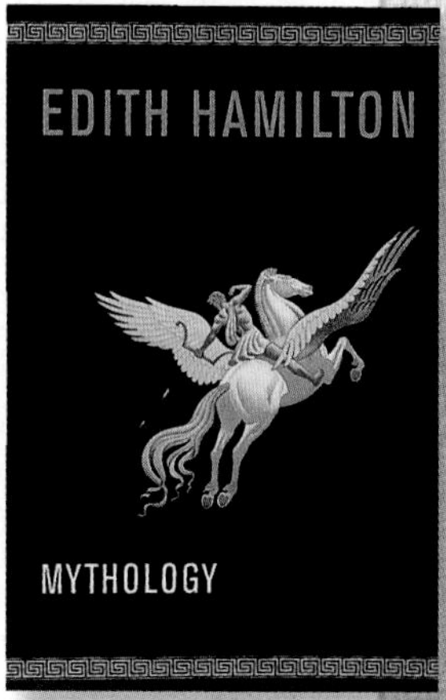

Aleta and the Queen
by Priscilla Galloway What was happening in Ithaca while Odysseus was away? This novel tells the story of Queen Penelope, who must defend the kingdom from take-over in her husband's absence. Among Penelope's few allies are Kleea, a faithful servant, and Aleta, Kleea's granddaughter. Despite many obstacles, Aleta summons courage and resourcefulness to help Penelope fend off greedy suitors.

Anpao: An American Indian Odyssey
by Jamake Highwater This book incorporates the folklore of Plains and Southwest Indians to tell the story of Anpao, a poor but brave young man who falls in love with the daughter of a chief. She agrees to marry him, but only after he attains the permission of the sun. Anpao undertakes a dramatic journey across mountains, deserts, and prairies to achieve his goal.

Standardized Test Practice

Read the following passage. Then read each question on page 901. Decide which is the best answer to each question. Mark the letter for that answer on your paper.

Leap of Faith

Alex Reardon leaned out of the plane's open cargo door and felt the wind tear at his hair. Eight thousand feet below him, the ground was a slowly drifting blotch of pastel colors. The drone of the plane's massive engines filled his ears like thunder, but Alex could still hear the nervous beating of his own heart. He'd never been so scared in his life.

Alex felt a hand grip his shoulder and pull him back into the plane. It was Susan, his skydiving instructor. "Ok, so it looks scary," she hollered. "You're ready for this, Alex."

Alex sighed and looked out the door at a passing cloud. He hoped Susan was right. It had been a long journey to get here, and he knew there was no turning back.

Skydiving was one of those things Alex had always sworn he'd never do. "Only a complete idiot would call jumping out of a high-flying airplane fun," he'd always said. He had argued with his father about this, but it had never made a difference. His dad would simply grin and snap himself into his jumpsuit. "Alex," he'd say, "some things in life worth doing will never make any sense."

"But this is ridiculous," Alex would protest, "sixty-four-year-old men do not freefall."

Alex's dad only shrugged. "I guess I'm the exception, then." And then he'd disappear into the sky. Alex would be left waiting on the ground, feeling powerless, straining his eyes for a glimpse of his father's billowing silk chute.

That was a year ago, before his father's heart attack. His dad recovered well with a little hospital time and a new diet, but the doctors had forbidden him to go skydiving again. Even though Alex's dad seemed physically healthy, Alex knew that the loss of his favorite hobby had dealt a crippling blow to his spirit.

Last Father's Day, Alex took his father aside and said, "I wanted to get you the perfect gift, but I couldn't find it in any store." Alex put on a big smile and tried to hide the fear creeping into his voice. "I've decided to freefall for you. It's my gift to you."

He saw his father try hard not to cry. His dad gave him a big hug. "That's great, son," he said. "But if you really want to do this, it'll actually be a gift to yourself."

A gift to myself, Alex thought, his palms starting to sweat.

The shrill buzzer that signaled final jump preparations shrieked, snapping Alex back to the present. Susan was checking the straps on his chute, testing the buckles, cinching and re-cinching the knots. "Just a few more seconds now," she yelled over the rising wind. "You're all set to go."

Alex looked down at the ground drifting far below. Somewhere down there, his father was waiting, smiling, proud of his son who now would learn to fly as he had once done. Alex took a deep breath and smiled. "Well," he said, "better get a move on, then."

He moved to the edge of the cargo door and leaned forward, letting the empty air accept his weight as he let go of his last hold on the plane and safety. "Some things in life worth doing will never make any sense."

The wind roared out a triumphant welcome. The rush of air on his face kissed him good-bye. A tiny lean forward . . . and he was gone! Alex Reardon was flying for the very first time in his life.

1 Why is Alex skydiving?

A Alex has always loved skydiving.

B His father asked him to try it.

C He promised Susan he would jump once.

D He is skydiving as a gift to his father.

2 In this passage, the word drone means —

F A quiet laugh

G A quick descent

H A loud humming noise

J A slow ascension

3 How does Alex feel about his first jump?

A Scared

B Angry

C Curious

D Confused

4 Which of these is a FACT from the passage?

F Alex's father is a great skydiver.

G It is dangerous for people over the age of sixty to skydive.

H Alex had never gone skydiving before.

J Alex's father was a professional skydiver.

5 When does Alex jump for the first time?

A On Father's Day

B On the day after his father's sixty-fourth birthday

C In the early afternoon

D About a year after his father's heart attack

6 Which was an OPINION previously held by Alex?

F Only idiots think jumping out of high-flying planes is fun.

G Alex had never jumped out of a plane before.

H It would be fine for Alex's father to go skydiving again.

J Skydiving is interesting and challenging.

STOP

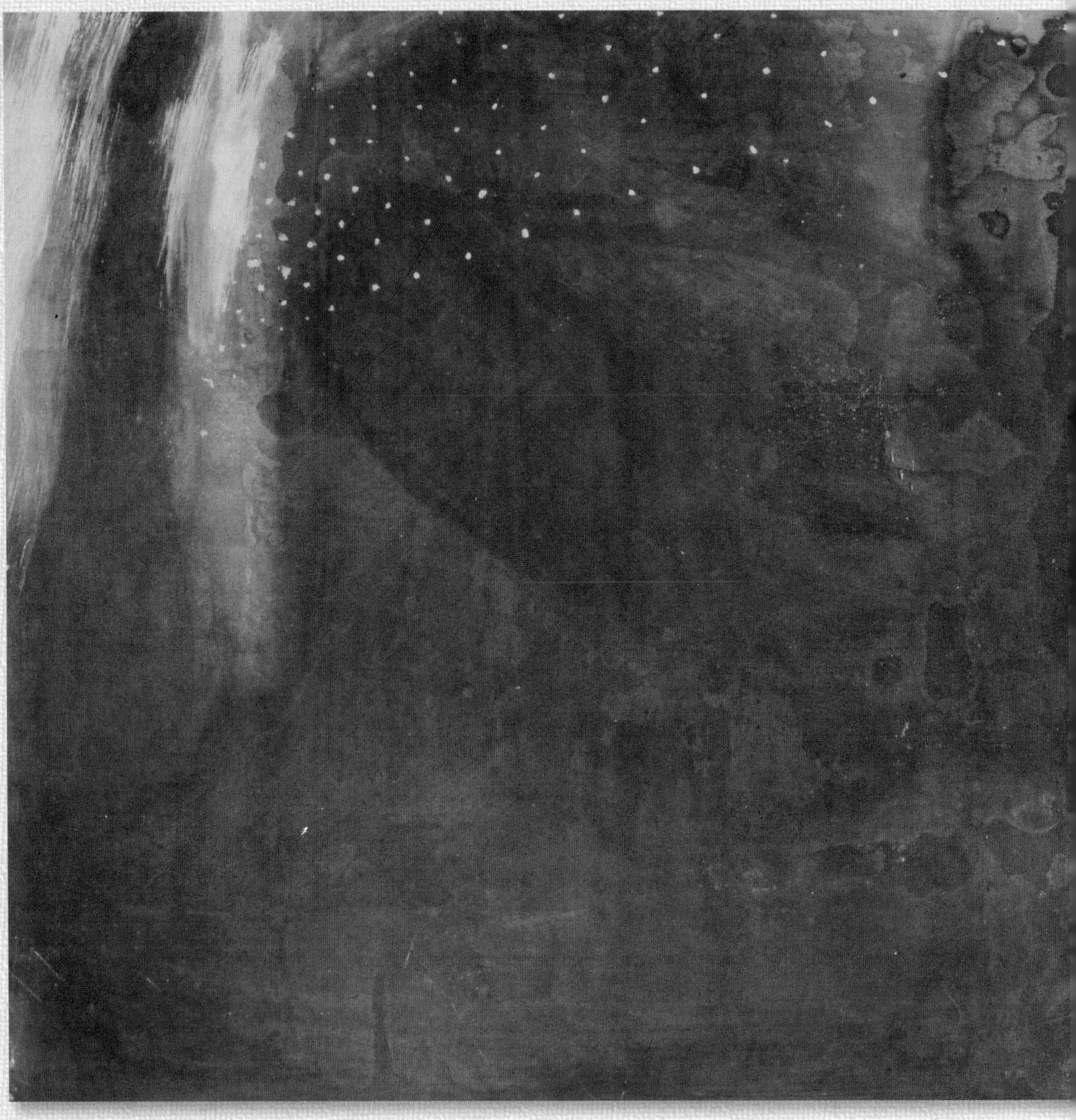

Purple Moon, 1997. Charlotte Johnstone. Oil and glaze on gesso board, 30.4 x 30.4 cm. Private collection.

UNIT SIX

Science Fiction and Fantasy

"Science fiction stories are extraordinary voyages into any of the infinite supply of conceivable futures."

—Isaac Asimov

Theme 12

In Other Worlds

Literature FOCUS

Science Fiction and Fantasy

What would happen if computers could program themselves? Might cloning one day lead to the end of death as we now understand it? In a **science fiction** story or novel, you might read a writer's answers to these and other questions that are beyond the scope of current human knowledge.

Real or imagined scientific and technological advancements form the basis of most science fiction. Isaac Asimov, one of the most famous writers in the genre, says that science fiction is about "life as we don't know it." But although artists and writers have been depicting strange lands and fantastic beings for thousands of years, science fiction didn't appear until science and technology began to play a major role in society.

Most scholars agree that the first science fiction novel is Mary Shelley's *Frankenstein*, published in 1818. At this time, the Industrial Revolution was in its early stages, and people were wondering what effect technology would have on everyday life. *Frankenstein*—which tells the story of a scientist who uses his knowledge to create life but instead creates a monster that destroys him and others—presents a pessimistic view of modern science. Later in the 1800s, French writer Jules Verne wrote a number of novels using scientific explanations to describe incredible adventures, such as traveling to the moon. Unlike Shelley, Verne was optimistic, or hopeful, about the future that technology would bring, and this attitude is reflected in his works. Even today, science fiction writers tend to be either optimistic or pessimistic about the impact technological and scientific change will have in the future.

Some early science fiction writers speculated about advancements that were actually realized decades later. The Czech author Karel Čapek, for example, wrote about robots and the atom bomb in the 1920s. Others, such as English author H. G. Wells, explored fantastical themes that continue to fascinate people today, such as time travel and Martian invasion.

After World War II, developments in nuclear and space technology drew the public's attention to science fiction, and the genre became more popular than ever. People were both afraid of and fascinated by new technologies; they saw that technology could be a benefit or a threat. However, the focus of science fiction shifted from the purely technological to the more social. Today, there is a division between "hard" science fiction, which emphasizes scientific explanations, and "soft" science fiction, which focuses on human action and responsibility.

Fantasy

Whereas a science fiction story or novel will include scientific explanations for its events, a work of **fantasy** breaks free from realistic depiction. Events happen as if by magic. Works of fantasy may include people, but they often take place in imaginary worlds and may include gnomes, elves, or other fantastical beings and forces.

ACTIVITY

Consider whether each selection in this unit is

- written in the tradition of optimism or pessimism.
- concerned more with technology or with human interests.
- drawn from a conventional science fiction theme.

Theme 12 In Other Worlds

Is there life on other planets or in other galaxies? The idea tempts the imagination. While scientists analyze data collected by the spaceships and satellites exploring the moons and planets in our solar system, dreamers fantasize about intergalactic time travel and futuristic species. By reading the selections in this theme, you'll discover the other worlds that result when reality and imagination collide.

THEME PROJECTS

Interdisciplinary Project

Art Imagine that you are on a tour of the alternative worlds referred to in this theme and that you want to send a postcard from each location to friends and family back home.

1. Use heavy watercolor paper or card stock to create a postcard from each location. Illustrate one side of each card with an important image from the selections.
2. On the back of each card, write a few sentences describing your experience.
3. "Mail" your postcards to your classmates, and discuss how your views of each world differ.

Listening and Speaking

Press Conference If the occurrences in this theme really happened, could a scientific explanation be offered to the public?

1. With a group, choose two events described in this theme.
2. Research what aspects of the events can be at least partially explained by modern scientific theory. For example, under what conditions might time travel, space travel, or life on other planets be possible?
3. Stage a press conference. Explain the scientific basis of each event to the public, and acknowledge the aspects of each event that cannot yet be scientifically explained.

Before You Read

The Sentinel

Reading Focus

What kind of evidence might convince someone that civilizations exist elsewhere in the universe?

List Ideas With a small group of classmates, discuss what specific pieces of evidence might lead someone to believe in alien civilizations. Then work together to make a "Top Ten List of Effective Alien Evidence."

Setting a Purpose Read to find out what evidence scientists discover during a futuristic moon expedition.

Building Background

The Time and Place

First published in 1951, this story looks ahead to the "future." It takes place on the surface of the moon during the late summer of 1996.

Did You Know?

Several years after writing "The Sentinel," Arthur C. Clarke expanded this short story into a screenplay for a major motion picture, *2001: A Space Odyssey,* which was released in 1968. Coauthored and directed by Stanley Kubrick, the movie stands as a milestone in science fiction filmmaking. Its special effects and realistic space-station interiors greatly influenced the science fiction movies that followed. Although both the short story and film were clearly within the realm of futuristic fiction when they were written, several "fantastic" elements have since become realities, including lunar landings, orbiting space stations, and computers with artificial intelligence.

Vocabulary Preview

tantalize (tant′ əl īz′) *v.* to torment or tease by tempting with something and then withholding it; p. 909

enigma (i nig′ mə) *n.* a mystery; a baffling person or thing; p. 910

exploit (eks′ ploit) *n.* a bold, daring deed; feat; p. 911

ebb (eb) *v.* to become less or weaker; decline; fail; p. 912

irrevocably (i rev′ ə kə blē) *adv.* in a way that cannot be revoked or undone; completely and hopelessly; p. 913

sentinel (sent′ ən əl) *n.* someone or something stationed to guard against and warn of danger; guard; p. 915

emissary (em′ ə ser′ ē) *n.* a person or agent sent, often in secret, on an official mission; p. 915

Meet Arthur C. Clarke

Unlike many science fiction authors, Arthur C. Clarke is truly a scientist. In fact, in 1945, when he was only twenty-eight years old, he developed the idea for orbital communication satellites, which are important to global communications today. He has written more than eighty science fiction books, many of which describe "fantastic" elements that later became reality. He has received numerous honors for his work, including nominations for both the Nobel Peace Prize and an Academy Award. Since 1956 Clarke has lived in Sri Lanka, keeping in touch with his international friends and colleagues by satellite, fax, and E-mail, all of which he predicted in his early science fiction.

Arthur C. Clarke was born in 1917 in England. This story was first published in 1951.

THE SENTINEL

Arthur C. Clarke

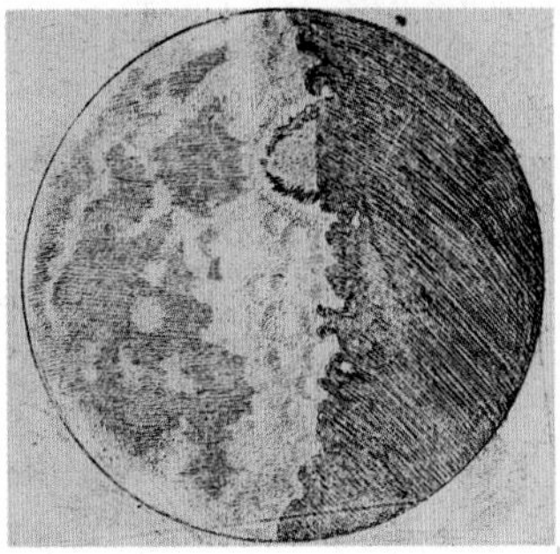

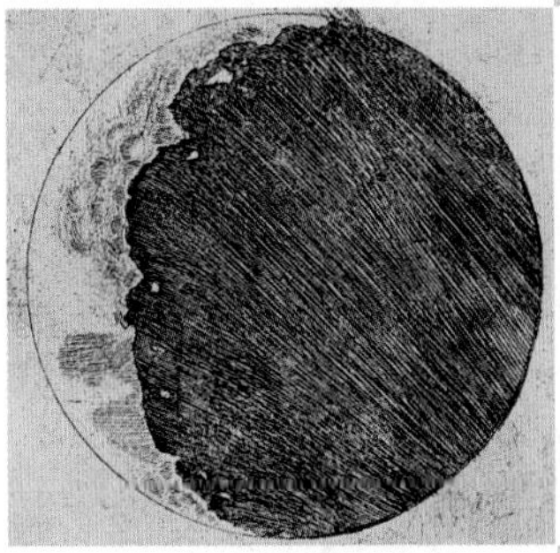
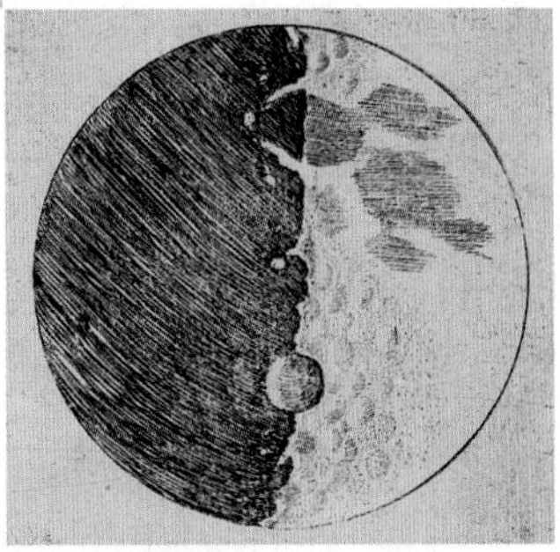

Sketches of the Moon. Galileo Galilei (1564–1642). Biblioteca Nazionale, Florence, Italy.

THE NEXT TIME YOU SEE the full moon high in the south, look carefully at its right-hand edge and let your eye travel upward along the curve of the disk. Round about two o'clock you will notice a small, dark oval: anyone with normal eyesight can find it quite easily. It is the great walled plain, one of the finest on the Moon, known as the Mare Crisium[1]—the Sea of Crises. Three hundred miles in diameter, and almost completely surrounded by a ring of magnificent mountains, it had never been explored until we entered it in the late summer of 1996.

---

1. *[Mare Crisium]* In 1609, when Italian scientist Galileo Galilei first viewed the moon's dark patches through an early telescope, he called them "seas." *Mare* (mär′ ā) is Latin for "sea." Today, these dark areas are known to be broad, lowland plains, but the Latin names given them in the 1600s are still used.

Our expedition was a large one. We had two heavy freighters which had flown our supplies and equipment from the main lunar base in the Mare Serenitatis,[2] five hundred miles away. There were also three small rockets which were intended for short-range transport over regions which our surface vehicles couldn't cross. Luckily, most of the Mare Crisium is very flat. There are none of the great crevasses[3] so common and so dangerous elsewhere, and very few craters or mountains of any size. As far as we could tell, our powerful caterpillar tractors would have no difficulty in taking us wherever we wished to go.

I was geologist—or selenologist, if you want to be pedantic[4]—in charge of the group exploring the southern region of the Mare. We had crossed a hundred miles of it in a week, skirting the foothills of the mountains along the shore of what was once the ancient sea, some thousand million years before. When life was beginning on Earth, it was already dying here. The waters were retreating down the flanks of those stupendous cliffs, retreating into the empty heart of the Moon. Over the land which we were crossing, the tideless ocean had once been half a mile deep, and now the only trace of moisture was the hoarfrost one could sometimes find in caves which the searing sunlight never penetrated.

We had begun our journey early in the slow lunar dawn, and still had almost a week of Earth-time before nightfall. Half a dozen times a day we would leave our vehicle and go outside in the space suits to hunt for interesting minerals, or to place markers for the guidance of future travelers. It was an uneventful routine. There is nothing hazardous or even particularly exciting about lunar exploration. We could live comfortably for a month in our pressurized tractors, and if we ran into trouble, we could always radio for help and sit tight until one of the spaceships came to our rescue.

I said just now that there was nothing exciting about lunar exploration, but of course that isn't true. One could never grow tired of those incredible mountains, so much more rugged than the gentle hills of Earth. We never knew, as we rounded the capes and promontories[5] of that vanished sea, what new splendors would be revealed to us. The whole southern curve of the Mare Crisium is a vast delta where a score of rivers once found their way into the ocean, fed perhaps by the torrential rains that must have lashed the mountains in the brief volcanic age when the Moon was young. Each of these ancient valleys was an invitation, challenging us to climb into the unknown uplands beyond. But we had a hundred miles still to cover, and could only look longingly at the heights which others must scale.

We kept Earth-time aboard the tractor, and precisely at 2200 hours the final radio message would be sent out to Base and we would close down for the day. Outside, the rocks would still be burning beneath the almost vertical sun, but to us it would be night until we awoke again eight hours later. Then one of us would prepare breakfast, there would be a great buzzing of electric razors, and someone would switch on the shortwave radio from Earth. Indeed, when the smell of frying sausages began to fill the cabin, it was sometimes hard to believe that we were not

2. *[Mare Serenitatis]* In the early 1970s, Apollo astronauts landed near the Sea of Serenity ("calmness").

3. A *crevasse* (kri vas′) is a deep, narrow crack.

4. One who is *pedantic* (pi dan′ tik) pays excessive attention to minor details and formal rules. Such a person would insist that a *geologist* studies the structure and history of the earth, while a *selenologist* studies the moon.

5. Points of land that project out into a body of water, *capes* are usually low and flat, whereas *promontories* are elevated.

back on our own world—everything was so normal and homely, apart from the feeling of decreased weight and the unnatural slowness with which objects fell.

It was my turn to prepare breakfast in the corner of the main cabin that served as a galley. I can remember that moment quite vividly after all these years, for the radio had just played one of my favorite melodies, the old Welsh air "David of the White Rock." Our driver was already outside in his space suit, inspecting our caterpillar treads. My assistant, Louis Garnett, was up forward in the control position, making some belated entries in yesterday's log.

As I stood by the frying pan, waiting, like any terrestrial[6] housewife, for the sausages to brown, I let my gaze wander idly over the mountain walls which covered the whole of the southern horizon, marching out of sight to east and west below the curve of the Moon. They seemed only a mile or two from the tractor, but I knew that the nearest was twenty miles away. On the Moon, of course, there is no loss of detail with distance—none of that almost imperceptible[7] haziness which softens and sometimes transfigures[8] all far-off things on Earth.

Those mountains were ten thousand feet high, and they climbed steeply out of the plain as if ages ago some subterranean eruption had smashed them skyward through the molten crust. The base of even the nearest was hidden from sight by a steeply curving surface of the plain, for the Moon is a very little world, and from where I was standing the horizon was only two miles away.

I lifted my eyes toward the peaks which no man had ever climbed, the peaks which, before the coming of terrestrial life, had watched the retreating oceans sink sullenly into their graves, taking with them the hope and the morning promise of a world. The sunlight was beating against those ramparts[9] with a glare that hurt the eyes, yet only a little way above them the stars were shining steadily in a sky blacker than a winter midnight on Earth.

I was turning away when my eye caught a metallic glitter high on the ridge of a great promontory thrusting out into the sea thirty miles to the west. It was a dimensionless point of light, as if a star had been clawed from the sky by one of those cruel peaks, and I imagined that some smooth rock surface was catching the sunlight and heliographing[10] it straight into my eyes. Such things were not uncommon. When the Moon is in her second quarter, observers on Earth can sometimes see the great ranges in the Oceanus Procellarum[11] burning with a blue-white iridescence[12] as the sunlight flashes from their slopes and leaps again from world to world. But I was curious to know what kind of rock could be shining so brightly up there, and I climbed into the observation turret and swung our four-inch telescope round to the west.

I could see just enough to tantalize me. Clear and sharp in the field of vision, the mountain peaks seemed only half a mile away,

6. *Terrestrial* means "of the earth; earthly."
7. *Imperceptible* means "not noticeable."
8. To *transfigure* a thing is to change its outward appearance, often into something glorious.

9. *Ramparts* are walls or embankments built for protection, as around a castle. Here, metaphorically, the ramparts are the mountain walls.
10. Here, *heliographing* means "reflecting." A *heliograph* is a signaling device that uses mirrors to reflect light from the sun.
11. *Oceanus Procellarum* is the (waterless) Ocean of Storms.
12. *Iridescence* is a display of shimmering and changing colors.

Vocabulary

tantalize (tant′ əl īz′) *v.* to torment or tease by tempting with something and then withholding it

Man and Space, 1971. Lepo Mikko. 200 x 200 cm. Tartu Art Museum, Estonia.

Viewing the painting: Which astronaut in this painting do you think best symbolizes the narrator? Give reasons for your answer.

but whatever was catching the sunlight was still too small to be resolved.[13] Yet it seemed to have an elusive[14] symmetry, and the summit upon which it rested was curiously flat. I stared for a long time at the glittering enigma, straining my eyes into space, until presently a smell of burning from the galley told me that our breakfast sausages had made their quarter-million-mile journey in vain.

All that morning we argued our way across the Mare Crisium while the western mountains reared higher in the sky. Even when we were out prospecting in the space suits, the discussion would continue over the radio. It was absolutely certain, my companions argued, that there had never been any form of intelligent life on the Moon. The only living things that had ever existed there were a few primitive plants and their slightly less degenerate[15] ancestors. I knew that as well as anyone, but there are times when a scientist must not be afraid to make a fool of himself.

"Listen," I said at last, "I'm going up there, if only for my own peace of mind. That mountain's less than twelve thousand feet high—that's only two thousand under Earth gravity—and I can make the trip in twenty hours at the outside. I've always wanted to go up into those hills, anyway, and this gives me an excellent excuse."

"If you don't break your neck," said Garnett, "you'll be the laughingstock of the expedition when we get back to Base. That mountain will probably be called Wilson's Folly from now on."

"I won't break my neck," I said firmly. "Who was the first man to climb Pico and Helicon?"[16]

13. Here, *resolved* means "made clearly visible."
14. The precise shape of the object was difficult to identify or grasp *(elusive).*
15. Here, *degenerate* (di jen′ ər it) means "having sunk below a former condition." The idea is that as water vanished, the moon's plant life gradually deteriorated in quality and finally died out.
16. Moon mountains are commonly named after Earth mountains. *Pico* is a mountain in the Azores, a group of islands in the northern Atlantic, and *Helicon* is a peak in Greece.

Vocabulary
enigma (i nig′ mə) *n.* a mystery; a baffling person or thing

"But weren't you rather younger in those days?" asked Louis gently.

"That," I said with great dignity, "is as good a reason as any for going."

We went to bed early that night, after driving the tractor to within half a mile of the promontory. Garnett was coming with me in the morning; he was a good climber, and had often been with me on such exploits before. Our driver was only too glad to be left in charge of the machine.

At first sight, those cliffs seemed completely unscalable, but to anyone with a good head for heights, climbing is easy on a world where all weights are only a sixth of their normal value. The real danger in lunar mountaineering lies in overconfidence; a six-hundred-foot drop on the Moon can kill you just as thoroughly as a hundred-foot fall on Earth.

We made our first halt on a wide ledge about four thousand feet above the plain. Climbing had not been very difficult, but my limbs were stiff with the unaccustomed effort, and I was glad of the rest. We could still see the tractor as a tiny metal insect far down at the foot of the cliff, and we reported our progress to the driver before starting on the next ascent.

Inside our suits it was comfortably cool, for the refrigeration units were fighting the sun and carrying away the body heat of our exertions. We seldom spoke to each other, except to pass climbing instructions and to discuss our best plan of ascent. I do not know what Garnett was thinking, probably that this was the craziest goose chase he had ever embarked upon. I more than half agreed with him, but the joy of climbing, the knowledge that no man had ever gone this way before, and the exhilaration of the steadily widening landscape gave me all the reward I needed.

I don't think I was particularly excited when I saw in front of us the wall of rock I had first inspected through the telescope from thirty miles away. It would level off about fifty feet above our heads, and there on the plateau would be the thing that had lured me over these barren wastes. It would be, almost certainly, nothing more than a boulder splintered ages ago by a falling meteor, and with its cleavage planes[17] still fresh and bright in this incorruptible, unchanging silence.

There were no handholds on the rock face, and we had to use a grapnel. My tired arms seemed to gain new strength as I swung the three-pronged metal anchor round my head and sent it sailing up toward the stars. The first time it broke loose and came falling slowly back when we pulled the rope. On the third attempt, the prongs gripped firmly and our combined weights could not shift it.

Garnett looked at me anxiously. I could tell that he wanted to go first, but I smiled back at him through the glass of my helmet and shook my head. Slowly, taking my time, I began the final ascent.

Even with my space suit, I weighed only forty pounds here, so I pulled myself up hand over hand without bothering to use my feet. At the rim I paused and waved to my companion, then I scrambled over the edge and stood upright, staring ahead of me.

You must understand that until this very moment I had been almost completely convinced that there could be nothing strange or unusual for me to find here. Almost, but not quite; it was that haunting doubt that had driven me forward. Well, it was a doubt no longer, but the haunting had scarcely begun.

17. Here, *planes* are rock surfaces, exposed as a result of the boulder's splitting, or *cleavage.*

Vocabulary

exploit (eks′ ploit) *n.* a bold, daring deed; feat

I was standing on a plateau perhaps a hundred feet across. It had once been smooth—too smooth to be natural—but falling meteors had pitted and scored its surface through immeasurable eons.[18] It had been leveled to support a glittering, roughly pyramidal structure, twice as high as a man, that was set in the rock like a gigantic, many-faceted jewel.

Probably no emotion at all filled my head in those first few seconds. Then I felt a great lifting of my heart, and a strange, inexpressible joy. For I loved the Moon, and now I knew that the creeping moss of Aristarchus and Eratosthenes[19] was not the only life she had brought forth in her youth. The old, discredited dream of the first explorers was true. There had, after all, been a lunar civilization—and I was the first to find it. That I had come perhaps a hundred million years too late did not distress me; it was enough to have come at all.

My mind was beginning to function normally, to analyze and to ask questions. Was this a building, a shrine—or something for which my language had no name? If a building, then why was it erected in so uniquely inaccessible a spot? I wondered if it might be a temple, and I could picture the adepts[20] of some strange priesthood calling on their gods to preserve them as the life of the Moon ebbed with the dying oceans, and calling on their gods in vain.

I took a dozen steps forward to examine the thing more closely, but some sense of caution kept me from going too near. I knew a little of archaeology, and tried to guess the cultural level of the civilization that must have smoothed this mountain and raised the glittering mirror surfaces that still dazzled my eyes.

The Egyptians could have done it, I thought, if their workmen had possessed whatever strange materials these far more ancient architects had used. Because of the thing's smallness, it did not occur to me that I might be looking at the handiwork of a race more advanced than my own. The idea that the Moon had possessed intelligence at all was still almost too tremendous to grasp, and my pride would not let me take the final, humiliating plunge.

And then I noticed something that set the scalp crawling at the back of my neck—something so trivial and so innocent that many would never have noticed it at all. I have said that the plateau was scarred by meteors; it was also coated inches deep with the cosmic dust that is always filtering down upon the surface of any world where there are no winds to disturb it. Yet the dust and the meteor scratches ended quite abruptly in a wide circle enclosing the little pyramid, as though an invisible wall was protecting it from the ravages of time and the slow but ceaseless bombardment from space.

There was someone shouting in my earphones, and I realized that Garnett had been calling me for some time. I walked unsteadily to the edge of the cliff and signaled him to join me, not trusting myself to speak. Then I went back toward the circle in the dust. I picked up a fragment of splintered rock and tossed it gently toward the shining enigma. If the pebble had vanished at that invisible barrier, I should not have been

18. An *eon* (ē′ ən) is an indefinitely long period of time.
19. Most moon craters are named for scientists and philosophers, such as these Greek astronomers of the third century B.C. (*Aristarchus* was among the first to say that the earth moves around the sun; *Eratosthenes* accurately calculated the earth's circumference.)
20. *Adepts* are experts; here, they're priests.

Vocabulary
ebb (eb) *v.* to become less or weaker; decline; fail

surprised, but it seemed to hit a smooth, hemispheric surface and slide gently to the ground.

I knew then that I was looking at nothing that could be matched in the antiquity of my own race. This was not a building, but a machine, protecting itself with forces that had challenged Eternity. Those forces, whatever they might be, were still operating, and perhaps I had already come too close. I thought of all the radiations man had trapped and tamed in the past century. For all I knew, I might be as irrevocably doomed as if I had stepped into the deadly, silent aura of an unshielded atomic pile.[21]

I remember turning then toward Garnett, who had joined me and was now standing

21. *Atomic pile* is another term for a nuclear reactor.

Vocabulary

irrevocably (i rev′ ə kə blē) *adv.* in a way that cannot be revoked or undone; completely and hopelessly

©Mario Sironi/Licensed by VAGA, New York, NY.

Three Mountains. Mario Sironi (1885–1961). Tempera on paper, 16 x 22.5 cm. Estorick Foundation, London.

Viewing the painting: How does this landscape compare to the moon's landscape as described in the story?

motionless at my side. He seemed quite oblivious to me, so I did not disturb him but walked to the edge of the cliff in an effort to marshal my thoughts.[22] There below me lay the Mare Crisium—Sea of Crises, indeed—strange and weird to most men, but reassuringly familiar to me. I lifted my eyes toward the crescent Earth, lying in her cradle of stars, and I wondered what her clouds had covered when these unknown builders had finished their work. Was it the steaming jungle of the Carboniferous,[23] the bleak shoreline over which the first amphibians must crawl to conquer the land—or, earlier still, the long loneliness before the coming of life?

Do not ask me why I did not guess the truth sooner—the truth that seems so obvious now. In the first excitement of my discovery, I had assumed without question that this crystalline apparition[24] had been built by some race belonging to the Moon's remote past, but suddenly, and with overwhelming force, the belief came to me that it was as alien to the Moon as I myself.

In twenty years we had found no trace of life but a few degenerate plants. No lunar civilization, whatever its doom, could have left but a single token of its existence.

I looked at the shining pyramid again, and the more I looked, the more remote it seemed from anything that had to do with the Moon. And suddenly I felt myself shaking with a foolish, hysterical laughter, brought on by excitement and overexertion: For I had imagined that the little pyramid was speaking to me and was saying, "Sorry, I'm a stranger here myself."

22. Garnett seemed unaware of, or *oblivious to,* the narrator. *To marshal one's thoughts* is to organize and make sense of them.

23. In geologic time, earth's *Carboniferous* (kär′ bə nif′ ər əs) Period was between 280 million and 345 million years ago, when land was covered with lush vegetation and swamps.

24. An *apparition* is a ghost or ghostly vision.

It has taken us twenty years to crack that invisible shield and reach the machine inside those crystal walls. What we could not understand, we broke at last with the savage might of atomic power and now I have seen the fragments of the lovely, glittering thing I found up there on the mountain.

They are meaningless. The mechanisms—if indeed they are mechanisms—of the pyramid belong to a technology that lies far beyond our horizon, perhaps to the technology of paraphysical forces.[25]

The mystery haunts us all the more now that the other planets have been reached and we know that only Earth has ever been the home of intelligent life in our Universe. Nor could any lost civilization of our own world have built that machine, for the thickness of the meteoric dust on the plateau has enabled us to measure its age. It was set there upon its mountain before life had emerged from the seas of Earth.

When our world was half its present age, *something* from the stars swept through the Solar System, left this token of its passage, and went again upon its way. Until we destroyed it, that machine was still fulfilling the purpose of its builders; and as to that purpose, here is my guess.

Nearly a hundred thousand million stars are turning in the circle of the Milky Way, and long ago other races on the worlds of other suns must have scaled and passed the heights that we have reached. Think of such civilizations, far back in time against the fading afterglow of Creation, masters of a universe so young that life as yet had come only to a handful of worlds. Theirs would have been a loneliness we cannot imagine, the

25. *Paraphysical forces* produce ordinary physical effects without using recognizable physical causes. Such effects might include the ability to float in midair, to materialize and dematerialize, and to move objects with the mind.

loneliness of gods looking out across infinity and finding none to share their thoughts.

They must have searched the star clusters as we have searched the planets. Everywhere there would be worlds, but they would be empty or peopled with crawling, mindless things. Such was our own Earth, the smoke of the great volcanoes still staining the skies, when that first ship of the peoples of the dawn came sliding in from the abyss[26] beyond Pluto. It passed the frozen outer worlds, knowing that life could play no part in their destinies. It came to rest among the inner planets, warming themselves around the fire of the Sun and waiting for their stories to begin.

Those wanderers must have looked on Earth, circling safely in the narrow zone between fire and ice, and must have guessed that it was the favorite of the Sun's children. Here, in the distant future, would be intelligence; but there were countless stars before them still, and they might never come this way again.

So they left a sentinel, one of millions they scattered throughout the Universe, watching over all worlds with the promise of life. It was a beacon that down the ages patiently signaled the fact that no one had discovered it.

Perhaps you understand now why that crystal pyramid was set upon the Moon instead of on the Earth. Its builders were not concerned with races still struggling up from savagery. They would be interested in our civilization only if we proved our fitness to survive—by crossing space and so escaping from the Earth, our cradle. That is the challenge that all intelligent races must meet, sooner or later. It is a double challenge, for it depends in turn upon the conquest of atomic energy and the last choice between life and death.

Once we had passed that crisis, it was only a matter of time before we found the pyramid and forced it open. Now its signals have ceased, and those whose duty it is will be turning their minds upon Earth. Perhaps they wish to help our infant civilization. But they must be very, very old, and the old are often insanely jealous of the young.

I can never look now at the Milky Way without wondering from which of those banked clouds of stars the emissaries are coming. If you will pardon so commonplace a simile, we have set off the fire alarm and have nothing to do but wait.

I do not think we will have to wait for long.

26. Here, *abyss* (ə bis′) refers to the immeasurably vast reaches of space.

Vocabulary

sentinel (sent′ ən əl) *n.* someone or something stationed to guard against and warn of danger; guard

emissary (em′ ə ser′ ē) *n.* a person or agent sent, often in secret, on an official mission

Responding to Literature

Personal Response

What does this story make you wonder about?

Analyzing Literature

Recall

1. Describe the setting of the story. Remember to include details about daily life, as well as about people's ideas and values at the time.
2. When the narrator makes breakfast, what does he see out the window? How do he and his crew members react to the vision?
3. Why did the narrator experience "a strange, inexpressible joy" upon making his discovery?
4. From the narrator's perspective, how and why, ultimately, was "the sentinel" nestled in the mountains of the Mare Crisium?
5. What is the effect of the atomic blast the scientists used against "the sentinel," and what does the narrator think will happen next?

Interpret

6. What can you infer about life on the moon from the setting's details?
7. "A scientist must not be afraid to make a fool of himself," says the narrator. How does this sentiment set him apart from his crew members?
8. Early in the story, the narrator states, "There is nothing hazardous or even particularly exciting about lunar exploration." Given his discovery, explain the **irony** in this statement. (See page R7.)
9. In your opinion, why did the scientists try for twenty years to crack the shield surrounding the machine?
10. What lines or details in the story indicate that the future is in jeopardy?

Evaluate and Connect

11. How might the narrator respond to the Reading Focus on page 906?
12. Clarke once wrote, "The only way of discovering the limits of the possible is to venture a little way past them into the impossible." In your opinion, do the narrator's actions and thoughts support this point of view? Do yours? Explain.
13. In your opinion, was the use of atomic power against "the sentinel" appropriate, or should the scientists have left it intact? Explain.
14. **Theme Connections** If this story were true, would you find its hypothesis reasonable—that "wanderers" from other worlds left sentinels to watch over all worlds that held the promise of life? Explain.
15. What adjectives would you use to describe this story?

Literary ELEMENTS

Suspense

Suspense is the growing interest and excitement readers experience while awaiting a climax or resolution in a work of literature. To build suspense, a writer may provide just enough information to keep the question *What will happen next?* burning in the reader's mind. Another technique for building suspense is the use of foreshadowing, which provides clues to future events and allows readers to guess at the outcome.

1. The narrator is cooking breakfast on the morning of his discovery. What specific events and details in this scene add to the suspense of the story?
2. Several times in the story, the narrator says that he and others believed that nothing "strange or unusual" would be found on top of the mountain and that intelligent life had never been on the moon. Why might these statements be considered foreshadowing of discoveries to come? What do they add to the overall suspensefulness of the story?

- See **Literary Terms Handbook**, p. R12.

Literature and Writing

Writing About Literature

How Great Is It? In his introduction to "The Sentinel" in the story collection *Science Fiction: Masters of Today,* Arthur Liebman writes that this story "did more to enhance the popularity of science fiction than perhaps any other short story of recent times. It remains 'must' reading for all science fiction fans." Write a critical review of "The Sentinel" in which you explain why the story might have made science fiction so popular and why you agree or disagree with Liebman's opinion that it is "must" reading.

Creative Writing

Keeping the Log Louis Garnett, the narrator's assistant, is responsible for keeping a log on the expedition to explore the Mare Crisium. From his point of view, write a log entry on the day the machine was first spotted in the mountains, on the day he climbed the mountain with the narrator, and on the day, twenty years later, atomic energy was used to reach the machine inside the crystal walls. Be sure to remain true to Garnett's character, and use details from the story in your entries.

Extending Your Response

Literature Groups

And the Future Is . . . ? With your group, discuss Arthur C. Clarke's vision of the future when he published this story in 1951. Does "The Sentinel" present the future as something to be anticipated or dreaded–or both? As you review the story, you might look for information about technological advancements as well as about human nature and social relationships. Make a list of details you find in the selection to support the viewpoints of your group members, and then share your conclusions with your classmates.

Interdisciplinary Activity

Science: Conditions on the Moon Clarke's descriptions of conditions on the moon were based on the scientific information that was available in 1951. List the physical details and scientific facts about the moon that he includes in his story regarding temperature, topography, gravitational force, degree of moisture, and so on. Then check those facts in current reference books. Report on any new information that was not available to Clarke when he wrote this story.

Performing

Do You Read Me, Houston? With a partner, create a skit in which one person plays the part of the narrator and the other person plays the part of a commander stationed at Mission Control at NASA headquarters in Houston. In your skit, present the dialogue that might have taken place as the narrator informs Mission Control about his discovery. Discuss together what should happen next: research "the sentinel" on the moon or make plans for transporting it back to Earth. Make sure that your dialogue is faithful to the story. For example, your narrator should express his caution about getting too close to the machine. Perform your skit for the class.

Reading Further

If you'd like to read more by Arthur C. Clarke, you might enjoy these works:

Novels: Two of Clarke's many novels, *The Fountains of Paradise* (1979) and *Rendezvous with Rama* (1973), have won both Hugo and Nebula awards.

Viewing: Arthur C. Clarke's award-winning 1968 movie *2001: A Space Odyssey,* a science fiction classic, is available on videocassette.

Save your work for your portfolio.

Skill Minilessons

GRAMMAR AND LANGUAGE • Commas to Separate Modifiers

When two or more coordinate adjectives precede a noun, use a comma to separate them, as in this example:

You will notice a small, dark oval.

To determine whether adjectives are coordinate, reverse their order or put the word *and* between them. If the sentence still sounds natural, the adjectives are coordinate. If reversing the order of the adjectives changes the meaning of the sentence, then you should not use a comma.

PRACTICE Copy the following sentences onto your paper. Add or delete commas where necessary. If a sentence does not require any changes, write *correct.*

1. The surface glistened in the bright searing sunlight.
2. The whole southern curve of the Mare Crisium is a vast delta.
3. At 2200 hours we sent the final, radio message.
4. I began to cook the hot, spicy sausages.
5. The pebble hit a smooth curved invisible barrier.

APPLY Write five sentences of your own in which two or more adjectives precede a noun. Punctuate the sentences correctly.

• For more information on using commas, see **Language Handbook,** pp. R47–R48.

READING AND THINKING • Identifying Assumptions

Like people in the real world, fictional narrators and characters often make assumptions based on their observations, experience, and knowledge. Identifying assumptions in a work of literature can help you understand why a narrator or character has drawn certain conclusions or has particular reactions to the outcome of events. For example, on the basis of scientific study and past exploration, the narrator and his colleagues assume that there has never been intelligent life on the moon. Identifying that assumption helps readers to understand why, later, they are so shocked to learn otherwise.

PRACTICE On your paper, identify the assumption that leads to each of the following conclusions.

1. Garnett concludes that the narrator will be the laughingstock of the expedition following their exploration of the mountain.
2. Upon seeing the machine up close for the first time, the narrator says, "Because of the thing's smallness, it did not occur to me that I might be looking at the handiwork of a race more advanced than my own."
3. The narrator concludes that the aliens will come to Earth in the near future.

• For more on analyzing what you read, see **Reading Handbook,** pp. R86–R92.

VOCABULARY • Analogies

An analogy is a type of comparison that is based on the relationship between things or ideas. To complete an analogy, begin by making up a sentence that expresses the relationship between the first pair of words. Then, look for another pair of words that, when put into the same sentence, also results in a true statement.

• For more on analogies, see **Communications Skills Handbook,** p. R77.

PRACTICE Choose a word to complete each analogy.

1. work : relax :: ebb :
   a. flatten b. struggle c. increase
2. puzzle : enigma :: rascal :
   a. clown b. scoundrel c. mischief
3. firmly : irrevocably :: similarly :
   a. closely b. differently c. identically

Grammar Link

Missing Comma in a Series

Whenever a sentence includes a list or series of three or more elements, use a comma after each element in the series that precedes the conjunction. You don't need to use commas if you use conjunctions to separate elements instead.

Problem 1 Missing commas in a series of words
Wilson was curious daring and energetic.

Solution A Use a comma after each word in the series that precedes the conjunction.
Wilson was curious, daring, and energetic.

Solution B Use a conjunction after each word in the series (except for the last word).
Wilson was curious and daring and energetic.

Problem 2 Missing commas in a series of phrases
Wilson halted above the plain sighted the tractor at the foot of the cliff and reported his progress to the driver.

Solution Use a comma at the end of each phrase preceding the conjunction.
Wilson halted above the plain, sighted the tractor at the foot of the cliff, and reported his progress to the driver.

Problem 3 Missing commas in a series of clauses
Each morning the lunar explorers awoke at 0600 hours one of their group prepared breakfast and another switched on the shortwave radio.

Solution Use a comma after each clause preceding the conjunction.
Each morning the lunar explorers awoke at 0600 hours, one of their group prepared breakfast, and another switched on the shortwave radio.

● For more on the use of commas, see **Language Handbook,** Mechanics, p. R47.

EXERCISE

Rewrite each sentence, adding commas or conjunctions as needed.

1. The freighters had flown supplies equipment and personnel to the Mare Crisium.
2. The explorers left their vehicle to examine the landscape to hunt for interesting minerals and to place markers for future travelers.
3. Wilson thought he would climb the mountain find the glittering object on top and unlock its secrets.
4. He gathered his strength swung the three-pronged metal anchor round his head and sent it sailing to the stars.
5. An ancient civilization could have thrived here its people could have raised this monument but the absence of cosmic dust on it raised unanswered questions.

MEDIA connection

Newspaper Article

Are unidentified flying objects (UFOs) strictly science fiction? In 1947 flying saucers made the headlines in the United States and around the world.

"Saucers" Listed in 39 States; Mustang Patrol Finds None

***New York Herald Times*, July 8, 1947, Paris edition**

NEW YORK, July 7—The mystery of the flying disks—whirling saucer-like objects skimming through the air at tremendous speeds—remained unsolved today, but reports poured in from all sections of the United States and eastern Canada that the phenomenon was observed again yesterday.

An Associated Press tabulation reported that the mystery objects had been seen in thirty-nine states. The disks were first reported to have been seen June 25 by Kenneth Arnold, a pilot, of Boise, Idaho, while flying over the Cascade Mountains.

He said he saw nine of them, flying in formation at a speed he estimated was at least 1,200 miles an hour. Then, he reported, they turned and eight minutes later disappeared. All other persons who have said they saw the disks concurred that they "disappeared" after a few minutes.

The Oregon National Guard, in an effort to

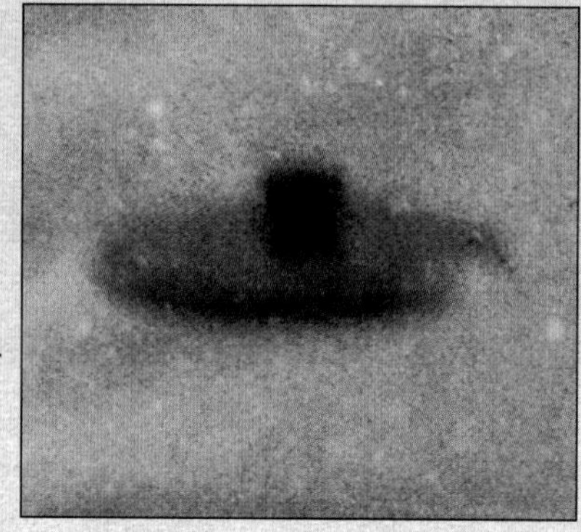

photograph the objects, sent a patrol of six Mustang fighter planes over the Cascade Mountains last night but nothing was seen. Government weather stations and astronomy students in the West have been watching nightly to no avail.

However, dozens of other citizens in the nation, many of them unusually dependable and considered unlikely to take part in any ruse, have sworn they witnessed the spectacle. Most observers agree that they are round or oval. Guesses as to their size ranged from that of a two-story house to a "silver ball six inches in diameter."

Army, Navy, and Atomic Energy Commission officials repeated their statements that they had no experimental work in progress that would be likely to send disks zipping through the sky or to create optical illusions of disks. Captain Tom Brown, of Army Air Forces Public Relations, in fact, expressed doubt that anything concrete existed anywhere able to travel in the way described.

"We don't believe anyone in this country or outside it," he said, "has developed a guided missile that will go 1,200 miles an hour."

Some scientists suggested that reflections of light on such objects as aircraft or water particles high in the sky might account for the bright objects. In some cases, the observers have insisted that the "saucers" have been accompanied by sound.

Analyzing Media

Would you have been likely to believe your eyes if you had seen the saucers in 1947? Or would you dismiss your vision and seek out a scientific explanation?

Before You Read

Visit to a Small Planet

Reading Focus

Do you think that it is human nature to want to engage in acts of war? Or is it human nature to want to live in peace?

Journal Write your answer in your journal. Give examples or reasons for your answer.

Setting a Purpose Read to discover how a visitor to Earth feels about the human capacity for war and peace.

Building Background

The Time and Place

This television play, which was first performed in 1955, takes place over a two-week period in an upper-middle-class home in Silver Glen, Maryland.

Did You Know?

A fearful reaction to aliens is fairly typical in science fiction from the 1930s through the 1950s, because most extraterrestrials were portrayed as frightening monsters, eerie spirits, or globs of slime that invaded, attacked, and ultimately controlled or destroyed civilization on Earth. In more recent times, a number of benevolent aliens have made their appearance in science fiction stories and movies, such as the shy creature that children befriend in the 1982 film *E.T.*

Vocabulary Preview

conjecture (kən jek′ cher) *n.* the drawing of a conclusion without definite or sufficient evidence; p. 922

patronizing (pā′ trə nīz′ ing) *adj.* being kind or helpful, but in a self important or snobbish way, as if dealing with an inferior; p. 927

perverse (pər vurs′) *adj.* determined to go against what is reasonable, expected, or desired; contrary; p. 933

malice (mal′ is) *n.* a desire to harm another; ill will; p. 934

lurid (loor′ id) *adj.* sensational; shocking; p. 939

inadvertently (in′ ad vurt′ ənt lē) *adv.* accidentally; unintentionally; p. 944

erratic (ə rat′ ik) *adj.* acting or moving irregularly or unpredictably; p. 946

Meet Gore Vidal

"The only thing I've ever really wanted in my life was to be President."

Gore Vidal (gôr vē däl′) comes to his passion for politics naturally. His grandfather was an Oklahoma senator, his father was a government official under President Franklin D. Roosevelt, and he is related to President Jimmy Carter and the late Jacqueline Kennedy Onassis. However, two unsuccessful campaigns for Congress crushed Vidal's political ambitions. In the mid-1950s, the witty and often sarcastic Vidal wrote screenplays as part of a plan to become financially independent. As a self-described "writer for hire," Vidal reached his goal, though it took about twice the time he had planned.

Gore Vidal was born in West Point, New York, in 1925.

Visit to a Small Planet

Gore Vidal

THE CAST		
KRETON	JOHN RANDOLPH	PRESIDENT OF PARAGUAY
ROGER SPELDING	GENERAL POWERS	SECOND VISITOR
ELLEN SPELDING	AIDE	
MRS. SPELDING	PAUL LAURENT	

Act 1

[Stock shot: The night sky, stars. Then slowly a luminous object arcs into view. As it is almost upon us, dissolve[1] *to the living room of the Spelding house in Maryland.*

Superimpose card: THE TIME: THE DAY AFTER TOMORROW.

The room is comfortably balanced between the expensively decorated and the homely. ROGER SPELDING *is concluding his TV broadcast. He is middle-aged, unctuous, resonant.*[2] *His wife, bored and vague, knits passively while he talks at his desk. Two technicians are on hand, operating the equipment.*

His daughter ELLEN*, a lively girl of twenty, fidgets as she listens.]*

SPELDING. [*Into microphone.*] . . . and so, according to General Powers—who should know if anyone does—the flying object which has given rise to so much irresponsible conjecture is nothing more than a meteor passing through the earth's orbit. It is not, as many believe, a secret weapon of this country. Nor is it a spaceship, as certain lunatic elements have suggested. General Powers has

1. In film, a *stock shot* is a standard image. A *dissolve* is the fading of one scene into another, with no blackout in between.
2. Spelding's manner is *unctuous,* or smug and falsely earnest, and his voice is *resonant,* or pretentiously loud and deep.

Vocabulary

conjecture (kən jek′ cher) *n.* the drawing of a conclusion without definite or sufficient evidence

assured me that it is highly doubtful there is any form of life on other planets capable of building a spaceship. "If any traveling is to be done in space, we will do it first." And those are his exact words. . . . Which winds up another week of news. [*Crosses to pose with wife and daughter.*] This is Roger Spelding, saying good night to Mother and Father America from my old homestead in Silver Glen, Maryland, close to the warm pulse beat of the nation.

TECHNICIAN. Good show tonight, Mr. Spelding.

SPELDING. Thank you.

TECHNICIAN. Yes, sir, you were right on time.

[*Technicians switch off microphone.* SPELDING *rises wearily, his mechanical smile and heartiness suddenly gone.*]

MRS. SPELDING. Very nice, dear. Very nice.

TECHNICIAN. See you next week, Mr. Spelding.

SPELDING. Thank you, boys.

[*Technicians go.*]

SPELDING. Did you like the broadcast, Ellen?

ELLEN. Of course I did, Daddy.

SPELDING. Then what did I say?

ELLEN. Oh, that's not fair.

SPELDING. It's not very flattering when one's own daughter won't listen to what one says while millions of people . . .

ELLEN. I always listen, Daddy, you know that.

MRS. SPELDING. We love your broadcasts, dear. I don't know what we'd do without them.

SPELDING. Starve, I suspect.

ELLEN. I wonder what's keeping John?

SPELDING. Certainly not work.

ELLEN. Oh, Daddy, stop it! John works very hard and you know it.

MRS. SPELDING. Yes, he's a perfectly nice boy, Roger. I like him.

SPELDING. I know, I know. He has every virtue except the most important one: he has no get-up-and-go.

ELLEN. [*Precisely.*] He doesn't want to get up and he doesn't want to go because he's already where he wants to be, on his own farm, which is exactly where *I'm* going to be when we're married.

SPELDING. More thankless than a serpent's tooth is an ungrateful child.

ELLEN. I don't think that's right. Isn't it "more deadly . . ."?[3]

SPELDING. Whatever the exact quotation is, I stand by the sentiment.

MRS. SPELDING. Please, don't quarrel. It always gives me a headache.

SPELDING. I never quarrel. I merely reason, in my simple way, with Miss Know-it-all here.

ELLEN. Oh, Daddy! Next you'll tell me I should marry for money.

SPELDING. There is nothing wrong with marrying a wealthy man. The horror of it has always eluded me. However, my only wish is that you marry someone hard-working, ambitious, a man who'll make his mark in the world. Not a boy who plans to sit on a farm all his life, growing peanuts.

ELLEN. English walnuts.

SPELDING. Will you stop correcting me?

ELLEN. But, Daddy, John grows walnuts . . .

[*JOHN enters, breathlessly.*]

JOHN. Come out! Quick! It's coming this way! It's going to land right here!

SPELDING. *What's* going to land?

JOHN. The spaceship. Look!

SPELDING. Apparently you didn't hear my broadcast. The flying object in question is a meteor, not a spaceship.

[*JOHN has gone out with ELLEN. SPELDING and MRS. SPELDING follow.*]

MRS. SPELDING. Oh, my! Look! Something *is* falling! Roger, you don't think it's going to hit the house, do you?

SPELDING. The odds against being hit by a falling object that size are, I should say, roughly, ten million to one.

JOHN. Ten million to one or not, it's going to land right here and it's *not* falling.

SPELDING. I'm sure it's a meteor.

MRS. SPELDING. Shouldn't we go down to the cellar?

SPELDING. If it's not a meteor, it's an optical illusion . . . mass hysteria.

ELLEN. Daddy, it's a real spaceship. I'm sure it is.

SPELDING. Or maybe a weather balloon. Yes, that's what it is. General Powers said only yesterday . . .

JOHN. It's landing!

SPELDING. I'm going to call the police . . . the army!

[*Bolts inside.*]

ELLEN. Here it comes . . . oh, look how it shines!

JOHN. How soft it lands!

MRS. SPELDING. Right in my rose garden!

---

3. Spelding and Ellen are referring to Shakespeare's *King Lear,* but the actual line is "How sharper than a serpent's tooth it is / To have a thankless child!"

ELLEN. Maybe it's a balloon.

JOHN. No, it's a spaceship and right there in your own back yard.

ELLEN. What makes it shine so?

JOHN. I don't know, but I'm going to find out. [*Runs off toward the light.*]

ELLEN. Oh, darling, don't! Darling, please. John, John come back!

[SPELDING, *wide-eyed, returns.*]

MRS. SPELDING. Roger, it's landed right in my rose garden.

SPELDING. I got General Powers. He's coming over. He said they've been watching this thing. They . . . they don't know what it is.

ELLEN. You mean it's nothing of ours?

SPELDING. They believe it . . . [*Swallows hard.*] . . . it's from outer space.

ELLEN. And John's down there! Daddy, get a gun or something.

SPELDING. Perhaps we'd better leave the house until the Army gets here.

ELLEN. We can't leave John.

SPELDING. I can. [*Peers nearsightedly.*] Why, it's not much larger than a car. I'm sure it's some kind of meteor.

ELLEN. Meteors are blazing hot.

SPELDING. This is a cold one.

ELLEN. It's opening . . . the whole side's opening! [*Shouts.*] John! Come back! Quick!

MRS. SPELDING. Why, there's a man getting out of it! [*Sighs.*] I feel much better already. I'm sure if we ask him, he'll move that thing for us. Roger, you ask him.

SPELDING. [*Ominously.*] If it's really a man?

ELLEN. John's shaking hands with him. [*Calls.*] John darling, come on up here . . .

MRS. SPELDING. And bring your friend.

SPELDING. There's something wrong with the way that creature looks . . . if it is a man and not a . . . not a monster.

MRS. SPELDING. He looks perfectly nice to me.

[*JOHN and the VISITOR appear. The VISITOR is in his forties, a mild, pleasant-looking man with side whiskers and dressed in the fashion of 1860. When he sees the three people, he pauses in silence for a moment. They stare back at him, equally interested.*]

VISITOR. I seem to've made a mistake. I *am* sorry. I'd better go back and start over again.

SPELDING. My dear sir, you've only just arrived. Come in, come in. I don't need to tell you what a pleasure this is . . . Mister . . . Mister . . .

VISITOR. Kreton. . . . This *is* the wrong costume, isn't it?

SPELDING. Wrong for what?

KRETON. For the country, and the time.

SPELDING. Well, it's a trifle[4] old-fashioned.

MRS. SPELDING. But really awfully handsome.

KRETON. Thank you.

MRS. SPELDING. [*To husband.*] Ask him about moving that thing off my rose bed.

[SPELDING *leads them all into the living room.*]

SPELDING. Come in and sit down. You must be tired after your trip.

KRETON. Yes, I am a little. [*Looks around delightedly.*] Oh, it's better than I'd hoped!

SPELDING. Better? What's better?

KRETON. The house . . . that's what you call it? Or is this an apartment?

SPELDING. This is a house in the state of Maryland, U.S.A.

---

4. ***A trifle*** (trī′ fəl) means "slightly."

KRETON. In the late twentieth century! To think this is really the twentieth century. I must sit down a moment and collect myself. The *real* thing! [*He sits down.*]

ELLEN. You . . . you're not an American, are you?

KRETON. What a nice thought! No, I'm not.

JOHN. You sound more English.

KRETON. Do I? Is my accent very bad?

JOHN. No, it's quite good.

SPELDING. Where *are* you from, Mr. Kreton?

KRETON. [*Evasively.*] Another place.

SPELDING. On this earth of course.

KRETON. No, not on this planet.

ELLEN. Are you from Mars?

KRETON. Oh dear no, not Mars. There's nobody on Mars . . . at least no one I know.

ELLEN. I'm sure you're teasing us and this is all some kind of publicity stunt.

KRETON. No, I really am from another place.

SPELDING. I don't suppose you'd consent to my interviewing you on television?

KRETON. I don't think your authorities will like that. They are terribly upset as it is.

This photograph is from a 1957 stage production of *Visit to a Small Planet,* as are all the photos on the following pages.

SPELDING. How do you know?

KRETON. Well, I . . . pick up things. For instance, I know that in a few minutes a number of people from your Army will be here to question me and they—like you—are torn by doubt.

SPELDING. How extraordinary!

ELLEN. Why did you come here?

KRETON. Simply a visit to your small planet. I've been studying it for years. In fact, one might say you people are my hobby. Especially this period of your development.

JOHN. Are you the first person from your . . . your planet to travel in space like this?

KRETON. Oh my no! Everyone travels who wants to. It's just that no one wants to visit you. I can't think why. *I* always have. You'd be surprised what a thorough study I've made. [*Recites.*] The planet Earth is divided into five continents with a number of large islands. It is mostly water. There is one moon. Civilization is only just beginning. . . .

SPELDING. Just beginning! My dear sir, we have had . . .

KRETON. [*Blandly.*] You are only in the initial stages—the most fascinating stages, as far as I'm concerned. . . . I do hope I don't sound patronizing.

ELLEN. Well, we are very proud.

KRETON. I know and that's one of your most endearing primitive traits. Oh, I can't believe I'm here at last!

[*GENERAL POWERS, a vigorous product of the National Guard, and his AIDE enter.*]

POWERS. All right, folks. The place is surrounded by troops. Where is the monster?

KRETON. I, my dear General, am the monster.

POWERS. What are you dressed up for, a fancy-dress party?

KRETON. I'd hoped to be in the costume of the period. As you see, I am about a hundred years too late.

POWERS. Roger, who is this joker?

SPELDING. This is Mr. Kreton . . . General Powers. Mr. Kreton arrived in that thing outside. He is from another planet.

POWERS. I don't believe it.

ELLEN. It's true. We saw him get out of the flying saucer.

POWERS. [*To AIDE.*] Captain, go down and look at that ship. But be careful. Don't touch anything. And don't let anybody else near it. [*AIDE goes.*] So you're from another planet.

KRETON. Yes. My, that's a very smart uniform, but I prefer the ones made of metal, the ones you used to wear. You know: with the feathers on top.

POWERS. That was five hundred years ago.

KRETON. As long ago as that!

POWERS. Are you *sure* you're not from Earth?

KRETON. Yes.

POWERS. Well, I'm not. You've got some pretty tall explaining to do.

KRETON. I am at your service.

POWERS. All right, which planet?

KRETON. None that you have ever heard of.

POWERS. Where is it?

KRETON. You wouldn't know.

POWERS. This solar system?

Vocabulary

patronizing (pā′ trə nīz′ ing) *adj.* being kind or helpful, but in a self-important or snobbish way, as if dealing with an inferior

KRETON. No.

POWERS. Another system?

KRETON. Yes.

POWERS. Look, I don't want to play twenty questions with you. I just want to know where you're from. The law requires it.

KRETON. It's possible that I *could* explain it to a mathematician, but I'm afraid I couldn't explain it to you, not for another five hundred years, and by then, of course, *you'd* be dead, because you people do die, don't you?

POWERS. What?

KRETON. Poor fragile butterflies, such brief little moments in the sun. . . . You see, *we* don't die.

POWERS. You'll die all right if it turns out you're a spy or a hostile alien.

KRETON. I'm sure you wouldn't be so cruel.

[*AIDE returns; he looks disturbed.*]

POWERS. What did you find?

AIDE. I'm not sure, General.

POWERS. [*Heavily.*] Then do your best to describe what the object is like.

AIDE. Well, it's elliptical,[5] with a fourteen-foot diameter. And it's made of an unknown metal which shines, and inside there isn't anything.

POWERS. Isn't anything?

AIDE. There's nothing inside the ship: no instruments, no food, nothing.

POWERS. [*To KRETON.*] What did you do with your instrument board?

KRETON. With my what? Oh, I don't have one.

POWERS. How does the thing travel?

KRETON. I don't know.

POWERS. You don't know! Now, look, mister, you're in pretty serious trouble. I suggest you do a bit of cooperating. You claim you traveled here from outer space in a machine with no instruments . . .

KRETON. Well, these cars are rather common in my world and I suppose, once upon a time, I must've known the theory on which they operate, but I've long since forgotten. After all, General, we're not mechanics, you and I.

POWERS. Roger, do you mind if we use your study?

SPELDING. Not at all. Not at all, General.

POWERS. Mr. Kreton and I are going to have a chat. [*To AIDE.*] Put in a call to the Chief of Staff.

AIDE. Yes, General.

[*SPELDING rises, leads KRETON and POWERS into next room, a handsomely furnished study, many books, globes of the world, and so forth.*]

SPELDING. This way, gentlemen.

[*KRETON sits down comfortably beside the globe, which he twirls thoughtfully. At the door, SPELDING speaks in a low voice to POWERS.*]

SPELDING. I hope I'll be the one to get the story first, Tom.

POWERS. There isn't any story. Complete censorship. And by the way, this house is under martial law.[6] I've a hunch we're in trouble.

[*He shuts the door. SPELDING turns and rejoins his family.*]

ELLEN. I think he's wonderful, whoever he is.

MRS. SPELDING. I wonder how much damage he did to my rose garden. . . .

---

5. *Elliptical* means "oval-shaped."

6. *Martial* (mär′ shəl) *law* is military rule forced on a civilian population in a time of war or during an emergency; constitutional rights and freedoms are temporarily suspended.

JOHN. It's sure hard to believe he's really from outer space. No instruments, no nothing . . . boy, they must be advanced scientifically.

MRS. SPELDING. Is he spending the night, dear?

SPELDING. What?

MRS. SPELDING. Is he spending the night?

SPELDING. Oh, yes, yes, I suppose he will be.

MRS. SPELDING. Then I'd better go make up the bedroom. He seems perfectly nice to me. I like his whiskers. They're so very . . . comforting. Like Grandfather Spelding's. [*She goes.*]

SPELDING. [*Bitterly.*] I *know* this story will leak out before I can interview him. I just know it.

ELLEN. What does it mean, we're under martial law?

SPELDING. It means we have to do what General Powers tells us to do. [*Goes to window. Soldier passes by.*] See?

JOHN. I wish I'd taken a closer look at that ship when I had the chance.

ELLEN. Perhaps he'll give us a ride in it.

JOHN. Traveling in space! Just like those stories. You know: intergalactic-drive stuff.

SPELDING. *If* he's not an impostor.

ELLEN. I have a feeling he isn't.

JOHN. Well, I better call the family and tell them I'm all right. [*He crosses to telephone by the door which leads into the hall.*]

AIDE. I'm sorry, sir, but you can't use the phone.

SPELDING. He certainly can. This is my house . . .

AIDE. [*Mechanically.*] This house is a military reservation until the crisis is over—order of General Powers. I'm sorry.

JOHN. Just how am I to call home to say where I am?

AIDE. Only General Powers can help you. You're also forbidden to leave this house without permission.

SPELDING. You can't do this!

AIDE. I'm afraid, sir, we've done it.

ELLEN. Isn't it exciting!

[*Cut to study.*]

POWERS. Are you deliberately trying to confuse me?

KRETON. Not deliberately, no.

POWERS. We have gone over and over this for two hours now and all that you've told me is that you're from another planet in another solar system . . .

KRETON. In another dimension. I think that's the word you use.

POWERS. In another dimension, and you have come here as a tourist.

KRETON. Up to a point, yes. What did you expect?

POWERS. It is my job to guard the security of this country.

KRETON. I'm sure that must be very interesting work.

POWERS. For all I know, you are a spy, sent here by an alien race to study us, preparatory to invasion.

KRETON. Oh, none of my people would *dream* of invading you.

POWERS. How do I know that's true?

KRETON. [*Blandly.*] You don't, so I suggest you believe me. I should also warn you: I can tell what's inside.

POWERS. What's inside?

KRETON. What's inside your mind.

POWERS. You're a mind reader?

KRETON. I don't really read it. I hear it.

POWERS. What am I thinking?

KRETON. That I am either a lunatic from the Earth or a spy from another world.

POWERS. Correct. But then you could've guessed that. [*Frowns.*] What am I thinking now?

KRETON. You're making a picture. Three silver stars. You're pinning them on your shoulder, instead of the two stars you now wear.

POWERS. [*Startled.*] That's right. I was thinking of my promotion.

KRETON. If there's anything I can do to hurry it along, just let me know.

POWERS. You can. Tell me why you're here.

KRETON. Well, we don't travel much, my people. We used to, but since we see everything through special monitors and re-creators, there is no particular need to travel. However, I am a hobbyist. I love to gad about.[7]

POWERS. [*Taking notes.*] Are you the first to visit us?

KRETON. Oh no! We started visiting you long before there were people on the planet. However, we are seldom noticed on our trips. I'm sorry to say I slipped up, coming in the way I did . . . but then this visit was all rather impromptu. [*Laughs.*] I am a creature of impulse, I fear. [*AIDE looks in.*]

AIDE. Chief of Staff on the telephone, General.

POWERS. [*Picks up phone.*] Hello, yes, sir. Powers speaking. I'm talking to him now. No, sir. No, sir. No, we can't determine what method of power was used. He won't talk. Yes, sir. I'll hold him here. I've put the house under martial law . . . belongs to a friend of mine, Roger Spelding, the TV commentator. Roger Spelding, the TV . . . What? Oh, no, I'm sure he won't say anything. Who . . . oh, yes, sir. Yes, I realize the importance of it. Yes, I will. Good-by. [*Hangs up.*] The President of the United States wants to know all about you.

KRETON. How nice of him! And I want to know all about him. But I do wish you'd let me rest a bit first. Your language is still not familiar to me. I had to learn them all. Quite exhausting.

POWERS. You speak *all* our languages?

KRETON. Yes, all of them. But then it's easier than you might think since I can see what's inside.

POWERS. Speaking of what's inside, we're going to take your ship apart.

KRETON. Oh, I wish you wouldn't.

POWERS. Security demands it.

KRETON. In that case *my* security demands you leave it alone.

POWERS. You plan to stop us?

KRETON. I already have. [*Beat.*] Listen.

[*Far-off shouting. AIDE rushes into the study.*]

AIDE. Something's happened to the ship, General. The door's shut and there's some kind of wall all around it, an invisible wall. We can't get near it.

KRETON. [*To camera.*] I hope there was no one inside.

POWERS. [*To KRETON.*] How did you do that?

KRETON. I couldn't begin to explain. Now, if you don't mind, I think we should go in and see our hosts.

[*He rises, goes into the living room. POWERS and AIDE look at each other.*]

POWERS. Don't let him out of your sight.

[*Cut to living room as POWERS picks up the telephone. KRETON is with JOHN and ELLEN.*]

7. To *gad about* is to move around restlessly or aimlessly, especially in search of fun or excitement.

KRETON. I don't mind curiosity but I really can't permit them to wreck my poor ship.

ELLEN. What do you plan to do, now you're here?

KRETON. Oh, keep busy. I have a project or two. . . . [*Sighs*.] I can't believe you're real!

JOHN. Then we're all in the same boat.

KRETON. Boat? Oh yes! Well, I should've come ages ago but I . . . I couldn't get away until yesterday.

JOHN. Yesterday? It only took you a *day* to get here?

KRETON. One of *my* days, not yours. But then you don't know about time yet.

JOHN. Oh, you mean relativity.[8]

KRETON. No, it's much more involved than that. You won't know about time until . . . now let me see if I remember . . . no, I don't, but it's about two thousand years.

JOHN. What do we do between now and then?

KRETON. You simply go on the way you are, living your exciting primitive lives . . . you have no idea how much fun you're having now.

ELLEN. I hope you'll stay with us while you're here.

KRETON. That's very nice of you. Perhaps I will. Though I'm sure you'll get tired of having a visitor under foot all the time.

ELLEN. Certainly not. And Daddy will be deliriously happy. He can interview you by the hour.

JOHN. What's it like in outer space?

8. In his theory of *relativity,* Albert Einstein discussed the interdependent, or interrelated, nature of time, space, energy, and gravity.

KRETON. Dull.

ELLEN. I should think it would be divine!

[*POWERS enters.*]

KRETON. No, General, it won't work.

POWERS. What won't work?

KRETON. Trying to blow up my little force field. You'll just plow up Mrs. Spelding's garden.

[*POWERS snarls.*]

ELLEN. Can you tell what we're *all* thinking?

KRETON. Yes. As a matter of fact, it makes me a bit giddy.[9] Your minds are not at all like ours. You see, we control our thoughts, while you . . . well, it's extraordinary the things you think about!

ELLEN. Oh, how awful! You can tell *everything* we think?

KRETON. Everything. It's one of the reasons I'm here, to intoxicate myself with your primitive minds . . . with the wonderful rawness of your emotions! You have no idea how it excites me! You simply seethe[10] with unlikely emotions.

ELLEN. I've never felt so sordid.[11]

JOHN. From now on I'm going to think about agriculture.

SPELDING. [*Entering.*] You would.

ELLEN. Daddy!

KRETON. No, no. You must go right on thinking about Ellen. Such wonderfully *purple* thoughts!

SPELDING. Now see here, Powers, you're carrying this martial law thing too far.

POWERS. Unfortunately, until I have received word from Washington as to the final disposition[12] of this problem, you must obey my orders: no telephone calls, no communication with the outside.

SPELDING. This is insupportable.

KRETON. Poor Mr. Spelding! If you like, I shall go. That would solve everything, wouldn't it?

POWERS. You're not going anywhere, Mr. Kreton, until I've had my instructions.

KRETON. I sincerely doubt if you could stop me. However, I put it up to Mr. Spelding. Shall I go?

SPELDING. Yes! [*POWERS gestures a warning.*] Do stay, I mean: want you to get a good impression of us . . .

KRETON. And of course you still want to be the first journalist to interview me. Fair enough. All right, I'll stay on for a while.

POWERS. Thank you.

KRETON. Don't mention it.

SPELDING. General, may I ask our guest a few questions?

POWERS. Go right ahead, Roger. I hope you'll do better than I did.

SPELDING. Since you can read our minds, you probably already know what our fears are.

KRETON. I do, yes.

SPELDING. We are afraid that you represent a hostile race.

KRETON. And I have assured General Powers that my people are not remotely hostile. Except for me, no one is interested in this planet's present stage.

SPELDING. Does this mean you might be interested in a *later* stage?

KRETON. I'm not permitted to discuss your future. Of course my friends think

9. Here, *giddy* means "dizzy."
10. *Seethe* (sēth) means "to suffer violent internal excitement."
11. Ellen feels degraded and wretched *(sordid).*
12. Here, *disposition* means "final outcome or settlement."

me perverse to be interested in a primitive society, but there's no accounting for tastes, is there? You are my hobby. I love you. And that's all there is to it.

POWERS. So you're just here to look around . . . sort of going native.

KRETON. What a nice expression! That's it exactly. I am going native.

POWERS. [*Grimly.*] Well, it is my view that you have been sent here by another civilization for the express purpose of reconnoitering[13] prior to invasion.

KRETON. That *would* be your view! The wonderfully primitive assumption that all strangers are hostile. You're almost too good to be true, General.

POWERS. You deny your people intend to make trouble for us?

KRETON. I deny it.

POWERS. Then are they interested in establishing communication with us? Trade? That kind of thing?

KRETON. We have always had communication with you. As for trade, well, we do not trade . . . that is something peculiar only to your social level. [*Quickly.*] Which I'm not criticizing! As you know, I approve of everything you do.

POWERS. I give up.

SPELDING. You have no interest then in . . . well, trying to dominate the earth?

13. An *express purpose* is clear and unmistakable, and *reconnoitering* means "gathering information, especially about enemy territory."

KRETON. Oh, yes! Didn't I tell you?

POWERS. I thought you just finished saying your people weren't interested in us.

KRETON. *They're* not, but *I* am.

POWERS. You!

KRETON. I, yes. You see, I've come here to take charge.

POWERS. Of the United States?

KRETON. No, of the whole world. I'm sure you'll be much happier and it will be great fun for me. You'll get used to it in no time.

POWERS. This is ridiculous. How can one man take over the world?

KRETON. [*Gaily.*] Wait and see!

POWERS. [*To* AIDE.] Grab him!

[*POWERS and AIDE rush KRETON, but within a foot of him they stop, stunned.*]

KRETON. Naughty! Naughty! See? You can't touch me. That's part of the game, too. [*Yawns and stretches.*] Now, if you don't mind, I shall go up to my room for a little lie-down.

SPELDING. I'll show you the way.

KRETON. That's all right. I know the way. [*Touches his brow.*] Such savage thoughts! My head is vibrating like a drum. I feel quite giddy, with all of you thinking at once. [*Starts to door, pauses beside* MRS. SPELDING.] No, it's not a dream, dear lady. I shall be here in the morning when you wake up. And now, good night, dear, wicked children.

[*He goes as we fade out.*]

Vocabulary

perverse (pər vurs′) *adj.* determined to go against what is reasonable, expected, or desired; contrary

Act 2

[*Fade in on* KRETON*'s bedroom next morning. He lies fully clothed on the bed with a cat on his lap.*]

KRETON. Poor cat! Of course I sympathize with you. Dogs *are* distasteful. What? Oh, I can well believe they do: yes, yes, how disgusting. They don't ever groom their fur! But you do *constantly*, such a fine coat. No, no, I'm not just saying that. I really mean it: exquisite texture. Of course, I wouldn't say it was *nicer* than skin, but even so . . . What? Oh, no! They *chase* you! Dogs chase you for no reason at all except pure malice? You poor creature. Ah, but you *do* fight back! That's right! Give it to them: slash, bite, scratch! Don't let them get away with a trick. . . . No! Do dogs really do that? Well, I'm sure *you* don't. What . . . oh, well, yes, I completely agree about mice. They *are* delicious! (Ugh!) Pounce, snap and there is a heavenly dinner. No, I don't know any mice yet . . . they're not very amusing? But after all, think how you must terrify them because you are so bold, so cunning, so beautifully predatory![14] [*Knock at the door.*] Come in.

ELLEN. [*Enters.*] Good morning. I brought you your breakfast.

KRETON. How thoughtful! [*Examines bacon.*] Delicious, but I'm afraid my stomach is not like yours, if you'll pardon me. I don't eat.

14. An animal that is *predatory* preys upon, or kills, other animals for food.

Vocabulary

malice (mal′ is) *n.* a desire to harm another; ill will

[*Removes pill from pocket and swallows it.*] This is all I need for the day. [*Indicates cat.*] Unlike this creature, who would eat her own weight every hour, given a chance.

ELLEN. How do you know?

KRETON. We've had a talk.

ELLEN. You can *speak* to the cat?

KRETON. Not speak exactly, but we communicate. I look inside and the cat cooperates. Bright red thoughts, very exciting, though rather on one level.

ELLEN. Does Kitty like us?

KRETON. No, I wouldn't say she did. But then she has very few thoughts not connected with food. Have you, my quadruped[15] criminal? [*He strokes the cat, which jumps to the floor.*]

ELLEN. You know, you've really upset everyone.

KRETON. I supposed that I would.

ELLEN. Can you really take over the world, just like that?

KRETON. Oh, yes.

ELLEN. What do you plan to do when you *have* taken over?

KRETON. Ah, that is my secret.

ELLEN. Well, I think you'll be a very nice President, *if* they let you, of course.

KRETON. What a sweet girl you are! Marry him right away.

ELLEN. Marry John?

KRETON. Yes. I see it in your head *and* in his. He wants you very much.

ELLEN. Well, we plan to get married this summer, if Father doesn't fuss too much.

KRETON. Do it before then. I shall arrange it all if you like.

ELLEN. How?

15. *Quadruped* (kwod′ rə ped′) means "four-footed."

KRETON. I can convince your father.

ELLEN. That sounds so ominous! I think you'd better leave poor Daddy alone.

KRETON. Whatever you say. [*Sighs.*] Oh, I love it here. When I woke up this morning I had to pinch myself to prove I was really here.

ELLEN. We were all doing a bit of pinching too. Ever since dawn we've had nothing but visitors and phone calls and troops outside in the garden. No one has the faintest idea what to do about you.

KRETON. Well, I don't think they'll be confused much longer.

ELLEN. How do you plan to conquer the world?

KRETON. I confess I'm not sure. I suppose I must make some demonstration of strength, some colorful trick that will frighten everyone . . . though I much prefer taking charge quietly. That's why I've sent for the President.

ELLEN. The President? *Our* President?

KRETON. Yes, he'll be along any minute now.

ELLEN. But the President just doesn't go around visiting people.

KRETON. He'll visit me. [*Chuckles.*] It may come as a surprise to him, but he'll be in this house in a very few minutes. I think we'd better go downstairs now. [*To cat.*] No, I will not give you a mouse. You must get your own. Be self-reliant. Beast!

[*Dissolve to the study.* POWERS *is reading a book entitled* The Atom and You. *Muffled explosions offstage.*]

AIDE. [*Entering.*] Sir, nothing seems to be working. Do we have the General's permission to try a fission bomb[16] on the force field?

POWERS. No . . . no. We'd better give it up.

AIDE. The men are beginning to talk.

16. A *fission bomb* is an atomic bomb.

POWERS. [*Thundering.*] Well, keep them quiet! [*Contritely.*][17] I'm sorry, Captain. I'm on edge. Fortunately, the whole business will soon be in the hands of the World Council.

AIDE. What will the World Council do?

POWERS. It will be interesting to observe them.

AIDE. You don't think this Kreton can really take over the world, do you?

POWERS. Of course not. Nobody can.

[*Dissolve to the living room.* MRS. SPELDING *and* SPELDING *are alone.*]

MRS. SPELDING. You still haven't asked Mr. Kreton about moving that thing, have you?

SPELDING. There are too many important things to ask him.

MRS. SPELDING. I hate to be a nag, but you know the trouble I have had getting anything to grow in that part of the garden . . .

JOHN. [*Enters.*] Good morning.

MRS. SPELDING. Good morning, John.

JOHN. Any sign of your guest?

MRS. SPELDING. Ellen took his breakfast up to him a few minutes ago.

JOHN. They don't seem to be having much luck, do they? [*To* SPELDING.] I sure hope you don't mind my staying here like this.

[SPELDING *glowers.*]

MRS. SPELDING. Why, we love having you! I just hope your family aren't too anxious.

JOHN. One of the G.I.'s[18] finally called them, said I was staying here for the weekend.

SPELDING. The rest of our lives, if something isn't done soon.

JOHN. Just how long do you think that'll be, Dad?

SPELDING. Who knows?

[KRETON *and* ELLEN *enter.*]

KRETON. Ah, how wonderful to see you again! Let me catch my breath. . . . Oh, your minds! It's not easy for me, you know: so many crude thoughts blazing away! Yes, Mrs. Spelding, I will move the ship off your roses.

MRS. SPELDING. That's awfully sweet of you.

KRETON. Mr. Spelding, if any interviews are to be granted, you will be the first, I promise you.

SPELDING. That's very considerate, I'm sure.

KRETON. So you can stop thinking *those* particular thoughts. And now where is the President?

SPELDING. The President?

KRETON. Yes, I sent for him. He should be here. [*Goes to terrace window.*] Ah, that must be he.

[*A swarthy*[19] MAN *in uniform with a sash across his chest is standing, bewildered, on the terrace.* KRETON *opens the glass doors.*]

KRETON. Come in, sir! Come in, Your Excellency. Good of you to come on such short notice.

[MAN *enters.*]

MAN. [*In Spanish accent.*] Where am I?

KRETON. You *are* the President, aren't you?

MAN. Of course I am the President. What am I doing here? I was dedicating a bridge and I find myself . . .

KRETON. [*Aware of his mistake.*] Oh, dear! *Where* was the bridge?

MAN. Where do you think, you idiot, in Paraguay!

---

17. When Powers speaks *contritely* (kən trīt′ lē), he expresses sorrowful regret for his wrongdoing (in this case, for losing his temper).
18. Here, *G.I.* means "soldier." The initials stand for "Government Issue," a term first used on U.S. Army supply lists.
19. *Swarthy* (swôr′ t͟hē) means "having a dark complexion."

KRETON. [*To others.*] I seem to've made a mistake. Wrong President. [*Gestures and the* MAN *disappears.*] Seemed rather upset, didn't he?

JOHN. You can make people come and go just like that?

KRETON. Just like that.

[POWERS *looks into room from the study.*]

POWERS. Good morning, Mr. Kreton. Could I see you for a moment?

KRETON. By all means. [*He crosses to the study.*]

SPELDING. I believe I am going mad.

[*Cut to study. The* AIDE *stands at attention while* POWERS *addresses* KRETON.]

POWERS. . . . and so we feel, the government of the United States feels, that this problem is too big for any one country. Therefore, we have turned the whole affair over to Paul Laurent, the Secretary-General of the World Council.

KRETON. Very sensible. I should've thought of that myself.

POWERS. Mr. Laurent is on his way here now. And may I add, Mr. Kreton, you've made me look singularly ridiculous.[20]

KRETON. I'm awfully sorry. [*Pause.*] No, you can't kill me.

POWERS. You were reading my mind again.

KRETON. I can't really help it, you know. And such *black* thoughts today, but intense, very intense.

POWERS. I regard you as a menace.

KRETON. I know you do and I think it's awfully unkind. I do mean well.

POWERS. Then go back where you came from and leave us alone.

20. To look *singularly ridiculous* would be to seem remarkably or extraordinarily silly.

KRETON. No, I'm afraid I can't do that just yet . . .

[*Telephone rings;* AIDE *answers it.*]

AIDE. He's outside? Sure, let him through. [*To* POWERS.] The Secretary-General of the World Council is here, sir.

POWERS. [*To* KRETON.] I hope you'll listen to *him.*

KRETON. Oh, I shall, of course. I love listening.

[*The door opens.* PAUL LAURENT, *middle-aged and serene, enters.* POWERS *and his* AIDE *stand at attention.* KRETON *goes forward to shake hands.*]

LAURENT. Mr. Kreton?

KRETON. At your service, Mr. Laurent.

LAURENT. I welcome you to this planet in the name of the World Council.

KRETON. Thank you, sir, thank you.

LAURENT. Could you leave us alone for a moment, General?

POWERS. Yes, sir.

[POWERS *and the* AIDE *go.* LAURENT *smiles at* KRETON.]

LAURENT. Shall we sit down?

KRETON. Yes, yes, I love sitting down. I'm afraid my manners are not quite suitable yet.

[*They sit down.*]

LAURENT. I'm sure they are more than suitable. But now, Mr. Kreton, in violation of all the rules of diplomacy,[21] may I come to the point?

KRETON. You may.

LAURENT. Why are you here?

21. *Diplomacy* means "tact" or "skill in negotiating with others without arousing anger." In international diplomacy, the unwritten rules say that one never comes directly to the point or asks straightforward questions.

KRETON. Curiosity. Pleasure.

LAURENT. You are a tourist, then, in this time and place?

KRETON. [*Nods.*] Yes. Very well put.

LAURENT. We have been informed that you have extraordinary powers.

KRETON. By your standards, yes, they must seem extraordinary.

LAURENT. We have also been informed that it is your intention to . . . to take charge of this world.

KRETON. That is correct . . . What a remarkable mind you have! I have difficulty looking inside it.

LAURENT. [*Laughs.*] Practice. I've attended so many conferences. . . . May I say that your conquest of our world puts your status of tourist in a rather curious light?

KRETON. Oh, I said nothing about *conquest*.

LAURENT. Then how else do you intend to govern? The people won't allow you to direct their lives without a struggle.

KRETON. But I'm sure they will if I ask them to.

LAURENT. You believe you can do all this without, well, without violence?

KRETON. Of course I can. One or two demonstrations and I'm sure they'll do as I ask. [*Smiles.*] Watch this. [*Pause. Then shouting. POWERS bursts into room.*]

POWERS. *Now* what've you done?

KRETON. Look out the window, Your Excellency.

[*LAURENT goes to window. A rifle floats by, followed by an alarmed soldier.*]

KRETON. Nice, isn't it? I confess I worked out a number of rather melodramatic tricks last night. Incidentally, all the rifles of all the soldiers in all the world are now floating in the air. [*Gestures.*] Now they have them back.

POWERS. [*To LAURENT.*] You see, sir, I didn't exaggerate in my report.

LAURENT. [*Awed.*] No, no, you certainly didn't.

KRETON. You were skeptical, weren't you?

LAURENT. Naturally. But now I . . . now I think it's possible.

POWERS. That this . . . gentleman is going to run everything?

LAURENT. Yes, yes I do. And it might be wonderful.

KRETON. You *are* more clever than the others. You begin to see that I mean only good.

LAURENT. Yes, only good. General, do you realize what this means? We can have one government . . .

KRETON. With innumerable bureaus, and intrigue . . .

LAURENT. [*Excited.*] And the world could be incredibly prosperous, especially if he'd help us with his superior knowledge. . . .

KRETON. [*Delighted.*] I will, I will. I'll teach you to look into one another's minds. You'll find it devastating but enlightening: all that self-interest, those lurid emotions . . .

LAURENT. No more countries. No more wars . . .

KRETON. [*Startled.*] What? Oh, but I like a lot of countries. Besides, at this stage of your development you're supposed to have lots of countries and lots of wars . . . innumerable wars. . . .

LAURENT. But you can help us change all that.

KRETON. *Change* all that! My dear sir, I am your friend.

LAURENT. What do you mean?

KRETON. Why, your deepest pleasure is violence. How can you deny that? It is the whole point to you, the whole point to my hobby . . . and you are my hobby, all mine.

LAURENT. But our lives are devoted to *controlling* violence, not creating it.

KRETON. Now, don't take me for an utter fool. After all, I can see into your minds. I can feel your emotions as though they were my own and your emotions are incredibly violent. My dear fellow, don't you *know* what you are?

LAURENT. No, what are we?

KRETON. You are savages. I have returned to the dark ages of an insignificant planet simply because I want the glorious excitement of being among you and reveling in your savagery! There is murder in all your hearts and I love it! It intoxicates me!

LAURENT. [*Slowly.*] You hardly flatter us.

KRETON. I didn't mean to be rude, but you did ask me why I came here and I've told you.

LAURENT. You have no wish, then, to . . . to help us poor savages.

KRETON. I couldn't even if I wanted to. You won't be civilized for at least two thousand years and you won't reach the level of my people for about a million years.

LAURENT. [*Sadly.*] Then you have come here only to . . . to observe?

KRETON. No, more than that. I mean to regulate your past times. But don't worry: I won't upset things too much. I've decided I don't want to be known to the people. You will go right on with your countries, your squabbles, the way you always have, while I will *secretly* regulate things through you.

Vocabulary
lurid (loor′ id) *adj.* sensational; shocking

LAURENT. The World Council does not govern. We only advise.

KRETON. Well, I shall advise you and you will advise the governments and we shall have a lovely time.

LAURENT. I don't know what to say. You obviously have the power to do as you please.

KRETON. I'm glad you realize that. Poor General Powers is now wondering if a hydrogen bomb might destroy me. It won't, General.

POWERS. Too bad.

KRETON. Now, Your Excellency, I shall stay in this house until you have laid the groundwork for my first project.

LAURENT. And what is that to be?

KRETON. A war! I want one of your really splendid wars, with all the trimmings, all the noise and the fire . . .

LAURENT. A war! You're joking. Why, at this moment we are working as hard as we know how *not* to have a war.

KRETON. But secretly you want one. After all, it's the one thing your little race does well. You'd hardly want me to deprive you of your simple pleasures, now would you?

LAURENT. I think you must be mad.

KRETON. Not mad, simply a philanthropist.[22] Of course I myself shall get a great deal of pleasure out of a war (the vibrations must be incredible) but I'm doing it mostly for you. Now, if you don't mind, I want you to arrange a few incidents, so we can get one started spontaneously.

LAURENT. I refuse.

KRETON. In that event, I shall select someone else to head the World Council. Someone who *will* start a war. I suppose there exist a few people here who might like the idea.

LAURENT. How can you do such a horrible thing to us? Can't you see that we don't want to be savages?

KRETON. But you have no choice. Anyway, you're just pulling my leg! I'm sure you want a war as much as the rest of them do and that's what you're going to get: the biggest war you've ever had!

LAURENT. [*Stunned.*] Heaven help us!

KRETON. [*Exuberant.*] Heaven won't. Oh, what fun it will be! I can hardly wait!

[*He strikes the globe of the world a happy blow as we fade out.*]

22. A ***philanthropist*** (fi lan′ thrə pist) **is someone who actively promotes the happiness and well-being of humanity.**

ACT 3

[*Fade in on the study, two weeks later.* KRETON *is sitting at a desk on which a map is spread out. He has a pair of dividers*[23] *and some models of jet aircraft. Occasionally he pretends to dive-bomb, imitating the sound of a bomb going off.* POWERS *enters.*]

POWERS. You wanted me, sir?

KRETON. Yes, I wanted those figures on radioactive fall-out.

POWERS. They're being made up now, sir. Anything else?

KRETON. Oh, my dear fellow, why do you dislike me so?

POWERS. I am your military aide, sir. I don't have to answer that question. It is outside the sphere of my duties.

KRETON. Aren't you at least happy about your promotion?

POWERS. Under the circumstances, no, sir.

23. A *divider* is an instrument for measuring distance and drawing circles. Also called a compass, it consists of two straight and equal legs connected at one end.

KRETON. I find your attitude baffling.

POWERS. Is that all, sir?

KRETON. You have never once said what you thought of my war plans. Not once have I got a single word of encouragement from you, a single compliment . . . only black thoughts.

POWERS. Since you read my mind, sir, you know what I think.

KRETON. True, but I can't help but feel that deep down inside of you there is just a twinge of professional jealousy. You don't like the idea of an outsider playing your game better than you do. Now confess!

POWERS. I am acting as your aide only under duress.[24]

KRETON. [*Sadly.*] Bitter, bitter . . . and to think I chose you especially as my aide. Think of all the other generals who would give anything to have your job.

24. To be *under duress* (doo res′) is to be operating in conditions of constraint or restriction.

POWERS. Fortunately, they know nothing about my job.

KRETON. Yes, I do think it wise not to advertise my presence, don't you?

POWERS. I can't see that it makes much difference, since you seem bent on destroying our world.

KRETON. I'm not going to destroy it. A few dozen cities, that's all, and not very nice cities either. Think of the fun you'll have building new ones when it's over.

POWERS. How many millions of people do you plan to kill?

KRETON. Well, quite a few, but they love this sort of thing. You can't convince me they don't. Oh, I know what Laurent says. But he's a misfit, out of step with his time. Fortunately, my new World Council is more reasonable.

POWERS. Paralyzed is the word, sir.

KRETON. You think they don't like me either?

POWERS. You *know* they hate you, sir.

KRETON. But love and hate are so confused in your savage minds and the vibrations of the one are so very like those of the other that I can't always distinguish. You see, we neither love nor hate in my world. We simply have hobbies. [*He strokes the globe of the world tenderly.*] But now to work. Tonight's the big night: first, the sneak attack; then, boom! [*Claps hands gleefully.*]

[*Dissolve to living room, to* JOHN *and* ELLEN.]

ELLEN. I've never felt so helpless in my life.

JOHN. Here we all stand around doing nothing while he plans to blow up the world.

ELLEN. Suppose we went to the newspapers . . .

JOHN. He controls the press. When Laurent resigned they didn't even print his speech.

[*A gloomy pause.*]

ELLEN. What are you thinking about?

JOHN. Walnuts.

[*They embrace.*]

ELLEN. Can't we do anything?

JOHN. No, I guess there's nothing.

ELLEN. [*Vehemently.*][25] Oh! I could kill him!

[*KRETON and POWERS enter.*]

KRETON. Oh, very good, Ellen, very good! I've never felt you so violent.

ELLEN. You heard what I said to John?

KRETON. Not in words, but you were absolutely bathed in malevolence.[26]

POWERS. I'll get the papers you wanted, sir. [*Exits.*]

KRETON. I don't think he likes me very much, but your father does. Only this morning he offered to handle my public relations and I said I'd let him. Wasn't that nice of him?

JOHN. I think I'll get some fresh air. [*Goes out through the terrace door.*]

KRETON. Oh, dear! [*Sighs.*] He doesn't like me either. Only your father is really entering the spirit of the game. He's a much better sport than you, my dear.

ELLEN. [*Exploding.*] Sport! That's it! You think we're sport. You think we're animals to be played with. Well, we're not. We're people and we don't want to be destroyed.

KRETON. [*Patiently.*] But *I* am not destroying you. You will be destroying one another of your own free will, as you have always done. I am simply a . . . a kibitzer.[27]

ELLEN. No, you are a vampire!

KRETON. A vampire? You mean I drink blood? Ugh!

ELLEN. No, you drink emotions, our emotions. You'll sacrifice us all for the sake of your . . . your vibrations!

KRETON. *Touché.*[28] Yet what harm am I really doing? It's true I'll enjoy the war more than anybody; but it will be *your* destructiveness, after all, not mine.

ELLEN. You could stop it.

KRETON. So could you.

ELLEN. I?

KRETON. Your race. They could stop altogether, but they won't. And I can hardly intervene in their natural development. The most I can do is help out in small, practical ways.

ELLEN. We are not what you think. We're not so . . . so primitive.

KRETON. My dear girl, just take this one household: your mother dislikes your father but she is too tired to do anything about it so she knits and she gardens and she tries not to think about him. Your father, on the other hand, is bored with all of you. Don't look shocked; he doesn't like you any more than you like him. . . .

ELLEN. Don't say that!

KRETON. I am only telling you the truth. Your father wants you to marry opportunistically;[29] therefore, he objects to John, while you, my girl . . .

[*With a fierce cry, ELLEN grabs a vase to throw.*]

ELLEN. You devil!

[*Vase breaks in her hand.*]

KRETON. You see? That proves my point perfectly. [*Gently.*] Poor savage, I cannot help

25. *Vehemently* (vē′ ə mənt lē) means "strongly; intensely; passionately."
26. *Malevolence* (mə lev′ ə ləns) means "malice."
27. Someone who looks on and gives unwanted advice or commentary is a *kibitzer* (kib′ it sər).
28. In conversation, the interjection *touché* (to͞o shā′) acknowledges a successful criticism, effective argument, or witty reply.
29. To act *opportunistically* is to take advantage of an opportunity to achieve some goal, regardless of the consequences or of morality.

what you are. [*Briskly.*] Anyway, you will soon be distracted from your personal problems. Tonight is the night. If you're a good girl, I'll let you watch the bombing.

[*Dissolve to study. Eleven forty-five.* POWERS *and the* AIDE *gloomily await the war.*]

AIDE. General, isn't there anything we can do?

POWERS. It's out of our hands.

[KRETON, *dressed as a hussar, with shako,*[30] *enters.*]

KRETON. Everything on schedule?

POWERS. Yes, sir. Planes left for their targets at twenty-two hundred.

KRETON. Good . . . good. I myself shall take off shortly after midnight to observe the attack firsthand.

POWERS. Yes, sir.

[KRETON *goes into the living room, where the family is gloomily assembled.*]

KRETON. And now, the magic hour approaches! I hope you're all as thrilled as I am.

SPELDING. You still won't tell us who's attacking whom?

KRETON. You'll know in exactly . . . fourteen minutes.

ELLEN. [*Bitterly.*] Are we going to be killed too?

KRETON. Certainly not! You're quite safe, at least in the early stages of the war.

ELLEN. Thank you.

MRS. SPELDING. I suppose this will mean rationing again.

30. A *hussar* (hə zär′) is a member of a cavalry regiment in any of several European armies, and a *shako* (shak′ ō) is a high, stiff military hat with a visor and, usually, a plume or feather attached in front.

SPELDING. Will . . . will we see anything from here?

KRETON. No, but there should be a good picture on the monitor in the study. Powers is tuning in right now.

JOHN. [*At window.*] Hey look, up there! Coming this way!

[ELLEN *joins him.*]

ELLEN. What is it?

JOHN. Why . . . it's *another* one! And it's going to land.

KRETON. [*Surprised.*] I'm sure you're mistaken. No one would dream of coming here. [*He goes to the window.*]

ELLEN. It's landing!

SPELDING. Is it a friend of yours, Mr. Kreton?

KRETON. [*Slowly.*] No, no, not a friend . . .

[KRETON *retreats to the study; on his way, he inadvertently drops a lace handkerchief beside the sofa.*]

JOHN. Here he comes.

ELLEN. [*Suddenly bitter.*] Now we have two of them.

MRS. SPELDING. My poor roses.

[*The new* VISITOR *enters in a gleam of light from his ship. He is wearing a most futuristic costume. Without a word, he walks past the awed family into the study.* KRETON *is cowering behind the globe.* POWERS *and the* AIDE *stare, bewildered, as the* VISITOR *gestures sternly and* KRETON *reluctantly removes shako and sword. They communicate by odd sounds.*]

VISITOR. [*To* POWERS.] Please leave us alone.

[*Cut to living room as* POWERS *and the* AIDE *enter from the study.*]

Vocabulary

inadvertently (in′ ad vurt′ ənt lē) *adv.* accidentally; unintentionally

POWERS. [*To* ELLEN.] Who on earth was that?

ELLEN. It's another one, another visitor.

POWERS. Now we're done for.

ELLEN. I'm going in there.

MRS. SPELDING. Ellen, don't you dare!

ELLEN. I'm going to talk to them. [*Starts to door.*]

JOHN. I'll go, too.

ELLEN. [*Grimly.*] No, alone. I know what I want to say.

[*Cut to interior of the study, to* KRETON *and the other* VISITOR *as* ELLEN *enters.*]

ELLEN. I want you both to listen to me . . .

VISITOR. You don't need to speak. I know what you will say.

ELLEN. That you have no right here? That you mustn't . . .

VISITOR. I agree. Kreton has no right here. He is well aware that it is forbidden to interfere with the past.

ELLEN. The past?

VISITOR. [*Nods.*] You are the past, the dark ages; we are from the future. In fact, we are *your* descendants on another planet. We visit you from time to time, but we never interfere because it would change *us* if we did. Fortunately, I have arrived in time.

ELLEN. There won't be a war?

VISITOR. There will be no war. And there will be no memory of any of this. When we leave here you will forget Kreton and me. Time will seem to turn back to the moment before his arrival.

ELLEN. [*To* KRETON.] Why did you want to hurt us?

KRETON. [*Heartbroken.*] Oh, but I didn't! I only wanted to have . . . well, to have a little fun, to indulge my hobby . . . against the rules, of course.

VISITOR. [*To* ELLEN.] Kreton is a rarity among us. Mentally and morally he is retarded. He is a child and he regards your period as his toy.

KRETON. A child, now really!

VISITOR. He escaped from his nursery and came back in time to you. . . .

KRETON. And *every*thing went wrong, everything! I wanted to visit 1860—that's my *real* period—but then something happened to the car and I ended up here; not that I don't find you nearly as interesting, but . . .

VISITOR. We must go, Kreton.

KRETON. [*To* ELLEN.] You did like me just a bit, didn't you?

ELLEN. Yes, yes I did, until you let your hobby get out of hand. [*To* VISITOR.] What is the future like?

VISITOR. Very serene, very different . . .

KRETON. Don't believe him: it is dull, dull, dull beyond belief! One simply floats through eternity: no wars, no excitement . . .

VISITOR. It is forbidden to discuss these matters.

KRETON. I can't see what difference it makes since she's going to forget all about us anyway.

ELLEN. Oh, how I'd love to see the future . . .

VISITOR. It is against . . .

KRETON. Against the rules. How tiresome you are. [*To* ELLEN.] But, alas, you can never pay us a call because you aren't born yet! I mean, where we are you are not. Oh, Ellen dear, think kindly of me, until you forget.

ELLEN. I will.

VISITOR. Come. Time has begun to turn back. Time is bending.

[*He starts to the door.* KRETON *turns conspiratorially to* ELLEN.]

KRETON. Don't be sad, my girl. I shall be back one bright day, but a bright day in 1860. I dote on[31] the Civil War, so exciting . . .

VISITOR. Kreton!

KRETON. Only next time I think it'll be more fun if the South wins! [*He hurries after the visitor.*]

[*Cut to clock as the hands spin backwards. Dissolve to the living room, exactly the same as the first scene:* SPELDING, MRS. SPELDING, ELLEN.]

SPELDING. There is nothing wrong with marrying a wealthy man. The horror of it has always eluded me. However, my only wish is that you marry someone hard-working, ambitious, a man who'll make his mark in the world. Not a boy who plans to sit on a farm all his life, growing peanuts . . .

ELLEN. English walnuts! And he won't just sit there.

SPELDING. Will you stop contradicting me?

ELLEN. But, Daddy, John grows walnuts . . .

[JOHN *enters.*]

JOHN. Hello, everybody.

MRS. SPELDING. Good evening, John.

ELLEN. What kept you, darling? You missed Daddy's broadcast.

JOHN. I saw it before I left home. Wonderful broadcast, sir.

SPELDING. Thank you, John.

[JOHN *crosses to window.*]

JOHN. That meteor you were talking about, well, for a while it looked almost like a spaceship or something. You can just barely see it now.

[ELLEN *joins him at window. They watch, arms about one another.*]

SPELDING. Spaceship! Nonsense! Remarkable what some people will believe, want to believe. Besides, as I said in the broadcast, if there's any traveling to be done in space we'll do it first, and we haven't done it yet. . . .

[*He notices* KRETON*'s handkerchief on sofa and picks it up. They all look at it, puzzled. Cut to a stock shot of the starry night, against which two spaceships vanish in the distance, one serene in its course, the other erratic, as we fade out.*]

31. To *dote on* is to show extreme affection for or pay excessive attention to.

Vocabulary

erratic (ə rat′ ik) *adj.* acting or moving irregularly or unpredictably

Responding to Literature

Personal Response

What is your reaction to Kreton? Share your response with a partner.

Analyzing Literature

Recall

1. What is happening at the Speldings' home just before Kreton arrives?
2. What reason does Kreton give at the beginning of act 1 for coming to Earth? What real reason is revealed at the end of the act?
3. Summarize how each of the characters reacts to Kreton.
4. What plan does Kreton reveal to Paul Laurent, and how does Laurent first react to it? What **conflict** arises when Kreton's ideas are fully revealed? (See Literary Terms Handbook, page R3.)
5. How is Kreton's plan thwarted? How does Kreton react?

Interpret

6. Briefly identify and describe Mr. and Mrs. Spelding, Ellen, and John. How would you characterize their relationships with one another?
7. How do Kreton's powers affect his assessment of, and attitude toward, people and life on Earth?
8. Explain why each character's response to Kreton is appropriate, given what you know about his or her personality, family role, job, or professional aspirations.
9. Why might Kreton think that people will go along with his plan?
10. Why does Kreton hate the idea of leaving? Which of Kreton's own mistakes are partly responsible for his inability to accomplish his goal?

Evaluate and Connect

11. How might Kreton and Laurent answer the question posed in the Reading Focus on page 921? Have your opinions broadened or changed after reading the play? How?
12. Why might Vidal have chosen to portray Kreton as calm, civilized, and polite? How did those qualities affect your initial impression of him, and how did your impression change as the play progressed?
13. Explain how Vidal uses the play's structure to build **suspense** and resolve the final conflict. (See Literary Terms Handbook, page R12.)
14. What would the characters in the play learn from Kreton's visit–if only they could remember it?
15. Do you agree with Kreton that life without conflict or wars would be boring? Why or why not?

Literary ELEMENTS

Comedy

A **comedy** is a type of drama that deals with light and amusing subjects or with serious and profound subjects in a light, familiar, or satirical manner. Comedies, which often have happy endings, amuse and entertain audiences through the use of verbal wit, physical humor, ridicule, or irony. Comedy writers sometimes poke fun at people's faults and limitations in order to teach something about the follies and foibles of human nature.

1. Why might *Visit to a Small Planet* be considered a comedy?
2. What weaknesses or faults of people or society does this play poke fun at? Cite examples from the play in your answer.
3. In your opinion, what were the funniest parts of the play? What made those parts funny to you?

- See **Literary Terms Handbook,** p. R3.

Literature and Writing

Writing About Literature

Focusing on Family Life Write an analysis of how Gore Vidal idealizes individual roles within the Spelding family in a way that was typical of his generation—where women were housewives, men went off to work each day and were in control of their families, and children were meant to be seen and not heard. How does Vidal still manage to create an atypical family, different from the stereotypes commonly seen during this era?

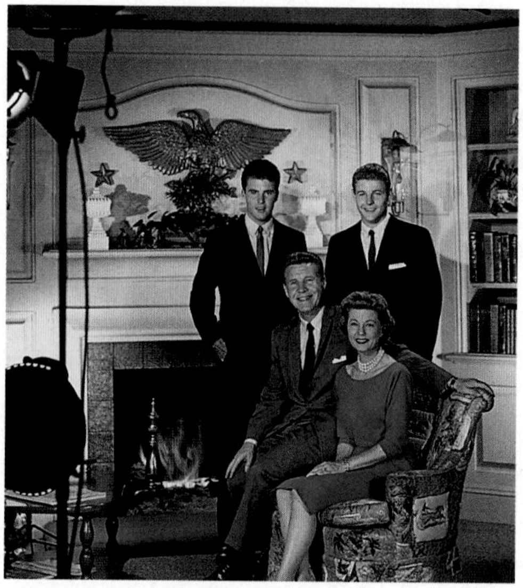

The television show *The Adventures of Ozzie and Harriet* depicted a stereotypical 1950s family.

Creative Writing

Broadcast News Roger Spelding is excited about the prospect of war—in part because of the journalistic possibilities wartime represents. Give what might be his final news broadcast to the world shortly before the bombing begins. Describe what's about to happen and why, including quotations from interviews with Powers or Laurent.

Extending Your Response

Literature Groups

Debating Human Nature Kreton says on page 933 that General Powers makes the "primitive assumption that all strangers are hostile." Kreton himself labels all society on Earth primitive, so he implies that most people think this way. Do you agree or disagree? Do you think that Gore Vidal also holds this point of view? Is wariness of strangers a basic human trait? Discuss these questions in your group, providing evidence from your own lives to support or dispute Kreton's assertion. Share a summary of the discussion with the class.

Performing

Act It Out With a small group, select a scene from the play to act out. Assign and practice the parts, using your own interpretations as well as the stage directions to guide your intonations, gestures, and movements. Have someone videotape the performance as if it were a television show, and play your videotape for the rest of the class.

Interdisciplinary Activity

Art: Storyboard Choose one of the play's three acts and create a storyboard—a series of sketches depicting the most important events in the order in which they occur. Include details of setting and character in your drawings, devoting one sketch to each scene or action. Display your sketches on posterboard.

Reading Further

If you liked this play, you might also enjoy these works:

Listening: *The War of the Worlds,* a classic science fiction novel by H.G. Wells, was adapted for the radio by actor and director Orson Welles. Audio cassettes of this 1938 radio broadcast capture the drama and suspense of the original program.

Viewing: *Visit to a Small Planet*, a movie on videocassette, was made in 1960 and stars Jerry Lewis as Kreton.

Save your work for your portfolio.

Skill Minilessons

GRAMMAR AND LANGUAGE • Exclamatory Sentences

Visit to a Small Planet contains many **exclamatory sentences,** which show strong feeling or indicate a forceful command. As these examples show, exclamatory sentences end with an exclamation point.

"Look! Something *is* falling!"

"It's landing!"

"Oh, how awful!"

Remember that an interjection at the beginning of a sentence may be followed by an exclamation point or a comma, depending on the force intended.

PRACTICE On your paper, write the following sentences. Add punctuation, including exclamation points or periods where they are needed.

1. Hey I told you to get that spaceship off my roses
2. What a strange costume he is wearing.
3. Yes I am the president of Paraguay
4. Take this breakfast tray upstairs to Mr. Kreton
5. Oh I can hardly wait

For more information on exclamatory sentences, see **Language Handbook,** p. R42.

READING AND THINKING • Analyzing Arguments

In *Visit to a Small Planet,* Kreton has a plan, and he attempts to persuade the other characters to agree with it and support it. In literary terms, he is presenting an argument–using facts and reasons to influence the ideas of others. Reading nonfiction articles and essays, as well as fictional pieces in which characters present strong arguments, requires careful thought. As you read, pause now and then to ask yourself questions such as these:

- How can I restate the author's or character's central argument?
- What facts or reasons does he or she use to support it?
- Which facts or reasons do I agree with?
- Do I feel the argument is fair and reasonable? Why or why not?
- How can I summarize my response?

PRACTICE Use the questions above to write an analysis of Kreton's argument.

For more on analyzing arguments, see **Reading Handbook,** pp. R102–R103.

VOCABULARY • The Prefix *mal-*

The prefix *mal-* or *male-,* meaning "bad, badly, wrong, or evil," comes from the Latin word *malus,* which means "bad" and from which we get *malice.* When *mal-* is attached to a familiar English word such as *formed* to make *malformed,* the meaning is easy to figure out simply by combining the meanings of the prefix and the base word. Even when the prefix is attached to an unfamiliar Latin root, its meaning of "badness," combined with context clues, will often reveal the new word's meaning.

PRACTICE Use what you know about context clues and the prefix *mal-* or *male-* to match each italicized word to one of the words listed after item number five.

1. What medicine is prescribed for that *malady?*
2. Was the fire an accident or the work of a *malefactor?*
3. It's hard to ignore the constant whining of a *malcontent.*
4. Found guilty of taking bribes, the mayor was removed from office for *malfeasance.*
5. I tried to apologize gracefully, but my *maladroit* statement made the situation worse.

a. clumsy
b. illness
c. dissatisfied person
d. evildoer
e. official misconduct

Before You Read

Scanning the Heavens for Signs of Life

Reading Focus

What would it mean to people on Earth if intelligent life were discovered beyond our solar system? What would it mean to you?

Discuss With a small group of classmates, discuss these questions. Then speculate why some people might choose to devote their lives to the search for extraterrestrial life.

Setting a Purpose Read to learn about scientific efforts to detect—and communicate with—extraterrestrial life.

Building Background

The Time and Place

In this article, William J. Broad reports on the work being done at the Project Phoenix headquarters in Arecibo (ä′ rə sē′ bō), Puerto Rico, in 1998.

Did You Know?

- A light-year is a unit of measure equal to the distance light can travel through a vacuum in one year—about 5.88 trillion miles. The speed of light is the fastest speed known to be possible.
- Scientists believe that any intelligent life forms that exist within our galaxy are likely to use technology to communicate the same way we do—by using electromagnetic radiation signals that travel at the speed of light. Therefore, scientists search for life by trying to detect these signals—which include radio waves, X rays, and gamma rays—in outer space.

Vocabulary Preview

enhance (en hans′) *v.* to make greater, as in strength, beauty, or value; intensify; p. 952

deride (di rīd′) *v.* to treat with scorn; mock; ridicule; p. 952

implication (im′ plə kā′ shən) *n.* suggestion; that which is logically indicated but not directly expressed; p. 952

comprehensive (kom′ pri hen′ siv) *adj.* covering completely or broadly; inclusive; p. 952

intact (in takt′) *adj.* entire; untouched, uninjured and having all parts; p. 954

Meet William J. Broad

As a reporter for the *New York Times*, William J. Broad is a regular contributor to its "Science Times" section and has won two Pulitzer Prizes as well as numerous awards for outstanding journalism. He has also written several scientific books, including a comprehensive overview of deep-sea exploration. To gather facts for his writing, Broad often travels throughout the world, observing scientists at work and participating in cutting-edge expeditions. When he is not probing into the mysteries of outer space or the ocean depths, he lives in Larchmont, New York, with his wife and three children.

William J. Broad was born in 1951. This article appeared in the New York Times *on September 29, 1998.*

Scanning the Heavens for Signs of Life

William J. Broad

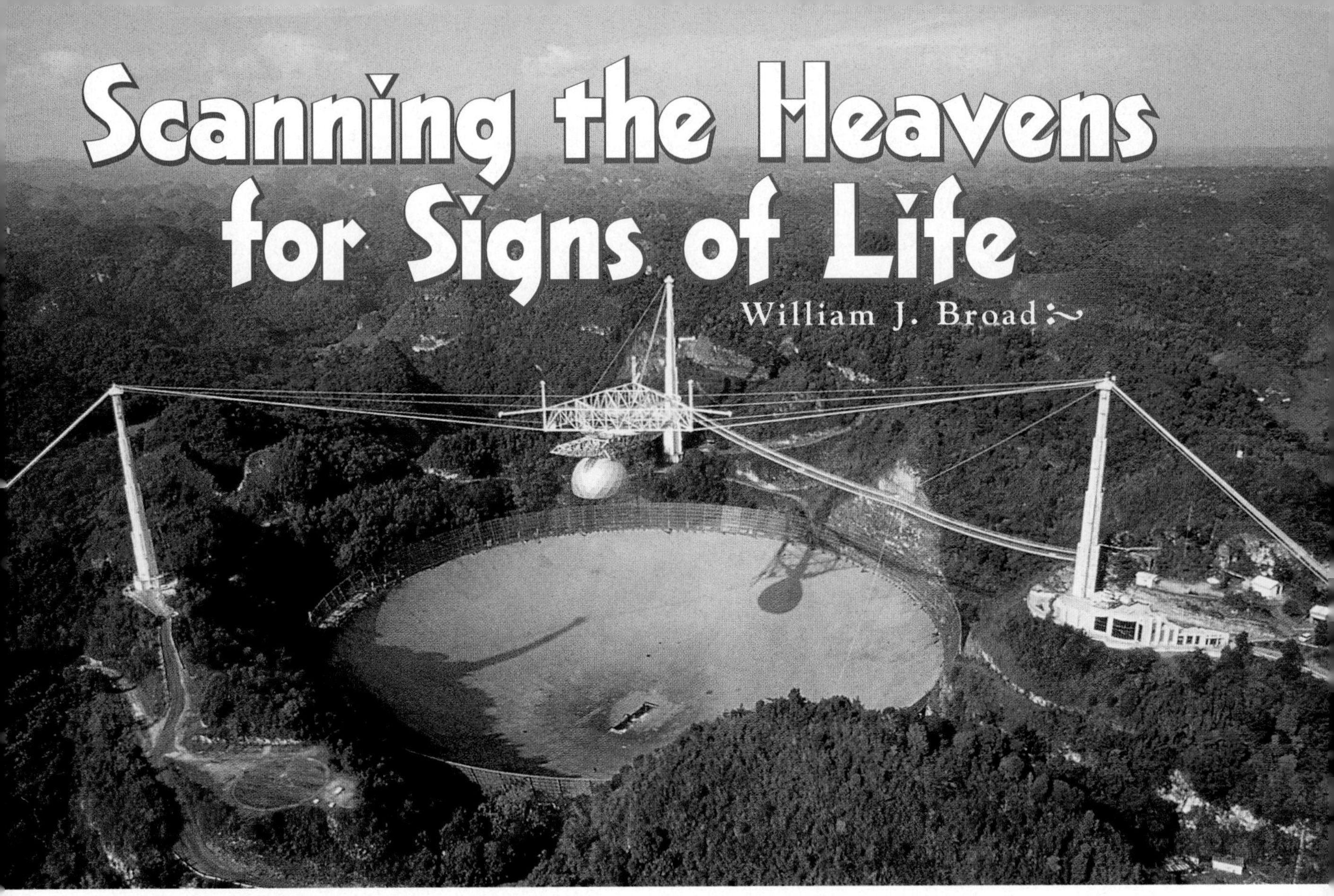

OUTSIDE IN THE FADING LIGHT, surrounded by dense jungle, the receiving dome on the world's largest radiotelescope wheeled into position. It fixed on Barnard's star, a scant six light-years away, the closest star to Earth in the Northern Hemisphere. Closeness meant it had been searched before. But now, the great dish antenna of the Arecibo[1] observatory began to gather in a riot of faint signals, giving the star its most discriminating[2] look yet for hints of invisible planets and intelligent life.

Tense with concentration, Dr. Jill C. Tarter, 54, closely examined the colored spikes[3] that slowly materialized on her monitor. Each was a candidate, a possible hello from afar. But in the next hour and a half, she, a colleague, and a nearby supercomputer rejected them, one by one. The signals turned out to be cosmic static and earthly interference.[4]

She showed no sign of frustration—no sigh, joke, or frown. A true believer, she just plowed ahead to examine a night full of stars, sure that some day there would be proof that humans were not alone in the universe.

The search for extraterrestrial intelligence, or SETI,[5] is at a turning point after nearly four decades of hard work. With the arrival here of Dr. Tarter and her crew from the SETI Institute in Mountain View, California, the field has reached a high point in terms of telescope sensitivity, a top goal of the alien hunters.

But it has found no extraterrestrials so far, despite forecasts that they should have been

1. *Arecibo* (ä′ rə sē′ bō) is a city in northern Puerto Rico.
2. Here, *discriminating* means "making distinctions accurately."
3. The signals are displayed in the form of a graph; each *spike* is a sharp rise followed by a sharp decline.
4. *Cosmic static* comes from natural sources of radiation in the universe, and *earthly interference* is the result of communication signals from the earth or from satellites.
5. In Latin, the prefix *extra-* means "beyond" or "outside," and the root *terra* means "earth." So anything *extraterrestrial* comes from beyond earth. *SETI* rhymes with *Betty.*

discovered by now. Instead, it has probed the heavens with regularity and heard nothing but a dead silence.

While pressing the hunt here at Arecibo, Dr. Tarter and her peers around the globe are engaged in quiet debate and soul searching over how to proceed. New ideas and strategies are being weighed, including expansions that would enhance telescope sensitivity and widen the hunt to more stars—perhaps 100,000 rather than the 1,000 now targeted.

"When you get far into a project and haven't found what you're looking for, it gives you pause," Seth Shostak, a SETI Institute scientist, said as he trudged down a hillside into the lush bowl that holds the telescope's huge receiving dish, the size of 26 football fields.

Does the silence bother him?

"It's a funny thing," Dr. Shostak replied. "You'd think it gets old. But it doesn't. The equipment keeps getting better and the odds keep getting better, which never happens in Vegas. Also, there are always new ideas. This is a field with new papers,[6] new meetings, new people—which is remarkable considering there is no data. So for me, it's not discouraging at all."

Close up, the great antenna was a grayish sea of thousands of perforated aluminum panels. High overhead, a cable car hauled engineers to the central receiving dome to do maintenance. Dr. Shostak strode under the dish into dim sunlight and surprisingly dense foliage.

Any boa constrictors down there?

"The worst thing is the mud," he called back confidently.

Like most SETI enthusiasts, Dr. Shostak and Dr. Tarter believe it is just a matter of time before earthlings use such antennas to make contact with aliens. Their faith is rooted in numbers, big ones. The Milky Way is estimated to have 400 billion stars, including the Sun. SETI scientists believe that many of these stars have planets orbiting them as well as advanced forms of life—an idea skeptics deride.

Alien civilizations in the galaxy are likely to number anywhere from 10,000 to one million, SETI enthusiasts say. If the higher density is right, that means advanced beings would inhabit about one in every 400,000 stars. The implication is that even a slow, detailed, comprehensive search from Earth would be mostly a wasteland of late nights, false leads, and frustration.

"It may look empty, but it's not," Dr. Shostak said as he sipped a root beer in the observatory's cafeteria, eager to cool off from the wet heat outside.

"O.K., maybe this is a hopeless task, maybe it's impossible," he conceded. "On the other hand, maybe it's like discussing the possibility of whether there's a continent between Europe and Asia in the cafés of Segovia[7] in the 1400s. Until you do the experiment, you don't know."

The first SETI hunt began in humble circumstances in the Allegheny Mountains of West Virginia. In 1960, Dr. Frank D. Drake, a young scientist at the National Radio Astronomy Observatory there, used an 85-foot antenna to listen around a few stars for

6. Here, *papers* refers to the formal compositions in which scientists present their theories and findings.

7. *Segovia* (sə gō′ vē ə) is a city in central Spain.

Vocabulary

enhance (en hans′) *v.* to make greater, as in strength, beauty, or value; intensify
deride (di rīd′) *v.* to treat with scorn; mock; ridicule
implication (im′ plə kā′ shən) *n.* suggestion; that which is logically indicated but not directly expressed
comprehensive (kom′ pri hen′ siv) *adj.* covering completely or broadly; inclusive

Jill Tarter and Seth Shostak.

alien transmissions. Ever since, a main SETI strategy has been to wield[8] increasingly big radiotelescopes, their size allowing them to gather increasingly faint signals. The dish antenna at Arecibo, 1,000 feet wide, is the biggest of them all.

SETI work started here with a bang. In 1974, at the urging of Dr. Drake, who then ran the observatory, the newly upgraded dish at Arecibo was used to beam a powerful, three-minute message at M13, a dense cluster of hundreds of thousands of stars orbiting the Milky Way. The message was a simple graphic showing the telescope as well as facts about the solar system and humans. The message is still zooming outward. At the speed of light, it will reach M13 in about 21,000 years. A reply from any aliens in that neighborhood would presumably take a similarly long time.

Dr. Tarter got hooked on the field in the mid-1970s, soon after the message was sent. She was then a young astronomer at the University of California at Berkeley. After reading a SETI report, she teamed up with another astronomer to hunt for aliens with the university's 85-foot telescope. "It was brave of Jill," Dr. Drake said in his autobiography, noting that SETI work back then could hurt a developing career.

By 1985, Dr. Tarter was a senior SETI scientist at the National Aeronautics and Space Administration. She and her colleagues built powerful computers to sift through cosmic and earthly interference and lined up many radiotelescopes, including Arecibo. Their goal was to survey 1,000 nearby stars, all within 200 light-years of Earth.

In 1992, the big search was ready to start. And Dr. Drake, the SETI pioneer, gave it a drum roll in his autobiography, *Is Anyone Out There?*, saying the find of all time was imminent.

"This discovery," he wrote, "which I fully expect to witness before the year 2000, will profoundly change the world."

But the plug was pulled suddenly in 1993 when Congress decided that SETI was a waste of public money.

Undeterred, Dr. Drake and Dr. Tarter took the hunt private at the SETI Institute. They won substantial support from a handful of silicon moguls, capitalized on[9] the $58 million the Government had invested in gear and forged ahead with the planned search. In 1995, they began roving from telescope to telescope.

Dr. Tarter, who heads Project Phoenix, as the hunt is known, is famous for her zeal. Wearing sandals, her hair tied in a pony tail, Dr. Tarter along with her institute colleagues

8. Here, *wield* (wēld) means "to handle or use, as a tool or weapon."

9. In being *undeterred,* Drake and Tarter were not discouraged from proceeding. They received funding from powerful businesspeople *(moguls)* who manufactured *silicon* chips for computers, and they took advantage of *(capitalized on)* equipment the government had already paid for.

started observing here Sept. 9 [1998]. It was the team's first return since the Federal plug was pulled. A new agreement gives them 2,000 hours of observing time, or about a half-year's worth of 12-hour night shifts, which they plan to spread over the next few years.

As always, the hunt focuses on close stars, since signals from their inhabited planets would be strongest. And it concentrates on ones similar to the Sun, the only star known to support life. Lastly, it tends to search older stars, since it assumes advanced life takes time to evolve.

At Arecibo, candidate alien signals are compared with readings from a radiotelescope nearly halfway around the world at Jodrell Bank in Britain. The comparison helps identify and rule out local earthly interference, which is exploding with the rise in satellites and cell phones.

"That is some hellacious thing," Dr. Tarter said as she glared at an interference spike. "It produces system indigestion."

Around midnight on Sept. 15, Dr. Tarter and Dr. Shostak were searching for aliens around EQ Pegasi, an unremarkable star 21 light-years away. Suddenly, the team's automatic search program started moving the telescope off the star, seeking to find out if a strong incoming signal was simply interference.

The signal died away, as it would if it originated from the star. And it returned when the telescope refocused on EQ Pegasi.

Rising out of their chairs, electrified by the drama, the two astronomers studied the signal's high rate of drift.[10] That suggested the transmitter was based on either a spinning satellite or a rapidly turning planet.

"Had Jill and I stared any harder at that display screen, we would have bored holes in the phosphor,"[11] Dr. Shostak recalled.

Again, the telescope was moved off target as the computer sought to double-check the signal's place of origin. This time the signal stayed on, meaning it was from a satellite.

"It was a big disappointment," Dr. Shostak admitted the next day. "I thought, 'Hey, this is the big one.'" Only a few times before had the team had such a sense of being on the verge of discovery.

Their faith apparently intact, despite the long hours and decades of failure, the alien hunters are planning in their spare time a new generation of strategies and gear. A committee based at the SETI Institute, including Dr. Tarter, Dr. Shostak, and 31 other experts, began meeting last year to chart a path into the future.

At the controls of the Arecibo search, Dr. Tarter became quite animated as she described futuristic arrays[12] of hundreds and perhaps even thousands of small dish antennas tied to one another electronically, scanning the sky for the advanced civilizations she knows are out there.

"We have to grow this," she said of untried gear that one day might dwarf Arecibo in sensitivity. "You have to crawl before you walk."

Her ultimate dream is to build an observatory on the far side of the Moon, free of earthly interference, scanning the heavens for an unfamiliar hello. She wants to be there herself, at the controls.

10. *[high rate of drift]* This indicates that the signal is changing rapidly.

11. *Phosphor* is the coating on the inside of a display screen.

12. An *array* is a large, orderly grouping or arrangement.

Vocabulary

intact (in takt′) *adj.* entire; untouched, uninjured and having all parts

Responding to Literature

Personal Response

Make a list of questions you would like to ask Dr. Tarter and Dr. Shostak.

Analyzing Literature

Recall and Interpret

1. What goal are Dr. Tarter, Dr. Shostak, and other SETI scientists pursuing at Arecibo, Puerto Rico? How do you know that the scientists feel it is a worthwhile goal? Use details from the selection in your answers.
2. After nearly forty years of work, why does it seem that SETI is at a "turning point"? What do you imagine will signal the next "turning point"?
3. Why might Dr. Frank Drake have written that Dr. Tarter was "brave" to become involved in SETI projects as a young scientist in the mid-1970s? Might he say the same thing of a scientist today? Why or why not?
4. What successes and failures have Drs. Tarter and Shostak experienced so far, and what do their reactions suggest about their personalities?

Evaluate and Connect

5. How might you change or expand your response to the Reading Focus on page 950 on the basis of this article? Explain.
6. What do you think of the scientists profiled in this article? What excites you–or bores you–about their work in Puerto Rico? Use details from the selection to help you explain why you feel as you do.
7. Identify the SETI scientists' arguments for why there is probably intelligent life beyond Earth. Do you think these arguments are logical? Explain why or why not.
8. Would you like to work in a scientific field that is laying the groundwork for potential success hundreds of years in the future? Why or why not?

Literary ELEMENTS

Analogy

An **analogy** is a comparison of two things that are alike in some way. An author will sometimes use an analogy to explain a concept that is complex or abstract by comparing it with something that will probably be more familiar to readers. In this article, for example, Dr. Shostak says that talking about the potential for life elsewhere in the galaxy is "like discussing the possibility of whether there's a continent between Europe and Asia in the cafés of Segovia in the 1400s."

1. Explain Dr. Shostak's analogy. How does it help explain the scientists' drive to continue their experiments?
2. Dr. Tarter says, "You have to crawl before you walk." What two situations or experiences is she comparing?

- See **Literary Terms Handbook,** p. R1.

Extending Your Response

Internet Connection

Who's Out There? Use the World Wide Web to find more information about SETI programs, organizations, and publications. Begin by searching the SETI Institute's Web site, and then branch out from there. Work with others to create a database of related Web sites, complete with names, addresses, and site descriptions.

Personal Writing

To Pay or Not to Pay Do you think that the United States government should pay to continue the search for extraterrestrial life? If you were a taxpayer, would you favor having your money spent on SETI programs? Write a letter to the editor of your local newspaper that expresses your point of view on this controversial subject.

Save your work for your portfolio.

COMPARING *selections*

Visit to a Small Planet and Scanning the Heavens for Signs of Life

COMPARE **FACT AND FICTION**

Compare the assumptions that the play and the article make about intelligent extraterrestrial life forms.

- Working with a small group, look through the selections and note the direct statements or subtle suggestions that are made about extraterrestrial beings and their goals, aspirations, and intentions.
- Use a Venn diagram like the one shown to chart the similarities and differences between the assumptions made by the two selections.

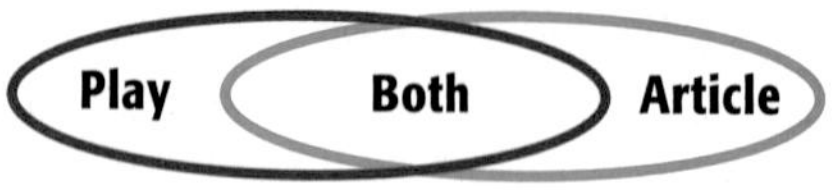

- Discuss which differences result from the fact that one selection is fiction and the other is nonfiction. Then come up with a theory to explain the similarities.

COMPARE **AUTHORS' ATTITUDES**

Gore Vidal wrote his play in the 1950s, long before humans ventured into space, whereas William J. Broad wrote his article in the 1990s, a decade of ongoing space exploration and the discovery of planets around other stars. Vidal is a playwright; Broad is a science reporter. How do the time periods in which they wrote and their purposes for writing affect the authors' stated or implied attitudes about their subjects? Write a two- or three-paragraph analysis of the differences between Vidal's and Broad's approaches to their subjects.

COMPARE **SPIN-OFFS**

Which selection would make a more popular television program–a documentary about SETI, based on Broad's article, or an adaptation of Vidal's play?

1. Write a paragraph supporting your choice. Explain why audiences would prefer it.
2. Create a "director's plan" for the program of your choice. For the TV spin-off of Vidal's play, suggest specific actors to play the major roles, and decide on costumes, props, and special effects. For the documentary based on Broad's article, suggest a narrator. Then make lists of shooting locations and sites, as well as people whom the narrator might interview.
3. Present your plan to the class.

Writing Skills

Organizing Logical Arguments

Do you believe that extraterrestrial life exists, or do you believe that we are alone in the universe? In either case, you must present a logical argument if you want to convince other people to share your view. A **logical argument** consists of a claim you make and the reasons, facts, statistics, and anecdotes you provide to support that claim and explain why you feel the way you do.

Before you begin to write, choose a topic, and gather the material you will use to support your viewpoint. Then think about how to organize the material logically. You will most likely want to state your thesis, or make your claim, in the introduction. This will help your readers know immediately what you're trying to prove.

In the body of your argument, you will probably want to organize your evidence in one of the following ways:

- **In order of importance.** Present your most convincing evidence first to capture the reader's attention, or present it last, so that it lingers in the reader's mind. In either case, the rest of your argument should follow from—or build to—the most convincing evidence.
- **By comparing your argument to opposing views.** You may want to show why an opposing argument is weaker than yours by stating its claims first and then refuting them with your own. Or you may want to show that your claim is stronger by stating your evidence first and then holding up the opposition's in comparison.

Conclude your argument by reaffirming your claim and, if it's appropriate, urging your audience to take action.

No matter how you organize your evidence, avoid making statements that distract the reader's attention from the central issue. In addition, make sure you consider all sides of the argument. Don't fall into simplistic either/or thinking that assumes an issue has only two sides.

EXERCISES

1. Using one of the above organizational strategies, write an outline for an argument on a topic of your choice. Use the World Wide Web, research books, or selections in this textbook to find evidence in support of your view.
2. Read the editorial page of a newspaper and find a letter or an article that presents an argument. Analyze the way the argument is organized. Where is the claim stated? How is the evidence presented? How effective do you think the argument is overall? Make a list of techniques you can use in your own writing.

Before You Read

The Flat of the Land

Reading Focus

Imagine that you looked out a window from your home and saw a river of mud oozing and inching steadily toward you.

Quickwrite What would you do? Jot down your ideas.

Setting a Purpose Read this short story to learn how a woman reacts when a bubbling mud hole next to her house runs amok.

Building Background

The Time and Place

This story is set in recent times near the small town of Pixley, California, which is located about sixty miles south of the city of Fresno. The events take place over a six-month period, from April to October.

Did You Know?

In California, mudflows are a fairly common and often serious effect of heavy spring rains; they have caused houses to become dislodged from their foundations and topple down hills. Mudflows also result from earthquakes and volcanic eruptions. In addition, the state has numerous hot springs, some of which have bubbling mud pools.

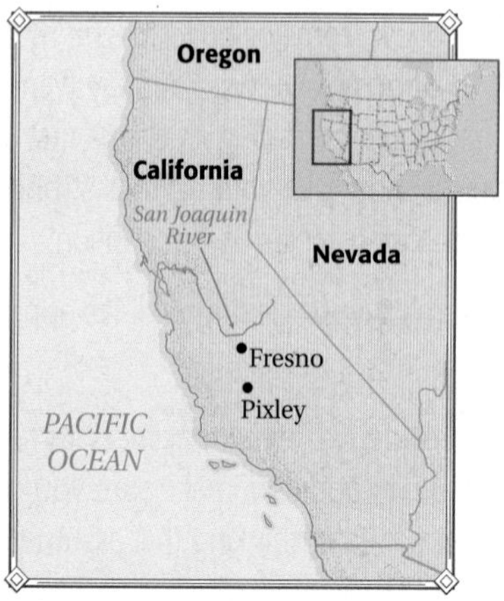

Vocabulary Preview

crevice (krev′ is) *n.* a narrow crack in or through something; p. 959

impenetrable (im pen′ ə trə bəl) *adj.* unable to be pierced, entered, or passed through; p. 960

indiscernible (in′ di sur′ nə bəl) *adj.* difficult or impossible to see; p. 964

lurk (lurk) *v.* to stay hidden, ready to attack; p. 965

belittle (bi lit′ əl) *v.* to cause to seem less important; to scorn; p. 965

skulk (skulk) *v.* to move in a sly or sneaky way so as to escape notice; p. 965

fluidity (flo͞o id′ ə tē) *n.* the ability, as of a liquid, to flow and change shape; p. 966

Meet Diana García

"For all would-be writers, begin now. Be alive to the swirl of life that surrounds you. Capture it in words and artwork."

This advice comes from an author who didn't begin writing until her mid-30s. Says Diana García, "Coming to writing has been the greatest blessing of my life." García says her fiction and poetry reflect her life: "Because of my own family's background, I often write about the experiences of migrant farm workers in California. I also write about . . . the San Joaquin Valley landscape."

Diana García was born in Merced, California, in 1950.

The Flat of the Land

Diana García

FROM THE ROOF OF HER HOUSE, Amparo[1] gauged the tilt of the old water tower with the name "Pixley" faintly outlined on the side. It was hard to say how long the tower would still be visible: another week or two, depending on the mud's flow. Not that a missing tower would make any difference in a place where the only off-ramp was at least five miles west and the combination store and restaurant with its dusty lunch counter was on the abandoned side of old Highway 99. Maybe the girl with the blonde hair and freckles who worked at the store or the girl's mother or grandmother would notice when Amparo stopped coming in for an occasional skinny hamburger and greasy fries.

The first time the mud caught Amparo's attention, it looked like a harmless bubble in the ground. It was an April morning, and she'd been hanging the wash out to dry on the clothesline behind her house. She had scarcely paid attention when the mud burped at her, distracted at the time by the breeze whipping the clothes on the line and thinking that the shadowy clouds overhead might contain some rain.

That had been almost six months ago. Amparo turned and studied the flat expanse to the east and the Sequoia foothills in the distance. At the point where the mud had first appeared, the bubble had grown to the size of a pond. Here the land sank into itself and followed the outline of some long-ago river, a few scattered cottonwoods the only clues to its crumbled banks. From this source, the mud had developed an easterly flow that skirted the stand of cottonwoods. Amparo wondered why the mud had left the trees untouched.

On the land next to hers, bulldozers had carved foundations for a style of house popular forty years earlier. From her roof, the excavations looked like archaeological digs.[2] By the time Amparo moved here, no one was left who could tell her why the development had been abandoned. All that remained of the original site was the water tower and the water main to her house. The only other trace of water was the mud; how else would the mud keep rising and spreading the way it did?

When the dimple of mud turned into a smile and then a six-inch wide crevice that threatened to swallow her clothesline,

1. *Amparo* (äm pär′ ō)

2. The word *archaeological* (är′ kē ə loj′ i kəl) refers to the scientific study of the past. Places where objects, such as bones, are dug up for study are called *digs* or *excavations*.

Vocabulary

crevice (krev′ is) *n.* a narrow crack in or through something

Amparo began to sense a possible threat to her hideaway. Up until now, she had kept her brothers and parents at bay[3] by giving them a Fresno post office box address. She visited them as often as twice a month so that they wouldn't press her for more information about where or how she was living. They seemed satisfied knowing she was living alone and that her disability income[4] was more than adequate for all her needs. She never talked about her son or her former husband, so they assumed she had laid those memories to rest. That damn mud, though, might spoil everything. At first she talked to it.

"What do you think you're doing? You have no business out here in this weather. The sun will bake you before the summer is over and then you'll have done all this work for nothing." When the sun didn't bake the oozing crack to a dry, light finish, she started asking, "Why don't you go downhill?"—indicating a direction opposite her house—"It's much easier than going uphill." The crack widened, its banks thickening and hardening, creating an impenetrable barrier within a few days' exposure to the sun.

Amparo trained herself not to think about the spreading mud. She listened to the Mexican stations on the radio. At night, she'd lie in bed and pretend the coyotes were talking to her instead of to the foothills and the jack rabbits. She'd answer, "Yes, manzanita[5] does make the best cover," and, "No, the easiest way to get yourself killed is to expose yourself." She rarely turned the lights on after dark, afraid someone might see the glow and learn she had discovered the house.

The house was no secret, really. A developer had built the two-story structure as a marketing device and then abandoned it as too expensive: adobe walls like those of a Pueblo ruin and energy supplied by an underground cable and a solar-powered generator. At one time, someone else must have lived here. Perhaps it had been a retired construction worker, some laborer or cement finisher destined to end his days sweeping dust from the compacted dirt floors and enjoying the cool feel of the dark tan walls, secure in the knowledge that no one would look for him here—no former wives or children with grandchildren to bother him.

Now it was Amparo's house. She washed her clothes in a wringer-washer like the one her mother had taught her to use when she was a little girl, like the one she had used when her son was born, the one in which she had washed his diapers. She admired, as if they were someone else's, the bookshelves carved into the sixteen-inch-thick walls of the living room and bedroom. When she felt the need for exercise, she'd run up and down the steps to the second floor loft and master bedroom, chanting "upstairs and downstairs and in my lady's chamber." And, of course, there was the six-inch plumbing throughout, wide enough to handle anything, even a pot of scorched beans.

Not that she ate much these days. She still enjoyed her plain Cream of Wheat for breakfast every morning—her *atole*,[6] she called it. For lunch and light snacks she had learned to eat seasonally, buying all her produce at the roadside stands along old

3. To keep *at bay* means to keep "at a distance."
4. *Disability income* is money paid by the government to people whose physical or mental impairment prevents them from holding jobs.
5. Several types of evergreen shrubs or small trees are known as *manzanita* (man′ zə nē′ tə).
6. *Atole* (ə tō′ lā) is a thin porridge or drink made with corn flour.

Vocabulary
impenetrable (im pen′ ə trə bəl) *adj.* unable to be pierced, entered, or passed through

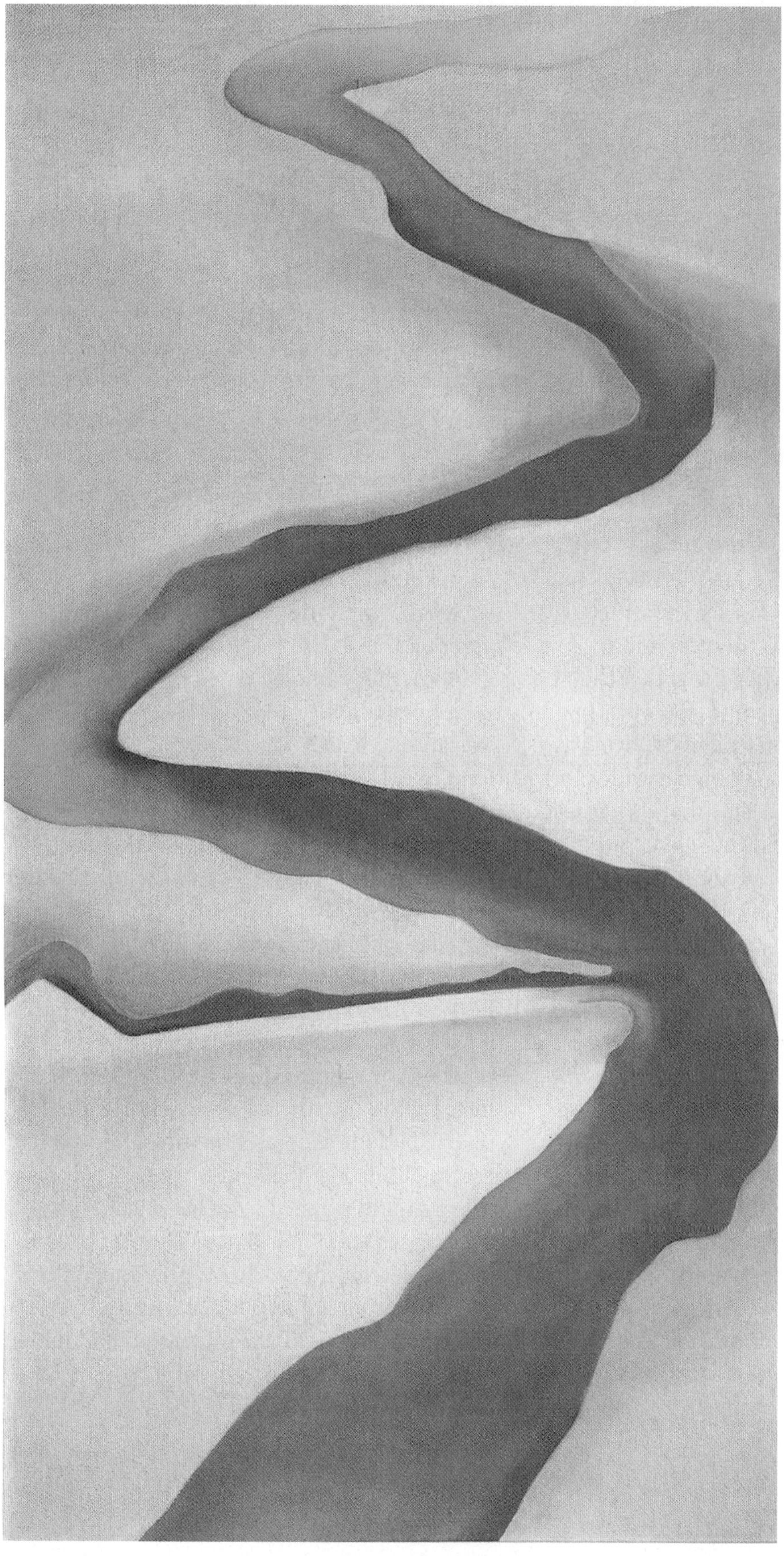

Pink and Green, 1960. Georgia O'Keeffe. Oil on canvas, 30 x 16 in. The Georgia O'Keeffe Museum, Santa Fe.

Viewing the painting: What similarities do you see between this painting and the story's setting?

Highway 99. There were almonds and raisins year-round; strawberries, peaches, tomatoes, and peppers during the summer. By early May she was tired of apples and oranges but with June came early corn and sometimes a melon or two. Dinner was always corn tortillas, beans, and rice. She made a pot of beans and another of rice every Sunday. Sometimes she'd toss some bits of chicken or beef along with a handful of garbanzos, some chopped onion, and cilantro[7] into the steaming rice. Her biggest craving was grease; once or twice a month she'd drive to Pixley for a hamburger and fries at the store's lunch counter.

The day the mud licked the left front tire of her old white Studebaker Lark station wagon, Amparo drove to the store for a "grease bomb"—that's what she called the hamburgers. It was the first official day of summer. By then, the mud-filled crevice was about twenty yards long, six inches wide, and about a foot-and-a-half deep. That day at the lunch counter she'd asked the young girl's mother, "Did they used to have a mud bath around here that you know of?"

"What do you mean, mud bath?" the woman had answered, poking a few loose strands of dark brown hair underneath one of the pink foam rollers on her head. At least the rollers worked better than the torn hair net the woman usually wore. "You mean the hot springs?"

Amparo checked her fries for stray hairs before she dipped them in ketchup. She knew about the dots on the map called Fountain Springs, California Hot Springs, and Miracle Springs. No water at any of them. "No, not water. Mud. Did they ever have mud baths over by the old water tower?" Amparo asked, trying not to sound too curious.

"No, no mud. This is a desert." The woman had a droning voice, like an old record player at slow speed. "The only water for mud would have to come from the creeks. We haven't had enough water for the creeks to run in almost ten years."

The woman's mother had interrupted, "The last time I saw the Chocolate River—that's the old riverbed over by your house—was when I was still a girl at home. That was about seventy years ago when the flash flood tore out the old road right after the war." Almost as an afterthought the old woman had added, "You know, a long time ago, when my grandmother's grandmother came here from Illinois, it was all tule marsh-land like Three Rivers."

Did You Know?
In the southwestern United States, *tule* (too͞′ lē) refers to bulrushes, which are swamp plants in the grass family.

That was when Amparo began parking her Studebaker on the side of the house away from the cottonwoods.

After the mud ate the clothesline and then the smallest manzanita bush, the one farthest from the house, Amparo consoled herself with the thought that at least the muddy flow didn't interfere with her sewer line. By the Fourth of July, when the crevice reached a foot wide and the dried banks on each side made a slick sidewalk cooler than the surrounding earth, she had made some allowances for its existence. That night, she lit sparklers in the starlight. She jumped and danced from bank to bank, playing a cheery game, a combination of hopscotch and jump rope, remembering incantatory[8] lyrics from first grade.

7. *Garbanzos* are chickpeas, and *cilantro* is an herb.

8. This nursery rhyme is *incantatory* (in kan′ tə tōr′ ē) in that it has the quality of words spoken in casting a spell or performing a sacred ceremony.

Mother, Mother, I am sick.
Call the doctor, quick, quick, quick.
In comes the doctor, in comes the nurse,
In comes the lady with the alligator purse.
Out goes the doctor, out goes the nurse,
Out goes the lady with the alligator purse.

In the morning, the crevice was fifty yards long—Amparo estimated this from the thirty-foot foundations on each side of her lot—and anywhere from three to four feet deep, depending on where she pushed an old mop handle into the ground. Much more than four feet deep and Amparo wouldn't have anything long enough to measure the depth. As it was, when she pushed the mop handle into the section closest to the biggest manzanita bush, her fingers could touch the slowly rising mud.

It was such fine, clean mud—no worms or sharp rocks. "How would you like some roses, an old grandiflora, a wine- or cinnamon-scented bush? Would you like that? I could plant a row on each side of the front yard, use some of your mud for fertilizer. I bet you'd make good fertilizer?" This last a question. It was hard to say what the mud wanted.

Did You Know?
Grandiflora (gran′ də flôr′ ə) is a kind of rosebush; the word is Latin for "great flower."

On July 15, her forty-fifth birthday, Amparo washed her bathtub and sprayed it with rosewater. When the sun was at its highest, she started dragging buckets of warm mud to the tub, climbing the stairs to the master bathroom, careful not to slosh too much onto the floor. Not that it mattered. Once the mud set, it was hard to tell where the original dirt floor ended and the new layer of mud began.

Amparo patted the mud to remove any air pockets, then took off all her clothes. She combed her long, still mostly black hair until it sparked with static electricity. Carefully she packed mud into her hair, arranged the entire mass into a turban on top of her head. Then she delicately dipped her right toes into the mud. Thick, lukewarm liquid squeezed between her toes. She lowered herself into the tub and let the mud ooze above her knees, her belly button. Eyes closed, she finally sank to her chest and leaned her head against the back of the tub.

She thrilled to the sensation, like that of someone holding her without making contact. It was as if she had lost half her body weight. She felt an unnatural buoyancy,[9] an inability to touch the very bottom of the tub. With smooth, even strokes, she massaged a thick layer of mud on her face and behind her ears.

She felt her skin tighten as the mud dried. When the mud grew cooler than her body, she pulled the plug and watched the mud make its way down the drain in small gulps. Then she padded downstairs, mud dribbling in small clumps wherever she stepped too hard.

Amparo sat outside in the late afternoon sun, her legs stretched in front of her, the heat baking her body mask to a glossy finish. She studied the effect in the hand mirror. As long as she kept her body perfectly still, she looked like an ancient statue. All the wrinkles were gone, the deep lines around her eyes and forehead, the cellulite.[10] And her back pain was gone.

Amparo stretched from her waist to touch her toes. Where the mud started to crack, she carefully peeled it away, conscious of the adhesive-like grip that caused her skin to

9. *Buoyancy* (boi′ ən sē) is the ability or tendency to float or rise.
10. Fatty deposits, especially around the thighs and hips, are called *cellulite* (sel′ yə līt′).

Modal Tide, 1940. Mark Tobey. Oil on canvas, 34½ x 47⅜ in. The Seattle Art Museum, WA.

Viewing the painting: In your opinion, what kind of movement is suggested by this painting? Do you think it reflects the movement of the mudflow? Why or why not?

redden wherever there was too much hair. Her skin had the firm smoothness of a ripened peach fresh from the tree. The pores on her nose had disappeared and her hair shone in the sunlight. She remembered how Sammy, her ex-husband, used to tell her that the first time he spotted her running her old black German shepherd in the park, the sun made her black-brown hair look like a comet. "How perfectly you've caught me," she told the mud, its slick surface stamped with the lines of her body. That night she fed the mud her leftover beans and rice.

In early August she spotted a possible hairline crack just to the right of the main crevice. She brushed the line with a manzanita branch and it seemed to go away. It was hard to say. By late August, when the hairline crack had lengthened to form a thin leg to a V, she was sure. This leg was aimed at the opposite corner of her house, and like the first leg, it pointed in the same direction. "Ahh, you want the foothills," she whispered.

At first, the mud's flow was indiscernible unless she sat for several minutes, her eyes focused on a mark she'd scratch into the

Vocabulary

indiscernible (in′ di sur′ nə bəl) *adj.* difficult or impossible to see still-damp sides of the widening cracks. Another trick she used to measure the mud's movement was to make little paper boats from old Christmas wrapping paper and watch them gently float and bob on the barely moving surface. By early October the mud flow was obvious—a steady movement east despite the three-year drought.

When she first found the house three years ago, its biggest attraction had been the roof, the easy access along the molded staircase that climbed in profile up the east wall of her second-floor bedroom to the roof escape. Amparo had always thought she would like to live in a house with a hidden staircase to some underground study; now she knew that her real dream had always been of such a skylight escape. She enjoyed climbing the stairs in the morning, sliding the double-construction skylights open. She'd clamber over the lip of the stairs and eat her *atole* on the roof, watching the day take hold. It was as if the house had been designed just for her.

Now she made the roof her lookout post; the mud would need guidance. "Foothills to the east, say 15 miles, straight flat land, hardly any sage," she announced her first day on the job. She listened to the mud's distinctive sound. She could hear it humming and swallowing, no longer baffled by its inability to lay claim to the house. There were no windows or doors on the east side of the first floor of the house. The mud waited at the weep holes[11] and joints, sensitive to the loosening of a corner as the house gave ground.

The coyotes' yips and cries grew more distinct. She counted how long it took their echoes to reach her, much as she would count the space between a thunderclap and a lightning flash. When they lurked too long she belittled them, smirking at their mangy coats, "Try a little mud in your fur. You'll kill a few fleas that way, I assure you," and "I once had a jacket with a red fox fur." She relented when they turned tail and skulked away. The next night she left a pile of freshly grilled chicken breasts seasoned with rosemary.

On the day of the harvest moon, Amparo drove to the Fruit Patch produce stand and bought the last of the zucchini, now over a foot long and four inches in diameter. She chose a pumpkin the size of her head, as well as a garland of dried red New Mexico chili pods and a selection of Indian corn tied with twine.

At sunset, Amparo climbed to the roof and arranged the offerings on favorite plates. She poured a mixture of *atole* topped with raisins and walnuts in a mixing bowl. When the moon was full overhead, she placed the plates and bowl in a star-shaped pattern, one for her head, the others for her hands and feet. Then she lay on the roof enjoying the cool breeze overhead.

To the mud she tossed an inconsequential aside.[12] "Isn't it nice not to have to worry about cleaning and cooking and washing and worrying about someone all the time?" When the mud withdrew like a sulky child and refused to respond to her chatter, she confessed, "Yes, I

11. On Amparo's adobe house, the outer walls extend above the roof line to provide a low wall around the flat roof. *Weep holes* in this wall allow rainwater to drain off.

12. Something that's *inconsequential* neither follows from nor leads to anything important; it's insignificant. An *aside* is a remark not meant to be heard by everyone–or anyone.

Vocabulary

lurk (lurk) *v.* to stay hidden, ready to attack
belittle (bi lit′ əl) *v.* to cause to seem less important; to scorn
skulk (skulk) *v.* to move in a sly or sneaky way so as to escape notice

give you credit for going uphill away from the riverbed. I never would have thought of that."

To the house she offered soothing counsel. "We'll ride it out together, the two of us. You'll see. I'll take good care of you." The mud hiccupped and poured a thick sheen over the lot. Amparo imagined how the land might have looked as an inland sea. "Just think of all that water." She felt the house shiver.

In Amparo's dreams that night, a stand of cottonwoods turned into a grove of ancient trees. Where a clothesline once twirled like a giant umbrella, clumps of tule rushes danced in the surge of a waxing moon.[13] In the distance, the flat roof of a house bobbed above the flat of the land that stretched toward the foothills.

And as she slept, the mud came close and caressed the base of the house. It told of the excitement of heat lightning cast on the horizon on summer evenings; of the tenderness of misty sighs heaved from a roiled[14] earth on snow-swept mornings; of a world best viewed from a height of 1500 feet.

In turn, the house recounted the thrill of water tumbling over a bed of smooth-ground gravel; of air so cold in autumn that spawning salmon gasped when they broke the surface.

House and mud lingered over shared secrets, reveling in this moment of discovery. The house openly admired the reflection of stars on the moist surface of the mud. In turn, the mud thrilled to the crusted surface of the house, each trowel-stroke another mystery to be explored.

In the predawn hours, Amparo awoke to the lurch of the house lifting and settling on a wide river of mud. House and mud paused as she clambered to the roof. They allowed her time to adjust her stance to the house's uncommon roll, then the house made a slow 180-degree turn from the old highway to the foothills.

Like a swimmer learning a new stroke, the house muscled through the mud, at first tentatively, then with increased fluidity. Loose pieces of masonry scattered as the house and mud picked up speed. The mud wash kicked up nearly one story high, flattening sage and manzanita.

"We're coming, we're coming, it won't be long before we're there," Amparo shouted to the hills. To the sun she complained, "We need some light over here. How do you expect us to see where we're going if you wait until six o'clock to get up?" To the house and mud she instructed, "Faster, go faster, we're almost there! Don't worry about me." As they drew closer, a cleft in the foothills parted, and house, mud, woman squeezed through in an eruption of closely contained forms, aiming for the tree-laced meadow above.

Through the temporary opening could be seen air so clear the sky looked like cut crystal, a passage so smooth that a traveler could press one hand against each side and never feel the moment of contact.

13. A *waxing moon* gradually increases in size and brightness until it's full.

14. Here, *roiled* means "disturbed; stirred up."

Vocabulary

fluidity (flo͞o id′ ə tē) *n.* the ability, as of a liquid, to flow and change shape

Responding to Literature

Personal Response
Do you like this story? Share your reaction to this story with a partner.

Analyzing Literature

Recall
1. Describe the **setting** of the story, including Amparo's house, the immediate surroundings, and the nearby town.
2. What kind of life does Amparo lead? Give details from the story.
3. What did the mud look like when Amparo first saw it, and how has it changed by the end of the story?
4. Summarize the changes in Amparo's reactions to the mud, and tell what uses she finds for it.
5. What happens to Amparo and her house at the end of the story?

Interpret
6. Does the setting seem realistic to you? Does it seem surreal or bizarre? Explain, using details from the story in your answer.
7. Why might Amparo have chosen to live as she does? What details in the story lead you to make these inferences?
8. Why is the formation and movement of the mud especially strange?
9. How would you characterize Amparo's relationship with the mud?
10. How do you explain the story's ending? Try to think not only about what is described as literally happening but also about a deeper, symbolic meaning.

Evaluate and Connect
11. How does García's use of **personification**–figurative language that gives human qualities or characteristics to animals, objects, or ideas–affect your perceptions of Amparo, the house, and the mud?
12. What is most appealing to you about Amparo's lifestyle? What seems most distasteful?
13. What images or events in this story did you find most memorable? Explain what was particularly striking about those images.
14. García writes, "Like a swimmer learning a new stroke, the house muscled through the mud. . . ." Describe the image this **simile** brings to mind. (See Literary Terms Handbook, page R11.) Create another simile to describe the flow of the mud or the movement of the house.
15. What purpose do you think García might have had for writing this story? Give reasons for your answer.

Literary ELEMENTS

Magical Realism
The term **magical realism** was originally used to describe a style of painting in which imaginary or improbable situations are presented in a realistic manner. The term is also used to describe a style of writing in which realistic details, events, settings, characters, and dialogue are interwoven with magical, bizarre, fantastic, or supernatural elements. This style of writing is especially prominent in Latin American literature.

1. How do you know that "The Flat of the Land" is an example of magical realism? Identify at least three realistic details and three fantastic elements in the story.
2. How does the use of magical realism affect your enjoyment of the story?

- See **Literary Terms Handbook,** p. R7.

Literature and Writing

Writing About Literature

A Bullet Review Imagine that you are a literary critic responsible for writing a "bullet review"–a review using not more than fifty words–on "The Flat of the Land." Make every word count as you write your review.

Personal Writing

Risking Absurdity Look back at what you wrote for the Reading Focus on page 958. Was your response practical or creative? Now that you have read this story, write another reaction to the situation, making it as bizarre or fantastic as you want.

Extending Your Response

Literature Groups

The Role of Isolation With your group, discuss the effect that Amparo's isolation has on the events and outcome of the story. How might the story have been different if Amparo had had a stronger relationship with the women at the store, or if she had had neighbors? Share your conclusions with other groups.

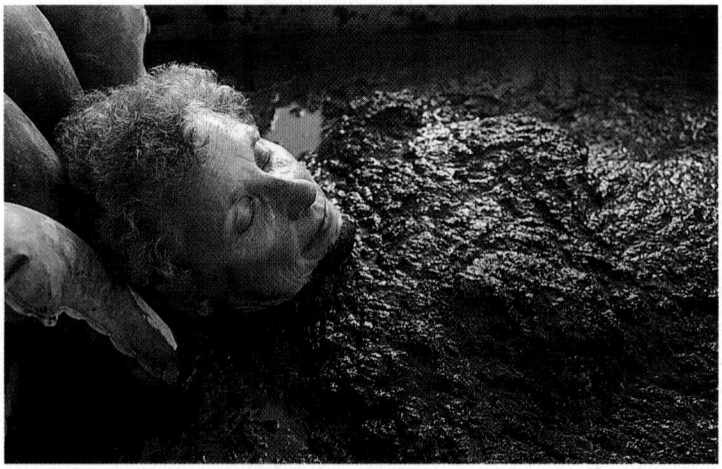

Interdisciplinary Activity

Mathematics: Sizing It Up Look through the story to find the dimensions of the mud on June 21, the first day of summer. Then find the dimensions of the mud on July 5 (assume that the mud is the same width as it was on July 4). What is the volume of the mud on each of those days? How many times greater is the mud's volume on July 5 than it was on June 21?

Reading Further

If you enjoyed this story, you might also like to read these poems by Diana García:

"La Curandera," a poem about a traditional Hispanic faith healer, and "When Living Was a Labor Camp Called Montgomery," a poem about the lives of migrant farm workers, both in *Paper Dance: 55 Latino Poets.*

Learning for Life

Pour on the Mud Do you think that stepping into a bathtub full of mud sounds horrible? Research why, since ancient times, some people have believed that mud baths and facial mud packs are advantageous for overall health and a feeling of well-being. Consider how for example, Amparo's experience with the mud bath affected her perception of herself and the oncoming mud. Draw conclusions about how and why mud might prove to be beneficial to the human body. Share your findings with the class.

Save your work for your portfolio.

Skill Minilessons

GRAMMAR AND LANGUAGE • Singular and Plural Possessive Nouns

Add an apostrophe and *-s* to form the possessive of a singular noun—even if it already ends in *-s*—and of any plural noun that does not end in *-s.* Use an apostrophe alone to form the possessive of a plural noun that ends in *-s.*

Singular noun: the mud's flow

Singular noun ending in *-s:* the grass's color

Plural noun not ending in *-s:* the women's restaurant

Plural noun ending in *-s:* the coyotes' cries

PRACTICE On your paper, write the correct possessive form of each noun in parentheses.

1. After three (weeks) flow, the mud formed a river.
2. The (mud) progress was slow but steady.
3. Amparo received her (parents) letters at a Fresno post office box.
4. The retired worker may have lived there to avoid his (children) visits.
5. The (dress) hem was covered with mud.

● For more about possessive nouns, see **Language Handbook,** p. R50.

READING AND THINKING • Creative Thinking

Some readers have difficulty understanding and interpreting works of magical realism because the stories include improbable or fantastic events. Sometimes, magical realism is used for comic effect. Other times, authors expand upon reality to help readers see everyday life in a new or different way. To understand such works, readers need to simply follow along on the journey the author sets out—and not worry about whether it's realistic. Like the author, the reader must think creatively and imagine the "What if?" questions the author poses and answers.

PRACTICE Review "The Flat of the Land," and write at least two "What if?" questions that may have inspired the story. Write the answers that the story gives to the questions.

APPLY As you read other works of fantasy or magical realism, identify the "What if?" questions the author poses and answers.

● For more about related reading strategies, see **Reading Handbook,** pp. R82–R83.

VOCABULARY • The Negating Prefixes *in-, im-, il-,* and *ir-*

In-, im-, il-, and *ir-* are all examples of "negating" prefixes. Usually, they mean "not," "without," or "the opposite of," and reverse the meaning of the words to which they are attached. When the mud created an *impenetrable* barrier, it made a barrier that could not be penetrated. The mud's flow was *indiscernible,* meaning that it could not be discerned, or seen. Sometimes, as in *impudent,* a negating prefix is attached to an unfamiliar Latin word or root, so recognizing the prefix isn't much help. Other times, what looks like a negating prefix, as in *income* or *illuminate,* isn't one at all. Often, though, negating prefixes are attached to familiar English base words.

PRACTICE For each sentence, list the underlined words in which *im-, in-, il-,* or *ir-* is a negating prefix.

1. Mother gave an <u>impassioned</u> speech against <u>illegible</u> handwriting.
2. I am <u>incapable</u> of explaining how <u>indebted</u> I feel to that teacher for the <u>impact</u> she had by <u>instilling</u> in me many <u>imperishable</u> values.
3. We received <u>information</u> only <u>irregularly</u>, but what we heard was that the <u>intolerable</u> conditions in that country had not changed.

● For information on adding prefixes, see **Language Handbook,** Spelling, p. R55.

INTERDISCIPLINARY CONNECTION
GEOLOGY

Ancient Seas and Bubbling Mud Holes

"The Flat of the Land" is a fantasy, but it is set in a real place—California's San Joaquin (san′ wä kēn′) Valley. What aspects of the story's fantastic elements are based in reality? Do mudflows occur in California? Does bubbling mud rise from the ground? Have huge water sources disappeared from the region?

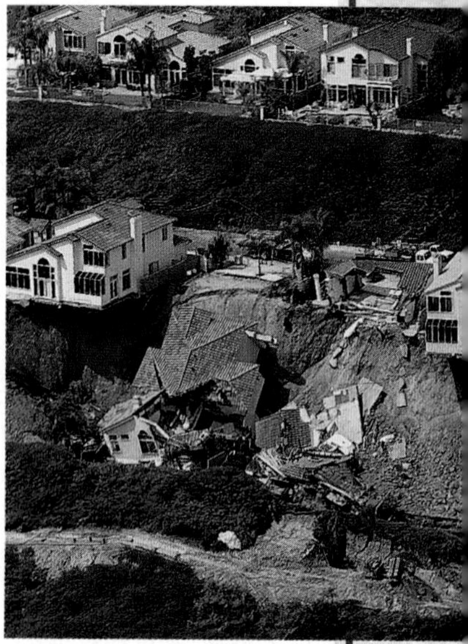

The answer to all these questions is *yes*. California abounds in geological oddities, some of which are described below.

An Inland Sea Several million years ago, an inland sea covered the San Joaquin Valley, its waves lapping against the western base of the Sierra Nevada mountains. As these mountains slowly rose, sediment carried down by mountain streams filled in the sea floor, and the sea water receded. Today, that sediment helps make the valley's soil incredibly fertile.

Landslides and Mudflows Landslides can occur wherever loose rock and soil exist on a sloping surface; heavy rainfall can also be a contributing factor. California has experienced thousands of landslides, due to earthquakes that result from the release of pressure from active fault lines. One type of landslide is the mudflow, a moving mass of soil made fluid by rain or melting snow. Mudflows, like other forms of landslides, can build up to speeds as high as three hundred miles per hour, or they might creep forward only a few inches per year.

Volcanoes Volcanic activity helped build up and shape California's mountains. Today, volcanic heat and pressure are released in the form of geysers, hot springs, and mud pots, which are holes that spout hot mud. Many popular spas are built near these natural wonders, and people flock to them to take mud baths and mineral water baths.

A Mud Bath Regimen

To soothe aching muscles, smooth skin, and relieve stress, take a mud bath at one of California's health spas! First, ease into a concrete tub full of thick, gooey, hot, black mud, and sink in until you're covered from your neck to your toes. After relaxing in the mud for ten to fifteen minutes, pull your arms, legs, and body free and step out. Take a shower and move on to the rest of the treatment: a whirlpool, steam bath, cooldown, and finally, a massage. Top it all off with a swim in a geyser-heated pool.

Activity

Conduct further research on one of the geological features mentioned above. Use the information you find to create a poster or other visual display that explains the phenomenon.

MEDIA connection

Magazine Article

After you eat lunch, what do you throw away? A milk carton? Ketchup packets? Napkins? Where will the trash go from there? As you'll see, it is not always easy to find a home for garbage—especially toxic waste.

A Stinking Mess

by John Langone—*Time*, January 2, 1989

Like the journey of the spectral *Flying Dutchman*, the legendary ship condemned to ply the seas endlessly, the voyage of the freighter *Pelicano* seemed destined to last forever. For more than two years, it sailed around the world seeking a port that would accept its cargo. Permission was denied and for good reason: the *Pelicano*'s hold was filled with 14,000 tons of toxic incinerator ash that had been loaded onto the ship in Philadelphia. At one point, the *Pelicano* brazenly dumped 4,000 lbs. of its unwanted cargo off a Haitian beach, then slipped back out to sea, trailing fresh reports that it was illegally deep-sixing the rest of its noxious cargo. Later, off Singapore, its captain announced that he had unloaded the ash in a country he refused to name.

The long voyage of the *Pelicano* is a stark symbol of the environmental exploitation of poor countries by the rich. It also represents the single most irresponsible and reckless way to get rid of the growing mountains of refuse, much of it poisonous, that now bloat the world's landfills. Indiscriminate dumping of any kind—in a New Jersey swamp, on a Haitian beach, or in the Indian Ocean—simply shifts potentially hazardous waste from one place to another. The practice only underscores the enormity of what has become an urgent global dilemma: how to reduce the gargantuan waste by-products of civilization without endangering human health or damaging the environment.

Man's effluent is more than an assault on the senses. When common garbage is burned, it spews dangerous gases into the air. Dumped garbage and industrial waste can turn lethal when corrosive acids, long-lived organic materials, and discarded metals leach

out of landfills into groundwater supplies, contaminating drinking water and polluting farmland.

The U.S., with its affluence and industrial might, is by far the most profligate offender. Each year Americans throw away 16 billion disposable diapers, 1.6 billion pens, 2 billion razors and blades and 220 million tires. They discard enough aluminum to rebuild the entire U.S. commercial airline fleet every three months. And the country is still struggling to clean up the mess created by the indiscriminate dumping of toxic waste.

Analyzing Media

1. Why might the countries visited by the *Pelicano* be opposed to taking the ship's cargo? In your opinion, should the countries have accepted the waste in return for a large sum of money? Explain why or why not.
2. Is it acceptable to send garbage into orbit in outer space, bury it in the desert, or store it in other seemingly empty places? Why or why not?

Before You Read

He—y, Come on Ou—t!

Reading Focus

Imagine that a method was discovered to rid the world of all its trash and other unwanted things.

List Ideas Make a list of things that people throw away, and describe methods that could be used to rid the world of these things. Jot down every idea that comes to mind.

Setting a Purpose Read this story to learn what happens when some people think that they have found the perfect solution to disposing of trash.

Building Background

The Time and Place

The events in this story take place in modern times near a fictional village in Japan.

Did You Know?

The disposal of waste materials is a serious environmental problem throughout the world. In the United States alone, people generate more than 200 million tons of trash each year, an average of more than four pounds per person each day. Unrecyclable solid wastes are incinerated (burned), buried in landfills, or sometimes illegally dumped in the oceans or rivers. All these disposal methods, however, contribute to air, water, and soil pollution, and many landfills are nearing their capacity. In addition, no safe method has ever been found for the disposal of nuclear wastes. The United States formerly dumped nuclear wastes into the sea, but this practice was stopped in 1970, and now these hazardous wastes are simply being stored at the sites where they are generated.

Vocabulary Preview

composure (kəm pō′ zhər) *n.* self-control; calmness; p. 974
plausible (plô′ zə bəl) *adj.* apparently true or acceptable; likely; p. 974
disperse (dis purs′) *v.* to go off in different directions; scatter; p. 974
cohort (kō′ hôrt′) *n.* a companion, associate, or member of the same group; p. 975
reverie (rev′ ər ē) *n.* fanciful thinking, especially of pleasant things; a daydream; p. 976

Meet Shinichi Hoshi

Shinichi Hoshi (shin ē chē ō shē) graduated from Tokyo University with a degree in agricultural chemistry, and at the age of twenty-three, took over as president of his family's pharmaceutical company when his father died. After selling the company, Hoshi joined the Japan Flying Saucer Research Club and began writing science fiction. He went on to become a prolific and popular writer of short stories, many of which are famous for the surprising twist at the end. After finishing his 1,001st story in 1983, he put down his pen, saying, "One thousand and one stories are enough."

Shinichi Hoshi was born in Tokyo in 1926 and died in 1997. This story was first published in the United States in 1978.

Sign of the Sun, 1957. Margaret Tomkins. Egg tempera on Masonite, 96½ x 38 in. Private collection.

He-y, Come on Out-t!

Shinichi Hoshi
translated by Stanleigh H. Jones

The typhoon had passed and the sky was a gorgeous blue. Even a certain village not far from the city had suffered damage. A little distance from the village and near the mountains, a small shrine[1] had been swept away by a landslide.

"I wonder how long that shrine's been here."

"Well, in any case, it must have been here since an awfully long time ago."

"We've got to rebuild it right away."

While the villagers exchanged views, several more of their number came over.

"It sure was wrecked."

"I think it used to be right here."

"No, looks like it was a little more over there."

Just then one of them raised his voice. "Hey, what in the world is this hole?"

Where they had all gathered there was a hole about a meter in diameter. They peered in, but it was so dark nothing could be seen. However, it gave one the feeling that it was so deep it went clear through to the center of the earth.

1. A *shrine* is any site or structure used in worship or devotion.

There was even one person who said, "I wonder if it's a fox's hole."

"He—y, come on ou—t!" shouted a young man into the hole. There was no echo from the bottom. Next he picked up a pebble and was about to throw it in.

"You might bring down a curse on us. Lay off," warned an old man, but the younger one energetically threw the pebble in. As before, however, there was no answering response from the bottom. The villagers cut down some trees, tied them with rope and made a fence which they put around the hole. Then they repaired[2] to the village.

"What do you suppose we ought to do?"

"Shouldn't we build the shrine up just as it was over the hole?"

A day passed with no agreement. The news traveled fast, and a car from the newspaper company rushed over. In no time a scientist came out, and with an all-knowing expression on his face he went over to the hole. Next, a bunch of gawking curiosity seekers showed up; one could also pick out here and there men of shifty glances who appeared to be concessionaires.[3] Concerned that someone might fall into the hole, a policeman from the local substation kept a careful watch.

One newspaper reporter tied a weight to the end of a long cord and lowered it into the hole. A long way down it went. The cord ran out, however, and he tried to pull it out, but it would not come back up. Two or three people helped out, but when they all pulled too hard, the cord parted at the edge of the hole. Another reporter, a camera in hand, who had been watching all of this, quietly untied a stout rope that had been wound around his waist.

Did You Know?
A *bullhorn* is a handheld microphone combined with a speaker that is used to communicate to a large group of people.

The scientist contacted people at his laboratory and had them bring out a high-powered bullhorn, with which he was going to check out the echo from the hole's bottom. He tried switching through various sounds, but there was no echo. The scientist was puzzled, but he could not very well give up with everyone watching him so intently. He put the bullhorn right up to the hole, turned it to its highest volume, and let it sound continuously for a long time. It was a noise that would have carried several dozen kilometers above ground. But the hole just calmly swallowed up the sound.

In his own mind the scientist was at a loss, but with a look of apparent composure he cut off the sound and, in a manner suggesting that the whole thing had a perfectly plausible explanation, said simply, "Fill it in."

Safer to get rid of something one didn't understand.

The onlookers, disappointed that this was all that was going to happen, prepared to disperse. Just then one of the concessionaires, having broken through the throng and come forward, made a proposal.

"Let me have that hole. I'll fill it in for you."

"We'd be grateful to you for filling it in," replied the mayor of the village, "but we

2. In this context, *repaired* means simply "went."
3. *Concessionaires* (kən sesh′ ə nārz′) are business owners or operators.

Vocabulary

composure (kəm pō′ zhər) *n.* self-control; calmness
plausible (plô′ zə bəl) *adj.* apparently true or acceptable; likely
disperse (dis purs′) *v.* to go off in different directions; scatter

can't very well give you the hole. We have to build a shrine there."

"If it's a shrine you want, I'll build you a fine one later. Shall I make it with an attached meeting hall?"

Before the mayor could answer, the people of the village all shouted out.

"Really? Well, in that case, we ought to have it closer to the village."

"It's just an old hole. We'll give it to you!"

So it was settled. And the mayor, of course, had no objection.

The concessionaire was true to his promise. It was small, but closer to the village he did build for them a shrine and an attached meeting hall.

About the time the autumn festival was held at the new shrine, the hole-filling company established by the concessionaire hung out its small shingle at a shack near the hole.

The concessionaire had his cohorts mount a loud campaign in the city. "We've got a fabulously deep hole! Scientists say it's at least five thousand meters deep! Perfect for the disposal of such things as waste from nuclear reactors."

Government authorities granted permission. Nuclear power plants fought for contracts. The people of the village were a bit worried about this, but they consented when it was explained that there would be absolutely no above-ground contamination for several thousand years and that they would share in the profits. Into the bargain, very shortly a magnificent road was built from the city to the village.

Trucks rolled in over the road, transporting lead boxes. Above the hole the lids were opened, and the wastes from nuclear reactors tumbled away into the hole.

From the Foreign Ministry and the Defense Agency boxes of unnecessary classified documents were brought for disposal. Officials who came to supervise the disposal held discussions on golf. The lesser functionaries,[4] as they threw in the papers, chatted about pinball.

The hole showed no signs of filling up. It was awfully deep, thought some; or else it might be very spacious at the bottom. Little by little the hole-filling company expanded its business.

Bodies of animals used in contagious disease experiments at the universities were brought out, and to these were added the unclaimed corpses of vagrants.[5] Better than dumping all of its garbage in the ocean, went the thinking in the city, and plans were made for a long pipe to carry it to the hole.

The hole gave peace of mind to the dwellers of the city. They concentrated solely on producing one thing after another. Everyone disliked thinking about the eventual consequences. People wanted only to work for production companies and sales corporations; they had no interest in becoming junk dealers. But, it was thought, these problems too would gradually be resolved by the hole.

Young girls whose betrothals[6] had been arranged discarded old diaries in the hole. There were also those who were inaugurating new love affairs and threw into the hole old photographs of themselves taken with former sweethearts. The police felt comforted as they used the hole to get rid of accumulations of expertly done counterfeit bills. Criminals breathed easier after throwing material evidence[7] into the hole.

4. *Functionaries* are also officials.
5. *Vagrants* (vā′ grənts) are people who, whether by choice or by circumstance, are without homes and jobs and who wander from place to place, often supporting themselves by begging.
6. Their parents had arranged the girls' *betrothals* (bi trō′ t͟həlz), or engagements to be married.
7. *Material evidence* would be any object that could directly connect a criminal to a crime.

Vocabulary

cohort (kō′ hôrt′) *n.* a companion, associate, or member of the same group

The Messenger. René Magritte (1898–1967). Private collection.

Viewing the painting: What might the objects in this sphere represent? In light of this story, what might the sphere itself symbolize? What connection can you draw between the title of the painting and the story's ending?

Whatever one wished to discard, the hole accepted it all. The hole cleansed the city of its filth; the sea and sky seemed to have become a bit clearer than before.

Aiming at the heavens, new buildings went on being constructed one after the other.

One day, atop the high steel frame of a new building under construction, a workman was taking a break. Above his head he heard a voice shout:

"He—y, come on ou—t!"

But, in the sky to which he lifted his gaze there was nothing at all. A clear blue sky merely spread over all. He thought it must be his imagination. Then, as he resumed his former position, from the direction where the voice had come, a small pebble skimmed by him and fell on past.

The man, however, was gazing in idle[8] reverie at the city's skyline growing ever more beautiful, and he failed to notice.

8. Here, *idle* means "useless."

Vocabulary

reverie (rev′ ər ē) *n.* fanciful thinking, especially of pleasant things; a daydream

Responding to Literature

Personal Response

What thoughts went through your mind as you finished reading this story? Describe them in your journal.

Analyzing Literature

Recall

1. Describe the hole. Where and how do the villagers discover it?
2. How do the villagers try to measure the hole? How does the scientist try to measure it? What does he then tell people to do?
3. How does the concessionaire gain control of the hole, and what does he do with it?
4. Make a list of the things people throw into the hole.
5. What mysterious event occurs at the end of the story?

Interpret

6. Of what significance, do you suppose, is the loss of the shrine to the villagers–and to the story?
7. The narrator says, "In his own mind the scientist was at a loss. . . ." In your opinion, why does he then give instructions to the villagers–and why do they follow his orders?
8. What do you think motivates the concessionaire to act as he does? Why might the villagers consent to the concessionaire's plans?
9. What is **ironic** about the officials' conversations upon disposing of materials into the hole? (See page R7.) Explain why the hole has positive effects on the village and on the people who live there.
10. How do you explain the story's ending? What do you predict will happen next?

Evaluate and Connect

11. Why might Hoshi have ended his story this way? In your opinion, what impact does the ending have on readers?
12. Do you find this story humorous, serious, or both? Explain.
13. As a general rule, Hoshi did not use proper nouns in his writing. How does this fact affect your interpretation of the story?
14. **Theme Connections** In what ways is the world Hoshi describes similar to and different from the world in which we live today?
15. Review your response to the Reading Focus on page 972. Compare the items in your list with the villagers' trash. How does the problem of waste disposal in today's society parallel the situation in the story?

Literary ELEMENTS

Moral

A **moral** is a practical lesson about right and wrong conduct, often found in an instructive story such as a fable or parable. Sometimes the moral of a story is explicitly stated, as in the well-known fable by Aesop, "The Tortoise and the Hare," which ends with the moral "Slow and steady wins the race." In other stories, however, the moral is implied rather than directly stated.

1. In your opinion, what is the implied moral of "He–y, Come On Ou–t!"?
2. How do you think the moral is demonstrated in the story?

- See **Literary Terms Handbook,** p. R8.

Literary Criticism

One critic writes, "Featuring a more satirical style than other writers in his genre, [Hoshi] often points out flaws in society through his short stories." Make a list of the flaws that Hoshi points out in "He–y, Come on Ou–t!" Then use your list to write a brief essay explaining how Hoshi satirizes modern society.

Literature and Writing

Writing About Literature

Analyzing Satire **Satire** is a form of writing that ridicules people, practices, or institutions in order to reveal their failings. Write a few paragraphs explaining why this story may be considered a satire. You might begin by analyzing the paragraph on page 975 that begins "The hole gave peace of mind to the dwellers of the city."

Personal Writing

Playing It Safe Hoshi explains the scientist's directive regarding the hole with the statement "Safer to get rid of something one didn't understand." In your journal, explain what this means in the context of the story. Then, describe a time when you might encounter this attitude today.

Extending Your Response

Literature Groups

Be a Social Critic The scientist, concessionaire, government officials, and villagers in this story represent types or groups of people, rather than individuals. In your group, discuss how Hoshi portrays the typical actions of each group and what criticism is implied. Share your conclusions with the class in an oral summary, or make a chart or poster to display in your classroom.

Interdisciplinary Activity

Environmental Science: Waste Solutions Investigate solutions to the problem of the disposal of solid and hazardous wastes. Make a list of possible solutions, and identify the advantages and limitations of each.

Listening and Speaking

A Scientific Explanation Imagine that the construction worker does *not* fail to notice the amazing occurrence at the end of the story. Instead, he reports to the scientist exactly what happened. As the scientist, develop a theory about what happened and explain it to the class. Advise others on what to do next!

Reading Further

You might enjoy these works in *The Best Japanese Science Fiction Stories,* edited by John L. Apostolov and Martin H. Greenberg:

"Take Your Choice," by Sakyo Komatsu, involves time travel. "The Road to the Sea," by Takashi Ishikawa, is about a boy who lives in the future.

Save your work for your portfolio.

Skill Minilesson

VOCABULARY • Analogies

An analogy is a type of comparison that is based on the relationships between things or ideas. Your task is to figure out the precise relationship represented by the first pair of words. Then find another pair of words that reflects the same relationship.

• For more on analogies, see **Communications Skills Handbook,** p. R77.

PRACTICE Choose the word pair that best completes each analogy.

1. gather : disperse ::
   a. collect : join
   b. create : destroy
   c. comment : criticize
   d. attach : follow
   e. attempt : fail

2. cohorts : group ::
   a. books : writer
   b. teammates : coach
   c. cars : highway
   d. siblings : family
   e. apples : tree

Vo•cab•u•lar•y Skills

Analyzing Words

When you come across a word that you don't understand, the first thing to do is to look for context clues–clues to a word's meaning that may exist in the sentence or passage in which the word is found. However, when there are no useful context clues available, analyzing the word itself by examining its separate parts may help you to discover its meaning.

The sentence "Everyone was glad to have a subterranean garbage dump" provides almost no information about the meaning of the word *subterranean.* Given how it is used, the word could mean "handy," "cheap," "huge," or many other things. The word itself, however, provides several clues to its meaning. The prefix *sub-,* meaning "under," may be familiar to you from such words as *submarine* and *subset.* If you are also familiar with the root *terra*–from *territory, extraterrestrial,* or *terra-cotta*–you know that it means *earth.* Therefore, the fact that *subterranean* means "under the earth" becomes clear.

Many unfamiliar words contain a familiar prefix, base word, root, or suffix. You have probably never seen *funniment,* but what could it mean except "humor"? Even if you don't know exactly what the suffix *-esque* means, you could guess that a *statuesque* person has something in common with a statue.

Although analyzing an unfamiliar word is not a substitute for looking it up in a dictionary, there are two reasons to try it. First, you may be able to get a good idea of what the word means. Second, breaking a word into pieces and putting it back together makes you notice its parts, and that can help you remember its meaning.

EXERCISE

Analyze the underlined words in the left column, using whatever clues they contain to help you. Match each one to its meaning on the right.

1. an inglorious act	a. likeness
2. initially successful	b. required
3. to boldly opine	c. at first
4. luxuriate in a bath	d. shameful
5. an obligatory response	e. like a snake
6. a trimonthly meeting	f. express a view
7. notice a similitude	g. inability to adapt
8. a serpentine appearance	h. study of poisons
9. the youth's maladjustment	i. four times a year
10. an interest in toxicology	j. take great delight in

Technology Skills

Database: Organizing Classes and Assignments

With so much information to keep track of, adjusting to the demands of high school can be difficult. You need to remember such things as your locker combination, class schedule, extracurricular activities, homework assignments, lunch period, bus number–the list goes on. Luckily, technology may offer a solution. Database software can help you organize your academic life.

Reviewing Database Tools

Take time to go over the major features of databases. If you have trouble at any time in this activity, browse through **Help** or consult with your teacher or lab instructor.

Term	Explanation
Database	A database is a collection of information arranged in predetermined ways and designed for a certain purpose.
Table	A table contains data about a particular subject.
Field	A field is a column of data in a table. Each field contains only one specific type of data.
Field name	Each column in a table is headed by a field name.
Record	A record is a row of data in a table. A single row can contain various types of data, but each row in a given table collects the data in the same order.
Database builder	A database builder is an interactive program that walks you through the creation of a database whose formats are partially preset.

Building a Class Organizer

In your journal, write everything you're expected to remember at school on a daily basis. Look at the events of your day as noted in your journal. To create a database that will organize these events in the form of a schedule of classes and assignments, follow the steps below.

1. To begin, open your database program. Go to the **File** menu and click on **New Database.** A typical database program will then ask you what sort of database you would like to create. Since you will need to define your own fields, select a blank database. Save it as "Class Organizer."
2. After you have saved your database, open a new table. You will be asked if you wish to see your table in **Design** or **Datasheet** view. Select **Design** view to name your own fields.

3. Once in **Design** view, you will be asked to create and describe field names. In the field name column, type the headings listed below:

   Period Class Location Start Time End Time Homework Work Done?

4. Select **number** as your data type for the Period field. Select **text** as your data type for the Class, Location, and Homework fields. For the Start Time and End Time fields, select the data type **date/time** and a time format that includes at least hours and minutes. Finally, select data type **yes/no** for the Work Done? field. Leave the description option blank for all of the fields.

5. Now switch to **Datasheet** view by clicking on the toggle icon under the **View** menu. You might be asked if you want the database program to set a primary key for you. For your purposes here, select **no.** You might also be asked if you want to save the table. Choose **yes,** and save to disk or to the shared directory of your network. As you name the file, include the day and date that the table reflects.

6. Open the table you just saved, and in the appropriate boxes enter the scheduling and assignment data for the day you are scheduling. Your table may end up looking something like this:

TECHNOLOGY TIP

If you have more than one table in your database, you can define one-to-one, one-to-many, or many-to-many relationships between any two, so that information appearing in one table will also appear in the other.

	Period	Class	Location	Start Time	End Time	Homework	Work Done?
	1	English	Room 222	9:00 AM	9:50 AM	The Sentinel	Yes
	2	Algebra 1	Room 302	9:55 AM	10:45 AM	p. 23, 1–31 odd	No
	3	World History	Mobile Unit 2	10:50 AM	11:40 AM	None	No
	4	Lunch		11:45 AM	12:30 PM		No
	5	PE	Gym	12:35 PM	1:20 PM	Wash uniform	No
	6	Band	Band Room	1:25 PM	2:15 PM	Bring clarinet	No
▶	7	Biology	Room 108	2:20 PM	3:10 PM	Cells, pp. 79–100	Yes
*							

7. At this point, save your schedule to disk for daily updating, and make a printout. You may want to print several copies of the schedule with the Homework and Work Done? fields left blank. Carry these with your notebooks, and update them regularly.

ACTIVITIES

1. Simple databases are useful tools for organizing tables of information. To practice database management, open your database program and select a database builder. Your options may include database builders designed to help you organize such things as your video, book, or music collection, addresses of friends and relatives, or your fitness schedule.

2. Think about ways the selections in this unit can be organized. You can arrange them by author, by genre, by publication date, or by class popularity. Ask your teacher for an extra-credit project arranging literature selections on a database.

Reading & Thinking Skills

Making Generalizations

When Mr. Kreton, the man who travels to Earth in *Visit to a Small Planet,* tells Earthlings, "Your deepest pleasure is violence. . . . It is the whole point of you," he is **making a generalization,** or forming a general opinion based on specific facts. Because making generalizations includes collecting and considering evidence, the process can help you arrive at a deeper understanding of what you read, see, and experience.

However, not all generalizations are valid, or logically correct. The criteria below can help you differentiate between valid generalizations and faulty ones.

Valid Generalizations	Faulty Generalizations
• draw on available evidence	• are based on limited evidence or on stereotypes
• are often qualified by such words as *most, rarely, usually*	• are absolute statements that use words such as *every, whole,* and *all*
• can be proved	• cannot be proved

According to the above criteria, Kreton's generalization about Earthlings is faulty. Kreton uses an absolute word, *whole,* which allows for no exceptions to his statement. Because we know that some people derive deeper pleasure from love and family than they do from violence, for example, his generalization is impossible to prove.

To make a valid generalization about humanity's attitude toward violence based on *Visit to a Small Planet,* consider all the evidence–implied or directly stated–that the play presents on the subject. You might use the following information to make a generalization:

- Kreton's interest in war draws attention to the fact that there have been many wars in human history.
- Powers keeps thinking of violent ways to kill Kreton.
- Laurent says, "We don't want to be savages."
- Ellen says, "We're people and we don't want to be destroyed."
- Ellen and John love each other and hope to marry.

Based on the evidence, you may form the following generalization: *Although human history includes violent episodes, many people deeply hope for peace.*

• For more on comprehension skills, see **Reading Handbook,** pp. R82–R94.

EXERCISE

Make a generalization that applies to another selection in this theme. Then list the evidence you used to make your generalization.

Before You Read

Prologue and *The Universe*

Reading Focus

What does the word *universe* make you think of?

Map It! Make a word web like this one and fill it in with the words and ideas that come to mind when you think about the universe. Continue branching out as you free-associate ideas. Then write a statement of how you see your place in the universe.

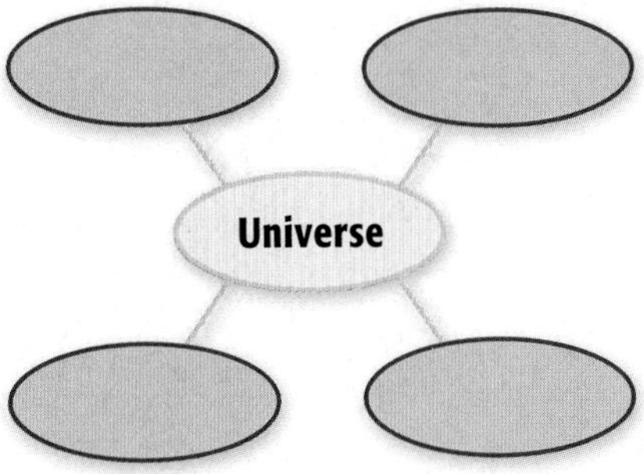

Setting a Purpose Read to learn the thoughts of two poets contemplating the universe–and their places within it.

Building Background

Did You Know?

- Astronomy is the study of stars, planets, and other material outside the earth's atmosphere. Although people have been studying astronomy since ancient times, it was only about three hundred years ago that a key fact was understood: the sun, not the earth, is the center of our solar system. The solar system is one small part of the Milky Way galaxy, and the Milky Way galaxy is part of a group of galaxies called the Virgo Cluster. The universe includes innumerable such clusters of galaxies and trillions of stars as bright as or brighter than the sun.
- Even after thousands of years of study, there are many questions astronomy hasn't answered. For example, the universe is considered to be the total amount of matter and energy in existence, as well as all the space that contains it, but astronomers don't know how large a space that may be. In order to study the universe so as to draw conclusions about it, scientists must assume that the same laws of physics operate throughout different solar systems and even different galaxies. Astronomers continue to work toward a better understanding of those laws.

Meet Edward Field

Edward Field worked as a laborer, an artist, a typist, and an actor; he published his first volume of poems in 1962. Noted for his conversational style, Field once wrote, "I see poetry as a mysterious force. Perhaps it's not meant to save the world, but maybe, if we are very true to its spirit, it can influence things in some way for the better."

Edward Field was born in Brooklyn, New York, in 1924.

Meet May Swenson

May Swenson has been described as "provocative," "vital," and "one of our few unquestionably major poets." Swenson was born, raised, and educated in Utah. She taught at numerous universities and produced nine volumes of poetry, receiving high honors for her work.

May Swenson was born in 1913 and died in 1989.

My World, 1993–1996. Derold Page. Acrylic on canvas, 91.5 x 91.5 cm. Private collection.

Prologue

Edward Field

Look, friend, at this universe
With its spiral clusters of stars
Flying out all over space
Like bedsprings suddenly busting free;
And in this galaxy, the sun
Fissioning itself away,°
Surrounded by planets, prominent in their dignity,
And bits and pieces running wild;
And this middling° planet
With a lone moon circling round it.

Look, friend, through the fog of gases at this world
With its skin of earth and rock, water and ice,
With various creatures and rooted things;
And up from the bulging waistline
To this land of concrete towers,
Its roads swarming like a hive cut open,
Offshore to this island, long and fishshaped,
Its mouth to a metropolis,
And in its belly, this village,
A gathering of families at a crossways,
And in this house, upstairs and through the wide open door
Of the front bedroom with a window on the world,
Look, friend, at me.

---

6 This line suggests the sun's abundant energy production. The word *fissioning,* however, refers to a nuclear reaction that releases energy when an atomic nucleus is split into two smaller fragments. The sun's energy actually comes from fusion, a reaction in which two nuclei combine to form one.

9 Something that's *middling* is medium, average, or ordinary. In this context, it also suggests the earth's position among the nine planets of the solar system.

THE UNIVERSE

May Swenson

What
is it about,
the universe,
the universe about us stretching out?
We, within our brains,
within it,
think
we must unspin
the laws that spin it.
We think *why*
because we think
because.
Because we think,
we think
the universe about us.

But does it think,
the universe?
Then what about?
About us?
If not,
must there be cause
in the universe?
Must it have laws?
And what
if the universe
is not about us?
Then what?
What
is it about?
And what
about *us*?

Responding to Literature

Personal Response

With whom would you want to share one or both of these poems, and why?

Analyzing Literature

Prologue

Recall and Interpret

1. What phrase does the speaker repeat to guide readers through the progression of ideas in this poem? How would you classify this progression?
2. Which lines in the poem describe Earth and its natural features? Which lines describe features created by people? Put the images in your own words.
3. What can you tell about the speaker? To whom might the speaker be addressing this poem? What evidence leads you to draw these conclusions?

Evaluate and Connect

4. A prologue is a preceding event or development or a preface to a literary work. Why might Field have chosen this **title?** What might this poem be a prologue to?
5. What would you say is the **mood** of this poem? (See page R8.) How is it similar to or different from your own mood when you think about your place in the universe?
6. On the basis of details and images in the poem, would you say that the speaker is content where he is? Why or why not? How does his perspective on his worldly environment compare with yours?

THE UNIVERSE

Recall and Interpret

7. Paraphrase three of the speaker's questions about the universe. What seems to be her overriding concern?
8. In your opinion, what is the meaning of the lines "We, within our brains, / within it, / think / we must unspin / the laws that spin it"? What seems to be the speaker's attitude about this idea?
9. Reread lines 10–15 and explain what you think the speaker is saying about cause-and-effect relationships and about people. In your opinion, why might people try to solve mysteries with cause-and-effect logic?

Evaluate and Connect

10. Swenson once remarked that she wanted readers to enjoy the sight as well as the sound of her poems. What effect does the poem's shape have on your reading of it?
11. Identify three instances of **rhyme,** and tell how the rhyme affects the mood of the poem. (See Literary Terms Handbook, page R10.)
12. In your opinion, which is more important to May Swenson and Edward Field—the big picture or the narrow one, the universe or the role of the individual in it? How are their views similar and different? Explain, using details from the poems in your answer.

Literary ELEMENTS

Denotation and Connotation

The **denotation** of a word or phrase is its literal, dictionary meaning. The **connotation** of the same term is what it implies or suggests in a particular context. For example, when Edward Field writes of "this middling planet," the denotation of the adjective *middling* is "medium-sized." The connotation of the word is richer, however. Given its context in lines nine and ten, *middling* makes Earth seem rather average and ordinary.

1. What is the denotation and connotation of the word *towers* in line 15? How would your reading of this line be different if Field had used the word *buildings* instead?
2. Find another term in "Prologue" that has a connotation different from its denotation. How does the context affect your understanding of the term's connotation?

- See **Literary Terms Handbook,** pp. R4 and R3.

Literature and Writing

Writing About Literature

Seeing Clearly Author and critic Stephen Stepanchev wrote that May Swenson is able to make "her reader see clearly what he [or she] has merely looked at before." To what extent was she successful in making you visualize or understand something new about the universe and about people's struggle to understand it? How might this quotation apply to Edward Field? What new awareness of your place in the world do you have after reading "Prologue"? Explain your answers in a few paragraphs.

Personal Writing

From Where I Stand . . . Do you think of outer space as near or far away? Do you wonder about the origin of all things? Does the planet resemble one huge living organism? Do you think people can use reason and logic to understand the universe? What do you think of or wonder about when you contemplate the universe? Select one or more of these topics to write about in your journal. You may wish to use the work you did for the Reading Focus on page 983 as a starting point for writing.

Extending Your Response

Literature Groups

Compare Philosophies In an 1899 volume of poetry entitled *War Is Kind,* Stephen Crane wrote: "A man said to the universe: / 'Sir, I exist!' / 'However,' replied the universe, / 'The fact has not created in me / A sense of obligation.'" With a group, interpret, compare, and contrast the views of Crane, Swenson, and Field regarding the relationship between the universe and human existence. Support your ideas with specific references to the poems. Share your conclusions with other groups.

Performing

Poetry Reading Work with a partner to prepare a dramatic reading of one of the poems. Experiment with different tones of voice to express what you consider to be the emotions suggested by the speaker's tone and the underlying theme of the poem. Also experiment with the emphasis you place on words, especially if you're reading "The Universe." Present your poetry reading to the class.

Interdisciplinary Activity

Geography: A Fishshaped Island Edward Field has lived in New York City most of his life. Therefore, his allusion to a "fishshaped" island may refer to New York's Long Island. Find maps of New York and Long Island, and locate the areas that Field describes as the "mouth to a metropolis" and "its belly." In what village might this poem be set? Explain your conclusion.

Save your work for your portfolio.

LISTENING, SPEAKING, and VIEWING

Evaluating Persuasive Techniques in Advertising

In her poem "The Universe," May Swenson asks hard questions about the role people play in the universe. As you view television commercials, listen to radio commercials, and take in other forms of advertising, you too should ask questions about what you see and hear. In order to make rational, informed choices about what you buy or believe, it's important that you evaluate the claims of advertisements.

One good way to evaluate advertising is to identify the type of appeal it is making. Watch and listen to ads carefully for the following appeals:

- **Emotional appeals** speak to people's desires to be loved, admired, happy, and safe, among other things. Emotional ads often use words and images designed to evoke particular feelings. You should question whether a product can fill an emotional need.
- **Rational appeals** speak to people as intelligent decision-makers. These ads may present important information, or they may just appear to do so by citing unrelated facts or making irrelevant or unfinished claims.
- **Appeals to authority** speak to people's faith in authority figures. These ads often feature an expert who recommends or praises a product. The problem is, the expert's statements may be influenced by the fact that he or she is getting paid, or the "expert" might actually be an actor hired to play a role.
- **Appeals by association** link a product to a desirable person or group of people. However, since a celebrity doesn't know any more about cars, fast food, or soft drinks than you do, you should think twice before letting his or her words influence your purchasing decision.

Once you've learned to identify an advertisement's appeal, you've taken the first step in becoming an informed consumer. You'll then be able to make appropriate buying decisions on the basis of true information rather than irrelevant or misleading information.

ACTIVITIES

1. Watch or listen to three television commercials or radio ads. For each one, write a brief summary and identify the type of appeal it uses.
2. With a small group, write three radio commercials for an existing product or one of your own invention. Use a different kind of appeal in each ad. Perform your commercials for the class, and ask your classmates to tell which appeal you are using.

Writing Workshop

Persuasive Writing: Essay

Persuasive writing tries to influence a reader to accept an idea, adopt a point of view, or perform an action. Advertisements, political speeches, and editorials are all examples of persuasion. By using evidence to create a logical argument, you too can convince others to share your views. **In this workshop, you will write a brief persuasive essay on the theme of other worlds.**

- As you write your persuasive essay, refer to the **Writing Handbook,** pp. R58–R71.

EVALUATION RUBRIC

By the time you complete this Writing Workshop, you will have

- written an introduction that includes a clearly stated claim
- provided clear and logical reasons for making your claim
- used appropriate evidence to support your reasons and to create a logical argument
- concluded by emphasizing why your readers should agree with or act on your claim
- presented a persuasive essay that is free of errors in grammar, usage, and mechanics

The Writing Process

PREWRITING

PREWRITING TIP

With a partner, brainstorm a list of things or ideas that you associate with the term "other worlds."

Explore ideas

What do you consider another world? The streets of a foreign city? The ocean floor? A planet in another galaxy? Try to identify some topics related to the places that come to mind. Controversial issues tend to make the best persuasive writing topics because you'll choose a single viewpoint and argue why it makes more sense than another viewpoint. Talk with friends, look through newspapers, or consider the suggestions below in order to find an other-worldly issue that you want to write persuasively about.

- Persuade people either that creatures from other worlds are likely to come to Earth in peace or that they are likely to come as enemies.
- Persuade people to support or oppose the continuation of the search for extraterrestrial intelligence (SETI).
- Persuade people to believe that reading science fiction about other worlds can help us better understand our own society–or not.

Consider your purpose

Decide what specific purpose you want your persuasive essay to accomplish. For instance, if you feel that people in the United States don't know enough about other countries, your specific purpose might be to persuade students in your school to form an armchair travelers' club to learn about other countries and cultures.

Choose an audience

Since there's no need to persuade people who already agree with you, your audience will consist of people who disagree with your view or are undecided. As you write, anticipate their reactions. Try to answer their objections before they can make them.

State a claim

A claim is a statement that asserts something. Think about your purpose and then state the claim that you want readers to accept. You'll probably want to include your claim in the introduction of your essay, and then use it to focus the rest of your argument. Because it plays such an important role, practice stating your claim before you begin writing.

STUDENT MODEL

Claim—The rain forest is a promising and largely unknown world, but unless we act fast to save it from destruction, we may never be able to explore its full potential.

Complete Student Model on p. R122.

Identify supporting evidence

You will need to cite strong evidence to support your claim. One way to start identifying evidence is to ask yourself questions that begin "What evidence do I have that ____ ?" Fill in the blank with assumptions that your claim rests upon. For example, if your claim states that we should preserve the promising but unknown world of the rain forest, one question you might ask is "What evidence do I have that the rain forests are worth saving?" Then look for answers to your questions.

A web like the one below is another good way to gather support for your claim. Print your claim at the center. Around that, print the reasons you believe that claim. Add circles or ovals for facts that could support each reason.

STUDENT MODEL

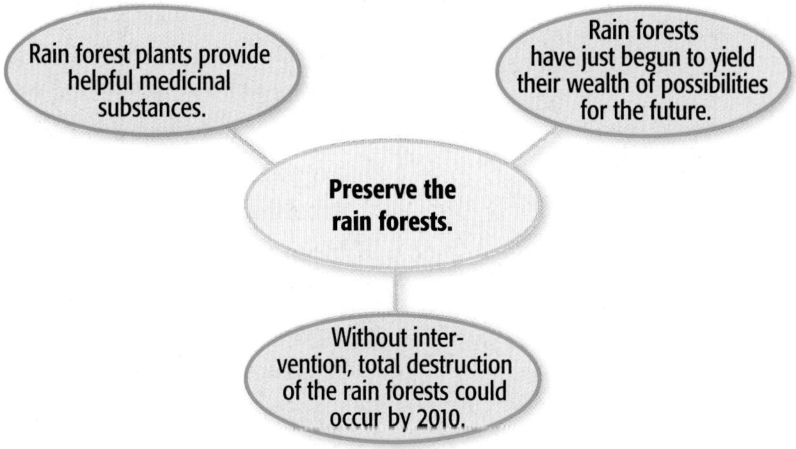
Rain forest plants provide helpful medicinal substances.
Rain forests have just begun to yield their wealth of possibilities for the future.
Preserve the rain forests.
Without intervention, total destruction of the rain forests could occur by 2010.

Construct a logical argument

Presented in the body of your essay, an argument consists of the evidence you use to support your claim. Select your strongest pieces of evidence and note how you can best explain them to your audience. What steps in your thinking will need to be explained? What connections will you need to point out? See the Writing Skill on page 957 for help with organizing a logical argument.

DRAFTING

DRAFTING TIP

Conclude your essay by reaffirming your claim. You might also explain how support for your claim could be put into action.

Use language to your advantage

Empty adjectives and wild promises fool no one. To avoid overgeneralizations, oversimplifications, or gross exaggerations of the facts, use limiting words, such as *many* or *most,* instead of words like *all* or *every.* Replace general words with specific ones. Choose words with connotations that reinforce your position.

Write your draft

Follow your prewriting notes as you write, but if you discover an interesting piece of evidence you hadn't planned to explore, set your notes aside and follow your hunch.

STUDENT MODEL

We have just started to uncover the benefits of the rain forests, but the forests are disappearing fast. The rain forests are being knocked down by the logging industry, and some old-growth forests will be totally destroyed within the next ten years.

Complete Student Model on p. R122.

REVISING

REVISING TIP

A thesaurus can help you find fresh synonyms for overused words. Remember, though, that the meanings of synonyms may vary slightly. Make sure you understand the exact definition of any new words you use.

Evaluate your work

Read your draft to yourself and make sure that what you've written fits your purpose and audience. Mark any weak spots that you want to strengthen and begin reworking those portions of the draft first.

Have a writing conference

Read your draft to a partner or small group. Use your audience's reactions to help you evaluate your work. Then use the **Rubric for Revising** to guide further revision.

RUBRIC FOR REVISING

Your revised persuasive essay should have

- ☑ an introduction that clearly states a claim
- ☑ evidence such as facts, examples, and anecdotes to support your claim
- ☑ a consistent organization that helps to build a logical argument
- ☑ transitions that help your audience follow the reasoning process
- ☑ answers to your audience's possible objections to your claim
- ☑ a conclusion that persuades readers to support your claim

Your revised persuasive essay should be free of

- ☑ details that do not support your claim
- ☑ overgeneralizations, oversimplifications, and exaggerations of evidence
- ☑ errors in grammar, usage, and mechanics

STUDENT MODEL

No one would argue the fact that the world ~~We can't keep using so much wood.~~ needs wood products to supply expanding ~~We've got to stop building wooden~~ building needs, but we ~~furniture. We~~ must pursue alternative sources of building material.

Complete Student Model on p. R122.

EDITING/PROOFREADING

At this stage, look closely at your writing, paying special attention to your use of language. As you proofread, check for errors in grammar, spelling, usage, and mechanics.

PROOFREADING TIP

Use the **Proofreading Checklist** on the inside back cover of this book to help you mark errors.

Grammar Hint

In general, for one-syllable or two-syllable modifiers, add *-er* to form the comparative form and *-est* to form the superlative form. For modifiers of three or more syllables, use *more* or *most*.

INCORRECT: *Knowledge of the rain forest is practicaler than knowledge of space.*

CORRECT: *Knowledge of the rain forest is more practical than knowledge of space.*

- For more about comparative and superlative forms, see **Language Handbook**, p. R37.

STUDENT MODEL

The distruction of the rain forest is the most criticalest environmental problem we now face on earth.

Complete Student Model on p. R122.

Complete Student Model

For a complete version of the model developed in this workshop, refer to **Writing Workshop Models**, p. R122.

PUBLISHING/PRESENTING

Where you publish or present your essay will depend on your audience and purpose. If you want to convince people your own age, you may want to submit your essay to the student newspaper. If you want to convince people in your local community, rework your essay into a petition or a leaflet and hand it out. You may even present it as a speech.

PRESENTING TIP

If you read your essay aloud, remember that your body language and tone of voice can make your argument even more convincing.

Reflecting

Now that you have used persuasive techniques to convince others, will it be harder or easier for others to persuade you? With a friend, discuss the reasons for your answer. Then record in your journal what you learned from sharing your persuasive essay with others. How can these lessons be applied toward your next piece of writing?

Save your work for your portfolio.

Unit Assessment

Personal Response

1. Which selection in this theme did you find most entertaining? Which did you find most thought-provoking? Which did you prefer, and why?
2. As a result of the work you did in this unit, what new ideas do you have about the following:
   - how to convince others to share your views
   - how to work with others to discover new ideas
   - how to make connections between fantasy and reality

Analyzing Literature

Compare Visions Some of the writers in this unit speculate about what life may be like in the future. Others write about a world where fantasy becomes reality–and anything can happen. Still others contemplate the nature of being alive in a vast universe. Compare and contrast two selections that suggest different attitudes about what the future may hold or about what life would be like in another world. Consider whether the selections are hopeful or whether they expect the worst. Also consider what role–if any–science and technology will play in the future. Use examples from the selections to support your conclusions.

Evaluate and Set Goals

Evaluate

1. What are your strongest accomplishments in each of the following areas?
   - reading
   - writing
   - working with others
   - working on your own
2. How successfully did you meet the goals you set for yourself before you began work on this unit?
3. How would you assess your work in this unit, using the following scale? Give at least two reasons for your assessment.
   4 = outstanding **3** = good **2** = fair **1** = weak

Set Goals

1. What aspect of your work in this unit were you disappointed with?
2. With your teacher, discuss ways to improve your performance in the future.
3. Write down several concrete goals that can help you improve. Then set checkpoints to monitor your progress.

Build Your Portfolio

Select What two pieces of writing from this unit do you want to include in your portfolio? The following questions may help you decide.
- Which piece demonstrates the greatest amount of imagination?
- Which piece is the most expertly polished?
- Which piece made you stretch your abilities?

Reflect Include a short written response with each piece. Your notes may address
- the ways in which you used outside knowledge to strengthen your writing.
- new ideas you generated by writing.
- goals you met by writing the piece.
- changes you would make if you rewrote the piece.

Reading on Your Own

You might also be interested in the following books.

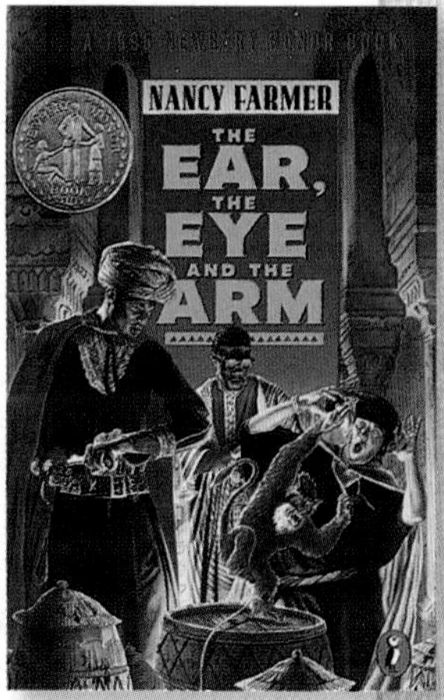

The Ear, the Eye and the Arm

by Nancy Farmer The place is Zimbabwe. The year is 2194. After sneaking into the city, three children are kidnapped by a monkey and forced into a life of hard labor. When the children's parents hire a trio of mutant detectives to retrieve them, trouble and adventure begin. This Newberry-award winning novel combines elements of both science fiction and traditional African culture.

A Midsummer Night's Dream

by William Shakespeare One of the most light-hearted of Shakespeare's plays, this fantasy follows young lovers into a magical forest, where the meddling of a mischievous elf causes comedy and chaos to ensue. Meanwhile, the king and queen of the fairies are having their own problems, and another group of humans are making humorous attempts to put on a play.

Nightfall

by Isaac Asimov and Robert Silverberg Two great science fiction writers collaborated on this suspenseful tale, which explores what happens when darkness slowly falls in a world that has seen nothing but sunlight for the last two thousand years. As a terrified society verges on chaos, only a few citizens are prepared to face a truth that reveals some of the most fundmental aspects of human experience.

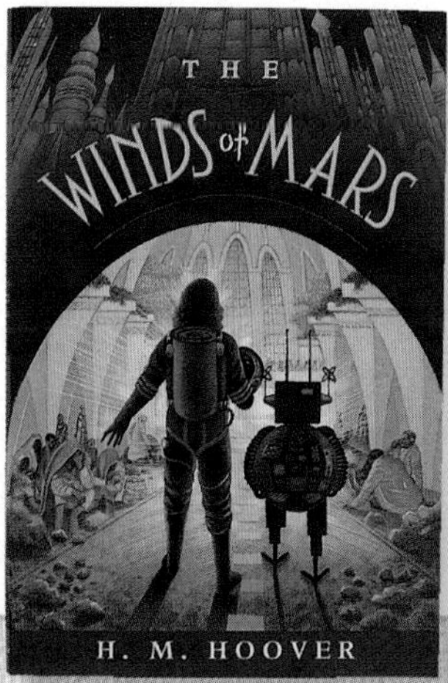

The Winds of Mars

by H. M. Hoover Annalyn Court's father is President of Mars. Or is he? Annalyn must decide whether or not her dad has been secretly replaced by an android, and in the meantime, a rebellion is threatening to tear the planet apart. The suspense mounts as battles rage in this exciting science fiction novel.

THE PRINCETON REVIEW

Standardized Test Practice

Read the passage. Some sections are underlined. The underlined sections may be one of the following:

- Incomplete sentences
- Run-on sentences
- Correctly written sentences that should be combined
- Correctly written sentences that do not need to be rewritten

Choose the best way to write each underlined section. Mark the letter for that answer on your paper. If the underlined section needs no change, mark the choice "Correct as is."

> Bionics is the science of designing artificial systems that imitate biological tissues and processes. It is also the science of constructing them. (1) It is not a pure strain of science. But rather an interdisciplinary field that incorporates chemistry, physics, physiology, and engineering. (2) In the field of medicine, bionics has allowed for major leaps in the development of life-saving devices. (3) For example, this modern science is responsible for the artificial heart.

1 A Bionics is the science of designing artificial systems that imitate biological tissues and processes; it is also the science of constructing them.

B Bionics is the science of designing and constructing artificial systems that imitate biological tissues and processes.

C Bionics is the science of designing artificial systems that imitate biological tissues and processes, therefore it is also the science of constructing them.

D Bionics is the science of designing artificial systems that imitate biological tissues and processes. And constructing them.

2 F It is not a pure strain. Of science, but rather an interdisciplinary field that incorporates chemistry, physics, physiology, and engineering.

G It is not a pure strain of science but rather an interdisciplinary field. That incorporates chemistry, physics, physiology, and engineering.

H It is not a pure strain of science, but rather an interdisciplinary field that incorporates chemistry, physics, physiology, and engineering.

J Correct as is.

3 A In the field of medicine. Bionics has allowed for major leaps in the development of life-saving devices.

B In the field of medicine and in the development of life-saving devices, bionics has allowed for major leaps.

C In the field of medicine, bionics has allowed for major leaps. In the development of life-saving devices.

D Correct as is.

Read the passage and decide which type of error, if any, appears in each underlined section. Mark the letter for your answer on your paper.

Ray walked into the animal shelter, slowly, (4) as Mary strode ahead. "hurry up, (5) Ray. They're going to close in half an hour."

"You know I think this is a waste of time" Ray responded. (6) "The last thing I need is a pet. They're messy, and they require too much attention."

"I know you're moving and will need some company. Let's find a friend for you."

As Ray reluctantly looked around he felt sorry for the many animals in cages. (7) He wasn't convinced that he could take care of any of them, though.

Then he spotted a young gray cat sitting in the play area. The cat had seperated himself from the other animals (8) that were playing and exploring, but he was not alone. He held a stuffed bunny firmly in his mouth as he sat there, (9) watching the others. Ray grinned as he realized that he wanted to share his new home with a playful pet.

4 F Spelling error
G Capitalization error
H Punctuation error
J No error

5 A Spelling error
B Capitalization error
C Punctuation error
D No error

6 F Spelling error
G Capitalization error
H Punctuation error
J No error

7 A Spelling error
B Capitalization error
C Punctuation error
D No error

8 F Spelling error
G Capitalization error
H Punctuation error
J No error

9 A Spelling error
B Capitalization error
C Punctuation error
D No error

STOP

Reference Section

Literary Terms Handbook

A

Act A major division of a play. Many long plays have several acts; short plays often have only one. An act may be divided into scenes.

See page 563.
See also SCENE.

Alliteration The repetition of sounds, most often consonant sounds, at the beginnings of words. Alliteration gives emphasis to words. Note the two examples of alliteration in the following line from Mary Oliver's "The Black Snake":

It is what sent the snake coiling and flowing
forward. . . .

See pages 417 and 437.
See also SOUND DEVICES.

Allusion A reference in a work of literature to a character, place, or situation from another work of literature, music, or art, or from history. For example, as Robert Horn describes a dilemma he faced during a chess game in his essay "The Child Is the Master," he makes an allusion to a famous Frank R. Stockton story that appears in this book: "The bishop or the knight. The lady or the tiger."

See page 892.

Analogy A comparison based on a similarity between things that are otherwise dissimilar. A writer may use an analogy to explain something abstract or unfamiliar.

See pages 788 and 955.
See also METAPHOR, SIMILE.

Anecdote A brief account of an interesting or amusing incident. An anecdote is often used as evidence to support or explain an idea, or it may be used to entertain readers or reveal the personality of the author or of another person. In "Field Trip," Naomi Shihab Nye's story about her time at camp is an anecdote.

See page 291.

Antagonist A person or force in society or nature that opposes the **protagonist**, or central character, in a literary work. In Gore Vidal's *Visit to a Small Planet*, the antagonist is Kreton, who intends to destroy the earth, using the Speldings' home as ground zero.

See pages 2, 234, and 760.
See also CONFLICT, PROTAGONIST.

Argument Nonfiction writing in which reason is used to influence people's ideas or actions.

See pages 949 and 957.

Aside In a play, a comment made by a character that is heard by the audience or another character but is not heard by the other characters onstage. Asides are frequently used to provide information to the audience and to reveal the private thoughts of characters. For example, in act 2, scene 2 of Shakespeare's *Romeo and Juliet,* page 610, Romeo makes two asides to the audience as he decides whether to make his presence known to Juliet, who is standing on the balcony above him.

See page 658.
See also SOLILOQUY.

Assonance The repetition of similar vowel sounds within nonrhyming words, especially in a line of poetry. The following stanza from Joan Fallert's poem "Wanderer" contains assonance in the repetition of the long *i* sound:

flying
south, south to feed
and nest, ride the thermals
mile after guileless mile without
resting.

See page 437.
See also SOUND DEVICES.

Atmosphere The mood or emotional quality of a literary work. Atmosphere often is created with details about people and setting. In "The Cask of Amontillado," Edgar Allan Poe creates atmosphere by describing the eerie setting. He writes, "We had passed through walls of piled bones, with casks and puncheons intermingling, into the inmost recesses of the catacombs."

See page 310.
See also MOOD.

Author's Purpose The author's reason for writing. For example, the purpose may be to persuade, to express an opinion, or to inform. Sometimes an author may have more than one purpose for writing. For example, Margaret Truman's purpose in writing "The United States vs. Susan B. Anthony" may have been both to inform readers about the life of this suffragist and to show that Anthony had a greater sense of humor than has been presumed.

See pages 281 and 317.

Autobiography The story of a person's life written by that person from the first-person point of view. An author typically focuses on the most significant events that happened to him or her. For example, in *All God's Children Need Traveling Shoes*, Maya Angelou writes about the time she was believed to be an African woman while visiting a Ghanaian village.

See pages 280 and 301.
See also BIOGRAPHY.

B

Ballad A song or poem that tells a story. Folk ballads, which typically tell of an exciting or dramatic event, were composed by an anonymous singer or author and passed on by word of mouth for generations before being written down. Literary ballads are written in imitation of folk ballads; they usually are attributed to an author.

See also NARRATIVE POETRY, ORAL TRADITION.

Biography The account of a person's life written by someone other than the subject. Biographies can be short or book-length or span several volumes. A biography may reflect the attitude that the author has toward his or her subject.

See pages 280 and 365.
See also AUTOBIOGRAPHY, MEMOIR, NONFICTION.

Blank verse Verse written in unrhymed lines of iambic pentameter, a rhythm pattern with five units, or feet, each of which has an unstressed syllable followed by a stressed syllable. Much of Shakespeare's work is written in blank verse. The following line from *Romeo and Juliet,* spoken by the friar, is an example of blank verse. The stressed and unstressed syllables are marked, as are the five **feet** in the meter:

FRIAR. Bĕ pá | tiĕnt, fór | thĕ wórld | ĭs bróad | ănd wíde.

See page 576.
See also METER, RHYTHM.

C

Character An individual in a literary work. Characters may be people, animals, robots, or whatever the author chooses. The most important characters in a work are called **main characters;** all others are called **minor characters.** In James Hurst's "The Scarlet Ibis," Brother and Doodle are main characters; Mama, Daddy, and Aunt Nicey are minor characters. The central conflict in a story always involves one or more of the main characters. A **round character,** such as Walter Mitty in James Thurber's "The Secret Life of Walter Mitty," shows varied and sometimes contradictory traits. A **flat character,** such as the obsessive, vengeful murderer in Edgar Allan Poe's "The Cask of Amontillado," reveals only one personality trait. A **stereotype** is a flat character of a familiar and often-repeated type. A **dynamic character,** such as Sarah in Joanne Greenberg's "And Sarah Laughed," develops and changes in the course of a literary work. This change may result from a conflict or from a newfound understanding of him- or herself or others. A **static character,** on the other hand, remains the same from the beginning to the end, such as the king in "The Lady, or the Tiger?" by Frank R. Stockton.

See pages 2, 163, 189, 562, and 779.
See also ANTAGONIST, CHARACTERIZATION, FOIL, PROTAGONIST.

Characterization The methods an author uses to reveal a character's personality. In **direct characterization,** the author or narrator makes direct statements about a character's traits, as in this description of Mr. Mathis from Grant Moss Jr.'s "Before the End of Summer": "He was a tall, rawboned man with a bullet-shaped head, and he looked exactly like what he was—a deacon in a church." In **indirect characterization** the author or speaker reveals a character's personality through the character's own words, thoughts, and actions and through the words, thoughts, and actions of other characters. In the same story, Grant Moss Jr. uses indirect characterization through the dialogue of another character: "He's a quiet child," his grand-mother said. "Sometimes I think he's too quiet, but he's a good child—at least when I got my eyes on him."

See pages 38 and 866.
See also CHARACTER.

Cinquain A five-line poem or stanza that follows a specific pattern of syllables. The first line has two syllables, the next line has four, then six, then eight, and the fifth line has two again.

See page 537.

Climax The point of greatest emotional intensity, interest, or suspense in the plot of a narrative. The climax typically comes at the turning point in a story or drama. For example, in Amy Tan's "Rules of the Game," the climax falls toward the end of the story when Meimei and her mother exchange harsh words and then Meimei runs away.

See pages 3, 22, and 881.
See also PLOT.

Comedy A type of drama that deals with light and amusing subjects or with serious and profound subjects in a light, familiar, or satirical manner. Comedies typically have happy endings, and they entertain audiences through the use of verbal wit, physical humor, ridicule, or irony. They often poke fun at people's faults and limitations in order to teach something about the follies and foibles of human nature. Gore Vidal's *Visit to a Small Planet* is a comedy.

See page 947.
See also DRAMA, FARCE, SATIRE.

Comic relief A short, funny episode that interrupts an otherwise serious or tragic work of drama. Such an episode may break the tension after a particularly intense scene, it may provide a bitterly humorous twist on the work's theme, or it may emphasize an unfolding tragedy. Many of Shakespeare's tragedies contain instances of comic relief.

See page 674.

Conclusion The ending of a piece of writing that provides closure to the piece and expresses the author's feelings about his or her experience. Toward the end of "Only Daughter," Sandra Cisneros describes how her father finally read and enjoyed one of her stories. Her conclusion states, "Of all the wonderful things that happened to me last year, that was the most wonderful." This comment emphasizes how much her father's opinion has always meant to her.

See pages 241 and 281.

Conflict The struggle between opposing forces in a story or play. An **external conflict** exists when a character struggles against some outside force, such as another character, nature, society, or fate. In Homer's *Odyssey,* Odysseus's conflicts—for example, with Polyphemus, Scylla and Charybdis, and the suitors—are all external. An **internal conflict** exists within the mind of a character who is torn between different courses of action. In W. D. Wetherell's "The Bass, the River, and Sheila Mant," the narrator is torn between reeling in the fish (and losing the potential affections of Sheila) and letting it go (and losing the catch of a lifetime).

See pages 3 and 51.
See also ANTAGONIST, PLOT, PROTAGONIST, RESOLUTION.

Connotation The unspoken or unwritten meanings associated with a word beyond its dictionary definition, or denotation. The context in which a word appears is critical to understanding its connotation.

See pages 311 and 988.
See also DENOTATION, FIGURATIVE LANGUAGE.

Consonance The repetition of consonant sounds before or after different vowel sounds, as in the line from "I Am Offering This Poem" by Jimmy Santiago Baca:

like a pair of thick socks

See also SOUND DEVICES.

D

Denotation The literal meaning or dictionary definition of a word.

See page 988.
See also CONNOTATION.

Description A detailed portrayal of a person, place, thing, or event. Description appeals to the senses, helping readers to see, hear, smell, taste, or feel the subject. Almost all writing contains elements of description. The opening paragraph of "The Scarlet Ibis" by James Hurst contains this rich description:

The last graveyard flowers were blooming, and their smell drifted across the cotton field and through every room of our house, speaking softly the names of our dead.

See page 381.
See also FIGURATIVE LANGUAGE, IMAGERY, SENSORY DETAILS.

Dialect A variation of a standard language spoken by a group of people, often within a particular region. Sentence structure, vocabulary, and pronunciation are all affected by dialect. For example, the following lines from "A Red, Red Rose" by Robert Burns make use of Scottish dialect:

Till a' the seas gang dry, my dear,
And the rocks melt wi' the sun!

See page 104.

Dialogue Conversation between characters in a literary work. Dialogue brings characters to life by revealing their personalities and by showing what they are thinking and feeling as they react to other characters. Dialogue also helps to advance the plot. The following passage from William Saroyan's "Gaston" is an example of dialogue in a work of fiction:

"Aren't you going to squash him?"
"No, of course not, why should I?"
"He's a bug. He's *ugh.*"

See pages 121 and 563.

Diction An author's choice of words and the arrangement of those words in phrases, sentences, or lines of a poem. An author will generally consider the literal meanings of words, or **denotation,** as well as the images or associations the words suggest, or **connotation.**

See page 152.
See also CONNOTATION, DENOTATION, STYLE, WORD CHOICE.

Drama A story written to be performed by actors in front of an audience. The script of a dramatic work, or play, includes **stage directions** that explain how characters should look, speak, move, and behave. They also might specify details of the **setting** and **scenery,** such as lighting, **props,** and sound effects. Plays are often divided into **acts,** which may also be divided into **scenes,** indicating a change in location or the passage of time.

See pages 562–563.
See also ACT, PROPS, SCENE, SETTING, STAGE DIRECTIONS.

Dramatic irony. See IRONY.

Dramatic poetry Poetry that uses elements of drama. One or more characters speak to other characters, to themselves, or to the reader. Dramatic poetry typically includes a tense situation or emotional conflict.

See also SPEAKER.

Dynamic character. See CHARACTER.

See page 779.

E

Epic A long narrative poem on a great and serious subject that is centered on the actions of a heroic figure. The epic hero has a goal and typically is embarked on a long journey that involves struggles with natural and supernatural beings–gods, monsters, and other human beings–which test the hero's bravery, wits, and skill in battle. The purpose of an epic poem is to entertain, teach, and inspire the listener or reader with examples of how people can strive and succeed against great odds.

See pages 804–806.
See also LEGEND, MYTH, NARRATIVE POETRY.

Epic simile An extended comparison using *like* or *as* to compare two seemingly unlike things. Also called a Homeric simile, the epic simile extends a comparison with elaborate descriptive details that can fill several lines of verse.

See page 829.
See also EPIC, SIMILE.

Essay A relatively short piece of informative nonfiction writing, usually on a single subject. **Expository essays** explain a topic or the steps in a process, report the news, or analyze a work of literature. **Narrative essays** relate true stories. **Persuasive essays** promote an opinion.

See pages 280–281.
See also NONFICTION.

Exaggeration. See HYPERBOLE.

Exposition The introduction of the characters, the setting, or the situation at the beginning of a story.

See pages 3, 22, and 132.

F

Fable A short, usually simple tale that demonstrates a moral and sometimes uses animal characters. Themes are typically stated outright, but sometimes they are not.

See also LEGEND, PARABLE, THEME.

Falling action In a play or story, the action that typically follows the climax and reveals its results.

See pages 3, 22, and 206.
See also PLOT, RESOLUTION, RISING ACTION.

Fantasy A highly imaginative type of fiction. The events depicted in works of fantasy could not really happen–they occur as if by magic. Fantasy stories may include people, but they commonly take place in imaginary worlds and may include gnomes, elves, or other fantastical beings and forces.

See page 904.
See also MAGICAL REALISM, SCIENCE FICTION.

Farce A type of comedy that provokes laughter by placing one-dimensional, or flat, characters in ridiculous situations. Gore Vidal's comedy *Visit to a Small Planet* has elements of farce.

See also COMEDY.

Fiction Literature in which situations and characters are invented by the writer. Aspects of a fictional work might be based on fact or experience. Fiction includes short stories, such as "The Winner," by Barbara Kimenye, and novels, such as *My Ántonia,* by Willa Cather.

See also FANTASY, NONFICTION, NOVEL, SCIENCE FICTION, SHORT STORY.

Figurative language Language used for descriptive effect, often to imply ideas indirectly. Although it may appear in all kinds of writing, figurative language is especially prominent in poetry. Figurative expressions are not literally true but express some truth beyond the literal level. A **figure of speech** is a specific device or kind of figurative language, such as **hyperbole, metaphor, personification, simile,** or **understatement.** For example, in his poem "Rain in My Heart," Edgar Lee Masters uses figurative language when he personifies memory:

. . . memory sleeps beneath the gray
And windless sky and brings no dreams
Of any well remembered day.

See pages 268 and 437.
See also CONNOTATION, HYPERBOLE, IMAGERY, METAPHOR, OXYMORON, PERSONIFICATION, SIMILE, SYMBOL, UNDERSTATEMENT.

First-person point of view. See POINT OF VIEW.

Flashback A literary device in which an earlier episode, conversation, or event is inserted into the chronological sequence of a narrative. Often presented as a memory of the narrator or of another character, a flashback may be sparked by one or more cues, such as a sound or odor associated with a prior experience or a visit to a related setting. In the story "And Sarah Laughed," author Joanne Greenberg uses flashback when she relates Sarah's memory of the day she first discovered that her baby was unable to hear.

See page 64.

Flat character. See CHARACTER.

See page 189.

Foil A character who provides a strong contrast to another character. A foil may emphasize another character's distinctive traits or make a character look better by comparison. For example, Mercutio is Romeo's foil in *Romeo and Juliet.*

See page 606.

Folklore The traditional beliefs, customs, stories, songs, and dances of a culture. Folklore is based in the concerns of ordinary people and is passed down through **oral tradition,** that is, passed from generation to generation by word of mouth.

See also EPIC, LEGEND, MYTH, ORAL TRADITION, TALL TALE.

Foreshadowing An author's use of clues that hint at events that will occur later in the plot. Foreshadowing often helps to build suspense as well as to prepare readers for what is to come. For example, in Gerald Haslam's "The Horned Toad," the death of the toad and its burial in its natural environment, the desert-like vacant lot from which it had come, foreshadow the death and burial of Grandma in the open country where she'd spent most of her life.

See also PLOT, SUSPENSE.

Free verse Poetry that has no fixed pattern of meter, rhyme, line length, or stanza arrangement. "I Was a Skinny Tomboy Kid," by Alma Luz Villanueva, is an example of free verse.

See page 496.
See also POETRY, RHYTHM.

G

Genre A category or type of literature characterized by a particular form or style. Prose–including fiction and nonfiction–poetry, and drama are examples of genres. The term also refers to subcategories of a particular type of literature. For example, science fiction and mystery are both genres of fiction. "He–y, Come On Ou–t!" by Shinichi Hoshi, for example, belongs to both the short story and science fiction genres.

H

Haiku Traditionally, a Japanese form of poetry that has three lines and seventeen syllables. The first and third lines have five syllables each, and the middle line has seven syllables. The purpose of a haiku is to capture a flash of insight that occurs during an observation of nature. "Peace," by Paula Yup, is a haiku.

See pages 498 and 500.

Hero The main character in a literary work, typically one whose character or deeds inspire the admiration of the reader. Although at one time *hero* was used to refer to males and *heroine* was used to refer to females, in contemporary usage, the term *hero* applies to both males and females.

See also EPIC, PROTAGONIST, TRAGEDY.

Hyperbole A figure of speech in which great exaggeration is used for emphasis or humorous effect. *You've asked me a million times* is an example of hyperbole.

See page 465.
See also FIGURATIVE LANGUAGE.

I

Iambic pentameter. See BLANK VERSE.

Idiom A work or phrase that has a special meaning different from its standard or dictionary meaning. For example, *burning the midnight oil* is an idiom that means "staying up late at night."

Imagery The "word pictures" that writers use to help evoke an emotional response in readers. In creating effective imagery, writers use sensory details, or descriptions that appeal to one or more of the five senses: sight, hearing, touch, taste, and smell.

See pages 437 and 469.
See also FIGURATIVE LANGUAGE.

Inversion Reversal of the usual word order in a prose sentence or line of poetry, for emphasis or variety. The following line from Shakespeare's *Romeo and Juliet* is an example of inversion.

JULIET. So Romeo would, were he not Romeo call'd.

Irony A contrast between appearance and reality. **Situational irony** exists when the actual outcome of a situation is the opposite of what is expected—as in the ending of O. Henry's "The Gift of the Magi." **Verbal irony** exists when a person says one thing and means another. For example, as Montresor leads Fortunato to his doom in the vaults, he says, "Come, we will go back ere it is too late. Your cough—," as if he were genuinely concerned about Fortunato's health. **Dramatic irony** exists when the reader knows something that a character does not know. For example, in Joanne Greenberg's "And Sarah Laughed," the reader knows that sign language is a means of communication and social inclusion long before Sarah herself realizes it.

See page 147.

L

Legend A story handed down from the past through the oral tradition and commonly believed to be based on historical events and an actual hero. Most legends are exaggerated, gaining elements of fantasy over the years.

See also EPIC, FABLE, FOLKLORE, MYTH, ORAL TRADITION, TALL TALE.

Line In a poem, a word or row of words that may or may not form a complete sentence.

See page 436.
See also STANZA.

Local color The use of specific details to re-create the language, customs, geography, and habits of a particular area. In her story "The Winner," for example, Barbara Kimenye brings the village of Kalasanda, Buganda, to life with many details about what the characters eat, drink, and wear.

Lyric poetry Poetry that expresses a speaker's personal thoughts and feelings. Lyric poems are usually short and musical. This broad category covers many poetic types and styles, including free verse and rhymed poetry. "I Wandered Lonely as a Cloud," by William Wordsworth, is an example of a lyric poem.

See pages 437 and 507.
See also POETRY.

M

Magical realism A style of writing in which realistic details, events, settings, characters, and dialogue are interwoven with magical, bizarre, fantastic, or supernatural elements. "The Flat of the Land," by Diana García, is an example of magical realism.

See page 967.

Main character. See CHARACTER.

See page 163.

Memoir A type of narrative nonfiction that presents the story of a period in a person's life and is usually written from the first-person point of view. A memoir often emphasizes a person's thoughts and feelings, the person's relationships with other people, or the impact of significant historical events on the person's life. *Night,* by Elie Wiesel, is an example of a memoir.

See pages 280 and 322.
See also AUTOBIOGRAPHY.

Metaphor A figure of speech that compares or equates two or more things that have something in common. A metaphor does not use *like* or *as.* The following lines from "I Am Offering This Poem," by Jimmy Santiago Baca, feature a metaphor:

[love] is a pot full of yellow corn
to warm your belly in winter

See pages 423, 437, and 452.
See also ANALOGY, FIGURATIVE LANGUAGE, SIMILE.

Meter A regular pattern of stressed and unstressed syllables that gives a line of poetry a predictable rhythm. The basic unit of meter is the **foot.** Typically, stressed syllables are marked with ′ and unstressed syllables with ˘. The meter is marked in the following lines from William Wordsworth's "I Wandered Lonely as a Cloud."

Ĭ wándĕred lónelў ás ă clóud
Thăt flóats ŏn hígh o'ĕr válеs ănd hílls

See pages 436 and 444.

Minor character. See CHARACTER.

See page 163.

Mood The feeling or atmosphere that an author creates in a literary work. The mood can suggest a specific emotion, such as excited or fearful. Mood can also suggest the quality of a setting, such as somber or calm. In a poem, word choice, line length, rhythm, and other elements contribute to its mood. Descriptive language and figures of speech also help to establish the mood. Richard Connell sustains a tense, eerie mood throughout much of the short story "The Most Dangerous Game."

An apprehensive night crawled slowly by like a wounded snake, and sleep did not visit Rainsford, although the silence of a dead world was on the jungle.

See pages 93 and 696.
See also ATMOSPHERE, SETTING.

Moral A practical lesson about right and wrong conduct. In fables, the moral is stated directly; in other stories, it is usually implied.

See page 977.

Myth A traditional story of anonymous origin that deals with goddesses, gods, heroes, and supernatural events. Homer's *Odyssey* incorporates some of the most famous traditional myths of ancient Greece, such as the myth of the Sirens.

See also FOLKLORE, LEGEND, ORAL TRADITION, TALL TALE.

N

Narration The kind of writing or speech that tells a story. Narration is not only used in novels, short stories, and narrative poetry but it can also be an important element in biographies, autobiographies, and essays.

See pages 280–281 and 374.
See also NARRATIVE POETRY, NARRATOR.

Narrative poetry Verse that tells a story. Narrative poetry includes ballads, epics, and shorter poems.

See pages 437 and 552–555.
See also BALLAD, EPIC, NARRATION.

Narrator The person who tells a story: a speaker, a character in the story, an outside observer, or even the author. In Truman Capote's "A Christmas Memory," for example, the narrator is Buddy, a character in the story. In Joanne Greenberg's "And Sarah Laughed," the narrator stands outside the story.

See also NARRATION, POINT OF VIEW, SPEAKER.

Nonfiction Prose writing about real people, places, and events. Nonfiction writers present information they consider true. Written in either the first- or third-person point of view, works of **narrative nonfiction** tell a story and often have characteristics of fiction, such as setting, characters, theme, or plot. Biographies, autobiographies, memoirs, and narrative essays are types of narrative nonfiction. The biographical essay "The United States vs. Susan B. Anthony," by Margaret Truman, is an example of narrative nonfiction. Works of **informative nonfiction** include essays, speeches, and articles that explain a topic or promote an opinion. Dennis Rodkin's newspaper article "Sunflowers Are as American as They Come" is an example of informative nonfiction.

See pages 280–281.
See also AUTOBIOGRAPHY, BIOGRAPHY, ESSAY, FICTION.

Novel A book-length, fictional prose narrative, typically having a plot that unfolds through the actions, speech, and thoughts of characters.

See also FICTION, SHORT STORY.

O

Onomatopoeia The use of a word or phrase that imitates or suggests the sound of what it describes. Eve Merriam bases an entire poem on this technique in "Onomatopoeia":

The rusty spigot
sputters,
utters
a splutter,
spatters a smattering of drops,
gashes wider;
slash,
splatters,
scatters,
spurts,
finally stops sputtering
and plash!
gushes rushes splashes
clear water dashes.

See page 437.
See also SOUND DEVICES.

Oral tradition Literature that passes by word of mouth from one generation to the next. Epics, such as Homer's *Odyssey,* were originally passed on in this manner.

See also BALLAD, FOLKLORE, LEGEND, MYTH, TALL TALE.

Oxymoron A figure of speech that is a combination of seemingly contradictory words. For example, the following lines from act 1, scene 1 of Shakespeare's *Romeo and Juliet* contain several oxymorons:

Why then, O brawling love, O loving hate,
O any thing, of nothing first create!
O heavy lightness, serious vanity,
Misshapen chaos of well-seeming forms,
Feather of lead, bright smoke, cold fire, sick health,
Still-waking sleep, that is not what it is!

See also FIGURATIVE LANGUAGE.

P

Parable A simple story pointing to a moral or religious lesson.

See also FABLE, MORAL.

Paradox A situation or statement that includes two parts, both of which are true but seem to contradict each other. It is a paradox, for example, if a person says that he gained back all the weight he lost following surgery but that his clothes still don't fit the way they did.

Parallelism The use of a series of words, phrases, or sentences that have similar grammatical form. Parallelism emphasizes the items that are arranged in the similar structures. The following is an example of parallelism in Margaret Truman's "The United States *vs.* Susan B. Anthony":

Daniel Anthony had a succession of homes, a succession of jobs, and a succession of financial ups and downs.

See pages 367, 392, and 607.
See also REPETITION.

Parody A literary or musical work that imitates the style of some other work in a satirical or humorous way. Behavior and customs can also be parodied.

Personification A figure of speech in which an animal, object, force of nature, or idea is given human qualities or characteristics, as in the following example from "Rain in My Heart" by Edgar Lee Masters:

And memory sleeps beneath the gray
And windless sky . . .

See pages 437, 479, and 846.
See also FIGURATIVE LANGUAGE.

Plot The sequence of events in a narrative work. The plot begins with the **exposition,** or the introduction of the **characters,** the **setting,** and the **conflict. Rising action** occurs as complications, twists, or intensifications of the conflict occur. This action leads up to the **climax,** or emotional high point. The climax gives way rapidly to its logical result in the **falling action,** and finally to the **resolution** in which the final outcome is revealed.

See pages 3, 22, and 563.
See also CLIMAX, CONFLICT, FALLING ACTION, RESOLUTION, RISING ACTION.

Poetry A form of literary expression that differs from prose in emphasizing the line as the unit of composition. Many other traditional characteristics of poetry apply to some poems but not to others: emotional, imaginative language; use of metaphor, simile; and other figures of speech, division into stanzas; rhyme; regular pattern of meter; and so on.

See pages 436–437.

Point of view The relationship of the narrator to the story. In a story with **first-person point of view,** the narrator is a character in the story, referred to as "I." The reader sees everything through that character's eyes. "A Christmas Memory," by Truman Capote, is told from the first-person point of view. In a story with **third-person limited** point of view, the narrator reveals the thoughts, feelings, and observations of only one character, referring to that character as "he" or "she," as in "The Flat of the Land," by Diana García. In a story with **third-person omniscient,** or all-knowing, point of view, the narrator is not a character in the story but someone who stands outside the story and comments on the action. A third-person omniscient narrator knows everything about the characters and the events and may reveal details that the characters themselves could not reveal. "The Most Dangerous Game," by Richard Connell, is told from the third-person omniscient point of view.

See pages 2 and 14.
See also NARRATOR, SPEAKER.

Props Theater slang (a shortened form of *properties*) for articles or objects used in a play or movie.

See also DRAMA.

Protagonist The central character in a literary work around whom the main conflict revolves. The protagonist is often the person with whom audience members or readers sympathize or identify. Walter Mitty is the protagonist in James Thurber's story "The Secret Life of Walter Mitty."

See pages 2, 234, and 760.

See ANTAGONIST, CHARACTER, CONFLICT, HERO.

Pun A humorous play on two or more meanings of the same word or on two different words with the same sound. Today, puns often appear in advertising headlines and slogans—for example, a movie theater might advertise its low prices by saying, "Get a reel deal."

See page 629.

R

Repetition A literary device in which sounds, words, phrases, lines, or stanzas are repeated for emphasis in a poem or other literary work. The use of repetition may lend a sense of unity and continuity to the writing. When a line or stanza is repeated in a poem, it is sometimes called a refrain.

See page 543.
See also PARALLELISM, RHYME.

Resolution The part of the plot that concludes the falling action by revealing or suggesting the outcome of the conflict.

See pages 3, 22, and 206.
See also CONFLICT, PLOT.

Rhyme The repetition of the same stressed vowel sounds and any succeeding sounds in two or more words. For example, *block* rhymes with *clock; weather* rhymes with *together.* In a poem, **internal rhyme** occurs within a line, while **end rhyme** occurs at the ends of lines. Slant rhymes occur when words include sounds that are similar but not identical. Slant rhyme usually involves some variation of **consonance** (the repetition of consonant sounds) or **assonance** (the repetition of vowel sounds).

See pages 326 and 437.
See also ASSONANCE, CONSONANCE, REPETITION, RHYME SCHEME, SOUND DEVICES.

Rhyme scheme The pattern that end rhymes form in a stanza or poem. The rhyme scheme is designated by the assignment of a different letter of the alphabet to each new rhyme. For example, the following lines from Edgar Lee Masters's poem "Rain in My Heart" have an *abcb* rhyme scheme:

There is a quiet in my heart *a*
Like one who rests from days of pain. *b*
Outside, the sparrows on the roof *c*
Are chirping in the dripping rain. *b*

See page 437.
See also RHYME, SONNET.

Rhythm The pattern of sound created by the arrangement of stressed and unstressed syllables, especially in poetry. Rhythm can emphasize certain words or ideas and give poetry a musical quality that can help convey meaning. Rhythm can be regular, with a predictable pattern or meter, or irregular.

See pages 436 and 511.
See also BLANK VERSE, METER, SCANSION.

Rising action The part of a plot that adds complications to the conflict and increases reader interest.

See pages 3 and 22.
See also FALLING ACTION.

Round character. See CHARACTER.

See page 189.

S

Satire A form of writing that ridicules people, practices, or institutions in order to reveal their failings. Satires vary in tone from mild amusement to boiling anger. They often aim to make people think critically about the subject at hand, but they can also be written for pure entertainment. Gore Vidal's *Visit to a Small Planet* may be considered a satire.

See page 572.
See also COMEDY.

Scansion The analysis of the rhythm of a line of verse. To scan a line of poetry means to note stressed and unstressed syllables and to divide the line into its feet, or rhythmical units.

See also METER, RHYTHM.

Scene A subdivision of an act in a play. Each scene usually takes place in a specific setting and time.

See page 563.
See also ACT.

Science fiction A type of fiction that is based on real or imagined scientific and technological advancements. Science fiction stories are sometimes set in futuristic worlds or on other planets, and they may include time travel or extraterrestrial beings. Some works of science fiction emphasize scientific explanations, while others focus on human action and responsibility, with technology in the background. "The Sentinel" by Arthur C. Clarke is an example of a science fiction story.

See page 904.
See also FANTASY.

Sensory details Evocative words that convey sensory experiences–seeing, hearing, tasting, touching, and smelling. Sensory details make writing come alive by helping readers experience what is being described.

See also IMAGERY.

Setting The time and place in which the events of a story, novel, or play occur. The setting often helps create an atmosphere or mood. Setting is not just physical, however; it includes ideas, customs, values, and beliefs of a particular time and place.

See pages 2, 84, and 563.
See also ATMOSPHERE, MOOD.

Short story A brief fictional narrative in prose. Elements of the short story include **plot, character, setting, point of view,** and **theme.**

See pages 2–3.

Simile A figure of speech using *like* or *as* to compare seemingly unlike things. The following similes come from Truman Capote's "A Christmas Memory":

She is small and sprightly, like a bantam hen.

Inside myself, I feel warm and sparky as those crumbling logs, carefree as the wind in the chimney.

See pages 437 and 452.
See also ANALOGY, FIGURATIVE LANGUAGE, IMAGERY, METAPHOR.

Situational irony. See IRONY.

Soliloquy A long speech delivered by a character who is alone onstage. A soliloquy typically reveals the private thoughts and emotions of the character. An example of a soliloquy may be found in act 2, scene 2 of Shakespeare's *Romeo and Juliet,* in the speech by Romeo that begins: "But soft! What light through yonder window breaks?"

See page 658.
See also ASIDE.

Sonnet A lyric poem of fourteen lines, almost always written in iambic pentameter and usually following strict patterns of stanza division and rhyme. Shakespeare's *Romeo and Juliet* includes several sonnets.

Sound devices Elements of poetry that appeal to the ear. In poetry, sound devices such as **alliteration** and **assonance** are used to emphasize certain words and underscore their meaning, to create or enhance rhythm, and to add a musical quality to the work.

See pages 437 and 551.
See also ALLITERATION, ASSONANCE.

Speaker Similar to the narrator in a work of prose, the speaker is the voice that communicates with the reader of a poem. A poet may invent a speaker with a particular identity in order to create a desired impact. For example, the speaker in Margaret Walker's poem "Lineage" is a granddaughter who is in awe of the strength of her grandmothers.

See pages 436 and 460.
See also NARRATOR, TONE.

Stage directions In a play, written instructions that explain how characters should look, speak, move, and behave. Stage directions also specify details of the setting and scenery, such as the sets, costumes, lighting, props, and sound effects. Examples of stage directions may be found in each of the plays in this book.

See pages 562–563 and 734.
See also DRAMA.

Stanza In a poem, a group of lines forming a unit. A stanza in a poem is similar to a paragraph in prose.

See page 436.
See also LINE.

Static character. See CHARACTER.

See page 779.

Stereotype A character who is not developed as an individual, but as a collection of traits and mannerisms supposedly shared by all members of a group.

See also CHARACTERIZATION.

Structure In poetry, the organization of images, ideas, words, and lines. The structure of a poem is sometimes created through the use of rhythm, rhyme, repetition, or stanzas.

See page 516.
See also STANZA.

Style The distinctive way in which an author uses language. Such elements as word choice, phrasing, sentence length, tone, dialogue, author purpose, and attitude toward the audience and subject can all contribute to an author's writing style.

See also AUTHOR'S PURPOSE, DICTION, TONE.

Suspense The growing interest and excitement readers experience while awaiting a climax or resolution in a work of literature. To build suspense, an author may use **foreshadowing**–or clues to what will happen next–as well as a number of other literary devices. "The Cask of Amontillado," by Edgar Allan Poe, is an example of an extremely suspenseful story. The reader, like Fortunato, is led through the catacombs and is kept "in the dark" until the very end about what sort of revenge the narrator will take.

See page 916.
See also FORESHADOWING, MOOD.

Symbol An object, a person, a place, or an experience that represents something else, usually something abstract. A symbol may have more than one meaning, or its meaning may change from the beginning to the end of a literary work. For example, to Mr. Shimada and his faithful employees in Yoshiko Uchida's "Of Dry Goods and Black Bow Ties," a bow tie is a symbol of dignity, honesty, and respectability.

See pages 176 and 485.
See also FIGURATIVE LANGUAGE.

T

Tall tale A wildly imaginative story, usually passed down orally, about the fantastic adventures or amazing feats of folk heroes in realistic local settings.

See also FOLKLORE, LEGEND, MYTH, ORAL TRADITION.

Theme The main idea or message of a literary work. Theme is not the subject of the work but instead is an insight about life or human nature. Some works have a **stated theme,** which is expressed directly and explicitly. Others have an **implied theme,** which is revealed gradually through such other literary elements as plot, character, setting, point of view, imagery, figures of speech, or symbolism.

See pages 3, 252, and 530.

Thesis The central idea or purpose of an essay or other work of nonfiction, commonly stated in one or more sentences.

See pages 281 and 344.

Third-person point of view. See POINT OF VIEW.

Title The name of a literary work.

See page 400.

Tone A reflection of a writer's or speaker's attitude toward a subject of a poem, story, or other literary work. Tone may be communicated through words and details that express particular emotions and that evoke an emotional response in the reader. For example, word choice or phrasing may seem to convey respect, anger, lightheartedness, or sarcasm. In the first paragraph of the excerpt from *West with the Night*, Beryl Markham conveys a mocking tone towards humans. "To an eagle or to an owl or to a rabbit, man must seem a masterful and yet a forlorn animal; he has but two friends. In his almost universal unpopularity, he points out, with pride, that these two are the dog and the horse. He believes, an innocence peculiar to himself, that they are equally proud of this alleged confraternity."

See pages 220, 474, and 850.
See also MOOD.

Tragedy A play in which a main character, called the **tragic hero,** suffers a downfall. The downfall may result from outside forces, as in the case of Romeo and Juliet, who are doomed by the external workings of bigotry and fear. Or the downfall may result from a weakness within the character, which is known as a **tragic flaw.**

See page 691.
See also DRAMA, HERO.

U

Understatement Language that makes something seem less important than it really is. In "Field Trip," for example, Naomi Shihab Nye uses understatement when she says that the woman who cut off her finger was "distracted."

V

Verbal irony. See IRONY.

Voice The distinctive use of language that conveys the writer's or narrator's personality to the reader. Voice is determined by elements of style such as word choice and tone.

W

Word choice The selection of words to convey meaning, suggest attitude, and create images. For example, in the essay "Walking," Linda Hogan chooses words that present the sunflower in a positive, almost magical light. "Over the summer this sunflower grew into a plant of incredible beauty, turning its face daily toward the sun in the most subtle of ways, the black center of it dark and alive with a deep blue light, as if flint had sparked an elemental fire there."

See page 335.
See also DICTION, STYLE.

Language Handbook

Troubleshooter

The Troubleshooter will help you recognize and correct errors that you might make in your writing.

Sentence Fragment

Problem: A fragment that lacks a subject

This new computer is fantastic. Is much faster than the old one. *frag*

Solution: Add a subject to the fragment to make it a complete sentence.

This new computer is fantastic. It is much faster than the old one.

Problem: A fragment that lacks a complete verb

The patrons poured from the theater. Theatergoers in excited groups. *frag*

The jet suddenly plunged. Passengers tumbling in the aisles. *frag*

Solution A: Add a complete verb or an auxiliary verb to make the sentence complete.

The patrons poured from the theater. The theatergoers chattered in excited groups.

The jet suddenly plunged. Passengers were tumbling in the aisles.

Solution B: Combine the fragment with another sentence. Add commas to set off a nonessential phrase, or a comma and a conjunction to separate two main clauses in a compound sentence.

The theatergoers, chattering in excited groups, poured from the theater.

The jet suddenly plunged, and passengers were tumbling in the aisles.

Problem: A fragment that is a subordinate clause

Tim scored the goal. Although he was injured in the attempt. *frag*

My term paper is about Robert Frost. Who is my favorite poet. *frag*

Solution A: Combine the fragment with another sentence. Add a comma to set off nonessential clauses.

Tim scored the goal, although he was injured in the attempt.

My term paper is about Robert Frost, who is my favorite poet.

Solution B: Rewrite the fragment as a complete sentence, eliminating the subordinating conjunction or the relative pronoun and adding a subject or other words necessary to make a complete thought.

Tim scored the goal. He was, however, injured in the attempt.

My term paper is about Robert Frost. He is my favorite poet.

Problem: A fragment that lacks both a subject and a verb

Keisha recited the poem. From memory. *frag*

Solution: Combine the fragment with another sentence.

Keisha recited the poem from memory.

Rule of Thumb: Sentence fragments can make your writing hard to understand. Make sure that every sentence has a subject and a verb.

Run-on Sentence

Problem: Comma splice—two main clauses separated by only a comma

We went canoeing last weekend, my shoulders still ache. *run-on*

Solution A: Replace the comma with an end mark of punctuation, such as a period or a question mark, and begin the new sentence with a capital letter.

We went canoeing last weekend. My shoulders still ache.

Solution B: Place a semicolon between the two main clauses.

We went canoeing last weekend; my shoulders still ache.

Solution C: Add a coordinating conjunction after the comma.

We went canoeing last weekend, and my shoulders still ache.

Problem: Two main clauses with no punctuation between them

The museum has a new exhibit of modern art we haven't seen it yet. *run-on*

Solution A: Separate the main clauses with an end mark of punctuation, such as a period or a question mark, and begin the second sentence with a capital letter.

The museum has a new exhibit of modern art. We haven't seen it yet.

Solution B: Separate the main clauses with a semicolon.

The museum has a new exhibit of modern art; we haven't seen it yet.

Solution C: Add a comma and a coordinating conjunction between the main clauses.

The museum has a new exhibit of modern art, but we haven't seen it yet.

Problem: Two main clauses with no comma before the coordinating conjunction

We washed cars all day and then we went out for Chinese food. *run-on*

Solution: Add a comma before the coordinating conjunction to separate the two main clauses.

We washed cars all day, and then we went out for Chinese food.

Rule of Thumb: It often helps to have someone else read your writing to see if it is clear. Since you know what the sentences are supposed to mean, you might sometimes miss the need for punctuation.

Lack of Subject-Verb Agreement

Problem: A subject that is separated from the verb by an intervening prepositional phrase

The bus with the band members leave at noon. *agr*

The peaks of the mountain range glistens with snow. *agr*

Solution: Ignore a prepositional phrase that comes between a subject and a verb. Make the verb agree with the subject, which is never the object of a preposition.

The bus with the band members leaves at noon.

The peaks of the mountain range glisten with snow.

Problem: A predicate nominative that differs in number from the subject

Raisins is a delicious snack. *agr*

Solution: Ignore the predicate nominative and make the verb agree with the subject of the sentence.

Raisins are a delicious snack.

Problem: A subject that follows the verb

Outside the mall stands six men. *agr*

Over there is several more. *agr*

Solution: In an inverted sentence, look for the subject *after* the verb. Then make sure the verb agrees with the subject.

Outside the mall stand six men.

Over there are several more.

Rule of Thumb: Reversing the order of an inverted sentence may help you decide on the correct verb form: "Several more are over there."

Problem: A collective noun as the subject

The committee meet at 3:30 every Wednesday afternoon. *agr*

The committee casts their votes for chairperson. *agr*

Solution A: If the collective noun refers to a group as a whole, use a singular verb.

The committee meets at 3:30 every Wednesday afternoon.

Solution B: If the collective noun refers to each member of a group individually, use a plural verb.

The committee cast their votes for chairperson.

Problem: A noun of amount as the subject

Thirty-five years are the average lifespan of a hippopotamus. *agr*

Fifty pennies fits into a coin roll. *agr*

Solution: Determine whether the noun of amount refers to one unit and is therefore singular, or whether it refers to a number of individual units and is therefore plural.

Thirty-five years is the average lifespan of a hippopotamus.

Fifty pennies fit into a coin roll.

Problem: A compound subject that is joined by *and*

Speakers and a joystick is plugged into my computer. *agr*

Cookies and cream are my favorite kind of ice cream. *agr*

Solution A: If the parts of the compound subject do not belong to one unit or if they refer to different people or things, use a plural verb.

Speakers and a joystick are plugged into my computer.

Solution B: If the parts of the compound subject belong to one unit or if both parts refer to the same person or thing, use a singular verb.

Cookies and cream is my favorite kind of ice cream.

Problem: A compound subject that is joined by *or* or *nor*

Neither the dictionaries nor the thesaurus are on the shelves. *agr*

Solution: Make the verb agree with the subject that is closer to it.

Neither the dictionaries nor the thesaurus is on the shelves.

Neither the thesaurus nor the dictionaries are on the shelves.

Problem: A compound subject that is preceded by *many a, every,* or *each*

Every student and teacher have passed through these halls. *agr*

Solution: Use a singular verb when *many a, each,* or *every* precedes a compound subject.

Every student and teacher has passed through these halls.

Problem: A subject that is separated from the verb by an intervening expression

My mother, as well as her brothers, were born in Sweden. *agr*

Solution: Certain expressions, such as *as well as, in addition to,* and *together with,* do not change the number of the subject. Ignore these expressions between a subject and its verb. Make the verb agree with the subject.

My mother, as well as her brothers, was born in Sweden.

Problem: An indefinite pronoun as the subject

Everyone enjoy mysteries. *agr*

Several of the top-seeded players is in the finals. *agr*

Solution: Determine whether the indefinite pronoun is singular or plural, and make the verb agree. Some indefinite pronouns are singular–*another, anyone, everyone, one, each, either, neither, anything, everything, something,* and *somebody.* Some are plural–*both, many, few, several,* and *others.* Some can be singular or plural–*some, all, any, more, most,* and *none*–depending on the noun to which they refer.

Everyone enjoys mysteries.

Several of the top-seeded players are in the finals.

Lack of Pronoun-Antecedent Agreement

Problem: A singular antecedent that can be either male or female

A lawyer often settles his clients' cases out of court. *ant*

Solution A: Traditionally, a masculine pronoun was used to refer to an antecedent that might be either male or female. This usage ignores or excludes females and is not acceptable in contemporary writing. Reword the sentence to use *he or she, him or her,* and so on.

A lawyer often settles his or her clients' cases out of court.

Solution B: Reword the sentence so that both the antecedent and the pronoun are plural.

Lawyers often settle their clients' cases out of court.

Solution C: Reword the sentence to eliminate the pronoun.

A lawyer often settles clients' cases out of court.

Problem: A second-person pronoun that refers to a third-person antecedent

Ms. Rivelli likes to travel to cities where you can get around by bus. *ant*

Solution A: Use the appropriate third-person pronoun.

Ms. Rivelli likes to travel to cities where she can get around by bus.

Solution B: Use an appropriate noun instead of a pronoun.

Ms. Rivelli likes to travel to cities where people can get around by bus.

Problem: A singular indefinite pronoun as an antecedent

Neither of the girls remembered to bring their gym clothes. *ant*

Solution: *Another, any, every, each, one, either, neither, anything, everything, something,* and *somebody* are singular and therefore require singular personal pronouns, even when followed by a prepositional phrase that contains a plural noun.

Neither of the girls remembered to bring her gym clothes.

> **Rule of Thumb:** To help you remember that pronouns such as *each, either,* and *neither* are singular, think *each one, either one,* and *neither one.*

Lack of Clear Pronoun Reference

Problem: A pronoun reference that is weak or vague

The players were elated, which was long overdue. *ref*

The fire was nearing our camp, and that made us nervous. *ref*

Solution A: Rewrite the sentence, adding a clear antecedent for the pronoun.

The players were elated by their victory, which was long overdue.

Solution B: Rewrite the sentence, substituting a noun for the pronoun.

The fire was nearing our camp, and the situation made us nervous.

Problem: A pronoun that could refer to more than one antecedent

Dad and Uncle Mark started a company, and he is the president. *ref*

Now that the actors have agents, they are getting more work. *ref*

Solution A: Rewrite the sentence, substituting a noun for the pronoun.

Dad and Uncle Mark started a company, and Dad is the president.

Solution B: Rewrite the sentence, making the antecedent of the pronoun clear.

The actors are getting more work now that they have agents.

Problem: The indefinite use of *you* or *they*

When a loon utters its eerie cry, you get goosebumps. *ref*

In Boston they call a submarine sandwich a grinder. *ref*

Solution A: Rewrite the sentence, substituting a noun for the pronoun.

When a loon utters its eerie cry, listeners get goosebumps.

Solution B: Rewrite the sentence, eliminating the pronoun entirely.

In Boston a submarine sandwich is called a grinder.

Shift in Pronoun

Problem: An incorrect shift in person between two pronouns

They enjoy gliding, a sport in which you try to catch thermals to stay aloft. *pro*

I believe in telling the truth, even when you will be punished for it. *pro*

Once you have tasted this salsa, everyone will be amazed. *pro*

Solution A: Replace the incorrect pronoun with a pronoun that agrees with its antecedent.

They enjoy gliding, a sport in which they try to catch thermals to stay aloft.

I believe in telling the truth, even when I will be punished for it.

Once you have tasted this salsa, you will be amazed.

Solution B: Replace the incorrect pronoun with an appropriate noun.

They enjoy gliding, a sport in which pilots try to catch thermals to stay aloft.

Shift in Verb Tense

Problem: An unnecessary shift in tense

The astronomers focus on the comet and compared observations. *shift t*

Justine glided onto the ice as the audience bursts into applause. *shift t*

Solution: When two or more events occur at the same time, be sure to use the same verb tense to describe each event.

The astronomers focus on the comet and compare observations.

Justine glided onto the ice as the audience burst into applause.

Problem: A lack of correct shift in tenses to show that one event precedes or follows another

By the time help arrived, we were stranded on the ledge for hours. *shift t*

Solution: When two events have occurred at different times in the past, shift from the past tense to the past perfect tense to indicate that one action began and ended before another past action began.

By the time help arrived, we had been stranded on the ledge for hours.

Rule of Thumb: When you need to use more than one verb tense in a sentence, it may help to first jot down the sequence of events you're writing about. Be clear in your mind which action happened first.

Incorrect Verb Tense or Form

Problem: An incorrect or missing verb ending

Last year my sister work on a ranch for the summer. *tense*

Has she decide what she would like to do this year? *tense*

Solution: Add *-ed* to a regular verb to form the past tense and the past participle.

Last year my sister worked on a ranch for the summer.

Has she decided what she would like to do this year?

Problem: An improperly formed irregular verb

We think our cat runned away last night. *tense*

I have teared an ad out of the "Lost Pets" section of the newspaper. *tense*

Solution: Irregular verbs form their past and past participle forms in some way other than by adding *-ed.* Memorize these forms, or look them up in a dictionary.

We think our cat ran away last night.

I have torn an ad out of the "Lost Pets" section of the newspaper.

Problem: Confusion between the past form and the past participle

We have occasionally beat their team. *tense*

Solution: Use the past participle form of an irregular verb, not the past form, when you use a form of the auxiliary verb *have.*

We have occasionally beaten their team.

Problem: Improper use of the past participle

Our glee club sung the national anthem at many games. *tense*

The thirsty picnickers drunk three cases of soda. *tense*

Solution A: The past participle of an irregular verb cannot stand alone as a verb. Add a form of the auxiliary verb *have* to the past participle to form a complete verb.

Our glee club has sung the national anthem at many games.

The thirsty picnickers have drunk three cases of soda.

Solution B: Replace the past participle with the past form of the verb.

Our glee club sang the national anthem at many games.

The thirsty picnickers drank three cases of soda.

Misplaced or Dangling Modifier

Problem: A misplaced modifier

Jenita got many compliments from her friends in her new outfit. *mod*

Dazed and terrified, we found the raccoon by the side of the road. *mod*

The birdwatchers spotted a yellow wagtail who had binoculars. *mod*

Solution: Modifiers that modify the wrong word or seem to modify more than one word in a sentence are called misplaced modifiers. Move the misplaced phrase as close as possible to the word or words it modifies.

In her new outfit, Jenita got many compliments from her friends.

We found the dazed and terrified raccoon by the side of the road.

The birdwatchers who had binoculars spotted a yellow wagtail.

Problem: Incorrect placement of the adverb *only*

Mustafa only collects stamps from island nations. *mod*

Solution: Place the adverb *only* immediately before the word or group of words it modifies.

Only Mustafa collects stamps from island nations.

Mustafa collects only stamps from island nations.

Mustafa collects stamps only from island nations.

Rule of Thumb: Note that each time *only* is moved, the meaning of the sentence changes. Check to be sure your sentence says what you mean.

Problem: A dangling modifier

After sandbagging for hours, the floodwaters finally began to recede. *mod*

Cutting the grass, a bee stung my arm. *mod*

Solution: Rewrite the sentence, adding a noun to which the dangling phrase clearly refers. Often you will have to add other words or change the form of the verb to complete the meaning of the sentence.

After sandbagging for hours, the residents watched the floodwaters finally begin to recede.

Cutting the grass, I was startled when a bee stung my arm.

Missing or Misplaced Apostrophe

Problem: Singular nouns

The duchess jewels were stolen by that airlines luggage handler. *poss*

Solution: Use an apostrophe and *-s* to form the possessive of a singular noun, even one that ends in *s.*

The duchess's jewels were stolen by that airline's luggage handler.

Problem: Plural nouns ending in *-s*

The veterans parade will be held next Monday. *poss*

Solution: Use an apostrophe alone to form the possessive of a plural noun that ends in *-s.*

The veterans' parade will be held next Monday.

Problem: Plural nouns not ending in *-s*

The womens department is located on the third floor. *poss*

Solution: Use an apostrophe and *-s* to form the possessive of a plural noun that does not end in *-s.*

The women's department is located on the third floor.

Problem: Pronouns

Please put everybodys potluck dishes on the table. *poss*

Their's is the biggest yacht I have ever seen. *poss*

Solution A: Use an apostrophe and *-s* to form the possessive of a singular indefinite pronoun.

Please put everybody's potluck dishes on the table.

Solution B: Do not use an apostrophe with any of the possessive personal pronouns.

Theirs is the biggest yacht I have ever seen.

Problem: Confusion between *its* and *it's*

One of the buffalo calves has wandered away from it's mother. *poss*

Its about time that someone spoke up about this problem. *cont*

Solution: Do not use an apostrophe to form the possessive of *it.* Use an apostrophe to form the contraction of *it is.*

One of the buffalo calves has wandered away from its mother.

It's about time that someone spoke up about this problem.

Missing Commas with Nonessential Elements

Problem: Missing commas with nonessential participles or participial phrases

The author smiling graciously signed copies of her books. com

Putting it bluntly I will not allow a potbellied pig in the house. com

Solution: Determine whether the participle or participial phrase is essential to the meaning of the sentence. If it is not essential, set off the element with commas.

The author, smiling graciously, signed copies of her books.

Putting it bluntly, I will not allow a potbellied pig in the house.

Problem: Missing commas with nonessential adjective clauses

Oklahoma which is rich in oil suffered a bad drought in the 1930s. com

Solution: Determine whether the clause is essential to the meaning of the sentence. If it is not essential, set off the clause with commas.

Oklahoma, which is rich in oil, suffered a bad drought in the 1930s.

Problem: Missing commas with nonessential appositives

Minstrels medieval singers entertained at royal banquets. com

Solution: Determine whether the appositive is essential to the meaning of the sentence. If it is not essential, set off the appositive with commas.

Minstrels, medieval singers, entertained at royal banquets.

Rule of Thumb: To determine whether a word, phrase, or clause is essential, try reading the sentence without it.

Problem: Missing commas with interjections and parenthetical expressions

Gee that was a beautiful ceremony. com

Your brother by the way has been waiting for you for an hour. com

Solution: Set off the interjection or parenthetical expression with commas.

Gee, that was a beautiful ceremony.

Your brother, by the way, has been waiting for you for an hour.

Missing Commas in a Series

Problem: Missing commas in a series of words, phrases, or clauses

The zoo's primate collection includes lemurs baboons and chimpanzees. com

Juan scowled turned on his heel and stomped off. com

The cat bounded out the window across the yard and over the fence. com

We videotaped the newlyweds walking down the aisle cutting the wedding cake and dancing. com

My sister is athletic my brother is musical and I am artistic. com

Solution: When there are three or more items in a series, use a comma after each item that precedes the conjunction.

The zoo's primate collection includes lemurs, baboons, and chimpanzees.

Juan scowled, turned on his heel, and stomped off.

The cat bounded out the window, across the yard, and over the fence.

We videotaped the newlyweds walking down the aisle, cutting the wedding cake, and dancing.

My sister is athletic, my brother is musical, and I am artistic.

Rule of Thumb: When you're having difficulty with a rule of usage, try rewriting the rule in your own words. Then check with your teacher to be sure you have grasped the concept.

Troublesome Words

This section will help you choose between words that are often confusing. It will also alert you to avoid certain words and expressions in school or business writing.

a, an

Use the article *an* when the word that follows begins with a vowel sound. Use *a* when the word that follows begins with a consonant sound. Therefore, use *a* when the word that follows begins with a long *u* sound ("yew").

An elephant stomped through **a** field.

An aunt of mine has **a** unique house.

Use the article *a* when the word that follows begins with a sounded *h.* Use *an* when the word that follows begins with an unsounded *h.*

A helmet from an ancient Roman soldier is quite **an** heirloom!

a lot, alot

This expression is always written as two words and means "a large amount." Some authorities discourage its use in formal English.

When the truck swerved, **a lot** of sand spilled from it.

When the truck swerved, **a large amount** of sand spilled from it.

accept, except

Accept is a verb meaning "to receive" or "to agree to." *Except* is occasionally used as a verb, but more often it is used as a preposition meaning "but."

Please **accept** my apologies.

All of the officers, **except** one, attended the meeting.

affect, effect

Affect is a verb meaning "to cause a change in; to influence." *Effect* may be a noun or a verb. As a noun it means "result." As a verb it means "to bring about or accomplish."

Exercise will **affect** your fitness level.

Exercise will have a beneficial **effect** on your fitness level.

Exercise will **effect** an improvement in your fitness level.

ain't

Ain't is never used in formal speaking and writing unless you are quoting the exact words of a character or real person. Instead of using *ain't,* use *am not, is not,* or a contraction such as *he isn't* or *I'm not.*

Muriel **isn't** coming to the party.

all ready, already

All ready is an adjective phrase that means "completely ready." *Already* is an adverb that means "before" or "by this time."

The climbers were **all ready** for their final ascent, but the storm was **already** upon them.

all right, alright

The expression *all right* should be written as two words.

Were the children **all right** after their frightening experience?

> **Rule of Thumb:** Dictionaries are good guides to the usage of a word. Even though some dictionaries do list the single word *alright,* they indicate that it is not a preferred spelling.

all together, altogether

Use *all together* to mean "in a group." Use the adverb *altogether* to mean "completely" or "on the whole."

The scholarship winners stood **all together** on the stage.

They seemed **altogether** thrilled with their awards.

amount, number

Use *amount* to refer to things that cannot be counted. Use *number* to refer to things that can be counted.

This recipe calls for a large **amount** of pepper.

This recipe calls for a large **number** of eggs.

anxious, eager

Anxious means "uneasy or worried about some event or situation." *Eager* means "having a keen interest" or "feeling impatient for something expected."

I am **anxious** about my dog's reaction to her shots.

The children are **eager** to go to the amusement park.

a while, awhile

A while is made up of an article and a noun. *In* and *for* often come before *a while,* forming a prepositional phrase. *Awhile* is an adverb.

I'll practice in **a while.** I'll practice for **a while.**

I'll rest **awhile** before practicing.

being as, being that

The expressions *being as* and *being that* are sometimes used instead of *because* or *since* in informal conversation. In formal speaking and writing, always use *because* or *since.*

Because Kendra has the flu, we'll need to find another debater.

Since it's already three o'clock, we'd better get ready to leave.

beside, besides

Beside means "at the side of." *Besides* usually means "in addition to."

The prime minister sat **beside** the president on the plane.

Besides playing hockey, the boys compete on the track team.

between, among

Use *between* to compare one person or thing with one other person or thing or with an entire group. Use *among* to show a relationship in which more than two persons or things are considered as a group.

When the twins dress alike, I can't see any difference **between** them.

There is quite a difference **between** Monet's painting and the others in the exhibit.

The members will settle the issue **among** themselves.

bring, take

Use *bring* to mean "to carry from a distant place to a closer one." Use *take* to mean the opposite: "to carry from a nearby place to a more distant one."

Please **bring** those videotapes over here.

When you go to the store, don't forget to **take** money with you.

can, may

Can indicates the ability to do something. *May* indicates permission to do something or the possibility of doing it.

May I wear your sweater if I **can** fix the button?

Rule of Thumb: Although *can* is sometimes used in place of *may* in informal speech, you should distinguish between them when speaking and writing formally.

can't hardly, can't scarcely

These terms are considered double negatives because *hardly* and *scarcely* by themselves have a negative meaning. Therefore, avoid using *hardly* and *scarcely* with *not* or *-n't.*

Our entire class **can hardly** fit into the new classroom.

Without my glasses, I **can scarcely** see the movie screen.

capital, capitol

Use *capital* to refer to the city that is the center of government of a state or country, to money or other assets, or to a capital letter. Use *capitol* to refer to the building or group of buildings in which a state legislature meets.

Sacramento is the **capital** of California.

The **capitol** in Boston, Massachusetts, has a gold dome.

complement, compliment

A *complement* is something that fills up, completes, or makes perfect. A *compliment* is an expression of praise or admiration.

This sauce is a great **complement** for the fish.

He blushes whenever anyone pays him a **compliment.**

compose, comprise

Compose often means "to form by putting together." *Comprise* means "to contain; embrace."

The sauce was **composed** of tomatoes, fresh garlic, and chopped onions.

Our state **comprises** twelve counties.

continual, continuous

Continual describes repetitive action with pauses between occurrences. *Continuous* describes an action that continues with no interruption in space or time.

The jackhammer's **continual** bursts of noise were irritating.

The development of language is a **continuous** process.

could of, might of, must of, should of, would of

After the words *could, might, must, should,* or *would,* use the helping verb *have,* not the preposition *of.*

I don't know what **could have** gone wrong with that dishwasher.

We **must have** looked pretty silly covered with all those soapsuds!

different from, different than

The expression *different from* is generally preferred to *different than.*

John Coltrane's jazz is quite **different from** Charlie Parker's.

emigrate, immigrate

Use *emigrate* to mean "to leave one country to settle in another." Use *immigrate* to mean "to come to a country to live there permanently." Use *from* with *emigrate,* and *to* or *into* with *immigrate.*

My friend Zhu **emigrated** from China five years ago.

In the 1800s, many Irish **immigrated** to the United States.

Rule of Thumb: Remember that the *e-* in *emigrate* comes from *-ex* ("out of"); the *im-* in *immigrate* comes from *in-* ("into").

ensure, assure, insure

Ensure means "to make sure of something or to guarantee it." *Assure* means "to reassure someone or to remove doubt." *Insure* means "to cover something with insurance or to secure it."

Excellent grades should **ensure** your acceptance by a college.

I **assure** you that I will be there to meet you at 4:30.

Mortgage contracts require home buyers to **insure** the property.

farther, further

Farther refers to physical distance. *Further* refers to degree or time.

I think the monument is **farther** north.

Maybe we should stop to ask for **further** directions.

fewer, less

Use *fewer* when referring to nouns that can be counted. Use *less* when referring to nouns that cannot be counted. *Less* may also be used with figures that are seen as single amounts or single quantities.

There were **fewer** snowstorms this winter than last.

Could we have a bit **less** noise, please?

I paid **less** than $10.00 for these jeans. [The amount of money is treated as a single sum, not as individual dollars.]

good, well

Use *good* as an adjective. *Well* may be used as an adverb of manner telling how ably or adequately something is done. *Well* also may be used as an adjective meaning "in good health."

Your hair looks **good** that way. [adjective after a linking verb]

Josie did **well** on her final exam. [adverb of manner]

Grandpa says he doesn't feel **well** enough to travel. [adjective meaning "in good health."]

had of

Do not use *of* between *had* and a past participle.

I wish I **had ordered** the shrimp instead of the salmon.

hanged, hung

Use *hanged* as the past tense when you mean "put to death by hanging." Use *hung* in all other instances.

In many countries, people were once **hanged** for minor offenses.

We **hung** a flag outside our house on Flag Day.

in, into

Use *in* to mean "inside" or "within." Use *into* to indicate movement or direction from outside to a point within.

After work, Mom soaks her feet **in** warm water.

I stepped backward and fell **into** the pool.

irregardless, regardless

Use *regardless.* The prefix *ir-* and the suffix *-less* both have negative meanings. When used together, they produce a double negative, which is incorrect.

Regardless of all my studying, I still got a bad grade.

lay, lie

Lay means "to put" or "to place"; it takes a direct object. *Lie* means "to recline" or "to be positioned"; it never takes an object.

Lay your towel under that beach umbrella.

The dog likes to **lie** on the sunny deck.

learn, teach

Learn means "to gain knowledge." *Teach* means "to give knowledge."

I was twelve before I **learned** how to swim.

Mrs. Murata **teaches** algebra at our high school.

leave, let

Leave means "to go away." *Let* means "to allow" or "to permit."

Do you think she will **leave** before the holidays?

Will you **let** me borrow your notes?

like, as

Like is a preposition and introduces a prepositional phrase. *As* is a subordinating conjunction and introduces a subordinate clause. (*As* can be a preposition in some cases, as in *He served as ambassador to Ireland.*) Many authorities say that it is incorrect to use *like* before a clause.

My two-year-old sister can swim **like** a fish.

The doctor is certain, **as** we all are, that you will recover.

loose, lose

The adjective *loose* (lo͞os) means "free," "not firmly attached," or "not fitting tightly." The verb *lose* (lo͞oz) means "to have no longer," "to misplace," or "to fail to win."

You're likely to **lose** your **loose** change if you have a hole in your pocket.

Remember, it's not who wins or **loses** that matters.

passed, past *Passed* is the past form and the past participle of the verb *pass. Past* may be an adjective, a preposition, an adverb, or a noun.	A truck **passed** us at a high rate of speed. [verb] Learn from your **past** mistakes. [adjective] Turn left just after you have gone **past** the church. [preposition] As we were walking **past,** we saw smoke coming from the roof. [adverb] The man's **past** was a mystery. [noun]
precede, proceed *Precede* means "to go before" or "to come before." *Proceed* means "to continue" or "to move along."	Kennedy's and Johnson's terms in office **preceded** Nixon's. Graduates will please **proceed** directly to the auditorium.
principal, principle As an adjective, *principal* means "most important." *Principal* can also be a noun that refers to the head of a school. The noun *principle* often refers to a fundamental truth or a rule.	Dad has been chosen to be the **principal** speaker at the convention. That **principle** is stated in the Bill of Rights.
raise, rise The verb *raise* means "to cause to move upward"; it always takes an object. The verb *rise* means "to go up"; it is intransitive and does not take an object.	I always **raise** the shades immediately after I wake up. The price of swimsuits will **rise** just before summer begins.
reason . . . is that, because *Because* means "for the reason that." Therefore, do not use *because* after *reason . . . is.* Use either *reason . . . is that* or *because* alone.	The **reason** I am not going **is that** I wasn't invited. I am not going **because** I wasn't invited.
respectfully, respectively Use *respectfully* to mean "with respect." Use *respectively* to mean "in the order named."	Always speak **respectfully** to the principal. Pines and maples are evergreen and deciduous, **respectively.**

says, said

Says is the present-tense, third-person singular form of the verb *say. Said* is the past tense of *say.* Be careful not to use *says* when you are referring to the past.

Marina now **says** her family is moving to Alaska.

Last week, she **said** her family was moving to Hawaii.

sit, set

Sit means "to place oneself in a sitting position." It rarely takes an object. *Set* means "to place" or "to put," and it usually takes an object. When *set* is used to mean "the sun is going down," it does not take an object.

Please **sit** in that chair.

Please **set** down that remote control.

What time will the sun **set** tonight?

than, then

Than is a conjunction. Use it in comparisons or to show exception. The adverb *then* usually refers to time and can mean "at that time," "soon afterward," "the time mentioned," "at another time," "for that reason," or "in that case."

I know that Rachel is a better swimmer **than** I am.

I would rather be anywhere else **than** here.

My parents didn't even know one another **then.**

I went home and **then** stopped by Dad's office.

I had almost finished my errands by **then.**

If you can solve the puzzle, **then** please speak up.

their, they're, there

Their is the possessive form of *they. They're* is the contraction of *they are. There* is an adverb that often means "in that place." *There* is also sometimes used as an interjection, expressing a sense of completion.

There! The packages are finally on **their** way!

Did the Jacksons say when **they're** going to China?

You'll find the book you want over **there** on that shelf.

toward, towards

These words are interchangeable. Both prepositions mean "in the direction of."

A meteor is heading **toward** the moon.

A meteor is heading **towards** the moon.

where . . . at

Do not use *at* after a question with *where.*

Can you tell me **where** the post office is?

whereas, while

Both *whereas* and *while* can be used as conjunctions meaning "although." *Whereas* can also mean "in view of the fact that." *While* can be used as a conjunction or noun indicating time.

Gil's favorite sport is rowing, **whereas** Dwyla's is tennis.

While I can read German well, I still can't speak it fluently.

Whereas all the tests are in, class is dismissed.

Mom worked nights **while** she went to school.

Rule of Thumb: The conjunction *whereas* is usually reserved for very formal occasions.

who, whom

Use the nominative pronoun *who* for subjects.

Who caught that line drive? [subject of the verb]

Did he mention **who** won first prize? [subject of the noun clause *who won first prize*]

Who did you say will be working at the refreshment stand? [subject of the verb *will be working*]

Rule of Thumb: When a question contains an interrupting expression such as *did you say* or *do you think,* it helps to omit the interrupting phrase to determine whether to use *who* or *whom.*

Use the objective pronoun *whom* for the direct or indirect object of a verb or verbal or for the object of a preposition.

Whom are you choosing as a partner? [direct object of the verb *are choosing*]

Whom did you hear Geoff tutored in math? [direct object of the verb *tutored*]

Naomi told **whom** my secret? [indirect object]

From **whom** did you borrow this book? [object of the preposition *from*]

Rule of Thumb: When speaking informally, people often use *who* instead of *whom* as the direct object in sentences like *Who should we call?* In writing and in formal speech, however, distinguish between *who* and *whom.*

Grammar Glossary

This glossary will help you quickly locate information on parts of speech and sentence structure.

A

Abstract noun. *See* Noun chart.

Action verb. *See* Verb.

Active voice. *See* Voice.

Adjective A word that modifies a noun or pronoun by limiting its meaning. An adjective tells *what kind, which one, how many,* or *how much.* Adjectives appear in various positions in a sentence. (The *graceful* dancer leapt to the stage. That dancer is quite *graceful.*)

Many adjectives have different forms to indicate **degree of comparison.**

The **comparative** form compares two persons, places, things, or ideas. *(wilder, more careful)*

The **superlative** form compares more than two persons, places, things, or ideas. *(wildest, most careful)* Some adjectives have completely different forms to show the comparative and superlative. *(bad, worse, worst)*

A **noun used as an adjective** tells *what kind* or *which one* about the noun modified. (*paper* carton, *sycamore* tree)

Possessive nouns can be considered adjectives because they modify nouns. (*Rachel's* pen)

A **proper adjective** is formed from a proper noun and begins with a capital letter. Proper adjectives are often created by using the following suffixes: *-an, -ian, -n, -ese,* and *-ish.* *(Californian, Taiwanese)*

Adjective clause. *See* Clause.

Adverb A word that modifies a verb, an adjective, or another adverb by making its meaning more specific. Adverbs answer the questions *How? When? Where?* and *To what degree?* When modifying a verb, an adverb may appear in various positions in a sentence. (*Occasionally,* we have seen them. We have seen them *occasionally.*) When modifying an adjective or another adverb, an adverb usually appears directly before the modified word. (Your input is *extremely* valuable.)

The word *not* and the contraction *-n't* are adverbs. (You may *not* want to believe it, but it's true.) Other negative words, such as *nowhere, hardly,* and *never,* can function as adverbs of time, place, and degree. (We might *never* know.)

Some adverbs have different forms to indicate degree of comparison. The **comparative** form of an adverb compares two actions. (lasts *longer;* cleans *more easily*)

The **superlative** form compares more than two actions. (lasts *longest;* cleans *most easily*) Some adverbs have completely different forms to show the comparative and superlative. *(little, less, least)*

Adverb clause. *See* Clause.

Antecedent. *See* Pronoun.

Appositive A noun or a pronoun placed next to another noun or pronoun to identify or give additional information about it. (My history teacher, *Mrs. Barrada,* makes learning enjoyable.)

Appositive phrase. *See* Phrase.

Article The adjective *a, an,* or *the.*

Indefinite articles (*a* and *an*) refer to one of a general group of persons, places, or things. (We saw *a* snake.)

The **definite article** *(the)* indicates that the noun is a specific person, place, or thing. (It slithered behind *the* rock.)

Auxiliary verb. *See* Verb.

B

Base form. *See* Verb tense.

LANGUAGE HANDBOOK

C

Clause A group of words that has a subject and a predicate and is used as part of a sentence. Clauses fall into two categories: *main clauses,* which are also called *independent clauses,* and *subordinate clauses,* which are also called *dependent clauses.*

A **main clause** has a subject and a predicate and can stand alone as a sentence. There must be at least one main clause in every sentence. (*The team scored,* and *the crowd cheered.*)

A **subordinate clause** has a subject and a predicate, but it cannot stand alone as a sentence. A subordinate clause makes sense only when attached to a main clause. Many subordinate clauses begin with subordinating conjunctions or relative pronouns. (Let's go out for pizza *after we finish rehearsing.*) The chart on this page shows the main types of subordinate clauses.

Collective noun. *See* Noun chart.

Common noun. *See* Noun chart.

Comparative. *See* Adjective, Adverb.

Complement A word or group of words that completes the meaning of a verb. The four kinds of complements are *direct objects, indirect objects, object complements,* and *subject complements.*

A **direct object** answers the question *What?* or *Whom?* after an action verb. (Mark chopped the *garlic* and *parsley.* His mother thanked *him.*)

An **indirect object** answers the question *To whom? For whom? To what?* or *For what?* after an action verb. (Keisha gave the *lilacs* some fertilizer.)

An **object complement** answers the question *What?* after a direct object. An object complement is an adjective, a noun, or a pronoun that completes the meaning of a direct object by identifying or describing it. (I think my friends find me *humorous.* Grandpa's illness made him an *invalid.* My brothers consider the computer *theirs.*)

A **subject complement** follows a subject and a linking verb. It identifies or describes a subject. The two kinds of subject complements are *predicate nominatives* and *predicate adjectives.*

A **predicate nominative** is a noun or pronoun that follows a linking verb and gives more information about the subject. (A tomato is a *fruit.* The girl in the shop was *she.*)

A **predicate adjective** is an adjective that follows a linking verb and gives more information about the subject. (The baby seems *lethargic.* Her skin feels *hot* and *damp.*)

Complex sentence. *See* Sentence.

Compound-complex sentence. *See* Sentence.

Compound noun. *See* Noun chart.

Compound sentence. *See* Sentence.

Conjunction A word that joins single words or groups of words.

A **coordinating conjunction** joins words or groups of words

TYPES OF SUBORDINATE CLAUSES

Clause	Function	Example	Begins with . . .
Adjective clause	Modifies a noun or pronoun in the main clause	The meal *that Wanda prepared* tasted delicious.	A relative pronoun such as *which, who, whom, whose,* or *that*
Adverb clause	Modifies a verb, an adjective, or an adverb in the main clause	I didn't eat lunch *until I got home.*	A subordinating conjunction such as *after, although, because, if, since, when,* or *where*
Noun clause	Serves as a subject, an object, or a predicate nominative in the main clause	*Whoever sails* knows the value of foul-weather gear.	Words such as *how, that, what, whatever, when, where, which, whichever, who, whom, whoever, whose,* or *why*

that have equal grammatical weight in a sentence. Coordinating conjunctions include *and, but, or, so, nor, for,* and *yet.* (We visited Venice, *but* we did not ride in a gondola.)

Correlative conjunctions work in pairs to join words and groups of words of equal importance. Correlative conjunctions include *both . . . and, just as . . . so, not only . . . but (also), either . . . or, neither . . . nor,* and *whether . . . or.* (Gymnasts are *not only* physically strong *but also* limber.)

A **subordinating conjunction** joins a dependent idea or clause to a main clause. Subordinating conjunctions include *after, although, as, as far as, because, before, if, in order that, since, so that, unless, until, when,* and *while.* (Mice were first kept as pets in Asia, *as far as* researchers can tell.)

Conjunctive adverb An adverb used to clarify the relationship between clauses of equal weight in a sentence. Conjunctive adverbs have several uses: to replace *and (also, besides, furthermore, moreover);* to replace *but (however, nevertheless, still, though);* to state a result *(consequently, therefore, so, thus);* or to state equality *(equally, likewise, similarly).* (Television is a great invention; *nevertheless,* watching too much TV can be harmful.)

Coordinating conjunction. *See* Conjunction.

Correlative conjunction. *See* Conjunction.

D

Declarative sentence. *See* Sentence.

Definite article. *See* Article.

Demonstrative pronoun. *See* Pronoun.

Direct object. *See* Complement.

E F

Emphatic form. *See* Verb tense.

Exclamatory sentence. *See* Sentence.

Future tense. *See* Verb tense.

G

Gerund A verb form that ends in *–ing* and is used as a noun. A gerund may function as a subject, the object of a verb, or the object of a preposition. (*Swimming* is my favorite sport. For fun and exercise, I recommend *swimming.*)

Gerund phrase. *See* Phrase.

I

Imperative sentence. *See* Sentence.

Indefinite article. *See* Article.

Indefinite pronoun. *See* Pronoun.

Indirect object. *See* Complement.

Infinitive A verb form that begins with the word *to* and functions as a noun, an adjective, or an adverb. (Sarah tried *to smile.* The hardest thing *to remember* is your own phone number.) When *to* precedes a verb, it is not a preposition but instead signals an infinitive.

Infinitive phrase. *See* Phrase.

Intensive pronoun. *See* Pronoun.

Interjection A word or phrase that expresses emotion or exclamation. An interjection has no grammatical connection to other words in the sentence. A comma follows a mild interjection; an exclamation point follows a strong one. (*Hey,* there's Beth. *Yuck!* This milk is sour.)

Interrogative pronoun. *See* Pronoun.

Interrogative sentence. *See* Sentence.

Intransitive verb. *See* Verb.

Inverted order In a sentence written in *inverted order*, the predicate comes before the subject. Some sentences are written in inverted order for variety or special emphasis. (Down the hill *sped* the sleigh *riders.*) The subject also generally follows the predicate in a sentence that begins with *there* or *here.* (There *was* a *crowd* of children on the hill. Here *is* the starting *gate.*) Questions, or interrogative sentences, are generally written in inverted order. In many questions, an auxiliary verb precedes the subject and the main verb follows it. (*Has anyone seen* the lost scarf?) Questions that begin with *who* or *what* follow normal word order.

Irregular verb. *See* Verb tense.

L M

Linking verb. *See* Verb.

Main clause. *See* Clause.

N O

Nominative pronoun. *See* Pronoun.

Noun A word that names a person, a place, a thing, or an idea. The chart on this page shows the main types of nouns.

Noun clause. *See* Clause.

Noun of direct address A noun that refers to the person being spoken to. (*John,* please help me.)

Number A noun, pronoun, or verb is *singular* in number if it refers to one person, place, thing, or idea. It is *plural* in number if it refers to more than one.

Object complement. *See* Complement.

Objective pronoun. *See* Pronoun.

P

Participial phrase. *See* Phrase.

Participle A verb form that can function as an adjective. Present participles always end in *–ing.* Most past participles end in *-ed,* although some are irregularly formed. (I will never see that *terrifying* movie again. This container is made from *recycled* plastics.)

Passive voice. *See* Voice.

Past tense. *See* Verb tense.

Perfect tenses. *See* Verb tense.

Personal pronoun. *See* Pronoun.

Phrase A group of words that acts as a single part of speech in a sentence.

An **appositive phrase** is an appositive plus any words that modify the appositive. If it is not essential to the meaning of the sentence, an appositive phrase is set off by commas. (Mrs. Fajardo's youngest child, *a boy of about nine,* is still in grade school.)

A **gerund phrase** contains a gerund and its complements and modifiers. (*Delivering newspapers before school* is one way to earn extra money.)

An **infinitive phrase** contains an infinitive and its complements and modifiers. (*To stand beneath the Eiffel Tower* is my fondest wish.)

A **participial phrase** contains a participle and its complements and modifiers. (Students *attending the woodworking workshop* will report to Room 115.) A participial phrase at the beginning of a sentence is usually followed by a comma. (*Crouched on the windowsill,* the cat eyed a sparrow.)

A **prepositional phrase** begins with a preposition and ends with a noun or a pronoun called the **object of the preposition.** A prepositional phrase can function as an adjective, modifying a noun or a pronoun. (Students must bring permission slips *from a parent or guardian.*) A prepositional phrase may also

TYPES OF NOUNS

Noun	Function	Examples
Abstract noun	Names an idea, a quality, or a characteristic	freedom, patience, cheerfulness
Collective noun	Names a group of things or people	batch, council
Common noun	Names a general type of person, place, thing, or idea	authors, desert
Compound noun	Is made up of two or more words	playground, mother-in-law, soap opera
Possessive noun	Shows possession, ownership, or the relationship between two nouns	the *plumber's* truck
Predicate noun	Follows a linking verb and gives information about the subject	Akira is the *winner.*
Proper noun	Names a particular person, place, thing, or idea	Amy Tan, Sahara

function as an adverb when it modifies a verb, an adverb, or an adjective. (At dusk, the mosquitoes arrive *in swarms.*)

A **verb phrase** consists of one or more auxiliary verbs followed by a main verb. (Mario *should have attended* the concert.)

A **verbal phrase** is a verbal plus any complements and modifiers. The three kinds of verbals are participles, gerunds, and infinitives.

Possessive noun. *See* Noun chart.

Predicate The part of a sentence or clause that says something about the subject. The predicate contains a verb and may contain objects, complements, or modifiers.

A **simple predicate** is a verb or verb phrase that tells something about the subject of a sentence. (The judge *spoke.*)

A **complete predicate** includes the simple predicate and all the words that modify it or complete its meaning. (The Supreme Court *was created by the Constitution.*)

A **compound predicate** is made up of two or more verbs or verb phrases that are joined by a conjunction and share the same subject. (The skater *stumbled and fell.*) In a compound predicate that contains verb phrases, do not repeat the auxiliary verb (or verbs) before the second verb. (The temperature *has risen and fallen* dramatically today.)

Predicate adjective. *See* Complement.

Predicate nominative. *See* Complement.

Preposition A word that shows the relationship of a noun or pronoun to some other word in a sentence. Some common prepositions are *aboard, about, above, across, after, against, along, amid, among, around, as, at, before, behind, below, beneath, beside, besides, between, beyond, by, concerning, despite, down, during, except, excepting, for, from, in, inside, into, like, near, of, off, on, onto, past, since, through, throughout, to, toward, under, underneath.* (The Donner party struggled *through* the pass.)

A **compound preposition** is made up of more than one word. These are common compound prepositions: *according to, ahead of, along with, apart from, aside from, as to, because of, by means of, in addition to, in front of, in spite of, instead of, next to, on account of, on top of, out of, owing to.* (Please bring a salad *in addition to* a dessert.)

Prepositional phrase. *See* Phrase.

Present tense. *See* Verb tense.

Progressive form. *See* Verb tense.

Pronoun A word that takes the place of a noun, a group of words acting as a noun, or another pronoun. The word or group of words to which a pronoun refers is called its **antecedent.** (In the following sentence, *tourists* is the antecedent of the pronoun *they. When the tourists first saw the Taj Mahal, they gasped.*)

A **demonstrative pronoun** points out specific persons, places, things, or ideas. *(this, that, these, those)* (*That* play was delightful!)

An **indefinite pronoun** refers to persons, places, or things in a more general way than a noun does. *(all, another, any, anybody, anyone, anything, both, each, either, enough, everything, few, many, most, much, neither, nobody, none, no one, nothing, one, other, others, plenty, several, some)* (Has *anybody* seen my math notebook?)

PERSONAL PRONOUNS

Case	Singular	Plural	Function in Sentence
Nominative	I, you, she, he, it	we, you, they	subject or predicate nominative
Objective	me, you, her, him, it	us, you, them	direct object, indirect object, or object of a preposition
Possessive	my, mine, your, yours, her, hers, his, its	our, ours, your, yours, their, theirs	replacement for the possessive form of a noun

An **intensive pronoun** adds emphasis to another noun or pronoun in the same sentence. Intensive pronouns have the same forms as reflexive pronouns. If an intensive pronoun is left out, the sentence still has the same meaning. (The governor *himself* answered my letter.)

An **interrogative pronoun** is used to form questions. *(who? whom? whose? what? which?)*

A **personal pronoun** refers to a specific person or thing. Personal pronouns have three cases: nominative, objective, and possessive. The case depends upon the function of the pronoun in the sentence. The chart on page R41 shows the case forms of the various personal pronouns.

A **reflexive pronoun** refers, or reflects back, to a noun or pronoun earlier in the sentence, indicating that the same person or thing is involved. (Wendy helped *herself* to the chips.)

A **relative pronoun** is used to begin a subordinate clause. *(who, whom, whose, whoever, whomever, whosoever, which, whichever, whatever, that, what)*

R

Reflexive pronoun. *See* Pronoun.

Regular verb. *See* Verb tense.

Relative pronoun. *See* Pronoun.

S

Sentence A group of words expressing a complete thought. Every sentence has a subject and a predicate. Sentences can be classified by function or by structure. The chart on this page shows the categories by function. Sentences can also be categorized by structure. *See also* Clause, Predicate, Subject.

A **simple sentence** has only one main clause and no subordinate clauses. *(DeVon sings.)* It can contain a compound subject or a compound predicate or both. *(DeVon and Marina sing. DeVon sings and dances. DeVon and Marina sing and dance.)* The subject and the predicate can be expanded with adjectives, adverbs, prepositional phrases, appositives, and verbal phrases. *(DeVon, a fine tenor, sings in the chorus at the opera.)* As long as the sentence has only one main clause, however, it remains a simple sentence.

A **compound sentence** has two or more main clauses. Each main clause of a compound sentence has its own subject and predicate. The main clauses are usually joined by a comma and a coordinating conjunction. *(DeVon sings, and Marina dances. DeVon sings, and Marina dances, but Germain teaches.)* A semicolon can also be used to join the main clauses in a compound sentence. *(Marina studied both ballet and modern dance; she prefers modern dance.)*

A **complex sentence** has one main clause and one or more subordinate clauses. *(Nomads value camel milk because it can be their main source of nourishment.)*

A **compound-complex sentence** has two or more main clauses and at least one subordinate clause. *(Camels can walk great distances, but they must be fed and rested often while they are on the move.)*

TYPES OF SENTENCES

Sentence Type	Function	Ends with . . .	Examples
Declarative sentence	Makes a statement	A period	The dock needs to be repaired.
Exclamatory sentence	Expresses strong emotion	An exclamation point	Look out for that fallen wire!
Imperative sentence	Gives a command or makes a request	A period or an exclamation point	Step over here for a minute.
Interrogative sentence	Asks a question	A question mark	Do you have a book of idioms?

A **declarative sentence** makes a statement. It usually ends with a period. *(The dock needs to be repaired.)*

An **imperative sentence** gives a command or makes a request. The subject "you" is understood. An imperative sentence usually ends with a period. *([You] Step over here for a minute.)*

An **interrogative sentence** asks a question. It ends with a question mark. *(Do you have a book of idioms?)*

An **exclamatory sentence** expresses strong emotion. It ends with an exclamation point. *(Look out for that fallen wire!)*

Simple predicate. *See* Predicate.

Simple sentence. *See* Sentence.

Simple subject. *See* Subject.

Singular. *See* Number.

Subject The part of a sentence that tells what the sentence is about.

A **simple subject** is the key noun or pronoun (or word or group of words acting as a noun) in the subject. (The lonely *wolves* howl.)

A **complete subject** consists of the simple subject and all the words that modify it. (*The main focus of the speech* was traffic congestion.)

A **compound subject** is made up of two or more simple subjects that are joined by a conjunction. The subjects share the same verb. (*Photos, posters, and sports awards* hang all around my room.)

Subject complement. *See* Complement.

Subordinate clause. *See* Clause.

Subordinating conjunction. *See* Conjunction.

T

Tense. *See* Verb tense.

Transitive verb. *See* Verb.

V

Verb A word that expresses action or a state of being and is necessary to make a statement.

An **action verb** tells what someone or something does. Action verbs can express either physical or mental action. (My mother *ran* in the marathon and *remembers* that stretch of the route.)

Auxiliary verbs, or helping verbs, are words that accompany the main verb of a sentence. The forms of *be (am, is, are, was, were, being, been)* and *have (has, have, had)* are common auxiliary verbs. (I *am* sleeping. I *have* slept.) Other auxiliary verbs include *can, could; do, does, did; may, might; must; shall, should;* and *will, would.*

An **intransitive verb** is an action verb that is *not* followed by a word that answers the question *What?* or *Whom?* (Bears *hibernate* during winter.)

A **linking verb** links, or joins, the subject of a sentence with a word or expression that identifies or describes the subject. A linking verb does not show action. The most commonly used linking verb is *be* in all its forms: *am, is, are, was, were.* (Scotland's glens *are* truly lovely.) Other linking verbs are *appear, become, feel, grow, look, remain, seem, smell, sound, stay,* and *taste.*

A **transitive verb** is an action verb that is followed by a word or words that answer the question *What?* or *Whom?* (I *stuffed* my dirty clothes into a pillowcase.)

Verb tense A verb has the ability to express time–present, past, and future–by means of tense. All the verb tenses are formed from the four principal parts of a verb–a base form *(freeze)*, a present participle *(freezing)*, a simple past form *(froze)*, and a past participle *(frozen)*.

A **regular verb** forms its simple past and past participle by adding *-ed* to the base form. *(pretend, pretended)*

An **irregular verb** forms its past and past participle in some way other than by adding *-ed* to the base form. *(fall, fell, fallen)*

The **present perfect tense** expresses an action or condition that occurred at some indefinite time in the past or began in the past and continues into the present. To form the present perfect tense, use *has* or *have* with the past participle of a verb. (The Kasugas *have lived* on our block for ten years.)

The **past perfect tense** indicates that one past action or condition began and ended before another past action started. To form the past perfect tense, use *had* with the past participle of a verb. (Dad *had painted* two rooms by the time I finished one.)

The **future perfect tense** indicates that one future action or condition will begin and end before another future event starts. To form the future perfect tense, use *will have* or *shall have* with the past participle of a verb. (In this weather, the fish *will have frozen* solid by the time I get it home.)

Each of the six tenses has a **progressive form** that expresses a continuing action. To make the progressive forms, use the appropriate tense of the verb *be* with the present participle of the main verb. (They *are running.* They *will have been running.*)

The present and past tenses have additional forms, called **emphatic forms,** that add special force, or emphasis, to the verb. To form the emphatic, use *do, does,* or *did* with the base form. (I *do study* hard every day.)

Verbal A verb form that functions in a sentence as a noun, an adjective, or an adverb. The three kinds of verbals are *participles, gerunds,* and *infinitives. See* Gerund, Infinitive, Participle.

Verbal phrase. *See* Phrase.

Voice The **voice** of a verb shows whether the subject performs the action or receives the action of a verb.

A verb is in the **active voice** when the subject of the sentence performs the action. (Robert Burns *wrote* this poem.)

A verb is in the **passive voice** when the action is performed on the subject. (This poem *was written* by Robert Burns.)

Mechanics

Capitalization

This section will help you recognize and use correct capitalization.

Rule	Example
Capitalize the first word in any sentence, including the first word of a direct quotation that is a complete sentence. Capitalize sentences in parentheses unless they are contained within another sentence.	The sign in the diner said, "Waitresses who are tipped don't spill." Texas is our second largest state. (Alaska is more than twice the size of Texas.)
Rule of Thumb: Since people do not always speak in complete sentences, written dialogue may contain sentence fragments. In dialogue, capitalize the first word of each fragment, as well as of each complete sentence. For example: "Time to go home," Mom called.	
Always capitalize the pronoun *I* no matter where it appears in a sentence.	I don't know if I can ever repay them for the kindnesses I've received.
Capitalize proper nouns, including **a.** names of individuals, titles used before a proper name, and titles used in direct address	King Hussein; Governor Jeanne Shaheen Thank you, General. [direct address]
b. names of ethnic groups, national groups, political parties and their members, and languages	Chinese Americans; Iraqis; the Republican Party; Democrats; Spanish
c. names of organizations, institutions, firms, monuments, bridges, buildings, and other structures	American Cancer Society; Field Museum; Hewlett-Packard Company; Statue of Liberty; Verrazano-Narrows Bridge; Chrysler Building; Wrigley Field
d. trade names and names of documents, awards, and laws	Levi's; Treaty of Versailles; Nobel Prize; Freedom of Information Act
e. geographical terms and regions or localities	Kenya; Tennessee; Lake Champlain; Fifth Avenue; Far East
f. names of planets and other heavenly bodies	Venus; Andromeda; Sirius; Io; Crab Nebula
g. names of ships, planes, trains, and spacecraft	HMS *Queen Elizabeth II;* the *Spruce Goose; Twentieth Century Limited; Challenger*

Rule	Example
h. names of most historical events, eras, calendar terms, and religious terms	Civil War; Great Depression; Age of Reason; Tuesday; March; Thanksgiving Day; Allah; Mormon; Hinduism; Christmas; Talmud
i. titles of literary works and publications, works of art, and musical compositions	*Beloved; Seventeen; The Thinker; American Gothic; Schindler's List;* "Kiss from a Rose"
j. specific names of school courses	Philosophy II
Capitalize proper adjectives (adjectives formed from proper nouns).	Central American governments; Elizabethan collar; Indian spices; Jewish synagogue

Punctuation

This section will help you use punctuation marks correctly.

Rule	Example
Use a **period** at the end of a declarative sentence or an imperative sentence (a polite command or request).	These prices are higher than I expected. Please hand me that spatula.
Use an **exclamation point** to show strong feeling or after a forceful command.	Wow! What a fantastic play that was!
Use a **question mark** to indicate a direct question.	What kind of computer do you have?
Use a **colon:** **a.** to introduce a list (especially after a statement that uses such words as *these, the following,* or *as follows*) and to introduce material that explains, illustrates, or restates preceding material	Noted American aviators include these: Wiley Post, Charles Lindbergh, and Amelia Earhart. Nathan must be feeling better: he asked to borrow my tennis racket.
Rule of Thumb: Do not use a colon between a verb and its complement. To be used correctly, a colon must follow a complete sentence.	
b. to introduce a long or formal quotation	Winston Churchill said this about public speaking: "If you have an important point to make, don't try to be subtle or clever. Use a pile driver. . . ."

Rule	Example
c. in statements of precise time, in biblical chapter and verse references, and after business-letter salutations	2:34 A.M. 2 Kings 11:12 Dear Mr. Fleming: Ladies and Gentlemen:
Use a **semicolon:**	
a. to separate main clauses that are not joined by a coordinating conjunction	Hawaii's climate is mild all year round; many travelers choose to visit the islands in summer.
b. to separate main clauses joined by a conjunctive adverb or by an expression such as *for example* or *that is*	There are 132 Hawaiian islands; however, nearly all residents live on seven of the islands. Hawaiian muumuus and aloha shirts are often colorful; that is, they are brightly patterned.
c. to separate the items in a series when these items contain commas	Hawaiian words familiar to many mainlanders include *luau,* which means "feast"; *aloha,* which can mean "love," "welcome," or "farewell"; and *hula,* which means "dance."
d. to separate two main clauses joined by a coordinating conjunction when such clauses already contain several commas	Travel ads often focus on Oahu's attractions, such as Waikiki Beach, Pearl Harbor, and Diamond Head; but the state has many other interesting sites.
Use a **comma:**	
a. between the main clauses of a compound sentence	I recognize her, but I can't think of her name.
b. to separate three or more words, phrases, or clauses in a series	Ayala is a member of the Debaters' Club, the Glee Club, and the swimming team.
c. between coordinate modifiers	She is a smart, athletic student.
d. to set off interjections, parenthetical expressions, and conjunctive adverbs	Max is, in fact, a sports fanatic.
e. to set off long introductory prepositional phrases	After several days of constant exposure to the sun, your skin will be dry and leathery.

Rule of Thumb: Use a comma after a short introductory prepositional phrase only if the sentence would be misread without it.

Rule	Example
f. to set off nonessential words, clauses, and phrases	
–introductory adverb clauses	Although Petra can read English well, her spoken English is not very fluent.
–internal adverb clauses that interrupt a sentence's flow	Those orange and black birds, unless I am mistaken, are Baltimore orioles.
–adjective clauses	Some of Frank Stella's paintings, which hang in many museums, have oddly shaped canvases.
–participles and participial phrases	The prize winners, beaming, rushed to the stage.
	Chasing after squirrels, the dog injured her foot.
–infinitive phrases	To speak frankly, I don't care for that design.
–appositives and appositive phrases	Dolphins and bats, both mammals, can hear much higher frequencies than humans can hear.

Rule of Thumb: Nonessential elements can be removed without changing the meaning of the sentence.

Rule	Example
g. to set off quotations in dialogue	"Yesterday," announced Kayla, "I won the debate."
h. to set off an antithetical phrase	Dawna, unlike Theresa, enjoys playing chess.
i. to set off a title after a person's name	Michael Todesca, M.S.W.; Delyna Smith, chair of the committee
j. to separate the various parts of an address, a geographical term, or a date	St. Louis, Missouri Saturday, July 4
	December 7, 1941 Cambridge, MA 02138
k. after the salutation of an informal letter and after the closing of all letters	Dear Mom and Dad, Sincerely,
l. to set off parts of a reference that direct the reader to the exact source	This rule is found in *The Chicago Manual of Style*, chapter 10, paragraph 83.
m. to set off words or names used in direct address and in tag questions	Keon, could you tutor me in algebra?
	You've never had chicken pox, have you?

Rule	Example
Use a **dash** to signal a change in thought or to set off and emphasize supplemental information or parenthetical comments. **Rule of Thumb:** A good test of the correct use of dashes is to delete the information that the dashes set off. If the remaining sentence retains its basic meaning, then the dashes were properly used. If the remaining sentence has lost crucial information, then the dashes were improperly used.	Mammoth Cave—its name is appropriate—has about 300 miles of tunnels. Hiroko went to college here—in the United States, I mean.
Use **parentheses** to set off supplemental material. A complete parenthetical sentence contained within another sentence is not capitalized and needs no period. If a parenthetical expression contained within another sentence requires a question mark or exclamation point, put the punctuation mark *inside* the parentheses.	Plain popcorn (lightly salted if desired) is a healthful and filling snack. Locusts form swarms (these insects are usually solitary) when their food supply is exhausted. I felt an incredible sense of relief (just think what might have happened!) when the plane landed.
Use **quotation marks:** **a.** to enclose a direct quotation, as follows:	Speaking of another writer's novel, Gore Vidal remarked, "This is not at all bad, except as prose."
When a quotation is interrupted, use two sets of quotation marks.	"All the really good ideas I ever had," said artist Grant Wood, "came to me while I was milking a cow."
Use single quotation marks around a quotation within a quotation.	Joe Namath, the legendary quarterback, said, "Till I was 13, I thought my name was 'Shut Up.'"
In writing dialogue, begin a new paragraph and use a new set of quotation marks every time the speaker changes.	"Dad, may I borrow five dollars?" I asked. "What for?" Dad replied. "Um, actually, it's for your Father's Day present," I answered sheepishly.
b. to enclose titles of short works, such as stories, poems, essays, articles, chapters, and songs	"Barometer Soup" is a song on that Jimmy Buffett CD.

Rule	Example
c. to enclose unfamiliar slang terms and unusual expressions	What does the slang word "dis" mean? Tom Wolfe coined the expression "radical chic."

Rule of Thumb: To tell whether question marks and exclamation points go inside or outside quotation marks, see how the quotation would be punctuated if it stood alone. If the quotation is a question or an exclamation, then the punctuation mark should go inside the quotation marks. If the quotation would end with a period, then the question mark or exclamation point should go outside the quotation marks.

Rule	Example
Use **italics:** **a.** for titles of books, lengthy poems, plays, films, television series, paintings and sculptures, long musical compositions, court cases, names of newspapers and magazines, ships, trains, airplanes, and spacecraft. Italicize and capitalize articles *(a, an, the)* at the beginning of a title only when they are part of the title.	*Beowulf* [long poem]; *Biography* [television series] *The Potato Eaters* [painting] *Appalachian Spring* [long musical composition] *Ebony* [magazine] *Eagle* [spacecraft] *Spirit of St. Louis* [airplane] *The Old Man and the Sea* [book] the *Boston Globe* [newspaper]
b. for foreign words and expressions that are not used frequently in English	The rider enjoyed the attention he got when he wore his *charro* costume.
c. for words, letters, and numerals used to represent themselves	The word *stationery*, with an *e*, refers to writing paper. I mistook your *3* for an *8*.
Use an **apostrophe:** **a.** to create a possessive form, as follows: Add an apostrophe and -*s* to all singular indefinite pronouns, singular nouns, plural nouns not ending in -*s*, and compound nouns. Add only an apostrophe to a plural noun that ends in -*s*.	nobody's fault — New Mexico's climate children's welfare — mass's density baby-sitter's duties — seat belt's buckle flowers' petals — Wongs' party
If two or more entities possess something jointly, use the possessive form for the last entity named. If they possess it individually, use the possessive form for each entity's name.	Aunt Ellie and Uncle Ed's house Microsoft's and Apple's operating systems

Rule	Example
b. to express amounts of money or time that modify a noun	a twelve dollars' savings a two weeks' delay [You can use a hyphenated adjective instead: a *two-week delay*.]
c. in place of omitted letters or numerals	can't [cannot] the crash of '29
d. with *-s* to form the plural of letters, numerals, symbols, and words used as words.	7's *p*'s and *q*'s +'s Your speech contains too many *whosoever*'s and *nevertheless*'s.
Use a **hyphen**: **a.** after any prefix joined to a proper noun or proper adjective	mid-July pre-Raphaelite
b. after the prefixes *all-*, *ex-*, and *self-* joined to any noun or adjective; after the prefix *anti-* when it joins a word beginning with *i;* after the prefix *vice-* (except in *vice president*); and to avoid confusion between words that begin with *re-* and look like another word	ex-husband self-conscious anti-inflammatory vice-regent re-mark the sale tags make a snide remark re-sign the document resign from her job

Rule of Thumb: Remember that the prefix *anti-* requires a hyphen when followed by a word that begins with *i* in order to prevent spelling words with two successive *i*'s. Otherwise, *anti-* does not require a hyphen except before a capitalized word.

Rule	Example
c. in a compound adjective that precedes a noun	a thirty-year career his tear-stained face
d. in any spelled-out cardinal or ordinal numbers up to *ninety-nine* or *ninety-ninth* and with a fraction used as an adjective	forty-nine twenty-third two-thirds cup
e. to divide a word at the end of a line between syllables or pronounceable parts	sur-face en-hanced

Abbreviations

Abbreviations are shortened forms of words. This section will help you learn how to use abbreviations correctly.

Rule	Example
Use only one period if an abbreviation occurs at the end of a sentence. If the sentence ends with a question mark or an exclamation point, use the period *and* the second mark of punctuation.	I addressed the letter to Jane Parsons, R.N. Do your friends live in the U.K.? It's already 11:00 P.M.!
Capitalize abbreviations of proper nouns and abbreviations related to dates and times.	George W. Bush; Morrissey Blvd. 767 B.C.; A.D. 1910; 6:15 A.M.
Use all capital letters and no periods for abbreviations of organization names that are pronounced letter by letter or as words.	IBM, SPCA, NOAA AMA, DOT, NYPD NFL, FBI, GSA
When addressing mail, use the official ZIP-code abbreviations of state names (two capital letters, no periods).	AZ (Arizona); CA (California) IL (Illinois); OK (Oklahoma) SC (South Carolina); DC (District of Columbia)
Use abbreviations for some personal titles.	Arthur Ashe Jr.; Dr. Caitlin Connor Maj. Jacob Stern; Olivia DiMario, A.R.N.P. Mrs. Anita Brown; Rev. Billy Graham
Abbreviate units of measure used with numerals in technical or scientific writing, but not in ordinary prose.	mi. (mile); oz. (ounce); tsp. (teaspoon) l (liter); kg (kilogram); cm (centimeter)

Rule of Thumb: In a letter it is appropriate to use a state abbreviation in the address. In other forms of writing, such as expository writing, spell out the name of a state.

Numbers and Numerals

This section will help you understand when to use numerals and when to spell out numbers.

Rule	Example
In general, spell out cardinal and ordinal numbers that can be written in one or two words.	I am one of twenty-nine students in Ms. Chung's algebra class. For the hundredth time, please turn the radio off.
Spell out any number that occurs at the beginning of a sentence.	Six thousand five hundred tickets were sold for the festival on Saturday.
In general, use numerals (numbers expressed in figures) to express numbers that would be written in more than two words. Extremely high numbers are often expressed as a numeral followed by the word *million* or *billion.*	There are 767 students in our high school. In 1977 a Soviet woman parachuted to the earth from an altitude of 48,556 feet. The federal deficit was about $350 billion that year.
If related numbers appear in the same sentence, use all numerals.	There are over 25,000 seats in the arena, but only about 1,000 have been reserved to date.
Use numerals to express amounts of money, decimals, and percentages.	$1.1 trillion 2.2 children per family 99.99 percent
Use numerals to express the year and day in a date and to express the precise time with the abbreviations *A.M.* and *P.M.*	Martin Luther King Jr. died on April 4, 1968. The carpenter said he'd be here by 8:30 A.M.
Spell out a number to express a century or when the word *century* is used, or to express a decade when the century is clear from the context. When a century and a decade are expressed as a single unit, use numerals followed by *-s.*	The United Kingdom of Great Britain—including England, Scotland, and Wales—was formed early in the eighteenth century. In the forties, however, England and Scotland were still fighting. American involvement in the Vietnam War in the 1960s and early 1970s became very controversial.
Use numerals for streets and avenues numbered above ten and for all house, apartment, and room numbers.	1422 West 31st Street 623 Third Avenue Room 273 Apartment 3B
Use numerals to express page and line numbers.	You'll find that reference on page 952, line 23.

Spelling

The following basic rules, examples, and exceptions will help you master the spellings of many words.

ie and *ei*

Many writers find the rules for certain combinations of letters, like *ie* and *ei,* difficult to remember. One helpful learning strategy is to develop a rhyme to remember a rule. Look at the following rhyme for the *ie* and *ei* rule.

Rule	Example
Put *i* before *e,*	pier, grief, shriek, yield
except after *c,*	deceive, conceit, conceive
or when sounded like *a,*	heiress, weight, skein
as in *neighbor* and *weigh.*	feint, unveiled, eighty

EXCEPTIONS: seize, leisure, weird, height, either, forfeit, protein.

-cede, -ceed, and *-sede*

Because different combinations of letters in English are sometimes pronounced the same way, it is often easy to make slight spelling errors. Except for the exceptions below, spell the *sēd* sound at the end of a word as *cede:*

recede **intercede** **secede**

EXCEPTION: One word uses *-sede* to spell the final *sēd* sound: supersede.

EXCEPTION: Three words use *-ceed* to spell the final *sēd* sound: proceed, exceed, succeed.

Unstressed vowels

Notice the vowel sound in the second syllable of the word *or-i-gin.* This is the unstressed vowel sound; dictionary respellings use the *schwa* symbol (ə) to indicate it. Because any of several vowels can be used to spell this sound, writers are often uncertain about which vowel to use. To help spell words with unstressed vowels correctly, try thinking of a related word in which the syllable containing the vowel sound is stressed.

Unknown Spelling	Related Word	Correct Spelling
pos_tive	position	positive
ess_nce	essential	essence
insp_ration	inspire	inspiration
emph_sis	emphatic	emphasis

Adding prefixes

When adding a prefix to a word, keep the original spelling of the word. If the prefix forms a double letter, keep both letters.

dis + obey = disobey
ir + rational = irrational
mis + laid = mislaid

Suffixes and the silent e

Many English words end in a silent letter *e.* Sometimes the *e* is dropped when a suffix is added. When adding a suffix that begins with a consonant to a word that ends in silent *e,* keep the *e.*

idle + ness = idleness
live + ly = lively

COMMON EXCEPTIONS: awe + ful = awful; judge + ment = judgment

When adding the suffix *-y* or a suffix that begins with a vowel to a word that ends in silent *e,* usually drop the *e.*

grime + y = grimy
sense + ible = sensible

COMMON EXCEPTION: mile + age = mileage

When adding a suffix that begins with *a* or *o* to a word that ends in *ce* or *ge,* keep the *e* so the word will retain the soft *c* or *g* sound.

outrage + ous = outrageous
notice + able = noticeable
salvage + able = salvageable

When adding a suffix that begins with a vowel to a word that ends in *ee* or *oe,* keep the *e.*

free + ing = freeing
canoe + able = canoeable
decree + ing = decreeing

Suffixes and the final *y*

When adding a suffix to a word that ends in a consonant + *y,* change the *y* to *i* unless the suffix begins with *i.* Keep the *y* in a word that ends in a vowel + *y.*

pry + ed = pried
betray + ed = betrayed
essay + ist = essayist

defy + ing = defying
annoy + ing = annoying
gray + ish = grayish

Doubling the final consonant

When adding a suffix to a word that ends in a consonant, double the final consonant if it is preceded by a single vowel and the word is one syllable, if the accent is on the last syllable and remains there even after the suffix is added, or if the word is made up of a prefix and a one-syllable word.

plug + ing = plugging	map + ed = mapped
propel + or = propellor	deter + ent = deterrent
recap + ing = recapping	disbar + ed = disbarred

Do not double the final consonant if the accent is not on the last syllable or if the accent shifts when the suffix is added. Also do not double the final consonant if it is preceded by two vowels or by another consonant. If the word ends in a consonant and the suffix begins with a consonant, do not double the final consonant.

alter + ed = altered	confer + ence = conference
contain + er = container	descend + ant = descendant
assess + ment = assessment	pain + ful = painful

Adding *-ly* and *-ness*

When adding *-ly* to a word that ends in a single *l,* keep the *l.* If the word ends in a double *l,* drop one *l.* When the word ends in a consonant + *le,* drop the *le.* When adding *-ness* to a word that ends in *n,* keep the *n.*

usual + ly = usually	shrill + ly = shrilly
crumble + ly = crumbly	plain + ness = plainness

Forming compound words

When joining a word that ends in a consonant to a word that begins with a consonant, keep both consonants.

class + mate = classmate	keep + sake = keepsake
book + store = bookstore	fiber + glass = fiberglass

Forming plurals

English words form plurals in many ways. Most nouns simply add *-s.* The following chart shows other ways of forming plural nouns and some common exceptions to the pattern.

GENERAL RULES FOR FORMING PLURALS		
If a noun ends in	**Rule**	**Example**
ch, s, sh, x, z	add *-es*	lynx, lynxes
a consonant + *y*	change *y* to *i* and add *-es*	calamity, calamities
o or a vowel + *y*	add *-s*	barrio, barrios; array, arrays
a consonant + *o* common exceptions	generally add *-es* but sometimes add only *-s*	tomato, tomatoes silo, silos; halo, halos
f or *ff* common exceptions	add *-s* change *f* to *v* and add *-es*	chef, chefs; cuff, cuffs leaf, leaves; loaf, loaves
lf	change *f* to *v* and add *-es*	calf, calves
fe	change *f* to *v* and add *-s*	wife, wives

A few plurals are exceptions to the rules in the previous chart, but they are easy to remember. The following chart lists these plurals and some examples.

SPECIAL RULES FOR FORMING PLURALS	
Rule	**Example**
To form the plural of proper names and one-word compound nouns, follow the general rules for plurals.	Shabazz, Shabazzes Friedman, Friedmans overleaf, overleaves
To form the plural of hyphenated compound nouns or compound nouns of more than one word, make the most important word plural.	mother-in-law, mothers-in-law chief of staff, chiefs of staff solicitor general, solicitors general
Some nouns have unusual plural forms.	foot, feet goose, geese louse, lice
Some nouns have the same singular and plural forms.	moose deer series

Writing Handbook

The Writing Process

Writing is a process with various stages: *prewriting*, *drafting*, *revising*, *editing/proofreading*, and *publishing/presenting*. Using these five stages of the writing process will allow you to investigate and write about any topic. Good writers move back and forth among stages in the writing process. For example, if you're having trouble drafting a paragraph, you might go back to the prewriting stage and outline it first. As you revise, you may find you need to redraft some of your writing. You may even need to gather more information or reevaluate your purpose.

The Writing Process

Prewriting → Drafting → Revising → Editing/Proofreading → Publishing/Presenting

Prewriting

The first stage, called prewriting, is the idea stage. By probing your thoughts, you can discover a topic and a purpose for writing about it. Prewriting includes exploring and gathering ideas and information, defining and refining the topic, and making a plan for a piece of writing.

Exploring ideas

The following suggestions will help you get started.

- Determine your purpose for writing (for a class assignment? to express your opinion?).
- Identify the audience (who you expect to read your writing).
- Think about what your purpose and audience suggest about the information you will provide and the way you will present your material.

The following techniques will help you find a topic to write about:

- Begin with an idea that interests you.
- Brainstorm for topics with a group of classmates.
- Look through your journals, scrapbooks, and photo albums for ideas.
- Check out the topics in a library catalog.
- Page through magazines and newspapers.

Gathering information

If you are writing to inform readers about a specific topic, now is the time to do research to find information. If you are writing about a topic based on personal experience, use techniques such as freewriting and listing to gather material.

- Freewriting is writing nonstop for a set time, usually only five or ten minutes. The idea is to keep pace with your thoughts, getting them on paper before they vanish. Freewriting can start anywhere and go anywhere.
- Listing involves starting with a key word or idea and then listing other ideas as they occur to you. When listing, don't worry about order or transitions; just let ideas flow freely from one to the next.

As you gather ideas and information, jot them down on note cards to use as you draft.

Organizing your material

Looking at the material you have gathered, define your topic. Then refine the scope of your topic so that it is neither too general nor too specific. Organize your information and ideas into a plan that serves as the basis for your writing.

- Choose an order in which to present your ideas. Some common organizing techniques include order of importance, spatial order, cause-and-effect order, and chronological order.
- Find and include missing information or ideas that might add interest or help accomplish the purpose of your writing.
- Develop a rough outline of your main points and supporting material, reflecting the order you have chosen.

Drafting

Translate the ideas and information you gathered during prewriting into a written draft. The goal during drafting is to let your writing flow without worrying about grammar or mechanics. Concentrate on your ideas at this point and evaluate your writing later.

Tips for drafting

- Follow the plan you made during prewriting, but remain flexible. Organize your material in the way that best accomplishes your purpose. Transform notes and ideas into related sentences and paragraphs.
- Make sure that each paragraph has a main idea that can be stated in a topic sentence. Also include supporting details such as sensory images, examples or anecdotes, quotations, facts, statistics, and reasons.
- Create logical links between sentences in a paragraph and between paragraphs by using transition words and phrases.
- Develop an introduction that will catch the interest of your intended audience.

Revising

After you finish your draft, put it aside and do something else for a while. Then look again at your draft to find ways to improve it. As you revise, review your draft to check that it accomplishes your purpose, and make whatever adjustments are necessary. At this stage you may add more information to clarify your ideas; you may also delete information that distracts from your overall purpose. Or you may decide to organize your information in a different way. Good writers often revise their writing several times before they are satisfied. Getting feedback from a peer is an important step in the revision process.

Using peer review

Ask one or more of your classmates to read your draft. You can direct their responses in some specific ways.

- Have readers tell you in their own words what they have read. If you do not hear your ideas restated, you will want to revise for clarity.
- Ask readers to tell you what parts of your writing they liked best and why. You may want to expand those elements as you revise.
- Discuss the ideas in your writing with your readers. Have them share their own ideas about the topic. Include in your revision any new insights you gain.
- Ask readers for their suggestions in specific areas, such as organization, word choice, or examples.

You may want to take notes on your readers' suggestions so you will have a handy reference as you revise. Finally, weigh your peer responses carefully. Compare them with your own insights. Use what is most helpful to revise your draft.

Tips for revising

Ask yourself the following questions.

- Have I said what I intended to say clearly and completely?
- Is my writing appropriate for my intended audience?
- Is the order of my information and ideas logical and effective?
- Have I developed my ideas clearly and with enough detail?
- Have I included examples that are meaningful to my intended audience?
- Do all of my details support my main idea? Have I included any irrelevant information or distracting details?
- Have I achieved my purpose in writing?

Editing/Proofreading

In the editing stage, you polish your revised draft and proofread it for errors in grammar and spelling. Use this proofreading checklist to help you check for errors, and use the proofreading symbols in the chart below to mark places that need corrections.

- ☑ Have I avoided run-on sentences and sentence fragments and punctuated sentences correctly?
- ☑ Have I used every word correctly, including plurals, possessives, and frequently confused words?
- ☑ Do verbs and subjects agree? Are verb tenses correct?
- ☑ Do pronouns refer clearly to their antecedents and agree with them in person, number, and gender?
- ☑ Have I used adverb and adjective forms and modifying phrases correctly?
- ☑ Have I spelled every word correctly, and checked the unfamiliar ones in a dictionary?

Proofreading Symbols

⊙	Lieut Brown	Insert a period.
∧	No one came the party.	Insert a letter or a word.
≡	I enjoyed paris.	Capitalize a letter.
/	The Class ran a bake sale.	Make a capital letter lowercase.
⁀ ‿	The campers are home sick.	Close up a space.
(sp)	They visited N.Y. (sp)	Spell out.
∧ ∧	Sue please come I need your help.	Insert a comma or a semicolon.
	He enjoyed feild day.	Transpose the position of letters or words.
#	alltogether	Insert a space.
ℊ	We went to to Boston.	Delete letters or words.
∨ ∨ ∨	She asked, Who's coming?	Insert quotation marks or an apostrophe.
/=/	mid January	Insert a hyphen.
¶	"Where?" asked Karl. "Over there," said Ray.	Begin a new paragraph.

Publishing/Presenting

There are a number of ways you can share your work. You could publish it in a magazine, a class anthology, or another publication, or read your writing aloud to a group. You could also join a writer's group and read one another's works.

Writing Modes

Writing can be classified under four basic headings: expository, narrative, descriptive, and persuasive. Each of these types, or modes, of writing has a specific purpose or cluster of purposes.

Expository Writing

Expository writing is writing that informs and explains. An essay response to an exam question may be expository. Other examples of expository writing include instructions, magazine articles, business reports, and textbooks.

The chart below lists five basic types of expository writing and a suggested way in which each type can be developed.

Use this checklist as you write.

- ☑ **Have I explained my subject thoroughly and clearly?**
- ☑ **Is the opening engaging and the conclusion effective?**
- ☑ **Is the information well organized?**
- ☑ **Do supporting details bring the subject to life?**
- ☑ **Are my comparisons complete and clearly stated?**

Type	Introduction	Body	Conclusion
Definition	Identify the item you are defining, and clearly state your purpose for writing.	Supply details that will give your readers a clear understanding of the item you are defining.	Summarize the definition, and explain its relevance to your readers.
Process	State the process you are explaining and its relevance.	List the steps of the process clearly, using transitions *(first, second, next, finally)* to show the relationships between the steps.	Emphasize the importance of the process, and identify its benefits to your audience.
Cause and effect	Write a thesis statement that makes the cause-and-effect relationship clear.	Organize the material into a cause-to-effect or an effect-to-cause pattern. Use transitions that point out causes and effects *(as a result, due to, therefore)* and that indicate degrees of certainty *(certainly, possibly, likely)*.	Summarize the cause-and-effect relationship, or extend the information you've presented.
Classification	Begin with a thesis statement or topic sentence, and a list of categories.	Explain each category, one by one, and include examples.	Summarize your classification and its significance.
Comparison and contrast	Identify the subjects you are comparing and your purpose for making the comparison.	List the similarities and differences among the subjects. Organize comparison-contrast by subject or by feature.	Summarize your discussion, and note its significance.

Descriptive Writing

Good descriptive writing depends on the creation of vivid word pictures and the organization of those pictures into an effective pattern. Writers may choose to describe a location, a character, an object, or an idea or feeling.

Use the checklist at the right for tips to help you revise your descriptive writing.

- ☑ Have I used details consistently to establish and maintain a believable mood?
- ☑ Did I select good details and organize them logically around a topic sentence?
- ☑ Have I kept the same kind of order throughout the description?
- ☑ Would adding transitional words and phrases help orient my readers?
- ☑ Have I chosen precise nouns and modifiers?

Narrative Writing

A narrative is a story—containing characters, setting, and plot—that relates a sequence of events. These events usually involve a conflict, or struggle, between a character and another person or a force of nature, or between ideas or values. Narratives may be true (nonfiction) or imagined (fiction).

Use this checklist to refine your narrative.

- ☑ Did I select and develop a conflict that can hold my readers' attention?
- ☑ Did I present background events and details that explain the basis of the conflict?
- ☑ Do my characters believably resolve the conflict?
- ☑ Does my narration present a clear and consistent point of view?
- ☑ Does the order in which I present the events in the narrative make sense?
- ☑ Did I use dialogue and anecdotes correctly?

Persuasive Writing

Persuasive writing is writing that tries to influence a reader to accept an idea, adopt a point of view, or take action on an issue. Effective persuasive writing uses strong, relevant evidence to support its claims. This kind of writing usually requires preparation, research, organization, note-taking, and careful consideration of language.

As you revise your persuasive writing, use this checklist as a guide.

- ☑ Have I presented my central claim clearly?
- ☑ Have I addressed opposing viewpoints?
- ☑ Is my evidence accurate and relevant?
- ☑ Is my reasoning sound?
- ☑ Have I clearly stated what action I want my readers to take?
- ☑ Have I presented my case in a way that will appeal to my audience?

Research Paper Writing

The research paper differs from many other kinds of writing because it includes factual information from a variety of sources. Careful planning and a step-by-step approach will result in a successful and engaging research paper.

Types of Research Papers

Research papers come in many types. This chart lists the most common.

Type	Description
Summary	The writer explores a topic by summing up the works and/or opinions of other writers and researchers.
Evaluative	The writer states an opinion and backs it up with evidence found in primary and/or secondary sources.
Original	The writer does original research that leads to new insights or information about the topic.
Combination	The writer combines approaches in one paper, such as summarizing opinions and then conducting original research.

Guidelines for Writing a Research Paper

After identifying the type of research paper you will write, you can begin the process of putting the paper together. Follow these guidelines when writing a research paper.

Make a schedule

Time before paper is due	Task
Four weeks	Begin planning, researching, and outlining
Three weeks	Start drafting the paper
Two weeks	Begin to revise
One week	Start editing

Choose a topic

Skim through books and encyclopedia articles to find an interesting topic or an intriguing aspect of an assigned topic that is neither too broad nor too narrow. A topic is probably too broad if the library has several books on it or if the encyclopedia gives it more than two pages. A topic may be too narrow if you can find only one or two articles on it and if the encyclopedia doesn't cover it.

Generate research questions

To help focus your research, frame three to seven questions to answer first. Base these questions on your central idea. As you research the answers to your questions, other questions may come up. Working with these questions and their answers will help you refine your topic.

Evaluate sources

There are two kinds of sources: primary and secondary.

A **primary source** is a firsthand account of an event–that is, one written by someone who actually experienced or observed the event. *Never Cry Wolf,* in which Farley Mowat describes his personal observations of a wolf family, is an example of a primary source.

A **secondary source** is one written by a person who has researched and interpreted primary sources.

Whether they are primary or secondary, make sure all your sources are

- authoritative–written by recognized authors in the field.
- reliable–published in reputable books, newspapers, Web sites, or periodicals.
- timely–the most recent available.
- suitable–appropriate and relevant to your topic and, if your topic is controversial, representative of differing views.

Develop a working bibliography

Your bibliography is a record of the books, articles, and other sources you will consult for your paper. Writing complete bibliography cards will make it easier to compile the final list of works cited. When you have found a source, skim it to see if it has any useful information. Look at tables of contents, indexes, chapter titles, and graphic aids to efficiently locate information. If the source looks promising, record the publication data–the title and author, the publishing company, the city, and date of publication–on a three-by-five index card. Number your cards in the upper right-hand corner so you can keep them in order. You might also include the name of the place where you found the source and any other information to help you locate that source again if you need it. You can also write yourself notes on the cards.

Sample bibliography, or source, cards

Book

- Source number: 1
- Author(s): *Kershaw, Alex.*
- Title: *Jack London: A Life.*
- City of publication/Publisher/Date of publication: *New York: St. Martin's, 1995.*
- Place: *Springfield Public Library*
- Call number: *B121.L*

Magazine

- Source number: 3
- Author: *Seaman, Donna.*
- Title of article: *"Review of Jack London: A Life."*
- Name of magazine/Date: *Booklist 1 Jan 1998:*
- Page: *764.*
- Place: *Springfield Public Library*

Online Article

- Source number: 14
- Author: *Stasz, Dr. Clarice.*
- Title: *"Jack [John Griffith] London."*
- Title of the database or project: *Berkeley Digital Library SunSITE.*
- Sponsoring organization/Date of access: *Library, U.C. Berkeley. 2 Mar. 2001*
- URL: <http://sunsite.berkeley.edu/London/jackbio.html>

Take notes

- As you find a piece of information that you can use, write it on a note card.
- In the upper right-hand corner of the note card, write the number of the source from the working bibliography.
- If you jot your own thoughts down on note cards, initial them so you will know they are yours.
- Place any direct quotations in quotation marks.
- Write the number of the page from which you have recorded or summarized information.

Sample Note Card

14

London's involvement with agriculture

London used terracing and manure spreading on his California ranch. He had observed these techniques in Japan. In America at this time they were considered unusual—almost revolutionary. (p. 43)

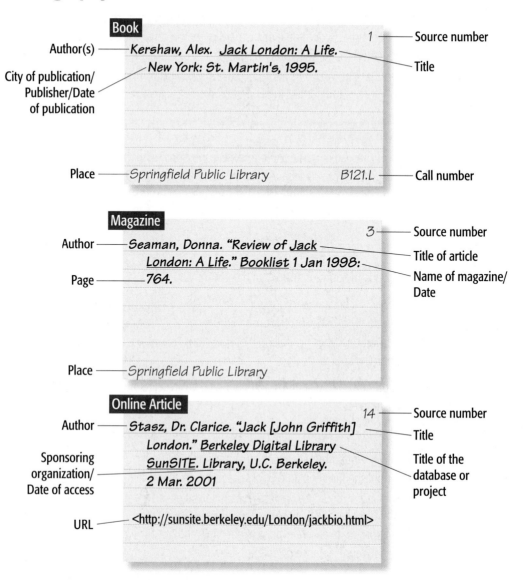

Create a working outline

Create a working outline to help you think about your topic critically and make your research efficient. The following tips will help you create your outline.

- Look for similarities in your notes; group note cards on similar topics together. Use each group as a main topic in your outline.
- Within groups cluster similar note cards into subgroups that elaborate on the larger and more general main topic. Use these subgroups as the subtopics in your outline.
- Arrange main topics to build on your central idea.
- As you continue your research and learn more, revise and elaborate your outline.
- Before you begin your first draft, prepare a final outline.

Sample Outline

Jack London—More than an Author

I. Childhood and youth
  A. Early years
  B. Young adulthood
II. Literary career
  A. Early efforts
  B. Great literary successes
III. Other interests
  A. Champion of social causes
    1. Woman suffrage
    2. Prohibition
  B. Agricultural accomplishments

Develop a thesis statement

A thesis statement is a concise idea that you try to prove, expand on, or illustrate in your writing. To write a thesis statement, rewrite your central idea into a clear, concise sentence. Make sure your sentence describes your topic and tells how you will approach the topic in the rest of the paper. This statement will help you keep on track as you write.

Draft your paper, using your outline and notes

After you have made an outline and written your thesis statement, you are ready to begin drafting. Concentrate on getting all your ideas and information down on paper. You can revise your draft later.

Cite your sources

To avoid plagiarism, which is presenting someone else's ideas or statements as your own, your research paper must indicate the sources of the information presented–including all ideas, statements, quotes, and statistics taken from sources and not considered common knowledge. The reference should precede the punctuation mark that concludes the sentence, clause, or phrase containing the material you are citing.

Parenthetical documentation If an author is obvious from the text of the paper (for example, if the text reads "As Ferguson points out . . ."), just insert the page number in parentheses. If the author is not obvious, however, use one of these forms of parenthetical documentation.

Type of Source	Style of Citation	Example
One author	Author's last name and page number in parentheses	(Kershaw 122)
Two or three authors	Authors' last names and page number in parentheses	(Gleiter and Thompson 112)
More than three authors	Name of only the first author	(Lincoln et al. 151)
No author or editor listed	Title shortened before page number	(Wildlife 72)
More than one work by an author is cited	Author and shortened book title	(Stasz American Dreamers 190)
More than one source cited	Semicolon after all but last source	(Finkelstein 201; Schroeder 98)

Create a bibliography

At the end of your paper, include a complete list of the sources used in your final version. This is your bibliography, or list of works cited.

From your bibliography cards, record the publishing information about the source.

- Alphabetize the source by the last name of the author or editor (use the name of the first author listed, if there is more than one).
- If the source has no author or editor, alphabetize it by the title of the book or article.
- If the source is a magazine or newspaper article that is not printed on consecutive pages, write only the first page number and a plus sign.

The proper bibliographic style for various sources is shown below. Note that in each entry, every line except the first is indented.

BIBLIOGRAPHY

Books with one author — Auerbach, Jonathan. Becoming Jack London. Durham, NC: Duke U.P. 1996.

Books with more than one author or editor — Cassuto, Leonard, and Jeanne Campbell Reesman, eds. Rereading Jack London. Stanford, CA: Stanford U.P., 1996. (Reverse only the first author's name.)

Magazine article — Lachtman, Howard. "Criticism of Jack London: A Selected Checklist." Modern Fiction Studies 22 (Spring 1976): 107–125. (Title of article and magazine; Volume, date, and page numbers)

Encyclopedia article — "London, Jack." The New Encyclopaedia Brittanica. 1998 ed. (Title of entry/Name of encyclopedia/Edition)

Online article — Stasz, Dr. Clarice. "Jack [John Griffith] London." Berkeley Digital Library SunSITE. Library, U.C. Berkeley. 2 Mar. 2001 <http://sunsite.berkeley.edu/London/jackbio.html>. (Title of database or project/Sponsoring organization/Date of access/URL)

Preparing a manuscript

Follow the guidelines of the Modern Language Association when you prepare the final copy of your research paper.

- Heading On separate lines in the upper left-hand corner of the first page, include your name, your teacher's name, the course name, and the date.
- Title Center the title on the line below the heading.
- Numbering Number the pages one-half inch from the top of the page in the right-hand corner. Include your last name before each page number after the first page.
- Spacing Use double-spacing throughout.
- Margins Leave one-inch margins on all sides of every page.

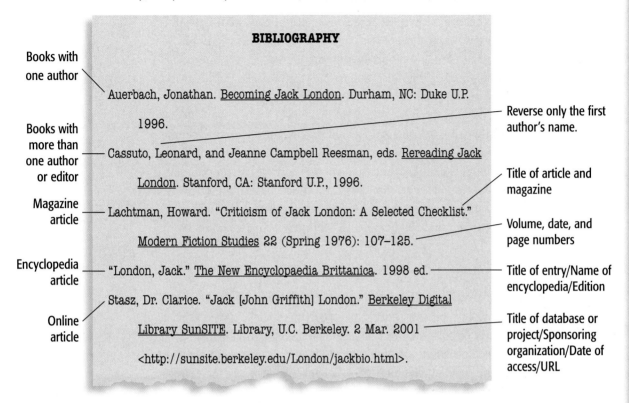

Business and Technical Writing

Business and technical writing are kinds of expository writing that explain information and processes to people within specific fields.

Business writing may include documents such as letters, memorandums, reports, briefs, proposals, and articles for business publications. Business writing must be clear, concise, accurate, and correct in style and usage.

Technical writing informs readers about specialized areas of science and technology. Technical writing is practical and objective, focusing on the technical content rather than on the author's perspective on the subject. User guides and manuals, data sheets describing software or equipment, business reports, and writing for newsletters in fields such as business, health, and science are all technical writing products.

Business letters

Whether you are writing a letter applying for a job, asking for information, or complaining about goods and services, be sure to use proper business letter form. Whenever possible, address your letter to a specific person rather than just to a company. Use a businesslike tone and explain exactly what you are requesting. The letter below illustrates the semiblock form, a popular style for a business letter that will help you get results.

36 Magnolia Place
Santa Rosa, CA 94097
April 18, 20___

Ms. Sarah Miller
Customer Service
Pebble Lane Clothing
4380 Industrial Park Drive
Quincy, MA 02345

Dear Ms. Miller:

On March 30 I ordered a cotton cardigan sweater (item number K7623, color navy) from your Spring catalogue. It arrived today, but it does not fit.

When I ordered the sweater, I followed the size chart provided in your catalogue. According to the chart, I should take a medium. However, the medium sweater I received is much too small.

I am enclosing the sweater and a copy of the invoice. Please send me the same sweater in the large size.

Sincerely,

Michael Weinstein

Memos

A memorandum is a concise means of communicating information to another person or to a group of people. A memo begins with a header that provides basic information, followed by the message. It does not have a formal closing.

TO: All Freshman Chorus members

FROM: Yvonne Clark

SUBJECT: Rehearsal for Spring Concert

DATE: May 2, 20___

Please note that the date, time, and place for the Spring Concert rehearsal have been changed. The rehearsal will be held in Room 22 on Tuesday, May 9, at 4:15 P.M. Please plan to attend.

Proposals

A proposal describes a project the writer wishes to undertake. It is presented to the person or persons responsible for making a decision in that area. A proposal includes the reasoning behind the plan (why this is a good idea) and an overview of the idea. The paragraphs below are from a proposal for a class dance.

Proposal

The officers of the freshman class propose a school dance to raise money for the class trip to Washington, D.C. The dance would be held in the gymnasium on Saturday, April 10, from 8:00 P.M. until midnight.

Proposed Schedule

January 8–20	Contact and hire DJ
January 27	Request Parents Club to provide refreshments and security
February 5	Arrange with computer and art classes to provide tickets and posters

Proposed Budget

Expenditures		
Security and refreshments	(donated by Parents Club)	$0.00
Tickets and publicity	(materials)	$15.00
Fee for DJ	(advanced from freshman class treasury)	$200.00
Income		
Anticipated revenue	(200 tickets @ $5)	$1000.00
Net Proceeds		***$785.00***

Using Electronic Resources

Computers and computer networks are changing the ways in which people gather information. If you have access to a personal computer at home or in school, you can find information in two ways—through CD-ROMs or through the Internet.

CD-ROM

CD-ROMs (compact disc-read-only memory), which store a variety of information, can be purchased at a store or through a mail-order catalog. CD-ROMs may include sound, photographs, and video, as well as text. Types of information available in this form include the following:

- general reference books–encyclopedias, almanacs, histories
- literature collections and biographies
- news reports from various sources
- back issues of magazines

The Internet

The Internet is, as its name implies, an extensive network that links computers. To access the Internet, you must purchase the services of an Internet service provider. Many Internet service providers are available.

The Internet gives you access to a wealth of information from universities, news organizations, researchers, government organizations, institutions, and individual experts in various fields. It also enables you to visit Web sites created by people who may or may not offer legitimate information and/or useful opinions.

Browsing the Web When you browse the Web, you search electronically for World Wide Web sites related to a particular subject.

Using a search engine Although you can browse the Web at large, you can narrow your search for selected information by using a search engine. When you select a specific search engine, it will identify a list of subject areas from which to choose.

Evaluating a Web site Consider the source of the material you locate when deciding whether the information on a Web site is reliable. Although many sites are maintained by educational institutions and other authorities, anyone can create a Web site and post information–or misinformation–on it. To evaluate a Web site, ask yourself these questions:

- Do I recognize the name of the author?
- Is the site associated with a well-known university or other reputable organization?
- Can the information be substantiated in another source?
- Is the writer citing a fact or offering an opinion?

Terms to know

Online information services are commercial services that provide many resources: chat forums; bulletin boards; databases; publications; reference materials; news, weather, and sports; and E-mail and Internet access.

The **World Wide Web (WWW)** is a global system that uses the Internet. It allows a user to create and link fields of information, to retrieve related documents, and to access the data in any order.

Downloading is using a computer modem to transfer a copy of a file from a distant computer to your computer.

A **Web site** is a group of one or more related Web pages that are accessible on the Internet. A **Web page** is a file that contains the information you view when you access a Web site. When you search the World Wide Web, you use a **Web browser** to access Web sites that carry the information you are searching for.

Computerized Library Resources

Electronic research is often faster than traditional methods and allows access to a wide spectrum of material. It has become an essential research tool. Public libraries, as well as school and university libraries, offer a variety of ways to do research electronically.

Catalogs Most libraries have computerized catalogs. By typing in a title or an author's name, you can find out if the library has the book, how many copies are in the library's collection, if the book is currently available, and if not, when it will be returned. In large library systems, the computer also provides the name of other libraries from which the desired book is available.

Electronic databases Your library may provide access to electronic databases through on-line information services. These databases are being continually updated. One helpful database available in many libraries is InfoTrac®, which provides an index and abstracts–short summaries–of articles from many periodicals. Other magazine indexes, some of which contain the full text of selected articles, may also be available.

Some libraries also have an extensive collection of CD-ROMs. Ask the librarian what is available at your library and how to access the information.

Study and Test-Taking Skills

Study Skills

Taking notes and budgeting study time are essential skills for success as a student.

Taking notes in class

Keeping notes based on classroom lectures and teachers' directions gives you a written record of important information. Try these tips for good note taking.

- Use loose-leaf paper if possible, so pages can be added and removed, and use a fresh page for every class. Write the name of the class and the date at the top of the page. Using a different notebook for each subject can help you organize your notes.
- Listen carefully for the main ideas and record them in your own words. Do not try to write down every word. Also, be alert for signal terms such as *most importantly, remember this,* and *to summarize.*
- Spend at least twice as much time listening as writing. Don't risk missing an important point while writing.
- Leave enough space around your notes to add more information later. Try leaving a wide left-hand margin to write in key points or an informal outline.
- As soon as possible after class, reread your notes and fill in any missing information. If possible, exchange notes with a peer and jot down any key points he or she has that you may have missed.
- Take notes not only on what your teacher presents in class, but also on your reading assignments. Your textbook can provide a framework to understand the context of the material presented by your teacher. You might use the headings and subheadings in your textbook to create a basic outline.
- Try reviewing your notes in an active way. Rewriting or typing them can help you commit key points to memory.

Using study time wisely

- Study in the same place each day. Choose a place that is quiet and free from distractions.
- If discussion helps you learn, find a study partner with whom you can work.
- Divide large assignments into smaller tasks. Reading four pages of a textbook each night is easier than trying to read twenty-eight pages every weekend.
- Make a monthly assignment calendar. By writing down due dates, test dates, and notes about upcoming assignments, you can see at a glance what work you need to do and when. It will also bring to your attention the times when you will be especially busy, allowing you to plan ahead.
- At the beginning of your study period, when your attention and energy are at their highest levels, work on the assignments you find hardest.

- Take a short break after completing each task. Stay alert by stretching, walking, or having a light snack.
- Review material before stopping. Even a short review will greatly increase the amount of material you are able to remember.

Preparing for Classroom Tests

This section will help you learn how to prepare for classroom tests.

Thinking ahead

- Write down information about an upcoming test–when it will be given, what it will cover, and so on–so you can plan your study time effectively.
- Review your quizzes, homework assignments, class notes, and handouts. Look at end-of-chapter review questions in your textbook.
- Develop your own questions about main ideas and important details, and practice answering them. Writing your own practice tests is an excellent way to get ready for a real test.
- Make studying into an active process. Rather than simply rereading your notes or a chapter in your textbook, try to create a summary of the material. This can be an outline, a list of characters, or a timeline. Try to include details from both your lecture notes and your textbook reading so you will be able to see connections between the two.
- Form study groups. Explaining information to a peer is one of the best ways to learn the material.
- Remember that students who are well rested and who eat a regular meal on the morning of a test generally score higher than others.

Taking objective tests

Objective tests ask questions that have specific, correct answers. Time is often limited for these tests, so be sure to use your time efficiently. First, read the directions carefully and ask questions if anything is unclear. Then try to respond to each item on the test, starting with the easier ones. You can always come back to the more difficult questions later. Finally, try to include some time to review your test before turning it in.

Below are tips for answering specific kinds of objective test items:

- **Multiple-choice** Read all the answer choices provided before choosing one; even if the first one seems nearly correct, a later choice may be a better answer. Be cautious about absolute words such as *always, never, all,* or *none.* Since most generalizations have exceptions, absolute statements are often incorrect.
- **True/False** If *any* part of the item is false, the correct answer must be "false."
- **Short-answer** Use complete sentences to help you write a clear response.
- **Fill-in** Restate fill-ins as regular questions to clarify what is being asked.
- **Matching** Note in the directions whether some responses can be used more than once, or not used at all.

Taking subjective (essay) tests

Typically, subjective tests ask questions that require you to write an essay. Your grade is based more on how well you are able to make your point than on whether you choose a correct answer.

- When you receive the test, first read it through. If there are several questions, determine how much time to spend on each question.
- Begin your answer by jotting down ideas on scratch paper for several minutes. Read the test question again to make sure you are answering it. Then create a rough outline from which you can create your essay.
- Start your essay with a thesis statement in the first paragraph, and follow with paragraphs that provide supporting evidence. Give as much information as possible, including examples and illustrations where appropriate.
- Finish your essay with a conclusion, highlighting the evidence you have provided and restating your thesis.
- You will probably not have time to revise and copy your essay. After you are finished writing, spend any remaining time proofreading your answer and neatly making any necessary corrections.

Preparing for Standardized Tests

Standardized tests are designed to be administered to very large groups of students, not just those in a particular class. Three of the most widely known standardized tests, part of the college application process, are the ACT (American College Testing), the PSAT (Preliminary Scholastic Assessment Test), and the SAT (Scholastic Assessment Test). The strategies in this handbook refer specifically to the PSAT and SAT tests, but they also can apply to preparing for the ACT and other standardized tests.

The PSAT is generally administered to students in the 11th grade, although some schools offer it to students in the 10th grade as well. This test is designed to predict how well you will do on the SAT. For most students, the PSAT is simply a practice test. Those who perform exceptionally well on the 11th grade PSAT, however, will qualify for National Merit Scholarship competition.

The Scholastic Assessment Tests consist of the SAT-I: Reasoning Test and a variety of SAT-II: Subject Tests. The SAT-I is a three-hour test that evaluates your general verbal and mathematics skills. The SAT-II: Subject Tests are hour-long tests given in specific subjects that are designed to show how much you have learned in a particular subject area.

The two primary skills tested by the verbal sections of the PSAT and the SAT-I are reading comprehension and vocabulary. You may not be immediately concerned with these tests, but you should begin to develop the long-term skills you will need in the upcoming years.

Reading comprehension

Start to read as much as you can. In addition to your reading assignments from school, get in the habit of reading newspapers and magazines whenever you can. The reading selections on the PSAT and SAT-I will cover some unfamiliar topics, so try to read articles about subjects that are new to you. The editorial pages of a local or national newspaper are a great place to get started.

Vocabulary

Nearly half of the items on the verbal sections of the PSAT and SAT are designed to test your vocabulary. Therefore, to put it simply, the more words you know, the higher your score will be. As you read, watch television, and listen to the radio, start to keep a stack of index cards on which you write down the words you do not know. Look up these words in your dictionary and use them, wherever possible, in your writing and in conversation. Just writing down the words and looking up their definitions won't help you remember them on the day of the test; you have to *use* them in order to learn them.

Analogies

One type of vocabulary-based question used on the PSAT and the SAT-I is the analogy. Analogy items test your ability to grasp the relationships between concepts. The best way to pinpoint the relationship between the words is to connect them with a simple sentence that defines one of the words. Some of the most common relationships seen on the PSAT and the SAT-I are shown below.

Relationship	Example
Cause and effect	heat : perspiration :: sadness : tears
User to tool	teacher : book :: carpenter : hammer
A person to the normal action of that person	artist : paint :: gardener : plant
Object to characteristic	water : wet :: brick : hard
Class to subclass (or subclass to class)	grain : rye :: music : rap

You will find answering analogy items on the PSAT and SAT-I easier if you understand some basic facts about them.

- Each group of analogy items is arranged in rough order of difficulty, from easiest to hardest.
- Many analogy items use only nouns. The rest involve a noun and an adjective, a noun and a verb, or a verb and an adjective.
- The key to improving your performance on analogies is to develop your vocabulary and practice identifying the relationship between two items.
- If you can eliminate even one answer choice, be sure to take a guess at the correct answer.

The Reading Process

Being an active reader is a very important part of being a lifelong learner. It is also an ongoing task. Good reading skills build on each other, overlap, and spiral around in much the same way that a winding staircase goes round and round while leading you to a higher place.

This handbook is designed to help you find and use the tools you'll need before, during, and after reading.

Vocabulary Development

Word identification and vocabulary skills are key building blocks in reading and in the comprehension process. By learning to use a variety of strategies to build your word skills and vocabulary, you will become a stronger reader.

Using context to determine meaning

The very best way to expand and extend your vocabulary is to read widely, listen carefully, and participate in a rich variety of discussions. When reading on your own, though, you can often figure out the meanings of new words by looking at their **context,** the other words and sentences that surround them. For example:

> *Contiguous* countries, such as the United States and Canada, usually have border patrols.

Although you may not know the meaning of *contiguous,* you can figure out from the phrase *such as the United States and Canada* that the word means "adjoining."

Tips for Using Context

- **Look for clues such as**
  - –a synonym or an explanation of the unknown word in the sentence.
    Elise's shop specialized in ***millinery,*** *or* ***hats for women.***
  - –a reference to what the word is or is not like.
    An ***archaeologist,*** *like a* ***historian,*** *deals with the past.*
  - –a general topic associated with the word.
    The ***cooking*** *teacher discussed the best way to* ***braise*** *meat.*
  - –a description or action associated with the word.
    He used the ***hoe*** *to* ***dig up*** *the garden.*
- **Predict a possible meaning.**

- **Determine whether the meaning makes sense in terms of the whole passage.**
- **Be aware the writer may be using**
  –a word with **multiple meanings.**
  Some of the group will play games; others will attend a play.
  –**figurative language,** such as **similes,** which use *like* or *as* to compare two unlike things and **metaphors,** which compare two unlike things without using *like* or *as.*
  The leaves rustled like silk as they drifted to the ground. (simile)
  The bullets of rain pelted the sidewalk. (metaphor)
  –**idioms,** expressions that have a meaning apart from the literal one.
  I'm just pulling your leg is an idiom used when joking with someone.
  Hint: If you come across an idiom with an unfamiliar meaning, look in the dictionary under the main word in the phrase. Many dictionaries list idioms after the definitions.
  –**technical vocabulary,** words that require an understanding of the specific terms of a specialized field.
  Be sure to clean your ***mouse*** *from time to time to make the* ***cursor*** *move smoothly.*

● For more on figurative language and idioms, see **Literary Terms Handbook,** pp. R5 and R6.

Using word parts and word origins

Another way to determine the meaning of a word is to take the word itself apart. If you understand the meaning of the **base,** or **root,** part of a word and also know the meanings of key syllables added either to the beginning or end of the base word, you can usually figure out what the word means.

Word Part	Definition	Example
Root	the most basic part of a word	*voc* means "call" *Convoke* means "call together."
Prefix	a syllable placed before a root word to change or add to its meaning	*inter-* means "between" *Intervene* means "come between."
Suffix	a syllable placed after a root word to create a new meaning	*-less* means "without" *Hopeless* means without hope

Word origins Since Latin, Greek, and Anglo-Saxon roots are the basis for much of our English vocabulary, having some background in one of these languages can be a useful vocabulary tool. For example, *astronomy* comes from the Greek root *astro,* which means "relating to the stars." *Stellar* also has a meaning referring to stars, but its origin is Latin. Knowing root words in other languages can help you determine meanings, derivations, and spellings in English.

Using vocabulary references

Dictionaries A dictionary provides the meaning or meanings of a word. Look at the sample dictionary entry below to see what other information it provides.

Forms of the word — Usage label — Part of speech — Examples of use — Numbered definitions — Idioms — Origin (etymology) — Synonyms

help (help) **helped** or *(archaic)* **holp, helped** or *(archaic)* **hol-pen, help-ing.** *v.t.* **1.** to provide with support, as in the performance of a task; be of service to: *He helped his brother paint the room.* ▲ also used elliptically with a preposition or adverb: *He helped the old woman up the stairs.* **2.** to enable (someone or something) to accomplish a goal or achieve a desired effect: *The coach's advice helped the team to win.* **3.** to provide with sustenance or relief, as in time of need or distress; succor: *The Red Cross helped the flood victims.* **4.** to promote or contribute to; further. *The medication helped his recovery.* **5.** to be useful or profitable to; be of advantage to: *It might help you if you read the book.* **6.** to improve or remedy: *Nothing really helped his sinus condition.* **7.** to prevent; stop: *I can't help his rudeness.* **8.** to refrain from; avoid: *I couldn't help smiling when I heard the story.* **9.** to wait on or serve (often with *to*): *The clerk helped us. The hostess helped him to the dessert.* **10. cannot help but.** *Informal* cannot but. **11. so help me (God).** oath of affirmation. **12. to help oneself to.** to take or appropriate: *The thief helped himself to all the jewels.* —*v.i.* to provide support, as in the performance of a task; be of service. —*n.* **1.** act of providing support, service, or sustenance. **2.** source of support, service, or sustenance. **3.** person or group of persons hired to work for another or others. **4.** means of improving, remedying, or preventing. [Old English *helpan* to aid, succor, benefit.]
Syn. *v.t.* **1. Help, aid, assist** mean to support in a useful way. **Help** is the most common word and means to give support in response to a known or expressed need or for a definite purpose: *Everyone helped to make the school fair a success.* **Aid** means to give relief in times of distress or difficulty: *It is the duty of rich nations to aid the poor.* **Assist** means to serve another person in the performance of his task in a secondary capacity: *The secretary assists the officer by taking care of his correspondence.*

Thesauruses These references provide synonyms and often antonyms. Some dictionaries and thesauruses are available on CD-ROM and on the Internet.

Glossaries Many textbooks and technical works contain condensed dictionaries that provide an alphabetical listing of words used in the text and their specific definitions. The example on page R81 is from a social studies textbook.

Glossary

A

abolitionist 1800s reformer who worked to end slavery (p. 342)
acid rain acid precipitation in the form of rain (p. 1016)
agribusiness large farming operation that includes the cultivation, processing, storage, and distribution of farm products (p. 869)
amendment alteration to the Constitution (p. 160)
amnesty act of a government by which pardon is granted to an individual or groups of persons (p. 445)
anarchism a belief in no direct government authority over society (p. 531)
anarchist one who opposes all forms of government (p. 616)

Identifying word relationships

Determining the relationships of words to each other also aids comprehension. Some special word relationships include analogies, synonyms, antonyms, denotation, and connotation.

- **Denotation** A denotation expresses the exact meaning of a word. A word may have more than one denotation, but all of its denotations will be listed in the dictionary. Notice, for example, all the denotations for the word *help* listed in the dictionary entry on page R80.
- **Connotation** Connotation refers to an emotion or an underlying value that accompanies a word's dictionary meaning. When the word *leper* is used, you know that the word refers to someone suffering from a specific disease, but its connotation includes feelings of disgust or pity and suggests separation from familiar surroundings.

TRY THE STRATEGIES

Play a game of Word Clues. Each player chooses a word that has been used in class in the past two weeks and coins a nonsense word to represent it. Player One writes a sentence on the board using his or her nonsense word in an appropriate context. Players who can identify the word from the context raise their hands. Each scores five points for a correct identification. If no one is able to identify the word, Player One supplies a synonym or antonym for it. Players who identify the word correctly after the second clue score three points. If no one identifies the word, Player One gets a one-point penalty and the next player repeats the procedure. When time is up, the player with the most points wins.

Comprehension Strategies

Reading comprehension means understanding—deriving meaning from—what you have read. Using a variety of strategies can help you improve your comprehension and make reading more interesting and more fun.

Previewing

Before beginning a selection, it's helpful to **preview** what you are about to read.

- **Read** the title, headings, and subheadings of the selection.
- **Look** at the illustrations and notice how the text is organized.
- **Skim** the selection; that is, take a quick glance at the whole thing.
- **Decide** what the author's purpose might be.
- **Predict** what a selection will be about.
- **Set a purpose** for your reading.

Establishing a purpose for reading

To get the greatest benefit from what you read, you should **establish a purpose for reading.** Some purposes for reading are

- to enjoy
- to find information, to discover
- to interpret
- to follow directions or take action
- to be persuaded about an issue
- to appreciate a writer's craft
- to find models for your own writing

Vary your reading strategies to fit the different purposes you have when you read. If you are reading for entertainment, you might read quickly, but if you read to gather information or follow directions, you might read more slowly, take notes, construct a graphic organizer, or reread sections of text.

TRY THE STRATEGIES

Look through a newspaper or a magazine at home or at the library. Preview three or four articles using the strategies listed under Previewing. Then decide what your purpose for reading would be for each of the articles selected. Which of the articles should you read slowly? Which might you read quickly? In a small group, discuss your purposes for reading and why your reading speed would differ from article to article.

Drawing on personal background

Good reading is an interactive process between the writer and each different person reading a selection. Even the youngest child has a body of information and personal experiences that are important and uniquely his or her own. When you draw on your personal background, combining it with the words on a page, you create meaning in a selection. Drawing on this personal background is also called activating prior knowledge. To expand and extend your prior knowledge, share it in active classroom discussions.

Ask yourself questions like these:

- What do I know about this topic?
- What familiar places have similar settings?
- What experiences have I had that compare or contrast with what I am reading?
- What characters from life or literature remind me of the characters or narrator in the selection?

Making and verifying predictions

As you read, take educated guesses about story events and outcomes; that is, make **predictions** before and during reading. Using your prior knowledge and the information you have gathered in your preview, you can predict what you will learn or what might happen in a selection. Then use information you gather as you read to adjust or **verify your predictions.** Have you ever read a mystery, decided who committed the crime, and then changed your mind as more clues emerged? You were adjusting your predictions. Or did you shriek with delight or smile smugly when you found out you guessed the murderer? You were verifying your predictions. Careful predictions and verifications increase your comprehension of a selection.

TRY THE STRATEGIES

Find a selection from your social studies or science textbook. First, preview the title, illustrations, and available heads and subheads to determine what the piece might be about, or what might happen. On your own paper, write your predictions about what you will read. Then, as you read, revise your predictions based on new information and your own background or prior knowledge.

Monitoring and modifying reading strategies

No matter what your purpose for reading, your most important task is to understand what you have read. Try having a conversation with yourself as you work through a selection. **Monitor,** or **check, your understanding,** using the following strategies:

- Summarize
- Clarify
- Ask questions
- Predict what will come next

This might be done once or twice in an easy, entertaining selection, or after every paragraph in a nonfiction selection, dense with new concepts.

One way of questioning yourself is to pretend that you are the teacher, trying to determine if your students have understood the main ideas of a selection. What questions would you ask? Be sure that you can answer those questions before you read on.

Tips for Monitoring Understanding

- Reread.
- Make a graphic organizer, such as a chart or a diagram, to help sort out your thoughts.
- Consult other sources, including text resources, teachers, and other students.
- Write comments or questions on another piece of paper for later review or discussion.

Use or modify whatever strategy fits your learning style, but don't settle for not understanding. Be an active reader.

Visualizing

Try to form a mental picture of scenes, characters, and events as you read. Use the details and descriptions the author gives you. According to your imagination and the text, what do the characters look like? What does the setting look like? Can you picture the steps in a process when you read nonfiction? If you can **visualize** what you read, selections will be more interesting. When someone reads aloud to you, try sketching what you're hearing–you'll be more likely to recall it later.

Constructing graphic organizers

Graphic organizers help you reconstruct ideas in a visual way, so you can remember them later on. You might make a **chart** or **diagram,** showing the information the author provides.

Venn diagrams When mapping out a comparison-and-contrast text structure, you can use a Venn diagram. The outer portions of the circles will show how two characters, ideas, or items contrast, or are different, and the overlapping part will compare two things, or show how they are similar.

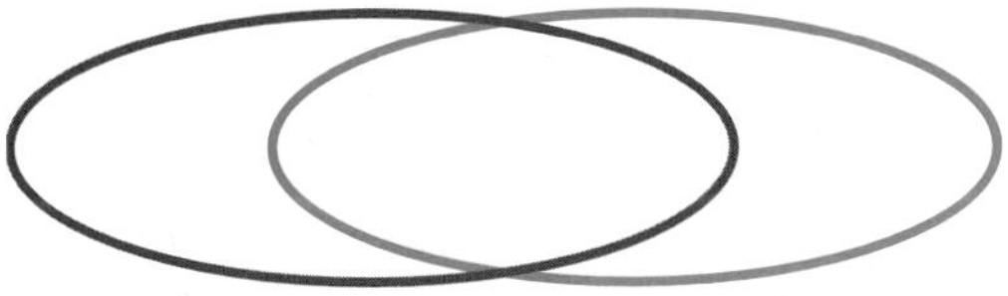

Flow charts To help you keep track of the sequence of events, use a flow chart. Arrange ideas or events in their logical, sequential order. Then draw arrows between your ideas to indicate how one idea or event flows into another. Look at the following flow chart to see how you can map out story events in chronological order, or show cause-and-effect relationships.

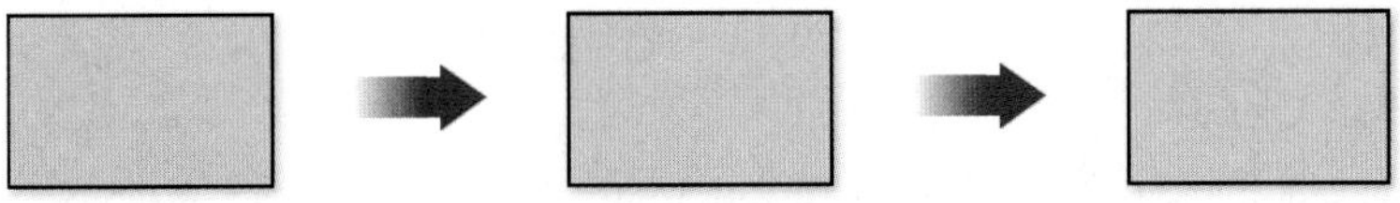

Web To help you determine a main idea and supporting details, use a web. Surround the main idea with examples or supporting details. Then create additional circles, branching off from the supporting details, to add related thoughts.

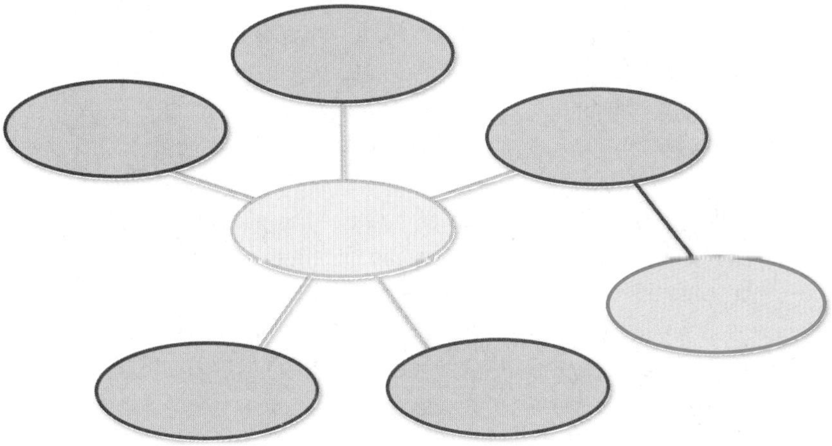

Analyzing text structures

Writers organize their written work in various ways, depending on their topic and purpose. Finding and analyzing that pattern of organization or **text structure** helps you to understand what an author is trying to say. Here are three important ways that writers structure or organize text:

Kind of Organization	Purpose	Clues
Comparison and contrast	To determine similarities and differences	Words and phrases like *similarly, on the other hand, in contrast to, but, however*
Cause and effect	To explore the reasons for something and to examine the results of events or actions	Words and phrases like *because* and *as a result*
Chronological order	To present events in time order	Words and phrases like *first, next, then, later,* and *finally*

Writers may embed one kind of structure within another, but it is usually possible to identify one main pattern of organization that will help you discover an author's purpose and will focus your attention on the important ideas in the selection.

Read the following example. Analyze the text structure used.

Seana and Tyra were identical twins, yet they were not identical in many ways. They looked exactly alike, tall and athletic, with long brown hair. Both girls played field hockey, and they both were in the school band. However, each girl had her own identity. Seana, for example, always kept her room neat and tidy, she did her homework on time, and she didn't mind helping around the house. On the other hand, Tyra's bed was piled so high with clothes, books, and her other possessions that she could barely get in it at night. She didn't mind doing her homework, but she could always find things she enjoyed more, so she put it off until the last minute. Her papers were usually smudged, and she often left out answers because she was in a hurry. Tyra didn't like chores. She put off cleaning her room as long as she could. In contrast, Seana liked to plan every minute of the day. Though the twins were very different, they understood each other and accepted each other. They were the best of friends.

What is the basic text structure in the preceding paragraph? How do you know? What words help you to see the structure? How could you show this information on a graphic organizer?

TRY THE STRATEGIES

Find a selection in your literature, social studies, or science textbook and determine its text structure. Look for important clues. Use the chart above to help you in your determination.

Interpreting graphic aids

Graphic aids provide an opportunity to see and analyze information at a glance. Some effective graphic aids include maps, charts, tables, and diagrams. To interpret any of these graphic aids, you need to understand how the information presented is organized.

Reading a map Maps are flat representations of land, with other features included. A **compass rose** helps a reader to determine direction. A **legend** explains the map's symbols, while a **scale** shows the relationship of the map size to the land represented. A map may show physical features, political divisions, or historical data.

Title shows kinds of information on the map.

Compass rose shows directional orientation.

Scale shows relationship to actual distances.

Legend explains colors or symbols on the map.

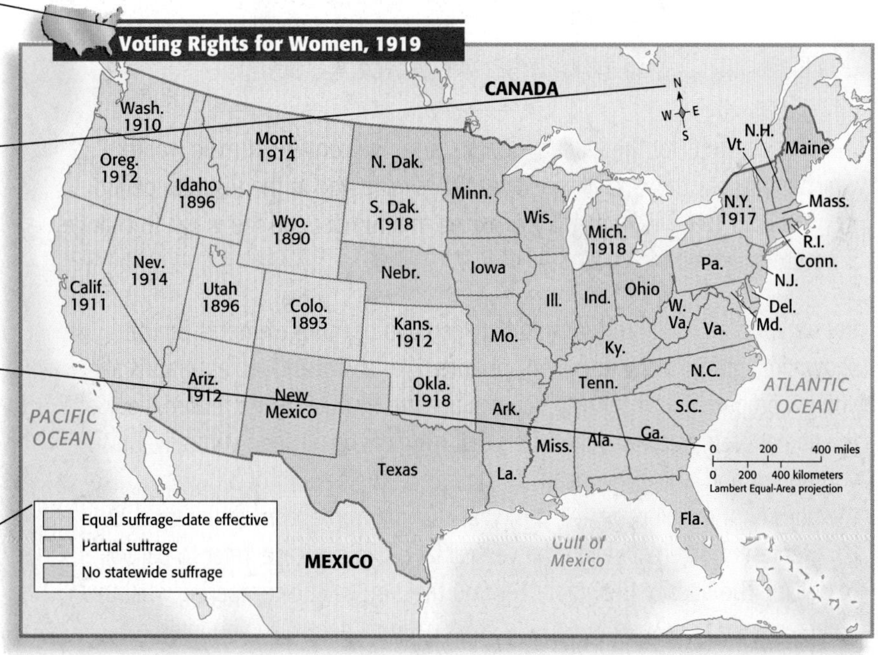

Refer to the map to answer these questions.

How many states did not have statewide woman suffrage in 1919?
What state was the first to grant women equal suffrage?

Reading a chart Charts help you compare and analyze information. In charts or tables, information is often presented in columns. These columns can run horizontally across the top of the chart, or vertically down the side of the chart.

The Labor Force, 1983–1993

	1983	1985	1990	1993
Total work-force (in thousands)	70,976	77,002	85,082	85,211
Percentage of total workforce				
Male	59.6	59.2	57.6	56.8
Female	40.4	40.8	42.4	43.2
White	87.0	86.3	85.4	85.0
Black	10.4	10.9	11.3	11.4
of Hispanic origin	NA	NA	8.2	8.3
Ratio of weekly median earnings				
Females to Males	66.7	68.2	71.8	76.8
Blacks to Whites	81.8	78.0	77.0	77.4
Hispanics to Whites	NA	NA	71.9	70.0

Source: *Statistical Abstract of the United States, 1994.*

Title of chart

Column heads

Subheads

Source of data

What accounts for the gradual decline in the percentage of male workers? In which group has the ratio of weekly earnings increased in the ten-year period from 1983 to 1993? How might you expect the numbers on the graph to change if it were extended to 2003?

Reading a graph The relationship between two or more elements can be shown in a graph, using dots, bars, or lines. Like charts and tables, graphs allow you to compare information so you can analyze how items are related. Look at the title of each graph and the labels that run horizontally and vertically. Be sure you understand what they mean. The labels on the bottom of bar graphs, like the ones on the next page, tell you what each bar represents. In this case, the bars represent different years. The vertical labels, in this case, refer to billions of dollars. The titles of the graphs tell you that you will be comparing what the federal government spends with the gross national debt. Can you interpret the information?

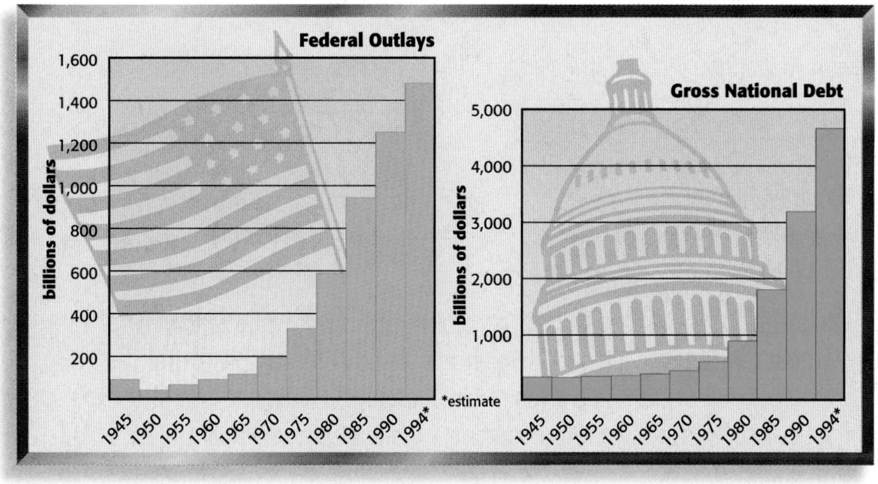

In what year did federal expenditures decrease? During what years did the national debt remain almost constant? During what periods did the national debt show the greatest increase? If the graphs were extended to the year 2004, would you project the gross national debt to be closer to 5,000 or 6,000 billion dollars?

Reading a diagram A diagram illustrates the parts of an item. You might see a diagram of a bicycle, for instance, with arrows identifying the name of each part. Diagrams can also illustrate how a process functions. For instance, the diagram below illustrates the steps used in writing an investigative report.

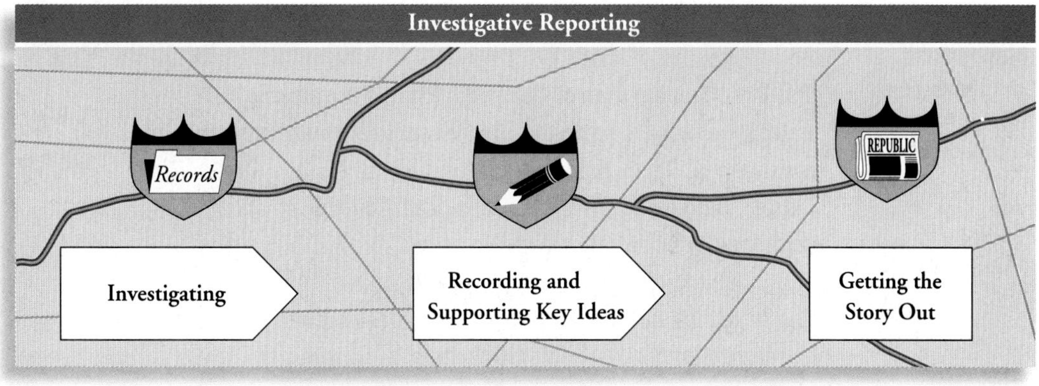

TRY THE STRATEGIES

In your social studies or science text, locate a section that uses a graphic aid. What kind of information is presented graphically? Read and interpret the information using the graphic aid, and then, on your paper, explain why the visual representation successfully presents the material.

Sequencing

The order in which thoughts are arranged is called **sequence.** A good sequence is one that is logical, given the ideas in a selection. Here are three common forms of sequencing:

- Chronological order
- Spatial order
- Order of importance

Recognizing the sequence of something is particularly important when **following complex written directions.** If a written sequence is illogical or incomplete, or if you fail to precisely follow steps in a given order, you may be unable to complete an important task such as taking a test or locating a destination when driving a car.

Identifying main ideas and supporting details

As you read, it is important to identify the **main idea** of a paragraph or passage. Overall, works of fiction and nonfiction can contain several main ideas. In a single paragraph, the main idea will be the thought that organizes the passage, and around which all other sentences are built. Some writers directly state main ideas in topic sentences, while others imply a main idea with examples and other clues.

Read a paragraph carefully. Then decide if one sentence contains the main organizing thought, or if that thought is implied. Once you identify the main idea, you can use the **supporting details** to learn additional information about the main idea.

Main idea — **The Four Corners area of Colorado, Utah, New Mexico, and Arizona is home to some of the most ancient dwellings on the continent of North America.** Places such as Chaco Canyon, New Mexico, Canyon de Chelly, Arizona, and Hovenweep on the Colorado-Utah borders are the locations for cliff houses built and inhabited by ancient people now known as the Anasazi. *The huge cliff houses, similar to apartment buildings, date back to before A.D. 500.* — Supporting details

The climate was very harsh—arid below 5,000 feet elevation and freezing above 7,000 feet elevation. **In order to live in the area, the Anasazi had to be a resourceful people.** — Main idea. *The Anasazi lived in communities so they could help each other. They grew their own crops and lived on such vegetables as corn, squash, and different varieties of beans. They managed to build dams to control water and eroding soil so that they could control crop growth. The earliest people are known as the Basket-makers because their only vessels were baskets, some woven tightly enough to hold water. Later cliff dwellers made pottery to use as vessels.* — Supporting details; Order of importance

Paraphrasing

When you **paraphrase,** you put something you've read into your own words. You might paraphrase just the main ideas or you might retell an entire story in your own words. You need to understand something thoroughly in order to put it into your own words, so paraphrasing is a useful strategy for reviewing and for judging if you've understood what you've read.

- Original In the three decades after the Civil War, the production of agricultural staples, such as wheat and cotton, nearly quadrupled while the supply of money increased very little.
- Paraphrase Although the amount of available cash remained about the same as before the Civil War, farmers produced almost four times as much wheat and other basic crops during the thirty-year postwar period.

Summarizing

When you **summarize**, you relate the main ideas of a selection in a logical sequence and in your own words. You are combining three skills in one. To create a good summary, include all the main ideas. Do not include anything that is not important. A good summary can be easily understood by someone who has not read the whole text or selection. If you're not sure if an idea is a main idea or a detail, try taking it out of your summary. Does your summary still sound complete?

Look at the following summary of the passage on the Anasazi.

> Huge cliff houses, built before A.D. 500, are located in the Four Corners area of Colorado, Utah, New Mexico, and Arizona. These ancient dwellings were built by the Anasazi. The resourceful Anasazi created farming communities in a harsh environment, growing and making what they needed to live.

Does this summary include all the important ideas? Does it answer who, what, where, why, and when?

TRY THE STRATEGIES

Read "The U.S. *vs.* Susan B. Anthony" on page 354 of your text. On separate paper, list the main ideas of the selection. Under each main idea, list the major supporting details that explain it. Use this information to write a summary of what you have read. Be sure that you do not use the writer's words. Paraphrase the writer's ideas in your own words.

Drawing and supporting inferences

Authors don't always directly state what they want you to understand in a selection. By providing clues and interesting details, they imply certain information. Whenever readers combine those clues with their own background and knowledge, they are drawing an inference. An **inference** involves using your reason and experience to come up with an idea, based on what an author implies or suggests. The following active reading behaviors help you infer:

- Predicting When you predict what a story will be about, or guess what will happen next, you are drawing an inference.
- Drawing conclusions A conclusion is a general statement you can make and explain with reasoning, or with supporting details from a text. If you read a story describing a sport where five players bounce a ball and throw it through a hoop, you may conclude that the sport is basketball.
- Making generalizations When readers make generalizations, they draw an inference that can apply to more than one item or group. This inference has a more general scope than a prediction or a conclusion. If you read articles about how the Sioux tribes revere the crane and how Cherokees believe strongly in protecting our natural resources, you might generalize that Native Americans respect nature.

What is most important when drawing inferences is to be sure that you have accurately based your guesses on supporting details from the text, as well as on your own knowledge. If you cannot point to a place in the selection to help back up your inference, you may need to rethink your guess.

> As Alice walked into the classroom, something struck her as odd. No one was talking, not even Lindsay, who was never at a loss for something to chat about. Daniel had a panic-stricken look on his face and was hurriedly looking through his bookbag in search of something important. Even the students who always hung around in the hall before class were now seated, poring over their open social studies books. Mr. Greising had that determined, teacher look he always wore when he was writing on the blackboard. "Oh, no," thought Alice. "He can't be doing this again!"

What inference might you draw from the paragraph above? What supporting details have you used to support your inference? Can you think of alternate inferences that might also be supported by the clues from the text?

TRY THE STRATEGIES

Together with several other students, silently read several pages from a selection none of you has previously read. On your own paper, write down any inferences you can draw from the material you read. Compare your inferences within your group.

Using study strategies

All students face important studying tasks at different points in their reading. Finding the right strategy will depend on the task you face. You may need to study for a quiz or a test, or make a class presentation with a group or by yourself. In each case you will want to pick the strategy which is most efficient and which helps you to organize and remember the material you need. Some useful study strategies include:

- Skimming and scanning If you want to refresh your memory about a passage you've read or get a general overview of new material, **skim** the pages by glancing quickly over the entire selection. It will focus your attention on the main ideas and the author's purpose. If you need to go back and find a particular piece of information, **scan** the selection, looking for key words or phrases that will point you to the specific information you need. You don't need to look at the whole selection. As you scan, look for section headings or terms in **boldfaced** type.
- Using and creating study guides It is often helpful to use end of chapter questions to guide you while you read. You can also create your own guide by turning headings and subheadings into questions to answer as you read. Don't forget to include captions underneath illustrations when thinking up questions to help focus your attention. Use the guide to help you review aloud or silently.
- Reviewing Active readers go back over selections again and again. They combine their notes, outlines, and study guides to provide themselves with different ways of approaching the same information. The more you review information from different angles, the better you'll recall it when you need to.
- Using KWL A KWL is a good device for charting expository information. Make three columns on a page. Label the first column *What I Know,* the second column *What I Want to Know,* and the third column *What I Learned.* You can also add more columns to record places where you found information and places where you can look for more information.

TRY THE STRATEGIES

Skim a few chapters in a history textbook to find examples of comparison and contrast, chronological order, and cause and effect. Make graphic organizers to create a visual presentation of the ideas you have just read. Use these organizers to study the material.

For more about study strategies, see **Communications Skills Handbook,** pp. R74–R75

Reading silently for sustained periods

What things keep you on track when you read? Do you need total silence to concentrate well, or does some soft background music help you stay focused? Whatever your preference, it is important to avoid distractions or interruptions when you have to read silently for any length of time.

Tips for Reading Silently

- Be sure you're comfortable, but not too comfortable.
- Once your external surroundings are set, it's important to maintain your concentration and check your comprehension regularly.
- Using a study guide or a concept web can help you get through difficult nonfiction passages. Your teacher may provide a guide, or you can use questions from the end of the material to guide you.
- When you read fiction, a story map or other graphic organizer will help you stay focused on the important elements of the selection.
- Take regular breaks when you need them, and vary your reading rate with the demands of the text.

TRY THE STRATEGIES

Choose one or more longer selections in this book. Block out a period of time during which you won't be interrupted. Make sure you are in a comfortable spot where you can concentrate. Read silently until you finish the selection. Then use the **Responding to Literature** questions that follow the selection to monitor your comprehension.

Reading Across Texts and Cultures

One of the most important student tasks is to read widely and to integrate information from different sources to create new knowledge. Throughout this text you have read both classic and contemporary works, looking at themes from different perspectives, from different cultures, and for different purposes. As a citizen of the world, and not just your own country, you have examined world literature through the eyes of history and with a view toward the future. Every time you discussed a selection, interpreted a theme, or analyzed a writer's purpose, you created new knowledge for yourself and your classmates.

Reading in varied sources

Writers in different sources can use a variety of styles and settings while telling the same story or covering the same subject. For instance, you might read several versions of the same folktale in order to appreciate different cultural themes or story elements. Whatever different sources you use, it's important to be able to organize and evaluate information, combining what you learn from varied sources to suit your purposes.

For instance, to learn about the history of your hometown or region, you might read and refer to a variety of texts:

- Consult a **map** to discover the boundaries and relative position of the geographical features of your town.
- Look up **diaries** and **journals** of long-time and former residents to gain valuable insights into different times and places.
- Find **speeches** made in the town on special occasions. These recorded public comments can showcase the style of the orator, as well as provide information about a topic, an area, or a group of people.
- Refer to the Internet and other **electronic media** that can lead you to a variety of sources and allow you to find a broader base of information about a subject.
- Try to find old **letters, memoranda, newspapers, magazines,** and **textbooks** that may provide valuable information not generally available in other sources.
- Ask a librarian or the curator of a local museum about **special collections** of posters or other resources that might offer information on your subject.

Read the following paragraphs from two kinds of sources. The purpose of this first paragraph is to provide information about national forests.

> Our national forests have gradually been turned into parks over the years because most of our population lives in cities, and many people want to enjoy the rare treat of getting out into a wilderness area. More and more people visit our national forests every year. The western portion of the United States contains most of our national forest land. Idaho, Montana, and Wyoming share a large forested area with Clearwater National Forest, Yellowstone National Park, Gallatin National Forest, Targhee National Forest, and Flathead National Forest.

This paragraph provides a personal perspective on the same topic.

As I topped the rocky crags towering over the valley below, I stood struck dumb with amazement. Below me lay the most beautiful sight I had ever seen. The lush green valley flowed into towering trees that were so huge I could not begin to reach around them. Sparkling streams flowed into water so clearly blue that it was startling. Giant waterfalls spewed down peaks into a lake that was clear as glass. As I proceeded down into the valley, I began to notice wildlife. The calls of unseen birds echoed through the treetops and bounced down through the clear air to strike my ears. I saw movements in the undergrowth which I took for small animals, hesitant to come out from their hiding places. A few larger animals, such as deer, seemed curious. Apparently, to them, I was just another animal and nothing to fear.

What do you find out about national forests from each source? How is the style of each source different? What kind of graphic organizer could you use to visually integrate the information in both sources?

TRY THE STRATEGIES

With a partner, select a topic that interests you, and look for information about it in several kinds of sources. Compare the information found in each source. Find a way to organize and combine your information in order to present it to the class in some new form.

Recognizing distinctive and shared characteristics of cultures

When reading literature from different world cultures, you will find common themes about human nature. You will also see the ways in which distinctive characteristics of cultures increase your appreciation of those themes while enriching the understanding, knowledge, and enjoyment you have for your own roots. Fairy tales, for example, often have counterparts in different cultures, so reading an Egyptian, a Native American, and an Asian version of "Cinderella" enhances your understanding of the story and also shows you the beauty and subtleties of different cultural traditions. Notice the similarities and differences in the elements of the Cinderella story in the four cultures charted at the top of page R97.

Culture	Heroine	Supernatural elements	Special clothing	Outcome
American/ European	Cinderella, mistreated stepchild	Fairy godmother	Glass slippers	Marries the prince
Zuni (Native American)	Turkey girl, turkey herder	Sacred turkeys	White doeskin robes	Breaks her promise and returns to rags
Egyptian	Rhodopis, Greek slave girl	Falcon	Rose-red slippers	Marries the Pharaoh
Hmong (Asian)	Jouanah, despised stepchild	Dead mother's spirit	Special sandals	Finds love and happiness

Literary Response

Whenever you share your thoughts and feelings about something you've read, you are responding to text. Since we are all different people, though, we respond in different ways. Everyone has a learning style. Some learn best when speaking and writing, while others enjoy moving around or creating something artistic. What you do when you read can take different forms. Some responses to reading can include discussions, journals, oral interpretations, and dramatizations.

Responding to informational and aesthetic elements

You respond to what you read with both your mind and your emotions. To respond intellectually, think about whether ideas are logical and well supported. To respond emotionally, ask yourself how you feel about a selection.

Tips for Interpreting and Responding to Literature

- **Discuss** what you have read and share your views of the selections with your teacher and other students in the class.
- **Keep a journal** about what you read. Record your thoughts, feelings, or what you have learned in a journal. Write down what impresses you as well as what questions you have.
- **Read aloud** to yourself or with others. Poetry and drama make particularly good read-aloud materials, but even nonfiction passages can become clearer if troublesome passages are read orally.
- **Take part in dramatizations** and **oral interpretations.** Present characters through actions and dialogue. Use your voice, facial expressions, and body language to convey meaning. A **readers theater** is one kind of dramatic presentation in which students take different parts and read through a play or other fictional work.

Using text elements to defend personal interpretations

Whatever your response to a selection or your interpretation of a theme, you must be sure to use elements of the text to support those responses and interpretations. You need to provide details given by the writer to back up your interpretation. If you can't provide those text proofs, you may need to rethink your response.

Often you are asked to write about the selections you read. It is not enough to say, "I really liked the main character." You must know why you liked him or her. Look for specific descriptions. What did you find interesting about a story's setting? What details created certain feelings in you?

Comparing personal responses with authoritative views

Critics' reviews may encourage you to read a book, see a film, or attend a performance. They may also warn you that whatever is reviewed is not acceptable entertainment or is not valued by the reviewer.

Ask yourself the following questions:

- Would I go to a movie if it got a bad review from critics?
- Would I read a book if a reviewer said that it was a waste of time?
- Do I ever disagree with reviewers?

Deciding whether or not to value a review depends on the credibility of the reviewer, and also on your own personal viewpoints and feelings. Be sure that as you read authoritative reviews, you determine if the writer's opinions are supported with adequate and accurate details. Read the following model.

Review of *The Mask of Zorro*

Producers: Doug Claybourne, David Foster

Holding out for a hero

Dashing *caballeros* in gleaming black-leather boots, cracking their bullwhips, flashing their swords and smoking disdainfully slim cigars: If stars Anthony Hopkins and Antonio Banderas had succumbed to the temptation to camp it up, this would be *The Phantom* all over again. But the Tonys swash their buckles straight—OK, with just the slightest hint of knowing smiles—and the result is old-fashioned fun. . . . The year is 1821, and the people of Alta California are caught in the war between Mexican revolutionary Santa Ana and the forces of Spanish oppression, embodied in brutal governor Don Rafael Montero (Stuart Smith). Their only hope: the avenger named Zorro

(Spanish for "fox"), who cuts a dashing figure in his black mask and cape while fighting for justice and the rights of the poor and defenseless. The man behind the mask is aristocratic Don Diego de la Vega (Hopkins), whom Montero ferrets out and imprisons; his wife is killed and his infant daughter Elena kidnapped to be raised as Montero's own child. Twenty years later, Elena is a beautiful and spirited young woman (Catherine Zeta-Jones), Montero has hatched a new plan to exploit Alta California to his own ends, and Don Diego has escaped and is training a successor, the bandit Alejandro Murieta (Banderas), who has his own unfinished business with Montero's minions. Rakishly handsome and a natural-born charmer, Banderas wears Zorro's slightly fetishistic getup with such graceful delight that the slate is wiped clean of such travesties as *Zorro, the Gay Blade.* But the movie's secret weapon is Hopkins, whose Don Diego is a grizzled bon vivant who can still break a lady's heart as smoothly as he can extinguish candles with his whip.

—Maitland McDonagh, *TV Guide*

If you have seen the film, answer these questions:

- Is the review balanced? Does it refer to both the positive and negative aspects of the film?
- What does the reviewer like best about the film?
- How does the reviewer evaluate weaker parts of the film?
- With what other film does he or she compare *The Mask of Zorro*?
- If you disagree with the reviewer, what do you think the reviewer failed to recognize in the film that might have influenced what he or she wrote?

If you have not seen the film, answer these questions:

- Based on this review, would you go to see this film? Why or why not?
- What evidence can you find that the reviewer is reliable?
- Does he or she back up opinions with facts?
- What bias, if any, does the reviewer reveal?

TRY THE STRATEGIES

In the weekend newspaper or on the Internet, find a review of a recent film. Use the questions and directives above to help you evaluate the review. If you have not seen the film, would the review influence you to see it? Why or why not? If you have seen the film, in what ways do you agree with the review? In what ways do you disagree?

Analysis and Evaluation

Active readers want to go beyond a simple understanding of the words on a page. They want to do more than recall information or interpret thoughts and ideas. When you read, you will want to read critically, forming opinions about characters and ideas and making judgments using your own prior knowledge and information from the text.

Analyzing characteristics of texts

To be a critical reader and thinker, start by analyzing the characteristics of the text. Some text characteristics can include

- Structure Writers use patterns of organization to clearly present main ideas or themes. By figuring out what text structure a writer has used–for instance, chronological order, comparison-contrast, or cause and effect–you can better understand a writer's message. Look at the structure to unlock the meaning.
- Word choices Authors select words according to their connotations, which carry emotional or implied meanings, as well as their denotations, or dictionary meanings. A writer who uses the words *blabbed, tattled,* or *gossiped* to describe what someone said has a different attitude than an author who uses the words *reported, narrated,* or *documented.* Looking at word choices helps you determine the writer's attitude about a topic and establishes a general mood within a piece of writing.
- Intended audience Most selections are written with a specific audience in mind. A speech at a pep rally would have a different style than one given by a diplomat at the United Nations. Writers must know their audiences in order to write material that is appropriate and interesting to the people who will read it.

As you read, look for the structure and word choices a writer uses to characterize his or her writing. Determine the intended audience for each selection you read.

Evaluating the credibility of sources

Would you take an article on nuclear fission seriously if you knew it was written by a comedic actor? If you need to rely on accurate information, it helps to know who wrote the selection and if that writer is qualified to speak with authority. How did the writer become informed?

Tips for Determining Credibility of a Source

- Look at the possible motivation of the author. If a reporter, for instance, writes an article about the rise in crime rate, you might find the story believable. If you found out, though, that the reporter has a close relative who is a police officer, and who wants a raise in pay, you might begin to question the truth, or credibility, of the article.

- Check on the background of the author. Do some research on the Internet, for example, to discover whether the writer is an authority in his or her field. Authors sometimes slant the facts in their work to convince readers to agree with them.
- Look at the statements the author makes. Is the author's information fact or opinion? Can the writer's statements be proved by other sources?
- Consider the publication in which an article appears. Is it a well-known journal or respected newspaper?
- Ask the opinion of a librarian or teacher–someone who is likely to be familiar with a particular author.

When you read for factual information, be sure to check on the credibility of your source.

Heart Disease and Diet: The University of Toronto Study

The current barrage of studies coming out points specifically to correlations between soy protein consumption and lower rates [of cholestorol and triglycerides]. In 1990 Lumen Foods proudly participated in a study at the University of Toronto, funded by Canada's National Institute of Health. The study . . . was published in the July 1993 issue of *The New England Journal of Medicine.* It concluded that ". . . very high intakes of foods rich in soluble fiber lower blood cholesterol levels even when the main dietary modifiers of blood limpids—namely, saturated fat and cholesterol—are greatly reduced." . . . Dr. Jenkins, the principal researcher, wrote that subjects who were served our Heartline products saw "very significant fall(s) in total serum cholesterol . . . irrespective of whether they were taking soluble or insoluble fiber supplements." Nonetheless, the final paper *(New England Journal of Medicine)* did not distinguish between vegetable protein and soy protein as such.

How would it affect your opinion about this article if you discovered that the author was employed by Lumen Foods, manufacturer of soybean products? Has the author included mostly factual statements or opinions? In your opinion, what effect does the final statement have on the credibility of the source?

TRY THE STRATEGIES

Read the selection entitled "Night," on page 305 of your text. Is this author credible? How do you know? Can you determine the author's motive for writing the selection? Is the information in the selection fact or opinion?

Analyzing logical arguments and modes of reasoning

When you analyze works you've read, ask yourself whether the reasoning behind an author's views are logical. Two kinds of logical reasoning are

Inductive Reasoning By observing a limited number of particular cases, a reader arrives at a general or universal statement. This logic moves from the specific to the general.

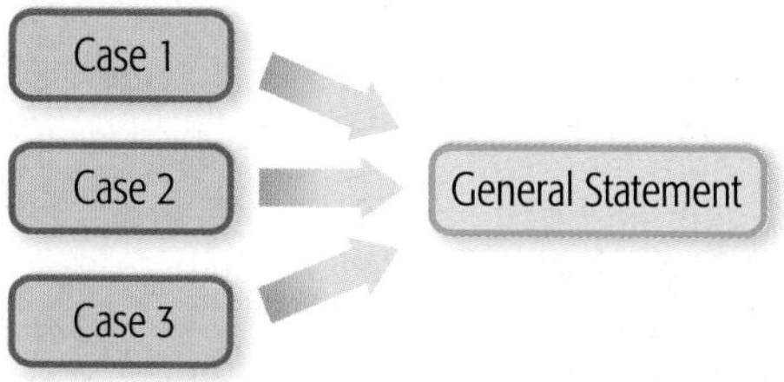

Deductive Reasoning This logic moves from that which is general to that which is specific. The reader takes a general statement and, through reasoning, applies it to specific situations.

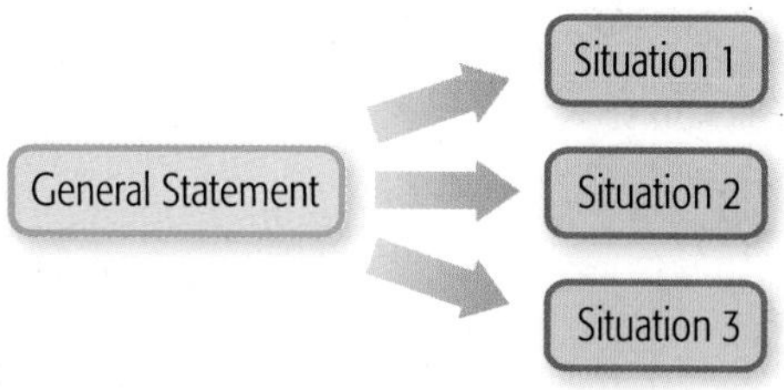

Identifying errors in logic

Whether reading an editorial, listening to a speech, or evaluating a commercial, watch out for these errors in logic:

- **Bare assertion** A claim is made and is not backed up with reasons.
  Go-Car-Go is the best gas on the market.
- **Oversimplifying** One cause or solution is given for a situation without the consideration of other factors.
  Annice wouldn't be so tired if she got to bed on time.
- **Begging the question** The writer assumes in a statement or definition the very point to be proved. Another name for this fallacy is circular reasoning.
  Teenagers cannot be trusted because they are irresponsible.
- **Either/or reasoning** This fallacy consists in reducing all options to two extremes.
  If you don't approve of capitalism, you must be a Communist.
- **Red herring** A highly controversial side issue is introduced that distracts from the issue under discussion.
  My political opponent is not a native of this state.

Sometimes writers neglect to support their arguments with facts, relying instead on opinions or generalizations. If ideas are not supported with facts, reasoning can become cloudy. When you interpret speeches and other persuasive writing, be sure to question the logic of the author to determine whether the reasoning is faulty.

Analyzing bias and persuasive techniques

A writer shows a **bias** when he or she demonstrates a strong, personal, and sometimes unreasonable opinion. An author who shows bias is inclined to a particular way of thinking. Editorials, documentaries, and advertisements commonly show bias. Writers use **persuasive techniques** when they try, through their writing, to get readers to believe a certain thing or to act in a particular way. A writer may have a strong personal bias and yet compose a persuasive essay that is logical and well supported. On the other hand, writers can be less than accurate in order to be persuasive. As a good reader, you'll need to judge whether a writer's bias influences his or her writing in negative or positive ways.

Look at some ways writers can misuse evidence in order to persuade:

- **Impressing with large numbers** Sometimes called the bandwagon appeal, this kind of argument relies on large numbers or references to *everybody* to be convincing.
  Over 5,000,000 satisfied customers have bought our product.
  Everybody raves about the new sports utility vehicle.
- **Irrelevant appeals to authority** An authority can only provide evidence in his or her own field. Dr. Joyce Brothers, for example, is not a competent authority in the field of breakfast cereals.
  Dr. Joyce Brothers says you won't be disappointed in the taste of Munchy Crunchies.
- **Appeal to popular sentiment** Some speakers or writers associate the point they are making with an item that enjoys popular appeal.
  Brushing with Toothful Polish is as important as drinking bottled water.

How well does the following paragraph persuade?

> There really is no need to build a new high school in our town. Another new school would only mean higher taxes for everyone. With all the new families moving into our community, it would be better to build more shopping malls. That would provide more jobs. Teachers have always been able to handle thirty or thirty-five students in a classroom. Besides, residents who no longer have children in school should not have to pay for all this fancy education. Vote "No" on the school referendum.

What bias does the writer show? With a partner, analyze the logic of the author's persuasive technique. How well are the writer's ideas supported?

TRY THE STRATEGIES

Find and read an editorial in the local newspaper. On your own paper, write a brief analysis of the writer's persuasive techniques. What kind of reasoning did the writer use? Was the writer biased?

Inquiry and Research

Asking and answering questions is at the very heart of being a good reader. You will need to read actively in order to research a topic assigned by a teacher. More often, you will need to generate an interesting, relevant, and researchable question on your own and locate appropriate print and nonprint information from a wide variety of sources. After you've done that, you'll need to categorize that information, evaluate it, and organize it in a new way in order to produce some kind of research project for a specific audience. Finally, you'll want to draw conclusions about your original research question, and in the best situations, that will lead you to other interesting questions and areas for further inquiry.

It sounds like a lot, but when you generate a question of strong interest to you, the process is fun and very worthwhile.

Generating relevant and interesting questions for research

Finding a good research question or topic is a very important first step and deserves your careful attention.

Tips for Generating Research Questions

- Think of a question or topic of interest to you.
- Choose a question that helps you focus your study on one main idea.
- Be sure your question is not too broad or too narrow.
  Too broad: How can we be ecologically more responsible?
  Better: What have Americans done in the last five years to preserve the Amazon rain forest?

Whether you are researching an assigned topic or a topic you have selected, start by generating questions.

Locating appropriate print and nonprint information

Because different sources present information in different ways, your research project will be more interesting and balanced when you read in a variety of sources. The following are some helpful print sources for research:

- Textbooks Texts include any book used as a basis for instruction or a source of information.
- Book indices A book index contains an alphabetical listing of books. Some book indices list books on specific subjects; others are more general. For example, H. W. Wilson's *Cumulative Book Index* lists hardcover and paperback books of fiction and nonfiction. Other indices list a variety of resources.
- Periodicals Magazines and journals are issued at regular intervals, but less frequently than daily. One way of locating information in magazines is to use the *Readers' Guide to Periodical Literature.* This guide is available in print form in most libraries. Here is a subject entry from the *Readers' Guide:*

DIGITAL TELEVISION
At war for 'eyeballs' [approved FCC standards for digital television] R. Coorsh. il *Consumers' Research Magazine* v80 p6 F '97
Battle lines [computer-televisions] J. Brinkley. il *Video* v21 p20 Jl/Ag '97
Bill Gates, the cable guy [wants to design set-top boxes and modems for digital TV] E. Lesly and A. Cortese. il *Business Week* p22-4 Jl 14 '97

- **Technical manuals** A manual is a guide or handbook intended to give instruction on how to perform a task or operate something. A vehicle owner's manual might give information on how to operate and service a car.
- **Reference books** These books include encyclopedias and almanacs, and are books used to locate specific pieces of information.
- **Electronic encyclopedias, databases, and the Internet** There are many ways to locate extensive information using your computer. Infotrac®, for instance, acts as an online readers guide. CD-ROM encyclopedias can provide easy access to all subjects.
- **Nonprint information** This includes anything that is not written down. Some good nonprint sources of information are films, videos, and recorded interviews.

Organizing and converting information

As you gather information from different sources, taking careful notes, you'll need to think about how to **synthesize** the information, that is, convert it into a unified whole, as well as how to change it into a form your audience will easily understand and that will meet your assignment guidelines.

First, ask yourself what you want your audience to know. Then, think about a pattern of organization, a structure that will best show your main ideas. You might ask yourself questions like the following:

- When comparing items or ideas, what graphic aids can I use?
- When showing the reasons something happened and the effects of certain actions, what text structure would be best?
- How can I briefly and clearly show important information to my audience?
- Would an illustration or even a cartoon help to make a certain point?

TRY THE STRATEGIES

Read a nonfiction selection from Unit 2 of your text. Based on a topic in the selection, create a question you would use as a focus for a research paper. Determine what kinds of sources you would use to gather information. Then plan how you would organize the material, including the graphic aids. Share your research plan with the class.

Adapting researched material for presentation

How should you present the material you've gathered? Before you decide, think about your audience and purpose. Who will receive this information? What is your purpose? When you change the information you've located in order to tell or show someone else, you are adapting your research material for presentation. There are many options you might consider:

- Written or oral report
- Interview
- Debate
- Dramatic presentation

● For more on publishing/presenting, see **Writing Handbook,** p. R61.

Drawing conclusions from gathered information

After you've spent considerable time looking at a research question, you will certainly form opinions about your topic. A conclusion is a general statement that you'll make about your research. It is important to explain your conclusions with good reasons and with supporting details from your sources.

Read the following excerpts and the conclusion that follows:

> Many scientists believe that acid deposition contributes to deforestation and soil degradation. It is known to dramatically accelerate the deterioration of buildings, including landmarks such as the Acropolis in Athens, the Taj Mahal in India, and the Statue of Liberty in New York City.
>
> —*National Geographic Information Central*

> It is not only plants and animals that suffer when the air is polluted. Buildings, sculptures, paintings, metal, glass, paper, leather, textiles, and rubber all deteriorate rapidly if exposed to sulphur dioxide, nitrogen oxides, or ozone.
>
> —*Norwegian Pollution Control Authority*

The chemical content of acid rain is in itself dangerous to fish and other freshwater organisms. Another, equally important reason why fish populations are depleted, impoverished, or, as is often the case, wiped out altogether, is that acid water leaches toxic aluminum from the soils and bedrock. . . .

—*Green Issues*

Conclusion: If acid rain is not controlled, both natural resources and manmade art treasures may be lost to future generations.

Tips for Drawing Conclusions

- Don't try to twist the facts to match your original idea.
- Don't make sweeping generalizations that go beyond the facts you've gathered.
- Be prepared to adjust your original question to reflect the information you've located. Recognize that your conclusions might be different from what you originally thought they might be.
- Be sure to accurately record where you've obtained your information.
- Never present ideas that aren't yours as if they were your own.
- Cite sources completely. If you're using a quote from someone, or if you present an idea taken from another source, be sure to use the proper notations.

TRY THE STRATEGIES

Read three or four articles about the same topic or current event. Compare the information and take careful notes. Then decide how you could organize and convert your information to support a reasonable conclusion, drawn from your reading.

● For more on citing sources and conducting research, see **Writing Handbook,** pp. R64–R69.

Writing Workshop Models

The following Writing Workshop Models are complete versions of the student models developed in the Writing Workshops at the end of each theme in this book. Use these models as examples of how one student might have responded to the assignments in the Writing Workshops.

Theme 1, pages 108-112

Personal Writing: Responding to a Short Story

My Response to "The Leap"

"The Leap," by Louise Erdrich, is about a remarkable woman who risks her life to save her daughter. The mother has lost her eyesight as a result of cataracts, but even without sight her life is a reflection of precise vision and courage. Her dexterity and skill achieved as a young trapeze artist saved a life not once, but twice. Reading this story left me stunned by her courage and physical skill, and it convinced me that even when you are terrified, you can and do make life-and-death decisions.

I can only imagine how the narrator's mother must have felt to lose the man she loved and the father of her unborn baby girl. I could feel the love and trust these two people shared. They were "like two sparkling birds" passing each other so high in the air, pausing and kissing "as they swooped past one another" during their trapeze act. When the storm struck and lightning destroyed the main pole of the circus tent, they began to fall to their death. This woman made a split-second decision not to cling to the man she loved, but to save herself and the child growing within her. She "changed direction" in midair, and her husband fell to his death.

The baby did not survive, but as the story continued, I became even more amazed by this courageous woman. Although talented and competent on the trapeze, she was illiterate. She was taught to read by her future husband during her recovery in the hospital. Books became a constant part of her life, and I found it tragic that life could be so unkind as to leave her without sight in the end. Yet, I somehow think she always had enough inner strength to handle whatever she encountered.

The mother remarried and had a daughter. Reading about how she saved her daughter from the fire in their home, when rescue seemed hopeless, left me with a feeling of awe. I couldn't believe it was possible to do something this brave. I was struck by how she took control of the situation. With no time to think about the consequences, this woman acted because it was necessary to save the life of her child. She climbed out on a tree branch near her daughter's window and jumped—flew—into the child's room. I could almost hear the tree branch as it broke, "so that it cracked in her hands, cracked louder than the flames as she vaulted with it toward the edge. . . ."

The story ends with a sentence that I needed to think about: "As you fall there is time to think." I guess there will be times in my life when I will have to make such quick, critical decisions. I just hope I will have as much strength and courage as the woman in this story when I need it most.

Descriptive Writing: Character Study

The Rainbow Lady

Before I moved here, I came from a small New England town where the days, the years, and even most of the people tended to blend together. But there was one woman in our town who stood out from all the rest, and her name was Vivian Esther. She stood very tall, and her silver gray hair was neatly braided, often with flowers. Her radiant complexion showed only the faintest hint of spider-like wrinkles around her eyes. We kids called her the "Rainbow Lady" because she wore dazzling green and yellow skirts, graced with cool pink and warm orange blouses. She turned out to be as kind as she was colorful.

The Rainbow Lady was best known around town as a keeper of cats—she had pet cats, stray cats, cats who were just visiting, and even cats she was asked to pet-sit. She held a special attraction for me because I loved cats and had never had one. My family often sat around our dinner table and talked about just how many cats really lived at her house.

I was soon to find out when our paths crossed early one October. She lived two blocks from us on the other side of the town green, where nearly all the houses were neat, white Victorians with black shutters, perfectly clipped lawns, and gardens that brimmed with appropriate seasonal blossoms. Her house stood on the corner lot, but it looked nothing like the neighboring Victorians. It was a crisp, yellow clapboard farmhouse with a sagging roofline. Ruby red shutters framed the glistening clean windows. The porch was filled with an array of multi-colored wicker furniture, laden with cushions and worn soft from sleeping cats.

That October day was cool and bright. As I walked by her house, I slowed down to see if I could spy her cats catching an afternoon snooze on the porch. I was so intent on trying to see the cats that I did not notice the Rainbow Lady sitting on the porch. Suddenly she stood up, dressed in several hues of green and blue, and smiled at me. "Hello," she called out, "would you like to come in for a visit?"

Well, of course I did, but I suddenly felt too shy to answer. As I walked up on the porch, I was disappointed when I didn't see any cats. The Rainbow Lady noticed the puzzled look on my face, smiled sweetly, and said, "They prefer the warmth of the parlor at this time of the day." She gently took me by the hand, and we walked into the parlor. The room was a reflection of its owner—vibrant with color and glowing in the sunlight. In contrast, on the couch were three black cats curled up together, looking almost like one. Overstuffed chairs held pairs of cats and kittens with their legs intertwined like knotted ropes. My eyes were drawn to a young orange tiger stretched out in solitude on the windowsill.

The Rainbow Lady moved ever so softly; I could barely hear the rustling of her skirt. She knelt and gave the tiger the softest kiss. Slowly he stirred, and she gave him a loving pet. As he stood to stretch, she picked him up and brought him over to me. My heart leaped. She sat me down, placed him gently in my lap, and patiently showed me how to pet him. I felt his contentment, and when he began to purr I looked into the Rainbow Lady's eyes.

"I think Muffin has found a new friend," she said warmly.

From then on the Rainbow Lady was more than a colorful character to me. She was Vivian, my new friend.

Theme 3, pages 270-273

Narrative Writing: Short Story

The Accident

Dad was not coming out of his coma, and my older brother, Chris, was finally on his way home after staying away from us for almost a year. I stared out at the runway. It was a crystal clear night, and I saw the approaching lights of the plane long before the wheels touched the ground. I looked through eyes that burned from having shed so many tears over the last two months. I usually enjoyed watching the delicate movement of these giant birds of steel as they came back to earth, but tonight I was filled only with an empty numbness; nothing seemed real.

As people exited the plane, everyone was greeted, kissed, and hugged by someone. I stood alone and waited. Then I saw him. The tattered green backpack was slung loosely over his left shoulder. His hair, which Dad always threatened to take a pair of scissors to, was still tucked behind his ears and secured with a rubber band, but that didn't matter anymore. Dad wouldn't be able to complain this time.

Chris pretty much quit talking to me last year, the same time he quit talking to Mom and Dad. Our eyes met as he got off the plane; he didn't say anything, just gave me a quick hug with one arm. We walked silently to the baggage claim area. I couldn't tell if he was still mad at us or if he was just sad. I couldn't tell if we were brothers again. His baggage came, and we went outside to catch a taxi.

The words automatically spilled from my mouth, "Columbia Presbyterian Hospital." How many more times these three dreadful words were to come out of my mouth, I didn't know. All I did know was that I had been living in their echo for the better part of two months. Since my mom was always at the hospital and there was no one home to drive me, I had to call taxis back and forth to the hospital all the time. Before the accident, I had never taken one.

Chris and I rode in silence as the taxi took us across the Kingstone Bridge. As we entered downtown, Chris finally spoke to me.

"It's gotten worse, not better, hasn't it?" he asked.

My palms began to sweat. "I think so," I answered. "They say the machines are the only thing keeping him alive." I reached out to Chris, but he only held my hand for a minute before he suddenly released his grip. Then he buried his head in his hands and started to cry.

"I shouldn't have," he said in between sobs. I felt my eyes well up. Did he mean he shouldn't have stayed away so long, or he shouldn't have come back at all? I reached out to him again, but he ignored my hand on his shoulder. When the taxi arrived at the hospital he had quit crying, but he still wasn't looking at me or talking.

The lobby, usually full of activity, was quiet tonight. We headed to the elevator, and I pushed the second-floor button. Our ride to the Intensive Care Unit, or ICU, was on its way. In coffin-like silence we rode the elevator to the second floor.

Landing on the ICU was like arriving on another planet. We stepped out of the elevator, and I saw Chris's eyes were riveted straight ahead to the ominous sliding glass doors that welcome people to the dreadful pain of the ICU. For some reason, I turned to him and said, "Don't move. I have to show you this." I went on to explain how the entrance doors to the ICU were highly sensitive and designed to open at the slightest human approach. "But I can beat the system," I said. At first Chris stood there wearing that "what are you talking about" expression, but then he crossed his arms over his chest, cocked his head, and, for the first time that night, grinned.

"O.K.," he said. "Prove it."

When I first figured out how to fool the doors a month ago, I thought of Chris. It was the kind of thing we used to do when we were little, when we were close. Would he think it was stupid now? As he watched, I inched my way along the wall and carefully stepped atop the gray plastic corner table strewn with magazines dating back to last Christmas. I ever so gently edged my way along the sagging fake leather couch and carefully slipped behind the five-foot palm tree. I found myself standing next to the ICU entrance doors. My heart was silently pounding, my mouth was dry, but the doors remained closed.

In silence, my eyes locked into my brother's. I was looking at a mirror image of myself. His crooked, half-bent grin burst into a full smile to match my own. Our father was still deathly ill, but I suddenly knew that whatever happened to him, I wouldn't be facing it alone. I had a brother. Chris walked toward me, the doors opened, and we walked together hand in hand into the ICU.

Theme 4, pages 346-350

Narrative Writing: Firsthand Account

The First Day

I lay awake in bed staring up at the ceiling, anxiously waiting for my alarm to go off. I had tossed and turned all night long and sleep was impossible. My stomach was doing flip-flops because it was the first day of school. My family had moved about a month ago, and although we had moved three times before, I still hated being the new kid. This time was different though. Not only was I starting at a new school where I didn't know anyone, it was high school and I was a freshman. They were two dreaded experiences rolled into one. I had heard so many horror stories of juniors and seniors picking on freshmen that I was scared to death.

The ringing of my alarm interrupted my thoughts. I threw off my covers, crawled out of bed, and stumbled into the bathroom. Every outfit I put on ended up in a heap on my floor. I had to look my best on the first day, but I was paranoid that the clothes that were cool back home wouldn't be cool here. Finally, I decided I couldn't go wrong with a T-shirt and jeans. My younger brother and sister inhaled their breakfast, but I was too nervous to eat. They had no idea what it was like to stress over high school.

My mom hurried the younger two outside to catch the bus and then drove me to school. During the ride, I imagined myself walking around and around the school, not finding any of my classes. I pictured a bunch of juniors and seniors knocking my books out of my hands and laughing when I bent down to pick them up. I heard my mother's comforting words of wisdom in the background as she drove, but they just came across as muffled sounds in my ears. As I got out of the car, my mom wished me luck. Thank goodness she didn't ask for a hug and kiss, since that would have been more than I could handle.

My heart was pounding so fast I thought it was going to burst out of my chest as I climbed the stairs into the school. It was a lot bigger than my old school, but, fortunately, my homeroom turned out to be the first room along the left wall. I would have rather died than ask someone where to go. I sat silently at the desk next to the door, smelling a fresh coat of paint. Next to me and behind me, kids I didn't know chatted excitedly about their summers or their after-school plans. We were all assigned lockers, the bell jangled in my ears, and we moved on to our next class. My classes all seemed to run together, with the teachers rambling on about rules, guidelines, and requirements.

The worst part of the day was lunch. Although I found my way to the cafeteria, I was mortified that I had no one to sit with. I waited in line for a bagel and iced tea. My stomach growled loudly since I had skipped breakfast, and I hoped that no one heard. I felt lost as I glanced around the lunchroom, but I managed to find an empty table and sat down. I was there by myself for what seemed like an eternity but was actually only a few minutes.

Eventually, other first-year students began to join me at my table. We were all pretty shy, but as we started to make small talk, I realized that everyone was just as unsure about this exciting, yet scary, environment as I was. I began to relax once I knew there were people sharing my own doubts and fears. While the end of the day could not come fast enough, and I still didn't really know anyone, none of the horror stories I had created in my head had come true, and I began to think that high school wasn't going to be that bad.

Theme 5, pages 426-429

Expository Writing: Biographical Essay

A Step Beyond

From the death of her beloved dog to the divorce of her parents, Heather was a target for bad luck. However, she never complained or whined, "Why me?" She had been challenged by many obstacles in her life, but her positive attitude and perseverance enabled her to succeed in spite of—or perhaps even because of—these hardships. Even when she had a catastrophic accident on the ski slope, she worked hard to bounce back and make the best of her situation. In fact, she worked so hard after the accident that she ended up achieving more than ever.

The accident happened on an unusually mild winter day in Vermont. The sun's reflection off the snow was blinding. The sky was a clear blue, with not even a cloud on the horizon. Almost everyone on the ski team had called it quits after a long day of hard training, but Heather wanted one more run. Her last slalom time had not been great, and she wanted to end with a good run. Standing at the top, she focused on the course and then sped through the starting gate. Just as she passed the halfway mark, her time looking promising, the tip of one of her new skis caught the stake of the blue gate. The sudden collision and her great momentum brought her tumbling to the ground. Only the outline of her skis and poles trailing her body could be seen sliding down the mountain under the giant spray of snow.

She had to be rushed to the hospital, where she learned that she had shattered the growth plate in her knee. Doctors informed her that she would need two major operations during the course of the next two years. Meanwhile, she would be unable to take part in any sort of strenuous physical activity, and it was doubtful she would ever downhill ski again. In one brief moment, all her hopes and dreams of being on the downhill ski team in college had been ruined. She stood on the sidelines and watched a teammate take away the state title she had wanted so much.

However, she never felt sorry for herself and refused to succumb to despair. After surgery, she fought through a great deal of pain and hardship, both emotion and physical. While she was heartbroken that she could no longer ski downhill, she worked with her physical therapist as hard as if she were training for an athletic event. She had to relearn simple things that she had always taken for granted, like how to climb stairs and how to get into and out of a chair. Many people would be frustrated and depressed under similar circumstances, but Heather approached the therapy as a challenge. In the process, she learned things about muscles, bones, and coordination that helped her when she was able to start training for a new sport—cross-country skiing. She battled to overcome what seemed insurmountable physical odds, but her dedication and perseverance finally paid off.

Three years after the accident, Heather confidently glided past her opponents in the last race of the season—the state finals. She saw the finish line in the near distance and was the first one to cross it—accompanied by the well-earned applause of hundreds of fans. Some were familiar faces and others were complete strangers, but they were all cheering on the new state champion. Because of Heather's perseverance and positive attitude, she achieved as a cross-country skier the goal she hadn't been able to achieve as a downhill skier before the accident.

Theme 6, pages 486-490

Persuasive Writing: Advice Essay

Getting Along

Parents and teenagers often have trouble getting along, and for a long time, my parents and I were no exception. Things have been a lot better between us this year, though. The reason is that we've each learned to try to understand where the other one is coming from, which makes it easier to compromise. I advise any parents and kids who are fighting a lot to try our approach: Identify the reasons the other person feels the way he or she does, take those into account, and then search for common ground.

I am a good example of how well this approach works because now I get along great with my parents, but up until last year, we used to argue all the time. It seemed like we fought over everything, but the main thing we disagreed on was what clothes, equipment, and food they would buy for me. My family isn't rich, but we are a long way from being poor. I didn't understand why almost every time I wanted something, from a four-dollar box of cereal to a two-hundred-dollar piece of computer hardware, they would tell me that it was unnecessary and wasteful.

Occasionally my parents compromised by letting me get a small or less expensive version of whatever I wanted, but this didn't stop the fights. Instead, I just thought that they were cheap and stingy. Finally, I got so frustrated that I yelled that at my father in the supermarket. Believe it or not, I actually screamed out, "Why are you always so stingy?" right in the cereal aisle. Needless to say, my father didn't appreciate that, and I got into trouble when I got home.

However, here's where we turned a corner: A few days later, my parents asked me to sit down with them. For the first time, they asked me in a calm and serious way why I wanted the things that I did. When they listened to my answer, they learned that not everything I asked for was just something I saw on TV. For example, I wanted a flat bed scanner for my computer because, as a future animator, I really felt I needed to learn more about how to manipulate art on the computer.

Then my parents told me a little bit about why they reacted the way they did when I asked for things. They said that before I was born, they had worked for two years in a country where people barely had enough to eat. They still volunteer at the soup kitchen every week. Being around people who couldn't count on having even the most basic things made my parents aware of how much so many people have and waste. They said that when they heard me saying that I "needed" this or that, all they could think about was the people who *really* needed something.

After this conversation, I started to think more carefully about what I asked for, and my parents became more willing to discuss those things instead of calling me wasteful. When we reached a compromise on whether or not I could get something, we all felt better about it. More importantly, we realized that the better we understood each other on any issue we fought over, the better chance we had of getting along.

Whether you're a parent or a teenager, you can try this approach next time there's a family fight. I'm not saying you'll always get what you want or that you'll never disagree again, but if you follow my advice, each person involved will feel less angry even if things don't go his or her way. First, wait a few days until the dust has settled—don't try to have this conversation when you're still angry—then invite the other person to sit down with you. Ask that person to explain what the issue means to him or her. Then, ask that person to listen while you explain yourself. Whether or not you can arrive at a compromise right away, you're on the road to understanding. The next time you get in a similar conflict, remind the person that you understand his or her position. A few moments later, ask if he or she understands you.

The important thing is that you try to understand each other before you try to convince the other person to agree with your point of view. This can sometimes be hard to do when tempers are flying, but take it from me, because I know from my own experience, a little understanding can go a long way.

Expository Writing: Extended Definition

Understanding Loyalty

What is loyalty? It's a word that's most often used in a positive sense. Most of us long for, and even expect, loyalty from our friends, families, and sweethearts, but do we always know what it means?

Loyalty is defined in the dictionary as a faithfulness that one feels and displays toward a person, cause, government, or duty. In other words, when you are loyal to something, you feel strongly about it, and your actions reflect that. However, loyalty is stronger than affection, which is an emotion that is not necessarily reflected in action. It is also stronger than gallantry, which is an act of kindness or bravery that does not necessarily have an emotion attached to it. Loyalty is both a feeling and a set of behaviors.

One type of loyalty is found between people. For example, my parents, my brothers and sister, and our dog all feel loyal to one another. The same thing goes for my best friends at school. My friend is a basketball player and he and his teammates are loyal to one another. My older brother has had the same girlfriend for a year, and their loyalty to one another is sweet and romantic. I'm lucky that my parents get along so well; I can see another kind of loyalty in their relationship.

Robert Burns's poem "A Red, Red Rose," which we read in class, is a great example of the intense loyalty that a lover can feel for his sweetheart. When I read the poem, I kept thinking about how great and deep this poet's love was for his girlfriend because he promised to be loyal to her "[t]ill a' the seas gang dry, . . . [a]nd the rocks melt wi' the sun!" Although he has to go away from his love, he is so loyal that he promises to come back to her "[t]ho' it were ten thousand mile!"

Loyalty can also be felt toward concepts or ideals. We hope our president and our senators and representatives do what's right for our country, and the world has the best chance for peace if countries remain loyal to the idea of true harmony.

Whether loyalty is felt toward an individual, a group, or an abstract idea, it always provides a sense of certainty in the person who is loyal; and it always provides a source of strength to the person or group who receives the loyalty. In this way, loyalty is like a security blanket—a source of security and comfort. It is also like a suit of armor—a source of protection and assurance.

Of course, all of us have seen ties of loyalty break: Some close friendships end; some of my friends' parents have had to get divorced. Loyalty can also have negative consequences. During wars, people use their loyalties to a cause to justify hurting or even killing others.

However, I want to think more about when loyalty works! Because loyalty is a feeling as well as a set of behaviors, you can really trust someone who is loyal to you. A loyal person won't claim to feel one way but act another way. Loyal people sincerely connect what they do with what they feel and say. The unswerving support that comes from loyalty can occasionally cause problems if the sentiment is misdirected, but without loyalty, the human race would be a scared, lonely, and vulnerable species.

Theme 8, pages 552-555

Creative Writing: Narrative Poem

I Feel Foreign, I Feel at Home

My parents speak a different native tongue
I hear Korean in our New Jersey home
And from relatives who call from Seoul, far-away.
But I prefer English—
The only language I think I'll need.

I've only seen pictures of this land,
My ancestors' country.
My parents worry I will never know
Those things they cannot forget.

On my thirteenth birthday, my parents tell me
Come summer, we are going to Korea for a month.
"My home is here!" I yell.
I blow up to my room like a storm.

July comes and we go, landing at Kimpo Airport in
Seoul.
The music flooding through my CD player
Is American, but the sights and sounds around me
Are distinctly Korean.
Everywhere I see Korean lettering,
Smiling Asian faces
Selling clothes, selling baby formula, selling cars.

I feel foreign, I feel at home.

Dad says the remains of ancient palaces
Still stand in each corner of the city.
In central Seoul, the department stores
Look like the ones we have in New Jersey.

Similar but different.
The young girls at the hotel wear white gloves with
Little hats that match their skirts.
They bow to my mother and father.

In a grocery store on a narrow side street
I see a giant container full of dried squid:
Hateful morsels, so chewy, so salty, so pungent.
My parents' favorite snack
Makes my lip curl and leaves me craving crackers.

While I stroll with my mother,
Kind old women with short, permed hair
Sell Korean delicacies on the street:
Airy rice cookies, dried beans, fruit, roasted
chestnuts.
I yearn for hamburgers and French fries.

My mother stops to greet a man selling fish-
shaped cookies from a wagon.
Her eyes light up as she tells me
How much she loves these cookies,
How she ate them as a child,
How popular they are among Koreans.
For her I will try one, and with baited breath,
She watches me eat a cookie,
This fish-shaped bean-paste cookie.
"Delicious!" I exclaim.
Mother is as delighted as I am surprised, and
I suddenly realize how important it is to my
parents that I learn to be Korean.

I feel foreign, I feel at home.

At Kimpo Airport, at journey's end,
Our relatives hug us and say
Come back soon!
When my aunt asks me if I liked Korea,
I tell her it is more beautiful than New Jersey!
Now my parents don't worry that I will never know
Those things they cannot forget.

We board the plane to New Jersey
And arrive at Newark Airport late at night.

I feel foreign, I feel at home.

Theme 9, pages 700-704

Expository Writing: Comparison-Contrast Essay

Comparing and Contrasting Romeo and Mercutio

Romeo and Mercutio, two characters in William Shakespeare's play *Romeo and Juliet*, are best friends. Like any pair of best friends, Romeo and Mercutio share differences as well as similarities. They have different attitudes toward romantic love, but they have similar attitudes about love and loyalty toward their friends and family. Shakespeare's portrayal of the friends' differences and similarities helps develop a major theme of the play—the constructive and destructive forces of love.

Romeo and Mercutio have very different ideas about romantic love. From the very beginning of the play, love is Romeo's entire motivation and the source of both his happiness and his suffering. For example, before Romeo meets Juliet at the beginning of the play, he tells Mercutio about his lovesickness for a young lady named Rosaline: "Under love's heavy burden do I sink" (1.4.22). Romeo then describes the emotional pain of love: "Is love a tender thing? It is too rough, / Too rude, too boist'rous and it pricks like thorn" (1.4.25-26). In contrast, Mercutio has a more practical attitude toward romantic love. He does not believe that someone should suffer because of romantic love. Mercutio offers Romeo sensible advice: "If love be rough with you, be rough with love" (1.4.27). In matters of romance, Mercutio does not believe in playing the helpless victim.

Romeo and Mercutio, however, do share similar views about the powerful bond of love and loyalty between friends and family. In act 3, scene 1, the strength of their friendship is put to the test. Tybalt challenges Romeo to a duel, but Romeo refuses to fight him. Tybalt does not know that Romeo has just secretly married Juliet and thus become Tybalt's cousin. Mercutio, seeing Romeo's refusal to fight as a threat to Romeo's reputation, feels compelled to save Romeo's honor and fights Tybalt in Romeo's place. As Romeo tries to stop the duel, Tybalt stabs and kills Mercutio. Romeo declares, "My very friend, hath got this mortal hurt / In my behalf—my reputation stain'd / With Tybalt's slander . . . " (3.1.106-108). Romeo then rises to defend Mercutio's honor by slaying Tybalt. This scene shows how both Romeo and Mercutio are willing to sacrifice their lives for the sake of their friendship.

The differences and similarities between Romeo's and Mercutio's attitudes toward love serve a dramatic purpose. The views and actions of these two friends help develop a major theme of the play—that love can be both a constructive and a destructive force. Out of love for Juliet, Romeo tries to end the feud between her family, the Capulets, and his family, the Montagues. Initially, he responds to Tybalt's challenge with love. When Tybalt challenges Romeo in act 3, Romeo says to him, "[I] love thee better than thou canst devise" (3.1.67). This shows that love can conquer hatred and bring about peace. However, love can also be destructive. Out of love for Romeo and loyalty to him, Mercutio insists on fighting Tybalt, but Mercutio's duel with Tybalt only intensifies the conflict between the feuding families and leads to a series of senseless deaths.

The differences and similarities between Romeo's and Mercutio's attitudes make the idea of love in *Romeo and Juliet* more complicated than it first appears. As one might expect in a love story, love is shown to be a powerful, wonderful thing, but love is also something that can encourage destructive behavior.

Theme 10, pages 794-797

Business Writing: Problem/Solution Report

Reclaiming Our Driveway

This is the second year we have lived in this house, and this spring, just like last year, our dirt driveway was almost impassable because of the spring thaw from the surrounding hills. To put it simply, for six weeks every year our driveway is a saturated bog. This situation creates two problems. The first is that the car gets stuck in the mud on a regular basis. The second is that we that can't pave the driveway and put up a permanent basketball hoop. I have a proposal that will solve both these problems.

The reason our driveway turns to mush in the spring is that hills rise immediately behind our house. When the snow on the hills melts, water rushes toward the lower ground. It heads right to our driveway, where it rises until the dirt becomes mud. Last year, after getting our car stuck so deeply that three people were needed to push it out of the driveway, we began parking on the side of the road. We put down planks so that we could walk up the driveway to get to our front door without sinking in mud, but the planks themselves started sinking. We couldn't go anywhere without mud caking our shoes and splashing on our pants.

In order to solve this problem, we need to channel the water away from the driveway and toward the side of our property. To do this, we should dig a ditch about six feet deep and two feet wide behind the house, making sure that the ditch gets slightly deeper as it goes farther away from the house. We should add drain tiles to the bottom of the ditch. Drain tiles are pipes with holes, which will take in any accumulated water and help redirect it. Finally, we should fill the ditch with large pieces of gravel, so any water that falls on it will trickle quickly down to the drain tiles and be whisked down the hill along the new, alternative route. If the water is rerouted around our house and away from the driveway, our driveway should be drier next spring, and we should be able to pave it without worrying that water from the spring thaw will crack the pavement.

Of course, if we reroute the water on our property, it might have consequences for our neighbors' property. Gravity always pulls water to lower ground, and their yards are a little bit lower than ours. If our new drainage system causes any problems for other families, we should help them set up their own drainage systems as well. That way, everyone will be able to get their cars out of their driveways, even in March and April when driveways typically have turned into tracts of mud. Perhaps more importantly, we'll have our choice of paved driveways on which to play basketball.

Expository Writing: Research Report

America's Betrayal and the Trail of Tears

Why would one group of people forcibly remove another group from their homeland? Could the relocated group ever recover from such a move? These questions must occur to anyone on first hearing about the forced march of the Cherokee. In 1838 Cherokee people living in Georgia were rounded up by federal troops and forced to walk eight hundred miles westward to an assigned section of Oklahoma. The Cherokee people call this sorrowful journey the "Trail Where They Cried" ("Brief"). Historians call it the "Trail of Tears." The events surrounding the Trail of Tears reveal a story of betrayal and injustice.

The Cherokee had strong and long-standing ties to their homeland. The early Cherokee people lived as warriors, hunters, and farmers in the southern area of the Appalachian Mountains. The territory of the Cherokee covered a vast region, including the present-day state of Georgia. When European explorers arrived during the mid-1500s, the Cherokee were the largest Native American group in North America. Most European explorers recognized the Cherokee's love for the land and respect of it (Fremon 12).

Around the beginning of the nineteenth century, the Cherokee started borrowing from the culture and customs of white settlers. For example, many Cherokee began to live in log cabins, raise cattle, and farm large fields. Some grew wealthy and set up large plantations. In 1821 a leader named Sequoya developed a written alphabet for the Cherokee. Using these letters, the Cherokee learned to read and write. They published an influential newspaper called the *Cherokee Phoenix*. By 1827 the Cherokee also had written a constitution that established a republican form of government, modeled after the U.S. government, for the Cherokee Nation. The Cherokee willingly adapted to many of the white settlers' ways and showed their trust for the country's political institutions. However, conflicts over land would undermine this trust.

The settlers' demand for Cherokee land in Georgia arose mainly from a struggle for political control. When the Cherokee adopted their constitution, Georgians felt threatened and declared that it violated the U.S. Constitution. The governor of Georgia asked President John Quincy Adams to support this position, while the state legislature took steps to force the Cherokee out of Georgia. In addition, the discovery of gold in Georgia in 1830 drew thousands of money-hungry settlers who were eager to make their fortunes (Fremon 56). White settlers and Southern cotton planters looked hungrily at the Cherokee Nation's rich land and pressured Cherokee leaders to exchange their traditional lands for territory in the West. However, the Cherokee resisted such demands.

In 1828, the year that Andrew Jackson was elected president of the United States, the Cherokee asked the U.S. Supreme Court to defend the rights of Native Americans in the Southeast. The state of Georgia claimed the right to make laws for the Cherokee. In response, the Cherokee claimed that federal treaties and the U.S. Constitution protected this Native American group as a self-ruling nation. In 1832 Chief Justice John Marshall sided with the Cherokee in their case against Georgia. The Supreme Court declared that Georgia's actions against the Cherokee were unconstitutional. In contrast, President Jackson sided with Georgia and vowed to defy the court ruling. Jackson reportedly said, "John Marshall has made his decision. Now let him enforce it" (Fremon 60).

While the Supreme Court debated the Cherokee Nation's claim to their land, Jackson persuaded his supporters in Congress to pass the Indian Removal Act of 1830. This act gave the federal government the authority to provide funds for negotiating treaties with Native Americans in the Southeast. The goal of these treaties would be to force Native Americans to move west. In 1835 the federal government persuaded a small group of Cherokee to sign the Treaty of New Echota. Under this treaty, the Cherokee were paid $5 million to exchange their lands in Georgia and Alabama for new territories in the West. Because the majority of Cherokee refused to sign the Treaty of New Echota, it was considered invalid by Cherokee law (Bealer 64). In a protest letter to the federal government and the people of the United States, a Cherokee who opposed the treaty clearly stated that the people wanted to stay on the land of their ancestors. Even former president John Quincy Adams, who was not always kind to the Cherokee when he was in office, called the treaty "infamous. . . . It brings eternal disgrace upon the country" (Fremon 71). This unfair treaty became the justification for removing the Cherokee from their homeland ("Brief").

The principal chief of the Cherokee, John Ross, appealed to the leaders in Washington, D.C., one last time. At first the new president, Martin Van Buren, agreed to let the Cherokee remain on their land for two more years, but then he changed his mind. On May 23, 1838, army troops under the command of General Winfield Scott stormed into Cherokee land. The troops invaded homes and dragged people from the fields. Thousands of Cherokee were put into stockades to wait for the long march to their new western lands ("Trail"). The Reverend James, who visited the stockades, wrote, "Many Cherokees who a few days ago were in comfortable circumstances are now victims of abject poverty. . . . It is a work of war in a time of peace" (Fremon 78). Some Cherokee escaped into the forest during this roundup. They hid in the Smoky Mountains, which lie between North Carolina and Tennessee. A brave Cherokee named Tsali escaped into the hills after killing a soldier who was harming his wife. Later Tsali and his sons turned themselves in and were executed in return for General Scott's guarantee that the rest of the Cherokee who had escaped into the mountains could remain there.

During October and November of 1838, the brutal forced march began. The Cherokee traveled an overland route that took them through Tennessee and Kentucky, the southern tip of Illinois, through Missouri and Arkansas, and finally to Oklahoma (Fremon 79). The conditions of the eight hundred-mile journey were horrendous. A doctor who accompanied the Cherokee estimated that more than four thousand of them, or almost one fifth of the entire Cherokee population, died. Illness, dehydration, malnutrition, and extreme weather conditions all contributed to the high mortality rate. Army private John Burnett recalled, "The sufferings of the Cherokees were awful. . . . They had to sleep in the wagons and on the ground without fire. And I have known as many as twenty-two of them to die in one night of pneumonia due to ill treatment, cold, and exposure" ("Trail"). John Ross's wife, Quatie Ross, was one of the thousands who perished on the Trail of Tears (Fremon 84).

The effects of the Trail of Tears on Cherokee life were devastating. The Cherokee were depleted in numbers and their cultural heritage nearly destroyed. In Oklahoma, old tensions reemerged and new ones surfaced. For example, the Cherokee who had opposed the Treaty of New Echota were still angry with those who had signed it. In fact, two of the men who had helped create the treaty were murdered by an anti-treaty group. Also, the new arrivals had to get along with another Native American group known as the Old Settlers, those who had migrated from the East as much as a generation earlier. For several years, brother was pitted against brother, and the new Cherokee land was the scene of violent conflicts. The feuding finally ended in 1846.

The descendants of the Cherokee who escaped the military roundup now number about six thousand. They have emerged as the Eastern Band of the Cherokee people. Today the Cherokee keep the memory of their ancestors' ordeal alive. Every year in Cherokee, North Carolina, a play called *Unto These Hills* is performed. This play tells the story of Tsali and the sacrifice he made so that at least a few Cherokee could remain on their true homeland (Fremon 90). In 1987, about 150 years after the forced removal of the Cherokee, Congress passed a bill designating the Trail of Tears as a National Historic Trail.

The Cherokee's claim to their land was justified and respected by many people of that time, including the chief justice of the United States and several senators. The Cherokee placed their trust in the American legal system, but that trust was betrayed. President Jackson's and President Van Buren's administrations used unfair strategies and policies to force the Cherokee from their land. The cruel treatment during the Trail of Tears is one of the saddest episodes in our nation's history. Such actions were betrayals of the democratic principles of the United States.

Works Cited

Bealer, Alex W. *Only the Names Remain*. New York: Little, 1996.

"Brief History of the Trail of Tears." *Cherokee Messenger*. The Cherokee Cultural Society of Houston. 11 Oct. 2000 <http://www.powersource.com/cherokee/history.html>.

Fremon, David K. *The Trail of Tears*. New York: New Discovery, 1994.

"The Trail of Tears." Cherokee Publishing. 11 Oct. 2000 <http://www.chota.com/cherokee/trail.html>.

Theme 12, pages 990-993

Persuasive Writing: Essay

Save the Rain Forest

People seem to enjoy speculating about what amazing discoveries might result from exploring other worlds. Researchers might find a cure for some terrible diseases! Well, you don't have to travel through deep space to find a promising but almost unknown world. There's one right here on Earth: It's called the rain forest. But unless we act to save the rain forest from destruction, we may never be able to explore its full potential.

We already know of many rain forest plants that provide substances useful in treating diseases. For example, the bark of plants called *curare lianas*, found in Latin America, contains an alkaloid used to treat diseases such as multiple sclerosis and Parkinson's disease. This same alkaloid has anesthetic qualities, making it useful in tonsillectomies, eye surgery, and other types of surgery. Madagascar's rosy periwinkle contains two important anti-tumor agents. If it weren't for wild yams from Mexico and Guatemala, we would not have cortisone, a drug used in the treatment of autoimmune disorders, inflammatory diseases, and certain cancers.

Scientists have only begun to uncover the treasures of the rain forest, yet those treasures are rapidly disappearing. The rain forests are being ravaged by the logging industry, and some old-growth forests will be completely destroyed by the early 2000s.

No one would dispute the fact that the world requires wood products to satisfy expanding building needs. There are no easy solutions to the problem, but there are helpful actions we can take. One important step is to increase public awareness of the value of the rain forests and the importance of continuing to use recycled wood pulp products. But first and foremost, we must not support companies that sell lumber harvested from old-growth forests. Instead, we need to support companies that have adopted strict policies prohibiting the use of old-growth pulp and have turned their energies toward developing lumber that is certified as having been harvested in a sustainable way.

If the destruction of the rain forests continues, it will bring about the destruction of plant life that could be a vital resource in fighting human diseases. Therefore, we must protect the rain forests by supporting the use of recycled wood-pulp products, the development of lumber that has been harvested in sustainable ways, and the pursuit of alternative sources of building materials.

Glossary

This glossary lists the vocabulary words found in the selections in this book. The definition given is for the word as it is used in the selection; you may wish to consult a dictionary for other meanings of these words. The key below is a guide to the pronunciation symbols used in each entry.

a	at	**ō**	hope	**ng**	sing
ā	ape	**ô**	fork, all	**th**	thin
ä	father	**oo**	wood, put	**<u>th</u>**	this
e	end	**o͞o**	fool	**zh**	treasure
ē	me	**oi**	oil	**ə**	ago, taken, pencil, lemon, circus
i	it	**ou**	out	**′**	indicates primary stress
ī	ice	**u**	up	**′**	indicates secondary stress
o	hot	**ū**	use		

A

accost (ə kôst′) *v.* to approach and speak to, especially in an aggressive manner; p. 88

adorn (ə dôrn′) *v.* to decorate; add beauty, honor, or distinction to; p. 84

adversary (ad′ vər ser′ ē) *n.* an opponent or enemy; p. 229

aghast (ə gast′) *adj.* filled with fear, horror, or amazement; p. 173

aloof (ə lo͞of′) *adj.* emotionally distant; uninvolved; disinterested; standoffish; p. 878

anguish (ang′ gwish) *n.* extreme mental or emotional suffering; p. 143

anthology (an thol′ ə jē) *n.* a collection of written works, such as poems, stories, or essays, in a single book or set; p. 314

antiquity (an tik′ wə tē) *n.* an ancient time or times; p. 214

apex (ā′ peks) *n.* the highest point; climax; p. 216

ardor (är′ dər) *n.* passion; intensity of emotion; enthusiasm; p. 835

articulate (ar tik′ yə lit) *adj.* able to express oneself well or effectively; p. 300

audible (ô′ də bəl) *adj.* capable of being heard; loud enough to be heard; p. 380

augment (ôg ment′) *v.* to become greater; increase; grow; p. 787

aversion (ə vur′ zhən) *n.* definite dislike combined with a desire to avoid whatever is disliked; p. 774

avert (ə vurt′) *v.* to turn away or aside; p. 237

avidly (av′ id lē) *adv.* eagerly; enthusiastically; p. 307

B

belittle (bi lit′ əl) *v.* to cause to seem less important; to scorn; p. 965

benevolently (bə nev′ ə lənt lē) *adv.* kindly; p. 230

bevy (bev′ ē) *n.* a group; p. 371

blighted (blīt′ əd) *adj.* damaged or spoiled; p. 264

bountiful (boun′ ti fəl) *adj.* overflowing with generosity; p. 773

C

careen (kə rēn′) *v.* to tilt or sway while moving, as if out of control; p. 256

cavort (kə vôrt′) *v.* to run and jump around playfully; p. 414

circuitous (sər kū′ ə təs) *adj.* roundabout; indirect; p. 354

cohort (kō′ hôrt′) *n.* a companion, associate, or member of the same group; p. 975

collective (kə lek′ tiv) *adj.* having to do with a group of persons or things; common; shared; p. 213

commandeer (kom′ ən dēr′) *v.* to seize by force or threats; p. 862

commemorate (kə mem′ ə rāt′) *v.* to preserve the memory of; p. 58

communal (kə mūn′ əl) *adj.* belonging to a community, society, or group; common; shared; p. 379

compassion (kəm pash′ ən) *n.* sympathy for another person's suffering or misfortune, combined with a desire to help; p. 753

compendium (kəm pen′ dē əm) *n.* a complete summary of the most important information on a subject; p. 319

comply (kəm plī′) *v.* to act in accordance with another's request; p. 63

composure (kəm pō′ zhər) *n.* self-control; calmness; p. 974

comprehensive (kom′ pri hen′ siv) *adj.* covering completely or broadly; inclusive; p. 952

concede (kən sēd′) *v.* to allow or grant, as a right or privilege; p. 387

condone (kən dōn′) *v.* to excuse or overlook an offense, usually a serious one, without criticism; p. 75

confidant (kon′ fə dant′) *n.* a person to whom secrets are entrusted; p. 396

conjecture (kən jek′ cher) *n.* the drawing of a conclusion without definite or sufficient evidence; p. 922

console (kən sōl′) *v.* to comfort or cheer someone experiencing sorrow or disappointment; p. 343

conspiracy (kən spir′ ə sē) *n.* the act of secretly planning together; p. 408

constricting (kən strikt′ ing) *adj.* restricting; limiting; p. 61

contemplate (kon′ təm plāt′) *v.* to give intense attention to; consider carefully; p. 725

contemptible (kən təmp′ tə bəl) *adj.* deserving of scorn; disgraceful; p. 865

contentious (kən ten′ shəs) *adj.* quarrelsome; argumentative; p. 845

conundrum (kə nun′ drəm) *n.* a puzzling or difficult problem; p. 371

converge (kən vurj′) *v.* to come together at a place; meet; p. 181

conviction (kən vik′ shən) *n.* a firmly established opinion or belief; p. 297

coveted (kuv′ i təd) *adj.* desired strongly; wished for longingly; p. 13

cower (kou′ ər) *v.* to crouch or shrink back, as in fear or shame; p. 853

craven (krā′ vən) *adj.* extremely cowardly; p. 118

crevice (krev′ is) *n.* a narrow crack in or through something; p. 959

D

declaim (di klām′) *v.* to speak as though giving a speech in a loud, formal manner; p. 321

deferential (def′ ə ren′ shəl) *adj.* respectful; p. 738

deflect (di flekt′) *v.* to cause to go off course; turn aside; p. 872

deplorable (di plôr′ ə bəl) *adj.* very bad; regrettable; p. 78

depreciate (di prē′ shē āt′) *v.* to lessen the price or value of; p. 9

deride (di rīd′) *v.* to treat with scorn; mock; ridicule; p. 952

din (din) *n.* loud, continuous noise; p. 309

dire (dīr) *adj.* dreadful; terrible; p. 46

discern (di surn′) *v.* to detect or recognize; make out; p. 71

disconsolate (dis kon′ sə lit) *adj.* so unhappy that nothing can comfort; hopeless and depressed; p. 169

discreet (dis krēt′) *adj.* showing good judgment; cautious; p. 158

disdainful (dis dān′ fəl) *adj.* showing scorn for something or someone regarded as unworthy; p. 120

disparity (dis par′ ə tē) *n.* inequality or difference; p. 356

disperse (dis purs′) *v.* to go off in different directions; scatter; p. 974

distraught (dis trôt′) *adj.* very upset; confused; p. 117

diverse (di vurs′) *adj.* markedly different; varied; p. 379

diverting (di vur′ ting) *adj.* amusing; entertaining; p. 78

doggedness (dô′ gid nəs) *n.* steady persistence; stubbornness; p. 264

dubious (do͞o′ bē əs) *adj.* skeptical; feeling doubt; p. 202

duly (do͞o′ lē) *adv.* rightfully; suitably; p. 19

dwindle (dwind′ əl) *v.* to gradually lessen; diminish; p. 835

E

ebb (eb) *v.* to become less or weaker; decline; fail; p. 912

elation (i lā′ shən) *n.* a feeling of great joy; ecstasy; p. 161

elemental (el′ ə ment′ əl) *adj.* of or like the forces of nature; ancient and powerful; p. 379

emaciated (i mā′ shē āt′ əd) *adj.* extremely thin; p. 307

emanate (em′ ə nāt′) *v.* to come forth; p. 46

embroider (em broi′ der) *v.* to make a written work more interesting with imaginary details or exaggerations; p. 314

emissary (em′ ə ser′ ē) *n.* a person or agent sent, often in secret, on an official mission; p. 915

enhance (en hans′) *v.* to make greater, as in strength, beauty, or value; intensify; p. 952

enigma (i nig′ mə) *n.* a mystery; a baffling person or thing; p. 910

enthrall (en thrôl′) *v.* to hold spellbound; fascinate; p. 159

ephemeral (i fem′ ər əl) *adj.* short-lived; temporary; passing quickly; p. 240

erratic (ə rat′ ik) *adj.* acting or moving irregularly or unpredictably; p. 946

evade (i vād′) *v.* to escape or avoid, often by cleverness; p. 379

excruciating (iks kro͞o′ shē ā′ ting) *adj.* agonizing; intensely painful; p. 342

exhilarated (ig zil′ ə rāt′ əd) *adj.* cheerful, lively, or excited; p. 398

expediency (iks pē′ dē ən sē) *n.* a means of achieving a particular goal; the quality of being appropriate to the end in view; p. 396

explicit (eks plis′ it) *adj.* definitely stated; clearly expressed; p. 89

exploit (eks′ ploit) *n.* a bold, daring deed; feat; p. 911

extricate (eks′ trə kāt′) *v.* to release from entanglement or difficulty; set free; p. 60

F

fervent (fur′ vənt) *adj.* having or showing great intensity of feeling; passionate; p. 47

filial (fil′ ē əl) *adj.* appropriate to a son or daughter; p. 203

finality (fī nal′ ə tē) *n.* the state of being settled; decisiveness; p. 245

flawed (flôd) *adj.* faulty; imperfect; blemished; p. 127

fluidity (flo͞o id′ ə tē) *n.* the ability, as of a liquid, to flow and change shape; p. 966

formidable (fôr′ mi də bəl) *adj.* causing fear, dread, awe, or admiration as a result of size, strength, power, or some other impressive quality; p. 815

fulfill (fool fil′) *v.* to measure up to, or satisfy; to bring to pass or make real; p. 315

futilely (fū′ til ē) *adv.* uselessly; vainly; hopelessly; p. 214

G

gamut (gam′ ət) *n.* the entire range or series of something; p. 174

genially (jēn′ yəl lē) *adv.* in a friendly way; pleasantly and cheerfully; p. 774

guile (gīl) *n.* slyness; craftiness; skillful deception; p. 815

guise (gīz) *n.* outward appearance; false appearance; p. 859

H

haggard (hag′ ərd) *adj.* having a worn and tired look; p. 117

harass (har′ əs) *v.* to bother or annoy repeatedly; p. 372

hover (huv′ ər) *v.* to remain suspended in the air in one place; p. 59

humility (hū mil′ ə tē) *n.* the quality of being humble or modest; p. 230

I

imminent (im′ ə nənt) *adj.* likely to happen soon; p. 21

impaired (im pārd′) *adj.* damaged; weakened; p. 737

impart (im pärt′) *v.* to make known; tell; p. 225

impartial (im pär′ shəl) *adj.* not favoring one side more than another; fair; p. 46

impassively (im pas′ iv lē) *adv.* in a way that shows no feeling; unemotionally; p. 736

impenetrable (im pen′ ə trə bəl) *adj.* unable to be pierced, entered, or passed through; p. 960

imperative (im per′ ə tiv) *adj.* absolutely necessary; p. 79

imperious (im pēr′ ē əs) *adj.* extremely proud and controlling; p. 47

impervious (im pur′ vē əs) *adj.* incapable of being passed through, affected, or disturbed; p. 331

implacable (im plak′ ə bəl) *adj.* impossible to satisfy or soothe; unyielding; p. 872

implication (im′ plə kā′ shən) *n.* suggestion; that which is logically indicated but not directly expressed; p. 952

implore (im plôr′) *v.* to ask earnestly; beg; p. 91

imposing (im pō′ zing) *adj.* impressive in appearance or manner; p. 397

impudence (im′ pyə dəns) *n.* speech or behavior that is aggressively forward or rude; p. 858

impunity (im pū′ nə tē) *n.* freedom from punishment, harm, or bad consequences; p. 87

imputation (im′ pyə tā′ shən) *n.* an accusation; p. 7

inadvertently (in′ ad vurt′ ənt lē) *adv.* accidentally; unintentionally; p. 944

inarticulate (in′ är tik′ yə lit) *adj.* not clearly expressed or pronounced; unclear; p. 716

inaugurate (in ô′ gyə rāt′) *v.* to make a formal beginning; p. 406

incessantly (in ses′ ənt lē) *adv.* endlessly; constantly; p. 169

incompetent (in kom′ pət ənt) *adj.* lacking ability, knowledge, or fitness; not capable; p. 356

incomprehensible (in′ kom pri hen′ sə bəl) *adj.* not understandable; p. 248

incongruously (in kong′ gro͞o′ əs lē) *adv.* in a way that does not fit; inappropriately; oddly; p. 246

incredulity (in′ krə do͞o′ lə tē) *n.* an unwillingness or inability to believe something; disbelief; p. 184

indiscernible (in′ di sur′ nə bəl) *adj.* difficult or impossible to see; p. 964

indulgence (in dul′ jəns) *n.* something granted or given; favor; privilege; p. 387

ineffectual (in′ i fek′ cho͞o əl) *adj.* not producing a desired result or effect; p. 285

infallibility (in fal′ ə bil′ ə tē) *n.* the state of being incapable of making an error; p. 262

infirmity (in fur′ mə tē) *n.* a weakness or ailment; p. 20

inflection (in flek′ shən) *n.* change or variation in the tone or pitch of the voice; p. 140

inhibition (in′ i bish′ ən) *n.* a restraint on one's natural impulses; p. 203

initiative (i nish′ ə tiv) *n.* the ability to lead or take the first step in an undertaking; p. 239

innuendo (in′ ū en′ dō) *n.* an insinuation or hint suggesting something unfavorable; p. 320

insidious (in sid′ ē əs) *adj.* slyly treacherous or deceitful; scheming; p. 841

insinuatingly (in sin′ ū āt′ ing lē) *adv.* in an indirect way; p. 118

insolent (in′ sə lənt) *adj.* so rude or proud as to be offensive; p. 118

instigate (in′ stə gāt′) *v.* to stir up or cause to happen; p. 7

intact (in takt′) *adj.* entire; untouched, uninjured and having all parts; p. 954

intimidate (in tim′ ə dāt′) *v.* to make timid or fearful; bully; p. 239

intuitive (in to͞o′ ə tiv) *adj.* rising from an impulse or natural tendency; instinctive; not learned; p. 297

irately (ī rāt′ lē) *adv.* in an enraged manner; angrily; p. 722

irreverent (i rev′ ər ənt) *adj.* showing a lack of proper respect; p. 399

irrevocably (i rev′ ə kə blē) *adv.* in a way that cannot be revoked or undone; completely and hopelessly; p. 913

J

jostle (jos′ əl) *v.* to bump, push, or shove roughly, as with elbows in a crowd; p. 870

justification (jus′ tə fə kā′ shən) *n.* a reason for an action that shows it to be just, right, or reasonable; p. 863

K

kilo (kē′ lō) *n.* short for kilogram, a unit of measure in the metric system equal to 1,000 grams (about 2.2 pounds); p. 127

L

languor (lang′ gər) *n.* a lack of spirit, interest, energy, or activity; mental or physical fatigue; p. 783

lavish (lav′ ish) *v.* to give generously; provide in abundance; p. 877

lithe (līth) *adj.* limber; bending easily; p. 205

lurid (loor′ id) *adj.* sensational; shocking; p. 939

lurk (lurk) *v.* to stay hidden, ready to attack; p. 965

M

malice (mal′ is) *n.* a desire to harm another; ill will; p. 934

malodorous (mal ō′ dər əs) *adj.* bad-smelling; stinky; p. 232

meager (mē′ gər) *adj.* inadequate in amount or quantity; p. 308

mediate (mē′ dē āt′) *v.* to settle a dispute between persons or sides by acting as a go-between; p. 775

millennium (mi len′ ē əm) *n.* one thousand years; *plural:* **millennia;** p. 246

moor (moor) *n.* a tract of open, rolling, wild land, often having marshes; p. 20

mortality (môr tal′ ə tē) *n.* the condition of being sure to die at some time; p. 342

mortified (môr′ tə fīd′) *adj.* deeply embarrassed, shamed, or humiliated; p. 859

muse (mūz) *v.* to think or reflect, especially in an idle, dreamy manner; p. 411

N

naive (nä ēv′) *adj.* innocent; unsophisticated; p. 300

nostalgia (nos tal′ jə) *n.* a sentimental longing for what is past or far away; p. 315

novel (nov′ əl) *adj.* new and unusual; p. 47

O

obliterated (ə blit′ ə rāt′ əd) *adj.* blotted or rubbed out; p. 183

oblivious (ə bliv′ ē əs) *adj.* unaware; not noticing; p. 733

obscure (əb skyoor′) *v.* to make difficult to understand; p. 229

obscurity (əb skyoor′ ə tē) *n.* the state of being undistinguished or not well known; p. 182

obstinate (ob′ stə nit) *adj.* stubborn; difficult to persuade; p. 716

omen (ō′ mən) *n.* a sign or event thought to foretell good or bad fortune; forewarning; p. 865

ominous (om′ ə nəs) *adj.* threatening; indicating harm or evil to come; p. 738

ostentatious (os′ tən tā′ shəs) *adj.* done with the intent of attracting notice; showy; p. 288

P

paltry (pôl′ trē) *adj.* practically worthless; insignificant; p. 321

pandemonium (pan′ də mō′ nē əm) *n.* wild uproar; p. 119

pang (pang) *n.* a sudden sharp feeling of pain or distress; p. 330

parched (pärcht) *adj.* severely dry; p. 343

parsimony (pär′ sə mō′ nē) *n.* stinginess; p. 7

patronizing (pā′ trə nīz′ ing) *adj.* being kind or helpful, but in a self-important or snobbish way, as if dealing with an inferior; p. 927

pauper (pô′ pər) *n.* a very poor person, especially one supported by public charity; p. 171

pensive (pen′ siv) *adj.* thinking deeply, often sadly; p. 200

peril (per′ əl) *n.* danger; risk; something that may cause injury or destruction; p. 836

periphery (pə rif′ ər ē) *n.* the surrounding area; outskirts; p. 246

perpetually (pər pech′ o͞o əl ē) *adv.* constantly; unceasingly; p. 61

perverse (pər vurs′) *adj.* determined to go against what is reasonable, expected, or desired; contrary; p. 933

picturesque (pik′ chə resk′) *adj.* having pleasing visual qualities suitable for a picture; pretty; p. 285

plaintive (plān′ tiv) *adj.* expressing sorrow; mournful; sad; p. 372

plait (plāt) *n.* a braid, as of hair; p. 31

plausible (plô′ zə bəl) *adj.* apparently true or acceptable; likely; p. 974

plunder (plun′ dər) *v.* to take (property) by force, especially in warfare; p. 813

pompous (pom′ pəs) *adj.* showing an exaggerated sense of self-importance; p. 288

ponderous (pon′ dər əs) *adj.* having great weight or bulk; heavy; p. 820

potent (pōt′ ənt) *adj.* having or exercising force, power, authority, or effectiveness; strong and powerful; p. 410

precariously (pri kār′ ē əs lē) *adv.* dangerously; insecurely; p. 265

precisely (pri sīs′ lē) *adv.* exactly; p. 128

preclude (pri klo͞od′) *v.* to prevent; make impossible; p. 87

precocious (pri kō′ shəs) *adj.* displaying maturity at an unusually early age; p. 717

prestigious (pres tē′ jəs) *adj.* having widely recognized importance and influence; p. 359

presume (pri zo͞om′) *v.* to take upon oneself without permission or authority; dare; p. 50

privation (prī vā′ shən) *n.* the lack of the comforts or basic necessities of life; p. 174

prodigious (prə dij′ əs) *adj.* extraordinary in size, number, or degree; enormous; p. 290

profound (prə found′) *adj.* significant; deep; intense; p. 156

profusion (prə fū′ zhən) *n.* plentiful amount; abundance; p. 821

prudence (pro͞od′ əns) *n.* cautious, good judgment; p. 10

purging (pur′ jing) *n.* a removal of whatever is unclean or undesirable; cleansing; p. 330

Q

quarry (kwôr′ ē) *n.* anything that is hunted or pursued, especially an animal; p. 70

quest (kwest) *v.* to seek; search or pursue in order to find something or achieve a goal; p. 838

R

ravage (rav′ ij) *n.* a destructive action or its results; p. 10

rawboned (rô′ bōnd′) *adj.* thin or very lean; p. 29

rebuke (ri būk′) *v.* to scold sharply; criticize; p. 859

reconcile (rek′ ən sīl′) *v.* make compatible or consistent; p. 240

reiterate (rē it′ ə rāt′) *v.* to say or do again; repeat; p. 265

relent (ri lent′) *v.* to become less harsh or strict; yield; p. 228

relinquish (ri ling′ kwish) *v.* to give up or surrender (something); p. 746

remorse (ri môrs′) *n.* a deep, painful feeling of guilt or sorrow for wrongdoing; p. 389

renowned (ri nound′) *adj.* famous; widely known; p. 861

restitution (res′ tə to͞o′ shən) *n.* compensation for something that has been lost, damaged, or taken away; p. 843

reticence (ret′ ə səns) *n.* the tendency to keep one's thoughts and feelings to oneself; p. 136

retrospect (ret′ rə spekt′) *n.* the act of looking back or thinking about the past; p. 314

revelry (rev′ əl rē) *n.* noisy festivity; merrymaking; p. 870

reverberate (ri vur′ bə rāt′) *v.* to echo; resound; p. 334

reverie (rev′ ər ē) *n.* fanciful thinking, especially of pleasant things; a daydream; p. 976

revulsion (ri vul′ shən) *n.* intense dislike, disgust, or horror; p. 872

ruefully (ro͞o′ fəl lē) *adv.* regretfully; p. 770

S

sage (sāj) *n.* a very wise person; p. 319

saunter (sôn′ tər) *n.* a slow, relaxed walk; stroll; p. 389

scruple (skro͞o′ pəl) *n.* an uneasy feeling or hesitancy to act that arises from moral or ethical considerations; p. 75

self-possessed (self′ pə zest′) *adj.* in control of oneself; composed; p. 19

sentinel (sent′ ən əl) *n.* someone or something stationed to guard against and warn of danger; guard; p. 915

serene (sə rēn′) *adj.* calm; peaceful; undisturbed; p. 262

severance (sev′ ər əns) *n.* the act of cutting off or apart; p. 341

shroud (shroud) *v.* to cover, as with a veil or burial cloth; conceal; p. 840

shun (shun) *v.* to keep away from; avoid; p. 834

simultaneously (sī′ məl tā′ nē əs lē) *adv.* at the same time; p. 725

skeptic (skep′ tik) *n.* one who tends to be doubtful or suspicious; p. 361

skulk (skulk) *v.* to move in a sly or sneaky way so as to escape notice; p. 965

solace (sol′ is) *n.* relief from sorrow or disappointment; comfort; p. 162

somnolence (som′ nə ləns) *n.* sleepiness; drowsiness; p. 373

sonorous (sə nôr′ əs) *adj.* rich and full sounding; p. 320

sporadically (spə rad′ i kəl lē) *adv.* irregularly; occasionally; p. 333

stoicism (stō′ ə siz′ əm) *n.* the ability to remain calm and unemotional, especially in spite of pain or suffering; p. 372

strident (strīd′ ənt) *adj.* loud, harsh, and shrill; p. 139

strive (strīv) *v.* to make an intense effort; p. 300

subtle (sut′ əl) *adj.* difficult to be perceived; not obvious; p. 240

suffuse (sə fūz′) *v.* to spread through or over; p. 330

sultrier (sul′ trē ər) *adj.* more hot and humid; p. 33

supplication (sup′ lə kā′ shən) *n.* earnest or humble request or prayer; p. 841

surreptitiously (sur′ əp tish′ əs lē) *adv.* secretly or slyly; p. 203

symmetrical (si met′ ri kəl) *adj.* exactly agreeing in size, form, and arrangement on both sides of something; p. 786

T

tangible (tan′ jə bəl) *adj.* capable of being touched or felt; p. 68

tantalize (tant′ əl īz′) *v.* to torment or tease by tempting with something and then withholding it; p. 909

tediously (tē′ dē əs lē) *adv.* in a bored and tiresome manner; dully; p. 341

temperance (tem′ pər əns) *n.* self-restraint or self-discipline in any kind of behavior; p. 736

tentative (ten′ tə tiv) *adj.* hesitant; uncertain; p. 63

throng (thrông) *n.* a large number of people or things crowded together; p. 329

transfixed (trans fikst′) *adj.* made motionless, as from awe or fear; p. 775

traverse (trə vurs′) *v.* to pass across or through; p. 786

tremulous (trem′ yə ləs) *adj.* characterized by trembling; shaky; p. 879

trepidation (trep′ ə dā′ shən) *n.* a feeling of nervous expectation; anxiety; p. 775

tumult (to͞o′məlt) *n.* commotion; uproar; p. 836

turbulent (tur′ byə lənt) *adj.* full of commotion, disorder, or violence; not calm or smooth; p. 288

U

ubiquitous (ū bik′ wə təs) *adj.* seeming to be everywhere at once; p. 214

ultimate (ul′ tə mit) *adj.* most significant; highest or final; p. 300

unkempt (un kempt′) *adj.* untidy; uncombed; messy; p. 711

unpretentious (un′ pri ten′ shəs) *adj.* modest; simple; not showy; p. 181

unprovoked (un′ prə vōkt′) *adj.* not incited or stirred to action (by something); p. 389

V

valor (val′ ər) *n.* great courage, especially in battle; p. 813

verbatim (vər bā′ tim) *adv.* word for word; in exactly the same words; p. 787

vexation (vek sā′ shən) *n.* anger, annoyance, or distress; p. 170

vigilant (vij′ ə lənt) *adj.* alert and watchful for danger or trouble; p. 159

vilify (vil′ ə fī′) *v.* to defame or malign someone with vicious and abusive statements; p. 358

vindictive (vin dik′ tiv) *adj.* wanting revenge; p. 144

vivacious (vi vā′ shəs) *adj.* full of life; lively; p. 711

vulnerable (vul′ nər ə bəl) *adj.* easily hurt or damaged; p. 373

W

whim (hwim) *n.* a sudden notion or fanciful idea; p. 387

wholesome (hōl′ səm) *adj.* promoting good health; healthful; p. 288

wily (wī′ lē) *adj.* tricky or sly; crafty; p. 870

wistful (wist′ fəl) *adj.* sadly longing; yearning; p. 764

Z

zealous (zel′ əs) *adj.* very eager; enthusiastic; p. 79

Spanish Glossary

A

accost/abordar *v.* acercarse o dirigirse a alguien de manera brusca; p. 88

adorn/adornar *v.* decorar; dar belleza, honrar o distinguir; p. 84

adversary/adversario *s.* oponente o enemigo; p. 229

aghast/estupefacto *adj.* lleno de temor, horror o sorpresa; p. 173

aloof/retraído *adj.* emocionalmente distante; desinteresado; reservado; p. 878

anguish/angustia *s.* extremo dolor emocional o mental; p. 143

anthology/antología *s.* colección de obras escritas, tales como poemas, cuentos o ensayos, en un solo texto; p. 314

antiquity/antigüedad *s.* época o épocas antiguas; p. 214

apex/ápice *s.* cima; cúspide; punto culminante; p. 216

ardor/ardor *s.* pasión; intensidad; entusiasmo; p. 835

articulate/elocuente *adj.* capaz de expresarse bien o efectivamente; p. 300

audible/audible *adj.* que se puede oír; con el suficiente volumen para escucharse; p. 380

augment/aumentar *v.* agrandar; acrecentar; p. 787

aversion/aversión *s.* fuerte antipatía, junto con el deseo de evitar lo que se detesta a toda costa; p. 774

avert/desviar *v.* apartar; alejar; p. 237

avidly/ávidamente *adv.* ansiosamente; con mucho entusiasmo; p. 307

B

belittle/empequeñecer; *v.* reducir; despreciar; menospreciar; p. 965

benevolently/benévolamente *adv.* amablemente; p. 230

bevy/bandada *s.* manada; grupo; p. 371

blighted/malogrado *adj.* dañado o arruinado; p. 264

bountiful/dadivoso *adj.* muy generoso; p. 773

C

careen/inclinar *v.* ladearse mientras se mueve, como cuando algo está fuera de control; p. 256

cavort/retozar *v.* correr y saltar juguetonamente; p. 414

circuitous/tortuoso *adj.* sinuoso; indirecto; p. 354

cohort/compañero *s.* socio o miembro de un grupo; secuaz; p. 975

collective/colectivo *adj.* relativo a un grupo de personas o cosas; común; compartido; p. 213

commandeer/confiscar *v.* adueñarse de algo mediante fuerza, autoridad o amenazas; p. 862

commemorate/conmemorar *v.* conservar el recuerdo de algo; p. 58

communal/comunal *adj.* que pertenece a una comunidad, sociedad o grupo; común; compartido; p. 379

compassion/compasión *s.* piedad por el sufrimiento de otra persona, junto con el deseo de ayudarla; p. 753

compendium/compendio *s.* resumen completo de la información más importante sobre un tema; p. 319

comply/obedecer *v.* actuar según la solicitud de otra persona; p. 63

composure/compostura *s.* autocontrol; calma; p. 974

comprehensive/completo *adj.* que cubre completa o ampliamente; exhaustivo; extenso; p. 952

concede/conceder *v.* permitir u otorgar, por ejemplo un derecho o privilegio; p. 387

condone/condonar *v.* excusar o ignorar una ofensa, por lo general grave, sin expresar crítica; p. 75

confidant/confidente *s.* persona a la que se confían los secretos; p. 396

conjecture/conjetura *s.* opinión que se forma sin tener evidencia definitiva o suficiente; p. 922

console/consolar *v.* animar o alentar a alguien que sufre o tiene un problema; p. 343

conspiracy/conspiración *s.* acto de planear secretamente en conjunto; p. 408

constricting/restrictivo *adj.* restringido; limitado; p. 61

contemplate/contemplar *v.* observar algo con gran atención; considerar cuidadosamente; p. 725

contemptible/despreciable *adj.* que merece desprecio; deshonroso; muy malo; p. 865

contentious/contencioso *adj.* conflictivo; peleador; p. 845

conundrum/acertijo *s.* problema complicado o difícil; p. 371

converge/converger *v.* reunirse en un lugar; p. 181

conviction/convicción *s.* opinión o creencia firmemente establecida; p. 297

coveted/codiciado *adj.* que se desea intensamente o por largo tiempo; p. 13

cower/acurrucarse *v.* agacharse o encogerse, como cuando se tiene miedo o vergüenza; p. 853

craven/pusilánime *adj.* muy cobarde; p. 118

crevice/grieta *s.* hendedura estrecha a través de algo; p. 959

D

declaim/declamar *v.* hablar en público con voz alta y de manera formal; p. 321

deferential/deferente *adj.* respetuoso; p. 738

deflect/desviar *v.* sacar de su curso; apartar; p. 872

deplorable/deplorable *adj.* muy malo; lamentable; p. 78

depreciate/depreciar *v.* reducir el valor o precio; p. 9

deride/mofarse *v.* burlarse; ridiculizar; p. 952

din/estrépito *s.* ruido fuerte y continuo; p. 309

dire/horrendo *adj.* espantoso; terrible; p. 46

discern/discernir *v.* detectar o reconocer; distinguir; p. 71

disconsolate/desconsolado *adj.* tan infeliz que nada lo puede consolar; desesperanzado y deprimido; p. 169

discreet/discreto *adj.* que muestra buen juicio; sensato; cauteloso; p. 158

disdainful/desdeñoso *adj.* que muestra fastidio o desprecio hacia algo o alguien; p. 120

disparity/disparidad *s.* desigualdad o diferencia; p. 356

disperse/dispersar *v.* despedir en diferentes direcciones; esparcir; p. 974

distraught/perturbado *adj.* muy molesto; confundido; p. 117

diverse/diverso *adj.* muy diferente; variado; p. 379

diverting/divertido *adj.* entretenido; ameno; p. 78

doggedness/obstinación *s.* gran persistencia; terquedad; p. 264

dubious/dudoso *adj.* que siente dudas; escéptico; p. 202

duly/debidamente *adv.* correctamente; apropiadamente; p. 19

dwindle/menguar *v.* reducir gradualmente; disminuir; p. 835

E

ebb/declinar *v.* reducir o debilitar; decaer; p. 912

elation/regocijo *s.* júbilo; sentimiento de inmensa alegría; p. 161

elemental/elemental *adj.* que sigue las fuerzas de la naturaleza; antiguo y poderoso; p. 379

emaciated/demacrado *adj.* extremadamente delgado; p. 307

emanate/emanar *v.* surgir; p. 46

embroider/adornar *v.* darle más interés a una narración escrita con detalles imaginarios o exageraciones; p. 314

emissary/emisario *s.* persona o agente que se envía, a menudo en secreto, a una misión oficial; p. 915

enhance/realzar *v.* aumentar, ya sea en fuerza, belleza o valor; intensificar; p. 952

enigma/enigma *s.* misterio; persona o cosa desconcertante; p. 910

enthrall/cautivar *v.* encantar; fascinar; p. 159

ephemeral/efímero *adj.* de corta vida; temporal; que pasa rápidamente; p. 240

erratic/errático *adj.* que actúa o se mueve de modo irregular o imprevisible; p. 946

evade/evadir *v.* escapar o evitar, a menudo usando la astucia; p. 379

excruciating/desgarrador *adj.* que causa inmenso dolor o pena; p. 342

exhilarated/alborozado *adj.* alegre, vivaz o emocionado; p. 398

expediency/conveniencia *s.* algo que permite alcanzar una meta; cualidad de ser apropiado para el fin deseado; p. 396

explicit/explícito *adj.* que se establece o expresa claramente; p. 89

exploit/proeza *s.* acto audaz e intrépido; hazaña; p. 911
extricate/desembrollar *v.* sacar de algo enredado o difícil; liberar; p. 60

F

fervent/ferviente *adj.* que demuestra gran intensidad o sentimiento; apasionado; p. 47
filial/filial *adj.* apropiado a un hijo o una hija; p. 203
finality/finalidad *s.* categórico; que no se puede cambiar; p. 245
flawed/dañado *adj.* defectuoso; imperfecto; deficiente; p. 127
fluidity/fluidez *s.* capacidad, como la de un líquido, de fluir y cambiar de forma; p. 966
formidable/formidable *adj.* que causa miedo, temor, asombro o admiración debido a su tamaño, fuerza u otra cualidad notoria; p. 815
fulfill/cumplir *v.* efectuar a cabalidad o cumplir; llevar a cabo o hacer realidad; p. 315
futilely/futilmente *adv.* inútilmente; en vano; p. 214

G

gamut/gama *s.* serie completa de algo; p. 174
genially/afablemente *adv.* de modo amistoso; agradable y amablemente; p. 774
guile/ardid *s.* trampa; falsedad; engaño muy bien planeado; p. 815
guise/encubrimiento *s.* disfraz; falsa apariencia; p. 859

H

haggard/demacrado *adj.* de aspecto cansado o enfermizo; p. 117
harass/acosar *v.* molestar o importunar repetidamente; p. 372
hover/suspender *v.* permanecer suspendido en el aire o en un mismo lugar; p. 59
humility/humildad *s.* cualidad de ser sencillo o modesto; p. 230

I

imminent/inminente *adj.* a punto de ocurrir; p. 21
impaired/deteriorado *adj.* dañado; debilitado; p. 737
impart/impartir *v.* comunicar; hacer saber; p. 225
impartial/imparcial *adj.* que no favorece a ningún lado; justo; p. 46
impassively/impasiblemente *adv.* sin mostrar sentimiento; indiferentemente; p. 736
impenetrable/impenetrable *adj.* que no se puede penetrar, entrar o atravesar; p. 960
imperative/imperativo *adj.* absolutamente necesario; p. 79
imperious/imperioso *adj.* extremadamente orgulloso y dominante; p. 47
impervious/imperturbable *adj.* que no se deja afectar o molestar; p. 331
implacable/implacable *adj.* imposible de satisfacer o calmar; inflexible; p. 872
implication/insinuación *s.* sugerencia; algo que se aconseja o sugiere indirectamente; p. 952
implore/implorar *v.* pedir desesperadamente; rogar; p. 91
imposing/imponente *adj.* impresionante en apariencia o actitud; p. 397
impudence/impudencia *s.* palabra o conducta descarada o en extremo inadecuada; p. 858
impunity/impunidad *s.* sin castigo, daño o consecuencias negativas; p. 87
imputation/imputación *s.* acusación; p. 7
inadvertently/inadvertidamente *adv.* accidentalmente; sin propósito o intención; p. 944
inarticulate/incapaz de expresarse *adj.* que no se expresa o pronuncia claramente; que no es claro; p. 716
inaugurate/inagurar *v.* iniciar algo formalmente; p. 406
incessantly/incesantemente *adv.* sin fin; constantemente; p. 169
incompetent/incompetente *adj.* que le falta habilidad, conocimiento o aptitud; incapaz; p. 356
incomprehensible/incomprensible *adj.* que no se entiende; p. 248
incongruously/incongruentemente *adv.* de un modo que no encaja o no se entiende; inapropiadamente; extrañamente; p. 246

incredulity/incredulidad *s.* incapacidad de creer algo; escepticismo; p. 184
indiscernible/indiscernible *adj.* difícil o imposible de ver; p. 964
indulgence/indulgencia *s.* algo que se otorga o concede; favor; privilegio; p. 387
ineffectual/ineficaz *adj.* que no produce el resultado o efecto deseado; p. 284
infallibility/infalibilidad *s.* condición de no cometer errores o fallas; p. 262
infirmity/dolencia *s.* debilidad o enfermedad; p. 20
inflection/inflexión *s.* cambio o variación en el tono de la voz; p. 140
inhibition/inhibición *s.* restricción de los impulsos o deseos naturales; p. 203
initiative/iniciativa *s.* capacidad de encabezar o dar el primer paso en un proyecto; p. 239
innuendo/indirecta *s.* insinuación o sugerencia de algo desfavorable; p. 320
insidious/insidioso *adj.* traicionero o engañoso; p. 841
insinuatingly/de modo insinuante *adv.* de modo indirecto; p. 118
insolent/insolente *adj.* tan grosero o altanero que ofende; p. 118
instigate/instigar *v.* hacer que algo ocurra; provocar; p. 7
intact/intacto *adj.* entero; sin lastimar; p. 954
intimidate/intimidar *v.* asustar; desafiar; p. 239
intuitive/intuitivo *adj.* que surge de un impulso o tendencia natural; instintivo; no aprendido; p. 297
irately/airadamente *adv.* rabiosamente; furiosamente; p. 722
irreverent/irreverente *adj.* que demuestra falta de respeto; p. 399
irrevocably/irrevocablemente *adv.* de un modo que no se puede cambiar o deshacer; inevitablemente; p. 913

J

jostle/empujar *v.* empellar o atropellar bruscamente, como cuando alguien se abre paso con los codos en medio de una multitud; p. 870
justification/justificación *s.* explicación de por qué una acción es justa, correcta o razonable; p. 863

K

kilo/kilo *s.* diminutivo de kilogramo, unidad de medida del sistema métrico equivalente a 1,000 gramos (aproximadamente 2.2 libras); p. 127

L

languor/languidez *s.* falta de vitalidad, interés, energía o actividad; fatiga mental o física; p. 783
lavish/prodigar *v.* dar generosamente; proporcionar en abundancia; p. 877
lithe/flexible *adj.* elástico; que se dobla fácilmente; p. 205
lurid/fenomenal *adj.* sensacional; impactante; p. 939
lurk/acechar *v.* permanecer escondido, listo para atacar; p. 965

M

malice/malicia *s.* deseo de lastimar a otro; mala intención; p. 934
malodorous/maloliente *adj.* de mal olor; pestilente; p. 232
meager/exiguo *adj.* muy escaso; limitado; p. 308
mediate/mediar *v.* tratar de arreglar una disputa entre dos partes; p. 775
millennium/milenio *s.* mil años; *plural:* **millennia;** p. 246
moor/marisma *s.* terreno bajo, anegadizo y silvestre que por lo común tiene pantanos; p. 20
mortality/mortalidad *s.* cualidad de mortal; dícese de lo que ha de morir o está sujeto a la muerte; p. 342
mortified/mortificado *adj.* profundamente apenado, avergonzado o humillado; p. 859
muse/meditar *v.* pensar o reflexionar, especialmente de modo soñador; p. 411

N

naive/ingenuo *adj.* inocente; inexperto; p. 300
nostalgia/nostalgia *s.* añoranza o deseo de lo que ya pasó o está lejano; p. 315
novel/novel *adj.* nuevo y original; p. 47

O

obliterated/arrasado *adj.* desvanecido o borrado; p. 183

oblivious/abstraído *adj.* distraído; que no se da cuenta; p. 733

obscure/confundir *v.* hacer que algo sea difícil de entender; p. 229

obscurity/obscuridad *s.* humildad; baja condición social; p. 182

obstinate/obstinado *adj.* terco; difícil de persuadir; p. 716

omen/presagio *s.* suceso que se considera signo de buena o mala suerte; augurio; p. 865

ominous/ominoso *adj.* siniestro; que indica que algo malo o diabólico está por llegar; p. 738

ostentatious/ostentoso *adj.* hecho con el fin de llamar la atención; llamativo; p. 288

P

paltry/insignificante *adj.* prácticamente sin valor; miserable; p. 321

pandemonium/pandemonio *s.* tumulto; alboroto; p. 119

pang/punzada *s.* sentimiento súbito de dolor o angustia; p. 330

parched/reseco *adj.* árido; extremadamente seco; p. 343

parsimony/parquedad *s.* tacañería; p. 7

patronizing/condescendiente *adj.* amable o útil, pero de un modo arrogante, como con alguien inferior; p. 927

pauper/indigente *s.* persona muy pobre que vive de la caridad pública; p. 171

pensive/pensativo *adj.* meditabundo; triste; p. 200

peril/peligro *s.* riesgo; algo que puede causar herida o destrucción; p. 836

periphery/periferia *s.* alrededores; extramuros; p. 246

perpetually/perpetuamente *adv.* de modo constante; incesantemente; p. 61

perverse/perverso *adj.* resuelto a ir en contra de lo razonable o deseado; contrario; p. 933

picturesque/pintoresco *adj.* que tiene características visuales placenteras como las de una pintura; bonito; p. 285

plaintive/quejumbroso *adj.* que expresa dolor; lastimero; triste; p. 372

plait/trenza *s.* arreglo del cabello; p. 31

plausible/plausible *adj.* aparentemente cierto o aceptable; probable; p. 974

plunder/saquear *v.* llevarse bienes ajenos a la fuerza, especialmente durante un disturbio o guerra; p. 813

pompous/pomposo *adj.* que muestra exagerado orgullo; petulante; p. 288

ponderous/voluminoso *adj.* que tiene gran peso o volumen; abultado; p. 820

potent/potente *adj.* que tiene mucha fuerza o efectividad; que ejerce poder o autoridad; fuerte y poderoso; p. 410

precariously/precariamente *adv.* inseguramente; deficientemente; p. 265

precisely/precisamente *adv.* exactamente; p. 128

preclude/imposibilitar *v.* impedir; hacer imposible; p. 87

precocious/precoz *adj.* que muestra madurez a temprana edad; p. 717

prestigious/prestigioso *adj.* que tiene amplio reconocimiento e influencia; p. 359

presume/osar *v.* hacer algo sin permiso o autoridad; atreverse; p. 50

privation/privación *s.* apuro; miseria; estrechez; p. 174

prodigious/prodigioso *adj.* extraordinario en tamaño, número o grado; enorme; p. 290

profound/profundo *adj.* significativo; intenso; p. 156

profusion/profusión *s.* en grandes cantidades; abundancia; p. 821

prudence/prudencia *s.* cautela; buen juicio; p. 10

purging/purga *s.* purificación de todo lo que no es limpio ni deseable; limpieza; p. 330

Q

quarry/presa *s.* cualquier cosa que se caza o busca, especialmente un animal durante una cacería; p. 70

quest/buscar *v.* ir en pos de algo con el fin de alcanzar una meta; p. 838

R

ravage/asolamiento *s.* acción destructiva o resultados de la misma; p. 10
rawboned/huesudo *adj.* muy flaco o enjuto; p. 29
rebuke/regañar *v.* reprender severamente; criticar; p. 859
reconcile/conciliar *v.* hacer compatible o uniforme; p. 240
reiterate/reiterar *v.* decir o hacer de nuevo; repetir; p. 265
relent/aplacarse *v.* volverse menos severo o estricto; ceder; p. 228
relinquish/rendir *v.* ceder o renunciar a algo; p. 746
remorse/remordimiento *s.* sentimiento profundo de culpa por una mala acción; p. 389
renowned/renombrado *adj.* famoso; muy conocido; p. 861
restitution/restitución *s.* compensación por algo que se ha perdido, dañado o que ha sido robado; p. 843
reticence/reserva *s.* tendencia a guardarse para sí mismo los pensamientos y emociones; p. 136
retrospect/retrospectiva *s.* acción de mirar hacia atrás o de pensar en el pasado; p. 314
revelry/parranda *s.* fiesta ruidosa; jolgorio; p. 870
reverberate/reverberar *v.* hacer eco; resonar; p. 334
reverie/ensueño *s.* pensamiento soñador, especialmente de cosas agradables; ilusión; p. 976
revulsion/repulsión *s.* repugnancia, aborrecimiento u horror; p. 872
ruefully/desconsoladamente *adv.* tristemente; p. 770

S

sage/sabio *s.* persona que sabe y conoce mucho; p. 319
saunter/caminata *s.* paseo lento y tranquilo; p. 389
scruple/escrúpulo *s.* sentimiento de aprensión o duda para actuar que surge de consideraciones morales o éticas; p. 75
self-possessed/dueño de sí mismo *adj.* controlado; tranquilo; p. 19
sentinel/centinela *s.* algo o alguien que vigila y advierte del peligro; guarda; p. 915
serene/sereno *adj.* calmado; pacífico; inalterado; p. 262
severance/ruptura *s.* acto de cortar o apartar; separación; p. 341
shroud/amortajar *v.* cubrir con una sábana de muerto o mortaja; p. 840
shun/esquivar *v.* mantenerse alejado de algo; evitar; p. 834
simultaneously/simultáneamente *adv.* al mismo tiempo; p. 725
skeptic/escéptico *s.* que tiende a dudar o a sospechar; p. 361
skulk/emboscarse *v.* permanecer oculto para no ser notado; p. 965
solace/solaz *s.* alivio de una pena o desilusión; consuelo; p. 162
somnolence/somnolencia *s.* sueño; sopor; letargo; p. 373
sonorous/sonoro *adj.* sonido fuerte y vibrante; p. 320
sporadically/esporádicamente *adv.* irregularmente; ocasionalmente; p. 333
stoicism/estoicismo *s.* dominio propio para mantener la calma ante el sufrimiento y el dolor; p. 372
strident/estridente *adj.* sonido fuerte y rechinante; p. 139
strive/pugnar *v.* hacer un gran esfuerzo; p. 300
subtle/sutil *adj.* difícil de percibir; que no es obvio; p. 240
suffuse/cubrir *v.* bañar; difundir; p. 330
sultry/sofocante *adj.* muy caliente y húmedo; p. 33
supplication/súplica *s.* ruego o plegaria; p. 841
surreptitiously/clandestinamente *adv.* secreta o furtivamente; p. 203
symmetrical/simétrico *adj.* que tiene el mismo tamaño, forma y disposición en ambos lados; p. 786

T

tangible/tangible *adj.* que se puede tocar o sentir; palpable; p. 68
tantalize/tentar *v.* provocar con algo prohibido o inalcanzable; ofrecer algo para luego negarlo; p. 909

tediously/tediosamente *adv.* de modo aburrido; monótonamente; p. 341
temperance/templanza *s.* moderación o autodisciplina en cualquier conducta; p. 736
tentative/tentativo *adj.* posible; incierto; p. 63
throng/aglomeración *s.* gran cantidad de personas o cosas reunidas en montón; gentío; p. 329
transfixed/paralizado *adj.* quedar inmóvil del miedo o asombro; p. 775
traverse/cruzar *v.* atravesar de un lugar a otro; p. 786
tremulous/trémulo *adj.* estremecido; tembloroso; p. 879
trepidation/turbación *s.* estado de angustia o ansiedad; p. 775
tumult/tumulto *s.* conmoción; alboroto; p. 836
turbulent/turbulento *adj.* lleno de conmoción, desorden o violencia; inquieto; p. 288

U

ubiquitous/ubicuo *adj.* que parece estar en todas partes al mismo tiempo; p. 214
ultimate/supremo *adj.* lo más significativo; principal o final; p. 300
unkempt/desaliñado *adj.* con aspecto descuidado; desgreñado o desaseado; p. 711
unpretentious/modesto *adj.* sencillo; p. 181
unprovoked/inmotivado *adj.* respuesta sin motivo o provocación; p. 389

V

valor/valor *s.* valentía, especialmente durante una batalla; p. 813
verbatim/textualmente *adv.* al pie de la letra; exactamente en las mismas palabras; p. 787
vexation/fastidio *s.* rabia, molestia o disgusto; p. 170
vigilant/vigilante *adj.* alerta ante el peligro o dificultad; p. 159
vilify/calumniar *v.* difamar o desacreditar; hacer comentarios mal intencionados; p. 358
vindictive/vengativo *adj.* que desea vengarse; p. 144
vivacious/vivaz *adj.* lleno de vida; animado; p. 711
vulnerable/vulnerable *adj.* que se lastima o daña fácilmente; p. 373

W

whim/capricho *s.* idea repentina; antojo; deseo súbito; p. 387
wholesome/saludable *adj.* que promueve una buena salud; p. 288
wily/taimado *adj.* tramposo; hipócrita; solapado; p. 870
wistful/nostálgico *adj.* que añora algo; melancólico; p. 764

Z

zealous/fervoroso *adj.* muy ansioso; entusiasta; p. 79

Index of Skills

References beginning with R refer to handbook pages.

Literary Concepts & Techniques

Reading & Thinking

Grammar and Language

Vocabulary

Writing

Listening, Speaking, and Viewing

Research and Study Skills

Media and Technology

Life Skills

Interdisciplinary Studies

Index of Authors and Titles

U

V

W

Y

Z

Index of Art and Artists

Acknowledgments

(Continued from page ii)

Literature

Unit 1

"Before the End of Summer" by Grant Moss Jr. Reprinted by permission, © 1960 The New Yorker Magazine, Inc. All rights reserved.

"The Leap," copyright © 1990 by Louise Erdrich. This story first appeared in *Harpers* magazine (March 1990) and was later adapted and made part of Ms. Erdrich's novel *Tales of Burning Love* (HarperCollins 1996). Reprinted by permission of the author.

"The Most Dangerous Game" by Richard Connell. Copyright © 1924 by Richard Connell. Copyright renewed © 1952 by Louise Fox Connell. Reprinted by permission of Brandt & Brandt Literary Agents, Inc.

From "To Protect Their Baby" by Liz Smith. Copyright © 1996 by Liz Smith. Reprinted by permission of William Morris Agency, Inc. on behalf of the author.

From "Secrets of the Paparazzi" reprinted with permission of *American Photo,* © 1992.

"Blues Ain't No Mockin' Bird" from *Gorilla, My Love* by Toni Bambara. Copyright © 1971 by Toni Cade Bambara. Reprinted by permission of Random House, Inc.

"The Secret Life of Walter Mitty" from *My World and Welcome To It* by James Thurber. Copyright © 1942 by James Thurber. Copyright © renewed 1970 by Helen Thurber and Rosemary A. Thurber. Reprinted by arrangement with Rosemary A. Thurber and the Barbara Hogenson Agency.

"Mystery Bugs" from the University of Kentucky Department of Entomology Web site, www.uky.edu/Agriculture/Entomology/enthp.htm. Reprinted by permission.

"Gaston" by William Saroyan. Permission granted by the Board of Trustees of Leland Stanford University.

"And Sarah Laughed" from *Rites of Passage* by Joanne Greenberg, published by Henry Holt & Co., 1972. Copyright ©1972 by Joanne Greenberg. Used by permission of the Wallace Literary Agency, Inc.

"Elena" by Pat Mora is reprinted with permission from the publisher of *Chants* (Houston: Arte Publico Press; University of Houston, 1985).

"American History" from *The Latin Deli: Prose & Poetry* by Judith Ortiz Cofer. Copyright © 1993 by Judith Ortiz Cofer. Reprinted by permission of The University of Georgia Press.

"The Winner" reprinted by permission of Barbara Kimenye.

"The Bass, the River and Sheila Mant" from *The Man Who Loved Levittown* by W. D. Wetherall, © 1985. Reprinted by permission of the University of Pittsburgh Press.

From "Courage That Runs in the Family" by Barbara Jones. GOOD HOUSEKEEPING, May 1996. Reprinted by permission of the author.

"Sweet Potato Pie" by Eugenia Collier, first published in *Black World,* August 1972. Reprinted by permission of the author.

"Rules of the Game," from THE JOY LUCK CLUB by Amy Tan. Copyright © 1989 by Amy Tan. Used by permission of Putnam Berkley, a division of Penguin Putnam Inc.

Reprinted courtesy of *Sports Illustrated,* March 2, 1992. Copyright © 1992, Time, Inc. "The Child Is Master" by Robert Horn. All rights reserved.

"The Horned Toad," copyright © 1983 by Gerald Haslam. Originally appeared in *New Arts Review* (January 1983). Reprinted by permission of the author.

Unit 2

Excerpt from "Pete Gray" by William C. Kashatus, author of ONE-ARMED WONDER: PETE GRAY, WARTIME BASEBALL AND THE AMERICAN DREAM (1995). Reprinted by permission.

Excerpt ("The Voodoo of Hell's Half-Acre") from *Black Boy* by Richard Wright. Copyright 1937, 1942, 1944, 1945 by Richard Wright. Copyright renewed 1973 by Ellen Wright. Reprinted by permission of HarperCollins Publishers, Inc.

From Elie Wiesel's Nobel Peace Prize acceptance speech, reprinted by permission of the Norwegian Nobel Institute.

Excerpt from *Night* by Elie Wiesel, translated by Stella Rodway. Copyright © 1960 by MacGibbon & Kee. Copyright renewed © 1988 by The Collins Publishing Group. Reprinted by permission of Hill & Wang, a division of Farrar, Straus & Giroux, Inc.

Untitled poem by Paulo Leminski, translated by Regina Alfarano. Revisions by Robert Creeley, from NOTHING THE SUN COULD NOT EXPLAIN. Sun & Moon Press, 1995. Reprinted by permission.

"Only Daughter" by Sandra Cisneros. Copyright © 1990 by Sandra Cisneros. First published in *Glamour,* November 1990. Reprinted by permission of Susan Bergholz Literary Services, New York. All rights reserved.

"Kipling and I" from *A Puerto Rican in New York* by Jesus Colon. Reprinted by permission of International Publishers.

Excerpt from *All God's Children Need Traveling Shoes* by Maya Angelou. Copyright © 1986 by Maya Angelou. Reprinted by permission of Random House, Inc.

"Field Trip" appears in *Never in a Hurry,* University of South Carolina Press, 1996. Reprinted by permission of the author, Naomi Shihab Nye.

From THE TRENTON PICKLE ORDINANCE by Dick Hyman. Copyright © 1976 by Dick Hyman. Used by permission of The Stephen Greene Press, an imprint of Penguin Putnam Inc.

"The United States vs. Susan B. Anthony" from *Women of Courage* by Margaret Truman. Copyright © 1976 by Margaret Truman Daniel. Reprinted by permission of HarperCollins Publishers.

"Good Old Uncle Albert," from *Never Cry Wolf* by Farley Mowat. Copyright © 1963 by Farley Mowat Ltd. By permission of Little, Brown and Company.

Excerpt from "Sunflowers are as American as they come" by Dennis Rodkin. *The Chicago Tribune,* August 10, 1997. Reprinted by permission of the author.

"Walking" by Linda Hogan, from *Dwellings: A Spiritual History of the Living World.* Copyright © 1995 by Linda Hogan.

Excerpt from "'Horse Whisperer' Takes a Different Tack in Training" by Dawn Hobbs. Copyright © 1998, Los Angeles Times. Reprinted by permission.

Excerpt from *West with the Night* by Beryl Markham. Copyright © 1942, 1983 by Beryl Markham. Reprinted by permission of North Point Press, a division of Farrar, Straus & Giroux, Inc.

"Of Dry Goods and Black Bow Ties" by Yoshiko Uchida. Reprinted courtesy of the Bancroft Library, University of California, Berkeley.

"A Christmas Memory" from *Breakfast at Tiffany's* by Truman Capote. Copyright © 1956 and renewed 1984 by Truman Capote. Reprinted by permission of Random House, Inc.

"Tia Chucha" from *The Concrete River,* copyright © 1991 by Luis J. Rodriguez. Reprinted with the permission of Curbstone Press, Inc.

Unit 3

"The Black Snake" from *Twelve Moons* by Mary Oliver. Copyright © 1979 by Mary Oliver. By permission of Little, Brown and Company.

"The Meadow Mouse," copyright © 1963 by Beatrice Roethke, Administratrix of the Estate of Theodore Roethke, from *The Collected Poems of Theodore Roethke* by Theodore Roethke. Used by permission of Doubleday, a division of Random House, Inc.

Excerpt from "Getting Her Kicks In: Butler's Earning Fame for Skill, Not Gender" by Michael Lee, *The Atlanta Journal-Constitution,* August 21, 1997. Reprinted with permission of *The Atlanta Journal* and *The Atlanta Constitution.*

"I Was a Skinny Tomboy Kid" from Bloodroot, copyright © 1977, 1982 by Alma Villanueva, Place of Heron Press, Austin, Texas. Reprinted by permission of the author.

"Purchase" from *Phantom Nightingale: Juvenilia* (Lotus, 1981), reprinted in *Remembrances of Spring: Collected Early Poems* (Michigan State University, 1993). Reprinted by permission of the author.

"Desmet, Idaho, March 1969" by Janet Cambell Hale. Copyright © 1975, 1993 by Kenneth Rosen. Reprinted from *Voices of the Rainbow,* edited by Kenneth Rosen, published by Arcade Publishing, Inc., New York, New York.

"The Funeral" FROM GORDON PARKS: WHISPERS OF INTIMATE THINGS, copyright © 1971 by Gordon Parks. Reprinted by permission of Penguin Putnam, Inc.

"The Space" from *New and Selected Poems* by Gary Soto. Copyright © 1995, published by Chronicle Books, San Francisco.

"Tears in Heaven" words and music by Eric Clapton and Will Jennings. Copyright © 1992 by E. C. Music Ltd. and Blue Sky Rider Songs. All rights for E. C. Music Ltd. administered by Unichappell Music Inc. International copyright secured. All rights reserved.

"who are you,little i," copyright © 1963, 1991 by the Trustees for the E. E. Cummings Trust, from *Complete Poems: 1904–1962* by E. E. Cummings. Edited by George J. Firmage. Reprinted by permission of Liveright Publishing Corporation.

"Goodnight Willie Lee, I'll See You in the Morning," copyright © 1975 by Alice Walker, from *Goodnight Willie Lee, I'll See You in the Morning* by Alice Walker. Used by permission of Doubleday, a division of Random House, Inc.

"The Reading" by Gabriel Gbadamosi. Reprinted by permission of the author.

"The World Is Not A Pleasant Place to Be" from *My House* by Nikki Giovanni. Copyright © 1972 by Nikki Giovanni. Reprinted by permission of HarperCollins Publishers.

"Serenity" by Gabriela Mistral, translated by Doris Dana. Copyright © 1971 by Doris Dana. Reprinted by arrangement with Doris Dana, c/o Joan Daves Agency as agent for the proprietor.

"Defining the Grateful Gesture" by Yvonne Sapia, appeared in *Valentine's Hair,* 1987, Northeastern University Press. Reprinted by permission of the author.

"My Mother Combs My Hair" by Chitra Banerjee Divakaruni, from *Black Candle,* copyright © 1991 by Chitra Banerjee Divakaruni. Reprinted by permission of CALYX Books.

"The Secret" by Denise Levertov, from *Poems 1960–1967.* Copyright © 1964 by Denise Levertov. Reprinted by permission of New Directions Publishing Corp.

"Mi Poesia/My Poetry" Copyright © 1980 by Maria Herrera-Sobek, from *Chasqui,* February–May 1980. Reprinted by permission of the author.

"Expression of Feelings, VII" by Yuan Mei, from *The Penguin Book of Chinese Verse,* translated by Robert Kotewall and Norman L. Smith, edited by A. R. Davis (Penguin Books, 1962). Translation copyright © Norman L. Smith and R. H. Kotewell, 1962.

"Peace" by Paula Yup, from *The Third Woman: Minority Writers of the United States,* Houghton Mifflin Company, 1980. Reprinted by permission of the author.

Haiku by Bashō, Haiku by Chiyo, from *Zen Art for Meditation* by Stewart W. Holmes and Chimyo Horioka. Copyright © 1973 by Charles E. Tuttle Co. Reprinted by permission.

Excerpt from The American Podiatric Medical Association Web site, reprinted by permission of the APMA.

"To the Foot from Its Child" from *A New Decade (Poems: 1958–1967)* by Pablo Neruda, translated by Alastair Reid. Copyright © 1969 by Alastair Reid. Used by permission of Grove/Atlantic.

"The Peace of Wild Things" from *Openings,* copyright © 1968 and renewed 1996 by Wendell Berry, reprinted by permission of Harcourt Brace & Company.

"Wanderer" by Joan Fallert, and "A Haiku" by Katy Peake, from *Shared Sightings,* edited by Sheila Golburgh Johnson, published by John Daniel & Co., Santa Barbara, CA, 1995.

From "How to Remember When You're Always Forgetting" by Dianne Hales. *Ladies Home Journal,* August 1995. Reprinted by permission of the author.

"Remember" from the book *She Had Some Horses* by Joy Harjo. Copyright © 1983 by Thunder's Mouth Press. Appears by permission of the publisher, Thunder's Mouth Press.

"You Will Forget" from *Red Hills of Home* by Chenjerai Hove, 1990. Reprinted by permission of Mambo Press.

From *Woven by the Grandmothers: Nineteenth-Century Navajo Textiles from the National Museum of the American Indian,* edited by Eulalie H. Bonar; copyright © 1996 by the Smithsonian Institution. Used by permission of the publisher.

"Lineage" from *This Is My Century: New and Collected Poems* by Margaret Walker Alexander. Copyright © 1989 by Margaret Walker Alexander. Reprinted by permission of The University of Georgia Press.

"Where Are Those Songs?" by Micere Githae Mugo. Reprinted by permission of the author.

Unit 4

"The Inspector-General" from *The Sneeze* by Anton Chekhov, adapted and translated by Michael Frayn. Copyright © 1989 by Michael Frayn. Reprinted by permission of Methuen.

"Wherefore Art Thou, Verona" by Gary Warner. Copyright © *Orange County Register.* Reprinted by permission.

"Counting the Beats" from *The Collected Poems 1975* by Robert Graves. Copyright © 1988 by Robert Graves. Used by permission of Carcanet Press, Ltd. and Oxford University Press, Inc.

Reprinted courtesy of *Sports Illustrated,* July 28, 1997. Copyright © 1997 Time, Inc. "Sign Language" by Tim Kurkjian. All rights reserved.

The Miracle Worker by William Gibson, reprinted with the permission of Scribner, a division of Simon & Schuster. Copyright © 1956, 1957 William Gibson. Copyright © 1959, 1960 Tamarack Productions, Ltd., and George S. Klein & Leo Grant as trustees under three separate deeds of trust.

"The Boy Who Talked With Dolphins" by Paula McDonald, reprinted with permission, from the April 1996 *Reader's Digest.*

Unit 5

Excerpts from *The Odyssey* by Homer, trans., R. Fitzgerald. Copyright © 1961, 1963 by Robert Fitzgerald and renewed 1989 by Benedict R. C. Fitzgerald. Reprinted by permission of Vintage Books, a Division of Random House, Inc.

"Jackie" words and music by Sinéad O'Connor. Copyright © 1991 EMI MUSIC PUBLISHING LTD. All rights for the United States and Canada controlled and administered by EMI BLACKWOOD MUSIC INC. All rights reserved. International copyright secured. Used by permission.

"Siren Song" from *Are You Happy: Selected Poems 1965–1975.* Copyright © 1976 by Margaret Atwood. Reprinted by permission of Houghton Mifflin Co. All rights reserved. "Siren Song" from *Selected Poems 1966–1984* by Margaret Atwood. Copyright © Margaret Atwood 1990. Reprinted by permission of Oxford University Press Canada.

"An Ancient Gesture" by Edna St. Vincent Millay. From *Collected Poems,* HarperCollins. Copyright © 1954, 1982 by Norma Millay Ellis. All rights reserved. Used by permission of Elizabeth Barnett, literary executor.

"Ithaca" from *The Complete Poems of Cavafy,* copyright © 1961 and renewed 1989 by Rae Dalven, reprinted by permission of Harcourt Brace & Company.

Unit 6

"The Sentinel" by Arthur C. Clarke. Reprinted by permission of the author and the author's agents, Scovil Chichak Galen Literary Agency, Inc.

"Visit to a Small Planet" from *United States Essays 1952–1992* by Gore Vidal. Copyright © 1957 by Gore Vidal. Reprinted by permission of Random House, Inc.

"Astronomers Revive Scan of the Heavens for Signs of Life" by William J. Broad. Copyright © 1998 by the New York Times Co. Reprinted by permission.

"The Flat of the Land," copyright © 1992 by Diana Garcia. Reprinted by permission of the author.

"Waste: What a Stinking Mess" by John Langone. Copyright © 1989 Time, Inc. Reprinted by permission.

"He-y, Come on Ou-t!" by Sinichi Hoshi. Reprinted by permission of the translator, Stanleigh H. Jones.

"Prologue" copyright © 1992 by Edward Field. Reprinted from *Counting Myself Lucky: Selected Poems 1963–1992,* with the permission of Black Sparrow Press.

"The Universe" by May Swenson. Used with permission of The Literary Estate of May Swenson.

"Onomatopoeia" from *A Sky Full of Poems* by Eve Merriam. Copyright © 1964, 1970, 1973, 1986 by Eve Merriam. Reprinted by permission of Marian Reiner.

Excerpt from "Acid Rain" on nationalgeographic.com/inforcentral, reprinted by permission of The National Geographic Society.

Maps

Ortelius Design, Inc.

Photography

Abbreviation key: **AH**=Aaron Haupt Photography; **AP**=Archive Photos; **AR**=Art Resource, New York; **BAL**=Bridgeman Art Library, London/New York; **CB**=Corbis/Bettmann; **CI**=Christie's Images; **SIS**=Stock Illustration Source; **LOC**=Library of Congress; **SS**=SuperStock; **TSI**=Tony Stone Images; **NWPA**=North West Picture Archives.

Cover (helmet)Courtesy Portsmouth Naval Shipyard Museum, Portsmouth VA. Photo by Bob Ander/Ander Commercial Photography, (painting) *On the Dogger Bank* by William Clarkson

Stanfield. Victoria & Albert Museum/E.T. Archive/SS; **vii** (t–b)Scala/AR, private collection/G.G. Kopilak/SS, BAL, Janet Atkinson/SIS, ©Kevin Flemming, National Optical Astronomy Observatories; **viii** Gallery Contemporanea, Jacksonville/SuperStock; **ix** (t)William J. Weber, (b)CB; **x** (t)CI, (b)Mark Burnett; **xi** ESM/AR; **xii** Daniel Wray/Natural Selections; **xiii** Gallery Contemporanea, Jacksonville/SS; **xiv** JAPACK/Corbis Los Angeles; **xv** (t)Cliff Riedinger/Natural Selections, (b)NC Museum of Art, Raleigh NC. Purchased with funds from the state of NC; **xvi** Daniel Nevins/SS; **xvii** (t)CB, (b)Everett Collection; **xvii** CB; **xviii** National Museum of American Art, Washington DC/AR; **xix** (t)Scala/AR, (b)©Kevin Flemming; **xx** BAL; **xxi** Scala/AR; **xxvi** Gallery Contemporanea, Jacksonville/SS; **4–5** AH; **6** CB; **8** Scala/AR; **10** CB; **11** Janet L. Adams; **12** Everett Shinn, *Cross Streets of New York, 1899,* in the collection of The Corcoran Gallery of Art. Gift of Margaret M. Hitchcock by exchange; **13** CB; **15** AP; **17** Courtesy of the artist; **18** (l)Tate Gallery,London/AR, (r)AP; **21** Erich Lessing/AR; **26** AP; **27** Mark Steinmetz; **28** National Museum of American Art, Washington DC, gift of the Harmon Foundation/AR; **30** AH; **32** Edward Owen/AR. Estate of Grant Wood, licensed by VAGA, New York NY; **33** CB; **35 36** AH; **37** The Newark Museum/AR; **39** AH; **41** Shao Feng Qiu/The Image Bank; **44** CB; **45** Art Wolfe/TSI; **46** Chris Hellier/Corbis; **48, 49** Tate Gallery, London/AR; **52** David Young-Wolff/TSI; **54** Bob Macklin; **56** (l)AP, (r)Nancy Crampton; **57** CI. ©1998 Artists Rights Society (ARS), New York/ADAGP, Paris; **59** Macduff Everton/Corbis; **61** George Hall/Corbis; **62** CI/SS. ©1998 Estate of Pablo Picasso/Artists Rights Society (ARS), New York; **66** (l)Bob Krist/Corbis, (r)*New York Times* Pictures; **67** Erich Lessing/AR; **69** Steve Lissau; **70** Paul Almasy/Corbis; **71** Thomas L. Kennedy, Client's Choice Ltd.; **76** CB; **77** (l)Stephen Derr/The Image Bank, (r)AH; **79** AH; **80** Neil Folberg/The Image Bank; **81** AH; **82** The Butler Institute of American Art; **86** CB; **87** Ian Shaw/TSI; **88** Scala/AR; **89** CB; **90** Tor Eigeland/Woodfin Camp & Assoc.; **91** Scala/AR; **92** NWPA; **94** Scala/AR; **96** Mark Burnett; **97** (l)William J. Weber, (r)©1998 Bill Gaskins; **99** Hampton University Museum, Hampton VA/©Elizabeth Catlett, licensed by VAGA; **101** Robert Franz/Corbis; **102** Private collection/Jessie Coates/SS; **103** Anthony Bannister/Corbis; **105** Rick Weber; **113** Tate Gallery, London/AR. Works by Hepworth ©Alan Bowness, Hepworth Estate; **115** CB; **116** SS; **118** AP; **120** The Minneapolis Institute of Arts; **125** (l)John D. Cunningham/Visuals Unlimited, (r)Gustav Verderber/Visuals Unlimited; **126** (l)David M. Dennis, (r)AP; **128** CI; **130** Tate Gallery, London/AR; **132** Chad Ehlers/TSI; **134** Courtesy Joanne Greenberg; **136** Kees van den Berg/Photo Researchers; **137** Collection of The Chase Manhattan Bank. Photo ©Zindman/Fremont; **139** Mark Burnett; **140** National Gallery of Canada, Ottawa; **142** Dallas Museum of Art, Allied Arts Civic Prize, Eighth Annual Dallas Allied Arts Exhibit, 1937; **145, 146** Reprinted from *Signing Made Easy.* ©1989 Rod R. Butterworth and Mickey Flodin. Permission granted by the Berkeley Publishing Group, a member of Penguin Putnam Inc. All rights reserved; **150** Pat Mora, Arte Publico Press; **151** CI; **153** (l)National Gallery of Canada, Ottawa, (r)CI; **155** (l)UPI/CB, (r)Miriam Berkley; **156–157** Larry Hamill; **157** AP; **158** Photo by Ivan Dalla Tanna, courtesyCecelia de Torres, Ltd., New York; **168** CB; **169** Alain Bemainous/Gamma Liaison; **170** Mark Steinmetz; **172** SS; **173** Courtesy Schwarz Gallery, Philadelphia; **175** Corbis; **177** CI; **180** Nation Foto; **181** Paul Kenward/TSI; **182** C. Bradley Simmons/Bruce Coleman Inc; **185** Courtesy Loïs Mailou Jones; **187** Charles Kennard/Stock Boston; **190** S. Webster; **197** Joel Peter Johnson/SIS; **198** (l)Roy Morsch/The Stock Market, (r)Celeste Wetherell and University of Pittsburgh Press; **199** John White/SIS; **200** Bob Daemmrich/Stock Boston; **201** Ed Labadie/SIS; **202** Collection of Brandywine River Museum; purchased for the museum by John T. Dorrance Jr., Mr. and Mrs. Felix duPont, Mr. and Mrs. James P. Mills, Mr. and Mrs. Bayard Sharp, two anonymous donors; **207** Mark Burnett; **210** DUOMO/Chris Trotman; **211** (l)AP, (r)file photo; **213** National Museum of American Art, Washington DC/AR; **214** Nancy Carter/NWPA; **217** Hirshhorn Museum and Sculpture Garden, Smithsonian Institution. Gift of Joseph W. Hirshhorn, 1966. Photographer: Ricardo Blanc; **219** file photo; **221** Mark Burnett; **224** (l)Giraudon/AR, (r)James Wilson/Woodfin Camp & Assoc.; **226** Winson Trang; **227** W.B. Finch/Stock Boston; **229** Popperfoto/AP; **230–231** Lou Jones/The Image Bank; **231** Charles Moore/Black Star; **236** (l)CB, (r)file photo; **238** Popperfoto/AP; **239, 240** Greg Spalenka; **243** Larry Moore/SIS; **244** Photo by B.J. Fundaro, Sonoma State University; **245** NPS photo by Richard Frear; **247** ©1998 The Museum of Modern Art, New York. Inter-American Fund; **248** CB; **250** Herbert Art Gallery, Bristol/E.T. Archive/SS; **255** Photofest; **256** Zefa Germany/The Stock Market; **258** Sylvia Martin/Photo Researchers; **260** CI; **262** Mark Steinmetz; **263** CI. ©1998 Artists Rights Society (ARS), New York/ADAGP, Paris; **264** Robert Finken/Photo Researchers; **265** CI/SS; **268** David Muench/Corbis; **275** AH; **278** ESM/AR; **280** AH; **284** Archivio G.B.B./G. Neri/Woodfin Camp & Assoc.; **285** AP; **286** CB; **289** Private collection/SS; **290** CB; **293** Peter Southwick/Stock Boston; **295** CB; **296** (l)Elliott Erwitt/Magnum Photos, (r)Globe Photos; **303** Ted Speigel/Corbis; **304** (l)CB, (r)Ulf Anderson/Gamma Liaison; **306** Collection of Yad Vashem Museum of Art, Jerusalem; **309** Courtesy Alfred Tibor; **312** Larry Moore/SIS; **313** Geoff Butler; **315** Kactus Foto, Santiago, Chile/SS; **318** (l)Culver Pictures, (r)International Publishers; **321** CI; **324** (l)National Portrait Gallery, Smithsonian Institution/AR, (r)AP; **325** Tony Garcia/TSI; **328** Wide World Photos; **329** UN/DPI Photo; **330** John Shaw/Tom Stack & Assoc.; **332** Charles Henry Hayden Fund, courtesy Museum of Fine Arts, Boston; **336** Mark Burnett; **340** (l)Mark Antman/The Image Works, (r)Gerardo Somoza/Outline; **343** TX State Library and Archives Commission; **351** Schalkwijk/AR; **353** (l)AP, (r)Harris & Ewing/Globe Photos; **355** American Stock/AP; **355–356** Jim Barber; **357** LOC/CB; **359** LOC; **362** file photo; **369** A. Ramey/Stock Boston; **370** (l)From *Trail of the Wolf* by R. D. Lawrence, (r)Wide World Photos; **371** Jim Brandenburg/Minden Pictures; **376** Lynn M. Stone; **377** (l)Sharon M. Kurgis, (r)Gary Isaacs, courtesy Scribner; **379** Charles W. Melton; **380** SS; **385** (l)Kristin Finnegan/TSI, (r)Wide World Photo; **386** Ernst Haas/TSI; **391** Kenwood House, Hampstead, London/BAL/SS; **394** UPI/CB; **397** CA Historical Society; **399** E.O. Hoppe/Corbis; **404** (l)Dewitt Jones/Corbis, (r)Hulton Deutsch Collection/Corbis; **405** Jeff Greenberg/dMRp/Photo Researchers; **406** Private collection/G.G. Kopilak/SS; **407** Holt Studios Int'l., Nigel Cattlin/Photo Researchers; **408** (l)Michael Freeman/Corbis, (r)C.G. Maxwell/Photo Researchers; **409** CB; **410** Matt Meadows; **412** Manfred Danegger/Photo Researchers; **413** The Metropolitan Museum of Art. Gift of Dr. and Mrs. Robert E. Carroll, 1979 (1979.138.2). Photograph ©1979 The Metropolitan Museum of Art; **414** (l)AP, (r)Holt Studios Int'l., Nigel Cattlin/Photo Researchers; **415** Munson-Williams-Proctor Institute Museum of Art, Utica NY, Edward W. Root Bequest; **416** Matt Meadows; **418** Geoff Butler; **420** (l)Werner Krutein/Liaison International, (r)courtesy Curbstone Press; **421** CI/SS; **424** (t)CB, (b)Mark Burnett; **431** AH; **434–435** Gallery Contemporanea, Jacksonville/SS; **435** Photograph ©1998 The Museum of Modern Art, New York. Advisory Committee Fund; **438** AH; **440** (t)CB; **441** Leeds Museums and Galleries (City Art Gallery) UK/BAL; **442–443** Manchester City Art Galleries/BAL; **445** Leeds Museum and Galleries (City Art Gallery) UK/BAL; **446** AP; **448** (l)Harvey Owens/Medichrome/The Stock Shop, (tr)Barbara Savage Cheresh, (br)Burt Glinn/Magnum; **449** Courtesy Ismael Frigerio; **450** Reprinted from *The Moon of the Owls* by Jean Craighead George, illustration ©1993 by Wendell Minor, published by HarperCollins Publishers; **454** *Atlanta Journal-Constitution*/ Jonathan Newton; **455** (t)Smithsonian Institution, (b)courtesy Naomi Long Madgett; **456–457** AH; **458** Courtesy the artist; **462** (l)Museum of North ID, (tr)Donna Matheson, (br)Roger W. Cowans/Ken Barboza Inc. **463** David Cain/Photo Researchers; **466** (t)courtesy Carolyn Soto, (b)National Portrait Gallery/CB; **467** Jim Brandenburg/Minden Pictures; **470** Ebet Roberts/The Everett Collection; **471** (t)Adam Scull/Globe Photos, (b)Andra Nelki; **476** Jim Corwin/Stock Boston; **476** (t)Judie Burstein/Globe Photos, (b)LOC/Corbis; **477** ©Elizabeth Catlett/Licensed by VAGA, New York NY; **480** (l)Stephanie Maze/Woodfin Camp & Assoc., (tr)courtesy Yvonne Sapia, (br)CALYX Books; **482** BAL; **491** Frank Herholdt/TSI; **492** (l)AP/David Lees, (tr)Christopher Felver/AP, (br)courtesy Maria Herrera-Sobek; **498** Asian Art & Archaeology, Inc./Corbis; **499** Japanese *No* Drama Costume (Nuihaku). Silk, plain weave; patterned with resist dyeing, impressed with gold leaf, and embroidered, Momoyama period, 16th century, 160.6 x 133.1 cm. Restricted gift; **501** Matt Meadows; **503** (l)Jacksonville Museum of Contemporary Art, FL/SS, (tr)CB, (br)Larry Ford/Outline; **504** JAPACK/Corbis Los Angeles; **505** The Lowe Art Museum, The University of Miami/SS; **508** (l)AH, (tr)Wide World Photos, (br)CB; **509** Courtesy Jack Tilton Gallery; **513** (l)©1998 Estate of Pablo Picasso/Artists Rights Society (ARS), New York NY/AR, (r)Hulton Getty/TSI; **514** Courtesy Museo Picasso, Barcelona. ©1999 Estate of Pablo Picasso/Artists Rights Society (ARS), New York; **525** Marc Garanger/Corbis; **526** (l)Tom Stock/TSI, (tr)CB, (br)file photo; **527** Wolfgang Kaehler/Corbis; **528** Thomas A. Schneider/Natural Selection; **531** Larry Moore/SIS; **532** (l)Breck Kent, (tr)National Portrait Gallery, Smithsonian Institution/AR, (br)courtesy John Daniel & Company; **533** Robert Noonan/Photo Researchers; **535–536** Cliff Riedinger/Natural Selection; **538** AH; **539** (t)©Hulleah J. Tsinhnahjinnie, courtesy Thunder Mouth Press, (b)photo by Jeremy Summerfield, courtesy Baobab Books, Harare, Zimbabwe; **540** ©Tim Nicola, courtesy Artistic Gallery, Santa Fe, photography by Jerry Jacka; **544** National Museum of the American Indian, Smithsonian Institution #9/1912; **545** (l)The American Red Cross, (tr)Nancy Crampton, (br)courtesy of Micere G.M. Mugo; **546** SS; **548–549** NC Museum of Art, Raleigh. Purchased with funds from the State of NC; **557** AH; **560–561** Andre Rouillard/SS; **562** CB; **566** Topham/The Image Works; **566** Hulton-Getty/Liaison Agency; **569** Scala/AR; **573** Daniel Nevins/SS; **574** Mary Evans Picture Library; **575** From *Shakespeare and His Theatre* by John Russell Brown. Illustrated by David Gentleman. Originally published by Penguin Books Ltd; **576** AP; **577** Paramount Pictures/AP; **578** Ted Spiegel/Corbis; **580** CI; **583** Palazzo Ducale, Mantua, Italy/SS; **588** Erich Lessing/AR; **597, 603, 611** CI; **616** Ashmolean Museum, Oxford; **623** CI; **626** Tate Gallery, London/AR; **630** Reprinted with permission of King Features Syndicate; **631** (l)NWPA, (r)SS; **634** CI; **639** By Permission of the Folger Shakespeare Library; **642** AR; **651, 657** BAL; **662** From the RSC Collection, with the permission of the Governors of the Royal Shakespeare Theatre, photo by Brian Glover; **668** SS; **671** Art Gallery of South Australia, Adelaide. Elder Bequest Fund 1899; **675** Larry Moore/SIS; **681** AR; **682** CI; **685** BAL; **690** From the collection of Agnes Scott College; **691** BAL; **694** (l)Joe Baker/SIS, (r)Topham/The Image Works; **695** Janet Atkinson/SIS; **697** CI; **705** Collection of the Kalamazoo Institute of the Arts. Blanche Hull Fund purchase. Courtesy George Adams Gallery, New York; **706** J. Daniel/Allsport; **707** Wide World Images; **708** Photofest; **709** (l)AP, (r)Photofest; **715, 719** Photofest; **723** The Everett Collection; **727, 729** AP; **741, 743, 752** The Everett Collection; **758** Photofest; **767** AP; **772, 776, 778** The Everett Collection; **782** Oscar White/Corbis; **783** Hulton Getty/TSI; **785** LOC/Corbis; **789** Courtesy the American Foundation for the Blind, Helen Keller Archives; **802** National Museum of American Art, Washington DC/AR; **804** SS; **805** Erich Lessing/AR; **807** Sotheby's Picture Library; **808** Brent Jones Photography; **809** CB; Kevin Flemming; **816** Mary Evans Picture Library; **822** Scala/AR; **825, 826** BAL; **831** Larry Moore/SIS; **832** P. Palagi/Mary Evans Picture Library; **834** file photo; **835** BAL; **837** Erich Lessing/AR; **842** Scala/AR; **845** Erich Lessing/AR; **848** (l)©1998 Museum of Fine Arts, Boston. Henry Lillie Pierce Fund, (r)Wyatt Counts/Outline; **849** BAL; **852** file photo; **853** BAL; **856** Mary Evans Picture Library; **859, 864** Erich Lessing/AR; **869** (t)Gianni Dagli Orti/Corbis, (c)Anestis Diakopoulos/Stock Boston, (b)Nimatallah/AR; **873** Ancient Art & Architecture Collection; **877** The Metropolitan Museum of Art, Fletcher Fund, 1956 (56.171.38). Photograph ©1989 The Metropolitan Museum of Art; **880** Mary Evans Picture Library; **882** Gail Mooney/Corbis; **884** Matt Bradley/Tom Stack & Assoc.; **888** (l)BAL, (tr)CB, (br)Margot Granitsas Archives/The Image Works; **889** Rosenwald Collection, ©1998 Board of Trustees, National Gallery of Art, Washington DC. ©1998 Artists Rights Society (ARS), New York/VG Bild-Kunst, Bonn; **899** AH; **902** BAL; **905** National Optical Astronomy Observatories; **906** Dana Fineman/Sygma; **907** Scala/AR; **910, 913** BAL; **917** NASA; **920** UPI/Corbis; **921** (l)Photofest, (r)AP; **923** UPI/CB; **926 through 945** Photofest; **946** CI/BAL. ©1998 Charly Herscovici, Brussels/ Artists Rights Society(ARS), New York; **948** ABC photo by John Engstead/Motion Picture & TV Archive; **950** Courtesy New York Times Company; **951, 953** ©Seth Shostak; **958** Courtesy Diana Garcia; **961** ©The Georgia O'Keeffe Museum. Gift of The Burnett Foundation; **962** Raymond Gehman/Corbis; **963** Amanda Merullo/Stock Boston; **964** The Seattle Art Museum, West Seattle Art Club, Katherine B. Baker Memorial Purchase Prize. ©Seattle Art Museum, photo: Paul Macapia. ©1998 Artists Rights Society (ARS), New York; **968** P. Menzel/Stock Boston; **970** A. Ramey/Stock Boston; **971** Stephan Ferry/Gamma Liaison; **972** (l)Greig Cranna/Stock Boston, (r)Japan Foreign-Rights Centre; **973** Fitzgerald Studio, photo ©1997 Eduardo Calderon; **974** Bob Daemmrich/Stock Boston; **983** (t)Black Sparrow Press, (b)Oscar White/Corbis; **984** BAL; **989** Larry Moore/SIS.

FCAT Test-Taking Strategies

What is the FCAT?

The FCAT is a test that measures your achievement of the Sunshine State Standards for reading, writing, science, and mathematics. The FCAT is also a graduation requirement. All Florida public school students must earn a passing score on the grade 10 FCAT to receive a high school diploma. Students who do not pass the FCAT in grade 10 can retake the test later in the school year. The FCAT can also be retaken in grades 11 and 12. This section of your textbook will help you prepare for FCAT Reading and FCAT Writing.

What is FCAT Reading?

FCAT Reading tests how well you comprehend what you read. This test asks you to read several passages and to answer questions about their meaning. Roughly 30 percent of the passages will be literary texts (such as poems, short stories, or play excerpts). The rest will be informational texts (such as biographies, magazine articles, or advertisements).

Each passage on FCAT Reading is followed by several multiple-choice questions. At some grades, short-response and extended-response questions are also included. Short- and extended-response questions ask for a written response to a question about the passage.

What is FCAT Writing?

FCAT Writing asks you to write an essay in response to an expository or persuasive writing prompt. You will not know which type of prompt will appear on the test until you are taking the test. It is important that you are prepared to respond to each type of prompt.

Why should you learn strategies for taking the FCAT?

Test-taking strategies can help you perform your best in the time that you are given to complete each part of the test. These strategies can also help you in taking other standardized tests, which have similar types of questions.

On the following pages, you will learn strategies for responding to each type of question and writing prompt on FCAT Reading and FCAT Writing. Each of these lessons provides

- a description of a strategy
- steps to follow in using the strategy
- a short practice exercise

You will be applying these strategies to the copy of "Scanning the Heavens for Signs of Life" (pages 951–954 of your book) that you will receive from your teacher.

Reading Actively

FCAT Reading tests not only your ability to understand what you read but also your ability to maintain that understanding over long reading passages. Reading actively can help your understanding by keeping you focused and involved as you read.

You might think that the best way to read a passage in FCAT Reading is to read slowly, trying to absorb every fact, but this is actually a poor use of your time. You will rarely need to remember specific facts to answer questions. The following strategies can help you to read actively.

Previewing the Passage

Before you read the passage, quickly preview it to get a sense of what the passage is about and to determine your purpose for reading. Look at the title, headings, illustrations, diagrams, captions, and other text features. Read the questions that follow the passage for clues to what information you should look for as you read. You might also skim the passage, or read over it quickly, to find the main idea or to get a general overview.

Labeling Paragraphs

After you preview, read the passage with the questions in mind. Keep track of the main ideas by selectively underlining key words and by writing short labels beside each paragraph or group of related paragraphs. (Paragraphs are related when they address a single main idea.) This strategy will help you to find important information easily when you need to look back at the passage to answer questions.

Here is an example of a labeled paragraph.

big telescope looks for intelligent life

> Outside in the fading light, surrounded by dense jungle, the receiving dome on the world's largest radiotelescope wheeled into position. It fixed on Barnard's star, a scant six light-years away, the closest star to Earth in the Northern Hemisphere. Closeness meant it had been searched before. But now, the great dish antenna of the Arecibo observatory began to gather in a riot of faint signals, giving the star its most discriminating look yet for hints of invisible planets and intelligent life.

Steps for Labeling Paragraphs

To label a paragraph like the one on the previous page, take the following steps.

Step 1 **Underline key words.**

As you read a paragraph, ask yourself, "Which words remind me of the questions I read?" and "Which words provide the most important information in this paragraph?" Words and phrases such as "Northern Hemisphere" and "Arecibo observatory" provide specific information, but the search for intelligent life is more important.

Step 2 **Summarize.**

Ask yourself, "What is this paragraph about?" Having underlined key words should help you answer this question. From the underlined words alone, you can get a sense that the paragraph deals with searching for intelligent life.

Step 3 **Label the paragraph.**

Preview your summary phrase next to the paragraph in as few words as possible. Don't bother to write a complete sentence. A phrase will do. For example, instead of the label shown, you could write "look for intelligent life."

PRACTICE

Preview "Scanning the Heavens for Signs of Life." To preview upcoming questions about the passage, look at the practice questions on pages FCAT5, FCAT7, and FCAT9 of this section of your book. Then read the passage. On your copy, underline key words and label the paragraphs or groups of paragraphs. Remember to underline and write just enough to help you recall the main ideas.

You will need to refer to your labels and underlining to practice the test-taking strategies discussed on the following pages.

Multiple-Choice Reading Questions

A multiple-choice question asks you to select the best answer from several possible choices. You can use the process of elimination to help you find the best answer choice.

The Process of Elimination

Each multiple-choice question on the FCAT provides four answer choices. When you read the choices, ask yourself, "Which choices are definitely wrong?" Eliminate those that you know are wrong and then choose the best answer from the remaining choices. Choosing the best answer from two or three choices is easier than choosing from four choices. You may even be able to use the process of elimination to get rid of three wrong choices. This would leave you with only one choice—the best answer to the question.

Now study how the process of elimination works. Read this example question.

● What is the biggest problem SETI scientists have encountered recently when searching their readings for incoming alien signals?

A. Too many alien signals are being picked up at SETI.

B. The government will not help the scientists repair the broken telescope.

C. Identification is difficult because the signals fade away too quickly.

D. Interference from satellites makes readings hard to decipher.

Steps in the Process of Elimination

To answer a multiple-choice question like this one, use the following steps.

Step 1 **Underline key words in the question and answer choices. Then look at your labels or key words in the passage to find the text that matches.**

Look for a label that is similar to "biggest problem" "alien signals," "broken telescope," or "satellites." **If you do not have a label that uses words from the question or the answer choices, skim the passage to see whether you have underlined any of these words as key words.** One of these methods—looking at labels or looking for key words—should lead you to the paragraph on page 954 that begins "At Arecibo, candidate alien signals are compared . . ."

Step 2 **Review your key words in the selected paragraph to get a good idea of what the paragraph is about.**

Key words in the paragraph might include *candidate alien signals, compared, earthly interference, exploding,* and *satellites and cell phones.*

Step 3 **Read each answer choice. Decide which answer choices are definitely wrong. Eliminate them by drawing a line through them in your test booklet (but NOT on your answer sheet).**

In the selected paragraph, there is no information to support the idea that the biggest problem with readings is that too many alien signals are being picked up at SETI or that the government will not help the scientists repair the broken telescope. Therefore, eliminate choices A and B.

Step 4 **Choose the best answer from the choices remaining.**

Although choice C seems possible—the signals may fade away very quickly—there is no information in the article to support this idea. Look at choice D to see whether it is a better choice. The paragraph states that earthly interference, which is on the rise because of satellites and cell phones, makes it difficult to identify alien signals. Therefore, choice D is the best answer.

PRACTICE

Answer questions 1 and 2 on a separate sheet of paper. Remember to use your paragraph labels and key words. Use the process of elimination to help you choose the best answer.

1. How does the author feel about the SETI project?

   A. The author believes the project will eventually enjoy success.
   B. The author believes the project is wasting investors' money.
   C. The author thinks there are gaps in the program's underlying logic.
   D. The author describes the project but does not state an opinion.

2. What does Seth Shostak mean by this comment?

   "When you get far into a project and haven't found what you're looking for, it gives you pause."

   F. His lack of success makes him wonder about his theories.
   G. He is being criticized by other scientists in the field.
   H. He is ready to give up and begin looking elsewhere.
   I. His telescope's receiving dish malfunctions occasionally.

Short-Response Reading Questions

Like a multiple-choice question, a short-response question asks you about a passage. However, instead of choosing the best answer, you use your own words to write an answer that is supported by details in the passage. Answering a short-response question should take about five minutes.

Read this example of a short-response question.

READ
THINK
EXPLAIN

Near the end of the article, why does Dr. Tarter comment, "You have to crawl before you walk"? Support your answer with information from the passage.

Steps for Answering the Question

To answer a short-response question, take the following steps.

Step 1 **Read all parts of the question carefully and underline key words. Make sure you completely understand what the question is asking before you answer it.**

The question above includes two important points. It asks why Dr. Tarter speaks of crawling before walking, and it tells you to use information from the passage.

Step 2 **Look back at the passage. Use your paragraph labels and underlined key words to find information that helps you answer the question.**

The quotation in the question appears in the next-to-last paragraph of the selection. Review the labels and underlined key words of the last few paragraphs to look for information to help you answer the question.

Step 3 **Use the information that you find in the passage to plan your answer.**

Dr. Tarter feels that the present methods of searching for life on other planets are primitive, like crawling, compared with the improved methods she thinks will be used in the future. That is the main idea of your answer. Supporting information from the passage could be quotations or facts that show what she expects in the future.

Step 4 **Write your response in the space provided.**

Your first sentence should provide a direct answer to the question. Support your answer by writing additional sentences that include relevant information from the passage.

Step 5 **Read over your response to make sure it answers the question and says what you intend to say.**

Here is an example of a response that received 2 points, which is the top score.

The topic sentence shows a complete understanding of the question.

Dr. Tarter said "You have to crawl before you walk" because she feels that the search for alien signals is a long process—like the process of learning to walk—that is just beginning. She looks forward to advances such as using "thousands of small dish antennas" to search for signals. She even dreams of an observatory on the dark side of the Moon. That would be a giant step that would make the present methods seem like crawling.

Supporting information from the passage elaborates on the main idea by showing Dr. Tarter's plans and dreams for the future.

By linking information from the passage to Dr. Tarter's words in the question,, the response answers the question correctly and completely.

PRACTICE

Now try this short-response question on your own. Write your answer on a separate sheet of paper. Be sure to use your key words and paragraph labels.

● **READ THINK EXPLAIN** What difficulty involving the U. S. Congress did SETI face? What was SETI's solution to the problem? Support your answer with information from the passage.

Extended-Response Reading Questions

An extended-response question is similar to a short-response question except that it requires a longer answer. The best answer is clear, correct, and complete. It also includes several examples from the passage for support. Answering an extended-response question should take ten to fifteen minutes.

Here is an example of an extended-response test item.

READ
THINK
EXPLAIN

How are Dr. Tarter's and Dr. Shostak's personalities similar? Support your answer with information from the passage.

Steps for Answering the Question

To answer an extended-response question like this one, take the following steps.

Step 1 **Read all parts of the question carefully and underline key words. Make sure you completely understand what the question is asking.**

The question above includes two important points. It asks how the personalities of the two scientists are alike, and it tells you to use information from the passage.

Step 2 **Look back at the passage for labels and key words that seem related to the question.**

If your labels seem unrelated to the question, focus on the key words you underlined. You can also skim the passage, looking for the scientists' names. Look for relevant information in any paragraph that mentions Dr. Tarter, Dr. Shostak, or both.

Step 3 **On a piece of scrap paper, write down the main idea of your response and list the details that support your main idea.**

Decide which details you want to include in your answer. You may also want to number them in the order you think they should appear.

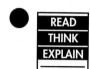

Step 4 **Write your response in the space provided.**

Begin with a statement that answers the question directly. You might even rephrase the question in your answer. For example, "How are Dr. Tarter's and Dr. Shostak's personalities similar . . ." becomes "Dr. Tarter's and Dr. Shostak's personalities are similar . . ." Then fully explain your answer, using the list of details from step 3 for support. Cross off each detail on your list as you use it.

Step 5 **Read over your response to make sure it answers the question and says what you intend to say.**

Here is an example of a response to the question about Dr. Tarter and Dr. Shostak on FCAT8. This response received 4 points, which is the top score.

The topic sentence shows a complete understanding of the question.

Dr. Tarter's and Dr. Shostak's personalities are similar because both scientists are very determined; they never give up looking for alien signals. Dr. Tarter concentrates tensely as she examines the scan signals; Dr. Shostak says that failing to find signs of intelligence on other planets is "not discouraging at all." Both are fascinated by a signal that may reveal an alien civilization, and although they are "disappointed" that the signal comes from a satellite, their faith in the search is "intact." Even though they have worked for many years on the project without seeing any alien signals, they are both certain that one day human beings will find intelligent alien life.

The writer uses several examples from the selection that clearly support the main idea of the response.

The writer answers the question completely and concludes by rephrasing the main idea.

PRACTICE

Now try this extended-response question on your own. Answer the question on a separate sheet of paper. Be sure to use your key words and paragraph labels from your practice in the Reading Actively lesson.

● READ THINK EXPLAIN

Briefly explain the history of the search for extraterrestrial intelligence (SETI). Support your answer with information from the passage.

Writing Expository and Persuasive Essays

FCAT Writing is a test of your ability. It includes a prompt that directs you to write an expository essay or a persuasive essay on an assigned topic. You will have forty-five minutes to plan and write your essay.

Expository Essays

An expository essay informs or explains by defining, classifying, or giving directions. The expository essay prompt will ask you to use facts or opinions to explain something. It will include words such as *explain, why,* or *how.*

Here is an example of a writing prompt for an expository essay.

> **Writing Situation**
>
> People tend to remember events that are significant for them.
>
> **Directions for Writing**
>
> Think about the people and places involved in a siginificant event from your childhood.
>
> Now describe that event and explain why it is significant to you.

Persuasive Essays

A **persuasive essay** tries to convince the reader of something. The persuasive essay prompt will ask you to try to convince readers to think or feel a certain way. It will include words such as *convince* or *persuade.*

Here is an example of a writing prompt for a persuasive essay.

> **Writing Situation**
>
> Your school has just announced that all music students must sell pizzas to raise money for new band uniforms and chorus robes.
>
> **Directions for Writing**
>
> Think about whether you would be for or against the proposed requirement.
>
> Now write a letter to the school newspaper in which you argue for or against the school's new fund-raising policy.

Steps for Writing an Essay

The best way to use your time and be successful in responding to FCAT Writing prompts is to plan ahead. Take time to think about what you want to write before you actually begin writing your response.

Use the following steps to write a high-scoring composition.

Step 1 **Make sure that you understand the prompt.**

- Study the prompt carefully and underline key words. Focus on the topic or issue presented in the prompt. Your score will be reduced if your essay strays from the topic.
- Notice whether the prompt asks for an expository essay or a persuasive essay.
- Keep your audience in mind. Unless the prompt states an audience for your writing, think of your audience as a group of adults whom you do not know well.
- Keep your purpose in mind. The purpose of an **expository essay** is to give information, to explain why or how, to clarify a process, or to define a concept.
  The purpose of a **persuasive essay** is to convince your audience to accept your position on an issue.

Step 2 **Before you start writing your essay, brainstorm for ideas and details that relate to the topic.**

- Jot notes on scratch paper as you think of ideas and important points to include in your essay.
- Use a graphic organizer such as a word web or Venn diagram to help you to generate ideas and to see your ideas more clearly.

Step 3 **Compose a thesis statement.**

- Refer to your notes and graphic organizer when determining your thesis.
- Be sure your statement responds directly to the prompt. In a **persuasive essay,** be sure to take a stand on the issue presented in the prompt.

Step 4 **Choose your main points or reasons and organize them in an order that makes sense.**

- Choose at least two main points or reasons to support your thesis.
- Decide what points best support your thesis and what details would help to explain those points. For an **expository essay,** choose points and details that make your explanation clear. For a **persuasive essay,** choose relevant arguments and evidence that will convince others to agree with you.
- Discard points that do not relate to your thesis statement.
- Arrange your main points or reasons in an order that is easy for your audience to follow. For an **expository essay,** consider using spatial, cause-and-effect, or chronological order. For a **persuasive essay,** organize your reasons to explain your position and to emphasize your best arguments.

Step 5 **Write your essay. Be sure to write neatly.**

- Include an introduction, at least two body paragraphs, and a conclusion.
- In your introductory paragraph, clearly express your thesis.
- Write a body paragraph for each of your main points or reasons. Begin each body paragraph with a topic sentence stating the main point or reason. Then provide appropriate details or convincing evidence to support the topic sentence.
- Conclude with a paragraph that restates and emphasizes your thesis.

Step 6 **Review your essay for focus, organization, and supporting details.**

- Make sure your writing is clearly focused on the topic. Delete sentences and ideas that don't support your thesis.
- Make sure you have an introduction, at least two body paragraphs that provide points in support of your thesis or your position, and a conclusion.
- Check that you have used relevant supporting details that extend and elaborate on your main points or reasons.
- Neatly cross out unwanted text and write in your revisions.

Step 7 **Proofread your essay for conventions of language and writing.**

- Make sure that your writing shows correct usage, sentence structure, spelling, punctuation, and capitalization.
- Neatly correct the errors that you find.

Sample Expository Essay

Now read this sample expository essay that responds to the writing prompt on page FCAT10. This essay would receive the best possible score of 6 points.

I'll never forget the first time I saw people juggling. I was only eight years old, but the magic of that day started me on a path that I hadn't dreamed of before then and that I haven't strayed from since.

The introduction engages the audience and provides a clear thesis statement.

My family and I had been in the Old City Market downtown. In the afternoon, we stopped to eat at our favorite pizza place, Tom's Pizzeria. We were almost done eating when a crowd began to gather across the street from the restaurant.

"Let's go see what's happening," Dad said. We paid the bill, gathered our bags, and walked across the cobblestone square.

An effective organizational pattern begins by setting the scene of the event.

The crowd had formed a wide circle around three street entertainers who were dressed in silver and purple costumes, like jesters. The entertainers had painted their faces with bright-colored greasepaint. They called "Hey now!" and "Look here!" across the circle as they juggled magnificently colored rings. They joked around and sometimes pretended they were going to drop their rings, but they never did.

The writer uses vivid details and precise language to describe the setting.

"How can they do that?" I asked my dad. I was in awe.

"Lots of practice," my dad replied.

Sentence variety and dialogue add interest to the essay.

One of the jugglers must have heard me, because right then she picked me out of the crowd. She came over and stood in front of me. As she leaned toward me, I could see where the red paint and the white paint were melting together on her face, making a fuzzy pink line down the middle of her nose.

The writing demonstrates proper use of grammar, punctuation, spelling, capitalization, and usage.

"I need a helper," she said. "Come on!"

(continued)

Dad gave me a nudge, and I reluctantly stepped into the circle. I was nervous, but I managed to listen to what she told me. Then, before I knew what was happening, I found myself throwing three rings to her, one at a time, until all of them were flying magically between us! Everybody clapped and I felt really good. I started to leave the circle, but it turned out my moment in the spotlight wasn't over. Before I knew it, she was giving me a lightning-fast lesson on how to juggle on my own. She was talking so fast and I was so happy and excited that I forgot about all the people watching me. The first time I tried, I dropped a ring, but on the very next try I was juggling two rings. I wished Grandpa could have seen me at that moment!

The writer extends support for the thesis by including a well-elaborated anecdote.

Then the crowd burst into applause.

"That's for you! Take a bow!" the smiling juggler told me. I don't think I had ever felt happier or more satisfied.

Then the jugglers put away their rings and got serious. They began juggling silver swords! With every "ooh" and "ahh" of the crowd, I became more entranced. I was still tingling with pride and exhilaration because of what had just happened to me. But I was excited about the future too. I knew I wanted someday to earn my own "oohs" and "ahhs" from a crowd. And that day, even as a little girl, I knew I could do it.

The lead sentence reinforces the chronological organization and signals a change of pace.

The parallels drawn between the jugglers and the writer effectively show how the event influenced her.

Well, I've been juggling, dancing, and acting ever since then. Stumbling onto those jugglers that afternoon with my family is a big part of why I'm in the drama club today and why I hope to go on to do much more.

The conclusion gives insight into the significance of the event by relating it to the present.

Sample Persuasive Essay

Now read this sample persuasive essay that responds to the writing prompt on page FCAT10. This essay would receive the best possible score of 6 points.

Everyone in the school has probably heard about the controversial new proposal requiring all music students to sell pizzas. While I agree that the music department does need new band uniforms and choir robes, I do not agree that requiring all music students to sell pizzas is an acceptable solution to the problem.

The writer presents the issue and takes a clear position.

The main reason I am against the proposal is that I believe a student's most important purpose in school should be to excel at his or her studies. Participation in all extracurricular activities, such as sports, clubs, and fund-raising, should come second to homework and test preparation. I think that most of this school's students and educators would agree that the grade point averages of our students could be better. If grades are ever going to improve, students need to concentrate all the more on their studies. It seems quite clear that the school's new fund-raising requirement would work against this goal and that grades would be more likely to drop than to improve.

The writer uses an effective organization by stating the most important reason first.

Relevant details and examples elaborate on the topic sentence.

Another important reason that the new fund-raising policy should be reconsidered is that many music students—a good number of whom are also involved in after-school sports and clubs—simply do not have time to sell products. Students participating in extracurricular activities often do not get home until after dinnertime, leaving just a few hours for eating and doing homework before bed. If fund-raising activities make students stay up late to complete their homework, students will not be getting the amount of rest they need to function properly in school. Of course, one might argue that students could fund raise on Saturdays or Sundays. But many teachers assign large projects for their students to complete over the weekend, and studies should always take priority.

The writer uses an effective transition to introduce a second reason.

To further elaborate on this reason, the writer shows a weakness in an opposing viewpoint.

(continued)

And what about spending time with the family? Most experts agree that during a person's teenage years it is extremely important to spend quality time with the family. The new fund-raising policy would require students to spend even more time away from home, depriving them of much-needed family interaction. In a few years, many students will leave home for college. It seems unfair to deprive them of precious family time in their teenage years, when a family's guidance and support are needed most.

The writer presents this reason and supporting evidence in an effective, logical order. The sentence structure is varied.

For all of these reasons, I feel that the school should seriously reconsider its decision to require all music students to participate in fund-raising. After all, there are more important issues at stake than a new set of polyester uniforms and robes.

The writer concludes by summing up his or her position.

PRACTICE

Now try responding to these writing prompts on your own.

1

Writing Situation

Your school board has proposed that students not be allowed to leave the school building during their lunch hour.

Directions for Writing

Think about whether you would favor the proposal or oppose it.

Now write a letter to persuade your school board to vote either for or against this proposal.

2

Writing Situation

People enjoy many different kinds of music—classical, jazz, rock, and country, to name a few.

Directions for Writing

Think about what kind of music you like best.

Now write to explain why that kind of music is your favorite.